NATIONAL GEOGRAPHIC
Reach

Language • Literacy • Content

Program Authors

Nancy Frey

Lada Kratky

Nonie Lesaux

Sylvia Linan-Thompson

Deborah Short

Jennifer Turner

NATIONAL GEOGRAPHIC

Hampton-Brown

NATIONAL GEOGRAPHIC
Reach
Language • Literacy • Content

Meet the Artist

Joel Sotelo grew up in Tijuana, Mexico and began coming to the United States with his mother as a young child. He now lives in San Diego where he works as an artist and designer. Sotelo loves to travel and integrates elements of many countries and cultures into his art.

Acknowledgments
Grateful acknowledgment is given to the authors, artists, photographers, museums, publishers, and agents for permission to reprint copyrighted material. Every effort has been made to secure the appropriate permission. If any omissions have been made or if corrections are required, please contact the Publisher.

Cover Design and Art Direction: Visual Asylum

Cover Illustration: Joel Sotelo

Text Credits

Unit One
Peachtree Publishers: *Martina the Beautiful Cockroach* by Carmen Agra Deedy. Text copyright © 2007 by Carmen Agra Deedy. Reprinted by permission of Peachtree Publishers.

Acknowledgments and credits continue on page Ack 1.

Program Authors
Nancy Frey
Lada Kratky
Nonie Lesaux
Sylvia Linan-Thompson
Deborah Short
Jennifer Turner

The National Geographic Society
John M. Fahey, Jr., President & Chief Executive Officer
Gilbert M. Grosvenor, Chairman of the Board

National Geographic School Publishing
Hampton-Brown
www.NGSP.com

Printed in the USA.
RR Donnelley, Menasha, WI

ISBN: 978-0-7362-7447-0
ISBN (TX): 978-0-7362-7449-4

10 11 12 13 14 15 16 17 18 19

10 9 8 7 6 5 4 3 2 1

Contents at a Glance

Authors

Program Authors

Nancy Frey

Nancy Frey, Ph.D., a Professor at San Diego State University, received the 2008 Early Career Achievement Award from the National Reading Conference. Dr. Frey has published in *The Reading Teacher, English Journal, Remedial and Special Education,* and *Educational Leadership.* She has co-authored more than fifty books on English Learners (*Language Learners in the English Classroom*), assessment (*Checking for Understanding*), writing (*Scaffolded Writing Instruction*), literacy (*Reading for Information in Elementary School*) and vocabulary (*Learning Words Inside and Out*). Dr. Frey teaches a variety of courses on reading instruction and literacy in content areas, classroom management, and supporting students with diverse learning needs. She also was a third grade classroom teacher.

Lada Kratky

Lada Kratky, M.A. in Spanish Literature, was a Spanish instructor at the Monterey Institute of International Studies and at the Defense Language Institute in Monterey. She has taught elementary bilingual programs and acted as a bilingual reading specialist. Kratky, a featured speaker at national educational conferences, presents strategies and techniques for effective literacy instruction and has authored several Spanish reading programs for National Geographic School Publishing/Hampton Brown including *Pan y canela* and *De canciones a cuentos; Elefonética,* K-2 leveled readers; *Phonics and Friends,* a K-2 English Phonics program; *Alfarrimas,* a Spanish reading program; and the ESL series, *Avenues.*

Nonie K. Lesaux

Nonie K. Lesaux, Ph.D., is Associate Professor at the Harvard Graduate School of Education. Her research and teaching focuses on reading development and preventing reading difficulties of children from linguistically diverse backgrounds. From 2002-2006, Dr. Lesaux was Senior Research Associate of the National Literacy Panel on Language Minority Youth and in 2007 was named one of five WT Grant scholars in support of her research on English-language learners in urban public schools. In 2009, Dr. Lesaux received a Presidential Early Career Award for Scientists and Engineers, the highest honor given by the United States government to young professionals beginning their independent research careers.

Deborah Short

Deborah J. Short, Ph.D., directs Academic Language Research & Training, and provides professional development on sheltered instruction and academic literacy to teachers. She is a senior research associate at the Center for Applied Linguistics where she co-developed the SIOP Model and has directed extensive research on English language learners. Publications include research articles in professional journals, such as *TESOL Quarterly, Journal of Educational Research, Educational Leadership, Education and Urban Society* and *Journal of Research in Education;* books on the SIOP Model; and several ESL series for National Geographic/Hampton-Brown including *Avenues, High Point, Edge, Inside,* and *Reach,* for K-12 students.

Sylvia Linan-Thompson

Sylvia Linan–Thompson, Ph.D., Associate Professor and Fellow at the University of Texas at Austin, is the associate director of the National Research and Development Center on English Language. Dr. Linan-Thompson has developed and examined reading interventions for struggling readers who are monolingual English speakers, English language learners and bilingual students acquiring Spanish literacy. She was a Kindergarten teacher in a bilingual classroom and has worked in Latin America, Africa, Asia, and Eastern Europe on projects related to literacy instruction and professional development and has authored articles, chapters and books on these topics.

Jennifer D. Turner

Jennifer D. Turner, Ph.D., Associate Professor at the University of Maryland, teaches reading education, and multicultural literature and instruction for reading specialists. She has published on exemplary literacy teachers and teaching for African American elementary students. Recently, Dr. Turner received the Elva Knight Research Grant from the International Reading Association for her work with new reading teachers in urban elementary schools. Turner has been elected to the Board of Directors for the National Reading Conference and serves as a co-editor of the literacy leaders department. Her newest book is *Looking Back to Move Forward in Educating African American Students.*

Consultant

John Seidlitz

John Seidlitz, independent education consultant, authored *Sheltered Instruction Plus: A Guide for Texas Teachers of English Learners, Navigating the ELPS: Using the New Standards to Improve Instruction for English Learners* and was a contributing author for *The SIOP Model for Teaching History-Social Studies for English Learners.* He co-developed the *7 Steps to Developing a Language Rich Interactive Classroom™* methodologies and has been a member of the SIOP® National Faculty and a guest lecturer for the LEP-SSI Initiative for the State of Texas. Seidlitz, a former social studies and ESL teacher, served as a secondary ESL program coordinator and founded Seidlitz Education which is dedicated to the mission of *Giving Kids the Gift of Academic Language™.*

Literature Reviewers

Carmen Agra Deedy
Carmen Agra Deedy came from Cuba as a refugee in the 1960s. Topics for her works are from Cuban folklore, such as the 2008 Pura Belpre Honor recipient, *Martina the Beautiful Cockroach*, to issues relating to human rights, as with the 2000 Jane Addams Honoree, *The Yellow Star: The Legend of King Christian X*. Her most recent work, *14 Cows For America*, was a New York Times Bestseller.

Jonda C. McNair
Jonda C. McNair, Ph. D., a former primary grade teacher, is an Associate Professor of Reading Education at Clemson University. Her work has appeared in numerous journals such as Language Arts, Young Children, and Children's Literature in Education.

Grace Lin
Grace Lin is the author and illustrator of more than a dozen picture books as well as middle grade novels. She believes, "Books erase bias, they make the uncommon everyday, and the mundane exotic. A book makes all cultures universal." Grace received a BFA from the Rhode Island School of Design in Providence, RI.

Anastasia Suen
Anastasia Suen, a former kindergarten ESL, first, fifth and sixth grade teacher, has authored numerous children's books and teaches writing to adults online and at Southern Methodist University in Dallas, Texas.

Teacher Reviewers

Kristin Blathras
Lead Literacy Teacher
Donald Morrill Elementary School
Chicago, IL

Irma Bravo Lawrence
Director II, District and English Learner
 Support Services
Stanislaus County Office of Education
Turlock, CA

Vicky Brioso-Saldala
Director of ESOL
Broward County Public Schools
Fort Lauderdale, FL

Blanca L. Campillo
Reading Coach
Chicago Public Schools
Chicago, IL

Sandy Cano
Bilingual Special Education Teacher/
 Case Manager
Pasteur Elementary School
Chicago, IL

Sina Chau-Pech
Elementary ELD Lead Teacher
Folsom Cordova Unified School District
Sacramento, CA

Carla Chavez
Language Arts Specialist
Galena Park Independent School District
Houston, TX

Anna Ciani
ESL Teacher
PS 291X
Bronx, NY

James M. Cleere
Teacher
Donald McKay School
Boston, MA

Judy H. Cole
ESL Teacher
Southwestern Randolph Middle School
Asheboro, NC

Jonathan Eversoll
International Baccalaureate
 Curriculum Coach
Park Center Senior High
Brooklyn Park, MN

Aimee R. Finley
Bilingual Teacher
C. A. Tatum Jr. Elementary School
Dallas, TX

Griselda E. Flores
Bilingual Instructional Coach
Chicago Public Schools
Chicago, IL

Julie Folkert
Language Arts Coordinator
Farmington Public Schools
Farmington, MI

Barbara Ann Genovese-Fraracci
District Program Specialist
Hacienda La Puente Unified
 School District
Hacienda Heights, CA

Norma Godina-Silva, Ph. D
Bilingual Education/ESL/
 Title III Consultant
ESL-BilingualResources.com
El Paso, TX

Vanessa Gonzalez
ESL Teacher/ESL Specialist
Rhoads Elementary
Katy, TX

Laura Hook
Elementary ESOL Resource Teacher
Howard County Public Schools
 Central Office Building
Ellicott City, MD

Leonila Izaguirre
Bilingual-ESL Director
Pharr – San Juan – Alamo
 Independent School District
Pharr, TX

Myra Junyk
Literacy Advocate and Writer
Toronto, ON, Canada

Lisa King
District Lead ESOL Teacher
Polo Road Elementary School
Columbia, SC

Keely Krueger
Director of Bilingual Education
Woodstock Community Unit School
 District 200
Woodstock, IL

Lore Levene
Coordinator of Language Arts, NBCT
Community Consolidated School
 District 59
Mt. Prospect, IL

Estee Lopez
Professor of Literacy Education and
 ELL Specialist
College of New Rochelle
New Rochelle, NY

Susan Mayberger
Coordinator of ESL, Migrant
 and Refugee Education
Omaha Public Schools
Omaha, NE

Annena Z. McCleskey
ELA Consultant/ Regional Literacy
 Training Center Director
Wayne RESA
Lathrup, MI

Michelle Navarro
Teacher on Special Assignment
Orange Unified School District
Orange, CA

Janie Oosterveen
Bilingual Teacher Specialist
San Antonio Independent School District
San Antonio, TX

Theresa Proctor-Reece
ELL Teacher
Windy River Elementary School
Boardman, OR

Sashi Rayasam
Director of ESL Services K-12
Durham Public Schools
Durham, NC

Robin Rivas
Curriculum Specialist ESL/FL
Milwaukee Public Schools
Milwaukee, WI

Shareeica Roberts
ESL Teacher
Carroll Academy for International Studies
Aldine, TX

Cynthia Rodriguez
Bilingual Teacher
Brill Elementary School
Spring, TX

Cristina Rojas, MS.Ed.
District Program Specialist, EL Programs
Hacienda La Puente Unified
 School District
Hacienda Heights, CA

Ana Sainz de la Peña
Director, ESOL and Bilingual Programs
The School District of Philadelphia
Philadelphia, PA

Julie Sanabria
ESOL Teacher
Mamaroneck Avenue School
White Plains, NY

Stephanie Savage Cantu
Bilingual Teacher
Stonewall Jackson Elementary School
Dallas, TX

Jennifer Skrocki Eargle
Elementary Language Arts Specialist
 & Contract Employee
Galena Park Independent
 School District
Houston, TX

Jennifer Slater-Sanchez
Educator
Palmdale School District
Palmdale, CA
Adjunct Professor
Brandman University
Antelope Valley, CA

Georgia Thompson
Literacy Coach
Esperanza Hope Medrano
 Elementary School
Dallas, TX

Dr. Annette Torres Elias
Assistant Professor
School of Education
Texas Wesleyan University
Fort Worth, TX

Sonia James Upton
ELL Consultant, Title III
Kentucky Department of Education
Frankfort, KY

Kathy Walcott
Spanish Immersion Specialist
Rockford Public Schools
Rockford, MI

Christine Kay Williams
ESOL Teacher
Baltimore County Public Schools
Baltimore, MD

Michelle Williams
ELL & Migrant Programs Director
West Ottawa Public Schools
Holland, MI

NATIONAL GEOGRAPHIC

Reach

Language • Literacy • Content

The next generation of language, vocabulary, reading, writing, and content for English language learners is within **Reach**.

- Actively engages and immerses students in a connected, expanding, and dynamic language environment

- Layers and scaffolds essential skills and strategies to move all learners to independence

- Easily adapts to meet your instructional priorities and requirements

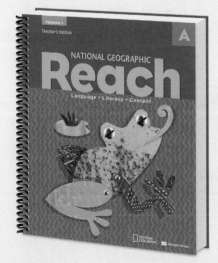

Level A
Kindergarten

Level B
Grade 1

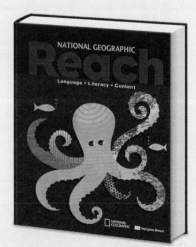

Level C
Grade 2

Level D

Grade 3

Level E

Grade 4

Level F

Grade 5

Active Learning

National Geographic Reach helps you provide English language learners with a robust and interactive learning environment to acquire and expand language.

Rich Academic Discussions

- Big Questions invite students to engage with content and each other
- Ongoing dialog encourages students to share knowledge experiences and cultural perspectives

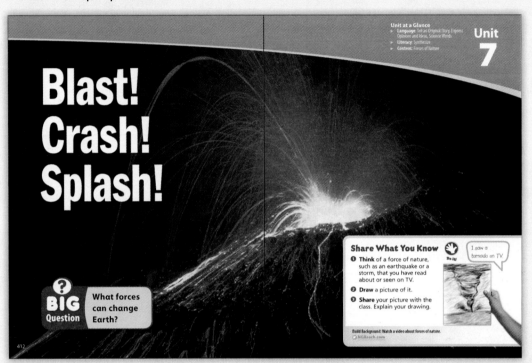

Interactive Learning Opportunities

- Hands-on activities build background knowledge and understanding
- Daily language practice builds proficiency
- Partner activities provide frequent opportunities to develop content and skills

Language of the Day

What interesting thing do you know about islands?

I know that islands are ____.

Tell an Original Story

Listen to Jenny's poem. Then use Language Frames to tell a story of your own.

Language Frames
- This story is about _____.
- It happens _____.
- First, _____.
- Then, _____.

A Scary Ride

Poem ((MP3))

This story is about a boy
With truly unruly hair.
It happens in a hot volcano.
You wouldn't think he'd dare!

First, he rides his tiny red cart
Down tunnels long and deep.
Soon, bubbling magma, thick as mud,
Begins to warm his feet.

Then, suddenly the place erupts!
Upward shoots his cart.
Bump! He lands—back on track,
In an amusement park.

414

Enriching Language and Content Experiences

- Engaging songs create risk-free environments for trying out new language
- Language frames provide valuable assistance to learning language functions
- *Teamwork Activities* boost language and content learning in centers

Accessible Visual Vocabulary

- Routines and supports accelerate vocabulary acquisition
- Materials focus learning on content and academic vocabulary
- Visuals assist students in the acquisition of grade-level vocabulary

EMPHASIS ON VOCABULARY

Going beyond story words, *National Geographic Reach* targets content and academic vocabulary. Abundant visual and text support makes the acquisition of high-utility vocabulary accessible to English language learners.

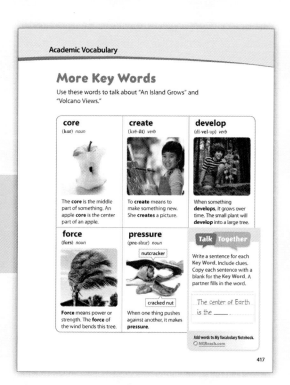

Academic Vocabulary

More Key Words

Use these words to talk about "An Island Grows" and "Volcano Views."

core
(kor) noun

The **core** is the middle part of something. An apple **core** is the center part of an apple.

create
(krē-āt) verb

To **create** means to make something new. She **creates** a picture.

develop
(di-vel-up) verb

When something **develops**, it grows over time. The small plant will **develop** into a large tree.

force
(fors) noun

Force means power or strength. The **force** of the wind bends this tree.

pressure
(pre-shur) noun

nutcracker

cracked nut

When one thing pushes against another, it makes **pressure**.

Talk Together

Write a sentence for each Key Word. Include clues. Copy each sentence with a blank for the Key Word. A partner fills in the word.

The center of Earth is the _____.

Add words to My Vocabulary Notebook.
NGReach.com

417

Engaging Technology

- Images and videos help students build background and context
- Games enhance the acquisition of language and vocabulary
- Multimedia resources empower students to reinforce and extend learning

Structured Support

National Geographic Reach delivers frequent and varied supports to meet the needs of all students.

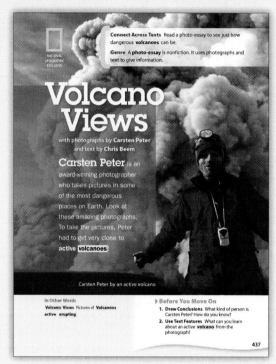

Paired Selections

- Reading across a variety of genres inspires leaning and discovery, and promotes engagement
- Selections include exclusive National Geographic nonfiction to motivate and prepare students for reading in the content areas

Valuable Pre-Reading Support

- Lessons equip students for reading success
- Layered instruction builds background, language, and vocabulary for students to access the reading with confidence

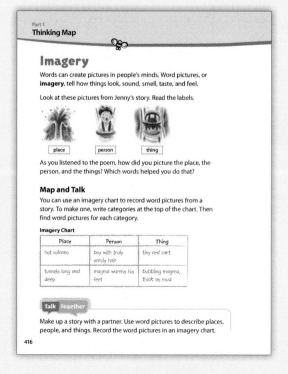

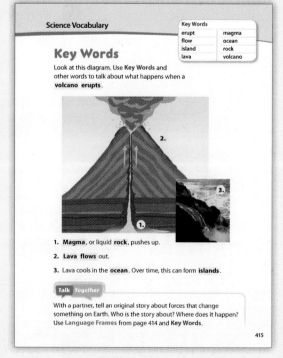

Focused Strategy Instruction

- Targeted lessons teach, model, and practice a reading strategy
- Application of pre-taught strategies elevates comprehension

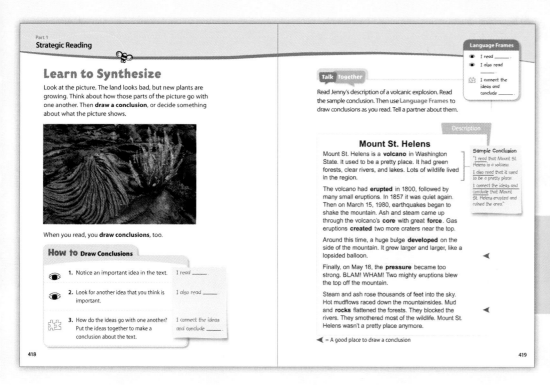

FOCUS AND REPETITION

Focus and repetition of one reading strategy per unit, aided by highly scaffolded instruction, help students succeed. Systematic application across genres promotes strategy transfer.

On-Page Reading Support

- Selections are divided into manageable chunks with frequent comprehension checks
- Highlighted key vocabulary and on-page assistance for idioms and other difficult words keeps students focused and moving through the reading

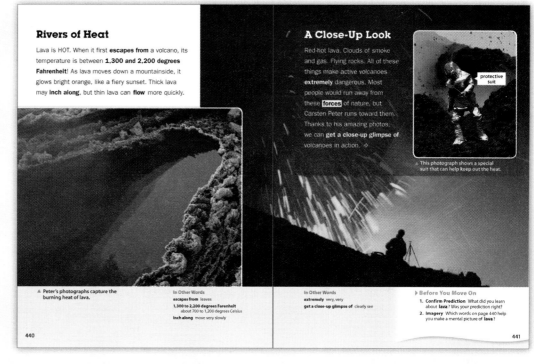

Multi-Level Assessment

- Differentiated assessments measure progress on skills and standards at students' appropriate language level
- A flexible set of assessments impact student learning

Instructional Flexibility

National Geographic Reach has been designed to enable you to tailor instruction to match your specific curriculum objectives, class setting, and the needs of your students.

Build Your Plan

The Online Lesson Planner allows you to easily create or customize plans and also includes a variety of ready-to-go plans.

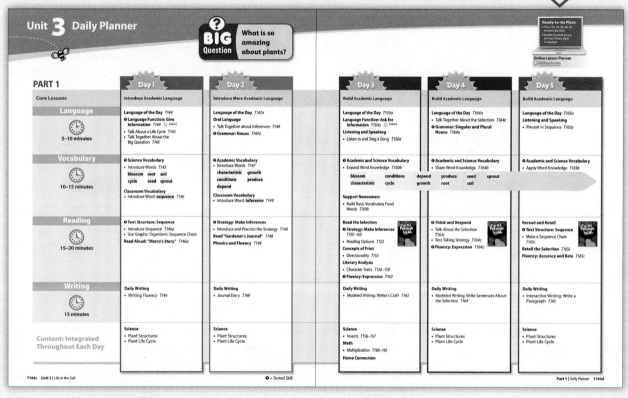

Clear Construction

- Week-at-a-glance planners clearly identify instructional activities by program strand
- Stated time allotments aid modification decisions

Focused Lesson Design

- Clearly identified objectives and tested skills inform instructional decisions
- Lessons are built to function in isolation or in the program's sequential path

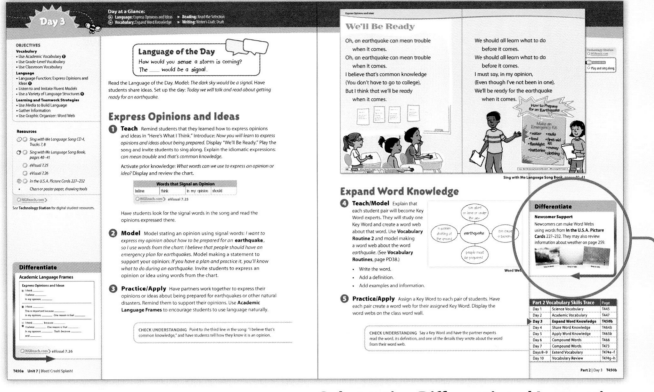

Substantive Differentiated Instruction

- Multi-level strategies within lessons support students at varying proficiency levels
- Print and online materials offer multiple learning pathways to making content comprehensible

Engaging Student Materials

Student Anthology

Fiction Library

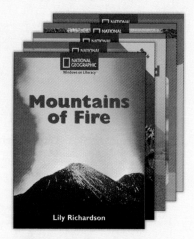

Nonfiction Library

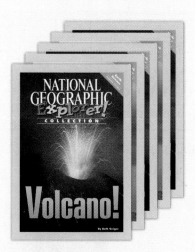

Explorer Books

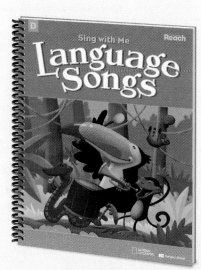

Big Book of Songs

Language Builder Picture Cards

NGReach.com

Build Background Videos
and Interactives

Online Student Books

Flexible Teaching Resources

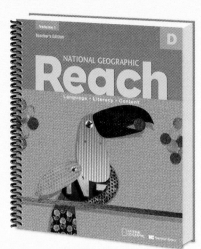

Teacher's Edition

Teamwork Activity Flip Charts

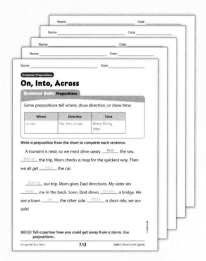

Practice Masters

Resources for Newcomers

Reach into Phonics

Comprehension Coach

Games for Learning

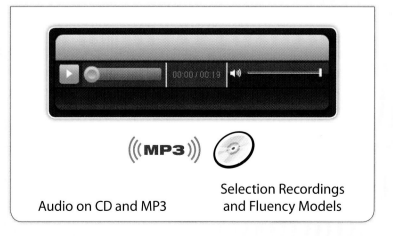

Audio on CD and MP3

Selection Recordings and Fluency Models

Multiple Measures to Assess Student Learning

Start the Year

English Language Proficiency Pretest

- Identify student ELP and complete profile to include Reading, Writing, Listening and Speaking
- Place students into Beginning, Intermediate, Advanced or Advanced High instructional groups

Monitor Progress

Part Tests

- Assess foundational skills taught within a part of a unit
- Flexibility for teacher to use as needed

Unit Tests

- Assess Reading, Writing, and Grammar skills
- Differentiated tests based on language level

- Flexibility for teacher to use as needed

Oral Fluency Benchmark Assessments

- Assess oral reading accuracy and rate 3x per year

Additional Assessments

- Unit Self-Assessments
- Writing Portfolio
- Affective and Metacognitive Measures
- Performance Rubrics

Ongoing Point-of-Use Informal Assessment

Variety of Reteaching Opportunities

End the Year

End-of-Level Assessment

- Assess standards and skills taught across the level
- Formats similar to state tests

English Language Proficiency Post Test

- Show growth in ELP from the beginning to the end of the year

Best Practices & Research Base

National Geographic Reach has been designed by experts in language and literacy. In this section, program authors present the best practices for teaching—practices that are grounded in current research and built into the listening, speaking, reading, writing, and content instruction presented in this program.

Big Questions and Big Ideas

How can I develop learners?
Base your ESL instruction in the content areas.

How can I encourage academic language?
Turn up the volume on academic talk!

How can I support diverse learning and language levels?
Extend your students' *reach* and move them toward independence.

How do I build a depth and breadth of vocabulary knowledge?
Focus on words that matter.

How can I monitor progress and adjust my instruction to maximize achievement and ensure all students succeed?
Know what they know.

How can I accomplish achievement goals with limited time and diverse learners?
Make every minute count!

How can I make teaching and learning relevant and impactful for all students?
Get to know your learners.

How can I help students build listening and reading comprehension?
Build strategic thinking.

How can I prepare students for life in a digital world?
Link to 21st century skills and resources.

How can I build strong writers?
Connect oral and written expression.

What is the role of fluency in instruction?
Make fluency more than just reading quickly.

How do I build foundational skills?
Reach into beginning reading.

Nancy Frey

Lada Kratky

Nonie K. Lesaux

Deborah J. Short

Sylvia Linan-Thompson

Jennifer D. Turner

Deborah Short, Ph.D., Center for Applied Linguistics

Deborah J. Short is a senior research associate who co-developed the SIOP Model and has directed quasi-experimental and experimental research on English language learners. Publications include articles in TESOL Quarterly, Journal of Educational Research, Educational Leadership; and several ESL series for National Geographic/Hampton-Brown including *Edge, Inside, High Point,* and *Avenues* for K-12 students.

NGReach.com > **Download Professional Development Podcasts**

((MP3)) Listen to Deborah Short share more information on content-based ESL instruction.

Base Your ESL Instruction in the Content Areas *by Deborah Short*

Schools across the United States are composed of ethnically and linguistically diverse students, and a growing number of them speak English as a new language. According to state-reported data, more than 5 million English language learners (ELLs) were enrolled in grades Pre-K through 12 in the 2005-2006 school year. From 1995-96 to 2005-06, their enrollment increased 57 percent although total enrollment increased by only 3 percent (NCELA, 2009). Most of the ELLs are in the elementary grades (Capps, et al., 2005). Unfortunately, these ELLs as a group are not succeeding as well as native English speakers on national and state assessments. On the 2007 National Assessment of Educational Progress (NAEP), for example, the average reading score for fourth grade ELLs was 36 points lower than that for English speakers. Moreover, 70 percent of these ELLs scored "below basic," the lowest level (Lee, Grigg, & Donahue, 2007). Similarly, ELLs on average scored 25 points lower on the fourth grade math test with 44 percent scoring "below basic" (Lee, Grigg, & Dion, 2007). ELLs clearly need support in acquiring academic English and in achieving success in content area classes.

The challenge of content-area learning Given the growth in the number of students who are not proficient in English, the language of instruction for most schools, classroom scenes like the following are common:

Loan wants to tell the teacher what she remembers about forests in her country but she doesn't have the words to explain. She isn't sure how her experiences relate to her science text. She sees photos of forests and the trees have red, orange, and yellow leaves. In other photos the trees look dead and the ground is white. Birds and other animals look different too. These aren't like the forests in Vietnam. Why not? Loan sits quietly and tries to follow what the teacher says, but he speaks quickly and doesn't write words on the board or show other pictures. She hears the word fall, but the trees didn't fall down, and cycle, but there is no bicycle. Loan

fears the teacher thinks she is a poor student, but she just doesn't know how to express her questions or describe the forests of her country.

Juan Miguel was born in the U.S. and is now in 4th grade. He is very social, speaks English and Spanish and contributes to group work in class. But when he has to read his social studies book and respond to teacher questions or write a summary, he falters. His writing consists of basic short sentences. He doesn't relate abstract concepts being studied to what's been learned. Juan Miguel was in a bilingual program for kindergarten and first grade and then moved to an English program for the past two years. He has been at the intermediate level of English proficiency since the start of third grade.

Many second language learners like Loan and Juan Miguel want to do well in school but struggle to participate actively in their subjects. Even when these students learn to speak some English, they may not have the necessary academic language skills and relevant background knowledge to complete many academic tasks, such as comparing two historical events, solving math word problems, writing observations for a science experiment, and summarizing a story. After one year in school, most ELLs are tested on grade-level curricula in English even though they are not proficient in their new language. This situation is not only difficult for the students but also for their teachers, few of whom have had professional development on effective approaches for integrating language and content instruction for students who are not proficient in English. Language is the key to learning in schools; we primarily learn through language and use language to demonstrate our knowledge. This fact rings particularly true for educators who work with students learning English as a new language while they are learning academic content. Without oral and written English language skills, students are hard pressed to learn and demonstrate their knowledge.

The solution: Content-based ESL instruction Many schools have offered English as a second language instruction (ESL) to ELLs like Loan and Juan Miguel. But traditionally this instruction has focused on survival language, storytelling, grammar drills, and basic vocabulary. It has often been unrelated to what's happening in other classes, and so hasn't been sufficient to help students succeed in school. Instead, educators need to consider ESL instruction as part of an overall program that develops language skills alongside, and in conjunction with, content area knowledge. This solution is frequently referred to as content-based ESL (CBESL). Content-based ESL classes are taught by language educators with two goals (Lyster, 2007; Short, 2006; Stoller, 2004):

- to develop English language proficiency
- to prepare ELLs for success in mainstream classes, especially in the content areas

Content-based ESL teachers develop students' English language proficiency by incorporating topics from the subject areas that students study in their grade level. This is often accomplished through thematic units, such as a plants or water cycle unit. Lessons can include objectives drawn from life sciences, social studies, language arts, and mathematics. Lessons target key content area vocabulary as well as the academic tasks ELLs need to become familiar with for the regular classroom (e.g., creating a timeline, taking notes from reference materials, making an oral presentation).

▲ Thematic units in National Geographic Reach link language skills to content area learning.

Integrate language skills with content learning

Content-based ESL teachers are responsible for addressing all the state ESL/English language proficiency (ELP) standards. Teachers must provide explicit instruction in the language skills (reading, writing, listening, speaking) and the elements of English (vocabulary, syntax, grammar, and conventions). However, CBESL teachers do not teach these skills in isolation, nor with a focus on conversational language. Rather they design lessons, select texts, and set assignments that reflect how those skills are applied in content classrooms. For example, if students are expected to record observations during a neighborhood walk in an upcoming social studies lesson, the CBESL teacher may teach descriptive adjectives, directional terms, and names of community resources beforehand. Or, if the students have to classify and compare animals, CBESL teachers may teach students academic language frames so they can use comparative expressions like "both . . . and. . . , neither . . . nor. . . "; ". . . are alike/different because. . .", and "on the one hand. . . , on the other hand. . . ."

It is particularly important that CBESL teachers incorporate many opportunities for oral language practice. During much of the school day, as Saunders and Goldenberg (in press) point out, students are engaged in content area instruction and reading and writing tasks, so an emphasis on listening and speaking in ESL/ELD time is crucial. In contrast to traditional ESL instruction, this listening and speaking time should develop skills needed for content learning. Keep in mind that in many content classes teachers don't take advantage of teachable moments for language development. They tend to correct students for content errors, not linguistic ones. They don't ask students to expand on their ideas or use elaborated speech. They don't encourage students to reformulate responses to negotiate meaning but provide the clarifications themselves (Musimeci, 1996, Swain, 1987). Effective content-based ESL teachers in contrast will do these things that advance second language acquisition.

Key Words	
blossom	produce
characteristic	root
conditions	seed
cycle	soil
depend	sprout
growth	

◀ **Vocabulary lessons include Key Words that are essential for student success in the content areas.**

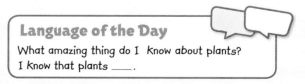

Language of the Day
What amazing thing do I know about plants?
I know that plants _____ .

▲ **Daily oral language activities develop students' ability to use academic language in talking about content area topics.**

In content-based ESL, teachers spend time helping students apply their growing knowledge base in strategic ways. For example, CBESL teachers introduce language learning strategies to students (e.g., using cognates to determine meanings of unknown words, rehearsing sentences before speaking, previewing headings and illustrations before reading) to help them continue their language development on their own and to assist them in other subjects. They also focus on reading comprehension strategies (e.g., making connections, determining importance) through a variety of authentic and meaningful texts related to the content topics.

Content-based ESL classes offer valuable opportunities to build students' background knowledge, which is critical for conceptual understanding and reading comprehension. For ELLs who are not familiar with American culture or who have had interrupted schooling, CBESL lessons can introduce students to academic topics their classmates know already. By tapping into what ELLs know, teachers make connections to new or related concepts and clear up misconceptions. Through simulations, video clips, field trips, and hands-on experiences, teachers also build foundational knowledge for these learners.

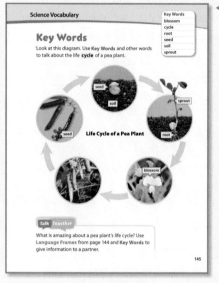

◀ **Science features support English learners in building academic knowledge and skills.**

National Geographic Reach has been designed specifically to support content-based ESL classes. The content-rich materials, student activities, and lesson plans promote academic language learning that is connected to the other subjects in a student's school day. *Reach* emphasizes major topics of science and social studies through thematic units that incorporate academic and content vocabulary and subject-specific tasks. The program also includes suggestions for relating themes to students' own experiences, cultures, and personal lives. Within a unit, each lesson builds on prior lessons to reinforce and extend the information students are learning and the language skills they are acquiring.

National Geographic Reach uses standards-based instruction as the medium for teaching English. The program is aligned with national and state curriculum standards for ESL/ELD, English language arts, science, and social studies. It addresses students' language development needs by providing:

- Daily oral language practice tied to content concepts and target language functions
- Attention to academic and content vocabulary through multimodal activities
- Comprehensive grammar instruction
- Authentic content reading selections drawn from diverse genres with built-in support
- Writing tasks for fluency, interactive writing, and independent writing with tools and resources

National Geographic Reach prepares ELLs for English-medium classes by giving them practice with key academic language, tasks, and topics. *National Geographic Reach* lessons give students opportunities to read varied fiction and nonfiction texts, to understand narrative structures like cause-effect and problem-and-solution, and to use text features to identify important information in science and social studies articles. Key vocabulary is taught to younger children through songs, games, role-play, and colorful visuals. Older children learn key vocabulary through graphics, word webbing, and other research-based word-learning strategies. Writing projects, such as writing a science article or a persuasive essay, mirror the assignments found in content classes.

Conclusion

Students need dedicated time for ESL/ELD instruction and that time needs to count (Saunders & Goldenberg, in press). Content-based ESL transforms a traditional ESL class into a forum for developing and applying subject knowledge, so CBESL instruction becomes an anchor for content classes. The material is relevant and meaningful to the students because it is aligned with their school subjects and standards. Infusing content in reading, writing, and oral language practice, as *National Geographic Reach* does, will equip our students with the academic language skills they need for success in school. And as ELLs strengthen these skills, they will interact more with English-speaking peers, demonstrate skills associated with academic uses of language, and improve their English reading comprehension.

Nonie K. Lesaux, Ph.D., Harvard Graduate School of Education

Nonie K. Lesaux is Associate Professor at the Harvard Graduate School of Education. Her research and teaching focuses on reading development and preventing reading difficulties of children from linguistically diverse backgrounds. Lesaux has received recognition for her work in Language Minority Youth, English-language learners and received a Presidential Early Career Award for Scientists and Engineers.

> **NGReach.com** **Download Professional Development Podcasts**

((MP3)) Listen to Nonie Lesaux share more information on developing academic language.

Turn up the Volume on Academic Talk!

by Nonie Lesaux

You might predict from this title that we are encouraging far more noise in classrooms across the country. In a way we are. But we're focusing on the other meaning of the word *volume*—the *amount* of talk we need in classrooms for optimal student learning. We need more talk and we need more productive noise—the sounds of students talking and working together; the sounds of learning.

One of the most effective tools in the classroom to promote learning and critical thinking is talk. Language reflects how we think, how we process and remember information; it is one of the most important ways that we represent and extend our thoughts and ideas (Vygotsky, 1978). Talk can be formal discussion or informal conversation. With language, we're able to go much beyond the here and now. We can discuss, compare, and justify present, past, and future events. We can describe what is happening around us or imagine what is taking place far away. Language opens up ideas and experiences that would otherwise not be possible to contemplate, understand, and learn about. We need to help learners to gain a curiosity and interest in language. They must become everyday language learners and users. We can do that by posing open-ended questions to our students and engaging in real dialogue with them, dialogue where we as teachers don't control all the turn-taking or know all the answers. By fostering and scaffolding academic talk, we will build language literacy and content skills and knowledge.

There are three guiding principles that teachers can incorporate in their classroom practices and curriculum to promote students' academic language.

- Students need more structured opportunities to talk
- Effective classroom talk is about more than asking questions
- Keep students reading for academic language skills

> *We need more talk—the sounds of students talking and learning together; the sounds of learning.*

1 Students need more structured opportunities to talk

We know that children living in poverty, including many English language learners (ELLs), are less likely to participate in academic conversations at home than children of higher socioeconomic status. They are less likely to be engaged in conversation where they make predictions about an upcoming outing, justify their claims with evidence, and articulate causes and effects. For these students to succeed academically, we need to teach these more sophisticated discourse patterns in classrooms. Yet when we look back on educational practices for hundreds of years past, we see that students have been taught to listen quietly as the teacher talked, so that they would learn. Unfortunately, that has not been a successful strategy for many children.

Across the nation, teachers dominate classroom talk (Cazden, 1988; Heath, 1978; Snow, Tabors, & Dickinson, 2001), yet they are not the ones who need practice talking. If we are going to close achievement gaps and develop *all* students' critical thinking and oral and written language skills, we need to provide them with significant opportunities to do so. Despite national calls for instructional frameworks that focus on *Reading, Writing, Listening*, and *Speaking*, instructional research tells us very clearly that speaking is the neglected standard. Students do very little speaking in classrooms and when they do, it qualifies as basic communication—it is not dynamic or engaging and it is not academic talk. Students answer low-level questions with one or two word replies, respond to directives, confirm information, and often repeat what the teacher says as part of a lesson. And if speaking is the neglected standard, listening is the misunderstood standard—*passive* listening, like following directions, is the norm. Developing *active* listening skills as part of our academic language requires instructional practices that force students into dialogue and debate that centers on rich concepts and builds up reasoning skills and background knowledge.

▲ Each unit includes a Big Question that spurs ongoing student discussion and dialogue and develops high levels of academic talk.

We need to infuse more opportunities for productive talk into our classrooms, especially in classrooms with ELLs and other at-risk students who need strong supports to develop their thinking and reading comprehension skills. *National Geographic Reach* is a program designed to address this need for ELLs and their classmates. In every unit, and across the lesson cycle, there are interesting things to talk about (i.e., big ideas on themes young learners can relate to) and structured opportunities to teach students how to participate in classroom talk effectively (i.e., language frames to help organize their thoughts and opinions, key vocabulary around the topic). *National Geographic Reach* presents, for example, collaborative learning activities to get students talking and practicing their active listening skills, and scaffolded support for teachers to lead effective discussions about big ideas. The wrap-up projects in each unit provide opportunities for oral presentation to practice academic talk.

② Effective classroom talk is about more than asking questions

One of the most common scenarios where students are given opportunities to speak in the elementary school classroom is the whole-group lesson. Consider the commonplace read-aloud. The teacher reads a story, pausing every now and again to pose a question to the group. Some students raise their hands with a candidate answer, and the teacher calls on a student to respond. In this whole-group scenario, the teacher directs the lessons and the opportunities for talk by students are quite limited.

To change the balance of talk in the classroom we need more than whole-group scenarios where the teacher controls a question-answer discussion and students answer one at a time. That practice hits upon only a small group of students and often those who are most proficient and high performing (Fisher, Frey & Rothenberg, 2008). We also can't rely almost exclusively upon the strategy of questioning

as a tool to promote classroom talk. Researchers have found explicit, "right there" questions—questions about the here and the now or questions where the answers are easily found in text—are used between 50 percent and 80 percent of the time in classrooms (Watson & Young, 1986; Zwiers, 2008). These questions serve primarily one purpose—to evaluate students' understanding about something relatively concrete and literal. Engaging students with talk that will promote their thought, language, and reading skills can't just be about assessment for the teacher's purpose (Cazden, 1988).

Effective instructional practices for classroom talk focus very seriously instead on dialogue to promote learning—it is the back and forth discussion that fosters critical thinking, develops verbal reasoning skills, and builds background knowledge. This discussion is also a way for students to work through and sharpen their ideas and informed opinions. Think about the times when you have sharpened and clarified your own thinking by talking something through with a peer. We need to provide similar opportunities to our students.

Good language instruction is at the core of the *National Geographic Reach* program. It is a program whereby instruction in academic language, including academic talk, centers on a big question featured in every unit. In order to grapple with big questions, students and teachers discuss the many answers to open-ended questions that ask students to imagine, plan, think, wonder, speculate, and articulate answers, which should lead to further dialogue. The program features instruction that draws significantly on the teacher's and the students' personal connections to the topic and promotes academic talk that is collaborative in nature. In many program lessons, students have to take a stance and debate a point of view, or do some research to role-play as part of a collaborative project, and report out to their peers as experts. In each one of these structured opportunities to talk, we ask students to learn from their peers by observing and listening, expose them to rich and engaging text that features academic language, and also use specialized language registers and vocabulary words to improve their academic language skills.

③ Keep students reaching for academic language skills

In planning instruction that will create classrooms filled with student academic talk, with dialogue and with open-ended questions that foster debate, deliberation, and wonder about big ideas and the world, we cannot simply meet students where they're at. We need to pull them along!

We need to teach the language of schooling through stimulating and challenging learning environments—classrooms filled with scaffolding opportunities to develop their language and thinking skills. Just as a toddler needs oral interaction with older siblings and adults who use more sophisticated language, language beyond the toddler's proficiency level, to develop his or her first language fully, so do our learners need exposure to more advanced levels of language use with scaffolding, modeling and frequent practice in the classroom.

Yet ironically just as the texts and the language needed for academic success become more difficult, less instructional time is devoted to student talk and oral language development.

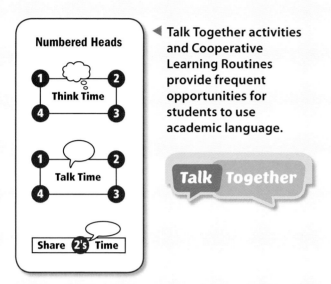

◀ Talk Together activities and Cooperative Learning Routines provide frequent opportunities for students to use academic language.

National Geographic Reach aims to shift the trends we see in standard practice; its design was guided by the principle that students need ongoing structured and scaffolded opportunities to develop their academic language skills. Its success in developing academic language depends upon good peer interaction and scaffolded discussions (August & Hakuta, 1997; Ellis, 1994). That means we teach students how to take turns, respect one another's ideas, and confirm their understandings of what a classmate said. We model what good conversations look like and how one builds on the ideas of others. The *National Geographic Reach* Teacher's Edition focuses on designing effective lessons and learning opportunities to increase academic talk in our classrooms, encouraging teachers to take advantage of built-in opportunities for peer scaffolding to push students forward, while paying careful attention to groupings. Every *National Geographic Reach* unit features multiple lessons and opportunities to foster academic language. At the end of each unit students participate in a collaborative project that encourages dialogue and discussion focused on the big question. Each unit also includes a writing project that provides opportunities for increased academic talk and scaffolded learning with peers, especially during the prewriting and editing phases when students share ideas with a partner, and when students edit each other's work and learn how to give feedback effectively. Throughout the program, language frames and Multi-Level Strategies provide scaffolded support to move students from forming basic sentences to making comparisons, giving opinions, and justifying choices to their peers.

Conclusion

If we are to close achievement gaps and support *all* students' academic development, especially that of ELLs, our classrooms should be filled with talk that centers on big ideas and complex concepts that are worthy of discussion and debate and engaging for our students. To do this we need to strike more of a balance between teacher talk and student talk—increasing student talk and decreasing teacher talk to provide more meaningful language learning opportunities (Cazden, 2001; Fisher, Frey, & Rothenberg, 2008; McIntyre, Kyle & Moore, 2006; Saunders & Goldenberg, 1992). It also means we need to expand teachers' repertoires to go beyond questioning and get students speaking. The lessons that promote students' academic and active listening skills are those that engage students to work and think together about a problem, see others' points of view, and better understand the knowledge and experiences they bring to the issue, as well as those lessons that engage students to think about big questions and ideas.

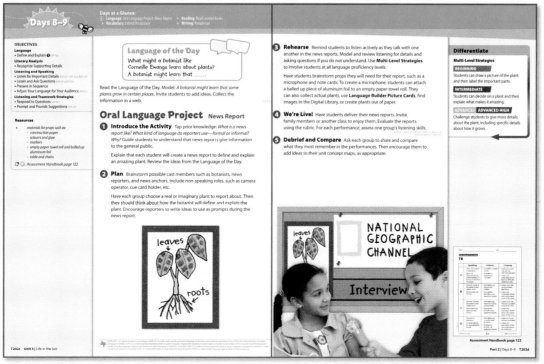

◀ Each lesson cycle includes a Theme Theater or Oral Language Project that engages students in using and elaborating their language skills.

Deborah Short, Ph.D., Center for Applied Linguistics

Deborah J. Short is a senior research associate who co-developed the SIOP Model and has directed quasi-experimental and experimental research on English language learners. Publications include articles in TESOL Quarterly, Journal of Educational Research, Educational Leadership; and several ESL series for National Geographic/Hampton-Brown including *Edge, Inside, High Point,* and *Avenues* for K-12 students.

NGReach.com **Download Professional Development Podcasts**

((MP3)) Listen to Deborah Short share more information on scaffolding instruction.

Extend Your Students' *Reach* and Move Them Toward Independence. *by Deborah Short*

When we get in our cars and drive away, we usually have a destination in mind. Furthermore, we have a route planned for getting there. Consider your students and your instruction. What is the destination you would like your students to reach at the end of their year with you? How far do they need to go to get there? How will you guide them along the way?

In the best of all possible worlds, our students would be proficient readers, writers and speakers of English after their time with us. That is rarely the case, unless we begin the school year with advanced learners. However, we can ensure that students make significant progress towards proficiency if we scaffold our instruction appropriately. And what is scaffolding? Simply put, it is meeting students where they are and leading them to where you want them to go.

Vygotsky (1978) asserted that students' language learning is promoted through social interaction and contextualized communication. Teachers can guide students to construct meaning from texts and classroom discourse and to understand complex content concepts by scaffolding instruction. When scaffolding, teachers pay careful attention to students' capacity for working in English. Teachers begin instruction at the current level of student understanding and move students to higher levels through tailored support.

Scaffolding strategies vary. One way they do so is by adjusting their speech (e.g., paraphrasing, giving examples, elaborating student responses) to help students comprehend and participate in discussions (Bruner, 1978). Another way teachers scaffold is by adjusting instructional tasks so they are incrementally more

Scaffolding is meeting students where they are and leading them to where you want them to go.

and more challenging (e.g., preteach vocabulary before a reading selection, have students draft an outline before writing an essay) and students learn the skills necessary to complete tasks on their own (Applebee & Langer, 1983). The acquisition of academic vocabulary also needs to be scaffolded. Many academic words are used infrequently, so teachers need to create motivating contexts in which students can use and become familiar with academic language (Corson, 1997). Teachers also scaffold by using visuals, context, gestures, and other ways of conveying information.

Without such teacher assistance, English language learners (ELLs) may fail to acquire fully their new language. It is important for teachers of ELLs to employ both verbal and instructional scaffolds to extend communication opportunities for students. Teachers need to be aware of students' proficiency and skill levels and plan instruction that provides comprehensible input yet moves the students further along the second language acquisition path. Effective scaffolding can increase the students' independence in performing a task or learning a new concept through the gradual release of responsibility (Echevarria, Vogt & Short, 2010; Fisher & Frey, 2008).

Teachers using **National Geographic Reach** have a wide array of scaffolding features to support students at their level of proficiency and to move them to higher levels of language use. These features enable teachers to:

- Adjust teacher speech to help students comprehend
- Support students in using language at increasingly higher levels
- Adjust instructional tasks so students are successfully challenged at their levels

Scaffolding

1 Adjust teacher speech to help students comprehend

Teachers play a critical role in language acquisition for students because they provide models of appropriate speech, word choice, intonation, and fluency. With *National Geographic Reach*, teachers use a variety of verbal scaffolds to help students understand new information and to advance students' English language use, comprehension, and thinking skills. They also regulate their speech according to the proficiency levels of their students, even when they have multiple levels in a class.

- **Think-alouds** By modeling and articulating their thought processes, teachers make their thinking apparent to children. They can explain the steps they go through to solve a problem, the reactions they have to a plot twist in a story, and the judgments they make to reject or accept possible answers to a question. Think-alouds are provided throughout the instructional plan; teachers can use them as provided or refer to them in developing their own think-alouds.

Think Aloud		Wr.
1. Plan		
I will make a RAFT to plan my writing. I will take the role of myself.		Role
Who is my audience? I will share my captions about sea turtles with the class.		Aud
Repeat the think aloud for audience (class) and form (captions). *I'd like to draw a picture of a sea turtle. I will write a caption to go w. about the picture.*		

- **Rate and Amount of Speech** Teachers adjust their rate of speech to the students' proficiency levels—speaking more slowly to beginners and at a more normal pace to advanced and transitional learners. They also moderate how much they say at any one time, speaking in phrases with pauses as needed.
- **Sophistication of Speech** For beginning level students, teachers use simple sentences and repeated terms. For more proficient learners, they use complex sentences, more synonyms, and more pronoun referents.
- **Repetition** By repeating what he or she has said, the teacher adds processing time for the students and a chance to double check what they heard. By repeating for the class what a student has said, the teacher can project the comment or response more clearly, and model correct pronunciation.
- **Restatement and Paraphrase** Restating and paraphrasing utterances by the teacher or other students also has value. It is a way to confirm or clarify what has been said, for example, appending a definition of a term or explanation of a statement, or rephrasing a statement using better known words.
- **Elaboration** When teachers elaborate and extend student responses, they model more sophisticated language use and how to connect ideas through conjunctions, comparisons, causation, and the like. Elaboration promotes rich discussion among students.

2 Support students in using language at increasingly higher levels

Students also learn through interaction with one another and with their teachers. Students need extensive oral language practice to deepen content and vocabulary knowledge and to practice academic language functions, such as clarifying information, negotiating meaning, and evaluating opinions. *National Geographic Reach* provides a rich array of verbal prompts, language frames, and other scaffolds that support students in generating academic talk. These include:

- **Providing models of good speech** Students using *National Geographic Reach* have access to a wide variety of good speech models in the Language of the Day, read alouds, songs and chants, and many other listening activities.
- **Elaborating responses** Teachers too often accept a brief answer and then add to it themselves. *National Geographic Reach* encourages students to extend their thoughts with prompts like:
  - *Tell me more.*
  - *What do you mean by that?*
  - *Who can add on?*
  - *Who has a different idea?*
- **Providing sentence starters and academic language frames** Language frames help students organize their thoughts and use academic vocabulary in meaningful ways. They provide the support for students to articulate their ideas and can be differentiated with more structure (or less) as needed. Examples include:
  - Phrases to agree or disagree (e.g., I agree with you but. . . , I disagree with you and think that. . . .)
  - Phrases to report on findings or evidence (e.g., We discovered that. . . , Our group found that. . . , The article explains that. . . .)
  - Phrases to use to ask for clarification (e.g., Could you say that again?, Could you say that another way?)

Differentiate

Academic Language Frames

Make Inferences
- I read _____.
  I know _____.
  And so _____.
- I read _____.
  Because I know _____, I can infer _____.
- The text says _____.
- That relates to what I know about _____.
  I can infer _____ because _____.

NGReach.com > eVisual 3.5

◀ Academic Language Frames provide multilevel support to help students express their ideas using academic vocabulary.

- **Cooperative learning** Proven cooperative learning techniques are embedded in lesson activities so students can discuss topics, accomplish roles, and apply their new knowledge collaboratively.

- **Providing extended speech activities** The amount of talking a student does can be adjusted by his or her proficiency level. Activities such as oral presentations, multi-day projects, and cooperative learning tasks generate richer, elaborated speech.

③ Adjust instructional tasks so students are successfully challenged at their levels

Instructional scaffolds help teachers make information accessible to students and teach procedures students can use to accomplish tasks.

- **Visuals** One of the easiest ways to convey information is through a visual format. *National Geographic Reach* makes extensive use of visuals including videos, whiteboard presentations, photographs, illustrations, tables and charts, and other graphics. This visual approach helps students with limited language proficiency to quickly assimilate new vocabulary, concepts, and processes.

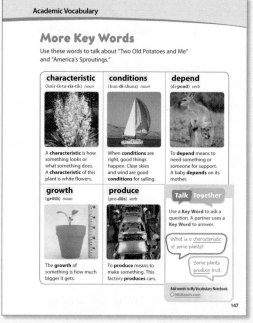

◀ **Visuals support instruction**

- **Graphic organizers** Graphic organizers are used extensively as tools for comprehending text, learning new vocabulary and concepts, and identifying important information and key points.
- **Comprehension strategy instruction** *National Geographic Reach* provides explicit instruction, modeling, and practice in learning strategies with authentic text. Teachers should capitalize on the cognitive and metacognitive strategies that students already use in their first language because these strategies will transfer to the new language (August & Shanahan, 2006) and students will use more effective strategies as they become more proficient in their second language (Riches & Genesee, 2006).

- **Process writing and writing frames** The writing process exemplifies scaffolded instruction (Rogers & Graham, 2008). In each unit of *National Geographic Reach*, students are assisted in creating their own texts. In the prewriting phase they generate ideas and talk them through with partners. When drafting, they begin to connect those ideas and often use writing frames for structured support. In the editing phase they receive feedback to strengthen their writing and they learn to give targeted feedback as well.
- **Peer tutoring** *National Geographic Reach* includes many opportunities for peer collaboration and tutoring. Students who have background knowledge about a topic can share their knowledge with classmates, explaining the content and modeling the language used to convey information. Students who have stronger literacy skills can assist others in reading and writing activities, explaining procedures or modeling tasks.
- **Cooperative learning** Cooperative activities are extremely useful for scaffolding instruction. Students support one another as they are learning the subject matter, and they practice their oral language skills as they interact verbally. *National Geographic Reach* provides many opportunities for students to interact using research-based Cooperative Learning Routines.

Conclusion

For students to have full access to the core curriculum, they need to be proficient in the language of schooling. Yet, the development of academic English is a complicated endeavor that involves more than just additional vocabulary development and grammar practice. Academic language is used in different ways in different contexts. The writing of a scientific lab report is not the same as the writing and delivery of a persuasive speech. The reading process used to follow steps in solving a math problem is not the same as those used to interpret a poem. Students need semantic and syntactic knowledge and facility with language functions. In their various classes, English learners must join their emerging understandings of the English language with the content they are studying in order to complete assigned academic tasks.

Regardless of proficiency level, all students can make progress in their language development. To achieve this, classroom communication and instruction need to be scaffolded so that tasks and discussions consistently move students along the pathway to second language acquisition and literacy knowledge. Teachers who scaffold appropriately shift responsibility for using new skills and strategies to students as quickly as they are able. However, students are not expected to leap to a new level of understanding and language use. Instead they are supported and guided along the way, reaching forward one step at a time towards their destination.

Nonie K. Lesaux, Ph.D., Harvard Graduduat School of Education

Nonie K. Lesaux is Associate Professor at the Harvard Graduate School of Education. Her research and teaching focuses on reading development and preventing reading difficulties of children from linguistically diverse backgrounds. Lesaux has received recognition for her work in Language Minority Youth, English-language learners and received a Presidential Early Career Award for Scientists and Engineers.

NGReach.com ▶ **Download Professional Development Podcasts**

(((MP3))) Listen to Nonie Lesaux share more information on research-based vocabulary instruction.

Focus Deeply on Words that Matter! *by Nonie Lesaux*

Vocabulary learning is an enormous task for all students; in order to be academically successful, students must leave high school with a working understanding of about 50,000 words. It's estimated that students reading at grade level learn 2,000 to 3,000 words a year in the context of reading print, which is not the case for students who are struggling. This relationship has major implications for instruction. For all learners, including English language learners (ELLs), vocabulary and reading comprehension have a reciprocal relationship—while greater vocabulary leads to greater comprehension, better comprehension also leads to learning more vocabulary words.

Research has found that academic vocabulary, the specialized and sophisticated language of text, is a particular source of difficulty for students who struggle with comprehension, especially ELLs. Many of these students have generally good foundational skills for word reading and many even read the print fluently, but don't understand deeply what they read. For example, a group of 8th grade Spanish-speaking ELLs enrolled in U.S. classrooms since the primary grades shows a common profile: grade-level word reading skills coupled with vocabulary and comprehension levels about two grade levels below.

Academic vocabulary is different from basic or conversational vocabulary and essential for academic success because it carries with it many important concepts that students need to know; but for many students, it must be explicitly taught. And in spite of the fact that gaps in reading performance are often associated with gaps in academic vocabulary knowledge and the conceptual knowledge that comes with it, deliberate, sustained instruction to develop students' academic vocabulary knowledge occurs infrequently in most classrooms across the U.S. and Canada. Estimates suggest that in kindergarten through second grade classrooms, only between 10 percent and 28 percent of academic

"Good vocabulary teaching involves a lot of talk and practice using language."

time focuses on explicit instruction in this area, while by the middle school years, this number is about 10 percent, and much of this instruction is incidental in nature, like providing a definition for a word in passing.

Much more instructional time is needed to build students' academic vocabulary skills, and during this teaching we have to give students lots of structured, planned opportunities to learn and use their oral language skills. Good vocabulary teaching involves a lot of talk and practice using language. It also involves giving students the language to talk about the concepts they know and to craft their explanations and arguments. Therefore, the problem for teachers and curricula to address, as soon as possible, is three-fold:

1. We need to spend more time on planned vocabulary teaching in our classrooms.
2. We need to focus carefully on the words we choose to teach.
3. We also need to teach word-learning strategies.

❶ We need to spend more time on planned vocabulary teaching in our classrooms

Students need to learn how to think about language and how words work. And in learning new words, students need to have a deep understanding of the concept that the word represents. This learning process takes time; this means an instructional plan that builds in opportunities to learn words over an extended period of time, providing multiple exposures across the lesson cycle, and using the words in different ways—reading, writing, listening, and speaking.

Our goal should be to help students attain the deep understanding that Beck and McKeown (1991) described as truly "knowing" a word: "a rich, decontextualized knowledge of each word's meaning, including its relationship to other words, and its extension to metaphorical use." Many students have only a narrow sense of a word, or what Graves calls "narrow-context bound knowledge." An example would be thinking that the concept of substitute is a teacher. These students need to develop a deep, decontextualized understanding of the concept behind the word to use it appropriately in academic discussion or writing. For example, understanding the concept of substitution and the many ways in which substitution can take place.

This means we need to carefully consider the number of words we teach and the time we allot to those words. In many classrooms it is common practice to teach a large number of words per week from a list or workbook, an approach that results in relatively shallow word knowledge that is rarely maintained for the long-term. Under these circumstances, students are often taught to look up words in the dictionary when they don't know their meanings. However, research tells us that dictionary definitions are inaccessible to most students. ELLs and other learners who need strong support to learn words need lots of relevant examples and explanations that use familiar language, yet dictionaries are organized with abbreviated definitions to conserve space and fit as many entries as possible.

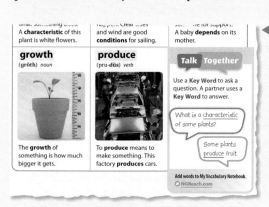

National Geographic Reach uses scaffolds word learning with
- visuals
- context
- student-friendly definitions
- oral language activities

In contrast with these common practices, *National Geographic Reach* emphasizes a much deeper and more sustained approach to vocabulary instruction. This approach is appropriate for all students, but is particularly suited and designed for English learners, many of whom lack deep knowledge of academic words and how to use them appropriately in academic discussion and writing.

Vocabulary instruction in *National Geographic Reach* features extended and multi-faceted exposure to support academic vocabulary learning. The program focuses on thematic units that incorporate academic vocabulary and content vocabulary in the domains of science, social studies and math. Using these content-rich materials, lessons promote vocabulary learning through rich oral language instruction and repeated opportunities for students to use the words in listening, speaking, reading and writing. A strong focus on collaborative learning ensures that students have many opportunities to incorporate the words as part of their overall developing English language skills.

This rich vocabulary instruction follows a step-by-step cycle to ensure that it is a cumulative process that provides multiple scaffolded exposures, across contexts, to vocabulary words. Key vocabulary is presented in colorful and motivating formats in the student

Part 1 Vocabulary Skills Trace		Page
Day 1	Social Studies Vocabulary	T5
Day 2	Academic Vocabulary	T7
Day 3	Expand Word Knowledge	T10b
Day 4	Share Word Knowledge	T24b
Day 5	Apply Word Knowledge	T25b
Day 6	Multiple-Meaning Words	T26
Day 7	Multiple-Meaning Words	T31
Days 8–9	Extend Vocabulary	T32e–f
Day 10	Vocabulary Review	T32h

A consistent 10-day plan provides frequent, varied opportunities for students to acquire and use vocabulary words and vocabulary strategies.

books. These words are introduced at the start of the 10-day lesson cycle using predictable routines in which students gain an initial understanding of the words and assess their own knowledge of them. As the lesson cycle progresses, students gain increasingly deeper knowledge of the words as they use them in multiple contexts.

Language learning is rich in songs, games, role-play, and colorful visuals. Older children learn key vocabulary through graphics, word webbing, and other research-based word-learning strategies. Oral language development and discussion plays an integral role in this teaching; *National Geographic Reach* focuses on oral language development to give students the words to talk about their ideas and about key academic information. Throughout the program, language frames are taught so students can use comparative expression. This practice using language helps with vocabulary learning and academic success.

Language Frames
- _____ is _____ .
- But _____ is _____ .
- _____ need _____ .
- And so do _____ .

In order to engage students with meaningful learning, throughout *National Geographic Reach* teachers are asked to encourage students to share what they already know about each word and how it relates to their experiences, while also asking teachers to model their own personal connections to words. By allowing students to practice using words in many contexts, in their speech and in writing, students will better understand all the ways that the words can be used and have time to grapple with shades of meaning.

❷ We need to focus carefully on the words we choose to teach

When we do spend time on vocabulary instruction, we need to make sure that we're making the most of that time to improve students' language and comprehension skills for success in all content areas. A crucial step to achieving this goal revolves around the words we choose to teach. This is especially important when teaching students, such as ELLs, with low vocabularies who need to learn lots of words deeply. Because truly knowing all levels and meanings of a word is a complex process, there is a growing consensus that vocabulary instruction should focus on deeply understanding a relatively small number of words.

We can't possibly "cover" or "teach" all the words students need to learn, but we can choose a set of words students need to be academically successful and then use those as a platform for teaching word-learning, for increasing academic talk, and for promoting more strategic reading of text. We call these words high-utility words.

This focus on high-utility words often represents a shift from current or past classroom practice and educational programs. Often these approaches have emphasized low-frequency, rare words (e.g., glint, burrowed) that appear in a given passage. These words can be relatively unimportant when we stack them up against all of the words that our ELLs and their classmates need to read for understanding.

For that reason, effective vocabulary instruction, such as that featured in *Reach*, must focus on high-impact academic words (e.g., debate, characteristic, observe) that are required for comprehending content and concepts. Spending precious instructional time on the deep learning of general-purpose academic words is much more valuable than targeting the low-frequency, rare words. In every unit, *Reach* focuses on teaching three sets of high-impact words, all of which represent key concepts:

- **Content vocabulary** The content words correspond with the unit's theme and are classified by subject area and are central to effective standards-based instruction. Examples of science vocabulary include habitat and root; examples of social studies vocabulary include immigration and globe; and examples of math vocabulary include equation and sum.
- **General-purpose academic words** These can be thought of as "delivery" words—the words that surround or are used to "deliver" the content. Examples of these words include balance, evidence, and solution.
- **Classroom vocabulary** In addition to high-utility academic and content area words, *Reach* focuses on important words that are specific to classroom procedures and skill instruction and that are essential for students to know for success in the classroom. Examples of these words are sequence and inference.

In addition to these three categories, *Reach* also provides support for teaching basic English words and concepts to newcomers and other students who are at the beginning levels of English acquisition.

❸ We also need to teach word-learning strategies

As noted above, we can't possibly "cover" or "teach" all the words students need to learn, so we also need to equip them with strategies to try to figure out the meaning of an unfamiliar word they encounter while reading. Students need to be directly instructed on how to figure out unfamiliar words. They are constantly coming up against words that they don't know in texts. They could skip them and potentially lose overall meaning, or be more constructive and pull the words apart, dig deeply enough to find a helpful context clue, think

of a related word that looks the same, or think about when they have heard the word before. What the student does at those crossroads will be determined by the strategies she has in her toolkit.

Teaching ELLs word-learning strategies provides them with an opportunity to develop their academic vocabulary skills and, in turn, to work through challenging text. *National Geographic Reach* texts, lessons, and student activities were designed with these principles in mind; the program includes a strong focus on word-learning strategies, so that students will gain the cognitive tools they need to learn a large number of words independently. The instruction focused on word-learning strategies takes many forms, including using context clues, analyzing word parts and root words for meaning, and practicing working with suffixes, prefixes, and affixes. These strategies need to become part of our ELLs' toolkits for oral language development and, ultimately, promote their reading comprehension skills.

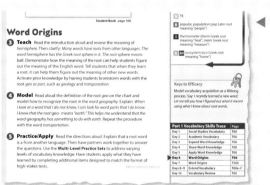

◄ **Word learning strategies give students the skills they need to learn a large number of words independently.**

Conclusion

In order to be academically successful, students must leave high school with a working understanding of about 50,000 words; greater vocabulary leads to greater comprehension, better comprehension also leads to learning more vocabulary words. Therefore, if we are to equip our ELLs for school success, a central part of instruction must focus on vocabulary learning. In the 21st century classroom, vocabulary teaching has to play a greater role and take up more instructional time than it has in years past (or than it typically has); this teaching must focus on a combination of direct instruction in high-utility words, across contexts and across a multi-day lesson cycle, and instruction in word-learning strategies. Good vocabulary teaching involves a lot of oral and written practice working with words, and it also involves giving students the language to talk about the concepts they know and to craft their explanations and arguments.

Jennifer D. Turner, Ph.D., University of Maryland

Jennifer D. Turner teaches reading education, and multicultural literature and instruction for reading specialists. She has published on exemplary literacy teachers and teaching for African American elementary students. Recently, Turner received the Elva Knight Research Grant from the International Reading Association for her work with new reading teachers in urban elementary schools. Jennifer serves as a co-editor of the Literacy Leaders department for *The Reading Teacher*.

NGReach.com ▸ **Download Professional Development Podcasts**

(((**MP3**))) Listen to Jennifer Turner share more information on assessment.

Know What They Know *by Jennifer Turner*

We all know that good assessment is the cornerstone of good instruction for English language learners (ELLs). Lately, however, teachers seem to have become increasingly frustrated with their current assessment systems. Teachers often collect huge amounts of data on their ELLs, but they don't know how to interpret it. Other teachers are overwhelmed by the data they collect, and they spend hours trying to figure out how the scores relate to the lessons that they are planning. It's not uncommon for teachers to say that they feel as if they are literally "drowning" in assessment data. So what can teachers do?

Conduct purposeful assessments

Assessment is not a one-size-fits-all process, so teachers need to know how to use assessment data for a number of different purposes. First, teachers use assessment data to diagnose students' needs and strengths (Schumm & Argüelles, 2006). Teachers can use assessments to determine areas of difficulty for students, including language, reading, and writing development, or to identify gaps in their content knowledge. In addition to identifying student needs, it is important that teachers gather and interpret assessment data in ways that illuminate the strengths that ELLs bring to the classroom (Au, 2006; Schumm & Argüelles, 2006). Dong (2006/2007) reminds us that ELLs are often extremely bright; however, they may have some difficulties expressing their knowledge because they are still learning to speak, write, and think in English. As a result, teachers must be careful not to interpret assessment results in ways that undermine ELLs' cultural background, or underestimate their cognitive, literacy, or linguistic capabilities (Au, 2006).

Second, and related to this first point, teachers need to use assessment data to inform their instructional planning and decision-making (Afflerbach, 2007; Edwards, Turner, & Mokhtari, 2008). Teachers assess students' background knowledge and strategies to make appropriate choices about materials and to form groups. Teachers use frequent, in-the-moment assessments to adjust their instruction based on students' understanding and engagement.

Teachers may also assess students' understanding after instructional lessons to determine if particular skills or concepts need to be retaught. Using assessment to guide classroom instruction is critical, because all students, including ELLs, learn within different zones of proximal development (Vygotsky, 1978). Teachers work with ELLs in their zones of proximal development by starting with children's independent level and moving them to higher levels of performance through scaffolding. To understand ELLs' learning levels, and the kinds of scaffolding needed to help them expand their reach, teachers must conduct comprehensive and systematic assessments.

Finally, teachers use assessments to monitor ongoing student learning. Teachers use a variety of formal and informal assessment measures to document ELLs' growth in English language, literacy, and content knowledge, as well as to highlight areas for improvement. Teachers use this data to provide useful information to parents about their child's achievement and development, which can strengthen home-school connections (Schumm & Argüelles, 2006). Teachers can also use this assessment data to communicate more effectively with ESL teachers and other specialists, and to create greater instructional coherence for ELLs across general and English language education programs.

How can teachers find out what ELLs know?

The ***National Geographic Reach*** program has been built on six research-based principles that help teachers assess what their English Language Learners know and need to learn:
1. Integrate English language and literacy assessments
2. Look at and listen to ELLs
3. Pair process and product measures to assess content knowledge
4. Identify learner differences
5. Integrate authentic and test-oriented assessments
6. Orchestrate opportunities for ELLs' self-assessment

1. **Integrate English language and literacy assessments.**
Assessing children's proficiency in English provides critical information for classroom teachers. Second language development is uneven, and teachers need to make certain that the learning environment and instruction are comprehensible to ELLs at their own proficiency levels (Au, 2006; August & Shanahan, 2006). Crosson and Lesaux (in press) recommend that teachers use English oral language proficiency assessments to generate an understanding of ELLs' development rather than to develop broad profiles based on skill level (e.g., students having "low" or "high" language skills).

In the literacy domain, teachers can use the same effective measures to assess ELLs because all children, including native English speakers, are developing phonemic awareness, phonics, comprehension, vocabulary, and fluency (Au, 2006; August & Shanahan, 2006). Assessing foundational skills with multiple measures is important because English literacy learning is both multidimensional and complex (Crosson & Lesaux, in press). For example, teachers may use early literacy assessments to gauge ELLs' print awareness, phonological awareness, and letter-word identification, but these measures do not provide adequate information about their oral language proficiency, vocabulary knowledge, and/or listening and reading comprehension levels (Crosson & Lesaux, in press). In addition, recent research has shown that text-reading fluency is not a reliable indicator of reading comprehension for ELLs, so teachers need to supplement fluency measures with vocabulary assessments to create a more comprehensive profile of students' English literacy skills (Lesaux & Kieffer, in press).

National Geographic Reach offers an English language assessment which teachers can use to determine ELLs' proficiency levels (i.e., beginner, intermediate, advanced, or advanced high) for differentiated instruction. By administering the language proficiency assessment as a pre- and post-measure, teachers can also evaluate the gains that ELLs make in their English language proficiency within a particular unit. In addition, every unit in *National Geographic Reach* incorporates a rich array of English literacy assessments. For example, the Comprehension Coach is an online tool which enables teachers to monitor students' oral reading fluency in English. Most importantly, teachers have multiple opportunities to gauge ELLs' comprehension and vocabulary knowledge before, during, and after the text is read. Because these literacy skills are embedded within rich, academic conversations and writing activities, teachers can also monitor ELLs' conversational and academic English language development.

2. **Look at and listen to ELLs.** Teachers can gather a wealth of information about ELLs by simply observing them and listening to them in the classroom. Goodman (2002) uses the term "kidwatching" to characterize the kind of ongoing, interpretive professional observations made by classroom teachers. By watching a young child who is learning English read a book, for example, teachers can determine his or her knowledge of concepts of print (e.g., reading from left to right, title). Teachers can also attain substantive information from ELLs by talking with them (Frey & Hiebert, 2002). Questioning, for example, is one form of assessment that many teachers are familiar with and constantly use in their classrooms. Research has shown that questions which are intended for specific purposes, use simplistic language and sentence structure, and provoke critical thinking are highly effective for assessing ELLs (Dong, 2006/2007; Schumm & Argüelles, 2006).

National Geographic Reach helps teachers to maximize the information obtained through observation and dialogue with ELLs. Each lesson includes questioning frameworks which support English language, literacy, and content learning. By asking a rich array of literal, inferential, personal and critical questions in the Talk Together sections, teachers can gauge ELLs' comprehension, vocabulary knowledge, and critical responses to fiction and informational texts. *National Geographic Reach* units are also structured to provide teachers with the flexibility to observe ELLs working independently, in pairs, small groups, and in whole group settings, and to listen in on their discussions.

3. **Pair process and product measures to assess content knowledge.** According to Afflerbach (2007), students' content knowledge can be gauged using two types of assessments. *Process assessments* help to illuminate the processes of student learning and development. Elementary teachers may use a K-W-L graphic organizer as a process assessment because it helps them to determine students' background knowledge about a topic, their interest level and motivation to read, and the reading strategies for comprehending and attaining new information. *Product assessments* demonstrate students' learning and mastery. Unit tests, written compositions, and projects may serve as product assessments because they help teachers to evaluate student learning.

National Geographic Reach offers a number of process and product assessments. Each unit incorporates process assessments, such as the Thinking Map and the Concept Map, to help teachers understand how ELLs are organizing and learning new content, and communicating their understanding in verbal and written form. Process assessments related to the Strategic Reading component give teachers information about the skills and strategies that ELLs are using to understand content-rich selections. In addition, Unit Wrap-Up projects serve as product assessments which highlight ELLs' mastery of important academic content and language.

4. **Identify learner differences.** ELLs are not a monolithic group. Children who are learning English often represent a number of cultural and ethnic groups. For example, while a number of children in a classroom may speak Spanish, they may have emigrated from countries as diverse as Mexico, Argentina,

and Spain. Research has demonstrated that students' English language and literacy attainment are shaped by a number of sociocultural factors, including family experience and schooling in the home country, immigration experiences, and heritage language proficiency (Goldenberg, Rueda, & August, 2006). In addition, children who are learning English have personal interests, preferences, and attitudes which shape their engagement in language and literacy learning (Krashen, 1987). Consequently, teachers can determine which instructional materials and activities are motivating for ELLs by using assessments to learn about their cultural and personal backgrounds.

National Geographic Reach helps teachers to learn more about ELLs' cultural and linguistic heritage. Units and lessons feature high-quality fiction and informational texts which focus on diversity. Global perspectives are also highlighted in a number of selections. As ELLs discuss these diverse texts, make personal connections, and share their family and community experiences, teachers can discover new insights about their cultural backgrounds. Affective measures in the *National Geographic Reach* program, such as interest surveys, also provide multiple opportunities for teachers to gather information about ELLs' reading preferences in and out of school.

Home Connection: Recipes

Explain that potatoes were developed thousands of years ago by native peoples of South America. Today potatoes are an important food everywhere in the world. Remind students about **Family Newsletter 3,** which asked them to collect favorite recipes for potatoes. Gather the recipes in a class Potato Cookbook.

◀ **Home Connection features help teachers understand students' cultural backgrounds and family experiences.**

5. **Integrate authentic and test-oriented assessments.** Teachers can glean a substantial amount of information about ELLs' language, literacy, and content development through authentic assessments. Authentic assessments are not only aligned with the curriculum, but they also emphasize real-world learning and task performance (Au, 2006). At the same time, ELLs need additional exposure to the "culture of testing" because they may not be familiar with the materials, procedures, and language demands related to high stakes testing (Afflerbach, 2007).

National Geographic Reach offers teachers a number of authentic measures, such as rubrics for performance-based projects (e.g., Theme Theater, writing projects), which help teachers gauge ELLs' reading, writing, and grammar development. Children who are learning English also have

multiple opportunities to engage with electronic print (e.g., emails, blogs), which teachers can use to ascertain their familiarity with technology. Equally important, teachers can evaluate their ELLs' knowledge about the questioning formats common in formal testing using the test-taking strategy components within each lesson, as well as the end-of-unit tests.

Describing a Story Rubric		
Scale	Content	Language
B	☐ Misses many characters ☐ Does not give details about characters	☐ Frequently hard to hear or understand ☐ Often seems uncomfortable with the describing task
I	☐ Covers some story characters ☐ Gives some details about characters	☐ Can be understood some of the time ☐ Seems somewhat comfortable with the describing task
A	☐ Covers most characters in the story ☐ Gives details about characters	☐ Can be understood most of the time ☐ Seems comfortable with the describing task
AH	☐ Covers all important story characters ☐ Gives many details about characters	☐ Speaks clearly and is easily understood ☐ Seems very comfortable with the describing task

◀ **Rubrics help teachers evaluate students' development in multiple areas including reading, and language. Rubrics also can be used to help students assess their own progress as learners.**

6. **Orchestrate opportunities for ELLs' self-assessment.** Sometimes teachers forget that students also need to assess their own learning in school. Self-assessments hold many important benefits for students. When ELLs and their classmates use self-assessments, they take control of their own language and literacy learning, and they achieve greater ownership of critical skills and strategies and build their confidence (Johnston, 2005; Turner & Kim, 2005).

Tools embedded within the *National Geographic Reach* program provide students the opportunity to document their growth in English language, literacy, and content. Each unit provides students with a rubric which enables them to determine what topics they know well and where they need continued support. Also, *National Geographic Reach* lessons include a number of activities (e.g., Writing Projects, Respond and Extend) and artifacts (e.g., Thinking Maps) which help ELLs develop metacognitive awareness.

Conclusion

It is not enough for teachers to assess ELLs for accountability purposes. Teachers not only need to know how to collect pertinent data on students' learning and development, but they must understand how to interpret the data and use it to make appropriate instructional decisions. Using the *National Geographic Reach* program, teachers can responsively assess the ELLs in their classroom, and use the information to design tailored and effective learning environments and instruction.

Lada Kratky, M.A.

Lada Kratky is a bilingual educator and featured national speaker. She has authored several Spanish reading programs including *Alfarrimas;* the phonics programs, *Phonics and Friends;* and the ESL series *Avenues.*

NGReach.com ▶ **Download Professional Development Podcasts**

(((**MP3**))) Listen to Lada Kratky share more about effective teaching routines and strategies.

Make Every Minute Count! *by Lada Kratky*

One great difficulty facing today's teachers of English language learners (ELLs) is lack of time. Juggling curriculum demands, which include large blocks of time for language arts, math, science, and social studies, teachers may find they have little time left to address the needs of their ELLs. However, if ELLs fall behind, the gap grows wider, making it difficult for them to catch up. How can teachers find enough time to teach everything their ELLs need? They can

1. Integrate ESL with content-area instruction
2. Use predictable routines
3. Plan and maintain the pace of instruction

❶ Integrate ESL with content-area instruction

Today's educators and districts have recognized an urgent need for a shift from traditional ESL programs to one that addresses concept and vocabulary development, especially in the content areas. Teaching social language basic English is not enough to improve student achievement. ESL programs must address the vocabulary needs that will enable ELLs to succeed in mainstream and content area classes. Language and literacy demands permeate every aspect of the school day. Instruction in language development must address the range of subjects and contexts ELLs experience to truly support and enhance their performance in the mainstream classroom.

National Geographic Reach features robust science and social studies units that also address the language needs of ELLs, with a strong concentration on vocabulary development. This content-based ESL approach merges needed language instruction with the content areas. Using *National Geographic Reach*, standards for language and for science or social studies can be addressed together during ESL time or during the content area block. Covering these standards together saves the teacher valuable classroom time and supports improved achievement for ELL students.

> *How can teachers find enough time to teach everything their ELLs need?*

❷ Use predictable classroom routines

Teaching time is often lost in classrooms when transitions and organizational tasks take more time than necessary. If students are unready to line up for lunch, the lining up process takes extra time. It may take five or six minutes for students to get ready for a writing task, when they could possibly be ready in a minute or two. These kinds of transitions may cost only a few minutes each, but over the course of a day or week they can add up to significant amounts of time lost. One way for teachers to save time is to establish consistent procedures or routines for transitions, so that when the teacher signals the transition, students know what is expected and can be ready promptly for the next activity.

Instructional routines also offer many opportunities to streamline classroom procedures and save time. When instruction follows predictable patterns, students can prepare themselves quickly for lessons. They don't need to spend time or attention figuring out the lesson process, so they are more able to focus on the content being taught. The instruction in *National Geographic Reach* follows predictable patterns. Lessons are consistently organized in the following steps:

Teach: The teacher explains what is to be learned
Model: The teacher models the skill students are expected to learn
Practice: Students practice the skill with support
Apply: Students apply the skill on their own.

National Geographic Reach also makes extensive use of instructional routines. These are simple learning procedures that follow a series of regular steps. Vocabulary, for example, is taught using a series of specific routines on successive days of the lesson cycle. As noted, *National Geographic Reach* emphasizes academic and content vocabulary. This focus implies a natural shift in methodology. It is no longer enough for students to simply hear the word followed by its definition and then use it in a sentence. Vocabulary instruction includes introducing the words, expanding word knowledge, sharing word knowledge, reteaching vocabulary, and providing additional vocabulary experiences.

Part 1 Vocabulary Skills Trace		Page
Day 1	Social Studies Vocabulary	T5
Day 2	Academic Vocabulary	T7
Day 3	Expand Word Knowledge	T10b
Day 4	Share Word Knowledge	T24b
Day 5	Apply Word Knowledge	T25b
Day 6	Multiple-Meaning Words	T26
Day 7	Multiple-Meaning Words	T31
Days 8–9	Extend Vocabulary	T32e–f
Day 10	Vocabulary Review	T32h

▶ **Vocabulary instruction makes use of a consistent set of research-based routines.**

- **Introduce the words** To introduce a word, the teacher pronounces it and points to a picture or diagram that depicts it. Immediately, students are asked to react to the word by rating it; they show if they know the word well, a little, or not at all, by showing one, two, or three fingers. They then share what they know about it. The teacher will give students a friendly definition of the word and use the picture dictionary to further illustrate the word. He/she then further elaborates the meaning of the word, relating it to personal experience, and encouraging the students to share their own experience. The students are motivated through questions or comments to discuss the word. This discussion will help students understand the word and its uses even further. In addition, the word will be analyzed by pointing out its parts and spelling patterns that will help the students recognize the word. Finally, the students can connect the word to other content areas, and the teacher can put it up on the Word Wall.

- **Expand word knowledge** On the next day, the students expand their word knowledge through the use of discussion, graphic organizers, drawing, and writing. The students are grouped in pairs, and each pair will become an expert on one word. The teacher then shows how to complete a graphic organizer. The graphic organizer is displayed, the teacher writes the word, adds a picture, definition, and content sentence. Each pair of students then completes the task using their Key Word and a similar graphic organizer. Becoming an expert builds depth of word knowledge, enhances word-learning strategies, and builds confidence and collaboration.

- **Share word knowledge** On the following day, students share their knowledge of the word they have been studying. Each students is paired with a partner who has been working on a different word than their own. They take turns reading to each other from their Graphic Organizers. As partners, they proceed to discuss and write sentence using both words they are studying. They write the sentences in their journal and underline the Key Words. The teacher forms cooperative learning groups and the activity is repeated until each Key Word has been entered into the students' journals. Once again, the activity provides opportunities for academic talk, practice with word-learning strategies, and increased opportunities for collaboration and a sense of ownership for learning.

- **Practice and reteach vocabulary** The words are then reviewed or retaught to students who did not master them. Content and Academic Vocabulary is embedded into reading, discussion, and teaching activities throughout the unit providing multiple exposures. During reteaching, the teacher says each word and asks the students to repeat it. Then he/she will teach the meaning, read the definition and use different words to elaborate on the meaning. He/she will make connections, giving examples of when the word can be used. The students record the word in their journal, discuss the sounds and spelling, and work further on the word by making a word map, drawing a picture to illustrate it, writing a definition, writing a sentence with the word, or writing its translation in the student's home language.

In addition to these steps, students can participate in a number of additional vocabulary practice and extension routines, including games such as Bingo! and activities such as word sorts and vocabulary skits.

Beyond vocabulary, *National Geographic Reach* uses consistent routines for reading, writing, structured responses, and cooperative learning. Many other steps in the lesson plan also follow predictable patterns; for example, **Language of the Day** and **Preview and Build Background** follow the same steps each time they occur. Features such as **Multi-Level Strategies** and **Academic Language Frames** appear in consistent places in the lesson plan. The content changes according to the instructional objective, but the format is consistent. Here again, because students know the format, they can concentrate on the content, and they need less time to get oriented to the task.

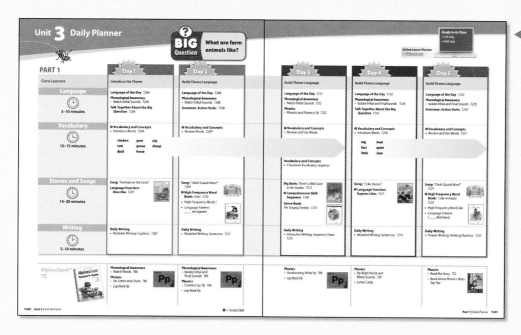

Day-by-day pacing and planning guides provide a clear pathway.

③ Plan and maintain the pace of instruction

Teachers of ELLs sometimes tend to slow down the pace of classroom instruction, thinking that their students need extra time. However, current research and practice suggest that most ELLs respond positively when teachers maintain an energetic classroom pace. Maintaining an energetic pace conveys valuable messages to students, including:

- The work of learning is important and engaging.
- The teacher has confidence in students' ability.
- There is a lot to cover and no time to waste.

Teachers who shift to a more energetic classroom pace frequently find that:

- Their ELL students are much better able to keep up with the pace than the teacher expected.
- Students who were disengaged often become more involved and interested.
- Teachers themselves enjoy the more rapid pace.

Picking up the pace of instruction means that there is more time to cover all the standards that ESL teachers are responsible for. It also often means a more enjoyable classroom experience for both students and teacher.

Planning a daily schedule is an important part of maintaining an appropriate classroom pace. The Lesson Planner in each unit of the *National Geographic Reach* Teacher's Editions clarifies the sequence of instruction and provides suggested time frames for each part of the lesson plan. Daily activities are related, and instruction flows naturally—which supports teachers in planning efficient use of time. For example, songs or chants introduce concepts and vocabulary. These lead to a formal introduction of vocabulary. Students work with graphic organizers and thinking maps to expand their understanding. They read, discuss, and further develop concepts. With teachers or peers, they engage in activities that improve academic and oral language proficiency, content knowledge, and reading comprehension.

The Online Planner makes it even easier for the teacher to organize and schedule lessons to suit the needs of her or his particular classroom. Using this tool, teachers can select specific activities, adapt the sequence of the lesson plan, or reorganize lessons to align with what students are learning in other classes.

The Online Planner includes pre-made lesson plans for various instructional models and can be personalized.

Conclusion

Most ESL teachers face the challenge of having too much to cover in the available class time. This article suggests three ways class time can be maximized:

- integrate ESL instruction with the content areas
- use predictable classroom routines
- plan and maintain the pace of instruction

National Geographic Reach provides resources to support teachers in each of these areas. With *Reach*, teachers are able to use class time more efficiently to achieve their ultimate goal: the academic success and growth of their students.

Jennifer D. Turner, Ph.D., University of Maryland

Jennifer D. Turner teaches reading education, and multicultural literature and instruction for reading specialists. She has published on exemplary literacy teachers and teaching for African American elementary students. Recently, Turner received the Elva Knight Research Grant from the International Reading Association for her work with new reading teachers in urban elementary schools. Jennifer serves as a co-editor of the Literacy Leaders department for *The Reading Teacher*.

NGReach.com ▶ **Download Professional Development Podcasts**

(((MP3))) Listen to Jennifer Turner share more information on meeting individual needs.

Get to Know Your Learners *by Jennifer Turner*

Every year, thousands of children who are learning English stream into elementary classrooms across the country. But not all classrooms are created equal. In some classrooms, English language learners (ELLs) seem to be lost; these students sit by themselves, rarely talk or interact with other students, make few attempts to open their books or join into classroom discussions, and gaze silently at the teacher during instruction. In other classrooms, however, ELLs seem to "fit into" the flow of classroom life; they are willing to communicate with other students and with the teacher, they take risks to participate in classroom conversations, and they are much more engaged with books and other reading materials during instruction.

What makes some classrooms inviting for ELLs and not others? A key factor is the classroom community that teachers and students work together to develop throughout the year. Classroom communities are dynamic learning environments that are rich in social relationships, promote collective agency and responsibility in learning, and foster collaborations involving talking, listening, reading, writing and thinking (Rousculp & Maring, 1992). Research has shown that while classroom communities are effective environments for all learners, they are particularly critical for the language and literacy development of ELLs. Classroom communities provide a safe environment for ELLs to take intellectual risks and to "play" with language (Fitzgerald, 1993; Turner & Kim, 2005). Consistent instructional routines, such as choral reading or interactive writing, help elementary ELLs to become familiar with the kinds of reading and writing valued within the classroom community, and to take ownership of those literate practices (Au, 2006; Kim & Turner, 2006). As a result, ELLs often want to "get into the action" of the classroom community, because they feel a sense of responsibility for their classmates' learning as well as their own (Day, 2002).

> *To build classroom community, teachers must take the initiative to establish and maintain strong social relationships with students.*

Personal relationships are the heart of vibrant classroom communities. To build classroom community, elementary teachers must take the initiative to establish and maintain strong social relationships with students (Kim & Turner, 2006). In these classrooms, teachers don't just learn about their ELLs on their first day of school; rather, they are committed to getting to know <u>all</u> their students throughout the year. Research has shown that teachers must get to know the ELLs in their classroom in five important ways:

1. Get to know them as **Language** Learners
2. Get to know them as **Literacy** Learners
3. Get to know them as **Content** Learners
4. Get to know them as **Cultural** Learners
5. Get to know them as **Digital** Learners

❶ Get to know them as language learners

It is important for elementary teachers to recognize that ELLs are acquiring proficiency in two forms of English language in classroom communities (Cummins, 2000). Conversational language enables students to communicate in a variety of informal ways, and represents the kinds of "social talk" that students use in the lunchroom and on the playground. In contrast, academic language is formalized English that is conceptual, abstract, and content-oriented. For ELLs, learning academic English language is much more cognitively demanding. Research has shown that while children can acquire conversational English language in 1–2 years, it can take 5–7 years for them to acquire proficiency in academic English (Collier, 1989).

Teachers not only need to know about their students' conversational and academic language knowledge, but they need to understand how these children have developed English language knowledge in schools. Some children may have been in Sheltered

English Immersion (SEI) classrooms, some may have been in English pullout programs in their schools, while others may have participated in bilingual programs that foster development in their home languages as well as English. Teachers may also discover that some of their students have had very little formal schooling in their home countries, or that their schooling in the United States has been extremely fragmented. As elementary teachers get to know the language histories of their ELLs, they can use this information to strategically build connections to these students' prior linguistic knowledge.

National Geographic Reach can help teachers to enhance their students' English language development. Instructional activities are implemented through a rich variety of collaborative formats, such as partner work, small groups, and whole class discussion, which build ELLs' conversational and academic English proficiency. *Reach* also provides scaffolding for students with a range of language proficiency levels in order to build their confidence and to support active participation within the classroom community.

◀ Literature includes a wide variety of fiction and nonfiction.

2 Get to know them as literacy learners

Good readers, including those who are learning English, need a variety of literacy skills, including phonemic awareness, phonics, vocabulary, oral reading fluency, comprehension, writing, and spelling (August & Shanahan, 2006; Shanahan & Beck, 2006). Elementary teachers, then, must get to know their students as literacy learners in order to orchestrate multiple opportunities for learning, developing, and mastering English literacy skills. For example, teachers must adjust their literacy instruction to accommodate children who are biliterate and can read and write in their primary language as well as those whose literacy skills are emergent in their home language (Fitzgerald, 1993).

We know that all elementary students have varied literacy preferences, learning styles, and literacy strengths and needs, and ELLs are no exception. Children may share similar home languages, such as Spanish or Korean, and yet their literacy backgrounds may be completely different. Some children who are learning English, for example, may prefer to read fairy tales or mysteries, while others may become engrossed with informational texts about volcanoes or insects. Outside of school, some ELLs may avidly read video game manuals, while others may enjoy writing letters to family members back in their home countries. Teachers must get to know the literacy interests of all children, including those who are learning English, in order to understand how to address their unique literacy strengths and needs, and to enhance their motivation to read, write, and talk within the classroom community.

National Geographic Reach offers elementary English learners a wide variety of fiction and nonfiction texts. Genres highlighted in *Reach* include realistic fiction, science articles, photo essays, poetry, and folktales. Lessons provide ELLs with multiple opportunities to experience the process of "becoming readers and writers in English" through text-based activities embedded within rich oral language contexts, such as singing songs, joining in choral reading, and composing texts. *Reach* also offers Libraries for additional

reading. Providing students with the ability to choose texts and extend reading and learning enhances motivation and accelerates the acquisition of new skills and knowledge. At the same time, lessons feature Language Frames, which offer children ways of thinking about and understanding higher-order comprehension skills and reading strategies, such as summarizing or visualizing, in English. Importantly, *National Geographic Reach* encourages ELLs to not only acquire new literacy skills that will help them to become strategic readers and writers, but this program encourages them to actively use these skills through performances like Theme Theater and other dramatic skits, and through collaborative writing projects.

3 Get to know them as content learners

Schools have not traditionally viewed children who are learning English as "content learners." In fact, the curriculum for children who are learning English has often emphasized low-level content, language, and literacy skills in English (Au, 2006). A number of programs for ELLs have focused on discrete parts of the English language (e.g., nouns, verbs) and/or isolated grammatical skills rather than on higher-order processes such as comprehension, summarization, or composition (Fitzgerald, 1993). Often schools have provided ELLs with a less demanding curriculum because their expectations for these children are extremely low, given that these students may have limited content knowledge or vocabulary knowledge in English (Fitzgerald, 1993).

However, students who are learning English need and deserve a curriculum that covers basic language and is content-rich and rigorous. Research has shown that ELLs can learn academic content when teachers effectively build their background knowledge and enhance their content vocabularies (Fitzgerald, 1993). When teachers get to know their ELLs, they begin to realize that while these students may have difficulty expressing their thoughts and ideas in English, they do have strong critical thinking skills, and are fully capable of mastering material in the content areas (Dong, 2006/2007).

The units in *National Geographic Reach* are designed with a strong content focus that integrates science and social studies topics with English language and literacy skills (e.g., reading, writing, speaking, listening). Each unit centers on a Big Question that not only aligns with core content standards, but also encourages elementary ELLs to think critically about new ideas and concepts, express their ideas and interests, and inquire about their world.

4 Get to know them as cultural learners

Although students may be learning English in our elementary classroom communities, they do not come to us as "blank slates." Rather, these students do have cultural knowledge and experiences that may serve as resources for their English language, literacy, and content learning (Goldenberg, Rueda, & August, 2006). Teachers must get to know what ELLs and their families are doing in their homes, because many daily activities, including cooking, paying bills, and making grocery lists, support young children's knowledge about the purposes, meanings, and uses of language and literacy (Anderson & Stokes, 1984). Even if families are not primarily speaking English, the home language and literacy environments that they create for their young children are still important. Research has shown that using their first language does not confuse young children who are learning English in schools, and may have positive contributions to their English language and literacy development (August & Shanahan, 2006).

Cultural Perspectives

Explain that haiku is a form of poetry that started long ago in Japan and now people from many countries write them. Ask students to find words in these haiku that tell the reader they are from a modern time and place. Possible responses include modern words (*yum*); foods from different countries and cultures.

◀ **Cultural Perspectives highlight the rich variety of cultures and emphasize the positive value of cultural diversity in the classroom.**

National Geographic Reach features high-quality literature that represents people and places within a wide variety of cultural, racial, and ethnic communities. Primary languages are often incorporated into the selections in ways that affirm students' linguistic backgrounds, and multiethnic characters and storylines build on students' cultural funds of knowledge. By tapping into students' cultural knowledge and home literacy experiences, units are designed to enhance students' English language proficiency, literacy acquisition, and writing development. Importantly, *Reach* also helps children who are learning English to expand their understanding of the world by including a number of fiction and nonfiction texts written from a global perspective.

5 Get to know them as digital learners

Like many elementary students, children who are learning English are often exposed to and use technology in a variety of ways, including surfing the internet, using computers, and communicating through email, text messaging, and other electronic formats. However, for young children who are learning English, technology may be a particularly useful educational tool. Researchers have found that technology can enrich ELLs' language, literacy, and content knowledge (Medina-Jerez, Clark, Medina, & Ramirez-Marin, 2007; Ybarra & Green, 2003). Case and Truscott (1999), for example, observed that when students used computers for reading instruction, their sight word vocabulary, fluency, and comprehension improved. Using technology enabled students to engage more actively with texts, to receive immediate feedback on reading performances, and to gain additional practice.

Children who are learning English have extensive access to technology through *National Geographic Reach*. The online Comprehension Coach offers ELLs opportunities to practice fluent reading. *Reach* units also include a rich digital library and Build Background videos, which teachers can use to build students' background knowledge and to promote interest in the topic. Games and the Vocabulary Notebook create personalized, interactive learning and practice opportunities. In addition, many lessons feature technology-based texts, such as emails and blogs, to promote student engagement and to help students understand how English language and literacy skills can be used to communicate diverse perspectives to diverse audiences.

Conclusion

Children who are learning English are not a homogenous group. They come to elementary classrooms with varying critical thinking skills, different instructional histories, and varied interests, cultural backgrounds, and family experiences. Elementary teachers must get to know their ELLs as individual learners with diverse language strengths and needs, literacy interests and preferences, content knowledge bases, and cultural and technological resources, and use that knowledge to build classroom communities which inspire children to learn English language, literacy, and content. *National Geographic Reach* provides a rich array of resources to help teachers accomplish this goal.

Sylvia Linan-Thompson, Ph.D., University of Texas

Sylvia Linan-Thompson is an associate director of the National Research and Development Center on English Language. She has developed and examined reading interventions for struggling readers who are monolingual English speakers, English language learners and bilingual students acquiring Spanish literacy. Linan-Thompson has authored articles, and books on literacy instruction and teacher professional development topics.

⊘ NGReach.com ❯ Download Professional Development Podcasts

(((**MP3**))) Listen to Sylvia Linan-Thompson share more information on comprehension.

Build Strategic Thinking *by Sylvia Linan-Thompson*

We engage students in comprehension-building activities because we know that to learn and succeed academically, students must be able to actively construct meaning on a regular basis—while talking, listening, viewing, doing activities, and while reading. Comprehension is more than just understanding what you read; you must transform that understanding, communicate it, and use it to build new knowledge. Therefore, students have to be aware of their own understanding and they must possess strategies for accessing and organizing information that is presented in text. Further, to be able to communicate and build knowledge, students need to acquire not only new content or information but also the vocabulary and language and text structures associated with it. This is true whether we are reading for information, to perform a task, or for literary experience.

What makes comprehension a challenge for ELLs?

Because the ability to comprehend text depends on language, English language learners (ELLs) often experience difficulty with comprehension tasks even when they are able to decode and have adequate reading speed. August, Francis, Hsu, & Snow (2006) identified the following challenges faced by ELLs when they are learning to read for understanding:
- smaller English vocabularies
- less background knowledge relevant to the texts they encounter in U.S. schools
- less familiarity with mainstream language patterns
- reduced motivation and limited interest in school-assigned reading materials

The good news is that these areas that can be addressed by robust instruction and the use of materials that tap into ELLs' interests and reflect their cultural background. *National Geographic Reach* is designed to address these specific needs of ELLs and enable them to reach high levels of comprehension.

Vocabulary Development Earlier papers in this section have emphasized the importance of vocabulary development for ELLs. In addition to needing foundational reading skills, and decoding skills in particular, students need to be able to access word meaning quickly (Perfetti & Mezynski, 1983). They must be able to recognize words, retrieve word meanings, and identify and use affixed word forms quickly. ELLs' limited knowledge of word meanings may make it difficult for them to comprehend what they read. *National Geographic Reach* focuses on developing important academic and content vocabulary through a systematic lesson plan and instructional routines that provide repeated exposure to key words, their varying meanings, and the contexts in which they are used.

Background Knowledge Comprehension may also be impacted by limited background knowledge. Our knowledge of specific topics and of the words used in talking about them facilitate our understanding of texts on those topics. Like many English-speaking striving students, ELLs may have limited knowledge of some academic and content area topics. *National Geographic Reach* fosters exposure to a wide range of topics and provides students with multiple opportunities to develop background knowledge in the process. These opportunities include
- multimedia resources for building background
- kinesthetic and cooperative activities that tap prior knowledge and experience
- concept-focused, visual, and contextualized vocabulary resources
- frequent opportunities to listen to and engage in oral language activities
- frequent use of graphic organizers to organize, build, and share knowledge

Visual and multimedia ▶ **resources build background.**

Mainstream Discourse The way language is used in school and in academic communication may be unfamiliar to ELLs. They may need explicit and systematic instruction to learn how English is used in academic conversations, discussions, presentations, and similar contexts. *National Geographic Reach* includes an extensive oral language strand that models the conventions of mainstream discourse and supports students in learning to use them. Lessons include a wide variety of language frames that demonstrate the appropriate use of academic English and coach students in developing these skills.

Motivating Materials ELLs need materials that expose them to new cultures and ideas through engaging text using rich vocabulary. With its emphasis on expository text and attention to diversity, *National Geographic Reach* provides reading material that will engage students, give some an opportunity to see their cultural background, and give others a chance to learn about new cultures, all the while exposing students to big ideas and rich vocabulary that build conceptual knowledge. To ensure that students engage with and understand the texts they read, lessons include collaborative oral-language and writing activities that are implemented prior to, during, and after reading.

Designing instruction to meet ELLs' needs

In addition to addressing the issues discussed above, an effective program for ELLs must provide instruction that meets these students at their level and moves them forward in ways that develop their confidence and success. Scaffolding must include:

- pre-teaching of key vocabulary and concepts
- the use of think-alouds that show students how to monitor their understanding
- questioning strategies that engage and extend learning
- teaching students to use graphic organizers as frames for thinking about and organizing information
- explicit instruction and extended practice in reading strategies

National Geographic Reach incorporates all of these scaffolding strategies in the lesson plans for each unit. Key vocabulary is concept-driven. Words are selected that relate to key ideas that underlie all activities, including reading. By selecting words based on the concept rather than on a particular text, knowledge schema are developed before reading and revisited throughout the unit. Ideas and words encountered through reading can be integrated into that larger schema. Students have multiple opportunities to explore and revisit words and ideas, expanding their understanding across the unit. Academic vocabulary extends that understanding beyond the unit, focusing on high-utility words that are commonly used across a range of subject areas. Instruction consistently uses think-alouds to model for students the thinking processes that expert learners use. Questioning strategies are explicitly taught, and graphic organizers are used throughout the program to support students in thinking about and organizing information they are learning.

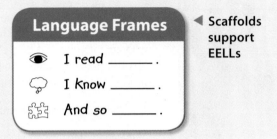

Focus on strategies

Strategies are plans we use and apply when hearing text that is read aloud or when reading independently. Strategies are not skills that can be taught by drill. They are complex procedures that provide an approach for completing a task. To use strategies effectively, students need to develop an awareness and understanding of the process, and then practice using the strategies with teacher assistance until they internalize the strategy and can master its application in reading, listening, viewing and other academic activities. They also need to learn when to use each strategy. *National Geographic Reach* focuses on seven key strategies to promote comprehension:

1. **Plan and Monitor Reading:** *Setting a clear purpose, predicting, checking predictions and understanding, and using "fix-up" strategies, if necessary*
2. **Determine Importance:** *identifying essential ideas and information*
3. **Ask Questions:** *interrogating texts for a variety of purposes*
4. **Visualize:** *forming sensory images*
5. **Make Connections:** *connecting information to yourself, the world, and connecting texts with other texts*
6. **Make Inferences:** *connecting ideas or information that the author does not explicitly link*
7. **Synthesize:** *putting ideas together to draw conclusions or make generalizations*

In the final unit of each level, *National Geographic Reach* focuses instruction on when and how to select strategies. Students who are strategic have tools that allow them to learn independently. Furthermore, strategic students learn to trust their own perceptions and to evaluate the quality of their products and the extent to which they have learned something. When they identify mistakes, they have tools to rectify them.

In addition to focused teaching of comprehension strategies, students need to learn about texts in order to understand them. Comprehension requires a full understanding of text structures, literary analysis skills, genre characteristics, and awareness of text features and how to use them. Building understanding of these skills before reading helps students know what to expect and better use the text to unlock key ideas and build understanding.

Teach with a gradual release of responsibility

According to Swanson (2001), successful teaching of strategies involves the following steps:

1. Explanation (systematic explanations, elaborations, and/or plans to direct task performance)
2. Modeling by teachers (verbal modeling, questioning, and demonstration)
3. Reminders to use specific strategies or procedures (cues, tactics, or procedures)
4. Step-by-step prompts or multi-process instructions
5. Dialogue (teacher and student talk back and forth)
6. Teacher asks questions to assure that students are applying the strategy
7. Teacher provides assistance or coaching only if necessary

As Fisher and Frey (2008) noted, this gradual release process involves a focus lesson ("I do it"), guided instruction ("We do it"), collaboration ("You do it together"), and finally independent application ("You do it alone").

Strategy instruction in *National Geographic Reach* follows these steps consistently.

Before reading, one strategy is introduced, helping students focus and develop the language and thinking to support strategic reading. They are connected to real-world examples to tap prior experience. They are then modeled by teachers. Clear instructions and language scaffolds are provided along with collaborative opportunities for students to practice and apply the steps of the strategy in short passages that integrate key vocabulary words. As students begin to read the selection, they are reminded to apply the strategy to the text.

As they read, supports are provided to build and apply reading strategies. **Before You Move On** questions scaffold the application of the strategy to the text. The gradual release model supports and scaffolds the application of the strategy through the Teacher's Edition. First the teacher models the strategy again, then he or she guides students in applying it, and finally students apply the strategy on their own, with support from the teacher only if needed. These steps include opportunities for students to discuss the application of the strategy with the teacher; further discussion takes place at the end of the unit when the class revisits the strategy learning experience. Companion selections and Leveled Library books are provided for further work with the strategy to help students apply strategies across multiple genres. In *National Geographic Reach*, strategies are taught in each level, so students' ability to use them grows increasingly sophisticated as they deal with more complex texts.

National Geographic Reach also uses the gradual release model for instruction in literary analysis skills and text structure. Before reading, concepts in literary analysis or text structure are tied to students' prior knowledge or experience and thinking maps (graphic organizers) are introduced, providing clear tools to scaffold the application of the skill. Guided practice and an opportunity for collaborative practice using a read aloud are provided before reading. During reading, the same scaffolds appear in the Student and Teacher materials, promoting gradual release of responsibility. After reading, students reread and use graphic organizers demonstrate their understanding of the literary analysis skill or text structure.

Conclusion

Reading comprehension presents significant challenges for many ELLs, who may have limited vocabulary and language knowledge that makes it harder for them to focus on the meaning of texts. Instructional materials for ELLs must be designed to provide the vocabulary, background, and language knowledge they need in order to comprehend their reading. In addition, materials must provide extensive instruction to help students develop reading skills and strategies that they can apply independently. *National Geographic Reach* provides motivational texts on a variety of topics, with rich vocabulary development and explicit instruction in comprehension strategies to assure that all ELLs can develop into skilled strategic readers and thinkers.

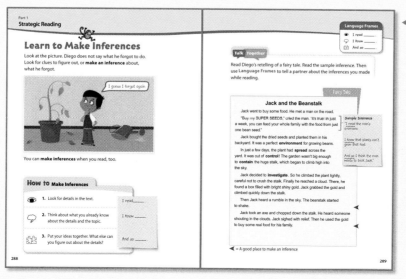

◀ Reading strategy instruction includes explanations, models, and scaffolded practice opportunities.

Nancy Frey, Ph.D., San Diego State University

Nancy Frey teaches in the San Diego State University teacher-credentialing and reading specialist programs focusing on reading instruction, content area literacy, and diverse student support. Frey has published in *The Reading Teacher, English Journal,* and *Educational Leadership.* Frey also co-authored *Checking for Understanding, Scaffolded Writing Instruction,* and *Learning Words Inside and Out.*

NGReach.com **Download Professional Development Podcasts**

(((**MP3**))) Listen to Nancy Frey share more information on technology.

Link to 21ˢᵗ Century Skills and Resources

by Nancy Frey

Peer over the shoulder of an elementary-aged child who is working on a computer and prepare to be amazed and a little intimidated. The children in today's classrooms have never known a time when the Internet did not exist, and have been raised in an environment where information is just as likely to be presented digitally as it is in print. When presented with an interesting question, they are as likely to turn to a computer or other device with a web browser as they are to look in a book. But this shift in learning is not confined to school-aged children. Increasingly, teachers of these same students have themselves experienced curriculum development as a digital process.

Professional organizations have united in their calls for a 21ˢᵗ century approach to education that broadens our approach to teaching, learning, and literacy. The International Reading Association (IRA) in 2009 called for literacy curricula that emphasize the use of print and digital technologies in learning. The IRA statement said that "students have the right to... teachers who use ICTs [information and communication technologies] skillfully for teaching and learning effectively" (IRA, 2009). The Partnership for 21ˢᵗ Century Learning Skills, a consortium of education and business organizations, states that the 21ˢᵗ century content must include "global awareness, financial, economic, business, and entrepreneurial literacy, civic literacy, and health and wellness awareness" (Partnership for 21ˢᵗ Century Learning Skills, 2009).

However, the development of 21ˢᵗ century learners who are also learning English can be complicated. Black (2008) asserts that "developing such proficiencies can pose an extra challenge for certain populations of students such as ELLs, if they are relegated to classroom contexts where the primary focus is mastery of traditional forms of print-based literacy." Access to 21ˢᵗ century learning experiences is also limited by access to the Internet. According to the Pew Internet and American Life Project, access to broadband is significantly lower in poorer households, among Hispanics, and in homes where English learners live, and access has declined in the last two years among this population due to cost (2008). This means that for English language learners (ELLs), the curriculum they use in school must focus on building the types of critical literacy needed for global communication. *National Geographic Reach* is designed to address this need in these important ways:

- building students' capacity for learning with technology
- supporting teachers' efforts in utilizing technology
- accentuating the content knowledge needed by 21ˢᵗ century learners

Student Learning in the 21ˢᵗ Century

Literacy and learning in the 21ˢᵗ century is shifting from an emphasis on the tools (e.g., computers, handheld devices, podcasts, networks) to processes. We know that the tools teachers and students use will continue to change at breathtaking speed. In fact, it is likely that by the time you read this paper, there will be new tools that did not exist when it was written. Today's educators understand the need to focus on the processes used by learners when utilizing technologies. All learners must know how to:

- search for information
- listen to and view information
- produce information
- store information
- share information
- present information (Fisher & Frey, in press)

National Geographic Reach is designed to develop these process skills with ELLs. Students using *Reach* search for information using both print-based and digital texts. They use print and technology to view and listen to information in a variety of formats, including videos, Digital Library images, eVisuals, interactive animations, digital and print versions of the Student Books, the Comprehension Coach, and other resources. Throughout the lessons in *National Geographic Reach*, students produce and store information through writing, graphic organizers, journals, tables, and charts. Writing genres include those needed for digital communication, such as emails and blogs. In each unit, students have many opportunities to share and present information with both small and large groups, in both formal and informal situations.

Social Learning in the 21st Century

Noted literacy researcher Paul Gee (2007) states that learning is socially constructed between people and requires them to probe, hypothesize, reprobe, and rethink. This process occurs in both face-to-face and digital environments. Evolving technology has made digital spaces increasingly interactive; users now expect to be able to dialogue, confer, and debate on any topic of interest. Whether in a classroom or a digital environment, students need the skills to ask questions, form opinions, ask more questions, and draw conclusions. Therefore, a curriculum designed to prepare 21st century learners must include ample opportunities for students to converse with their peers, ask questions, disagree, and formulate their own opinions.

The lessons in *National Geographic Reach* continually promote this kind of active learning and engagement. Students are involved daily in verbal and written discourse about ideas and information that impact their local communities and the world at large. *Reach* focuses on developing the academic language skills students need to discuss and exchange ideas, express opinions, and understand and present important concepts, in oral, written and digital formats.

Communication in the 21st Century

Both on- and offline experiences are necessary for students to become thoroughly literate in the 21st century. *National Geographic Reach* emphasizes the skills necessary for students to communicate and collaborate in both face-to-face and digital environments. Lessons include a variety of features that support ELLs in developing the academic language and academic vocabulary needed in effective verbal and written communication. These features include Academic Language Frames, Multi-Level Strategies, multiple exposures to important content area and academic vocabulary, and a scaffolded writing strand that models for students how to develop their ideas and express them in writing.

As Leu and colleagues (2009) note, "[o]nline reading and writing are so closely connected it is not possible to separate them; we read online as authors and write online as readers". The ability to do this requires that learners be immersed in the rich oral and written dialogue with others that *National Geographic Reach* embodies.

Reading and Writing in the 21st Century

Leu et al. (2009) state that the "self-directed text construction" of online reading experiences represents a shift from traditional print-based literacy. Students in an online environment move freely between texts to form understandings. Today's students need experiences with moving among a group of texts in order to develop the ability to synthesize information.

Each unit in *National Geographic Reach* is organized around a Big Question. Students explore this question as they move through a set of informational and narrative texts to construct understanding. The Big Questions are designed to defy easy answers, and learners are prompted to use both their background knowledge and what they have learned from their readings to draw conclusions and formulate answers.

Print and online resources are available to explore these questions. The robust print materials build print-based literacy. Multimedia resources support the new skills and formats Leu referenced. These include

- Build Background Videos and Interactive animations
- Multimedia resources in the National Geographic Digital Library
- Audio resources in multiple formats including MP3s
- Online games for learning
- Interactive eEditions
- Hypertext supports and guides in the Comprehension Coach

This organization encourages students to engage in the kinds of nonlinear multi-text explorations needed when reading and researching online.

Conclusion

It is imperative that we prepare students for their future as members of a global community where information is shared, produced, and understood across space and people. The challenge is great, especially because the past decades have taught us that we are not able to predict the tools students will be using as adults. Rather, our best approach is to ensure that students know how to communicate and collaborate with one another in both face-to-face and digital environments. They must be provided with daily opportunities to read, write, speak, listen, and view using many kinds of visual and written texts. Students must become increasingly comfortable searching for information, storing it, sharing it, producing it, and presenting it to a variety of audiences. Learners who are able to do these things are well prepared for a new century.

Nancy Frey, Ph. D., San Diego State University

Nancy Frey teaches in the San Diego State University teacher-credentialing and reading specialist programs focusing on reading instruction, content area literacy, and diverse student support. Frey has published in *The Reading Teacher, English Journal,* and *Educational Leadership.* Frey also co-authored *Checking for Understanding, Scaffolded Writing Instruction,* and *Learning Words Inside and Out.*

NGReach.com > **Download Professional Development Podcasts**

(((MP3))) Listen to Nancy Frey share more information on writing.

Connect Oral and Written Expression *by Nancy Frey*

The ability to read and write to convey information, provoke thought, and inspire others has long been considered a hallmark of an educated person (Manguel, 1996). More importantly, reading and writing are tools for empowerment, providing a voice and a forum for those who would otherwise be silent (Freire, 2000). For English language learners (ELLs), the ability to be heard, both verbally and in writing, is especially vital. Children who are learning to write while learning another language are challenged to acquire both the skills and the academic vocabulary and language necessary for effective writing. Recent research emphasizes that writing is a social act, not just a strictly cognitive one, and that the social act of writing is fueled by the conversations that occur among writers (Au, 1997; Dyson, 1989).

National Geographic Reach capitalizes on this interaction of oral language development and writing development. Students regularly engage in research-based instructional routines that invite them to compose orally in the company of their peers (Lapp, Flood, & Tinajero, 1994). In addition, teachers deliver writing lessons designed to scaffold student learning using a gradual release of responsibility model of instruction (Pearson & Gallagher, 1983). Students using *Reach* write daily to build writing fluency and skills. The intensification of learning that comes from daily writing is key to consistent growth in students' writing skills.

> *Using a scaffolded approach to writing instruction, children learn not only what and how to write, but why we write.*

Language Frames

Tell Your Ideas	Respond to Ideas
I think _____ would be interesting.	I like that idea because _____.
A story about _____ would be _____.	The main character should be someone who _____.
_____ would make a great _____ for my story.	A better _____ might be _____.

◀ **Language frames support peer conferences.**

① Talk is Essential to Writing

Writing researcher James Britton stated, "writing floats on a sea of talk" (Britton, 1983). Indeed, the art of written composition invariably arises from the conversations we have with others. These acts of oral composition are an essential, yet often overlooked, element of writing. In their study of the writing practices of elementary ELLs, Bicais and Correira (2008) noted that "[c]hildren used peer talk to share their experiences, abilities, skills, and knowledge in interactions that contributed to their learning" and further observed that some students who were quiet during whole class instruction became engaged when discussing their writing with peers.

The challenge in any classroom is to establish an environment where spoken language is fostered in ways that contribute to learning. This is accomplished first psychologically, in a classroom that honors the homes and cultures of the children (Turner, 2007). Toward this end, the literature featured in *National Geographic Reach* highlights the experiences of people from all over the world. In addition to creating a sense of psychological safety, these readings provide students with a bridge to write about their own experiences as well as those of others. In addition, *Reach* provides a framework that encourages students to speak, listen, read, and write in the company of others. While some of this is accomplished in a large group format, much student talk and its associated writing occurs with partners and in small groups. These frequent small group interactions promote language development and provide young writers with the opportunity to compose orally before doing so on paper (Fisher, Frey, & Rothenberg, 2008).

② Scaffolded Instruction Builds Writing Skills

Scaffolded instruction is a principle of teaching dating back to the early 20th century. Vygotsky's (1938/1978) observations of the interactions of children who were learning together gave him insight into the possibilities of what could occur when a competent other (teacher or peer) was present to offer support. Over time, Vygotsky's insights about a learner's zone of proximal development were reinterpreted as the teacher practice of scaffolding (Wood, Bruner, & Ross, 1976). Scaffolding in turn has been further explained in reading as a gradual release of responsibility model of instruction (Pearson & Gallagher, 1983). More recently, this model has been expanded for reading and writing instruction to include a collaborative learning phase where students engage in productive group work in the company of peers (Fisher & Frey, 2007, 2008). Students benefit from time to write together through guided instruction as well as from skill-building exercises such as writing specific types of sentences, power writing, and close examination and replication of writing models (Fisher & Frey, 2007).

Writing instruction in *National Geographic Reach* is scaffolded through writing routines that are used consistently throughout the lesson cycle. These routines include:

- **Modeled Writing** In Modeled Writing the teacher uses a think aloud approach to model and explain the decision making process used by a writer (Davey, 1983). Students are able to observe what the teacher writes as she explains how she decides what to include and how to express it. For many students, witnessing and participating in the modeling process is essential for understanding the act of writing.

Say	Write
The girl and her father planted the sprouting potatoes in soil.	I think the girl learned that you can plant sprouting potatoes in soil.
The potato plants produced many new potatoes.	She also learned that potato plants produce many new potatoes.

▲ In Modeled Writing, the teacher first thinks aloud, showing students how she decides what to write. She then models how to turn her thinking into written text.

- **Interactive Writing** In Interactive Writing the teacher and students work together to discuss what they will write, and then students take turns adding to the written product on the board or chart paper. This discussion may proceed one word at a time, with frequent rereading of what has already been written, so that students have extended opportunities to think about and take part in the construction of a piece of writing.

- **Independent Writing** Students using *National Geographic Reach* also have many opportunities to write independently. They write in response to literature or to class discussions of

Big Questions, and in many other contexts. However, they are not asked to write independently without support. The lessons in *National Geographic Reach* consistently provide teacher models, language frames, sentence starters, or other supports so students can write successfully on their own.

- **Power Writing** Writing fluency is critical to the development of young writers. Students including ELLs may find it difficult to begin and continue a writing task. As with reading instruction, where it is understood that a steady daily diet of texts nourishes young readers and contributes to fluency, so it is with writing. *Reach* uses an approach called Power Writing (Fearn & Farnan, 2001; Fisher & Frey, 2007) to build the writing stamina of young writers. These brief, timed writing events encourage children to put their ideas down on paper in order to build writing fluency. Over time, as they track the amount they write, students can see their own developing fluency and writing skill. Other approaches, such as specific sentences, invite students to use newly acquired vocabulary to create grammatically and semantically correct sentences (Fisher & Frey, 2007). Importantly, these original sentences are further extended into longer pieces so that students move quickly from word, to sentence, to paragraph.

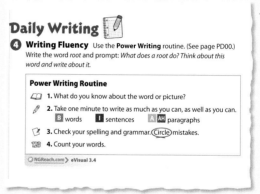

Daily Writing ✏️

④ **Writing Fluency** Use the **Power Writing** routine. (See page PD00.) Write the word *root* and prompt: *What does a root do? Think about this word and write about it.*

Power Writing Routine

📖 1. What do you know about the word or picture?

✏️ 2. Take one minute to write as much as you can, as well as you can.
   B words   **I** sentences   **A AH** paragraphs

✎ 3. Check your spelling and grammar. Circle mistakes.

123 4. Count your words.

◯ NGReach.com ▸ eVisual 3.4

◀ The Power Writing Routine encourages students to put their ideas down on paper to build writing fluency.

- **Writing on Demand** *National Geographic Reach* lessons also include opportunities for students to write on demand. These activities resemble the kinds of writing students frequently encounter on tests. *National Geographic Reach* lessons provide models of how to analyze and interpret writing prompts and how to write effectively in response.

- **Developing Vocabulary for Writing** Schleppegrell and Go (2007) examined the writing of fourth and fifth grade English learners who had generated lists of possible academic language and vocabulary prior to writing and found that the young writers utilized these lists to strengthen the structure and content of their writing. Vocabulary instruction in *National Geographic Reach* includes multiple opportunities for students to explore, list, and write about new academic and content vocabulary, and they are consistently encouraged to use these new words in discussion and in their writing.

- **Writing Projects** In addition to daily writing activities, *National Geographic Reach* includes more extended writing projects, in which students the writing process to create and publish a more developed piece of written work. Students study a model, plan, draft, revise, and edit their work, and then publish it for their peers. The writing projects include many opportunities for students to learn from each as they collaborate, share, and review each others' work. Writing projects include a wide variety of writing forms, including narratives, articles, persuasive essays, descriptive writing, and others.
- **Unit Wrap-Up Projects** Engaging, creative projects connect many modes of communication—oral, visual, kinesthetic—and connect learning back to the central idea via the Big Question.

Conclusion

While writing is often viewed as an independent activity, the research on the importance of collaboration before and after writing is compelling. Writing is ultimately about audience, so conversation and response are integral to the process. As noted earlier, writers typically begin to compose orally before they put pencil to paper. Therefore, it is essential for young writers to convey their own ideas, listen to the ideas of others, and dialogue about both. Children also need opportunities to discuss what they have written with fellow writers in order to obtain peer responses. Students meet the authors of many of the readings in *National Geographic Reach* and learn how these professionals approach their craft. These author conversations are intended to model the kind of thinking that writers of all ages engage in. And finally, the act of writing is far too important to leave to chance. We know that merely "causing" writing through writing prompts is not enough. Young writers must be taught about the structures and conventions of the language, as well as the craft. Purposeful attention to building the fluency, content knowledge, and art of writing are woven together into a compelling program. Using a scaffolded approach to writing instruction, children learn not only what and how to write, but most importantly, why we write. In discovering the art of writing, they also discover themselves.

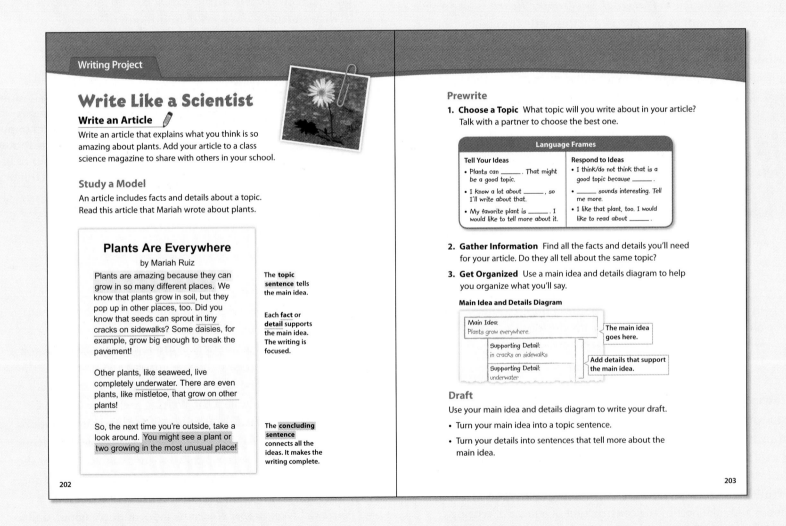

Sylvia Linan-Thompson, Ph.D., University of Texas

Sylvia Linan-Thompson is an associate director of the National Research and Development Center on English Language. She has developed and examined reading interventions for struggling readers who are monolingual English speakers, English language learners and bilingual students acquiring Spanish literacy. Linan-Thompson has authored articles, and books on literacy instruction and teacher professional development topics.

NGReach.com ➤ **Download Professional Development Podcasts**

(((**MP3**))) Listen to Sylvia Linan-Thompson share more information on fluency.

Fluency is More than Reading Quickly!

by Sylvia Linan-Thompson

Fluent reading is important because it represents effortless reading. If a task is easy and enjoyable we are more likely to engage in it. Conversely, if a task is difficult we are less likely to voluntarily engage in it. The implication for English language learners (ELLs) extends beyond fluency since we learn most of our new vocabulary from wide reading.

Thanks to the increased attention to reading instruction most of us are able to define reading fluency as involving three skills: reading accurately, at a good rate, and with prosody. To best promote students' achievement, it is important to understand why each of these components is critical for fluent reading as well as comprehension.

Accuracy Students who can read accurately have developed decoding skills, can read a substantial number of high frequency words automatically, and have strategies for reading unknown words when they encounter them in text (Tumner & Chapman, 1995). Accurate reading is also important to comprehension. Although it may not affect comprehension if we read *home* for *house*, it will if we read *horse* for *house*. Therefore, it is important to ensure that students develop adequate decoding skills. Exposure to and practice reading high frequency and decodable words both in isolation and in text will help students develop automaticity in reading words. Students also need to learn to monitor their understanding of what they read. This monitoring will help them self-correct if a word they read incorrectly affects their comprehension of what they are reading.

> *"If students pause appropriately, use correct phrasing, or change their intonation and expression in response to the text, we can usually assume that they understand what they are reading."*

Rate Students who have developed automaticity in reading words will be able to read at an appropriate rate. To help you understand why automaticity at the word level is important in reading, remember what it was like to learn to ride a bike. When we are first learning to ride most of our attention is on maintaining our balance and keeping the bicycle moving forward. We are not able to admire the scenery or to hold a conversation. As our ability to maintain our balance becomes automatic, we can begin to enjoy the scenery and can hold conversations with other riders. If we are daring, we may even ride with "no hands". LaBerge and Samuels (1974) explained that because we are only able to attend to one thing at a time, we alternate our attention between activities when we have to attend to two or more activities. However, if one activity is so well learned that it is automatic, we can give another activity our undivided attention. If we apply this analogy to reading fluency it becomes clear that to maximize comprehension, word reading has to be automatic.

A bike-riding analogy can help us understand the challenge of vocabulary for ELLs. We know from cognitive studies that people can retain seven items for twelve seconds in short-term memory. After twelve seconds we have to do something with the information or we lose the memory. Readers must be able to hold information in working memory while constructing meaning from text (Francis, Rivera, et al., 2006). When learning to read in a second language, students frequently encounter words they can decode but may not know the meaning of. Their attention becomes diverted and working memory taxed as they try to make sense of these words. By the time they figure out the meaning of the words, they may have lost the thread of the text, with a resulting loss of both fluency and comprehension.

Prosody Equally important to automaticity, reading with prosody, or the rhythm of natural language, can serve as an indicator that students are processing the text as they read. Reading with prosody includes several elements:

- Phrasing: Phrasing is how you use your voice to group words together. When students speak with correct phrasing, they have a smooth rhythm and meter and don't read too fast or too slow. Sentences are smooth, not choppy. As they learn about phrasing, students use punctuation to guide them in when to stop, pause, or emphasize words or phrases.
- Intonation: Good readers change their voice as they read. As students learn to read with good intonation, they use rise in fall of the pitch or tone of voice as they read. They change the sound of their voice to match the text, stressing words or phrases as appropriate.
- Expression: Expression is how you use your voice to show feeling. As students learn to read with expression, they focus on matching the sound and volume of their voice to the text.

If students pause appropriately, use correct phrasing, or change their intonation and expression in response to the text, we can usually assume that they understand what they are reading. Their response to the text is a reflection of their processing of the text as they read. If they are unable to comprehend the text, or if they are still developing decoding skills, their reading of the text may resemble reading a list of unrelated words—reading in a monotone. If there is some comprehension of the text, their reading may be uneven—halting and monotone at some points, and fluid and with expressive at others.

❶ Fluent reading involves more than speed

In the last few years we have seen an increased emphasis on the assessment of oral reading fluency (ORF). Evidence clearly demonstrates that oral reading fluency is related to reading comprehension. As a result, much of the fluency instruction in classrooms has focused on increasing students' reading rate so that they can meet the benchmark for the grade level and time of year.

However, if teachers base their instructional decisions solely on students' ORF scores, they may over-estimate students' ability to comprehend what they read. Recent research tells us that for linguistically diverse students—faced with the challenge of reading in a language in which they're not typically fully proficient—text-reading fluency is *not* a reliable indicator of reading comprehension. For example, across four studies conducted with linguistically diverse learners and/or low-performing learners, from the primary grades to grade 6, text-reading fluency scores were in the average range, yet the mean score for reading comprehension was well below average. This may be the case not just for ELLs, but also for many of their peers who are from low-income backgrounds with underdeveloped language and world knowledge.

Goals such as ORF benchmarks are useful tools for educators, but teachers must keep in mind that there is variation among students and that the same reading rate may lead to different results. For example, Kung (2009) found that:

- A third grade ELL with an ORF score of 130 words correct per minute (wcpm) has a 61 percent chance of passing the Minnesota state test.
- A third grade monolingual English speaker with the same ORF score has an 80 percent chance of passing the state test.
- ELLs must read 150 wcpm to have an 80 percent chance of passing the third grade test.
- An ELL with high English proficiency and a score of 130 wcpm has a 68 percent chance of passing the test while one with low English proficiency has a 29 percent chance of passing.

The answer in response to the data presented here is not to work on getting students to read faster but also to build and monitor their language skills and develop their background knowledge so that they can understand what they read when they are reading at an appropriate rate. Strong accuracy and rate are important measures and must be combined with other key measures of reading to ensure the ultimate goal of building a strong understanding of text and enjoyment of reading.

❷ Language factors can influence fluency

Research with ELLs indicates that many ELLs are able to develop good word-level decoding skills. However, they may continue to lag behind their peers on measures of reading fluency and comprehension. Research shows that language skills often play a significant role in these students' reading fluency. Students unfamiliar with English syntax are less likely to be able to anticipate what will come next in a sentence and therefore, approach each word as an independent word rather than as part of a sentence with meaning. Even when decoding is automatic, these language based factors may impact fluency:

- Limited English vocabulary;
- Divergent background knowledge;
- Limited knowledge of English syntax and grammar and language transfer challenges;
- Phonics transfer issues; and
- Lack of familiarity with English morphology (word parts and the way words work).

These challenges are often balanced by benefit of oral fluency in students' home language. As we work to help students succeed, instruction must leverage the strengths ELLs bring to the classroom to gain knowledge of vocabulary, background, linguistic, phonetic, and morphological knowledge of English.

3 Instruction is designed to build fluency and comprehension

From the information above, we can see that it is not enough to make sure that ELLs have adequate decoding skills and practice in oral reading rates. To become fully fluent readers and enhance comprehension in English, ELLs need to develop rich vocabulary and knowledge of the world. They need to become increasingly familiar with English syntax, grammar, and morphology. And they need to develop deep knowledge of the meanings of words.

National Geographic Reach is designed to address all of these needs that impact ELLs' achieving full reading fluency and comprehension. As we have seen from the earlier articles in this section, *Reach* focuses on building students' academic and content vocabulary, increasing their background knowledge, teaching them the structure of English, and building strong comprehension strategies. Vocabulary lessons in *National Geographic Reach* provide extensive exposure to key words. When students have developed deep familiarity with words, they will be able to read and comprehend them in text. Content, language, grammar, vocabulary, and decoding skills are aligned around interesting academic topics that motivate students and support them in achieving high levels of comprehension.

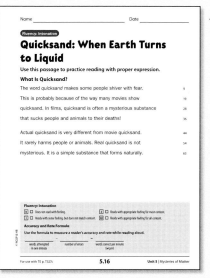

◀ Fluency lessons develop students' reading accuracy, rate, intonation, and expression.

In addition to this rich foundation of vocabulary and language, *National Geographic Reach* also provides specific practice to help students develop fluency. Resources include:
- Professional modeled readings and teacher read-alouds.
- Fluency models focusing on specific prosody skills.
- Frequent opportunities for oral reading, which is beneficial because it forces students to attend to each word (Francis, Rivera, et al. 2006).

- Repeated reading activities give students practice in reading texts multiple times until they are able to read them fluently and with good prosody.
- Multiple texts of varying genres and lengths on similar topics, which provides the opportunity to see and read words used in similar contexts across different texts.
- A rich array of Leveled Books, which offer additional opportunities to develop fluency as students read on topics of their choice.

These instructional resources provide a rich array of tools to support accuracy, rate, and prosody.

Finally, the components of *National Geographic Reach* include the online **Comprehension Coach**—an interactive, personalized computer application. This resource supports fluency development by allowing students to
- hear modeled, fluent readings
- record repeated readings and keep track of wcpm scores
- access coaching for pronunciation and point-of-use vocabulary and comprehension supports.

The **Comprehension Coach** can highlight text as it is read, identify mis-readings and provide feedback and tools to coach students. The speech recognition provides automatic assessment of accuracy and rate, saving instructional time and allowing teachers to focus on building comprehension skills. Students can use the **Comprehension Coach** to track their developing comprehension and fluency via an online resource. They can practice listening and reading anytime, anywhere. This creates a non-threatening environment that promotes more frequent practice and builds confidence.

Conclusion

For ELLs, the development of reading fluency involves more than automatic decoding and reading rate. Many ELLs need to develop more extensive vocabulary, wider background knowledge, and greater familiarity with English grammar, syntax, and word meanings in order to read with full comprehension and fluency. *National Geographic Reach* addresses these foundation needs and also provides extensive practice in oral and repeated reading to help ELLs achieve the highest level of understanding and fluency.

Lada Kratky, M.A.

Lada Kratky is a bilingual educator and featured national speaker. She has authored several Spanish reading programs including *Alfarrimas;* the phonics programs, *Phonics and Friends;* and ESL series *Avenues.*

NGReach.com **Download Professional Development Podcasts**

(((MP3))) Listen to Lada Kratky share more information on beginning reading.

Reach into Beginning Reading *by Lada Kratky*

A classroom filled with beginning readers is typically made up of students from a wide range of backgrounds and with varying strengths. The teacher's task is to discover those strengths and build on them. It is generally said that one third of the students in such a classroom will learn how to read relatively easily; another third will have to work harder; and for the last third, reading will be one of the most difficult skills they will ever have to master. English language learners (ELLs) may face even greater challenges, as they will have to master both language and literacy skills at the same time, since reading is not just decoding, but working through text to arrive at its message.

The report of the National Reading Panel in 2000 identified five key components of reading instruction: phonological awareness, phonics, vocabulary, comprehension, and fluency. As teachers of ELLs, we must add another component – that of language. ELLs who are learning to read in English must also learn how English works – its grammar and syntax, language functions, and the meanings of many new words. An effective reading program for ELLs will focus on all these skills. As students develop their phonological awareness, phonics, vocabulary, and language, they will also develop increasing reading fluency. And as fluency develops, it will in turn strengthen comprehension—the ultimate goal of reading.

National Geographic Reach provides explicit and systematic instruction in all these areas to assure success for ELLs who are learning to read.

1. **Phonological awareness** Phonological awareness is the ability to hear, identify and manipulate sounds in words. It is an essential skill for emergent readers; children must be able to distinguish sounds in words before they can link the sounds to the letters that represent them. Explicit instruction in phonological awareness significantly improves students' reading (National Reading Panel, 2000). Phonological awareness is generally included in classrooms from Kindergarten to Grade 2, but it is appropriate and necessary in any classroom, with students of any age, where beginning reading is taught.

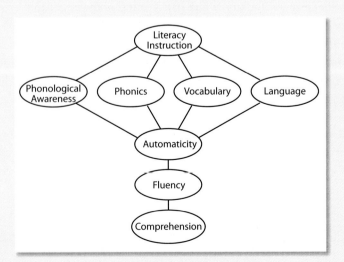

As in all areas of learning, students bring to the classroom different strengths which will affect the sequence in which phonological awareness skills are taught. For those children with little awareness of the sounds they articulate while speaking, Yopp (2000) recommends starting with activities that focus on rhyme. Playful poems will naturally engage young learners, and encourage them to focus on repeating sounds in words.

National Geographic Reach begins phonological awareness instruction with identifying rhyming words. As instruction continues, children become aware of word parts by clapping or tapping syllables. After syllables, lessons shifts to teaching students to hear individual sounds, focusing first on those that are easiest to hear—the vowels and continuous consonants (*f, h, l, m, n, r, s, w, y, z*). *National Geographic Reach* makes extensive use of Elkonin boxes, or sound boxes – a row of rectangles (first developed by the Russian psychologist Elkonin) that visually represent the sounds children listen for. These boxes help children distinguish separate sounds and identify which sounds come first, last, or in the middle of a word.

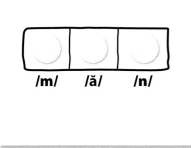

◀ Sound boxes help beginning readers visualize the distinct sounds they hear in words, in this case the word *m-a-n*.

After some practice with sound boxes, children can start to identify the sounds without visual support. Phonological awareness then continues developing sound awareness skills like changing initial, medial, and final sounds in words to make new words. As children start to associate letters with sounds, phonological awareness activities can begin to also include letters.

2. **Phonics** Explicit and systematic phonics instruction is an essential part of a successful classroom reading program (National Reading Panel, 2000). Phonics instruction teaches students to map sounds to letters and then to blend the sounds to decode words. Some students will begin to sound out words as soon as they have learned letter-sound correspondences. Other students, however, need explicit and repeated coaching to blend sounds and recognize the words they are decoding. *Reach into Phonics*, the phonics component of *National Geographic Reach*, uses consistent routines to teach letter-sound correspondences and word blending. Children are first taught to blend using the sound-by-sound blending routine; additional routines (vowel-first blending; whole word blending) are included for children who need additional support.

Reach into Phonics includes a wide variety of engaging activities that support children in practicing their decoding skills. Word building activities reinforce sound/spellings. Word sorting helps familiarize ELLs with the many ways some English sounds (such as long o) can be spelled. After learning and practicing phonics skills in individual words and sentences, children read the **Read on Your Own Books**. These decodable texts focus on content area topics linked to the instructional units of *National Geographic Reach*. They provide practice with the phonics skills that have been taught, but unlike many decodable texts, they feature meaningful and engaging text that children want to read, illustrated with outstanding photographs.

Flamingos
by Kate Baker

What kind of bird is this?
It's a flamingo.

nest

A mother flamingo has an egg in a mud nest. The mother will watch over the egg almost all of the time.

3. **High Frequency Words** Typical English text includes a large number of High Frequency Words—common words that appear very frequently and are often phonetically irregular, such as *a, one, are,* and *of.* Readers must learn to recognize High Frequency Words on sight. To teach instant recognition of these words, *National Geographic Reach* uses a research-based High Frequency Word Routine in which children look at the word, hear it pronounced, hear it used in a sentence, then say the word, spell it, and say it again. Children have multiple opportunities to read the words after they are taught, including in context in the **Read On Your Own Books.** High frequency words are reviewed as part of language function lessons, reinforcing the meaning and pronunciation of these essential words.

4. **Vocabulary and Language** Lessons in phonological awareness, phonics, and high frequency words support beginning readers in developing effective decoding skills, which are essential to becoming a fluent reader. However, while these skills are necessary, they are not sufficient. As we have seen above, many children, and ELLs especially, need robust vocabulary and language instruction to achieve their potential as readers.

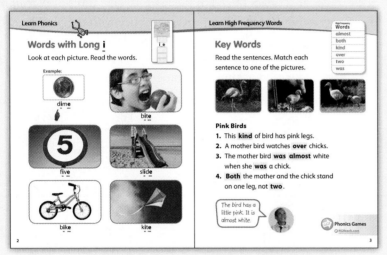

▲ **Pages include visual and contextual supports.**

Earlier papers in this section have detailed the research basis of vocabulary and language instruction in *National Geographic Reach*. These same strengths are built in to all levels of the program. Visual and contextual visual supports are also a key part of beginning reading instruction to ensure that all shell support and develop English language proficiency growth.

5. **Comprehension** Building meaning and understanding is central to all parts of the program. As they learn to read children are challenged to think and talk about ideas and concepts.

Children don't spend time reading simplistic decodable texts. **Read on Your Own Book** topics are grade level science and social studies concepts, topics which relate to real life, texts that are worth reading and interest the students. Beginning readers read for meaning and are then asked to think about their reading. They give opinions, hold discussions, ask questions and answer them.

Content-based texts provide opportunities to develop comprehension and early literacy skills. ▶

Beginning readers benefit from the same robust and systematic vocabulary and language instruction as in later grades *National Geographic Reach*. Key vocabulary words are carefully selected for high academic and content utility. They are initially taught using a consistent research-based routine for introducing words. The words are then revisited each day of the lesson plan, so that children have multiple opportunities to explore the words and deepen their knowledge of them, to learn additional meanings, and to use the words many times in discussion, writing, games, graphic organizers, and skits or dramas. This repeated and varied exposure to words is what makes it possible for children to internalize and "own" the words and to use them effectively in academic discourse.

The same is true of language instruction in *National Geographic Reach*. Throughout each day, children are continually involved in learning and using language. In **Language of the Day** activities, language function lessons, grammar lessons, discussions with the teacher and with peers, **Theme Theater**, and daily writing, children are constantly encouraged and motivated to practice using new academic language and to make it part of their lives.

Conclusion

As we have seen, many ELLs are able to decode text rapidly, but often their limited vocabulary and language skills interfere with their ability to comprehend. As ELLs develop more extensive vocabulary, comprehension, and language skills, they are increasingly able to combine decoding skills, language structures, and vocabulary knowledge to work their way through meaningful texts. Repeated exposure to content vocabulary helps develop reading fluency, which in turn leads to increased comprehension. With the repeated, focused practice encouraged in *National Geographic Reach*, students become fluent readers and develop strong comprehension skills, leading to enjoyment of learning and high levels of academic success.

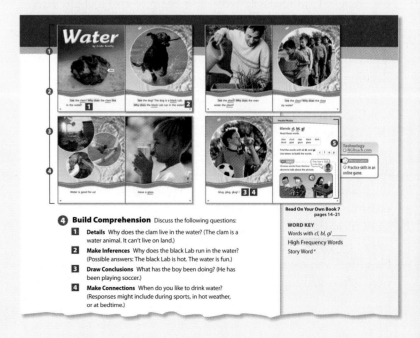

Teaching Routines & Strategies

Routines   Instructional routines are simple learning procedures that follow consistent steps. Routines benefit both you and your students in many ways. Use these guidelines to introduce and conduct routines.

- **Support student learning.**   When students know a routine, they can focus more clearly on the content to be learned. They don't have to focus on how to conduct the activity because the learning procedure is familiar and understood. You can gradually release responsibility for conducting the routines in *National Geographic Reach:*

    1. When introducing a new routine, give clear instructions. Then, model how to conduct the routine. Monitor students to ensure they follow instructions.

    2. As students begin to be familiar with classroom routines, invite classroom volunteers to restate the procedures for a routine. This provides practice in oral language and allows students to use known and new classroom language patterns and academic vocabulary words.

    3. As students become more familiar with classroom routines, have classroom volunteers give instructions. Other classmates can clarify, restate, or reinforce important steps in a routine.

- **Save transition time.**   Once your students know a routine, they can apply it to new content quickly and easily, saving valuable classroom time for teaching and learning. Providing appropriate visual and contextual supports will help students quickly focus on key tasks.

- **Set clear expectations.**   Routines help students know what you expect of them. Post examples of model student work to help students recognize examples of the results you are seeking. Have students save examples of their work in their portfolios and monitor growth through the year. In addition to reinforcing expectations for learning, set clear expectations for teamwork and collaboration.

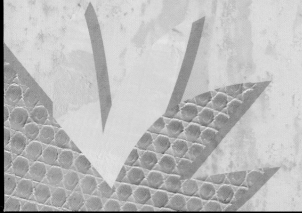

Teaching Routines & Strategies

Table of Contents

Introduce the Words

Purpose: Students engage in learning concepts and acquire background knowledge as they learn new key words and develop a deeper understanding of the words.

Research Basis: Decades of research have confirmed the important role that vocabulary plays in reading comprehension and in students' overall academic success (Hiebert & Kamil 2005). Immersing students in rich and varied language experiences permits them to learn words through listening, speaking, reading, and writing. In this new view of robust, explicit instruction, vocabulary is introduced using consistent, predictable routines (Beck et al. 2002). Follow these steps to help students make words fully their own, so that vocabulary can be accessed at will in a variety of situations.

1. **Pronounce the word.** Model the pronunciation of the key word and point to the accompanying picture; have students pronounce the word.

2. **Rate the word.** Have students hold up their fingers to show how well they know the word:

   Ask: *What do you know about this word?* Encourage students to share their ideas about the word.

  I have never seen or heard this word before

 I have seen the word before but I can't use it in a sentence

I can use it in a sentence or give a definition

3. **Define the word.** Use a student-friendly definition to explain the meaning. (Definitions are provided in the Picture Dictionary at the back of the Student Book.)

4. **Elaborate the meaning.** Generate discussion of the word. Use one or more of the following strategies:
   - Relate the word to your personal experience.
   - Encourage students to use the word as they talk about their own experience.
   - Using questions or comments, motivate students to engage in discussion about the word. Extended discussion will help all students understand the word and how it is used.
   - Point out word parts and spelling patterns that will help students recognize the word.
   - Challenge students to connect the word across content areas.
   - Post the words on the word wall.

5. **Post the words on a word wall.**
   - Reserve a section of the classroom wall or bulletin board for the Word Wall.
   - As new vocabulary is introduced, write the words on cards and add them to the wall. Words can be arranged in random order, or alphabetically, by similar topic, or in other ways as you choose.
   - Tell students that they will add definitions, sentences, drawings, and more to the word wall as they learn more about each word.
   - Periodically have students read the Word Wall or portions of it chorally. Encourage students to tell about how they have used the words in class or outside of school.

Application

DAY 1
- Introduce new Content Vocabulary (Day 1 of each lesson plan)

DAY 2
- Introduce new Academic Vocabulary (Day 2 of each lesson plan)

Teacher: When I was growing up, my parents marked my **growth** on the wall every year.

Student 1: My mom says I'm having a **growth** spurt.

Student 2: I want my **growth** to keep going until I'm seven feet tall.

Teacher: What could we say about our city's **growth**?

Student 3: The city's **growth** has made a traffic problem.

Expand Word Knowledge

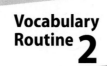

Purpose: Students use graphic organizers, illustrations, and writing to expand their knowledge of the meaning and usage of new words.

Research Basis: Research confirms that students need to use a word multiple times in different contexts to become fully familiar with the word and its meaning or meanings. Exploring the word through the use of graphic organizers, writing, and illustrations provides a rich array of experiences with the word that helps students develop deep word knowledge (Beck et al. 2002; Carlo et al. 2004; Marzano et al. 2005).

1. **Group students in pairs.** Explain that each pair will become experts on one vocabulary word.

2. **Display the graphic organizer.** Use the graphic organizer or three-dimensional graphic organizer specified in the Teacher's Edition lesson, or another graphic organizer from the examples in Vocabulary Routine 4.

3. **Select a key word.** Display the vocabulary word and model for students how to locate information about the word and complete the graphic organizer.
   - Find the word in the Picture Dictionary in the Student Book or in another dictionary and read the information about the word.
   - Write the word.
   - Add a definition, context sentence, and picture.

4. **Assign key words.** Assign a word to each student pair and have them create a similar graphic organizer for their word.

Application

DAY 3
- Expand Word Knowledge (Day 3 of each lesson plan)

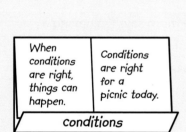

4-Corner Vocabulary

Word	Picture
property	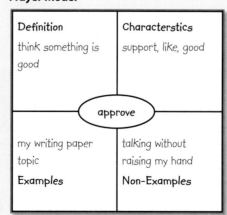
Word in Context	**Definition**
My parents have owned property for many years.	a piece of land or real estate

Frayer Model

Definition	Characterstics
think something is good	support, like, good
my writing paper topic	talking without raising my hand
Examples	**Non-Examples**

approve

Share Word Knowledge

Purpose: Students deepen word knowledge by sharing their deeper understandings of words for which they have become class experts. For variations on this routine, use Cooperative Learning Routines.

Research Basis: Talking about words and sharing their knowledge of words provides additional opportunities for students to use new words in different contexts and to become increasingly familiar with how the words are used. Taking the role of the class expert on a word motivates students to continue exploring words and their meanings (Beck et al. 2002; Blachowicz et al. 2005).

1. **Establish partners.** Pair each student with a partner who studied a different vocabulary word for Vocabulary Routine 2 (Expand Word Knowledge).

2. **Share.** Partners take turns reading to each other their graphic organizers from Vocabulary Routine 2.

3. **Discuss.** Partners discuss and create sentences using both vocabulary words. If needed give students sentence starters.

4. **Write.** Students write their sentences in their journals and draw a line under each vocabulary word.

5. **Repeat.** Repeat steps 1–4 above until each student has a journal entry for each vocabulary word.

Application

DAY 4
- Share Word Knowledge
  (Day 4 of each lesson plan)

Student 1: My word is cycle.

Student 2: The word I studied is depend.

Student 1: Let's make a sentence using both words.

Student 2: How about, "Plants and animals depend on the water cycle for the water they drink."

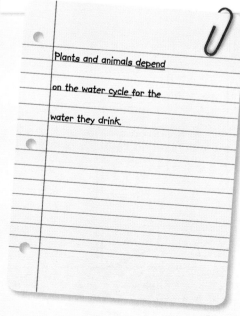

Plants and animals depend
on the water cycle for the
water they drink.

Review, Extend, or Reteach Using Graphic Organizers

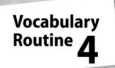
Purpose: Extend the use of graphic organizers (described in Vocabulary Routine 2) to provide instruction and practice with vocabulary words and other important words used in classroom directions and discussion.

Research Basis: In addition to learning key words that are important for selection comprehension and understanding content-area concepts, English learners are often exposed to many new words used in classroom directions, explanations, and discussion. Examples are words such as *sequence, inference, dialogue,* and *routine.* Research demonstrates that graphic organizers are an effective tool for introducing these words and giving students experience in using them and exploring their meanings (Hiebert & Kamil 2005). Graphic organizers are also effective tools for reteaching and providing additional practice. By creating visuals that show word meanings and relationships, students gain varied experiences that support different pathways to understanding.

1. **Display the word.** Write the word on the board or chart paper. Check prior knowledge.

2. **Display the graphic organizer.** Use the graphic organizer specified in the Teacher's Edition or select another graphic organizer from those shown on the following pages.

3. **Model.** Think aloud as you model partially completing the graphic organizer.

4. **Involve students.** Engage students in discussing the word and in adding information about the word to the graphic organizer. Information can include a definition, context sentence, picture, examples and non-examples, and multiple meanings.

5. **Independent work.** Have students create their own graphic organizers for the word.

Application

DAYS 1 & 2
- Classroom Vocabulary (Days 1 and 2 of each lesson plan, as needed)
- Reteaching vocabulary
- Vocabulary practice

Three-Dimensional Graphic Organizers

Window

Portrait

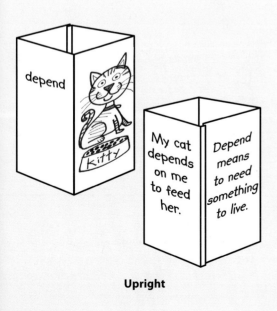

Upright

Fold-Up Tab

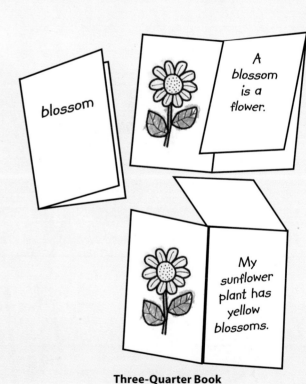

Three-Quarter Book

Other Graphic Organizers

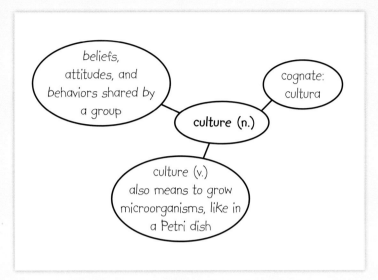

Word Web

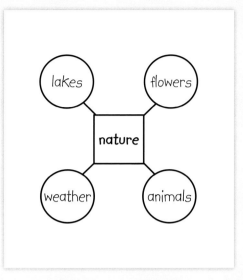

Word Web of Examples

Wordbench

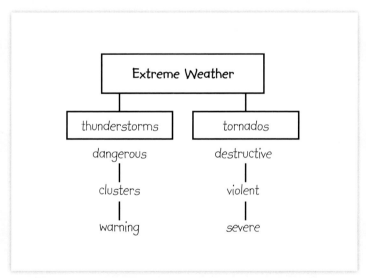

Semantic Web

Word	Definition	My Example
strategy	a plan	my football team's plan to win

Example Chart

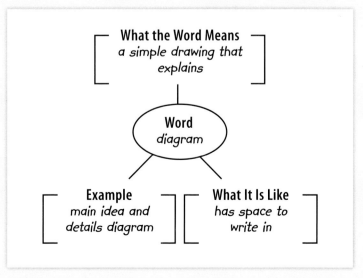

Word Map

Text-Talk Read Aloud

Vocabulary Routine 5

Purpose: The text-talk method teaches text-specific vocabulary after a selection has been read aloud to students.

Research Basis: Research demonstrates that reading aloud to students is most effective when the teacher engages students in discussion about words, concepts, and events in the selection both during and after reading aloud. The text-talk method provides a framework for guiding discussion and focusing on important key words (Beck et al. 2002; Gambrell et al. 1996).

1. **Display the key words.**

2. **Read aloud.** As you read, pause to provide a short explanation of each key word as you come to it. For example, if you are teaching the word *otherwise* you might say: *You can use the word* otherwise *when you are explaining what might happen. For example, I hope I catch the bus today after school, otherwise I will be late.*

3. **Elaborate meanings.** After reading, activate prior knowledge: *What do you know about this word?* Explain the meanings of the key words more fully, using the steps of Vocabulary Routine 1.

4. **Discuss.** Create discussion prompts that encourage students to use the words together. For example, for the word *otherwise*, you may display the following frame and ask students to use the word as they tell about an upcoming weekend activity, holiday, or school event.

   > I hope _____, otherwise _____.

5. **Extend.** Encourage students to think about and use the key words at other times in classroom discussion, and in their lives beyond the classroom. Invite them to tell about how they have used the target words outside of class and to tell about how they have heard friends and family use the target words.

Application

DAYS 3–4 & 6
- Use with **In Other Words** and to extend understanding of Content, Classroom, and Academic Vocabulary. (Days 3–4 and 6 of each lesson plan)

DAYS 8–9
- Use with Guided Reading groups (Days 8–9 of each lesson plan)

In July, when the plants were as tall as my waist, we picked potato beetles off the leaves. I dropped them into a pail of soapy water.

"Gross."

"We have to do this," Dad said. "**Otherwise**, the bugs will eat the leaves and the potatoes won't grow."

potato beetle

In Other Words
Otherwise If we don't

156

> Otherwise, the bugs will eat the leaves and the plants won't grow. In other words, if we don't, the bugs will eat the leaves..."

Reteaching Vocabulary

Purpose: Review or reteach vocabulary that has been previously introduced.

1. **Establish groups.** Group students who did not master vocabulary, or who will benefit from reviewing the words. Follow the following steps for each word to be retaught or reviewed.

2. **Focus on the key word.** Point out the word on the Picture Dictionary page of the Student Book.

3. **Pronounce the word.** Say the word and have students repeat it after you.

4. **Teach the meaning.** Read the definition of the word, and then elaborate the meaning using different words and giving additional examples. For example, for the word *depend* you might say: *You depend on something when you need it to live or to do something. Some students depend on the school bus to get to school. We all depend on each other to make our school a healthy, happy place.*

5. **Make connections.** Discuss with students when they might use the word. Model an example. Then have students use Think, Pair, Share (PD59) to make connections.

6. **Write and remember.** Have students record each word on a separate page in their journals. Ask them what they note about the word's sounds and spelling. Then have them do one or more of the following:

   - Make a Word Map to help them remember the word. (See Word Map, page PD41).
   - Make a drawing to illustrate the word's meaning.
   - Write a definition.
   - Write a context sentence.
   - Write the translation of the word in their home language. Go to NGReach.com to find translations of vocabulary words in eight languages.

Application

DAY 10
- Review or reteaching (Day 10 of each lesson plan)

You depend on something when you need it to live or to do something. Some students depend on the school bus to get them to school. Can you think of a way you might use depend?

Animals and plants depend on water to live.

Vocabulary Practice and Extension Activities

Purpose: These routines can be used to give students more experience in recognizing, remembering, learning and extending the meaning of key words and other new vocabulary.

Research Basis: Research confirms that hands-on activities, games, and other kinesthetic and interactive instructional techniques are effective in helping students acquire and remember new information including vocabulary.

Application

DAY 5
- Vocabulary lessons (Day 5)

DAY 10
- Reteaching and vocabulary review (Day 10)

Vocabulary Bingo

1. **Distribute cards.** Hand out Bingo cards. (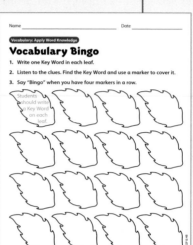 available at NGReach.com).

2. **Fill out cards.** Have students write the key words in random order on the card.

3. **Give clues.** Provide oral clues or questions about the key words. For example, for the word *produce* you might say: *This word means to make or give.*

4. **Mark the words** Have students place a marker on each word as they identify it.

5. **Bingo!** When a student has a complete row of markers, he or she calls, "Bingo." Ask the student to review his or her answers and pair answers with the clues.

Picture It

1. **Write the words.** On the board, write several vocabulary words.

2. **Group students.** Arrange students in small groups, each with chart paper and a marker.

3. **Teams plan.** Have each group:
   - Choose a key word (without telling what the word is)
   - Decide how they can show the word's meaning in a drawing
   - Choose one member of the group who will create the drawing.

4. **Students create drawings.** Call on a group, and allow the drawer 15 to 30 seconds to complete the picture.

5. **Students identify the word.** Have other groups talk quietly about the picture. When they agree on the key word, they designate one member to raise his or her hand and give their answer.

6. **Award points.** When a group guesses the key word correctly, award 1 point to the group and have that group's drawer take the next turn. Continue until one group has collected 3 points.

Yes or No?

1. **Ask questions.** Pose yes or no questions using two vocabulary words. You or your students can make up the questions. For example, the following questions might be asked using words to do with plants: *Do roots grow in the soil? Are blossoms a characteristic of rose plants?*

2. **Students respond.** Students can respond orally, in writing, or they can use thumbs up or thumbs down. Have students compare responses and pair their answers with the clue. Remind students to use complete sentences and restate the question. For example: *Yes, roots grow in the soil.*

Word Sorts

1. **Students write words.** Have students write the words on 3x5 cards or strips of paper, one word per card or strip.

2. **Establish categories.** For a closed sort, provide the category of how the words should be sorted, such as:
   - Related meanings or concepts
   - Synonyms
   - Part of speech
   - Connotation
   - Formal or informal
   - Spelling patterns
   - Words with multiple meanings
   - Words with Spanish cognates

   For an open sort, have students work together to determine the sort categories.

3. **Explain sorts.** When students have sorted the words, have them explain their sorts. Have them create a chart or web to record the word relationships they found.

4. **Sort again.** Have students sort the words again using different categories. Have them record the information in a graphic organizer.

Part of Speech Sort

Nouns	Verbs	Adverbs
abstract (n.)	adhere (v.)	ethically (adv.)
dilemma (n.)	advocate (v.)	desolately (adv.)
	reinforce (v.)	deliberately (adv.)

Number of Syllable Sort

2	3	4	5
ab-stract	ad-vo-cate	des-o-lae-ly	de-lib-er-ate-ly
ad-here	di-lem-ma		
e-thi-cal	re-in-force		

Word Poems

1. **Concrete Poems** Students draw a meaningful shape or object and write words along the outline of the shape, so words look like the physical shape. For example, a student may draw a volcano and along the outline write: *lava, magma, cone, flow, ash, erupt.*

2. **Diamante Poems** Diamante Poems are 7 lines long. To begin, have students think of two words that are opposites (antonyms).
   - Line 1: Write a noun
   - Line 2: Add two adjectives that describe line 1
   - Line 3: Add three action verbs that relate to line 1
   - Line 4: Add two nouns that relate to line 1, and two nouns that relate to line 7
   - Line 5: Add three action verbs that relate to line 7
   - Line 6: Add two adjectives that describe line 7
   - Line 7: Write a noun that is the opposite of or contrasts with line 1

3. **Cinquain Poems** Cinquain poems have different patterns. Have students work together to complete the pattern below with a key word.
   - Line 1: A noun
   - Line 2: Two adjectives
   - Line 3: Three related words ending in –ing
   - Line 4: A related phrase
   - Line 5: Another word for the noun

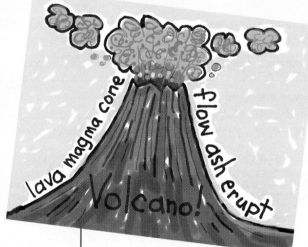

Vocabulary Practice and Extension Activities (continued)

Stump the Expert

1. **Name the expert.** Designate one student to be the expert.

2. **Challenge the expert.** Another student (the stumper) presents a definition. The expert has 10 seconds to produce the term.

3. **Continue the challenges.** If the expert responds accurately, the next stumper offers a challenge. This continues until the expert is stumped or answers a set number of challenges and earns applause.

4. **Name a new expert.** The student who stumps the expert becomes the new expert.

Multiple Key Word Skit

1. **Group students.** Organize students in small groups and give each group a list of five or more vocabulary words.

2. **Brainstorm.** Allow time for groups to brainstorm how the words relate to each other and to create a skit with dialogue that includes all the words.

3. **Discuss.** After students present their skits, discuss with them which skit was most original, most humorous, or used the words most accurately.

Around the World

1. **Choose a traveler.** A student designated as the traveler moves from his or her seat to stand by a neighboring student, the challenger.

2. **Provide a definition.** The teacher gives the traveler and the challenger a definition; whoever responds first with the correct word becomes the new traveler and challenges a new student.

3. **Continue the challenge.** A traveler who continues to respond first and returns to his or her own seat has gone "around the world."

Vocabulary Concentration

1. **Prepare pairs of cards.** Write each key word on two cards or slips of paper.

2. **Spread the cards.** Turn the cards over and spread them randomly on a table.

3. **Students look for matches.** Students take turns turning over two cards. When a student turns over two cards that have same word, he or she keeps the cards.

4. **The winner!** The student with the most cards is the winner.

Rivet

1. **Select a key word.** For this variation of the game Hangman, choose a key word.

2. **Write a blank for each letter.** On the board, write a blank for each letter of the word. For example, for *ecosystem,* write _ _ _ _ _ _ _ _ _ .

3. **Fill in letters one by one.** Fill in the blanks one letter at a time: <u>e</u> <u>c</u> <u>o</u> _ _ _ _ _ _ .

4. **Have students guess the word.** Pause briefly after you write each letter. Encourage the class to guess the word.

5. **Complete the word.** When someone identifies the word correctly, have that student fill in the remaining blanks.

Guided Reading

Reading Routines

Purpose: Guide and support students as they read texts at their instructional reading level.

Research Basis: Research demonstrates the importance of teachers providing support for decoding and comprehension as students read text at their instructional level. Guided reading helps students negotiate increasingly difficult text (Pinnell & Fountas 1996).

Before Reading

1. **Form groups.** Organize groups of 4–6 students of similar reading ability.

2. **Choose books.** Select a leveled text. Use one of the National Geographic Reach leveled library books or go to NGReach.com and use the leveled book finder. Provide a copy for each student.

3. **Prepare students for reading.** Adapt the preparation to the text, student language level, and student performance. Monitor progress and select and instructional focus. Preparation may involve the following steps:
   - Preview the book. Talk about the cover and title page. Page through it and discuss illustrations and other features to build background about the book and its topic.
   - Lead a discussion about the book's topic to build further background and vocabulary.
   - Ask students to make predictions about what will happen or what will learn.

4. **Read aloud.** In some cases, you may wish to read part of the text or all of the text aloud before students read.

During Reading

5. **Have students read the text.** Students can read softly to themselves (whisper reading) or silently, you may want to read portions of the text aloud and then have students echo read, or you may want to have partners take turns reading portions of the text aloud to each other.

6. **Observe students.** Circulate to observe students as they read. Provide guidance as needed by asking questions, prompting, and coaching students to apply strategies to decode difficult words or to improve their comprehension. Monitor progress and select an instructional focus for questions. Here are examples of questions you might ask (and the instructional focus):
   - *What sound does this letter make?* (phonics)
   - *What would you do if you were this character? How do you think this character is feeling?* (comprehension, literary analysis)
   - *Why do you think that happened?* (comprehension, literary analysis)
   - *What's happening in the picture?* (comprehension, text features)
   - *What do you think will happen next?* (comprehension)

After Reading

7. **Discuss the reading.** Select strategies to address challenge areas, extension opportunities, or individual interests. After-reading activities can include:
   - Have students summarize the book and make connections.
   - Have students tell about how they applied reading strategies to the text.
   - Have students discuss how new information or ideas relate to the Big Question.

8. **Extend the reading.** If time allows, encourage students to engage in activities that extend their understanding, such as:
   - Rewrite the story with different or additional characters, a new ending, or other changes.
   - Create a short play or pantomime based on the book.
   - Write a letter to the author or to one of the book's characters.
   - Draw a picture about something related to the book.
   - Research and report on something mentioned in the book.

9. **Review your observations.** Check your notes of students' reading and comprehension to identify areas where they need additional instruction. Use a mini-lesson format to provide needed lessons in decoding, word structure, comprehension strategies, and other skills.

Application

DAYS 8 & 9
- Reading leveled books (Days 8 and 9)

Additional Reading Routines

Purpose: These reading routines provide support for students in accessing text that may be difficult for them to read independently; they also help develop fluent oral reading.

Research Basis: Research confirms the importance of all students being exposed to grade-level text for concept and vocabulary development. These routines provide support for students who are not yet able to read grade-level selections on their own. Listening to a recording of the selection provides the most support.

Echo reading has been shown to contribute to the reading growth of low-achieving readers (Mathes et al 2001). Echo reading, choral reading, and paired or partner reading provide increasingly lower levels of support and encourage students to develop toward independent reading of grade-level text. In addition, the added comprehension focus that teachers provide before, during, and after reading provide additional opportunity to rehearse reading skills and strategies. Observe students as they read, with the goal of providing the lowest level of support that will enable students to access the text being read.

Application

DAYS 3 & 6
- Options for Reading (Day 3 or Day 6)

Listening Center

1. **Choose a space.** A good space is a quiet corner, where students using the center will not be distracted or disturb others.

2. **Gather resources.** Resources can include CD players, headphones, books recorded onto a computer, audio CD, or other electronic device, and one or more copies of books students will listen to. You may also want to provide response sheets, pencils and markers, and baskets to hold books and materials.

3. **Assign text.** Students can listen to books on their own or in groups, depending on interest and reading level. Encourage students to follow along in the text as they listen.

4. **Provide ways to respond.** Have students illustrate their favorite part of the story, complete a response sheet, write about what they heard, or respond in some other way.

Echo Reading

1. **Select a text.** The text can be a complete selection or a portion of text. Passages for echo reading are best when they are short and motivating for students.

2. **Select students.** Echo reading can be used with a small group or an individual student. It is most appropriate for students who are not yet able to process the text on their own but can track the print as you read aloud and as they repeat the sentences after you.

3. **Have students listen and repeat.** The teacher reads a sentence aloud, modeling good intonation and rhythm. Students then read the sentence aloud following the teacher's model. Encourage students to track the print as they listen and repeat.

4. **Correct errors.** The teacher provides immediate feedback to correct student mistakes.

5. **Have students reread.** After reading aloud with the teacher, have students reread the text in pairs until they can read it fluently.

Choral Reading

1. **Select a text.** The text can be a complete selection or a portion of a text. Passages for choral reading are best when they are short and motivating for students. Predictable text works well for choral reading.

2. **Select students.** Choral reading is most appropriate for students who are hesitant to read aloud independently but can join in reading the text in unison with other students with the teacher leading. Choral reading helps build students' motivation, confidence, and fluency.

3. **Read the text aloud first.** Model fluent reading and good intonation.

4. **Read the text in unison with students.** Have all students in the group read the passage aloud in unison with you. Encourage them to use good intonation.

5. **Have students reread.** After reading with the teacher, have students reread the text in pairs until they can read it fluently.

Paired Reading

1. **Select a text or portion of text.** Passages for paired reading are best when they include strong emotions or dialogue.

2. **Pair students.** You may wish to pair students of similar reading ability, or pair a high level reader with a lower level reader.

3. **Explain the procedure.** Tell students if you want them to:
   - Read the passage aloud in unison.
   - Take turns with each person reading a sentence, paragraph, or page.
   - Have one student listen while the other reads.

4. **Model error correction.** Demonstrate how students should support each other by rereading misread words, and asking for and giving help when needed.

5. **Encourage fluent reading.** Partners should practice good prosody (phrasing, expression, and intonation) as they read.

6. **Encourage discussion.** Have the reader pause at the end of a paragraph of section. The listener can then summarize or make a connection. Pairs can ask each other questions about what was read, such as:
   - *What was your favorite part of the story?*
   - *What was your page about?*
   - *Were there any parts that were hard to read?*

Independent Reading Support

Purpose: Support students in making effective and successful use of independent reading time.

Research Basis: Independent reading can help students develop fluency, vocabulary, comprehension, and background knowledge. Teachers can support students as independent readers by assisting with book selection and encouraging students to share information about what they have read (Cunningham & Stanovich 1998).

1. **Select topics.** Support students in selecting books of interest for independent reading. These may be leveled books, books from the library, or other books by familiar authors or on topics students are interested in. Discussing books in advance with individual students or groups can motivate readers and help them determine what they want to read.

2. **Select reading level.** Support students in choosing books of appropriate difficulty. In most cases, the student should know 95 percent of the words in a text in order to read it independently with success. However, students may be able to handle more challenging text if they are highly motivated, if they possess or can build background knowledge, or if they can get help with challenging vocabulary from you or from a peer.

3. **Apply strategies.** Encourage students to apply the strategies they are learning as they read independently. You may wish to teach a strategy mini-lesson, such as visualizing or making connections, to a small group of students before they begin reading. As they read, they should then jot down how they use the strategy in their journals, on sticky notes, or on a graphic organizer.

4. **Conduct conferences.** Hold short conferences with students during independent reading time. Engage students in talking about what they are reading, how it interests them, and any questions they have about the text. Listen and observe carefully, and coach students as needed with vocabulary development, comprehension strategies, word skills, or other areas.

5. **Share reading.** Bring students together to share their reading experiences. Students who have read different books can summarize what they read, and share how they used strategies and what they found most interesting in their reading. Students who have read the same or similar books can share what they have learned about the topic and what more they would like to learn.

6. **Extend understanding.** Encourage students to extend their understanding of the book with an activity such as one of the following:
   - Rewrite the story with different or additional characters, a new ending or other changes.
   - Create a short play or pantomime based on the book.
   - Write a letter to the author or to one of the book's characters.
   - Draw a picture about something related to the book.
   - Research and report on something mentioned in the book.

Application

DAYS 3 & 6
- Options for Reading (Day 3 or Day 6)

DAYS 8 & 9
- Reading leveled books (Days 8 and 9)

Introduce High Frequency Words

Purpose: Introduce high frequency words to students.

Research Basis: High frequency words are the most common words in printed English. About 100 words make up 50 percent of most English text. Many of these words are phonetically irregular, so students must learn to recognize them on sight without needing to sound them out. Many high frequency words are abstract, and English learners may need helping understanding their meanings. The following routine encourages students to look carefully at new high frequency words as they begin to commit them to memory; it also encourages students to explore the words' meanings.

1. **Display the word.** Display the word on the board or whiteboard and have students look at it carefully.

2. **Pronounce the word.**

3. **Use the word.** Pronounce the word in a sentence, and explain what it means. Example: *The moon is very far from the earth.* Far *means a long way away.*

4. **Have students say the word aloud.**

5. **Have students spell the word chorally.**

6. **Have students say the word again.**

7. **Use the word in sentences.** Encourage students to make up sentences and to have a discussion using the word.

Application

- Use **Reach into Phonics** for instruction in High Frequency Words

---

More Beginning Reading Routines

For these routines, see the Teacher's Edition for Reach into Phonics

- Phonological Awareness
- Introduce a Sound/Spelling
- Vowel First Blending
- Continuous Blending
- Reading Decodable Text

Repeated Reading Routines

Fluency Routines

Purpose: Develop reading fluency.

Research Basis: Research has shown that repeated reading (3–4 readings) of texts at an appropriate instructional level can increase reading fluency for students who struggle with reading (Chard et al. 2002; Dowhower 1987; Kuhn & Stahl 2003; O'Shea et al. 1985; Samuels 1979), and that it can enhance comprehension (Daly & Martens 1994; Dowhower 1987; Freeland et al. 2000). As described on pages PD48–PD49, repeated readings also build comprehension.

Application

- Daily fluency lessons

Choral or Echo Reading/Marking the Text

1. **Select a passage.** Choose an appropriate text and provide copies for students. Keep passages short and use a variety of texts: narrative, expository, poems, songs, student writing. Choose text that is motivating.

2. **Provide a model.** Have students listen to a fluent reading of the text. This can be read aloud by the teacher or a recorded version. Use the fluency models provided on the selection recordings audio CD or in MP3 format at NGReach.com.

3. **Have students mark the text.** As they listen to the model, have students mark the reader's phrasing (/ for a short pause; // for a longer pause) or intonation (rising or falling inflections) on a copy of the text.

4. **Have students read the text.** Students can echo or choral read the text with you, following markings for phrasing and intonation. Coach phrasing and intonation as needed.

5. **Repeated readings.** Have partners practice reading the same text in its unmarked version until they can read it fluently.

Paired Reading

1. **Select a passage.** Choose an appropriate text and provide copies for participants. Paired reading works best with a selection that contains strong emotions.

2. **Establish pairs.** Pairs can be peer-to-peer or student-adult groupings. Note that performance tends to be better when students read aloud to an adult as opposed to a peer.

3. **Read alternate sentences.** Have partners alternate reading sentences, checking each other's readings as they go.

4. **Monitor fluency.** Encourage students to attend to prosody (phrasing, expression, and intonation) as they read.

Recording and Tracking  Comprehension Coach

1. **Read and record.** Have students use the Comprehension Coach to record and analyze their readings.

2. **Re-record as needed.** Encourage students to repeat their recording until they are satisfied with their reading and rate.

3. **Note progress.** Have students note their accuracy and rate as measured by the Comprehension Coach. They should see increases in both rate and accuracy over time.

Timed Reading 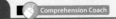 Comprehension Coach

Use this technique to help students develop an appropriate reading rate with good accuracy. Research suggests this technique is highly motivational if students have a clear target for words read correct per minute (WCPM) and then chart their progress.

1. **Read and record.** Have students use the Comprehension Coach to record their readings. The Comprehension Coach encourages students to read carefully and thoughtfully, repairing miscues, thinking about vocabulary, and actively comprehending as they read.

2. **Graph results.** Have students record their WCPM on a graph or chart each time they use the Comprehension Coach.

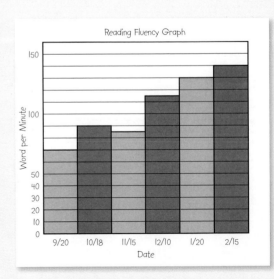

Reading Fluency Graph

Power Writing

Writing Routine 1

Purpose: Develop students' writing fluency; provide an opportunity for students to record their progress in writing fluency.

Research: Research shows that expert writers write longer strings of words before stopping to think than less skilled writers. Power writing practice helps students learn to get their words down on paper quickly. It also helps them overcome the tendency to stall before starting to write (Fisher & Frey 2007). While power writing can focus on any word or concept, this routine is most effective when key words and ideas relate to the topic or theme of a unit.

 1. **Display a word or picture.** Choose a word or picture that will be motivating for students to write about. Invite them to think about the word or picture and what they know about the word or concept. Activate prior knowledge or experiences: *What do you think of when you hear/see?*

2. **Set the timer.** The timer is usually set for one minute. In some cases you may want to vary the amount of time.

 3. **Have students write.** Ask students to write as much as they can, as well as they can in one minute. If students at different proficiency levels need support, use the following multi-level strategies:

   B Beginning-level students can write single word as a list. Ask: *Write all the words you know.*

   I Intermediate students write sentences.

   A **AH** Encourage Advanced and Advanced High students to write paragraphs.

 4. **Check work.** Have students check their spelling and grammar and circle any mistakes.

 5. **Count words.** Have students count the number of words they wrote and record the number on their papers.

6. **Repeat the procedure.** If time allows, have students create more than one passage. Repeat steps 2–5 one or two times.

7. **Record results.** Have students record their best result and create a writing fluency graph. Over time, the graph will show students' growth in fluency and help motivate their progress as writers.

8. **Adjust the time.** To develop fluency further, vary the amount of writing time from 30 seconds to two minutes or more in separate Power Writing sessions.

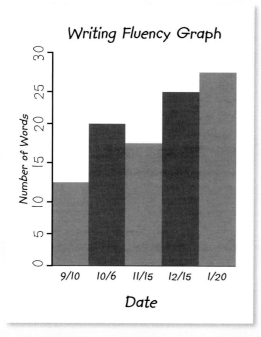

Modeled Writing

Purpose: Model the process of composing to help students learn the writing process, writing strategies and writer's craft.

Research: Many students, may not understand the process of recording their thoughts or conversation in writing. Modeled writing demonstrates the process of how language is represented in written form. Modeling the process often is effective in improving students' attitude toward writing as well as their writing skills (Fisher & Frey 2007). Modeled writing also helps deepen vocabulary, language, and concept development through frequent exposure to clear models and think-alouds.

1. **Develop a RAFT.** Think aloud to model how to develop a RAFT for what you will write. For example:

   Role: *I will take the role of a reporter writing an article for the newspaper.*
   Audience: *My audience is the readers of the newspaper.*
   Form: *My form is a news article.*
   Topic: *I will write about some new puppies.*

2. **Model thinking about the first sentence.** Think aloud as you decide what you will include in your first sentence. For example: *I want to tell about some new puppies that were born last week at my neighbor's house. I'll write a news article to tell about the puppies. I'll begin by telling the most important facts.*

3. **Write the first sentence.** Read aloud what you have written. For example: *Last week six new puppies were born on Davis Street.*

4. **Continue thinking aloud as you write.** Think aloud to model how you plan and write additional sentences. For example: *Next I'll tell what the puppies looked like. I'll write:* The puppies were brown and white and had soft fur. Their eyes were closed.

5. **Involve students.** Encourage students to help write additional sentences. Discuss their ideas with them, and add the new ideas to the writing as appropriate.

6. **Add a title.** When the writing is complete, think aloud as you add a title, and as you review the writing and make any needed corrections.

Puppies Born

Last week six new puppies were born on Davis Street. The puppies were brown and white and had soft fur. Their eyes were closed. They were born under the porch at the Marino's house. Mrs. Marino fixed a bed for the puppies and their mother in the hall. Mrs. Marino said she would look for new homes for the puppies in a few weeks.

Interactive Writing

Purpose: Scaffold students to turn collaborative oral composition into written form.

Research: Expert writers make many decisions as they write. Students may not understand all of the decisions involved. Interactive writing makes these decisions part of the conversation between teacher and students. It also demonstrates for students how expert writers think about word choice and constantly review to maintain syntax and meaning as they write (Fisher & Frey 2007).

1. **Establish a purpose.** Discuss with students the purpose and audience you will be writing for. For example: *Let's write a letter to Mayor Wheeler to thank her for visiting our class last week.*

2. **Talk through the text.** Lead a discussion with students about how to word each sentence, and then support individual students as they write letters or entire words in sentences on the board or chart paper. For example: *How will we begin our letter? . . . Good, Alana, let's start with* Dear Mayor Wheeler: *Can you come up and write that for us?* Continue the discussion having different members of the class take turns writing.

3. **Problem solving.** Use questions or prompts to help students solve problems as they write. For example: *So far this sentence says:* Thank you for coming to . . . *What did we say comes next in the sentence? . . . That's right, Duwayne, next we're going to write* Lincoln School. . . . *Can you come up and write the next word? What letter does* Lincoln *begin with?*

4. **Reread frequently.** Reread the entire message after each word is added. This will help students see how each word fits into the overall process.

Application

DAY 5
- Daily Writing (Day 5 of each lesson plan).

Dear Mayor Wheeler:
   Thank you for coming to **Lincoln School** to tell us about your job. We think you really like being the Mayor. We are sorry you don't get to ride on fire trucks.
   Yesterday there was a cat on the playground. We think she was lost. Can you help us find a home for her?

Thank you,
Mrs. Bonilla's Class

Independent Writing

Purpose: Provide support to help students achieve success as independent writers.

Research: Most elementary students need continued support as they become independent writers. They are most successful when the teacher provides effective prompts, a collaborative context, and effective coaching (Fisher & Frey 2007).

Application

DAY 5
- Daily Writing (Day 5 of each lesson plan)

1. **Provide appropriate writing prompts.** Make sure that writing prompts are motivating and appropriate. Prompts should:
   - Encourage a variety of responses
   - Allow for a range of writing abilities
   - Be appropriate for the writers' experiences
   - Include topics that interest students

2. **Use RAFTs.** Have students use the RAFT structure to make sure writing assignments have a clear purpose and authenticity. Students should understand their Role, Audience, Form, and Topic before they begin to write. Here is a sample RAFT:

   Role: A student who wants to clean up a vacant lot.
   Audience: Neighbors who could help clean up the lot.
   Form: An email message
   Topic: Please come on Saturday to help clean up the lot.

3. **Support peer response.** Teach students how to be effective peer reviewers of each others' writing. Strategies may include:
   - Use the language frames to scaffold conversation.
   - Encourage writers to invite responses from peers, but don't compel them.
   - Encourage students to talk with each other as readers, not as critics. If something makes them laugh, or feel sad, or catches their interest, they should tell the writer so. If something isn't clear, they should tell that, too. However, details of word choice, organization, sentence structure, etc. are best dealt with in teacher-student conferences.

4. **Conference.** Confer with students about their writing. Conferences should be short and focused. Include the following steps:
   - **Inquiry:** Ask about, the topic, how the work is coming, and areas of difficulty.
   - **Decision:** Based on student responses, decide on the focus for the conference.
   - **Instruction:** Choose a point for teaching. This may be any of the writing traits, writer's craft, grammar, usage, spelling, capitalization, and punctuation. Refer to records of student performance on grammar, revising and editing, and spelling lessons and assessments. Writing traits rubrics and other resources for conferences are provided in the **Assessment Handbook**.
   - **Recording:** Record anecdotal notes of the conference for follow-up. Include next steps for the writer.

Student Journals

Journaling is a good way to help students move from note taking and assigned writing to writing independently. Lessons in **National Geographic Reach** include many opportunities for students to make notes about vocabulary, language, and grammar, and to write in response to their reading or their thoughts about Big Questions. Journals help students remember what they have learned and see their progress over time.

- **Set up journals.** Journals can take many forms. You may wish to have students keep a journal with separate sections for vocabulary, language, grammar, and writing. Or students can just add cumulatively to their journals as they learn. In either case, encourage students to decorate their journals and maintain them with care.

- **Coach.** Observe students as they write and look for opportunities to coach them with spelling, word skills, strategies, and their thinking about topics and Big Questions.

- **Review journals.** Have students review their journals with you at conference time. Reviewing their work over time helps students recall what they've learned and see how they have progressed. It can also help you focus on areas where a student may need reteaching or additional support.

Routines for Structured Responses

Purpose: To support all students in participating actively in daily lessons.

Research Basis: Structured response formats are instructional practices that can be incorporated into daily lessons and allow all students to participate productively (Heward, 2006). Carefully planned structured response routines can ensure that every student participates in a lesson, and that participation remains focused and on task. They also allow for immediate feedback to support correct answers and to address incorrect ones.

> ### Application
> - Daily Lessons, whenever student response is called for

Choral Responses

Choral responses allow students to join in on important academic words, expressions, or ideas. They allow the teacher to determine immediately which students understand a presentation.

1. **Cue students in advance.** Use an established spoken cue (e.g., *Everybody; Look at me; Eyes up*) to focus students' attention.

2. **Give a prompt or ask a question.** Use prompts or questions that can be answered with one or two words or an academic phrase.

3. **Allow wait time.** Use a visual cue (e.g., holding up a hand as a "stop sign," then dropping it quickly) to provide wait time for students to think before they answer (and to keep some students from blurting out the answer). This use of wait time allows students to think about and form their answers and increases their confidence to join in class interactions.

4. **Provide feedback.** Acknowledge correct responses. For example: *That's right. Good work, everyone!* If some students give the wrong answer or say nothing, provide immediate corrective feedback. For example: *The correct answer is _____. Let's all say that together.*

Response cards

Response cards can be used to ensure participation by every student. Response cards work best when the answer is short; for example, students are asked to change a verb in a sentence from present to past tense. Response cards can be index cards, small white boards, or small pieces of paper.

1. **Use simple prompts.** Give students a prompt or ask them a question that can be answered with one or two words, *yes/no*, or *true/false*.

2. **Allow wait time.** Tell students to think about their answers. Silently count to 5, then say: *Write your answer.*

3. **Students display their cards.** After students have had time to write, say: *Hold up your cards.*

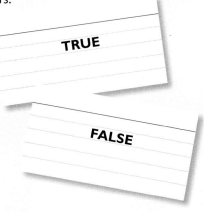

4. **Give feedback.** Quickly check all of the cards and provide feedback, such as: *Good work! Almost everyone wrote* true, *which is the correct answer.* If some students give an incorrect answer, provide immediate corrective feedback, such as: *I see some of you wrote* Sammy, *which is the name of the main character in the passage. The correct answer is _____.*
Say it with me, _____.

5. **Continue with other prompts and questions.**

Cooperative Learning Routines

Purpose: These routines provide consistent opportunities for students to work together and learn from one another.

Research Basis: Cooperative learning routines take advantage of classroom diversity and make it a vital resource for helping all students acquire challenging academic content and language. These routines promote active engagement and social motivation for all students. For English language learners, they also create opportunities for purposeful communication. Regular use of such routines has been shown to be effective (Johnson & Johnson 1986; Kagan 1986; Slavin 1988).

Application

DAYS 4, 6 & 7
- Day 4 Vocabulary; Day 4 Fluency; Day 6 Language; Day 6 Respond and Extend; Day 7 Vocabulary; Day 7 Reread

STRUCTURE & GRAPHIC	DESCRIPTION	BENEFITS & PURPOSE
CORNERS	• Corners of the classroom are designated for focused discussion of four aspects of a topic. • Students individually think and write about the topic for a short time. • Students group into the corner of their choice and discuss the topic. • At least one student from each corner shares about the corner discussion.	• By "voting" with their feet, students literally take a position about a topic. • Focused discussion develops deeper thought about a topic. • Students experience many valid points of view about a topic.
FISHBOWL	• Part of a group sits in a close circle, facing inward; the other part of the group sits in a larger circle around them. • Students on the inside discuss a topic while those outside listen for new information and/or evaluate the discussion according to pre-established criteria. • Groups reverse positions.	• Focused listening enhances knowledge acquisition and listening skills. • Peer evaluation supports development of specific discussion skills. • Identification of criteria for evaluation promotes self-monitoring.
INSIDE-OUTSIDE CIRCLE	• Students stand in concentric circles facing each other. • Students in the outside circle ask questions; those inside answer. • On a signal, students rotate to create new partnerships. • On another signal, students trade inside/outside roles.	• Talking one-on-one with a variety of partners gives risk-free practice in speaking skills. • Interactions can be structured to focus on specific speaking skills. • Students practice both speaking and active listening.
JIGSAW	• Group students evenly into "expert" groups. • Expert groups study one topic or aspect of a topic in depth. • Regroup students so that each new group has at least one member from each expert group. • Experts report on their study. Other students learn from the experts.	• Becoming an expert provides in-depth understanding in one aspect of study. • Learning from peers provides breadth of understanding of over-arching concepts.

STRUCTURE & GRAPHIC	DESCRIPTION	BENEFITS & PURPOSE
NUMBERED HEADS TOGETHER	• Students number off within each group. • Teacher prompts or gives a directive. • Students think individually about the topic. • Groups discuss the topic so that any member of the group can report for the group. • Teacher calls a number and the student from each group with that number reports for the group.	• Group discussion of topics provides each student with language and concept understanding. • Random recitation provides an opportunity for evaluation of both individual and group progress.
ROUNDTABLE	• Seat students around a table in groups of four. • Teacher asks a question with many possible answers. • Each student around the table answers the question a different way.	• Encouraging elaboration creates appreciation for diversity of opinion and thought. • Eliciting multiple answers enhances language fluency.
TEAM WORD WEBBING	• Provide each team with a single large piece of paper. Give each student a different colored marker. • Teacher assigns a topic for a word web. • Each student adds to the part of the web nearest to him/her. • On a signal, students rotate the paper and each student adds to the nearest part again.	• Individual input to a group product ensures participation by all students. • By shifting point of view, students develop broad and in-depth understanding of concepts.
THINK, PAIR, SHARE	• Students think about a topic suggested by the teacher. • Pairs discuss the topic. • Students individually share information with the class.	• The opportunity for self-talk during the individual think time allows the student to formulate thoughts before speaking. • Discussion with a partner reduces performance anxiety and enhances understanding.
THREE-STEP INTERVIEW	• Students form pairs. • Student A interviews student B about a topic. • Partners reverse roles. • Student A shares with the class information form student B; then B shares information from student A.	• Interviewing supports language acquisition by providing scripts for expression. • Responding provides opportunities for structured self-expression.
MIX AND MATCH	• Prepare cards that can be matched as pairs, such as a word and its definition. • Hand one card to each student. • Students mingle and talk about their cards. • Teacher calls "Match," and each student finds the partner whose card matches with his or her own. Students exchange cards and mingle again.	• The mixing process encourages students to have multiple conversations with an academic focus. • Discussions provide each student with language and concept understanding. • Cards can be traded, so students don't know who their partner is until the end.

Research Base and Bibliography

Language and Literacy

Asher, J., & Price, B. (1967). The learning strategy of total physical response: Some age differences. *Child Development*, 38, 1219–1227.

Asher, J. (1969). The total physical response approach to second language learning. *The Modern Language Journal*, 53, 1.

Au, K. (2006). *Multicultural issues and literacy achievement*. Mahwah, NJ: Lawrence Erlbaum.

August, D., & Hakuta, K. (1998). *Educating language-minority children*. Washington, DC: National Research Council.

August, D., & Shanahan, T. (Eds.). (2006). *Developing literacy in second-language learners: Report of the National Literacy Panel on Language-Minority Children and Youth*. Mahwah, NJ: Erlbaum.

August, D. L., & Shanahan, T. (2006). Synthesis: Instruction and professional development. In D. L. August & T. Shanahan (Eds.), *Developing literacy in a second language: Report of the National Literacy Panel*. Mahwah, NJ: Lawrence Erlbaum Associates.

Bailey, A. (Ed.). (2006). *The language demands of school: Putting academic English to the test*. New Haven, CT: Yale University Press.

Bauman, J. F., Russell, N.S., & Jones, L. A. (1992). Effects of think-aloud instruction on elementary students' comprehension abilities. *Journal of Reading Behavior*, 24 (2), 143–172.

Berg, C. (1999). The effects of trained peer response on esl students' revision types and writing quality. *Journal of Second Language Writing*, 8 (3), 215–241.

Bicais, J., & Correira, M. G. (2008). Peer-learning spaces: A staple in the English learner's tool kit for developing language and literacy. *Journal of Research in Childhood Education*, 22(4), 363–375.

Biemiller, A. (1999). *Language and reading success*. Newton Upper Falls, MA: Brookline Books.

Blum-Kulka, S., & Snow, C. E. (2004). Introduction: The potential of peer talk. *Discourse Studies*, 6(3), 291–306.

Brice, A., & Roseberry-McKibben, C. (1999). Turning frustration into success for English language learners. *Educational Leadership*, 56(7), 53–55.

Brown, A., Campoine, J., and Day, J. (1981). Learning to learn: On training students to learn from texts. *Educational Researcher*, 10, 14–24.

Bruner, J., Goodnow, J, & Austin, G. A. (1967). *A study of thinking*. New York: Science Editions.

Callow, J. (2008, May). Show me: principles for assessing students' visual literacy. *The Reading Teacher*, 61(8), 616–626.

Celce-Murcia, M., Brinton, D., & Goodwin, J. (1996). *Teaching pronunciation: A reference for teachers of English to speakers of other languages*. Cambridge: Cambridge University Press.

Chamot, A. U., & O'Malley, J. M. (1994) *The calla handbook: implementing the cognitive academic language learning approach*. White Plains, NY: Addison Wesley Longman.

Collier, V. P. (1995). *Promoting academic success for ESL students: Understanding second language acquisition for school*. Elizabeth, NJ: New Jersey Teachers of English to Speakers of Other Languages-Bilingual Educators.

Collier, V. P., & Thomas, W. P. (1989). How quickly can immigrants become proficient in school English? *Journal of Educational Issues of Language Minority Students*, 5, 26–38.

Crandall, J. (Ed.). 1987. *ESL through content area instruction: mathematics, science, social studies*. Englewood Cliffs, NJ: Prentice Hall.

Cummins, J. (2000). *Language, power and pedagogy: Bilingual children in the crossfire*. Buffalo, NY: Multilingual Matters.

Cunningham-Flores, M. (1998). *Improving adult esl learners' pronunciation skills*. National Center for ESL Literacy Education.

Day, J. P. (2002). We learn from each other: Collaboration and community in a bilingual classroom. In R. Allington & P. H. Johnston (Eds.), *Reading to learn: Lessons learned from exemplary fourth-grade classrooms* (pp. 99–122). New York: Guildford Press.

Diaz-Rico, L. T., & Weed, K. Z. (2002). *The crosscultural, language, and academic development handbook: A complete K–12 reference guide*. Boston, MA: Allyn & Bacon.

Dickinson, D. K., & Tabors, P. (Eds.). (2001). *Beginning literacy with language*. Baltimore: Brookes.

Dong, Y. R. (2006/2007). Learning to think in English. *Educational Leadership, Best of 2006–2007*, 9–13.

Dressler, C. (2006). First and second-language literacy. In D. L. August & T. Shanahan (Eds.), *Developing literacy in a second language: Report of the National Literacy Panel*. Mahwah, NJ: Lawrence Erlbaum Associates.

Droop, M., & Verhoeven, L. (2003). Language proficiency and reading ability in first- and second-language learners. *Reading Research Quarterly*, 38(1), 78–103.

Dutro, S., & Moran, C. (2002), Rethinking English language instruction: An architectural approach. In G. Garcia (Ed.), *English learners reading at the highest level of English literacy*. Newark, DE: International Reading Association.

Echevarria, J., Short, D., & Vogt, M. (2008). *Making content comprehensible. The sheltered instruction observation protocol*. Boston, MA: Pearson.

Echevarria, J., Vogt, M. A., & Short, D. J. (2004). *Making content comprehensible for English learners: The SIOP model* (2nd ed.). Boston, MA: Allyn & Bacon.

Feldman, K., & Kinsella, K. (2005). *Create an active participation classroom. The CORE Reading Expert*. Retrieved from www.core-learn.com/pdfs/Newsletters/CORE%202005%20Spring%20Newsletter.pdf.

Fillmore, L. W. (2004). *The role of language in academic development*. In Excerpts from a presentation by Lily Wong Fillmore at the Closing the Achievement Gap for EL Students conference. Santa Rosa: CA: Sonoma County Office of Education. Retrieved from www.scoe.k12.ca.us/aiming_high/docs/AH_language.pdf.

Fitzgerald, J. (1995). English-as-a-second-language learners' cognitive reading processes: A review of research in the United States. *Review of Educational Research*, 65, 145–190.

Fitzgerald, J. (1993). Literacy and students who are learning English as a second language. *The Reading Teacher*, 46, 638–647.

Francis, D., Lesaux, N., & August, D. (2006). Language instruction. In D. August & T. Shanahan (Eds.), *Developing literacy in second-language learners: Report of the National Literacy Panel on Language-Minority Children and Youth* (pp. 365–413). Mahwah, NJ: Erlbaum.

Francis, D. J., Rivera, M., Lesaux, N., Kieffer, M., & Rivera, H. (2006). *Practical guidelines for the education of English language learners: Research-based recommendations for instruction and academic interventions.* Retrieved from www.centeroninstruction.org/files/ELL1-Interventions.pdf.

Gambrell, L. B., Morrow, L. M., & Pressley, M. (Eds.). (2007) *Best Practices in Literacy Instruction.* New York: Guilford.

Garcia, G., & Beltran, D. (2005) Revisioning the blueprint: Building for the academic success of English learners. In G. Garcia (Ed.). *English learners: Reaching the highest levels of English literacy.* Newark: DE: International Reading Association.

Genesee, F., Lindholm-Leary, K., Saunders, W., & Christian, D. (2006). *Educating English language learners: A synthesis of research evidence.* New York: Cambridge University Press.

Genesee, F. & Geva, E. (2006). Cross-linguistic relationships in working memory, phonological processes, and oral language. In D. L. August & T. Shanahan (Eds.), *Developing literacy in a second language: Report of the National Literacy Panel.* Mahwah, NJ: Lawrence Erlbaum Associates.

Gersten, R., & Baker, S. (2000). What we know about effective instructional practices for English-language learners. *Exceptional Children, 66,* 454–470.

Gibbons, P. (2002). *Scaffolding language, scaffolding learning: Teaching second language learners in the mainstream classroom.* Portsmouth, NH: Heinemann.

Girard, V. (2005). English learners and the language arts. In V. Girard (Ed.), *Schools moving up: A WestEd initiative.* Retrieved November 8, 2006, from www.schoolsmovingup.net/cs/wested/view/e/140

Goldenberg, C. (2006). *Improving achievement for English learners: Conclusions from 2 research reviews.* Retrieved from www.colorincolorado.org/article/12918

Goldenberg, C. (2004). *Successful school change: Creating settings to improve teaching and learning.* New York: Teachers College Press.

Goldenberg, C. (1992–1993). Instructional conversations: promoting comprehension through discussion, *The Reading Teacher, 46* (4), 316–326.

Goldenberg, C., Rueda, R., & August, D. (2006). Sociocultural influences on the literacy attainment of language-minority children and youth. In D. August & T. Shanahan (Eds.), *Developing literacy in second-language learners: Report of the National Literacy Panel on Language-Minority Children and Youth* (pp. 269–318). Mahwah, NJ: Erlbaum.

High, J. (1993). *Second language learning through cooperative learning.* San Clemente, CA: Kagan Publishing.

Hill, J., & Flynn, K. (2006). *Classroom instruction that works with English language learners.* Alexandria, VA: Association for Supervision and Curriculum Development.

Johnson, D., & Johnson, R. (1995). *Creative controversy: Intellectual challenge in the classroom* (3rd ed.). Edina, MN: Interaction Book Company.

Kagan, S. (1990). Cooperative learning for students limited in language proficiency. In M. Brubacker, R. Payne & K. Rickett (Eds.), *Perspectives on small group learning.* Oakville, Ontario, Canada.

Kagan, S. (1992). *Cooperative learning.* San Juan Capistrano, CA: Kagan Cooperative Learning.

Kim, Y., & Turner, J. D. (2006). Creating literacy communities in multicultural and multilingual classrooms: Lessons learned from two European American elementary teachers. In R.T. Jimenez & V.O. Pang (Eds.), *Race, Ethnicity, and Education Volume 2: Language and Literacy in Schools* (pp.219–236). Westport, CT: Praeger Publishing Group.

Kirschner, P. A., Sweller, J., and Clark, R. E. (2006). Why minimal guidance during instruction does not work: An analysis of the failure of constructivist, discovery, problem-based, experiential, and inquiry-based teaching. *Educational Psychologist, 41,* 75–86.

Krashen, S. (1987). *Principles and practices in second language acquisition.* New York: Prentice-Hall.

Leeman, J. (2003). Recasts and second language development: Beyond negative evidence. *Studies in Second Language Acquisition, 25,* 37–63.

Lesaux, N. K. (2006). Development of literacy of language minority learners. In D. L. August & T. Shanahan (Eds.), *Developing literacy in a second language: Report of the National Literacy Panel.* Mahwah, NJ: Lawrence Erlbaum Associates.

Lesaux, N., & Siegel, L. (2003). The development of reading in children who speak English as a second language. *Developmental Psychology, 39,* 1005–1019.

Lesaux, N. K., Lipka, O., & Siegel, L.S. (2006). Investigating cognitive and linguistic abilities that influence the reading comprehension skills of children from diverse linguistic backgrounds. *Reading and Writing: An Interdisciplinary Journal, 19*(1), 99–131.

Lesaux, N. K. & Crosson, A.C. (2005). Addressing variability and vulnerability: Promoting the academic achievement of English learners in San Diego. In R. Hess (Ed.), *Urban reform: Lessons from San Diego* (pp. 263–281). Cambridge, MA: Harvard Education Press.

Lyman, F. T. (1981). The responsive classroom discussion: The inclusion of all students. In A. Anderson (Ed.), *Mainstreaming Digest* (pp. 109–113). College Park: University of Maryland Press.

Marzano, R. J., Pickering, D. J., & Pollock, J. E. (2001). *Classroom instruction that works: Research-based strategies for increasing student achievement.* Alexandria, VA: Association for Supervision and Curriculum Development.

Marzano, R. (2004). *Building academic background.* Alexandria, VA: MCREL, ASCD.

Mayer, R. (2003). *Learning and instruction.* New Jersey: Pearson Education, Inc.

Medina-Jerez, W., Clark, D.B., Medina, A., & Ramirez-Marin, F. (2007). Science for ELLs: Rethinking our approach. *The Science Teacher, 74,* 52–56.

Miller, J. F., Heilmann, J., Nockerts, A., Iglesias, A., Fabiano, L., & Francis, D. J. (2006). Oral language and reading in bilingual children. *Learning Disabilities Research & Practice, 21*, 30–43.

Morrison Institute for Public Policy. (2006). *Why some schools with Latino children beat the odds and others don't.* Tempe, AZ: Author.

National Research Council. (2000). *How people learn: Brain, mind, experience, and school.* Washington, DC: National Academies Press.

Novak, J. D. (1995). Concept mapping: a strategy for organizing knowledge. In S. M. Glynn & R. Duit (eds.), *Learning Science in the Schools: Research Reforming Practice.* Mahwah, NJ: Lawrence Erlbaum Associates.

Pearson, P. D., & Gallagher, G. (1983). The gradual release of responsibility model of instruction. *Contemporary Educational Psychology, 8*, 112–123.

Powell, M. (1996). *Presenting in English.* Hove: Language Teaching Publications.

Saenz, L. M., Fuchs, L. S., & Fuchs, D. (2005). Peer-assisted learning strategies for English language learners with learning disabilities. *Exceptional Children, 71*, 231–247.

Rousculp, E. E., & Maring, G. H. (1992). Portfolios for a community of learners. *Journal of Reading, 35*, 378–385.

Samway K., & McKeon, D. (2007). *Myths and realities: best practices for English language learners.* Portsmouth NH: Heineman.

Saunders, W. M., & Goldenberg, C. (1999). Effects of instructional conversations and literature logs on limited- and fluent-English proficient students' story comprehension and thematic understanding. *Elementary School Journal, 99*(4), 277–301.

Saunders, W. M., Foorman, B. P., & Carlson, C. D. (2006). Do we need a separate block of time for oral English language development in programs for English learners? *The Elementary School Journal, 107*, 181–198.

Scarcella, R. (2003). *Academic English: A conceptual framework.* Los Angeles: Language Minority Research Institute.

Scarcella, R. (2003). *Accelerating academic English: A focus on the English learner.* Oakland, CA: Regents of the University of California.

Schleppegrell, M. J. (2001). Linguistic features of the language of schooling. *Linguistics and Education, 12*, 431–459.

Schleppegrell, M. J. (2004). *The language of schooling: A functional linguistics perspective.* Mahwah, NJ: Erlbaum.

Seidlitz, J. (2008) *Navigating the ELPS: Using the new standards to improve instruction for English language learners.* San Antonio, TX: Canter Press.

Seidlitz, J. & Perryman, B., (2008) *Seven steps to building an interactive classroom: Engaging all students in academic conversation.* San Antonio TX: Canter Press.

Shanahan, T. & Beck, I.L. (2006). Effective literacy teaching for English-language learners. In D. L. August & T. Shanahan (Eds.), *Developing literacy in a second language: Report of the National Literacy Panel.* Mahwah, NJ: Lawrence Erlbaum Associates.

Snow, C. E., & Fillmore, L. W. (2000). *Clearinghouse on languages and linguistics.* Retrieved from www.cal.org/ericcll/teachers/teacher.pdf.

Tabors, P., Paez, M., & Lopez, L. (2003). Dual language abilities of bilingual four- year olds: Initial findings from the Early Childhood Study of language and literacy development of Spanish-speaking children. *NABE Journal of Research and Practice, 1*(1), 70–91.

Taba, H. (1962). *Curriculum development: Theory and practice.* New York: Harcourt Brace & World.

Thornburry, S. (2005). *How to teach speaking.* Essex, England: Pearson.

Turner, J. D., & Kim, Y. (2005). Learning about building literacy communities in multicultural and multilingual communities from effective elementary teachers. *Literacy Teaching and Learning, 10*, 21–42.

Turner, J. (2007). Beyond cultural awareness: Prospective teachers' visions of culturally responsive teaching. *Action in Teacher Education, 29*(3), 12–24.

Uchikoshi, Y. (2005). Narrative development in bilingual kindergarteners: Can Arthur help? Developmental Psychology, 41, 464–478.

Vail, N. J. and Papenfuss, J. (1993). *Daily oral language plus.* Evanston, IL: McDougal, Littell.

Vaughn, S., Cirino, P. T., Linan- Thompson, S., Mathes, P. G., Carlson, C. D., Cardenas-Hagan, E., et al. (2006). Effectiveness of a Spanish intervention and an English intervention for English language learners at risk for reading problems. *American Educational Research Journal, 43*, 449–487.

Weaver, C. (1996). *Teaching grammar in context.* Portsmouth, NH: Boynton, Cook Publishers.

Wennerstrom, A. (1993). Content-based pronunciation. *TESOL Journal, 1*(3), 15–18.

Wong-Fillmore, L. & Snow, C. (2000). *What teachers need to know about language.* Washington, DC: ERIC Clearinghouse on Languages and Linguistics.

Zwiers, J. (2008). *Building Academic Language.* Newark, DE: Jossey-Bass/International Reading Association.

Vocabulary

August, D., Carlo, M., Dressler, C., & Snow, C. (2005). The critical role of vocabulary development for English language learners. *Learning Disabilities Research and Practice, 20*, 50–57.

Bauman, J. F., & E. Kame'enui (Eds.). (2004). *Vocabulary Instruction: Research to Practice.* New York: Guilford.

Bear, D. R., Invernizzi, M., Templeton, S., & Johnson, F. (2004). *Words their way: Word study for phonics, vocabulary, and spelling instruction (2nd Ed.).* Upper Saddle River, NJ: Merrill Prentice Hall.

Beck, I. L., McKeown, M.G., & Kucan, L. (2002). *Bringing words to life.* New York: The Guilford Press.

Beck, I. L., & McKeown, M. G. (1991). Conditions of vocabulary acquisition. In R. Barr, M. L. Kamil, P. B. Mosenthal, & P. D. Pearson (Eds.), *Handbook of reading research* (Vol. 2, pp. 789–814). White Plains, NY: Longman.

Beck, I. L., McKeown, M. G., & Omanson, R. C. (1987). The effects and uses of diverse vocabulary instructional techniques. In M.G. McKeown & M.E. Curtis (Eds.), *The nature of vocabulary acquisition* (pp.147–163). Mahwah, NJ: Lawrence Erlbaum Associates.

Biemiller, A. (2004). Teaching vocabulary in the primary grades: Vocabulary instruction needed. In J.F. Baumann & E. Kame'enui (Eds.), *Vocabulary instruction: Bringing research to practice* (pp.209–242). Mahwah, NJ: Lawrence Erlbaum Associates.

Blachowicz, C. L. Z., & Fisher, P. J. L. (2000). Vocabulary instruction. In M. L. Kamil, P. B. Mosenthal, P. D. Pearson, & R. Barr (Eds.), *Handbook of reading research* (Vol. 3, pp. 503–523). White Plains, NY: Longman.

Blachowicz, C. L. Z., Fisher, P. J. L., Ogle D., & Watts-Taffe, S. (2006). Vocabulary: Questions from the classroom. *Reading Research Quarterly,* 41, 524–539.

Carlo, M. S., August, D., McLaughlin, B., Snow, C. E., Dressler, C., Lippman, D. N., Lively, T. J., & White, C. E. (2004). Closing the gap: Addressing the vocabulary needs of English-language learners in bilingual and mainstream classrooms. *Reading Research Quarterly,* 39, 188–215.

Carlo, M. S., August, D., & Snow, C. E. (2005). Sustained vocabulary-learning strategies for English language learners. In E. H. Hiebert & M. Kamil (Eds.), *Teaching and learning vocabulary: Bringing research to practice* (pp.137–153). Mahwah, NJ: Lawrence Erlbaum Associates.

Coxhead, A. (2000). A new Academic Word List. *TESOL Quarterly,* 34(2): 213–238.

Eyraud, K., Giles, G., Koenig, S., & Stoller, F. (2000). The word wall approach: Promoting L2 vocabulary learning. *English Teaching Forum,* 38, pp. 2–11.

Graves, M. F. (2006). *The vocabulary book: Learning and instruction.* New York: Teacher's College Press.

Harrington, M. J. (1996). Basic instruction in word analysis skills to improve spelling competence. *Education,* 117, 22. Available at: www. questia.com.

Kieffer, M. J., & Lesaux, N. K. (in press). Breaking down words to build meaning: Morphology, vocabulary, and reading comprehension in the urban classroom. *The Reading Teacher.*

Lehr, F., Osborn, J., & Hiebert, E. H. (2004). *A focus on vocabulary.* Honolulu, HI: Pacific Regional Educational Laboratory. Available at: www.prel.org/programs/rel/vocabularyforum.asp.

Nagy, W. E., & Scott, J. A. (2000). Vocabulary processes. In R. Barr, M. L. Kamil, P. Mosenthal, & P. D. Pearson (Eds.), *Handbook of reading research: Vol. 3* (pp. 269–284). New York: Longman.

Nagy, W. E., & Stahl, S. A. (2006). *Teaching word meanings.* Mahwah, NJ: Lawrence Erlbaum Associates.

Roser, N., & Juel, C. (1982). Effects of vocabulary instruction on reading comprehension. In J.A. Niles & L.A. Harris (Eds.), *Yearbook of the National Reading Conference: Vol. 31. New inquiries in reading research and Instruction* (pp. 110–118). Rochester, NY: National Reading Conference.

Ruddell, M. R., & Shearer, B. A. (2002). "Extraordinary," "tremendous," exhilarating," "magnificent": Middle school at-risk students become avid word learners with the vocabulary-self collection strategy (VSS). *Journal of Adolescent and Adult Literacy,* 45(4), 352–363.

Stahl, S. A. (1999). *Vocabulary development.* Cambridge, MA: Brookline Books.

Stahl, S. A., & Nagy, W. E. (2006). *Teaching word meanings.* Mahwah, NJ: Lawrence Erlbaum Associates.

White, T., Sowell, J., & Yanagihara, A. (1989). Teaching elementary students to use word-part clues. *The Reading Teacher,* 42, 302–308.

Wixson, K. K. (1986). Vocabulary instruction and children's comprehension of basal stories. *Reading Research Quarterly,* 21(3) 317–329.

Reading

Allington, R. L. (2001). *What really matters for struggling readers: Designing research-based programs.* New York, NY: Addison Wesley Educational Publishers Inc.

Baker, L. (2004). Reading comprehension and science inquiry: Metacognitive connections. In E.W. Saul (Ed.), *Crossing borders in literacy and science instruction: Perspectives on theory and practice.* Newark, DE: International Reading Association; Arlington, VA: National Science Teachers Association (NSTA) Press.

Beck, I. L. (2006). *Making sense of phonics: The hows and whys.* New York: Guilford Press.

Beck, I. L., & McKeown, M. G., (2001). Inviting students into the pursuit of meaning. *Educational Psychology Review,* 13(3), 225–241.

Beck, I. L., McKeown, M. G., Hamilton, R. L., and Kucan, L. (1997). *Questioning the Author: An approach for enhancing student engagement with text.* Delaware: International Reading Association.

Boulware, B. J., & Crow, M. (2008, March). Using the concept attainment strategy to enhance reading comprehension. *The Reading Teacher,* 61(6), 491–495.

Cain, K. & Oakhill, J. (1998). Comprehension skill and inference-making ability: Issues and causality. In C. Hulme and R.M. Joshi (Eds.), *Reading and spelling: Development and disorders.* London: Lawrence Erlbaum.

Cain, K. & Oakhill, J. (2000). Inference making ability and its relation to comprehension failure in young children. *Reading and Writing: An Interdisciplinary Journal,* 11,489–503.

Calhoon, M. B., Al Otaiba, S., Cihak, D., King, A., & Avalos, A. C. (2006). *Effects of a peer-mediated program on reading skill acquisition for two-way bilingual first grade classrooms.* Manuscript submitted for publication.

Cirino, P. T., Vaughn, S., Linan-Thompson, S., Cardenas-Hagan, E., Fletcher, J. M., & Francis, D. J. (2007). *One year follow-up outcomes of Spanish and English interventions for English language learners at-risk for reading problems.* Manuscript submitted for publication.

Crawford, E. C., & Torgesen, J. K. (2006). *Teaching all students to read: Practices from Reading First schools with strong intervention outcomes.* Tallahassee, FL: Florida Center for Reading Research. Available at: www.fcrr.org.

Cunningham, A. E., & Stanovich, K. (1998). *What reading does to the mind.* American Educator, 22 (1), 8–15.

Denton, C. A., Anthony, J. L., Parker, R., & Hasbrouck, J. E. (2004). Effects of two tutoring programs on the English reading development of Spanish-English bilingual students. *The Elementary School Journal,* 104, 289–305.

Dole, J., Duffy, G., Roehler, L., & Pearson, P. (1991). Moving from the old to the new: Research in reading comprehension instruction. *Review of Educational Research,* 61, 239–264.

Duke, N. K., & Pearson, P. D. (2002). Effective practices for developing reading comprehension. In A. E. Farstrup & S. J. Samuels (Eds.), *What research has to say about reading instruction* (3rd ed.) (pp. 205–242). Newark, DE: International Reading Association.

Fielding, L., Kerr, N., & Rosier, P. (2007). *Annual growth for all students, catch-up growth for those who are behind.* Kennewick, WA: The New Foundation Press.

Garcia, G. E. (2000). Bilingual children's reading. In M. L. Kamil, P. B. Mosenthal, P. D. Pearson, & R. Barr (Eds.), *Handbook of reading research: Volume III* (pp. 813–834). Mahwah, NJ: Lawrence Erlbaum Associates.

Gerber, M., Jimenez, T., Leafstedt, J., Villaruz, J., Richards, C., & English, J. (2004). English reading effects of small-group intensive instruction in Spanish for K–1 English learners. *Learning Disabilities Research & Practice,* 19(4), 239–251.

Head, M., & Readence, J. (1986). Anticipation guides: Meaning through prediction. In E. Dishner, T. Bean, J. Readence, & D. Moore (Eds.), *Reading in the Content Areas,* Dubuque, IA: Kendall/Hunt.

Kosanovich, M., Ladinsky, K., Nelson, L., & Torgesen, J. (2006). *Differentiated reading instruction: Small group lesson structures for all students.* Tallahassee, FL: Florida Center for Reading Research. Available at: www.fcrr.org.

Lehr, F. & Osborne, J. (2006). *Focus on comprehension.* Honolulu, HI: Pacific Regional Educational Laboratory. Available at: www.prel.org/programs/rel/comprehensionforum.asp.

Lesaux, N. K., & Kieffer, M. J. (in press). Sources of reading comprehension difficulties for language minority learners and their classmates in early adolescence. *American Educational Research Journal.*

Lesaux, N. K., & Siegel, L. S. (2003). The development of reading in children who speak English as a second language. *Developmental Psychology,* 39(6), 1005–1019.

Lesaux, N. K., Lipka, O., & Siegel, L. S. (2006). Investigating cognitive and linguistic abilities that influence the reading comprehension skills of children from diverse linguistic backgrounds. *Reading and Writing: An Interdisciplinary Journal,* 19, 99–131.

Linan-Thompson, S., & Hickman-Davis, P. (2002). Supplemental reading instruction for students at risk for reading disabilities: Improve reading 30 minutes at a time. *Learning Disabilities Research and Practice,* 17(4), 242–251.

Linan-Thompson, S., Vaughn, S., Hickman-Davis, P., & Kouzekanani, K. (2003). Effectiveness of supplemental reading instruction for second-grade English language learners with reading difficulties. *The Elementary School Journal,* 103(3), 221–238.

McMaster, K. L., Kung, H., Han, I., & Cao, M. (in press). Peer-assisted learning strategies: A "tier 1" approach to promoting responsiveness to beginning reading instruction for English learners. *Exceptional Children.*

McKeown, M. G., Beck, I. L., & Worthy, M. J. (1993). Grappling with text ideas: Questioning the author. *Reading Teacher,* 46, 560–66.

National Reading Panel. (2000). *Report of the National Reading Panel: Teaching children to read.* Bethesda, MD: National Institute of Child Health and Human Development.

Ogle, D. S. (1986). K-W-L group instructional strategy. In A. S. Palincsar, D. S. Ogle, B. F. Jones, & E. G. Carr (Eds.), *Teaching reading as thinking.* Alexandria, VA: Association for Supervision and Curriculum Development.

Palincsar, A. S., & Brown, A. L. (1985). Reciprocal teaching: Activities to promote reading with your mind. In T. L. Harris & E. J. Cooper (Eds.), *Reading thinking and concept development: Strategies for the classroom.* New York: The College Board.

Pressley, M. (2000). What should comprehension instruction be the instruction of? In M. Kamil, P. B. Mosenthal, P. D. Pearson, & R. Barr (Eds.), *Handbook of Reading Research: Vol. 3* (pp. 545–561). Mahwah, NJ: Lawrence Erlbaum Associates.

Pressley, M., & Afflerbach, P. (1995). *Verbal protocols of reading: The nature of constructively responsive reading.* Hillsdale, NJ: Erlbaum.

Proctor, C. P., Carlo, M., August, D., & Snow, C. (2005). Native Spanish-speaking children reading in English: Toward a model of comprehension. *Journal of Educational Psychology,* 97, 246–256.

Quiroga, T., Lemos-Britton, Z., Mostafapour, E., Abbott, R. D., & Berninger, V. W. (2002). Phonological awareness and beginning reading in Spanish-speaking ESL first graders: Research into practice. *Journal of School Psychology,* 40, 85–111.

Riedel, B. W. (2007). The relation between DIBELS, reading comprehension, and vocabulary in urban, first grade students. *Reading Research Quarterly,* 42, 460–466.

Saunders, W. M., & Goldenberg, C. (1999). Effects of instructional conversations and literature logs on limited- and fluent- English-proficient students' story comprehension and thematic understanding. *Elementary School Journal,* 99, 277–301.

Schlick Noe, K., & Johnson, N. (1999). *Getting started with literature circles.* Norwood, MA: Christopher-Gordon Publishers, Inc.

Slavin, R., & Cheung, A. (2005). A synthesis of research on language of reading instruction for English language learners. *Review of Educational Research,* 75, 247–284.

Snow, C. E., Burns, M. S., & Griffin, P. (Eds.). (1998). *Preventing reading difficulties in young children.* Washington, DC: National Academy Press.

Swanson, H. L., Sáez, L., & Gerber, M. (2004). Do phonological and executive processes in English learners at risk for reading disabilities in grade 1 predict performance in grade 2? *Learning Disabilities Research & Practice,* 19, 225–238.

Taylor, W. (1953). Close procedure a new tool for measuring readability. *Journalism Quarterly,* 30, 415–433.

Torgesen, J. K. (2006). *A principal's guide to intensive reading interventions for struggling readers in early elementary school.* Portsmouth, NH: RMC Research Corporation, Center on Instruction. Available at: www.centeroninstruction.org.

Tumner, J., & Chapman, J. (1995). Context use in early reading development: Premature exclusion of a source or individual differences? *Issues in Education,*1, 97–100.

Vaughn, S., Cirino, P. T., Linan-Thompson, S., Mathes, P. G., Carlson, C. D., Cardenas-Hagan, E., et al. (2006). Effectiveness of a Spanish intervention and an English intervention for English language learners at risk for reading problems. *American Educational Research Journal, 43,* 449–487.

Vaughn, S., Mathes, P., Linan-Thompson, S., Cirino, P., Carlson, C., Pollard-Durodola, S., et al. (2006). Effectiveness of an English intervention for first-grade English language learners at risk for reading problems. *Elementary School Journal, 107,* 153–180.

Vaughn, S., Linan-Thompson, S., & Hickman-Davis, P. (2003). Response to treatment as a means for identifying students with reading/learning disabilities. *Exceptional Children, 69,* 391–410.

Vaughn, S., Mathes, P., Linan-Thompson, S., & Francis, D. (2005). Teaching English language learners at risk for reading disabilities to read: Putting research into practice. *Learning Disabilities Research and Practice, 20*(1), 58–67.

Verhoeven, L. (1990). Acquisition of reading in a second language. *Reading Research Quarterly, 25,* 90–114.

Verhoeven, L. T. (2000). Components in early second language reading and spelling. *Scientific Studies of Reading, 4,* 313–330.

Willhelm, J. (2002). *Action strategies for deepening comprehension.* New York: Scholastic.

Writing

Britton, J. (1983). Writing and the story of the world. In B. Kroll & E. Wells (Eds.), *Explorations in the development of writing theory, research, and practice* (p. 3–30). New York: Wiley.

Calderón, M., Hertz-Lazarowitz, R., & Slavin, R. (1998). Effects of bilingual cooperative integrated reading and composition on students transitioning from Spanish to English reading. *Elementary School Journal, 99,* 153–165.

Celce-Murcia, M. (2002). On the use of selected grammatical features in academic writing. In M. C. Colombi & M. J. Schleppegrell (Eds.), *Developing advanced literacy in first and second languages* (pp. 143–158). Mahwah, NJ: Erlbaum.

Cunningham, P., & Allington, R. (2003). *Classrooms that work.* New York: Pearson Education, Inc.

Dyson, A. H. (1989). *Multiple worlds of child writers: Friends learning to write.* New York: Teachers College Press.

Elbow, P. (1998). *Writing with power.* Oxford: Oxford University Press.

Fisher, D., & Frey, N. (2008). Releasing responsibility. *Educational Leadership, 66*(3), 32–37.

Fisher, D., & Frey, N. (2007). *Scaffolded writing instruction: Teaching with a gradual-release framework.* New York: Scholastic.

Fisher, D., Frey, N., & Rothenberg, C., (2008). *Content area conversations: How to plan discussion-based lessons for diverse language learners.* Alexandria, VA: Association for Supervision and Curriculum Development.

Fearn, L., & Farnan, N. (2001). *Interactions: Teaching writing and the language arts.* Boston: Houghton Mifflin.

Kirby, D., Kirby, D. L., & Liner, T. (2004). *Inside out: Strategies for teaching writing.* Portsmouth, NH: Heinemann.

McCarrier, A., Pinnell, G. S., & Fountas, I. C. (2000). *Interactive writing: How language and literacy come together, K–2.* Portsmouth, NH: Heinemann.

Samway, K. (2006). *When English language learners write: connecting research to practice.* Portsmouth: Heineman.

Schleppegrell, M. J., & Go, A. L. (2007). Analyzing the writing of English learners: A functional approach. *Language Arts, 84*(6), 529–538.

Strong, W. (2001). Coaching writing: *The power of guided practice.* Portsmouth, NH: Heinemann-Boynton/Cook.

Fluency

Breznitz, Z. (2006). *Fluency in reading.* Mahwah, NJ: Lawrence Erlbaum Associates.

Crosson, A. C., & Lesaux, N. K. (in press). Revisiting assumptions about the relationship of fluent reading to comprehension: Spanish-speakers' text-reading fluency in English. *Reading and Writing: An Interdisciplinary Journal.*

Downhower, S. L. (1987). Effects of repeated reading on second grade transitional readers' fluency and comprehension. *Reading Research Quarterly, 22*(4), 389–406.

Geva, E., & Yaghoub-Zadeh, Z. (2006). Reading efficiency in native English-speaking and English-as-a-second-language children: The role of oral proficiency and underlying cognitive-linguistic processes. *Scientific Studies of Reading, 10,* 31–57.

Kuhn, M. R. (2005). Helping students become accurate, expressive readers: Fluency instruction for small groups. *The Reading Teacher, 58,* 338–344.

Kung, S. H. (2009). *Predicting the success on a state standards test for culturally and linguistically diverse students using curriculum-based oral reading measures.* Unpublished doctoral dissertation, University of Minnesota.

LaBerge, D., & Samuels, S. J. (1974). Toward a theory of automatic information processing in reading. *Cognitive Psychology, 6,* 293–323.

Maurice, K. (1983). The fluency workshop. *TESOL Newsletter, 17,* 4.

Osborn, J., Lehr, F., & Hiebert, E. H. (2003). *A Focus on Fluency.* Honolulu, HI: Pacific Resources for Education and Learning. Available at www.prel.org/programs/rel/rel.asp.

Pikulski, J., & Chard, D. (2005). Fluency: the bridge between decoding and reading comprehension. *The Reading Teacher, 58,* 510–521.

Samuels, S. J., & Farstrup, A. E. (2006). *What research has to say about fluency instruction.* Newark, DE: International Reading Association.

Schilling, S. G., Carlisle, J. F., Scott, S. E., & Zeng, J. (2007). Are fluency measures accurate predictors of reading achievement? *The Elementary School Journal, 107,* 429–448.

Research Base and Bibliography, continued

Vaughn, S., Chard, D. J., Bryant, D. P., Coleman, M., Tyler, B. J., Linan-Thompson, S., & Kouzekanani, K. (2000). Fluency and comprehension interventions for third-grade students. *Remedial and Special Education, 21*(6), 325–335.

Technology

Fisher, D., & Frey, N. (in press). *Literacy 2.0: Language, literacy and learning in a new century* [working title]. Bloomington, IN: Solution Tree.

Gee, J. P. (2007). *What video games have to teach us about learning and literacy.* New York: Palgrave Macmillan.

International Reading Association. (May 2009). *New literacies and 21st century technologies: A position statement of the International Reading Association.* Newark, DE: Author. Used with permission.

Leu, D. J., O'Byrne, W. I., Zawilinski, L., McVerry, J. G., & Everett-Cacopardo, H. (2009). Expanding the new literacies conversation. *Educational Researcher, 38*(4), 264–269.

Mayer, R. E. (2001). Multimedia learning. New York: Cambridge University Press. Partnership for 21st Century Skills. (2009). *Framework for 21st century learning.* Retrieved from www.21stcenturyskills.org/index.php?option=com_content&task=view&id=254&Itemid=120.

Ybarra, R. & Green, T. (2003). Using technology to teach ESL/EFL students to develop language skills. *The Internet TESL Journal, 9,* n.p.

Assessment

Afflerbach, P. (2007). *Understanding and using reading assessment K–12.* Newark, DE: International Reading Association.

Carpenter, S. K., Pashler, H., Cepeda, N. J., and Alvarez, D. (2007). Applying the principles of testing and spacing to classroom learning. In D. S. McNamara and J. G. Trafton (Eds.), *Proceedings of the 29th Annual Cognitive Science Society* (p. 19). Nashville, TN: Cognitive Science Society.

Carpenter, S. K., Pashler, H., Wixted, J. T., and Vul, E. (in press). The effects of tests on learning and forgetting. *Memory & Cognition.*

Dempster, F. N., & Perkins, P. G. (1993). Revitalizing classroom assessment: Using tests to promote learning. *Journal of Instructional Psychology, 20,* 197–203.

Dominguez de Ramirez, R., & Shapiro, E. S. (2006). Curriculum-based measurement and the evaluation of reading skills of Spanish-speaking English language learners in bilingual education classrooms. *School Psychology Review, 35,* 356–369.

Edwards, P., Turner, J. D., & Mokhtari, K. (2008). Balancing the assessment of and the assessment for learning in support of student literacy achievement. *Reading Teacher, 61,* 682–684.

Fisher, D., & Frey, N. (2007). *Checking for understanding: Formative assessment techniques for your classroom.* Alexandria, VA: Association for Supervision and Curriculum Development.

Frey, N., & Heibert, E. (2002). Teacher-based assessment of literacy learning. In J. Flood, D. Lapp, J. R. Squire, & J. M. Jensen (Eds.). *Handbook of Research on the Teaching of English Language Arts* (2nd ed.), pp.608–618. Mahwah, NJ: Lawrence Erlbaum.

Gersten, R., Dimino, J., & Jayanthi, M. (in press). Development of a classroom observational system. In B. Taylor & J. Ysseldyke (Eds.), *Reading instruction for English language learners: The Bond symposium.* New York: Teachers College.

Goodman, Y. (2002). Informal methods of evaluation. In J. Flood, D. Lapp, J. R. Squire, & J. M. Jensen (Eds.). *Handbook of Research on the Teaching of English Language Arts* (2nd ed.), pp. 600–607. Mahwah, NJ: Lawrence Erlbaum.

Johnston, P. (2005). Literacy assessment and the future. *The Reading Teacher, 58*(7), 684–686.

Limbos, M. (2006). Early identification of second language students at risk for reading disability. *Dissertation Abstracts International, 66* (10-A), 3566A.

Schumm, J. S. & Arguelles, M. E. (2006). No two learners are alike: The importance of assessment and differentiated instruction. In J. S. Schumm (Ed.), *Reading assessment and instruction for all learners.* New York: Guilford Press.

Torgesen, J. K. (2006). *A comprehensive K–3 reading assessment plan: Guidance for school leaders.* Portsmouth, NH: RMC Research Corporation, Center on Instruction. Available at: www.centeroninstruction.org.

Townsend, D., Lee, E., & Chiappe, P. (2006). *English or Spanish? The efficacy of assessing Latino/a children in Spanish for risk of reading disabilities.* Paper presented at the meeting of the Society for the Scientific Study of Reading, Vancouver, BC, Canada.

Wiley, H. I., & Deno, S. L. (2005). Oral reading and maze measures as predictors of success for English learners on a state standards assessment. *Remedial and Special Education, 26,* 207–214.

Living Traditions

BIG Question

How important are traditions?

Part 1   How can traditions shape who we are?

Part 2   How do traditions help guide us?

Curriculum Connections

Content Connection
- Cultural Traditions, Customs, and Celebrations

Unit 1

Theme Connection
- Artistic Traditions
- Family Traditions

Student Book

Unit 1

Living Traditions

(?) BIG QUESTION

How important are traditions?

Social Studies
▸ Cultural Traditions, Customs, and Celebrations

NGReach.com **REACH ONLINE FOR LEARNING** Sing with Me Audio (((MP3)) • Read with Me Audio (((MP3)) • National Geographic Digital Library • Interactive eEdition • Games for learning • My Vocabulary Notebook • Online Resources

REACH ONLINE FOR TEACHING Presentation Tool • Online Lesson Planner • Leveled Book Finder • eAssessment • Word Builder • Professional Development Podcasts (((MP3))

Animal Intelligence

(?) **BIG QUESTION**

Just how smart are animals?

Science
▸ Animal Behavior

⊕ NGReach.com   REACH ONLINE FOR LEARNING Sing with Me Audio (((MP3))) ▪ Read with Me Audio (((MP3))) ▪ National Geographic Digital Library
▪ Interactive eEdition ▪ Games for learning ▪ My Vocabulary Notebook ▪ Online Resources
REACH ONLINE FOR TEACHING Presentation Tool ▪ Online Lesson Planner ▪ Leveled Book Finder ▪ eAssessment ▪ Word Builder
▪ Professional Development Podcasts (((MP3)))

Unit 3

Amazing Places

(?) BIG QUESTION

Why learn about other places?

Social Studies
▸ Geographic Tools and Features

🌐 NGReach.com REACH ONLINE FOR LEARNING Sing with Me Audio (((MP3))) ▪ Read with Me Audio (((MP3))) ▪ National Geographic Digital Library
▪ Interactive eEdition ▪ Games for learning ▪ My Vocabulary Notebook ▪ Online Resources
REACH ONLINE FOR TEACHING Presentation Tool ▪ Online Lesson Planner ▪ Leveled Book Finder ▪ eAssessment ▪ Word Builder
▪ Professional Development Podcasts (((MP3)))

Power of Nature

(?) **BIG QUESTION**

How do we relate to nature?

Science
▸ Natural Resources
▸ Wind, Water, Earth, and Air

NGReach.com **REACH ONLINE FOR LEARNING** Sing with Me Audio ((MP3)) ▪ Read with Me Audio ((MP3)) ▪ National Geographic Digital Library ▪ Interactive eEdition ▪ Games for learning ▪ My Vocabulary Notebook ▪ Online Resources

REACH ONLINE FOR TEACHING Presentation Tool ▪ Online Lesson Planner ▪ Leveled Book Finder ▪ eAssessment ▪ Word Builder ▪ Professional Development Podcasts ((MP3))

Unit 5

Invaders!

(?) **BIG QUESTION**

When do harmless things become harmful?

Science
▸ Science Process: Collect, Record, and Analyze Data
▸ Animal Habitats and Migration

NGReach.com REACH ONLINE FOR LEARNING Sing with Me Audio (((MP3))) ▪ Read with Me Audio (((MP3))) ▪ National Geographic Digital Library
▪ Interactive eEdition ▪ Games for learning ▪ My Vocabulary Notebook ▪ Online Resources
REACH ONLINE FOR TEACHING Presentation Tool ▪ Online Lesson Planner ▪ Leveled Book Finder ▪ eAssessment ▪ Word Builder
▪ Professional Development Podcasts (((MP3)))

Treasure Hunters

? BIG QUESTION

Why do we seek treasure?

Social Studies
▸ Exploration

NGReach.com REACH ONLINE FOR LEARNING Sing with Me Audio (((MP3))) ▪ Read with Me Audio (((MP3))) ▪ National Geographic Digital Library
▪ Interactive eEdition ▪ Games for learning ▪ My Vocabulary Notebook ▪ Online Resources

REACH ONLINE FOR TEACHING   Presentation Tool ▪ Online Lesson Planner ▪ Leveled Book Finder ▪ eAssessment ▪ Word Builder
▪ Professional Development Podcasts (((MP3)))

Unit 7

Moving Through Space

(?) BIG QUESTION

What does it take to explore space?

Science
- ▸ Solving Problems
- ▸ Speed
- ▸ Space

NGReach.com **REACH ONLINE FOR LEARNING** Sing with Me Audio (((MP3))) ▪ Read with Me Audio (((MP3))) ▪ National Geographic Digital Library ▪ Interactive eEdition ▪ Games for learning ▪ My Vocabulary Notebook ▪ Online Resources

REACH ONLINE FOR TEACHING Presentation Tool ▪ Online Lesson Planner ▪ Leveled Book Finder ▪ eAssessment ▪ Word Builder ▪ Professional Development Podcasts (((MP3)))

Saving a Piece of the World

(?) BIG QUESTION

What's worth protecting?

Social Studies
▸ Preserving Species
▸ Preserving Culture

Genres at a Glance

Reading

Student Anthology
Pages 2–71

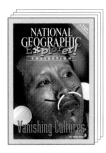

Explorer Books Collection
Vanishing Cultures
Culture Clash

Non-Fiction Library

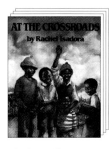

Fiction Library

Sing with Me Language Songs
Pages 4–7

Assessment

Assessment Handbook
Pages 1–54

Practice Masters and Manipulatives

Language and Literacy Teamwork Activities
Pages 5–10
Cross-Curricular Teamwork Activities
Pages 5–10

Practice Masters
Pages 1.1–1.24

Language Builder Picture Cards
Pages E1–E13

Newcomer

In The U.S.A.
Resources for Newcomers

Phonics

Reach into Phonics
See Teacher's Edition
Pages T2–T27

NGReach.com

Reach into Teaching

- Online Lesson Planner
- Teaching Resources
- Presentation Tool
- eEdition NG Digital Library
- eAssessment: Online Tests Scan and Score Reports

Reach into Learning

- My Vocabulary Notebook
- Vocabulary Games
- Personalized Dictionaries
- NG Digital Library
- Comprehension Coach

Recordings

- Songs and Chants CD
- Selection Recordings CD
- Fluency Models CD

Unit **1** Planner

Living Traditions

BIG Question: How important are traditions?

Student Book

- Build Background Video
- Introduce the  **BIG** Question

	LANGUAGE	VOCABULARY	READING
PART 1 **Weeks 1 and 2** **Focus:** Cultural Traditions	**Language Function** ❶ Express Feelings • Agree and Disagree **Grammar** ❶ Complete Sentences ❶ Simple Subjects and Predicates **Listening & Speaking** • Listen for Implicit Ideas **How to Learn Language** • Use Nonverbal Clues **Oral Language Project** • Interview	**Key Words** ❶ Social Studies Vocabulary craft perform tradition musical pottery weave ❶ Academic Vocabulary create express style culture medium ❶ Basic Vocabulary: The Arts act in a play play the guitar dance to the play the piano music draw a picture sing a song paint a picture take a picture play the drums write a story ❶ Use a Dictionary	**Reading Strategy** ❶ Plan and Monitor **Genre** • Interview **Text Structure** ❶ Main Idea and Details **Test Features** • Questions and Answers JOSH PONTE A Musical Journey **Genre** • Biography **Test Features** • Biography Shaped by Tradition **Leveled Library** **Reading Fluency** ❶ Phrasing ❶ Accuracy and Rate
PART 2 **Weeks 3 and 4** **Focus:** Family Traditions and Customs	**Language Function** ❶ Ask for and Give Information **Grammar** ❶ Compound Subjects ❶ Compound Predicates • Subject-Verb Agreement **Listening & Speaking** ❶ Give Instructions **How to Learn Language** • Self-Monitor and Self-Correct **Theme Theater** • Perform a Skit	**Key Words** ❶ Social Studies Vocabulary ancestor marriage ritual ceremony occasion ❶ Academic Vocabulary belief influence role custom relationship ❶ Basic Vocabulary: Family aunt niece cousin family father daughter grandfather granddaughter grandmother grandson mother son sister brother uncle nephew ❶ Idioms and Expressions	**Reading Strategy** ❶ Plan and Monitor **Genre** • Folk Tale Martina the Beautiful Cockroach A CUBAN FOLK TALE **Text Structure** ❶ Plot **Literary Analysis** • Character and Setting **Genre** • Magazine Article Coming of Age **Literary Analysis** • Narrator **Leveled Library** **Reading Fluency** ❶ Expression ❶ Accuracy and Rate

Ready-to-Go Plans
▶ Time (20, 30, 40, 60, 90 minutes per day)
▶ Model (Content Focus, Literacy Focus, Dual Language)

Online Lesson Planner

NGReach.com >

WRITING	LEARNING STATIONS	REVIEW, ASSESS, RETEACH
Daily Writing • Writing Fluency • Journal Entry • Writer's Craft: Visuals • Advertisement • Interview Questions • Biographic Article	Make a Musical Instrument Rhythm Patterns Same and Different Words and Music Use Text to Ask Questions Continue the Interview	**Oral Language Rubrics** • Express Feelings • Retell a Selection • Oral Language Project: Listening, Speaking, Content **Vocabulary Test** • Key Words: Content Vocabulary • Key Words: Academic Vocabulary
Daily Writing • Writing Fluency • Writer's Craft: Humorous Paragraph • Friendly Letter • Paragraph • Journal Entry • Writing Project: Interview	Who Else Would Have Eaten Martina? Write Word Problems Create a Family Tree What I Mean Is … Tell About a Holiday You're Invited!	**Oral Language Rubrics** • Ask for and Give Information • Retell a Story • Theme Theater: Listening, Speaking, Content **Vocabulary Test** • Key Words: Content Vocabulary • Key Words: Academic Vocabulary **Reading Test** ❶ Reading Strategy: Plan and Monitor

UNIT WRAP-UP

Answer the

Unit 1 Assessment
• Self-Assessment
• Reading B I A AH
• Grammar B I A AH
• Writing I A AH

Resources

- Unit 1 Build Background Video
- Family Newsletter 1
- eVisual 1.1
- Practice Master 1.1

NGReach.com

See **Technology Station** for digital student resources.

Home Connection

Send home **Family Newsletter 1.**

Students discuss their traditions with their families. With family permission, students bring in items to share that represent these traditions.

Living Traditions

1 Preview and Predict Read the unit title aloud and encourage students to flip through the unit. Ask: *What do you think you will learn? What makes you think that?*

2 Introduce the Big Question Ask: *What do you think the word* tradition *means?* (a special way of doing something that a family or group has) *What is a holiday tradition that your family has?* (Answers will vary.)

Read aloud the Big Question. Have students share possible answers. Encourage them to provide details. List the answers.

3 Build Background Preview the video: *Now we will play a video that tells us about traditions. We'll learn about traditions of different cultures and why those traditions are important.*

▶ Play the video.

NGReach.com **Build Background Video**

Discuss the video:

- *What are some examples of traditions?*

- *How do traditions help pass on ideas, beliefs, and customs to people in the future?*

- *What traditions in the video are similar to traditions in our community?*

- *How do the images in the video help you understand that traditions can change?*

4 Share What You Know Review the three steps of the directions. Explain: *To complete the activity, you will need to think about:*

- *a holiday you celebrate*
- *the special things you do to celebrate that holiday*

Make a four-column chart on the board. Use the seasons as headings for the columns. Ask students about the holidays celebrated in each season. List them in the chart. Suggest that students choose a holiday from the chart and show how they celebrate it.

Display the drawings, clustering together those that depict the same holiday. Discuss the similarities and differences in how the holidays are celebrated.

Living Traditions

1
2

BIG Question

How important are traditions?

Unit at a Glance
▶ **Language**: Express Feelings, Ask for and Give Information, Social Studies Words
▶ **Literacy**: Plan and Monitor
▶ **Content**: Culture and Traditions

Unit 1

Technology Station
○ NGReach.com

Digital Library
○ Watch the video.

Share What You Know ✋

Do it!

❶ **Think** of your favorite holiday of the year. Draw a picture to show how your family celebrates it. How is the celebration the same every year?

❷ **Share** your picture with a partner.

❸ **Explain** what makes the holiday special for you.

Build Background: Watch a video about traditions.
○ NGReach.com

4
3

Student Book pages 2–3

❺ **Begin the Unit Concept Map** Introduce the concept map: *As you go through this unit, it will be helpful to organize your thinking in a concept map.*

Display the unit concept map for the Big Question. Explain: *The Big Question is restated in the middle. We'll write our answers inside the people pictured on the map.*

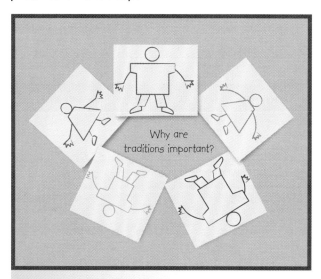

Why are traditions important?

○ NGReach.com ▸ eVisual 1.1

Have students add the ideas they already listed, and any other ideas they may have, to **Practice Master 1.1**. Explain that they will add more to the concept maps as they read through the unit and learn more about why traditions are important.

Name _____ Date _____

Unit Concept Map

Living Traditions

Make a concept map with the answers to the Big Question: How important are traditions?

For use with TE p. T3   1.1   Unit 1 | Living Traditions

○ ○ **Practice Master 1.1**

Talk About the **BIG Question**	Page
Begin the Unit Concept Map	T2–T3
Link to Content Vocabulary	T5
Link to "Josh Ponte: A Musical Journey"	T27
Link to "Shaped by Tradition"	T34a
Link to Content Vocabulary	T37
Link to "Martina the Beautiful Cockroach"	T59
Link to "Coming of Age"	T64a
Share Your Ideas	T71

Unit 1 | Launch   T3

BIG Question How important are traditions?

PART 1

Days 1–5

▶ **Main Selection**
Josh Ponte: A Musical Journey, by Ramona Jafar

▶ **Genre**
Interview

▶ **Selection Summary**
This interview is with Josh Ponte, an English man who traveled to Gabon, Africa in order to help gorillas. While he was there, he discovered the unique music performed by the people of Gabon. Ponte learned that the music and instruments are handed down from generation to generation, connecting the people with their culture, nature, and with each other.

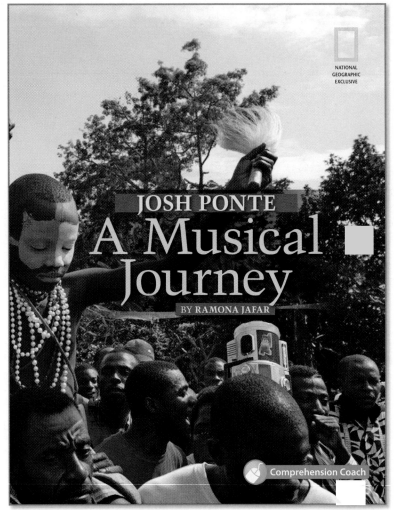

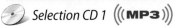
Selection CD 1 (((**MP3**)))

Skills at a Glance	
Language	Express Feelings; Agree and Disagree; Oral Language Project
Grammar	Complete Sentences; Simple Subjects and Predicates
Vocabulary	Social Studies Vocabulary: *craft, musical, perform, pottery, tradition, weave* Academic Vocabulary: *create, culture, express, medium, style* Use a Dictionary
Reading Strategy	Learn to Plan and Monitor
Literary Analysis	Main Idea and Details
Writing	Writing Fluency; Journal Entry; Writer's Craft: Visuals; Advertisement; Interview Questions; Biographic Article
Newcomer Support	Use *In the USA:* arts words

Days 6–10

▶ **Companion Selection**
Shaped by Tradition, by Patricia Millman

▶ **Genre**
Biography

▶ **Selection Summary**
Michael Naranjo, a Native American sculptor, has been working with clay since he was a child. Losing his sight and partial use of one hand while fighting in the Vietnam War, Naranjo had to "relearn" how to sculpt. Now, he "sees with his hands," and his sculptures are displayed around the United States and Europe.

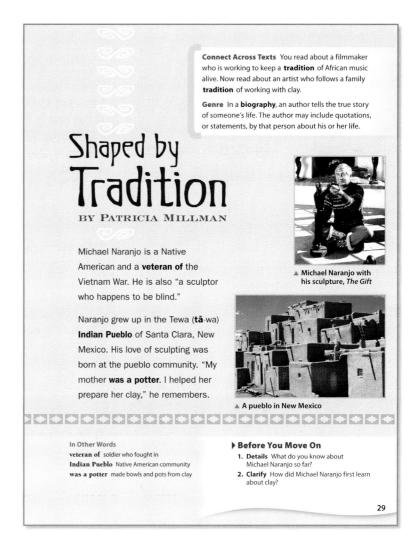

Connect Across Texts You read about a filmmaker who is working to keep a **tradition** of African music alive. Now read about an artist who follows a family **tradition** of working with clay.

Genre In a **biography**, an author tells the true story of someone's life. The author may include quotations, or statements, by that person about his or her life.

Shaped by Tradition
BY PATRICIA MILLMAN

Michael Naranjo is a Native American and a **veteran of** the Vietnam War. He is also "a sculptor who happens to be blind."

Naranjo grew up in the Tewa (**tā**-wa) **Indian Pueblo** of Santa Clara, New Mexico. His love of sculpting was born at the pueblo community. "My mother **was a potter**. I helped her prepare her clay," he remembers.

▲ Michael Naranjo with his sculpture, *The Gift*

▲ A pueblo in New Mexico

In Other Words
veteran of soldier who fought in
Indian Pueblo Native American community
was a potter made bowls and pots from clay

▶ **Before You Move On**
1. **Details** What do you know about Michael Naranjo so far?
2. **Clarify** How did Michael Naranjo first learn about clay?

29

Leveled Library Books

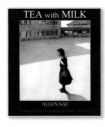

Unit 1 Daily Planner

BIG Question How important are traditions?

PART 1

Core Lessons	**Day 1**	**Day 2**
	Introduce Academic Language	Introduce More Academic Language
Language 🕐 5–10 minutes	**Language of the Day** *T4* ❶ **Language Function: Express Feelings** *T4* 🔊 ((MP3)) **Oral Language** • Talk About Festivals and Street Fairs *T5* • Talk Together About the Big Question *T5*	**Language of the Day** *T7a* ❶ **Grammar: Complete Sentences** *T7a* **Oral Language** • Talk Together About Planning and Monitoring *T8*

Vocabulary
 🕐 10–15 minutes
	❶ **Social Studies Vocabulary**
	 • Introduce Words *T5*
	    craft perform tradition
	    musical pottery weave
	 Classroom Vocabulary
	 • Introduce Word: **detail** *T6*
		❶ **Academic Vocabulary**
		 • Introduce Words *T7*
		    create medium
		    culture style
		    express
		 Classroom Vocabulary
		 • Introduce Word: **preview** *T9*

Reading 🕐 15–20 minutes	❶ **Text Structure: Main Idea and Details** • Introduce Main Idea and Details *T6a* • Use Graphic Organizers: Main Idea Diagram *T6* **Read Aloud: "The Family Party"** *T6a*	❶ **Strategy: Plan and Monitor** • Introduce and Practice the Strategy *T8* **Read "Perla's Journal"** *T9* **Phonics and Fluency** • Words with Short ă *T8*
Writing 🕐 15 minutes	**Daily Writing** • Writing Fluency *T6*	**Daily Writing** • Journal Entry *T9*
Content: Integrated Throughout Each Day	**Social Studies** • Explore Customs and Traditions • Geography	**Social Studies** • Explore Customs and Traditions • Geography

❶ = Tested Skill

Ready-to-Go Plans
▶ Time (20, 30, 40, 60, 90 minutes per day)
▶ Model (Content Focus, Literacy Focus, Dual Language)

Online Lesson Planner
⊙ NGReach.com

Day 3

Build Academic Language

Language of the Day *T10a*
Language Function: Agree and Disagree *T10a* 🔊 ((MP3))
Listening and Speaking
• Listen to and Sing a Song *T10a*

⊙ Academic and Social Studies Vocabulary
• Expand Word Knowledge *T10b*

| craft | culture |
| create | express |

Support Newcomers
• Build Basic Vocabulary: The Arts Words *T10b*

Read the Selection
⊙ Strategy: Plan and Monitor *T10—T24–25*
• Reading Options *T12*
Concepts of Print
• Hold a Book and Turn Pages *T13*
Literary Analysis
• Fact or Opinion; How to Paraphrase *T14–15*
Text Features • Photos *T16–17*
⊙ Fluency: Phrasing *T24–25*

Daily Writing
• Modeled Writing: Writer's Craft *T24–25*

Social Studies
• Musical Traditions *T18–19*
Math
• Rhythm and Pattern *T20–21*

Day 4

Build Academic Language

Language of the Day *T26a*
⊙ Grammar: Simple Subjects and Predicates *T26a*
Oral Language
• Talk About the Selection *T26c*

⊙ Academic and Social Studies Vocabulary
• Share Word Knowledge *T26b*

| medium | perform | style |
| musical | pottery | tradition |

Think and Respond
• Talk About the Selection *T26c*
• Test-Taking Strategy *T26c*
⊙ Fluency: Phrasing *T26c*

Daily Writing
• Independent Writing: Write About It *T26*

Social Studies
• Explore Customs and Traditions
• Geography

Day 5

Build Academic Language

Language of the Day *T27a*
Listening and Speaking
• Listen for Implicit Ideas *T27a*
How to Learn Language
• Use Nonverbal Clues *T27a*
Oral Language
• Talk Together About the Big Question *T27*

⊙ Academic and Social Studies Vocabulary
• Apply Word Knowledge *T27b*

| weave |

Reread and Retell
⊙ Text Structure: Main Idea and Details
• Make a Main Idea Diagram *T27c*
Retell a Selection *T27c*
⊙ Fluency: Accuracy, Rate, and Phrasing *T27c*

Daily Writing
• Interactive Writing: Interview Questions *T27*

Social Studies
• Explore Customs and Traditions
• Geography

Unit 1 Daily Planner continued

PART 1

Core Lessons	Day 6 — Expand Academic Language	Day 7 — Expand Academic Language

Language
🕐 5–10 minutes

Day 6

Language of the Day *T28a*
- ❶ **Language Function: Express Feelings** *T28a*

Oral Language
- Talk Together About the Big Question *T34a*

Day 7

Language of the Day *T35a*
- ❶ **Grammar: Complete Sentences** *T35a*

Vocabulary
🕐 10–15 minutes

Day 6

❶ **Use a Dictionary** *T28*

Support Newcomers:
- Additional Practice Using a Dictionary *T28*

Day 7

❶ **Use a Dictionary** *T35*
- Dictionary Entries *T35*

Reading
🕐 15–20 minutes

Day 6

Read the Biography *T29a*
- Reading Options *T29a*
- ❶ **Strategy: Plan and Monitor** *T29a—T32–33*

Text Feature
- Quotations *T30–T31*
- ❶ **Fluency: Accuracy and Rate** *T34*

Respond and Extend
- Compare Author's Purpose *T34a*

Day 7

Reread the Selection: Focus on Biography *T36a*

Writing
🕐 15 minutes

Day 6

Daily Writing
- Writing Fluency *T34*

Day 7

Daily Writing
- Modeled Writing: Biographic Article *T36b*

Content: Integrated Throughout Each Day

Day 6

Social Studies
- Explore Customs and Traditions
- Geography

Day 7

Social Studies
- Explore Customs and Traditions
- Geography

❶ = Tested Skill

Days 8–9

Apply Academic Language

Oral Language Project
- Introduce the Activity *T36c*
- Plan *T36c*
- Practice *T36d*
- Entertainment Today! *T36d*
- Debrief and Compare T36d

Read Leveled Books

Fiction *T36e*

 **B**

Key Words

crossroads   rumble

distant   waiting

guitar

 I

Key Words

department   marry

foreigner   worst

homeland

 **A** **AH**

Key Words

festival   parade

lanterns   tradition

palace

Nonfiction *T36f*

 **B**

Key Words

celebrate   graves

cemetery   spirit

glow

 **I**

Key Words

cactus   peace

dozens   toad

Easter

 **A** **AH**

Key Words

celebrate   important

feast   worship

festival

Daily Writing
- Journal Entry *T36f*

Day 10

Review and Assess

Interactive Review *T36g–T36h*
- ❶ Language Function: Express Feelings
- ❶ Grammar: Complete Sentences
- ❶ Vocabulary: Social Studies and Academic Vocabulary
- ❶ Vocabulary Strategy: Use a Dictionary
- ❶ Reading Strategy: Plan and Monitor
- ❶ Literary Analysis: Interview
- ❶ Text Structure: Main Idea and Details
- ❶ Fluency: Phrasing

Assessment *T36g–T36h*

Same Book, Different Levels

 **B** **I** **A** **AH**

Key Words

anthropologist   famine   jungle

arrow   forest   nomads

cultures   habitat   tribe

Reading Station

EXPLORER! COLLECTION
Ladder Text:
• Pioneer edition for below level readers
• Pathfinder edition for on and above level readers

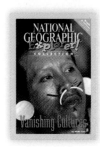 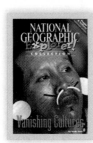

DECODABLE TEXTS

TRADE BOOK COLLECTION
Use the **Leveled Book Finder** at
NGReach.com

Content Stations

Download complete lesson plans **NGReach.com ›**

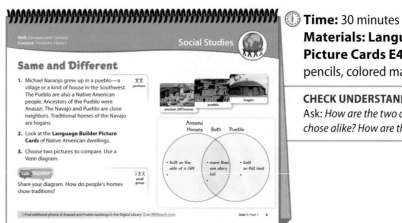

Skill: Explore Sound
Content: Traditions, Customs

Science

Make a Musical Instrument

1. Talk about musical instruments. Think of the different ways they make sound. ★★ partners

2. Design a musical instrument that you can make yourself. Use ordinary items you can find at home or in the classroom, or use items found in nature.

3. Make your instrument. Write sentences to explain how you made it and how it works.

Talk Together ★★★ small group
Share your musical instrument. Discuss the materials you used.

> I used a shoebox. I cut a hole in the lid. I stretched rubber bands across it. I placed pencils at each end to hold the rubber bands above the surface of the lid. When I strum the rubber bands, they make a sound. The sound is louder because of the hollow space inside the shoebox.

Digital Option Use graphics software to design your instrument.
Unit 1 | Part 1   5

Time: 30 minutes
Materials: home or classroom objects, paper, pencils

CHECK UNDERSTANDING
Have students explain how their instruments make sound.

Skill: Compare and Contrast
Content: Traditions, Homes

Social Studies

Same and Different

1. Michael Naranjo grew up in a pueblo—a village or a kind of house in the Southwest. The Pueblo are also a Native American people. Ancestors of the Pueblo were Anasazi. The Navajo and Pueblo are close neighbors. Traditional homes of the Navajo are hogans. ★★ partners

2. Look at the **Language Builder Picture Cards** of Native American dwellings.

3. Choose two pictures to compare. Use a Venn diagram.

Talk Together ★★★ small group
Share your diagram. How do people's homes show traditions?

Anasazi Houses / Both / Pueblo
• built on the side of a cliff • more than one story tall • built on flat land

Find additional photos of Anasazi and Pueblo buildings in the Digital Library on NGReach.com.
Unit 1 | Part 1   6

Time: 30 minutes
Materials: Language Builder Picture Cards E4–E6, paper, pencils, colored markers

CHECK UNDERSTANDING
Ask: *How are the two dwellings you chose alike? How are they different?*

Skill: Patterns
Content: Patterns in Different Cultures

Math

Rhythm Patterns

1. Look at the patterns on the **Language Builder Picture Cards.** ★★ partners

2. Choose a pattern. Assign a different sound to each part of a pattern, such as hand clapping, finger snapping, or foot stomping.

3. Make the sounds to "play" your pattern.

4. Choose another pattern and repeat the activity.

5. Practice your patterns and then play them together.

Navajo blankets / Hopi baskets / Pueblo pottery

Talk Together ★★★ large group
Share your rhythm patterns. Talk about how you assigned sounds to each part of your pattern.

> This rhythm matches my pattern: SNAP, STOMP, CLAP, SNAP, SNAP, STOMP, CLAP, SNAP

Digital Option Use a media player to record your patterns.
Unit 1 | Part 1   7

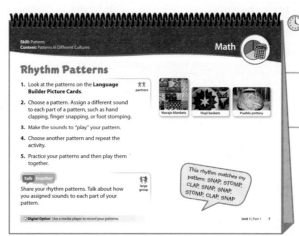

Time: 20 minutes
Materials: Language Builder Picture Cards E1–E3

CHECK UNDERSTANDING
Ask students to tell which sound they assigned to each part of a pattern.

Use these resources to provide daily opportunities for students to work individually or in groups at learning stations around the classroom.

Language Stations

Download complete lesson plans @NGReach.com >

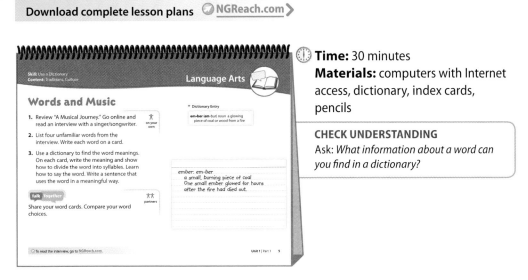

Time: 30 minutes

Materials: computers with Internet access, dictionary, index cards, pencils

CHECK UNDERSTANDING
Ask: *What information about a word can you find in a dictionary?*

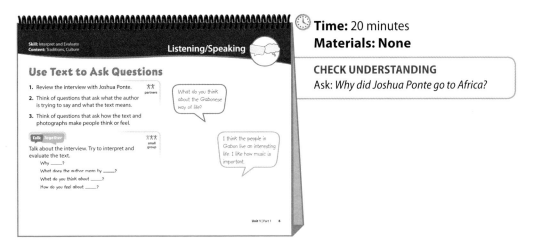

Time: 20 minutes
Materials: None

CHECK UNDERSTANDING
Ask: *Why did Joshua Ponte go to Africa?*

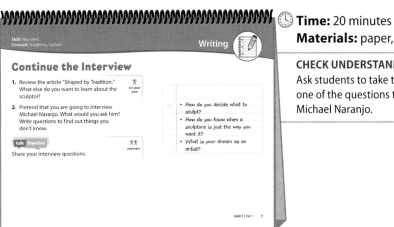

Time: 20 minutes
Materials: paper, pencils

CHECK UNDERSTANDING
Ask students to take turns reading aloud one of the questions they would ask Michael Naranjo.

Technology Station

Access resources @NGReach.com >

((MP3)) Recordings

- Fresh Hot Corn Tamales
- Too Many Tamales!
- A Musical Journey

Digital Library

Learn vocabulary and practice language

- Key Word Images
- Language Builder Picture Cards

My Vocab Notebook

- Add Words

Comprehension Coach

- Use interactive library support. Automatically measure fluency.

Online Assessment

- Practice items in standardized test format.

Day at a Glance:
▶ **Language:** Express Feelings   ▶ **Reading:** Main Idea and Details
▶ **Vocabulary:** Social Studies Vocabulary   ▶ **Writing:** Writing Fluency

OBJECTIVES

Vocabulary
- Acquire and Use Grade-Level Vocabulary 🕐

Language
- Language Function: Express Feelings 🕐
- Listen to and Imitate Fluent Models
- Use a Variety of Sentence Types
- Participate in Discussion

Learning and Teamwork Strategies
- Activate Prior Knowledge
- Use Media to Build Language
- Use Context to Build Concepts and Language

Social Studies
- Explore Customs and Traditions

Resources

🎵 🔊 *Sing With Me Language Song Book page 4*

💿 🔊 *Sing With Me Language Song CD 1 Tracks 1, 2*

🔊 *eVisual 1.2*

🔊 *eVisual 1.3*

🔊 *Key Word Images*

🎴 🔊 *Language Builder Picture Cards E7–E13*

◯ NGReach.com >

See **Technology Station** for digital student resources.

Differentiate

Academic Language Frames

Express Feelings
- I feel _____.
  I am _____.

- I feel so _____.
  I am very _____.

- I feel so _____ when _____.
- I am very _____ when _____.

◯ NGReach.com > eVisual 1.3

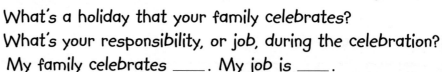

Language of the Day

What's a holiday that your family celebrates?
What's your responsibility, or job, during the celebration?
My family celebrates ____. My job is ____.

Read the Language of the Day. Model: *My family celebrates Kwanzaa. My job is to light the candles.* Then, invite students to tell about their own duties and responsibilities at family celebrations. Then explain that students will be listening, speaking, and writing more about **traditions** today.

Express Feelings

1 Teach/Model Display "Fresh Hot Corn Tamales." Read the introduction aloud and play the song. Invite students to follow along as you play the song a second time. Model how to echo and chime in as the audio prompts.

Point out the **Language Frames** and model using these structures to express and talk about feelings.

How to Express Feelings	
1. Say *I feel* and add a feeling word.	I feel so excited.
2. Say *I am* and add a feeling word.	I am very happy.

◯ NGReach.com > eVisual 1.2

With students, generate a list of words that show feelings and emotions, such as: *amazed, grateful, lazy, nervous, peaceful,* and *surprised.*

2 Practice/Apply Invite students to share about feelings at different holidays and celebrations. To prompt more detail, model how to make sentences such as: *I feel so proud when my parents ask me to sing.* Use **Academic Language Frames** to encourage students to use language naturally to express feelings with different kinds of sentences.

> **CHECK UNDERSTANDING** Display **Language Builder Picture Cards E7–E13** (Thanksgiving, Children's Day, Night of the Radishes, Earth Day, Teuila Festival, Carnival). Have students express their feelings about the holidays shown on these cards, and/or any other special occasions that they celebrate with their families.

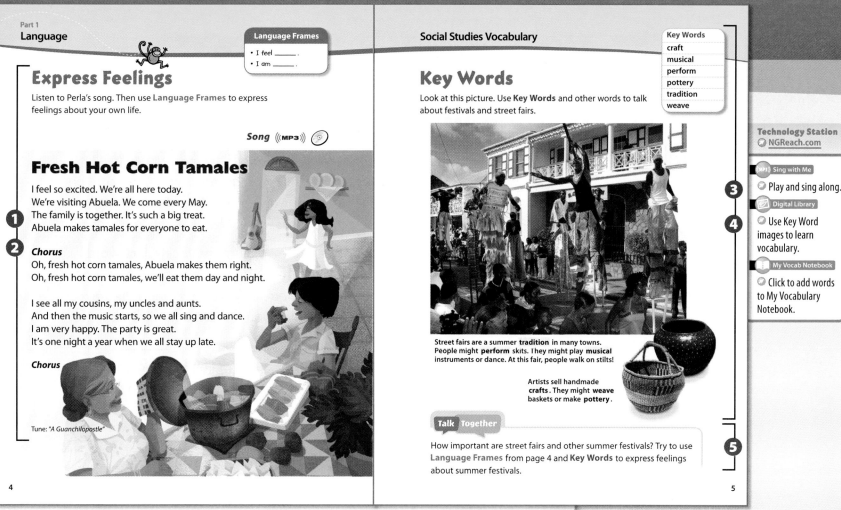

Student Book pages 4–5

Social Studies Vocabulary

3 **Teach/Model** Read the introduction and the captions. Use **Vocabulary Routine 1** (See **Vocabulary Routines** on page PD37) and **Key Word Images** to teach the words. Access definitions on pages 616–639.

1. **Pronounce** the word and point to its picture: **perform**.

2. **Rate** the word. Have students hold up their fingers to show how well they know the word. (1 = very well, 2 = a little, 3 = not at all) Ask: *What do you know about this word?*

3. **Define** the word: *To perform means to present an artistic work such as a play or piece of music.*

4. **Elaborate** Relate the word to your experience: *The group will perform my favorite song.*

4 **Practice/Apply** Have partners take turns repeating the routine for each word, using complete sentences for steps 2, 3, and 4.

5 **Talk Together About the Big Question**
Check Understanding and Connect Concepts Review the **Language Frames** on page 4 and provide an example:

> *I am amazed at all the beautiful handmade **crafts**. I like the baskets and **pottery** best. I feel lucky that I found the perfect vase.*

Add the ideas to your unit concept map.

Differentiate

Spanish Cognates ▸
*musical/musical;
tradition/tradición*

Part 1 Vocabulary Skills Trace		Page
Day 1	**Social Studies Vocabulary**	**T5**
Day 2	Academic Vocabulary	T7
Day 3	Expand Word Knowledge	T10b
Day 4	Share Word Knowledge	T26b
Day 5	Apply Word Knowledge	T27b
Day 6	Use a Dictionary	T28
Day 7	Use a Dictionary	T35
Days 8–9	Extend Vocabulary	T36e–f
Day 10	Vocabulary Review	T36g–h

Day 1
continued

Day at a Glance:
▶ **Language:** Express Feelings
▶ **Vocabulary:** Social Studies Vocabulary
▶ **Reading:** Main Idea and Details
▶ **Writing:** Writing Fluency

OBJECTIVES

Vocabulary
• Acquire and Use Classroom Vocabulary ❶
• Use Grade-Level Vocabulary

Comprehension and Literary Analysis
• Demonstrate Listening Comprehension
• Recognize Main Idea and Details ❶

Listening and Speaking
• Adjust your volume, pitch and tone

Learning and Teamwork Strategies
• Use Graphic Organizers: Main Idea Diagram
• Reason Deductively

Writing
• Develop Writing Fluency
• Monitor and Self-Correct Writing

Social Studies
• Explore Customs and Traditions

Resources

 eVisual 1.4

 Practice Master 1.2

eVisual 1.5

Differentiate

Multi-Level Strategies

BEGINNING

Help students identify a main idea and copy it onto their charts. Have them point to details in the photo and label them.

INTERMEDIATE

Have students look at the picture and write down the details. Then ask students to think of the main idea for those details.

ADVANCED

Have students write complete sentences for the main idea and details.

ADVANCED HIGH

Encourage students to create more details that are not shown in the picture but could be details about the street fair.

Main Idea and Details

❶ Teach Connect concepts: *What Key Words have you learned to help you express feelings about* **traditions** *? You saw those words in a caption describing the photo of the street fair. Now you will learn how to make a graphic organizer to show the main idea and details of different traditions.*

Read the first paragraph and teach the Classroom Vocabulary word *detail*. Use the picture on page 6 to teach how to look for a main idea and details. Ask students: *What is happening in the picture? Why are they all together?* Have volunteers describe what different family members are doing.

Read aloud the explanation about making a main idea diagram. Clarify the purpose. Remind students to listen for the main idea and details as you read "The Family Party" aloud.

> **Read Aloud**
>
> ### The Family Party
>
> Everyone has gathered at Perla's abuela's house for a family party. Perla helps her grandmother make and serve the food. Some of the other kids dance while Perla's cousin plays a guitar. Music and people fill the room. Everyone is having a great time.
>
> 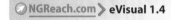 **NGReach.com** ▶ eVisual 1.4

❷ Model Review the first two sentences of "The Family Party." Have volunteers tell what the main idea is. Model the process: Abuela has a party *is the main idea. Let's write that on the left side of the diagram.* Ask: *What is a detail about the party?* (Perla helps with the food.) Say: *We will write that on the right side of the diagram.* Ask volunteers to read the other details listed in the diagram. Have them suggest other details that could be added.

❸ Practice/Apply Read aloud the instructions. Distribute **Practice Master 1.2** for students to use as they complete their diagrams. Use **Multi-Level Strategies** to help students at all proficiency levels talk about the main idea and details. Monitor students' developing proficiency. (See page R2 for Proficiency Level Descriptions.)

> **CHECK UNDERSTANDING** *Act out one of the details from "The Family Party."* (Students should pretend to make food, dance, or pretend to play the guitar.)
>
>

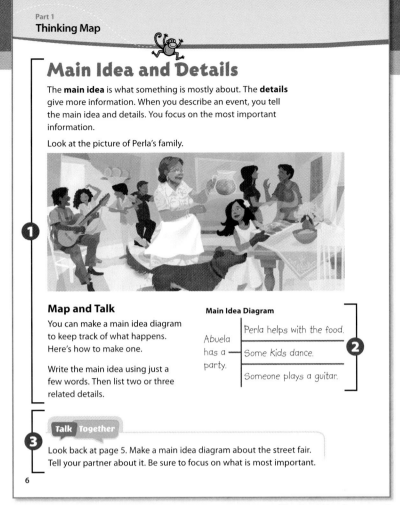

Main Idea and Details

The **main idea** is what something is mostly about. The **details** give more information. When you describe an event, you tell the main idea and details. You focus on the most important information.

Look at the picture of Perla's family.

①

Map and Talk

You can make a main idea diagram to keep track of what happens. Here's how to make one.

Write the main idea using just a few words. Then list two or three related details.

Main Idea Diagram

Abuela has a party. — Perla helps with the food.

— Some kids dance.

— Someone plays a guitar.

②

③

 Talk Together

Look back at page 5. Make a main idea diagram about the street fair. Tell your partner about it. Be sure to focus on what is most important.

6

Student Book page 6

Daily Writing

④ **Writing Fluency** Use the **Power Writing routine**. (See **Writing Routines** on page PD53.) Write the word *tradition* and prompt: *Name a tradition of your family. What do you do?* Think about this word and write about it.

Power Writing Routine

 1. What do you know about the word or picture?

 2. Take one minute to write as much as you can, as well as you can.
B words   **I** sentences   **A AH** paragraphs

 3. Check your spelling and grammar. Circle mistakes.

 4. Count your words.

NGReach.com eVisual 1.5

CLOSE AND ASSESS

- **Language** *Express feelings about a family tradition.* (Students should use sentences such as *I am _____, I feel _____.*)
- **Reading** *Name the main idea and details of your drawing for Share What You Know on page 3.* (Answers will vary.)
- **Vocabulary** *What Key Words can you use to tell about your family traditions?* (Answers will vary.)

Classroom Vocabulary

Use **Vocabulary Routine 4** to teach **detail**. (See **Vocabulary Routines**, PD40.)

Upright

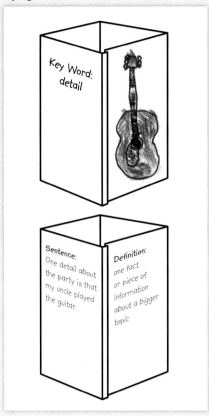

Key Word: detail

Sentence: One detail about the party is that my uncle played the guitar.

Definition: one fact or piece of information about a bigger topic

Name _____ Date _____

Thinking Map: Main Idea Diagram

Street Fair

Make a main idea diagram about the photo of a street fair on page 5.

Main Idea Diagram

Possible answer: Artists sell handmade crafts.

Possible answer: Street fairs are a summer tradition in some towns.

Possible answer: They sell baskets.

Possible answer: They sell clay pots.

Use your main idea diagram to tell your partner about the street fair picture.

For use with TE p. T6a   1.2   Unit 1 | Living Traditions

Practice Master 1.2

Day 2

Day at a Glance:
- ▶ **Language:** Complete Sentences
- ▶ **Vocabulary:** Academic Vocabulary
- ▶ **Reading:** Learn to Plan and Monitor
- ▶ **Writing:** Journal Entry

OBJECTIVES

Vocabulary
- Acquire and Use Academic Vocabulary
- Use Grade-Level Vocabulary ❶

Grammar
- Identify Complete Sentences

Learning and Teamwork Strategies
- Make Connections Across Content Areas

Resources

 Practice Master 1.3

Key Word Images

⊙ NGReach.com ▶

See **Technology Station** for digital student resources.

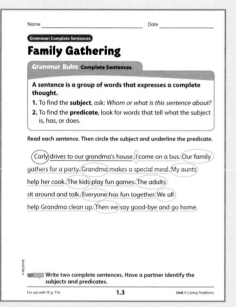

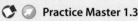 **Practice Master 1.3**

Language of the Day

When does your family have traditional foods?
My family has _____ on_____ .

Read the Language of the Day. Model: *My family has rice cakes on New Year's Day.* Invite students to take turns telling about the traditional foods they eat on special occasions and holidays. Explain that students are going to learn how they can make complete sentences to tell about these foods and **traditions**.

Grammar Complete Sentences [B] [I] [A] [AH]

❶ Teach/Model Write the sample sentences and read them aloud.

> 1. Perla is a good helper.
> 2. Perla's abuela has dough and filling.
> 3. Together, they make tamales for the party.

Define complete sentences: *A sentence expresses a complete thought. It has two parts, a subject and a predicate.* Explain: *The subject tells whom or what the sentence is about. The predicate tells what the subject is, has, or does.* Point to sentence 1. Ask: *Who is this sentence about?* (Perla) Circle *Perla.* Say: *Perla is the subject. What do we learn about her?* (She is a good helper.) Underline *is a good helper.* Identify it as the predicate. Ask: *Does the predicate tell us what Perla is, has, or does?* (is)

Ask: *Who is sentence 2 about?* (Perla's abuela) Circle *Perla's abuela. Does the predicate tell us what her abuela is, has, or does?* (has) Underline *has dough and filling.*

Continue with sentence 3. Then create sentence frames with missing subjects or predicates and have students offer suggestions for completing them.

- *The tamales _____.* (Examples: steam on the stove, are for a party)
- *_____ cannot wait to eat.* (Examples: Uncle Ramón, Perla, Her brother.)

❷ Practice/Apply Have partners talk about family traditions and write two sentences each about them on sentence strips. Partners cut the sentences into subjects and predicates and trade with another pair who reassembles and reads them aloud. Then assign **Practice Master 1.3**.

> **CHECK UNDERSTANDING** Write the sentence *My brother and sister ate tamales.* Have students circle the complete subject and underline the complete predicate.

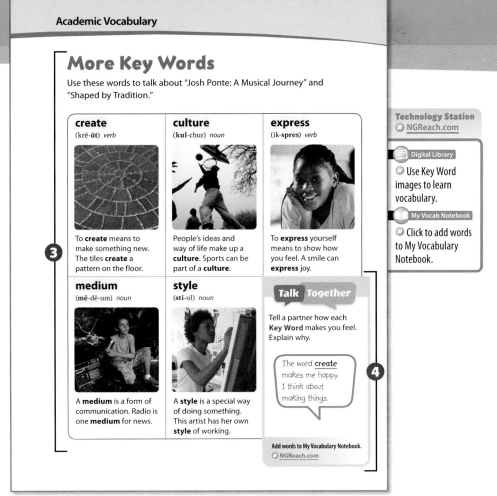

Student Book page 7

Academic Vocabulary

③ Teach/Model Invite students to discuss each photograph on the page. Use **Vocabulary Routine 1** (See **Vocabulary Routines,** page PD37) and **Key Word Images** to teach the words. Access definitions on pages 616–639.

1. **Pronounce** the word and point to its picture: **create** .

2. **Rate** the word. Have students hold up their fingers to show how well they know the word. (1 = very well, 2 = a little, 3 = not at all) Ask: *What do you know about this word?*

3. **Define** the word: *To create means to make something new.*

4. **Elaborate** Relate the word to your experience; for example: *I create music to* **express** *my feelings.*

④ Practice/Apply Use the ratings from step 2 to form pairs. Have partners take turns telling how each Key Word makes them feel. Encourage them to explain why the word makes them feel that way.

> **CHECK UNDERSTANDING AND CONNECT CONCEPTS** Point to each **Key Word Image** and ask students to explain what it means.

Keys to Efficacy

Prompt students to use content, academic, and/or classroom vocabulary by asking questions such as:. *How can you use the word create to tell about something you've made?*

Differentiate

Spanish Cognates ▶
create/crear; culture/cultura; express/expresar; medium/medio; style/estilo

Part 1 Vocabulary Skills Trace		Page
Day 1	Social Studies Vocabulary	T5
Day 2	**Academic Vocabulary**	**T7**
Day 3	Expand Word Knowledge	T10b
Day 4	Share Word Knowledge	T26b
Day 5	Apply Word Knowledge	T27b
Day 6	Use a Dictionary	T28
Day 7	Use a Dictionary	T35
Days 8–9	Extend Vocabulary	T36e–f
Day 10	Vocabulary Review	T36g–h

Day 2
continued

Day at a Glance:
▶ **Language:** Complete Sentences   ▶ **Reading:** Learn to Plan and Monitor
▶ **Vocabulary:** Academic Vocabulary   ▶ **Writing:** Journal Entry

OBJECTIVES

Vocabulary
- Acquire and Use Classroom Vocabulary
- Acquire and Use Academic Vocabulary ➊
- Use Grade-Level Vocabulary

Learning to Read
- Words with Short *a*

Reading Strategy
- Learn to Plan and Monitor ➊

Learning and Teamwork Strategies
- Use Personal Experience
- Use Visuals

Writing
- Write a Journal Entry

Resources

  🌀 eVisual 1.6

   Reach Into Phonics TE page T4

Learn to Plan and Monitor

❶ Teach   Read the introduction aloud and discuss the picture. Say: *Perla and her grandmother invited 30 people. In order to plan, they must preview what they think the event will be like. They need to predict how many people will come and how much each person will eat. Later, they can check to see how their plan worked out.* Teach the Classroom Vocabulary word *preview*.

❷ Model   Connect: *You also preview a story before you read it and predict what it will be about it.* Read the chart aloud. Model how to preview and predict about the picture. Say:

- *I read that Perla and her grandmother are getting ready for a family party.*
- *I see her grandmother making tamales.*
- *I predict that they are preparing tamales for their party.*
- *I'll have to read the story to see if my prediction is correct.*

❸ Practice/Apply   Read aloud the directions. Point out the **Language Frames**. Chorally read "Perla's Journal" and the sample student prediction.

Direct students' attention to the How to steps and **Academic Language Frames** to help students at each proficiency level preview and predict. Students should make a prediction at each red arrow and confirm if it was correct when they read the journal entries for Saturday and Sunday.

> **CHECK UNDERSTANDING**   Ask students to think about Perla's journal. Say: *Predict where Perla's family will go next year. Explain your prediction.* (Students should note that Perla's family makes a yearly trip to Mexico.)

Differentiate

Academic Language Frames

Learn to Plan

- ■ I read _____.
  I see _____.
  I predict that _____.
  My prediction _____.

- ■ I read _____.
  I predict that _____.
  I keep reading and learn _____.
  My prediction _____.

- ■ The text says _____.
- ■ That tells me _____, so I predict _____.
  As I read, I learn _____.
  My prediction _____.

🌀 **NGReach.com** ▸ eVisual 1.6

Phonics and Fluency

Words with Short /ă/

Display these words: *mad, bat, ham.* Say the words and have students repeat them. Point out the vowel sound /ă/, heard in each word. Blend /m/ /ă/ /d/. Have students repeat. Have students blend *bat* and *ham.* Display **Transparency 11** from **Reach Into Phonics** and work through the lesson.

Practice   Display these sentences from "Perla's Journal."
- The car trip wasn't bad.
- Marla and I are pen pals.
- I added the filling.

Have partners read the sentences chorally several times to develop fluency.

Learn to Plan and Monitor

Look at the picture. Perla and Abuela are getting ready for a family party. When you prepare for an event, you have to plan. You **preview**, or look ahead to, the event. You **predict** what might happen.

1

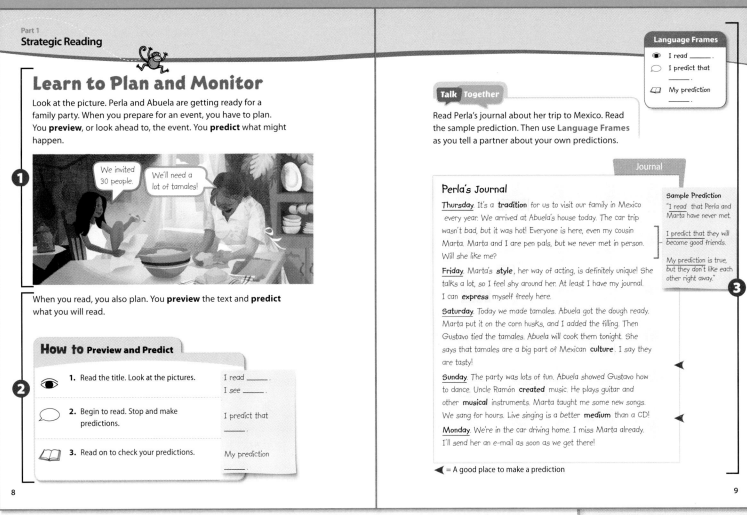

> We invited 30 people.

> We'll need a lot of tamales!

When you read, you also plan. You **preview** the text and **predict** what you will read.

How to Preview and Predict

2

1. Read the title. Look at the pictures.

   I read _____.
   I see _____.

2. Begin to read. Stop and make predictions.

   I predict that _____.

3. Read on to check your predictions.

   My prediction _____.

8

Language Frames

- 👁 I read _____.
- 💬 I predict that _____.
- 📖 My prediction _____.

Talk Together

Read Perla's journal about her trip to Mexico. Read the sample prediction. Then use **Language Frames** as you tell a partner about your own predictions.

Journal

Perla's Journal

Thursday. It's a **tradition** for us to visit our family in Mexico every year. We arrived at Abuela's house today. The car trip wasn't bad, but it was hot! Everyone is here, even my cousin Marta. Marta and I are pen pals, but we never met in person. Will she like me?

Friday. Marta's **style**, her way of acting, is definitely unique! She talks a lot, so I feel shy around her. At least I have my journal. I can **express** myself freely here.

Saturday. Today we made tamales. Abuela got the dough ready. Marta put it on the corn husks, and I added the filling. Then Gustavo tied the tamales. Abuela will cook them tonight. She says that tamales are a big part of Mexican **culture**. I say they are tasty!

Sunday. The party was lots of fun. Abuela showed Gustavo how to dance. Uncle Ramón **created** music. He plays guitar and other **musical** instruments. Marta taught me some new songs. We sang for hours. Live singing is a better **medium** than a CD!

Monday. We're in the car driving home. I miss Marta already. I'll send her an e-mail as soon as we get there!

◀ = A good place to make a prediction

Sample Prediction

"I read that Perla and Marta have never met.

I predict that they will become good friends.

My prediction is true, but they don't like each other right away."

3

9

Daily Writing

4 **Journal Entry** Point out the features of the journal entries in "Perla's Journal": a date, the first-person point of view, and the informal language. Then write a RAFT for students to follow:

- Role: Perla
- Audience: herself
- Form: journal entry
- Topic: what happens next

Adjust the prompt to include students at all proficiency levels.

B Have students make a visual journal.

A Have students write paragraphs

I Have students write sentences.

AH Have students create multiple entries.

Invite students to share their entries with the class.

CLOSE AND ASSESS

- **Language** Write this sentence and have students circle the complete subject and underline the complete predicate: *My grandma makes the best tamales.* (Subject: My grandma; Predicate: makes the best tamales)

- **Reading** *Read Monday's entry in "Perla's Journal." Predict what will happen next.* (Possible answer: *Perla will e-mail Marta. They will get together again.*)

- **Vocabulary** *What Key Words did you use in your journal entry?*

Classroom Vocabulary

Use **Vocabulary Routine 4** to teach **preview**. (See **Vocabulary Routines, PD40**.) Have students make a **Three-Fold Tab** to record what they learn about the word *preview*.

Three-Fold Tab

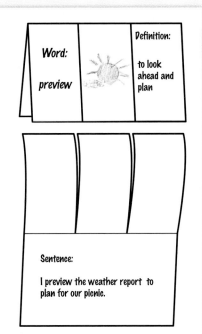

Word: preview

Definition: to look ahead and plan

Sentence:

I preview the weather report to plan for our picnic.

Day 3

Day at a Glance:
▶ **Language:** Agree and Disagree ▶ **Reading:** Read the Selection
▶ **Vocabulary:** Expand Word Knowledge ▶ **Writing:** Writer's Craft

OBJECTIVES

Vocabulary
• Use Grade-Level Vocabulary
• Use Academic Vocabulary

Language
• Language Function: Agree and Disagree
• Listen to and Imitate Fluent Models
• Use a Variety of Strategic Learning Techniques

Learning and Teamwork Strategies
• Use Media to Build Language
• Gather Information
• Use Graphic Organizer: Dictionary Entry

Resources

🎵 💿 *Sing With Me Language Song CD 1 Tracks 3, 4*

📖 💿 *Sing With Me Language Song Book, page 5*

💿 *eVisual 1.7*

🗂 *In the U.S.A. Picture Cards 111–120*

🌐 **NGReach.com**

See **Technology Station** for digital student resources.

Differentiate

Multi-Level Strategies

Pair students of mixed proficiency levels. Have students participate according to their proficiency level.

BEGINNING

Students can express thoughts and opinions using simple sentences that start with *I like* or *I don't like.* They can use the sentences in the chart to agree or disagree with their partners' statements.

INTERMEDIATE

Prompt students to state their thoughts and opinions with complete sentences. Remind them to give reasons for disagreeing.

ADVANCED **ADVANCED HIGH**

When agreeing, have students form sentences that include the verb and a pronoun that refers to the original speaker's statement, as in the song (*I love them, too*).

Language of the Day

Do you agree it's important to keep traditions alive? Why or why not?

I agree/disagree that it's important to keep traditions alive. I think _____ .

Read the Language of the Day. Model: *I agree that it's important to keep traditions alive. I think traditions connect us to our roots.* Invite students to share their opinions in small groups. When the groups have finished their discussion, tell students that they will practice making similar kinds of statements showing agreement and disagreement.

Agree and Disagree

1 **Teach** Remind students that they learned how to **express** feelings from "Fresh Hot Corn Tamales." Introduce: *Now you will learn how to agree and disagree.* Play the song "Too Many Tamales" and invite students to sing along.

Activate prior experience: *When you agree with somebody, you think or feel the same way as the other person. When you disagree, you don't think or feel the same way.* Call on volunteers to locate where in the song Gustavo agrees with Perla and where he disagrees. Say: *Here are some ways you can show you agree or disagree with somebody.* Then review the chart:

Agree	Disagree
I agree.	I don't agree./I disagree.
So do I./I do, too.	I don't.
So am I./I am, too.	I'm not.

🌐 **NGReach.com** ▶ **eVisual 1.7**

2 **Model** With a volunteer, role-play a short discussion in which one of you expresses a thought, feeling, or opinion, and the other agrees or disagrees. Point out that it's important to give the reason for disagreeing. For example, one of you might say *I love fortune cookies,* and the other could respond *I don't. I think they're too hard and crunchy.*

3 **Practice/Apply** Have partners work together. Ask one to express a thought, feeling, or opinion; his or her partner can agree or disagree. Partners can then reverse roles. Use **Multi-Level Strategies** to encourage students to support students at all proficiency levels.

CHECK UNDERSTANDING Ask: *What does "agree" mean? What does "disagree" mean?* (Agree is when you think or feel the same thing as another person. Disagree is when you think or feel something different.)

Too Many Tamales!

🎤 I love corn tamales.

🎤 Yes, I love them, too.
We helped to make tamales,
 and then I ate a few.

🎤 Now I feel so hungry!

🎤 Oh, I don't agree!
I'm full of tamales.
 I ate twenty-three!

Chorus:

Oh, fresh hot corn tamales, I ate one, two, three, four.
Oh, fresh hot corn tamales, I couldn't eat one more.

| Technology Station |
| ⬤ NGReach.com |

(MP3) Sing with Me
⬤ Play and sing along.

Tune: "A Guanchilopostle" | MP3 or Song CD 1 Tracks 3–4 **Song** 5

Sing With Me Language Song Book page 5

Expand Word Knowledge

4 Teach/Model Explain that each student pair will become Key Word experts. They will study one Key Word and create a dictionary entry poster about that word. Use **Vocabulary Routine 2** and model making a dictionary entry about the word **culture**. (See **Vocabulary Routines**, page PD38.)

- Write the word.
- Add the part of speech
- Add a definition.
- Add a context sentence.

| culture | **Noun** |
| | People's ideas and way of life. Clothing, language, and traditions are all part of a country's culture. |

Dictionary Entry

5 Practice/Apply Assign a Key Word to each pair of students. Have each pair create a dictionary entry poster for their assigned Key Words. Display the posters on the class word wall.

> **CHECK UNDERSTANDING** Say a Key Word and have the partner experts read their definition and sentence from their dictionary entry posters.

Key Words	
craft	perform
create	pottery
culture	style
express	tradition
medium	weave
musical	

Differentiate

Newcomer Support

Newcomers can make dictionary entries using words from **In the U.S.A. Picture Cards** 111–120.

Part 1 Vocabulary Skills Trace		Page
Day 1	Social Studies Vocabulary	T5
Day 2	Academic Vocabulary	T7
Day 3	**Expand Word Knowledge**	**T10b**
Day 4	Share Word Knowledge	T26b
Day 5	Apply Word Knowledge	T27b
Day 6	Use a Dictionary	T28
Day 7	Use a Dictionary	T35
Days 8–9	Extend Vocabulary	T36e–f
Day 10	Vocabulary Review	T36g–h

Day 3
continued

Day at a Glance:
▶ **Language:** Agree and Disagree
▶ **Vocabulary:** Expand Word Knowledge
▶ **Reading:** Read the Selection
▶ **Writing:** Writer's Craft

OBJECTIVES

Vocabulary
• Use Academic Vocabulary ⊕
• Use Grade-Level Vocabulary ⊕

Reading Strategy
• Plan: Preview

Comprehension and Literary Analysis
• Analyze Text Features: Interview
• Analyze Genre: Interview

Learning and Teamwork Strategies
• Use Prereading Supports
• Build Background Knowledge

Resources

⊙ *Comprehension Coach*

Keys to Efficacy

Use wait time—give students a chance to think before rephrasing a question, moving on, or answering it yourself.

Preview the Interview

❶ Introduce Tell students to look at the photograph on pages 10 and 11 and read the selection title. *What do you see in the photograph? What do you predict this selection will be about?* Connect to personal experience by asking: *Does this celebration remind you of a celebration that you have seen or attended? Tell about it.*

❷ Genre and Text Feature Read aloud the definitions. *An interview is a kind of conversation. In this interview, Ramona is asking the questions; Mr. Ponte is the answering them.* Connect to the genre: *As you read the interview, use the text features to help you figure out who is speaking.*

❸ Preview and Build Background Use sheltering strategies as you conduct a picture walk.

Pages	Say (and Do)
12–13	*This is Josh Ponte, a filmmaker and music producer. He took a trip to Gabon, in West Africa.* (Point to the map, then point to the photos.) *What did he do there?* (He made movies about **traditional** dances and music.)
14–15	*What can you tell about Gabon from these photos?* (Music is important to the people of Gabon. They **perform** songs and dances at celebrations, and even when they are doing chores.)
16–17	*Here are some traditional dances of Gabon. Look at the first photo. What are the dancers wearing?* (traditional costumes) *How are their bodies decorated?* (Their faces are painted.) *What about the singers in the bottom picture?* (They are wearing red cloth, and they have red powder smeared on their bodies.)
18–19	*What can you tell about the **musical** instruments of Gabon?* (They make their own instruments from things they find in nature. One instrument looks like an animal horn. Another looks like a harp with one string.)
20–21	*Look at the first photo. This instrument is called a pluri arc, because it is shaped like an arc.* (Trace the shape of the instrument with your finger.) *Describe the instrument in the next photo.* (It looks like a harp, but it has more strings than the one on page 19.)
22–25	*What can you tell about Gabonese **culture**, based on these pictures?* (Gabonese people live in villages in the forest. They make their own houses, tools, and toys. They fish and get their own food.)

CHECK UNDERSTANDING Ask: *What's an interview?* (An interview is a recorded conversation. One person asks questions and the other person answers.)

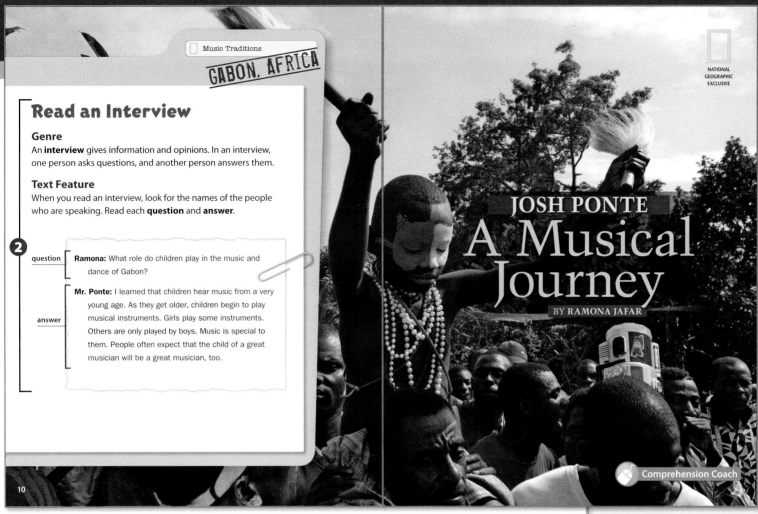

Music Traditions

GABON, AFRICA

Read an Interview

Genre
An **interview** gives information and opinions. In an interview, one person asks questions, and another person answers them.

Text Feature
When you read an interview, look for the names of the people who are speaking. Read each **question** and **answer**.

2

question — **Ramona:** What role do children play in the music and dance of Gabon?

answer — **Mr. Ponte:** I learned that children hear music from a very young age. As they get older, children begin to play musical instruments. Girls play some instruments. Others are only played by boys. Music is special to them. People often expect that the child of a great musician will be a great musician, too.

NATIONAL GEOGRAPHIC EXCLUSIVE

JOSH PONTE

A Musical Journey

BY RAMONA JAFAR

 Comprehension Coach

10

 ## Comprehension Coach

Build Reading Power
Assign students to use the software, based on their instructional needs.

Read Silently	**Listen** 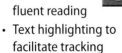	**Record**
• Comprehension questions with immediate feedback • Vocabulary support	• Process model of fluent reading • Text highlighting to facilitate tracking • Vocabulary support	• Oral reading fluency practice • Speech recognition for oral fluency assessment with immediate feedback

 ### Cultural Perpectives

Remind students that this selection tells about music in Gabon, a country in West Africa. Explain to students that many cultures have traditional forms of music. Sometimes it is the **style** of music, like the Caribbean reggae. Sometimes it is the instruments used, for example, the bagpipe of Scotland or the ukulele of Hawaii. Ask the class to share traditional forms of music from other cultures that they know about.

OBJECTIVES

Vocabulary
• Use Academic Vocabulary 🅣
• Use Grade-Level Vocabulary 🅣

Learning to Read
• Phonics: Words with Short *o*

Reading Strategies
• Plan: Set a Purpose, Predict, Confirm Predictions
• Learn to Plan and Monitor 🅣

Fluency
• Phrasing 🅣

Comprehension and Literary Analysis
• Identify Main Idea and Details
• Use Text Structure: Interview

Learning and Teamwork Strategies
• Use Reading Supports

Writing
• Connect Reading and Writing
• Analyze a Professional Model: Interview
• Develop Writer's Craft

Social Studies
• Geography

Resources

💿 🅢 *Read with Me Selection*

🅒 🅢 *Practice Master 1.4*

🅒 🅢 *Reach into Phonics TE page T6*

🌐 NGReach.com ▶

See **Technology Station** for digital student resources.

Name _____ Date _____

Key Points Reading

Josh Ponte: A Musical Journey

❶ Josh Ponte traveled to Gabon to help save gorillas. He learned that the Gabonese have one of the world's oldest cultures. Their music, dance, and storytelling are thousands of years old.

❷ Their music sounds like birds and animals in the forest. The villagers sing and dance all day long. It is a tradition that connects the people as they work and play.

❸ Many people in Gabon cannot read or write, so they tell stories through music. Their traditions and lives are connected to each other and to nature. They respect the world around them.

For use with TE p. T12   1.4   Unit 1 | Living Traditions

🅒 🅢 **Practice Master 1.4**

Read the Interview

Suggested Pacing

• Day 3: Read Section 1, pages 12–13
• Day 4: Read Sections 2 and 3, pages 14–25

Reading Options Scaffold the support for varied reading levels.

BELOW LEVEL	ON LEVEL	ABOVE LEVEL
Listen and Read Along	**Read Together**	**Read and Adjust Rate**
• Read **Key Points Reading** aloud, while students track the print. Reread in phrases and have students echo the phrases building up to reading the entire sentence. • Use the photographs to support English vocabulary. • Check understanding with selected Build Comprehension questions.	• Have students set a purpose for reading. Then select passages to read chorally or aloud in partners. Pause to ask the Build Comprehension questions. • At the end of each section, have students summarize what they learned.	• Have students set a purpose for reading each section. Then read silently. • Have students discuss each section with partners and point out illustrations that helped them understand the text. • Ask the Build Comprehension Questions to check understanding.

Phonics and Fluency

Words with Short /ŏ/

Teach/Model Display the words *log* and *hot*. Point out the *o* in each word and explain: *The* o *in these words makes the short* o *sound /ŏ/.* Have students repeat the sound. Display **Transparency 12** from **Reach into Phonics** and work through the lesson.

Practice/Apply Display these sentences from "Josh Ponte: A Musical Journey."
• Combining new songs with old songs creates a cultural melting pot.
• I want a world that still has gorillas—and lots of music.

Underline the words *pot* and *lots*. Have partners write the words and circle the letter that makes the short *o* sound. Then have partners read the words chorally several times to develop fluency in reading words with short vowels.

1 ▸ Set a Purpose
Find out why music and nature are important to the cultural **traditions** of Gabon.

The Journey Begins

One morning in 2001, Josh Ponte read something that changed his life forever. A newspaper **ad** grabbed his attention: "Gorillas in Africa Need Help." One week later, he was in the forests of Gabon (ga-**bon**) with sixteen gorillas.

Soon, he fell in love with Gabon's unique **culture**. Ponte, who is also a filmmaker and music producer, found that people in Gabon have **traditions** of music that he had never seen or heard. He decided to help share these **rare** cultural traditions with the world.

I spoke with Mr. Ponte to learn about Gabon's music traditions and how those traditions tie to nature.

AFRICA

2 Gabon

In Other Words
ad advertisement
rare unusual

Ramona: Mr. Ponte, tell me why you left your home in England to travel to Gabon, a country in Central Africa.

Mr. Ponte: When I saw the newspaper ad to help Gabon wildlife, I wanted to help. I grew up in England, playing outdoors whenever I could. I have always been interested in nature. I enjoy learning about other places in the world. I wanted to see with my own eyes what was going on in Gabon. **3**

▲ Josh Ponte films people **performing** traditional music and dance in Gabon.

▸ **Before You Move On**
4
1. **Plan and Monitor** Look at the title and the photos on pages 12 and 13. What do you think this interview will be about?
2. **Use Text Features** Who is interviewing Mr. Ponte? Explain how you know.

12   13

Build Comprehension, pages 12–13

1 **Set a Purpose** Read the introduction to help students set a purpose.

2 **Use Visuals** Look at the map on page 12. Where is Gabon? (in western Africa) What can you tell about it? (It is a small country near the coast.)

3 **Main Idea and Details** MODEL | GUIDE | APPLY Why does Mr. Ponte go to Gabon? Model how to tell about the main idea: *I think about Ramona's question: Why did you leave England? Then I know that the details will be in his answer: He left because he saw an ad to help Gabon wildlife. He is interested in nature and enjoys learning about other places in the world.*

4 **Answers to Before You Move On**

1. Plan and Monitor MODEL | GUIDE | APPLY Use the Language Frames from page 8 to model how to preview and predict.

- *I read the title, "The Journey Begins."*
- *I see photos of Mr. Ponte in the forest with a gorilla and taking pictures.*
- *I predict that this interview will be about Mr. Ponte's trip to Gabon.*
- *I read the purpose and the introduction. It tells me that Mr. Ponte will talk about music and nature in Gabon's traditions.*

2. Use Text Features Ramona is interviewing Mr. Ponte. The bold type names the speakers and Ramona asks the question.

N B

Concepts of Print: Hold a Book and Turn Pages

Teach/Model Model holding the book correctly. Turn to pages 10–11. Point to the page numbers as you say: *This is page 10. This is page 11.* Repeat for pages 12–13.

Practice/Apply Ask students to turn to the next two pages and identify the page numbers. Have partners practice holding the book correctly and turning the pages. Call out instructions for students to follow: *Turn to page 14.* Pause for students to find the corresponding page and hold up their books. Ask volunteers to take turns calling out page numbers for their classmates to find.

Keys to Efficacy

Prompt students to support their thinking with evidence (personal experience, quote from text, photograph, etc.). *How do you know that? How can we check?*

Music and People

Ramona: After your time with Gabonese wildlife, you traveled around the country. This is where you first saw and heard the music of Gabon. What did you think?

Mr. Ponte: To me, their music sounds perfect. Many sounds work together like the different birds and animals in the forest. For example, one person claps in one **rhythm**, while another hits a can with a stick in a different rhythm. These sounds come together to **create** beautiful songs. It was very different from **what I knew**. I wanted to record this music.

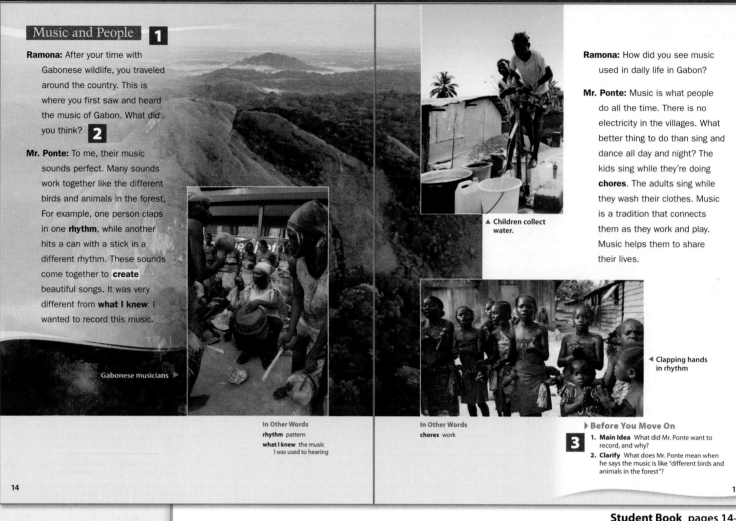

Gabonese musicians ▶

▲ Children collect water.

◀ Clapping hands in rhythm

Ramona: How did you see music used in daily life in Gabon?

Mr. Ponte: Music is what people do all the time. There is no electricity in the villages. What better thing to do than sing and dance all day and night? The kids sing while they're doing **chores**. The adults sing while they wash their clothes. Music is a tradition that connects them as they work and play. Music helps them to share their lives.

In Other Words
rhythm pattern
what I knew the music I was used to hearing

In Other Words
chores work

▶ **Before You Move On**
1. **Main Idea** What did Mr. Ponte want to record, and why?
2. **Clarify** What does Mr. Ponte mean when he says the music is like "different birds and animals in the forest"?

14

15

Student Book pages 14–15

Literary Analysis: Fact or Opinion

Explain that Ramona's question, "What did you think?" asks for Mr. Ponte's opinion. *What is his response?* ("Their music sounds perfect.") *Why is this an opinion?* (It is how he feels, not something he can prove.) *A fact is information that you can prove.* Have students identify other examples of fact and opinion on these pages and as you continue to read the interview.

Literary Analysis: How to Paraphrase

Tell students that when you paraphrase, you say something in your own words. Explain: *It is important to keep the meaning of the text when you restate it. For example, how would you say this quotation on page 15 in your own words: "Music helps them to share their lives."*

Build Comprehension, pages 14–15

1 **Plan and Monitor: Preview** [MODEL | GUIDE | APPLY] Guide students in previewing the pages.

- *What do the title and captions say?* (I read that this is about music and people; people make music in many ways.)

- *What do you see in the photos?* (I see children and adults working and making music together.)

- *What do you learn from Ramona's questions?* (I read that she asks him about what he thought of their music and how it is part of their daily life.)

2 **Sequence** After Mr. Ponte spent time with the wildlife, what did he do next? (He traveled around the country and heard the music of Gabon.)

3 **Answers to Before You Move On**

1. **Main Idea** [MODEL | GUIDE | APPLY] The main idea is that Mr. Ponte wants to record the Gabonese music. What details support this? (Possible answers: Their music is different. He thinks it sounds perfect.)

2. **Clarify** In the forest, animals make many different sounds. All these sounds together make the sounds of the forest just as all the instruments together make the Gabonese music.

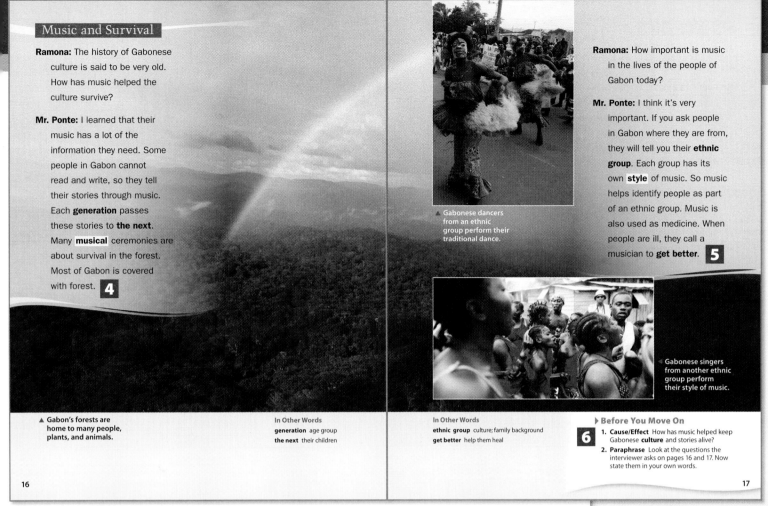

Music and Survival

Ramona: The history of Gabonese culture is said to be very old. How has music helped the culture survive?

Mr. Ponte: I learned that their music has a lot of the information they need. Some people in Gabon cannot read and write, so they tell their stories through music. Each **generation** passes these stories to **the next**. Many **musical** ceremonies are about survival in the forest. Most of Gabon is covered with forest. **4**

▲ Gabon's forests are home to many people, plants, and animals.

▲ Gabonese dancers from an ethnic group perform their traditional dance.

Ramona: How important is music in the lives of the people of Gabon today?

Mr. Ponte: I think it's very important. If you ask people in Gabon where they are from, they will tell you their **ethnic group**. Each group has its own **style** of music. So music helps identify people as part of an ethnic group. Music is also used as medicine. When people are ill, they call a musician to **get better**. **5**

◀ Gabonese singers from another ethnic group perform their style of music.

In Other Words
generation age group
the next their children

In Other Words
ethnic group culture; family background
get better help them heal

▶ **Before You Move On**
6
1. **Cause/Effect** How has music helped keep Gabonese **culture** and stories alive?
2. **Paraphrase** Look at the questions the interviewer asks on pages 16 and 17. Now state them in your own words.

16

17

Student Book pages 16–17

Build Comprehension, pages 16–17

4 **Draw Conclusions** Why do you think many of Gabon's musical ceremonies are about survival? (Most of Gabon is covered with forest. The people use singing to share their experiences about surviving in the forest.)

5 **Identify Details** `MODEL | GUIDE | APPLY` Besides telling stories, in what other ways is music important to the people of Gabon? (The **style** of music identifies people as part of an ethnic group. They also use music as medicine.)

6 **Answers to Before You Move On**

1. **Cause/Effect** Since many of the people do not read or write, they use music to tell their stories and pass them on to the next generation.

2. **Paraphrase** Answers will vary. Possible response: Do you think music has helped the Gabonese **culture** survive? Explain. How is music important to the Gabonese people today?

B **I** **A** **AH**

Text Feature: Photos

Teach/Model Point to the top photo on page 17. Say: *Text features such as photographs support the text. They add details and help readers. Compare the two pictures on page 17. How do these photos support the text?* (They show how each ethnic group has its own style.)

Practice/Apply Have students work with partners to review other photographs as they read the selection. Ask them to tell how the photographs support the text.

Part 1 | Days 3–4 **T16–17**

Playing Music

Ramona: What role do children play in the music and dance of Gabon?

Mr. Ponte: I learned that children hear music from a very young age. As they get older, children begin to play musical instruments. Girls play some instruments. Others are only played by boys. Music is special to them. People often expect that the child of a great musician will be a great musician, too. **1**

A Gabonese child plays an instrument made from the horn of a forest antelope.

2

▲ The *mongongo* is an instrument made from a vine stretched across a bent branch.

Ramona: How do you think the forests and nature help people **express** their music?

Mr. Ponte: Gabonese people make instruments from natural resources. People who live in the villages and forests use the natural materials around them, such as trees. There are no stores where they can buy instruments. When you hear their music, it's like listening to the sounds of the forest. **3**

▶ **Before You Move On**

4 1. **Confirm Prediction** Based on the photos and what you have read so far, was your prediction about the interview correct? Explain.

2. **Analyze** Why is the *mongongo* a good example of a Gabonese instrument?

18   19

Student Book pages 18–19

B I A AH

Social Studies: Music

People have created music and made musical instruments for centuries. The people of Gabon use natural materials such as branches as **musical** *instruments. Can you think of other natural materials that are used in this way?* (seashells, gourds, etc). Have students find examples of other instruments that different **cultures** use, especially those using natural materials. Ask students to brainstorm things they could use to make instruments.

Build Comprehension, pages 18–19

1 **Make Inferences** Why do you think people expect the child of a great musician will be a great musician too? (Possible response: People think that if a parent is a musician the child will inherit that talent.)

2 **Make Connections** Point to the photos. *What instruments do these instruments remind you of?* (Possible response: The one on page 18 reminds me of a flute or harmonica. The one on page 19 reminds me of a harp).

3 **Main Idea and Details** MODEL | GUIDE | APPLY What is the main idea of the text on page 19? What details support this? (Main idea: Nature helps people **express** their music. Details: The people make the instruments from things they find in nature. Hearing the music is like listening to the forest.)

4 **Answers to Before You Move On**

1. Confirm Prediction MODEL | GUIDE | APPLY Answers will vary. Students can explain what they based their original predictions on.

2. Analyze The mongongo is a good example of a Gabonese instrument because it is made from natural resources; a vine is stretched across a bent branch.

Student Book (pages 20–21)

Music Traditions

Ramona: Did you learn about any Gabonese music traditions that are slowly being forgotten?

Mr. Ponte: Yes. Sometimes when we looked for one particular dance, song, or instrument to record, we could not find anyone left alive who knew it. The *pluri arc*, for example, is an instrument that is not seen or played very often.

pluri arc

◄ A rare musical instrument

Ramona: Do you think that new music traditions are replacing older ones?

Mr. Ponte: Traditional music can change every time it is played because nothing is written down. **5**

They say when an **elder** dies in Gabon, it's like a library burning. As time passes, the same songs may be told in different ways.

Also, many young Gabonese people now know about the world through travel and the Internet. The young people start to mix new styles of music with traditional ones. Combining new songs with old songs creates a cultural **melting pot**. **6**

▲ These Gabonese musicians combine traditional styles with modern styles of music.

In Other Words
elder older person
melting pot mixture of many different things

▶ **Before You Move On**
7 1. **Problem/Solution** What problem did Mr. Ponte sometimes have when trying to record Gabonese music?
2. **Clarify** Why is an elder's death like a library burning? Explain.

20   21

Build Comprehension, pages 20–21

5 **Details** `MODEL | GUIDE | APPLY` Why can traditional music in Gabon keep changing? (Nothing is written down so songs may be told in different ways from generation to generation.)

6 **Plan and Monitor: Predict** Predict how you think the music of Gabon may change in the future. (Answers will vary. Possible response: I think the music will start sounding more modern and similar to other music because young people from Gabon are traveling and using the Internet to listen to other types of music.)

7 **Answers to Before You Move On**

1. **Problem/Solution** Sometimes when Mr. Ponte looked for a particular dance or song to record, he couldn't find anyone alive who knew it.

2. **Clarify** An elder has a lot of knowledge, just as books in a library are full of information. When an elder dies, the information is lost, just as library books would be lost if the library burned down.

Math: Rhythm and Pattern

Have students explore rhythmic patterns using simple instruments, such as wood sticks and shakers. Working in pairs, have one student **create** a series of patterns while the partner listens carefully. Then have partners switch, so the second partner tries to recreate the patterns. Students can also record their patterns using a series of simple dots and dashes for short and long sounds.

Respect for the Natural World

Ramona: In addition to the unique culture, Gabon has unique and amazing wildlife. How important is the natural world to the people of Gabon?

Mr. Ponte: It's very important. In 2002, the government of Gabon created thirteen national parks. They were created to protect Gabon's people and wildlife. Gabon's forests have stayed almost the same for thousands of years. People such as the pygmies (**pig**-mĕz) live in the forest. They understand the forest better than anyone. They help scientists keep track of a park's animals to make sure they are safe. **1**

▲ Loango National Park was one of the thirteen national parks created in 2002.

22

Ramona: You've said that the people of Gabon seem to have more time in their daily lives than most people have. What do you mean?

Mr. Ponte: I believe that in the villages of Gabon, life is very simple. I saw children make amazing toys from trash they found in the village. Adults spend much of the day making one hot meal. Watches, computers, and cell phones are not part of their lives. They have time to notice every leaf and every cloud in the sky. **2 3**

◄ A handmade toy

▶ **Before You Move On**

4
1. **Details** In what year were the national parks of Gabon created? How many parks were **created**?
2. **Clarify** What did Mr. Ponte learn about how people in the villages of Gabon spend their time?

23

Student Book pages 22–23

Keys to Efficacy

Ask supporting questions when students need to be more specific or concentrate on less material. *Tell me more about what you do in your daily life.*

Build Comprehension, pages 22–25

1 **Identify Details** MODEL | GUIDE | APPLY How do the pygmies help the scientists? (They keep track of animals to make sure they are safe.)

2 **Make Connections** Music and the natural world are important to the Gabonese people. What is important to you? (Answers will vary.)

3 **Make Comparisons** Why do you think the people of Gabon have more time in their daily lives than you do? (Answers will vary.)

4 **Answers to Before You Move On**
1. **Details** MODEL | GUIDE | APPLY Thirteen parks were created in 2002.
2. **Clarify** Possible response: He learned that they have a lot of free time. Adults may spend the day making one hot meal.

5 **Use Visuals** Why does Mr. Ponte film the musician on page 25? (Possible: To help preserve Gabonese music.)

6 **Answers to Before You Move On**
1. **Clarify** A Gabonese village is like family because their lives are connected. They look out for one another and help another.
2. **Paraphrase** Possible response: Mr. Ponte learned to respect the world around him and to take care of our natural world.

Caring About the Natural World

Ramona: Why do you think people in Gabon care so deeply about their natural world?

Mr. Ponte: I think it is because their traditions and lives are connected to the natural world. The village is like a family. The natural world provides them with everything they need to live. They get their food from nature. They build their musical instruments and homes from natural materials.

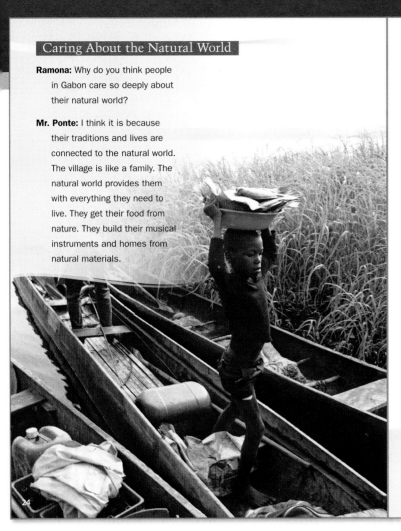

◄ Many people in Gabon catch fish for food. Here, a boy in Gabon unloads fish from a boat.

Ramona: What do you think we can learn from the people of Gabon?

Mr. Ponte: We all depend on each other and on nature. In Gabon, I learned that you can have a great life by respecting the world around you. My time in the villages and the forests taught me how important it is to keep our natural world healthy. Twenty-five years from now, I want a world that still has gorillas—and lots of music! ❖

▲ Ponte films a musician playing the *mongongo*, an instrument made from natural materials.

▲ A Gabonese man helps orphaned young gorillas and a chimp.

▶ **Before You Move On**

1. **Clarify** How is a Gabonese village "like a family," according to Mr. Ponte?
2. **Paraphrase** How does Mr. Ponte answer the question on this page? State his answer in your own words.

24 / 25

Student Book pages 24–25

Daily Writing A AH

1 Writer's Craft Explain: *Like Ramona Jafar, you can use pictures and maps to support your writing. Think about what visuals would help the reader better understand the information.* Use the **Modeled Writing Routine** to write sentences about a place you have visited or would like to visit. (See **Writing Routines,** page PD54.)

Think Aloud	Write
I want to go to Paris because it is pretty. I can show the Eiffel Tower.	Paris, France, is a beautiful city. The photo shows Eiffel Tower, a Paris landmark.
I can show a map with Paris on it.	The map shows Paris is located in central France.
I know Paris is a center for art. I can show the Louvre Museum.	Paris is a center for art. Its Louvre Museum has many famous paintings.

Have students write their sentences in their journals.

CLOSE AND ASSESS

- **Language** *What feelings did Mr. Ponte express about Gabonese music?* (Their music sounds perfect. They create beautiful songs. He wanted to record it.)
- **Vocabulary** *How would you use the word* medium *to talk about Gabon?*
- **Reading** *How did previewing the title and photos help you to predict what the text would be about?* (Answers will vary.)

I A AH

Fluency: Phrasing

Teach/Model Explain the concept: *Fluent readers read with the correct phrasing. They pause at the end of a natural phrase in a sentence, and they stop at the end of a sentence.* Direct students' attention to page 24. Say: *If we do not pause and stop briefly as we read, the words will seem to run together and the meaning will be hard to figure out.* Play the selection recording or read aloud page 24 with correct phrasing.

Practice Have partners read the page aloud together several times, mimicking the phrasing you modeled.

Day 4

Day at a Glance:
- ▶ **Language:** Simple Subjects and Predicates
- ▶ **Vocabulary:** Share Word Knowledge
- ▶ **Reading:** Think and Respond
- ▶ **Writing:** Write About It

OBJECTIVES

Vocabulary
- Use Academic Vocabulary ❶
- Use Grade-Level Vocabulary ❶

Grammar
- Identify Simple Subjects and Predicates ❶

Learning and Teamwork Strategies
- Review
- Collaborate with Peers

Resources

- ⊙ *eVisual 1.8*
- ✂⊙ *Practice Master 1.5*

Differentiate

Language Transfer

Issue In Chinese languages, Haitian Creole, Hmong, Korean (generally), and Vietnamese, the verb is not inflected for person and number. Speakers of these languages may create sentences such as *She play the guitar* instead of *She plays the guitar*.

Strategy Write sentence pairs such as these on sentence strips for students to cut apart and reassemble:

He sings all the time.

They sing all the time.

Part 1 Grammar Skills Trace		Page
Day 2	Complete Sentences	T7a
▶ Day 4	**Simple Subjects and Predicates**	**T26a**
Day 7	Complete Sentences	T35a
Day 10	Review Complete Sentences	T36g

Language of the Day

What did you learn about music in Gabonese culture?
I learned that _____.

Read the Language of the Day. Model: *I learned that music is a* **tradition** *that connects the people of Gabon as they work and play.* As students share, take notes to record what they have learned. Then explain that students will have the opportunity to share more thoughts and impressions about the selection.

Grammar Simple Subjects and Predicates B I A AH

❶ Teach/Model Write and read aloud these sentences.

> *Each generation tells its stories through music.*
> *Many old stories tell about survival in the forest.*

Have volunteers identify and circle the complete subject of each sentence. (Each generation, Many old stories) Point to sentence 1. Ask: *What is the most important word in the subject?* (generation) Underline *generation*. Repeat with sentence 2. (stories) Say: *The circled words are called the simple subject.*

Have volunteers identify the complete predicates. (tells its stories through music, tell about survival in the forest) Have volunteers find the most important word in each predicate. (tells, tell) Underline the words and say: *The underlined words are called the simple predicate, or "the verb."*

Ask: *Why does sentence 1 use the verb* tells *while sentence 2 uses the verb* tell? Have partners use **Think, Pair, Share** to come up with answers. Then display the Grammar Rules box to confirm the correct answer.

Grammar Rules Subject-Verb Agreement

1. The simple subject must agree with the simple predicate, the verb.
2. Use *-s* at the end of verbs that tell about one person or thing.
3. Do not use *-s* at the end of verbs that tell about more than one person or thing.

⊙ NGReach.com ▶ eVisual 1.8

❷ Practice/Apply Organize students into small groups. One student gives a subject; others complete the sentence with predicates. The group selects one sentence and records the simple subject and simple predicate. Then students change roles. Assign **Practice Master 1.5**.

CHECK UNDERSTANDING Write this sentence: *Mr. Ponte photographs the Gabonese people.* Have students identify the simple subject and the simple predicate.

Share Word Knowledge

3 **Teach/Model** To connect concepts, say: *Yesterday you became Key Word experts. Today you will share what you know about your Key Words.* Pair each student with a partner who studied a different word. Have partners follow the steps of **Vocabulary Routine 3** to share their word knowledge. (See **Vocabulary Routines**, page PD39.)

- Take turns reading dictionary entry posters.
- Talk about how the pictures on the posters show the meanings of the Key Words.
- Create sentences using the Key Words and write them in your journals.
- Draw a line under each Key Word.

4 **Practice/Apply** Have students form an **Inside-Outside Circle** with numbered partners on the inside and lettered partners on the outside. Have students outside the circle share their knowledge of a Key Word. On signal, have students rotate to create new partnerships. Then have students trade inside/outside roles. (See **Cooperative Learning Routines**, pages PD58–PD59.)

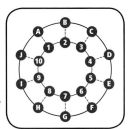

Inside-Outside Circle

Rotate and repeat until each student has a journal entry for each Key Word. Have students take turns reading the dictionary entry posters again. All students should echo the pronunciation. Correct any mispronunciations.

> **CHECK UNDERSTANDING** Give definitions of words and have students hold up the dictionary entries that match the definitions.

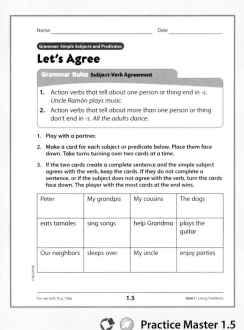

Name _____ Date _____

Let's Agree

Grammar Rules Subject-Verb Agreement

1. Action verbs that tell about one person or thing end in *-s*. *Uncle Ramón plays music.*
2. Action verbs that tell about more than one person or thing don't end in *-s*. *All the adults dance.*

1. Play with a partner.
2. Make a card for each subject or predicate below. Place them face down. Take turns turning over two cards at a time.
3. If the two cards create a complete sentence and the simple subject agrees with the verb, keep the cards. If they do not complete a sentence, or if the subject does not agree with the verb, turn the cards face down. The player with the most cards at the end wins.

Peter	My grandpa	My cousins	The dogs
eats tamales	sing songs	help Grandma	plays the guitar
Our neighbors	sleeps over	My uncle	enjoy parties

For use with TE p. T26a **1.5** Unit 1 | Living Traditions

Practice Master 1.5

Part 1 Vocabulary Skills Trace		Page
Day 1	Social Studies Vocabulary	T5
Day 2	Academic Vocabulary	T7
Day 3	Expand Word Knowledge	T10b
▶ **Day 4**	**Share Word Knowledge**	**T26b**
Day 5	Apply Word Knowledge	T27b
Day 6	Use a Dictionary	T28
Day 7	Use a Dictionary	T35
Days 8–9	Extend Vocabulary	T36e–f
Day 10	Vocabulary Review	T36g–h

Day 4
continued

Day at a Glance:
▶ **Language:** Simple Subjects and Predicates
▶ **Vocabulary:** Share Word Knowledge
▶ **Reading:** Think and Respond
▶ **Writing:** Write About It

OBJECTIVES

Vocabulary
• Use Grade-Level Vocabulary
• Use Academic Vocabulary

Language
• Use Language Function: Express Feelings

Fluency
• Phrasing

Literary Analysis
• Analyze Genre: Interview
• Use Text Structure: Details

Test-Taking Strategies
• Know the Test Format
• Practice and Apply Strategies

Writing
• Write a Paragraph

Resources

 eVisual 1.9

 NGReach.com ❯

See **Technology Station** for digital student resources.

I | A | AH

Fluency: Phrasing

Review Review phrasing (page T24–25). Display this reminder: *Phrasing is how you use your voice to group words together.*

Apply Challenge pairs to a phrasing face-off. Have partners practice reading page 24. Then organize teams of four and have pairs give each other feedback about their reading.

Think and Respond

1 Talk About It Prompt students to cite evidence from the text. Remind students to use Key Words in their answers. If students have difficulty, help them use the sentence starters to form their answers.

1. **Interview** Possible answer: An interview gives information and opinions. You read the questions that one person asks and the answers another person gives.

2. **Express Feelings** Possible answer: This journey made me feel excited and interested. I liked the music and was interested in learning more about the Gabonese **culture**.

3. **Details** Possible answer: The mongongo is the **musical** instrument that interests me the most. It looks like a very simple version of a harp. I think the instrument makes a sound similar to what you hear when you pluck a guitar string.

2 Test-Taking Strategies: Know the Test Format Explain: *When taking a test, it is important to know the test format. You can use appropriate strategies for certain formats. For example, if the format is multiple choice, you should read the question before looking at the answers, eliminate answers you know are not correct, and then read all the remaining choices before choosing your answer.*

Say: *I read the question first. I think I know the answer but I will review all the answer choices.*

> **Which of the following is a musical instrument that is not seen or played very often any more in Gabon?**
> A. mongongo
> B. pluri arc
> C. violin
> D. Gabonese harp
>
> ⬤ NGReach.com ❯ eVisual 1.9

I know that the violin is not a Gabonese instrument, so I can eliminate that as my answer choice. I remember that the pluri arc is no longer played, and that is an answer choice. (B. pluri arc)

Display the remaining practice items. Have students look at the test format to decide how to answer the questions.

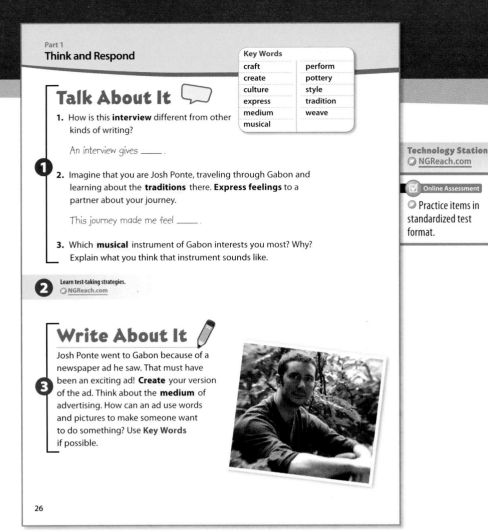

Part 1
Think and Respond

Key Words

craft	perform
create	pottery
culture	style
express	tradition
medium	weave
musical	

Talk About It

1. How is this **interview** different from other kinds of writing?

An interview gives _____ .

2. Imagine that you are Josh Ponte, traveling through Gabon and learning about the **traditions** there. **Express feelings** to a partner about your journey.

This journey made me feel _____ .

3. Which **musical** instrument of Gabon interests you most? Why? Explain what you think that instrument sounds like.

2 Learn test-taking strategies.
NGReach.com

Write About It

Josh Ponte went to Gabon because of a newspaper ad he saw. That must have been an exciting ad! **Create** your version of the ad. Think about the **medium** of advertising. How can an ad use words and pictures to make someone want to do something? Use **Key Words** if possible.

26

Technology Station
NGReach.com

☑ Online Assessment
○ Practice items in standardized test format.

Student Book page 26

Daily Writing

3 **Write About It** Read the directions aloud. Use the **Independent Writing Routine** to help students put their thoughts in writing, using the Key Words. (See **Writing Routines**, page PD56.)

Say	Write
The title of the newspaper ad grabbed Mr. Ponte's attention. I must have an exciting title.	Discover Gabon's unique culture and traditions!
Seeing photos can make people interested in visiting a place. I need interesting photos and captions.	Enjoy the musical style of Gabonese music and dance. (photo of musicians)

Point out Key Words you used: *tradition, culture, musical,* and *style.* Have students use these ideas or their own to write their ads in their journals.

CLOSE AND ASSESS

• **Language** *Write a sentence. Trade sentences with a partner. Partners change the subject or predicate and then underline the simple subject and simple predicate.*

• **Reading** *Which Gabon tradition interested you most?* (Answers will vary.)

• **Vocabulary** *How do the Key Words help you understand the interview? Give an example from the text.* (Answers will vary.)

Keys to Efficacy

Narrow the focus when students need to be more specific or concentrate on less material. *Pick one idea about the Gabonese people to write about. What makes this idea interesting?*

Day 5

Day at a Glance:
- **Language:** Listen for Implicit Ideas
- **Vocabulary:** Apply Word Knowledge
- **Reading:** Reread and Retell
- **Writing:** Write a Paragraph

OBJECTIVES

Vocabulary
- Use Academic Vocabulary
- Use Grade-Level Vocabulary

Listening and Speaking
- Listen for Implicit Ideas

Media and Technology
- Build Concepts from Media

Learning and Teamwork Strategy
- Use Nonverbal Clues
- Restate Instructions
- Review
- Use Patterns in Language
- Collaborate with Peers

Resources

- index cards
- eVisual 1.10
- Build Background Video

Differentiate

N B I

How to Learn Language

Use Nonverbal Clues Tell students: *If you do not know how to say something in words, show what you mean with your body.*

- Use gestures to show that you do not understand.
- Nod your head to show you do understand.

Have students use body language to let you know whether or not they understand what you read.

Language of the Day

Why are musical traditions a part of every culture? Musical traditions are part of every culture because _____.

Read the Language of the Day. Have students recall what they learned about traditions in the **Build Background Video** for the unit when they complete the sentence frame. Add their ideas to the unit concept map.

Listen for Implicit Ideas

1 Teach/Model Introduce the concept: *When you listen for implicit ideas, you need to listen to the "message behind the message."* Display the how to card and model how to listen for implicit ideas.

How to Listen for Implicit Ideas

1. Listen carefully for important details.	The bouzouki is a **musical** instrument from Greece. It has 8 strings. A guitar has only 6.
2. Think about the speaker's message. What's the idea that's not actually put into words?	It takes a long time to learn how to play the bozouki well.
3. Put the "unsaid message" into words.	The bouzouki is like a guitar, but it's even harder to play than a guitar.

NGReach.com > eVisual 1.10

Ask students how they can figure out the implicit idea. Confirm: *The speaker doesn't say the bouzouki is harder to play but you can tell that's what he means. It's an implicit part of his message.*

2 Practice/Apply Pair students, and have students practice making and listening for implicit ideas. Explain to the speakers: *Think of a message or idea. How can you hint at the idea without actually saying it?* Then tell the listeners: *Listen for the implicit idea. Put the clues together and figure out what the "unsaid message" is.* After they have practiced, invite partners to reenact their discussions for the class.

CHECK UNDERSTANDING Ask: *How sure can you be that you've understood an implicit idea?* (You can never be totally sure, because the speaker didn't actually say it. But you can make a good guess.)

Apply Word Knowledge

3 **Teach/Model** Tell students that today they will play a game. Explain how to play "Yes or No."

- *I look at the Key Words.*
- *I write a yes/no question with a Key Word. For example: Is* **pottery** *a musical tradition?*
- *The answer is no. Pottery is not a musical tradition. It's an artistic tradition.*
- *The team that correctly answers the question scores one point.*
- *The team with the most points wins the game.*

4 **Practice/Apply** Write the Key Words on the board. Distribute index cards to each team. Clarify: *Make sure each question includes at least one Key Word.* Have each team write three or four questions for the game.

Explain that the answer to each question must be *yes* or *no*. Monitor students as they write their questions.

Collect the question cards to play the game with the class. Remind teams to raise their hands when they want to answer a question.

Monitor students as they follow your instructions. Restate instructions as required.

For vocabulary games, go to NGReach.com.

> **CHECK UNDERSTANDING** Repeat a question and have students explain how they used their knowledge of the Key Words to decide if the answer was *yes* or *no*.

Day 5
continued

Day at a Glance:
- ▶ **Language:** Listen for Implicit Ideas
- ▶ **Vocabulary:** Apply Word Knowledge
- ▶ **Reading:** Reread and Retell
- ▶ **Writing:** Write Questions

OBJECTIVES

Vocabulary
- Use Academic Vocabulary ❶
- Use Grade-Level Vocabulary ❶

Language
- Compare Genres
- Participate in Discussion
- Retell the Selection

Learning and Teamwork Strategies
- Use Graphic Organizers: Main Idea Diagram

Fluency
- Read with Accuracy and Rate ❶
- Read with Phrasing ❶

Writing
- Write Questions

Resources

📄🖥 *Practice Master 1.6*

📄🖥 *Practice Master 1.7*

🖥 *Comprehension Coach*

🌐 **NGReach.com** ›

See **Technology Station** for digital student resources.

Reread and Retell

❶ Teach Read aloud the introduction and reinforce: *The main ideas and the details can help you tell what the text is about.* Read through the example Main Idea Diagram and callouts. Then explain: *I state the main idea then I give details about that idea.*

Have students complete **Practice Master 1.6**.

❷ Retell Read aloud the directions and language frames. Display the **Retell a Selection Rubric**. Have students retell the selection to their partners using the sentence frame: *This part of the interview is mainly about.* Remind them to tell the main ideas and the details about each section of the interview. Partners reverse roles and repeat.

Retell a Selection		
Scale	**Content**	**Language**
B	☐ Misses or confuses main ideas. ☐ Included few or unrelated details.	☐ Frequently hard to hear or understand. ☐ Often seems uncomfortable with the task.
I	☐ Correctly identifies some of the main ideas. ☐ Some details relate to the important parts.	☐ Can be understood most of the time ☐ Seems somewhat comfortable with the task.
A	☐ Correctly identifies most of the main ideas of the selection. ☐ Details mostly relate to the important parts.	☐ Is almost always understood. ☐ Seems comfortable with the task.
AH	☐ Correctly identifies all main ideas. ☐ Details relate to the important parts.	☐ Is easily understood. ☐ Is very comfortable with the task.

Fluency Accuracy, Rate, and Phrasing ▮I▮ ▮A▮ ▮AH▮

❸ Fluency Have students record their reading on the **Comprehension Coach** to assess each student's progress for rate and accuracy.

Have students use the passage on **Practice Master 1.7** to record their reading for phrasing. Listen to each recording and assess children's ability to read with appropriate phrasing.

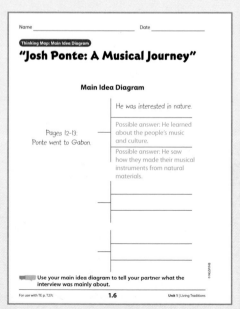

Practice Master 1.6

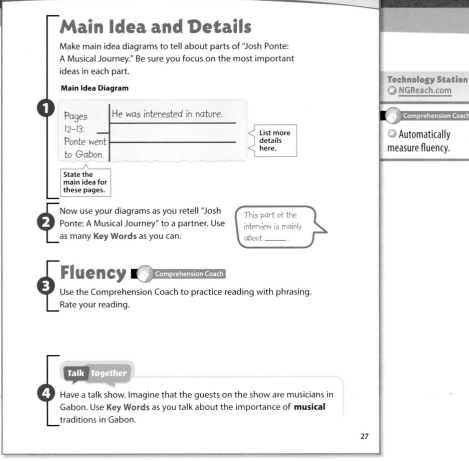

Student Book page 27

4 Talk Together Read aloud the directions and have students role-play an interview. Encourage students to talk about the importance of **musical traditions** in Gabon. Students should add their ideas to their unit concept map.

Daily Writing

5 Write Interview Questions Use the **Interactive Writing** routine to write interview questions students would pose to Mr. Ponte. Help students frame the questions to show that they have a knowledge of Mr. Ponte's work. (See **Writing Routines** page PD55.)

- As a class, discuss which aspects of Mr. Ponte's work interested them most.
- Have students take turns building the questions, one word at a time.
- Offer corrective feedback.

Have students copy the questions into their journals.

CLOSE AND ASSESS

- **Language** *Complete the sentence: When I listen for implicit ideas, I _____.* (Answers will vary.)
- **Reading** *How does a main idea diagram help you retell a selection?* (It helps you focus on the most important information.)
- **Vocabulary** *What Key Words did you use to tell about the interview?* (Answers will vary.)

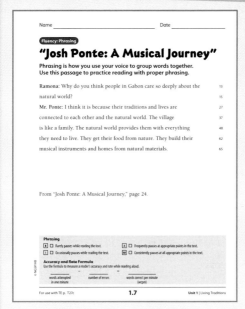

Keys to Efficacy

Encourage elaboration, for example: *Tell me why the mongongo was your favorite instrument.*

Practice Master 1.7

Day 6

Day at a Glance:
Language: Express Feelings   **Reading:** Read the Selection
Vocabulary: Use a Dictionary   **Writing:** Writing Fluency

OBJECTIVES

Vocabulary
- Use Academic Vocabulary ❶
- Use Grade-Level Content Vocabulary ❶
- Strategy: Use Reference Sources: Dictionary ❶

Language
- Language Function: Express Feelings ❶
- Use a Variety of Language Structures

Learning and Teamwork Strategies
- Make Appropriate Contributions
- Prompt and Provide Suggestions
- Build on Ideas

Resources

- ⊙ *eVisual 1.11*
- • *eVisual 1.12*
- 📖 ⊙ *Language Builder Picture Card E11*

Language of the Day

What is an instrument or **craft** that you know? What's an instrument or craft that you would like to learn?
I know _____. I would like to learn _____.

Read the Language of the Day. Model: *I know how to play the guitar. I would like to learn how to make* **pottery**. Invite students to share about any musical instruments they play or crafts they enjoy and to express their feelings about instruments or crafts they would like to learn. Explain that today students will talk, read, and write about other arts and crafts.

Express Feelings

❶ Teach/Model Review how to express feelings (page T4). Explain: *When you express feelings, you let other people know how you feel. To help the other person understand, tell when, where, and why you have those feelings. For example, you might say: I feel nervous before I play the guitar in front of other people.* Display the chart and work with a volunteer to model this language function. Invite students to make variations of these sentences.

How to Express Feelings	
1. Tell about times you have a particular feeling.	I feel nervous before a concert. I'm excited when I'm about to walk on stage.
2. Tell why you have different feelings at different times.	I'm satisfied after a good performance. I know did my best. I'm disappointed if the performance is bad, because I know it could have been better.

⊙ NGReach.com > *eVisual 1.11*

❷ Practice/Apply Have students participate in group discussions, sharing about the feelings they have when they participate in musical performances and/or arts and crafts. Use **Academic Language Frames** to provide ideas to support every language level.

> **CHECK UNDERSTANDING** Display **Language Builder Card E11** and have students tell how they would feel if they were one of the people in the photo.

Differentiate

Academic Language Frames

Express Feelings
- ■ I am _____.
  I feel _____.
  _____
- ■ I feel _____ when _____.
  I am _____ if _____.
  _____
- ■ I am _____ before _____.
  I feel _____ when _____.
  I am _____ if _____.
  I feel _____ after _____.

⊙ NGReach.com > *eVisual 1.12*

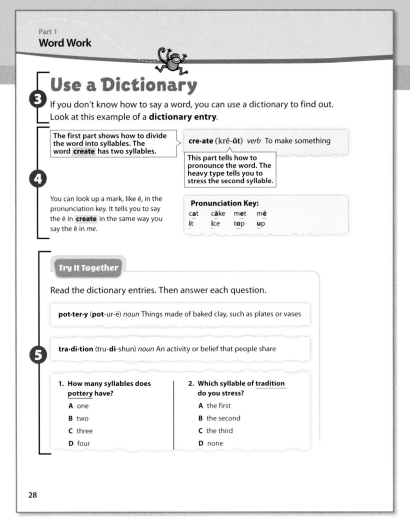

Use a Dictionary

3 If you don't know how to say a word, you can use a dictionary to find out. Look at this example of a **dictionary entry**.

The first part shows how to divide the word into syllables. The word **create** has two syllables.

cre·ate (krē-**āt**) *verb* To make something

This part tells how to pronounce the word. The heavy type tells you to stress the second syllable.

4 You can look up a mark, like ē, in the pronunciation key. It tells you to say the ē in **create** in the same way you say the ē in *me*.

Pronunciation Key:

cat	cāke	met	mē
it	īce	top	up

Try It Together

Read the dictionary entries. Then answer each question.

pot·ter·y (**pot**-ur-ē) *noun* Things made of baked clay, such as plates or vases

5 **tra·di·tion** (tru-**di**-shun) *noun* An activity or belief that people share

1. How many syllables does **pottery** have?
   A one
   B two
   C three
   D four

2. Which syllable of **tradition** do you stress?
   A the first
   B the second
   C the third
   D none

28

Student Book page 28

Use a Dictionary

3 **Teach** Read the first sentence. Then write the dictionary entry for **express**. Use heavy strokes to show boldface. Say: *Let's look at how a word might look in a dictionary.*

ex·press (ek-**spres**) *verb* To put your thoughts and feelings into words

Explain: *A dictionary entry shows how to divide a word into syllables.* Have students count the syllables. Say: *A dictionary entry also tells how to pronounce a word. The bold print tells you which syllable to stress, or say loudest.* Say *express,* emphasizing the second syllable.

4 **Model** Guide students through the dictionary entry for **create**. Have a volunteer count the syllables. Ask: *How do you know which syllable to stress?* (The syllable is in bold print.) Model how to use the Pronunciation Key, calling attention to the marks above the vowels to indicate long vowel sounds. Have volunteers read the long and short vowel words.

5 **Practice/Apply** Read the directions aloud. Have students use the dictionary entries to examine the syllables in *pottery* and **tradition**. Then have partners work together to answer the questions. Use the **Multi-Level Practice Sets** to address varying levels of vocabulary knowledge.

> CHECK UNDERSTANDING Write: **na·tive** (**nā**-tiv). Ask: *How do you pronounce this word? How many syllables does it have? Which syllable do you stress?*

Differentiate

Multi-Level Practice Sets

N **clay** (klā) *noun* Dirt that can be molded into shapes when wet

B **wild·life** (**wīld**-līf) *noun* Animals and plants living in their natural environment

I **eth·nic** (**eth**-nik) *adjective* Having to do with groups of people who share the same culture

A **go·ril·la** (guh-**ril**-uh) *noun* A very large, strong ape

AH **e·lec·tric·i·ty** (i-lek-**triss**-uh-tē) *noun* A form of energy

Part 1 Vocabulary Skills Trace		Page
Day 1	Social Studies Vocabulary	T5
Day 2	Academic Vocabulary	T7
Day 3	Expand Word Knowledge	T10b
Day 4	Share Word Knowledge	T26b
Day 5	Apply Word Knowledge	T27b
Day 6	**Use a Dictionary**	**T28**
Day 7	Use a Dictionary	T35
Days 8–9	Extend Vocabulary	T36e–f
Day 10	Vocabulary Review	T36g–h

Day 6
continued

Day at a Glance:
Language: Express Feelings
Vocabulary: Use a Dictionary

Reading: Read the Selection
Writing: Writing Fluency

OBJECTIVES

Vocabulary
- Use Academic Vocabulary ❶
- Use Grade-Level Content Vocabulary ❶

Language
- Listen to a Preview

Reading Strategies
- Learn to Plan: Preview and Predict ❶
- Make Connections: Text to Text

Comprehension and Literary Analysis
- Recognize Genre: Biography
- Interpret Visuals

Learning and Teamwork Strategies
- Use Prereading Supports
- Build Background Knowledge
- Use Reading Supports

Resources

 Practice Master 1.8

Read the Biography

❶ Connect Across Texts Read aloud the introduction and explain: *You read about how* **musical tradition** *shapes, or influences, the people of Gabon. As you read this biography of an artist, think about how a family tradition shaped him.*

❷ Genre Read aloud the explanation. Clarify: *A biography tells about the life of a real person. It describes the person's experiences and achievements.* Elaborate: *Main events are usually presented in time order.*

❸ Preview and Build Background Use sheltering strategies as you conduct a picture walk.

Pages	Say (and Do)
29	(Point to the picture of Michael Naranjo.) *This artist, Michael Naranjo, uses clay to make sculptures, or figures.* (Point to the picture of Taos Pueblo.) *Michael Naranjo grew up in a pueblo community. What details tell you about his* **culture**?
30–31	*Look at the photos on page 30. They show Naranjo making* **pottery**. *What are some of the steps he follows?* (First he presses the clay. Then he shapes it.) *Look at the photos on page 31. What does it show?* (His family.)
32–33	*Look at the sculptures and describe them.* (One shows a human face. Another one shows a bird. Some of them show people dressed in animal skins.)

❹ Read "Shaped by Tradition" Scaffold the support for varied reading levels.

BELOW LEVEL	ON LEVEL	ABOVE LEVEL
Listen and Read Along	**Read Together**	**Plan and Read Silently**
• Have students track the print as you read aloud. Stop occasionally and model how to paraphrase. • Check understanding with selected Build Comprehension and Before You Move On questions.	• Before reading, guide students through the **Strategy Planner**. • Have partners take turns reading aloud. Then check understanding with the Build Comprehension questions. • After reading, ask students how the strategy planner helped them.	• Before reading, have partners complete the **Strategy Planner**. • Have partners read silently. Then use the Build Comprehension and Before You Move On questions to check understanding. After reading, have partners explain how the strategy planner helped them.

CHECK UNDERSTANDING Ask: *How is a biography of an artist who* **creates** *pottery different from a fiction story about an artist?*

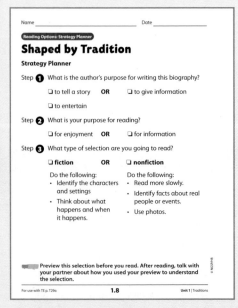

Practice Master 1.8

Shaped by Tradition
BY PATRICIA MILLMAN

Michael Naranjo is a Native American and a **veteran of** the Vietnam War. He is also "a sculptor who happens to be blind."

Naranjo grew up in the Tewa (tā-wa) **Indian Pueblo** of Santa Clara, New Mexico. His love of sculpting was born at the pueblo community. "My mother **was a potter**. I helped her prepare her clay," he remembers.

▲ Michael Naranjo with his sculpture, *The Gift*

▲ A pueblo in New Mexico

In Other Words
veteran of soldier who fought in
Indian Pueblo Native American community
was a potter made bowls and pots from clay

▶ **Before You Move On**
1. **Details** What do you know about Michael Naranjo so far?
2. **Clarify** How did Michael Naranjo first learn about clay?

29

Student Book page 29

Build Comprehension, page 29

1 **Plan and Monitor** RETEACH What do you predict you will learn about in this selection? Review how to preview and predict on page T8. First, read the title. Next, look at the pictures. Then make a prediction. Remember to check your prediction after you read. (Possible response: I predict I'll learn about an artist who discovered how to make things because he followed traditions.)

2 **Main Idea and Details** Identify the main idea and details in the second paragraph. Offer a possible response: Main Idea: Naranjo got his love of sculpting from his family and his community. Details: His mother was a potter. He helped her prepare her clay.

3 **Answers to Before You Move On**
1. **Details** Michael Naranjo is a Native American and a veteran of the Vietnam War. He is a sculptor who is blind. He grew up in the Tewa Indian Pueblo of Santa Clara, New Mexico.

2. **Clarify** His mother was a potter. When he was young, Michael helped his mother prepare her clay.

Cultural Perpectives

Many cultures create pottery or art that is unique and represents their culture. Review that Michael Naranjo grew up in the Tewa Indian Pueblo. Explain that the Pueblo people are made up of many different Native American communities in the Southwest. Point out that each Pueblo community has its own culture—and its own style of pottery.

Have groups of students research pottery from different Pueblo communities. *What features identify each group's pottery? Do they have different shapes, colors, or designs?*

1 Preparing the Clay

Naranjo's mother would put brown clay on a **canvas** cloth and sprinkle white clay on top of it. Next, she would fold the canvas and press the clay into a log shape.

"Then I would take off my shoes and **perform** a little dance on the clay," Naranjo says. "I could feel the **moist** clay between my toes. When I **reached** the other end, I'd step off the canvas."

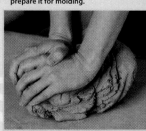

▼ Pressing clay helps prepare it for molding.

After the clay is prepared, an artist can mold it. Here, the artist molds the clay to make a pot. ▶

In Other Words
canvas cotton
moist wet
reached danced all the way to

30

Naranjo's dance served an important purpose. He was **blending** the white clay and the brown clay to make it stronger. With this clay, his mother could make pots that would last a long time.

"Playing with clay—that's probably how I started sculpting," Naranjo says. "Not long after that, I wanted to make **figures** of animals. Even then, I knew that I wanted to be an artist someday."

Rose Naranjo (seated at right) passed along the art of **pottery**-making to her son Michael, her daughter Dolly (seated at left), and her granddaughter Jody (holding her baby). ▶

In Other Words
blending mixing
figures shapes; forms

▶ **Before You Move On**
3
1. **Describe** How did Naranjo's mother prepare clay?
2. **Clarify** How do you think Naranjo knew he wanted to be an artist?

31

Student Book pages 30–31

Text Feature: Quotations

Teach/Model Point out that although this selection isn't like the interview with Josh Ponte, "Shaped by Tradition" does include quotations from Michael Naranjo. Explain: *We know what Naranjo said by looking at the quotation marks. The words between the quotation marks show Naranjo's exact words.* Point out the quotation marks and read Naranjo's quotations in the second paragraph on page 30.

Practice/Apply Have students identify other quotes from Naranjo.

Build Comprehension, pages 30–31

1 **Plan and Monitor** MODEL | GUIDE | APPLY Preview the pages. Then predict what you will read about on pages 30–31. (Possible response: I predict I will read how Naranjo helped his mother prepare her clay.) Now read the two pages to check your prediction.

2 **Visualize: Sensory Images** When you read about Naranjo's little dance, what pictures do you see in your mind? What do you hear? What do you feel? (Possible response: I see Naranjo dancing a funny dance. I hear *squish, squish, squish.* I feel wet clay all over my toes.)

3 **Answers to Before You Move On**

1. **Describe** Naranjo's mother puts brown clay on a canvas cloth and sprinkles white clay on top of it. Next, she folds the canvas and presses the clay into a log shape. Then, she has Michael dance on the clay to blend it and make it stronger.

2. **Clarify** Naranjo liked playing with clay, and he liked to make figures of animals from clay.

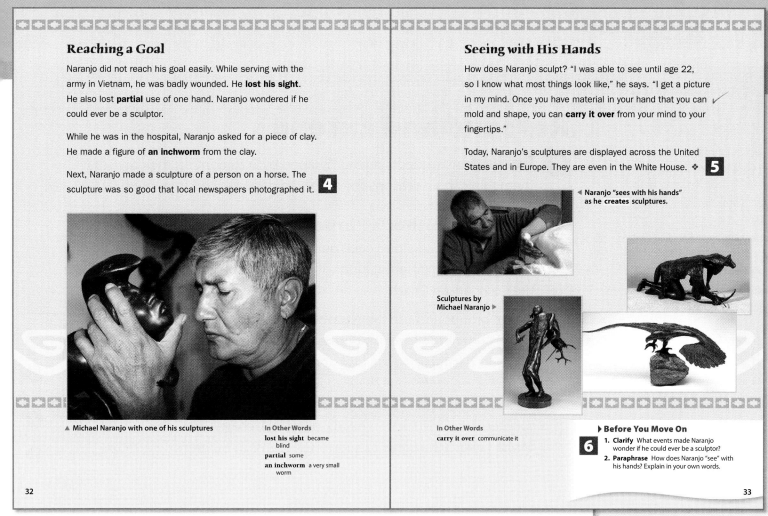

Reaching a Goal

Naranjo did not reach his goal easily. While serving with the army in Vietnam, he was badly wounded. He **lost his sight**. He also lost **partial** use of one hand. Naranjo wondered if he could ever be a sculptor.

While he was in the hospital, Naranjo asked for a piece of clay. He made a figure of **an inchworm** from the clay.

Next, Naranjo made a sculpture of a person on a horse. The sculpture was so good that local newspapers photographed it. **4**

▲ Michael Naranjo with one of his sculptures

In Other Words
lost his sight became blind
partial some
an inchworm a very small worm

32

Seeing with His Hands

How does Naranjo sculpt? "I was able to see until age 22, so I know what most things look like," he says. "I get a picture in my mind. Once you have material in your hand that you can mold and shape, you can **carry it over** from your mind to your fingertips."

Today, Naranjo's sculptures are displayed across the United States and in Europe. They are even in the White House. ❖ **5**

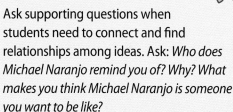
◄ Naranjo "sees with his hands" as he **creates** sculptures.

Sculptures by Michael Naranjo ▶

In Other Words
carry it over communicate it

▶ Before You Move On
1. **Clarify** What events made Naranjo wonder if he could ever be a sculptor?
2. **Paraphrase** How does Naranjo "see" with his hands? Explain in your own words.

33

Student Book pages 32–33

Build Comprehension, pages 32–33

4 **Draw Conclusions** Why do you think the newspapers photographed Naranjo's sculpture? How did this affect him? (Possible response: They were surprised that someone who was blind could **create** such a good sculpture. The publicity convinced Michael that he could become a sculptor.)

5 **Make Connections** What did you learn from Michael Naranjo's biography? (Possible response: I learned that no matter how difficult life is or how hard a goal is to reach, if I work hard, I can do anything I want to do.)

6 **Answers to Before You Move On**
1. **Clarify** Naranjo lost his sight and partial use of one hand while serving in the army in Vietnam.

2. **Paraphrase** (Possible response: Michael remembers what things look like, so he gets a picture in his mind. Then when he has clay in his hands, he uses his hands to shape what he sees in his mind.)

Keys to Efficacy

Ask supporting questions when students need to connect and find relationships among ideas. Ask: *Who does Michael Naranjo remind you of? Why? What makes you think Michael Naranjo is someone you want to be like?*

Home Connection

Have students share the family items they brought from home that reflect a family **tradition**. It may be an item that has been passed down or photos of an event that the family celebrates. Students can talk about the tradition, how it started, and describe how it is celebrated or continued.

Day 6
continued

Day at a Glance:
Language: Express Feelings   **Reading:** Respond and Extend
Vocabulary: Use a Dictionary   **Writing:** Writing Fluency

OBJECTIVES

Vocabulary
• Use Academic Vocabulary
• Use Grade-Level Content Vocabulary

Language
• Participate in Discussion

Fluency
• Read with Accuracy and Rate

Literary Analysis
• Compare Author's Purpose

Learning and Teamwork Strategies
• Use Graphic Organizer: Chart

Writing
• Develop Writing Fluency
• Monitor and Self-Correct Writing

Resources

Practice Master 1.9

eVisual 1.13

Respond and Extend

1 **Reread** As students reread "Shaped by Tradition" on their own, have them think about reasons the author might have had for writing it.

2 **Compare Author's Purpose** Read the introduction. Ask volunteers to read aloud each purpose for writing. Have students share examples of the different kinds of writing. Then explain how to complete the Comparison Chart.

Create groups and use the **Numbered Heads**. Help focus student thinking: *If a purpose isn't clearly stated in the selection, it is implied. First, look at the genre of the selection. Is it fiction or nonfiction? Think about the language the author uses. What are some features you see in articles that inform?* (photos, captions, section heads, diagrams, charts) Provide **Multi-Level Strategies** to support students at different levels.

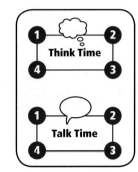

Numbered Heads

Focus	Questions
1. What clues tell you the author's purpose?	Does the author tell a story or provide facts? Does the author give opinions?
2. What is the author's purpose?	Did the author write to entertain, to inform, or to express ideas or persuade?

As students report their group's ideas, students should record them on **Practice Master 1.9.**

3 **Talk Together About the Big Question**
Read aloud the question and directions. Remind students that each selection told about important **traditions**. Ask a follow-up question to prompt students to use newly acquired vocabulary and to focus discussion.

Have students add their ideas to the unit concept map.

> **CHECK UNDERSTANDING** *What are the main reasons that authors write? How can you identify the author's purpose if it isn't stated?*

Differentiate

Multi-Level Strategies

BEGINNING

Help students find the purpose for the interview on page 12. Tell them the purpose for the biography and have them find features that support it.

INTERMEDIATE

Have students use a checklist of features to help them identify the author's purpose for the biography. Have them cite examples from the text to support their answers.

ADVANCED ADVANCED HIGH

Engage students in a discussion. Ask: *Does the author achieve the purpose you identified? Determine if you think the author met the purpose. Explain how he or she did so.*

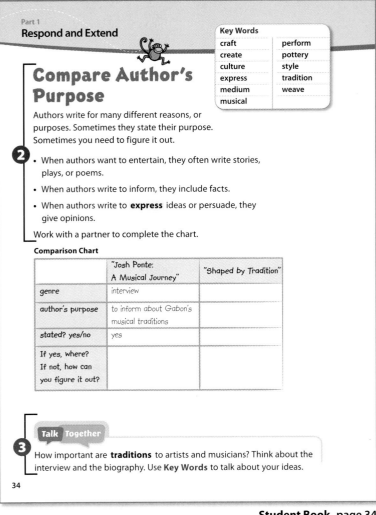

Key Words	
craft	perform
create	pottery
culture	style
express	tradition
medium	weave
musical	

Compare Author's Purpose

Authors write for many different reasons, or purposes. Sometimes they state their purpose. Sometimes you need to figure it out.

2
- When authors want to entertain, they often write stories, plays, or poems.
- When authors write to inform, they include facts.
- When authors write to **express** ideas or persuade, they give opinions.

Work with a partner to complete the chart.

Comparison Chart

	"Josh Ponte: A Musical Journey"	"Shaped by Tradition"
genre	interview	
author's purpose	to inform about Gabon's musical traditions	
stated? yes/no	yes	
If yes, where? If not, how can you figure it out?		

Talk Together

3
How important are **traditions** to artists and musicians? Think about the interview and the biography. Use **Key Words** to talk about your ideas.

34

Student Book page 34

Daily Writing

4 **Writing Fluency** Use the **Power Writing Routine** (see page PD53). Write the word *craft* and prompt: *What crafts have you made? Think about this word and write about it.*

Power Writing Routine

 1. What do you know about the word or picture?

 2. Take one minute to write as much as you can, as well as you can.
B words   **I** sentences   **A** **AH** paragraphs

 3. Check your spelling and grammar. Circle mistakes.

 4. Count your words.

 NGReach.com  eVisual 1.13

Fluency: Accuracy and Rate

To activate prior knowledge and practice fluency, conduct timed readings of "Josh Ponte: A Musical Journey." Select an option for recording

- Use the automatic speech recognition on the **Comprehension Coach** to track word count per minute for the entire passage.

- Use **Practice Master 1.7**.

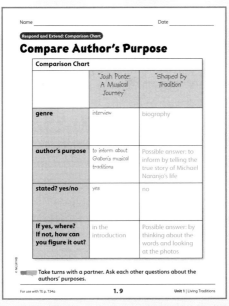

Name _____ Date _____

Respond and Extend: Comparison Chart
Compare Author's Purpose

Comparison Chart

	"Josh Ponte: A Musical Journey"	"Shaped by Tradition"
genre	interview	biography
author's purpose	to inform about Gabon's musical traditions	Possible answer: to inform by telling the true story of Michael Naranjo's life
stated? yes/no	yes	no
If yes, where? If not, how can you figure it out?	in the introduction	Possible answer: by thinking about the words and looking at the photos

Take turns with a partner. Ask each other questions about the authors' purposes.

For use with TE p. T34a   1.9   Unit 1 | Living Traditions

 **Practice Master 1.9**

Day 7

Day at a Glance:
- ▶ **Language:** Complete Sentences
- ▶ **Vocabulary:** Use a Dictionary
- ▶ **Reading:** Reread the Selection
- ▶ **Writing:** Biographic Article

OBJECTIVES

Vocabulary
- Use Academic Vocabulary **⊤**
- Use Grade-Level Vocabulary **⊤**
- Strategy: Use Reference Sources: Dictionary **⊤**

Grammar
- Identify Complete Sentences

Learning and Teamwork Strategies
- Relate to Prior Knowledge
- Make Contributions

Resources

 Practice Master 1.10

eVisual 1.14

Differentiate

Language Transfer

Issue In many languages, the subject of a sentence may come before or after the predicate, or it may even be omitted, if it is implied from context. Some English language learners may be unsure of where to place the subject within a sentence, or they may even duplicate the subject with a pronoun, creating sentences such as *Michael he make pottery* instead of *Michael makes pottery*.

Strategy Have students copy each of the following sentences on sentence strips. Then have them cut the strips apart, separating the subject from the predicate. Shuffle the strips and have students reassemble them to create correctly formed sentences.

Rose sprinkles white clay.

Dolly and Jody fold the canvas.

Michael dances in the clay.

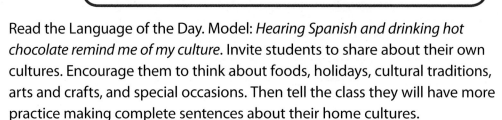

Language of the Day

What reminds you of your culture?

____ and ____ remind me of my culture.

Read the Language of the Day. Model: *Hearing Spanish and drinking hot chocolate remind me of my culture.* Invite students to share about their own cultures. Encourage them to think about foods, holidays, cultural traditions, arts and crafts, and special occasions. Then tell the class they will have more practice making complete sentences about their home cultures.

Grammar Complete Sentences **I** **A** **AH**

1 **Teach/Model** Read the introduction and the first rule. Write: *All over the world, Native artists.* Ask: *Do these words express a complete thought?* (no) Call on a volunteer to read aloud the second rule. Then write: *honor their cultures.* Ask: *Do these words express a complete thought?* (no)

Say: *The first group of words is missing a predicate. The second group is missing a subject.*

Ask students to read the third rule aloud. Have a student rewrite the two groups of words to form a complete sentence:

> *All over the world, Native artists honor their cultures.*

Say: *This is a complete sentence. It has two parts. It has a complete subject.* Have a volunteer underline the complete subject in blue. (All over the world, Native artists) Say: *It has a complete predicate.* (honor their cultures) Have a volunteer underline the complete predicate in red.

2 **Practice** Read aloud the directions and the sentences from "Josh Ponte: A Musical Journey." If necessary, help students identify subjects and predicates with prompts such as: *Who or what is the sentence about? Find the part that tells what the subject is, has, or does.*

3 **Apply in Writing** Read aloud the directions and have students work independently. Provide support as necessary. Assign **Practice Master 1.10.**

> **CHECK UNDERSTANDING** Write: *Michael's sculptures are in the White House.* Say: *Point out the complete subject and complete predicate in the sentence.*

Complete Sentences

A sentence expresses a complete thought. A **complete sentence** has two parts, a subject and a predicate.

Grammar Rules   Complete Sentences

❶

• The **complete subject** tells whom or what the sentence is about. It includes all the words that tell about the subject.	**My older brother**
• The **complete predicate** tells what the subject is, has, or does. It includes all the words that tell about the predicate.	**plays flute in the school band**
• A complete sentence needs both a **complete subject** and a **complete predicate**.	**My older brother plays flute in the school band.**

Read Complete Sentences

❷ Read these sentences with a partner. What is the complete subject in each sentence? What is the complete predicate?

Many people in Gabon tell their stories through music. Each generation passes these stories to the next. Many musical rituals are about survival in the forest.

Write Complete Sentences

❸ Write a paragraph about Josh Ponte's musical journey. Be sure to include a complete subject and a complete predicate in each sentence. Read your paragraph aloud to a partner.

35

Student Book   page 35

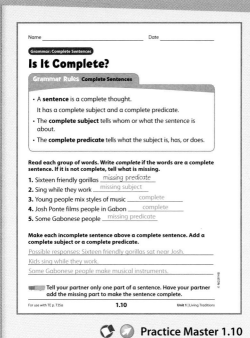

Name _____ Date _____

Grammar: Complete Sentences

Is It Complete?

Grammar Rules   Complete Sentences

• A **sentence** is a complete thought.
  It has a complete subject and a complete predicate.
• The **complete subject** tells whom or what the sentence is about.
• The **complete predicate** tells what the subject is, has, or does.

Read each group of words. Write *complete* if the words are a complete sentence. If it is not complete, tell what is missing.

1. Sixteen friendly gorillas ___missing predicate___
2. Sing while they work ___missing subject___
3. Young people mix styles of music ___complete___
4. Josh Ponte films people in Gabon ___complete___
5. Some Gabonese people ___missing predicate___

Make each incomplete sentence above a complete sentence. Add a complete subject or a complete predicate.

Possible responses: Sixteen friendly gorillas sat near Josh.
Kids sing while they work.
Some Gabonese people make musical instruments.

▭▭▭ Tell your partner only one part of a sentence. Have your partner add the missing part to make the sentence complete.

For use with TE p. T35a   **1.10**   Unit 1 | Living Traditions

✏ 🔄 **Practice Master 1.10**

Dictionary Entries

an·i·mal (**an**-ə-məl) *noun* Any living creature that can move about and eat food

can·vas (**can**-vəs) *noun* A strong, heavy cloth

com· mu· ni· ty (kə-**myü**-nə-tē) *noun* A group of people living in the same place

dis·play (dis-**plā**) *verb* To put something out where people can see it

me·di·um (**mē**-dē-əm) *noun* A way to communicate such as sculpture, writing, or music

pho·to·graph (**fō**-tə-graf) *verb* To take a picture with a camera

🌐 NGReach.com ▷ **eVisual 1.14**

Use a Dictionary

❹ Review/Model Review the Day 6 Lesson Plan (See page T28.) Model how to use a dictionary to pronounce a word. Spell the Key Word **medium** and have students find it in the Dictionary Entries. Ask: *How many syllables does this word have?* Students may hold up fingers to show the number. Say: *Yes, three is correct and we stress the first syllable.* Ask: *Is the e in this word like the e in* met *or in* me? (me) *What sound does the letter* i *make?* (ē) Have students chorally pronounce the word.

❺ Practice/Apply Write the words below. For each word, ask students to use the Dictionary Entries to identify the number of syllables. Next, have a volunteer point out the syllable that is stressed: first, second, third, fourth. Then have partners turn and talk about how the word is pronounced and its meaning.

1. display   (2, second syllable)
2. photograph   (3, first syllable)
3. community   (4, second syllable)
4. animal   (3, first syllable)
5. canvas   (2, first syllable)

CHECK UNDERSTANDING Write: **examine** (ig-**zam**-in) Ask: *How do you pronounce this word? What can you tell me about the syllables?*

Part 1 Vocabulary Skills Trace		Page
Day 1	Social Studies Vocabulary	T5
Day 2	Academic Vocabulary	T7
Day 3	Expand Word Knowledge	T10b
Day 4	Share Word Knowledge	T26b
Day 5	Apply Word Knowledge	T27b
Day 6	Use a Dictionary	T28
Day 7	**Use a Dictionary**	**T35**
Days 8–9	Extend Vocabulary	T36e–f
Day 10	Vocabulary Review	T36g–h

Day 7
continued

Day at a Glance:
▶ **Language:** Complete Sentences
▶ **Vocabulary:** Use a Dictionary

⊙ **Reading:** Reread the Selection
⊙ **Writing:** Biographic Article

OBJECTIVES

Vocabulary
• Use Academic Vocabulary ⊙
• Use Grade-Level Vocabulary ⊙

Literary Analysis
• Genre: Recognize Biography

Learning and Teamwork Strategies
• Participate in Discussion
• Use Graphic Organizers: Web

Writing
• Reproduce Modeled Writing
• Write a Biographic Article

Reread Focus on Biography

1 Teach Remind students that a biography tells about the life of a real person. Explain: *A biography is usually written in time order, and it has certain features.* Elaborate: *One feature of a biography is that it can include quotations from the person. A biography tells about important people and events in the person's life. It also describes the person's talents and achievements.*

Introduce the concept: *Today you will read "Shaped by Tradition" again. This time, think about the features of a biography. Think about how the author uses these features to help readers get to know Michael Naranjo.*

2 Model Have volunteers read the first page of "Shaped by Tradition" aloud. Ask: *Where did Michael spend his childhood?* (Tewa Indian Pueblo of Santa Clara, New Mexico) *The author gives details about Michael that help us know what he is like.* Ask: *What is one of Michael's achievements?* (veteran of the Vietnam War) *What is one of his talents?* (sculpting)

Display a web. Work with students to organize features of a biography on the web.

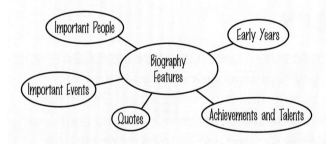

3 Practice/Apply in Reading Have small groups copy the Biography Features web. Then instruct them to reread "Shaped by Tradition" and use **Team Word Webbing** to create a web about Michael Naranjo. (See **Cooperative Learning Routines**, pages PD58–PD59.) Have them add details from the selection under the appropriate features of on the web.

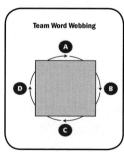

Team Word Webbing

Daily Writing

Modeled Writing: Biographic Article Review features of a biography (pages T29a and T36a.) Then use the **Modeled Writing** routine to illustrate how to write a biographic article about a musician. (See **Writing Routines**, on page PD54.)

Think Aloud	Write
1. Plan	
I will make a RAFT to plan my writing. I will take on the role of a reporter.	Role: reporter
Who is my audience? I want people who like music to learn about my favorite musician. My audience will be music lovers.	Audience: music lovers
Repeat the think aloud for form (biographic article) and topic (your favorite musician and your opinion of his/her latest song).	
2. Write	
Since this is a biographic article, I will give some true details about my favorite musician's life. I'll use complete sentences in my article.	David Archuleta is my favorite musician. David was born on December 28, 1990 in Miami, Florida. He grew up in Murray, Utah. David speaks English and Spanish.
I plan to tell why I like or do not like this musician's latest song. I'll remember to give reasons for my opinion.	David's latest songs are on a holiday CD. I like this CD because I can compare David's songs with other holiday songs from different religions and **cultures**.
Repeat the think aloud to add more biographic details or opinions.	
3. Read and Reflect	
I will read aloud my final article and check it one more time. Have I met the plan I made during my RAFT? Yes! Do I want to make more changes? No. Now I can share it with music lovers.	Read the article, checking for points addressed during the modeling.

Use **Multi-Level Strategies** to support students at all proficiency levels in writing a biographic article.

CLOSE AND ASSESS

- **Language** Write a sentence about a favorite musician. Circle the complete subject, and underline the complete predicate.
- **Vocabulary** Are there words that are difficult to pronounce in your article? How can you help your readers know how to say these words?
- **Reading** What details about your favorite musician's life did your readers learn? What details about Michael Naranjo's life did you learn?

Days 8–9

Day at a Glance:
▶ **Language:** Oral Language Project: Interview
▶ **Vocabulary:** Extend Vocabulary
▶ **Reading:** Read Leveled Books
▶ **Writing:** Paraphrase

OBJECTIVES

Vocabulary
• Use Academic and Grade-Level Vocabulary

Language
• Language Function: Express Feelings ❶

Listening and Speaking
• Listen for Implicit Ideas
• Listen and Ask Questions
• Make Eye Contact
• Speak at the Right Pace

Learning and Teamwork Strategies
• Respond to Questions

Resources
•   *materials for props, such as:*
   – *clipboards*
   – *cardboard tubes*
   – *construction paper*
   – *boxes*
   – *markers*
   – *tape*

 Assessment Handbook *page 6*

Language of the Day

How would you summarize what you learned about **traditions**?
I know that traditions _____ .

Read the Language of the Day. Model: *I know that traditions can be passed down from parents to their children. If you make art or music with a family member, it can become a tradition.* Have each student give a brief summary of what they have learned.

Oral Language Project Interview

❶ Introduce the Activity Tap prior knowledge by reviewing: *Ramona conducted an interview with Josh Ponte.* Ask: *What happened during this interview?* (Ramona asked Mr. Ponte questions and Mr. Ponte answered them.)

Prompt brainstorming: *Imagine that one of the most popular singing groups in the country is performing in our community. You are part of a group of student reporters who will interview the performers before the concert.* Ask: *What will you ask the musicians about their lives? What questions will you ask about their music? What will you ask about their latest CD?* Record students' questions on a chart paper.

❷ Plan Form groups of seven students each. Explain that each group will conduct an interview: four students can role play reporters who ask questions and three students can role play the performers who answer questions. Guide students at different proficiency levels to select appropriate roles.

> When did you start singing?
> What do you like about being a musician?
> How do you feel when you perform?

3 **Practice** Have students select a real or imaginary singing group. Then have groups use the question chart for ideas as they plan the interview. Mention that questions and answers should be in the form of complete sentences. Suggest that reporters practice keeping their voices natural, as if they were asking the questions for the first time. Encourage performers to express their feelings as they answer questions. Remind both reporters and performers to make eye contact and listen for implicit ideas during the interviews. Model and review:

- As you listen, watch gestures and take notes on important details.
- Think about what the gestures and words mean together.

Use **Multi-Level Strategies** to involve students at all proficiency levels.

Provide reporters with clipboards. Students can make microphones from cardboard tubes and balls of crumpled foil. Have students use boxes, markers, construction paper, and tape to create musical instruments for the singing group.

4 **Entertainment Today!** Have students conduct the interviews. Invite family members or another class to enjoy them.

Evaluate the interviews using the rubric.

5 **Debrief and Compare** Ask each group to share what they most remember from the interviews. Have them compare the questions each group asked. Then encourage them to add their ideas to the unit concept maps, as appropriate.

Differentiate

Multi-Level Strategies

BEGINNING

Have students draw a picture of the musical instruments the musicians play. Provide sentence frames:

- Do you like playing the _____?
- When did you learn to _____?

INTERMEDIATE

Encourage students to take notes during the interview.

ADVANCED **ADVANCED HIGH**

Challenge students to come up with additional questions during the interview.

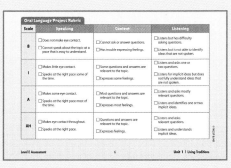

 Assessment Handbook page 6

Days 8–9
continued

Day at a Glance:
- **Language:** Oral Language Project: Interview
- **Vocabulary:** Extend Vocabulary
- **Reading:** Read Leveled Books
- **Writing:** Paraphrase

OBJECTIVES

Vocabulary
- Extend Vocabulary through Wide Reading

Language
- Participate in Discussion

Reading
- Read Independently
- Summarize Reading
- Make Connections: Text to Text
- Apply Reading Strategies Varied Texts

Writing
- Paraphrase Maintaining Meaning

Social Studies
- Explore Customs and Traditions

Resources

 Leveled Books:
- *At the Crossroads*
- *Tea with Milk*
- *The Red Lantern Festival*
- *El Dia De Los Muertos*
- *In My Family/En Mi Familia*
- *Harvest Festivals*

Reach Leveled Library Lesson Plans

Find more leveled readers about this topic.

Differentiate Read Leveled Books

Group students based on their reading abilities and interests. Use the **Guided Reading** routine (See page PD47) for books at students' instructional level. Use the **Independent Reading Support** (see page PD50) for books at students' independent reading level.

After reading, organize the students into heterogeneous groups to discuss what they read and to use the new information to answer the Big Question. Use these prompts to guide your discussion:

- What new information did you learn about how traditions shape us?

- What surprised you?

- How did new information change your answer?

Fiction

BEGINNING LEVEL

At the Crossroads
by Rachel Isadora

- **Genre:** Realistic Fiction

The fathers of the village are coming home after months away working in the mines. The children wait all night to welcome them home.

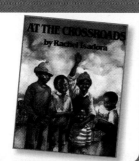

Key Words

crossroads

distant

guitar

rumble

waiting

INTERMEDIATE LEVEL

Tea with Milk
by Allen Say

- **Genre:** Biographical Fiction

The author shares the story of his mother's childhood in San Francisco, her problems upon returning to Japan, and how she met his father.

Key Words

department

foreigner

homeland

marry

worst

ADVANCED   ADVANCED HIGH LEVELS

The Red Lantern Festival
by Janet Stutley

- **Genre:** Play/Folktale

Yuan goes to work in the Emperor's palace, but she misses her family. Yuan's friend helps her by creating a new festival, so she can leave the palace one night.

Key Words

festival

lanterns

palace

parade

tradition

Nonfiction

BEGINNING LEVEL

El Dia De Los Muertos
by Mary Dodson Wade

- **Genre:** Expository Nonfiction

This beginning reader explains how Mexican families celebrate the lives of their deceased loved ones by sharing pictures and stories, preparing feasts, and lighting candles.

Key Words

celebrate

cemetery

glow

graves

spirit

INTERMEDIATE LEVEL

In My Family/En Mi Familia
by Carmen Lomas Garza

- **Genre:** Memoir

In both English and Spanish, the author shares special moments and traditions from her childhood and family.

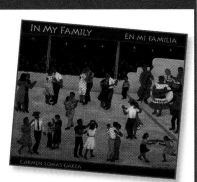

Key Words

cactus

dozens

Easter

peace

toad

ADVANCED   ADVANCED HIGH LEVELS

Harvest Festivals
by Gare Thompson

- **Genre:** Expository Nonfiction

Giving thanks for the crops is important in many cultures. Learn about how people celebrate harvest festivals all over the world.

Key Words

celebrate

feast

festival

important

worship

Daily Writing A AH

Journal Entry Have students write a journal entry in their reading journals. Use "Josh Ponte: A Musical Journey" to model how to write a journal entry. Focus on how to paraphrase maintaining meanings. Say: *Singing while doing chores is a new tradition in Gabon. Is that right?* (no). Then work with students to restate: *Music has been part of Gabon culture for a long time.*

Same Book / Different Levels

B I A AH

Vanishing Cultures
by Wade Davis

Travel to remote areas of the world and learn about the people who live there. Discover why their unique cultures are struggling to survive.

Pioneer Edition
Fountas and Pinnell: P-R

- **B** Conduct a Picture Walk.
- **I** Read text and captions.

Key Words

arrow	cultures
forest	jungle
nomads	tribe

Pathfinder Edition
Fountas and Pinnell: Q-S

- **A** Read text and captions.
- **AH** Read and write responses to questions.

Key Words

anthropologist	cultures
famine	habitat
nomads	tribe

Day 10

OBJECTIVES

Language
- Review Language Function: Express Feelings ⓣ

Language
- Review Complete Sentences

Vocabulary
- Review and Use Grade-Level Vocabulary ⓣ
- Review Dictionary Skills ⓣ

Reading Strategy
- Learn to Plan and Monitor ⓣ

Comprehension and Literary Analysis
- Review Genre: Interview
- Review Main Idea and Details ⓣ

Fluency
- Phrasing

Resources

- *Language Builder Picture Cards E8, E10, and E12*
- *Key Word Images*
- *Assessment Handbook*
- *eVisuals 1.15*
- *Comprehension Coach*

Part 1 Grammar Skills Trace		Page
Day 2	Complete Sentences	T7a
Day 4	Simple Subject and Predicate	T26a
Day 7	Complete Sentences	T35a
Day 10	**Review Complete Sentences**	**T36g**

Language of the Day

What did you learn? How does it help you in school? I learned how to ____. ____ means ____. For example, ____.

Read the Language of the Day. Model: *I learned how to express my feelings. This means I can tell people how I feel. For example, I can tell my students that I am proud of all their hard work.* Review the list of skills students learned in Part 1. Prompt students to talk about a skill they learned: *How did you use that skill? How do you think you can use that skill again?*

Review and Assess

Use these interactive review activities to reinforce concepts covered in Part 1. Then use the assessment tools to evaluate students' progress. For more details about assessment, see page T71a.

Language Function

Express Feelings

Use a **Think, Pair, Share** to have students engage in a conversation about traditions. Show **Language Builder Picture Cards E8, E10**, and **E12**. Have students discuss the traditions shown in the pictures and express their feelings about them. Have students share some of their feelings with the group.

- **Assessment:** Language Function Rubric on page 2 of the Assessment Handbook.

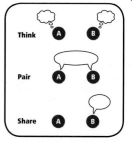

Think, Pair, Share

Language

Complete Sentences

Assign each group of students a topic. Have students write as many complete sentences as they can on that topic. Ask groups to circle the complete subject and underline the complete predicate as they check their sentences. Then tally the sentences.

Vocabulary

Social Studies and Academic Vocabulary

Form two teams. Show **Key Word Images**. Have one player from the first team silently choose one image. Give the player one minute to draw clues that help his or her team identify the selected Key Word. Once the word has been identified, have the team use it in a sentence.

- **Assessment:** Key Word tests on pages 3–5 of the Assessment Handbook.

Key Words	
craft	perform
create	pottery
culture	style
express	tradition
medium	weave
musical	

Vocabulary Strategy

Word Work: Use a Dictionary

Form teams. Tell students they will compete in a "dictionary hunt." Have teams take turns identifying elements in a dictionary entry. Use prompts such as:

- *Find the entry for the word* **musical**.
- *Tell how many syllables are in the word.*
- *Pronounce the word using the respelling.*
- *Use the word in an oral sentence.*

The team that gives the most correct answers wins.

Reading Strategy

Plan and Monitor

Read the title, introduction, and first question and answer of "A Greek New Year's Tradition." Have students tell how they can plan and predict for the interview using the **Academic Language Frames**: *I read/hear _____. I predict that _____. My prediction _____.*

Comprehension

Literary Analysis

Read the rest of "A Greek New Year's Tradition." Have students tell what facts or information they learned from the interview, using the frame: *One fact I learned is _____.*

Text Structure

Have students identify the main idea and details, using these frames: *The main idea of the interview is _____. One detail is _____. Another detail is _____.*

Fluency

Phrasing

Have students review their own recordings of "Josh Ponte: A Musical Journey" in the Comprehension Coach. Then have students practice reading **Leveled Library Books** that are appropriate for their reading levels, focusing on accuracy and phrasing.

- **Assessment:** Reading Fluency Benchmark Assessment on pages 441–447 of the Assessment Handbook.

Read Aloud

A Greek New Year's Tradition

Jamie Sample interviews Gus Stamos about his Greek New Year's tradition.

Jamie: Why is January 1st such an important day for your family?

Gus: January 1st is St. Basil's Day. On this day, we remember St. Basil for his kindness and generosity to the poor. We honor him by giving gifts to family, friends, and those in need.

Jamie: Do you have any special traditions for this day?

Gus: One tradition is for children to go from house to house singing. The first child to enter your home brings good luck and receives a coin.

Jamie: Are there any special foods you have on St. Basil's Day?

Gus: An important food is *Vassilopitta* or St Basil's Bread. Inside this sweet bread is a silver or gold coin. The first slice is for St. Basil, the second for the home, the third for the oldest family member, and so on down to the youngest. Whoever finds the coin will be lucky for the next year.

Jamie: What happens if the coin is in the slice for the home?

Gus: That's easy. Then the whole family will be lucky!

NGReach.com > eVisual 1.15

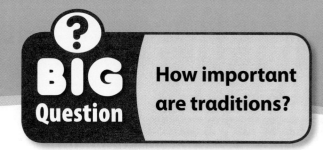

BIG Question How important are traditions?

PART 2

Days 1–5

▶ **Main Selection**
Martina the Beautiful Cockroach, A Cuban Folk Tale, by Carmen Agra Deedy, illustrated by Eugenia Nobati

▶ **Genre**
Human Interest Feature

▶ **Selection Summary**
Martina, a cockroach, is getting ready to choose a husband. Her grandmother tells her that a "Coffee Test"—spilling coffee on her suitors to see how they control their temper—is how to find a good husband. After some suitors fail the test, Martina meets the mouse Pérez. Pérez, having been told about the Coffee Test from his grandmother, ends up performing the test on her.

SELECTION AWARDS

- *American Library Association:* Pura Belpré Award Honor Book, 2008
- *Bank Street College of Education:* Best Children's Books of the Year, 2008

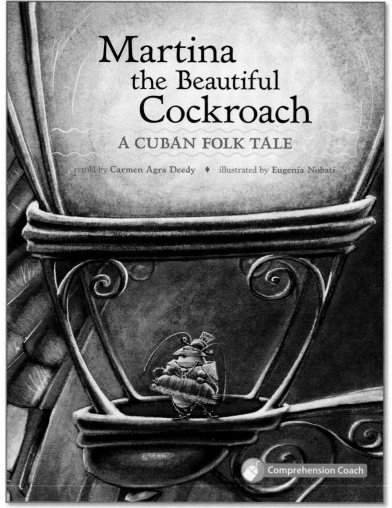

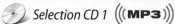
Selection CD 1 (((**MP3**)))

Skills at a Glance	
Language	Ask for and Give Information; Theme Theater
Grammar	Compound Subjects; Compound Predicates; Subject-Verb Agreement
Vocabulary	Social Studies Vocabulary: *ancestor, ceremony, marriage, occasion, ritual*
	Academic Vocabulary: *belief, custom, influence, relationship, role*
	Idioms and Expressions
Reading Strategy	Plan and Monitor
Literary Analysis	Plot
Writing	Writing Fluency; Prewrite; Writer's Craft: Humor; Friendly Letter; Edit and Proofread; Paragraph; Journal Entry
Newcomer Support	Use *In the USA:* family words

▶ Companion Selection

Coming of Age, adapted from *Skipping Stones,* illustrated by Shannon Brady

▶ Genre

Magazine Article

▶ Selection Summary

In this coming-of-age story, an Indian-American girl named Jyotsna goes through her sari ceremony. This ceremony celebrates the turning of the girl into a young woman. Traditional events that are part of the ceremony are mentioned.

Connect Across Texts Read about a family **custom** from India that celebrates a girl's coming of age.

Genre A **magazine article** is nonfiction. It gives facts about real people, places, or events.

Coming of Age

adapted from *Skipping Stones* ❀ illustrated by Shannon Brady

Many Hindus celebrate important **phases in life** with special **ceremonies** called *samskaras*. For Jyotsna Grandhi, one important *samskara* happened when she **turned** eleven. The ceremony, called a sari ceremony, welcomed her into adulthood. During the ceremony, Jyotsna received her first half sari, or *voni*. In some Indian traditions, this is meant to be the **outfit** worn by young women until **marriage**.

Here is what Jyotsna had to say about her sari ceremony.

full sari

half sari

◄ A sari is a traditional garment worn by some women in India.

In Other Words
phases in life times in a person's growth and development
turned reached the age of
outfit clothing

▶ **Before You Move On**
1. **Use Text Features** How do the title, illustration, and caption help you understand what this article is about?
2. **Main Idea** What does the sari **ceremony** celebrate?

61

Leveled Library Books

Differentiated Instruction

B | BEGINNING

A Picnic in October

by Eve Bunting

Tony's family visits the Statue of Liberty every year to celebrate his grandparents' arrival in the United States and the statue's birthday.

This Is the Way We Eat Our Food

by Laine Falk

In this book, students read about various mealtime customs from around the world.

I | INTERMEDIATE

How My Parents Learned to Eat

by Ina R. Friedman

An American man and a Japanese woman learn the proper way to eat in each other's cultures. They teach both customs to their daughter.

I Am Indian American

by Pamela Graham

In this book, students are introduced to Karim, an American boy whose family is from New Delhi. Students read about East Indian heritage, including clothes, food, holidays, and beliefs.

A | ADVANCED **AH | ADVANCED HIGH**

The Big Catch

by Gare Thompson

In this chapter book, a Vietnamese-American family struggles to fit into a Texas fishing community.

Mexico: Cultures and Celebrations

by Greg Banks

Read all about Mexican culture. Students learn about Mexico's food, customs, clothing, art, and celebrations, as well as the ways past and modern cultures have influenced everyday life in Mexico.

Unit **1** Daily Planner

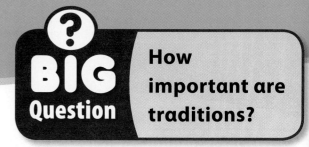

BIG Question — How important are traditions?

PART 2

Core Lessons

Content: Integrated Throughout Each Day

	Day 1	**Day 2**
	Introduce Academic Language	Introduce More Academic Language
Language ⏰ 5–10 minutes	**Language of the Day** *T36* ❶ **Language Function: Function: Ask for and Give Information** *T36* 🔊 ((MP3)) **Oral Language** • Talk About Traditions *T37* • Talk Together About the Big Question *T37*	**Language of the Day** *T39a* ❶ **Grammar: Compound Subjects** *T39a* **Oral Language** • Talk Together About Planning and Monitoring *T40*

Vocabulary ⏰ 10–15 minutes	❶ **Social Studies Vocabulary**
	 • Introduce Words *T37*
	    ancestor marriage ritual
	    ceremony occasion
		❶ **Academic Vocabulary**
		 • Introduce Words *T39*
		    belief relationship
		    custom role
		    influence
		 Classroom Vocabulary
		 • Introduce Words *T41*
		    monitor clarify

Reading ⏰ 15–20 minutes	❶ **Text Structure: Plot** • Introduce Plot *T38a* • Use Graphic Organizers: Story Map *T38* **Read Aloud: "Peter's New Tooth"** *T38a*	❶ **Strategy: Plan and Monitor** • Introduce and Practice the Strategy *T40* **Read "Luka's Grandparents"** *T41* **Phonics and Fluency** • Words with Short ĭ, ŭ *T40*
Writing ⏰ 15 minutes	**Daily Writing** • Writing Fluency *T38*	
	Social Studies • Explore Customs and Traditions • Geography	**Social Studies** • Explore Customs and Traditions • Geography

Ready-to-Go Plans
▶ Time (20, 30, 40, 60, 90 minutes per day)
▶ Model (Content Focus, Literacy Focus, Dual Language)

Online Lesson Planner
NGReach.com

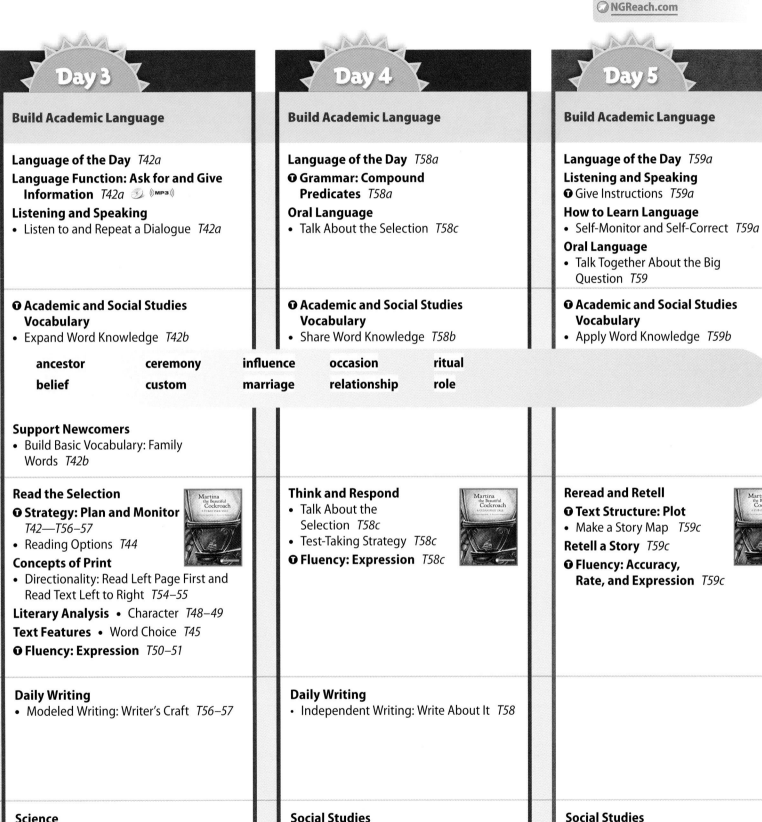

Day 3

Build Academic Language

Language of the Day *T42a*
Language Function: Ask for and Give Information *T42a*
Listening and Speaking
• Listen to and Repeat a Dialogue *T42a*

❶ Academic and Social Studies Vocabulary
• Expand Word Knowledge *T42b*

| ancestor | ceremony | influence | occasion | ritual |
| belief | custom | marriage | relationship | role |

Support Newcomers
• Build Basic Vocabulary: Family Words *T42b*

Read the Selection
❶ Strategy: Plan and Monitor *T42—T56–57*
• Reading Options *T44*
Concepts of Print
• Directionality: Read Left Page First and Read Text Left to Right *T54–55*
Literary Analysis • Character *T48–49*
Text Features • Word Choice *T45*
❶ Fluency: Expression *T50–51*

Daily Writing
• Modeled Writing: Writer's Craft *T56–57*

Science
• Color-Changing Lizards *T52–53*

Day 4

Build Academic Language

Language of the Day *T58a*
❶ Grammar: Compound Predicates *T58a*
Oral Language
• Talk About the Selection *T58c*

❶ Academic and Social Studies Vocabulary
• Share Word Knowledge *T58b*

Think and Respond
• Talk About the Selection *T58c*
• Test-Taking Strategy *T58c*
❶ Fluency: Expression *T58c*

Daily Writing
• Independent Writing: Write About It *T58*

Social Studies
• Explore Customs and Traditions
• Geography

Day 5

Build Academic Language

Language of the Day *T59a*
Listening and Speaking
❶ Give Instructions *T59a*
How to Learn Language
• Self-Monitor and Self-Correct *T59a*
Oral Language
• Talk Together About the Big Question *T59*

❶ Academic and Social Studies Vocabulary
• Apply Word Knowledge *T59b*

Reread and Retell
❶ Text Structure: Plot
• Make a Story Map *T59c*
Retell a Story *T59c*
❶ Fluency: Accuracy, Rate, and Expression *T59c*

Social Studies
• Explore Customs and Traditions
• Geography

PART 2

Core Lessons

	Day 6	**Day 7**
Language 5–10 minutes	**Expand Academic Language** **Language of the Day** *T60a* ❶ **Language Function: Ask for and Give Information** *T60a* **Oral Language** • Talk Together About the Big Question *T64a*	**Expand Academic Language** **Language of the Day** *T65a* ❶ **Grammar/Spelling: Subject-Verb Agreement** *T65a*
Vocabulary 10–15 minutes	❶ **Idioms and Expressions** *T60* **Support Newcomers:** • Additional Idioms and Expressions *T60*	❶ **More Idioms and Expressions** *T65* • Idioms and Expressions *T65*
Reading 15–20 minutes	**Read the Magazine Article** *T61a* • Reading Options *T61a* ❶ **Strategy: Plan and Monitor** *T61a–T63* ❶ **Fluency: Accuracy and Rate** *T64* **Respond and Extend** • Compare Content *T64a*	**Reread the Selection: Focus on Narrator** *T66a*
Writing 15 minutes	**Daily Writing** • Writing Fluency *T64*	**Daily Writing** • Modeled Writing: Paragraph *T66b*
Content: Integrated Throughout Each Day	**Social Studies** • Explore Customs and Traditions • Geography	**Social Studies** • Explore Customs and Traditions • Geography

❶ = Tested Skill

Apply Academic Language

Theme Theater
- Introduce the Activity *T66c*
- Plan *T66c*
- Rehearse *T66d*
- Here Comes the Bride! *T66d*
- Debrief and Compare *T66d*

Read Leveled Books

Fiction *T66e*

 **B**

Key Words

braid	October
dock	statue
millions	

 **I**

Key Words

chopsticks	restaurant
fork	taught
knives	

A **AH**

Key Words

ancestors	neighborhood
catch	tradition
customer	

Nonfiction *T66f*

 **B**

Key Words

around	sip
finished	tool
fork	

 **I**

Key Words

actually	respect
continent	spices
patterns	

 **A** **AH**

Key Words

ancestors	pottery
language	victory
national	

Daily Writing
- Journal Entry *T66f*

Review and Assess

Interactive Review *T66g–T66h*
- ⊕ Language Function: Ask and Give Information
- ⊕ Grammar: Subject-Verb Agreement
- ⊕ Vocabulary: Social Studies and Academic Vocabulary
- ⊕ Vocabulary Strategy: Idioms and Expressions
- ⊕ Reading Strategy: Plan and Monitor
- ⊕ Literary Analysis: Folk Tale
- ⊕ Text Structure: Plot
- ⊕ Fluency: Expression

Assessment *T66g–T66h*

Same Book, Different Levels

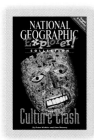 **I** **A** **AH**

Key Words

conquistador	explorers	language
culture	guest	migrated
empire	immunity	prisoner

Reading Station

EXPLORER! COLLECTION
Ladder Text:
- Pioneer edition for below level readers
- Pathfinder edition for on and above level readers

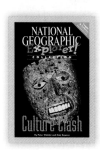 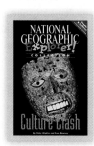

DECODABLE TEXTS

TRADE BOOK COLLECTION
Use the **Leveled Book Finder** at
NGReach.com

Content Stations

Download complete lesson plans ⦿ **NGReach.com** ➤

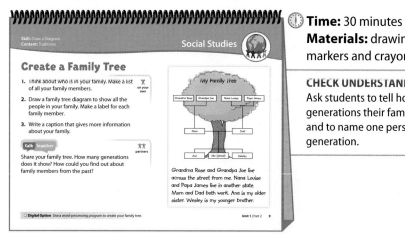

Skill: Research
Content: Insects
Science

Insect Eaters
1. Review "Martina the Beautiful Cockroach." What does the lizard say after Martina spills coffee on him? ★ *on your own*
2. Go online and read about animals and the insects they eat.
3. Think about what you have learned about insect eaters. Write a few sentences to describe how the other suitors would have treated Martina.

Talk Together ★★★ *small group*
Share your sentences.

> The article says that mice eat insects. In fact, it says that mice eat cockroaches. In real life, Martina's marriage would not be a happy one. Pérez the mouse would probably eat her.

☐ To read about insect-eating animals, go to NGReach.com.
Unit 1 | Part 2   8

🕐 **Time:** 20 minutes
Materials: computers with Internet access, paper, pencils

CHECK UNDERSTANDING
Ask: *Would Don Gallo have eaten Martina? Why or why not?*

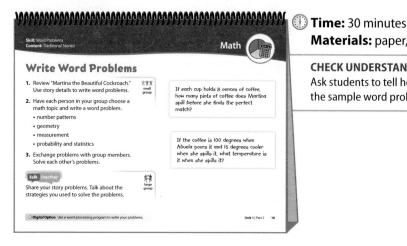

Skill: Draw a Diagram
Content: Traditions
Social Studies

Create a Family Tree
1. Think about who is in your family. Make a list of all your family members. ★ *on your own*
2. Draw a family tree diagram to show all the people in your family. Make a label for each family member.
3. Write a caption that gives more information about your family.

Talk Together ★★ *partners*
Share your family tree. How many generations does it show? How could you find out about family members from the past?

My Family Tree

> Grandma Rose and Grandpa Joe live across the street from me. Nana Louise and Papa James live in another state. Mom and Dad both work. Ana is my older sister. Wesley is my younger brother.

☐ **Digital Option** Use a word-processing program to create your family tree.
Unit 1 | Part 2   9

🕐 **Time:** 30 minutes
Materials: drawing paper, colored markers and crayons, paper, pencils

CHECK UNDERSTANDING
Ask students to tell how many generations their family trees show and to name one person from each generation.

Skill: Word Problems
Content: Traditional Stories
Math

Write Word Problems
1. Review "Martina the Beautiful Cockroach." Use story details to write word problems. ★★★ *small group*
2. Have each person in your group choose a math topic and write a word problem.
   - number patterns
   - geometry
   - measurement
   - probability and statistics
3. Exchange problems with group members. Solve each other's problems.

Talk Together ★ *large group*
Share your story problems. Talk about the strategies you used to solve the problems.

> If each cup holds 8 ounces of coffee, how many pints of coffee does Martina spill before she finds the perfect match?

> If the coffee is 100 degrees when Abuela pours it and 15 degrees cooler when she spills it, what temperature is it when she spills it?

☐ **Digital Option** Use a word-processing program to write your problems.
Unit 1 | Part 2   10

🕐 **Time:** 30 minutes
Materials: paper, pencils

CHECK UNDERSTANDING
Ask students to tell how they would solve the sample word problems.

Use these resources to provide daily opportunities for students to work individually or in groups at learning stations around the classroom.

Language Stations

Download complete lesson plans ⊘NGReach.com ❯

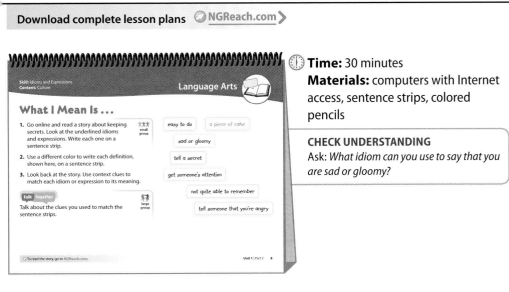

Skill: Idioms and Expressions
Content: Culture

Language Arts 📖

What I Mean Is ...

1. Go online and read a story about keeping secrets. Look at the underlined idioms and expressions. Write each one on a sentence strip. ⭐⭐⭐ small group

2. Use a different color to write each definition, shown here, on a sentence strip.

3. Look back at the story. Use context clues to match each idiom or expression to its meaning.

Talk Together 👫 large group
Talk about the clues you used to match the sentence strips.

easy to do | a piece of cake
sad or gloomy
tell a secret
get someone's attention
not quite able to remember
tell someone that you're angry

⊘To read the story, go to NGReach.com. | Unit 1 | Part 2 | 8

🕐 **Time:** 30 minutes
Materials: computers with Internet access, sentence strips, colored pencils

CHECK UNDERSTANDING
Ask: *What idiom can you use to say that you are sad or gloomy?*

Skill: Ask for and Give Information
Content: Traditions, Holidays

Listening/Speaking 🎧

Tell About a Holiday

1. Look at the **Language Builder Picture Cards**. What do you know about each holiday? ⭐ on your own

2. Think about holidays you celebrate and traditions that you and your family share.

Talk Together ⭐⭐⭐ small group
Place the **Language Builder Picture Cards** in a pile. Choose one. Tell what you know or want to know about the holiday. Ask for and give information about different traditions.
What happens on ____?
How can you ____?
We can ____.

Noche de Rabanos (Night of the Radishes)
Children's Day
Earth Day
Thanksgiving
Tequila Festival
Loy Krathong Festival
Carnival

What happens on Earth Day?

⊘Find additional holiday photos in the Digital Library ⊘on NGReach.com. | Unit 1 | Part 2 | 9

🕐 **Time:** 20 minutes
Materials: Language Builder Picture Cards E7–E13

CHECK UNDERSTANDING
Ask: *What happens on Earth Day?*

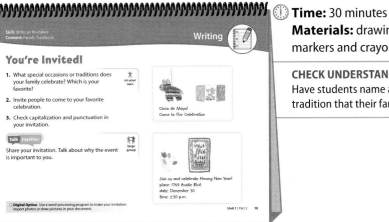

Skill: Write an Invitation
Content: Family Traditions

Writing ✏️

You're Invited!

1. What special occasions or traditions does your family celebrate? Which is your favorite? ⭐ on your own

2. Invite people to come to your favorite celebration.

3. Check capitalization and punctuation in your invitation.

Cinco de Mayo!
Come to Our Celebration

Talk Together 👫 large group
Share your invitation. Talk about why the event is important to you.

Join us and celebrate Hmong New Year!
place: 1769 Austin Blvd.
date: December 30
time: 2:30 p.m.

⊘ **Digital Option** Use a word-processing program to make your invitation. Import photos or draw pictures in your document. | Unit 1 | Part 2 | 10

🕐 **Time:** 30 minutes
Materials: drawing paper, colored markers and crayons

CHECK UNDERSTANDING
Have students name a special occasion or tradition that their family celebrates.

Technology Station

Access resources ⊘NGReach.com ❯

((MP3)) Recordings

🔊 A Tooth Tradition

🔊 What Happened to Your Tooth?

🔊 Martina the Beautiful Cockroach

Digital Library

Learn vocabulary and practice language

🔊 Key Word Images

🔊 Language Builder Picture Cards

My Vocab Notebook

🔊 Add Words

Comprehension Coach

🔊 Use interactive library support. Automatically measure fluency.

Online Assessment

🔊 Practice items in standardized test format.

Day 1

Day at a Glance:
- ▶ **Language:** Ask for and Give Information
- ▶ **Vocabulary:** Social Studies Vocabulary
- ▶ **Reading:** Plot
- ▶ **Writing:** Writing Fluency ; Study a Model

OBJECTIVES

Vocabulary
- Acquire and Use Grade-Level Key Vocabulary **ⓣ**

Language
- Language Function: Ask for and Give Information **ⓣ**
- Listen to and Imitate Fluent Models
- Use a Variety of Sentence Types
- Participate in Discussion

Learning and Teamwork Strategies
- Activate Prior Experience
- Use Media to Build Language
- Use Context to Build Concepts and Language

Social Studies
- Explore Customs and Traditions

Resources

- 📖 🔊 *Sing With Me Language Song Book,* page 6
- 💿 🔊 *Sing With Me Language Song CD 1* Tracks 5, 6
- 🔊 *eVisual 1.16*
- 🔊 *eVisual 1.17*
- 🔊 *Key Word Images*

Ⓝ NGReach.com ❯

See **Technology Station** for digital student resources.

Differentiate

Academic Language Frames

Ask for and Give Information
■ How can I _____?
You can _____.
■ How can I _____?
You can _____.
Or, you can _____.
▨ How can I _____?
■ You can _____.
Or, you can _____.
You can also _____.

Ⓝ NGReach.com ❯ eVisual 1.17

Language of the Day

What are some important events and traditions that show you are growing up?
_____ shows that you are growing up.

Read the Language of the Day. Model: *Turning ten shows that you are growing up.* Invite students to share their own responses, and encourage them to elaborate on their ideas. If it is not mentioned by any of the students, suggest that losing your first tooth also shows that you are growing up. Tell students that today they will learn a song about a boy who loses his first tooth.

Ask for and Give Information

❶ Teach/Model Display "A Tooth Tradition." Read the introduction aloud and play the song. Invite students to sing along as you play the song again. Model how to echo and chime in as the audio prompts.

Point out the **Language Frames** and model using these structures to ask for and give information about losing a tooth.

How to Ask for and Give Information	
1. Ask a question. Start with *How can I.*	How can I get rid of a loose tooth?
2. Answer the question. Start with *You can.*	You can wiggle it gently. Or, you can pull it out. You can also wait for it to come out by itself.

Ⓝ NGReach.com ❯ eVisual 1.16

With volunteers, practice asking and answering other questions related to different **cultural** traditions; for example: *How can I make a birthday cake?* or *How can I decorate my house for a party?* Help volunteers form responses with *You can,* modeling correct usage as necessary.

❷ Practice/Apply Have partners practice asking and answering questions with *How can I.* Use **Academic Language Frames** to encourage students at all proficiency levels.

> **CHECK UNDERSTANDING** Ask: *How do you answer a question that starts with "How can I"?* (Start with the words *You can*).

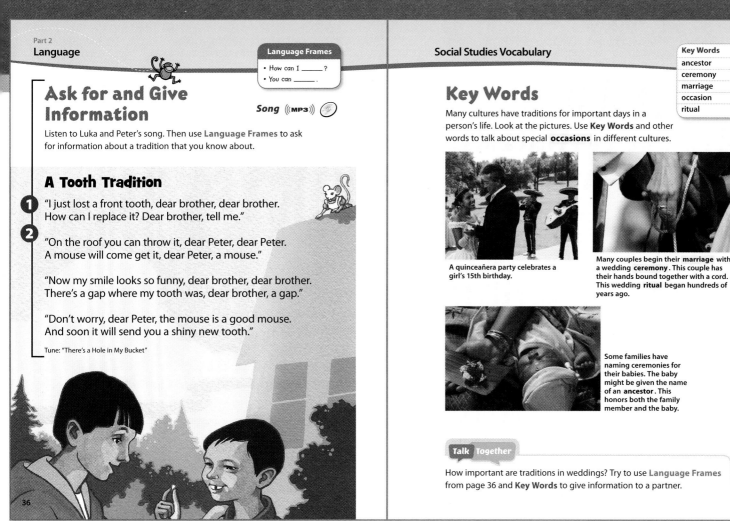

Student Book pages 36–37

Social Studies Vocabulary

❸ Teach/Model Read the introduction and the photo captions. Use **Vocabulary Routine 1** (See page PD37.) and **Key Word Images** to teach the words. Access definitions on pages 616–639.

1. **Pronounce** the word and point to it in the caption: **ancestor**.

2. **Rate** the word. Have students hold up their fingers to show how well they know the word. (1 = very well, 2 = a little, 3 = not at all) Ask: *What do you know about this word?*

3. **Define** the word: *An ancestor is a member of your family who lived a long time ago.*

4. **Elaborate** Relate the word to your experience: *I want to learn the language and visit the country of my ancestors.*

❹ Practice/Apply Have partners take turns repeating the routine for each word, using complete sentences for steps 2, 3, and 4.

❺ Talk Together About the Big Question

Check Understanding and Connect Concepts Review the **Language Frames** on page 36 and provide an example:

> **Question:** *How can I celebrate a special* **occasion***, such as a* **marriage***?*

> **Answer:** *You can have a big party and invite family and friends. You can celebrate the happiness of the bride and groom.*

Add the ideas to your unit concept map.

Differentiate

Spanish Cognates ▶

ancestor/ancestro; ceremony/ceremonia; occasion/ocasión; ritual/ritual

Part 2 Vocabulary Skills Trace		Page
Day 1	**Social Studies Vocabulary**	**T37**
Day 2	Academic Vocabulary	T39
Day 3	Expand Word Knowledge	T42b
Day 4	Share Word Knowledge	T58b
Day 5	Apply Word Knowledge	T59b
Day 6	Idioms and Expressions	T60
Day 7	More Idioms and Expressions	T65
Days 8–9	Extend Vocabulary	T66e–f
Day 10	Vocabulary Review	T66g–h

Day 1
continued

Day at a Glance:
▶ **Language:** Ask for and Give Information
▶ **Vocabulary:** Social Studies Vocabulary
▶ **Reading:** Plot
▶ **Writing:** Writing Fluency; Study a Model

OBJECTIVES

Vocabulary
• Acquire and Use Grade-Level Key Vocabulary **T**

Comprehension and Literary Analysis
• Demonstrate Listening Comprehension
• Identify Plot **T**

Learning and Teamwork Strategies
• Use Graphic Organizers: Story Map
• Reason Deductively

Writing
• Develop Writing Fluency
• Monitor and Self-Correct Writing
• Writing Project: Study a Model

Social Studies
• Explore Customs and Traditions

Resources

 eVisual 1.18

 Practice Master 1.11

eVisual 1.19

Differentiate

Multi-Level Strategies

BEGINNING

Allow students to draw a visual story map to represent the plot of their partner's story. Encourage them to list words and phrases that tell about each event.

INTERMEDIATE

Refer to the instruction at the top of the page. Remind students that the middle of the story usually has the most events. Ask them to include all the important events in the story.

ADVANCED ADVANCED HIGH

Encourage students to use their story map to retell their partner's story to another student.

Plot

① **Teach** Connect concepts: *What Key Words have you learned to help you give information about family traditions? You saw those words in the captions of photos showing special* **occasions** *in different cultures. Now you will learn how to make a graphic organizer that shows the series of events in a story.*

Read aloud the first sentence and the bulleted text. Use the illustrations on page 38 to model the parts of the plot. Point to each illustration as you reinforce: *The plot is the series of events in a story. Most stories have a beginning, a middle, and an end.*

Read aloud the explanation about making a story map. Clarify the purpose: *I can make a story map to help me show the order of events in a story.* Remind students to listen for the series of events as you read "Peter's New Tooth" aloud.

> **Read Aloud**
>
> ### Peter's New Tooth
>
> Peter is smiling. It is a special occasion. He has lost a tooth. Peter throws his old tooth on the roof. A mouse catches the tooth and puts it in her apron. Now Peter grows a new tooth. What a beautiful smile he has!

⊘ NGReach.com ▶ eVisual 1.18

② **Model** Review the first three sentences of "Peter's New Tooth." Have a volunteer read the first box in the story map. Model: *I make a box for the event that happens at the beginning of the story. What happens first?* Review the next two sentences. Have volunteers read the next two boxes and explain what to do.

③ **Practice/Apply** Read aloud the instructions. Distribute **Practice Master 1.11** for students to use as they complete their story maps. Use **Multi-Level Strategies** to help students at all proficiency levels talk about the plot of their partner's story. Monitor students' developing proficiency. (See page R2 for Proficiency Level Descriptions.)

> **CHECK UNDERSTANDING** *What happens at the beginning of "Peter's New Tooth"?* Point to the first illustration. (Peter loses a tooth.) Have students use the illustrations to tell what happens at the beginning, middle, and end of the story, "Peter's New Tooth."

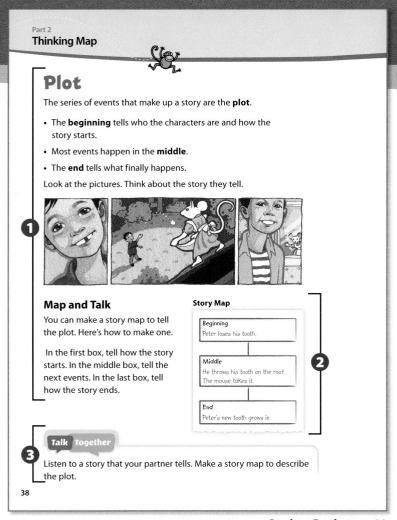

Plot

The series of events that make up a story are the **plot**.

- The **beginning** tells who the characters are and how the story starts.
- Most events happen in the **middle**.
- The **end** tells what finally happens.

Look at the pictures. Think about the story they tell.

1

Map and Talk

You can make a story map to tell the plot. Here's how to make one.

In the first box, tell how the story starts. In the middle box, tell the next events. In the last box, tell how the story ends.

Story Map

Beginning
Peter loses his tooth.

Middle
He throws his tooth on the roof. The mouse takes it.

End
Peter's new tooth grows in.

2

Talk Together

3 Listen to a story that your partner tells. Make a story map to describe the plot.

38

Student Book page 38

Daily Writing

4 **Writing Fluency** Use the **Power Writing Routine**. (See page PD 53.)
Write the word **occasion** and prompt: *How does your family celebrate special occasions?* Think about this word and write about it.

Power Writing Routine

 1. What do you know about the word or picture?

 2. Take one minute to write as much as you can, as well as you can.
B words   **I** sentences   **A** **AH** paragraphs

 3. Check your spelling and grammar. Circle mistakes.

 4. Count your words.

 NGReach.com > eVisual 1.19

5 **Writing Project: Study a Model** Have students review a model
of the writing form for their Writing Projects. (See pages T66k–T66.)

CLOSE AND ASSESS

- **Language** *What information can you give about Peter's tooth tradition?*
(Students should use information from the song in their answers.)

- **Reading** *How can a story map help you retell a story?*

- **Vocabulary** *What Key Words did you use to write about special occasions
your family celebrates?*

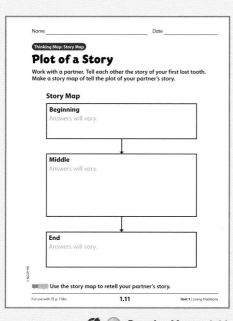

Name _____ Date _____

Thinking Map: Story Map
Plot of a Story
Work with a partner. Tell each other the story of your first lost tooth.
Make a story map of tell the plot of your partner's story.

Story Map

Beginning
Answers will vary.

Middle
Answers will vary.

End
Answers will vary.

Use the story map to retell your partner's story.

For use with TE p. T38a   1.11   Unit 1 | Living Traditions

 **Practice Master 1.11**

Day 2

OBJECTIVES

Vocabulary
- Acquire and Use Academic Vocabulary ❶
- Use Grade-Level Vocabulary

Grammar
- Identify Compound Subjects ❶

Learning and Teamwork Strategies
- Make Connections Across Content Areas

Resources

- Practice Master 1.12
- Key Word Images

NGReach.com

See **Technology Station** for digital student resources.

Name _____ Date _____

Grammar: Compound Subjects

The Twins' Birthday Party

Grammar Rules Compound Subjects

A compound subject is made up of two simple subjects that share the same verb.
Join the two subjects with *and* or *or*.

The bride (and) groom cut the cake.

Cara (and) John are sitting at my table.

Flowers (or) candles decorate each table.

Adults (and) children dance to the music.

Read each sentence. If the sentence has a compound subject, underline the subjects. Circle the word that joins the subjects.

1. Kara (and) Kayla are twins.
2. Today is the twins' birthday.
3. Balloons (and) streamers decorate the yard.
4. Pink plates (and) cups are on the tables.
5. Grandmother puts candles on the cake.
6. Mom (or) Dad will light the candles.
7. Kara (and) Kayla will make a wish.

Tell a partner about a birthday party or other celebration. Use a compound subject in one of your sentences.

For use with TE p. T39a   1.12   Unit 1 | Living Traditions

Practice Master 1.12

Language of the Day

What happens at a wedding **ceremony**?

At a wedding ceremony, _____.

Read the Language of the Day. Model: *At a wedding ceremony, people bring gifts for the bride and groom.* Create a web for the answers and encourage students to share their ideas. Then explain that today students will look at sentences they can use to talk about ceremonies.

Grammar Compound Subjects B I A AH

1 Teach/Model Write the sample sentences and read them aloud.

> 1. Amy and Mike plan their wedding.
> 2. Family and friends will attend the **marriage** ceremony.
> 3. Either Anahita or Logan will play music.

Ask: *Who is planning their wedding?* (Amy and Mike) *If both of them are planning it, what is the simple subject?* Provide time for students to discuss the question. Then say: *We call this kind of subject a compound subject.* Ask: *Do sentences 2 and 3 have compound subjects too?* (Yes) Have volunteers underline the two subjects and circle the word joining them. (Family (and) friends, Anahita (or) Logan)

Say: *Compound subjects share the same verb.* Have volunteers identify the verbs. (plan, will attend, will play) Then explain that sentences can be combined by forming a compound subject. Write: *The bride cuts the cake. The groom cuts the cake.* Provide a think-aloud: *These sentences sound too short. Can I combine them? Yes. I can combine the two subjects into a compound subject.* Then write: *The bride and groom cut the cake.*

2 Practice/Apply Have partners complete these frames with compound subjects: _____ *bring presents;* _____ *take pictures;* _____ *enjoy the* **occasion** . Then assign **Practice Master 1.12** for more practice.

> **CHECK UNDERSTANDING** Write the following sentences: *The graduation ceremony was long. Parents and teachers cheered the students.* Ask students to identify the sentence with a compound subject.

Part 2 Grammar Skills Trace		Page
▶ Day 2	Compound Subjects	T39a
Day 4	Compound Predicates	T58a
Day 7	Subject-Verb Agreement	T65a
Day 10	Review Subject-Verb Agreement	T66g

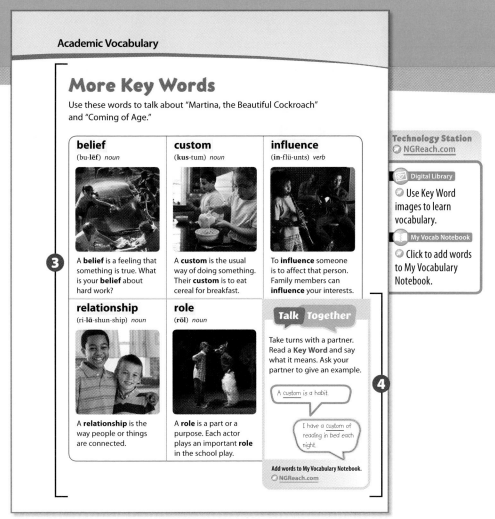

Student Book page 39

Academic Vocabulary

3 Teach/Model Invite students to discuss each photograph on the page. Read the directions aloud and use **Vocabulary Routine 1** (See page PD37.) and **Key Word Images** to teach the words.

1. **Pronounce** the word and point to its picture: **custom**.

2. **Rate** the word. Have students hold up their fingers to show how well they know the word. (1 = very well, 2 = a little, 3 = not at all) Ask: *What do you know about this word?*

3. **Define** the word: *A custom is the usual way of doing something. At our school, it is a custom to say the Pledge of Allegiance every morning.*

4. **Elaborate** Relate the word to your experience: *In my family, our custom is to watch a movie together and eat popcorn on Friday night.*

4 Practice/Apply Use the ratings from step 2 to form pairs. Have partners take turns reading each Key Word aloud and saying what it means.

> **CHECK UNDERSTANDING** Point to the **Key Word Image** of each word and ask students to use the word in a new sentence.

Differentiate

Spanish Cognates ▸
custom/costumbre;
influence/influenciar;
relationship; relación

Part 2 Vocabulary Skills Trace		Page
Day 1	Social Studies Vocabulary	T37
Day 2	**Academic Vocabulary**	**T39**
Day 3	Expand Word Knowledge	T42b
Day 4	Share Word Knowledge	T58b
Day 5	Apply Word Knowledge	T59b
Day 6	Idioms and Expressions	T60
Day 7	Idioms and Expressions	T65
Days 8–9	Extend Vocabulary	T66e–f
Day 10	Vocabulary Review	T66g–h

Day 2
continued

Day at a Glance:
▶ **Language:** Compound Subjects
▶ **Vocabulary:** Academic Vocabulary
▶ **Reading:** Plan and Monitor
▶ **Writing:** Prewrite

OBJECTIVES

Vocabulary
• Use Classroom Vocabulary
• Use Academic Vocabulary ❶
• Acquire and Use Grade-Level Vocabulary ❶

Learning to Read
• Phonics: Read Words with Short *i, u*

Reading Strategy
• Plan and Monitor ❶

Learning and Teamwork Strategies
• Use Personal Experience
• Use Visuals

Writing
• Writing Project: Prewrite

Social Studies
• Explore Customs and Traditions

Resources

 eVisual 1.20

 Reach Into Phonics TE pages T16, T18

Differentiate

Academic Language Frames

Monitor and Clarify

■ What does _____ mean?
I will _____ . It means _____ .

_____

■ What does _____ mean?
I will _____ . It means _____ .
I know this because _____ .

_____

■ When I do not understand something, I can _____ .
■ I do not understand what _____ means, so I will
_____ .
I think it means _____ because _____ .

⊘NGReach.com ▶ eVisual 1.20

Plan and Monitor

❶ Teach Read the introduction aloud and display the picture. Ask students if there is anything in the picture they do not understand. Make the connection: *When you do not understand something, stop and think about what it means. Sometimes, things you see or read will help make the meaning clear.* Teach Classroom Vocabulary words *monitor* and *clarify*.

❷ Model Read the chart chorally with students. Model clarifying your understanding of the picture:

• What does this picture mean?

• I will look carefully at the picture. The woman wears a traditional Japanese kimono and holds a cup of tea.

• It means that the picture shows a tea ceremony.

❸ Practice/Apply Read the directions aloud. Point out the **Language Frames**. Read aloud *Luka's* interview and the sample student question and response. Direct students to monitor their reading of the interview. At each red arrow, they should ask a question and then clarify anything they do not understand. Use **Academic Language Frames** to help students at each proficiency level share their questions and answers with a partner. Encourage them to identify information in the text that helps them clarify their understanding.

> **CHECK UNDERSTANDING** Ask: *How did monitoring your reading help you better understand the interview?*

Phonics and Fluency

Words with Short /ĭ/i; /ŭ/u

Display these words: *big* and *hug*. Point out the CVC spelling pattern and explain: *When a vowel comes between two consonants, it has a short sound.* Blend /b/ /ĭ/ /g/. Have students repeat. Have students blend *hug*. Display **Transparency 18** from **Reach Into Phonics** and work through the lesson.

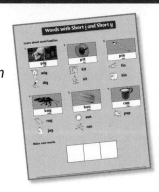

Practice Display these sentences:
• I hug the bride and groom.
• The guests sit at tables.
• They cut the big cake.

Have partners read the sentences chorally several times to develop fluency. Listen as partners read. Correct pronunciation.

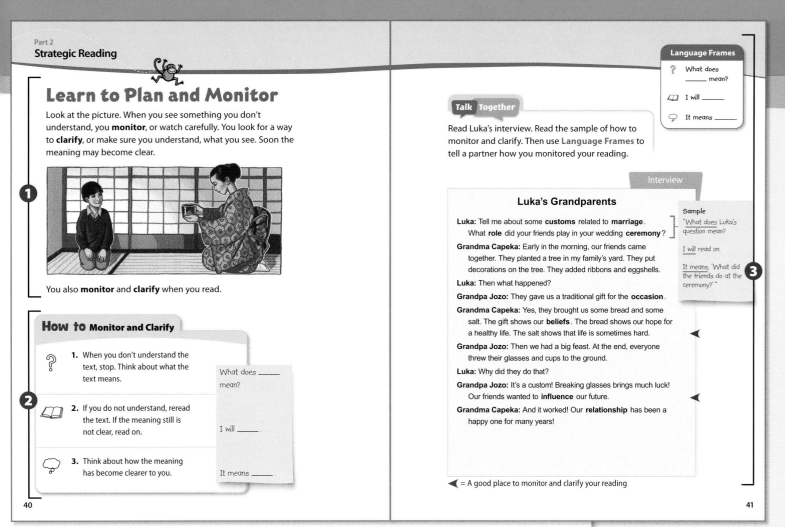

Learn to Plan and Monitor

Look at the picture. When you see something you don't understand, you **monitor**, or watch carefully. You look for a way to **clarify**, or make sure you understand, what you see. Soon the meaning may become clear.

1

You also **monitor** and **clarify** when you read.

How to Monitor and Clarify

2

1. When you don't understand the text, stop. Think about what the text means.

What does _____ mean?

2. If you do not understand, reread the text. If the meaning still is not clear, read on.

I will _____ .

3. Think about how the meaning has become clearer to you.

It means _____ .

40

Language Frames

? What does _____ mean?

📖 I will _____

💭 It means _____

Talk Together

Read Luka's interview. Read the sample of how to monitor and clarify. Then use **Language Frames** to tell a partner how you monitored your reading.

Interview

Luka's Grandparents

Luka: Tell me about some **customs** related to **marriage**. What **role** did your friends play in your wedding **ceremony**?

Grandma Capeka: Early in the morning, our friends came together. They planted a tree in my family's yard. They put decorations on the tree. They added ribbons and eggshells.

Luka: Then what happened?

Grandpa Jozo: They gave us a traditional gift for the **occasion**.

Grandma Capeka: Yes, they brought us some bread and some salt. The gift shows our **beliefs**. The bread shows our hope for a healthy life. The salt shows that life is sometimes hard. ◄

Grandpa Jozo: Then we had a big feast. At the end, everyone threw their glasses and cups to the ground.

Luka: Why did they do that?

Grandpa Jozo: It's a custom! Breaking glasses brings much luck! Our friends wanted to **influence** our future. ◄

Grandma Capeka: And it worked! Our **relationship** has been a happy one for many years!

Sample

"What does Luka's question mean?

I will read on.

It means, 'What did the friends do at the ceremony?' "

3

◄ = A good place to monitor and clarify your reading

41

Student Book pages 40–41

Daily Writing

4 **Writing Project: Prewrite an Interview** Have students plan their Writing Projects. (See pages T67a–T67b.)

CLOSE AND ASSESS

- **Language** *Use a sentence with a compound subject to tell about Luka's interview. Provide sentence frames: _____ and _____ are Luka's grandparents. _____ and _____ were two gifts they received.*
- **Reading** *How did you monitor your reading? How did you clarify your understanding of something you did not understand in Luka's interview?*
- **Vocabulary** *What Key Words did you use in your description of a family tradition?* (Answers will vary.)

Classroom Vocabulary

Use **Vocabulary Routine 4** to teach **clarify**. (See **Vocabulary Routines**, page PD40.) Repeat with **monitor**.

Word Map

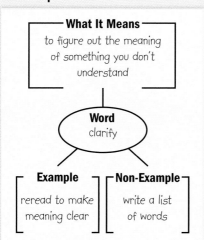

What It Means
to figure out the meaning of something you don't understand

Word
clarify

Example
reread to make meaning clear

Non-Example
write a list of words

Day 3

Day at a Glance:
▶ **Language:** Ask for and Give Information   ▶ **Reading:** Read the Selection
▶ **Vocabulary:** Expand Word Knowledge   ▶ **Writing:** Writer's Craft; Draft

OBJECTIVES

Vocabulary
- Use Academic Vocabulary
- Use Grade-Level Vocabulary

Language
- Language Function: Ask for and Give Information
- Listen to and Imitate Fluent Models
- Use a Variety of Sentence Types

Learning and Teamwork Strategies
- Use Media to Build Language
- Collaborate with Peers
- Gather Information
- Use Graphic Organizer: 4-Corner Poster

Resources

- ℗ ⊙ *Sing With Me Language Song CD 1 Tracks 7, 8*
- ⊙ *Sing With Me Language Song Book, page 7*
- ⊙ *eVisual 1.21*
- ▣ *In the U.S.A. Picture Cards 5–14*
- • *chart or poster paper*

◎ NGReach.com ▶

See **Technology Station** for digital student resources.

Differentiate

Multi-Level Strategies

BEGINNING

Pair these students with more proficient students, and have them answer their partners' questions.

INTERMEDIATE

Have these students ask questions with *what, when, where,* and *who.*

ADVANCED   ADVANCED HIGH

Have these students ask and answer questions with *what, when, where,* and *who.* Encourage them to elaborate on their answers.

Language of the Day

What are some different **customs** and **beliefs** from around the world about losing your first tooth?
In ____, kids ____.

Read the Language of the Day. Model: *In the United States, some kids put their teeth under their pillows. In the morning they find some money.* Invite students to share about similar traditions in their home cultures, for example: *In my culture, kids plant a lost tooth in the garden. Later on a flower will grow in the same place.*

Ask for and Give Information

1 **Teach** Remind students that they learned how to ask for information with the words *How can I* and practiced giving answers with *You can.* Continue: *What other words can you use to ask questions?* Confirm that the words *what, when, where,* and *who* are all words that can be used to ask for information.

Then display "What Happened to Your Tooth?" Play the dialogue.

Asking for Information	Giving Information
What did Peter lose?	He lost his **tooth.**
When did his tooth fall out?	It fell out **last night.**
Where is he going to throw his tooth?	He is going to throw it **on the roof.**
Who is going to replace his tooth?	**The mouse** is going to replace his tooth.

◎ NGReach.com ▶ eVisual 1.21

Circle the words in boldface and explain how the answers relate to the questions: *When you give an answer, make sure you give the information the other person wants.*

2 **Model** Asking for and giving information: *What did Peter lose? He lost his tooth. When did his tooth fall out? It fell out last night.* Invite volunteers to ask and answer similar kinds of questions about the dialogue.

3 **Practice/Apply** Form pairs of students, and have students take turns asking and answering questions about a traditional celebration, **ceremony,** or special **occasion** they have attended or know about. Use **Multi-Level Strategies** to support students at all proficiency levels.

CHECK UNDERSTANDING *The word "what" asks about a thing. What do the other question words ask about? ("When" asks about time; "Where" asks about a place; "Who" asks about a person.)*

Sing With Me Language Song Book page 7

Expand Word Knowledge

4 **Teach/Model** Explain that each student pair will become Key Word experts. They will study one Key Word and create a Key Word poster about that word. Use **Vocabulary Routine 2** and model making a 4-corner poster about the word **occasion**. (See **Vocabulary Routines,** page PD38.)

- Write the word.
- Add a picture
- Add a definition.
- Add a context sentence.

occasion	
Sentence: A birthday party is a special occasion.	**Definition:** a special or important event

4-Corner Poster

5 **Practice/Apply** Assign a Key Word to each pair of students. Have each pair create a poster for their assigned Key Word. Display the posters on the class word wall.

> **CHECK UNDERSTANDING** Say a Key Word and have the partner experts for the word read the definition and sentence from their poster.

Key Words

ancestor	marriage
belief	occasion
ceremony	relationship
custom	ritual
influence	role

Differentiate

Newcomer Support

Newcomers can make 4-Corner Posters using words from **In the U.S.A. Picture Cards** 5–14.

Part 2 Vocabulary Skills Trace		Page
Day 1	Social Studies Vocabulary	T37
Day 2	Academic Vocabulary	T39
Day 3	**Expand Word Knowledge**	**T42b**
Day 4	Share Word Knowledge	T58b
Day 5	Apply Word Knowledge	T59b
Day 6	Idioms and Expressions	T60
Day 7	Idioms and Expressions	T65
Days 8–9	Extend Vocabulary	T66e–f
Day 10	Vocabulary Review	T66g–h

Day 3

continued

Day at a Glance:
▶ **Language:** Ask for and Give Information
▶ **Vocabulary:** Expand Word Knowledge
▶ **Reading:** Read the Selection
▶ **Writing:** Writer's Craft ; Draft

OBJECTIVES

Vocabulary
- Use Academic Vocabulary
- Use Grade-Level Vocabulary ❶

Reading Strategies
- Plan: Preview
- Make Inferences

Comprehension and Literary Analysis
- Recognize Genre: Folk Tale
- Analyze Elements of Fiction: Character and Setting
- Interpret Text Features: Illustrations

Learning and Teamwork Strategies
- Use Prereading Supports
- Build Background Knowledge

Resources

 Comprehension Coach

Keys to Efficacy

Refocus when student responses are off topic: *Tell me more about that. What makes you say that?*

Preview the Folk Tale

❶ Introduce Ask students to describe the character on page 43. Tell them that the character is a cockroach, a kind of bug. Read the title and ask: *Do you think this story is about a real cockroach? Why or why not?* Confirm responses: *Real cockroaches don't wear clothes. Plus, most people think cockroaches are ugly, not beautiful.* Ask students to predict what the story might be about.

❷ Genre, Characters, and Setting Point out that the selection has a subtitle, *A Cuban Folk Tale.* Read aloud the definition of a folk tale. Elaborate: *Folk tales tell about the values,* **beliefs**, *and* **customs** *of a culture.*

Read aloud the definitions of character and setting. Point to the map and pictures. Explain: *The main character of the story is a cockroach named Martina. The story takes place in Havana, a city in the country of Cuba.*

❸ Preview and Build Background Use sheltering strategies as you conduct a picture walk.

Pages	Say (and Do) 💬 ✋
44–45	*Look at the first picture. It shows Martina with her aunt and grandmother. They are giving her presents. I wonder what the special* **occasion** *is. May be Martina is having a birthday, or maybe she's going to get married. The next picture shows Martina with her grandmother. What do you think her grandmother is saying?*
46–47	*This picture shows a parrot on one side. He is making some big announcement. On the other side, I can see Martina and her relatives on the balcony. A rooster is spreading his wings and acting important. What do you think he's saying? Maybe he wants to marry Martina. A man who wants to marry a woman is called her suitor.*
48–49	*Look, Martina spilled her coffee on the rooster. Maybe it was some kind of test. Why do you think she is testing the rooster? Do you think he passed the test? I guess not, because now a pig is at the balcony. Do you think the pig will pass the test?*
50–51	*Martina did it again. She poured coffee on the pig. I guess he didn't pass the test, because now a lizard is at the balcony. What do you think will happen next?*
52–53	*Guess what? Martina poured coffee on the lizard, too. She looks very upset. She's probably tired of having so many suitors. Do you think she will have another suitor?*
54–55	*Here we go again. This time a mouse wants to be Martina's suitor. What does he have to do to pass the test?*
56	*What's happening in this picture? How do you think the story will end?*

CHECK UNDERSTANDING *What are the characters of a story?* (the people or animals in it) *What is the setting of a story?* (where and when the story takes place)

Read a Story

Genre

A **folk tale** is a story that people share and tell again and again. Folk tales usually reflect the culture they come from.

Character and Setting

Characters are the people or animals in a story. Setting is where and when the story takes place.

▲ Martina

▲ The setting of this story is Havana, a city in Cuba. The story is set in the past.

42

Martina
the Beautiful
Cockroach
A CUBAN FOLK TALE

retold by **Carmen Agra Deedy** ◆ illustrated by **Eugenia Nobati**

Comprehension Coach

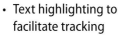 **Comprehension Coach**

Build Reading Power

Assign students to use the software, based on their instructional needs.

Read Silently	**Listen**	**Record**
• Comprehension questions with immediate feedback • Vocabulary support	• Process model of fluent reading • Text highlighting to facilitate tracking • Vocabulary support	• Oral reading fluency practice • Speech recognition for oral fluency assessment with immediate feedback

---

B I A AH

Cultural Perspectives

Explain that folk tales began as oral stories that were meant to entertain listeners. Folk tales are often set in a far-off time and place, and they usually tell about everyday life. The characters in the folk tales are often animals with human characteristics. Folk tales usually have some kind of lesson or moral to be learned. Ask students to share examples of folk tales from different cultures and identify the lessons these stories teach.

OBJECTIVES

Vocabulary
- Use Academic Vocabulary ⊕
- Use Grade-Level Vocabulary ⊕

Learning to Read
- Phonics: Words with Digraph /ch/: *ch, tch*
- Concepts of Print: Use Directionality: Read Left Page First and Read Text Left to Right to Bottom

Reading Strategies
- Plan: Set a Purpose, Predict, Confirm Predictions
- Plan and Monitor ⊕

Fluency
- Expression ⊕

Comprehension and Literary Analysis
- Recognize Genre: Folk Tale
- Analyze Plot ⊕
- Analyze Text Features: Word Choice

Writing
- Develop Writer's Craft
- Writing Project: Draft

Social Studies
- Explore Customs and Traditions

Resources

 Read with Me Selection

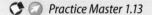 *Practice Master 1.13*

Reach into Phonics TE page 22

Ⓝ NGReach.com ▸

See **Technology Station** for digital student resources.

Name _____ Date _____

Key Points Reading

Martina the Beautiful Cockroach

❶
Martina the Cockroach was ready to get married. Her grandmother told her to spill coffee on a suitor's shoes. She could see how he would act when he was angry that way.

❷
From the balcony, Martina greeted her suitors—a rooster, a pig, and a lizard. The Coffee Test showed her that they were the wrong suitors.

❸
Then Martina saw a mouse and went to meet him. She didn't want to use The Coffee Test for him. Her grandmother said she had to. Martina reached for a cup, but the mouse got one first. He splashed Martina's shoes. He knew he was her perfect match.

For use with TE p. T44   **1.13**   Unit 1 | Living Traditions

🖉 ⊙ Practice Master 1.13

Read the Folk Tale

Suggested Pacing

- Day 3: Read Section 1, pages 44–47
- Day 4: Read Sections 2 and 3, pages 48–57

Reading Options   Scaffold the support for varied reading levels.

BELOW LEVEL	ON LEVEL	ABOVE LEVEL
Listen and Read Along	**Read Together**	**Read Independently**
• Ask students to set a purpose for listening. Then read aloud the **Key Points Reading** while students track the print. • Check understanding with selected Build Comprehension questions. Then include students in Talk Together (page T59c.)	• Have groups set a purpose for reading—to get information or enjoy a story—and read silently. Then select passages to read chorally. Pause to ask the Build Comprehension questions. • At the end of each section, have students summarize what has happened so far in the story.	• Have students set a purpose for reading—to get information or enjoy a story. Have them choose and use an appropriate reading rate for the purpose as they read silently. • Pause during the oral rereading to ask the Build Comprehension questions. Also discuss the effectiveness of the rate students chose, and adjust, if necessary.

Phonics and Fluency

Digraph /ch/: *ch, tch*

Teach/Model Explain that the /ch/ sound can be made by the letters *ch* or *tch*. Write *touch* and *switch* on the board. Say the words, emphasizing the /ch/ sound as you underline the spellings. Say: Touch *and* switch *both have the /ch/ sound, but it is spelled in different ways.* Display **Transparency 19** from **Reach into Phonics** and work through the lessons.

Practice/Apply Display these sentences:

- Martina is a cockroach.
- Her family looks on with watchful eyes.
- She found the perfect match.

Underline the words *cockroach, watchful,* and *match.* Have partners write the words and circle the letters that stand for the /ch/ sound. Then have partners read the words chorally several times to develop fluency in reading the words.

▶ Set a Purpose

1 Martina is ready to get married. Find out how she chooses a husband.

Martina Josefina Catalina Cucaracha was a beautiful cockroach. She lived in a cozy street lamp in Old Havana with her big, lovable family.

Now that Martina was 21 days old, she was ready to **give her leg in marriage**. The Cucaracha household was crawling with excitement! Every **señora** in the family had something to offer. **2**

Tia Cuca gave her *una peineta*, a seashell comb. *Mamá* gave her *una mantilla*, a lace shawl. But *Abuela*, her Cuban grandmother, gave her *un consejo increíble*, some shocking advice.

peineta

mantilla

"You want me to do WHAT?" Martina was **aghast**.

"You are a beautiful cockroach," said *Abuela*. "Finding husbands to choose from will be easy—picking the right one could be **tricky**."

"B-b-but," stammered Martina, "how will spilling COFFEE on **a suitor's shoes** help me find a good husband?" **3**

Her grandmother smiled. "It will make him angry! Then you'll know how he will speak to you when he **loses his temper**. Trust me, Martina. The Coffee Test never fails." **4**

Martina wasn't so sure.

In Other Words
give her leg in marriage get married (a joke based on the expression *give her hand in marriage*)
señora woman (in Spanish)
Tia Aunt (in Spanish)

In Other Words
aghast shocked; amazed
tricky difficult
a suitor's shoes the shoes of a person who wants to marry me
loses his temper gets angry

44

45

Student Book pages 44–45

Build Comprehension, pages 44–45

1 **Set a Purpose** Read the introduction at the top of page 44 to set the purpose.

2 **Key Words** Why is Martina's turning 21 days old a special **occasion**? (She is old enough to get married.) What **custom** do the women in Martina's family follow when a woman is old enough for **marriage**? (Each woman gives the bride-to-be a gift.)

3 **Plan and Monitor** MODEL GUIDE APPLY Remind students to stop and think about what the text means if they do not understand something they read. Model:

- *What does Martina's grandmother mean when she tells her that spilling coffee on her suitors will help her find a good husband?*
- *I will read on in the text.*
- *She means that this will show Martina how they act when they are angry.*

4 **Make Inferences** Why would Martina want to make her suitors angry? (The suitors will act nice as they try to impress Martina. They will show their true character when they are angry.)

B **I** **A** **AH**

Text Feature: Word Choice

Teach/Model Explain that authors often use words from other languages to enhance the setting of the story. This story is set in Havana, Cuba, so the author includes words in Spanish. Read aloud and translate the Spanish words on page 44. Explain that in this story the Spanish words and phrases are in italic type. Say: *The author uses Spanish words and phrases throughout the story to help the readers hear how the characters from Havana sound when they talk. Hearing them speak in their own language gives us a better understanding of Cuban culture.*

Practice/Apply Have students find other examples of Spanish words and phrases in the story. Show them how to use the In Other Words section at the bottom of the page to find out the meaning of the Spanish words. Have partners discuss how these words add interest to the story and enhance the setting.

Technology Station
NGReach.com

(MP3) Read with Me
● Play and read along.

Comprehension Coach
● Use interactive vocabulary support. Automatically measure fluency.

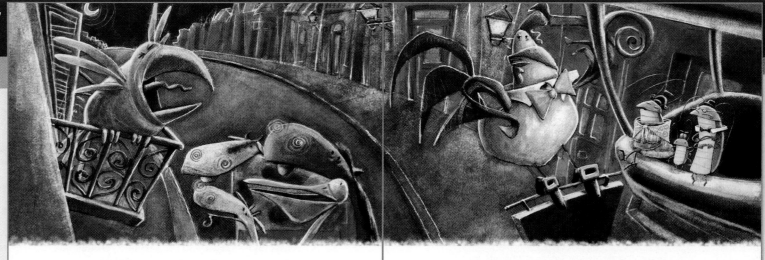

Meanwhile, *Papá* sent *el perico*, the parrot, to **spread the word**.

Soon all Havana—from the busy sidewalks of El Prado to El Morro castle—was **abuzz with** the news. Martina the beautiful cockroach was ready to choose a husband.

As was the **custom**, Martina would greet her suitors from the balcony, under her family's many watchful eyes.

Daintily, she sat down and crossed her legs, and crossed her legs, and crossed her legs.

She didn't have long to wait.

1

In Other Words
spread the word tell everyone
abuzz with talking about
Daintily Carefully

46

Don Gallo, the rooster, strutted up first. Martina tried not to stare at his splendid shoes.

Keeping one eye on his reflection, Don Gallo greeted her with a sweeping bow. "*¡Caramba!* You really are a beautiful cockroach. I will look even more fabulous with you on my wing!"

With that, he leaned forward and crooned,
"Martina Josefina Catalina Cucaracha,
Beautiful *muchacha*,
Won't you be my wife?"

Martina hesitated only for an instant. "Coffee, *señor*?"

In Other Words
¡Caramba! Wow! (in Spanish)
muchacha girl (in Spanish)
señor sir (in Spanish)

▶ **Before You Move On**
2 1. **Plot** What is *Abuela's* advice to Martina at the beginning of the story?
2. **Character** What is Don Gallo like? How can you tell?

47

Student Book pages 46–47

Keys to Efficacy

Narrow the focus when students need to be more specific or concentrate on less material. Tell me more about how Don Gallo acts.

Build Comprehension, pages 46–47

1 **Use Key Words** Describe the **custom** for Martina to meet her suitors. (Martina would greet them from the balcony. Her family would watch as they met.)

2 **Answers to Before You Move On**

1. Plot MODEL | GUIDE | APPLY Model for students how to tell what happened at the beginning of the story. Say: *At the beginning of the story, we meet Martina and learn that she is ready to get married. Her Abuela gives her some advice. She tells her to test her suitors by pouring coffee on their shoes to see if they get mad. Now Martina is meeting her first suitor.*

2. Character Possible answer: Don Gallo is self-centered. He struts. He is always looking at himself. I can tell he only wants Martina because she will sit on his wing and make him look better.

▸ **Predict**

3 What will the Coffee Test show Martina about her suitors?

Right on cue, *Abuela* appeared. With a quick glance at her grandmother, Martina nervously splattered coffee onto the rooster's spotless shoes.

"Oh my!" she said **with mock dismay**. "I'm **all feelers** today!"

"*¡Ki-ki-ri-kiiii!*" The rooster was furious. "Clumsy cockroach! I will teach you better manners when you are my wife."

Martina was stunned. The Coffee Test had worked!

"A most humble offer, *señor*," she said coolly, "but I cannot accept." **4**

Don Cerdo, the pig, hoofed up next. His smell curled the little hairs on Martina's legs.

"What an **unimaginable** scent," Martina wheezed. "Is it some new pig cologne?"

"Oh, no, **señorita**. It's the **sweet aroma** of my **pig sty**. Rotten eggs! Turnip peels! Stinky cheese!" Don Cerdo licked his chops and sang,

"Martina Josefina Catalina Cucaracha,
Beautiful *muchacha*,
Won't you be my wife?"

Martina had already left in search of coffee. She wasted no time with the pig. **5**

In Other Words
Right on cue Just as planned
with mock dismay pretending to be sorry
all feelers clumsy

In Other Words
unimaginable awful
señorita Miss (in Spanish)
sweet aroma good smell
pig sty pigpen; home

48

49

Build Comprehension, pages 48–49

3 **Predict** Read aloud the question on page 48 and have students make predictions: How might Martina's suitors react when she pours coffee on them? (Possible answer: They might get angry.)

4 **Draw Conclusions** Why does Martina decide not to accept Don Gallo's offer of marriage? (Possible answer: She realizes he has a bad temper and only wants her as a wife because she is beautiful.)

5 **Character's Actions** Why do you think Martina hurries off to get the coffee after the pig asks her to marry him? (She wants to get rid of him quickly because he smells bad to her. She knows the test works.)

B I A AH

Literary Analysis: Character

Teach/Model Remind students that a character is a person or an animal in a story. Point out that we learn about characters through their appearance as well as through what they say, do, and think. Explain that we can also learn about characters by how they interact with one another. Say: *Martina and her grandmother have a close and trusting relationship. I can tell this because when Martina's grandmother told her about the Coffee Test, Martina was shocked, but she still followed her grandmother's advice.*

Practice/Apply Have students look for other evidence in the story that shows the relationship between Martina and her grandmother. Ask: *How does Martina feel about her grandmother's advice now? How can you tell?*

"*¡Gronc! ¡Gronc!*" squealed Don Cerdo as he dabbed at the coffee on his shoes. "What a tragedy for my poor loafers!"

He really is quite a **ham**, thought Martina.

"Calm yourself, *señor*. I'll clean them for you!"

"I'll say you will!" he snorted. "When you are my wife, there'll be no end to cleaning up after me!"

Martina rolled her eyes in disbelief.

"A most charming offer, *señor*," she said **drily**, "but I must **decline**. You are much too **boorish** for me." **1**

The Coffee Test had saved her from yet another **unsuitable** suitor.

The pig was scarcely out of sight when Don Lagarto, the lizard, crept over the railing. His oily fingers brushed the little cockroach's lovely *mantilla*.

"You shouldn't **sneak up on** a lady like that!"

"I don't sneak. I creep," he said, circling Martina.

For some reason this fellow really **bugged** her. "I've had enough of creeps for one day," said Martina. "*Adiós*." **2**

In Other Words
ham bad actor
drily calmly
decline say no
boorish rude (a joke based on the fact that a *boar* is another name for a pig)

In Other Words
unsuitable bad choice for a
sneak up on surprise
bugged bothered
Adiós Goodbye (in Spanish)

▸ **Before You Move On**

3 1. **Plot** What does the Coffee Test show Martina about her first two suitors? How do these characters change?

2. **Clarify** Why is it funny that Martina thinks Don Cerdo is "a ham?"

50

51

Student Book pages 50–51

I **A** **AH**

Fluency: Expression

Teach/Model Explain the concept: *Fluent readers read with expression. They change their voices to show feelings they get from the text.* Direct students' attention to page 50. Say: *Think about what the text is saying. Don Cerdo is angry because Martina poured coffee his shoes. Martina does not like Don Cerdo and has no desire to marry him.* Play the selection recording or read aloud page 50, emphasizing the rhythm and rhyme and the feeling of each character.

Practice Have partners read the page aloud together several times, mimicking the expression you modeled.

Build Comprehension, pages 50–51

1 **Confirm Predictions** Think about your prediction about how Martina's suitors will react when she pours coffee on them. Was your prediction correct? (Answers about predictions will vary.)

2 **Character's Feelings** Why do you think Martina dislikes Don Largato? (He brushes her shawl with his oily fingers. He sneaks up on her.)

3 **Answers to Before You Move On**

1. **Plot** MODEL | GUIDE | APPLY Guide students in retelling what happened in the middle of the story. Say:

   • *How did Don Gallo and Don Cerdo act before Martina poured coffee on their shoes?* (They were nice and complimented her beauty.)

   • *How did Don Gallo and Don Cerdo react when Martina poured coffee on their shoes?* (They both got very angry.)

   • *What did the Coffee Test show Martina?* (These two suitors would not make good husbands for her.)

2. **Clarify** MODEL | GUIDE | APPLY What does it mean when Martina calls Don Cerdo a ham? (He is acting badly.) What have you read about Don Cerdo? (He is a pig.) What do you know about pigs? (They give us ham.) Why is it funny that she calls him a ham? (Because ham comes from pigs!)

"**B**ut I need you! Wait!" The lizard fell on one scaly knee and **warbled**,

"Martina Josefina Catalina Cucaracha,
Beautiful *muchacha*,
Won't you be my wife?"

Martina sighed. "Let me see if there's any coffee left."

This time she **wasn't taking any chances**. Martina returned with TWO cups for the lizard.

"*¡Psssst! ¡Psssst!*" he spat. Don Lagarto was **livid**. He changed colors three times before he finally found his true one. "And to think," he hissed. "I was going to eat—er—MARRY you!" **5**

Martina stared at the lizard. You could have heard a breadcrumb drop.

"**Food for thought**, *señor*," Martina said **icily**, "but I must refuse. You are much too cold-blooded for me." **6**

When her grandmother returned to collect the day's coffee cups, Martina was still **fuming**.

"I'm going inside, *Abuela*."

"So soon?"

"*¡Sí!* I'm afraid of whom I might meet next!" **7**

Abuela drew Martina to the railing and pointed to the garden below. "What about him?"

In Other Words
warbled sang
wasn't taking any chances
      would make sure the test worked
livid very angry

In Other Words
Food for thought That's something to think about
icily in an unfriendly way
fuming very angry
¡Sí! Yes! (in Spanish)

52   53

Build Comprehension, pages 52–53

4 **Predict** Read the question on page 52 and have students make predictions: What are some other ways suitors could react to the Coffee Test? Sample: A suitor might laugh.

5 **Character's Feelings** Was Martina right to dislike Don Lagarto? (Possible: Yes, he wanted to eat her not marry her.)

6 **Clarify Language** What does the idiom *food for thought* mean? Guide students to use the In Other Words section at the bottom of page 53 to find the meaning. (*Food for thought* means "something to think about.")

7 **Make Comparisons** How are Martina's suitors alike? (Possible: They are not being themselves; they pretend to be someone different.)

I **A** **AH**

Science:
Color-Changing Lizards

A chameleon is a lizard that can change its color. Chameleons cannot change to every color. Most turn green, brown, or gray. Light, temperature and mood can cause a chameleon to change color. The chameleon has layers of cells under its skin. To change color, it makes these cells bigger or smaller.

Challenge students to research other animals that change color, such as the octopus and the squid.

Martina looked down at the tiny brown mouse, and her cockroach heart began to beat faster.

Ti-ki-tin, ti-ki-tan.

"Oh, *Abuela*, he's **adorable**. Where has he been?"

"Right here all along."

"What do I do?"

"Go talk to him . . . and just be yourself."

Martina **handed** *Abuela* her *peineta* and *mantilla*, then **scurried** down to the garden. The mouse was waiting.

Ti-ki-tin, ti-ki-tan.

"*Hola*, hello." His voice was like warm honey. "My name is Péréz."

In Other Words
adorable very cute; charming
handed gave
scurried hurried

54

"*Hola*," she whispered shyly. "I'm Martina—"

"—the beautiful cockroach," he finished for her.

"You think I'm beautiful?"

The little mouse turned pink under his fur. "Well, my eyes are rather weak, but I have excellent EARS. I know you are strong and good, Martina Josefina Catalina Cucaracha." Then he **squinted sweetly**. "Who cares if you are beautiful?"

TI-KI-TIN, TI-KI-TAN.

"Martina-a-a-a-a! Don't forget the coffee!" It was *Abuela*.

No, thought Martina. No coffee for Péréz!

"Martina Josefina Catalina Cucaracha!"

In Other Words
squinted sweetly narrowed his eyes in a cute way, to try to see better

55

N **B**

Concepts of Print: Directionality: Read Left Page First and Read Text Left to Right

Teach/Model Model turning to page 44, the first page of the story. Show students that this page is a left-hand page. Explain: *When you read a book, you always read the left page first. The story begins on this left page.* Next, point to the first word on page 44 and say: *You read the words on a page from left to right, too.* Then model reading the sentence in left-to-right order, tracking the print with a finger as you do so.

Practice/Apply Have students point to the first word on page 45. Read aloud the first sentence and have students run a finger under the text in their copies.

Keys to Efficacy

Cite evidence from the text: *Point to the visual that shows that or read me the sentence that helped you answer that question.*

Build Comprehension, pages 54–55

1 **Theme** Martina's grandmother told her "just be yourself." How does this relate to the lesson or theme of the story? (Possible answer: Martina learns that it is better to be yourself instead of pretending to be someone you are not.)

2 **Figurative Language** Why do you think the author compares the mouse's voice to "warm honey"? (His voice is sweet and pleasant.)

3 **Make Comparisons** How is Péréz different from Martina's other suitors? (Péréz does not pretend to be someone he is not. He values Martina because she is strong and good not because she is beautiful.)

Build Comprehension, page 56

4 **Answers to Before You Move On**

1. **Clarify** MODEL | GUIDE | APPLY Not only did he change color three times as he got angrier, he also revealed his true character. He had planned to eat her.

2. **Plot** MODEL | GUIDE | APPLY Students should realize that while Peréz is Martina's perfect match, it is really Martina that passes the Coffee Test because Peréz spills coffee on her and she is surprised, not angry.

"Sí, Abuela." Martina knew better than to argue with her Cuban grandmother.

With a heavy heart, she reached for the cup.

But Pérez got there first. Quick as a mouse, he splashed *café cubano* onto Martina's shoes.

Now **the coffee was on the other foot**.

Martina was too delighted to be angry. At last, she'd found her perfect match. But she had to ask, "How did you know about the Coffee Test?"

Pérez grinned. "Well, *mi amor*, my love . . . I too have a Cuban grandmother." ❖

In Other Words
café cubano Cuban coffee (in Spanish)
the coffee was on the other foot
they switched places (a joke based on the expression *the shoe was on the other foot*)

▶ **Before You Move On**
4
1. **Clarify** What does the author mean when she says that Don Lagarto found his true color?
2. **Plot** Which character passes the Coffee Test? Explain.

56

Meet the Author

Carmen Agra Deedy

AWARD WINNER

Carmen Agra Deedy was born in Cuba. When she was young, she moved to the United States. Carmen says the two cultures have taught her that people everywhere are alike.

One example is that people everywhere enjoy funny stories! One day, Carmen was invited to tell a story in Spanish to a gym full of students. Suddenly a huge cockroach flew across the gym. As the students began squealing, Carmen decided to tell one of her favorite Cuban folk tales about a cockroach. That tale became *Martina the Beautiful Cockroach.*

▲ A Cuban cockroach

Carmen says that when writing *Martina the Beautiful Cockroach,* "I told it just as I remembered my mother telling it." ▶

Writer's Craft 🖉
Find examples of humor in the story. It might be funny things that happen, or the way the author uses funny sayings. Then write a short paragraph that includes humor.

57

Student Book pages 56–57

Meet the Author, page 57

Have students chorally read the Meet the Author copy.

1 **Writer's Craft** Read aloud the Writer's Craft. Ask students for examples of humor in the story, such as: *Daintily, she sat down and crossed her legs, and crossed her legs, and crossed her legs* (page 46.) *For some reason this fellow really bugged her,* (page 51.)

Daily Writing 📝 Ⓐ ⒶⒽ

2 **Writer's Craft** Explain: *Like Carmen Agra Deedy, you can add humor to your stories.* Use the **Modeled Writing Routine** to write a humorous paragraph. (See **Writing Routines,** page PD54.)

Think Aloud 💬	**Write** 🖉
The main character is a rabbit with long, floppy ears. He always trips over his ears.	Robby tried to step over the puddle, but he tripped over his ears and fell in the mud. What a mess!

Have students write their sentences in their journals.

3 **Writing Project: Draft an Interview** Have students draft their Writing Projects. (See pages T67c–T67.)

> **CLOSE AND ASSESS**
> • **Language** *I want to know about the story you read. How can I ask for information?*
> • **Vocabulary** *Explain how the coffee test* **influences** *Martina's decision.*
> • **Reading** *How did you monitor your understanding as you read?*

Keys to Efficacy

Use a student's response, even if correct, to guide follow-up questions and prompt further dialogue: *How can we check? How did you know?*

Author Study

Encourage students to read more books written by Carmen Agra Deedy.

-*The Last Dance*
-*The Library Dragon*
-*The Secret of Old Zeb*

 **Day 4**

Day at a Glance:
- ▶ **Language:** Compound Predicates
- ▶ **Vocabulary:** Share Word Knowledge
- ▶ **Reading:** Think and Respond
- ▶ **Writing:** Write About It; Revise

OBJECTIVES

Vocabulary
- Use Academic Vocabulary ●
- Use Grade-Level Vocabulary ●

Grammar
- Identify Compound Predicates ●

Learning and Teamwork Strategies
- Review
- Collaborate with Peers

Resources

 Practice Master 1.14

Language Builder Picture Card E13

Differentiate

Language Transfer

Issue In Chinese languages, Haitian Creole, Hmong, Korean (generally), and Vietnamese, the verb is not inflected for person and number. Speakers of these languages sometimes have the tendency to say *She walk in the rain* instead of *She walks in the rain*.

Strategy Write sentence pairs such as these on sentence strips for students to cut apart and reassemble:

Martina sips coffee with her suitors.

The suitors sip coffee with Martina.

Part 2 Grammar Skills Trace		Page
Day 2	Compound Subjects	T39a
▶ Day 4	Compound Predicates	T58a
Day 7	Subject-Verb Agreement	T65a
Day 10	Review Subject-Verb Agreement	T66g

T58a Unit 1 | Living Traditions

Language of the Day

What did Martina learn about customs and tradition?

She learned that _____ .

Read the Language of the Day. Model: *The coffee test will show Martina what her* **relationship** *with her husband will be like.* Have each student repeat your sentence and add their ideas to create a cumulative sentence. Then explain that today students will talk and write about the selection.

Grammar Compound Predicates B I A AH

1 Teach/Model Write and read aloud these sentences:

> *Martina's family gave her presents.*
> *Martina's family offered her advice.*
> *Martina's family gave her presents <u>and</u> offered her advice.*

Point to sentence 1. Say: *This sentence has one simple subject:* family. *The family gave Martina presents. There is one simple predicate, or verb:* gave. Repeat for sentence 2. (family, offered)

Point to sentence 3 and ask: *What did the family do?* (They gave Martina presents and offered her advice.) Underline the subject and verbs as you explain: *This sentence has one simple subject* (family), *but two verbs* (gave *and* offered). *It has a compound predicate. You can combine verbs in a compound predicate with the word* and *or the word* or. Write:

> *Martina wears her comb and puts on her mantilla for the* **occasion** .
> *Martina's aunts may sing or dance during the* **ceremony** .
> *Martina sat, smiled sweetly, and greeted her suitors.*

Ask: *How many verbs does the last sentence have?* (3) *What are they?* (sat, smiled, greeted) Say: *When a compound predicate has three or more verbs, use a comma between them.*

2 Practice/Apply Partners write two sentences with the same subject but different verbs, then exchange sentences with another student pair. The new pair combines the sentences using a compound predicate. Then assign **Practice Master 1.14**.

> **CHECK UNDERSTANDING** Have students explain how to combine these sentences: *Martina's grandmother gave her advice. Her grandmother made her follow it.*

Share Word Knowledge

③ Teach/Model To connect concepts, say: *Yesterday you became Key Word experts. Today you will share what you know about your Key Words.* Pair each student with a partner who studied a different word. Have partners follow the steps of **Vocabulary Routine 3** to share their word knowledge. (See **Vocabulary Routines**, page PD39.)

- Take turns reading the 4-Corner posters.
- Talk about how the content sentences help show the meanings of the Key Words.
- Create sentences using both Key Words and write them in your journals.
- Draw a line under each Key Word.

④ Practice/Apply Have student experts learn about two different words and interview each other about their word using the **Three-Step Interview**. Then have them report about each other's words to the group. (See **Cooperative Learning Routines,** pages PD58–PD59.)

Repeat until all the words are discussed.

Three-Step Interview

> **CHECK UNDERSTANDING** Display the **Language Builder Picture Card E13** (Carnival) and ask students to use Key Words to tell about it.

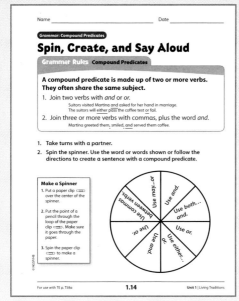

Name _____ Date _____

Grammar: Compound Predicates

Spin, Create, and Say Aloud

Grammar Rules Compound Predicates

A compound predicate is made up of two or more verbs. They often share the same subject.
1. Join two verbs with *and* or *or*.
   Suitors visited Martina and asked for her hand in marriage.
   The suitors will either pass the coffee test or fail.
2. Join three or more verbs with commas, plus the word *and*.
   Martina greeted them, smiled, and served them coffee.

1. Take turns with a partner.
2. Spin the spinner. Use the word or words shown or follow the directions to create a sentence with a compound predicate.

Make a Spinner
1. Put a paper clip over the center of the spinner.
2. Put the point of a pencil through the loop of the paper clip. Make sure it goes through the paper.
3. Spin the paper clip to make a spinner.

For use with TE p. T58a   **1.14**   Unit 1 | Living Traditions

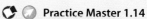

Practice Master 1.14

Day 4
continued

Day at a Glance:
- ▶ **Language:** Compound Predicates
- ▶ **Vocabulary:** Share Word Knowledge
- ▶ **Reading:** Think and Respond
- ▶ **Writing:** Write About It; Revise

OBJECTIVES

Vocabulary
- Use Academic Vocabulary ⊕
- Use Grade-Level Vocabulary ⊕

Language
- Use Language Function: Ask for and Give Information ⊕

Fluency
- Expression ⊕

Literary Analysis
- Analyze Genre: Folk Tale
- Identify Plot ⊕

Test-Taking Strategies
- Practice and Apply Strategies: Know the Test Format
- Practice and Apply Strategies

Writing
- Write a Paragraph
- Writing Project: Revise

Resources

 eVisual 1.22

 NGReach.com ▶

See **Technology Station** for digital student resources.

 I A AH

Fluency: Phrasing

Review Review expression (pages T50–51). Provide this reminder: *Expression is using your voice to show feeling.*

Apply Challenge pairs to use expression to practice reading page 50. Encourage them to react the way the characters might respond. Then organize teams of four and have pairs give each other feedback about their reading.

Think and Respond

1 **Talk About It** Prompt students to cite evidence from the text. Remind students to use Key Words in their answers. If students have difficulty, help them use the sentence starters to form their answers.

1. **Genre: Folk Tale** Possible answers: The folk tale has animal characters that act like people, and it shows the culture of the Cuban people.

2. **Ask for and Give Information** Responses should focus on Abuela and Martina's **relationship**. Possible answer: How can you tell that Abuela cares for Martina? I can tell because she gives good advice on how to choose a husband.

3. **Plot** Answers will vary. Have students decide if the characters act like real people. Would people get angry if you spilled coffee on them?

2 **Test-Taking Strategies: Know the Test Format** Explain: *When taking a test, it is important to know the test format. Plan and preview the test. Look for the important parts such as the directions and questions. You may also see an introduction, a title, and a passage.*

Model: *I read the directions first.* Have a student read the directions. *Then I read the introduction and the passage.* Ask a volunteers to read the introduction and the passage. Point out the additional directions. *Now I read the question. I know I need to find an incomplete sentence. I can reread the passage to find the answer.* Have students reread and identify the correct answer.

> **Directions:** Read the introduction and passage. Then read each question and fill in the correct answer.
>
> *Help Carlos revise and edit a paragraph. Read the paragraph and think about the changes Carlos should make. Then answer the questions.*
>
> The Coffee Test
>
> (1) In the folk tale "Martina the Beautiful Cockroach." (2) Abuela gives Martina advice about choosing a husband. (3) She tells Martina to spill coffee on her suitors' shoes. (4) A suitor who reacts badly will not make a good husband.
>
> **Which group of words is an incomplete sentence?**
>
> A. Group 1
>
> B. Group 2
>
> C. Group 3
>
> D. Group 4
>
> NGReach.com ▶ eVisual 1.22

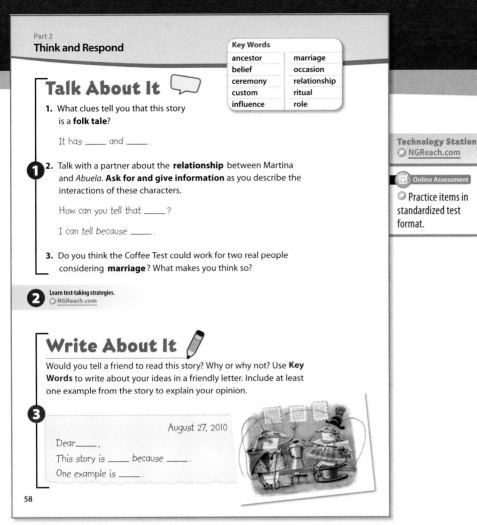

Part 2
Think and Respond

Key Words

ancestor	marriage
belief	occasion
ceremony	relationship
custom	ritual
influence	role

Talk About It

1. What clues tell you that this story is a **folk tale**?

   It has _____ and _____ .

2. Talk with a partner about the **relationship** between Martina and *Abuela*. **Ask for and give information** as you describe the interactions of these characters.

   How can you tell that _____ ?

   I can tell because _____ .

3. Do you think the Coffee Test could work for two real people considering **marriage**? What makes you think so?

Learn test-taking strategies.
NGReach.com

Write About It

Would you tell a friend to read this story? Why or why not? Use **Key Words** to write about your ideas in a friendly letter. Include at least one example from the story to explain your opinion.

August 27, 2010

Dear_____,
This story is _____ because _____ .
One example is _____ .

58

Technology Station
NGReach.com

☑ Online Assessment

Practice items in standardized test format.

Student Book page 58

Daily Writing

3 **Write About It** Read the directions aloud. Use the **Supported Independent Writing** routine to help students put their thoughts in writing, using the Key Words and the sentence frames. (See **Writing Routines**, page PD56.)

Say	Write
The author has fun with words in this story. For example, she uses animal words and expressions to tell what Don Cerdo is like.	This story is funny because the author has fun with words. One example is in the relationship with Don Cerdo. Martina calls him a "ham."

Point out the Key Word that you used to complete the sentence frame: *relationship*. Have students use these ideas or their own to write sentences in their journals.

4 **Writing Project: Revise an Interview** Have students revise their Writing Project compositions. (See pages T68a–T68.)

> **CLOSE AND ASSESS**
>
> - **Language** *Combine these sentences: Don Cerdo acts like a pig. Don Cerdo smells like one, too.* (Don Cerdo acts like a pig and smells like one, too.)
> - **Reading** *Which animal suitor did you think was the funniest? Explain.*
> - **Vocabulary** *How did you use Key Words in your writing?* (Answers will vary.)

Keys to Efficacy

Remind students to use formal language during classroom disscussions: *You have a great idea. Here is a way to say what you mean in a class discussion: _____ .*

Day 5

Day at a Glance:
- ▶ **Language:** Give Instructions
- ▶ **Vocabulary:** Apply Word Knowledge
- ▶ **Reading:** Reread and Retell
- ▶ **Writing:** Edit and Proofread Interview

OBJECTIVES

Vocabulary
- Use Academic Vocabulary 🅣
- Use Grade-Level Vocabulary 🅣

Listening and Speaking
- Give Instructions 🅣
- Listen Actively 🅣

Learning and Teamwork Strategy
- Self-Monitor and Self Correct
- Follow Instructions
- Review

Social Studies
- Explore Customs and Traditions

Resources

- 🄯 eVisual 1.23
- 🄯 🄯 Practice Master 1.15
- · coin for Vocabulary game

Differentiate

N B I How to Learn Language
Self-Monitor and Self-Correct

Tell students: If the other person doesn't understand your directions, you probably need to give the directions again. Try giving them in a different way. Provide an example, showing how the same directions can be given two different ways:

> Put the books on the shelf in alphabetical order.

> Put the books on the shelf. Put the books that start with A in the front.

Language of the Day

What's a custom or tradition you want to learn more about? Why?

I want to learn more about ___ because ___.

Read the Language of the Day. Model: *Customs and traditions are important because they bring families together.* Have all students complete the sentence frame, trying not to repeat a previous suggestion. Explain that today students will give instructions, play a word game, retell the story, and write about it.

Give Instructions

1 **Teach/Model** Introduce the concept: *When you give instructions, you tell someone how to do something. It is important to tell the steps in the correct order and tell exactly what to do.*

Display the how to card. Read aloud the card and model giving instructions for blowing up a balloon.

How to Give Instructions

1. State the purpose.	Here's how to blow up a balloon.
2. Give the steps in the order. Use sequence words.	First, stretch the balloon. Next, blow air into the balloon until it is full.
3. Use commands to tell exactly what to do.	Finally, tie a knot in the open end of the balloon.

🄯 NGReach.com ▶ eVisual 1.23

2 **Practice/Apply** Have students work with partners to give classroom-related instructions. They might tell how to straighten up an area, for example, or how to set up a learning center. Have listeners offer feedback. Were the instructions easy to understand? Were the steps in order? Teach the **How to Learn Language** strategy to help students as they speak.

> **CHECK UNDERSTANDING** Ask: What words show the steps when you give instructions? (*First, next, finally*)

Apply Word Knowledge

3 **Teach/Model** Display **Practice Master 1.15** and explain how to play "Word Race":

- *Write the Key Words in any order on the card. Use every Key Word at least once.*

- *Flip a coin to see how many spaces to move your marker. Move 1 space for Heads and 2 spaces for Tails.*

- *Read the word on the space. Tell what the word means and use it in a sentence. For example: The word is **ritual**. A ritual is part of a ceremony or special occasion. An example of a marriage ritual is the bride and groom exchanging rings.*

- *Your partner will check to see if you used the word correctly. If you did, you can stay where you are. If you didn't use the word correctly, move back one space.*

- *Take turns with your partner. The first one to reach the finish, wins.*

4 **Practice/Apply** Distribute **Practice Master 1.15**. Have students write the Key Words on their copies. Clarify: *Make sure you write every Key Word on your sheet. If you have an extra space, you can use a word again.*

Explain that as partners play the game, they should verify their partner's definitions and sentences. Encourage them to offer help or advice in reading, defining, or using Key Words correctly.

Monitor students as they follow your instructions. Restate the instructions as required.

For vocabulary games, go to NGReach.com.

> **CHECK UNDERSTANDING** Call out a definition and have students name the Key Word.

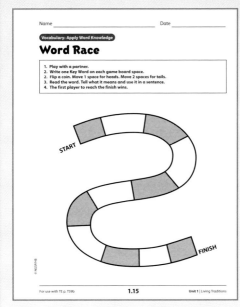

Practice Master 1.15

Day 5
continued

Day at a Glance:
► **Language:** Give Instructions
► **Vocabulary:** Apply Word Knowledge
▶ **Reading:** Reread and Retell
▶ **Writing:** Edit and Proofread

OBJECTIVES

Vocabulary
• Use Academic Vocabulary ❶
• Use Grade-Level Vocabulary ❶

Language
• Compare Genres
• Participate in Discussion
• Retell the Story

Reading Fluency
• Read with Accuracy and Rate ❶
• Read with Expression ❶

Literary Analysis
• Identify the Plot

Writing
• Write a Paragraph Response
• Writing Project: Edit and Proofread

Social Studies
• Explore Customs and Traditions

Resources

📀 💿 *Practice Master 1.13*

📀 💿 *Practice Master 1.16*

📀 💿 *Practice Master 1.17*

💿 *Comprehension Coach*

🌐 **NGReach.com** ❯

See **Technology Station** for digital student resources.

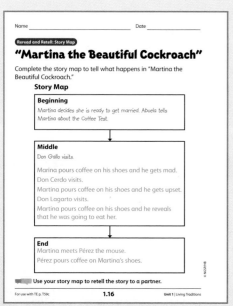

Practice Master 1.16

Reread and Retell

❶ Plot Read aloud the introduction. Reinforce: *The plot is the series of events in a story.* Read through the example story map and callouts. Explain: *A story map lists what happens at the beginning, the middle, and the end of the story. Most of the events happen in the middle of the story.*

Have students complete **Practice Master 1.16**.

❷ Retell Read aloud the directions and language frames. Have partners take turns retelling the story. Remind them to tell about all the main events in the order they happened. Provide the Key Points Reading (**Practice Master 1.13**) for students who need additional support.

To evaluate student's proficiency levels, use the Retelling a Story Rubric.

Retelling a Story Rubric		
Scale	**Content**	**Language**
B	☐ Main events of the plot are missing or out of order. ☐ Fails to use sequence words.	☐ Frequently hard to hear or understand. ☐ Is uncomfortable with the retelling task.
I	☐ Includes events of the plot in the correct order. ☐ Uses few sequence words.	☐ Is often hard to hear or understand. ☐ Seems somewhat uncomfortable with the retelling task
A	☐ Relates most of the main events of the plot in the correct order. ☐ Reinforces order with sequence words.	☐ Can be understood most of the time. ☐ Is fairly comfortable with the retelling task.
AH	☐ Tells all the events of the plot in the correct order. ☐ Uses sequence words to reinforce order.	☐ Speaks clearly and is easily understood ☐ Is comfortable with the retelling task.

Fluency Accuracy, Rate, and Expression **I** **A** **AH**

❸ Fluency Have students record their reading on the **Comprehension Coach** to assess each student's progress for rate and accuracy. Have students use the passage on **Practice Master 1.17** to record their reading for expression. Listen to each recording and assess students' ability to read with expression.

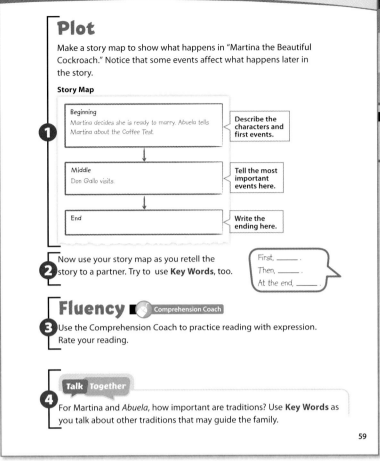

Plot

Make a story map to show what happens in "Martina the Beautiful Cockroach." Notice that some events affect what happens later in the story.

Story Map

1

| Beginning |
| Martina decides she is ready to marry. Abuela tells Martina about the Coffee Test. |

→ Describe the characters and first events.

↓

| Middle |
| Don Gallo visits. |

→ Tell the most important events here.

↓

| End |

→ Write the ending here.

2 Now use your story map as you retell the story to a partner. Try to use **Key Words**, too.

First, _____ .
Then, _____ .
At the end, _____ .

Fluency ■ Comprehension Coach

3 Use the Comprehension Coach to practice reading with expression. Rate your reading.

Talk Together

4 For Martina and *Abuela*, how important are traditions? Use **Key Words** as you talk about other traditions that may guide the family.

59

Student Book page 59

Technology Station
NGReach.com

Comprehension Coach

○ Automatically measure fluency.

Name _____ Date _____

Fluency: Expression

"Martina the Beautiful Cockroach"

Expression in reading is how you use your voice to express feeling. Use this passage to practice reading with proper expression.

"¡Gronc! ¡Gronc!" squealed Don Cerdo as he dabbed at the coffee on his shoes. "What a tragedy for my poor loafers!"

He really is quite a ham, thought Martina.

"Calm yourself, señor. I'll clean them for you!"

"I'll say you will!" he snorted. "When you are my wife, there'll be no end to cleaning up after me!"

Martina rolled her eyes in disbelief.

"A most charming offer, señor," she said dryly, "but I must decline. You are much too boorish for me."

From "Martina the Beautiful Cockroach," page 50

Expression

Accuracy and Rate Formula
Use the formula to measure a reader's accuracy and rate while reading aloud.

For use with TE p. T59c   1.17   Unit 1 | Living Traditions

Practice Master 1.17

4 Talk Together Ask students what **rituals** and **customs** are important to Martina and her family in "Martina the Beautiful Cockroach." Read aloud the directions and have students jot down notes for their responses. Then have students share their ideas. Students should add their ideas to their unit concept maps.

Daily Writing

5 Writing Project: Edit and Proofread an Interview
Have students edit and proofread their Writing Project compositions. (See pages T69c–T69.)

Keys to Efficacy

Remind students to use content, academic, and/or classroom vocabulary: *How can you use the word* **marriage** *in your response? How could you use the word* **belief**?

CLOSE AND ASSESS

- **Language** *Complete this sentence: When I give instructions, I _____ .* (state the purpose, tell the steps in order, use sequence words, tell exactly what to do)

- **Reading** *Briefly retell the plot of "Martina the Beautiful Cockroach." What happens at the beginning, the middle, and the end of the story?*

- **Vocabulary** *What Key Words did you use to talk about the importance of rituals and customs for Martina and Abuela?* (Answers will vary.)

Day 6

Day at a Glance:
Language: Ask for and Give Information **Reading:** Read the Selection
Vocabulary: Idioms and Expressions **Writing:** Writing Fluency; Publish and Share

OBJECTIVES

Vocabulary
• Use Academic Vocabulary ⊙
• Use Grade-Level Content Vocabulary ⊙
• Strategy: Use Context Clues for Idioms ⊙

Language
• Language Function: Ask for and Give Information
• Use a Variety of Language Structures ⊙

Learning and Teamwork Strategies
• Collaborate with Peers
• Speak When Recognized
• Respond to Questions

Resources

🔘 eVisual 1.24
🔘 eVisual 1.25
📱🔘 Language Builder Picture Card E11

Language of the Day

What **role** does tradition play in Martina's life?
What role does it play in your life?
Tradition plays _____ role in Martina's life.
It plays _____ in my life.

Read the Language of the Day. Model: *Tradition plays an important role in Martina's life. It plays an important role in my life, too.* Invite students to share about the role of tradition in their own lives as well.

Ask for and Give Information

1 Teach/Model Review how to ask for and give information (page T36). Name the question words with students. Say: *To answer, give information that goes with the question word. Then you can give more details to make your answer even more complete.*

Display the chart and work with a volunteer to model this language function. Reverse roles.

Ask for Information	Give Information
What kind of a story is "Martina the Beautiful Cockroach"?	"Martina the Beautiful Cockroach" is a Cuban folk tale. People in Cuba tell this folk tale again and again.
Where does this folk tale take place?	This folk tale takes place in Havana, Cuba. Cuba is a country in the Caribbean.

🔘 NGReach.com ▶ eVisual 1.24

Invite students to ask for information about the characters in the folk tale. Record the questions. Help students use the question to begin their responses.

2 Practice/Apply Have students conduct a **Three-Step Interview**, taking turns asking and answering questions about the author Carmen Agra Deedy. (See Cooperative **Learning Routines**, pages PD58–PD59.) Use **Academic Language Frames** to provide ideas to support every language level.

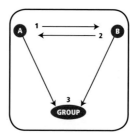

Three-Step Interview

CHECK UNDERSTANDING Display **Language Builder Card E11** and have partners ask for and give information about the picture.

Differentiate

Academic Language Frames

Ask for and Give Information
■ Who is _____? She is _____.
  Where was _____? She was _____.
_____
■ How can you tell that _____?
  I can tell _____ because _____.
  Where was the _____?
  Who _____?
_____
■ What happened when _____?
■ _____ happened _____.
  Why did _____?
    _____ because _____.

🔘 NGReach.com ▶ eVisual 1.25

Idioms and Expressions

3 **Idioms** and **expressions** are colorful ways to say something. The words that make up an idiom mean something different from what they mean by themselves. Use clues from the sentence to figure out what an idiom or expression means.

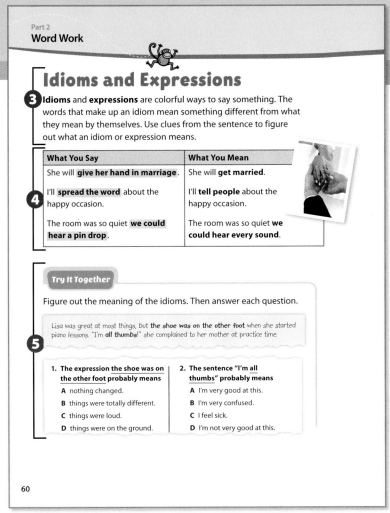

What You Say	What You Mean
She will **give her hand in marriage**.	She will **get married**.
4 I'll **spread the word** about the happy occasion.	I'll **tell people** about the happy occasion.
The room was so quiet **we could hear a pin drop**.	The room was so quiet **we could hear every sound**.

Try It Together

Figure out the meaning of the idioms. Then answer each question.

5 Lisa was great at most things, but **the shoe was on the other foot** when she started piano lessons. "I'm **all thumbs**!" she complained to her mother at practice time.

1. The expression **the shoe was on the other foot** probably means
   A nothing changed.
   B things were totally different.
   C things were loud.
   D things were on the ground.

2. The sentence "I'm all thumbs" probably means
   A I'm very good at this.
   B I'm very confused.
   C I feel sick.
   D I'm not very good at this.

60

Student Book page 60

Idioms and Expressions

3 **Teach** Read the introduction. Write: *We planned a surprise party for Mom, but someone spilled the beans so she found out about it.*
Say: *We can use context clues to figure out the meaning of the idiom,* spilled the beans. *I know that the speaker wanted to have a surprise party but Mom wasn't surprised. I think* spilled the beans *means "to tell beforehand."*

4 **Model** Have a volunteer read the first example. Model determining the meaning of *give her hand in* **marriage**. Say: *When you get married, you hold hands so I think* give her hand in marriage *means "get married."* Repeat the procedure for the idioms *spread the word* and *hear a pin drop*. Have students tell about times when they've heard these idioms used.

5 **Practice/Apply** Read the directions aloud. Have a volunteer read the example. Then have partners answer the questions. Have them talk about the context clues they used to figure out the meanings. Use the **Multi-Level Practice Sets** to address varying levels of vocabulary knowledge.

> **CHECK UNDERSTANDING** Say: *Tell me what* gave it her best shot *means in this sentence: Martina felt funny about doing the Coffee Test, but she gave it her best shot, and it worked!* (*Gave it her best shot* means "she tried her hardest to do well.")

Differentiate

Multi-Level Practice Sets

I The photographer wanted the children to smile. "*Say cheese,*" he said. (smile)

B Everyone was surprised by the news. It came *out of the blue.* (completely unexpected)

N Pedro laughed. "I don't believe your story. Are you *pulling my leg?* (joking)

A Inez was tired after soccer practice. She said, "I'll *catch forty winks* and start my homework after I rest. (take a nap)

AH I got to school *just in the nick of time.* Five more minutes and I would have been late. (not too late, but close)

Part 2 Vocabulary Skills Trace		Page
Day 1	Social Studies Vocabulary	T37
Day 2	Academic Vocabulary	T39
Day 3	Expand Word Knowledge	T42b
Day 4	Share Word Knowledge	T58b
Day 5	Apply Word Knowledge	T59b
Day 6	**Idioms and Expressions**	**T60**
Day 7	Idioms and Expressions	T65
Days 8–9	Extend Vocabulary	T66e–f
Day 10	Vocabulary Review	T66g–h

Day 6
continued

Day at a Glance:
Language: Ask for and Give Information
Vocabulary: Idioms and Expressions
Reading: Read the Selection
Writing: Writing Fluency; Publish and Share

OBJECTIVES

Vocabulary
• Use Academic Vocabulary ●
• Use Grade-Level Vocabulary ●

Learning to Read
• Concepts of Print: Recognize Paragraphs

Reading Strategy
• Plan: Preview ●
• Read the Selection
• Make Connections: Text to Self
• Monitor Reading: Clarify Ideas
• Ask Questions

Comprehension and Literary Analysis
• Recognize Genre: Magazine Article
• Analyze Plot
• Use Text Features to Preview
• Interpret Visuals
• Recognize Topic

Learning and Teamwork Strategies
• Use Prereading Supports
• Build Background Knowledge
• Use Reading Supports

Resources

Practice Master 1.18

Practice Master 1.18

Read the Magazine Article

1 Connect Across Texts Read aloud the introduction. Say: *Tell about some* **occasions** *when you have seen or taken part in family traditions and* **customs**.

2 Genre Read aloud the explanation. Explain that magazine articles can be written about many topics. Ask students to share the topics of magazine articles or magazines that they have seen. Encourage a range of responses, such as crafts, fashion, sports, news, history, cars, and computers. Explain that all these types of articles are about real people, places, or events.

3 Preview and Build Background Use sheltering strategies as you conduct a picture walk.

Pages	Say (and Do)
61	*In India, when a girl turns 11, she is seen as an adult. That is a big deal.* (Make a facial expression that shows you are impressed.) *In a special* **ceremony**, *called a sari ceremony, she is given a new outfit called a half sari.* (Point to the half sari and say: *How pretty.*) *After another special ceremony—a wedding—a woman can wear a full sari.* (Point to the girls wearing half saris in the illustration, then to the women in full saris.) *How is a half sari different from a full sari?*
62–63	*A girl named Jyotsna had her sari ceremony at her aunt's house.* (Point to the girl in the first photograph.) *She was excited for the ceremony. She dressed up and got to sit on a chair decorated with flowers.* (Point to the girl seated in the second photograph.) *Then her relatives brought her a half-sari, some jewelry, and other gifts.* (Point to the illustrations.) *Do you think you would enjoy that?!*

4 Read "Coming of Age" Scaffold the support for varied reading levels.

BELOW LEVEL	ON LEVEL / ABOVE LEVEL
Listen and Learn	**Read Together**
• Ask students to set a purpose for listening—to get information or to enjoy a story. Have them track the print as you read aloud.	• Have students use a **Double-Entry Log** as they read. Students should write each page number in column 1, at least two details from each page in column 2, and their thoughts about each detail in column 3.
• Check understanding with selected Build Comprehension questions.	• Review students' log and discuss the Build Comprehension and Before You Move On questions.

CHECK UNDERSTANDING Ask: *What* **ritual** *did Jyotsna take part in at age 11?* (getting a half sari to show that she was an adult)

Coming of Age

adapted from *Skipping Stones* ❀ illustrated by Shannon Brady

Connect Across Texts Read about a family **custom** from India that celebrates a girl's coming of age. **1**

Genre A **magazine article** is nonfiction. It gives facts about real people, places, or events. **2**

Many Hindus celebrate important **phases in life** with special **ceremonies** called *samskaras*. For Jyotsna Grandhi, one important *samskara* happened when she **turned** eleven. The ceremony, called a sari ceremony, welcomed her into adulthood. During the ceremony, Jyotsna received her first half sari, or *voni*. In some Indian traditions, this is meant to be the **outfit** worn by young women until **marriage**.

Here is what Jyotsna had to say about her sari ceremony.

full sari

half sari

◀ A sari is a traditional garment worn by some women in India.

In Other Words
phases in life times in a person's growth and development
turned reached the age of
outfit clothing

▶ **Before You Move On**
3 1. **Use Text Features** How do the title, illustration, and caption help you understand what this article is about?
2. **Main Idea** What does the sari **ceremony** celebrate?

61

Student Book page 61

Build Comprehension, page 61

1 **Monitor** RETEACH Review with students how to monitor as they read. What does coming of age mean? I will read on in the text to find out. I learn that coming of age means when a child is considered an adult. (See page T40.)

2 **Relate to Personal Knowledge** When a woman wears a full sari, like in this illustration, others know she is married. What other customs do you know of that show that a person is married? (Students may suggest wedding rings or other customs that they know of.)

3 **Answers to Before You Move On**

1. Use Text Features The title tells that this is an article about something that happens at a certain age. The picture and caption tell that in India, single girls and married women wear different clothes. These all give clues about the topic of the article: coming of age for Indian girls.

2. Main Idea The sari ceremony celebrates a girl becoming an adult.

B I A AH

Cultural Perpectives

Explain that "Coming of Age" ceremonies are important for younger teens and their families in many cultures and religions. These ceremonies mean that a child is becoming an adult. They also can mean increased responsiblity. For example, Jewish boys and girls have a bar mitzvah or a bat mitzvah at age 12 or 13 to mark their transition to adulthood. Girls from Hispanic cultures may celebrate becoming a woman at age 15 with a celebration called a *quinceañera*. Invite students to share their knowledge of or experience with "Coming of Age" ceremonies.

Jyotsna's Sari Ceremony

I celebrated my sari ceremony at my aunt's home in India. I wore my best silk skirt, blouse, and jewelry. I sat on a chair decorated with flowers.

My uncle and his wife presented my first *voni* to me, along with jewelry. I was asked to put on the new clothes and the jewelry.

All our relatives took turns **blessing me** by putting yellow-colored rice grains on my head. They also handed me gifts. **1 2 3**

▲ Surrounded by family, Jyotsna Grandhi prepares to celebrate her sari ceremony.

▲ In *Jyotsna's* sari ceremony, she received her first *voni*, or half sari.

In Other Words
blessing me wishing me good luck and good health

62

Student Book page 62

Build Comprehension, page 62

1 **Monitor** MODEL | GUIDE | APPLY After students finish reading page 62, have them write a question about something they do not understand. Then have them reread the pages to figure out the answer to the question. (Questions and answers will vary.)

2 **Make Inferences** Explain to students that the rice often symbolizes prosperity. Then ask: *Why do you think Jyotsna's relatives put rice on her head?* (They want her to have a prosperous life as an adult.)

3 **Use Key Words** What are some of the **customs** that the family followed for Jyotsna's ceremony? (Sample responses: She sat on a chair decorated with flowers; they gave her gifts; they put rice on her head.)

▼ Jyotsna during her sari ceremony

Before the ceremony started, I was excited. I knew that afterwards people would think of me as a young woman. I also was partly sad because I would miss **being pampered** as the **baby of** the house.

During the ceremony, I felt uncomfortable when everybody was looking at me. All I could think of was taking the dress off and changing into my regular outfit. I liked the gift-giving part of the ceremony best! **4**

—Jyotsna Grandi, 11, Indian-American, New Jersey ❖

▲ Family and friends gave Jyotsna presents to celebrate her coming of age.

In Other Words
being pampered getting special treatment
baby of youngest person in

▶ **Before You Move On**

5 1. **Clarify** What parts of the text help you understand why Jyotsna felt uncomfortable during the **ceremony**?

2. **Details** What special **customs** are part of the **ceremony**?

63

Student Book page 63

Build Comprehension, page 63

4 **Sequence** Have students tell the sequence of events of Jyotsna's Sari Ceremony. (First Jyotsna gets dressed for her sari ceremony. Second she sits on a flowered chair and receives a half sari and jewelry, gifts, and blessings. Afterward, she tells how she felt before and during the **ceremony**.)

5 **Answers to Before You Move On**

1. **Clarify** MODEL | GUIDE | APPLY I reread the text to find out why Jyotsna felt uncomfortable. In the last paragraph I read that she was uncomfortable when everyone was looking at her. I also read that she wanted to be wearing her regular clothes.

2. **Details** Some special **customs** include dressing up, sitting on a flower-decorated chair, receiving gifts, receiving a half sari and jewelry, and receiving blessings.

**Home Connection:
Family Traditions**

Have students recall Family Newsletter 1 in which they were asked to bring from home items that represent family traditions, such as art work, crafts, fabrics, photographs, and musical recordings. Encourage discussion about what the items represent and how they might sort the items to represent different kinds of traditions.

Day 6
continued

Day at a Glance:
▶ **Language:** Ask for and Give Information
▶ **Vocabulary:** Idioms and Expressions
▶ **Reading:** Read the Selection
▶ **Writing:** Writing Fluency; Publish and Share

OBJECTIVES

Vocabulary
• Use Academic Vocabulary ⊕
• Use Grade-Level Content Vocabulary ⊕

Language
• Participate in Discussion

Fluency
• Read with Accuracy and Rate ⊕

Literary Analysis
• Compare Content

Learning and Teamwork Strategies
• Use Graphic Organizer: Venn diagram

Writing
• Develop Writing Fluency
• Monitor and Self-Correct Writing

Resources

⊘ eVisual 1.26

↻ ⊘ Practice Master 1.19

⊘ eVisual 1.27

Respond and Extend

1 **Reread** As students reread "Coming of Age," have them think about how it is the same as and different from "Martina the Beautiful Cockroach."

2 **Compare Content** Read the instructions. Explain that a Venn diagram is used to compare and contrast the content of the folk tale with the content of the magazine article. Use the instruction to explain how to complete the Venn diagram.

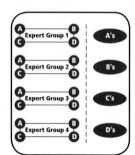

Jigsaw

Create groups for **Jigsaw**. (See Cooperative **Learning Routines**, pages PD 58–PD59.) Help focus students' thinking: *Pay attention to what happens in each selection. Think about the big ideas.* Ask questions to help guide discussion. Provide **Academic Language Frames** to support students' at different levels.

Focus	Questions
1. Events	Could the events happen in real life?
2. Place	Where do the events take place?
3. Time	When do the events happen?
4. Characters/People	Who is this selection about?
5. Theme	What is the big idea?

As students report their group's ideas, students should record them on **Practice Master 1.19**.

3 **Talk Together About the Big Question**

Read aloud the question and directions. Prompt students to use newly acquired vocabulary and to focus discussion: *Do you think Martina will pass on the tradition of The Coffee Test to her own daughter? Explain. How do you know that the sari* **ceremony** *was important to Jyotsna and her family?*

Have students add ideas to the unit concept map.

> **CHECK UNDERSTANDING** Have students tell why the folk tale and the magazine article are both included in the unit "Living Traditions."

Differentiate

Academic Language Frames

Make Comparisons

■ A thing that is the same is _____ .
   A thing that is different is _____ .

■ _____ and _____ are alike because both have _____ .
   _____ is different from _____ because it has _____ .

■ Both _____ and _____ have _____ , but only
■ _____ has _____ .

⊘ NGReach.com ▶ eVisual 1.26

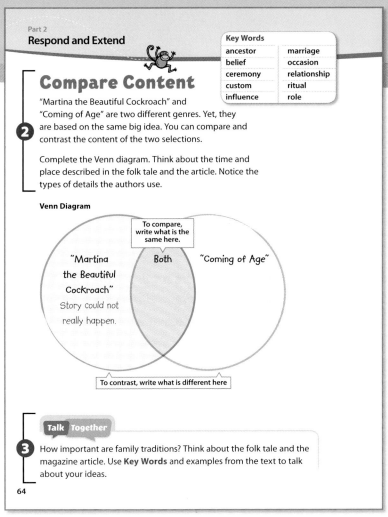

Key Words	
ancestor	marriage
belief	occasion
ceremony	relationship
custom	ritual
influence	role

Compare Content

"Martina the Beautiful Cockroach" and "Coming of Age" are two different genres. Yet, they are based on the same big idea. You can compare and contrast the content of the two selections.

Complete the Venn diagram. Think about the time and place described in the folk tale and the article. Notice the types of details the authors use.

Venn Diagram

To compare, write what is the same here.

"Martina the Beautiful Cockroach" Both "Coming of Age"

Story could not really happen.

To contrast, write what is different here.

Talk Together

3 How important are family traditions? Think about the folk tale and the magazine article. Use **Key Words** and examples from the text to talk about your ideas.

64

Student Book page 64

Daily Writing

4 **Writing Fluency** Use the **Power Writing Routine** (See page PD53.) Write the word **relationship** and prompt: *How would you describe your relationship with your good friend? Think about this word and write about it.*

Power Writing Routine

 1. What do you know about the word or picture?

 2. Take one minute to write as much as you can, as well as you can.
  B words   **I** sentences   **A** **AH** paragraphs

 3. Check your spelling and grammar. Circle mistakes.

 4. Count your words.

NGReach.com eVisual 1.27

5 **Writing Project: Publish and Share an Interview** Have students publish and share their Writing Project compositions. (See page T69.)

Fluency: Accuracy and Rate

To activate prior knowledge and practice fluency, conduct timed readings of "Martina the Beautiful Cockroach." Select an option for recording:

- Use the automatic speech recognition on the **Comprehension Coach** to track word count per minute for the entire passage.
- Use **Practice Master 1.17**.

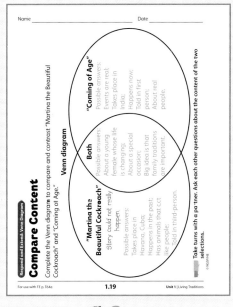

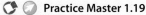 **Practice Master 1.19**

Day 7

Day at a Glance:
- ▶ **Language:** Subject-Verb Agreement
- ▶ **Vocabulary:** More Idioms and Expressions
- ▶ **Reading:** Reread the Selection
- ▶ **Writing:** Writing on Demand: Paragraph

OBJECTIVES

Vocabulary
- Use Academic Vocabulary ●
- Use Grade-Level Vocabulary ●
- Strategy: Use Context Clues for Idioms ●

Grammar
- Demonstrate Subject-Verb Agreement

Learning and Teamwork Strategies
- Relate to Prior Knowledge
- Make Contributions

Resources

 Practice Master 1.20

eVisual 1.28

Differentiate

Language Transfer

Issue In African-American Vernacular English, sometimes a singular verb is used with a plural subject. The student may say, for example, *We was there* instead of *We were there*.

Strategy Write sentence pairs on strips for students to cut apart between the subject and verb and then reassemble. Have them read aloud each sentence.

> She sees a rooster.
> They see a rooster.
> He is funny.
> They are funny.

Language of the Day

What's the difference between a custom, ritual, and tradition?
Customs are ____. A ritual is ____.
Traditions are ____.

Read the Language of the Day. Model: *Customs are small gestures like handshakes. A ritual is a wedding or some other ceremony. Traditions are cultural patterns.* Invite students to give their own definitions and examples of each word.

Grammar/Spelling Subject-Verb Agreement Ⓘ Ⓐ ⒶⒽ

1 Teach/Model Read the introduction and examples aloud. Have students point to the subjects. Then read the first rule in the box. Say: *A plural verb does not end in –s.* Write examples: *My cousins perform. The boys play drums. The girls dance.* Have students choral read the sentences.

Have a volunteer read the first rule and sentence. Say: *Both subjects* (Uncle Leo *and* Aunt Flora) *are singular, but there are two subjects joined by* and. *So we use a plural verb* (sing). Clarify grammar terms: *When we use the right verb with the right subject, we say that the subject and verb "agree."*

Read the rules in the second row one at a time, followed by the sample sentences. Point out that *sings* agrees with Uncle Leo, the last subject.

Say: *A singular verb ends in –s.* Write examples and have students choral read them: *My cousin performs. The boy plays drums. The girl dances.* Point to the second sample sentence. Say: Sing *agrees with* our cousins, *the last subject.* Repeat: *A plural verb does not end in –s.*

Write these sentences and guide students in circling the right verbs.

> *Jyotsna's cousins or her sister* bless/blesses *her with rice.* (blesses)

> *Jyotsna or her cousins* smile/smiles *the biggest.* (smile)

2 Practice Read aloud the directions and sentences. Guide students in identifying subjects. Point out the compound predicate. Encourage volunteers to explain why the verbs agree with their subjects.

3 Apply in Writing Read aloud the directions and have students work independently. Provide support as necessary. Assign **Practice Master 1.20**.

> **CHECK UNDERSTANDING** Have each student name a compound subject with *or* for a partner to use in a complete sentence with correct subject-verb agreement.

Part 1 Grammar Skills Trace		Page
Day 2	Compound Subjects	T39a
Day 4	Compound Predicates	T58a
Day 7	Subject-Verb Agreement	T65a
Day 10	Review Subject-Verb Agreement	T66g

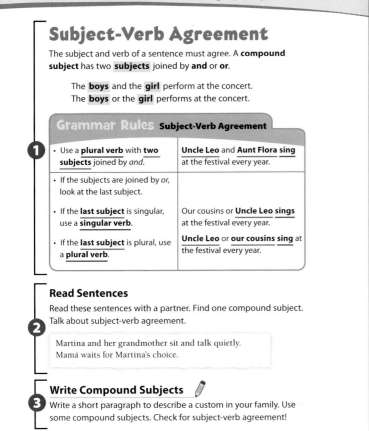

Subject-Verb Agreement

The subject and verb of a sentence must agree. A **compound subject** has two **subjects** joined by **and** or **or**.

The **boys** and the **girl** perform at the concert.
The **boys** or the **girl** performs at the concert.

Grammar Rules Subject-Verb Agreement

1

• Use a **plural verb** with **two subjects** joined by *and*.	**Uncle Leo** and **Aunt Flora sing** at the festival every year.
• If the subjects are joined by *or*, look at the last subject.	
• If the **last subject** is singular, use a **singular verb**.	Our cousins or **Uncle Leo sings** at the festival every year.
• If the **last subject** is plural, use a **plural verb**.	**Uncle Leo** or **our cousins sing** at the festival every year.

Read Sentences

2 Read these sentences with a partner. Find one compound subject. Talk about subject-verb agreement.

Martina and her grandmother sit and talk quietly.
Mamá waits for Martina's choice.

Write Compound Subjects 🖉

3 Write a short paragraph to describe a custom in your family. Use some compound subjects. Check for subject-verb agreement!

65

Student Book page 65

More Idioms and Expressions

4 **Review/Model** Review the Day 6 Lesson Plan (page T60). Write this sentence and model using context clues to determine the meaning of *true blue*:

All my true blue relatives traveled long distances to attend my sari **ceremony**. (loyal)

Display the Idioms and Expressions sentences and have volunteers read them aloud. Have students turn and talk about the meaning of *on cloud nine* in the first sentence. (extremely happy)

5 **Practice/Apply** Have students use the **Numbered Heads** routine to figure out the meaning of the underlined words using context clues. (See **Cooperative Learning Routines** pages PD58–PD59.)

2. a frog in my throat   (a hoarse voice)

3. a red-letter day   (an important day)

4. tickled pink   (very pleased)

5. heart of gold   (very kind)

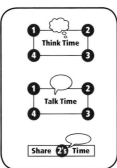

Numbered Heads

CHECK UNDERSTANDING Say: *Tell me what the lion's share means in this sentence: Everyone helped to clean up after the ceremony, but my uncle was amazing and did the lion's share of the work.* (largest amount)

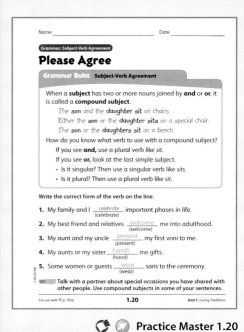

Grammar: Subject-Verb Agreement

Please Agree

Grammar Rules Subject-Verb Agreement

When a **subject** has two or more nouns joined by **and** or **or**, it is called a **compound subject**.

The **son** and the **daughter sit** on chairs.
Either the **son** or the **daughter sits** on a special chair.
The **son** or the **daughters sit** on a bench.

How do you know what verb to use with a compound subject?
If you see **and**, use a plural verb like *sit*.
If you see **or**, look at the last simple subject.
• Is it singular? Then use a singular verb like *sits*.
• Is it plural? Then use a plural verb like *sit*.

Write the correct form of the verb on the line.

1. My family and I ___celebrate___ important phases in life.
   (celebrate)

2. My best friend and relatives ___welcome___ me into adulthood.
   (welcome)

3. My aunt and my uncle ___present___ my first voni to me.
   (present)

4. My aunts or my sister ___hands___ me gifts.
   (hand)

5. Some women or guests ___wear___ saris to the ceremony.
   (wear)

Talk with a partner about special occasions you have shared with other people. Use compound subjects in some of your sentences.

For use with TE p. T65a   **1.20**   Unit 1 | Living Traditions

Practice Master 1.20

Idioms and Expressions

1 Jyotsna was <u>on cloud nine</u> during the gift-giving part of the ceremony.

2 I could hardly speak at the ceremony because I had <u>a frog in my throat</u>.

3 The day of the sari ceremony was <u>a red-letter day</u>, and Jyotsna would never forget it.

4 Jyotsna was excited and <u>tickled pink</u> that people would think of her as a young lady.

5 My aunt gave me a voni and jewelry because she has <u>a heart of gold</u>.

NGReach.com eVisual 1.28

Day 7
continued

Day at a Glance:
▶ **Language:** Subject-Verb Agreement
▶ **Vocabulary:** More Idioms and Expressions
▶ **Reading:** Reread the Selection
▶ **Writing:** Writing on Demand: Paragraph

OBJECTIVES

Vocabulary
• Use Academic Vocabulary ❶
• Use Grade-Level Vocabulary ❶

Literary Analysis
• Recognize Literary Elements: First-Person/Third-Person Point of View

Learning and Teamwork Strategies
• Reproduce Modeled Writing
• Respond to Questions

Writing
• Reproduce Modeled Writing
• Writing on Demand: Write a Paragraph

Reread Focus on Narrator

❶ Teach Introduce the concept: *A narrator tells the events of a story or article. It is the narrator's voice that speaks to readers.* Continue: *Authors usually choose between a third-person narrator and a first-person narrator.*

Display this chart and guide students to explore the differences.

Third-Person Narrator	First-Person Narrator
Gives background which includes facts and details	Describes his/her own feelings
Uses pronouns *he, his, she, her*	Uses pronouns *I, my, me*

Continue: *Today you will read "Coming of Age" again. This time think about who is the narrator.*

❷ Model Have volunteers read the introduction page aloud. Ask students what this page tells about? (It is presenting facts about special **ceremonies**.) Ask: *What pronouns does the narrator use?* (she, her). I can figure out that this page uses a third-person narrator.

❸ Practice/Apply in Reading Have students reread the rest of "Coming of Age." Have them use a **Roundtable** and give examples of how they know this part of the article uses a first-person narrator. (See **Cooperative Learning Routines,** pages PD58–PD59.) Students may, for example, note that on page 63, the first-person narrator, Jyotsna, describes her feelings. "I felt uncomfortable when everybody was looking at me." The pronouns *I* and *me* are clues about the narrator. Then have students turn and talk about how the introduction would be different if it used a first-person narrator.

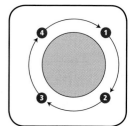

Roundtable

Daily Writing

Writing on Demand: Paragraph   Display the writing prompt and have a volunteer read it aloud.

> Write a paragraph that describes a favorite family tradition. Explain what you do and why.

Unpack the Prompt   Ask: *What is the purpose for writing?* (to write about a favorite family tradition and explain what I do and why) Say: *What form does the writing need to be?* Circle *paragraph* in the prompt.

Explain that a good test-taking strategy is to list ideas you might write about. Ask: *What family traditions do you like? Do you have a birthday or tooth tradition to share. How does your family celebrate a special* **occasion**?

Use the **Modeled Writing Routine** to illustrate how to write a paragraph. (See **Writing Routines** on page PD54.)

Think Aloud	Write
1. Prewrite	
First I plan my writing. I will make a web. I'll put the topic of my paragraph in the center circle.	Favorite Family Tradition
2. Write	
I will start my paragraph with the main idea that tells what the paragraph is all about.	My favorite family tradition is our Thanksgiving Thank-You tree.
Next, I'll add details that support or tell more about the main idea. I will make sure that I use complete sentences. I'll check that the subjects and verbs agree.	Dad and Mom set up a tree. Each person makes a paper ornament. We draw or write on the ornament to tell why we are thankful.
Add a few more sentences to complete the paragraph.	
3. Read and Reflect	
Model how to proofread the paragraph. Check spelling, grammar, punctuation, and capitalization with students, one feature at a time. Have students confirm that you have used correct subject-verb agreement.	

Display the finished paragraph to use as a model. Use **Multi-Level Strategies** to support students at all proficiency levels in writing a paragraph. Have students read their completed paragraphs to a partner.

CLOSE AND ASSESS

- **Language** *Where did you use subject-verb agreement correctly? Read the sentence or sentences. Identify any compound subjects or predicates.*
- **Vocabulary** *Did you have an opportunity to use idioms? What were they? What Key Words did you use?*
- **Reading** *Compare your paragraph with a paragraph in "Coming of Age." Remember to include the narrator's viewpoint in your comparison.*

Differentiate

Multi-Level Strategies

BEGINNING

Have students first draw the favorite tradition they plan to write about. Help students label their drawings to identify vocabulary they may need when writing. Encourage students to refer to the drawings as they write.

INTERMEDIATE

Have partners work in pairs to plan their paragraphs. Have them ask each other questions about the family tradition. Encourage students to use the answers as they write sentences that give details.

ADVANCED

Have students write the paragraph independently. Then have partners offer feedback on the paragraph form. *Was the main idea clear? Did the other sentences support the main idea? Were there sentences that did not support the main idea?*

ADVANCED HIGH

Have students focus on the narrator. Ask: *Will you write from a first-person narrator point of view as in the model? How will your paragraph be different if you use a third-person narrator?*

Days 8-9

Day at a Glance:
- ▶ **Language:** Theme Theater: Perform a Skit
- ▶ **Vocabulary:** Extend Vocabulary
- ▶ **Reading:** Read Leveled Books
- ▶ **Writing:** Paraphrase

OBJECTIVES

Language
- Language Function: Ask for and Give Information ❶

Literary Analysis
- Compare Characters

Listening and Speaking
- Use Context and Visuals
- Determine the Purpose for Listening
- Stay on Topic
- Adjust Your Language for Your Audience

Learning and Teamwork Strategies
- Connect Ideas

Resources

- materials for props, such as:
  - construction paper
  - craft items (bendable sticks, buttons, beads)
  - boxes
  - markers
  - scissors
  - glue
  - tape
- 🔖 ⏱ *Assessment Handbook* page 10

Language of the Day

What character in the folk tale made you laugh? ____ made me laugh because ____ .

Read the Language of the Day aloud. Model: *Don Cerdo, the pig, made me laugh because he thought his pig sty smelled sweet.* As students respond, keep a tally to find the class favorite.

Theme Theater Perform a Skit

❶ Introduce the Activity Ask a few volunteers to retell "Martina the Beautiful Cockroach." Say: *Tell about the main events in your own words. Be sure to describe the characters.*

Brainstorm: *Imagine that more suitors came to ask for Martina's hand in marriage. Which animals might come to the balcony this time?* Have students brainstorm a list of animal suitors. Record their responses in a list.

Continue the discussion: *What do these new suitors look like? What do they say and do? How do they react to the Coffee Test?* Allow time for students to share their ideas.

❷ Plan Form casts of five to six students each. Have each cast create a skit about Martina's new suitors. Guide students at different proficiency levels to select appropriate roles, such as Martina, Abuela, and the suitors.

As students plan, have casts work together to create character webs for two or three animals on the list. Each web will show details about what the character looks like, says, does, and how he reacts. Tell students to refer to the webs as they develop dialogue. Remind them to stay on topic and use informal language in the conversations.

③ Rehearse As students rehearse, encourage them to incorporate actions, gestures, and expressions. Prompt with questions, for example: *How will a monkey show he is silly? How will an alligator show he is hungry?* Use **Multi-Level Strategies** to help students at each proficiency level.

Have students create or bring props from home. They can use construction paper and craft items to make headgear for Martina and Abuela. Provide boxes, construction paper, markers, scissors, glue, and tape for students to use in making the suitors' costumes.

④ Here Comes the Bride! Clear space and let the skits begin. Invite family members or another class to enjoy the performances. For each performance, select a group to assess for listening skills.

⑤ Debrief and Compare Ask each group to share what they enjoyed in the performance. Then have students compare and contrast their animal suitor characters with the characters in "Martina the Beautiful Cockroach." Have them add any ideas they learned about traditions to their unit concept map.

Differentiate

Multi-Level Strategies

BEGINNING

Provide language frames to help students plan one character's dialogue:

- The _____ looks like _____.
- He wants _____.
- He says, " _____."

Guide them to use the frames as they rehearse.

INTERMEDIATE

Provide a list of character traits, such as silly, hungry, frisky, scary, sleepy, and sneaky. Have students practice using actions, gestures, and expressions to show the traits.

ADVANCED ADVANCED HIGH

Challenge students to use idioms in their dialogue that reflect the suitors. A monkey, for example, might "monkey around" or act like an ape. A alligator might snap its jaws causing Martina to say, "See you later, alligator." A dog might be "barking up the wrong tree."

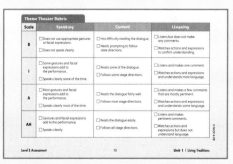

 Assessment Handbook page 10

Days 8-9
continued

Day at a Glance:
▶ **Language:** Theme Theater: Perform a Skit
▶ **Vocabulary:** Extend Vocabulary
▶ **Reading:** Read Leveled Books
▶ **Writing:** Paraphrase

OBJECTIVES

Vocabulary
• Extend Vocabulary through Wide Reading

Language
• Participate in Discussion

Reading
• Read Independently
• Summarize Reading
• Make Connections: Text to Text
• Apply Reading Strategies Varied Texts

Writing
• Paraphrase in Logical Order

Social Studies
• Explore Customs and Traditions

Resources

 Leveled Books:
- *A Picnic in October*
- *How My Parents Learned to Eat*
- *The Big Catch*
- *This Is the Way We Eat Our Food*
- *I Am Indian American*
- *Mexico: Culture and Celebrations*

Reach Leveled Library Lesson Plans

NGReach.com ›

Find more leveled readers about this topic.

Differentiate Read Leveled Books

Group students based on their reading abilities and interests. Use the **Guided Reading** routine (See page PD47) for books at students' instructional level. Use the **Independent Reading Support** (see page PD50) for books at students' independent reading level.

After reading, organize the students into heterogeneous groups to discuss what they read and to use the new information to answer the Big Question. Use these prompts to guide your discussion:

• What new information did you learn about how traditions help guide us?

• What surprised you?

• How did new information change your answer?

Fiction

BEGINNING LEVEL

A Picnic in October
by Eve Bunting

• **Genre:** Realistic Fiction

Tony's family visits the Statue of Liberty every year to celebrate his grandparents' arrival in the United States and the statue's birthday.

Key Words

braid

dock

millions

October

statue

INTERMEDIATE LEVEL

How My Parents Learned to Eat
by Ina R. Friedman

• **Genre:** Realistic Fiction

In World War II Japan, an American sailor and a Japanese woman learn the proper way to eat food in each other's cultures. Once they are married, they practice both customs with their daughter.

Key Words

chopsticks

fork

knives

restaurant

taught

ADVANCED   ADVANCED HIGH LEVELS

The Big Catch
by Gare Thompson

• **Genre:** Realistic Fiction

In this chapter book, a Vietnamese-American family struggles to fit into a Texas fishing community.

Key Words

ancestors

catch

customer

neighbor-hood

tradition

Nonfiction

BEGINNING LEVEL

This Is the Way We Eat Our Food
by Laine Falk

- **Genre:** Expository Nonfiction

Some kids eat with their hands. Others use a piece of bread like a spoon! In this book, students read about various mealtime customs from around the world.

Key Words

around

finished

fork

sip

tool

INTERMEDIATE LEVEL

I Am Indian American
by Lawrence Pelhan

- **Genre:** Expository Nonfiction

In this book, students are introduced to Karim, an American boy whose family is from New Dehli. Students read about East Indian heritage, including clothes, food, holidays, and beliefs.

Key Words

actually

continent

patters

respect

spices

ADVANCED   ADVANCED HIGH LEVELS

Mexico: Cultures and Celebrations
by Greg Banks

- **Genre:** Expository Nonfiction

Read all about Mexican culture. Students learn about Mexico's food, customs, clothing, art, and celebrations, as well as the ways past and modern cultures have influenced everyday life in Mexico.

Key Words

ancestors

language

national

pottery

victory

Daily Writing A AH

Journal Entry Have students write a journal entry in their reading journals. Use "Martina the Beautiful Cockroach" to model how to paraphrase in logical order. Present an example that does not maintain order by telling the end first. Have students share their journal entries with others, recommending books they enjoyed.

Same Book / Different Levels
B I A AH

Culture Clash
by Peter Winkler and Fran Downey

Experience what happened when the Spanish came to Mexico and collided with the powerful Aztecs and how the world was changed.

Pioneer Edition
Fountas and Pinnell: P–R

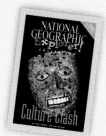

- **B** Conduct a Picture Walk.
- **I** Read text and captions.

Key Words

culture	empire
explorers	guest
language	prisoner

Pathfinder Edition
Fountas and Pinnell: Q–S

- **A** Read text and captions.
- **AH** Read and write responses to questions.

Key Words

conquistador	culture
explorers	immunity
language	migrated

Part 2 Vocabulary Skills Trace	Page
Day 1	Social Studies Vocabulary	T37
Day 2	Academic Vocabulary	T39
Day 3	Expand Word Knowledge	T42b
Day 4	Share Word Knowledge	T58b
Day 5	Apply Word Knowledge	T59b
Day 6	Idioms and Expressions	T60
Day 7	Idioms and Expressions	T65
Days 8–9	Extend Vocabulary	T66e–f
Day 10	Vocabulary Review	T66g–h

OBJECTIVES

Language
- Review Language Function: Ask for and Give Information ⊕

Language
- Review Compound Subjects, Compound Predicates, and, Subject-Verb Agreement

Vocabulary
- Review and Use Grade-Level Key Vocabulary ⊕
- Review Idioms and Expressions

Reading Strategy
- Review Monitor and Clarify ⊕

Comprehension and Literary Analysis
- Review Plot ⊕
- Review Genre: Folk Tale

Fluency
- Expression

Content Area
- Explore Customs and Traditions

Resources

- 🔊 *Key Word Images*
- ↻ 🔊 *Assessment Handbook*
- ↻ 🔊 *eVisual 1.29*
- 🔊 *Comprehension Coach*

Part 2 Grammar Skills Trace		Page
Day 2	Compound Subjects	T39a
Day 4	Compound Predicates	T58a
Day 7	Subject-Verb Agreement	T65a
▶ Day 10	Review Subject-Verb Agreement	T66g

Language of the Day

What did you learn? How does it help you in school?
I learned how to ____. ____ means to ____.
For example, ____.

Read the Language of the Day. Model: *I learned how to monitor my reading. It means to ask questions about what I don't understand. For example, if I am confused about something I read, I can reread or read on to see if the meaning becomes clear.* Prompt students to talk about a skill they learned.

Review and Assess

Use these interactive review activities to reinforce concepts covered in Part 2. Then use the assessment tools to evaluate students' progress. For more details about assessment, see page T71a.

Language Function

Ask for and Give Information

Use an **Inside-Outside Circle** to have students ask for and give information. Students outside the circle ask for information about students on the inside. Students inside the circle give the information. Have students rotate through the circle and then trade inside and outside roles.

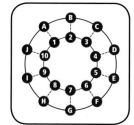
Inside-Outside Circle

- **Assessment:** Language Function Rubric on page 2 of the Assessment Handbook.

Grammar

Subject-Verb Agreement

Have students put their names and these subjects in a hat: *the boys, the girls, my sister, my brother.* Have students take turns drawing two names from the hat to form a compound subject. Then have them use that compound subject in a complete sentence with correct subject-verb agreement.

- **Assessment:** Grammar and Spelling Unit Test on pages 41–45 of the Assessment Handbook.

Vocabulary

Social Studies and Academic Vocabulary

Show **Key Word Images**. Have pairs prepare clues to the meaning of each word. Then ask pairs to present their clues one at a time to another pair. Have listeners try to guess the word. See which pair guesses the word with the fewest clues.

- **Assessment:** Key Word tests on pages 7–9 of the Assessment Handbook.

Key Words	
ancestor	marriage
belief	occasion
ceremony	relationship
custom	ritual
influence	role

Vocabulary Strategy

Word Work: Idioms and Expressions

Have partners find the meanings of these idioms: *all ears, eat your words, hit the books,* and *keep a straight face.* Challenge them to use the words in context sentences that reveal the meaning of each idiom. Students then present their sentences to another group for those students to figure out the meanings.

> When Dad said he had exciting news, I was all ears.

> Does all ears mean "listening carefully"?

• **Assessment:** Reading Unit Test on pages 14–39 of the Assessment Handbook.

Reading Strategy

Monitor and Clarify

Read aloud the first two paragraphs of "The Next to Be Married." Pause for students to monitor and clarify their understanding. Encourage the use of **Academic Language Frames,** for example: *What does* <u>bouquet</u> *mean? It means* <u>"a bunch of flowers."</u> Continue reading, pausing after each paragraph for students to ask questions.

• **Assessment:** Reading Strategy Test on page 11 of the Assessment Handbook.

Comprehension

Literary Analysis

Read aloud "The Next to Be Married." Have each student identify the features that help make this a folk tale.

Text Structure

Have the student relate the events of the plot. Remind him or her to tell what happens in the beginning, the middle, and at the end.

• **Assessment:** Reading Unit Test on pages 14–39 of the Assessment Handbook.

Fluency

Expression

Have students review their own recordings of "Martina the Beautiful Cockroach" in the Comprehension Coach. Then have students practice reading **Leveled Library Books** that are appropriate for their reading levels, focusing on accuracy, rate, and expression.

 Read Aloud

The Next to Be Married

Rena Rabbit had five sisters. They were all married with families. Only Rena remained unmarried and without bunnies of her own.

Rena's friends tried to help. Francie Fox said, "Whoever catches my bouquet is the next to be married." Francie threw the bouquet right at Rena, but Rena hopped too high. Tina Turtle caught the bouquet.

At Tina Turtle's wedding, Tina said, "Write your name on the bottom of my shoe. If your name is still there after the wedding, you are the next to be married." That night, only Greta Goose's name was on the shoe.

At Greta Goose's wedding, each guest got a tiny pin. Greta said, "Put the pin on your dress. If you lose the pin during the wedding, you are the next to marry."

Rena pinned the pin on her dress. She danced, jumped, and twirled. She forgot about the pin until Greta said, "Excuse me, everyone! Sammy Squirrel has found a pin."

Everyone was looking at Rena. She blushed as Sammy handed her the pin. Rena was finally getting married!

NGReach.com **eVisual 1.29**

Part 2 Vocabulary Skills Trace

Day		Page
Day 1	Social Studies Vocabulary	T37
Day 2	Academic Vocabulary	T39
Day 3	Expand Word Knowledge	T42b
Day 4	Share Word Knowledge	T58b
Day 5	Apply Word Knowledge	T59b
Day 6	Idioms and Expressions	T60
Day 7	Idioms and Expressions	T65
Days 8–9	Extend Vocabulary	T66e–f
▶ Day 10	Vocabulary Review	T66g–h

Mode and Form

An article based on an interview presents a conversation in question-and-answer form. For this project, students will interview a neighbor or family member about a tradition that interests them. Then students will write an article that tells about the person and describes the tradition.

Writing Checklist

A good article based on an interview

✔ begins by introducing the person interviewed and the topic

✔ lists the exact questions and answers in an order that makes sense

✔ ends with a interesting quotation from the person interviewed.

Ⓝ NGReach.com ❭ eVisual 1.30

Connect Reading to Writing Use "Josh Ponte: A Musical Journey" as a professional model of an article based on an interview. Reread the text and point out features of the form.

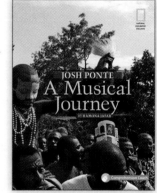

Writing Trait: Focus and Coherence

Students will learn how good writers maintain focus and create an article based on an interview in which:

- the beginning introduces the person being interviewed and the topic
- all questions and answers are about the same topic and flow from one to the next
- the article ends with a memorable quotation from the person being interviewed.

Lesson Overview and Pacing

Each lesson in the Writing Project provides detailed instruction. Teach the Writing Project during Part 2 of the unit with this suggested daily sequence and pacing plan, or adjust as your schedule and student needs require.

- Day 1: Introducing the Writing Prompt, Study a Model
- Day 2: Prewrite
- Day 3: Draft
- Day 4: Revise
- Day 5: Edit and Proofread
- Day 6: Publish

Classroom Vocabulary

Use **Vocabulary Routine 4** to teach focus and coherence . (See **Vocabulary Routines**, page PD40.)

Word Map

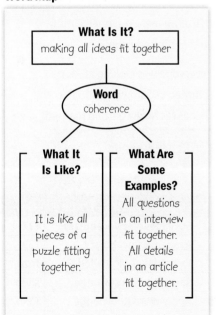

What Is It?
making all ideas fit together

Word
coherence

What It Is Like?
It is like all pieces of a puzzle fitting together.

What Are Some Examples?
All questions in an interview fit together. All details in an article fit together.

Rubric: Interview

Students use **Practice Master 1.21** to score their own writing on the trait of focus and coherence. You can then use the *Reach* Writing Rubric to score each student's project on all traits.

Writing Rubric

Score Point	Focus and Coherence	Organization	Development of Ideas	Voice and Style	Written Conventions
4	**Focus** Paragraphs and the writing as a whole are focused. Ideas are related. Details are relevant. **Completeness** The writing feels complete. The introduction and conclusion are meaningful.	**Structure** The organizing strategy is well-suited to the writer's purpose. **Progression of Ideas** Ideas flow logically and smoothly, with meaningful transitions.	**Content Quality** The writer takes a risk and treats the topic in an interesting way, with insight and thoughtfulness. **Elaboration** Ideas are developed in depth.	**Individuality** The writing sounds genuine and unique. **Word Choice** Words and phrases are interesting and appropriate to the writer's purpose and audience.	**Grammar, Usage, Mechanics, and Spelling** There are only a few errors. **Sentence Fluency** Sentences are varied and effective.
3	**Focus** Paragraphs and the writing as a whole are mostly focused, but there are a few sudden shifts between ideas. Most details are relevant. **Completeness** The writing feels mostly complete. The introduction and conclusion add some meaning.	**Structure** The organizing strategy is generally suited to the writer's purpose. **Progression of Ideas** Most ideas flow logically and smoothly, but there are a few gaps.	**Content Quality** The writer does not take much of a risk, but does treat the topic in a thoughtful way. **Elaboration** Some ideas are more developed than others.	**Individuality** For the most part, the writing sounds genuine and unique. **Word Choice** Words and phrases are mostly interesting and appropriate to the writer's purpose and audience.	**Grammar, Usage, Mechanics, and Spelling** Errors are minor and/or infrequent. **Sentence Fluency** There is some sentence variety. Sentences are generally effective.
2	**Focus** Paragraphs and the writing as a whole are somewhat focused, but there are a number of sudden shifts between ideas. Some details are relevant. **Completeness** The writing feels somewhat complete. The introduction and conclusion may be superficial.	**Structure** The organizing strategy is not clear or does not suit the writer's purpose. **Progression of Ideas** There are breaks in logic and very few transitions.	**Content Quality** The topic is covered, but in an uninteresting way. **Elaboration** Ideas are listed or mentioned superficially.	**Individuality** A few passages sound genuine and unique. **Word Choice** Words and phrases are somewhat interesting and appropriate to the writer's purpose and audience.	**Grammar, Usage, Mechanics, and Spelling** Errors are frequent, but the meaning is clear. **Sentence Fluency** Sentences are somewhat awkward and have simple or inaccurate words.
1	**Focus** The writing is not focused. Ideas are unrelated. Many details are irrelevant. **Completeness** The writing feels incomplete. If there is an introduction and conclusion, they may be perfunctory.	**Structure** No organizing strategy is evident. **Progression of Ideas** Writing is illogical, wordy, and/or repetitious.	**Content Quality** The topic is not really covered. **Elaboration** There is little or no development of ideas.	**Individuality** There is little or no sense of the writer. **Word Choice** Words and phrases are not appropriate to the writer's purpose and audience.	**Grammar, Usage, Mechanics, and Spelling** Errors are severe and/or frequent and are a barrier to understanding. **Sentence Fluency** Sentences are awkward and have missing or misused words.

OBJECTIVES
Writing

- Analyze a Student Model: Interview
- Trait: Evaluate for Focus and Coherence ❶
- Use a Rubric to Analyze Writing

Resources

 eVisual 1.30

 Practice Master 1.21

eVisual 1.31

Introduce the Writing Project

❶ Analyze the Prompt Ask a volunteer to read aloud the title of the project and the prompt. As the student reads, have the rest of the class begin to fill out the first three sections of a RAFT:

Role: reporter
Audience: classmates
Form: article based on interview
Topic: _____

Remind students that although they haven't decided on a specific topic, the prompt gives them a broad subject to begin thinking about. Ask them what that subject is. (a tradition that interests the student) Explain that they will be choosing a topic for their writing when they do the Prewrite step.

Focus on language: *Who is the audience?* (classmates) Ask them how that will affect the language they use. (It will be more informal, with words that are familiar to kids their age.)

Study a Model

❷ Focus on Features Read aloud the directions and then have the students read the model silently. Remind students to notice how the questions flow smoothly from one to the next and that the interview ends with an interesting quotation.

Chorally reread the model, stopping to discuss each callout. Display the **Writing Checklist** and have students find examples of each feature in the model.

Writing Checklist

A good article based on an interview

- ✔ begins by introducing the person interviewed and the topic
- ✔ lists the exact questions and answers in an order that makes sense
- ✔ ends with a interesting quotation from the person interviewed.

NGReach.com ⟩ **eVisual 1.30**

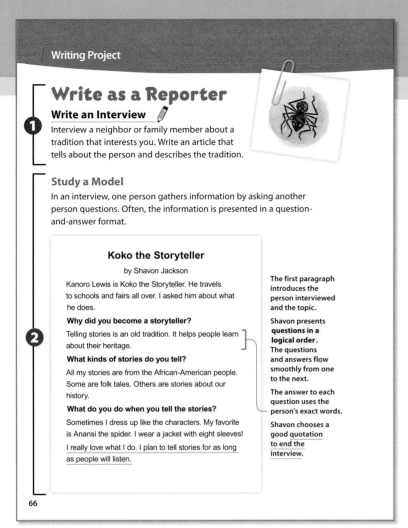

Write as a Reporter

① Write an Interview

Interview a neighbor or family member about a tradition that interests you. Write an article that tells about the person and describes the tradition.

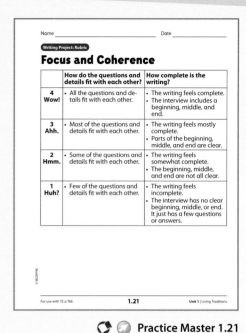

Study a Model

In an interview, one person gathers information by asking another person questions. Often, the information is presented in a question-and-answer format.

②

Koko the Storyteller

by Shavon Jackson

Kanoro Lewis is Koko the Storyteller. He travels to schools and fairs all over. I asked him about what he does.

Why did you become a storyteller?

Telling stories is an old tradition. It helps people learn about their heritage.

What kinds of stories do you tell?

All my stories are from the African-American people. Some are folk tales. Others are stories about our history.

What do you do when you tell the stories?

Sometimes I dress up like the characters. My favorite is Anansi the spider. I wear a jacket with eight sleeves! I really love what I do. I plan to tell stories for as long as people will listen.

The first paragraph introduces the person interviewed and the topic.

Shavon presents **questions in a logical order**. The questions and answers flow smoothly from one to the next.

The answer to each question uses the person's exact words.

Shavon chooses a good **quotation** to end the interview.

66

Student Book page 66

Name _____ Date _____

Writing Project: Rubric

Focus and Coherence

	How do the questions and details fit with each other?	How complete is the writing?
4 Wow!	• All the questions and details fit with each other.	• The writing feels complete. • The interview includes a beginning, middle, and end.
3 Ahh.	• Most of the questions and details fit with each other.	• The writing feels mostly complete. • Parts of the beginning, middle, and end are clear.
2 Hmm.	• Some of the questions and details fit with each other.	• The writing feels somewhat complete. • The beginning, middle, and end are not all clear.
1 Huh?	• Few of the questions and details fit with each other.	• The writing feels incomplete. • The interview has no clear beginning, middle, or end. It just has a few questions or answers.

For use with TE p T66   1.21   Unit 1 | Living Traditions

Practice Master 1.21

---

③ Teach the Trait

Ask: *When you are focused on doing something, such as playing basketball really well, how are you thinking?* (I am thinking only about basketball. Nothing is distracting me.) Define: *When an interview has focus and coherence, the introduction and all the questions and answers are related, and the writing feels complete.* Find examples in the model:

- *What is the focus of the interview?* (why Koko is a storyteller and how he tells stories)

- *Why is the introduction important to the focus of the interview?* (It gives background about the person interviewed.)

- *How do the questions help give focus and coherence to the interview?* (They are all related to the topic.)

④ Present the Rubric

Distribute **Practice Master 1.21** Read aloud the questions and features of each score point. Assign partners the task of telling you the difference between a paper with a score of 2 and one with a score of 4. Allow time for the partners to review the rubric and then report. (Students' responses should indicate that a 4-point paper has clearer focus and coherence.) Use the **Academic Language Frames** to support students of all proficiency levels.

> **CHECK PROGRESS** Ask students to explain how questions in dark print help them understand the focus of the interview.

Differentiate

Academic Language Frames

Discuss the Rubric

■ 1. It   has   focus and coherence.
                does not have

   2. The article   has   an introduction,
                     does not have questions, and strong
                                    end.

▬ 1. A four-point interview has _____.
■ 2. The first paragraph introduces _____ and _____.
   3. The questions are in a _____ order.

▬ A 4-point interview has a clear _____, but the _____
■ of the 2-point paper is unclear.

   In a 2-point interview, the questions _____, but in a
   4-point paper, the questions _____.

NGReach.com > eVisual 1.31

OBJECTIVES

Learning and Teamwork Strategies
- Generate Ideas through Brainstorming
- Use Graphic Organizers: 5Ws Chart

Writing
- Writing Process (Prewrite): Select a Topic, Organize Ideas

Resources

 eVisual 1.32

 Practice Master 1.22

Prewrite

1 Choose a Topic Review: *What is the subject of our interview?* (a tradition each of us finds interesting) *Now we will brainstorm traditions to select a specific topic. When you brainstorm, you write down all your ideas.* Display and discuss the following guidelines:

> - Say or write whatever you are thinking about traditions.
> - Use words, phrases, details from a selection, details that your family and friends have shared, and pictures.
> - Don't think about whether an idea is strong or weak. Just write it.

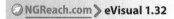 **NGReach.com > eVisual 1.32**

With a volunteer, model using the **Language Frames** to brainstorm traditions and take notes of your ideas. Then have partners brainstorm and select a tradition. To help narrow the topics, remind students that they also have to identify a neighbor or family member to interview about the tradition.

2 Gather Information Remind students that they must talk to a neighbor or family member to gather information. Also remind them that they should write the questions in a logical order and write answers in the person's exact words.

> Discuss the 5Ws Chart on page 67 with students. Then have them use the chart as a model to create their own chart to develop interview questions with a logical flow.

Have students work with a partner to rehearse asking their questions. Partners can then revise or delete any as necessary. For the actual interview, provide students with recording devices, if possible. Remind students to take careful notes. Encourage them to ask for clarification if the person being interviewed says a word, phrase, or special term they don't understand. Also remind students to thank the person for the interview.

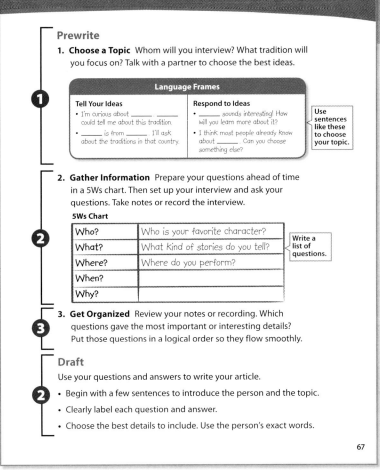

Prewrite

1. **Choose a Topic** Whom will you interview? What tradition will you focus on? Talk with a partner to choose the best ideas.

Language Frames	
Tell Your Ideas	**Respond to Ideas**
• I'm curious about _____ _____ could tell me about this tradition.	• _____ sounds interesting! How will you learn more about it?
• _____ is from _____ . I'll ask about the traditions in that country.	• I think most people already know about _____ . Can you choose something else?

Use sentences like these to choose your topic.

2. **Gather Information** Prepare your questions ahead of time in a 5Ws chart. Then set up your interview and ask your questions. Take notes or record the interview.

5Ws Chart

Who?	Who is your favorite character?
What?	What kind of stories do you tell?
Where?	Where do you perform?
When?	
Why?	

Write a list of questions.

3. **Get Organized** Review your notes or recording. Which questions gave the most important or interesting details? Put those questions in a logical order so they flow smoothly.

Draft

Use your questions and answers to write your article.

• Begin with a few sentences to introduce the person and the topic.

• Clearly label each question and answer.

• Choose the best details to include. Use the person's exact words.

67

Student Book page 67

Name _____ Date _____

Writing Project: Prewrite

5Ws Chart

Complete the 5Ws Chart for your interview.

Who?	
What?	
Where?	
When?	
Why?	

© NGSP&HB

For use with TE p. T67b **1.22** Unit 1 | Living Traditions

Practice Master 1.22

---

3 Get Organized Remind students that an article based on an interview begins with interesting information about the person interviewed and then includes interesting questions and answers in a logical order.

Briefly review the 5Ws Chart on page 67. Reinforce the trait of focus and coherence by reminding students that all the questions fit together; they all ask about Koko's work as a storyteller.

Distribute **Practice Master 1.22.** Ask: *What is the word that will begin your question on the first line?* (Who) Have students provide examples of questions that begin with *Who.* (example: *Who taught you how to cook?*) Continue with the remaining question words.

Have students review their interview notes or recording to complete their own 5Ws Charts. Use **Multi-Level Strategies** to support students at each proficiency level.

CHECK PROGRESS Check 5Ws charts. Then ask students to trade charts and discuss whether each question is interesting—and whether all questions have focus and coherence. Have them circle the most interesting question.

Differentiate

Multi-Level Strategies

BEGINNING

Have students dictate simple questions for their interviews.

INTERMEDIATE

Have students record the most important question they asked for each category and its answer.

ADVANCED ADVANCED HIGH

Ask students to record both their main questions and answers and the follow-ups. Tell them to include any interesting details they learned.

OBJECTIVES
Writing

- Writing Process (Drafting): Write an Interview
- Use Writing Strategies: Write a Strong Beginning
- Develop Writer's Craft: Use Precise Words

Draft

1 Introduce Drafting Use the **Modeled Writing Routine** (See **Writing Routines**, page PD54.) to show students show how to turn their 5Ws charts and interview notes into a draft. Students will focus on:

- **Writer's Craft: Use Precise Words** Introduce: *Good writers use precise words to tell readers exactly what they mean.* Have students look at the model on page 66 and read the second sentence. Then write the following: *He travels all over.* Ask students to compare the two sentences and explain which is more precise. (He travels to schools and fairs all over.) Discuss the importance of precise words to show the reader exactly what the writer means. Tell students to be sure to use precise words in their drafts.

- **Writing Strategy: Write a Strong Beginning** Explain: *A strong beginning for an interview introduces the person interviewed and explains the interview's purpose. It catches the readers attention and makes the reader want to read on.* Have students look at the model on page 66 and explain why this interview has a strong beginning.

Say	Write
My first paragraph should introduce the person interviewed and explain the interview's purpose. I interviewed Koko.	Kanoro Lewis is Koko the Storyteller. He travels to schools and fairs all over. I asked him about what he does.
I have asked my questions, but I need to organize the ideas in a logical order. First I need to have a question and answer that explain why Koko became a storyteller.	Why did you become a storyteller?
I know my readers will want to know what kinds of stories Koko tells. I write that question next.	What kinds of stories do you tell?
Finally, I want to know tell readers about what Koko does when telling stories.	What do you do when you tell stories?
Pause to review focus and coherence. Ask: *Is the interview focused so far?* (yes) *Do all the questions s fit together?* (yes) *Now I will record Koko's answers from my notes. These are Koko's exact words. I will choose a good quote to end the interview.*	
How do I finish my interview? (with an interesting quotation from Koko)	I really love what I do. I plan to tell stories for as long as people will listen.

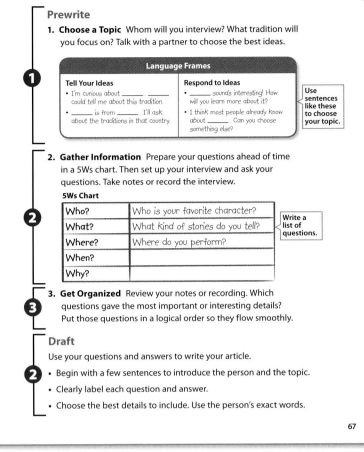

Prewrite

1. **Choose a Topic** Whom will you interview? What tradition will you focus on? Talk with a partner to choose the best ideas.

> **Language Frames**
>
> **Tell Your Ideas**
> - I'm curious about _____ . _____ could tell me about this tradition.
> - _____ is from _____ . I'll ask about the traditions in that country.
>
> **Respond to Ideas**
> - _____ sounds interesting! How will you learn more about it?
> - I think most people already know about _____ . Can you choose something else?

Use sentences like these to choose your topic.

2. **Gather Information** Prepare your questions ahead of time in a 5Ws chart. Then set up your interview and ask your questions. Take notes or record the interview.

5Ws Chart

Who?	Who is your favorite character?
What?	What kind of stories do you tell?
Where?	Where do you perform?
When?	
Why?	

Write a list of questions.

3. **Get Organized** Review your notes or recording. Which questions gave the most important or interesting details? Put those questions in a logical order so they flow smoothly.

Draft

Use your questions and answers to write your article.

- Begin with a few sentences to introduce the person and the topic.
- Clearly label each question and answer.
- Choose the best details to include. Use the person's exact words.

67

Student Book page 67

2 Write the Draft Have students begin their own drafts. Use **Multi-Level Strategies** to support writers at all levels of language proficiency.

Drafting Tip: Drafting can sometimes go more smoothly when you work with a partner. The partner can give you ideas as you work.

Remind students: *Your chart and notes may contain fragments or incomplete ideas. Check that every sentence in your draft is a complete sentence.*

> **CHECK PROGRESS** Have students circle precise words in their drafts. Ask them to explain why each is a precise word.

Differentiate

Multi-Level Strategies

BEGINNING

Have students point to each question in the draft. Then have them point to each answer. If they are confused as to which blocks of text are questions and which are answers, point out examples in the "Koko" model as you guide them in developing their drafts.

INTERMEDIATE

Provide sentence frames to guide students in requesting help with drafting:
- I need help with ____.
- I think I should ____.
- Could you show me how to ____.

ADVANCED   ADVANCED HIGH

Tell partners to show their drafts to one another and discuss any problems they are experiencing. Suggest they use the Koko model to point out ways to help one another properly develop the drafts.

OBJECTIVES

Listening, Speaking, and Teamwork Strategies
- Conduct a Peer Conference
- Prompt and Provide Suggestions

Writing
- Writing Process (Revise)
- Revise Drafts for Focus and Coherence ❶
- Revise Drafts for Logical Order and Sufficient Detail
- Use Revising Marks (Insert, Transpose)

Resources

- 🧭 eVisual 1.33
- 🔄 🧭 Practice Master 1.23
- 🧭 eVisual 1.34

Differentiate

Multi-Level Strategies

BEGINNING

Hold individual conferences with these students. Check to be sure each one has included sufficient detail and placed question-answer sets in a logical order.

INTERMEDIATE

Tell partners to ask and answer:
- *Have I included enough detail?*
- *Are all my questions in an order that makes sense?*

ADVANCED ADVANCED HIGH

Have these students hold complete peer conferences. Direct them to point out strengths, as well as problems. Also, tell them to provide suggestions for improvement.

Revise

❶ Read, Retell, Respond Review the trait on **Practice Master 1.23**. Then use **eVisual 1.33**. to model how to conduct a peer conference. Have students read the paragraph aloud.

> ### Koko the Storyteller
>
> Kanoro Lewis is Koko the Storyteller. He travels all over.
>
> Q: What kinds of stories do you tell?
>
> A: All my stories are from the African-American people.
>
> Q: Why did you become a storyteller?
>
> A: Telling stories is an old tradition. It helps people learn about their heritage.
>
> Q: What do you do when you tell stories?
>
> A: Sometimes I dress up like the characters. My favorite is Anasi the spider. I wear a jacket with eight sleeves.

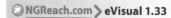

NGReach.com ❯ eVisual 1.33

Point to the **Language Frames** as you retell the story and make suggestions:

- *Your interview is about Koko the storyteller. The tradition that Koko talked about was telling stories. The most interesting thing I learned was that Koko sometimes dresses up like the characters.*

- *I'd like to know more about the kinds of stories Koko tells. Could you check Koko's answers to add details Koko gave you when you asked this question?*

- *The sequence of questions doesn't seem logical. Could you move the question "Why did you become a storyteller" to the beginning?*

Have pairs discuss their drafts. Use **Multi-Level Strategies** to support students at all proficiency levels.

❷ Make Changes Read through the samples. Then use **eVisual 1.33** to model how to revise a draft. Display and use the Revising Marks as you work through the example.

Explain: *During the peer conference, my reader gave me a lot of suggestions. I've also looked at the rubric again to see what a Score 4 should contain.*

Model the first change: *I could add more detail to the first paragraph to better introduce the topic and explain the purpose of the interview.*

Call on students to suggest additional changes that would turn the model into a 4. Have students use **Practice Master 1.23** for additional practice.

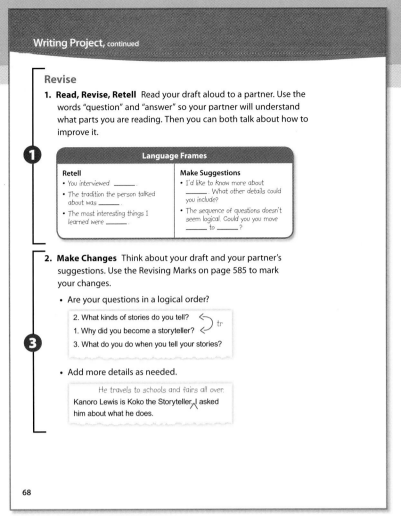

Revise

1. Read, Revise, Retell Read your draft aloud to a partner. Use the words "question" and "answer" so your partner will understand what parts you are reading. Then you can both talk about how to improve it.

Language Frames	
Retell	**Make Suggestions**
• You interviewed _____ .	• I'd like to know more about _____ . What other details could you include?
• The tradition the person talked about was _____ .	
• The most interesting things I learned were _____ .	• The sequence of questions doesn't seem logical. Could you move _____ to _____ ?

2. Make Changes Think about your draft and your partner's suggestions. Use the Revising Marks on page 585 to mark your changes.

• Are your questions in a logical order?

> 2. What kinds of stories do you tell?
> 1. Why did you become a storyteller?
> 3. What do you do when you tell your stories?   tr

• Add more details as needed.

> He travels to schools and fairs all over.
> Kanoro Lewis is Koko the Storyteller. I asked him about what he does.

68

Student Book page 68

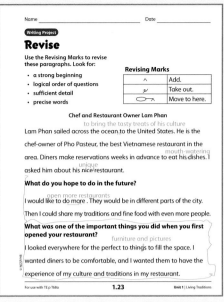

Practice Master 1.23

---

3 Revise the Draft Tell students to use the Revising Marks and begin revising their own drafts. Remind them to review the rubric and notes from their peer conference.

Post examples as a reminder to include precise words and enough detail in their first paragraph:

Weak Beginning

Bich Trang has a restaurant. I asked her about what she does.

Strong Beginning

Bich Trang is the chef-owner of Pho Pasteur, the best Vietnamese restaurant in the area. Diners reserve weeks in advance to eat her mouth-watering dishes. I asked her about what she does.

 **NGReach.com** ▸ **eVisual 1.34**

CHECK PROGRESS As students revise, check to make sure that they have used precise words in their interviews and that they have ordered the questions in a logical way. The beginning should introduce the person interviewed and the topic.

OBJECTIVES

Listening and Speaking

- Adjust Volume, Pitch, and Tone
- Use Visuals
- Visualize
- Make Connections

Writing

- Writing Process (Edit and Proofread): Edit for Spelling, Grammar, and Mechanics
- Writing Process (Publish and Share): Create a Final Copy; Read Writing Aloud

Grammar, Spelling, and Mechanics

- Use Complete Sentences
- Subject-Verb Agreement
- Check Spelling (Compound Words)
- Capitalize Sentences
- Use End Marks (Avoid Comma Splices)

Resources

  Practice Master 1.24

eVisual 1.35

Focus on Grammar: Compound Subjects: Subject-Verb Agreement

Review: *The verb in a sentence must agree with the subject.* Write: *Luz goes.*

Circle *Luz*. Say: *Luz is the subject of the sentence.* Underline *goes*, and draw an arrow from *goes* to *Luz*. Say: *The verb* goes *agrees with the subject* Luz. Luz *is one person, so* goes *is the correct verb.*

Repeat the procedure with the sentence *Luz and Kam go.*

Write the following sentences. Have students write the correct verb for each sentence.

Jo _____ . see/sees (sees)

Jo and Tia _____ see/sees (see)

Yoko _____ . say/says (says)

Yoko and Ian _____ . say/says (say)

Assign **Practice Master 1.24** for additional practice.

Edit and Proofread

1 **Focus on Spelling: Compound Words** Remind students that a compound word is a word made of two or more smaller words. Tell students they can sometimes, but not always, tell the meaning of a compound word based on the smaller words that form it. Suggest students check a dictionary if they are not certain of the meaning of a compound word.

Write *airplane* on the board. Ask: *What are the two smaller words that form the word* airplane? *(air plane)* Repeat with *indoor (in door)* and *cannot (can not).*

Display the following words. Have partners work together to write the two words that form each compound word.

everywhere (every where)	forever (for ever)
snowflake (snow flake)	doorknob (door knob)
homework (home work)	popcorn (pop corn)

Assign **Practice Master 1.24** for additional practice.

2 **Focus on Mechanics: Avoiding Comma Splices** Explain: *Each complete sentence must express a complete thought. It must have a subject and a predicate. You should not combine two complete sentences with a comma. Instead, you should write a period at the end of the first sentence and begin a second sentence with a capital letter.*

Guide students in correcting the following comma splices. Reinforce the concept: *Do not use a comma to separate two complete sentences.*

We like yogurt, we also like pizza.
(We like yogurt. We also like pizza.)

There are lists, you can sign up now.
(There are lists. You can sign up now.)

Assign **Practice Master 1.24** for additional practice.

3 **Edit and Proofread** Display the **Editing Marks** as partners work together to edit and proofread their articles.

Provide and model the editing tip: *Notice the highlights in the model. Use the highlights and the information about this text to make a checklist. Check off the items on your checklist while you edit. Pause to correct each error when you see it.*

Editing Marks

∧	Add
⌒	Take out
⊙∧	Move to here.
sp	Check spelling.

NGReach.com > eVisual 1.35

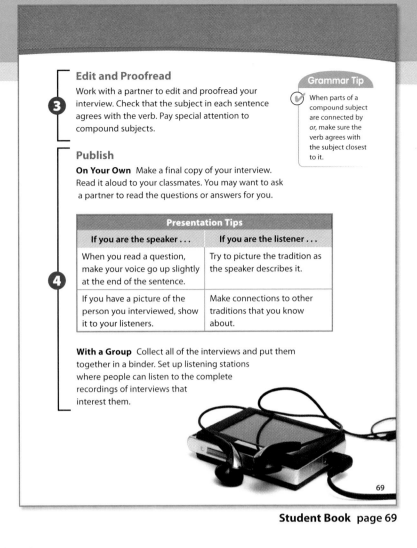

Edit and Proofread

3 Work with a partner to edit and proofread your interview. Check that the subject in each sentence agrees with the verb. Pay special attention to compound subjects.

Grammar Tip

When parts of a compound subject are connected by *or*, make sure the verb agrees with the subject closest to it.

Publish

On Your Own Make a final copy of your interview. Read it aloud to your classmates. You may want to ask a partner to read the questions or answers for you.

4

Presentation Tips	
If you are the speaker . . .	**If you are the listener . . .**
When you read a question, make your voice go up slightly at the end of the sentence.	Try to picture the tradition as the speaker describes it.
If you have a picture of the person you interviewed, show it to your listeners.	Make connections to other traditions that you know about.

With a Group Collect all of the interviews and put them together in a binder. Set up listening stations where people can listen to the complete recordings of interviews that interest them.

69

Student Book page 69

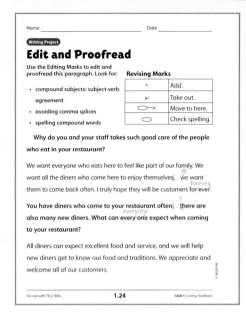

Practice Master 1.24

Publish

3 Share Your Interview Encourage students to make a neat final copy of the interview. Then they may read it aloud or illustrate it and give it to another student to read.

- **Speak with Expression:** Help your listener better understand your article by making your voice rise at the end of each question. This will help the listener understand that you have just finished reading a question and you will next be reading the answer.

- **Use Visuals:** Show a picture of the person interviewed—if you have one. If not, try to find other pictures that show something important mentioned in the interview. This will help readers better understand and enjoy the reading.

- **Visualize:** As you listen, try to picture the tradition as the speaker describes it. This will help the tradition become clear and alive for you.

- **Make Connections:** As you listen, make connections to other traditions you know. The tradition in the interview can become more interesting and easier to understand when you connect it to something you already know.

Have students include photos or illustrations with their interviews. If students have recorded their interviews, set up listening stations in the classroom and keep a copy of the final interviews nearby. Then put the interviews together and copy or scan them.

Add a copy of each interview in the appropriate student's Writing Portfolio.

OBJECTIVES

Concepts and Vocabulary
- Use Grade-Level Vocabulary ❶
- Use Academic Vocabulary ❶
- Use Learning Strategies: Graphic Organizers

Language
- Language Function: Express Opinions; Express Ideas; Ask for and Give Information
- Discuss Ideas

Social Studies
- Explore Customs and Traditions

Resources

- pens or pencils
- colored markers, colored pencils, or crayons
- paper
- supplies to make a time capsule container

Community Connection

Discuss with students cultural festivals or ceremonies that take place in your community. Ask students who have attended these events to describe sights, sounds, tastes, and smells they experienced. Encourage students to attend one of these occasions with friends or families.

Language of the Day

What have you learned about the importance of traditions?

I have learned ＿＿＿＿.

Read the Language of the Day. Model: *I have learned that* **traditions** *are important because they help people pass on their* **culture**. Have students share other answers to the question.

Talk Together

① **Complete the Unit Concept Map** Read aloud the introduction. Encourage students to skim the selections in the unit, review the **Leveled Library** books they read, and think about class discussions.

Use these possible answers to the unit concept map to guide the discussion.

Concept Map

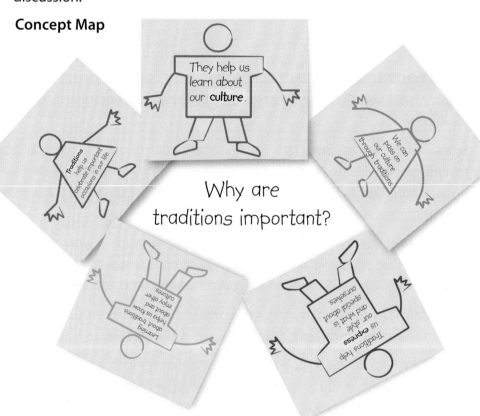

② **Write a Description** Read aloud the directions. Have students look back at Luka's interview on page 41 to reread the description of a tradition. Remind students to include interesting details in their descriptions.

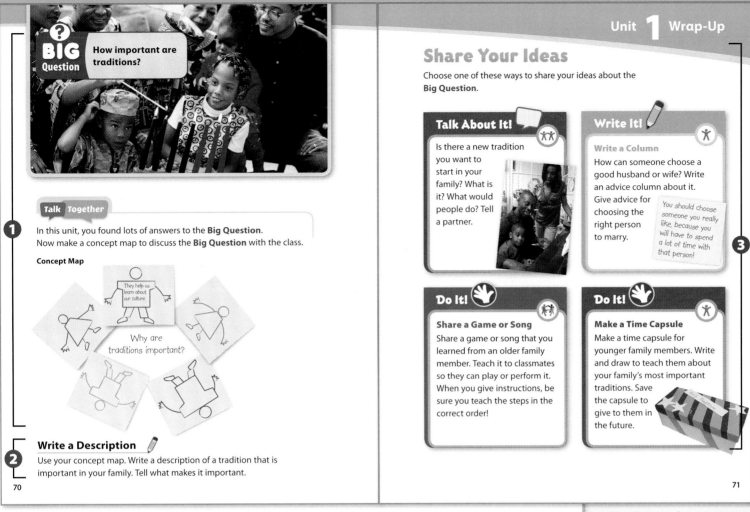

BIG Question How important are traditions?

Talk Together

1 In this unit, you found lots of answers to the **Big Question**. Now make a concept map to discuss the **Big Question** with the class.

Concept Map

They help us learn about our culture

Why are traditions important?

Write a Description

2 Use your concept map. Write a description of a tradition that is important in your family. Tell what makes it important.

70

Share Your Ideas

Choose one of these ways to share your ideas about the **Big Question**.

Talk About It!

Is there a new tradition you want to start in your family? What is it? What would people do? Tell a partner.

Write It!

Write a Column

How can someone choose a good husband or wife? Write an advice column about it. Give advice for choosing the right person to marry.

You should choose someone you really like, because you will have to spend a lot of time with that person!

Do It!

Share a Game or Song

Share a game or song that you learned from an older family member. Teach it to classmates so they can play or perform it. When you give instructions, be sure you teach the steps in the correct order!

Do It!

Make a Time Capsule

Make a time capsule for younger family members. Write and draw to teach them about your family's most important traditions. Save the capsule to give to them in the future.

3

71

Student Book pages 70–71

Share Your Ideas

3 **Select and Present** Read aloud the presentation options. Explain that some options can be completed alone, but that others involve working in groups. You may choose to assign students to specific activities or allow them to self-select.

Oral Activity: Talk About It! **B** **I** Remind students that traditions often involve food, music, decorations, games, and special clothing. Encourage students to incorporate at least two of these into their tradition.

Writing Activity: Write a Column **I** **A** **AH** Suggest that students create a cause-and-effect chart showing good qualities for partners and reasons those traits are important. Encourage students to include some of these ideas in their writing.

Kinesthetic Activity: Share a Game or Song **B** **I** **A** **AH** Demonstrate how to teach a song or the steps of a game bit by bit. For example, sing one line and have students echo it after you. Then go on to the next line. Encourage students to teach their song or game in a similar manner.

Kinesthetic Activity: Make a Time Capsule **I** **A** **AH** Encourage students to label their drawings with phrases or sentences to identify and explain each tradition.

4 **Respond and Close** Have students share what they think is the most important reason we have traditions.

Keys to Efficacy

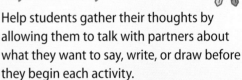

Help students gather their thoughts by allowing them to talk with partners about what they want to say, write, or draw before they begin each activity.

Administer the assessments below to monitor progress and identify which students will benefit from review, reteaching, or additional practice.

Tested Skills	Assessment Tools	Review and Reteaching
Oral Language		
❶ Express Feelings ❶ Ask for and Give Information	• Part 1, Day 10 TE page T36g; 🔁 💿 page 2 • Part 2, Day 10 TE page T66g; 🔁 💿 page 2	💿 Reteaching and Review Activities
❶ Retell a Story	• Part 1, Day 5 TE page T27c; 🔁 💿 page 6 • Part 2, Day 5 TE page T59c; 🔁 💿 page 10	Preview and model how to complete the graphic organizers. Provide additional books for practice and re-testing. • Leveled Library • Explorer Book Collection 💿 Leveled Book Finder
Vocabulary		
❶ Content Vocabulary ❶ Academic Vocabulary ❶ Use a Dictionary ❶ Idioms and Expressions	🔁 💿 ☑ 💿 Part 1 Key Words Test, page 3 🔁 💿 ☑ 💿 Part 2 Key Words Test, page 7 🔁 💿 ☑ 💿 Reading Unit Test, page 14 **B** **I** **A** **AH**	Use the Vocabulary Reteaching Routine (PD43). 💿 Vocabulary Games 💿 Reteaching and Review Activities 💿 My Vocabulary Notebook
Reading		
Reading Comprehension ❶ Strategy: Plan and Monitor ❶ Text Structure: Main Idea and Details ❶ Literary Analysis: Plot **Reading Fluency** ❶ Phrasing ❶ Expression ❶ Accuracy and Rate	🔁 💿 Reading Strategy Test, page 11 🔁 💿 ☑ 💿 Reading Unit Test, page 14 **B** **I** **A** **AH** **Comprehension Coach** 🔁 💿 Fluency Practice Masters, pages 1.7 and 1.17 🔁 💿 ☑ Fluency Benchmark Assessment, page 441	**Review Comprehension** Review the test items. Point out the correct response for each item and discuss why it is correct. 💿 Leveled Library lesson plans **Review Fluency** Use Fluency Routines (PD52) and Fluency Passages from Unit 1. Have students listen to the fluency model as they follow along in the text.
Grammar and Writing		
Grammar ❶ Complete Sentences ❶ Simple Subjects and Predicates ❶ Compound Subjects ❶ Compound Predicates ❶ Subject-Verb Agreement **Writing** ❶ Writing Trait: Organization	🔁 💿 ☑ 💿 Grammar Unit Test, page 41 **B** **I** **A** **AH** 🔁 💿 ☑ 💿 Writing Unit Test, page 47 **I** **A** **AH** 🔁 💿 Writing Rubrics, Forms, and Checklists, page 469 🔁 💿 Writing Self-Assessment and Peer Assessments, page 482	**Grammar** Review Grammar Rules boxes and eVisuals from this unit. Use Handbook pages to reteach with additional examples. 💿 Reteaching and Review Activities **Writing** To reteach the writing process or writing traits, use Handbook pages. 💿 Reteaching and Review Activities
Other Measures		

🔁 💿 Unit Self-Assessment, page 13   🔁 💿 Affective Measures, pages 462–465   🔁 💿 Metacognitive Measures, pages 466–468

Key: ❶ Tested Skill   🔁 Assessment Handbooks   💿 NGReach.com   ☑ eAssessment   💿 ExamView

Animal
Intelligence

BIG Question Just how smart are animals?

Part 1 What can we learn from animals?

Part 2 How do animals show their intelligence?

Curriculum Connections

Content Connection	Unit 2	Theme Connection
• Animal Behavior		• Learning and Intelligence

Reading

Student Anthology
Pages 72–143

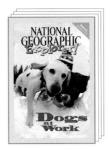

Explorer Books Collection
Dogs at Work
Do Elephants Talk?

Non-Fiction Library

Fiction Library

Sing with Me Language Songs
Pages 8–11

Assessment

Assessment Handbook
Pages 55–108

Practice Masters and Manipulatives

Language and Literacy Teamwork Activities
Pages 11–16
Cross-Curricular Teamwork Activities
Pages 11–16

Practice Masters
Pages 2.1–2.22

Language Builder Picture Cards
Pages E14–E26

Newcomer

In The U.S.A.
Resources for Newcomers

Phonics

Reach into Phonics
See Teacher's Edition
Pages T28–T53

NGReach.com

Reach into Teaching

- Online Lesson Planner
- Teaching Resources
- Presentation Tool
- eEdition NG Digital Library
- eAssessment: Online Tests Scan and Score Reports

Reach into Learning

- My Vocabulary Notebook
- Vocabulary Games
- Personalized Dictionaries
- NG Digital Library
- Comprehension Coach

Recordings

- Songs and Chants CD
- Selection Recordings CD
- Fluency Models CD

Unit 2 Planner

Student Book

UNIT LAUNCH

- Build Background Video
- Introduce the  **BIG** Question

	LANGUAGE	VOCABULARY	READING

PART 1

Weeks 1 and 2
Focus: Animal Behavior

LANGUAGE

Language Function
- ❶ Express Ideas
- Engage in Discussion

Grammar
- ❶ Kinds of Sentences
- ❶ Questions

Listening & Speaking
- Listen Actively

How to Learn Language
- Find Patterns in Language

Theme Theater
- Extend the Story

VOCABULARY

Key Words
- ❶ Science Vocabulary

  adaptation   predator   trait
  defend   prey

- ❶ Academic Vocabulary

  behavior   response   survival
  characteristic   strategy

- ❶ Basic Vocabulary: Food

  chicken   hot dog   soup
  chips, salsa   pizza   taco
  egg   salad
  hamburger   sandwich

- ❶ Homophones

READING

Reading Strategy
- ❶ Make Connections

Genre
- Trickster Tale

Text Structure
- ❶ Analyze Characters

Literary Analysis
- ❶ Characters

Genre
- Trickster Tale

Literary Analysis
- Dialogue

Leveled Library

Reading Fluency
- ❶ Expression
- ❶ Accuracy and Rate

PART 2

Weeks 3 and 4
Focus: Animal Intelligence

LANGUAGE

Language Function
- ❶ Engage in Conversation
- Tell an Original Story

Grammar
- ❶ Compound Sentences
- ❶ Complex Sentences
- ❶ Understand Compound Sentences

Listening & Speaking
- ❶ Use Gestures and Expressions

How to Learn Language
- Relate to Personal Experience

Oral Language Project
- TV Talk Show

VOCABULARY

Key Words
- ❶ Science Vocabulary

  command   memory   skill
  imitate   pattern   tool

- ❶ Academic Vocabulary

  ability   inherit   learn
  communication   language

- ❶ Basic Vocabulary: Greetings and Good-Byes

  Hi. /Hey.
  Hello./Hello.
  Hi there./Hello.
  Hello./Good morning.
  Bye./See you later.

  Good-bye.
  Have a nice day./Good-bye.
  See you soon./Bye.
  Good-bye./Good-bye.

- ❶ Use a Dictionary

READING

Reading Strategy
- ❶ Make Connections

Genre
- Science Article

Text Structure
- ❶ Main Idea and Details

Text Feature
- Photographs and Captions

Genre
- Science Article

Literary Analysis
- Writer's Style

Leveled Library

Reading Fluency
- ❶ Intonation
- ❶ Accuracy and Rate

❶ = Tested Skill

WRITING	LEARNING STATIONS	REVIEW, ASSESS, RETEACH
Daily Writing • Writing Fluency • Fanciful Story • Writer's Craft: Characteristics • E-Mail • Journal Entry • Short Story with Dialogue	Animal Sense Write Your Own Investigate an Animal Trickster Tale Research an Animal A Tricky Story	**Oral Language Rubrics** • Express Ideas • Analyze a Character • Theme Theater: Listening, Speaking, Content **Vocabulary Test** • Key Words: Content Vocabulary • Key Words: Academic Vocabulary
Daily Writing • Writing Fluency • List • Paragraph • Journal Entry • Writing Project: Business Letter	Design a Test Animal Math Facts About Service Animals Shades of Meaning Listen and Respond Make an Animal Album	**Oral Language Rubrics** • Engage in Conversation • Explain a Story • Oral Language Project: Listening, Speaking, Content **Vocabulary Test** • Key Words: Content Vocabulary • Key Words: Academic Vocabulary **Reading Test** • Reading Strategy: Make Connections

UNIT WRAP-UP

Answer the
 **BIG Question**

Unit 2 Assessment
• Self-Assessment
• Reading B I A AH
• Grammar B I A AH
• Writing I A AH

Home Connection

Send home **Family Newsletter 2**.

Students talk with family members about the benefits and responsibilities of being a pet owner. Together, st write and illustrate a short essay about how to care for a pet.

Animal Intelligence

1 Preview and Predict Read the unit title aloud and encourage students to flip through the unit. Ask: *What do you think you will learn? What makes you think that?*

2 Introduce the Big Question Ask: *What are some other words for* smart? (bright, intelligent, clever) *There are many ways to be smart. What ways can you think of?* (solving problems, remembering facts, knowing how to make things)

Read aloud the Big Question. Have students share possible answers. Encourage them to provide details. List the answers.

3 Build Background Preview the video: *Now we will play a video that tells us about animal intelligence. We'll see examples of smart things animals can do.*

▶ Play the video.

⊙ NGReach.com › **Build Background Video**

Discuss the video:

• *What are some smart things animals do?*

• *What is an example of something an animal is born knowing how to do?*

• *What is an example of something an animal can learn from its parents or a human?*

• *Tell about something smart that an animal you know can do.*

• *Do you think the ideas in this video would be harder or easier to learn if the author presented it as a magazine article? Why?*

4 Share What You Know Review the three steps of the directions. Explain: *To complete the activity, you will need to think about:*

• *animals you know or have seen*

• *how the animal you choose looks and acts*

Have students take a few moments to list animals they know. Then ask them to look at the list and identify the animal they think is most special. Next, have them list words to describe that animal. Tell students to circle at least three of those traits to show in their drawing.

Provide sentence frames students may use to discuss their drawing: *This is _____. [She/He] is special because _____. [She/He] can _____.*

Animal Intelligence

Student Book pages 72–73

5 **Begin the Unit Concept Map** Introduce the concept map: *As you go through this unit, it will be helpful to organize your thinking in a concept map.*

Display the unit concept map for the Big Question. Explain: *The Big Question is restated in the mother duck. We'll write our answers in the baby ducks.*

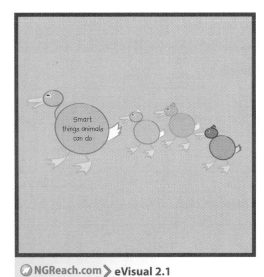

NGReach.com > eVisual 2.1

Have students add the ideas they already listed, and any other ideas they may have, to **Practice Master 2.1.** Explain that they will add more to the concept maps as they read through the unit and learn more about the smart things that animals do.

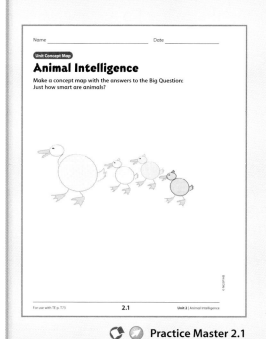

Practice Master 2.1

Talk About the **BIG** Question	Page
Begin the Unit Concept Map	T72–T73
Link to Content Vocabulary	T75
Link to "Love and Roast Chicken"	T97
Link to "Mouse Deer and Farmer"	T104a
Link to Content Vocabulary	T107
Link to "Animal Smarts"	T129
Link to "The Clever Chimps of Fongoli"	T136a
Share Your Ideas	T143

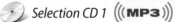
PART 1

Days 1–5

▶ Main Selection
Love and Roast Chicken, a Trickster Tale from the Andes Mountains, written and illustrated by Barbara Knutson

▶ Genre
Trickster Tale

▶ Selection Summary
This tale follows the adventures of Cuy the Guinea Pig as he outsmarts Tío Antoni the Fox and prevents Tío Antoni from eating him. Tío Antonio swears revenge on Cuy, but after being tricked by Cuy more than once, Tío Antonio vows to stay away from Cuy.

SELECTION AWARDS

- *Foreword Magazine:* Book of the Year Award, Bronze Finalist, 2004
- *Society of School Librarians:* International Book Awards Honor Book, 2005
- *Bank Street College of Education:* Best Children's Books of the Year, 2004
- *American Library Association:* Notable Children's Books, 2005

Selection CD 1 (((MP3)))

Skills at a Glance	
Language	Express Ideas; Engage in Discussion; Theme Theater
Grammar	Kinds of Sentences; Questions
Vocabulary	Science Vocabulary: *adaptation, defend, predator, prey, trait*
	Academic Vocabulary: *behavior, characteristic, response, strategy, survival*
	Homophones
Reading Strategy	Make Connections
Literary Analysis	Analyze Characters
Writing	Writing Fluency; Fanciful Story; Writer's Craft: Human Characteristics; E-mail; Journal Entry; Short Story with Dialogue
Newcomer Support	Use *In the USA:* food words

▶ Companion Selection

Mouse Deer and Farmer, a Trickster Tale from Southeast Asia, adapted from a story told by Aaron Shepard, illustrations by Meilo So

▶ Genre

Trickster Tale

▶ Selection Summary

This tale follows the adventures of Mouse Deer as he steals vegetables from Farmer's garden. He escapes the Farmer once, but gets locked up the second time. In the end, the clever Mouse Deer tricks the Farmer's dog into letting him go.

 AUTHOR AWARDS

Aaron Shepard
- ***Storytelling World Magazine:*** Storytelling World Resource Award, Honor, 2008
- ***American Folklore Society:*** Aesop Accolade, 1996, 1997

Connect Across Texts You read about a guinea pig who outwits a fox. Now read another trickster tale and compare **survival** skills.

Genre **Trickster tales** often reflect the culture or place they come from.

Mouse Deer and Farmer
A Trickster Tale from Southeast Asia

adapted from a story told by **Aaron Shepard** • *illustrations by* **Meilo So**

Mouse Deer loved to eat the fruits, roots, and **shoots** of the forest, but he loved the vegetables in Farmer's garden even more. One day, he stepped into the garden and sniffed a **juicy cucumber**.

In Other Words
shoots young, soft plants
juicy cucumber tasty green vegetable ▶

▶ **Before You Move On**
1. **Character's Motive** Why does Mouse Deer step into the vegetable garden?
2. **Setting** Describe Farmer's garden.

99

Leveled Library Books

Differentiated Instruction

B BEGINNING

An Interview with Harry the Tarantula

by Leigh Ann Tyson

Katy Did of KBUG radio interviews Harry the Tarantula, who tells about his fascinating life as one of the world's creepiest spiders.

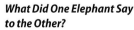

What Did One Elephant Say to the Other?

by Becky Baines

Elephants don't need words to communicate. They use their whole bodies to "talk" to each other and other animals.

I INTERMEDIATE

Dolphin Rescue

by Glen Phelcan

In this chapter book, students learn about dolphin intelligence when an injured baby dolphin is rescued and successfully returned to its parents.

Creepy Creatures

by Sneed B. Collard III

In this book, students read about some creatures that seem scary (and may even be dangerous), but will quickly discover that they are trying to survive just like we are.

A ADVANCED **AH ADVANCED HIGH**

The World According to Humphrey

by Betty G. Birney

A substitute teacher brings a hamster named Humphrey to school. Humphrey explains what you can learn about yourself by taking care of another species.

Do Animals Have Feelings Too?

by David L. Rice

True animal stories show examples of animals that experience feelings of compassion, joy, love, and grief.

Unit 2 Daily Planner

BIG Question — Just how smart are animals?

PART 1

Core Lessons

	Day 1 Introduce Academic Language	**Day 2** Introduce More Academic Language
Language 5–10 minutes	**Language of the Day** *T74* ❶ **Language Function: Express Ideas** *T74* **Oral Language** • Talk About Animal Behavior *T75* • Talk Together About the Big Question *T75*	**Language of the Day** *T77a* ❶ **Grammar: Kinds of Sentences** *T77a* **Oral Language** • Talk Together About Making Connections *T78*

Vocabulary
10–15 minutes
	❶ **Science Vocabulary**
	• Introduce Words *T75*
	  adaptation predator trait
	  defend prey
	Classroom Vocabulary
	• Introduce Word: **analyze** *T76*
		❶ **Academic Vocabulary**
		• Introduce Words *T77*
		  behavior strategy
		  characteristic survival
		  response

Reading 15–20 minutes	❶ **Literary Analysis: Analyze Characters** • Introduce Analyzing Character *T76a* • Use Graphic Organizers: Character Chart *T76* **Read Aloud: "Raccoon Run-in"** *T76a*	❶ **Strategy: Make Connections** • Introduce and Practice the Strategy *T78* **Read "Three City Raccoons"** *T79* **Phonics and Fluency** • Short ĕ *T78*
Writing 15 minutes	**Daily Writing** • Writing Fluency *T76*	**Daily Writing** • Fanciful Story *T79*
Content: Integrated Throughout Each Day	**Science** • Explore Animal Intelligence • Investigate Animal Adaptation	**Science** • Explore Animal Intelligence • Investigate Animal Adaptation

Ready-to-Go Plans
▶ Time (20, 30, 40, 60, 90 minutes per day)
▶ Model (Content Focus, Literacy Focus, Dual Language)

Online Lesson Planner
🖉 NGReach.com

Day 3

Build Academic Language

Language of the Day T80a
Language Function: Engage in Discussion T80a ((MP3))
Listening and Speaking
• Listen to and Chant T80a

❶ Academic and Science Vocabulary
• Expand Word Knowledge T80b

adaptation   characteristic

behavior   defend

Support Newcomers
• Build Basic Vocabulary: Food Words T80b

Read the Selection
❶ Strategy: Make Connections T80–95
• Reading Options T82
Concepts of Print
• Directionality T83
Literary Analysis
• Use of Spanish Words T90–93
❶ Fluency: Expression T94

Daily Writing
• Modeled Writing: Writer's Craft T95

Home Connection
• Animal Stories T84–85
Math
• Word Problems T86–87
Science
• Eucalyptus Trees T88–89

Day 4

Build Academic Language

Language of the Day T96a
❶ Grammar: Questions T96a
Oral Language
• Talk About the Selection T96c

❶ Academic and Science Vocabulary
• Share Word Knowledge T96b

predator   response   survival

prey   strategy   trait

Think and Respond
• Talk About the Selection T96c
• Test-Taking Strategy T96c
❶ Fluency: Expression T96c

Daily Writing
• Independent Writing: Write About It T96

Science
• Explore Animal Intelligence
• Investigate Animal Adaptation

Day 5

Build Academic Language

Language of the Day T97a
Listening and Speaking
• Listen Actively T97a
How to Learn Language
• Find Patterns in Language T97a
Oral Language
• Talk Together About the Big Question T97

❶ Academic and Science Vocabulary
• Apply Word Knowledge T97b

Reread and Retell
❶ Literary Analysis: Analyze Characters
• Make a Character Chart T97c
❶ Analyze a Character T97c
❶ Fluency: Accuracy, Rate, and Expression T97c

Daily Writing
• Interactive Writing: Journal Entry T97

Science
• Explore Animal Intelligence
• Investigate Animal Adaptation

PART 1

Core Lessons	Day 6	Day 7
	Expand Academic Language	**Expand Academic Language**
Language 5–10 minutes	**Language of the Day** T98a ❶ **Language Function: Express Ideas and Engage in Discussion** T98a **Oral Language** • Talk Together About the Big Question T104a	**Language of the Day** T105a ❶ **Grammar: Kinds of Sentences** T105a
Vocabulary 10–15 minutes	❶ **Homophones** T98 **Support Newcomers:** • Additional Homophones T98	❶ **More Homophones** T105 • Dictionary Entries T105
Reading 15–20 minutes	**Read the Trickster Tale** T99a • Reading Options T99a ❶ **Strategy: Make Connections** T99a—T102–103 **Literary Analysis** • Genre T100–T101 **Literary Analysis** • Sound Words T100–T101 ❶ **Fluency: Accuracy and Rate** T104 **Respond and Extend** • Compare Characters' Adventures T104a	**Reread the Selection: Focus on Dialogue** T106a
Writing 15 minutes	**Daily Writing** • Writing Fluency T104	**Daily Writing** • Modeled Writing: Short Story with Dialogue T106b
Content: Integrated Throughout Each Day	**Science** • Explore Animal Intelligence • Investigate Animal Adaptations	**Science** • Explore Animal Intelligence • Investigate Animal Adaptations

Apply Academic Language

Theme Theater
- Introduce the Activity *T106c*
- Plan *T106c*
- Rehearse *T106d*
- Curtains Up! *T106d*
- Debrief and Compare *T106d*

Read Leveled Books

Fiction *T106e*

 **B**

 **I**

 **A** **AH**

Key Words

breathe   hind
burrow   poison
cricket

Key Words

blowhole   shark
echo   surface
mammal

Key Words

according   humans
anxious   stroked
creatures

Nonfiction *T106f*

 **B**

 **I**

 **A** **AH**

Key Words

calves   grumble
danger   trumpet
greet

Key Words

control   shark
prey   tentacles
scales

Key Words

devotion   loyalty
grief   mate
happiness

Daily Writing
- Journal Entry *T106f*

Review and Assess

Interactive Review *T106g–T106h*
- ❶ Language Function: Express Ideas
- ❶ Grammar: Kinds of Sentences
- ❶ Vocabulary: Science and Academic Vocabulary
- ❶ Vocabulary Strategy: Homophones
- ❶ Reading Strategy: Make Connections
- ❶ Literary Analysis: Trickster Tale
- ❶ Text Structure: Analyze Characters
- ❶ Fluency: Accuracy, Rate, and Expression

Assessment *T106g–T106h*

Same Book, Different Levels

 **I** **A** **AH**

Key Words

breed   disease   search
commands   impaired   service
disabilities rescue   skills

Reading Station

EXPLORER! COLLECTION
Ladder Text:
- Pioneer edition for below level readers
- Pathfinder edition for on and above level readers

DECODABLE TEXTS

TRADE BOOK COLLECTION
Use the **Leveled Book Finder** at
NGReach.com

Content Stations

Download complete lesson plans NGReach.com ›

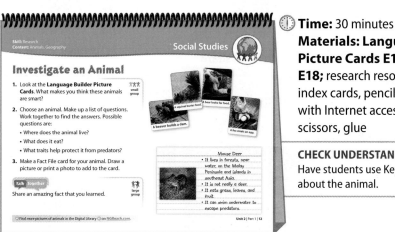

Skill: Research, Classify
Content: Animal Adaptations

Science

Animal Sense

1. Go online to watch videos of animals. Find out about adaptations for survival. ★★ partners
2. Take notes. Identify an adaptation that helps the animal survive. Identify the animal, too.

Talk Together ★★★ small group

Share your notes. What are some different ways that animals survive? Make a chart. List animals for each category.

	Make Warning Sound	Use Tools	Hide	Move Fast
snow				
monkeys				
whales				
crickets				

To view videos of animal adaptations, go to NGReach.com.

Unit 2 | Part 1 | 11

Time: 40 minutes
Materials: computers with Internet access, paper, pencils

CHECK UNDERSTANDING
Ask students to name an animal and tell how the animal adapts to survive.

Skill: Research
Content: Animals, Geography

Social Studies

Investigate an Animal

1. Look at the **Language Builder Picture Cards.** What makes you think these animals are smart? ★★★ small group
2. Choose an animal. Make up a list of questions. Work together to find the answers. Possible questions are:
   - Where does the animal live?
   - What does it eat?
   - What traits help protect it from predators?
3. Make a Fact File card for your animal. Draw a picture or print a photo to add to the card.

Talk Together ★★ large group

Share an amazing fact that you learned.

Mouse Deer
- It lives in forests, near water, on the Malay Peninsula and islands in southeast Asia.
- It is not really a deer.
- It eats grass, leaves, and fruit.
- It can swim underwater to escape predators.

Find more pictures of animals in the Digital Library on NGReach.com.

Unit 2 | Part 1 | 12

Time: 30 minutes
Materials: Language Builder Picture Cards E14, E15, E17, E18; research resources; lined index cards, pencils, computers with Internet access and printer, scissors, glue

CHECK UNDERSTANDING
Have students use Key Words to talk about the animal.

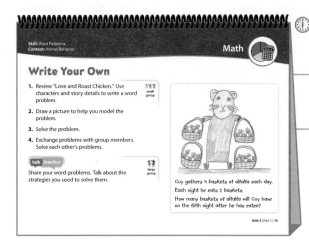

Skill: Word Problems
Content: Animal Behavior

Math

Write Your Own

1. Review "Love and Roast Chicken." Use characters and story details to write a word problem. ★★★ small group
2. Draw a picture to help you model the problem.
3. Solve the problem.
4. Exchange problems with group members. Solve each other's problems.

Talk Together ★★ large group

Share your word problems. Talk about the strategies you used to solve them.

Cuy gathers 4 baskets of alfalfa each day. Each night he eats 2 baskets.
How many baskets of alfalfa will Cuy have on the fifth night after he has eaten?

Unit 2 | Part 1 | 13

Time: 30 minutes
Materials: paper, pencils, colored markers and crayons

CHECK UNDERSTANDING
Ask students to use their pictures to talk about the math problem.

Use these resources to provide daily opportunities for students to work individually or in groups at learning stations around the classroom.

Language Stations

Download complete lesson plans **@NGReach.com** >

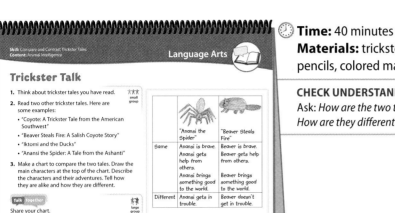

Time: 40 minutes
Materials: trickster tales, paper, pencils, colored markers and crayons

CHECK UNDERSTANDING
Ask: *How are the two trickster tales alike? How are they different?*

Time: 30 minutes
Materials: research resources

CHECK UNDERSTANDING
Have students tell what they know about their partner's animal.

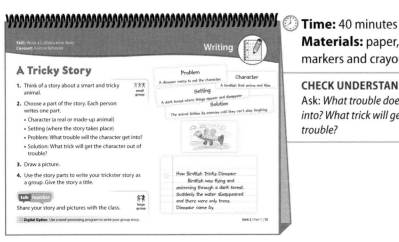

Time: 40 minutes
Materials: paper, pencils, colored markers and crayons

CHECK UNDERSTANDING
Ask: *What trouble does the character get into? What trick will get the character out of trouble?*

Technology Station

Access resources **@NGReach.com** >

 **Recordings**

- Raccoon Talk
- A Discussion
- Love and Roast Chicken

 **Digital Library**

Learn vocabulary and practice language

- Key Word Images
- Language Builder Picture Cards

 **My Vocab Notebook**

- Add Words

 **Comprehension Coach**

- Use interactive library support. Automatically measure fluency.

Online Assessment

- Practice items in standardized test format.

Day 1

Day at a Glance:
- ▶ **Language:** Express Ideas
- ▶ **Vocabulary:** Science Vocabulary
- ▶ **Reading:** Analyze Characters
- ▶ **Writing:** Writing Fluency

OBJECTIVES

Vocabulary
- Acquire and Use Grade-Level Key Vocabulary: predator, trait ⊙

Language
- Language Function: Express Ideas ⊙
- Listen to and Imitate Fluent Models
- Use a Variety of Language Structures
- Participate in Discussion ⊙

Learning and Teamwork Strategies
- Activate Prior Experience
- Use Media to Build Language
- Use Context to Build Concepts and Language

Science
- Examine Animal Intelligence
- Identify Animal Adaptations

Resources

- 📖 🔊 *Sing With Me Language Song Book page 8*
- 💿 🔊 *Sing With Me Language Song CD 1, Tr 9,10*
- 🔊 *eVisual 2.2*
- *eVisual 2.3*
- 🔊 *Key Word Images*
- 📧 *Language Builder Picture Card E19*

ⓃNGReach.com ›

See **Technology Station** for digital student resources.

Differentiate

Academic Language Frames

Express Ideas

I'm going to talk about _____.
- ■ I think _____
  I know _____.

_____

I'm going to say a few things about _____.
- ■ I think _____
  I know _____
  I also know that _____.

_____

I'm going to say a few things about _____.
- ■ I think _____ and _____.
- ■ I know _____.
  I also know that _____.
  That's why I think that _____.

ⓃNGReach.com › eVisual 2.3

Language of the Day

What's your favorite animal? What do you know about it?

_____ are my favorite animal. _____ are _____.

Read aloud the Language of the Day. Say: *Tigers are my favorite animal. Tigers are big and have stripes.* Invite students to share about their favorite animals. Make a class chart or collage of favorite animals. Explain that students will be listening, speaking, and writing more about animals today.

Express Ideas

① **Teach/Model** Point out the dialogue on page 74. Read the introduction aloud and play the song. Invite students to listen for the voices of the two speakers as you play the selection a second time. Model how to echo and chime in as the audio prompts.

Display the how to card. Point out the **Language Frames** and model using these structures to express ideas about an animal you have seen.

How to Express Ideas	
1. Name the topic.	I'm going to say a few things about parrots.
2. Tell what you think.	I think that parrots are beautiful.
3. Tell what you know.	I know parrots live in South America. I also know that parrots make good pets.

ⓃNGReach.com › eVisual 2.2

Prompt students to share information they know about an animal. Point to each step on the How to card as the students express ideas.

② **Practice/Apply** Have students express ideas about the pictures shown on the Unit Opener or about the work they did in Share What You Know. Use **Academic Language Frames** to encourage students to use language naturally to express ideas with different kinds of sentences.

CHECK UNDERSTANDING Display **Language Builder Card E19** (cat) and have students express ideas about it.

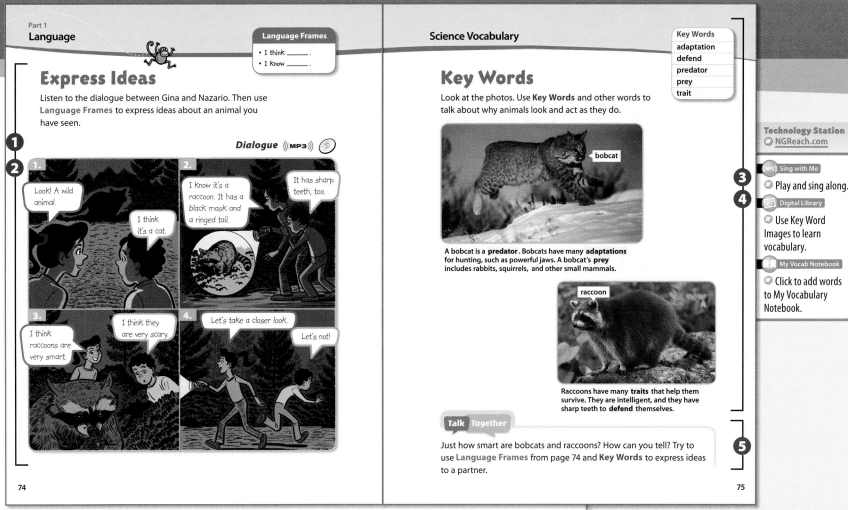

Student Book pages 74–75

Science Vocabulary

3 **Teach/Model** Read the introduction and discuss the photographs. Use **Vocabulary Routine 1** and **Key Word Images** to teach the words. Access definitions on page pages 616–639.

1. **Pronounce** the word and point to the picture of the bobcat: **predator**.

2. **Rate** the word. Have students hold up their fingers to show how well they know the word. (1 = very well, 2 = a little, 3 = not at all) Ask: *What do you know about this word?*

3. **Define** the word: *A predator is an animal that hunts other animals for food.*

4. **Elaborate** Relate the word to your experience; for example: *My cat thinks she is a predator. She hunts for birds, but she hasn't caught one yet!*

4 **Practice/Apply** Have partners take turns repeating the routine for each word, using complete sentences for steps 2, 3, and 4.

5 **Talk Together About the Big Question**
Check Understanding and Connect Concepts Review the **Language Frames** on page 74 and provide an example:

> *I think that chimpanzees are very intelligent. They have many of the same* **traits** *as humans. I know chimps take care of their young. They can also make and use tools. That's why I think they are very smart.*

Add the ideas to your Unit concept map.

Differentiate

Spanish Cognates ▶

adaptation/adaptación; defend/ defender; predator/depredador; prey/presa

Part 1 Vocabulary Skills Trace		Page
Day 1	**Science Vocabulary**	**T75**
Day 2	Academic Vocabulary	T77
Day 3	Expand Word Knowledge	T80b
Day 4	Share Word Knowledge	T96b
Day 5	Apply Word Knowledge	T97b
Day 6	Homophones	T98
Day 7	Homophones	T105
Days 8–9	Extend Vocabulary	T106e–f
Day 10	Vocabulary Review	T106g–h

Day 1
continued

Day at a Glance:
▶ **Language:** Express Ideas
▶ **Vocabulary:** Science Vocabulary
▶ **Reading:** Analyze Character
▶ **Writing:** Writing Fluency

OBJECTIVES

Vocabulary
- Acquire and Use Classroom Vocabulary: **analyze**
- Acquire and Use Grade-Level Vocabulary: **trait** ⊕

Comprehension and Literary Analysis
- Demonstrate Listening Comprehension
- Analyze Character

Learning and Teamwork Strategies
- Use Graphic Organizers: Character Chart Reason Deductively

Writing
- Develop Writing Fluency
- Monitor and Self-Correct Writing

Science
- Explore Animal Intelligence
- Investigate Animal Adaptations

Resources

- eVisual 2.4
- eVisual 2.5
- Practice Master 2.2

Differentiate

Multi-Level Strategies

BEGINNING

Provide a sentence starter for each section of the chart, for example:

- Gina does _____.
- Gina says _____.
- Gina is _____.

INTERMEDIATE

Remind students to look at the dialogue for examples of what the character says. Point out that dialogue appears inside quotation marks.

ADVANCED   ADVANCED HIGH

Encourage students to discuss each character's traits and to give examples of words and actions that show those traits.

Analyze Characters

1 Teach Connect concepts: *What Key Words have you learned to help you express ideas about animals? You learned that each animal has unique traits, or characteristics. Characters in stories have traits, too. Now you will learn how to make a character chart to help you identify a character's traits.* Teach Classroom Vocabulary word *analyze*.

Read the first paragraph. *When you analyze characters, look at what they say and do. A character's words and actions show what the character is like.* Have a pair of students read the cartoon. Ask: *What do you learn about Nazario and Gina from their words and actions?* (Gina finds raccoons interesting; Nazario is scared of them.)

Read aloud the explanation about making a graphic organizer. Clarify the purpose: *I can make a character chart to help me identify each character's traits.* Remind students to listen for the characters' words and actions as you read "Raccoon Run-in" aloud.

> **Read Aloud**
>
> ### Raccoon Run-in
>
> Gina loves exploring the backyard at night. She sees a raccoon. Gina shines a flashlight on the animal so she can get a better look at it. "Raccoons are interesting," says Gina. Nazario hides behind Gina. He trembles and says, "Raccoons are scary." *CRACK!* "AAAAAA!" screams Nazario as he runs inside the house.
>
> ● NGReach.com ▶ eVisual 2.4

2 Model Review the first four sentences of "Raccoon Run-in." Have volunteers read the second row of boxes in the character chart and model the process: *I record what the character does and says. This helps me figure out the character's traits. Gina watches the raccoon. She wants to get a closer look at it. She says it is interesting. This shows me Gina is curious and brave.* Have volunteers repeat for the third row of boxes.

3 Practice/Apply Read aloud the instructions. Distribute **Practice Master 2.2** for students to use as they complete their charts. Use **Multi-Level Strategies** to help students at all proficiency levels talk about character traits. Monitor students' develop proficiency. (See page R2 for Proficiency Level Descriptions.)

> **CHECK UNDERSTANDING** *What are Nazario's traits?* (shy, scared) *How does Nazario show he is scared?* (He screams and runs away.)

Analyze Characters

Writers describe **characters**. You can also tell what characters are like by:

- what they say or do
- how they act with each other.

Read the cartoon. Find out more about Nazario and Gina.

Map and Talk

You can make a character chart to analyze characters. Write each name. Then fill in what the character does and says. Tell what these details show about the character.

Character Chart

Character	What the Character Does	What the Character Says	What It Shows
Gina	watches a raccoon	Raccoons are interesting.	She is curious. She is brave.
Nazario	screams, runs away	Raccoons are scary.	He is shy. He is scared.

Talk Together

Tell your partner about another character you have read about. Describe the character's **traits**. Make a character chart with your partner.

76

Student Book page 76

Daily Writing

 Writing Fluency Use the **Power Writing Routine**. (See page PD53.) Write the word traits and prompt: *What traits do you have? Think about this word and write about it.*

Power Writing Routine

 1. What do you know about the word or picture?

 2. Take one minute to write as much as you can, as well as you can.
   B words   **I** sentences   **A** **AH** paragraphs

 3. Check your spelling and grammar. (Circle) mistakes.

 4. Count your words.

NGReach.com ▸ eVisual 2.5

CLOSE AND ASSESS

- **Language** *Express your ideas about raccoons. What do you know about this animal?* (Students should use information from the dialogue in their answers.)

- **Reading** *Think about Gina and Nazario. What does each character say? What does this tell you about their traits?* (Gina wants a closer look. Nazario says raccoons are scary. Gina is brave and Nazario is scared.)

- **Vocabulary** *What Key Words did you use in your answers?* (Answers will vary.)

Classroom Vocabulary

Use **Vocabulary Routine 4** to teach **analyze**. (See **Vocabulary Routines, page PD40.**)

Three-Fold Tab

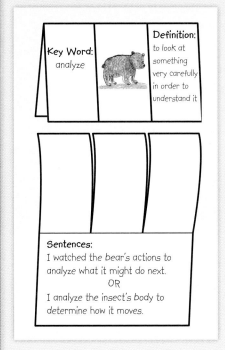

Key Word: analyze

Definition: to look at something very carefully in order to understand it

Sentences:
I watched the bear's actions to analyze what it might do next.
OR
I analyze the insect's body to determine how it moves.

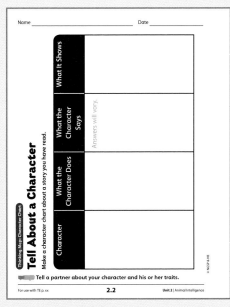

Name _____ Date _____

Tell About a Character
Make a character chart about a story you have read.

Character	What the Character Does	What the Character Says	What It Shows
		Answers will vary.	

Tell a partner about your character and his or her traits.

For use with TE p. xx   2.2   Unit 2 | Animal Intelligence

 **Practice Master 2.2**

Day 2

Day at a Glance:
- ▶ **Language:** Kinds of Sentences
- ▶ **Vocabulary:** Academic Vocabulary
- ▷ **Reading:** Make Connections
- ▷ **Writing:** Fanciful Story

OBJECTIVES

Vocabulary
- Acquire and Use Academic Vocabulary: **behavior** ❶
- Use Grade-Level Vocabulary: **defend**

Grammar
- Recognize Kinds of Sentences ❶

Learning and Teamwork Strategies
- Make Connections Across Content Areas

Resources

- ⊘ eVisual 2.6
- ⟳ ⊘ Practice Master 2.3
- ⊘ Key Word Images

◯NGReach.com❯

See **Technology Station** for digital student resources.

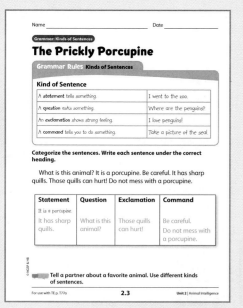

⟳ ⊘ **Practice Master 2.3**

> ## Language of the Day
> How do animals defend themselves?
> Some animals defend themselves with _____ .

Read the Language of the Day. Model: *Some animals defend themselves with sharp teeth.* Create a web and encourage students to share their ideas. Then explain that students will look at words they can use to talk about animals.

Grammar Kinds of Sentences 🅱 🅘 🅐 🄰🄷

❶ **Teach/Model** Write these sentences. Have students identify the subject and predicate in sentences 1 and 2. (bobcats/find; they/are)

> 1. Bobcats find food in the wild.
> 2. They are predators.
> 3. Don't pet wild animals.

Ask: *What is the subject in sentence 3?* Have students suggest answers. Then say: *This kind of sentence is called a "command." The subject is not named, but it is the person you are speaking to.* Display the chart and say: *Actually, there are four different kinds of sentences.* Read the explanations and sentences. Have students suggest other sentences for each type.

Kinds of Sentences	Example
A statement tells something.	Raccoons have sharp teeth.
A question asks something.	Do raccoons bite?
An exclamation shows strong feeling.	Those teeth are sharp!
A command tells you to do something.	Stay away from raccoons.

◯NGReach.com❯ **eVisual 2.6**

Point out the end punctuation in each sentence. Then say: Some sentences mean "no." Write: *You should never touch a wild raccoon. Raccoons are not tame.* Ask: *What words mean "no" in these sentences?* (never, not)

❷ **Practice/Apply** Have partners identify the kinds of sentences in the dialogue on page 74. Then assign **Practice Master 2.3** for more practice.

> **CHECK UNDERSTANDING** Display several sentences. Have students identify each kind of sentence and the end punctuation.

> This is
> my dog.

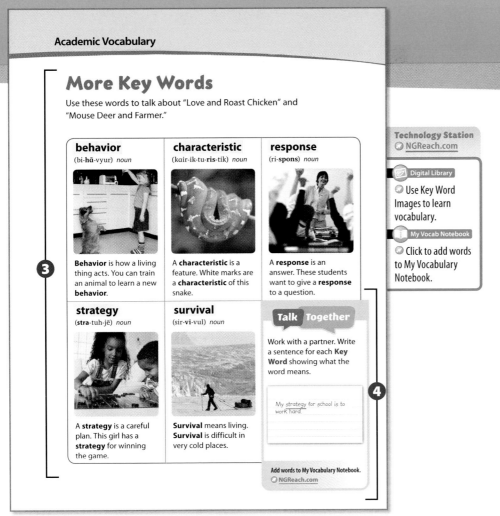

Student Book page 77

Academic Vocabulary

3 **Teach/Model** Invite students to discuss each photograph on the page. Read the directions aloud and use **Vocabulary Routine 1** and **Key Word Images** to teach the words.

1. **Pronounce** the word and point to its picture: **behavior**.

2. **Rate** the word. Have students hold up their fingers to show how well they know the word. (1 = very well, 2 = a little, 3 = not at all) Ask: *What do you know about this word?*

3. **Define** the word: *Behavior is how a living thing acts.*

4. **Elaborate** Relate the word to your experience: *I give my dog a treat when he shows good behavior.*

4 **Practice/Apply** Use the ratings from step 2 to form pairs. Have partners work together in making sentences with the Key Words. Have a volunteer from each pair share one of the pair's sentences with the class.

> **CHECK UNDERSTANDING** Point to the **Key Word Image** of each Key Word and ask students to explain what each word means.

Keys to Efficacy

Ask processing questions if a student's answer is incomplete: *Yes,* survival *means living. What else do you know about survival?*

Differentiate

Spanish Cognates ▶
characteristic/característica; response/ respuesta; strategy/estrategia

Part 1 Vocabulary Skills Trace	Page
Day 1	Social Studies Vocabulary	T75
Day 2	**Academic Vocabulary**	**T77**
Day 3	Expand Word Knowledge	T80b
Day 4	Share Word Knowledge	T96b
Day 5	Apply Word Knowledge	T97b
Day 6	Homophones	T98
Day 7	Homophones	T105
Days 8–9	Extend Vocabulary	T106e–f
Day 10	Vocabulary Review	T106g–h

Day 2
continued

Day at a Glance:
▶ **Language:** Different Kinds of Sentences
▶ **Vocabulary:** Academic Vocabulary
▶ **Reading:** Make Connections
▶ **Writing:** Fanciful Story

OBJECTIVES

Vocabulary
• Acquire and Use Academic Vocabulary ⊕
• Use Grade-Level Vocabulary ⊕

Learning to Read
• Read Words With Short *e*

Reading Strategy
• Make Connections ⊕

Learning and Teamwork Strategies
• Use Personal Experience
• Use Visuals

Writing
• Write a Fanciful Story

Resources

⊘ *eVisual 2.7*

⟲ ⊘ *Reach Into Phonics TE page T30*

Make Connections

1 Teach Read the introduction aloud. Ask students how they can make a connection between the picture and something in their own lives. Make the connection: *When you think about how a story relates to your life or another story, you make a connection.* Point out that students can make connections between a text and themselves, the world, or another text.

2 Model Read the How to card aloud. To model making a connection about the picture, say:

• *It's about a raccoon that has knocked over some garbage cans.*
• *The raccoon reminds me of a skunk I saw in our yard.*
• *Now I understand what the skunk was doing. It was looking for food!*

Have students do a turn and talk about the connections they would make.

3 Practice/Apply Read the directions aloud. Point out the Language Frames. Read chorally "Three City Raccoons" and the sample student connection.

Direct students' attention to the raccoon family's discussion of whether or not they should move to the city. Use **Academic Language Frames** to help students at each proficiency level make connections. Encourage them to make connections to other stories as well.

> **CHECK UNDERSTANDING** Reread the sentences that tell what the family found in the city. Ask: *What connections can you make to this part of the story?*

Differentiate

Academic Language Frames

Make Connections

■ It's about _____.
   _____ reminds me of _____.
   Now I understand _____.

■ It's about _____.
   _____ reminds me of _____.
   Now I understand _____ because _____.

■ It's about _____.
■ _____ reminds me of _____ because _____.
   Now I understand _____ and _____.

Phonics and Fluency

Short /ĕ/

Display these words: *bed, let, web.* Point out the CVC spelling pattern and explain: *When a one-syllable word ends in a consonant and has only one vowel, the vowel has a short sound.* Blend /b/ /ĕ/ /d/. Have students repeat. Have students blend *let* and *web.* Display **Transparency 21** from **Reach Into Phonics** and work through the lesson.

Practice Display these sentences:
• This is my bed.
• They let us stay.
• The bug is in the web.

Have partners read the sentences chorally several times to develop fluency. Listen as partners read. Correct pronunciation.

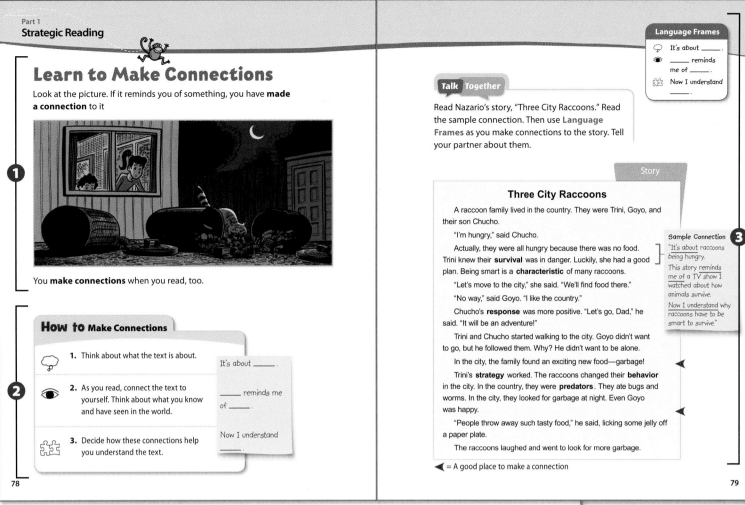

Learn to Make Connections

Look at the picture. If it reminds you of something, you have **made a connection** to it

You **make connections** when you read, too.

How to Make Connections

1. Think about what the text is about.

   It's about _____ .

2. As you read, connect the text to yourself. Think about what you know and have seen in the world.

   _____ reminds me of _____ .

3. Decide how these connections help you understand the text.

   Now I understand _____ .

Language Frames

- It's about _____ .
- _____ reminds me of _____ .
- Now I understand _____ .

Talk Together

Read Nazario's story, "Three City Raccoons." Read the sample connection. Then use **Language Frames** as you make connections to the story. Tell your partner about them.

Story

Three City Raccoons

A raccoon family lived in the country. They were Trini, Goyo, and their son Chucho.

"I'm hungry," said Chucho.

Actually, they were all hungry because there was no food. Trini knew their **survival** was in danger. Luckily, she had a good plan. Being smart is a **characteristic** of many raccoons.

"Let's move to the city," she said. "We'll find food there."

"No way," said Goyo. "I like the country."

Chucho's **response** was more positive. "Let's go, Dad," he said. "It will be an adventure!"

Trini and Chucho started walking to the city. Goyo didn't want to go, but he followed them. Why? He didn't want to be alone.

In the city, the family found an exciting new food—garbage!

Trini's **strategy** worked. The raccoons changed their **behavior** in the city. In the country, they were **predators**. They ate bugs and worms. In the city, they looked for garbage at night. Even Goyo was happy.

"People throw away such tasty food," he said, licking some jelly off a paper plate.

The raccoons laughed and went to look for more garbage.

◀ = A good place to make a connection

Sample Connection ③
"It's about raccoons being hungry.
This story reminds me of a TV show I watched about how animals survive.
Now I understand why raccoons have to be smart to survive."

78   79

Student Book pages 78–79

Daily Writing

④ Fanciful Story Discuss the features of Nazario's story with students, pointing out the animal characters and the dialogue. Discuss how students can use Nazario's story to write their own fanciful story. Then write a RAFT for students to follow:

- Role: Narrator
- Audience: Friends, Family
- Form: fanciful story
- Topic: Animals in the city

B Have students draw and label storyboards.

A Have students write sentences.

I Have students write a paragraph.

AH Have students write multiple paragraphs.

Invite students to share their stories with the class.

CLOSE AND ASSESS

- **Language** Ask students to identify sentences in "Three City Raccoons" as statements, questions, or exclamations, and name the end punctuation of each sentence.
- **Reading** *At the end of "Three City Raccoons," the raccoons are learning to live in a new place. What connections can you make to this?* (Answers will vary.)
- **Vocabulary** *How would you use the Key Word* **behavior** *to describe the raccoons in the story?* (Answers will vary.)

Day 3

Day at a Glance:
▶ **Language:** Engage in Discussion
▶ **Vocabulary:** Expand Word Knowledge
▶ **Reading:** Read the Selection
▶ **Writing:** Writer's Craft

OBJECTIVES

Vocabulary
- Use Academic Vocabulary: strategy ●
- Use Grade-Level Vocabulary: defend, predator ●
- Use Classroom Vocabulary: dialogue

Language
- Language Function: Engage in Discussion ●
- Listen to and Imitate Fluent Models

Learning and Teamwork Strategies
- Identify and Express Points of Agreement
- Identify and Express Points of Disagreement
- Use Media to Build Language
- Use Graphic Organizer: Frayer Model Poster

Resources

- *Sing With Me Language Song CD 1, Tr 11,12*
- *Sing With Me Language Song Book, page 9*
- *eVisual 2.8*
- *eVisual 2.9*
- *Chart or poster paper*
- *In the USA Picture Cards 130–140*

NGReach.com▸

See **Technology Station** for digital student resources.

Differentiate

Academic Language Frames

Engage in Discussion
- I think _____.
- I like what you said about _____.
- I feel _____.

- I think _____.
  I believe this because _____.
  Tell me more about _____.
  I agree/disagree because _____.

NGReach.com▸ eVisual 2.9

T80a   **Unit 2 | Animal Intelligence**

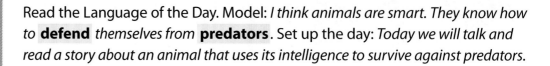

Language of the Day

Do you think animals are smart? Why or why not?
I think _____.

Read the Language of the Day. Model: *I think animals are smart. They know how to **defend** themselves from **predators**.* Set up the day: *Today we will talk and read a story about an animal that uses its intelligence to survive against predators.*

Engage in Discussion

❶ Teach Review Gina and Nazario's dialogue on page 74, emphasizing how they expressed different ideas on the same topic. Conclude by saying: *Like Gina and Nazario, people express different ideas when they engage in discussion.* Display "A Discussion." Play the chant and invite students to chant along.

Activate prior knowledge: *What are important rules to follow when you engage in discussion?* (ask questions, show you are listening, give your opinions, and respect others' opinions) Connect: *These are the same rules that we follow when we discuss things in school.* Review the chart:

Rules of Discussion			
Ask Questions.	**Show you are listening.**	**Give your opinions.**	**Respect others' opinions.**
What do you think?	I like what you said. Tell me more.	I think _____ I feel _____	I understand what you are saying but I disagree.

NGReach.com▸ eVisual 2.8

❷ Model Invite students to think of other expressions to add to the chart. Model how to use these expressions in a short discussion with a volunteer, similar to the one between Gina, Nazario, and their grandmother. Start by asking: *What do you think about raccoons? Are they interesting or scary?*

❸ Practice/Apply Have students engage in a discussion about the pictures they made in Share What You Know (page 73). Use **Academic Language Frames** to encourage students to use language naturally.

CHECK UNDERSTANDING Invite discussion about which animal might make a better pet, a cat or a dog. Monitor students to see that they follow the rules of discussion.

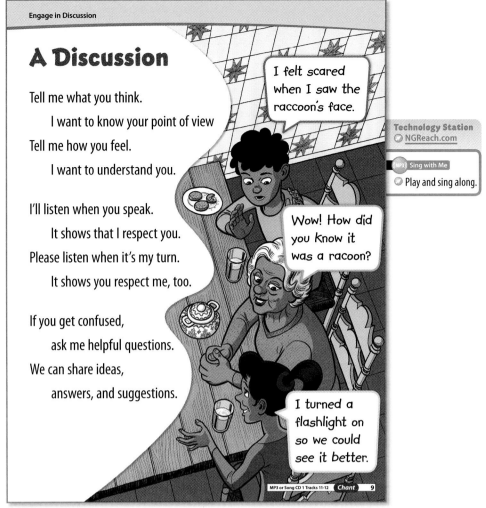

A Discussion

Tell me what you think.
    I want to know your point of view

Tell me how you feel.
    I want to understand you.

I'll listen when you speak.
    It shows that I respect you.

Please listen when it's my turn.
    It shows you respect me, too.

If you get confused,
    ask me helpful questions.

We can share ideas,
    answers, and suggestions.

I felt scared when I saw the raccoon's face.

Wow! How did you know it was a racoon?

I turned a flashlight on so we could see it better.

MP3 or Song CD 1 Tracks 11-12 **Chant** 9

Technology Station
◎ NGReach.com

(MP3) **Sing with Me**
◎ Play and sing along.

Sing With Me Language Song Book page 9

Expand Word Knowledge

4 **Teach/Model** Explain that each student pair will become Key Word experts. They will study one Key Word and create a Key Word poster about that word. Use **Vocabulary Routine 2** and model making a Frayer Model poster about the word **strategy**. (See **Vocabulary Routines,** page PD38.)

- Write the word in the center.
- Add a definition.
- Add characteristics.
- Add an example and a non-example.

Definition	Characteristics
A careful plan.	A careful plan
strategy	
A plan to win the game.	Playing the game without a plan
Example	Non Example

Frayer Model Poster

5 **Practice/Apply** Assign a Key Word to each pair of students. Have each pair create a poster for their assigned Key Words. Display the posters on the class word wall.

CHECK UNDERSTANDING Say a Key Word and have the partner experts for the word read the definition and sentence from their poster.

Key Words

adaption	prey
behavior	response
characteristic	strategy
defend	survival
predator	trait

Differentiate

Newcomer Support
Newcomers can make Frayer Model posters using words from **In the USA Picture Cards** 131–140.

Part 1 Vocabulary Skills Trace		Page
Day 1	Science Vocabulary	T75
Day 2	Academic Vocabulary	T77
Day 3	**Expand Word Knowledge**	**T80b**
Day 4	Share Word Knowledge	T96b
Day 5	Apply Word Knowledge	T97b
Day 6	Homophones	T98
Day 7	Homophones	T105
Days 8–9	Extend Vocabulary	T106e–f
Day 10	Vocabulary Review	T106g–h

Day 3

continued

Day at a Glance:
▶ **Language:** Engage in Discussion
▶ **Vocabulary:** Expand Word Knowledge
▶ **Reading:** Read the Selection
▶ **Writing:** Writer's Craft

OBJECTIVES

Vocabulary
- Use Academic Vocabulary: characteristic **T**
- Use Grade-Level Vocabulary: defend **T**

Reading Strategy
- Plan: Preview

Comprehension and Literary Analysis
- Analyze Elements of Fiction: Character
- Analyze Genre: Trickster Tale

Learning and Teamwork Strategies
- Use Prereading Supports
- Build Background Knowledge

Resources

Comprehension Coach

Keys to Efficacy

Promote collaborative thinking. Have students build on one another's ideas.

Preview the Story

1 **Introduce** Tell students to look at pages 80–81 as you read the title of the story. Prompt students to talk about the illustration: *Where does this story take place, in the city or the country? I see mountains and a field, so it must be the country. Look at the animals. What kind of animals are they? That's right, one is a guinea pig and the other is a fox.* Talk about the **characteristics** of these animals, providing any necessary vocabulary, such as *fur* and *paws*. Then connect to personal experience: *Have you ever seen a fox or guinea pig? What do you know about these animals?*

2 **Genre and Character** Read aloud the definition of *characters* and point to the pictures of the characters and their labels. Explain: *The characters in the story are Cuy the Guinea Pig and Tío Antonio the Fox.* Read aloud the genre definition. Connect the genre to the characters: *We know that one animal is going to outwit the other. Which do you think it will be, Cuy or Tío Antonio? Why do you think that?*

3 **Preview and Build Background** Use sheltering strategies as you conduct a picture walk.

Pages	Say (and Do)
82–83	*Tío Antonio is growling at Cuy.* (Make a growling sound.) *Cuy is holding up a rock.* (Hold up your arms as if supporting a rock.) *Do you think Cuy will be able to* **defend** *himself if he is holding a rock? What do you think Cuy will do next?*
84–85	*It looks like Cuy tricked the fox. Now Tío Antonio is holding the rock. How do you think Cuy got the fox to do that? Look at the next picture. Cuy has put on a hat and poncho. He's talking to the farmer. What do you think he's saying?*
86–87	*Cuy is now working in the farmer's garden. What do you think he told the farmer? He sure is tricky, isn't he? When the farmer isn't looking, Cuy takes off his disguise and eats all the farmer's alfalfa.*
88–89	*The farmer is making a person out of clay. He put the clay person in the field. Look! Cuy is talking to the clay person. He touches the sticky clay.* (Pantomime touching the clay figure.) *Oh, no! Cuy is stuck.*
90–91	*Now the farmer knows that Cuy has been eating his alfalfa. The farmer is angry. He ties Cuy to a tree.* (Pantomime being angry.) *Once again, Cuy cannot defend himself? What do you think Tío Antonio will do?*
92–94	*Look at Tío Antonio's thought bubble. What do you think Cuy is telling him? Will Cuy fool Tío Antonio again? Yes, he does. Now the fox is tied to the tree. What happens when Tío Antonio tells the farmer what happened?* (The farmer laughs.)

CHECK UNDERSTANDING Ask: *Who are the characters in this story?* (Cuy the Guinea Pig, Tío Antonio the Fox, farmer) *What kind of story is this?* (It's a trickster tale. That means it's about a character that outwits another character.)

Read a Story

Genre

① A **trickster tale** is a story in which the main character tries to outwit, or outsmart, the other characters. The main character is almost always a clever animal.

② **Characters**

Characters are the people or animals in a story.

Cuy the Guinea Pig

Tío Antonio the Fox

LOVE AND ROAST CHICKEN

A Trickster Tale from the Andes Mountains

written and illustrated by
Barbara Knutson

Comprehension Coach

80

Student Book pages 80–81

Comprehension Coach

Build Reading Power

Assign students to use the software, based on their instructional needs.

Read Silently	**Listen**	**Record** 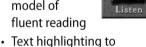
• Comprehension questions with immediate feedback • Vocabulary support	• Process model of fluent reading • Text highlighting to facilitate tracking • Vocabulary support	• Oral reading fluency practice • Speech recognition for oral fluency assessment with immediate feedback

Cultural Perspectives

Ask students if they know the difference between farm animals and wild animals. In many parts of the world, wild animals are a problem for farmers and farm animals. In North America, wild foxes and dogs attack farm animals. In parts of Africa, South America, and Asia, for example, tigers and other wild cats are especially dangerous. Other animals and insects eat the farmer's crops. Invite students to share what they know about these problems and the ways that farmers deal with them.

OBJECTIVES

Vocabulary
- Use Academic Vocabulary: characteristic, strategy ⊕
- Use Grade-Level Vocabulary: predator, prey ⊕

Learning to Read
- Phonics: Words with Digraphs *ck* /k/; *sh* /sh/
- Concepts of Print: Directionality

Reading Strategies
- Plan: Set a Purpose, Predict, Confirm Predictions
- Make Connections ⊕

Fluency
- Expression ⊕

Comprehension and Literary Analysis
- Analyze Character

Learning and Teamwork Strategies
- Use Reading Supports

Writing
- Develop Writer's Craft: Characters

Resources

 Read with Me Selection CD

 Practice Master 2.4

 Reach Into Phonics TE pages T34, T36

⊙ NGReach.com ▶

See **Technology Station** for digital student resources.

Key Points Reading

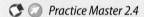

Name _____ Date _____

(Key Points Reading)

Love and Roast Chicken: A Trickster Tale from the Andes Mountains

① Cuy the Guinea Pig saw Tío Antonio the Fox and had no time to hide. He told Tío Antonio that the sky was falling. Tío Antonio began to hold up the rock. He got tired and let go. The sky didn't fall. Tío Antonio was angry at Cuy, but Cuy had gone to the farmer's house.

② Cuy helped the farmer during the day. At night, Cuy ate the alfalfa. The farmer noticed someone was stealing his alfalfa. He made a sticky gum doll. Cuy got stuck to the doll. The farmer found Cuy.

③ The farmer tied Cuy to a tree. Tío Antonio saw Cuy and wanted to eat him. Cuy told Tío Antonio that the farmer's daughter wanted to marry him. Cuy would have to eat roast chicken. Tío Antonio took Cuy's place. When the farmer found Tío Antonio, he told him what Cuy said. The farmer laughed. Tío Antonio escaped. He said Cuy would never trick him again. He stayed far away from Cuy.

For use with TE p. T82   **2.4**   Unit 2 | TK

Practice Master 2.4

Read the Story

Suggested Pacing

- Day 3: Read Section 1, pages 82–85
- Day 4: Read Sections 2 and 3, pages 86–94

Reading Options Scaffold the support for varied reading levels.

BELOW LEVEL	ON LEVEL	ABOVE LEVEL
Listen and Read Along	**Read Together**	**Read Silently and Aloud**
• Have students track the print on the **Key Points Reading** while you read the text aloud. Pause and have them pantomime the characters' actions as they read along. • Check understanding with selected Build Comprehension questions.	• Have groups set a purpose for reading—to get information or enjoy a story—and read silently. Then select passages to read chorally. Pause to ask the Build Comprehension questions. • At the end of each section, have students summarize what Cuy does.	• Have students set a purpose for reading. Have them read silently and study the illustrations to clarify the text. • Then have students read the selection aloud and analyze the characters' actions and dialogue for meaning. Ask and discuss the Build Comprehension questions.

Phonics and Fluency

Words with Digraphs *ck* (/k/) and *sh* (/sh/)

Teach/Model Display these words: *stick, dish, rack, shut*. Point out the *ck* and *sh* digraphs and explain: *The digraph* ck *makes the /k/ sound, the* sh *digraph makes the /sh/ sound*. Have students repeat the sounds. Circle the digraphs. Display **Transparency 23** from **Reach into Phonics** and work through the lesson.

Practice/Apply Display these sentences from "Love and Roast Chicken."

- He crouched under the rock and pushed up.
- He ducked and let go.
- He feasted on fresh alfalfa.

Underline the words *rock, pushed, ducked,* and *fresh*. Have partners write the words and circle the digraphs *ck* or *sh* in each word. Then have partners read the words chorally several times to develop fluency.

▶ Set a Purpose

1 A clever guinea pig meets a hungry fox. Find out how he **defends** himself.

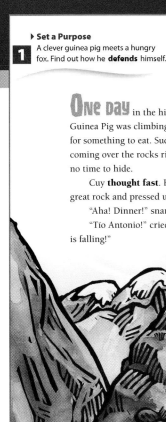

One Day in the high Andes Mountains, Cuy the Guinea Pig was climbing up and down the paths looking for something to eat. Suddenly, he saw Tío Antonio the Fox coming over the rocks right in front of him, and there was no time to hide.

Cuy **thought fast**. He **squeezed** under the edge of a great rock and pressed up with his arms.

"Aha! Dinner!" snarled Fox.

"Tío Antonio!" cried Cuy. "Haven't you heard? The sky is falling!"

2

In Other Words
thought fast quickly thought of an idea
squeezed pushed himself

"**Nonsense!**" growled Tío Antonio, but he **couldn't help looking up**. "It looks the same as always!"

"That's because I'm holding it up with this rock," said Cuy. "I've been here all day, and I need to go to the bathroom. Please, will you hold the rock for just a moment?"

Fox looked up again. It would be terrible if the sky fell. He **crouched** under the rock and pushed up with his front legs.

3

"Don't let go," warned Cuy, "or we will all be squashed flat." Then he **scurried off** to look for more food.

In Other Words
"**Nonsense!**" That's not true!
couldn't help looking up looked up anyway
crouched lowered his body
scurried off ran away

▶ **Before You Move On**

4 1. **Plot** How does Cuy **protect** himself from Tío Antonio?

2. **Character** Which character is a **predator** and which is **prey**? How do you know?

82

Student Book pages 82–83

Build Comprehension, pages 82–83

1 **Set a Purpose** Read aloud the introduction at the top of page 82 to set a purpose for reading.

2 **Setting** How would you describe the setting of the story? (It is in the mountains. It is very rocky. Some mountains have snow at the top.)

3 **Draw Conclusions** What would Cuy have done if he had more time? (He would hide from the fox.)

4 **Answers to Before You Move On**

1. Plot Cuy holds up a rock and tells the fox that the sky is falling. Then he tricks the fox into holding up the rock.

2. Character MODEL | GUIDE | APPLY As you model the answer, remind students of the definitions of **predator** and **prey**. Say: *Tío Antonio says "Aha, dinner," when he sees Cuy. He shows his teeth and looks hungrily at Cuy in the illustration on page 83. This shows that Tío Antonio wants to eat Cuy, so he is the predator and Cuy is his prey.*

N **B**

Concepts of Print: Directionality

Teach/Model Use pages 82–83 to model reading text that turns a line and continues at the left. On page 82, demonstrate tracking print from left to right for the first line, then sweeping from the end of the line to the beginning of the next line. Then model reading the second line from left to right. Have students follow along in their copies as you repeat the process.

Practice/Apply On page 83, read the first line of the text, tracking the print. Stop at the end of the line and ask students to name the word that comes next (looking). Read the second line as you track the text. Then have partners practice the process with the text on both pages.

Technology Station
📀 NGReach.com

(MP3) Read with Me

▶ Play and read along.

Comprehension Coach

▶ Use interactive vocabulary support. Automatically measure fluency.

▶ **Predict**
1 What will Tío Antonio do?

By sunset, Tío Antonio couldn't hold his arms up any longer. "I have to let go, even if the sky falls!" He **ducked** and let go.

Nothing happened. The rock and the sky stayed where they had always been.

"I'll get that guinea pig!" barked Fox as he **bounded** **2** down the trail.

In Other Words
ducked bent down quickly
bounded ran

84

But Cuy had a plan. "I'm going where there's **plenty** of food and someone who always chases Fox away," he decided. **3**

Cuy knew that a farmer and his daughter lived down in the valley. So he put on a hat and a poncho and went down the mountain to knock on the farmer's door.

In Other Words
plenty a lot

▶ **Before You Move On**
4
1. **Confirm Prediction** What did Tío Antonio do?
2. **Make Connections** How would you feel if you were the fox?

85

Student Book pages 84–85

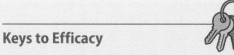

B I A AH

Home Connection:
Animal Stories

Discuss how clever Cuy was to trick Tío Antonio. Compare Cuy's cleverness to the intelligence of real animals. Remind students of **Family Newsletter 2**, which asked them to collect stories from family or community members about the intelligent things pets or other animals have done. Have them draw pictures of these stories and use the pictures to retell the story to their peers. Gather the drawings to make a classroom book of Intelligent Animals.

Keys to Efficacy

Remind students to use content, academic, and/or classroom vocabulary: *How can you use a key word to explain your answer?*

Build Comprehension, pages 84–85

1 **Predict** Read aloud the introduction. Model using the illustrations to predict what will happen. Ask: *What else can you predict from the illustrations?*

2 **Plot** What is Cuy's problem? What's his solution? (Possible response: Cuy tricked Tío Antonio, and he knows that the fox will come looking for him. That's why Cuy is wearing a disguise. He wants to hide from the fox.)

3 **Make Inferences** Who does Cuy mean when he says "someone who always chases Fox away"? (he is talking about the farmer)

4 **Answers to Before You Move On**

1. **Confirm Prediction** Tío Antonio held up the rock until sunset. Then his arms got tired, so he put his arms down and ducked. Nothing happened.

2. **Make Connections** MODEL | GUIDE | APPLY As you model the answer, remind students to think about how they would feel if they were tricked by someone. Say: *It's about how Cuy tricks Tío Antonio. It reminds me of a time that someone tricked me, and I was mad. I would be mad if I held up the rock for a long time. Now I understand how Tío Antonio feels.*

"**Buenos días,** *Papay*," said Cuy. "Need any help with the alfalfa?"

"What a small man," thought the farmer, "but I do need help."

"*Bueno*," he said. "You can start **right away**."

All day Cuy helped Florinda, the farmer's daughter, weed and hoe and water the fields. But all night he feasted on fresh alfalfa. **6**

alfalfa

86

"All this food and **no Fox in sight**. I'm going to stay here **the rest of my life**!" Cuy decided.

By the third day, the farmer noticed something was wrong. "Who is stealing all my alfalfa?" he wondered. "**I'd better** make it look like someone is guarding the field." **7 8**

87

Build Comprehension, pages 86–87

5 **Predict** Read aloud the prediction. Why is Cuy at the farm? What do you think he will do there? Use the illustrations to help you predict.

6 **Make Connections** MODEL GUIDE APPLY Say: *Cuy weeded, hoed, and watered the fields all day. How would you feel if you worked hard all day? How is this different from the way that Cuy feels?* To guide students in making connections, have them tell what they would do at night if they had worked all day. *What does this tell you about how much Cuy likes alfalfa?* (He must like it a lot.)

7 **Problem and Solution** *What problem does the farmer have soon after Cuy starts working at the farm?* (Someone is eating his alfalfa.) *What's the farmer's solution?* (He decides to make it look like someone is guarding the field.)

8 **Predict** *What will the farmer do next?* (Answers will vary. I think the farmer might watch the field at night. Perhaps the farmer will make a scarecrow.)

Student Book pages 86–87

I **A** **AH**

Math: Word Problems

Pose this word problem to the class: *Tío Antonio said he would eat one chicken every day of the year. If the farmer had 388 chickens, how many chickens would be left at the end of the year?* On the board, express the problem with numbers and math symbols, prompting students to provide the answer. (388 − 365 = 23) Encourage students, in pairs or in small groups, to formulate their own word problems involving characters from the story. They can then pose their problems to the class, providing answers as necessary.

He shaped a little person out of clay and covered it with **sticky sap** from the eucalyptus tree. He **propped it up** in the field and went to bed.

In the middle of the night, Cuy crept out for a snack, but someone had gotten there before him.

"**¡Buenas noches!** Are you a friend of Florinda's?" he said. The visitor said nothing. "I said, hello!" When Cuy reached out to shake her hand, his paw stuck.

In Other Words
sticky sap liquid that is like glue
propped it up stood it up
¡Buenas noches! Good evening (in Spanish)

88

"**Oho,** so you want to hold my hand!" said Cuy. He patted her on the shoulder with his other paw, but that one stuck too.

"**¡Caramba!** Let go!" Guinea Pig said. "If you don't let go, I'll kick you!" But the person didn't say a word, and she didn't let go.

Cuy kicked hard with his right foot, which stuck. Then he kicked with his left foot, and that stuck too. "LET ME GO!" shouted Cuy so loudly that the farmer woke up and ran outside.

In Other Words
Oho Oh
¡Caramba! Goodness, stop it! (in Spanish)

▶ **Before You Move On**
1. **Confirm Prediction** What happened to Cuy at the farm?
2. **Make Connections** Does Cuy remind you of anyone you know? Explain.

89

Student Book pages 88–89

Build Comprehension, pages 88–89

1 **Revise Prediction** Read the first paragraph on page 88. Model how to revise your prediction: *The farmer is making a person out of clay. I change my prediction; I think he will put the clay person in the garden to look like a guard.*

2 **Details** Cuy tries to shake hands with the clay person. Show me what happens. (students pantomime having hand stuck.)

3 **Key Words** What is one **characteristic** of Cuy? (Answers will vary: He is friendly because he keeps trying to talk to the clay person.)

4 **Answers to Before You Move On**

1. Confirm Prediction Answers about predictions will vary. First, Cuy was stealing the farmer's alfalfa. But then the farmer tricked Cuy and caught him.

2. Make Connections MODEL | GUIDE | APPLY Answers about making connections will vary. Cuy reminds me of my friend Sal. He always knows how to get out of a sticky situation.

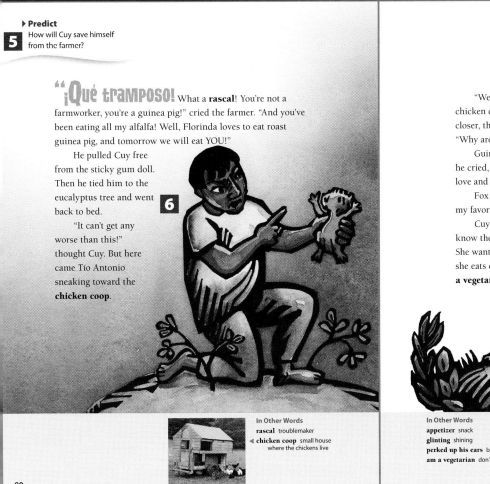

"**¡Qué tramposo!** What a **rascal**! You're not a farmworker, you're a guinea pig!" cried the farmer. "And you've been eating all my alfalfa! Well, Florinda loves to eat roast guinea pig, and tomorrow we will eat YOU!"

He pulled Cuy free from the sticky gum doll. Then he tied him to the eucalyptus tree and went back to bed.

"It can't get any worse than this!" thought Cuy. But here came Tío Antonio sneaking toward the **chicken coop**.

In Other Words
rascal troublemaker
◄ **chicken coop** small house where the chickens live

90

"Well, well!" said Fox. "I was looking for chicken dinner, but here is my **appetizer**!" He came closer, the moonlight **glinting** on his sharp teeth. "Why are you tied up?"

Guinea Pig gulped. "Oh, Tío Antonio!" he cried, thinking fast. "It's all because of love and roast chicken."

Fox **perked up his ears**. "Those are my favorite subjects."

Cuy put his paw over his heart. "You know the farmer's daughter, Florinda? She wants to marry me. But the trouble is, she eats chicken every day. And I **am a vegetarian**!"

In Other Words
appetizer snack
glinting shining
perked up his ears became interested
am a vegetarian don't eat meat

91

Build Comprehension, pages 90–91

5 Predict Read aloud the question. Think about what Cuy has already done in the story. Predict how he will save himself from the farmer.

6 Summarize What has happened in the story so far? (Cuy protected himself from Tío Antonio by tricking him to hold the rock. Then Cuy went to the farm and ate the farmer's alfalfa. The farmer tricked Cuy with a clay person. The farmer caught Cuy and tied him to a tree.)

7 Clarify Language Look at the third paragraph on page 91. It says, "Fox perked up his ears." I'm not sure what that means so I can look at the bottom of the page where it says In Other Words. *Perked up his ears* is another way of saying "became interested." Fox became interested because love and roast chicken were his favorite subjects.

8 Key Words Is a **predator** a vegetarian? Explain. (No, predators eat meat or other animals; vegetarians don't eat meat.)

B I A AH

Literary Analysis: Use of Spanish Words

The story takes place in the Andes Mountains in South America. The author included Spanish words to give a sense of their culture. Have students compare the Spanish phrase on page 90 with its English meaning. Do the English words give the same feeling as the Spanish words? Have students compare other examples of Spanish words used in the story.

"They've tied me up until I promise to marry Florinda and eat big plates of roast chicken every day! What am I going to do?"

"*Pobrecito*," said Tío Antonio, licking his lips. "I hate to see you **1** suffer. Just to help you, I will take your place."

"Really?" said Cuy. "You are very kind."

So Fox untied Cuy. Then Cuy tied Tío Antonio to the tree and **slipped** back into the alfalfa field for one last feast.

In Other Words
Pobrecito Poor little thing (in Spanish)
slipped went quietly

92

The next morning, the farmer came out to untie his dinner. To his surprise, he found a fox.

"What now? **Another disguise?**" The farmer picked up a stick.

"Oh no, *Papay*, don't hit me!" said Tío Antonio. "I promise to eat one of your chickens every day of the year!"

"*¿Cómo?*" cried the farmer.

"Of course, *Papay*," Tío Antonio added quickly, "I also plan to marry your daughter."

"*¿CÓMO?*" spat the farmer, and he raised the stick over his head. **2**

In Other Words
Another disguise? Are you pretending to be someone else again?
¿Cómo? What? (in Spanish)

93

Student Book pages 92–93

I A AH

Fluency: Expression

Teach/Model Explain the concept: *Fluent readers read with expression. They change their voices to show feelings they get from the text.* Direct students' attention to page 90. Say: *Think about what this text is saying. The farmer is angry when he finds out Cuy is eating his alfalfa. When you read this, show anger in your voice.* Play the selection recording or read aloud page 90, emphasizing the rhythm and rhyme and the anger of finding out someone tricked you.

Practice Have partners read the page aloud together several times, mimicking the expression you modeled.

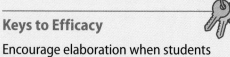

Keys to Efficacy

Encourage elaboration when students provide an answer or express an opinion: *Tell me more …*

Build Comprehension, pages 92–94

1 **Make Inferences** Why do you think Tio Antonio agrees to take Cuy's place? (He believes he will get to eat chicken every day. Cuy has fooled him again.)

2 **Plot** How does the farmer react when he finds the fox? (First he is surprised. Then he picks up a stick. He is angry because he thinks he is being tricked again.

3 **Answers to Before You Move On**

1. Confirm Prediction Cuy makes up a story and gets Tío Antonio to untie him. Then he ties Tío Antonio to the tree.

2. Character MODEL | GUIDE | APPLY The farmer laughs because he thinks it is funny how Cuy tricked Tío Antonio. The farmer thinks the story Cuy told Tío Antonio is ridiculous.

Meet the Author, page 95

Have students chorally read the Meet the Author copy.

1 **Writer's Craft** Say: *In "Love and Roast Chicken," Barbara Knutson gives her animal characters many human characteristics.* Point out an example on page 85: *So he put on a hat and a poncho and went down the mountain to knock on the farmer's door. Have students find other examples in the text.*

As fast as he could, Tío Antonio explained what Cuy had said.

"You believed a story like that? How foolish!" The farmer laughed until the tears ran down his cheeks. *"¡Qué ridículo!"*

While the farmer laughed, Fox bit **clean** through the rope and scrambled over the field wall. "CUY!" he howled. "You will never trick me again!"

And to make sure that was true, he stayed away from Cuy for a long, long time. ❖

In Other Words
"¡Qué ridículo!" That's ridiculous! (in Spanish)
clean completely

▶ **Before You Move On**

3
1. **Confirm Prediction** How does Cuy trick Tío Antonio to escape the farmer?
2. **Character** Why is the farmer laughing?

94

Meet the Author and Illustrator
Barbara Knutson

When Barbara Knutson was young, she loved drawing pictures of animals. When she grew up, she started writing and illustrating books for children.

Barbara also loved to travel. Her adventures around the world gave her many story ideas. No matter where she went, she always brought her sketchbook with her. "I could write and draw what I learned along the way, including many stories about the fox, and one special story about Cuy the Guinea Pig."

◀ Barbara Knutson traveled to many parts of the world. People would often be interested in her sketches.

Writer's Craft
1
2 Find places in the story where Barbara Knutson gives human qualities to the animals in the story. Then write a few sentences of your own. Describe what your favorite animal would say and do if it was a character in a story.

95

Student Book pages 94–95

Daily Writing A AH

2 **Writer's Craft** Explain: *Like Barbara Knutson, you can use words to give animals human* **characteristics**. *Think about an animal you know and how it acts. Then think of the words that show human characteristics.* Use the **Modeled Writing** routine to write sentences about human characteristics of an animal or pet. (See **Writing Routines,** page PD54.)

Think Aloud	Write
My dog shakes hands and gives me high-fives.	When I say, "Give me five," my dog slaps his paw against my hand.
When my dog closes his eyes, he thinks I can't see him.	My dog is like a little kid. When I catch him on my bed, he closes his eyes and pretends he's asleep.

Have students write their sentences in their journals.

CLOSE AND ASSESS
- **Language** *How can I express my ideas about the character Cuy?* (Encourage students to share what they know about Cuy and their opinions of him.)
- **Vocabulary** *How did the story help you better understand the meaning of the Key Word* **strategy**?
- **Reading** *What connections did you make as you read the story?* (Students should cite the Reading Strategy lessons on pages T84–85, T88–89, and T94.

Meet the Author

Encourage students to read more books written by Barbara Knutson.
- *How the Guinea Fowl Got Her Spots*
- *Sungura and Leopard*
- *Why the Crab Has No Head*

Day 4

Day at a Glance:
▶ **Language:** Questions
▶ **Vocabulary:** Share Word Knowledge
▶ **Reading:** Think and Respond
▶ **Writing:** Write About It

OBJECTIVES

Vocabulary
• Use Academic Vocabulary: response ⊤
• Use Grade-Level Vocabulary: defend, predator ⊤

Grammar
• Recognize and Understand Questions ⊤

Learning and Teamwork Strategies
• Review
• Collaborate with Peers

Resources

⊘ *eVisual 2.10*

⟡⊘ *Practice Master 2.5*

▤⊘ *Language Builder Picture Cards E20, E21*

Differentiate

Language Transfer

Issue In Japanese, a statement can be turned into a **yes/no** question by adding **ka** to the end of the statement. The particle **ka** is, in effect, a vocalized question mark. In other languages, such as Spanish, a statement can be turned into a **yes/no** question by simply raising the pitch of the voice: **A raccoon eats meat?** Speakers of other languages may try to transfer such rules when forming questions in English.

Solution To reinforce English word order, have students copy sentences like the ones below, cut the words apart, mix them up, then reassemble each sentence.

Is Barbara Knutson a writer?

Do you read books?

What do raccoons like to eat?

When does class start?

T96a   Unit 2 | Animal Intelligence

Language of the Day

Do you think Cuy was an intelligent animal?
I think ____.

Read the Language of the Day. Model: *I think Cuy was an intelligent animal because he could think quickly to get out of tough situations.* Have students read your sentence. Then invite them to share and express their ideas about Cuy.

Grammar Questions B I A AH

1 **Teach/Model** Say: *Some questions ask for a "yes" or "no" answer. Fox asked Cuy, "Why are you tied up?" Could Cuy answer with a "yes" or "no"?* (no) Say: *Some questions need longer answers.* Display the chart.

Sentence begins with	Question	Answer
Do? Does? Is? Are? Have? Will? and others	Does Cuy like alfalfa? Did Fox eat Cuy?	Yes. No.
Who? What? When? Where? How? Why?	Where is the story from? Why does the farmer laugh?	It is from the Andes. Cuy tricked Fox.

⊘ **NGReach.com** ▶ *eVisual 2.10*

Read the words that begin short-answer questions. Invite a student to read each question and another to answer it. Underline the verbs in the questions. Say: *In most sentences, the subject comes before the predicate. Where is the subject in these sentences?* (in the middle) Underline the verbs. (Does like, Did eat) Then read the words that begin longer-answer questions. One student reads the question; another answers.

Explain: *Sometimes a question comes at the end of a statement. The question often includes a contraction like* isn't, aren't, *or* wasn't. Write:

• Cuy was smart, wasn't he?

• You liked the story, didn't you?

Circle the contractions. Have students answer the questions. Say: *These kinds of questions often have short answers.*

2 **Practice/Apply** Have small groups ask and answer questions about "Love and Roast Chicken." Tell them to list the question words they hear. Then assign **Practice Master 2.5** for more practice.

CHECK UNDERSTANDING Display this sentence: *Do you like carrots?* Ask: *Will this question need a longer answer or a "yes or no" answer?* (yes or no)

Share Word Knowledge

3 **Teach/Model** To connect concepts, say: *Yesterday you became Key Word experts. Today you will share what you know about your Key Words.* Group each student with a partner who studied a different word. Have partners follow the steps of **Vocabulary Routine 3** to share their word knowledge. (see **Vocabulary Routines,** page PD39.)

- Take turns reading Key Word posters.
- Talk about how the pictures on the posters show the meanings of the Key Words.
- Create sentences using both Key Words and write them in your journals.
- Draw a line under each Key Word.

4 **Practice/Apply** Have each set of partners self-identify as Partner A and Partner 1. Group lettered partners together; group numbered partners together. Form an **Inside-Outside Circle** with numbered partners on the inside and lettered partners on the outside (see **Cooperative Learning Routines,** pages PD58–PD59.)

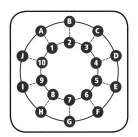

Inside-Out Circle

Students share the two words they studied and copy the information they learn into their vocabulary journals. Rotate and repeat until each student has a journal entry for each Key Word. Have students take turns reading the Key Words posters again. All students should echo the pronunciation. Correct any mispronunciations.

> **CHECK UNDERSTANDING** Display **Language Builder Picture Cards E20 and E21** (dog, ant) and ask students to use Key Words to tell about each one.

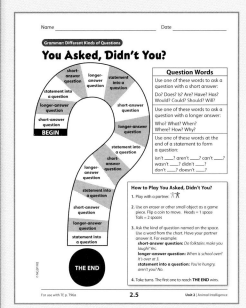

C ◯ **Practice Master 2.5**

Part 1 Vocabulary Skills Trace		Page
Day 1	Science Vocabulary	T75
Day 2	Academic Vocabulary	T77
Day 3	Expand Word Knowledge	T80b
▶ Day 4	**Share Word Knowledge**	**T96b**
Day 5	Apply Word Knowledge	T97b
Day 6	Homophones	T98
Day 7	More Homophones	T105
Days 8–9	Extend Vocabulary	T106e–f
Day 10	Vocabulary Review	T106g–h

Day 4
continued

Day at a Glance:
▶ **Language:** Questions ▶ **Reading:** Think and Respond
▶ **Vocabulary:** Share Word Knowledge ▶ **Writing:** Write About It

OBJECTIVES

Vocabulary
- Use Academic Vocabulary: behavior, characteristic strategy ❶
- Use Grade-Level Vocabulary: trait ❶

Language
- Use Language Function: Express Ideas ❶

Fluency
- Expression ❶

Literary Analysis and Comprehension
- Make Connections
- Analyze Genre: Trickster Tale
- Analyze Characters

Test-Taking Strategies
- Practice and Apply Strategies: Read Directions Carefully

Writing
- Write Responses to Trickster Tale

Resources

⊘ *eVisual 2.11*

 **NGReach.com**

See **Technology Station** for digital student resources.

 I **A** **AH**

Fluency: Expression

Review Review expression (page T88). Display this reminder: *Change your voice to match what you are reading.*

Apply Challenge pairs to an expressive reading face-off. Have partners practice reading page 90. Then organize teams of four and have pairs give each other feedback about their reading.

Think and Respond

❶ **Talk About It** Prompt students to cite evidence from the text. Remind students to use Key Words in their answers. If students have difficulty, help them use the sentence starters to form their answers.

1. **Trickster Tale** Possible answers: One trick that Cuy plays is having Tío Antonio hold up the rock. A trick that Tío Antonio plays is biting through the rope and escaping while the farmer is laughing. One trick that the farmer plays is putting a clay person in the garden.

2. **Express Ideas** Answers will vary. Possible answer: I think Cuy is smarter because he manages to escape each time he is caught.

3. **Describe Relationships** Tío Antonio is always trying to catch Cuy, but he's not clever enough. Cuy may be small, but he's a lot smarter than Tío Antonio, and he can outwit Tío Antonio pretty easily.

❷ **Test-Taking Strategies: Read Directions Carefully**
Explain: *Tests have directions that tell you what to do. A good test-taking* **strategy** *is to read directions carefully so you know what the question is asking you to do.*

> **Read the sentences. Which sentence tells about a character's traits? Circle the letter of the correct answer.**
>
> A. Cuy lives on a farm.
> B. The farmer has a daughter named Florinda.
> C. Cuy plays tricks and tells a lot of stories.
> D. Tío Antonio is a fox, not a guinea pig.

⊘ **NGReach.com** ❭ **eVisual 2.11**

Ask: *What do the directions ask you to do first?* (Find a sentence that tells about a character's **traits**.) *I need to identify words that describe traits.*

Directions	What to do
Read the sentences.	Read the answer choices. Eliminate choices that don't describe a character.
Which sentence tells about a character's traits?	Find words that describe traits, such as smart, friendly, etc.
Circle the letter.	Circle the correct choice.

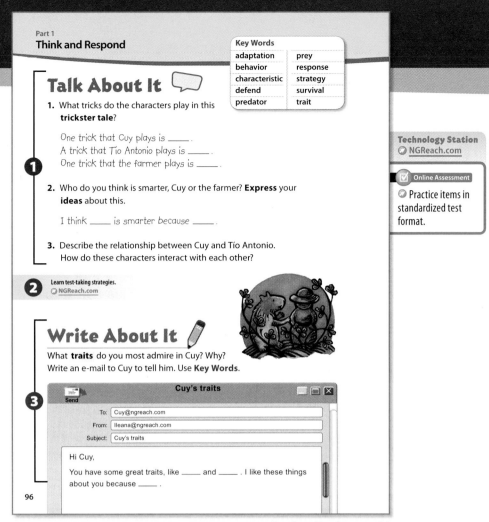

Part 1
Think and Respond

Key Words

adaptation	prey
behavior	response
characteristic	strategy
defend	survival
predator	trait

Talk About It

1. What tricks do the characters play in this **trickster tale**?

   One trick that Cuy plays is _____ .
   A trick that Tío Antonio plays is _____ .
   One trick that the farmer plays is _____ .

2. Who do you think is smarter, Cuy or the farmer? **Express** your **ideas** about this.

   I think _____ is smarter because _____ .

3. Describe the relationship between Cuy and Tío Antonio. How do these characters interact with each other?

Learn test-taking strategies.
◯ NGReach.com

Technology Station
◯ NGReach.com

☑ Online Assessment
◯ Practice items in standardized test format.

Write About It

What **traits** do you most admire in Cuy? Why? Write an e-mail to Cuy to tell him. Use **Key Words**.

```
                              Cuy's traits                    ▢ ▢ ✖
  Send
        To:    Cuy@ngreach.com
        From:  Ileana@ngreach.com
        Subject: Cuy's traits

        Hi Cuy,
        You have some great traits, like _____ and _____ . I like these things
        about you because _____ .
```

96

Student Book page 96

Daily Writing Ⓘ Ⓐ Ⓐ̲Ⓗ̲

3 Write About It Read the directions aloud. Point out the sentence frame: *You can use this sentence to begin an e-mail.* Use the **Independent Writing** routine to help students put their thoughts in writing, using the Key Words and the sentence frame. (See **Writing Routines,** page PD56.)

Say	Write
Cuy thought fast to think of holding up the rock.	You have some great traits. You can think fast. I like this about you because it shows me how smart you are.
Cuy told the fox a story about the farmer's daughter and eating chicken. The fox believed it.	You are a good storyteller. I like this about you because it shows that you are creative.

Point out the Key Word that you used to complete the sentence frame: *trait.* Have students use these ideas or their own to write an e-mail to Cuy.

Keys to Efficacy

Focus on the process of making meaning, not right answers. *What are some other opinions?*

CLOSE AND ASSESS

- **Language** *Express your ideas about Tío Antonio's **behavior*** (Opinions will vary.)

- **Reading** *How was the farmer smart like Cuy?* (Answers will vary.)

- **Vocabulary** *What Key Words can you use to talk about the way a character acts, speaks, and looks?* (trait, **characteristic**, behavior)

Day 5

Day at a Glance:
▶ **Language:** Listen Actively   ▶ **Reading:** Reread and Analyze
▶ **Vocabulary:** Apply Word Knowledge   ▶ **Writing:** Write a Paragraph

OBJECTIVES

Vocabulary
• Use Academic Vocabulary ⊕
• Use Grade-Level Vocabulary: **defend** ⊕

Listening and Speaking
• Listen Actively

Learning and Teamwork Strategies
• Review
• Use Patterns in Language
• Collaborate with Peers

Media and Technology
• Unit Launch Video

Resources

   ⊙ *Unit 2 Build Background Video*

   ⊙ *eVisual 2.12*

 •   *Student dictionaries, index cards*

Differentiate

How to Learn Language

Find Patterns in Language Explain:
Listen for patterns in language. The articles
a, an, *and the often come before nouns.*

You hear:

An elephant has a trunk.

You say:

An elephant has a tail.

Form student pairs with mixed proficiency
so that students can listen for language
patterns as they talk about the animals they
heard about.

Language of the Day

What makes animals special?
Animals are special because ____.

Read the Language of the Day. Have students watch the **Unit 2 Build Background Video** again then complete the sentence frame. Add their ideas to the unit concept map. Then explain that today they will learn how to listen actively, play a word game, retell the story, and write about it.

Listen Actively

1 **Teach/Model** Introduce the concept: *When you know how to listen actively, you can better remember information you hear.* Display a picture of an animal and share several facts about it. Then ask a volunteer to share information about the animal. Display the How to card and model how to listen actively as the volunteer talks.

How to Listen Actively	
☁ 1. **Make a picture in your mind of what you hear.**	I see an elephant with a long trunk.
👂 2. **Listen for important details.**	I hear that elephants have two tusks, or long, pointed teeth.
❓ 3. **Ask questions if you do not understand.**	Does that mean elephants eat with their tusks?
👂 4. **Listen for answers to your questions.**	Elephants use their tusks to **defend** themselves.

⊙ NGReach.com ＞ eVisual 2.12

2 **Practice/Apply** Present information about another animal, pausing frequently to practice the steps. Have students tell what new information they heard. Teach the **How to Learn Language** strategy to help students as they talk about what they heard.

> **CHECK UNDERSTANDING** Have students switch partners. One partner listens actively while the other relates new information learned about the animal.

Apply Word Knowledge

③ Teach/Model Tell students they will play a vocabulary game called "You Made That Up!" Guide students in following oral instructions as you explain how to play the game.

- *First, I choose one Key Word.*
- *I write three definitions for the word. One definition is real and two definitions are fake, or not real.*
- *I read aloud my word and all three definitions. For example: The word is* **strategy**. *My definitions are (1) a narrow body of water, (2) a careful plan, and (3) a quick response to a problem.*
- *Which definition is correct, 1, 2, or 3? (2) The student who answers correctly reads his or her word and definitions.*

④ Practice/Apply Give each student a dictionary and an index card. Clarify: *Make sure you include the real definition of the word and two definitions that are not correct.*

Explain that students should number their definitions. They can make the correct definition any number from 1 to 3. Have students circle the number of the correct choice on their card.

Ask students to read aloud their word and the numbered definitions. Remind students to raise their hand if they want to give an answer.

Monitor students as they follow your instructions. Restate the instructions as required.

For vocabulary games, go to NGReach.com

> **CHECK UNDERSTANDING** Call out a word and three definitions. Ask students to explain how they knew which definition was the correct one.

Day 5
continued

Day at a Glance:
▶ **Language:** Listen Actively
▶ **Vocabulary:** Apply Word Knowledge
▶ **Reading:** Reread and Analyze
▶ **Writing:** Write a Paragraph

OBJECTIVES

Vocabulary
- Use Academic Vocabulary ❶
- Use Grade-Level Vocabulary: predator, trait ❶

Language
- Analyze Characters ❶
- Participate in Discussion

Learning and Teamwork Strategies
- Use Graphic Organizers (Character Chart)
- Reason Deductively

Fluency
- Read with Accuracy and Rate ❶
- Read with Expression ❶

Writing
- Write a Paragraph Response

Resources

- ⟳ ⊘ *Practice Master 2.4*
- ⟳ ⊘ *Practice Master 2.6*
- ⟳ ⊘ *Practice Master 2.7*
- ⊘ *Comprehension Coach*

Reread and Analyze

❶ Talk About It Read aloud the introduction and reinforce: *What characters do and say tells us about their* **traits**, *or personality.* Read through the example character chart. Then explain: *Cuy runs into a* **predator**, *Tío Antonio. Cuy tells him the sky is falling. This shows Cuy thinks fast and tricks the fox so he won't eat Cuy.*

Have students complete **Practice Master 2.6**.

❷ Analyze Read aloud the directions and sentence frames. Have students analyze the characters in the story with their partners. Remind them to tell what each character did and said. One partner analyzes a character then the partners reverse roles and repeat with a different character. Provide the Key Points Reading (**Practice Master 2.4**) for students who need additional support.

To evaluate students' proficiency levels, use the Analyze a Character Rubric.

Analyze a Character Rubric

Scale	Content	Language
B	☐ Misses many important characters. ☐ Does not know the characters well.	☐ Frequently hard to hear or understand. ☐ Often seems uncomfortable with the retelling task.
I	☐ Misses some important characters. ☐ Tells one character's words and actions.	☐ Is often hard to hear or understand. ☐ Seems somewhat uncomfortable with the retelling task.
A	☐ Covers most important characters. ☐ Tells most characters' words, actions, and traits.	☐ Can be understood most of the time. ☐ Seems somewhat comfortable with the retelling task.
AH	☐ Covers all important characters. ☐ Tells each character's words, actions, and traits.	☐ Speaks clearly and is easily understood. ☐ Is very comfortable with the retelling task.

Fluency Accuracy, Rate, and Expression I A AH

❸ Fluency Have students record their reading on the **Comprehension Coach** to assess each student's progress for rate and accuracy.

Have students use the passage on **Practice Master 2.7** to record their reading for expression. Listen to each recording and assess students' ability to read with expression.

Reread and Analyze Character Chart

Love and Roast Chicken

Fill in what the character says and does. Write what this shows about the character.

Character Chart

Character	What the Character Does	What the Character Says	What It Shows
Cuy	runs into a fox	"The sky is falling."	thinks fast tricky
Tío Antonio	holds up the rock	"I have to let go, even if the sky falls!"	foolish easily tricked
the farmer	makes a clay person	"I'd better make it look like someone is guarding the field."	clever inventive

▭▭ Use your character chart to retell the story to a partner.

For use with TE p. T97c — **2.6** — **Unit 2** | Animal Intelligence

⟳ ⊘ **Practice Master 2.6**

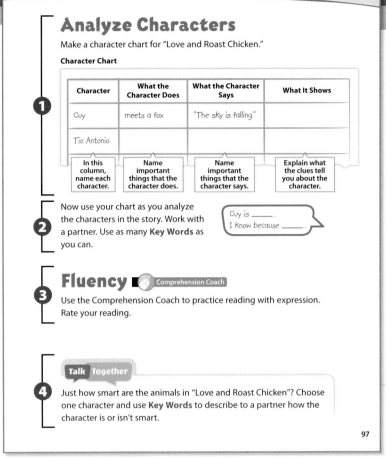

Analyze Characters

Make a character chart for "Love and Roast Chicken."

Character Chart

1

Character	What the Character Does	What the Character Says	What It Shows
Cuy	meets a fox	"The sky is falling."	
Tío Antonio			
In this column, name each character.	Name important things that the character does.	Name important things that the character says.	Explain what the clues tell you about the character.

2 Now use your chart as you analyze the characters in the story. Work with a partner. Use as many **Key Words** as you can.

> Cuy is _____.
> I know because _____.

Fluency Comprehension Coach

3 Use the Comprehension Coach to practice reading with expression. Rate your reading.

Talk Together

4 Just how smart are the animals in "Love and Roast Chicken"? Choose one character and use **Key Words** to describe to a partner how the character is or isn't smart.

97

Student Book page 97

Name _____ Date _____

Fluency Passage

"Love and Roast Chicken"

Expression in reading is how you use your voice to express feeling. Use this passage to practice reading with proper expression.

"Qué tramposo! What a rascal! You're not a farmworker,   9
you're a guinea pig!" cried the farmer. "And you've been eating   20
all my alfalfa! Well, Florinda loves to eat roast guinea pig,   31
and tomorrow we will eat YOU!"   37

He pulled Cuy free from the sticky gum doll. Then he tied him   50
to the eucalyptus tree and went back to bed.   59

"It can't get any worse than this!" thought Cuy. But here came   71
Tío Antonio sneaking toward the chicken coop.   78

From "Love and Roast Chicken," page 90

Expression

AH □ Changes voice to match all the content		B □ Changes voice, but it does not match content	
A □ Changes voice to match some of the content		N □ Does not change voice	

Accuracy and Rate Formula

| words attempted in one minute | – | number of errors | = | words correct per minute (wcpm) |

For use with TE p. T97c   2.7   Unit 2 | Animal Intelligence

 **Practice Master 2.7**

4 **Talk Together** Discuss the smart or foolish things the animals in the story do. Read aloud the directions and have students choose one character to describe. Then have students share their ideas with the class.

Daily Writing ✏️

5 **Write a Journal Entry** Use the **Interactive Writing** routine to write a journal entry from Cuy's point of view to tell how he outsmarted Tío Antonio. (See **Writing Routines** page PD55.)

- As a class, decide how Cuy should sound in his journal entry. Will he be boastful or modest?
- Have students take turns building the journal entry one word at a time.
- Offer corrective feedback.

Have students copy the paragraph into their journals.

Keys to Efficacy

Ask supporting questions when students need to connect and find relationships among ideas and statements: *What makes you think this character is _____?*

What did the character do or say to make you think _____?

CLOSE AND ASSESS

- **Language** *Complete this sentence: When I listen actively, I _____.* (make a picture in my mind, listen for important details, ask questions and listen for answers to my questions)
- **Reading** *In a story, what gives us clues about a character's traits?* (the character's words and actions)
- **Vocabulary** *What Key Words did you use in your answers?* (Answers will vary.)

Day 6

Day at a Glance:
Language: Express Ideas and Engage in Discussion
Vocabulary: Homophones
Reading: Read the Selection
Writing: Writing Fluency

OBJECTIVES

Vocabulary
- Use Academic Vocabulary: behavior ⓣ
- Use Grade-Level Content Vocabulary ⓣ
- Use Context Clues for Homophones

Language
- Language Function: Express Ideas and Engage in Discussion
- Use a Variety of Sentence Lengths

Learning and Teamwork Strategies
- Identify and Express Points of Agreement
- Identify and Express Points of Disagreement
- Collaborate with Peers

Resources

- ⊙ eVisual 2.13
- ⊙ eVisual 2.14

Differentiate

Academic Language Frames

Express Ideas and Engage in Discussion

■ What do you think about _____?
  I think that _____.
_____

■ Let's talk about _____.
  I know that _____ because _____.
  I heard you say that _____.
_____

■ Let's talk about _____.
■ I think that _____ because _____.
  I like your idea about _____.
  I don't think that _____.

⊙ NGReach.com > eVisual 2.14

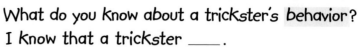

Language of the Day

What do you know about a trickster's behavior?
I know that a trickster _____.

Read the Language of the Day. Model: *I know that a trickster thinks fast.* Create a web for the answers and encourage students to share their ideas. Then explain that today students will read another tale about a trickster.

Express Ideas and Engage in Discussion

❶ Teach/Model Review the list of expressions that the class generated for asking questions and expressing ideas (page T80a). Connect concepts: *You also express your ideas when you engage in a discussion.* Explain concepts: *When you express ideas, you tell what you know or what you think. When you engage in a discussion, you express your ideas and listen to and respect the ideas of others.*

Display the chart and work with a volunteer to model how to express ideas as you engage in a discussion. Reverse roles.

Ask a Question	Express Ideas
What do you know about tricksters?	I know tricksters are smart.
What do you think about a trickster's behavior?	I think a trickster's behavior is funny.

⊙ NGReach.com > eVisual 2.13

Invite students to engage in a discussion about a trickster's behavior. Guide them to express their ideas using a variety of sentence types.

❷ Practice/Apply Have students participate in a **Think, Pair, Share** based on what people can learn from smart animals like tricksters. Use **Academic Language Frames** to provide ideas to support every language level.

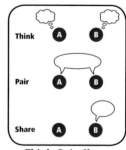

Think, Pair, Share

CHECK UNDERSTANDING Have students use the illustration on page 80 to express ideas about Cuy, using the Key Word **behavior**.

Cuy the Guinea Pig

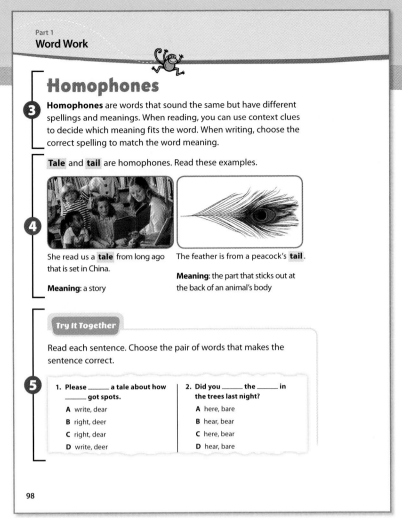

Homophones

3 **Homophones** are words that sound the same but have different spellings and meanings. When reading, you can use context clues to decide which meaning fits the word. When writing, choose the correct spelling to match the word meaning.

Tale and **tail** are homophones. Read these examples.

4

She read us a **tale** from long ago that is set in China.

Meaning: a story

The feather is from a peacock's **tail**.

Meaning: the part that sticks out at the back of an animal's body

Try It Together

Read each sentence. Choose the pair of words that makes the sentence correct.

5

1. Please _____ a tale about how _____ got spots.
   A write, dear
   B right, deer
   C right, dear
   D write, deer

2. Did you _____ the _____ in the trees last night?
   A here, bare
   B hear, bear
   C here, bear
   D hear, bare

98

Student Book page 98

Homophones

3 **Teach** Read the introduction aloud. Write the homophones *tale* and *tail*. Have students tell what is the same (the sounds) and what is different (the spelling and meanings). Discuss the meanings (*tale*: a story; *tail*: an animal part). Display this sentence: My teacher read a trickster _____. Have students tell which homophone makes sense and why.

4 **Model** Read the explanation about *tail* and *tale* and model how to use context to determine which homophone to use. Point to the photo of the children and say: *I see children listening to a story.* Then read the caption and say: *The word* tale *means "story." The children are listening to* a tale. Invite a volunteer to repeat with the word *tail*.

5 **Practice/Apply** Read the directions aloud. Discuss the meanings of the homophone pairs *right/write, dear/deer, here/hear,* and *bare/bear.* Then have partners work together to complete the sentences. Use the **Multi-Level Practice Sets** to address varying levels of vocabulary knowledge.

> **CHECK UNDERSTANDING** Say: *Choose a homophone pair. Use each word correctly in a sentence.* (Possible answer: I sent an email to a friend. I don't have a cent in my pocket.

Differentiate

Multi-Level Practice Sets

N *for* (as in: This is for him.) *four* (a number)

B *here* (in this place), *hear* (sense with the ears)

I *hour* (60 minutes), *our* (belonging to us)

AH *paws* (animal feet), *pause* (stop)

A *I'll* (I will), *isle* (island), *aisle* (path)

Keys to Efficacy

Model how to focus on meaning. *When a sentence with a homophone doesn't make sense, I check to be sure I'm using the correct meaning. How can we check the meaning?*

Day 6
continued

Day at a Glance:
- **Language:** Express Ideas and Engage in Discussion
- **Vocabulary:** Homophones
- **Reading:** Read the Trickster Tale
- **Writing:** Writing Fluency

Read the Trickster Tale

1 **Connect Across Texts** Read aloud the introduction. Explain: *Cuy the Guinea Pig used his wits to survive, or stay alive. In this story, you will read about another animal who does the same. Think about how the stories are similar and how they are different.*

2 **Genre** Review what students have learned about trickster tales. Then, read aloud the explanation. Elaborate: *Most trickster tales are folk tales. A folk tale is traditional story that has been told and retold. It often shows the values of the people in that place. What folk tales do you know?*

3 **Preview and Build Background** Use sheltering strategies as you conduct a picture walk.

Pages	Say (and Do)
99	*What an interesting animal!* (Point to the mouse deer.) *It is very small, but it looks like a deer. That's why it's called a mouse deer. What can you tell about a mouse deer from this picture?* (It likes to eat plants. It lives in the forest close to where people live.)
100–101	*Oh, no! Mouse Deer comes too close to the farmer's garden. What happens?* (He *gets* caught in a trap.) *Mouse Deer gets away, but he goes back to the farm later on. What happens then?* (He *kicks* a scarecrow and his leg *gets* stuck. Maybe the scarecrow is sticky, like the little clay person in "Love and Roast Chicken.")
102–103	*The farmer is holding Mouse Deer upside down by the legs. I guess Mouse Deer got stuck on the scarecrow, and that's how the farmer caught him. What do you see in the next picture?* (Mouse Deer is in a cage.) *The dog looks like he wants to eat Mouse Deer! Is that what happens?* (No, Mouse Deer gets away.) *I wonder how Mouse Deer gets away? We'll have to read the story to find out!*

4 **Read "Mouse Deer and Farmer"** Scaffold the support for varied reading levels.

BELOW LEVEL	ON/ABOVE LEVEL
Listen and Read Along	**Read Silently and Interact with Text**
• Have students act out events and feelings as you read the text aloud.	• Have students take notes as they read the tale silently. Focus on similarities and differences between the two tales.
• Check understanding with selected Build Comprehension questions.	• After reading, have them use their notes to engage in discussion.

CHECK UNDERSTANDING Ask: *What makes a trickster tale different from other stories?*

Student Book page 99

Build Comprehension page 99

1 **Set a Purpose** What would you like to find out as you read this trickster tale? (Answers will vary. Possible answer: I want to find out if Mouse Deer is as smart as Cuy.)

2 **Make Inferences** Where does Mouse Deer live? How do you know? (Mouse Deer lives in the forest. I read that Mouse Deer loved to eat fruits, roots, and shoots in the forest. I know that animals find foods to eat where they live. So I know that Mouse Deer lives in a forest.)

3 **Answers to Before You Move On**
1. **Character's Motive** Mouse Deer loves to eat vegetables because they are different from the foods in the forest.
2. **Setting** Farmer's garden has lots of different kinds of vegetables. The illustration shows juicy cucumbers, tomatoes, peppers, and eggplants in Farmer's garden.

Cultural Perpectives: Trickster Tales

Explain that tales about tricksters come from many cultures. Provide students with picture books about tricksters from different cultures, such as the Anansi tales from Africa and the Caribbean. Have partners browse the illustrations to find out about the culture. Have them talk about what they notice about the place and way of life. Ask: *What is the weather like? What plants grow there? What do the people or animals wear?*

Snap! Mouse Deer's leg was caught in a **snare**! When he saw Farmer coming, Mouse Deer lay down and made his body **stiff**.

"Look what I caught," said Farmer. "But this mouse deer looks dead. Maybe he's been dead a long time. I guess we can't eat him."

Farmer freed Mouse Deer from the snare and tossed him back into the forest. Mouse Deer landed with a soft *plop*, then jumped up and ran away.

"Hey! You tricked me!" Farmer yelled, but Mouse Deer just laughed.

In Other Words
snare trap
stiff not move

100

A few days passed, but Mouse Deer kept thinking about those vegetables. When he went back to the garden, he saw something new. It looked like a man, but its head was a coconut and its body was rubber.

"**A scarecrow!**" said Mouse Deer. "Farmer can't scare me with that!"

Mouse Deer kicked the scarecrow, but his foot stuck to its body. The scarecrow was covered with sticky sap from a rubber tree!

"Let me go!" Mouse Deer cried.

In Other Words
"A scarecrow!" That isn't a real person!

▶ **Before You Move On**
1. **Character's Motive** Why does Farmer make a scarecrow?
2. **Make Connections** Compare how the farmer in this story and the farmer in "Love and Roast Chicken" outsmart the main character.

101

I A AH

Literary Analysis: Genre

Teach/Model Remind students that a trickster tale often shows the culture or way of life of people in a certain place. Point to the illustration and model: *Farmer wears a hat. He wears light clothing. This shows me what people in Southeast Asia wear. It tells me that the sun is hot in this place.*

Practice/Apply Have students use the illustrations and text to find other examples that show the way of life in Southeast Asia. Say: *What foods do the people eat?* (vegetables and mouse deer) *What are their houses like?* (The houses are above the ground on boards.)

Literary Analysis: Sound words

Onomatopoeia is the use of words that stand for sounds. On page 100, the writer uses the word "snap" when the snare traps Mouse Deer's leg. Find another example of a sound word on the page. (*plop*)

Build Comprehension, page 100–101

1 **Analyze Character** Remind students that they can figure out what a character is like by what the character does or says. Ask: *What does Mouse Deer do when he sees Farmer coming? What does this show you about Mouse Deer?* (Mouse Deer makes his body stiff. He plays dead. This shows that Mouse Deer is smart and thinks fast.)

2 **Draw Conclusions** *Why do you think Farmer opens the snare?* (Farmer wants to eat Mouse Deer, but he thinks Mouse Deer is dead. Farmer doesn't want to eat a dead mouse deer so he opens the snare.)

3 **Answers to Before You Move On**
1. **Character's Motive** Farmer wants to catch Mouse Deer.
2. **Make Connections** RETEACH Guide students to make connections:

Say: *In this story, the farmer makes a scarecrow to catch the Deer Mouse. It reminds me of the clay doll that the farmer in* Love and Roast Chicken *made.*

Ask: *What did each farmer do to make sure he caught the trickster?* (They each added sticky sap.)

Then Farmer appeared. "Welcome back," he said. Then he pulled Mouse Deer off the scarecrow and locked him in a chicken coop.

"You'll stay here tonight," said Farmer, "and tomorrow you'll be our dinner."

That night Mouse Deer couldn't sleep. When the sun **rose**, he just lay there sadly. Then he heard a voice.

"So Farmer finally caught you," said Farmer's dog.

Mouse Deer thought fast. "What do you mean, Dog? Farmer didn't catch me." **4**

"Then why are you in the coop?" asked Dog.

"Because there aren't enough beds in the house. You see, tomorrow Farmer is holding a **feast**, and I'm the **guest of honor**."

"That's not fair!" said Dog. "I've been his loyal friend for years, so I should be the guest of honor!"

"You're right. Why don't you take my place?"

So Dog lifted the latch and opened the door. Mouse Deer ran toward the forest, laughing.

"Farmer will have to find a different dinner now, because he can't catch me!" ❖ **5**

In Other Words
rose came up in the morning

In Other Words
feast big, special meal
guest of honor most important guest there

▶ **Before You Move On**

6
1. **Make Connections** How is Mouse Deer like Cuy?
2. **Character** Why does Dog think he should be the guest of honor?

102

103

Student Book pages 102–103

Build Comprehension, pages 102–103

4 **Summarize** What has happened since Mouse Deer got stuck on the scarecrow? (Farmer pulled Mouse Deer off the scarecrow. He locked Mouse Deer in a chicken coop. Mouse Deer told Dog that Farmer didn't catch him.)

5 **Plot** If Mouse Deer hadn't tricked Dog, do you think he could have still escaped? How? (Answers will vary. Possible answer: Yes, he would have found a way to trick the farmer again.)

6 **Answers to Before You Move On**
1. **Make Connections** APPLY Remind students how to make connections: Possible answers: Both Mouse Deer and Cuy tricked other animals. Mouse Deer and Cuy tried to steal food from the farmers. Mouse Deer and Cuy are clever.

2. **Character** Dog thinks he should be the guest of honor because he has been Farmer's loyal friend for years.

Keys to Efficacy

Too many questions can lead to a loss of comprehension. Select questions wisely.

Science: Mouse Deer

Display photos or computer images of the small mouse deer of Southeast Asia.

Have students create a "**Characteristic**" web that shows the features of the small mouse deer. Students can use pictures and/or words.

Day 6
continued

Day at a Glance:
Language: Express Ideas and Engage in Discussion
Vocabulary: Homophones
Reading: Respond and Extend
Writing: Writing Fluency

OBJECTIVES

Vocabulary
• Use Academic Vocabulary: behavior, **T**
• Use Grade-Level Content Vocabulary: predator, prey trait, survival **T**

Language
• Participate in Discussion

Fluency
• Read with Accuracy and Rate **T**

Literary Analysis
• Compare Characters' Adventures

Learning and Teamwork Strategies
• Use Graphic Organizer: Venn Diagram
• Collaborate with peer

Writing
• Develop Writing Fluency
• Monitor and Self-Correct Writing

Resources

⊘ eVisuals 2.15

⊘ eVisual 2.1

✎⊘ Practice Master 2.8

Differentiate

Academic Language Frames

Make Comparisons
■ Here is a list of things that are the same: _____.
  Here is a list of things that are different: _____.

_____

■ _____ and _____ are alike because both _____.
  _____ is different from _____ because _____.

■ While _____ and _____ both have adventures,
  _____ had _____ while _____ had _____.
■ Both characters were _____, but _____ was the
  most _____ because _____.

⊘NGReach.com > eVisual 2.15

Respond and Extend

1 **Reread** As students reread "Mouse Deer and Farmer" on their own, have them think about what happens to the characters.

2 **Compare Characters' Adventures**
Remind students that a Venn diagram compares two things. Say: *You can use a Venn diagram to compare two plots. You can show how the stories are alike and how they are different.* Read the instructions.

Create groups and use the **Numbered Heads.** Help focus students' thinking: *Think about each character's adventures, or exciting experiences.* Ask questions to help guide discussion. Provide **Academic Language Frames** to support students at different levels.

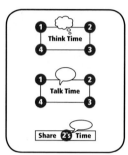

Numbered Heads

Focus	Questions
1. Behavior	What does the character say and do?
2. Events	What risks did each character take? What tricks did each character play to save himself?
3. Results	What were the results of the characters' actions?

As students report their group's ideas, students should record them on **Practice Master 2.8**.

3 **Talk Together About the Big Question** Read aloud the question and directions. Remind students that the animals they read about are not real animals because these animals talk and act like people. Guide students to focus on the animals' intelligence by describing their **survival** skills.

Have students add ideas to the Unit concept map.

CHECK UNDERSTANDING Have students make Cuy and Mouse Deer cards. Have them hold up a card(s) when you describe one or both characters.

Mouse Deer

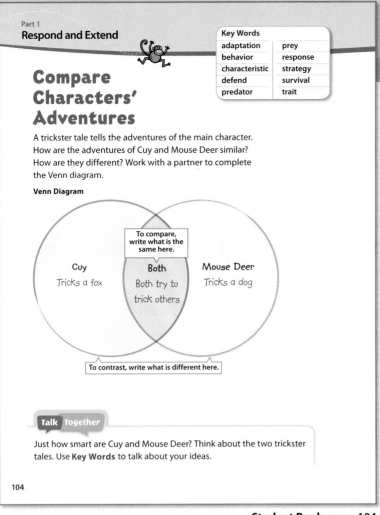

Compare Characters' Adventures

Key Words

adaptation	prey
behavior	response
characteristic	strategy
defend	survival
predator	trait

A trickster tale tells the adventures of the main character. How are the adventures of Cuy and Mouse Deer similar? How are they different? Work with a partner to complete the Venn diagram.

Venn Diagram

Cuy
Tricks a fox

To compare, write what is the same here.

Both
Both try to trick others

Mouse Deer
Tricks a dog

To contrast, write what is different here.

Talk Together

Just how smart are Cuy and Mouse Deer? Think about the two trickster tales. Use **Key Words** to talk about your ideas.

104

Student Book page 104

Daily Writing

4 **Writing Fluency** Use the **Power Writing** routine (see page PD53). Write the word **survival** and prompt: *Both trickster tales were about survival. What do you need for survival? Think about this word and write about it.*

Power Writing Routine

 1. What do you know about the word or picture?

 2. Take one minute to write as much as you can, as well as you can.
B words   **I** sentences   **A** **AH** paragraphs

 3. Check your spelling and grammar. (Circle) mistakes.

123 **4.** Count your words.

 eVisual 2.16

Fluency: Accuracy and Rate

To activate prior knowledge and practice fluency, conduct timed readings of "Love and Roast Chicken." Select an option for recording.

- Use the automatic speech recognition on the **Comprehension Coach** to track word count per minute for the entire passage.

- Use **Practice Master 2.7.**

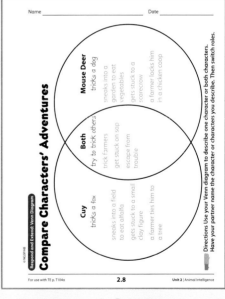

Practice Master 2.8

CLOSE AND ASSESS

- **Language** *Why do you think people like to read trickster tales? Express your ideas. I think* _____ .

- **Reading** *How does* Mouse Deer and Farmer *connect to a story you already read?*

- **Vocabulary** *Create a food chain that indicates the* **predator/prey** *retain relationships in* Mouse Deer. _____ .

Day 7

Day at a Glance:
- ▶ **Language:** Kinds of Sentences
- ▶ **Vocabulary:** Homophones
- ▶ **Reading:** Reread the Selection
- ▶ **Writing:** Short Story with Dialogue

OBJECTIVES

Vocabulary
- Use Academic Vocabulary ❶
- Use Grade-Level Vocabulary ❶
- Use Context Clues for Homophones ❶

Grammar
- Identify Kinds of Sentences ❶

Learning and Teamwork Strategies
- Relate to Prior Knowledge
- Make Contributions

Resources

  Practice Master 2.9

eVisual 2.17

Differentiate

Language Transfer

Issue In Chinese languages, Hmong, and Korean, a question can be formed by adding *yes* or *no* to the end of a statement. Students who speak this language may say *The trickster tale is interesting, yes?* instead of *Is the trickster tale interesting?* They may say *You like that character, no?* instead of *Do you like that character?*

Solution Provide language frames for students to use for practicing questions:

Is that _____?

Do you _____?

Was she _____?

Are they _____?

Part 1 Grammar Skills Trace	Page
Day 2	Kinds of Sentences	T77a
Day 4	Questions	T96a
▶ Day 7	**Kinds of Sentences**	**T105a**
Day 10	Review Kinds of Sentences	T106g

Language of the Day

What questions can you ask about the words tail and tale?

Do these words ____?

Model: *I know that tail and tale are homophones. Homophones sound alike. I could ask: Do these words sound alike?* Have students devise their questions based on what they know about homophones.

Grammar Kinds of Sentences Ⅰ A AH

❶ Teach/Model Read the introduction and the rules for the first two sentences. Say: *Notice the punctuation at the end of each sentence. What ends sentence 1?* (a period) *What ends sentence 2?* (an exclamation mark) Write:

> *That's not fair* (exclamation mark);

> *Farmer can't catch Mouse Deer* (period);

Ask students which is a statement and which is an exclamation. Have a volunteer add the end mark to each one. Read the next two rules and examples. Write:

> *Will Dog listen to Mouse Deer* (question mark);

> *Go home* (period);

> *Where is Mouse Deer* (question mark);

Ask volunteers to identify the kinds of sentences and add the end marks. Say: *Each kind of sentence has its own kind of end punctuation. A command can end with a period or an exclamation point.*

❷ Practice Read the directions and the excerpt from "Love and Roast Chicken." If necessary, help students identify the question by pointing out the end mark. Provide time for students to answer the question. Then say: *When you see the word* Who, *you know that the speaker is asking you to name a person.*

❸ Apply in Writing Read aloud the directions and have students work with a partner. Provide support, as necessary. Then assign **Practice Master 2.9** for practice with capitalization and end punctuation.

CHECK UNDERSTANDING Ask: *What words might you see at the beginning of a question?* (Possible answers: *Who, What, When, Where, Why, How, Is, Are, Was, Were, Do, Does*)

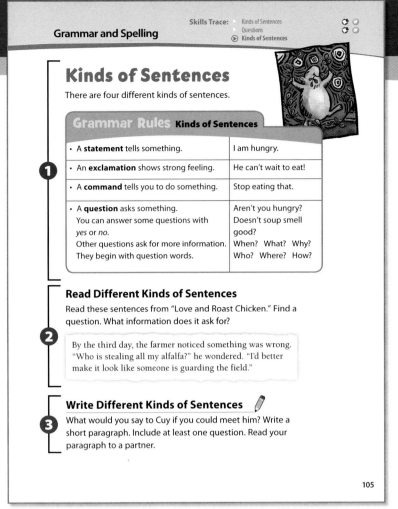

Kinds of Sentences

There are four different kinds of sentences.

① Grammar Rules Kinds of Sentences

• A **statement** tells something.	I am hungry.
• An **exclamation** shows strong feeling.	He can't wait to eat!
• A **command** tells you to do something.	Stop eating that.
• A **question** asks something. You can answer some questions with *yes* or *no*. Other questions ask for more information. They begin with question words.	Aren't you hungry? Doesn't soup smell good? When? What? Why? Who? Where? How?

② Read Different Kinds of Sentences

Read these sentences from "Love and Roast Chicken." Find a question. What information does it ask for?

> By the third day, the farmer noticed something was wrong. "Who is stealing all my alfalfa?" he wondered. "I'd better make it look like someone is guarding the field."

③ Write Different Kinds of Sentences ✏️

What would you say to Cuy if you could meet him? Write a short paragraph. Include at least one question. Read your paragraph to a partner.

105

Student Book page 105

More Homophones

④ Review/Model Review the Day 6 lesson (page T98). Write these sentences and use the **Dictionary Entries** to model using the definitions to identify which homophone makes sense in the first sentence. Have students do a **Think, Pair, Share** to determine which homophone makes sense in the remaining sentences. (See **Cooperative Learning Routines**, pages PD58–PD59.)

I wrote a letter to my _____ grandmother. (dear; much loved)

My dad is my grandmother's _____ . (son; male child)

I told Grandmother about a _____ we read. (tale; story)

⑤ Practice/Apply Write each sentence. Have students spell the homophone that makes sense in each sentence. Then have students turn and talk to explain how they determined the meaning that made sense.

1. The fox has a bushy _____ . (tail; an animal part)
2. Some animals sleep when the _____ is out. (sun; a star that gives Earth light and heat)
3. The mouse _____ tricked the dog. (deer; an animal)
4. Most dogs are _____ to their owners. (dear; much loved)
5. A trickster _____ is fun to read. (tale; story)

> **CHECK UNDERSTANDING** Say: *Say and spell an example of a homophone pair.*

Name _____ Date _____

Grammar: Kinds of Sentences

It's Not So Tricky

Grammar Rules Kinds of Sentences

There are four kinds of sentences.

Name	Definition	Example
statement	tells something	Mouse Deer is smart.
question	asks something	Where is Mouse Deer?
exclamation	shows strong feeling	What a trick!
command	tells you to do something	Bring me some food. Be careful!

Name each sentence. Then write each sentence correctly.

1. where does Mouse Deer go
   question Where does Mouse Deer go?
2. he is in the garden
   statement He is in the garden.
3. what a big mistake
   exclamation What a big mistake!
4. tell Mouse Deer to run
   command Tell Mouse Deer to run.

▬ Tell a partner what you know about trickster tales. Use different kinds of sentences.

For use with TE pT105a   **2.9**   Unit 2 | Animal Intelligence

🔄 ▶ **Practice Master 2.9**

Dictionary Entries

dear *adj.* much loved *My aunt is dear to me.*
deer *n.* an animal *A deer lives in the forest.*

son *n.* male child *My dad's son is my brother.*
sun *n.* a star that gives Earth light and heat *The sun is high in the sky.*

tail *n.* an animal part *The dog will wag its tail.*
tale *n.* a story *The author wrote a tale about animals.*

NGReach.com ⟩ eVisual 2.17

Part 1 Vocabulary Skills Trace		Page
Day 1	Science Vocabulary	T75
Day 2	Academic Vocabulary	T77
Day 3	Expand Word Knowledge	T80b
Day 4	Share Word Knowledge	T96b
Day 5	Apply Word Knowledge	T97b
Day 6	Homophones	T98
Day 7	**More Homophones**	**T105**
Days 8–9	Extend Vocabulary	T106e–f
Day 10	Vocabulary Review	T106g–h

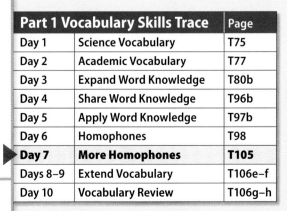

Day 7
continued

Day at a Glance:
▶ **Language::** Kinds of Sentences
▶ **Vocabulary:** Homophones

▶ **Reading:** Reread the Selection
▶ **Writing:** Short Story with Dialogue

OBJECTIVES

Vocabulary
- Use Academic Vocabulary 🅣
- Use Grade-Level Vocabulary: prey 🅣
- Use Classroom Vocabulary: dialogue 🅣

Literary Analysis
- Identify and Use Dialogue

Learning and Teamwork Strategies
- Relate to Prior Knowledge
- Make Contributions

Writing
- Reproduce Modeled Writing
- Write a Short Story with Dialogue

Reread Focus on Dialogue

1 **Teach** Remind students that in this trickster tale, they read a conversation or **dialogue** between characters. Write *dialogue* and explain: *Readers can get to know a character better by reading dialogue, the characters' words and thoughts. In dialogue, each character's words are surrounded by quotation marks.* Introduce the concept: *Today you will reread the trickster tale "Mouse Deer and Farmer." This time, think about how the author uses dialogue to show how one character tricks another.*

2 **Model** Have two volunteers read the dialogue between Mouse Deer and Dog on page 102. Ask: *What does Dog think when he says, "So farmer finally caught you."* (Mouse Deer will not escape this time.) *What does Mouse Deer's answer mean?* (He's thinking fast again.) Explain: *The author uses their dialogue to show that Mouse Deer is outsmarting Dog.*

Make a chart. Have volunteers read the next lines of dialogue and point out the quotation marks. Show how to use dialogue to compare what the two characters are like. What do their words show about them?

Dog	Mouse Deer
"So farmer finally caught you."	"What do you mean, Dog? Farmer didn't catch me."
"Then why are you in the coop?"	"Because there aren't enough beds in the house."

3 **Practice/Apply in Reading** Have students read "Mouse Deer and Farmer." Then have them participate in a **Roundtable**. Have students use dialogue to compare and contrast the characters. Support students by adding dialogue to the chart for them to discuss. *Dog: "I should be the guest of honor." Mouse Deer: "You're right. Why don't you take my place?"*

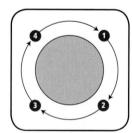

Roundtable

Daily Writing

Modeled Writing: Short Story with Dialogue   Review the story form, trickster tale, (page T80). Remind students to use different kinds of sentences and quotation marks for dialogue. Then use the **Modeled Writing** routine to illustrate how to write a short story with dialogue in which one character tricks another. (See Writing Routines, on page PD54.)

Think Aloud	Write
1. Plan	
I will make a RAFT to plan my writing. I will take on the role of a storyteller.	Role: storyteller
I think my classmates will enjoy another trickster tale.	Audience: class of children
Repeat the think aloud for form (short story) and topic (a good trick).	
2. Write	
My story will happen in the rain forest. Both characters will be animals who talk and act like people. The beginning of my story will tell the problem. I'll use dialogue to show what the characters say and think.	Bird was hungry. He knew that the juiciest fruit was in Monkey's tree. "You can't have my fruit!" said Monkey. "The best fruit is mine because I'm the smartest animal in the rain forest!" So Bird flew away.
Now I'll write the middle of the story. It will tell what Bird does to trick Monkey. I remember how the author used dialogue so I'll write what Bird says to trick Monkey. I'll remember to use quotation marks.	Bird flew through the rain forest calling to all the birds. "Come to a surprise party for Monkey! There will be lots of fruit!"
I'll finish by writing the ending of this story. It tells what happens when Bird tricks Monkey.	Monkey saw all the birds. He said, "What a surprise! I'm happy you came to honor me!" Then the birds began to eat the fruit. What could Monkey do? "Great fruit!" said Bird. "I think I'll have a second helping!"
3. Read and Reflect	
I will read aloud my final story and check it one more time. *Have I met the plan I made during my RAFT? Yes! Do I want to make more changes? No.* *Now I can share it with my classmates.*	Read the beginning, middle, and end of the story.

Display the finished short story as a model. Circle end punctuation and quotation marks. Use **Multi-Level Strategies** to support students at all proficiency levels.

CLOSE AND ASSESS
- **Language** *Identify example of different kinds of sentences you used in your story. Point out the punctuation for each sentence type.* (Sample response: "You can't have my fruit!" is an exclamation.)
- **Reading** *How did the dialogue in the tale help you analyze the characters?* (Possible: It helped me to know what the character was thinking. It showed me how clever or foolish a character was.)
- **Vocabulary** *Did you use any Key Words in your story? Which words did you use?* (Answers will vary.)

Differentiate

Multi-Level Strategies

BEGINNING

Use these sentence starters and allow beginners to draw and/or write short story events in order.
- At the beginning, _____.
- In the middle, _____.
- At the end, _____.

INTERMEDIATE

Have students work with partners to compose a short story. Have them use color for the quotation marks in the draft.

ADVANCED

Encourage students to use at least one statement, question, exclamation, and command in the story. Have them read dialogue just as they think the characters would speak.

ADVANCED HIGH

Have students focus on each character's intelligence as they write dialogue. Ask: *How would a smart animal solve the problem? What might the animal say to show he/she is smart?*

Days 8–9

Day at a Glance:
▶ **Language:** Theme Theater: Extend the Story ▶ **Reading:** Read Leveled Books
▶ **Vocabulary:** Extend Vocabulary ▶ **Writing:** Paraphrase

OBJECTIVES

Language
• Language Function: Express Ideas ❶

Literary Analysis
• Analyze Characters

Listening and Speaking
• Listen Actively
• Watch Actions and Expressions
• Speak Clearly
• Use Gestures and Expressions

Learning and Teamwork Strategies
• Prompt and Provide Suggestions

Resources

• materials for costumes and props, such as:
  - construction paper
  - scissors and glue
  - paper plates
  - crayons and markers

 Assessment Handbook page 60

Language of the Day

What do you think about characters who play tricks on others?
I thought ____. Now I think ____.

Read the Language of the Day. Model: *I thought the characters were silly. Now I think they are smart.* Have students share answers to the question.

Theme Theater Extend the Story

❶ Introduce the Activity Remind students of how Cuy used his intelligence to avoid being eaten in "Love and Roast Chicken." Then, ask: *What if Cuy meets a new character who wants to eat him? What might this new character be like?* Allow time for students to offer suggestions.

Brainstorm a scene that would extend the story: *Imagine that Cuy wants to trick the new character to avoid being eaten. What kind of trick might Cuy play?* Collect ideas. *Now imagine that the farmer and Florinda are nearby. Will they help Cuy trick the new character?*

❷ Plan Form casts of four students each. Have each cast choose a story extension. Guide students at different proficiency levels to select appropriate roles.

3 **Rehearse** Have casts work together to create dialogue that involves Cuy, the new character, the farmer, and Florinda. Have group members give one another feedback as they rehearse. Remind students to provide specific ideas, such as *You can lick your lips and rub your stomach to show that you are hungry.* As students rehearse use **Multi-Level Strategies** to help students at each proficiency level.

Students can make masks or headbands to represent their characters. Have the class make simple props for all the groups to use, such as a eucalyptus tree or a drawing of the farmer's house.

4 **Curtains Up!** Have casts present their story extensions to another class. For each performance, assess one group's listening skills. Afterward, evaluate each performance using the rubric.

5 **Debrief and Compare** Ask each group to share what they enjoyed about the performances. Encourage them to compare and contrast the dialogue in the story extension with the dialogue in "Love and Roast Chicken."

Differentiate

Multi-Level Strategies

BEGINNING

Show students how to use facial expressions, gestures, and props to express ideas.

INTERMEDIATE

Coach students to practice speaking their lines in a clear voice that is loud enough for an audience to hear.

ADVANCED

Encourage students to change their voice to speak as they think the character would. Ask: *Does Cuy have a squeaky voice? Does the farmer have a deep voice?*

ADVANCED HIGH

As they practice lines, encourage students to use tone of voice to show statements, questions, and exclamations.

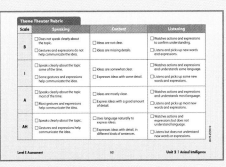

  Assessment Handbook page 60

Days 8–9
continued

Day at a Glance:
▶ **Language:** Theme Theater: Extend the Story
▶ **Vocabulary:** Extend Vocabulary
▶ **Reading:** Read Leveled Books
▶ **Writing:** Paraphrase

OBJECTIVES

Vocabulary
• Extend Vocabulary through Wide Reading

Language
• Participate in Discussion

Reading
• Read Independently
• Summarize Reading
• Make Connections: Text to Text
• Apply Reading Strategies Varied Texts

Writing
• Paraphrase Maintaining Meaning

Science
• Examine Animal Intelligence
• Identify Animal Adaptations

Resources

 Leveled Books:
  - *An Interview with Harry the Tarantula*
  - *Dolphin Rescue*
  - *The World According to Humphrey*
  - *What Did One Elephant Say to the Other?*
  - *Creepy Creatures*
  - *Do Animals Have Feelings Too?*

  Reach Leveled Library Lesson Plans

NGReach.com

Find more leveled readers about this topic.

Differentiate   Read Leveled Books

Group students based on their reading abilities and interests. Use the **Guided Reading** routine (See page PD47) for books at students' instructional level. Use the **Independent Reading Support** (see page PD50) for books at students' independent reading level.

After reading, organize the students into heterogeneous groups to discuss what they read and to use the new information to answer the Big Question. Use these prompts to guide your discussion:

• What new information did you learn about animal intelligence?

• What surprised you?

• How did new information change your answer?

Fiction

BEGINNING LEVEL

An Interview with Harry the Tarantula
by Leigh Ann Tyson

• **Genre:** Animal Fantasy

Katy Did of KBUG radio interviews Harry the Tarantula, who tells her all about his fascinating life as one of the world's creepiest spiders.

Key Words

breathe

burrow

cricket

hind

poison

INTERMEDIATE LEVEL

Dolphin Rescue
by Glen Phelan

• **Genre:** Realistic Fiction

In this chapter book, students learn about dolphin intelligence when an injured baby dolphin is rescued and successfully returned to its parents.

Key Words

blowhole

echo

mammal

shark

surface

ADVANCED   ADVANCED HIGH LEVELS

The World According to Humphrey
by Betty G. Birney

• **Genre:** Animal Fantasy

A substitute teacher brings a hamster named Humphrey to school. Told from the hamster's perspective, Humphrey explains what you can learn about yourself by taking care of another species.

Key Words

according

anxious

creatures

humans

stroked

Nonfiction

BEGINNING LEVEL

What Did One Elephant Say to the Other?
by Becky Baines

- **Genre:** Expository Nonfiction

Elephants don't need words to communicate. They use their whole bodies to "talk" to each other and other animals.

Key Words

calves

danger

greet

grumble

trumpet

INTERMEDIATE LEVEL

Creepy Creatures
by Sneed B. Collard III

- **Genre:** Expository Nonfiction

In this book, students read about some creatures that seem scary (and may even be dangerous), but will quickly discover that they are trying to survive just like we are.

Key Words

control

prey

scales

shark

tentacles

ADVANCED   ADVANCED HIGH LEVELS

Do Animals Have Feelings Too?
by David L. Rice

- **Genre:** Expository Nonfiction

True animal stories show examples of animals that experience feelings of compassion, joy, love, and grief.

Key Words

devotion

grief

happiness

loyalty

mate

Daily Writing A AH

Journal Entry Have students write a journal entry in their reading journals. Use "Love and Roast Chicken" to model how to write a journal entry. Focus on how to paraphrase maintaining meaning. Say: *The sky will fall if Cuy does not hold up the rock. Is this right?* (no). Then work with students to restate: *Cuy tells Tío Antonio that he is holding up the sky so that the fox won't eat him.*

Same Book / Different Levels
B I A AH

Dogs at Work
by Terrell Smith

Discover how service dogs are trained and how these dogs help people.

Pioneer Edition
Fountas and Pinnell: P–R

B Conduct a Picture Walk.

I Read text and captions.

Key Words

breed	disease
rescue	search
service	skills

Pathfinder Edition
Fountas and Pinnell: Q–S

A Read text and captions.

AH Read and write responses to questions.

Key Words

breed	commands
disabilities	impaired
rescue	service

Part 1 Vocabulary Skills Trace		Page
Day 1	Science Vocabulary	T75
Day 2	Academic Vocabulary	T77
Day 3	Expand Word Knowledge	T80b
Day 4	Share Word Knowledge	T96b
Day 5	Apply Word Knowledge	T97b
Day 6	Homophones	T98
Day 7	Homophones	T105
▶ Days 8–9	Extend Vocabulary	T106e–f
Day 10	Vocabulary Review	T106g–h

OBJECTIVES

Language
- Review Language Function: Express Ideas **T**

Grammar
- Review Kinds of Sentences

Vocabulary
- Review and Use Grade-Level Key Vocabulary **T**
- Review Homophones **T**

Reading Strategy
- Review Make Connections **T**

Comprehension and Literary Analysis
- Review Characters **T**
- Review Character Chart

Fluency
- Read with Expression, Rate, and Accuracy

Resources

- *Assessment Handbook*
- *Key Word Images*
- *eVisual 2.18*
- *Comprehension Coach*

Language of the Day

What did you learn? How does it help you in school? I learned how to ____. ____ means to ____. For example, ____.

Model: *I learned how to express ideas. Expressing ideas means to tell what you think about something. For example, I think lions are amazing animals.* Review the list of skills students learned in Part 1. Prompt students to talk about a skill they learned: *How did we use that skill? How do you think you can use that skill again?*

Review and Assess

Use these interactive review activities to reinforce concepts covered in Part 1. Then use the assessment tools to evaluate students' progress. For more details about assessment, see page T143a.

Language Function

Express Ideas

Use a **Roundtable** to have students express ideas about animals. Show **Key Word Images**. Have the students in each group express ideas about each image.

- **Assessment:** Language Function Rubric on page 56 of the Assessment Handbook.

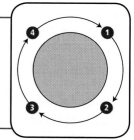

Round table

Grammar

Kinds of Sentences

Write examples of different kinds of sentences on the board. Have partners identify each one as a statement, command, question, or exclamation. Challenge partners to write sentences and read them aloud to the class.

Vocabulary

Science and Academic Vocabulary

Form two teams. Show **Key Word Images**. Give clues to one of the Key Words. Have each team take turns identifying the correct word based on the clues. Have teams use each word in a sentence.

- **Assessment:** Key Word Tests on pages 57–59 of the Assessment Handbook.

Key Words	
adaptation	prey
behavior	response
characteristic	strategy
defend	survival
predator	trait

Vocabulary Strategy

Word Work: Homophones

Conduct a team competition. Each team uses a pair of homophones in two different sentences that show the different meanings of the words. The opposing team must give a definition of the homophone as it is used in each sentence. Then teams change roles and repeat the process. The team that gives the most correct definitions wins.

> I read a fairy tale.

> In that sentence, tale means "story."

Reading Strategy

Read Aloud

Make Connections

Read the first two paragraphs of "The Sneaky Squirrel." Have students make connections to the text using the **Academic Language Frames**: *It's about _____. _____ reminds me of _____.*

Comprehension

Read Aloud

Literary Analysis

Read the rest of "The Sneaky Squirrel." Have students tell what characteristics of a trickster tale they see in the story, using the frame: *I can tell this is a trickster tale because _____.*

Text Structure

Have students analyze the characters by telling what they say and do, using these frames: *The squirrel says _____. The squirrel does _____. This shows me that the squirrel _____.*

Fluency

Accuracy, Rate, and Expression

Have students review their own recordings of "Love and Roast Chicken" in the Comprehension Coach. Then have students practice reading **Leveled Library Books** that are appropriate for their reading levels, focusing on accuracy, rate, and expression.

Read Aloud

The Sneaky Squirrel

A hungry squirrel scurried through the grass. He found a nut at the base of a tree.

Just then, a crow swooped down to the ground. The crow tried to take away the nut.

"What are you doing?" asked the squirrel.

"Stand back," said the crow. "I am going to eat this nut."

"Nut?" said the squirrel. "This is not a nut. It is just a rock."

The crow looked puzzled. "Are you sure?" he asked.

"Watch," said the squirrel as he tapped the nut on the tree. "It's just a rock."

The crow flew off, and the squirrel rushed home with the nut.

NGReach.com > eVisual 2.18

Part 1 Vocabulary Skills Trace		Page
Day 1	Science Vocabulary	T75
Day 2	Academic Vocabulary	T77
Day 3	Expand Word Knowledge	T80b
Day 4	Share Word Knowledge	T96b
Day 5	Apply Word Knowledge	T97b
Day 6	Homophones	T98
Day 7	More Homophones	T105
Days 8–9	Extend Vocabulary	T106e–f
Day 10	**Vocabulary Review**	**T106g–h**

BIG Question — Just how smart are animals?

PART 2

Days 1–5

▶ **Main Selection**
Animal Smarts, by Leslie Hall

▶ **Genre**
Science Article

▶ **Selection Summary**
This selection discusses how animals are intelligent beings that can communicate with each other, and some can even communicate with humans. Animals included in the selection are chimpanzees, meerkats, and parrots. Some scientists study animals to better understand the depth of their intelligence.

Selection CD 1 (((MP3)))

Skills at a Glance	
Language	Engage in Conversation; Tell an Original Story; Oral Language Project
Grammar	Compound Sentences; Complex Sentences
Vocabulary	Science Vocabulary: *command, imitate, memory, pattern, skill, tool*
	Academic Vocabulary: *ability, communication, inherit, language, learn*
	Use a Dictionary
Reading Strategy	Make Connections
Literary Analysis	Main Idea and Details
Writing	Writing Fluency; Prewrite; Draft; List; Edit and Proofread; Paragraph; Journal Entry
Newcomer Support	Use *In the USA:* greetings and good-byes words

▶ Companion Selection

The Clever Chimps of Fongoli, by Elizabeth Sengel

▶ Genre

Science Article

▶ Selection Summary

Chimpanzees in Fongoli, an area in Senegal, have learned a new method of finding food. Because large male chimps do not share the food they find, female and young male chimps have to be more resourceful. They take a broken-off tree branch, sharpen it with their teeth, and use it as a spear to hunt for prey in tree hollows.

NATIONAL GEOGRAPHIC EXCLUSIVE

Connect Across Texts
Read this article to **learn** what one scientist discovered while studying chimpanzees.

Genre A **science article** can tell about a new discovery in science.

THE CLEVER CHIMPS OF
Fongoli

by Elizabeth Sengel

It's hard to get a meal in Fongoli. The **harsh** landscape offers only **patches of greenery**. The sun burns like a 200-watt bulb. By eight o'clock in the morning, the rocky, treeless ground **bakes** in 90-degree heat.

▲ Chimps walk across dry ground in Fongoli.

In Other Words
harsh dry and hot
patches of greenery a few places with trees and plants
bakes gets really hot

▶ **Before You Move On**
1. **Make Connections** What does Fongoli remind you of? Explain.
2. **Use Text Features** What can you tell about this article from the title, the photo, and the caption?

131

Leveled Library Books

Differentiated Instruction

B | BEGINNING

Mouse-Deer Must Be Quick

by Constance Foland

Tiger wants to eat Mouse-Deer! Mouse-Deer must be quick to trick the Tiger out of a meal.

Good Dog!

by Susan Ring

This easy reader provides students an introduction to service animals and how dogs can help people.

I | INTERMEDIATE

My Buddy

by Audrey Osofsky

Buddy is a service dog. He helps a boy with muscular dystrophy have an active, independent life.

Animal Masterminds

by Catherine Nichols

In this chapter book, learn more about smart animals that can count, learn sign language, and identify colors.

A | ADVANCED / AH | ADVANCED HIGH

Animal Trainer

by Susan Koehler

Hillary visits her cousin at the Ocean City Dolphin Arena and learns more about the job of an animal trainer.

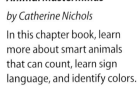

Koko's Kitten

by Dr. Francine Patterson

Koko the gorilla uses sign language to talk to her handlers. When she asks for a pet, her handlers search high and low for the perfect companion.

Unit 2 Daily Planner

PART 2

Core Lessons

	Day 1 Introduce Academic Language	**Day 2** Introduce More Academic Language
Language 🕐 5–10 minutes	**Language of the Day** *T106* ❶ **Language Function: Engage in Conversation** *T106* 💿 ((MP3)) **Oral Language** • Talk About Dog Training *T107* • Talk Together About the Big Question *T107*	**Language of the Day** *T109a* ❶ **Grammar: Compound Sentences** *T109a* **Oral Language** • Talk Together About Making Connections *T110*
Vocabulary 🕐 10–15 minutes	❶ **Science Vocabulary** • Introduce Words *T107* command memory skill imitate pattern tool **Classroom Vocabulary** • Introduce Word: **diagram** *T108*	❶ **Academic Vocabulary** • Introduce Words *T109* ability language communication learn inherit **Classroom Vocabulary** • Introduce Word: **remind** *T110*
Reading 🕐 15–20 minutes	❶ **Text Structure: Main Idea and Details** • Introduce Main Idea and Details *T108a* • Use Graphic Organizers: Thinking Map *T108* **Read Aloud: "James and Millie "** *T108a*	❶ **Strategy: Make Connections** • Introduce and Practice the Strategy *T110* **Read "Train Your Dog to Be Terrific"** *T111* **Phonics and Fluency** • Words with Digraphs /th/*th,* /ng/*ng* *T110*
Writing 🕐 15 minutes	**Daily Writing** • Writing Fluency *T108*	
	Science • Explore Animal Intelligence	**Science** • Explore Animal Intelligence

Content: Integrated Throughout Each Day

Day 3

Build Academic Language

Language of the Day *T112a*
Language Function: Tell an Original Story *T112a* 🔊 ((MP3))
Listening and Speaking
• Listen to and Sing a Song *T112a*

❶ Academic and Science Vocabulary
• Expand Word Knowledge *T112b*

ability	communication
command	imitate

Support Newcomers
• Build Basic Vocabulary: Greetings and Good-Byes Words *T112b*

Read the Selection
❶ Strategy: Make Connections *T112—T126–127*
• Reading Options *T114*
Literary Analysis
• Text Features *T115*
❶ Fluency: Intonation *T122–123*

Home Connection
• Pet Photographs *T116–117*
Science
• Intelligence *T118–119*
Math
• Patterns *T120–121*

Day 4

Build Academic Language

Language of the Day *T128a*
❶ Grammar: Complex Sentences *T128a*
Oral Language
• Talk About the Selection *T128c*

❶ Academic and Science Vocabulary
• Share Word Knowledge *T128b*

inherit	learn
language	memory

Think and Respond
• Talk About the Selection *T128c*
• Test-Taking Strategy *T128c*
❶ Fluency: Intonation *T128c*

Daily Writing
• Modeled Writing: Write About It *T128*

Science
• Explore Animal Intelligence

Day 5

Build Academic Language

Language of the Day *T129a*
❶ Listening and Speaking
• Use Gestures and Expressions *T129a*
How to Learn Language
• Relate to Personal Experience *T129a*
Oral Language
• Talk Together About the Big Question *T129*

❶ Academic and Science Vocabulary
• Apply Word Knowledge *T129b*

pattern tool	
skill	

Reread and Explain
❶ Text Structure: Main Idea and Details
• Make a Main Idea Diagram *T129c*
Explain a Story *T129c*
❶ Fluency: Accuracy, Rate, and Intonation *T129c*

Science
• Explore Animal Intelligence

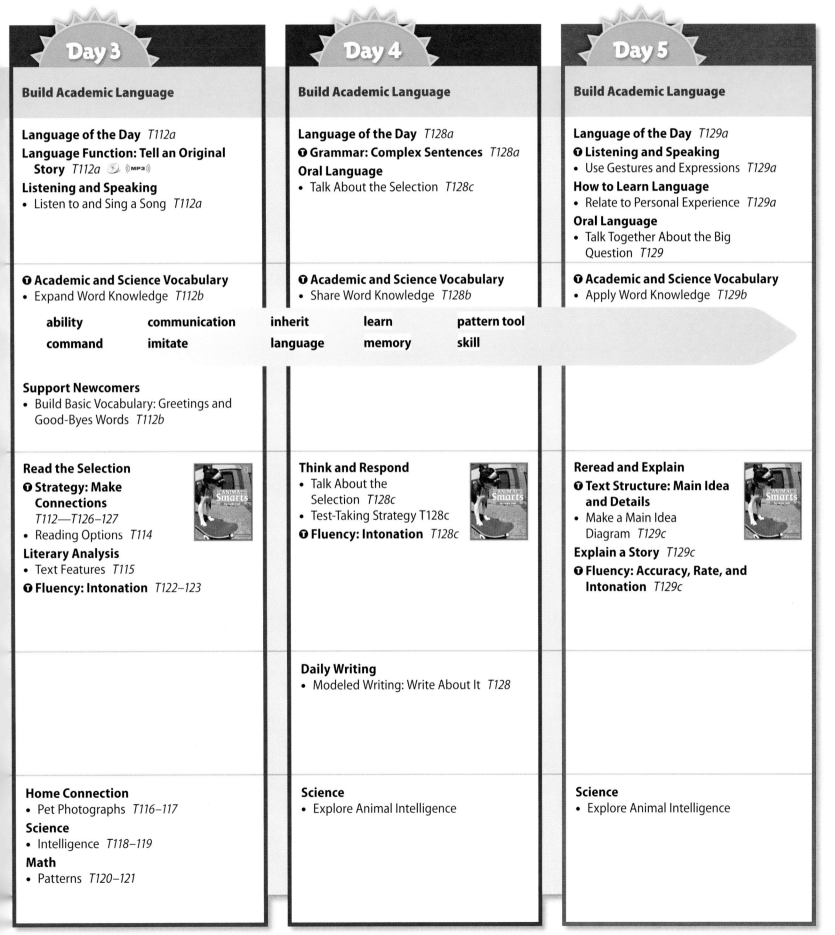

Unit 2 Daily Planner continued

PART 2

Core Lessons

	Day 6	**Day 7**
Language 5–10 minutes	Expand Academic Language **Language of the Day** *T130a* **Language Function: Tell an Original Story** *T130a* **Oral Language** • Talk Together About the Big Question *T136a*	Expand Academic Language **Language of the Day** *T137a* **❶ Grammar: Understand Compound Sentences** *T137a*
Vocabulary 10–15 minutes	**❶ Use a Dictionary** *T130* **Support Newcomers:** • Additional Practice Using a Dictionary *T130*	**❶ More Dictionary Skills** *T137* • Dictionary Entry Structure *T137*
Reading 15–20 minutes	**Read the Science Article** *T131a* • Reading Options *T131a* **❶ Strategy: Make Connections** *T131a–T135* **Literary Analysis** • Analyze Visuals *T134–T135* **Fluency: Accuracy and Rate** *T136* **Respond and Extend** • Compare Facts *T136a*	**Reread the Selection: Focus on Writer's Style** *T138a*
Writing 15 minutes	**Daily Writing** • Writing Fluency *136*	**Daily Writing** • Modeled Writing: Paragraph *T138b*
Content: Integrated Throughout Each Day	**Science** • Explore Animal Intelligence	**Science** • Explore Animal Intelligence

❶ = Tested Skill

Days 8–9

Apply Academic Language

Oral Language Project
- Introduce the Activity *T138c*
- Plan *T138c*
- Rehearse *T138d*
- Lights, Camera, Action! *T138d*
- Debrief and Compare *T138d*

Read Leveled Books

Fiction *T138e*

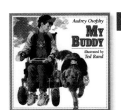

Key Words

angry	tiger
guarding	trick
licked	

Key Words

commands	service
disease	wheelchair
obey	

Key Words

behavior	target
dolphin	trainer
perform	

Nonfiction *T138f*

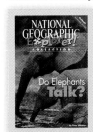

Key Words

contest	missing
energy	roam
guide	

Key Words

chimpanzee	scientist
experiments	squawk
parrot	

Key Words

communicate	language
gorilla	understand
kitten	

Daily Writing
- Journal Entry *T138f*

Day 10

Review and Assess

Interactive Review *T138g–T138h*
- 🔊 Language Function: Engage in Conversation
- 🔊 Grammar: Compound Sentences
- 🔊 Vocabulary: Science and Academic Vocabulary
- 🔊 Vocabulary Strategy: Use a Dictionary
- 🔊 Reading Strategy: Make Connections
- 🔊 Literary Analysis: Science Article
- 🔊 Text Structure: Main Idea and Details
- 🔊 Fluency: Accuracy and Intonation

Assessment *T138g–T138h*

Same Book, Different Levels

Key Words

calves	herd	scientists
extinction	language	tusks
habitat	regions	wilderness

Reading Station

EXPLORER! COLLECTION
Ladder Text:
- Pioneer edition for below level readers
- Pathfinder edition for on and above level readers

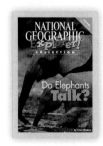
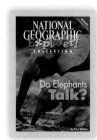

DECODABLE TEXTS

TRADE BOOK COLLECTION
Use the **Leveled Book Finder** at
 NGReach.com

Content Stations

Download complete lesson plans 🌐 **NGReach.com** ❯

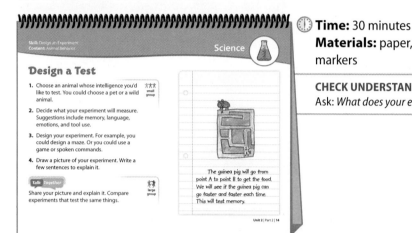

Skill: Design an Experiment
Content: Animal Behavior

Science 🧪

Design a Test

1. Choose an animal whose intelligence you'd like to test. You could choose a pet or a wild animal. ★★★ small group
2. Decide what your experiment will measure. Suggestions include memory, language, emotions, and tool use.
3. Design your experiment. For example, you could design a maze. Or you could use a game or spoken commands.
4. Draw a picture of your experiment. Write a few sentences to explain it.

Talk Together 👫 large group
Share your picture and explain it. Compare experiments that test the same things.

The guinea pig will go from point A to point B to get the food. We will see if the guinea pig can go faster and faster each time. This will test memory.

Unit 2 | Part 2 | 14

🕐 **Time:** 30 minutes
Materials: paper, pencils, colored markers

CHECK UNDERSTANDING
Ask: *What does your experiment measure?*

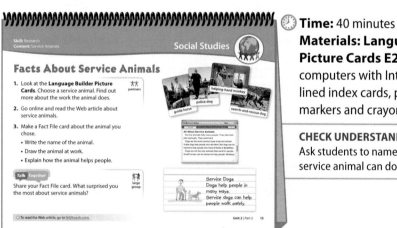

Skill: Research
Content: Service Animals

Social Studies 🌎

Facts About Service Animals

1. Look at the **Language Builder Picture Cards.** Choose a service animal. Find out more about the work the animal does. ★★ partners
2. Go online and read the Web article about service animals.
3. Make a Fact File card about the animal you chose.
   - Write the name of the animal.
   - Draw the animal at work.
   - Explain how the animal helps people.

Talk Together 👫 large group
Share your Fact File card. What surprised you the most about service animals?

To read the Web article, go to NGReach.com

Unit 2 | Part 2 | 15

🕐 **Time:** 40 minutes
Materials: Language Builder Picture Cards E23–E26, computers with Internet access, lined index cards, pencils, colored markers and crayons, scissors, glue

CHECK UNDERSTANDING
Ask students to name something that a service animal can do.

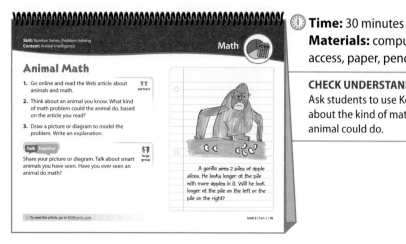

Skill: Number Sense, Problem Solving
Content: Animal Intelligence

Math 🔢

Animal Math

1. Go online and read the Web article about animals and math. ★★ partners
2. Think about an animal you know. What kind of math problem could the animal do, based on the article you read?
3. Draw a picture or diagram to model the problem. Write an explanation.

Talk Together 👫 large group
Share your picture or diagram. Talk about smart animals you have seen. Have you ever seen an animal do math?

To read the article, go to NGReach.com

A gorilla sees 2 piles of apple slices. He looks longer at the pile with more apples in it. Will he look longer at the pile on the left or the pile on the right?

Unit 2 | Part 2 | 16

🕐 **Time:** 30 minutes
Materials: computer with Internet access, paper, pencils, colored markers

CHECK UNDERSTANDING
Ask students to use Key Words to talk about the kind of math problem their animal could do.

Use these resources to provide daily opportunities for students to work individually or in groups at learning stations around the classroom.

Language Stations

Download complete lesson plans NGReach.com >

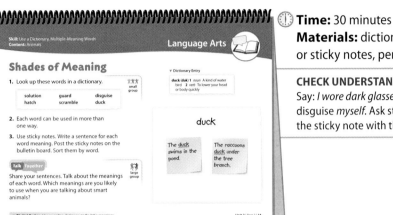

Time: 30 minutes
Materials: dictionary, paper strips or sticky notes, pencils

CHECK UNDERSTANDING
Say: *I wore dark glasses and a wig to disguise myself.* Ask students to hold up the sticky note with this meaning.

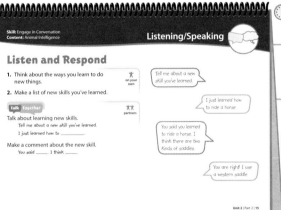

Time: 20 minutes
Materials: paper, pencils

CHECK UNDERSTANDING
Ask students to talk about a new skill that their partner has just learned.

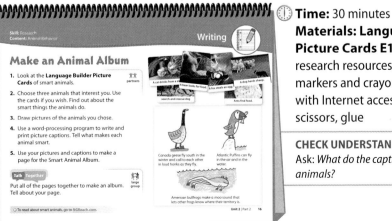

Time: 30 minutes
Materials: Language Builder Picture Cards E14–E26, research resources, paper, colored markers and crayons, computers with Internet access and printer, scissors, glue

CHECK UNDERSTANDING
Ask: *What do the captions tell us about the animals?*

Technology Station

Access resources NGReach.com >

(MP3) Recordings

- Let's Talk About Pets
- The Smartest Dog
- Animal Smarts

Digital Library

Learn vocabulary and practice language

- Key Word Images
- Language Builder Picture Cards

My Vocab Notebook

- Add Words

Comprehension Coach

- Use interactive library support. Automatically measure fluency.

Online Assessment

- Practice items in standardized test format.

Day 1

Day at a Glance:
▶ **Language:** Engage in Conversation ▶ **Reading:** Main Idea and Details
▶ **Vocabulary:** Science Vocabulary ▶ **Writing:** Writing Fluency; Study a Model

OBJECTIVES

Vocabulary
• Acquire and Use Grade-Level Vocabulary: command, memory, skill ⊕

Language
• Language Function: Engage in Conversation ⊕
• Listen to and Imitate Fluent Models
• Use a Variety of Language Structures
• Participate in Discussion

Learning and Teamwork Strategies
• Activate Prior Experience
• Use Media to Build Language
• Use Context to Build Concepts and Language

Science
• Explore Animal Intelligence

Resources

🔊 ⦿ *Sing With Me Song Book* page 10

⦿ ⦿ *Sing With Me Language Song CD 1,* Tracks 13, 14

⦿ *eVisuals 2.19, 2.20*

⦿ *Key Word Images*

⦿ *Language Builder Picture Card E23*

⦿ **NGReach.com** ⟩

See **Technology Station** for digital student resources.

Differentiate

Academic Language Frames

> **Engage in Conversation**
> ■ I think _____.
>   I agree./I don't agree.
> _____
> ■ I think _____ because _____.
>   I agree/disagree because _____.
>   You said _____. I think _____.
> _____
> ■ I think _____ because _____.
> ■ I agree/disagree because _____.
>   You said _____ and _____.
>   I think _____ and _____.

⦿ **NGReach.com** ⟩ **eVisual 2.20**

> ## Language of the Day
>
> What are some commands that we give animals?
> We command _____.

Read the Language of the Day. Model: *We command dogs to sit.* Have each student repeat your sentence and add their own ideas to create a cumulative sentence. Then explain that students will be listening, speaking, and writing more today about what animals can learn.

Engage in Conversation

❶ Teach/Model Display the dialogue "James and His Dog" on page 106. Read the introduction aloud and play the dialogue. Invite students to read aloud chorally as you play the dialogue a second time.

Point out the **Language Frames** and model using these structures to engage in conversation about animals. Display the how to card.

How to Engage in Conversation	
1. Tell your point of view or opinion.	James: I think dogs are smarter than cats. Kirsten: I don't agree.
2. Wait for your turn to talk. Ask and answer questions.	James: Why do you think that? Kirsten: I taught my dog to sit and roll over.

⦿ **NGReach.com** ⟩ eVisual 2.19

Model this language function with a volunteer. Ask the volunteer if he or she thinks that dogs are smarter than cats. Engage the volunteer in a short conversation, modeling the turn-taking and listening skills explained in the How to card.

❷ Practice/Apply Have students engage in conversation about the pictures they made in Share What You Know (page 73). Use **Academic Language Frames** to provide support for students at all levels they exchange ideas about what makes animals special.

> **CHECK UNDERSTANDING** Display **Language Builder Card E23** (search-and-rescue dog) and have students give information about it.

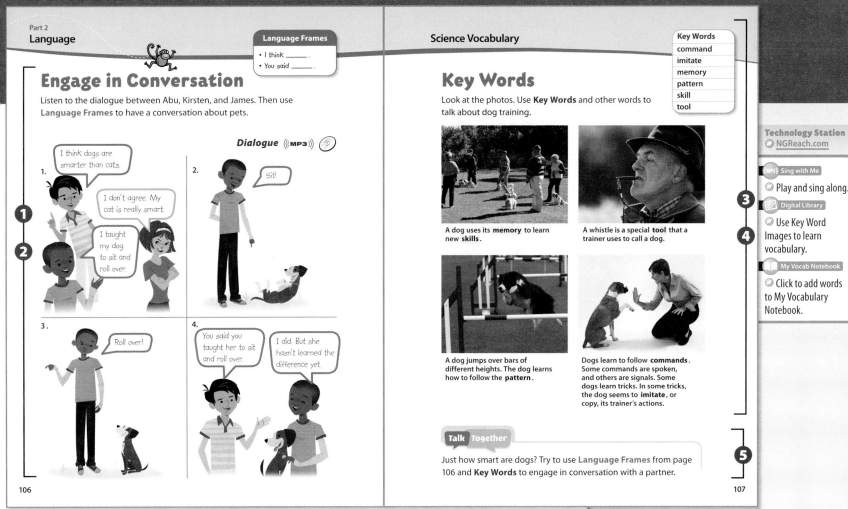

Science Vocabulary

3 Teach/Model Read the introduction and the captions for the photos. Use **Vocabulary Routine 1** and **Key Word Images** to teach the words. Access definitions on pages 616–639.

1. **Pronounce** the word and point to its picture: command.

2. **Rate** the word. Have students hold up their fingers to show how well they know the word. (1 = very well, 2 = a little, 3 = not at all) Ask: *What do you know about this word?*

3. **Define** the word: *A command is an order to do something.*

4. **Elaborate** Relate the word to your experience; for example: *When the principal gives me a command, I must do what she says.*

4 Practice/Apply Have partners take turns repeating the routine for each word, using complete sentences for steps 2, 3, and 4.

5 Talk Together About the Big Question
Check Understanding and Connect Concepts Review the **Language Frames** on page 106 and provide an example:

> *You said that dogs use **memory** to learn new **skills**. Then they can follow the trainer's commands. I think that dogs must be very smart and have good memories.*

Add the ideas to your unit concept map.

Differentiate

Spanish Cognates ▶

imitate/imitar;
memory/memoria;
pattern/patrón

Part 2 Vocabulary Skills Trace		Page
Day 1	**Science Vocabulary**	**T107**
Day 2	Academic Vocabulary	T109
Day 3	Expand Word Knowledge	T112b
Day 4	Share Word Knowledge	T128b
Day 5	Apply Word Knowledge	T129b
Day 6	Use a Dictionary	T130
Day 7	Use a Dictionary	T137
Days 8–9	Extend Vocabulary	T138e–f
Day 10	Vocabulary Review	T138g–h

Day 1
continued

Day at a Glance:
▶ **Language:** Engage in Conversation ⊙ **Reading:** Main Idea and Details
▶ **Vocabulary:** Science Vocabulary ⊙ **Writing:** Writing Fluency; Study a Model

OBJECTIVES

Vocabulary
- Acquire and Use Classroom Vocabulary: **diagram**
- Use Grade Level Vocabulary: skill

Comprehension and Literary Analysis
- Demonstrate Listening Comprehension
- Understand Main Idea and Details ❶
- Listening and Speaking

Learning and Teamwork Strategies
- Use Graphic Organizers: Main Idea Diagram Reason Deductively

Writing
- Develop Writing Fluency
- Monitor and Self-Correct Writing
- Study a Model

Science
- Explore Animal Intelligence

Resources

⊙ ⊙ *eVisuals 2.21, 2.22*

⊙ ⊙ *Practice Master 2.10*

Differentiate

Multi-Level Strategies

BEGINNING

Provide sentence starters:

- The main idea is _____.

- One detail is _____.

INTERMEDIATE

Refer to the instruction at the top of the page. Remind students that details are examples or facts about the main idea. Ask them to give examples of commands that dogs can follow.

ADVANCED ADVANCED HIGH

Encourage students to elaborate on each detail that they provide: *Dogs can sit and give a paw to their owner.*

Main Idea and Details

❶ Teach Connect concepts: *What Key Words have you learned to help you talk about animals? The captions and photographs showed dogs learning new* **skills** *. Now you will learn how to make a Main Idea Diagram to identify a main idea and details about how animals learn.* Teach the Classroom Vocabulary word *diagram.*

Read the first paragraph. Use the illustrations on page 108 to model how to identify the main idea and suppporting details. What idea do you get from the three pictures? (A boy is teaching his dog a trick.) That is the main idea. The first caption states this idea. Each picture and caption then give details about how he does this. Have volunteers read the other captions.

Have students point to the diagram. Ask a volunteer to read aloud the explanation about making a main idea diagram. Clarify the purpose: *I can make a main idea diagram to show how ideas are related.* Remind students to listen for the main idea and details as you read "James and Millie" aloud.

> **Read Aloud**
>
> ### James and Millie
>
> James taught his dog to shake hands. They practiced after school every day for three weeks. It was hard for Millie to learn the new skill. First, James gave a **command**. "Give me your paw, Millie." Then he took Millie's paw. Finally, she learned to give him the paw. Then Millie got a treat!
>
> ⊙ NGReach.com ❯ **eVisual 2.21**

❷ Model Review the first two sentences of "James and Millie." Have volunteers read the first two boxes in the main idea and details diagram. Model the process: *I make a box for the main idea. It is the first sentence. I make another box for the first detail and write it.* Ask: *Why is the third sentence a better supporting detail than the second sentence?* (It tells how he taught his dog.) Have a volunteer repeat the process for the last detail.

❸ Practice/Apply Read aloud the instructions. Distribute **Practice Master 2.10** for students to use as they complete their diagrams. Use **Multi-Level Strategies** to help students at all proficiency levels identify main ideas and details. Monitor students' developing proficiency. (See page R2 for Proficiency Level Descriptions.)

> **CHECK UNDERSTANDING** *What is the main idea of "James and Millie"? What is another detail you can give to support the main idea?* (He gave a command; he took her paw.)

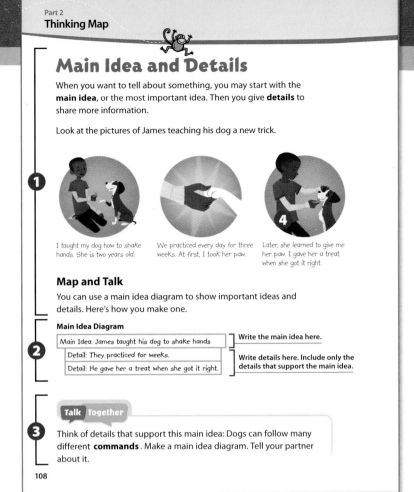

Main Idea and Details

When you want to tell about something, you may start with the **main idea**, or the most important idea. Then you give **details** to share more information.

Look at the pictures of James teaching his dog a new trick.

1

I taught my dog how to shake hands. She is two years old.

We practiced every day for three weeks. At first, I took her paw.

Later, she learned to give me her paw. I gave her a treat when she got it right.

Map and Talk

You can use a main idea diagram to show important ideas and details. Here's how you make one.

Main Idea Diagram

2

Main Idea: James taught his dog to shake hands.
Detail: They practiced for weeks.
Detail: He gave her a treat when she got it right.

Write the main idea here.

Write details here. Include only the details that support the main idea.

Talk Together

3 Think of details that support this main idea: Dogs can follow many different **commands**. Make a main idea diagram. Tell your partner about it.

108

Student Book page 108

Daily Writing

4 **Writing Fluency** Use the **Power Writing** routine. (see page PD53). Write the word **memory** and prompt: What does your *memory* do? Think about this word and write about it.

Power Writing Routine

 1. What do you know about the word or picture?

 2. Take one minute to write as much as you can, as well as you can.
   B words   **I** sentences   **A** **AH** paragraphs

 3. Check your spelling and grammar. Circle mistakes.

 4. Count your words.

 **NGReach.com** > eVisual 2.22

5 **Writing Project: Study a Model Business Letter** Have students review a model of the writing form for their Writing Projects. See T138k–T138.

CLOSE AND ASSESS

- **Language** *Which do you think are smarter, cats or dogs? Explain.* (Students should use information from the dialogue in their answers.)

- **Reading** *Dogs can follow many commands. What is one command that dogs can learn?* (They can learn to shake hands.)

- **Vocabulary** *Which Key Words did you use to talk about what animals can learn to do?* (Answers will vary.)

Classroom Vocabulary

Use **Vocabulary Routine 4** to teach **diagram**. (See **Vocabulary Routines**, page PD40.)

Word Map

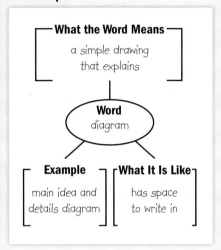

What the Word Means
a simple drawing that explains

Word
diagram

Example	**What It Is Like**
main idea and details diagram	has space to write in

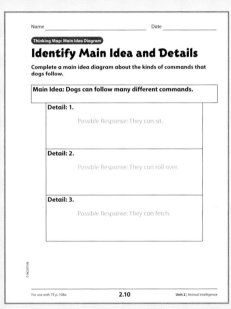

Name _____ Date _____

Thinking Map: Main Idea Diagram

Identify Main Idea and Details

Complete a main idea diagram about the kinds of commands that dogs follow.

Main Idea: Dogs can follow many different commands.
Detail: 1. *Possible Response: They can sit.*
Detail: 2. *Possible Response: They can roll over.*
Detail: 3. *Possible Response: They can fetch.*

For use with TE p. 108a   2.10   Unit 2 | Animal Intelligence

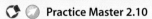 **Practice Master 2.10**

Day 2

Day at a Glance:
▶ **Language:** Compound Sentences   ▶ **Reading:** Make Connections
▶ **Vocabulary:** Academic Vocabulary   ▶ **Writing:** Prewrite: Business Letter

OBJECTIVES

Vocabulary
- Acquire and Use Academic Vocabulary ⊕
- Use Grade-Level Vocabulary: **ability**, **command**, **memory**

Language
- Compound Sentences ⊕

Learning and Teamwork Strategies
- Make Connections Across Content Areas

Resources

🔄 🌐 *Practice Master 2.11*

🔊 🌐 *Key Word Images*

🅝 **NGReach.com** ▶

See **Technology Station** for digital student resources.

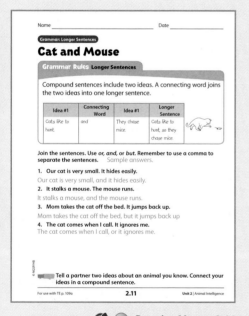

Practice Master 2.11

Language of the Day

How do animals use their memory?
_____ use their memory _____.

Read the Language of the Day. Model: *Elephants use their memory to find water.* Create a T-chart for the answers and encourage students to share their ideas. Then explain that today students will look at sentences they can use to talk about animals.

Grammar Compound Sentences 🅑 🅘 🅐 🅐🅗

1 **Teach/Model** Write the sample sentences and read them aloud.

> 1. A horse can jump, and it can run fast.
> 2. Mark's horse likes to run, but it does not like to jump.
> 3. Mark can train his horse to jump, or he can just let it run.

Ask about the sample sentences.

- *Could "A horse can jump" stand alone as a complete sentence?* (yes)
- *Could "It can run fast" stand alone as a sentence?* (yes)
- *What word connects the two sentences?* (and)
- *What does the comma do?* (It separates the two sentences.)

Say: *You can combine two short sentences into one compound sentence. Use* and *to join two ideas that are alike.* Say: *A horse can do two similar things: It can jump, and it can run. Combine similar ideas with* and.

Ask: *What word combines two sentences in sentence 2?* (but) Say: *Use* but *to combine sentences that show a difference.* Repeat with sentence 3. (or) Say: *Use* or *to show a choice between ideas.* Define *and, but,* and *or* as conjunctions. Say: *Put a comma before the conjunction.* Write this chart.

Coordinating Conjunctions		
and	**but**	**or**
similar ideas	different ideas	choice of ideas

2 **Practice/Apply** Partners take turns saying short sentences about an animal. The partner combines them into one compound sentence and writes it. Circulate and check for commas. Then assign **Practice Master 2.11**.

> **CHECK UNDERSTANDING** Display the sentences. Have students combine them into a compound sentence. (Students should use *or.*)

> Dogs may bite. They may be nice.

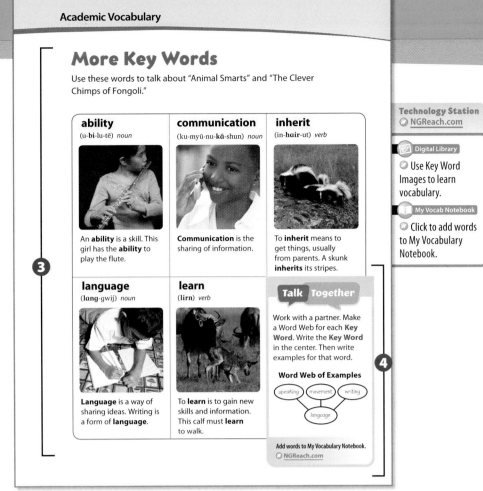

Student Book page 109

Academic Vocabulary

❸ Teach/Model Invite students to discuss each photograph on the page. Read the directions aloud and use **Vocabulary Routine 1** and **Key Word Images** to teach the words.

1. **Pronounce** the word and point to its picture: **ability**.

2. **Rate** the word. Have students hold up their fingers to show how well they know the word. (1 = very well, 2 = a little, 3 = not at all) Ask: *What do you know about this word?*

3. **Define** the word: *Ability is a skill. This girl has the ability to play the flute. To have an ability means you are able to do something well.*

4. **Elaborate** Relate the word to your experience: *I went to college for four years. Now I have the ability to teach.*

❹ Practice/Apply Use the ratings from step 2 to form pairs. Have partners work together in making word webs for each of the Key Words. Have volunteers share one word web with the class.

> **CHECK UNDERSTANDING** Point to the **Key Word Image** of each Key Word and ask students to use the word in a new sentence.

N B I A AH
Keys to Efficacy

Represent vocabulary acquisition as a lifelong process: *I just learned a new word the other day. I try to learn words as often as I can.*

Differentiate

Spanish Cognates ▶
*ability/habilidad;
inherit/heredar;
communication/comunicación;
language/lenguaje*

Part 2 Vocabulary Skills Trace		Page
Day 1	Science Vocabulary	T107
Day 2	**Academic Vocabulary**	**T109**
Day 3	Expand Word Knowledge	T112b
Day 4	Share Word Knowledge	T128b
Day 5	Apply Word Knowledge	T129b
Day 6	Use a Dictionary	T130
Day 7	Use a Dictionary	T137
Days 8–9	Extend Vocabulary	T138e–f
Day 10	Vocabulary Review	T138g–h

Day 2
continued

Day at a Glance:
- ▶ **Language:** Compound Sentences
- ▶ **Vocabulary:** Academic Vocabulary
- ▷ **Reading:** Make Connections
- ▷ **Writing:** Prewrite: Business Letter

OBJECTIVES

Vocabulary
- Acquire and Use Classroom Vocabulary: **remind** ⊙
- Use Academic Vocabulary: **communication** ⊙
- Use Grade-Level Vocabulary ⊙

Learning to Read
- Read Words with Digraphs /th/ th, /ng/, ng

Reading Strategy
- Make Connections: Text to World ⊙

Learning and Teamwork Strategies
- Use Personal Experience
- Use Visuals

Writing
- Writing Project: Prewrite

Resources

 eVisual 2.23

 Reach Into Phonics TE page T44

Make Connections

1 Teach Read the introduction aloud and display the picture. Ask students what the picture reminds them of. Discuss aspects of the scene that could be familiar, such as where it is and what events or actions it shows. Make the connection: *You can use what you already know to make connections to the things you see and read.*

2 Model Read the chart chorally with students and teach the Classroom Vocabulary word *remind*. To model making a connection about the picture, ask:

- *What is the picture about?* It's about <u>a dog that is running away from James.</u>
- *What does it remind you of?* <u>The dog</u> reminds me of <u>a time my neighbor's dog got out. We were afraid it would get lost.</u>
- *How does that help you understand the picture?* Now I understand <u>why James look worried.</u>

3 Practice/Apply Read the directions aloud. Point out the Language Frames. Have students read aloud the first paragraph of James's report and the sample student connection.

Direct attention to the second and third paragraphs. Use **Academic Language Frames** to help students at each proficiency level make connections. Students should make connections about being consistent and patient with pets and explain how they made each connection.

> **CHECK UNDERSTANDING** Reread the third paragraph. *Think about times you have learned something new. How can you make a connection to a dog learning a skill?*

Differentiate

Academic Language Frames

Make Connections
- ■ It's about _____.
  - _____ reminds me of _____.
  - Now I understand _____.

- ■ The text is about _____.
  - Because it has _____ reminds me of _____.
  - The connections help me understand _____.

- ■ The _____ is about _____ and _____.
- ■ That reminds me of what I know about _____.
  - Because I connected to what I know,
  - I understand _____.

NGReach.com ▶ eVisual 2.23

Phonics and Fluency

Words with Digraphs /th/ *th*, /ng/, *ng*

Display these words: *then* and sing. Point out the digraphs *th* and *ng* and explain: *Sometimes two consonants work together to make a single sound.* Point to letters as you say each sound in *then*: /th/ /ĕ/ /n/. Have students repeat. Repeat the procedure for *sing*. Display **Transparency 26** from **Reach Into Phonics** and work through the lesson.

Practice Display the sentences from James' report:

- Dog trai<u>n</u>i<u>ng</u> takes time.
- You will need to repeat <u>th</u>i<u>ng</u>s over and over.
- "Bri<u>ng</u> me <u>th</u>e ball."

Have partners read the sentences chorally several times to develop fluency. Listen as partners read. Correct pronunciation.

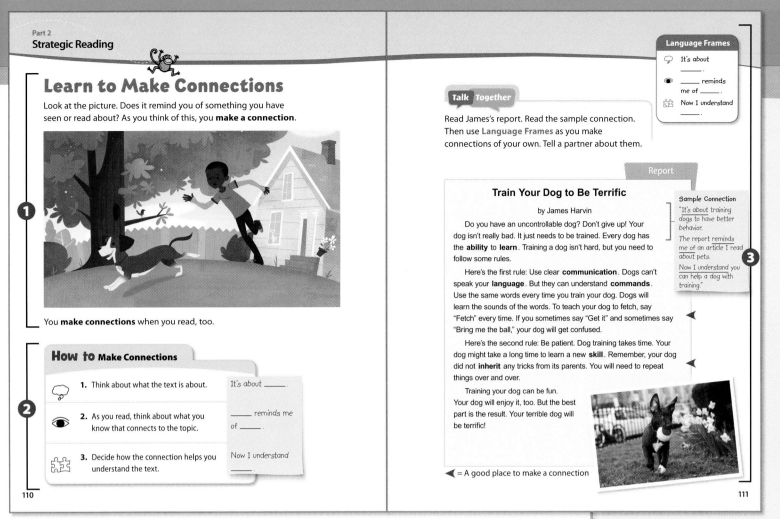

Learn to Make Connections

Look at the picture. Does it remind you of something you have seen or read about? As you think of this, you **make a connection**.

1

You **make connections** when you read, too.

How to Make Connections

2

🗨️ 1. Think about what the text is about.   It's about _____.

👁️ 2. As you read, think about what you know that connects to the topic.   _____ reminds me of _____.

🧩 3. Decide how the connection helps you understand the text.   Now I understand _____.

110

Language Frames

🗨️ It's about
_____.

👁️ _____ reminds
me of _____.

🧩 Now I understand
_____.

Talk Together

Read James's report. Read the sample connection. Then use Language Frames as you make connections of your own. Tell a partner about them.

Report

Train Your Dog to Be Terrific

by James Harvin

Do you have an uncontrollable dog? Don't give up! Your dog isn't really bad. It just needs to be trained. Every dog has the **ability** to **learn**. Training a dog isn't hard, but you need to follow some rules.

Here's the first rule: Use clear **communication**. Dogs can't speak your **language**. But they can understand **commands**. Use the same words every time you train your dog. Dogs will learn the sounds of the words. To teach your dog to fetch, say "Fetch" every time. If you sometimes say "Get it" and sometimes say "Bring me the ball," your dog will get confused. ◄

Here's the second rule: Be patient. Dog training takes time. Your dog might take a long time to learn a new **skill**. Remember, your dog did not **inherit** any tricks from its parents. You will need to repeat things over and over. ◄

Training your dog can be fun. Your dog will enjoy it, too. But the best part is the result. Your terrible dog will be terrific!

Sample Connection

"It's about training dogs to have better behavior.

The report reminds me of an article I read about pets.

3

Now I understand you can help a dog with training."

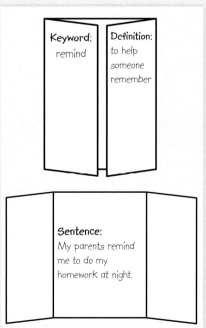

◄ = A good place to make a connection

111

Student Book pages 110–111

---

4 ## Writing Project: Prewrite: Business Letter Have students plan their Writing Projects. See pages T39a–T39b.

CLOSE AND ASSESS

- **Language** *Use a compound sentence to tell me the two rules in James's report.* (Students should use the conjunction *and* to join the two rules from the report.)
- **Reading** *The last paragraph in James's report says:* Training your dog can be fun. *What connections can you make with this statement?* (Answers will vary.)
- **Vocabulary** *What kinds of communication can you use when teaching animals?* (Answers will vary.)

Classroom Vocabulary

Use **Vocabulary Routine 4** to teach **remind**. (See Vocabulary Routines, page PD40.)

Window

Keyword:	Definition:
remind	to help someone remember

Sentence:
My parents remind me to do my homework at night.

Day 3

Day at a Glance:
- ▶ **Language:** Tell an Original Story
- ▶ **Vocabulary:** Expand Word Knowledge
- ▶ **Reading:** Read the Selection
- ▶ **Writing:** Draft a Business Letter

OBJECTIVES

Vocabulary
- Use Academic Vocabulary: **learn** ❶
- Use Grade-Level Vocabulary ❶

Language
- Language Function: Tell an Original Story
- Listen to and Imitate Fluent Models
- Use a Variety of Language Structures

Learning and Teamwork Strategies
- Use Media to Build Language
- Gather Information
- Use Graphic Organizers: 4-Corner Poster

Resources

- Sing with Me Language Song CD 1, Tracks 15, 16
- Sing with Me Language Song Book page 11
- eVisual 2.24
  Language Builder Picture Card E24
- • Chart or poster paper
- In the U.S.A. Picture Cards 1–4

Ⓝ **NGReach.com** ▶

See **Technology Station** for digital student resources.

Differentiate

Multi-Level Strategies

Tell an Original Story

B Have these students draw pictures to represent their stories.

I Have these students draw pictures and tell a story that goes with their picture.

A Encourage students at advanced levels to include more detail in their stories. They may also want to use pictures for support, but their stories may have details that elaborate and go beyond the scenes depicted in their pictures.

Language of the Day

What do I know about animal intelligence?
I know that some animals ____.

Read the Language of the Day. Say: *I know that some animals can* **learn** *to do tricks.* Have each student repeat your sentence and add their ideas to create a cumulative sentence. Then explain that today students will tell stories about animals that are very smart.

Tell an Original Story

❶ Teach Tell students they are going to practice telling original stories. Explain: *An original story is a story that you make up. The story can be short and simple.*

Display "The Smartest Dog." Play the song and invite students to sing along. Point out that the song tells a story. Ask students: *What does every story need to have?* Then, review the following chart:

Parts of a Story		
Characters	**Events**	**Dialogue**
The people in a story	What happens in a story	What the characters say to each other

Ⓝ **NGReach.com** ▶ **eVisual 2.24**

❷ Model Telling a story: *I saw a dog and its owner in the park. They were playing fetch by the lake, and the ball went into the lake. The dog went into the water to get the ball. It came back and dropped the ball on the ground. The dog said, "Here's the ball." The owner said. "That's the wrong ball. Go back and try again." The dog had to fetch four different balls. Finally, the last ball was the right one.*

❸ Practice/Apply Have students tell stories about other smart animals. Use **Multi-Level Strategies** to support students at all proficiency levels.

CHECK UNDERSTANDING Display **Language Builder Picture Card E24** (police dog) and have students tell an impromptu story about it.

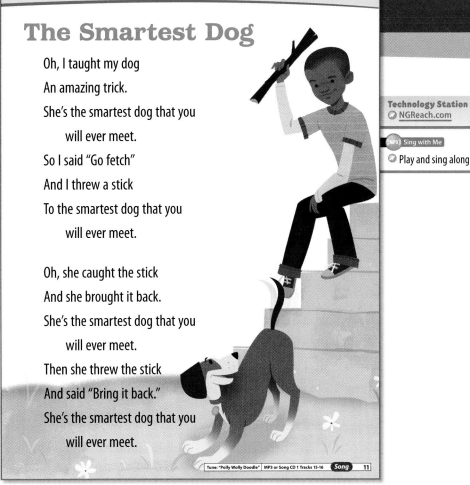

The Smartest Dog

Oh, I taught my dog
An amazing trick.
She's the smartest dog that you
    will ever meet.
So I said "Go fetch"
And I threw a stick
To the smartest dog that you
    will ever meet.

Oh, she caught the stick
And she brought it back.
She's the smartest dog that you
    will ever meet.
Then she threw the stick
And said "Bring it back."
She's the smartest dog that you
    will ever meet.

Tune: "Polly Wolly Doodle"   MP3 or Song CD 1 Tracks 15-16   **Song**   11

Sing With Me Language Song Book   page 11

Technology Station
○ NGReach.com

(MP3) Sing with Me
○ Play and sing along.

Key Words

ability	learn
command	memory
communication	pattern
imitate	skill
inherit	tool
language	

Expand Word Knowledge

4 **Teach/Model** Explain that each student pair will become Key Word experts. They will study one Key Word and create a Key Word poster about that word. Use **Vocabulary Routine 2** and model making a 4-Corner Poster about the word **command**. (See **Vocabulary Routines,** page PD54.)

- Write the word.
- Add a picture.
- Add a definition.
- Add a context sentence.

5 **Practice/Apply** Assign a Key Word to each pair of students. Have each pair create a poster for their assigned Key Words. Display the posters on the class word wall.

command	*(drawing of girl and dog)*
Sentence: The girl is giving the dog a command to sit.	Definition: A command is an order or demand to do something.

4-Corner Poster

Differentiate

Newcomer Support

Newcomers can make 4-corner posters using words from In the USA Picture Cards 1–4.

CHECK UNDERSTANDING Say a Key Word and have the partner experts for the word read the definition and sentence from their poster.

Part 2 Vocabulary Skills Trace		Page
Day 1	Science Vocabulary	T107
Day 2	Academic Vocabulary	T109
▶ **Day 3**	**Expand Word Knowledge**	**T112b**
Day 4	Share Word Knowledge	T128b
Day 5	Apply Word Knowledge	T129b
Day 6	Use a Dictionary	T130
Day 7	Use a Dictionary	T137
Days 8–9	Extend Vocabulary	T138e–f
Day 10	Vocabulary Review	T138g–h

Day 3
continued

Day at a Glance:
▶ **Language:** Tell an Original Story   ⏵ **Reading:** Read the Selection
▶ **Vocabulary:** Expand Word Knowledge   ⏵ **Writing:** Draft a Business Letter

OBJECTIVES

Vocabulary
- Use Academic Vocabulary: **ability**, **communication**, **learn** ⊙
- Use Grade-Level Vocabulary: **pattern**, **tool** ⊙

Reading Strategy
- Plan: Preview

Comprehension and Literary Analysis
- Interpret Visuals
- Analyze Genre: Science Article

Learning and Teamwork Strategies
- Use Prereading Supports
- Build Background Knowledge

Resources

   Comprehension Coach

Keys to Efficacy

Give students a chance to think before rephrasing a question, moving on, or answering it yourself.

Preview the Selection

❶ Introduce Ask students to look at the picture of the dog on page 113. Say: *Have you ever seen a dog that can ride a skateboard?* Have a volunteer read the title aloud and ask students to predict what they think the selection will be about, based on the title and picture.

❷ Genre and Text Features Read aloud the text about science articles on page 112. Talk about how photographs and captions help the reader to better understand an article. Ask students to explain how the caption on page 112 helps to describe the picture of the chimpanzee.

❸ Preview and Build Background Use sheltering strategies as you conduct a picture walk.

Pages	Say (and Do) 💬 ✋
114–115	*A girl is eating spaghetti with a fork.* (Pantomime eating with a fork.) *The chimpanzee is holding a stick. What do you think he is doing with it?* (digging) *Both the girl and the chimpanzee are using* **tools**.
116–117	*Baby animals* **learn** *from their mothers. What do you think the baby orangutan is learning?* (to call out) *What did this orangutan learn to do with a leaf?* (make a hat) *Do you see another baby animal?* (tadpole)
118–119	*Some animals* **communicate** *with people. How do you think the woman and gorilla talk to each other?* (with hand signals) *What do you think these meerkats are listening for?* (Maybe they are listening for signs of danger.) *How do you think they communicate?* (with barks or yelps)
120–121	*This dog is learning a trick. Have you ever trained an animal? Can other animals learn tricks? This parrot can make* **patterns**. *How do you think the parrot can pick up these blocks?* (point to claws or beak)
122–123	*Look at the elephant's long trunk.* (Pantomime an elephant's trunk with your arm.) *What do you think the elephant can pick up with its trunk? Can you guess what this elephant learned to do?* (how to unlock its cage)
124–125	*What is the woman doing?* (training the dolphin to jump) *Do you know how dolphins communicate?* (with clicking sounds)
126–127	*The woman here is writing about the gorilla.* (Pantomime writing notes in a small notebook.) *She wants to learn how gorillas communicate. What would you like to learn about* **animal communication**?

CHECK UNDERSTANDING Have students look again at the photo on page 113. Ask: *What caption can you write to go with this picture?* (Answers will vary but should describe what is happening in the photo.)

Read a Science Article

2

Genre
A **science article** is nonfiction. It gives facts about a science topic such as animal behavior.

Text Features
Look at **photographs** and **captions** in science articles. They help you understand the text better.

photograph

◀ Koko uses sign language to communicate. Here, she uses the sign for *eat*.

caption

112

ANIMAL Smarts
by Leslie Hall

Comprehension Coach

Student Book pages 112–113

Comprehension Coach

Build Reading Power
Assign students to use the software, based on their instructional needs.

Read Silently
- Comprehension questions with immediate feedback
- Vocabulary support

Listen
- Process model of fluent reading
- Text highlighting to facilitate tracking
- Vocabulary support

Record
- Oral reading fluency practice
- Speech recognition for oral fluency assessment with immediate feedback

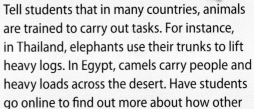

Cultural Perpectives

Tell students that in many countries, animals are trained to carry out tasks. For instance, in Thailand, elephants use their trunks to lift heavy logs. In Egypt, camels carry people and heavy loads across the desert. Have students go online to find out more about how other cultures train and employ animals.

OBJECTIVES

Vocabulary
- Use Academic Vocabulary: ability, language, learn **O**
- Use Grade-Level Vocabulary: pattern, memory, skill, tool **O**

Learning to Read
- Phonics: Differentiate Consonant Blends

Reading Strategies
- Plan: Set a Purpose, Predict, Confirm Predictions
- Make Connections: Text to World **O**

Fluency
- Intonation **O**

Learning and Teamwork Strategies
- Use Reading Supports

Comprehension and Literary Analysis
- Main Idea and Details **O**
- Use Text Structure: Photos and Captions

Writing
- Connect Reading and Writing
- Writing Project: Draft

Science
- Explore Animal Behavior

Math
- Patterns

Resources

- Read with Me Selection
- Practice Master 2.12
- Reach Into Phonics TE T46, T48

NGReach.com

See **Technology Station** for digital student resources.

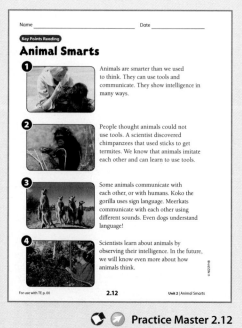

Name _____ Date _____

Key Points Reading

Animal Smarts

1 Animals are smarter than we used to think. They can use tools and communicate. They show intelligence in many ways.

2 People thought animals could not use tools. A scientist discovered chimpanzees that used sticks to get termites. We know that animals imitate each other and can learn to use tools.

3 Some animals communicate with each other, or with humans. Koko the gorilla uses sign language. Meerkats communicate with each other using different sounds. Even dogs understand language!

4 Scientists learn about animals by observing their intelligence. In the future, we will know even more about how animals think.

For use with TE p. 00   **2.12**   Unit 2 | Animal Smarts

Practice Master 2.12

Read the Science Article

Suggested Pacing

- Day 3: Read Section 1, pages 114–117
- Day 4: Read Sections 2 and 3, pages 118–127

Reading Options   Scaffold the support for varied reading levels.

BELOW LEVEL	ON LEVEL	ABOVE LEVEL
Read Together	**Read Together**	**Read Independently**
• Have students track the print on the **Key Points Reading** while you read the text aloud. • Have students use photos and captions to understand main ideas. • Check understanding with selected Build Comprehension questions.	• Have groups set a purpose for reading and read with a partner. Then choose passages to read aloud together. • Use Build Comprehension questions to check understanding. • At the end of each section, have students summarize the main ideas.	• Have students read each section silently and write down the main idea for each section as they read. Have them study the illustrations to clarify the text. • Students can discuss their main ideas as you ask the Build Comprehension questions.

Phonics and Fluency

Consonant Blends

Teach/Model Explain that two consonants can blend together to make one sound. Write these consonant blends on the board and say them aloud for children: -nd, -st, -lt, -mp, -nt, fr-, sm-, sn-, sl, cl-, tr-, st-, pl-, dr-. Display words that use these blends, such as: and, mist, melt, jump, and went. Write each word on the board and ask students to underline the consonant blend. Display **Transparencies 27–29** from **Reach into Phonics** and work through the lesson (pages T46, T48.)

Practice/Apply Display this sentence from "Animal Smarts."

- From sharing information to using tools and even playing tricks on people, it turns out that animals are smarter than we thought.

Have partners write the words that have consonant blends and underline the letters that make up the blends. Have students trade papers when they are finished to see if their answers agreed with each other.

Set a Purpose
Find out how animals
demonstrate their intelligence.

2 What can animals do? From sharing information to using **tools** and even playing tricks on people, **it turns out** that animals are smarter than we thought.

Cool Tools

Using tools **takes smarts**. When you need to **sort out** a problem, you have to figure out why it is a problem. Then you find or make a tool to help you solve it. Think of the tools you use every day: a fork, a pair of scissors, even a cell phone.

◀ A fork is a useful tool. You can use it in many different ways. ▶

For many years, no one thought animals could use tools. Then in 1960, scientist Jane Goodall saw chimpanzees taking leaves off sticks and using the sticks to **"fish"** for food in **termite** nests. It was the first time anyone had seen wild animals making tools. Now we know that many animals use tools in smart ways. **3**

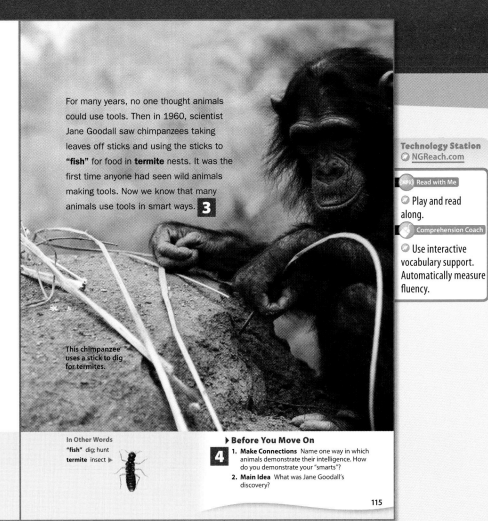

This chimpanzee uses a stick to dig for termites.

In Other Words
it turns out we know
takes smarts requires intelligence
sort out solve

In Other Words
"fish" dig; hunt
termite insect ▶

▶ **Before You Move On**
4 1. **Make Connections** Name one way in which animals demonstrate their intelligence. How do you demonstrate your "smarts"?
2. **Main Idea** What was Jane Goodall's discovery?

114

115

Student Book pages 114–115

Build Comprehension, pages 114–115

1 **Set a Purpose** Read the Set a Purpose at the top of page 114.

2 **Make Predictions** Before you read, predict how you think animals show their intelligence. (Accept all reasonable predictions.)

3 **Use Key Words** What other kinds of **tools** from nature might help the chimpanzee get food from the termite nest on page 115? (Possible response: long blades of grass)

4 **Answers to Before You Move On**

1. Make Connections MODEL | GUIDE | APPLY As you model, try to make the connection between the text and the students' world. *The text tells us how chimpanzees use sticks to fish for termites. I've seen birds use small sticks and twigs to build their nests, so I think they use tools, too.* The second question must be answered from students' own experiences.

2. Main Idea MODEL | GUIDE | APPLY Model how to find the main idea of the paragraph on page 115. Remind students that the main idea is what a paragraph or article is mostly about. Explain that the main idea is not always the first sentence in a paragraph. Say: *The main idea of this paragraph is the last sentence, "Now we know that many animals use tools in smart ways."* Help students identify the details that support the main idea.

B I A AH

**Literary Analysis:
Text Features**

Remind students that photos and captions can help to illustrate the main idea and details of a page. The main idea on pages 114 and 115 is that animals can use tools. Ask students to look at the photos on these pages and read the captions. How do they support the main idea? Do you think the chimpanzee might use the stick in a different way?

Technology Station
NGReach.com

Read with Me
Play and read along.
Comprehension Coach
Use interactive vocabulary support. Automatically measure fluency.

How Animals Learn

Animals already know how to do some things when they are born. For example, a baby orangutan can **grasp** a leaf with its hands. It doesn't need to **learn** how. It **inherits** the **ability**.

Orangutans also learn things from their parents. A young orangutan may see its mother use a leaf as a napkin or a rain hat. It may then copy her actions. The ability to learn shows intelligence. **1** **2**

▼ Young orangutans sometimes copy the actions of their parents.

▼ Orangutans may learn from their parents how to use a leaf as a hat.

In Other Words
◄ **grasp** hold

116

Memory and Smarts

To remember something also takes smarts. Female poison dart frogs have **incredible memories**. After a frog's eggs hatch, the female carries each tadpole to its own leafy **spot** somewhere in the rainforest. **3**

She returns every few days to bring food to each tadpole. That means the frog has to remember **the location of** as many as 30 tiny tadpoles!

▼ tadpole

A female poison dart frog can remember the location of many tadpoles. ▼

In Other Words
incredible very good
spot place
the location of where she put

▶ **Before You Move On**
4
1. **Use Text Features** Which orangutan photo shows **learned** behavior? Explain.
2. **Details** How does the poison dart frog show intelligence?

117

Student Book pages 116–117

Build Comprehension, pages 116–117

1 **Summarize** How do young ways that animals learn? (Animals already know how to do some things when they are born, but they can also **learn** to do things some things by watching their parents.)

2 **Make Inferences** How can you tell if someone learned something or if they knew how to do it since the time they were born? (Think about whether the action is something that babies can do, such as eat, sleep, or laugh.)

3 **Use Key Words** Why do you think **memory** is important for babies? (Accept all reasonable responses and encourage a conversation.)

4 **Answers to Before You Move On**

1. **Use Text Features** Point to each photo of the orangutan and ask students to talk about what is happening in each one. A baby is born being able to make sounds. It must learn to use a tool.

2. **Details** MODEL | GUIDE | APPLY Help students find details to answer the question. Say: *The main idea is that memory shows intelligence.* Then have students answer the question. (I think it shows a lot of intelligence to remember where so many tadpoles are. That is why the poison dart frog is smart.)

Home Connection

Have students bring in photos of their pets doing different things. Post these pictures and have students write captions for them.

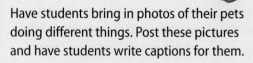

A Way with Words

5 It takes brains to talk. Scientists have found ways to talk with some of Earth's smartest animals. Koko the gorilla was one of the first animals to learn to communicate with human beings.

Scientists taught Koko sign **language**. That is a way to talk with your hands. When people talk, Koko answers in sign language. She can **sign** more than 1,000 words.

Sometimes Koko makes up a new sign. This tells us that Koko can **think on her own**. It also shows that she wants to communicate. **6**

◄ Koko uses sign language to communicate. Here, she uses the sign for *eat*.

In Other Words
sign use sign **language** to say
think on her own create new signs by herself

118

Sound Signals

Meerkats don't communicate with people. Yet they do communicate with each other. These **chattering** animals make sounds that mean different things. Meerkats live in groups. While the group looks for food, one meerkat **stands guard**. It makes little peeps to tell the others that everything is safe. When danger is near, the guard meerkat changes the sound. It yelps, barks, or whistles. **7**

When meerkats are in danger, they give a warning. They make sounds when predators are near.

In Other Words
chattering noisy
stands guard watches for danger

▶ **Before You Move On**
8 1. **Make Connections** Compare and contrast Koko with another animal you know or have read about. How does each one communicate?
2. **Details** How do meerkats communicate with each other?

119

Build Comprehension, pages 118–119

5 **Figurative Language** What does the term *It takes brains to talk* mean? (I think it means that you have to be able to think to learn to talk, because the brain helps you to learn language and not just make sounds.

6 **Make Inferences** Why does it make sense to teach sign **language** to animals like Koko? (Animals cannot speak words like we do, so we can **communicate** with them by using signs.)

7 **Ask Questions** What questions can you ask about how animals communicate with each other and with us? Sample: what kinds of words did Koko learn?)

8 **Answers to Before You Move On**
1. **Make Connections** `MODEL | GUIDE | APPLY` Ask: *How does Koko communicate?* (She uses sign language.) Ask: *What is another animal you know that communicates with people?* (Students may mention a parrot that can talk or a dog that barks, etc.) Ask: *Do these animals communicate in the same way?*
2. **Details** `MODEL | GUIDE | APPLY` Have students scan the page with their finger to locate words such as *communicate* and to find words that indicate sounds such as *peeps, yelps, barks,* and *whistles.* Have students tell when each kind of sound is used.

Student Book pages 118–119

I **A** **AH**

Science: Intelligence

Introduce the concept: *Intelligence is how smart someone is. What do you think the smartest animal on Earth is?* Encourage students to speculate and support their responses. After a brief discussion, tell students, if they do not mention it, that humans are the most intelligent animals.

Look and Fetch

What can a dog do? It can stay, sit, roll over, and maybe a few other things. A pet dog may seem pretty smart to its owner. Yet some dogs have shown amazing **skill** at understanding language and pictures.

▲ Many dogs can follow commands.

1 Betsy is a clever border collie. She understands 340 **spoken words**. Many dogs can follow **commands**, but Betsy **takes it a step further**. When someone shows her a picture of an object, she goes and **fetches** that object. Betsy can fetch hundreds of different things.

Betsy can understand hundreds of spoken words. ▶

In Other Words
spoken words words that people say to her
takes it a step further does more
fetches gets

120

A Brainy Bird

Do you think a bird can **recognize patterns**? An African gray **3** parrot named Alex could. He amazed scientists by figuring out patterns and then talking about them.

A scientist showed Alex a green cup and a green key. Then she asked the parrot what was the same about the objects. Alex said, "Color." Then the scientist asked what was different. Alex said, "Shape." Now that's a **brainy** bird!

Alex could figure out patterns based on different shapes and colors.

In Other Words
recognize find; notice
brainy smart

▶ **Before You Move On**
4 1. **Make Connections** Compare another animal you know to Betsy. How does each animal show its intelligence?
2. **Main Idea** How do Alex's actions **demonstrate** intelligence?

121

Student Book pages 120–121

Math: Patterns

Remind students that the Australian gray parrot Alex could recognize shapes and patterns. Ask them why it is important for people to be able to recognize shapes and patterns, such as the shape of a stop sign or the patterns of a traffic light? Discuss shapes students know that have a special meaning to them.

Build Comprehension, pages 120–121

1 **Confirm Word Meaning** Reread the sentence "Betsy is a clever border collie." What is another word for *clever*? (smart) Who do you know that is clever? Use the word to tell about that person or animal.

2 **Cause and Effect** What happens when someone shows Betsy the border collie a picture of an object? (She goes to fetch the object.)

3 **Author's Purpose** Why did the author write about Betsy the border collie and Alex the parrot in this selection? (They are both good examples of how intelligent an animal can be.)

4 **Answers to Before You Move On**

1. **Make Connections** MODEL | GUIDE | APPLY Students should say that Betsy can recognize a picture and match it to an object. Then guide them to talk about another animal they know and explain how that animal shows intelligence. Ask if the two animals are intelligent in similar ways or different ways.

2. **Main Idea** MODEL | GUIDE | APPLY Encourage students to look at the photo and caption to help them figure out what is unique about Alex the parrot. Students should respond that Alex can identify a **pattern** and then match the pattern to its name.

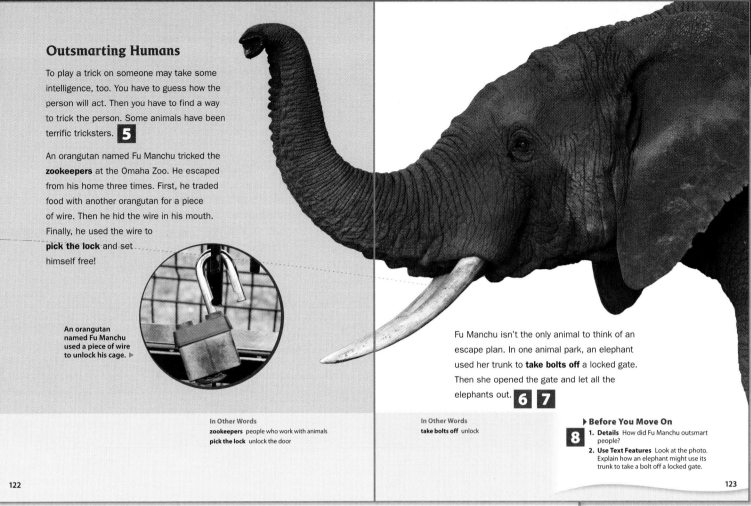

Outsmarting Humans

To play a trick on someone may take some intelligence, too. You have to guess how the person will act. Then you have to find a way to trick the person. Some animals have been terrific tricksters. **5**

An orangutan named Fu Manchu tricked the **zookeepers** at the Omaha Zoo. He escaped from his home three times. First, he traded food with another orangutan for a piece of wire. Then he hid the wire in his mouth. Finally, he used the wire to **pick the lock** and set himself free!

◀ An orangutan named Fu Manchu used a piece of wire to unlock his cage. ▶

Fu Manchu isn't the only animal to think of an escape plan. In one animal park, an elephant used her trunk to **take bolts off** a locked gate. Then she opened the gate and let all the elephants out. **6** **7**

In Other Words
zookeepers people who work with animals
pick the lock unlock the door

In Other Words
take bolts off unlock

▶ **Before You Move On**
8
1. **Details** How did Fu Manchu outsmart people?
2. **Use Text Features** Look at the photo. Explain how an elephant might use its trunk to take a bolt off a locked gate.

122

123

Build Comprehension, pages 122–123

5 **Paraphrase** How do you trick someone? (You guess how they will act then you plan a trick.)

6 **Make Comparisons** How were the actions of the orangutan and the elephant similar? (They both used their intelligence to let themselves out of cages.)

7 **Adjust Reading Rate** When you read, you will come across more difficult words, such as *Fu Manchu* and *Omaha*. What should you do when you see words like this? (Read slower and pronounce the words carefully.)

8 **Answers to Before You Move On**

1. **Details** MODEL | GUIDE | APPLY Fu Machu picked a lock on his cage to let himself free. He did this without the humans seeing him. He traded an orangutan food for a wire, then hid the wire until he could use it without being seen.

2. **Use Text Features** An elephant can use its trunk to grasp things. It can use its trunk to hold the bolts and turn them until they are loose and come off.

Student Book pages 122–123

I **A** **AH**

Keys to Efficacy

Encourage full sentences as students paraphrase the information about the elephant.

I **A** **AH**

Fluency: Intonation

Teach/Model Explain the concept: *Intonation is the rise and fall of your voice as you speak.* Direct students' attention to the first paragraph on page 122. Say: *Read this paragraph and then imagine you were saying to a friend instead of reading it. How would your voice sound different from the way it sounds when reading? Where does your voice go up and down?* Play the selection recording or read aloud the first paragraph of page 122, emphasizing the correct intonation as you read.

Practice Have partners read the page aloud together several times, mimicking the intonation you modeled.

124

Tricking the Trainers

A clever dolphin named Kelly knows how to get what she wants. Her trainers taught her to collect the trash that fell into her pool. When she gave it to a **keeper**, she got **a treat**. In this way, her pool stayed clean. Yet the tricky dolphin figured out how to trick her trainers. **1**

Now when paper drops into her pool, she hides it. When the trainers come, she swims down and tears off a piece of the paper. She gives it to the trainers **in exchange for** a fish treat. Then she goes back and tears off another piece. She gets the same treat for small pieces as she gets for big pieces. So she tears off small pieces to make the paper last longer. That way, **the treats keep coming!** **2**

◄ Dolphins are smart and playful animals. They can also learn tricks.

In Other Words
keeper worker
a treat food as a reward
in exchange for and gets
the treats keep coming she gets more treats

▶ **Before You Move On**
3
1. **Details** How does Kelly outsmart her trainers?
2. **Make Connections** Which of Kelly's actions are **learned** behaviors?

125

Student Book pages 124–125

I A AH

Keys to Efficacy

Encourage students to support their responses: *Where did you read about that?*

N B

Concepts of Print: Identify Letters and Words

Teach/Model Frame this sentence on page 125: *Now when the paper drops in her pool, she hides it.* Point to the first letter in *Now* and identify it. Point to the remaining letters in the word and have students identify them. Ask: *How many letters are in this word?* (3) Point to the space between *Now* and *when*. Have students do the same in their books. Explain: *This space shows where the word* Now *ends and the word* when *begins.* Have students count the words in the sentence. (11)

Practice/Apply Frame the final sentence on page 125. Invite students to choose a word in the sentence and tell how many letters are in the word. Have students count the number of words in the sentence.

Build Comprehension, pages 124–125

1 **Sequence** What did Kelly's trainers teach her to do before she **learned** to trick them? (They taught her to pick up trash that fell into her pool.)

2 **Draw Conclusions** What does Kelly's trick tell you about a dolphin's **ability** to learn and be an intelligent animal? (Dolphins can not only learn something but they can then figure out a new way to use the same information.)

3 **Answers to Before You Move On**

1. **Details** MODEL | GUIDE | APPLY She tears up the pieces of paper that fall into the pool so that she can get more treats.

2. **Make Connections** MODEL | GUIDE | APPLY The behavior of returning an object to the trainer for a treat is learned. Another learned behavior is tricking the trainer by giving more pieces of paper for more treats. Kelly learned how to collect trash to get a treat. She figured out on her own how to get more treats.

Learning About Animals

When scientists **observe** animals, they learn more about their behavior. They learn more about how the animals think and what they think about.

You may be amazed by the memory of a mother poison dart frog. You may be surprised that a parrot can talk about shapes, or that an elephant can plan a clever escape. Yet in the future, these **feats** may seem simple when we know even more about animals. Whether you **chat** with gorillas or **tidy** up with dolphins, it's clear that we have a lot more to learn about animals. ❖ **4**

5

Scientists learn about animals by observing their behavior. ▷

In Other Words
observe study
feats actions
chat talk
tidy clean

126

▶ **Before You Move On**
6 1. **Main Idea** What do scientists **learn** by studying animal behavior?
2. **Use Text Features** Describe what is happening in the photo on this page.

127

Student Book pages 126–127

Build Comprehension, pages 126–127

4 **Author's Purpose** What was the author's purpose for writing the selection? (To inform readers about how intelligent animals can be.)

5 **Form Opinions** Do you think it is important to study animal behavior? (Accept all answers that form an opinion about the topic.)

6 **Answers to Before You Move On**
1. **Main Idea** MODEL | GUIDE | APPLY They learn how animals think and what they can be taught to do.
2. **Use Text Features** MODEL | GUIDE | APPLY The woman is observing the gorilla and writing down information about its behavior.

Daily Writing A AH

1 **Writing Project: Draft a Business Letter** Have students draft their Writing Projects. See pages T139c–T139

CLOSE AND ASSESS
- **Make Connections** *Give an example of ways that animals help people.*
- **Use Text Features** *Which photo best describes animal intelligence?*
- **Main Idea and Details:** *What details support the main idea that animals are intelligent?* (they use tools, they learn language, etc.)

Day 4

Day at a Glance:
▶ **Language:** Complex Sentences   ▶ **Reading:** Think and Respond
▶ **Vocabulary:** Share Word Knowledge   ▶ **Writing:** Write About It; Revise a Business Letter

OBJECTIVES

Vocabulary
• Use Academic Vocabulary ⊕
• Use Grade-Level Vocabulary ⊕

Language
• Complex Sentences ⊕

Learning and Teamwork Strategies
• Review
• Collaborate with Peers

Resources

⊘ *eVisual 2.25*

⬙⊘ *Practice Master 2.13*

⬚⊘ *Language Builder Picture Card E15*

Differentiate

Language Transfer

Issue English Language Learners often feel that complex sentences are too long to understand clearly.

Strategy Break apart complex sentences into their separate clauses. Instead of reading the connecting word between the two clauses, read the first clause as if it ends in a period. Then read the second clause as an individual sentence. Ask students if they understand the meaning of the sentences any better now.

Language of the Day

What things from nature can *be used* as tools? _____ *can be used as a tool.*

Read the Language of the Day. Model: *Rocks can be used as a tool. People can use rocks to pound something, like a hammer. Otters use a rock to crack open shells.* Have each student repeat your sentence. Have students give examples of other natural materials that can be used as tools by either people or animals. Then explain that today students will talk and write about the selection.

Grammar Complex Sentences

1 **Teach/Model** Remind students that a compound sentence is made by joining two complete sentences with conjunctions like *and, but,* and *or.* Then display the subordinating conjunctions chart.

Subordinating Conjunctions	
when	because
relates ideas in time	explains why something happens
When they are born, animals already know some things.	Kelly tears the paper because she wants more treats.

⊘ NGReach.com ❯ **eVisual 2.25**

Ask: *Imagine if I came into the room and said, "When I was young," and didn't say anything else. Would that make sense?* (no) *What if I only said, "because I like you." Would you be waiting for me to say more?* (yes)

Read the dependent clauses in the chart. (when they are born, because she wants more treats) Say: *In a complex sentence, one half of the sentence can not stand alone as a complete sentence. It needs the other half to complete the thought.* Read the sample sentences in the chart and ask: *Do they make sense?* (yes) Then explain the uses of *when* and *because.*

2 **Practice/Apply** Have partners turn and talk, using *when* and *because* in authentic sentences. Check that they are using *when* and *because* correctly. Have pairs write one complex sentence. Assign **Practice Master 2.13**.

> **CHECK UNDERSTANDING** Say these sentences: *The horse jumps over the fences.* and *The horse jumps over a fence when its trainer blows a whistle.* Have students identify which of the sentences is a complex sentence and explain why.

Share Word Knowledge

3 **Teach/Model** To connect concepts, say: *Yesterday you became Key Word experts. Today you will share what you know about your Key Words.* Pair each student with a partner who studied a different word. Have partners follow the steps of **Vocabulary Routine 3** to share their word knowledge. (see page PD39.)

- Take turns reading Key Word posters.
- Talk about how the pictures on the posters show the meanings of the Key Words.
- Create sentences using both Key Words and write them in your journals.
- Draw a line under each Key Word.

4 **Practice/Apply** Group students who know different words and have them use the **Jigsaw** to share their words. Have them work together to do a word sort. Ask students to write each of their words on an index card or strip of paper. Then have them sort the words by parts of speech. Then encourage students to sort the words in categories of their own choosing. (See **Cooperative Learning Routines,** pages PD58–PD59

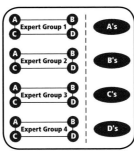

Jigsaw

> **CHECK UNDERSTANDING** Display the **Language Builder Picture Card E15** (bear looking for food) and ask students to use Key Words to tell about it.

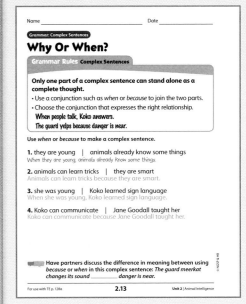

Name _____ Date _____

Grammar: Complex Sentences

Why Or When?

Grammar Rules Complex Sentences

Only one part of a complex sentence can stand alone as a complete thought.
- Use a conjunction such as *when* or *because* to join the two parts.
- Choose the conjunction that expresses the right relationship.
  When people talk, Koko answers.
  The guard yelps because danger is near.

Use *when* or *because* to make a complex sentence.

1. they are young | animals already know some things
When they are young, animals already know some things.

2. animals can learn tricks | they are smart
Animals can learn tricks because they are smart.

3. she was young | Koko learned sign language
When she was young, Koko learned sign language.

4. Koko can communicate | Jane Goodall taught her
Koko can communicate because Jane Goodall taught her.

Have partners discuss the difference in meaning between using *because* or *when* in this complex sentence: *The guard meerkat changes its sound _____ danger is near.*

For use with TE p. 128a   2.13   Unit 2 | Animal Intelligence

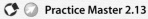 **Practice Master 2.13**

Day 4
continued

Day at a Glance:
▶ **Grammar:** Complex Sentences
▶ **Vocabulary:** Share Word Knowledge
▶ **Reading:** Think and Respond
▶ **Writing:** Write About It; Revise a Business Letter

OBJECTIVES

Vocabulary
- Use Academic Vocabulary: communication, language, learn ⊤
- Use Grade-Level Vocabulary: imitate, tool ⊤

Language
- Use Language Function: Engage in Conversation

Fluency
- Intonation

Literary Analysis
- Analyze Genre: Science Article

Test-Taking Strategies
- Practice and Apply Strategies: Read Directions Carefully

Writing
- Write Responses to Science Article
- Writing Project: Revise

Resources

⟳ eVisual 2.26

⟳ NGReach.com ⟩

See **Technology Station** for digital student resources.

Fluency: Intonation

Teach/Model Review intonation (page T122–123). Display this reminder: *Use natural highs and lows in your voice as you read.*

Practice Have students model proper intonation for each other. Ask partners to practice reading page 122. Then have them take turns reading it to each other with the correct intonation. Have them offer feedback to each other about their reading.

Think and Respond

❶ Talk About It Prompt students to cite evidence from the text. Remind students to use Key Words in their answers. If students have difficulty, help them use the sentence starters to form their answers.

1. **Genre** Talk with students about the facts they **learned**. Students may mention that they learned that animals can use **tools**, learn things from their parents, communicate, remember things, and learn to do different tricks and tasks.

2. **Engage in Conversation** Have students review rules for engaging in a conversation. (They should tell their point of view, respect others, wait their turn to talk, ask and answer questions, listen for key ideas, and summarize what they hear.)

3. **Compare/Contrast** Have students use the language frames to compare animal and human **communication**. How is it similar; how is it different? Ask students to cite examples from the selection. (Animals and humans both use sounds. Some animals bark, but humans talk.)

❷ Test-Taking Strategies: Read Directions Carefully

Explain: *When taking a test, read directions carefully before answering. You may have to write the correct answer or circle the correct answer. Look for important words that tell you how to follow the directions and how to show your answer. These words can also give you a clue as to what kind of question you are being asked.*

Important Word	Look for...
circle	Multiple choice or true/false questions
Fill in, write, choose	Sentences with missing words
Write, explain, describe	Answers that require a long response

Ask: *Which word in the directions tells you how to answer?* (circle) *What kind of question is this?* (multiple choice)

> **What did Jane Goodall observe chimpanzees do in the wild? Circle the correct answer.**
>
> A. learn to speak
>
> B. use tools
>
> C. trick humans
>
> D. count objects
>
> ⟳ NGReach.com ⟩ eVisual 2.26

Display the remaining practice items. Have partners take turns reading the directions carefully and answering the items.

Share Word Knowledge

3 **Teach/Model** To connect concepts, say: *Yesterday you became Key Word experts. Today you will share what you know about your Key Words.* Pair each student with a partner who studied a different word. Have partners follow the steps of **Vocabulary Routine 3** to share their word knowledge. (see page PD39.)

- Take turns reading Key Word posters.
- Talk about how the pictures on the posters show the meanings of the Key Words.
- Create sentences using both Key Words and write them in your journals.
- Draw a line under each Key Word.

4 **Practice/Apply** Group students who know different words and have them use the **Jigsaw** to share their words. Have them work together to do a word sort. Ask students to write each of their words on an index card or strip of paper. Then have them sort the words by parts of speech. Then encourage students to sort the words in categories of their own choosing. (See **Cooperative Learning Routines**, pages PD58–PD59

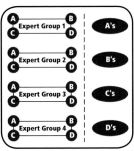

Jigsaw

> **CHECK UNDERSTANDING** Display the **Language Builder Picture Card E15** (bear looking for food) and ask students to use Key Words to tell about it.

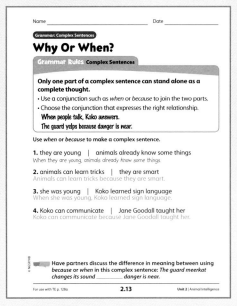

Name _____ Date _____

Grammar: Complex Sentences

Why Or When?

Grammar Rules Complex Sentences

Only one part of a complex sentence can stand alone as a complete thought.
- Use a conjunction such as *when* or *because* to join the two parts.
- Choose the conjunction that expresses the right relationship.
  When people talk, Koko answers.
  The guard yelps because danger is near.

Use *when* or *because* to make a complex sentence.

1. they are young | animals already know some things
When they are young, animals already know some things.

2. animals can learn tricks | they are smart
Animals can learn tricks because they are smart.

3. she was young | Koko learned sign language
When she was young, Koko learned sign language.

4. Koko can communicate | Jane Goodall taught her
Koko can communicate because Jane Goodall taught her.

Have partners discuss the difference in meaning between using *because* or *when* in this complex sentence: *The guard meerkat changes its sound _____ danger is near.*

For use with TE p. 128a   **2.13**   Unit 2 | Animal Intelligence

 Practice Master 2.13

Day 5

Day at a Glance:
▶ **Language:** Use Gestures and Expression ▶ **Reading:** Reread and Explain
▶ **Vocabulary:** Apply Word Knowledge ▶ **Writing:** Edit and Proofread a Business Letter

OBJECTIVES

Vocabulary
• Use Grade-Level Vocabulary: **tool** ❶
• Use Academic Vocabulary ❶

Listening and Speaking
• Use Gestures and Expression ❶

Learning and Teamwork Strategies
• Relate to Personal Experience
• Use Patterns in Language
• Review

Media and Technology
• Build Concepts from Media

Science
• Explore Animal Intelligence

Resources

• *Markers for Picture It*

▶ *Unit 2 Build Background Video*

▶ *eVisual 2.27*

Differentiate

How to Learn Language

Relate to Personal Experience Explain:
Personal experience can help you understand unfamiliar gestures and expressions.

You See and Hear:
Somebody holds his or her hand up and says "Stop!"

You Think:
"One time I saw a police officer show this same gesture to a driver. The driver stopped."

You Know:
The gesture and expression mean the speaker wants you to stop.

Have mixed proficiency partners practice, using gestures and expressions that they have learned from experience.

Language of the Day

What are some skills animals have? How do these skills show intelligence?
I know that animals can ____.
These skills show that animals ____.

Read the Language of the Day. Have students view the **Unit 2 Build Background Video** before completing the sentence frame. Add their ideas to the unit concept map. Then explain that today they will learn how to use gestures and expressions in speaking, play a word game, retell the selection, and write about it.

Use Gestures and Expressions

❶ **Teach/Model** Introduce the concept:
When you speak, use gestures and expressions to keep your listeners interested. Model gestures and expressions appropriate to a sentence or two. Ask a volunteer to repeat the procedure with the next two sentences. Display the How to card and identify each step as the volunteer talks.

▶ Play the video.

NGReach.com > **Digital Library**

How to Use Gestures and Expressions

👄	1. Tell about the topic.	I think animals are really good at communication.
😮	2. Use words that show how you feel about the topic. Show feeling on your face.	I'm amazed by their communication skills.
👄	3. Give more information and details.	Animals can hear very well.
🧑	4. Use expressions and hand gestures that help your listener understand.	They hear sounds people cannot hear.

NGReach.com > eVisual 2.27

❷ **Practice/Apply** Pair students, and have partners talk about animal communication. Encourage them to use gestures and expressions while they talk.

CHECK UNDERSTANDING Ask: *What's the difference between a gesture and an expression?* (A gesture is something you do with your hands or body; an expression is a feeling that you show on your face.)

Apply Word Knowledge

3 **Teach/Model** Organize students in small groups and situate each group in a separate part of the room. Post several Key Words and explain how to play "Picture It."

- *Groups choose one of the posted Key Words and decide a way to show its meaning in a drawing. One member is assigned as the artist on each turn.*
- *At each group's turn, the artist completes a drawing and displays it for the class.*
- *Viewing groups must figure out what word the drawing shows. One member of each group raises a hand to give the answer.*
- *The correct group gets a point and gets to show its drawing next. The game ends when one group earns 3 points. Members should take turns drawing and giving answers.*

4 **Practice/Apply** Distribute markers and have groups create their first drawing. Clarify: *Make sure you only show the word. Do not write the word on the drawing anywhere.* Provide an example with a drawing of a homework list: *This drawing shows a note. Which Key Word is this an example of?* (**language**)

Have students follow the agreed upon rules as they play the game. Monitor students as they complete the activity. Restate instructions as needed.

For vocabulary games, go to NGReach.com.

> **CHECK UNDERSTANDING** Display several completed drawings and have students explain how the pictures helped them identify Key Words.

Part 2 Vocabulary Skills Trace		Page
Day 1	Science Vocabulary	T107
Day 2	Academic Vocabulary	T109
Day 3	Expand Word Knowledge	T112b
Day 4	Share Word Knowledge	T128b
Day 5	**Apply Word Knowledge**	**T129b**
Day 6	Use a Dictionary	T130
Day 7	Use a Dictionary	T137
Days 8–9	Extend Vocabulary	T138e–f
Day 10	Vocabulary Review	T138g–h

Day 5
continued

Day at a Glance:
▶ **Language:** Use Gesture and Expression
▶ **Vocabulary:** Apply Word Knowledge
▶ **Reading:** Reread and Explain
▶ **Writing:** Edit and Proofread a Business Letter

OBJECTIVES

Vocabulary
- Use Academic Vocabulary: communication, language ⊕
- Use Grade-Level Vocabulary: skill, tool ⊕
- Use Classroom Vocabulary: diagram, remind ⊕

Language
- Use Gesture and Expression ⊕
- Participate in Discussion

Learning and Teamwork Strategies
- Use Graphic Organizers: Main Idea Diagram
- Reason Deductively

Fluency
- Read with Accuracy Rate and Intonation ⊕

Writing
- Writing Project: Edit and Proofread

Science
- Explore Animal Intelligence

Resources

🔘 *Comprehension Coach*

🔗🔘 *Practice Masters 2.14, 2.15*

🔗 **NGReach.com** ❯

See **Technology Station** for digital student resources.

Name _____ Date _____

Reread and Explain: Main Idea Diagram

"Animal Smarts"
Make a Main Idea Diagram for "Animal Smarts."

Main Idea Diagram

Main Idea: Animals are.
Detail: Chimpanzees can use tools.
Detail: Frogs can remember.
Detail: Some animals can communicate with people.
Detail: Meerkats can communicate with each other.
Detail: Dogs can learn tricks.
Detail: Parrots can sort blocks.
Detail: Elephants and dolphins can trick humans.

▬▬▬ Use your main idea diagram to explain the selection to a partner.

For use with TE p. T129c   2.14   Unit 2 | Animal Intelligence

 Practice Master 2.14

Reread and Explain

1 **Main Idea and Details** Reinforce: *The main idea is what a selection is mostly about. Details are facts or examples that tell more about that idea.* Review the main idea diagram and call outs. Ask: *What would you say is the main idea of "Animal Smarts"?* (Animals are smart in many ways.) Then ask: *What are two examples in the article that show how animals are smart?* Tell students they will complete the chart by adding more supporting details. Encourage students to look at section heads for supporting details.

Have students complete **Practice Master 2.14**.

2 **Explain** Read aloud the directions and language frames. Have students explain the ideas in the selection to their partners. Remind them to tell how each detail supports the main idea. Partners reverse roles and repeat. Provide the Key Points Reading (**Practice Masters 2.12**) for students who need additional support.

To evaluate student's proficiency levels, use the following rubric:

Explain a Story Rubric		
Scale	**Content**	**Language**
B	☐ Misses many important main ideas. ☐ Includes few details.	☐ Frequently hard to hear or understand. ☐ Rarely uses Key Words correctly and frequently.
I	☐ Misses some important main ideas. ☐ Includes some details.	☐ Is often hard to hear or understand. ☐ Sometimes uses Key Words correctly and frequently.
A	☐ Covers most important main ideas. ☐ Includes most supporting details.	☐ Can be understood most of the time. ☐ Often uses Key Words correctly and frequently.
AH	☐ Covers all main ideas in the selection. ☐ Includes all supporting details.	☐ Speaks clearly and is easily understood. ☐ Uses Key Words correctly and frequently.

Fluency Accuracy, Rate, and Intonation ▊I▊ ▊A▊ ▊AH▊

3 **Fluency** Have students record their reading on the **Comprehension Coach** to assess each student's progress for rate and accuracy. Have students use the passage on **Practice Master 2.15** to record their reading for intonation. Listen to each recording and assess students' ability to read with intonation.

Main Idea and Details

Make a main idea diagram for "Animal Smarts."

Main Idea Diagram

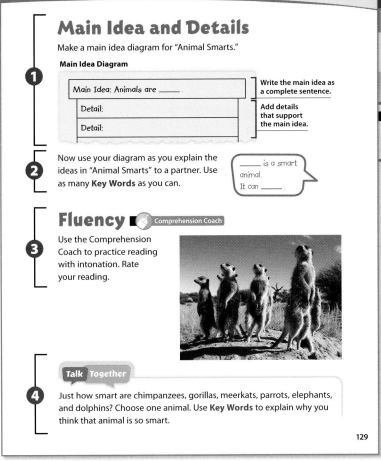

①

Main Idea: Animals are _____.

Detail:

Detail:

Write the main idea as a complete sentence.

Add details that support the main idea.

② Now use your diagram as you explain the ideas in "Animal Smarts" to a partner. Use as many **Key Words** as you can.

_____ is a smart animal. It can _____.

Technology Station
🖱 NGReach.com

▶ Comprehension Coach

⏺ Automatically measure fluency.

Fluency ▮ Comprehension Coach

③ Use the Comprehension Coach to practice reading with intonation. Rate your reading.

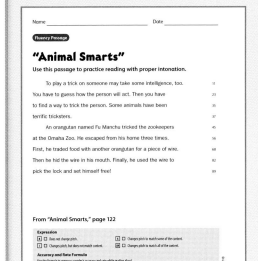

Talk Together

④ Just how smart are chimpanzees, gorillas, meerkats, parrots, elephants, and dolphins? Choose one animal. Use **Key Words** to explain why you think that animal is so smart.

129

Student Book page 129

Name _____ Date _____

Fluency Passage

"Animal Smarts"

Use this passage to practice reading with proper intonation.

To play a trick on someone may take some intelligence, too.	11
You have to guess how the person will act. Then you have	23
to find a way to trick the person. Some animals have been	35
terrific tricksters.	37
An orangutan named Fu Manchu tricked the zookeepers	45
at the Omaha Zoo. He escaped from his home three times.	56
First, he traded food with another orangutan for a piece of wire.	68
Then he hid the wire in his mouth. Finally, he used the wire to	82
pick the lock and set himself free!	89

From "Animal Smarts," page 122

Expression
- ▢ Does not change pitch.
- ▢ Changes pitch, but does not match content.
- ▢ Changes pitch to match some of the content.
- ▢ Changes pitch to match all of the content.

Accuracy and Rate Formula
Use the formula to measure a reader's accuracy and rate while reading aloud.

words attempted in one minute	–	number of errors	=	words correct per minute (wcpm)

For use with TE p. T129   **2.15**   Unit 2 | Animal Intelligence

 Practice Master 2.15

---

④ Talk Together Discuss some of the **skills** and **tools** used by animals in "Animal Smarts." Read aloud the directions and have students work independently to organize their explanation. Then have them take turns sharing their ideas before adding them to their unit concept maps.

Daily Writing 📝

⑤ Writing Project: Edit and Proofread a Business Letter
Have students edit and proofread their Writing Project compositions. See pages T141a–T141.

Keys to Efficacy

Provide prompts students can use to help one another: *I agree with you because _____. How can we build that idea into something bigger?*

CLOSE AND ASSESS

- **Language** Use gestures and expression as you *Tell me something you liked about "Animal Smarts."*
- **Reading** *Share a detail that supports the main idea: animals can **communicate** in many ways.* (Possible answer: Gorillas can learn sign **language**.)
- **Vocabulary** *How do the Key Words skills and tools help you give details?* (Answers will vary.)

Day 6

Day at a Glance:
○ **Language:** Tell an Original Story   ► **Reading:** Read the Selection
○ **Vocabulary:** Use a Dictionary   **Writing:** Writing Fluency; Publish and Share

OBJECTIVES

Vocabulary
• Use Academic Vocabulary ⊕
• Use Grade-Level Content Vocabulary ⊕
• Use Reference Sources (Dictionary) ⊕

Language
• Language Function:
  Tell an Original Story

Learning and Teamwork Strategies
• Prompt and Provide Suggestions
• Build on Ideas

Resources

⊘ eVisual 2.28

⊘ eVisual 2.29

⊘ Language Builder Picture Cards

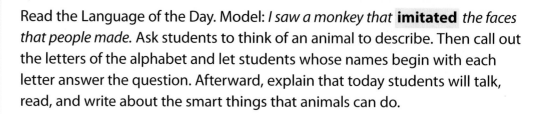

Language of the Day

How do animals learn new skills?
I saw a/an _____ that _____.

Read the Language of the Day. Model: *I saw a monkey that **imitated** the faces that people made.* Ask students to think of an animal to describe. Then call out the letters of the alphabet and let students whose names begin with each letter answer the question. Afterward, explain that today students will talk, read, and write about the smart things that animals can do.

Tell an Original Story

1 **Teach/Model** Define an original story. Say: *An original story has made-up characters, events, and dialogue. The story usually tells about a problem and the solution to the problem.*

Display the chart and model using these structures to tell a story.

How to Tell An Original Story	
Tell who the story is about and where it takes place.	This is a story about a young penguin named Pagoo.
Tell about a problem.	Pagoo is lost and needs to find his way home.
Tell what the characters do to solve the problem.	Pagoo asks an old penguin to give him directions.
Tell how the problem is solved.	Pagoo follows the directions and finds his way home.

⊘ NGReach.com ▷ eVisual 2.28

Invite a volunteer to tell another impromptu story. Point to each step on the How to card to help the volunteer include each key element.

2 **Practice/Apply** Give students time to think of a story they want to tell. Suggest to them that they tell another story about an animal that gets lost. They can take notes and/or draw pictures to help generate ideas.

Use **Academic Language Frames** to help students at every proficiency level.

Differentiate

Academic Language Frames

Tell an Original Story
■ This is a story about _____.

■ This is a story about _____.
  The problem is that _____.
  The problem is solved when _____.

■ This is a story about _____.
■ The problem is that _____.
  The problem is solved when _____.
  In the end, _____.

⊘ NGReach.com ▷ eVisual 2.29

CHECK UNDERSTANDING Have each pair of students select a **Language Builder Picture Card** and tell a story about the picture.

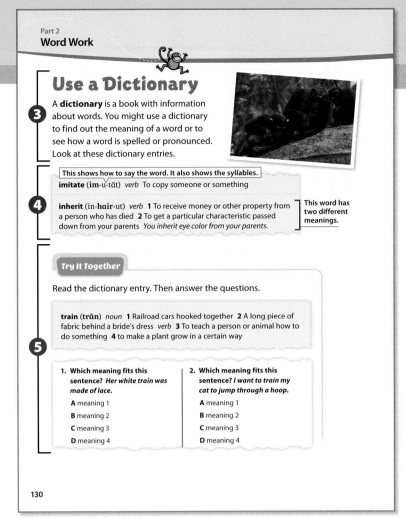

Use a Dictionary

3 A **dictionary** is a book with information about words. You might use a dictionary to find out the meaning of a word or to see how a word is spelled or pronounced. Look at these dictionary entries.

4

> This shows how to say the word. It also shows the syllables.
>
> **imitate** (**im**-u-tāt) *verb* To copy someone or something
>
> **inherit** (in-**hair**-ut) *verb* **1** To receive money or other property from a person who has died **2** To get a particular characteristic passed down from your parents *You inherit eye color from your parents.*
>
> This word has two different meanings.

Try It Together

5 Read the dictionary entry. Then answer the questions.

> **train** (**trān**) *noun* **1** Railroad cars hooked together **2** A long piece of fabric behind a bride's dress *verb* **3** To teach a person or animal how to do something **4** to make a plant grow in a certain way

1. Which meaning fits this sentence? *Her white train was made of lace.*
   A meaning 1
   B meaning 2
   C meaning 3
   D meaning 4

2. Which meaning fits this sentence? *I want to train my cat to jump through a hoop.*
   A meaning 1
   B meaning 2
   C meaning 3
   D meaning 4

130

Student Book page 130

Use a Dictionary

3 **Teach** Read the introduction aloud. Activate prior knowledge by having students think of words for which they would like to know the pronunciation, meaning, or spelling. List the words.

4 **Model** Guide students through an examination of the dictionary entry, *imitate*. Point to the callout and explain the features. Ask volunteers to use the features for the second word, **inherit**. *How do you pronounce it? How many syllables? How many meanings?* Choose a word from the list just created. Model finding it in a student dictionary. Point out features.

5 **Practice/Apply** Read the directions aloud. Then have partners work together to answer the questions. Have partners study the **Multi-Level Practice Sets**. Challenge them to use each meaning in a sentence. Have students with extra time choose words from the class list, look them up in a dictionary, and share findings with the class.

> **CHECK UNDERSTANDING** Say: *Look up the word* peep *in a dictionary and give two meanings for the word.*

Differentiate

Multi-Level Practice Sets

N **spot** (**spot**) *noun* **1** A small part of a surface that is different from the rest: *a white dog with black spots* **2** A stain or ugly mark **3** A particular place *verb* **4** To see or locate

B **bolt** (**bōlt**) *noun* **1** A pin or rod for holding something in place **2** A sliding bar for locking a door **3** A stroke of lightning *verb* **4** To fasten with a bolt **4** To move very quickly

I **sign** (**sīn**) *noun* **1** A symbol that stands for something else **2** A poster or board with information on it **3** A hint or warning *verb* **4** to use sign language to say **5** To write one's name in cursive

A **observe** (ub-**zurv**) *verb* **1** To see or notice **2** to examine carefully: *We observed the animal's behavior*

AH **study** (**stud**-ē) *verb* **1** To attempt to learn, know, or understand **2** To take classes in: *to study music* **3** To examine carefully *noun* **4** An area of knowledge **5** A room set aside for reading or studying

Day 6
continued

Day at a Glance:
Language: Tell an Original Story
Vocabulary: Use a Dictionary
Reading: Read the Selection
Writing: Writing Fluency; Publish and Share

OBJECTIVES

Vocabulary
• Use Grade-Level Vocabulary: **imitate**, **skills**, **tool** ⊕
• Use Academic Vocabulary: **ability**, **learn** ⊕

Language
• Listen to a Preview

Reading Strategies
• Plan: Preview
• Read the Selection
• Make Connections: Text to Text
• Strategy: Make Connections ⊕

Literary Analysis
• Analyze Visuals
• Analyze Genre: Science Article

Learning and Teamwork Strategies
• Use Prereading Supports
• Build Background Knowledge
• Use Reading Supports

Resources

 Practice Masters 2.16

Read the Science Article

❶ Connect Across Texts Read aloud the introduction and explain: *As you read the science article, think about the Big Question. Animals show their* **ability** *to* **learn** **skills** *in different ways.*

❷ Genre Read aloud the definition. Ask: *Does this article tell a story or give information?* (It gives information.) *Look at the picture and read the title. What do you think this discovery is about?* (It has something to do with chimpanzees. Maybe it tells what the chimps can do.)

❸ Preview and Build Background Use sheltering strategies as you conduct a picture walk.

Pages	Say (and Do) 💬 ✋
131	*Fongoli is a very hot, dry place.* (Pretend to fan yourself.) *It can be hard to find food in a place like this. What would you do?*
132–133	*Fongoli is in Africa.* (Point to a Fongoli chimp.) *Many chimpanzees live there. They wander around looking for food.* (Point to Jill Pruetz.) *Jill Pruetz watches them to learn how they live.*
134–135	*The chimps make a* **tool** *to hunt other animals. They find a tree branch and pull off its leaves.* (Pretend to break off a branch and pull off the leaves.) *Many chimps make this tool.* (Point to the photo of Teva.) *Do you think this young chimp will learn too?*

❹ Read "The Clever Chimps of Fongoli" Scaffold the support for various reading levels.

BELOW LEVEL	ON LEVEL	ABOVE LEVEL
Listen and Learn	**Read Together**	**Use a Dialogue Journal**
• Ask students to set a purpose for listening—to get information or to enjoy an article. Have them track the print while you read the text aloud. Then have students read the article chorally. • Guide children in blending multisyllabic words.	• Have students read with partners, pausing after each page to individually complete column 1 of the Dialogue Journal. • After reading, have partners trade journals to read their partner's comments and write responses in column 2. • Meet with students to discuss the journals and ask the Build Comprehension questions.	• Have students use the **Dialogue Journal** as they read silently. Students write page numbers and record their thoughts in column 1. • Partners trade journals, read column 1, and write responses in column 2. Then students compare the two columns of their journals. Meet with students to discuss the Build Comprehension questions.

CHECK UNDERSTANDING Ask: *What's the difference between a science article and a story?* (A story doesn't give information, but a science article does. A science article tells about a discovery.)

Connect Across Texts
Read this article to **learn** what one scientist discovered while studying chimpanzees.

Genre A **science article** can tell about a new discovery in science.

1

THE CLEVER CHIMPS OF Fongoli

by Elizabeth Sengel

1

It's hard to get a meal in Fongoli. The **harsh** landscape offers only **patches of greenery**. The sun burns like a 200-watt bulb. By eight o'clock in the morning, the rocky, treeless ground **bakes** in 90-degree heat.

▲ Chimps walk across dry ground in Fongoli.

In Other Words
harsh dry and hot
patches of greenery a few places with trees and plants
bakes gets really hot

▶ **Before You Move On**
2
1. **Make Connections** What does Fongoli remind you of? Explain.
2. **Use Text Features** What can you tell about this article from the title, the photo, and the caption?

131

Student Book page 131

Build Comprehension, page 131

1 **Make Predictions** As you read the first page of the article, make a prediction about what this article will teach you about how smart chimps are. What problem might these clever chimps solve? (I predict that the article will teach me how the chimps find food in such a hot and dry place.)

2 **Answers to Before You Move On**

1. Make Connections RETEACH Remind students that when they read, they should think about how the text relates to what they know. Have them think about similar places they may have seen or read about. Then have them answer the question. (Answers will vary. Possible response: Fongoli reminds me of a place we learned about in social studies class.)

2. Use Text Features Possible response: I can tell that the article is about chimps in a place called Fongoli. The word *clever* tells me that the chimps are smart and the article may explain this.

Cultural Perpectives: Animal Stories

Science articles tell us facts about animals. Students can also learn about animals from the stories of cultures around the world. They tell us how people in different places think and feel about animals. Have students share examples of animal stories they know from different places around the world. Have students research stories about an animal that interests them from one or more cultures. Ask them to share their findings with the class.

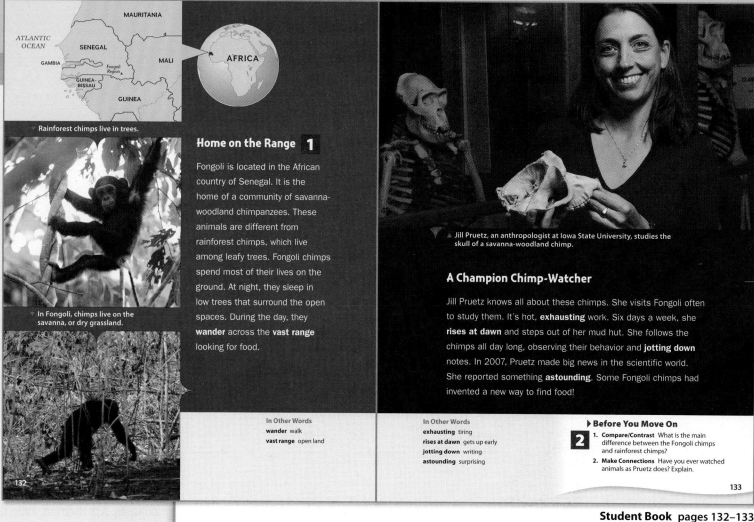

Rainforest chimps live in trees.

In Fongoli, chimps live on the savanna, or dry grassland.

Home on the Range 1

Fongoli is located in the African country of Senegal. It is the home of a community of savanna-woodland chimpanzees. These animals are different from rainforest chimps, which live among leafy trees. Fongoli chimps spend most of their lives on the ground. At night, they sleep in low trees that surround the open spaces. During the day, they **wander** across the **vast range** looking for food.

▲ Jill Pruetz, an anthropologist at Iowa State University, studies the skull of a savanna-woodland chimp.

A Champion Chimp-Watcher

Jill Pruetz knows all about these chimps. She visits Fongoli often to study them. It's hot, **exhausting** work. Six days a week, she **rises at dawn** and steps out of her mud hut. She follows the chimps all day long, observing their behavior and **jotting down** notes. In 2007, Pruetz made big news in the scientific world. She reported something **astounding**. Some Fongoli chimps had invented a new way to find food!

In Other Words
wander walk
vast range open land

In Other Words
exhausting tiring
rises at dawn gets up early
jotting down writing
astounding surprising

▶ **Before You Move On**
2
1. **Compare/Contrast** What is the main difference between the Fongoli chimps and rainforest chimps?
2. **Make Connections** Have you ever watched animals as Pruetz does? Explain.

132

133

Student Book pages 132–133

B I A AH

Home Connection:
Intelligent Animal Stories

Send home a copy of **Family Newsletter 2** from the **Teacher's Resource Book.** Students collect stories from family or community members about the intelligent things pets or other animals can do.

I A AH

Science: Animal Observations

Explain that chimpanzees are not the only animals Jill Pruetz studies, nor is Fongoli the only place she observes animals. Have students go online to learn more about Jill Pruetz's work with animals. Ask them to report their findings to the class.

Build Comprehension, pages 132–133

1 **Main Idea and Details** Review Main Idea and Details from page 108 with students. What is the main idea of the text on page 132?

- The title and text help me to identify that the main idea of page 132 is that Fongoli chimps live on the ground.

- The details that support this are that the Fongoli chimps live on a savanna, or dry grassland. They spend most of their day on the ground looking for food.

2 **Answers to Before You Move On**

1. **Compare/Contrast** Fongoli chimps spend most of their time on the ground. Rain forest chimps live in the trees.

2. **Make Connections** APPLY Answers will vary. Students should explain about when they did this and provide details of what they observed.

Whittling Weapons

The clever chimps had figured out how to make a spear-like **tool**. First, they break a branch off a tree and rip away the leaves. Then they **sharpen** one end of the stick with their teeth. They use the spears to hunt bush babies. These are small animals that sleep in **hollow** tree trunks during the day. The chimps look for an opening in a hollow tree **limb**. Then they **jab** the weapon through the opening to try to kill their prey. **4** **5**

▲ A chimp pushes a sharpened stick into a tree hole.

▲ A bush baby in a hollow tree trunk

▲ Pruetz holds the sharp tool made by a Fongoli chimp.

In Other Words
sharpen make a sharp point at
hollow holes in
limb branch
jab push

Getting Creative

In Fongoli, the chimps **compete for** limited amounts of food. When big males find food, they have very bad manners! Like greedy children, they **refuse to** share. Females and young males have to find their own food. Pruetz believes that this situation has forced them to become creative. That's what led to their tool-making.

Teva is a young chimp in Fongoli. Her mother is one of the best hunters. Will Teva's mother teach her how to make spears? "It will be interesting to see if Teva **picks it up**," Pruetz says.

If Teva learns this **skill**, she will find it easier to eat in Fongoli.

Teva, a young chimp in Fongoli, learns from her mother. ▶

In Other Words
compete for fight over
refuse to will not
picks it up learns

▶ Before You Move On
6
1. **Problem/Solution** How have the Fongoli chimps solved the problem of finding food? Explain.
2. **Draw Conclusions** Why do the chimps of Fongoli have to be creative?

134

135

Build Comprehension, pages 134–135

3 **Steps in a Process** What are the steps that Fongoli chimps follow to make weapons to hunt for food? Write sentences or draw a picture to show each step. (1. Break a branch off a tree. 2. Rip off the leaves. 3. Sharpen one end of the branch.)

4 **Use Key Words** Write sentences using the Key Word **ability** to describe the intelligence of Fongoli chimps. (Possible answer: The chimps show intelligence by their **ability** to make **tools**.)

5 **Main Idea and Details** What discovery did Jill Pruetz make about the chimpanzees of Fongoli? (That the chimpanzees know how to make a tool to help them hunt.) Knowing this, how would you state the main idea? (The main idea is that chimpanzees are smart animals because they have **learned** to make a tool.)

6 **Answers to Before You Move On**
1. **Problem/Solution** The chimps discovered a way to make tools to catch food.
2. **Draw Conclusions** The chimps of Fongoli have to be creative because there is limited food in the area and the bigger apes do not share.

B **I** **A** **AH**

Literary Analysis: Analyze Visuals

Teach/Model Explain that photographs are a visual element of an article. They can either show information described in the text or add new information. Point to the photograph of the chimp's tool. Say: *This photograph shows me what the chimps' weapon looked like.*

Practice/Apply Have students review all the photographs in the science article. Then ask them to identify one that they find most helpful in understanding the selection and explain why.

Day 6
continued

Day at a Glance:
Language: Tell an Original Story
Vocabulary: Use a Dictionary
Reading: Read the Selection
Writing: Writing Fluency Publish and Share

OBJECTIVES

Vocabulary
• Use Academic Vocabulary ⊕
• Use Grade-Level Content Vocabulary: **skill, tool** ⊕

Language
• Participate in Discussion

Fluency
• Read with Accuracy and Rate

Literary Analysis
• Compare Facts

Learning and Teamwork Strategies
• Use Graphic Organizer: Comparison Chart

Writing
• Develop Fluency
• Monitor and Self-Correct Writing
• Writing Project: Publish and Share

Resources

  eVisual 2.30

Practice Master 2.17

Comprehension Coach

Differentiate

Multi-Level Strategies

BEGINNING

Demonstrate how these students can use photos to locate facts listed on the chart.

INTERMEDIATE

Demonstrate how these students can use section heads to locate facts. Encourage them to write one additional fact.

ADVANCED ADVANCED HIGH

Encourage students to find additional facts about chimps in the articles and write them on the chart using complete sentences.

Respond and Extend

1 Reread As students reread "The Clever Chimps of Fongoli" on their own, have them think about how the facts of the two science articles fit together.

2 Compare Facts Remind students that a comparison chart compares information from two sources. Say: *You can use a comparison chart to compare which facts about chimpanzees are presented in both articles.*

Read the instructions. Create two groups and use the **Fishbowl** cooperative learning strategy. Have students inside the circle identify facts about chimpanzees that are in one article while those outside the circle listen and complete their charts. Then have students reverse roles for the other article. Ask questions to help guide students in completing their charts. Provide **Multi-Level Strategies** to support students at different language levels.

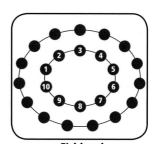

Fishbowl

Focus	Questions
1. Tools	What tools used by chimps does each article discuss?
2. Skills	What skills of chimps does each article discuss?
3. Roles of People	What roles does each article say people play?

Have partners record their ideas on **Practice Master 2.17**.

3 Talk Together About the Big Question
Read aloud the questions and the directions. Ask follow-up questions to prompt students as they use newly acquired vocabulary and to focus discussion.

• What skills have scientists seen in chimps?
• How do you think young chimps learn these skills?

> **CHECK UNDERSTANDING** Make cards with either animal names or animal smarts on them. Have students play Memory with a partner, taking turns to match the animal smart with the appropriate animal.
> ▶ If students have difficulty, have them look back at the facts in the selections.

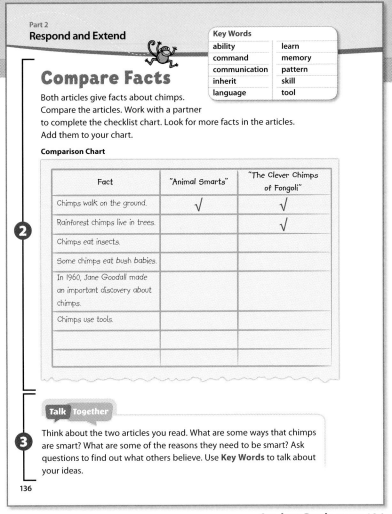

Key Words

ability	learn
command	memory
communication	pattern
inherit	skill
language	tool

Compare Facts

Both articles give facts about chimps.
Compare the articles. Work with a partner
to complete the checklist chart. Look for more facts in the articles.
Add them to your chart.

Comparison Chart

②

Fact	"Animal Smarts"	"The Clever Chimps of Fongoli"
Chimps walk on the ground.	√	√
Rainforest chimps live in trees.		√
Chimps eat insects.		
Some chimps eat bush babies.		
In 1960, Jane Goodall made an important discovery about chimps.		
Chimps use tools.		

Talk Together

③ Think about the two articles you read. What are some ways that chimps
are smart? What are some of the reasons they need to be smart? Ask
questions to find out what others believe. Use **Key Words** to talk about
your ideas.

136

Student Book page 136

Daily Writing

④ Writing Fluency Use the **Power Writing** routine (see page PD53).
Write the word **communication** and prompt: *What is communication like
for animals? Think about this word and write about it.*

Power Writing Routine

1. What do you know about the word or picture?

2. Take one minute to write as much as you can, as well as you can.
B words   **I** sentences   **A** **AH** paragraphs

3. Check your spelling and grammar. Circle mistakes.

4. Count your words.

NGReach.com ▸ eVisual 2.30

⑤ Writing Project: **Publish and Share** Have students publish and
share their Writing Project compositions. See page T141.

CLOSE AND ASSESS

• **Language** *Tell a story about an animal that imitates another animal.*

• **Vocabulary** *Use a dictionary to look up a word from the class list. Share
what you learn.*

• **Reading** *How do scientists learn about chimps?* (They observe and take notes.)

Fluency: Accuracy and Rate

To activate prior knowledge and practice
fluency, conduct timed readings of "The
Clever Chimps of Fongoli." Select an option
for recording:

• Use the automatic speech recognition on
the **Comprehension Coach** to track word
count per minute for the entire passage.

• Use Practice Master 2.15.

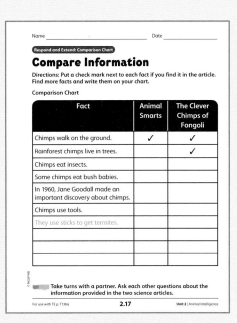

Name _____ Date _____

Respond and Extend: Comparison Chart

Compare Information

Directions: Put a check mark next to each fact if you find it in the article.
Find more facts and write them on your chart.

Comparison Chart

Fact	Animal Smarts	The Clever Chimps of Fongoli
Chimps walk on the ground.	✓	✓
Rainforest chimps live in trees.		✓
Chimps eat insects.		
Some chimps eat bush babies.		
In 1960, Jane Goodall made an important discovery about chimps.		
Chimps use tools.		
They use sticks to get termites.		

Take turns with a partner. Ask each other questions about the
information provided in the two science articles.

For use with TE p. T136a   **2.17**   Unit 2 | Animal Intelligence

Practice Master 2.17

Day 7

OBJECTIVES

Vocabulary
- Use Academic Vocabulary ❶
- Use Grade-Level Vocabulary ❶
- Use Reference Sources (Dictionary) ❶

Grammar
- Compound Sentences ❶

Learning and Teamwork Strategies
- Make Contributions

Resources

 Practice Master 2.18

 eVisual 2.31

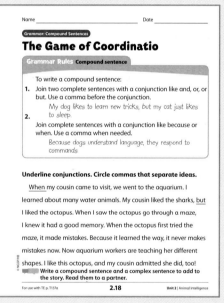

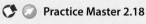 **Practice Master 2.18**

Language of the Day

What do I know about animal communication?
I know that _____.

Model: *I know that birds communicate by singing.* Have each student repeat your sentence and then share ideas about other types of animal communication. Then explain that students will be learning more about compound sentences like today's question.

Grammar Understand Compound Sentences I A AH

❶ Teach/Model Read the introduction and example sentence. Point out the comma before the conjunction. Say: *The comma can help you identify the two sentences that have been combined.*

Read aloud the first rule and the example. Ask: *How are these two ideas alike?* (The second sentence tells one way animals can solve problems.) Write this sentence, and have students tell how the two ideas are alike: *I like to swim, and I love to ride my bike.*

Read aloud the second rule and example. Ask: *How are these two ideas different?* (One sentence tells about what animals know. The other tells about what they must **learn**.) Write: *I want to play baseball, but I have to do my homework.* Have students tell how the two ideas are different. Ask a volunteer to say another compound sentence using *but*.

Have volunteers read the third rule and example aloud. Ask: *What are the two choices?* (Animals may use sounds or signs.) Write: *I could play fullback, or I could be the goalie.* Have students tell how the two ideas are choices. Then have a volunteer say another compound sentence using *or*.

❷ Practice Read aloud the passage from "Animal Smarts." Ask a volunteer to find and read the compound sentence. (the last sentence) Ask another volunteer to identify the conjunction in the sentence. (but)

❸ Apply in Writing Read aloud the directions and then have students write independently. Provide support as necessary. Assign **Practice Master 2.18**.

> **CHECK UNDERSTANDING** Ask: *What makes the following statement a compound sentence? Meercats do not talk, but they do communicate.* (It has two complete sentences connect by the word *but*.)

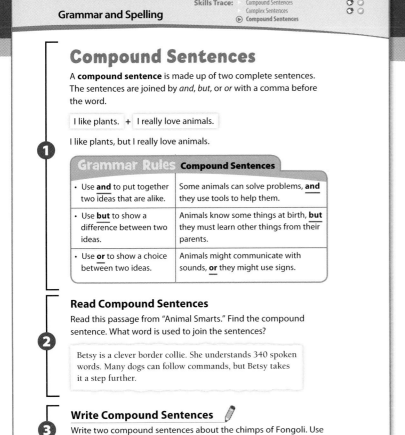

Student Book page 137

More Dictionary Skills

4 **Review/Model** Review the Day 6 lesson (page T130). Read the Dictionary Entries with students. Point out the word spellings and pronunciations. Call on volunteers to tell how many syllables are in each word. Then read aloud the first sentence. Use the dictionary entry to determine the meaning of the underlined word. Have student pairs determine the meaning of the word in the second sentence.

1. *Fongoli chimps do not have a wide <u>range</u> of food to choose from.*

2. *Fongoli chimps must wander the dry <u>range</u> looking for food.*

5 **Practice/Apply** Have partners take turns determining the meaning of the underlined words in the sentences below. Remind students to refer to the Dictionary Entries for help.

3. *Many animals make their homes in <u>hollow</u> trees and logs.* (1)

4. *The cabin is in a small <u>hollow</u> between the mountains.* (4)

5. *Betsy can follow a <u>command</u>.* (3)

6. *The pirate captain <u>commands</u> his ship.* (2)

> **CHECK UNDERSTANDING** *Tell me the meaning of* range *in this sentence:* The two countries are separated by a range of mountains. (a group of things in a row)

Dictionary Entry Structure

> **Dictionary Entries**
>
> **hollow** (**hol•ō**) *adjective* **1** Empty on the inside, not solid **2** Echoing, as if coming from a cave *noun* **3** An opening or hole **4** A small valley
>
> **range** (**rānj**) *noun* **1** A set, selection, or variety **2** An open area of land for animals to graze and find food **3** A group of things in a row, as of mountains
>
> **command** (cu-**mand**) *verb* **1** To order or direct *noun* **2** To be in control of *noun* **3** An order

🌐 NGReach.com ▶ eVisual 2.31

Day 7
continued

Day at a Glance:
▶ **Language:** Compound Sentences
▶ **Vocabulary:** Use a Dictionary

▶ **Reading:** Reread the Selection
▶ **Writing:** Writing on Demand: Paragraph

OBJECTIVES

Vocabulary
• Use Academic Vocabulary ❶
• Use Grade-Level Vocabulary: **memory**, **tool** ❶
• Use Classroom Vocabulary: **diagram**
• Use Dictionary Skills ❶

Literary Analysis
• Summarize Main Ideas
• Identify Main Ideas and Details

Learning and Teamwork Strategies
• Relate to Prior Knowledge
• Make Contributions

Writing
• Reproduce Modeled Writing
• Write a paragraph

Reread   Focus on Writer's Style

❶ Teach   Good writers vary their writing to keep it interesting. A writer chooses words carefully. A writer will also use different kinds of sentences and sentences of that are different lengths.

Today, you will read "The Clever Chimps of Fongoli" again. This time you will look at the kinds of words and sentences the writer used.

❷ Model   Read aloud the first page of the selection. Ask: *What words and phrases does the writer use to let you know it is hot?* (burns like a 200-watt bulb, bakes)

What kind of sentences did the writer use? (statements) *Are all the sentences the same length?* (No) Point out that the last sentence is longer than the rest.

Read pages 132 and 133. Make a T-chart to list vivid words and phrases and sentence types.

Vivid Words and Phrases	Kinds of Sentences
burns like a 200-watt bulb	It's hard to get a meal in Fongoli.

❸ Practice/Apply in Reading   Have students read the section of "The Clever Chimps of Fongoli" titled "Whittling Weapons." Use Team Word Webbing to allow students to identify examples of vivid or specific word choices and kinds of sentences the writer used. Have students discuss these and write the examples on their T charts. Then have students share with the class.

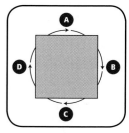

Team Word Webbing

Daily Writing

Writing on Demand: Paragraph Write the prompt and have a volunteer read it aloud.

> Write a paragraph that includes examples of how animals show their intelligence.

Unpack the Prompt Ask: *What is the purpose for writing?* (to give information about animal intelligence in response to a test question) *What form does the writing need to be?* Circle *a paragraph* in the prompt. Have volunteers underline important words (examples, animals, intelligence).

Explain: *A good test-taking strategy is to write your main idea sentence first then add details.*

Use the **Modeled Writing** routine to illustrate how to write a paragraph (See Writing Routes on page PD54.)

Think Aloud	Write
1. Plan	
First I want to plan my writing. I can use a Main Idea diagram to organize my ideas. I start with the main idea.	Animals show their intelligence in different ways.
What details do I want to add? I put them in the cells beneath the main idea. Add detail cells to the **diagram**.	chimps make **tools** orangutans copy their parents poison dart frogs have great **memories**
2. Write	
I will start my paragraph with my main idea.	There are many smart animals, and they show their intelligence in different ways.
Next, I will add details about the topic.	Chimps use tools to get food.
Go through the remaining details to finish the paragraph. Then write a concluding sentence.	
3. Read and Reflect	
Model how to proofread the paragraph. Have students confirm that they used connecting words and commas to separate ideas.	

Display the finished paragraph to serve as a model. Use **Multi-Level Strategies** to support students at all proficiency levels. After students complete their writing, have them read their paragraphs aloud to partners.

CLOSE AND ASSESS
- **Language** Ask: *What are three words you can use to combine two sentences into one?* (and, but, or)
- **Vocabulary** Write this dictionary entry and have students explain each feature. **figure** (fig-yur) *noun* **1** A written number **2** A shape or outline *verb* **3** To think or predict
- **Reading** *How can a writer make the text more interesting to read?* (Use vivid or specific words and phrases, vary the kinds of sentences and the sentence length.)

Differentiate

Multi-Level Strategies

BEGINNING

Provide frames, such as:
- One animal is ___. It shows its intelligence by ___.
- Another animal, the ___, shows its intelligence by ___.

INTERMEDIATE

Have students work with a partner to write paragraphs. Have them begin by brainstorming animals they read about in this unit or knew about already then list an example of each animal's intelligence. As they write, encourage them to ask: *Are we answering the prompt?*

ADVANCED **ADVANCED HIGH**

Have students brainstorm and write paragraphs independently. Then have them work in small groups to tell how one other person in the group answered the writing prompt.

Days 8–9

Day at a Glance:
- ▶ **Language:** Oral Language Project: TV Panel
- ▶ **Vocabulary:** Extend Vocabulary
- ▶ **Reading:** Read Leveled Books
- ▶ **Writing:** Paraphrase

OBJECTIVES

Vocabulary
- Use Academic Vocabulary ⓣ
- Use Grade-Level Vocabulary ⓣ

Language
- Language Function: Engage in Conversation ⓣ

Listening and Speaking
- Listen and Take Notes
- Listen Critically
- Use Correct Speech
- Stay on Topic

Learning and Teamwork
- Support/Defend Ideas

Resources

- *materials for props, such as:*
  - *table and chairs*
  - *scissors and glue*
  - *magazines with animal pictures*
  - *construction paper*
  - *crayons and markers*
  - *note cards*
  - *empty paper towel rolls and empty tissue boxes*
  - *aluminum foil*

- 🔾 ◐ *Assessment Handbook page 64*

HOST: How do you know that dogs are intelligent?

SCIENTIST: Some dogs guide people who cannot see. That takes intelligence.

Language of the Day

What do you still wonder about animals and the intelligent things they do?
I wonder if _____ .

Read the Language of the Day. Model: *I wonder if animals like snakes and fish can* **learn** **skills** *too.* Invite students to share their own sentences stating what they still wonder about animals.

Oral Language Project TV Talk Show

1 Introduce the Activity Set up a panel of participants for a TV Talk Show about animal intelligence. Tap prior knowledge: *What do you know about panel discussions?* Lead students to understand that all panelists speak, either by starting a discussion or by answering questions.

2 Plan Form groups of six students. Roles should include talk show host, scientists, and non-speaking roles, such as camera operator and cue card holder. Assign roles according to proficiency levels.

Dog Expert   Bird Expert   Chimpanzee Expert   Elephant Expert

3 **Rehearse** Have each group choose an animal for the panel to discuss. Students should think about what the scientists will share about the animal's intelligence. Then, have students write questions, answers, and simple dialogue for a script involving the host and the scientists. Use **Multi-Level Strategies** to involve students at all proficiency levels.

Help students set up a desk or table for the TV talk show host and chairs for the scientists to use. Students can create props, such as microphones and camera equipment using construction paper, paper towel rolls, aluminum foil and empty tissue boxes. Students can also draw pictures of their animals or cut animal photos out of magazines to display during the talk show.

4 **Lights, Camera, Action!** Have groups take turns presenting. Students in the audience should ask questions and take notes on information that is new to them. Invite family members or another class to enjoy the discussions. Evaluate the panel discussions using the rubric.

5 **Debrief and Compare** Ask each group to share what they learned from the panels. Have them compare the information each group shared. Then encourage them to add ideas to their unit concept maps, as appropriate.

Differentiate

Multi-Level Strategies

BEGINNING

Provide sentence frames:

• ___ are smart.

• They can ___.

INTERMEDIATE

Provide sentence frames:

• I am an expert on ___.

• I know that ___ are smart because they ___.

ADVANCED ADVANCED HIGH

Challenge students to answer the audience's questions during the panel and come up with additional questions of their own.

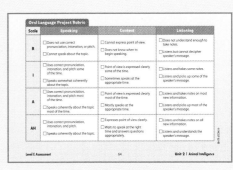

Assessment Handbook page 64

OBJECTIVES

Vocabulary
• Extend Vocabulary through Wide Reading

Language
• Participate in Discussion

Reading
• Read Independently
• Summarize Reading
• Make Connections: Text to Text
• Apply Reading Strategies Varied Texts

Writing
• Paraphrase in Logical Order

Science
• Explore Animal Intelligence

Resources

 Leveled Books:
- *Mouse-Deer Must Be Quick*
- *My Buddy*
- *Animal Trainer*
- *Good Dog!*
- *Animal Masterminds*
- *Koko's Kitten*

   Reach Leveled Library Lesson Plans

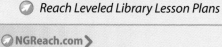

Find more leveled readers about this topic.

Differentiate Read Leveled Books

Group students based on their reading abilities and interests. Use the **Guided Reading** routine (See page PD47) for books at students' instructional level. Use the **Independent Reading Support** (see page PD50) for books at students' independent reading level.

After reading, organize the students into heterogeneous groups to discuss what they read and to use the new information to answer the Big Question. Use these prompts to guide your discussion:

• What new information did you learn about animal intelligence?

• What surprised you?

• How did new information change your answer?

Fiction

BEGINNING LEVEL

Mouse-Deer Must Be Quick
by Constance Foland

• **Genre:** Animal Fantasy

Tiger wants to eat Mouse-Deer! Mouse-Deer must be quick to trick the Tiger out of a meal.

Key Words

angry

guarding

licked

tiger

trick

INTERMEDIATE LEVEL

My Buddy
by Audrey Osofsky

• **Genre:** Realistic Fiction

Buddy is a service dog. He helps a boy with muscular dystrophy have an active, independent life.

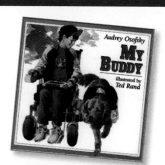

Key Words

commands

disease

obey

service

wheelchair

ADVANCED   ADVANCED HIGH LEVELS

Animal Trainer
by Susan Koehler

• **Genre:** Graphic Novel

Hillary visits her cousin at the Ocean City Dolphin Arena and learns more about the job of an animal trainer.

Key Words

behavior

dolphin

perform

target

trainer

Nonfiction

BEGINNING LEVEL

Good Dog!
by Susan Ring

- **Genre:** Expository Nonfiction

This easy reader provides students an introduction to service animals and how dogs can help people. Also available in Spanish.

Key Words

contest

energy

guide

missing

roam

INTERMEDIATE LEVEL

Animal Masterminds
by Catherine Nichols

- **Genre:** Expository Nonfiction

In this chapter book, learn more about smart animals that can count, learn sign language, and identify colors.

Key Words

chimpanzee

experiments

parrot

scientist

squawk

ADVANCED   ADVANCED HIGH LEVELS

Koko's Kitten
by Dr. Francine Patterson

- **Genre:** Narrative Nonfiction

Koko the gorilla uses sign language to talk to her handlers. When she asks for a pet, her handlers search high and low for the perfect companion.

Key Words

communicate

gorilla

kitten

language

understand

Daily Writing   A AH

Journal Entry Have students write a journal entry in their reading journals. Use "Animal Smarts" to model how to paraphrase in logical order. Provide an example that does not maintain order by telling facts from the middle out of order. Have students share their journal entries with others, recommending books they enjoyed.

Same Book / Different Levels
B I A AH

Do Elephants Talk?
by Peter Winkler

Explore the secret language of elephants and why these huge animals are struggling to survive in the wild.

Pioneer Edition
Fountas and Pinnell: P-R

B Conduct a Picture Walk.

I Read text and captions.

Key Words

calves   habitat

herd   language

regions   wilderness

Pathfinder Edition
Fountas and Pinnell: Q-S

A Read text and captions.

AH Read and write responses to questions.

Key Words

calves   extinction

scientists   language

tusks   wilderness

OBJECTIVES

Language
• Review Language Function: Engage in Conversation ⬥

Grammar
• Review Compound Sentences

Vocabulary
• Review and Use Grade-Level Key Vocabulary ⬥
• Review Dictionary Skills

Reading Strategy
• Review Make Connections

Comprehension and Literary Analysis
• Review Genre: Science Article
• Review Main Idea and Details

Fluency
• Intonation

Science
• Explore Animal Intelligence

Resources

⬥ ⬥ *Key Word Images*

⬥ ⬥ *Assessment Handbook*

⬥ *eVisual 2.32*

⬥ ⬥ *Comprehension Coach*

Part 2 Grammar Skills Trace		Page
Day 2	Compound Sentences	T109a
Day 4	Complete Sentences	T128a
Day 7	Compound Sentences	T137a
▶ Day 10	Review Compound Sentences	T138g

Language of the Day

What did you learn? How does it help you in school?

I learned how to ____. For example, ____.

It helps me ____.

Model: *I learned how to engage in conversation. It helps me share my ideas with other people.* Review the skills students learned in Part 2. Prompt students to talk about a skill they learned.

Review and Assess

Use these interactive review activities to reinforce concepts covered in Part 2. Then use the assessment tools to evaluate students' progress. For more details about assessment, see page T143a.

Language Function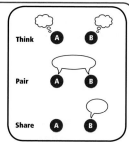

Engage in Conversation

Use a **Think, Pair, Share** to have students engage in a conversation about animals. Show the **Key Word Images**. Have students think about which animal they like best and why then discuss their ideas with a partner. Have students share their information with the class.

• **Assessment:** Language Function Rubric on page 56 of the Assessment Handbook.

Think, Pair, Share

Grammar

Compound Sentences

For each pair of students, write a compound sentence on a sentence strip. Cut the strip on either side of the conjunction to create three pieces. Have partners arrange the text to form the compound sentence. Have pairs trade strips with other pairs and see if they can form new sentences.

• **Assessment:** Grammar and Spelling Unit Test on pages 95–100 of the Assessment Handbook.

Vocabulary

Science and Academic Vocabulary

Form two teams. Show **Key Word Images**. Have one player from the first team silently choose one image. Give the player one minute to draw clues that help his or her team identify the selected Key Word. Then have the team use it in a sentence.

• **Assessment:** Key Word Tests on pages 57–63 of the Assessment Handbook.

Key Words	
ability	learn
command	memory
communication	pattern
imitate	skill
inherit	tool
language	

Vocabulary Strategy

Use a Dictionary

Form teams. Tell students they will compete in a "dictionary hunt." Have teams take turns identifying elements in a dictionary entry. Use prompts such as:

Find two definitions for **command**.

Find the number of syllables in *command*.

Find an example sentence for one meaning of *command*.

Find the meaning of *command* that fits this sentence: I *command* you to clean your room.

• **Assessment:** Reading Unit Tests on pages 68–94

Reading Strategy

Read Aloud

Make Connections

Read the first paragraph of "Animals in Action." Have students make a connection to the text using the **Academic Language Frames**: *It's about _____. _____ reminds me of _____. Now I understand _____.*

• **Assessment:** Reading Strategy Test on page 65 of the Assessment Handbook.

Comprehension

Read Aloud

Literary Analysis

Read the rest of "Animals in Action." Have students tell what facts or information they learned from the article, using the frame: *One fact I learned is _____.*

Text Structure

Have students identify the main idea and details in the selection, using these frames: *The main idea of the article is _____. One detail is _____. Another detail is _____.*

• **Assessment:** Reading Unit Tests on pages 68–94 of the Assessment Handbook.

Fluency

Accuracy and Intonation

Have students review their own recordings of "Animal Smarts" in the Comprehension Coach. Then have students practice reading **Leveled Library Books** that are appropriate for their reading levels, focusing on accuracy and intonation.

Read Aloud

Animals in Action

Animals can be trained to do many different things. A dolphin can learn to do flips, jump through a hoop, and hit a ball. The dolphin receives a reward each time it performs the trick.

Many dogs are trained to work as service animals. They learn to perform tasks for people with physical challenges. These dogs guide people who are blind and pull wheelchairs. They help people with everyday tasks around the home, such as opening and closing doors, and turning lights on and off.

Even a four-ton elephant can be trained! For thousands of years, elephants have been trained to carry people and cargo. They can also learn to work with loggers, carrying and pulling heavy logs.

NGReach.com > eVisual 2.32

Part 2 Vocabulary Skills Trace		Page
Day 1	Science Vocabulary	T107
Day 2	Academic Vocabulary	T109
Day 3	Expand Word Knowledge	T112b
Day 4	Share Word Knowledge	T128b
Day 5	Apply Word Knowledge	T129b
Day 6	Use a Dictionary	T130
Day 7	Use a Dictionary	T137
Days 8–9	Extend Vocabulary	T138e–f
Day 10	**Vocabulary Review**	**T138g–h**

Mode and Form

A letter of inquiry or request is a formal business letter. For this project, students will write a business letter to a scientist to ask for information about a specific animal.

> ## Writing Checklist
>
> **A good business letter**
>
> ✔ states the reason for writing
>
> ✔ includes a heading, an inside address, a formal greeting, a body, and a closing
>
> ✔ uses formal language.
>
> ◯ NGReach.com ❯ eVisual 2.33

Writing Trait: Development of Ideas

Students learn how good writers fully develop their ideas and create writing in which:

- the topic is treated in an interesting way
- ideas are developed in depth.

Lesson Overview and Pacing

Each lesson in the Writing Project provides detailed instruction. Teach the Writing Project during Part 2 of the unit with this suggested daily sequence and pacing plan, or adjust as your schedule and student needs require.

- Day 1: Introducing the Writing Prompt, Study a Model
- Day 2: Prewrite
- Day 3: Draft
- Day 4: Revise
- Day 5: Edit and Proofread
- Day 6: Publish

Classroom Vocabulary

Use **Vocabulary Routine 4** to teach **development** and **idea** . (See **Vocabulary Routines**, page PD40.)

Word Web

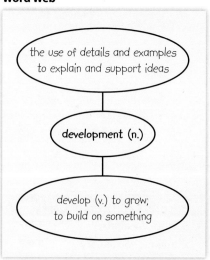

the use of details and examples to explain and support ideas

development (n.)

develop (v.) to grow; to build on something

Rubric: Business Letter

Students use **Practice Master 2.19** to score their own writing on the trait of development of ideas. You can then use the *Reach* Writing Rubric to score each student's project on all traits.

Writing Rubric

Score Point	Focus and Coherence	Organization	Development of Ideas	Voice and Style	Written Conventions
4	**Focus** Paragraphs and the writing as a whole are focused. Ideas are related. Details are relevant. **Completeness** The writing feels complete. The introduction and conclusion are meaningful.	**Structure** The organizing strategy is well-suited to the writer's purpose. **Progression of Ideas** Ideas flow logically and smoothly, with meaningful transitions.	**Content Quality** The writer takes a risk and treats the topic in an interesting way, with insight and thoughtfulness. **Elaboration** Ideas are developed in depth.	**Individuality** The writing sounds genuine and unique. **Word Choice** Words and phrases are interesting and appropriate to the writer's purpose and audience.	**Grammar, Usage, Mechanics, and Spelling** There are only a few errors. **Sentence Fluency** Sentences are varied and effective.
3	**Focus** Paragraphs and the writing as a whole are mostly focused, but there are a few sudden shifts between ideas. Most details are relevant. **Completeness** The writing feels mostly complete. The introduction and conclusion add some meaning.	**Structure** The organizing strategy is generally suited to the writer's purpose. **Progression of Ideas** Most ideas flow logically and smoothly, but there are a few gaps.	**Content Quality** The writer does not take much of a risk, but does treat the topic in a thoughtful way. **Elaboration** Some ideas are more developed than others.	**Individuality** For the most part, the writing sounds genuine and unique. **Word Choice** Words and phrases are mostly interesting and appropriate to the writer's purpose and audience.	**Grammar, Usage, Mechanics, and Spelling** Errors are minor and/or infrequent. **Sentence Fluency** There is some sentence variety. Sentences are generally effective.
2	**Focus** Paragraphs and the writing as a whole are somewhat focused, but there are a number of sudden shifts between ideas. Some details are relevant. **Completeness** The writing feels somewhat complete. The introduction and conclusion may be superficial.	**Structure** The organizing strategy is not clear or does not suit the writer's purpose. **Progression of Ideas** There are breaks in logic and very few transitions.	**Content Quality** The topic is covered, but in an uninteresting way. **Elaboration** Ideas are listed or mentioned superficially.	**Individuality** A few passages sound genuine and unique. **Word Choice** Words and phrases are somewhat interesting and appropriate to the writer's purpose and audience.	**Grammar, Usage, Mechanics, and Spelling** Errors are frequent, but the meaning is clear. **Sentence Fluency** Sentences are somewhat awkward and have simple or inaccurate words.
1	**Focus** The writing is not focused. Ideas are unrelated. Many details are irrelevant. **Completeness** The writing feels incomplete. If there is an introduction and conclusion, they may be perfunctory.	**Structure** No organizing strategy is evident. **Progression of Ideas** Writing is illogical, wordy, and/or repetitious.	**Content Quality** The topic is not really covered. **Elaboration** There is little or no development of ideas.	**Individuality** There is little or no sense of the writer. **Word Choice** Words and phrases are not appropriate to the writer's purpose and audience.	**Grammar, Usage, Mechanics, and Spelling** Errors are severe and/or frequent and are a barrier to understanding. **Sentence Fluency** Sentences are awkward and have missing or misused words.

OBJECTIVES
Writing

- Analyze a Student Model: Business Letter
- Trait: Evaluate for Development of Ideas ⓣ
- Use a Rubric to Analyze Writing

Resources

 Practice Master 2.19

 eVisual 2.33

 *eVisual 2.34*

Introduce the Writing Project

❶ Analyze the Prompt Ask a volunteer to read aloud the title of the project and the prompt. As the student reads, have the rest of the class begin to fill out the first three sections of a RAFT:

Role: researcher

Audience: scientist

Form: business letter

Topic: _____

Remind students that although they haven't decided on a specific topic, the prompt gives them a broad subject to begin thinking about. Ask them what that subject is. (How smart is a certain animal and how much can it learn?) Explain that they will be choosing a topic for their writing when they do the Prewrite step.

Focus on language: *Who is the audience?* (a scientist) Ask them how that will affect the language they use. (It will be formal, with words they would use to talk with an adult who is not a relative.)

Study a Model

❷ Focus on Features Read aloud the directions and then have the students read the model silently. Remind students to look for the parts of a business letter as they read.

Chorally reread the model, stopping to discuss each callout. Display the **Writing Checklist** and have students find examples of each feature in the model.

Writing Checklist

A good business letter

- ✔ states the reason for writing
- ✔ includes a heading, an inside address, a formal greeting, a body, and a closing
- ✔ uses formal language.

NGReach.com ⟩ eVisual 2.33

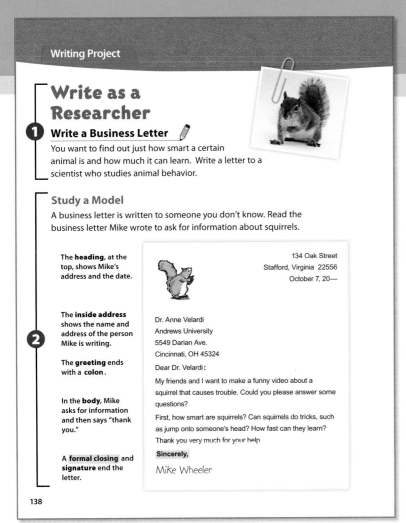

Write as a Researcher

1 **Write a Business Letter**
You want to find out just how smart a certain animal is and how much it can learn. Write a letter to a scientist who studies animal behavior.

Study a Model
A business letter is written to someone you don't know. Read the business letter Mike wrote to ask for information about squirrels.

2

The **heading**, at the top, shows Mike's address and the date.

The **inside address** shows the name and address of the person Mike is writing.

The **greeting** ends with a **colon**.

In the **body**, Mike asks for information and then says "thank you."

A **formal closing** and **signature** end the letter.

> 134 Oak Street
> Stafford, Virginia 22556
> October 7, 20—
>
> Dr. Anne Velardi
> Andrews University
> 5549 Darian Ave.
> Cincinnati, OH 45324
>
> Dear Dr. Velardi:
>
> My friends and I want to make a funny video about a squirrel that causes trouble. Could you please answer some questions?
>
> First, how smart are squirrels? Can squirrels do tricks, such as jump onto someone's head? How fast can they learn? Thank you very much for your help.
>
> **Sincerely,**
>
> *Mike Wheeler*

138

Student Book page 138

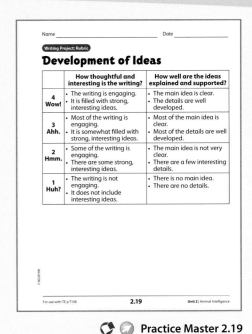

Name _____ Date _____

Writing Project: Rubric
Development of Ideas

	How thoughtful and interesting is the writing?	How well are the ideas explained and supported?
4 Wow!	• The writing is engaging. • It is filled with strong, interesting ideas.	• The main idea is clear. • The details are well developed.
3 Ahh.	• Most of the writing is engaging. • It is somewhat filled with strong, interesting ideas.	• Most of the main idea is clear. • Most of the details are well developed.
2 Hmm.	• Some of the writing is engaging. • There are some strong, interesting ideas.	• The main idea is not very clear. • There are a few interesting details.
1 Huh?	• The writing is not engaging. • It does not include interesting ideas.	• There is no main idea. • There are no details.

For use with TE p T138   **2.19**   Unit 2 | Animal Intelligence

Practice Master 2.19

3 **Teach the Trait** *Which is more developed—an outline or a finished paper?* (a finished paper) *If an idea is developed, what is it like?* (The idea is fully explained.) Define: *Well-developed ideas use details and examples to fully explain the ideas in an interesting way.* Find examples in the model:

- *What does the writer want to know?* (How smart are squirrels?)
- *How does the writer develop his idea in an interesting way?* (asks engaging questions about what squirrels can learn)
- *What are the examples that develop the main idea?* (Can squirrels do tricks? Can they jump onto someone's head? How fast can they learn?)

4 **Present the Rubric** Distribute **Practice Master 2.19**. Read aloud the questions and features of each score point. Assign partners the task of telling you the difference between a paper with a score of 2 and 4. Allow time for the partners to review the rubric and then report out. (Students' responses should indicate that a 4-point paper has a strong development of ideas.) Use the **Academic Language Frames** to support students of all proficiency levels.

> **CHECK PROGRESS** Name each part of a business letter, and have students point to the correct section of the model. Ask volunteers to tell about the features of each part.

Differentiate

Academic Language Frames

Discuss the Rubric
trait: development of ideas

■ 1. It   does   engage the reader.
      does not
   2. The ideas   are   explained/
      are not   supported.
   3. The writer   includes   details/examples.
      does not include

■ 1. A 4-point paper _____.
   2. The writing _____.
   3. The ideas are supported with _____ and _____.

■ In a 4-point paper, the writing _____, but in a
■ 1-point paper the writing _____.
   The ideas in a 4-point paper are, but in a 1-point paper they are _____.

NGReach.com ▶ **eVisual 2.34**

OBJECTIVES

Writing

Learning and Teamwork Strategies

- Generate Ideas through Listing
- Use Graphic Organizers: Main Idea Diagram

Writing

- Writing Process (Prewrite): Select a Topic, Organize Ideas

Resources

 eVisual 2.35

 Practice Master 2.20

Prewrite

1 Choose a Topic Review: *What is the subject of our business letter?* (what can animals learn) *You will work with a partner to choose an animal to ask about. Together you will write questions in a list. You will ask a scientist about things your animal could learn.* Display and discuss the guidelines:

> · Think about your topic. Make a list of questions about this topic.
>
> · Begin each question with a question word and end it with a question mark.

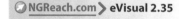 NGReach.com > **eVisual 2.35**

With a volunteer, model using the **Language Frames** to discuss ideas and make a list of questions. Then have partners select a topic.

2 Gather Information Remind students that their questions should relate to the idea of what animals can learn and should develop this main idea.

> The main idea is what the letter is mostly about. *How smart are pigs?*
>
> The other questions should develop the main idea. *What commands can I teach a pig? How hard is it to housebreak a pig? What unusual things are pigs able to do?*

Encourage students to think about the animal they want to learn more about and list questions they could ask a scientist about this animal. Then have them review the list and cross out any questions that do not relate to the idea of animal intelligence.

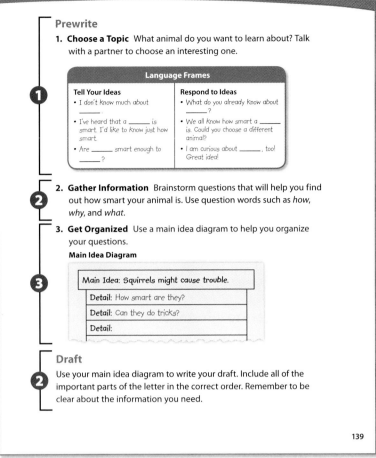

Prewrite

1. Choose a Topic What animal do you want to learn about? Talk with a partner to choose an interesting one.

Language Frames	
Tell Your Ideas	**Respond to Ideas**
• I don't know much about _____.	• What do you already know about _____?
• I've heard that a _____ is smart. I'd like to know just how smart.	• We all know how smart a _____ is. Could you choose a different animal?
• Are _____ smart enough to _____?	• I am curious about _____, too! Great idea!

2. Gather Information Brainstorm questions that will help you find out how smart your animal is. Use question words such as *how, why,* and *what.*

3. Get Organized Use a main idea diagram to help you organize your questions.

Main Idea Diagram

Main Idea: Squirrels might cause trouble.

Detail: How smart are they?
Detail: Can they do tricks?
Detail:

Draft

Use your main idea diagram to write your draft. Include all of the important parts of the letter in the correct order. Remember to be clear about the information you need.

139

Student Book page 139

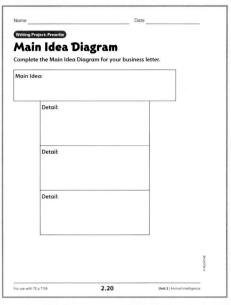

Practice Master 2.20

③ **Get Organized** Remind students that business letters are written in a logical order that begin with a main idea followed by details. Review the main idea and details diagram they created for "Animal Smarts" (see page T129c).

Work through the diagram. Reinforce the trait of development of ideas by reminding students that each supporting detail should relate to and develop the main idea.

Distribute **Practice Master 2.20**. Ask: *What goes in the top box?* (the main idea) *What goes in each smaller box?* (details or questions that support and develop the main idea) Have students complete their own diagrams, using the questions they listed earlier. Use **Multi-Level Strategies** to support students at each proficiency level.

> **CHECK PROGRESS** Check main idea diagrams. Then ask students to trade papers. Students should check to see that all questions in their partner's diagram are related to the main idea.

Differentiate

Multi-Level Strategies

BEGINNING

Students can write simple words in each detail box. They may wish to add pictures to support their ideas.

INTERMEDIATE

Encourage students to write simplified questions in the detail boxes.

ADVANCED **ADVANCED HIGH**

Challenge students to write some questions that relate to specific tricks or tasks animals could learn.

OBJECTIVES

- Writing Process (Drafting): Write a Business Letter
- Use Writing Strategies: Organize Information
- Develop Writer's Craft: Use a Voice Appropriate to the Audience

Draft

① **Introduce Drafting** Use the **Modeled Writing Routine** (see **Writing Routines**, page PD54) to show how to turn the main idea diagram into a draft. Students will focus on:

- **Writer's Craft: Use a Voice Appropriate for the Audience** Introduce: _Most business letters are written to someone you do not know._ Have students look at the model on page 138. Ask: _How is this letter different from a letter you would write to your best friend?_ (It includes an inside address. It uses a formal greeting and closing.) Remind students to use formal language in their drafts.

- **Writing Strategy: Organize Information** Explain that most business letters state the purpose of the letter or the main idea at the beginning of the body. Details and specific information tell more about the main idea. Have students identify questions that relate to the main idea in the model on page 138.

Say	Write
A business letter is a formal letter. I am writing to someone I do not know. I start with my address and the date. Then I write the name and address of the person I am writing to.	134 Oak Street Strafford, Virginia 22556 October 7, 20— Dr. Anne Velardi Andrews University 5549 Darian Ave. Cincinnati, OH 45324
I write a greeting below the inside address. I begin with a formal word, such as Dear. I use the scientist's title. I end with a colon.	Dear Dr. Velardi:
I begin the body by explaining why I am writing. I want to find out how smart squirrels are. I am asking the scientist to answer some questions.	My friends and I want to make a funny video about a squirrel that causes trouble. Could you please answer some questions?
Now I develop my idea. I begin with my main idea question. Then I write questions that develop that idea.	First, how smart are squirrels? Can squirrels do tricks, such as jump onto someone's head? How fast can they learn?
I end by thanking the person for his or her help. How do I end a formal letter? (with a formal closing followed by a signature)	Thank you very much for your help. Sincerely,

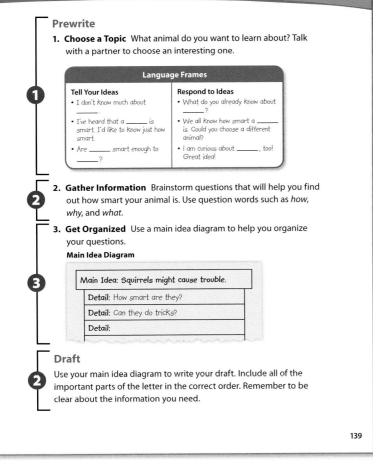

Prewrite

1. **Choose a Topic** What animal do you want to learn about? Talk with a partner to choose an interesting one.

Language Frames	
Tell Your Ideas	**Respond to Ideas**
• I don't know much about _____.	• What do you already know about _____?
• I've heard that a _____ is smart. I'd like to know just how smart.	• We all know how smart a _____ is. Could you choose a different animal?
• Are _____ smart enough to _____?	• I am curious about _____, too! Great idea!

2. **Gather Information** Brainstorm questions that will help you find out how smart your animal is. Use question words such as *how*, *why*, and *what*.

3. **Get Organized** Use a main idea diagram to help you organize your questions.

Main Idea Diagram

Main Idea: Squirrels might cause trouble.

Detail: How smart are they?

Detail: Can they do tricks?

Detail:

Draft

Use your main idea diagram to write your draft. Include all of the important parts of the letter in the correct order. Remember to be clear about the information you need.

139

Student Book page 139

2 **Write the Draft** Have students begin their own drafts. Use **Multi-Level Strategies** to support writers at all levels of language proficiency.

Explain that it is important to have everything you need before you begin your draft. This helps writers stay focused on their writing; they do not have to get up and look for something they need. Writers who have all their materials can write letters that are clear and well organized. Encourage students to identify all the materials they need to write their draft. (paper, pencil, RAFT chart, list of questions, graphic organizer)

Remind students: *Your diagram and notes may contain fragments or incomplete ideas. Check that every sentence in your draft is a complete sentence.*

CHECK PROGRESS Have students look at their drafts. Have them number the parts of their letter. Have they included all the parts? Is each part correctly formatted? Does it contain the correct information?

Differentiate

Multi-Level Strategies

BEGINNING

Use the model on page 138 to review the parts of a business letter. Help students generate information for the heading and inside address.

INTERMEDIATE

Have these students focus on using appropriate formal language in their draft.

ADVANCED

Ask these students to try to include at least three questions in the body of their letter.

ADVANCED HIGH

Have these students focus on including each part of a business letter and formatting it correctly.

OBJECTIVES

Listening, Speaking, and Teamwork Strategies
- Conduct a Peer conference
- Prompt and Provide Suggestions

Writing
- Writing Process (Revise)
- Revise Drafts for Development of Ideas ●
- Revise Drafts for Clarity of Purpose and Clarity of Wording
- Use Revising Marks (Insert, Take Out, Transpose)

Resources

 eVisual 2.36

 Practice Master 2.21

eVisual 2.37

Differentiate

Multi-Level Strategies

BEGINNING

Hold individual conferences with these students. Check to be sure each one has included all five parts of a business letter.

INTERMEDIATE

Have partners ask and answer:

Did I include all the parts of a business letter?

Did I use formal language?

ADVANCED ADVANCED HIGH

Have these students hold complete peer conferences. Direct them to point out strong parts as well as problems. Ask them to provide suggestions for improvement.

Revise

1 Read, Retell, Respond Review the trait on **Practice Master 2.21**. Then use **eVisual 2.36**. to model how to conduct a peer conference. Have students read the paragraph aloud.

> Dear Dr. Taylor:
>
> My family wants to get a pot-bellied pig. Do pigs make good house pets? Could you answer some questions to help us decide?
>
> What commands can I teach a pig? How is it to housebreak a pig? What unusual things are pigs able to do? Do they really eat a lot?
>
> Thanks a bunch.
> Your friend,

NGReach.com > eVisual 2.36

Point to the **Language Frames** as you retell the letter and make suggestions. Remind students that business letters use formal, not informal, language.

- *You want to know about pigs. You want to know if they make good house pets. Your family will use the information to decide whether or not to get a pet pig.*

- *The heading and inside address are missing from your letter. I don't understand the question about housebreaking a pig. Can you ask it a different way? The question "Do pigs make good house pets?" seems out of order.*

Have pairs discuss their drafts. Use **Multi-Level Strategies** to support students at all proficiency levels.

2 Make Changes Read through the samples. Then use **eVisual 2.36** to model how to revise a draft. Display and use the Revising Marks as you work through the example.

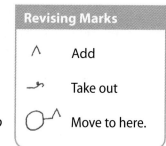

Explain: *During the peer conference, my reader gave me many of suggestions. I've also looked at the rubric again to see what a Score 4 should contain.*

Model the first two changes: *The heading and inside address are missing from the letter. I will add them. Then I will check to see if all the other parts of the letter are there.*

Call on students to suggest additional changes that would turn the model into a 4. Have students use **Practice Master 2.21** for additional practice.

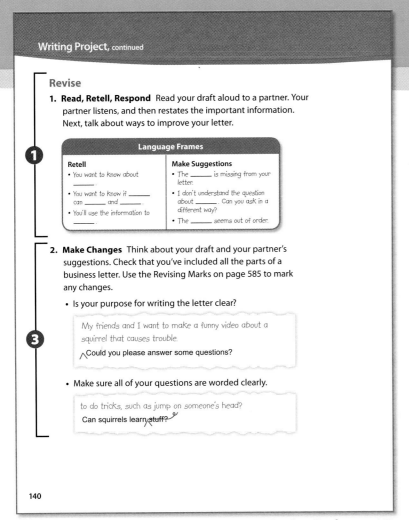

Revise

1. **Read, Retell, Respond** Read your draft aloud to a partner. Your partner listens, and then restates the important information. Next, talk about ways to improve your letter.

Language Frames	
Retell	**Make Suggestions**
• You want to know about _____.	• The _____ is missing from your letter.
• You want to know if _____ can _____ and _____.	• I don't understand the question about _____. Can you ask in a different way?
• You'll use the information to _____.	• The _____ seems out of order.

2. **Make Changes** Think about your draft and your partner's suggestions. Check that you've included all the parts of a business letter. Use the Revising Marks on page 585 to mark any changes.

• Is your purpose for writing the letter clear?

> My friends and I want to make a funny video about a squirrel that causes trouble.
> ∧Could you please answer some questions?

• Make sure all of your questions are worded clearly.

> to do tricks, such as jump on someone's head?
> Can squirrels learn stuff?

140

Student Book page 140

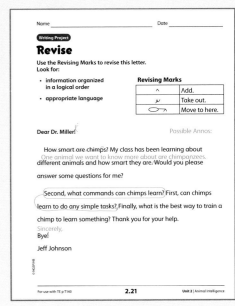

Practice Master 2.21

---

③ Revise the Draft Tell students to use the Revising Marks and begin revising their own drafts. Remind them to review the rubric and notes from their peer conferences.

Post examples as a reminder to use formal language.

Inappropriate Language	**Appropriate Language**
Hi Doctor T! My family wants a pig. Isn't that cool? I want you to answer all my questions.	Dear Dr. Taylor: My family has heard that pigs make excellent pets. Would you please answer some questions for me?

NGReach.com > eVisual 2.37

CHECK PROGRESS As students revise, check to make sure each letter has a clear purpose. Also check that all questions are worded clearly.

OBJECTIVES

Listening and Speaking
- Monitor Understanding
- Listen and Make/Take Notes
- Adjust Language to Audience
- Adjust Intonation

Writing
- Writing Process (Edit and Proofread): Edit for Spelling, Grammar, and Mechanics
- Writing Process (Publish and Share): Create a Final Copy; Read Writing Aloud

Grammar, Spelling, and Mechanics
- Write a Variety of Sentences
- Write Compound Sentences
- Check Spelling (Abstract Vowels)
- Capitalize and Punctuate Addresses

Resources

  Practice Master 2.22

eVisual 2.38

Review Grammar: Different Kinds of Sentences

Display these sentences:

> How smart are cats
>
> Cats are very smart
>
> They can learn simple tricks
>
> That's an amazing trick

Have students identify each type of sentence and tell what punctuation mark goes at the end. Point out the question word *How*. Ask students to name other question words and use them to ask questions.

Explain that related sentences can be joined to create a compound sentence. Model using a comma and the word *and* to join the second and third sentences.

Ask students to identify the contraction. Ask them to name other examples of contractions.

Assign **Practice Master 2.22** for additional practice.

Edit and Proofread

❶ Focus on Abstract Vowels Remind students that some vowel sounds can be spelled in more than one way. Display these words. Read them aloud and have students identify the letters that make each vowel sound.

au { cause, autumn, because aw { jaw, law, awful al { walk, fall, almost ou { bought, thought

oi { join, soil oy { boy, enjoy

ou { cloud, proud ow { clown, down

Display these words: *town, pause, talk, toy, pounce, draw, point*. Have students work in pairs. One student says a word, and the other student tells which list the word would go in. Ask students if they know other words for each list.

Assign **Practice Master 2.22** for additional practice.

❷ Focus on Mechanics: Capitalization and Punctuation of Addresses Review the parts of an address, using the student model on page 138. Explain the following rules:

The first letter of the name of a person, school, street, city, and a state should be capitalized. Capitalize an abbreviation for a state. Use a comma between the name of a city and a state abbreviation.

Write your name and the school's address on the board. Include errors in capitalization and punctuation. Ask students to identify errors and tell how to fix them. Model using editing marks to make the changes.

Assign **Practice Master 2.22** for additional practice.

❸ Edit and Proofread Display the editing marks as partners work together to edit and proofread their articles.

Provide and model the editing tip: *As you edit, read the text aloud, as if you were doing a speech. This helps you focus on the words. When you locate an error, pause to correct it.*

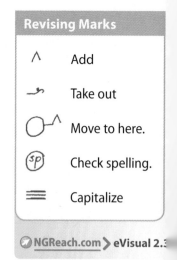

Revising Marks

∧	Add
⤴	Take out
◯—∧	Move to here.
ⓢⓅ	Check spelling.
≡	Capitalize

NGReach.com > eVisual 2.3

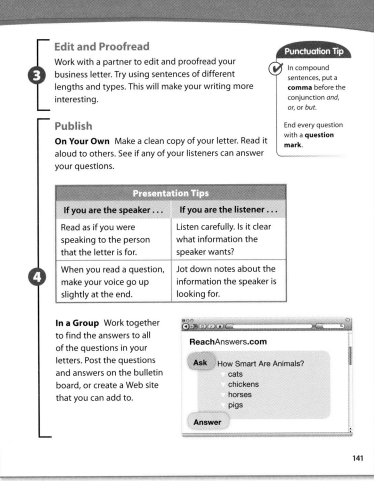

Edit and Proofread

3 Work with a partner to edit and proofread your business letter. Try using sentences of different lengths and types. This will make your writing more interesting.

Publish

On Your Own Make a clean copy of your letter. Read it aloud to others. See if any of your listeners can answer your questions.

Punctuation Tip

In compound sentences, put a **comma** before the conjunction *and*, *or*, or *but*.

End every question with a **question mark**.

Presentation Tips	
If you are the speaker . . .	**If you are the listener . . .**
Read as if you were speaking to the person that the letter is for.	Listen carefully. Is it clear what information the speaker wants?
When you read a question, make your voice go up slightly at the end.	Jot down notes about the information the speaker is looking for.

4 **In a Group** Work together to find the answers to all of the questions in your letters. Post the questions and answers on the bulletin board, or create a Web site that you can add to.

ReachAnswers.com

Ask How Smart Are Animals?
- cats
- chickens
- horses
- pigs

Answer

141

Student Book page 141

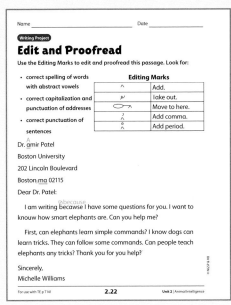

Practice Master 2.22

Publish

4 **Share Your Business Letter** Encourage students to make a clean copy of their business letter. They may choose to type it with a word processing program. Then let students decide if they will share their writing with the class by reading it aloud. Go through the **Presentation Tips** and model the skills for the class:

- **Adjust Language to Audience:** Remind students that their letter is written to an adult they do not know. Demonstrate the difference in the way you speak to a friend and to someone you do not know.

- **Adjust Intonation:** Model saying different types of sentences. Have students listen to the difference in the way you read a statement and a question.

- **Monitor Understanding:** Remind students to think about what they hear and ask questions about anything they do not understand.

- **Take Notes:** Have a volunteer read one of the Presentation Tips and illustrate how to make a note about it.

Have students work in small groups to do research and find answers to the questions in their letters. Have them take notes to create question and answer cards. Then display the cards on a bulletin board, or have students use the information to create a Web site for other students.

Add a copy of each letter to the appropriate student's Writing Portfolio.

CHECK PROGRESS Have partners share ideas about why it is important to use formal language and be clear and concise in a business letter.

Unit 2 Wrap-Up

OBJECTIVES

Concepts and Vocabulary
- Use Grade-Level Vocabulary ⊕
- Use Academic Vocabulary ⊕
- Use Learning Strategies: Graphic Organizers

Language
- Language Function: Express Ideas; Engage in Discussion and Conversation; Tell an Original Story ; Retell a Story
- Discuss Ideas

Science
- Examine Animal Intelligence
- Identify Animal Adaptations
- Explore Animal Intelligence

Resources

- art materials for the maze (string, glue, etc.)
- pens or pencils
- lined and unlined paper
- art materials to make puppets

Community Connection

Suggest that students start an Animal Log. Tell them to keep a small notebook and pen with them and record intelligent behaviors of animals in their neighborhood. Encourage students to share their observations with family and friends.

Language of the Day

What have you learned about animal intelligence?
I have learned ____ .

Read the Language of the Day. Model: *I learned that animals use* **traits** *they are born with to survive, and they can also* **imitate** *their parents to* **learn skills** *they need.* Have students share other answers to the question.

Talk Together

1 **Complete the Unit Concept Map** Read aloud the introduction. Encourage students to skim the selections in the unit, review the **Leveled Library** books they read, and think about class discussions.

Use these possible answers to the unit concept map to guide the discussion.

Concept Map

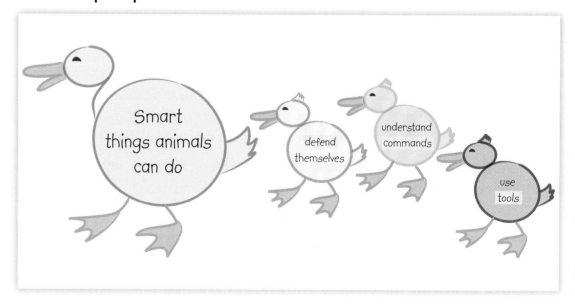

2 **Write an E-Mail** Read aloud the directions. Have students refer back to the Write About It activity on page 96 to remind them of how to se up an e-mail.

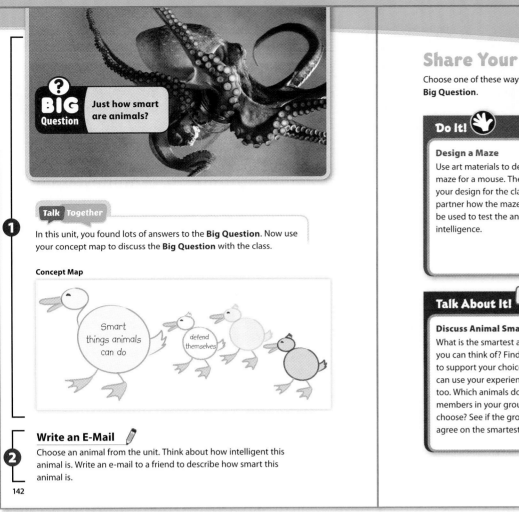

Share Your Ideas

Choose one of these ways to share your ideas about the **Big Question**.

BIG Question

Just how smart are animals?

Talk Together

In this unit, you found lots of answers to the **Big Question**. Now use your concept map to discuss the **Big Question** with the class.

Concept Map

Smart things animals can do

defend themselves

Write an E-Mail

Choose an animal from the unit. Think about how intelligent this animal is. Write an e-mail to a friend to describe how smart this animal is.

142

Do It!

Design a Maze

Use art materials to design a maze for a mouse. Then display your design for the class. Tell a partner how the maze might be used to test the animal's intelligence.

Write It!

Write a Comic

Write a comic strip that tells a trickster tale. Include a main character that plays tricks on others. Draw pictures to go with your story. Share your comic with the class.

You can't catch me!

Talk About It!

Discuss Animal Smarts

What is the smartest animal you can think of? Find facts to support your choice. You can use your experiences, too. Which animals do other members in your group choose? See if the group can agree on the smartest animal.

Do It!

Put on a Puppet Show

Make puppets for the characters in "Love and Roast Chicken." Then perform a puppet show to retell the story.

Student Book pages 142–143

Share Your Ideas

❸ Select and Present Read aloud the presentation options. Explain that some options can be completed alone, but that others involve working in groups. You may choose to assign students to specific activities or allow them to self-select.

 Kinesthetic Activity: Design a Maze **B I** Have students describe kinds of mazes that are familiar to them, such as corn mazes or paper and pencil maze puzzles. If students are unfamiliar with mazes, draw a simple maze on the board.

Writing Activity: Write a Comic **B I A AH** Have students use a story map to plan their comic strips:

- *Characters* _____
- *Trick* _____
- *Beginning* _____
- *Middle* _____
- *End* _____

Oral Activity: Discuss Animal Smarts **I A AH** Provide time for each group to share the results of its discussion with the class. Suggest that they use the frame: *We think _____ is the smartest animal. We think that because _____.*

 Kinesthetic Activity: Put on a Puppet Show **B I** Have students revisit the illustrations. Explain that this will help them remember important things for their puppet show.

❹ Respond and Close Have students share something they learned that animals can do that shows animal intelligence.

Keys to Efficacy

Have samples and models of the products you want students to create available for them to examine. However, emphasize that students should use their own ideas for the activities, not copy the samples.

Administer the assessments below to monitor progress and identify which students will benefit from review, reteaching, or additional practice.

Tested Skills	Assessment Tools	Review and Reteaching
Oral Language		
❶ Express Ideas ❶ Engage in Conversation	• Part 1, Day 10 TE page T106g; 🔄 ⊘ page 56 • Part 2, Day 10 TE page T138g; 🔄 ⊘ page 56	⊘ Reteaching and Review Activities
❶ Analyze a Character ❶ Explain a Story	• Part 1, Day 5 TE page T97c; 🔄 ⊘ page 60 • Part 2, Day 5 TE page T129c; 🔄 ⊘ page 64	Preview and model how to complete the graphic organizers. Provide additional books for practice and re-testing. • Leveled Library • Explorer Book Collection ⊘ Leveled Book Finder
Vocabulary		
❶ Content Vocabulary ❶ Academic Vocabulary ❶ Homophones ❶ Use a Dictionary	🔄 ⊘ ☑ 💿 Part 1 Key Words Test, page 57 🔄 ⊘ ☑ 💿 Part 2 Key Words Test, page 61 🔄 ⊘ ☑ 💿 Reading Unit Test, page 68 B I A AH	Use the Vocabulary Reteaching Routine (PD43). ⊘ Vocabulary Games ⊘ Reteaching and Review Activities ⊘ My Vocabulary Notebook
Reading		
Reading Comprehension ❶ Strategy: Make Connections ❶ Literary Analysis: Analyze Characters ❶ Text Structure: Main Idea and Details **Reading Fluency** ❶ Expression ❶ Intonation ❶ Accuracy and Rate	🔄 ⊘ Reading Strategy Test, page 65 🔄 ⊘ ☑ 💿 Reading Unit Test, page 68 B I A AH **Comprehension Coach** 🔄 ⊘ Fluency Practice Masters, pages 2.7 and 2.15 🔄 ⊘ ☑ Fluency Benchmark Assessment, page 441	**Review Comprehension** Review the test items. Point out the correct response for each item and discuss why it is correct. ⊘ Leveled Library lesson plans **Review Fluency** Use Fluency Routines (PD52) and Fluency Passages from Unit 1. Have students listen to the fluency model as they follow along in the text.
Grammar and Writing		
Grammar ❶ Kinds of Sentences ❶ Questions ❶ Compound Sentences ❶ Complex Sentences **Writing** ❶ Writing Trait: Organization	🔄 ⊘ ☑ 💿 Grammar Unit Test, page 95 B I A AH 🔄 ⊘ ☑ 💿 Writing Unit Test, page 101 I A AH 🔄 ⊘ Writing Rubrics, Forms, and Checklists, page 469 🔄 ⊘ Writing Self-Assessment and Peer Assessments, page 482	**Grammar** Review Grammar Rules boxes and eVisuals from this unit. Use Handbook pages to reteach with additional examples. ⊘ Reteaching and Review Activities **Writing** To reteach the writing process or writing traits, use Handbook pages. ⊘ Reteaching and Review Activities
Other Measures		
🔄 ⊘ Unit Self-Assessment, page 67	🔄 ⊘ Affective Measures, pages 462–465	🔄 ⊘ Metacognitive Measures, pages 466–468

Key: ❶ Tested Skill   🔄 Assessment Handbooks   ⊘ NGReach.com   ☑ eAssessment   💿 ExamView

Amazing Places

BIG Question

Why learn about other places?

Part 1 **What helps us imagine the world?**

Part 2 **What makes a place amazing?**

Curriculum Connections

Content Connection
• Maps
• Geographic Features

Unit 3

Theme Connection
• Imagining New Places
• Going to Extremes

Reading

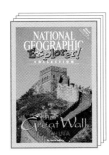

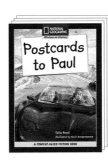

**Student
Anthology**
Pages 144–213

**Explorer Books
Collection**
*The Great Wall of
   China
Climbing to Success*

**Non-Fiction
Library**

Fiction Library

**Sing with Me
Language
Songs**
Pages 12–15

Assessment

**Assessment
Handbook**
Pages 109–165

Practice Masters and Manipulatives

**Language and Literacy
Teamwork Activities**
Pages 17–22
**Cross-Curricular Teamwork
Activities**
Pages 17–22

Practice Masters
Pages 3.1–3.24

**Language Builder
Picture Cards**
Pages E27–E39

Newcomer

In The U.S.A.
Resources for Newcomers

Phonics

Reach into Phonics
*See Teacher's Edition
   Pages T54–T77*

NGReach.com

Reach into Teaching

- Online Lesson Planner
- Teaching Resources
- Presentation Tool
- eEdition NG Digital Library
- eAssessment:
  Online Tests Scan and
  Score Reports

Reach into Learning

- My Vocabulary Notebook
- Vocabulary Games
- Personalized Dictionaries
- NG Digital Library
- Comprehension Coach

Recordings

- Songs and Chants CD
- Selection Recordings CD
- Fluency Models CD

Unit **3** Planner

Amazing Places

Student Book

UNIT LAUNCH

- Build Background Video
- Introduce the

LANGUAGE	VOCABULARY	READING

PART 1

Weeks 1 and 2
Focus: Visualizing Other Places

Language Function
- ❶ Give and Follow Directions
- Give, Restate, and Follow Directions

Grammar
- ❶ Plural Nouns with -s, -es
- ❶ Nouns and Articles a, an, the

Listening & Speaking
- ❶ Listen for Important Details

How to Learn Language
- Ask for Clarification

Theme Theater
- Step Into the Scene

Key Words
- ❶ Social Studies Vocabulary

continent	globe	map
country	hemisphere	
equator	inhabitant	

- ❶ Academic Vocabulary

| border | range | transport |
| imagine | suggest | |

- ❶ Basic Vocabulary: Places in the World

China	Guatemala	Peru
Colombia	Haiti	Philippines
Cuba	India	Russia
Dominican Republic	Jamaica	South Korea
El Salvador	Mexico	Vietnam
Ethiopia	Pakistan	Iran

- ❶ Word Origins

Reading Strategy
- ❶ Visualize

Genre
- Fictional Tale

Text Structure
- ❶ Theme

Literary Analysis
- Setting

Genre
- Free Verse

Literary Analysis
- Elements of Poetry

Leveled Library

Reading Fluency
- ❶ Intonation
- ❶ Accuracy and Rate

PART 2

Weeks 3 and 4
Focus: Amazing Places

Language Function
- ❶ Describe Places
- ❶ Make and Respond to Requests

Grammar
- ❶ Irregular Plurals: Count/Noncount
- ❶ Capitalization of Proper Nouns
- ❶ More Plural Nouns

Listening & Speaking
- Adjust Speech for Purpose

How to Learn Language
- Analyze Expressions

Oral Language Project
- Oral Report

Key Words
- ❶ Social Studies Vocabulary

canyon	ocean	valley
elevation	plain	
landform	plateau	

- ❶ Academic Vocabulary

| feature | physical | surface |
| locate | region | |

- ❶ Basic Vocabulary: Seasons, Months, and Activities

winter	sled down a hill
spring	plant seeds
summer	swim in a lake
fall	rake leaves

- ❶ Compound Words

Reading Strategy
- ❶ Visualize

Genre
- Social Studies Article

Text Structure
- ❶ Main Idea and Details

Text Feature
- Graphs and Diagrams

Genre
- Profile

Literary Analysis
- Genre: Profile

Leveled Library

Reading Fluency
- ❶ Phrasing
- ❶ Accuracy and Rate

❶ = Tested Skill

Online Lesson Planner
NGReach.com ›

WRITING	LEARNING STATIONS	REVIEW, ASSESS, RETEACH
Daily Writing • Writing Fluency • Friendly Letter • Writer's Craft: Figurative Language • Letter • Paragraph Response • Free Verse Poem • Journal Entry	Study a Place Find Your Way Natural Features Map Figurative Language Classroom Map My Special Place	**Oral Language Rubrics** • Give and Follow Directions • Summarize a Story • Theme Theater: Listening, Speaking, Content **Vocabulary Test** • Key Words: Content Vocabulary • Key Words: Academic Vocabulary
Daily Writing • Writing Fluency • Experience • Writing on Demand: Description • Journal Entry • Writing Project: Research Report	Extreme Environments My Place, Your Place Create a Relief Map Place to Place Explore Extremes Go to Extremes	**Oral Language Rubrics** • Describe Places • Summarize a Selection • Oral Language Project: Listening, Speaking, Content **Vocabulary Test** • Key Words: Content Vocabulary • Key Words: Academic Vocabulary **Reading Test** • Reading Strategy: Visualize

UNIT WRAP-UP

Answer the

 Question

Unit 3 Assessment
• Self-Assessment
• Reading
• Grammar
• Writing

OBJECTIVES

Listening, Speaking, and Viewing
• Respond to a Video
• Participate in a Discussion

Learning and Teamwork Strategies
• Preview and Predict
• Relate to Personal Experience
• Use Graphic Organizers
• Use Media to Build Concepts

Media
• View and Discuss a Video
• Analyze Media

Resources

○ *Unit 3 Build Background Video*

○ *Family Newsletter 3*

○ *eVisual 3.1*

○ *Practice Master 3.1*

○ NGReach.com ❯

See **Technology Station** for digital student resources.

Home Connection

Send home **Family Newsletter 3**.
Students interview an adult family member or community member about the most interesting place the interviewee has been. Students then collect or create some kind of memento about this place and share it with the class.

Amazing Places

① Preview and Predict Read the unit title aloud and encourage students to flip through the unit. Ask: *What do you think you will learn? What makes you think that?*

② Introduce the Big Question Ask: *Where are some places you have lived or visited? What are some things you learned about these places?* (Answers will vary.)

Read aloud the Big Question. Have students share possible answers. Encourage them to provide details. List the answers.

③ Build Background Preview the video: *Now we will play a video that tells us about other places. We'll learn about why it is important to explore and learn about other places.*

Discuss the video:

• *Why is it fun and useful to learn about other places?*

• *What are some ways places can be different from one another?*

• *What can maps show us about other places?*

• *How does the creator of the video use images to show us that it is important to learn about other places?*

▶ Play the video.

○ NGReach.com ❯ **Build Background Video**

④ Share What You Know Review the three steps of the directions. Explain: *To complete the activity, you will need to think about:*

• *which place you will choose*

• *how you will show what is special about the place*

If some students have not traveled, provide time for them to look at visuals in books about other regions, states, or countries. Help them notice ways that those places are different from their own community. Ask students to choose one of the places for the topic of their story strip.

Post students' story strips around a world map. Have them attach strings from their story strips to the approximate location they have depicted.

Unit at a Glance
► **Language:** Give and Follow Directions, Describe Places, Social Studies Words
► **Literacy:** Visualize
► **Content:** Geography

Unit
3

Amazing Places

BIG Question

Why learn about other places?

Share What You Know ✋ *Do It!*

❶ **Make** a story strip about a place you have visited or would like to visit.

❷ **Display** your story strip in the classroom.

❸ **Tell** the class the best things about the place.

Build Background: Watch a video about amazing places.
○ NGReach.com

144

Student Book pages 144–145

❺ **Begin the Unit Concept Map** Introduce the concept map: *As you go through this unit, it will be helpful to organize your thinking in a concept map.*

Display the unit concept map for the Big Question. Explain: *The Big Question is restated at the top of the pyramid. We'll add our answers to the blocks under the top block.*

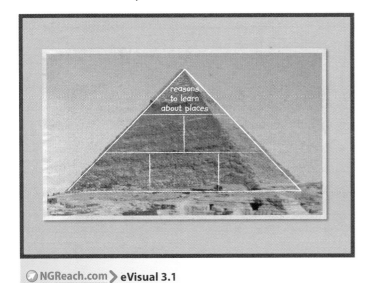

reasons to learn about places

○ NGReach.com ▷ eVisual 3.1

Have students add the ideas they already listed, and any other ideas they may have, to **Practice Master 3.1**. Explain that they will add more to concept maps as they read through the unit and learn more about the benefits of learning about other places.

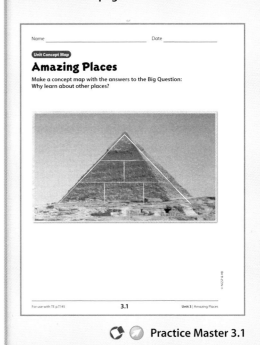

Name _____ Date _____

Unit Concept Map

Amazing Places

Make a concept map with the answers to the Big Question: Why learn about other places?

For use with TE p.T145   **3.1**   Unit 3 | Amazing Places

○ ○ **Practice Master 3.1**

Talk About the **BIG Question**	Page
Begin the Unit Concept Map	T144–T145
Link to Content Vocabulary	T147
Link to "How I Learned Geography"	T167
Link to "Tortillas Like Africa"	T172a
Link to Content Vocabulary	T175
Link to "Extreme Earth"	T197
Link to "Photographing the World"	T204a
Share Your Ideas	T213

BIG Question Why learn about other places?

PART 1

Days 1–5

▶ **Main Selection**
How I Learned Geography, by Uri Shulevitz

▶ **Genre**
Fictional Tale

▶ **Selection Summary**
A boy and his parents flee their war-torn country and settle in an area where they were poor and had little food. One day, the father brings home a map instead of bread. The boy and his mother are upset, but soon the boy is captivated by all the names he sees on the map. The boy uses his imagination thinking of the places on the map, and so he forgets his hunger.

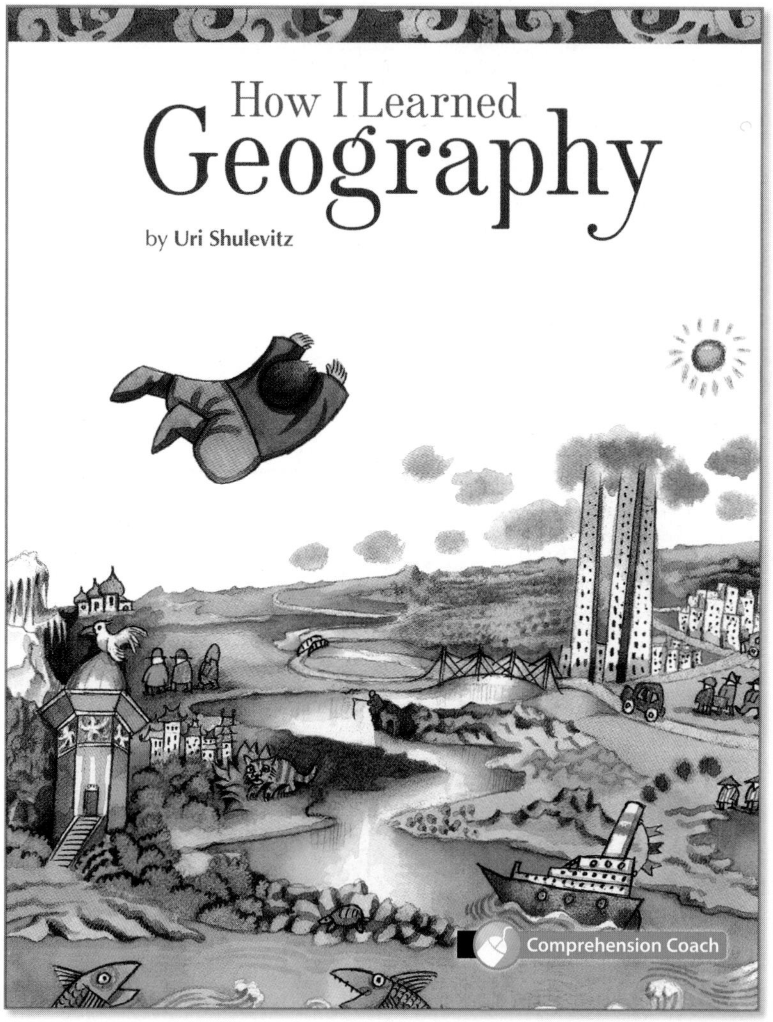

SELECTION AWARDS

- *American Library Association:* Charlotte Zolotow Award Honor Book, 2009
- *American Library Association:* Randolph Caldecott Medal Honor Book, 2009
- *Children's and Young Adult Bloggers' Literary Awards:* Cybil Award for Fiction Picture Book nominee, 2008
- *School Library Journal:* Best Books, 2008

Selection CD 1 (((**MP3**)))

Skills at a Glance	
Language	Give, Restate, and Follow Directions; Theme Theater
Grammar	Plural Nouns with *-s, -es;* Nouns and Articles *a, an, the*
Vocabulary	Social Studies Vocabulary: *continent, country, equator, globe, hemisphere, inhabitant, map*
	Academic Vocabulary: *border, imagine, range, suggest, transport*
	Word Origins
Reading Strategy	Visualize
Literary Analysis	Theme
Writing	Writing Fluency; Friendly Letter; Writer's Craft: Figurative Language; Free Verse Poem; Journal Entry
Newcomer Support	Use *In the USA:* places in the world words

► **Companion Selection**

Tortillas Like Africa, by Gary Soto, illustrated by Joel Nakamura

► **Genre**

Free Verse

► **Selection Summary**

A boy and his brother Isaac are rolling out dough to make tortillas. The boy and his brother see the shapes of countries from all over the world in their dough. Descriptions of the countries' shapes are included.

 SELECTION AWARDS

- *University of Wisconsin-Milwaukee Center for Latin American and Caribbean Studies:* Américas Award for Children's and Young Adult Literature, 1995
- *Commonwealth Club:* California Book Awards Winner, 1995
- *School Library Journal Book Review:* Starred Review, 1995
- *Kirkus Book Review:* Starred Review, 1995

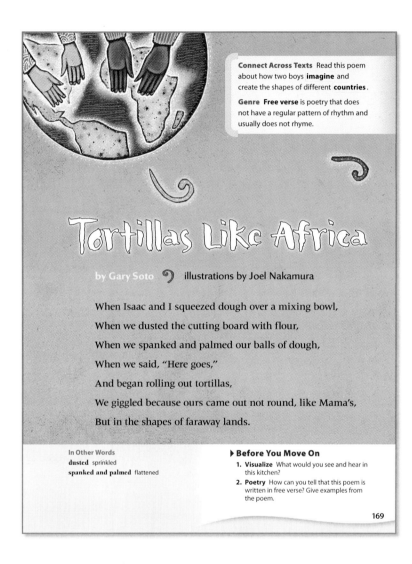

Connect Across Texts Read this poem about how two boys **imagine** and create the shapes of different **countries**.

Genre Free verse is poetry that does not have a regular pattern of rhythm and usually does not rhyme.

Tortillas Like Africa

by Gary Soto   illustrations by Joel Nakamura

When Isaac and I squeezed dough over a mixing bowl,
When we dusted the cutting board with flour,
When we spanked and palmed our balls of dough,
When we said, "Here goes,"
And began rolling out tortillas,
We giggled because ours came out not round, like Mama's,
But in the shapes of faraway lands.

In Other Words
dusted sprinkled
spanked and palmed flattened

▶ **Before You Move On**
1. **Visualize** What would you see and hear in this kitchen?
2. **Poetry** How can you tell that this poem is written in free verse? Give examples from the poem.

169

Leveled Library Books

Differentiated Instruction

 BEGINNING | 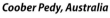 **INTERMEDIATE** | **ADVANCED** | **AH ADVANCED HIGH**

Postcards to Paul

by Talia Reed

Ari and his dad drive across the country to visit Ari's cousin Paul. Along the way, they send postcards to Paul of all the things they see and places they visit.

A Look at Mexico

by Helen Frost

Learn more about Mexico, their geography, and their culture. Maps and photographs support early readers in understanding the text.

Somewhere in the World Right Now

by Stacey Schuett

A girl lies in bed dreaming about tomorrow. Around the world, some days are ending while others are beginning.

Coober Pedy, Australia

by Elspeth Leacock

The people of Coober Pedy, Australia live in a hot, dry climate, but they have found a way to escape the heat. They live underground!

The Flying Doctor

by Alan Horsfield

When Randall falls from a horse, he needs medical attention. In rural Australia, the Royal Flying Doctor Service is there to help.

Galway, Ireland

by Elspeth Leacock

Galway is a community on the coast of Ireland. Students will read all about this interesting town and the people who live there.

Unit 3 Daily Planner

BIG Question Why learn about other places?

PART 1

Core Lessons

	Day 1	**Day 2**
	Introduce Academic Language	**Introduce More Academic Language**
Language 5–10 minutes	**Language of the Day** *T146* **❶ Language Function: Give and Follow Directions** *T146* ((MP3)) **Oral Language** • Talk About Geography *T147* • Talk Together About the Big Question *T147*	**Language of the Day** *T149a* **❶ Grammar: Plural Nouns with -s and -es** *T149a* **Oral Language** • Talk Together About Visualizing *T150*

Vocabulary 10–15 minutes	**❶ Social Studies Vocabulary**
	• Introduce Words *T147*
	  continent globe map
	  country hemisphere
	  equator inhabitant
	Classroom Vocabulary
	• Introduce Word: **theme** *T148*
		❶ Academic Vocabulary
		• Introduce Words *T149*
		  border suggest
		  imagine transport
		  range
		Classroom Vocabulary
		• Introduce Word: **visualize** *T151*

Reading 15–20 minutes	**❶ Text Structure: Theme** • Introduce Theme *T148a* • Use Graphic Organizers: Theme Chart *T148* **Read Aloud: "No Place Like Home"** *T148a*	**❶ Strategy: Visualize** • Introduce and Practice the Strategy *T150* **Read "Vanita's Letter"** *T151* **Phonics and Fluency** • Long *e, o, i* *T150*
Writing 15 minutes	**Daily Writing** • Writing Fluency *T148*	**Daily Writing** • Friendly Letter *T151*
Content: Integrated Throughout Each Day	**Social Studies** • Explore Maps • Investigate Geography	**Social Studies** • Explore Maps • Investigate Geography

Ready-to-Go Plans
▸ Time (20, 30, 40, 60, 90 minutes per day)
▸ Model (Content Focus, Literacy Focus, Dual Language)

Online Lesson Planner
NGReach.com

Day 3

Build Academic Language

Language of the Day *T152a*
Language Function: Give, Restate, and Follow Directions *T152a* (MP3)
Listening and Speaking
• Listen to a Poem *T152a*

❶ Academic and Social Studies Vocabulary
• Expand Word Knowledge *T152b*

| border | country | globe |
| continent | equator | hemisphere |

Support Newcomers
• Build Basic Vocabulary: Places in the World Word *T152b*

Read the Selection
❶ Strategy: Visualize *T152–165*
• Reading Options *T154*
Concepts of Print
• Directionality *T155*
Literary Analysis
• Setting *T162–163*
❶ Fluency: Intonation *T164*

Daily Writing
• Modeled Writing: Writer's Craft *T165*

Home Connection
• Interesting Places *T156–157*
Social Studies
• Markets *T158–159*
Social Studies
• Maps *T160–161*

Day 4

Build Academic Language

Language of the Day *T166a*
❶ Grammar: Nouns and Articles *a, an, the* *T166a*
Oral Language
• Talk About the Selection *T166c*

❶ Academic and Social Studies Vocabulary
• Share Word Knowledge *T166b*

| imagine | map |
| inhabitant | range |

Think and Respond
• Talk About the Selection *T166c*
• Test-Taking Strategy *T166c*
❶ Fluency: Intonation *T166c*

Daily Writing
• Modeled Writing: Write About It *T166*

Social Studies
• Explore Maps
• Investigate Geography

Day 5

Build Academic Language

Language of the Day *T167a*
❶ Listening and Speaking
• Listen for Important Details *T167a*
How to Learn Language
• Ask for Clarification *T167a*
Oral Language
• Talk Together About the Big Question *T167*

❶ Academic and Social Studies Vocabulary
• Apply Word Knowledge *T167b*

| suggest |
| transport |

Reread and Summarize
❶ Text Structure: Theme
• Make a Theme Chart *T167c*
Summarize a Story *T167c*
❶ Fluency: Accuracy, Rate, and Intonation *T167c*

Daily Writing
• Interactive Writing: Paragraph Response *T167*

Social Studies
• Explore Maps
• Investigate Geography

PART 1

Core Lessons

	Day 6	Day 7
Language 5–10 minutes	**Expand Academic Language** **Language of the Day** *T168a* ❶ **Language Function: Give, Restate, and Follow Directions** *T168a* **Oral Language** • Talk Together About the Big Question *T172a*	**Expand Academic Language** **Language of the Day** *T173a* ❶ **Grammar/Spelling: Plural Nouns with -s, -es** *T173a*
Vocabulary 10–15 minutes	❶ **Word Origins** *T168* **Support Newcomers:** • Additional Word Origins *T168*	❶ **More Word Origins** *T173* • **Word Roots** *T173*
Reading 15–20 minutes	**Read the Free Verse Poem** *T169a* • Reading Options *T169a* ❶ **Strategy: Visualize** *T169a–T170* **Concepts of Print** • Identify Letters and Identify a Word *T169* **Literary Analysis** • Line Breaks *T171* ❶ **Fluency: Accuracy, Rate and Intonation** *T172* ❶ **Respond and Extend** • Compare Figurative Language *T172a*	**Reread the Selection: Focus on Elements of Poetry** *T174a*
Writing 15 minutes	**Daily Writing** • Writing Fluency *172*	**Daily Writing** • Modeled Writing: Free Verse Poem *T174b*
Content: Integrated Throughout Each Day	**Social Studies** • Explore Maps • Investigate Geography	**Social Studies** • Explore Maps • Investigate Geography

Apply Academic Language

Theme Theater
- Introduce the Activity *T174c*
- Plan *T174c*
- Rehearse *T174d*
- Enjoy the Show! *T174d*
- Debrief and Compare *T174c*

Read Leveled Books

Fiction *T174e*

 B

 **I**

 **A** **AH**

Key Words

forest	traveling
houseboats	yesterday
ranch	

Key Words

darkness	shoulders
morning	tomorrow
murmurs	

Key Words

climate	landmarks
directions	range
emergency	

Nonfiction *T174f*

 **B**

 **I**

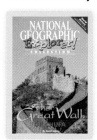 **A** **AH**

Key Words

coyote	million
desert	popular
factories	

Key Words

climate	kangaroo
continent	underground
equator	

Key Words

community	peaceful
famine	traditions
language	

Review and Assess

Interactive Review *T174g–T174h*
- 🔧 Language Function: Give and Follow Directions
- 🔧 Grammar: Nouns and Articles *a, an, the*
- 🔧 Vocabulary: Social Studies and Academic Vocabulary
- 🔧 Vocabulary Strategy: Word Origins
- 🔧 Reading Strategy: Visualize
- 🔧 Literary Analysis: Setting
- 🔧 Text Structure: Theme
- 🔧 Fluency: Accuracy and Intonation

Assessment *T174g–T174h*

Same Book, Different Levels

 **I** **A** **AH**

Key Words

China	emperor	protect
dragon	invaders	soldiers
dynasty	nomads	steppe

Daily Writing
- Journal Entry *T174f*

Reading Station

EXPLORER! COLLECTION

Ladder Text:
- Pioneer edition for below level readers
- Pathfinder edition for on and above level readers

 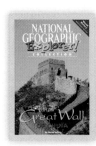

DECODABLE TEXTS

TRADE BOOK COLLECTION

Use the **Leveled Book Finder** at
NGReach.com

Content Stations

Download complete lesson plans **NGReach.com ›**

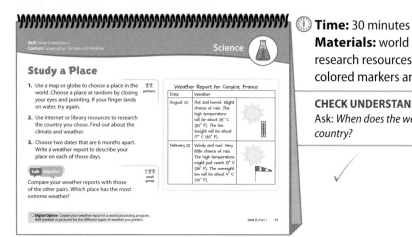

Study a Place

1. Use a map or globe to choose a place in the world. Choose a place at random by closing your eyes and pointing. If your finger lands on water, try again.
2. Use Internet or library resources to research the country you chose. Find out about the climate and weather.
3. Choose two dates that are 6 months apart. Write a weather report to describe your place on each of those days.

Time: 30 minutes
Materials: world map or globe, research resources, paper, pencils, colored markers and crayons

CHECK UNDERSTANDING
Ask: *When does the weather get hot in your country?*

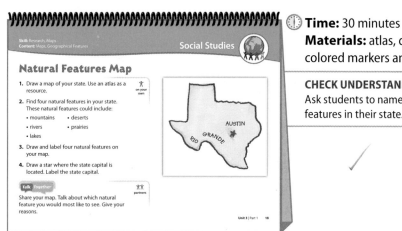

Natural Features Map

1. Draw a map of your state. Use an atlas as a resource.
2. Find four natural features in your state. These natural features could include:
   - mountains
   - deserts
   - rivers
   - prairies
   - lakes
3. Draw and label four natural features on your map.
4. Draw a star where the state capital is located. Label the state capital.

Time: 30 minutes
Materials: atlas, drawing paper, colored markers and crayons

CHECK UNDERSTANDING
Ask students to name two natural features in their state.

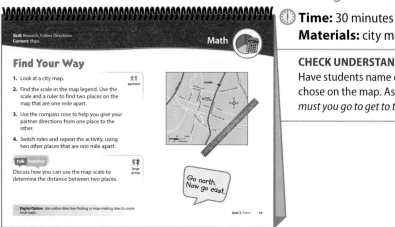

Find Your Way

1. Look at a city map.
2. Find the scale in the map legend. Use the scale and a ruler to find two places on the map that are one mile apart.
3. Use the compass rose to help you give your partner directions from one place to the other.
4. Switch roles and repeat the activity, using two other places that are one mile apart.

Time: 30 minutes
Materials: city maps, rulers

CHECK UNDERSTANDING
Have students name one place that they chose on the map. Ask: *In which direction must you go to get to the other place?*

Use these resources to provide daily opportunities for students to work individually or in groups at learning stations around the classroom.

Language Stations

Download complete lesson plans NGReach.com >

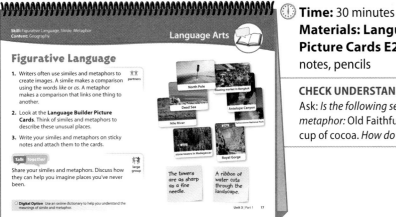

Skill: Figurative Language, Simile, Metaphor
Content: Geography

Language Arts

Figurative Language

1. Writers often use similes and metaphors to create images. A simile makes a comparison using the words *like* or *as*. A metaphor makes a comparison that links one thing to another.
2. Look at the **Language Builder Picture Cards.** Think of similes and metaphors to describe these unusual places.
3. Write your similes and metaphors on sticky notes and attach them to the cards.

Talk Together
Share your similes and metaphors. Discuss how they can help you imagine places you've never been.

Digital Option Use an online dictionary to help you understand the meanings of simile and metaphor.

Unit 3 | Part 1   17

Time: 30 minutes
Materials: Language Builder Picture Cards E27–E39, sticky notes, pencils

CHECK UNDERSTANDING
Ask: *Is the following sentence a simile or a metaphor:* Old Faithful is like a steaming cup of cocoa. *How do you know?*

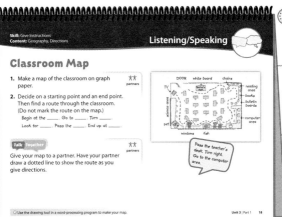

Skill: Give Instructions
Content: Geography, Directions

Listening/Speaking

Classroom Map

1. Make a map of the classroom on graph paper.
2. Decide on a starting point and an end point. Then find a route through the classroom. (Do not mark the route on the map.)
   Begin at the _____. Go to _____. Turn _____.
   Look for _____. Pass the _____. End up at _____.

Talk Together
Give your map to a partner. Have your partner draw a dotted line to show the route as you give directions.

Use the drawing tool in a word-processing program to make your map.

Unit 3 | Part 1   18

Time: 30 minutes
Materials: graph paper, pencils, colored markers and crayons

CHECK UNDERSTANDING
Give commands, such as, *turn right, turn left, go straight,* and ask students to act them out.

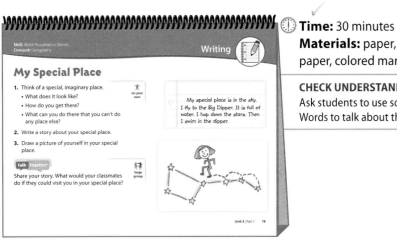

Skill: Write Imaginative Stories
Content: Geography

Writing

My Special Place

1. Think of a special, imaginary place.
   - What does it look like?
   - How do you get there?
   - What can you do there that you can't do any place else?
2. Write a story about your special place.
3. Draw a picture of yourself in your special place.

Talk Together
Share your story. What would your classmates do if they could visit you in your special place?

Unit 3 | Part 1   19

Time: 30 minutes
Materials: paper, pencils, drawing paper, colored markers and crayons

CHECK UNDERSTANDING
Ask students to use some of the Key Words to talk about their imaginary place.

Technology Station

Access resources NGReach.com >

 **Recordings**
- A Map to My Home
- One Way to Make a Map
- How I Learned Geography

 **Digital Library**
Learn vocabulary and practice language
- Key Word Images
- Language Builder Picture Cards

 **My Vocab Notebook**
- Add Words

 **Comprehension Coach**
- Use interactive library support. Automatically measure fluency.

 **Online Assessment**
- Practice items in standardized test format.

Day 1

OBJECTIVES

Vocabulary
• Acquire and Use Grade-Level Vocabulary ❶

Language
• Language Function: Give and Follow Directions ❶
• Listen to and Imitate Fluent Models
• Use a Variety of Language Structures
• Participate in Discussion

Learning and Teamwork Strategies
• Activate Prior Knowledge
• Use Media to Build Language
• Use Context to Build Concepts and Language

Social Studies
• Explore Maps
• Investigate Geography

Resources

🎵 🔊 *Sing with Me Language Song Book 12*

💿 🔊 *Sing with Me Language Song CD 2 Tr 1,2*

📀 *eVisuals 3.2*

📀 *eVisual 3.3*

📀 *Key Word Images*

🌐 **NGReach.com** ▶

See **Technology Station** for digital student resources.

Differentiate

Academic Language Frames

Give and Follow Directions
■ Where's the _____ ?

_____

■ Go to _____ .
Look for _____ .
Turn _____ . Follow _____ .

_____

■ Go to _____ .
■ Look for _____ .
Turn _____ at the/down the _____ .
Follow _____ past the/until _____ .
The _____ is at the _____ .

🌐 **NGReach.com** ▶ eVisual 3.3

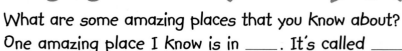

Language of the Day

What are some amazing places that you know about? One amazing place I know is in ____. It's called ____.

Read the Language of the Day. Model: *One amazing place I know is in Mexico. It's called the Pyramid of the Moon.* Encourage students to share about other amazing places they know, telling where they are and what they are called. Then tell students they are going to learn how to ask for and give directions.

Give and Follow Directions

① **Teach/Model** Display the chant. Read the introduction aloud and play the chant. Invite students to chant along as you play it a second time. Model how to echo and chime in as the audio prompts.

Point out the **Language Frames** and model using these structures to give and follow directions to find a specific location.

How to Give and Follow Directions	
1. **Ask for directions using the word** *where*.	Where's the nurse's office?
2. **Give directions using words and phrases such as** *go to, look for, turn,* **and** *follow*.	Go to the courtyard. Look for the library. Turn right down the hallway. Follow the hallway past the drinking fountain. The nurse's office is at the end of the hallway.

🌐 **NGReach.com** ▶ eVisual 3.2

Prompt one or two students to name locations at school. Point to each step on the How to card as the students give directions to each location. To prompt more detail say: *Which way do I go next?*

② **Practice/Apply** Form pairs of students. Have students ask for and give directions to different places that they know. Use **Academic Language Frames** to encourage students to use language naturally when giving directions.

CHECK UNDERSTANDING Have partners take turns giving and following directions from one location inside the classroom to another.

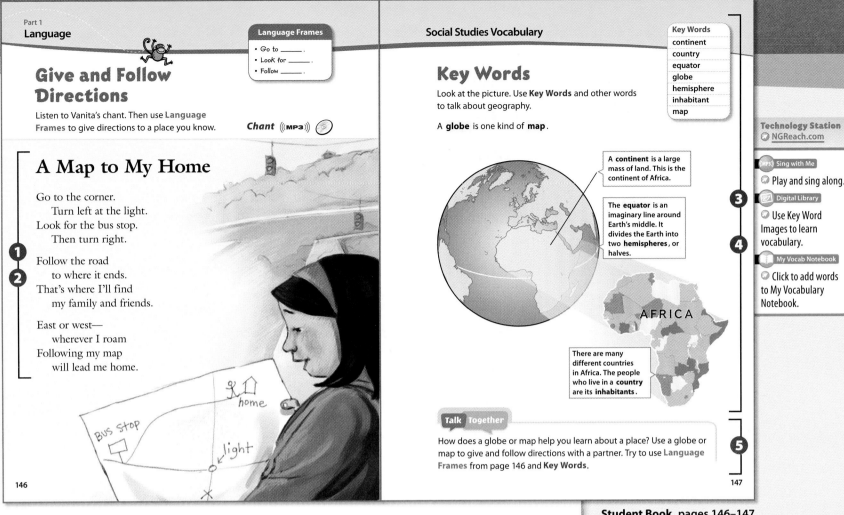

Social Studies Vocabulary

3 **Teach/Model** Read the introduction and work through the diagram. Use **Vocabulary Routine 1** and **Key Word Images** to teach the words. Access definitions on pages 616–639.

1. **Pronounce** the word and point to its picture: **globe**.

2. **Rate** the word. Have students hold up their fingers to show how well they know the word. (1 = very well, 2 = a little, 3 = not at all) Ask: *What do you know about this word?*

3. **Define** the word: *A globe is one kind of* **map**.

4. **Elaborate** Relate the word to your experience: *I can use a globe to find the location of different places on Earth.*

4 **Practice/Apply** Have partners take turns repeating the routine for each word, using complete sentences for steps 3 and 4.

5 **Talk Together About the Big Question**
Check Understanding and Connect Concepts Review the **Language Frames** on page 146 and provide an example:

> *You can use a map to give somebody directions. A map tells where to turn and what streets to follow.*

Add the ideas to your unit concept map.

Differentiate

Spanish Cognates ▶

continent/continente; equator/ecuador; globe/globo; hemisphere/hemisferio; inhabitant/habitante; map/mapa

Part 1 Vocabulary Skills Trace		Page
Day 1	**Social Studies Vocabulary**	**T147**
Day 2	Academic Vocabulary	T149
Day 3	Expand Word Knowledge	T152b
Day 4	Share Word Knowledge	T166b
Day 5	Apply Word Knowledge	T167b
Day 6	Word Origins	T168
Day 7	Word Origins	T173
Days 8–9	Extend Vocabulary	T174e–f
Day 10	Vocabulary Review	T174g–h

Day 1
continued

Day at a Glance:
▶ **Language:** Give and Follow Directions
▶ **Vocabulary:** Social Studies Vocabulary
▶ **Reading:** Theme
▶ **Writing:** Writing Fluency

OBJECTIVES

Vocabulary
- Acquire and Use Classroom Vocabulary ✿
- Use Grade-Level Vocabulary ✿

Comprehension and Literary Analysis
- Demonstrate Listening Comprehension
- Understand Theme ✿

Listening and Speaking
- Listen for Implicit Ideas

Learning and Teamwork Strategies
- Use Graphic Organizers: Theme Chart
- Reason Deductively

Writing
- Develop Writing Fluency
- Monitor and Self-Correct Writing

Social Studies
- Explore Maps
- Investigate Geography

Resources

- ⟳ eVisuals 3.4
- · eVisual 3.5
- ✂ ⟳ Practice Master 3.2

Differentiate

Multi-Level Strategies

BEGINNING

Provide a sentence starter for each part of the chart:

- The title is ___.
- The story takes place ___.
- The characters are ___.
- In the story ___.
- The theme is ___.

INTERMEDIATE

Encourage students to use complete sentences to summarize the plot and state the theme.

ADVANCED ADVANCED HIGH

Encourage students to use the words from the chart headings when they discuss their chart with a partner: *The character in the story is Vanita.*

Theme

❶ Teach Connect concepts: *You learned Key Words that help you give information about places around the world. When you give information, you usually have a main message, or theme, that ties the information together. Stories that you read also have a theme. Now you will learn how to make a theme chart to help you identify the theme of a story.*

Read the first paragraph and teach the Classroom Vocabulary word *theme*. Use the illustrations on page 148 to teach the clues to figure out a story's theme. Ask students: *What is the story's title? Who was the story about? What happened in the story? What did the girl learn?*

Read aloud how to make a theme chart. Ask students to clarify the purpose. Remind students to listen for clues to theme as you read "No Place Like Home" aloud.

> **Read Aloud**
>
> ### No Place Like Home
>
> Vanita read a story called "No Place Like Home." I asked Vanita what the story was about. She told me that it was about a girl who wanted to see the world. The girl went many different places, but she couldn't wait to get home. The girl learned that home is a good place to be. "It's about why home is good," said Vanita.
>
> ⟳ NGReach.com ▸ eVisual 3.4

❷ Model Remind students that Vanita is describing a book that she read. Have volunteers read the first two boxes in the theme chart and model the process: *I write the title in the top left box. I tell who the story is about in the top right box.* Have students continue with the remainder of the chart.

❸ Practice/Apply Read aloud the instructions. Distribute **Practice Master 3.2** for students to use as they complete their charts. Use **Multi-Level Strategies** to help students at all proficiency levels talk about the story clues for the theme. Monitor students' developing proficiency. (See page PD15 for Proficiency Level Descriptions.)

> **CHECK UNDERSTANDING** *What was Vanita's book about?* (a girl who wanted to travel but couldn't wait to get home) *What was the theme of Vanita's book?* (Home is good place.)

Theme

The main message of a story is its **theme**. Use clues in the story to figure out its theme. Look for clues in the title, the characters, and the plot or events in the story.

Find out about a story that Vanita read.

1

"What's this about?" | "A girl couldn't wait to see the world." | "Then she couldn't wait to get home." | "It's about why home is good."

Map and Talk

You can make a theme chart to help you identify the message of a story. Write the title, setting, characters, and plot. Think about how these parts work together to give a message. Then write a sentence that tells the theme of the story.

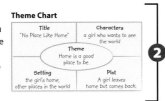

Theme Chart

Title	Characters
"No Place Like Home"	a girl who wants to see the world

Theme
Home is a good place to be.

Setting	Plot
the girl's home, other places in the world	A girl leaves home but comes back.

2

 Talk Together

Make a theme chart about a story you know. List the title, setting, characters, and plot. Use the chart to explain the theme to a partner.

148

Student Book page 148

Daily Writing

4 **Writing Fluency** Use the **Power Writing** routine. (see page PD 53). Write the word **globe** and prompt: *What information can you find on a globe? Think about this word and write about it.*

Power Writing Routine

 1. What do you know about the word or picture?

 2. Take one minute to write as much as you can, as well as you can.
B words **I** sentences **A** **AH** paragraphs

 3. Check your spelling and grammar. (Circle) mistakes.

 4. Count your words.

NGReach.com eVisual 3.5

Classroom Vocabulary

Use **Vocabulary Routine 4** to teach **theme**. (See **Vocabulary Routines, Page PD40**).

Word Map

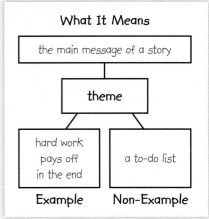

What It Means

the main message of a story

theme

hard work pays off in the end

Example

a to-do list

Non-Example

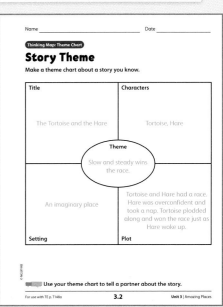

Name _____ Date _____

Thinking Map: Theme Chart
Story Theme

Make a theme chart about a story you know.

Title	Characters
The Tortoise and the Hare	Tortoise, Hare

Theme
Slow and steady wins the race.

Setting	Plot
An imaginary place	Tortoise and Hare had a race. Hare was overconfident and took a nap. Tortoise plodded along and won the race just as Hare woke up.

Use your theme chart to tell a partner about the story.

For use with TE p. T148a 3.2 Unit 3 | Amazing Places

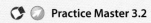 **Practice Master 3.2**

Day 2

Day at a Glance:
▶ **Language:** Plural Nouns with -s, -es   ▶ **Reading:** Visualize
▶ **Vocabulary:** Academic Vocabulary   ▶ **Writing:** Personal Narrative

OBJECTIVES

Vocabulary
• Acquire and Use Academic Vocabulary ❶
• Use Grade-Level Vocabulary ❶

Language
• Plural Nouns with -s, es ❶

Learning and Teamwork Strategies
• Make Connections Across Content Areas

Resources

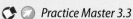 *Practice Master 3.3*

  Key Word Images

⟨ NGReach.com **⟩**

See **Technology Station** for digital student resources.

Language of the Day

What are the names of different [countries] you know about?

I know about _____ .

Read the Language of the Day. *I know about Afghanistan.* Encourage students to add the names of other countries, creating a cumulative sentence. As an added challenge you can have students add the names of places in alphabetical order: *I know about Afghanistan, Bolivia, China,* etc.

Grammar Plural Nouns with -s, -es

❶ Teach/Model Review: *The simple subject tells who or what the sentence is about.* Say: *The simple subject is often a noun: a word that names a person, place, thing or idea.* Then, write these sentences: *Derek has two big* **maps** *of Africa. A* **globe** *shows all the countries of the world.*

Help students identify the simple subjects. (Derek, globe) Say: *These words name a person, place, thing or idea. They are nouns.* Ask: *What other words in the sentences name a person, place, thing or idea?* Have volunteers underline the other nouns. (maps, Africa, countries, world)

Say: *A noun can name one person, place, thing or idea, or more than one.* Circle the nouns *maps* and *countries.* Say: *These nouns name more than one. We call them "plural nouns."* Create a Grammar Rules chart.

Grammar Rules

1. To make most nouns plural, just add **-s**.
2. If the noun ends in **s, z, sh, ch,** or **x,** add **-es**.
3. If the noun ends in **y** after the consonant, change the **y** to **i** and add **-es**.

Read the grammar rules aloud. Then, write these nouns and model forming plurals: **inhabitant**, *glass, lunch, fox, country*. For example, say: *Glass ends in -s; I will make it plural by adding -es. I have five glasses.*

❷ Practice/Apply Have partners use the grammar rules to decide how to form plurals of *globe, family, dish, box*. Then assign **Practice Master 3.3.**

> **CHECK UNDERSTANDING** Write this sentence: *I found shells on the beaches and put them in boxes.* Have students identify plural nouns. (shells, beaches, boxes)

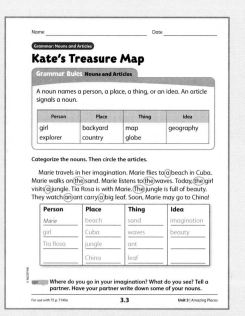

Practice Master 3.3

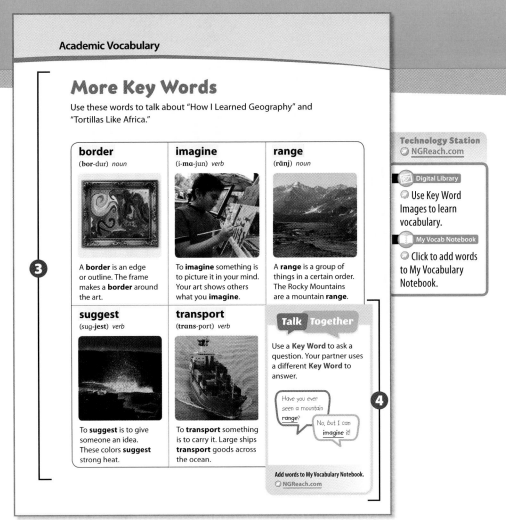

More Key Words

Use these words to talk about "How I Learned Geography" and "Tortillas Like Africa."

border (**bor**-dur) noun	**imagine** (i-**ma**-jun) verb	**range** (rănj) noun
A **border** is an edge or outline. The frame makes a **border** around the art.	To **imagine** something is to picture it in your mind. Your art shows others what you **imagine**.	A **range** is a group of things in a certain order. The Rocky Mountains are a mountain **range**.

suggest (sug-**jest**) verb	**transport** (**trans**-port) verb
To **suggest** is to give someone an idea. These colors **suggest** strong heat.	To **transport** something is to carry it. Large ships **transport** goods across the ocean.

Talk Together

Use a **Key Word** to ask a question. Your partner uses a different **Key Word** to answer.

> Have you ever seen a mountain **range**?

> No, but I can **imagine** it!

Add words to My Vocabulary Notebook.
NGReach.com

Technology Station
NGReach.com

Digital Library
Use Key Word Images to learn vocabulary.

My Vocab Notebook
Click to add words to My Vocabulary Notebook.

Student Book page 149

Academic Vocabulary

3 **Teach/Model** Invite students to discuss each photograph on the page. Read the directions aloud and use **Vocabulary Routine 1** and **Key Word Images** to teach the words.

1. **Pronounce** the word and point to its picture: **border**.

2. **Rate** the word. Have students hold up their fingers to show how well they know the word. (1 = very well, 2 = a little, 3 = not at all) Ask: *What do you know about this word?*

3. **Define** the word: *A border is an edge of something.*

4. **Elaborate** Relate the word to your experience: *I put colorful strips of paper around the border of my bulletin board.*

4 **Practice/Apply** Use the ratings from step 2 to form pairs. Have partners take turns asking and answering questions. Have volunteers share one question and answer with the class.

CHECK UNDERSTANDING Point to the **Key Word Image** of each word and ask students to explain what each word means.

Keys to Efficacy

Building your vocabulary should be a lifelong process: *I recently learned a new word. I figured out what it meant by ___.*

Differentiate

Spanish Cognates ▶
imagine/imaginar; range/rango; suggest/sugerir; transport/transportar

Part 1 Vocabulary Skills Trace		Page
Day 1	Social Studies Vocabulary	T147
Day 2	**Academic Vocabulary**	**T149**
Day 3	Expand Word Knowledge	T152b
Day 4	Share Word Knowledge	T166b
Day 5	Apply Word Knowledge	T167b
Day 6	Word Origins	T168
Day 7	Word Origins	T173
Days 8–9	Extend Vocabulary	T174e–f
Day 10	Vocabulary Review	T174g–h

Day 2
continued

Day at a Glance:
▶ **Language:** Nouns and Articles *a, an, the* ▶ **Reading:** Visualize
▶ **Vocabulary:** Academic Vocabulary ▶ **Writing:** Write a Friendly Letter

OBJECTIVES

Vocabulary
• Use Academic Vocabulary ❶
• Use Grade-Level Vocabulary ❶
• Acquire and Use Classroom Vocabulary

Learning to Read
• Long *e, i, o*

Reading Strategy
• Learn to Visualize ❶

Learning and Teamwork Strategies
• Use Personal Experience
• Use Visuals

Writing
• Write a Friendly Letter

Resources

🔘 *eVisual 3.6*

💿 *Reach Into Phonics TE page T56*

Visualize

❶ Teach Read the introduction aloud. When you visualize, you use all your senses to imagine what something is like. Discuss details in the picture that relate to the five senses. Make the connection: *I see Vanita's hair blowing. I visualize how it feels when the wind blows.* Point out that students also visualize when they read. Teach the Classroom Vocabulary word *visualize.*

❷ Model Read the chart aloud. To model visualizing details in the picture, say:

• *I see a hot-air balloon.*
• *I picture myself floating through the sky.*
• *I feel excited to be so high up in the air.*

❸ Practice Read the directions aloud. Point out the **Language Frames.** Read aloud Vanita's letter and the sample student visualization.

Direct students' attention to the third paragraph and use **Academic Language Frames** to help students at each proficiency level visualize. Students may describe the heat or the bugs and how each makes them feel. Encourage them to identify words that help to visualize the scene. Ask volunteers to share what they visualize in the last paragraph.

> **CHECK UNDERSTANDING** Reread the third paragraph. Ask: *What details help you see and feel what you read about?*

Differentiate

Academic Language Frames

Visualize

■ I read _____ .
 I picture _____ .
 I feel _____ .

■ I read _____ .
 The word _____ makes me picture _____ .
 _____ makes me feel _____ .

■ I read _____ and _____ .
■ The words _____ and _____ make me picture
 _____ .
 I feel _____ because _____ .

🌐 NGReach.com > *eVisual 3.6*

Phonics and Fluency

Long *e, o, i*
Display these words: *me, hi, no.* Point out the CV spelling pattern and explain: When a vowel is at the end of a word or a syllable, it has a long sound. Blend /m/ /ē/. Have students repeat. Have students blend *hi* and *no.* Display **Transparency 31** from **Reach Into Phonics** and work through the lesson.

Practice Display the sentences:
• We live near the ocean.
• The **equator** divides the **globe** into two *equal* parts.
• Visiting a new place is a good *idea.*

Have partners read the sentences chorally several times to develop fluency.

Learn to Visualize

Look at the picture. Imagine, or **visualize**, what Vanita sees from the balloon. Imagine what she hears and feels.

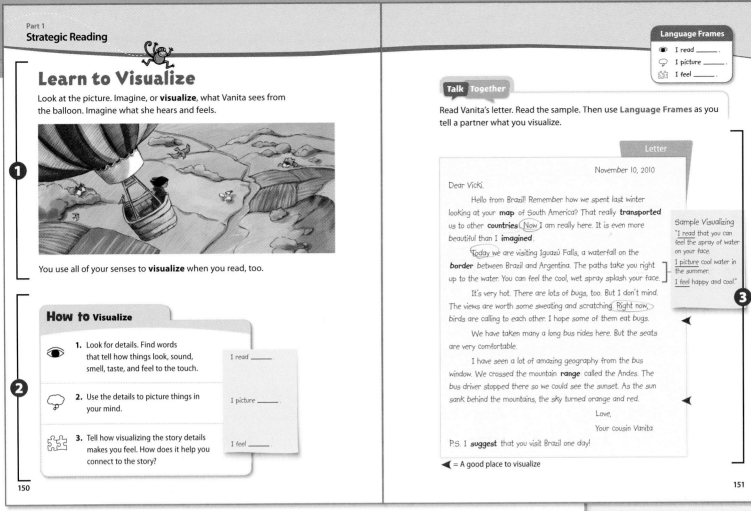

You use all of your senses to **visualize** when you read, too.

How to Visualize

1. Look for details. Find words that tell how things look, sound, smell, taste, and feel to the touch.

   I read _____ .

2. Use the details to picture things in your mind.

   I picture _____ .

3. Tell how visualizing the story details makes you feel. How does it help you connect to the story?

   I feel _____ .

150

Language Frames

👁 I read _____ .
💭 I picture _____ .
🧩 I feel _____ .

Talk Together

Read Vanita's letter. Read the sample. Then use **Language Frames** as you tell a partner what you visualize.

Letter

November 10, 2010

Dear Vicki,

Hello from Brazil! Remember how we spent last winter looking at your **map** of South America? That really **transported** us to other **countries**. Now I am really here. It is even more beautiful than I **imagined**.

Today we are visiting Iguazú Falls, a waterfall on the **border** between Brazil and Argentina. The paths take you right up to the water. You can feel the cool, wet spray splash your face.

It's very hot. There are lots of bugs, too. But I don't mind. The views are worth some sweating and scratching. Right now, birds are calling to each other. I hope some of them eat bugs.

We have taken many a long bus rides here. But the seats are very comfortable.

I have seen a lot of amazing geography from the bus window. We crossed the mountain **range** called the Andes. The bus driver stopped there so we could see the sunset. As the sun sank behind the mountains, the sky turned orange and red.

Love,

Your cousin Vanita

P.S. I **suggest** that you visit Brazil one day!

◄ = A good place to visualize

Sample Visualizing

"I read that you can feel the spray of water on your face.

I picture cool water in the summer.

I feel happy and cool."

151

Student Book pages 150–151

Daily Writing

4 Friendly Letter Point out the features of a friendly letter in Vanita's letter: personal opinions about an event, informal language, a date, and the salutation and closing. Then write a RAFT for students to follow:

- Role: Yourself
- Audience: A friend
- Form: Friendly Letter
- Topic: A place you have visited

Adjust the prompt to include students at all proficiency levels.

B Have students use a letter form.

I Have students write sentences.

A Have students write a paragraph.

AH Have students write multiple paragraphs.

Invite students to share their letters with the class.

CLOSE AND ASSESS
- **Language** *Name a noun.* (Answers will vary.)
- **Reading** *In her letter, Vanita describes the sunset. What words help you visualize the sunset?* (the sky turned orange and red)
- **Vocabulary** *What Key Words did Vanita use? Make a sentence of your own with each of these words.* (Answers will vary.)

Classroom Vocabulary

Use **Vocabulary Routine 4** to teach **visualize**. (See **Vocabulary Routines, Page PD40**.)

Wordbench

> visualize
> [vi-zhe[schwa]-we[schwa]-liz]
> visual   visualization
> vis= sight   ize=to cause
> Meaning: to form a mental picture

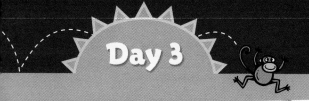

Day 3

OBJECTIVES

Vocabulary
- Use Academic Vocabulary ⊕
- Use Grade-Level Vocabulary ⊕

Language
- Language Function: Give, Restate, and Follow Directions ⊕
- Listen to and Imitate Fluent Models
- Use a Variety of Language Structures

Learning and Teamwork Strategies
- Use Media to Build Language
- Gather Information
- Use Graphic Organizers: Upright

Resources

- 🎵 🔵 *Sing With Me Language Song CD 2 Tr 3, 4*
- 📀 🔵 *Sing With Me Language Song Book,* page 13
- 🔵 eVisual 3.7
- 📖 *In the U.S.A. Picture Cards 15–24*
- • *Chart or poster paper*

🌐 **NGReach.com** ▸

See **Technology Station** for digital student resources.

Differentiate

Academic Language Frames

Give, Restate, and Follow Directions

■ Look for the _____ .
  Go to the _____ .
  Follow the _____ .

■ Look for the _____ . Turn _____ .
  Go to the _____ . Then go _____ .
  Follow the _____ .

■ Look for the _____ . Turn _____ at the _____ .
■ Go to the _____ next to _____ . Then go _____ .
  Follow the _____ , until _____ and _____ .

🌐 **NGReach.com** ▸ **eVisual 3.7**

Language of the Day

What do maps show? What don't they show?
Maps show _____ . They don't show _____ .

Read the Language of the Day. Model: *Maps show* **countries**. *They don't show the* **inhabitants** *of those countries.* Invite students to take turns sharing their own ideas.

Give, Restate, and Follow Directions

1 Teach Remind students that they learned how to give and follow directions from Vanita's chant. Introduce: *Now you will learn to give, restate, and follow directions using a map.* Display "One Way to Make a Map." Say the poem and invite students to follow along.

Ask: *How did Vanita draw her map?* (She **imagined** what it looked like from a bird's point of view.) *Now we'll draw a map of our neighborhood, too.*

2 Model Draw a map of the school and its immediate vicinity from "a bird's point of view." Model how to give directions to a nearby location: *I want to give someone directions to go to the library. I use the direction word* west: *Go out of the school and go west.* Ask volunteers to restate your directions. A way of restating the given sample would be: *Go past the school entrance and turn left.* Point out that restating directions in their own words will help them remember the directions.

3 Practice/Apply Have partners work together to give, restate, and follow directions using the map you drew on the board. Use **Academic Language Frames** to encourage students to use language naturally.

CHECK UNDERSTANDING Point out the map and have students give, restate, and follow directions, using their finger to show the path on the map.

One Way to Make a Map

First, you imagine what a bird sees
Looking down
At your town.
You are flying high, up above the trees.

Next, you show the world that the birds know.
You add a street
And repeat.
Then you add some little houses in a row.

> First, I'll pretend I'm a bird flying above my town. Then, I'll draw a map that shows my town from the bird's point of view.

MP3 or Song CD 2 Tracks 3–4 **Chant** 13

Sing With Me Language Song Book page 13

Technology Station
NGReach.com

MP3 Sing with Me
Play and sing along.

Expand Word Knowledge

④ Teach/Model Explain that each student pair will become Key Word experts. They will study one Key Word and create a Key Word poster about that word. Use **Vocabulary Routine 2** and model making an Upright Visual Organizer for the word **hemisphere**. (See **Vocabulary Routines,** page PD38.)

- Write the word.
- Add a picture.
- Add a definition.
- Add a context sentence.

⑤ Practice/Apply Assign a Key Word to each pair of students. Have each pair create an Upright for or their assigned Key Word. Display the Uprights in the classroom.

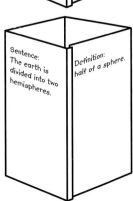

Key Word: hemisphere

Sentence: The earth is divided into two hemispheres.

Definition: half of a sphere.

Upright Visual Organizer

> **CHECK UNDERSTANDING** Say a Key Word and have the partner experts read the word, definition, and sentence from their Uprights.

Key Words

border	imagine
continent	inhabitant
country	map
equator	range
globe	suggest
hemisphere	transport

Differentiate

Newcomer Support

Newcomers can make Uprights using words from **In the U.S.A. Picture Cards** 15–24.

Part 1 Vocabulary Skills Trace		Page
Day 1	Social Studies Vocabulary	T147
Day 2	Academic Vocabulary	T149
Day 3	**Expand Word Knowledge**	**T152b**
Day 4	Share Word Knowledge	T166b
Day 5	Apply Word Knowledge	T167b
Day 6	Word Origins	T168
Day 7	More Word Origins	T173
Days 8–9	Extend Vocabulary	T174e–f
Day 10	Vocabulary Review	T174g–h

Day 3
continued

Day at a Glance:
▶ **Language:** Give, Restate, and Follow Directions
▶ **Vocabulary:** Expand Word Knowledge
▶ **Reading:** Read the Selection
▶ **Writing:** Writer's Craft

OBJECTIVES

Vocabulary
• Use Academic Vocabulary ⓣ
• Use Grade-Level Vocabulary ⓣ

Reading Strategy
• Plan Preview

Comprehension and Literary Analysis
• Analyze Elements of Fiction: Setting

Learning and Teamwork Strategies
• Use Prereading Supports
• Build Background Knowledge

Resources

ⓒ *Comprehension Coach*

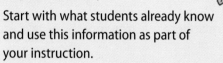

Keys to Efficacy

Start with what students already know and use this information as part of your instruction.

Preview the Story

❶ Introduce Tell students to look at the art on pages 152–153 as you read aloud the title of the story. Have students predict: *What do you think this story will be about? What do you see in the picture?* Encourage students to use key words to describe what they see. Point out that the boy is looking down on buildings, people, boats, and cars. Then connect to personal experience: *Have you ever flown in an airplane or stood on the top floor of a high building and looked down? What did you see?*

❷ Genre and Setting Read aloud the definition of a fictional tale. Elaborate: *This story tells how a boy used his* **imagination**.

Read aloud the definition of setting and point to the picture of the city. Explain: *The setting of this story is Turkestan.* Connect to the genre: *As we read this story, think about the places where the story occurs.*

❸ Preview and Build Background Use sheltering strategies as you conduct a picture walk.

Pages	Say (and Do) 💬 ✋
154–155	*A family is running away.* (Pretend to walk quickly and say, "Hurry!") *Have you ever left a place quickly? What might the red and black sky suggest?* (a fire) *Now we see a town with many buildings close together. Do you think the family went to this place?*
156–157	*The boy sits outside his house. How does he look?* (Act out being sad.) *Look at the crowd of people on the next page. What does it look like they are doing?* (buying and selling things) *What kind of place is this?* (a marketplace)
158–159	*Dad brings home a package.* (Pretend to carry something.) *What do you think it could be? The mother and little boy have their hands out, waiting for something. Oh, now the boy lies under his blanket and watches the man eat. Do you think the boy is hungry?*
160–161	*Father hangs up a* **map** *while the boy watches. Do you have a map at home? Wow! Now the boy is flying over the map.* (Put your arms out like you're flying.) *Do you think this is real or is he imagining this?*
162–164	*Look at all the places the boy goes. What are some of the places you see?* (beach, snow, etc.) (Pantomime running on the beach or climbing a mountain.) *I think he will let his imagination take him many more places.*

CHECK UNDERSTANDING *Why do we call this a fictional tale?* Some of it happens in the boy's imagination.

Read a Story

Genre
A **fictional tale** is an imaginative account of a series of events.

Setting
The setting of a story is where and when the events happen.

This story takes place about 1940 in Turkestan, a city in Central Asia.

2

152

How I Learned Geography

by Uri Shulevitz

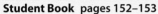

Comprehension Coach

Student Book pages 152–153

Comprehension Coach

Build Reading Power
Assign students to use the software, based on their instructional needs.

Read Silently	Listen	Record
• Comprehension questions with immediate feedback • Vocabulary support	• Process model of fluent reading • Text highlighting to facilitate tracking • Vocabulary support	• Oral reading fluency practice • Speech recognition for oral fluency assessment with immediate feedback

Cultural Perpectives

Explain that the boy in the story imagined going to many different **countries**. Invite students to share different places they have lived or visited. Encourage them to describe their first impressions upon arriving. You can help initiate the discussion by sharing about your own experiences moving or travelling to new places.

OBJECTIVES

Vocabulary
- Use Academic Vocabulary **T**
- Use Grade-Level Vocabulary **T**

Learning To Read
- Phonics: Multisyllabic Words

Reading Strategies
- Plan: Set a Purpose, Predict, Confirm Predictions
- Read the Selection
- Visualize **T**

Fluency
- Intonation **T**

Comprehension and Literary Analysis
- Recognize Setting
- Theme **T**

Learning and Teamwork Strategies
- Use Reading Supports

Writing
- Connect Reading and Writing
- Analyze a Professional Model
- Develop Writer's Craft

Resources

⊘ ◎ *Read with Me Selection CD* 0

♺ ◎ *Practice Master 3.4*

◎ *Reach Into Phonics TE pages T182, T184*

⊘ **NGReach.com** >

See **Technology Station** for digital student resources.

Key Points Reading

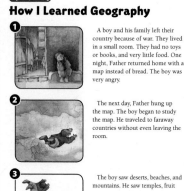

Name _____ Date _____

Key Points Reading

How I Learned Geography

① A boy and his family left their country because of war. They lived in a small room. They had no toys or books, and very little food. One night, Father returned home with a map instead of bread. The boy was very angry.

② The next day, Father hung up the map. The boy began to study the map. He traveled to faraway countries without even leaving the room.

③ The boy saw deserts, beaches, and mountains. He saw temples, fruit groves, and tall buildings. He spent many hours away from his hunger. He understood that his father was right after all.

For use with TE p. T154   **3.4**   Unit 3 | Amazing Places

♺ ◎ **Practice Master 3.4**

Read the Story

Suggested Pacing

- Day 3: Read Section 1, pages 154–155
- Day 4: Read Sections 2 and 3, pages 156–164

Reading Options Scaffold the support for various reading levels.

BELOW LEVEL	ON LEVEL	ABOVE LEVEL
Listen and Read Along	**Read Together**	**Read Independently**
• Have students track the print on the **Key Points Reading** while you read the text aloud. • Check understanding with selected Build Comprehension questions. • Have students share details in the illustrations that help them understand the text.	• Have students set a purpose for reading—to get information or enjoy a story—and read silently. Then select passages to read aloud or chorally in partners. Pause to ask the Build Comprehension questions. • At the end of each section, have students summarize how the boy felt and why.	• Have students set a purpose for reading. Have them read silently and study the illustrations to clarify the text. • Then students read the story aloud. Discuss meaning as you ask the Build Comprehension questions. Have students share illustration details that help them understand the text.

Phonics and Fluency

Multisyllabic Words

Teach/Model Explain that students can read long words if they know how to divide them into syllables: Display these words: **country**, **border**, **transport**. Pronounce each word and have students clap the two syllables with you. Ask: *How many syllables do you hear in each word?* (two) Display **Transparency 34** from **Reach Into Phonics** and work through the lesson.

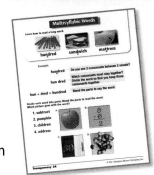

Practice/Apply Display these sentences from "How I Learned **Geography**":

- Mother and I were worried and hungry.
- I didn't think I would ever forgive him.

Underline the words *hungry* and *forgive*. Then have partners read the words chorally several times to develop fluency in decoding multisyllabic words. Listen as partners read and correct pronunciation.

▶ Set a Purpose

1 A family must leave home. Find out what happens.

When war **devastated** the land, buildings crumbled to dust. Everything we had was **lost**, and we **fled empty-handed**. **2**

because the summers were hot, the sun burned the ground

We traveled far, far east to another **country**, where summers were hot and winters were cold, to a city of houses made of clay, straw, and camel dung, surrounded by dusty **steppes**, burned by the sun. **3**

In Other Words
devastated destroyed; ruined
lost gone
fled empty-handed left with nothing

In Other Words
steppes plains; flat lands ▼

▶ **Before You Move On**

4
1. **Setting** Where does the family go after leaving their home?
2. **Figurative Language** What would a place "burned by the sun" look like?

Technology Station
▶ NGReach.com

(MP3) Read with Me
○ Play and read along.

Comprehension Coach
○ Use interactive vocabulary support. Automatically measure fluency.

154

155

Student Book pages 154–155

Build Comprehension, pages 154–155

1 **Set a Purpose** Read aloud the introduction at the top of page 154 to help students set a purpose for reading.

2 **Draw Conclusions** What might be some reasons the family have to leave their home? (The war ruined their land. They lost everything.)

3 **Confirm Purpose** What is the purpose for reading this story? (To find out why the family leaves their home and what happens to them after they leave.)

4 **Answers to Before You Move On**

1. **Setting** The family traveled east to another country.

2. **Figurative Language** A place burned by the sun would probably feel very hot, almost like it's on fire. The writer used the phrase to help you **imagine** how hot it is.

> **Predict**
> **1** What will the family's life be like in this new **country**?

handwritten: We lived in a small room with others; therefore we slept on the floor.

We lived in a small room with a **couple** we did not know. We slept on a dirt floor. I had no toys and no books. Worst of all, **food was scarce**. **3**

In Other Words
couple husband and wife
food was scarce there was not much food

156

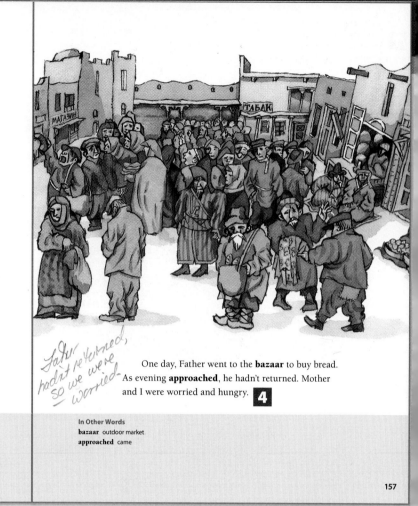

handwritten: Father hadn't returned, so we were worried.

One day, Father went to the **bazaar** to buy bread. As evening **approached**, he hadn't returned. Mother and I were worried and hungry. **4**

In Other Words
bazaar outdoor market
approached came

157

Student Book pages 156–157

Home Connection: Interesting places

Remind students about **Family Newsletter 3**, which asked them to interview an adult about the most interesting place the interviewee has been. Have students talk about their interview and share something with the class that represents an interesting aspect of the place (photos, drawings, realia, etc.).

Keys to Efficacy

Give students a chance to think about an answer before you rephrase a question, move on, or answer it yourself.

Build Comprehension, pages 156–157

1 **Predict** Read aloud the introduction. Model using the illustrations to predict what will happen. Ask: *What else can you predict from the illustrations?*

2 **Character's Feeling** What does the illustration suggest about how the boy is feeling about his new home? (Students can act out a response.)

3 **Make Inferences** Do you think the boy's family has a lot of money to spend? (No, they lost everything in the war and now they have to share a small room with a couple. The boy has no toys or books).

4 **Make Connections** The boy is worried when his father doesn't return home. Have you ever felt worried? Tell about that time. (Answers will vary.) Be careful with raising sensitive issues.

It was nearly dark when he came home. He carried a long roll of paper under his arm.

"I bought a **map**," he **announced triumphantly**.

"Where is the bread?" Mother asked.

"I bought a map," he said again.

Mother and I said nothing.

"I had enough money to buy only a tiny piece of bread, and we would still be hungry," he explained apologetically.

"No supper tonight," Mother said **bitterly**. "We'll have the map instead."

[handwritten margin note:] Father brought home a map, not food. As a result, we had no dinner

[handwritten margin note:] I covered my head so I wouldn't hear him chew.

I was **furious**. I didn't think I would ever forgive him, and I went to bed hungry, while the couple we lived with ate their **meager supper**.

The husband was a writer. He wrote in silence, but oh how loudly he chewed! He chewed a small crust of bread with such enthusiasm, as if it were the most delicious morsel in the **world**. I **envied him** his bread and wished I were the one chewing it. I covered my head with my blanket so I would not hear him smacking his lips with such noisy delight.

In Other Words
announced triumphantly said proudly
bitterly quietly with anger

In Other Words
furious very angry
meager supper small dinner
envied him wanted

▶ **Before You Move On**

1. **Confirm Prediction** Describe the family's life in this new place.
2. **Visualize** What sounds do you think the boy heard as he tried to sleep that night?

158

159

Build Comprehension, pages 158–159

5 **Key Words** What does Father bring home? (a **map**)

6 **Character's Feelings** How do Mother and the boy feel towards Father? (Angry) Why? (They are hungry and expected him to buy food.)

7 **Cause/Effect** What was the effect of Father's buying the map? (The family had nothing to eat and were still hungry.)

8 **Answers to Before You Move On**

1. **Confirm Predictions** Answers about predictions will vary. (Their life in the new **country** is hard. They live in a small room and do not have any food to eat.)

2. **Visualize** MODEL | GUIDE | APPLY Use the Language Frames from page 151 to model visualizing what the boy hears:

   • *I read that the boy is hungry and that the writer chews loudly.*

   • *I picture the man chewing loudly and smacking his lips noisily as he eats the bread.*

   • *I feel sad for the boy because he has nothing to eat.*

Student Book pages 158–159

I **A** **AH**

Social Studies: Markets

In many countries, people shop at outdoor markets or buy from street vendors. Father visited an outdoor market on page 157. How is this market different from a grocery store? Ask students if they have been to an outdoor market or bazaar. Have them describe what it was like.

▸ **Predict**

1 How will the **map** affect the boy?

The next day Father hung the map. It **took up** an entire wall. Our cheerless room was **flooded** with color.

I became fascinated by the map and spent long hours looking at it, studying its every detail, and many days drawing it on any scrap of paper that **chanced my way**. **2**

I found strange-sounding names on the map and **savored their exotic sounds**, making a little rhyme out of them:

Fukuoka Takaoka Omsk,
Fukuyama Nagayama Tomsk,
Okazaki Miyazaki Pinsk,
Pennsylvania Transylvania Minsk!

I repeated this rhyme and was **transported** far away without ever leaving our room. **3**

In Other Words
took up covered
flooded filled
chanced my way I found

In Other Words
savored their exotic sounds enjoyed
the unusual way they sounded

▸ **Before You Move On**

4
1. **Theme** What does the **map** mean to the boy?
2. **Visualize** How does the rhyme **transport** the boy?

160

161

Student Book pages 160–161

I **A** **AH**

Social Studies: Maps

Maps are used to show the location of places. Look at the illustration on page 160, what do the colors on the map show? (**countries,** ocean) How else might colors be used on a map? (to show **continents**, to show different regions or features) Look up examples of some different kinds of maps online to see how color is used, e.g., topographic, population, etc.

Build Comprehension, pages 160–161

1 **Predict** Read aloud the first paragraph on page 160. Model using illustrations to predict what will happen. Ask: *Which illustrations help you predict how the* **map** *affects the boy?*

2 **Sequence** What does the boy do once the map is hung up? (look at it and study its every detail)

3 **Key Words** What does the boy **imagine**? (that he is **transported** to other places)

4 **Answers to Before You Move On**

1. **Theme** MODEL | GUIDE | APPLY Model how to use the clues in the story to figure out the theme. Point out important details that show what the map means to the boy: He is fascinated with it. He spends hours looking at it and drawing it. What does the map let the boy do? (It lets him imagine other places.) How does this help the boy? (It helps him forget about his present life.)

2. **Visualize** MODEL | GUIDE | APPLY *What do you read about the names?* (They were strange-sounding.) *What do you picture as the boy reads the names?* (I picture him closing his eyes and imagining himself in the faraway places.) *How does it make you feel?* (I feel happy and excited for him because he can forget his hard life for awhile.)

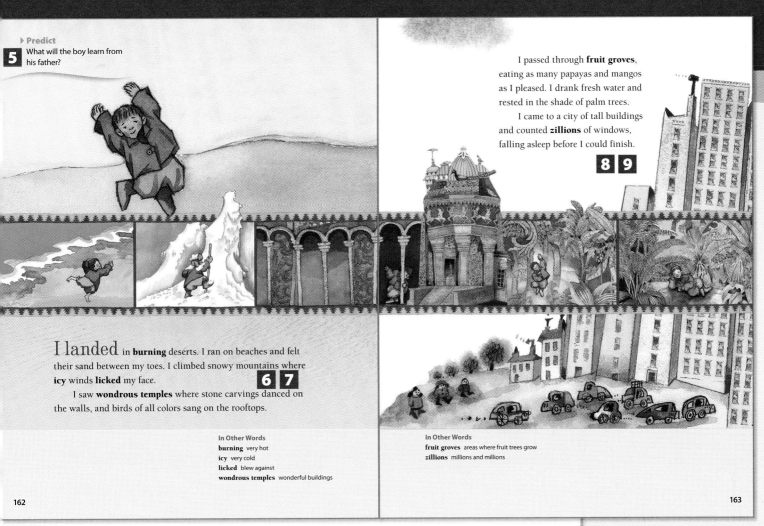

I passed through **fruit groves**, eating as many papayas and mangos as I pleased. I drank fresh water and rested in the shade of palm trees.

I came to a city of tall buildings and counted **zillions** of windows, falling asleep before I could finish.

8 9

I **landed** in **burning** deserts. I ran on beaches and felt their sand between my toes. I climbed snowy mountains where **icy** winds **licked** my face. **6 7**

I saw **wondrous temples** where stone carvings danced on the walls, and birds of all colors sang on the rooftops.

In Other Words
burning very hot
icy very cold
licked blew against
wondrous temples wonderful buildings

In Other Words
fruit groves areas where fruit trees grow
zillions millions and millions

162

163

Build Comprehension, pages 162–163

5 **Confirm Prediction** Was your prediction about how the map affects the boy correct? (Answers about predicting will vary.)

6 **Predict** Read aloud the first paragraph on page 162. Ask: *What has happened in the story so far that will help me to predict what the boy learns from his father?*

7 **Role-Play** What did the boy imagine doing? Show me how you would do those things. (Responses will vary. Students might pantomime running on the beach or climbing a mountain.)

8 **Visualize** MODEL | GUIDE | APPLY Use the **Language Frames** to visualize one of the places the boy imagined. Remember to look for details that help you visualize. (Answers will vary. Students should include sensory details and images for each place.)

9 **Theme** MODEL | GUIDE | APPLY Guide students to explain how the author's descriptions help them better understand how the map helped the boy. Ask students to point to places the boy imagined. How did going to these different settings help him?

B I A AH

Literary Analysis: Setting

Teach/Model Remind students that setting refers to the place and time a story happens.

Practice/Apply Have students review the illustrations and text to look at other settings the boy imagined. Have students pick a setting, such as the desert, that they might have seen or visited. How would they describe it? Use picture cards of real places similar to those shown in the story. What are other places you could visit?

I **A** **AH**

Fluency: Intonation

Teach/Model Explain the concept: *Fluent readers read with correct intonation. They raise and lower their voices as they read text. Raise your voice at the end of a question. When you tell something, let your voice go down at the end.* Display page 158. Model reading the page with intonation.

Practice Have partners read the page aloud together several times, mimicking the intonation you modeled.

Keys to Efficacy

Give students a chance to think before rephrasing a question, moving on, or answering it yourself.

Build Comprehension, page 164

1 **Character's Feelings** Does the boy feel the same now as he did at the beginning of the story? (No) Explain. (Now he is grateful his father bought the **map** because it helps him forget his troubles.)

2 **Answers to Before You Move On**

1. Theme MODEL | GUIDE | APPLY Say: *Use the events and the setting to help you decide what the boy learned.* (From his father, the boy learned that you can use your **imagination** to help you live with a bad situation. You don't have to be miserable even if your life is miserable.)

2. Figurative Language An icy wind is cold. A lick is wet, so an icy wind licking my face would feel cold and wet against my face.

Meet the Author

Have students chorally read the Meet the Author copy. Point out that Uri Shulevitz is an author and an illustrator. He combined his colorful illustrations with vivid words to show how the boy took imaginary trips to forget his hard life.

1 **Writer's Craft** Have students open their books to pages 162 and 163 of the story. The author uses figurative language to help you visualize the places the boy imagines. Say: *Look at these examples.* Point out an example on the page.

. . . burning deserts

Ask students to identify other examples from these pages. Students may cite the following examples:

. . . icy winds licked my face

… stone carvings danced on the walls

… rested in the shade of palm trees

… counted zillions of windows, falling asleep before I could finish

Then read aloud the Writer's Craft on page 165 with students.

And so I spent **enchanted hours** far, far away from our hunger and **misery**. I forgave my father. He was right, after all. ❖

In Other Words
enchanted hours hours filled with wonder
misery sadness

 ▶ **Before You Move On**
1. **Theme** What does the boy learn from his father?
2. **Figurative Language** What would it feel like if an icy wind licked your face?

164

Meet the Author and Illustrator

Uri Shulevitz

Imagine what it would be like to wander for ten years without a real home. That's how Uri Shulevitz spent ten years of his childhood.

Shulevitz was born in Poland in 1935. World War II began when he was just four years old. A bomb fell on his family's apartment. Soon after, the family moved to Central Asia, where this story is set. Later, the family moved to France. Shulevitz explains, "I changed schools and languages frequently because of the war years. The only constant in my life was my drawing."

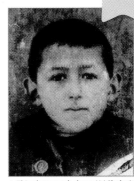

▲ This photograph shows Uri Shulevitz as a boy, when he lived in Central Asia.

Writer's Craft ✏
Look at the way the author describes the places the boy imagines on pages 162 and 163. Now imagine a place you have been or would like to visit. Write a brief paragraph that uses figurative language to describe what this place is like.

165

I A AH

Meet the Author

Encourage students to read more books written by Uri Shulevitz.

- *One Monday Morning*
- *Rain Rain Rivers*
- *Snow*
- *So Sleepy Story*

Daily Writing  A AH

2 Writer's Craft Explain: *Uri Shulevitz used figurative language to help readers visualize the places the boy visits in his imagination. Think about a place you have visited or would like to visit. Use figurative language to help your readers visualize the place.* Use the **Modeled Writing** routine to write sentences about the characteristics of the place. (See **Writing Routines**, page PD54).

Think Aloud 💬	**Write** ✏
I would like to visit Lalaria, a beach my father went to as a child. It is not sandy. It has smooth, white pebbles and stones. The rocks seem to sing when the waves washed over them.	As a child, my father's favorite beach was Lalaria in Greece. Here, rocks fall from the white cliffs and are polished smooth by the sea. The pebbles and stones sing as the waves dance onto the shore and back—la-la ria, la-la ria.

Have students write their sentences in their journals.

CLOSE AND ASSESS

- **Language** *Use a map to give directions to get from one place to another.* (Encourage students to use the words *east, west, north,* and *south* in their directions.)
- **Vocabulary** *What Key Words did you use in your answers?* (Answers will vary.)
- **Reading** *What did you visualize as you read the story?* (Students may cite the three Reading Strategy lessons presented in Build Comprehension.)

Day 4

Day at a Glance:
▶ **Language:** Nouns and Articles *a, an, the* ▶ **Reading:** Think and Respond
▶ **Vocabulary:** Share Word Knowledge ▶ **Writing:** Write About It

OBJECTIVES

Vocabulary
• Use Academic Vocabulary ⊕
• Use Grade-Level Vocabulary ⊕

Language
• Nouns and Articles *a, an, the* ⊕

Learning and Teamwork Strategies
• Review
• Collaborate with Peers

Resources

🔊 *eVisual 3.8*

✏️🔊 *Practice Master 3.5*

🖼️🔊 *Language Builder Picture Card E39*

Differentiate

Language Transfer

Issue In Spanish, plurals are formed by adding -s to nouns that end in a vowel and -es to nouns ending in a consonant or *y*.

Strategy Create a chart with examples.

English		Spanish	
Singular	Plural	Singular	Plural
desert	deserts	desierto	desiertos
temple	temples	templo	templos
hotel	hotels	hotel	hoteles
color	colors	color	colores

As you write each plural form, point out the ending. Compare the differences between the English endings and the Spanish endings. Have students copy the chart and practice with additional cognates, writing both singular and plural forms. Be sure to include cognates from the Key Words (*continent/continente; globe-globo; inhabitant/habitante; map/mapa;* etc.).

Language of the Day

In "How I Learned Geography," the boy uses his imagination to visit many different countries. Where do you go in your imagination? I imagine going ____ .

Read the Language of the Day. Model: *I imagine going to a cave.* Invite students to share about the places they visit in their imaginations. Write the names of these places on the board, including the articles. Go back and circle the articles. Tell students that today they will learn about articles like these.

Grammar Nouns and Articles *a, an, the* ⬛B ⬛I ⬜A ⬜AH

1 **Teach/Model** Review: A noun names a person, place, thing, or idea. Display the chart. Call upon a different student to read each column of the chart. Invite students to add more nouns to the chart.

Noun Chart			
People	**Places**	**Things**	**Ideas**
man	city	**map**	geography
Uri	France	supper	delight

🔊 **NGReach.com** ▶ eVisual 3.8

Write the following sentences and have volunteers read them aloud.

1. The man put a map on the wall.

2. The boy pretended to be an **inhabitant** of many countries.

Underline these phrases: *The man, a map, the wall, The boy, an inhabitant.* Say: *Some words help to identify a noun. They show that the next word is a noun. We call these little words "articles."* Write and discuss the following rules. Have students copy them into their journals.

• Use *a* and *an* when you talk about something in general.

• Use *a* before a noun that begins with a consonant. Use *an* before a noun that begins with a vowel.

• Use *the* to talk about something specific.

2 **Practice/Apply** Have partners find *a* and *the* in the selection and discuss why the writer used the general (*a*) or the specific (*the*) article. Then have them list nouns that would follow *an*. Assign **Practice Master 3.5.**

CHECK UNDERSTANDING Display the words. Have students tell which words are nouns and which are articles.

state
the
pencil
a

Share Word Knowledge

③ Teach/Model To connect concepts, say: *Yesterday you became Key Word experts. Today you will share what you know about your Key Words.* Group each student with a partner who studied a different word. Have partners follow the steps of **Vocabulary Routine 3** to share their word knowledge. (See **Vocabulary Routine 3,** page PD39.)

- Take turns reading Key Word organizers.
- Talk about how the pictures on the organizer show the meanings of the Key Words.
- Create sentences using both Key Words and write them in your journals.
- Draw a line under each Key Word.

④ Practice/Apply Use a Three-Step Interview. Have student experts learn about two different words and interview each other about their words. Then have them report about each other's words to the group. (see **Cooperative Learning Routines,** pages PD58–PD59).

Repeat until all the words are discussed.

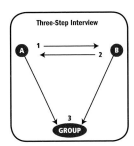

Three-Step Interview

CHECK UNDERSTANDING Display the **Language Builder Picture Card E39** (the floating market in Bangkok) and ask students to use Key Words to tell about it.

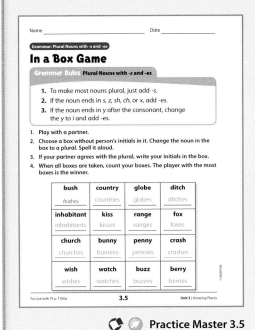

Practice Master 3.5

Part 1 Vocabulary Skills Trace		**Page**
Day 1	**Social Studies Vocabulary**	**T147**
Day 2	**Academic Vocabulary**	**T149**
Day 3	**Expand Word Knowledge**	**T152b**
▶ **Day 4**	**Share Word Knowledge**	**T166b**
Day 5	**Apply Word Knowledge**	**T167b**
Day 6	**Word Origins**	**T168**
Day 7	**Word Origins**	**T173**
Days 8–9	**Extend Vocabulary**	**T174e–f**
Day 10	**Vocabulary Review**	**T174g–h**

Day 4
continued

Day at a Glance:
▶ **Language:** Plural Nouns with -*s*, -*es*   ▶ **Reading:** Think and Respond
▶ **Vocabulary:** Share Word Knowledge   ▶ **Writing:** Write About It

OBJECTIVES

Vocabulary
• Use Academic Vocabulary
• Use Grade-Level Vocabulary

Language
• Use Language Function: Give and Follow Directions

Reading Fluency
• Intonation

Literary Analysis
• Analyze Genre: Fictional Tale

Test-Taking Strategies
• Practice and Apply Strategies: Look for Important Words

Writing
• Write Responses to Fictional Tale

Resources

 eVisual 3.9

 NGReach.com

See **Technology Station** for digital student resources.

I A AH

Fluency: Intonation

Review Review intonation (page T164). Display this reminder: *Lift your voice at the end of a question. When you tell something, let your voice go down at the end.*

Apply Challenge pairs to an intonation reading face-off. Have partners practice reading page 158. Then organize teams of four and have pairs give each other feedback about their reading.

Think and Respond

1 **Talk About It** Prompt students to cite evidence from the text. Remind students to use Key Words in their answers. If students have difficulty, help them use the sentence starters to form their answers.

1. **Fictional tale** The story tells about events that the character imagines. It has real events combined with imagined events.

2. **Give and Follow Directions** You can play a game on a **map**. I think of a place on the map but do not tell my partner. Then I give clues such as *It's in the northern* **hemisphere**. *It is a* **country**. I keep giving clues until my partner guesses the place. Then we switch giving directions and finding the place.

3. **Analyze** Possible answer: The boy was sad because he left behind everything he knew. I would not like to leave my home and friends.

2 **Test-Taking Strategies: Look for Important Words** Explain: *Test questions have important words that tell you what to look for to answer a question.* List these words and discuss them: *before, after, best, who, what, where, when, why.* Display the sample question.

Important Word	Look for...
before, after	the order things happen
best	the best answer choice—more than one may seem right
who, what, when, where, or why	a person, thing, time, place, or reason

Ask: *What important word do you see in this question?* (after) *I need to find the answer choice that tells what happens after the dad hangs the map.* Ask students what the answer to the question is. (Answer choice B)

> **What happens after the dad hangs up the map?**
> A. The boy feels sad.
> B. The boy studies the map.
> C. The dad takes the map down.
> D. The dad buys the map.

 NGReach.com eVisual 3.9

Display the remaining practice items. Have partners look for important words in the question and then answer the items.

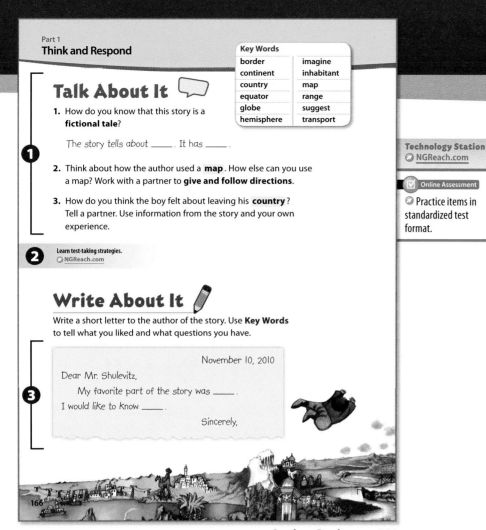

Part 1
Think and Respond

Talk About It

1. How do you know that this story is a **fictional tale**?

   The story tells about _____. It has _____.

2. Think about how the author used a **map**. How else can you use a map? Work with a partner to **give and follow directions**.

3. How do you think the boy felt about leaving his **country**? Tell a partner. Use information from the story and your own experience.

2 Learn test-taking strategies.
   NGReach.com

Key Words

border	imagine
continent	inhabitant
country	map
equator	range
globe	suggest
hemisphere	transport

Technology Station
NGReach.com

☑ Online Assessment
○ Practice items in standardized test format.

Write About It ✏

Write a short letter to the author of the story. Use **Key Words** to tell what you liked and what questions you have.

> November 10, 2010
>
> Dear Mr. Shulevitz,
>   My favorite part of the story was _____.
> I would like to know _____.
>   Sincerely,

Student Book page 166

Daily Writing ✏

3 **Write About It** Read the directions aloud. Point out the sentence frames. You can use these frames to begin your writing. Use the **Independent Writing** routine to help students write a letter to the author using the Key Words and the sentence frames. (See Writing Routines, page PD56.)

Say 💬	Write ✏
*The boy was **transported** far away without ever leaving his room.*	My favorite part of the story was when the boy was transported to amazing places.
The boy landed in burning deserts, ran on beaches, and climbed snowy mountains.	I would like to know which countries he describes.

Point out the Key Words that you used to complete the sentence frames: *transport* and *country*. Have students use these ideas or their own to write a letter in their journals.

> **CLOSE AND ASSESS**
> • **Language** *Say the plural form of each word: horse, sash, watch* (horses, sashes, watches.)
> • **Reading** *Why do you think reading and **imagination** were so important to Uri Shulevitz?* (Answers will vary.)
> • **Vocabulary** *What Key Words did you use in your answers?* (Answers will vary.)

N **B** **I** **A** **AH**

Keys to Efficacy

Remind students to use content, academic, and/or classroom vocabulary. *How can you use a Key Word to explain your idea?*

Day 5

Day at a Glance:
▶ **Language:** Listen for Important Details   ▶ **Reading:** Reread and Retell
▶ **Vocabulary:** Apply Word Knowledge   ▶ **Writing:** Write a Paragraph

OBJECTIVES

Vocabulary
• Use Academic Vocabulary ❶
• Use Grade-Level Vocabulary ❶

Listening and Speaking
• Listen for Important Details ❶

Learning and Teamwork Strategies
• Ask for Clarification
• Ask for Help
• Restate Instructions
• Review

Media and Technology
• Build Concepts from Media

Resources

🎬 *Unit 3 Build Background Video*

💿 🎬 *eVisual 3.10*

Differentiate

N B I

How to Learn Language

Ask for Clarification Explain: *Sometimes we have questions about or do not fully understand something we hear. When that happens, you can ask others to repeat or explain what they said.* Create a chart of ways students can ask for help.

What does this word mean?
Can you explain this sentence to me?
Can you restate this idea for me?

Have students suggest other questions and add them to the chart.

Form pairs of students at different proficiency levels so that newcomers and beginners can practice asking intermediate- and advanced-level students for clarification about the content of the video.

> ## Language of the Day
> Why should we learn about other places?
> We learn about other places because _____.

Read the Language of the Day. Have students recall the information they learned in the unit launch video and complete the sentence frame. Add their ideas to the unit concept map. Then explain that today they will learn how to listen actively, play a word game, retell the story, and write about it.

Listen for Important Details

❶ Teach/Model Introduce the concept: *When you know how to listen for important details, you can better understand information you hear.* Play the first part of the video. Then ask a volunteer to give information from it. Display the How to card and model how to listen for important details as the volunteer talks.

▶ Play the animation

NGReach.com ▶ ■ Digital Library

How to Listen for Important Details

☁	1. Identify the subject or main idea.	The subject is a **globe**, which is a **map** of Earth.
👂	2. Listen for details that tell about the main idea.	I hear that Earth has two **hemispheres**.
❓	3. Ask questions if you do not understand.	What is a hemisphere?
👂	4. Listen for key words and answers to your questions.	I hear that the **equator** divides Earth into two halves, or hemispheres.

NGReach.com ▶ eVisual 3.10

---

❷ Practice/Apply Play the next part of the video, pausing frequently to allow partners to practice the steps. Have students tell what important details they heard. Teach the **How to Learn Language** strategy to help students as they talk about the video.

> **CHECK UNDERSTANDING** Have students switch partners. One partner listens for important details while the other relates new information learned.

Apply Word Knowledge

③ Teach/Model Tell students they are going to play a game called "Yes or No." Guide them in following these oral instructions:

- *I look at the Key Words.*
- *I write a yes/no question that includes at least one Key Word. For example: Is a globe a kind of map?*
- *The answer is yes. The team that correctly answers the question scores one point.*
- *The team with the most points wins the game.*

④ Practice/Apply Write the Key Words on the board. Distribute index cards to each team. Clarify: *Make sure each question includes at least one Key Word.* Have each team write three or four questions for the game.

Explain that the answer to each question must be *yes* or *no.* Monitor students as they write their questions.

Collect the question cards to play the game with the class. Remind teams to raise their hands when they want to answer a question.

Monitor students as they follow your instructions. Restate the instructions as required.

For vocabulary games, go to NGReach.com.

> **CHECK UNDERSTANDING** Repeat a question and have students explain how they used their knowledge of the Key Words to decide if the answer was *yes* or *no.*

Day 5
continued

Day at a Glance:
▶ **Language:** Listen for Important Details
▶ **Vocabulary:** *Yes* or *No*
▶ **Reading:** Reread and Summarize
▶ **Writing:** Write a Paragraph

OBJECTIVES

Vocabulary
• Use Academic Vocabulary **T**
• Use Grade-Level Vocabulary **T**

Language
• Summarize the Story
• Participate in Discussion

Learning and Teamwork Strategies
• Use Graphic Organizers: Theme Chart
• Reason Deductively

Reading Fluency
• Read with Accuracy and Rate **T**
• Read with Intonation **T**

Literary Analysis
• Understand Theme

Writing
• Write a Paragraph Response

Social Studies
• Investigate Geography

Resources

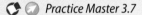 *Practice Master 3.6*

Practice Master 3.7

eVisual 3.11

Comprehension Coach

NGReach.com >

See **Technology Station** for digital student resources.

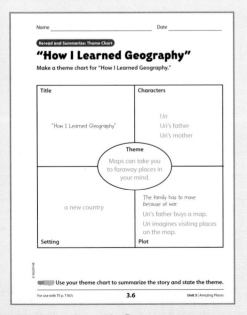

Name _____ Date _____

Reread and Summarize: Theme Chart
"How I Learned Geography"
Make a theme chart for "How I Learned Geography."

Title	Characters
"How I Learned Geography"	Uri Uri's father Uri's mother
Theme Maps can take you to faraway places in your mind.	
a new country	The family has to move because of war. Uri's father buys a map. Uri imagines visiting places on the map.
Setting	Plot

Use your theme chart to summarize the story and state the theme.

For use with TE p. T167c   3.6   Unit 3 | Amazing Places

Practice Master 3.6

T167c   **Unit 3 |** Amazing Places

Reread and Summarize

1 **Theme** Read aloud the introduction and reinforce: *We can look for clues that tell us the main message of the story. Look at the title, setting, characters, and events in the story.* Read through the example theme chart. Then explain: *I think about what happens in the story. This helps me figure out what the theme is.*

Have students complete **Practice Master 3.6**.

2 **Summarizing** Read aloud the directions and language frames. Display the **Summarizing a Story Rubric**. Have students summarize the story for their partners. Remind them to include important details such as the setting and characters. Partners reverse roles and repeat. Provide the **Key Points Reading (Practice Master 3.4)** for students who need additional support.

Summarizing a Story Rubric		
Scale	**Content**	**Language**
B	☐ Misses many important story events. ☐ Does not state the story's theme.	☐ Is often hard to hear and understand. ☐ Is uncomfortable with the summarizing task.
I	☐ Includes many story events. ☐ Makes a general statement about the story's theme.	☐ Is understood most of the time. ☐ Seems somewhat comfortable with the summarizing task.
A	☐ Covers the main story events. ☐ Is able to identify the story's theme.	☐ Is clearly and easily understood. ☐ Is comfortable summarizing the story.
AH	☐ Relates all important parts of the story. ☐ Expresses the story's theme clearly.	☐ Speaks clearly and expressively. ☐ Employs eye contact and gestures when relating events.

Fluency Accuracy, Rate, and Intonation **I** **A** **AH**

3 **Fluency** Have students record their reading on the **Comprehension Coach** to assess each student's progress for rate and accuracy. Have students use the passage on **Practice Master 3.7** to record their reading for intonation. Listen to each recording and assess students' ability to read with intonation.

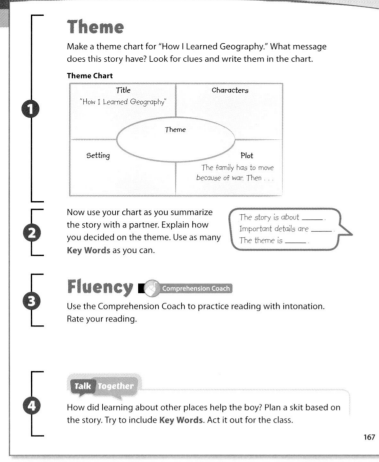

Theme

Make a theme chart for "How I Learned Geography." What message does this story have? Look for clues and write them in the chart.

Theme Chart

1

Title "How I Learned Geography"	Characters
Theme	
Setting	Plot The family has to move because of war. Then . . .

2 Now use your chart as you summarize the story with a partner. Explain how you decided on the theme. Use as many **Key Words** as you can.

> The story is about _____.
> Important details are _____.
> The theme is _____.

Fluency 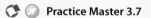 Comprehension Coach

3 Use the Comprehension Coach to practice reading with intonation. Rate your reading.

Talk Together

4 How did learning about other places help the boy? Plan a skit based on the story. Try to include **Key Words**. Act it out for the class.

167

Student Book page 167

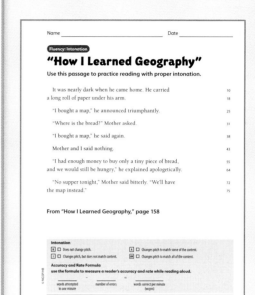

Technology Station
NGReach.com

Comprehension Coach
Automatically measure fluency.

Name _____ Date _____

Fluency: Intonation

"How I Learned Geography"
Use this passage to practice reading with proper intonation.

It was nearly dark when he came home. He carried	10
a long roll of paper under his arm.	18
"I bought a map," he announced triumphantly.	25
"Where is the bread?" Mother asked.	31
"I bought a map," he said again.	38
Mother and I said nothing.	43
"I had enough money to buy only a tiny piece of bread,	55
and we would still be hungry," he explained apologetically.	64
"No supper tonight," Mother said bitterly. "We'll have	72
the map instead."	75

From "How I Learned Geography," page 158

Intonation

Accuracy and Rate Formula
use the formula to measure a reader's accuracy and rate while reading aloud.

For use with TE p. T167c   **3.7**   Unit 3 | Amazing Places

 **Practice Master 3.7**

4 **Talk Together** Discuss how learning about other places helped the boy escape from his misery. Read aloud the directions and have students work in pairs or small groups to create their skits. Then have students share their skits with the class. Students should add their ideas to their Unit concept maps.

Daily Writing

5 **Write a Paragraph Response** Use the **Interactive Writing** routine to write a short class description of an **imaginary** place the students would like to visit. (See **Writing Routines**, page PD55.)

- As a class, discuss what this place might look like.
- Have students take turns building the paragraph, one word at a time.
- Offer corrective feedback.
- Have students copy the paragraph into their journals.

N B I A AH

Keys to Efficacy

Remind students to use content, academic, and/or classroom vocabulary: *How can you use a Key Word to explain your idea?*

CLOSE AND ASSESS

- **Language** *Complete this sentence: When I listen for important details, I _____.* (identify the subject or main idea, listen for important details, ask questions, listen for key words and answers to my questions)
- **Reading** *What clues helped you figure out the theme of the story?* (I thought about the story's title, setting, characters, and events.)
- **Vocabulary** *What Key Words did you use in our discussion?* (Answers will vary.)

Day 6

Day at a Glance:
- **Language:** Give, Restate, and Follow Directions
- **Vocabulary:** Word Origins
- **Reading:** Read the Selection
- **Writing:** Writing Fluency

OBJECTIVES

Vocabulary
- Use Academic Vocabulary ⊕
- Use Grade-Level Vocabulary ⊕
- Strategy: Word Origins ⊕

Language
- Language Function: Give, Restate, and Follow Directions ⊕
- Use a Variety of Sentence Types

Learning and Teamwork Strategies
- Use Prior Knowledge
- Prompt and Provide Suggestions

Resources

- ⊙ eVisual 3.11
- ⊙ eVisual 3.12

Language of the Day

What are the similarities and differences between a *globe* and a **map**?

A map _____. A globe _____. They both _____.

Read the Language of the Day. Model: *A map is flat. A globe is round. They both show the borders of* **countries**. Pair students and have partners complete the frames on their own. Then invite partners to share their complete sentences with the class. Record their ideas on the board in the form of a Venn diagram.

Give, Restate, and Follow Directions

1 **Teach/Model** Review how to give and follow directions. Say: *When you give directions, you tell how to get to a place or how to do something. When you restate directions, you repeat the information to be sure your listener understands what to do. When you follow directions, you do exactly what you hear or read in order.* Display the chart and work with a volunteer to model this language function. Reverse roles.

Give Directions	Restate Directions	Follow Directions
Look for the light.	Look for the traffic light.	I see the traffic light.
Turn left.	Turn left onto Main Street.	I turn left onto Main Street.

⊙ NGReach.com ▶ eVisual 3.11

Invite students to give directions to a location in the school building without naming the location, such as: *Turn left out of our classroom. Follow the hallway to the end. Look for the blue door. Turn right. Where are you?* Then guide students in recognizing where the directions led.

2 **Practice/Apply** Have students form an **Inside-Outside Circle**. Students in the inside circle give brief directions for students in the outside circle to follow. Use **Academic Language Frames** to provide ideas to support every language level.

CHECK UNDERSTANDING Hide a small object and let half of the students see the location. Have them take turns giving directions to the other students to find it.

If students have difficulty, provide a model: *Follow the aisle between the desks. Turn right at Marc's desk. Look under the book on the shelf.*

Differentiate

Academic Language Frames

Give, Restate, and Follow Directions

■ Look for the _____.
  Yes, look for the _____.
  Go to the _____.
  Follow the _____.

■ Look for the _____.
  Go to the _____.
  Yes, go to the _____.
  Follow the _____ to the _____.

■ Go to the _____ and look for the _____.
■ Turn at the _____.
  Yes, turn at the _____.
  Follow the _____ until you _____.

⊙ NGReach.com ▶ eVisual 3.12

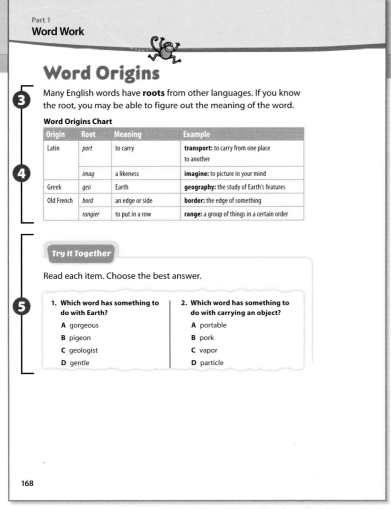

Word Origins

Many English words have **roots** from other languages. If you know the root, you may be able to figure out the meaning of the word.

Word Origins Chart

Origin	Root	Meaning	Example
Latin	*port*	to carry	**transport:** to carry from one place to another
	imag	a likeness	**imagine:** to picture in your mind
Greek	*geo*	Earth	**geography:** the study of Earth's features
Old French	*bord*	an edge or side	**border:** the edge of something
	rangier	to put in a row	**range:** a group of things in a certain order

Try It Together

Read each item. Choose the best answer.

1. Which word has something to do with Earth?
   A gorgeous
   B pigeon
   C geologist
   D gentle

2. Which word has something to do with carrying an object?
   A portable
   B pork
   C vapor
   D particle

168

Student Book page 168

Word Origins

3 **Teach** Read the introduction aloud and review the meaning of **hemisphere**. Then clarify: *Many words come from other languages. The word* hemisphere *has the word part* sphere *in it.* Sphere *comes from a Greek word, meaning "ball."* Demonstrate how the meaning of the root can help students figure out the meaning of the English word. Say: *When you learn a root, it can help you figure out the meaning of new words.* Have students brainstorm words with the root *geo* or *port,* such as *geology* and **transportation**.

4 **Model** Read aloud the definition of the root *geo* on the chart and model how to recognize the root in the word **geography**. Explain: *When I look at a word that I do not know, I can look for word parts that I do know. I know that the root* geo- *means "earth." This helps me understand that the word* geography *has something to do with earth.* Repeat the procedure with the word *transport.*

5 **Practice/Apply** Read the directions aloud. Then have partners work together to answer the questions. Use the **Multi-Level Practice Sets** to address varying levels of vocabulary knowledge.

CHECK UNDERSTANDING Say: *Tell what the root is in this word:* arrange. *(rangier) What does the root mean? ("to put in a row")*

Differentiate

Multi-Level Practice Sets

N *thermometer* (*therm* Greek root meaning "heat"; *meter* Greek root meaning "measure")

B *popular, population* (*pop* Latin root meaning "people")

I **equator** (*equa* Latin root meaning "to make equal")

A AH *ecosystem* (*eco* Greek root meaning "home")

Keys to Efficacy

Model vocabulary acquisition as a lifelong process. Say: *I recently learned a new word. Let me tell you how I figured out what it meant using what I knew about word roots.*

OBJECTIVES

Vocabulary
- Use Academic Vocabulary
- Use Grade-Level Content Vocabulary

Language
- Listen to a Preview

Learning to Read
- Concepts of Print: Identify Letters and Identify a Word

Reading Strategies
- Plan: Preview
- Make Connections: Text to Text

Literary Analysis
- Analyze Genre: Free Verse
- Use Text Features: Line Breaks and Repeated Words

Learning and Teamwork Strategies
- Use Prereading Supports
- Use Reading Supports

Resources

- *Practice Master 3.8*
- *eVisual 3.13*

Double-Entry Log

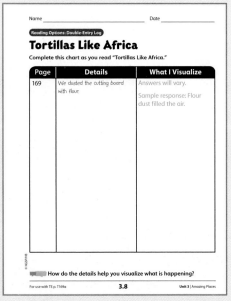

Practice Master 3.8

Read the Free Verse Poem

1 **Connect Across Texts** Read aloud the introduction and explain: *As you read the story, think about the Big Question. The boys in this poem make tortillas with funny shapes. They* **imagine** *each tortilla is shaped like a different* **continent** *or* **country**.

2 **Genre** Read aloud the explanation. Clarify: *Free verse is a kind of poetry. It usually does not have words that rhyme like other poems. Instead, free verse may use repetition, or words that are repeated. The lines of the poem are different lengths. A long sentence may be separated into more than one line of the poem.*

3 **Preview and Build Background** Use sheltering strategies as you conduct a picture walk.

Pages	Say (and Do)
169	*A boy and his brother make tortillas. First they get the dough ready.* (Pretend to make a ball of dough.) *Then they roll it and flatten it with their hands.*
170–171	*Have you seen tortillas? They are round and flat. Look at the shapes on the pages. What do some of the boys' tortillas look like?* (a boot, etc.) *What do you think the boys will do with their tortillas when they are done?* (eat them)

4 **Read "Tortillas Like Africa"** Scaffold the support for various reading levels.

BELOW LEVEL	ON LEVEL	ABOVE LEVEL
Listen and Read Along	**Read Together**	**Read Silently**
• Have students track the print while you read the text aloud. Then have students read the selection chorally. • Guide students in blending multisyllabic words.	• Have students use a **Double-Entry Log** as they read in pairs. Students should write at least two details from each page and tell what they visualize. • Review students' logs and discuss the Build Comprehension and Before You Move On questions.	• Have students complete a **Double-Entry Log** as they read silently. Students should add how the details helped them visualize. • Review students' logs as they read the poems aloud. • Check understanding with the Build Comprehension questions.

CHECK UNDERSTANDING Ask: *What form of writing is free verse?* (a poem) *What makes it different from some other poems?* (It does not rhyme. It has lines with different lengths)

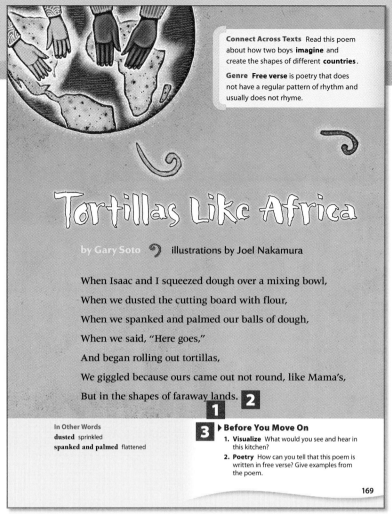

Connect Across Texts Read this poem about how two boys **imagine** and create the shapes of different **countries**.

Genre **Free verse** is poetry that does not have a regular pattern of rhythm and usually does not rhyme.

Tortillas Like Africa

by Gary Soto　　illustrations by Joel Nakamura

When Isaac and I squeezed dough over a mixing bowl,
When we dusted the cutting board with flour,
When we spanked and palmed our balls of dough,
When we said, "Here goes,"
And began rolling out tortillas,
We giggled because ours came out not round, like Mama's,
But in the shapes of faraway lands.

In Other Words
dusted sprinkled
spanked and palmed flattened

3 ▶ **Before You Move On**
1. **Visualize** What would you see and hear in this kitchen?
2. **Poetry** How can you tell that this poem is written in free verse? Give examples from the poem.

169

Student Book page 169

Build Comprehension, page 169

1 **Cause** Why do the boys giggle after rolling out their tortillas? (They giggle because their tortillas are not round, but in the shapes of countries.)

2 **Sequence** Tells what happens first, next, and last as the boys make tortillas shaped like faraway lands.

3 **Answers to Before You Move On**

1. **Visualize** RETEACH Review how to visualize (page T150). Offer a possible response: I read about two boys making tortillas. I see them working at the counter or table. I picture flour, dough, a rolling pin, and a cutting board. The air would be dusty from the flour. It says they spanked and palmed the dough, so I would hear clapping noises and laughter as they make their tortillas.

2. **Poetry** Possible answer: It does not rhyme. It has lines that are different lengths. It has line breaks at different places.

I **A** **AH**

Cultural Perpectives: Traditional Foods

Explain that the tortilla is a traditional food of Mexico. It is a kind of flatbread made from corn. Tell students that many other cultures have similar kinds of flatbreads, such as Indian nan, Greek pita, French crepe, and so on. Invite students to give additional examples of traditional breads or foods from other cultures.

N **B**

Concepts of Print: Identify Letters and Identify a Word

Teach/Model Direct students' attention to the first line *When Isaac and I squeezed dough over the mixing bowl* on page 169. Point out the first letter in the first word and identify it. Repeat with the remaining letters in *When*. Read *When* together, then have students put their fingers on the space between *When* and *Isaac*. Explain: *This space shows where the word* When *ends and the word* saac *begins.*

Practice/Apply Have partners count the letters in each remaining word in the line. Have them count the total amount of words in the line.

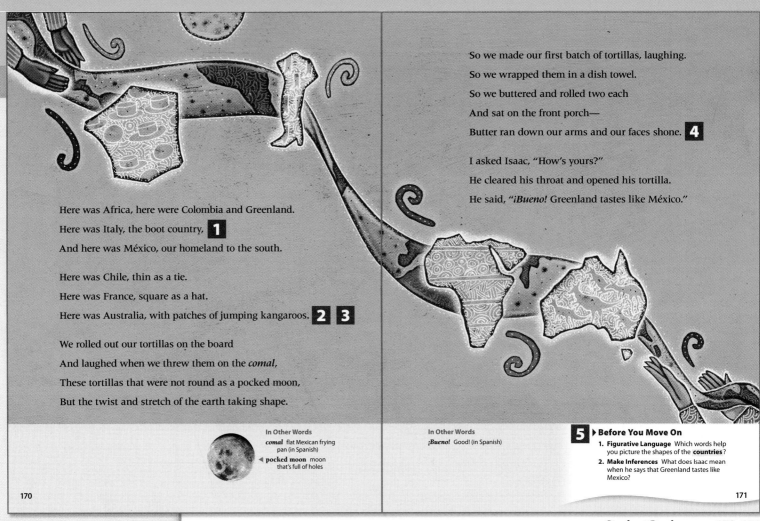

Here was Africa, here were Colombia and Greenland.
Here was Italy, the boot country, **1**
And here was México, our homeland to the south.

Here was Chile, thin as a tie.
Here was France, square as a hat.
Here was Australia, with patches of jumping kangaroos. **2** **3**

We rolled out our tortillas on the board
And laughed when we threw them on the *comal*,
These tortillas that were not round as a pocked moon,
But the twist and stretch of the earth taking shape.

So we made our first batch of tortillas, laughing.
So we wrapped them in a dish towel.
So we buttered and rolled two each
And sat on the front porch—
Butter ran down our arms and our faces shone. **4**

I asked Isaac, "How's yours?"
He cleared his throat and opened his tortilla.
He said, "*¡Bueno!* Greenland tastes like México."

In Other Words
comal flat Mexican frying
    pan (in Spanish)
◄ **pocked moon** moon
    that's full of holes

In Other Words
¡Bueno! Good! (in Spanish)

5 ▶ **Before You Move On**
1. **Figurative Language** Which words help
   you picture the shapes of the **countries**?
2. **Make Inferences** What does Isaac mean
   when he says that Greenland tastes like
   Mexico?

170

171

Student Book pages 170–171

Geography: Maps

Have students look at the description of the different countries and their shapes on the page. Then use a world map (or go online) and have students compare the shapes of the actual countries with their descriptions in the poem.

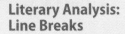

Literary Analysis: Line Breaks

Teach/Model Explain: *In free verse poems, the poet breaks, or stops, lines in different places to create a certain rhythm or feeling.* Point out how lines on the first page are all part of one sentence. Explain that some of the lines are broken before they reach the end of the space on the page. Discuss with students how the writer chose to break the lines. (by steps in making tortillas, where connecting words (*and, but*) occur).

Build Comprehension, pages 170–171

1 **Make Inferences** Why does the narrator call Italy "the boot **country**"? (It is shaped like a boot.)

2 **Visualize** **APPLY** How do the words "patches of jumping kangaroos" help you visualize Australia? (You can imagine these animals hopping around the dry plains of Australia.) **O**

3 **Key Words** What are the names of some of the countries and **continents** the boys mention on this page? (Africa is a continent. Australia is a country and a continent. Colombia, Greenland, Mexico, Chile, and France are countries.)

4 **Characters' Feelings** How do you think the brothers feel about making tortillas? How do you know? (They enjoy it. They think it is fun They giggle and laugh.)

5 **Answers to Before You Move On**

1. **Figurative Language** Possible responses: Italy is the boot country; Chile is thin as a tie; France is square as a hat.

2. **Make Inferences** Possible response: He means that even though it is shaped like Greenland, it tastes like Mexico because tortillas are a traditional Mexican food. Tortillas remind the boys of Mexico, the country they came from.

Make a Continent Map

Social Studies

Materials: *paper markers or crayons, tape, map for reference, computers for research*

1 **Teach**   Activate prior knowledge: *Raise your hand if you have used a map. Why are maps useful?* (maps show a place in relation to other places) Explain: *A map is a visual representation of a larger area.* Connect concepts: *To be useful, a map must show areas on a smaller scale.*

Raise your hand if you think a full-size map would be useful. How many think it would not be useful? If you were riding your bicycle through a park, could you use a full size map? (no) *It would be too large to handle. So, the measurements are scaled down to make a map that can be easily used.*

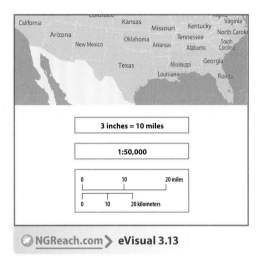

3 inches = 10 miles

1:50,000

2 **Model**   Display **eVisual 3.13**. Explain: *Mapmakers show scale in different ways. The first example uses words to describe the ratio between the map's scale and the real world. In the second example, one unit of distance is 50,000 of the same unit in the real world. So, one inch on the map is 50,000 inches in the real world, one foot on the map is 50,000 feet, and so on.* Point to the last example. *What is this called?* (a map scale) *How does it work?* (it uses a unit of measure to represent a real distance on earth)

Think aloud: *So, I want to make a map of a town. The town is 20 miles wide and 10 miles long. I can write* 1 inch = 2 miles *or I can use a map scale. It could look like this.*

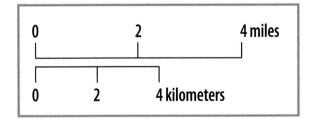

What size would my map be? (10 in. wide, by 5 in. long)

3 **Practice/Apply**   Divide students into groups. Assign each group a continent (Africa, Antarctica, Asia, Australia, Europe, North America, South America). Each group will draw a scale map of their assigned continent. As a class, decide on a map scale that all groups will use. Have each group post their map on the wall and give a presentation about the continent.

Make more content connections with Cross-Curricular Teamwork Activities (Pages T146g and T174o)   ▶

Day 6
continued

Day at a Glance:
Language: Give, Restate, and Follow Directions
Vocabulary: Word Origins
Reading: Respond and Extend
Writing: Writing Fluency

OBJECTIVES

Vocabulary
• Use Academic Vocabulary ⓣ
• Use Grade-Level Content Vocabulary ⓣ

Reading Fluency
• Read with Accuracy and Rate

Literary Analysis
• Compare Figurative Language ⓣ

Learning Strategy
• Use Graphic Organizer: T chart

Writing
• Writing Fluency

Resources

🔘 eVisual 3.14

• eVisual 3.15

🔘 Practice Master 3.9

🔘 Comprehension Coach

Differentiate

Academic Language Frames

Compare Figurative Language

■ This simile compares _____ to _____.
  It uses the word _____.
  This metaphor compares _____ to _____.

■ This simile compares _____ to _____.
  It uses the word _____.
  This metaphor compares _____ to _____.
  This _____ helps me picture _____.

■ While this _____ and this _____ both _____,
■ the _____ uses the word _____, while the _____
  does not _____.

🔘 NGReach.com ▸ eVisual 3.14

Respond and Extend

❶ Reread As students reread "Tortillas Like Africa" on their own, have them think about the language the poet uses.

❷ Compare Figurative Language Read the instructions. Explain to students that a T chart can be used to compare the language used in different types of literature. Use the instruction to explain how to complete the Figurative Language Chart.

Create groups and use **Jigsaw** routine. Have two groups become experts in finding metaphors and two groups become experts in finding similes. Help focus student thinking: *Both metaphors and similes compare things. A metaphor suggests what two things are being compared but doesn't state it.* Ask questions to help guide discussion. Provide **Academic Language Frames** to support students at different language levels.

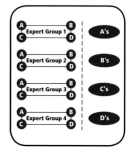

Jigsaw

Focus	Questions
1. Metaphors	What two things are being compared? Is the comparison made without using the words *like* or *as*?
2. Simile	What two things are being compared? Does the comparison use the words *like* or *as*?

As students report their group's ideas, students should record them on **Practice Master 3.9.**

❸ Talk Together

Read aloud the question and the directions. Remind students that each selection told about how young boys **imagined** places around the world. Ask follow-up questions to prompt students to use newly acquired vocabulary and to focus discussion. *What helped the boys imagine different places? What words did the characters use to describe these places?*

Have students add their ideas to the Unit concept map.

> **CHECK UNDERSTANDING** Have partners choose a place mentioned in either selection. Ask them to tell the words the author used to help them make a picture in their minds.

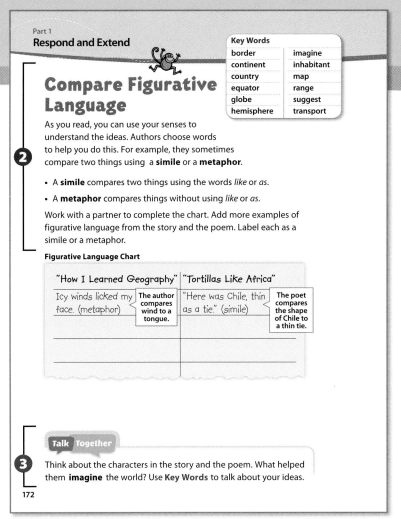

Compare Figurative Language

As you read, you can use your senses to understand the ideas. Authors choose words to help you do this. For example, they sometimes compare two things using a **simile** or a **metaphor**.

- A **simile** compares two things using the words *like* or *as*.
- A **metaphor** compares things without using *like* or *as*.

Work with a partner to complete the chart. Add more examples of figurative language from the story and the poem. Label each as a simile or a metaphor.

Figurative Language Chart

"How I Learned Geography"	"Tortillas Like Africa"
Icy winds licked my face. (metaphor) — The author compares wind to a tongue.	"Here was Chile, thin as a tie." (simile) — The poet compares the shape of Chile to a thin tie.

Talk Together

3 Think about the characters in the story and the poem. What helped them **imagine** the world? Use **Key Words** to talk about your ideas.

172

Student Book page 172

Daily Writing

4 **Writing Fluency** Use the **Power Writing** routine (see page PD53). Write the word **equator** and prompt: *What kinds of things might you see, feel, and hear in a place that is on the equator?* Think about this word and write about it.

Power Writing Routine

 1. What do you know about the word or picture?

 2. Take one minute to write as much as you can, as well as you can.
 B words   **I** sentences   **A** **AH** paragraphs

 3. Check your spelling and grammar. Circle mistakes.

123 **4.** Count your words.

NGReach.com eVisual 3.15

CLOSE AND ASSESS

- **Language** *Give me directions from our classroom to the lunch room.*
- **Reading** *Describe free verse poetry. Tell what makes it different from other kinds of writing.* (It has line breaks in different places to create rhythm. It has lines with different lengths. It does not rhyme. It sometimes has repeated words.)
- **Vocabulary** *Tell me what the root of this word is:* **transport**. *What does the root mean?* (port; "to carry")

Fluency: Accuracy, Rate, and Intonation

To activate prior knowledge and practice fluency, conduct timed readings of "How I Learned **Geography**." Select an option for recording:

- Use the automatic speech recognition on the **Comprehension Coach** to track word count per minute for the entire passage.
- Use **Practice Master 3.7**

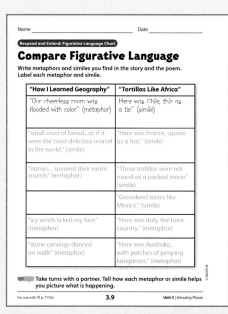

Name _____ Date _____

Respond and Extend: Figurative Language Chart

Compare Figurative Language

Write metaphors and similes you find in the story and the poem. Label each metaphor and simile.

"How I Learned Geography"	"Tortillas Like Africa"
"Our cheerless room was flooded with color." (metaphor)	"Here was Chile, thin as a tie." (simile)
"small crust of bread...as if it were the most delicious morsel in the world." (simile)	"Here was France, square as a hat." (simile)
"names...savored their exotic sounds" (metaphor)	"These tortillas were not round as a pocked moon" (simile)
	"Greenland tastes like Mexico." (simile)
"icy winds licked my face" (metaphor)	"Here was Italy, the boot country." (metaphor)
"stone carvings danced on walls" (metaphor)	"Here was Australia, with patches of jumping kangaroos." (metaphor)

Take turns with a partner. Tell how each metaphor or simile helps you picture what is happening.

For use with TE p. T172a   **3.9**   Unit 3 | Amazing Places

  Practice Master 3.9

Day 7

Day at a Glance:
▶ **Language:** Plural Nouns with *-s* and *-es* ▶ **Reading:** Reread the Selection
▶ **Vocabulary:** Word Origins ▶ **Writing:** Free Verse Poem

OBJECTIVES

Vocabulary
• Use Academic Vocabulary ❶
• Use Grade-Level Vocabulary
• Strategy: Word Origins

Grammar
• Plural Nouns with *-s*, *-es* ❶

Learning and Teamwork Strategies
• Use Context

Resources

 Practice Master 3.10

eVisual 3.16

Differentiate

Language Transfer

Issue In French, Spanish, and other European languages, plurals are often (but not always) formed by adding *-s* to the end of the singular form of a noun, as in English. In these languages, a plural noun must be accompanied by a plural article.

Strategy Write the following chart on the board, asking speakers of Spanish and French to help you complete the corresponding columns. Draw students' attention to the definite articles, reminding students that, in English, *the* keeps the same form, whether it goes with a singular noun or a plural noun.

English	Spanish	French
the colors	los colores	les couleurs
the continents	los continentes	les continents
the deserts	los desiertos	les déserts
the inhabitants	los habitantes	les habitants
the hotels	los hoteles	les hôtels
the temples	los templos	les temples

T173a **Unit 3** | Amazing Places

Language of the Day

What words have you learned related to **geography**?
I learned the words _____ .

Read the Language of the Day. Model: *I learned the words* **equator** *and* **hemisphere**. Invite students to name the words that they have learned throughout the course of the last seven days. Record the words that they name on the board. Keep the list handy, as you may use nouns from the list to practice forming plurals during the Grammar lesson.

Grammar/Spelling   Plural Nouns with *-s*, *-es*   B I A AH

❶ Teach/Model Read aloud the introduction and the first rule. Then write these nouns and add *-s* to make the plural forms.

> **map** ➝ *maps*   **continent** ➝ *continents*   **inhabitant** ➝ *inhabitants*

Read aloud the second rule. Then write these nouns and invite volunteers to add *-es* to make the plural forms.

> *box* ➝ *boxes*   *dish* ➝ *dishes*
>
> *tornado* ➝ *tornadoes*   *patch* ➝ *patches*

Have a volunteer read aloud the third rule. Then write these nouns. Model changing the final *y* to *i* and adding *-es* to make the plural forms.

> *city* i ➝ *cities*   *story* i ➝ *stories*

Read the last part of the explanation aloud. Then write these nouns. Circle the *a* and the *o* and remind students that they are vowels. Then invite volunteers to add *-s* to make the plural forms.

> *day* ➝ *days*   *toy* ➝ *toys*

❷ Practice Read aloud the directions and the excerpt from "How I Learned Geography." If necessary, help students identify the plural nouns, pointing out the *-s* endings. (temples, carvings, walls, birds, colors, rooftops)

❸ Apply in Writing Read aloud the directions and have students work independently. Provide support as necessary. Assign **Practice Master 3.10.**

> **CHECK UNDERSTANDING** Ask: *How do you form the plural of* **globe**? (add *-s*) *How do you form the plural of* batch? (add *-es*) *How do you form the plural of* sky? (change the *y* to *i* and add *-es*)

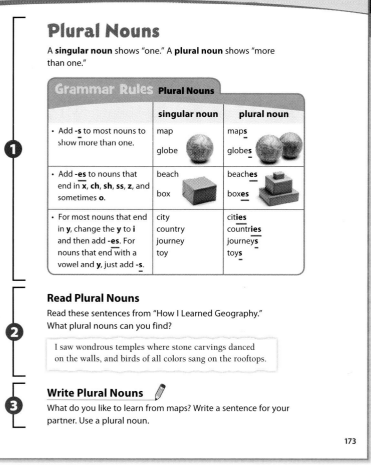

Plural Nouns

A **singular noun** shows "one." A **plural noun** shows "more than one."

Grammar Rules Plural Nouns

	singular noun	plural noun
• Add **-s** to most nouns to show more than one.	map globe	map**s** globe**s**
• Add **-es** to nouns that end in **x**, **ch**, **sh**, **ss**, **z**, and sometimes **o**.	beach box	beach**es** box**es**
• For most nouns that end in **y**, change the **y** to **i** and then add **-es**. For nouns that end with a vowel and **y**, just add **-s**.	city country journey toy	cit**ies** countr**ies** journey**s** toy**s**

Read Plural Nouns

Read these sentences from "How I Learned Geography." What plural nouns can you find?

> I saw wondrous temples where stone carvings danced on the walls, and birds of all colors sang on the rooftops.

Write Plural Nouns 🖉

What do you like to learn from maps? Write a sentence for your partner. Use a plural noun.

173

Student Book page 173

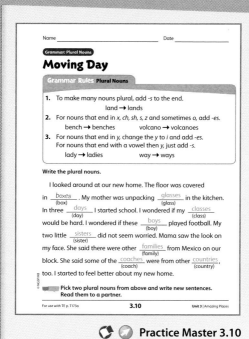

Practice Master 3.10

More Word Origins

4 **Review/Model** Review the Day 6 lesson (page T168). Use the list of **Word Roots** to model identifying roots in words. Write the word *population* on the board. Say: *I will look for a root in the word* population. *The root is* pop. *It means "people." This tells me that the meaning of the whole word has something to do with people.*

5 **Practice/Apply** Read each word and write it on the board. Have students identify the root using the Word Roots chart as reference. Have partners turn and talk about how the meaning of the root gives clues to the meaning of the whole word.

1. **cycle** (cyc; "circle")
2. **photograph** (graph; "draw, write")
3. **equator** (equa; "equal")
4. **populous** (pop; "people")
5. **bicycle** (cyc; "circle")

CHECK UNDERSTANDING Say: *Give me an example of another word you know that has a root from another language. What is the root? How does it help you understand the meaning of the whole word?*

Word Roots

Root	Origin	Meaning
pop	Latin	people
equa	Latin	equal
graph	Greek	draw, write
cyc	Greek	circle

NGReach.com ❯ **eVisual 3.16**

Part 1 Vocabulary Skills Trace		Page
Day 1	Social Studies Vocabulary	T147
Day 2	Academic Vocabulary	T149
Day 3	Expand Word Knowledge	T152b
Day 4	Share Word Knowledge	T166b
Day 5	Apply Word Knowledge	T167b
Day 6	Word Origins	T168
▶ Day 7	**More Word Origins**	**T173**
Days 8–9	Extend Vocabulary	T174e–f
Day 10	Vocabulary Review	T174g–h

Day 7
continued

Day at a Glance:
▶ **Language:** Plural Nouns with -s and -es
▶ **Vocabulary:** Word Origins
⏵ **Reading:** Reread the Selection
⏵ **Writing:** Free Verse Poem

OBJECTIVES

Vocabulary
- Use Academic Vocabulary ❶
- Use Grade-Level Vocabulary ❶

Literary Analysis
- Identify the Structure of Poetry ❶
- Describe Sensory Language

Learning and Teamwork Strategies
- Make Appropriate Contributions
- Connect Ideas

Writing
- Reproduce Modeled Writing
- Write a Free Verse Poem
- Use Figurative Language

Reread Focus on Elements of Poetry

❶ Teach Explain that poets make many choices about how a poem will look and sound. Write *free verse.* Ask a student to read the definition on the genre opener. Ask students what is meant by rhyme and rhythm. *Today you will read "Tortillas Like Africa" again. This time think about how the poem is set up. Pay attention to line breaks, repeated words, and the kinds of words the poet chose to describe things.*

❷ Model Have volunteers read aloud the first page of "Tortillas Like Africa." Ask students what they notice about the first four lines (Each line begins with *When*; they are different lengths.) Say: *The poet repeats words to create a kind of rhythm.* Ask students if they remember how the poet breaks these lines on the page. (Each line is a step in making tortillas.)

Make a web. Ask students to describe what they see, hear, smell, etc. and fill in the chart with their answers. Explain that some words may fit in more than one category. Point out that the poet uses both sensory words and figurative language.

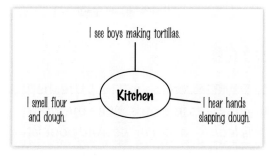

❸ Practice/Apply Have students read "Tortillas Like Africa" chorally. After reading, Use **Corners** to form groups to discuss these elements in the poem: word choice, line length, line breaks, repetition.

A word I saw repeated was _____.
The author may have done this to _____.
The lines in this poem _____.

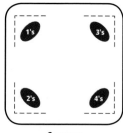

Corners

Ask each group to share what they learned about the elements of the poem.

> **CHECK UNDERSTANDING** Ask students to name one of the structural elements in the poem and give an example of it.

Daily Writing

Modeled Writing: Free Verse Poem Review the free verse form (page T169a) and how writers use details to help readers visualize (page T150). Then use the **Modeled Writing** routine to illustrate how to write a free verse poem. (See **Writing Routines** on page PD54.)

Think Aloud	Write
1. Plan	
I will make a RAFT to plan my writing. I will take on the role of a poet writing about a place I would like to go.	Role: a poet writing about a favorite place
Who is my audience? I have a group of friends who would like to hear about where I would like to go. I will write for them.	Audience: a group of friends
Repeat the think aloud for form (free verse poem) and topic (imagining a place you'd like to go).	
2. Write	
I am going to write my poem in the first person, so I will be writing using pronouns such as I and my.	I **imagine** the Andes Mountains.
I remember how Gary Soto used metaphors and similes to help the reader picture the tortillas in the poem. I will do the same thing to help my readers picture the place in my poem.	mountain peaks as sharp as arrows snow as white as sugar
Now, I'll try to think of words I can repeat in a group of lines.	I imagine
Repeat the think aloud for other elements of free verse, repeating - where to break lines in order to create feeling or rhythm	
3. Read and Reflect	
I will read aloud my final poem and check it one more time. *Have I met the plan I made during my RAFT? Yes! Do I want to make more changes? No. Now I can share it with my friend.*	I imagine the Andes Mountains. I imagine peaks as sharp as arrows. I compare the white snow to sugar. I imagine the cold stinging my nose like a bee.

Display the finished free verse poem to serve as a model and circle punctuation and capital letters. Use **Multi-Level Strategies** to support students at all proficiency levels in writing a free verse poem.

Differentiate

Multi-Level Strategies

BEGINNING

Use this frame and allow beginners to draw or write familiar words to complete the poem.

- I imagine ___.
- I imagine it ___.
- I imagine it is ___ as a ___.

INTERMEDIATE

Have students work in small groups to write a free verse poem together. Then have them share their poem with the class. Have each student read aloud at least one line.

ADVANCED

Ask students to write their poems independently. Then have partners offer feedback about their language.

ADVANCED HIGH

Have students focus on figurative language. Encourage them to include both a simile and a metaphor in their poems.

CLOSE AND ASSESS
- **Language** Name some plural nouns from the poem. Do they end with -s or -es? (Possible answers: *Balls, lands, shapes, kangaroos,* and *tortillas* end with -s. *Patches* ends with -es.)
- **Reading** How does the poet help you visualize the different shapes of the tortillas? (He compares them to the shapes of different **countries**.)
- **Vocabulary** Did you use any Key Words in your poem? What were they? (Answers will vary.)

Days 8-9

Day at a Glance:
▶ **Language:** Theme Theater: Step Into the Scene
▶ **Vocabulary:** Extend Vocabulary
▶ **Reading:** Read Leveled Books
▶ **Writing:** Paraphrase

OBJECTIVES

Vocabulary
• Use Grade-Level Vocabulary

Language
• Language Function: Give, Restate, and Follow Directions ⓣ

Listening and Speaking
• Listen for Important Details
• Focus on Pronunciation
• Speak at the Right Pace

Learning and Teamwork Strategies
• Build on Ideas

Resources

• materials for props such as:
  - construction paper
  - markers
  - chairs

📄🔊 Assessment Handbook page 114

Language of the Day

What did you learn about **countries**?
What do you still want to learn?
I learned that different countries ____. I still want to learn ____.

Read the Language of the Day. Model: *I learned that different countries have amazing places to visit. I still want to learn about the languages and cultures of other countries, too.* Invite students to share their own answers to the question as well. Explain that, during the next two days, students will act out a skit about a trip to another country.

Theme Theater Step Into the Scene

① **Introduce the Activity** Tap prior knowledge by brainstorming a list of countries that students would like to visit. Next to the name of each country, record two or three things that students already know about it. Ask: *What places can you visit in this country? What languages are spoken there? What else do you know about this place?* Use responses to identify which students could benefit from reviewing the audio recording or rereading the selection.

② **Plan** Form groups of six students. Assign the acting roles: three travelers, a taxi driver, and a tour guide. Guide students at different proficiency levels to select appropriate roles.

Explain the premise of the skit: *Two travelers get into a taxi. They tell the driver where they want to go. The driver doesn't know the city, and has to ask them for directions. They use their* **map** *to give the driver directions and the driver repeats the directions. When they get to their destination, a tour guide shows them around.*

3 Rehearse Have casts create a script based on the premise you presented to the class. Students can use language frames on page 146 to help create the script. Encourage students to work together and help them build on one another's ideas. Students may want to role-play the skit first, and then rehearse and memorize their lines. Use **Multi-Level Strategies** as groups rehearse, to help students at each proficiency level.

Guide students in gathering any props they need. For example, students can place two chairs side by side to represent the backseat of a taxi, with another chair in front for the taxi driver. Students may also create a map with simple details and a steering wheel.

4 Enjoy the Show! Arrange for family members or another class to enjoy the performance. When the audience is ready, invite the director of each skit to introduce the scene and give credit to the scriptwriter. As students present their skits, evaluate their skills using the rubric.

5 Debrief and Compare Ask each group to share what they enjoyed in the performances. Encourage them to compare the skits with "How I Learned Geography."

Differentiate

Multi-Level Strategies

BEGINNING

Students can point to places on the map to show where they want to go. Provide sentence frames:

Turn ___.

Go to the ___.

INTERMEDIATE

Students can decide on a destination and then give, follow, and restate detailed directions.

ADVANCED **ADVANCED HIGH**

Challenge students to give more details to their directions, including specific descriptions of the destination.

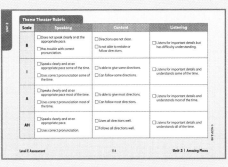

 Assessment Handbook page 114

Days 8-9
continued

Day at a Glance:
▶ **Language:** Theme Theater: Step Into the Scene
▶ **Vocabulary:** Extend Vocabulary
▶ **Reading:** Read Leveled Books
▶ **Writing:** Paraphrase

OBJECTIVES

Vocabulary
• Extend Vocabulary through Wide Reading

Language
• Participate in Discussion

Reading
• Read Independently
• Summarize Reading
• Make Connections: Text to Text
• Apply Reading Strategies Varied Texts

Writing
• Paraphrase Maintaining Meaning

Social Studies
• Explore the World's Regions

Resources

 Leveled Books:
- *Postcards to Paul*
- *Somewhere in the World Right Now*
- *The Flying Doctor*
- *A Look at Mexico*
- *Coober Pedy, Australia*
- *Galway, Ireland*

🔊 *Reach Leveled Library Lesson Plans*

🌐 NGReach.com ▶

Find more leveled readers about this topic.

Differentiate Read Leveled Books

Group students based on their reading abilities and interests. Use the **Guided Reading** routine (See page PD47) for books at students' instructional level. Use the **Independent Reading Support** (see page PD50) for books at students' independent reading level.

After reading, organize the students into heterogeneous groups to discuss what they read and to use the new information to answer the Big Question. Use these prompts to guide your discussion:

• What new information did you learn about what helps us imagine the world?

• What surprised you?

• How did new information change your answer?

Fiction

BEGINNING LEVEL

Postcards to Paul
by Talia Reed

• **Genre:** Realistic Fiction

Ari and his dad drive across the country to visit Ari's cousin Paul. Along the way, they send postcards to Paul of all the things they see and places they visit.

Key Words
forest
houseboats
ranch
traveling
yesterday

INTERMEDIATE LEVEL

Somewhere in the World Right Now
by Stacey Schuett

• **Genre:** Realistic Fiction

A little girl lies in bed dreaming about tomorrow. Around the world, some days are ending while others are just beginning.

Key Words
darkness
morning
murmurs
shoulders
tomorrow

ADVANCED   ADVANCED HIGH LEVELS

The Flying Doctor
by Alan Horsfield

• **Genre:** Realistic Fiction

When Randall falls from a horse, he needs medical attention. In rural Australia, the Royal Flying Doctor Service is there to help.

Key Words
climate
directions
emergency
landmarks
range

Nonfiction

BEGINNING LEVEL

A Look at Mexico
by Helen Frost

- **Genre:** Expository Nonfiction

Learn more about Mexico, their geography, and their culture. Maps and photographs support early readers in understanding the text.

Key Words

coyote

desert

factories

million

popular

INTERMEDIATE LEVEL

Coober Pedy, Australia
by Elspeth Leacock

- **Genre:** Expository Nonfiction

The people of Coober Pedy, Australia live in a hot, dry climate, but they have found a way to escape the heat. They live underground!

Key Words

climate

continent

equator

kangaroo

under-ground

ADVANCED   ADVANCED HIGH LEVELS

Galway, Ireland
by Elspeth Leacock

- **Genre:** Expository Nonfiction

Galway is a community on the coast of Ireland. Students will read all about this interesting town and the people who live there.

Key Words

community

famine

language

peaceful

traditions

Daily Writing   A AH

Journal Entry Have students write a journal entry in their reading journals. Use "How I Learned Geography" to model how to write a journal entry. Focus on how to paraphrase maintaining meaning. Say: *The boy's family brought all their possessions to their new home. Is that right?* (no). Then work with students to restate: *The boy's family left most of their things behind.*

Same Book / Different Levels

B I A AH

The Great Wall of China
by David Jeffery

Discover how and why the Great Wall of China was built and why it needs protecting today.

Pioneer Edition
Fountas and Pinnell: P–R

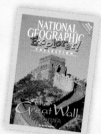

B Conduct a Picture Walk.

I Read text and captions.

Key Words

China   dragon

emperor   invaders

protect   soldiers

Pathfinder Edition
Fountas and Pinnell: Q–S

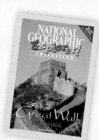

A Read text and captions.

AH Read and write responses to questions.

Key Words

dragon   dynasty

emperor   invaders

nomads   steppe

OBJECTIVES

Language
• Review Language Function: Give and Follow Directions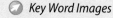

Grammar
• Review Nouns and Articles *a, an, the* T

Vocabulary
• Review Grade-Level Vocabulary T
• Review Word Origins

Reading Strategy
• Review Visualization T

Comprehension and Literary Analysis
• Review Setting
• Review Theme T

Fluency
• Accuracy, Rate, and Intonation T

Social Studies
• Investigate Geography

Resources

🔲 ◯ *Assessment Handbook*

◯ *Key Word Images*

◯ *eVisuals 3.18*

◯ ◯ *Comprehension Coach*

Language of the Day

What did you learn? How does it help you in school?

I learned how to ____. ____ means to ____. For example, ____.

Read the language of the day. Model: *I learned how to give directions. To give directions means to tell someone how to get to a specific place. For example, I can give directions to the cafeteria.* Review the list of skills students learned in Part 1. Prompt students to talk about a skill they have learned: *How did we use that skill? When might you use that skill in your everyday life?*

Review and Assess

Use these interactive review activities to reinforce concepts covered in Part 1. Then use the assessment tools to evaluate students' progress. For more details about assessment, see page T213a.

Language Function

Give and Follow Directions

Have students form pairs. Student A asks Student B for directions to a specific location at school. Then partners reverse roles. Have students share their directions with the class. Challenge students to identify the ending location.

• **Assessment:** Language Function Rubric on page 110 of the Assessment Handbook.

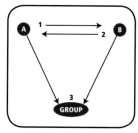

Three-Step Interview

Grammar

Nouns and Articles *a, an, the*

Display these words: *map, apple, beach, egg, box, city, wish.* Have partners determine whether *a* or *an* goes before each noun. Then have partners write the plural form of each noun and use it in a sentence with *the.*

Vocabulary

Social Studies and Academic Vocabulary

Form two teams. Show **Key Word Images**. Point to an image and define one of the Key Words. Have teams take turns identifying the Key Word and telling whether the Key Word matches the image. If the word and definition match the image, have teams use the Key Word in a sentence. If they do not match the image, challenge teams to identify the correct image.

• **Assessment:** Use the Key Word tests on pages 111–113 of the Assessment Handbook.

Key Words

border	imagine
continent	inhabitant
country	map
equator	range
globe	suggest
hemisphere	transport

Part 1 Grammar Skills Trace		Page
Day 2	Plural Nouns with *-s* and *-es*	T149a
Day 4	Nouns and Articles *a, an, the*	T166a
Day 7	Plural Nouns with *-s* and *-es*	T173a
▶ Day 10	**Review Nouns and Articles**	T174g

Vocabulary Strategy

Word Work: Word Origins

Display these roots and their meanings: *port, imag, geo, equa, bord, rangier.* Display **Key Word Images**. Ask teams to identify which Key Word contains each root. Challenge teams to list additional words for each root. The team that gives the most correct answers wins.

> The word **imagine** contains the root **imag**. Another word that contains this root is **imagination**.

Reading Strategy

Read Aloud

Visualize

Read the first two paragraphs of "Life in the Desert." Have students tell how they visualize what is described in the text using the **Academic Language Frames**: *I read _____. I picture _____. I feel _____.*

Comprehension

Read Aloud

Literary Analysis

Read the rest of "Life in the Desert." Have students describe the setting of the story using these frames: *The setting of the story is _____. This place is _____. This place has _____.*

Text Structure

Have students tell about the theme of the story using these frames: *The title is _____. The story takes place in _____. The story is about _____. The theme of the story is _____.*

Fluency

Accuracy and Intonation

Have students review their own recordings of "How I Learned Geography" in the Comprehension Coach. Then have students practice reading **Leveled Library Books** that are appropriate for their reading levels, focusing on accuracy and intonation.

Read Aloud

Life in the Desert

I love learning about new places. I visited my cousin in Phoenix, Arizona. I couldn't believe how hot it was. It was 110 degrees during the day. My skin felt like it was on fire.

Arizona is a very dry place. I only saw a few trees. Many homes have rocks instead of green grass in front. I did see many tall, green cactuses. One was taller than my cousin's house! Its sharp spines were shiny needles in the sun, but it had pretty yellow flowers, too.

I didn't think anything could live in that intense heat, but my cousin showed me a lizard sunning on a rock. I felt a warm breeze on my face and looked up. A hawk circled high above, looking for mice on the ground.

I enjoyed my trip to Arizona. I learned that plants and animals can thrive even in extreme conditions.

🌐 **NGReach.com** ⟩ eVisual 3.18

BIG Question — Why learn about other places?

PART 2

Days 1–5

▶ **Main Selection**
Extreme Earth, by Beth Geiger

▶ **Genre**
Social Studies Article

▶ **Selection Summary**
This article discusses the "extreme" places on Earth—the tallest, hottest, and coldest of places, for example. Included in the article are the Great Barrier Reef, Mt. Everest, the Sahara, the Amazon River, Antarctica, Angel Falls, the Grand Canyon, and Lechuguilla Cave. Sidebars contain helpful diagrams and photographs.

Selection CD 1 (((MP3)))

Skills at a Glance	
Language	Describe Places; Make and Respond to Requests; Oral Language Project
Grammar	Irregular Plurals: Count/Noncount; Capitalization of Proper Nouns
Vocabulary	Social Studies Vocabulary: *canyon, elevation, landform, ocean, plain, plateau, valley*
	Academic Vocabulary: *feature, locate, physical, region, surface*
	Compound Words
Reading Strategy	Visualize
Literary Analysis	Main Idea and Details
Writing	Writing Fluency; Research Report; Draft; Experiences; Edit and Proofread; Description; Journal Entry
Newcomer Support	Use *In the USA:* seasons, months, and activities words

Days 6–10

▶ **Companion Selection**
Photographing the World, by Kristin Cozort

▶ **Genre**
Profile

▶ **Selection Summary**
Jimmy Chin is an extreme photographer and mountain climber who travels the world taking pictures of nature. His pictures are often shot in dangerous places, such as from mountaintops. By putting himself in dangerous situations, he is able to take pictures of things that might not otherwise get photographed.

Connect Across Texts Would you like to visit amazing places? Find out about a person who photographs amazing places.

Genre A **profile** briefly describes a person. It tells what the person does and cares about.

NATIONAL
GEOGRAPHIC
EXCLUSIVE

Photographing the
WORLD
by KRISTIN COZORT

▲ Jimmy Chin

GROWING UP in the **flatlands** of southern Minnesota, Jimmy Chin dreamed of places with high, snowy mountains and tall rock towers.

He was 12 when he first **fell in love with** the outdoors. Chin explains that after a family trip to Glacier National Park, "I was changed forever. Spending time in the mountains and rock climbing became **my passions**."

In Other Words
flatlands plains
fell in love with began to like
my passions the things I liked the most

▶ **Before You Move On**
1. **Make Connections** Picture the place where Jimmy Chin grew up. Now picture the mountains. Which do you prefer? Why?
2. **Analyze** How did a trip to Glacier National Park change Chin? How do you know?

199

Leveled Library Books

Differentiated Instruction

B BEGINNING

In the Dark Cave

by Richard Watson

Some animals are adapted to living in darkness. Alexander encounters some of these during a visit to a cave.

Places to Visit

by Nick Bruce

Learn more about some of America's beautiful natural landmarks. Maps help to geographically orient students.

I INTERMEDIATE

My Little Island

by Frane Lessac

Two boys visit the Caribbean island where one of them was born. Students learn about the island's culture along with them.

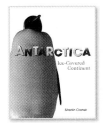

Antarcticca: Ice-Covered Continent

by Sherilin Chanek

Learn more about the coldest continent on Earth—Antarctica, a land of ice and wind.

A ADVANCED   AH ADVANCED HIGH

Antarctic Adventure

by Rebecca L. Johnson

In this chapter book, four interns travel to icy Antarctica to study Adelie penguins. While they're there, they learn all about the world's coldest continent.

Matthew Henson

by Maryann N. Weidt

In this chapter book, students read about Matthew Henson, an African-American explorer and one of the first people to reach the North Pole.

BIG Question Why learn about other places?

PART 2

Core Lessons

	Day 1	Day 2
	Introduce Academic Language	**Introduce More Academic Language**
Language 5–10 minutes	**Language of the Day** *T174* ❶ **Language Function: Describe Places** *T174* 🔊 ((MP3)) **Oral Language** • Talk About Landforms *T175* • Talk Together About the Big Question *T175*	**Language of the Day** *T177a* ❶ **Grammar: Irregular Plurals: Count/Noncount** *T177a* **Oral Language** • Talk Together About Visualizing *T178*

Vocabulary 10–15 minutes	❶ **Social Studies Vocabulary**
	 • Introduce Words *T175*
	    canyon ocean valley
	    elevation plain
	    landform plateau
	 Classroom Vocabulary
	 • Introduce Words: **outline** *T176*
		❶ **Academic Vocabulary**
		 • Introduce Words *T177*
		    feature region
		    locate surface
		    physical
		 Classroom Vocabulary
		 • Introduce Words: **describe** *T179*

Reading 15–20 minutes	❶ **Text Structure: Main Idea and Details** • Introduce Main Idea and Details *T176a* • Use Graphic Organizers: Description Chart *T176* **Read Aloud: "Ethan's Story"** *T176a*	❶ **Strategy: Visualize** • Introduce and Practice the Strategy *T178* **Read "My Trip Down"** *T179* **Phonics and Fluency** • Long *a, i, o, u* in VCe Form; Words with Long and Short Vowel Sounds *T178*
Writing 15 minutes	**Daily Writing** • Writing Fluency *T176*	
Content: Integrated Throughout Each Day	**Social Studies** • Explore Landforms • Investigate Landmarks	**Social Studies** • Explore Landforms • Investigate Landmarks

Ready-to-Go Plans
► Time (20, 30, 40, 60, 90 minutes per day)
► Model (Content Focus, Literacy Focus, Dual Language)

Online Lesson Planner
NGReach.com

Day 3

Build Academic Language

Language of the Day *T180a*
Language Function: Make and Respond to Requests *T180a* ((MP3))
Listening and Speaking
• Listen to and Sing a Song *T180a*

❶ Academic and Social Studies Vocabulary
• Expand Word Knowledge *T180b*

canyon   feature

elevation   landform

Support Newcomers
• Build Basic Vocabulary: Seasons, Months, and Activities Words *T180b*

Read the Selection
❶ Strategy: Visualize
T180—T194–195
• Reading Options *T182*
Concepts of Print
• Capitalization *T183*
Literary Analysis
• Social Studies Article *T188–189*
❶ Fluency: Phrasing *T192–193*

Home Connection
• Family Trips *T184–185*
Social Studies
• Geography *T186–187*
Math
• Make a Graph *T190–191*
Geography
• Research *T194–195*

Day 4

Build Academic Language

Language of the Day *T196a*
❶ Grammar: Capitalization of Proper Nouns *T196a*
Oral Language
• Talk About the Selection *T196c*

❶ Academic and Social Studies Vocabulary
• Share Word Knowledge *T196b*

locate   physical   plateau

ocean   plain   region

Think and Respond
• Talk About the Selection *T196c*
• Test-Taking Strategy *T196c*
❶ Fluency: Phrasing *T196c*

Daily Writing
• Independent Writing: Write About It *T196*

Social Studies
• Explore Landforms
• Investigate Landmarks

Day 5

Build Academic Language

Language of the Day *T197a*
Listening and Speaking
• Adjust Speech for Purpose *T197a*
How to Learn Language
• Analyze Expressions *T197a*
Oral Language
• Talk Together About the Big Question *T197*

❶ Academic and Social Studies Vocabulary
• Apply Word Knowledge *T197b*

surface

valley

Reread and Summarize
❶ Text Structure: Main Idea and Details
• Make an Outline *T197c*
Retell a Story *T197c*
❶ Fluency: Accuracy, Rate, and Phrasing *T197c*

Social Studies
• Explore Landforms
• Investigate Landmarks

PART 2

Core Lessons	Day 6	Day 7
	Expand Academic Language	Expand Academic Language
Language 🕐 5–10 minutes	**Language of the Day** *T198a* ❶ **Language Function: Describe Places** *T198a* **Oral Language** • Talk Together About the Big Question *T204a*	**Language of the Day** *T205a* ❶ **Grammar: More Plural Nouns** *T205a*
Vocabulary 🕐 10–15 minutes	❶ **Compound Words** **T198** **Support Newcomers:** • Additional Compound Words *T198*	❶ **More Compound Words** *T205*
Reading 🕐 15–20 minutes	**Read the Profile** *T199a* • Reading Options *T199a* ❶ **Strategy: Visualize** *T199a—T202–203* **Concepts of Print** • Identify Letters and Identify a Word *T199* **Text Features** • Captions *T200–201* **Fluency: Accuracy and Rate** *T204* **Respond and Extend** • Compare Text Features *T204a*	**Reread the Selection: Focus on Genre: Profile** *T206a*
Writing 🕐 15 minutes	**Daily Writing** • Writing Fluency *T204*	**Daily Writing** • Modeled Writing: Description *T206b*
Content: Integrated Throughout Each Day	**Social Studies** • Explore Landforms • Investigate Landmarks	**Social Studies** • Explore Landforms • Investigate Landmarks

Days 8–9

Apply Academic Language

Oral Language Project
- Introduce the Activity *T206c*
- Plan *T206c*
- Practice *T206d*
- Explore the World! *T206d*
- Debrief and Compare *T206d*

Read Leveled Books

Fiction *T174m*

 B

 **I**

 **A** **AH**

Key Words

creatures	depths
cricket	shaft
darkness	

Key Words

dozens	square
folktales	volcano
gobble	

Key Words

icebergs	scientists
penguin	survival
predators	

Nonfiction *T174n*

 B

 **I**

 **A** **AH**

Key Words

areas	national
canyon	volcano
marsh	

Key Words

coldest	icebergs
continent	penguin
explored	

Key Words

adventure	journey
expedition	servant
friendships	

Daily Writing
- Journal Entry *T206f*

Day 10

Review and Assess

Interactive Review *T206g–T206h*
- 🔆 Language Function: Describe Places
- 🔆 Grammar: Irregular Plurals
- 🔆 Vocabulary: Social Studies and Academic Vocabulary
- 🔆 Vocabulary Strategy: Compound Words
- 🔆 Reading Strategy: Visualize
- 🔆 Literary Analysis: Main Idea and Details
- 🔆 Text Structure: Description
- 🔆 Fluency: Phrasing

Assessment *T206g–T06h*

Same Book, Different Levels

 I **A** **AH**

Key Words

avalanche	guide	Sherpa
dangerous	migrated	skills
expeditions	scale	summit

Reading Station

EXPLORER! COLLECTION
Ladder Text:
- Pioneer edition for below level readers
- Pathfinder edition for on and above level readers

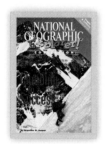 

DECODABLE TEXTS

TRADE BOOK COLLECTION
Use the **Leveled Book Finder** at
⊙ NGReach.com

Content Stations

Download complete lesson plans ⊙ **NGReach.com** >

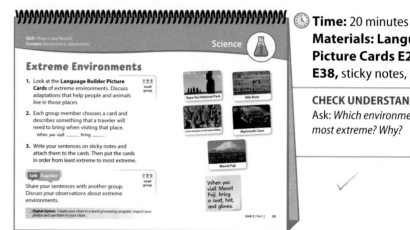

Skill: Observe and Record
Content: Environments, Adaptations

Science

Extreme Environments
1. Look at the **Language Builder Picture Cards** of extreme environments. Discuss adaptations that help people and animals live in those places. ★★★ small group
2. Each group member chooses a card and describes something that a traveler will need to bring when visiting that place.
   When you visit _____ bring _____.
3. Write your sentences on sticky notes and attach them to the cards. Then put the cards in order from least extreme to most extreme.

Talk Together ★★★ small group
Share your sentences with another group. Discuss your observations about extreme environments.

◻ **Digital Option** Create your chart in a word-processing program. Import your photos and use them in your chart.

Unit 3 | Part 2   **20**

🕐 **Time:** 20 minutes
Materials: Language Builder Picture Cards E27, E28, E31, E35, E38, sticky notes, pencils

CHECK UNDERSTANDING
Ask: *Which environment do you think is the most extreme? Why?*

✓

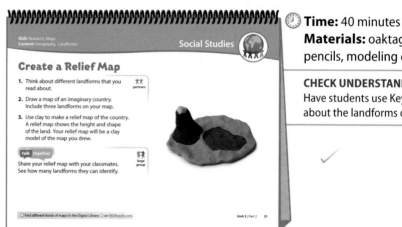

Skill: Research, Maps
Content: Geography, Landforms

Social Studies

Create a Relief Map
1. Think about different landforms that you read about. ★★ partners
2. Draw a map of an imaginary country. Include three landforms on your map.
3. Use clay to make a relief map of the country. A relief map shows the height and shape of the land. Your relief map will be a clay model of the map you drew.

Talk Together large group
Share your relief map with your classmates. See how many landforms they can identify.

◻ Find different kinds of maps in the Digital Library ⊙ on NGReach.com.

Unit 3 | Part 2   **21**

🕐 **Time:** 40 minutes
Materials: oaktag or cardboard, pencils, modeling clay

CHECK UNDERSTANDING
Have students use Key Words to talk about the landforms on their relief maps.

✓

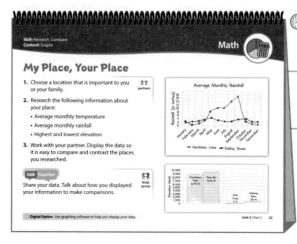

Skill: Research, Compare
Content: Graphs

Math

My Place, Your Place
1. Choose a location that is important to you or your family. ★★ partners
2. Research the following information about your place:
   - Average monthly temperature
   - Average monthly rainfall
   - Highest and lowest elevation
3. Work with your partner. Display the data so it is easy to compare and contrast the places you researched.

Average Monthly Rainfall

Talk Together large group
Share your data. Talk about how you displayed your information to make comparisons.

◻ **Digital Option** Use graphing software to help you display your data.

Unit 3 | Part 2   **22**

🕐 **Time:** 40 minutes
Materials: research resources, paper, pencils, colored markers and crayons

CHECK UNDERSTANDING
Ask: *What is the highest elevation in the place you chose?*

✓

Use these resources to provide daily opportunities for students to work individually or in groups at learning stations around the classroom.

Language Stations

Download complete lesson plans **NGReach.com**

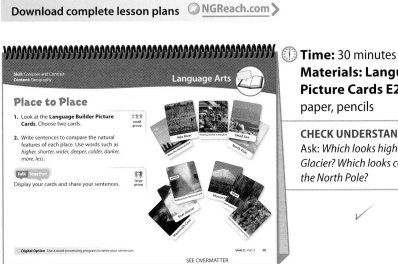

Time: 30 minutes
Materials: Language Builder Picture Cards E27–E39, paper, pencils

CHECK UNDERSTANDING
Ask: *Which looks higher, Mt. Fuji or Bear Glacier? Which looks colder, Madagascar or the North Pole?*

Time: 30 minutes
Materials: Language Builder Picture Cards E27–E39, lined index cards, pencils

CHECK UNDERSTANDING
Ask questions using superlatives, such as: *What is the coldest place you've been? What is the highest mountain you've climbed?*

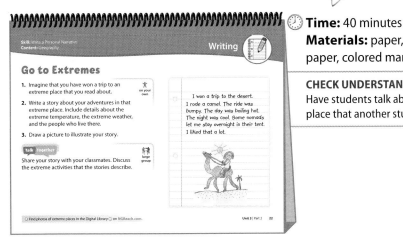

Time: 40 minutes
Materials: paper, pencils, drawing paper, colored markers and crayons

CHECK UNDERSTANDING
Have students talk about an extreme place that another student wrote about.

Technology Station

Access resources **NGReach.com**

 **Recordings**

- My Travels
- Please Tell Me
- Extreme Earth

 **Digital Library**

Learn vocabulary and practice language

- Key Word Images
- Language Builder Picture Cards

 **My Vocab Notebook**

- Add Words

 **Comprehension Coach**

- Use interactive library support. Automatically measure fluency.

Online Assessment

- Practice items in standardized test format.

Day at a Glance:
- ▶ **Language:** Describe Places
- ▶ **Vocabulary:** Social Studies Vocabulary
- ▶ **Reading:** Main Idea and Details
- ▶ **Writing:** Writing Fluency; Study a Model

OBJECTIVES

Vocabulary
- Acquire and Use Grade-Level Vocabulary ⊙

Language
- Language Function: Describe Places ⊙
- Listen to and Imitate Fluent Models
- Use a Variety of Language Structures
- Participate in Discussion

Learning and Teamwork Strategies
- Activate Prior Knowledge
- Use Media to Build Language
- Use Context to Build Concepts and Language

Social Studies
- Investigate Landforms
- Explore Well-Known Landmarks

Resources

- 📘 🔵 *Sing With Me Language Song Book 14*
- 🔵 🔵 *Sing With Me Language Song CD 2 Tr 5,6*
- 🔵 *eVisuals 3.19*
- • *eVisual 3.20*
- 🔵 *Key Word Images*
- 📄 *Language Builder E30*

🌐 **NGReach.com** ›

See **Technology Station** for digital student resources.

Differentiate

Academic Language Frames

Describe Places

- ■ I went to _____ .
  The _____ has _____ .
  This _____ is _____ .

_____

- ■ I went to _____ .
  The _____ has _____ .
  This _____ is _____ .

_____

- ■ I went to _____ .
- ■ The _____ has _____ .
  It is/They are _____ .
  It feels/They feel _____ .

🌐 **NGReach.com** › eVisual 3.20

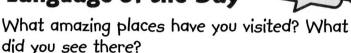

Language of the Day

What amazing places have you visited? What did you see there?

I went to _____ . I saw. _____ .

Read the Language of the Day. Model: *I went to New York City. I saw the Empire State Building.* Invite students to tell about memorable places they have visited and what they saw there. Tell students they will learn how to describe these places in more detail.

Describe Places

❶ Teach/Model Display "My Travels." Read the introduction aloud and play the song. Invite students to sing along as you play the song a second time. Model how to echo and chime in as the audio prompts.

Point out the **Language Frames** and model using these structures to describe the Great Wall.

How to Describe Places	
1. Tell about a place you know.	I went to the Great Wall of China. This place is amazing.
2. Name one of its features.	The wall has many towers.
3. Give details about that feature.	The towers are twenty feet tall. They are made out of stone. The stone is very beautiful. It feels hard and rough.

🌐 NGReach.com › eVisual 3.19

Prompt one or two students to share information about places they know. Point to each step on the How to card as the students give information. To prompt more detail say: *Tell me more.*

❷ Practice/Apply Have students draw a picture of a place they have visited. Encourage them to list words that help describe the place. Then have students share a description of the place. Use **Academic Language Frames** to encourage students to use language naturally to describe the places they have chosen.

CHECK UNDERSTANDING Display **Language Builder Card E30** (Royal Gorge Bridge, Arkansas River) and have students describe it.

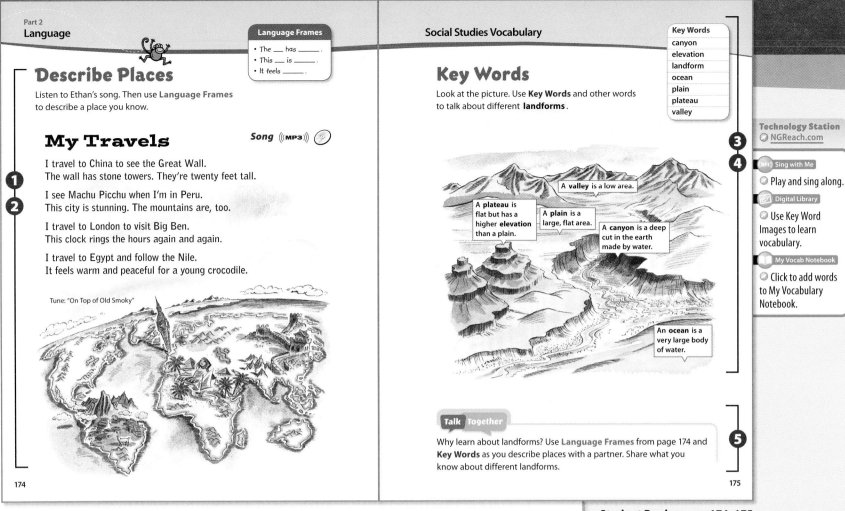

Language Frames
- The ___ has ___.
- This ___ is ___.
- It feels ___.

Describe Places

Listen to Ethan's song. Then use **Language Frames** to describe a place you know.

My Travels

Song ((MP3))

I travel to China to see the Great Wall.
The wall has stone towers. They're twenty feet tall.

I see Machu Picchu when I'm in Peru.
This city is stunning. The mountains are, too.

I travel to London to visit Big Ben.
This clock rings the hours again and again.

I travel to Egypt and follow the Nile.
It feels warm and peaceful for a young crocodile.

Tune: "On Top of Old Smoky"

174

Social Studies Vocabulary

Key Words
canyon
elevation
landform
ocean
plain
plateau
valley

Key Words

Look at the picture. Use **Key Words** and other words to talk about different **landforms**.

A **valley** is a low area.

A **plateau** is flat but has a higher **elevation** than a plain.

A **plain** is a large, flat area.

A **canyon** is a deep cut in the earth made by water.

An **ocean** is a very large body of water.

Talk Together

Why learn about landforms? Use **Language Frames** from page 174 and **Key Words** as you describe places with a partner. Share what you know about different landforms.

175

Technology Station
○ NGReach.com

(MP3) Sing with Me
○ Play and sing along.

Digital Library
○ Use Key Word Images to learn vocabulary.

My Vocab Notebook
○ Click to add words to My Vocabulary Notebook.

Student Book pages 174–175

Social Studies Vocabulary

3 **Teach/Model** Read the introduction and work through the diagram. Use **Vocabulary Routine 1** and **Key Word Images** to teach the words. Access definitions on pages 616–639.

1. **Pronounce** the word and point to its picture: **plain**.

2. **Rate** the word. Have students hold up their fingers to show how well they know the word. (1 = very well, 2 = a little, 3 = not at all) Ask: *What do you know about this word?*

3. **Define** the word: *A plain is a large, flat area of land.*

4. **Elaborate** Relate the word to your experience: *One time I walked across a plain. It was covered with tall grass.*

4 **Practice/Apply** Have partners take turns repeating the routine for each word, using complete sentences for steps 2, 3, and 4.

5 **Talk Together About the Big Question**
Check Understanding and Connect Concepts Review the **Language Frames** on page and provide an example:

> *I went to the Grand Canyon last year. This place is beautiful. The* **canyon** *has steep walls. The walls have red dirt. The dirt is like sand. It feels hard and grainy.*

Add the ideas to your unit concept map.

Differentiate

Spanish Cognates ▶

canyon/cañón; elevation/ elevación; ocean/océano valley/valle

Part 2 Vocabulary Skills Trace		Page
Day 1	Social Studies Vocabulary	T175
Day 2	Academic Vocabulary	T177
Day 3	Expand Word Knowledge	T180b
Day 4	Share Word Knowledge	T196b
Day 5	Apply Word Knowledge	T197b
Day 6	Compound Words	T198
Day 7	Compound Words	T205
Days 8–9	Extend Vocabulary	T206e–f
Day 10	Vocabulary Review	T206g–h

Day 1
continued

OBJECTIVES

Vocabulary
• Acquire and Use Classroom Vocabulary
• Use Grade-Level Vocabulary ⊙

Comprehension and Literary Analysis
• Identify Main Idea and Details
• Demonstrate Listening Comprehension
• Describe Places

Listening and Speaking
• Listen for Important Details

Learning and Teamwork Strategies
• Use Graphic Organizers: Main Idea and Details
• Reason Deductively

Writing
• Develop Writing Fluency
• Monitor and Self-Correct Writing

Social Studies
• Investigate Landforms
• Explore Well-Known Landmarks

Resources

⊘ eVisual 3.21

• eVisual 3.22

✂⊘ Practice Master 3.11

Differentiate

Multi-Level Strategies

BEGINNING

Have students write each main idea. Ask them to point to the illustration and identify a supporting detail about what Ethan saw in each place.

INTERMEDIATE

Have students write each main idea. Ask questions to help them identify supporting details, e.g., What is Big Ben? What does it do?

ADVANCED   ADVANCED HIGH

Encourage students to give specific details about each place and to write complete sentences.

Main Idea and Details

1 Teach Connect concepts: *The Key Words you learned give you* information about **landforms**. *You can use these words to describe details about different places. Now you will learn to make an outline that will help you organize information about places.* Teach Classroom Vocabulary word *outline.*

Read the first paragraph. Have students look at the photographs as volunteers read the captions. *Where have you heard of these places before?* Reread the song on page 174.

Read aloud how to make an outline. Clarify the purpose: *I can make an outline to help me identify main ideas and details.* Ask students to point to each photo as you read "Ethan's Story." Remind them to listen for words that describe the different places.

> **Read Aloud**
>
> ### Ethan's Story
>
> Ethan likes to travel to faraway places. What has he learned about these places? He went to China and saw the Great Wall. This long wall has stone towers that are twenty feet tall. He also went to Peru and visited Machu Picchu. It is an old city that sits high on a mountain. It was built long ago by the Incas.
>
> ⊘ NGReach.com ▶ eVisual 3.21

2 Model Review the first three sentences in Ethan's Story. Have a volunteer point to the first line on the outline. Model the process: *I write a Roman numeral 1 and then a sentence that tells where Ethan went first.* Ask students which country Ethan visited first. *Then I write two details about the place that Ethan visited.* Have volunteers read the details and then repeat the process for the rest of the outline.

3 Practice/Apply Read aloud the instructions. Distribute **Practice Master 3.11** for students to complete their outlines. Use **Multi-Level Strategies** to help students at all proficiency levels outline the main ideas and details of Ethan's travels on page 174. Monitor students' developing proficiency.

> **CHECK UNDERSTANDING** *What was the second place that Ethan visited? What are two details that describe that place?*

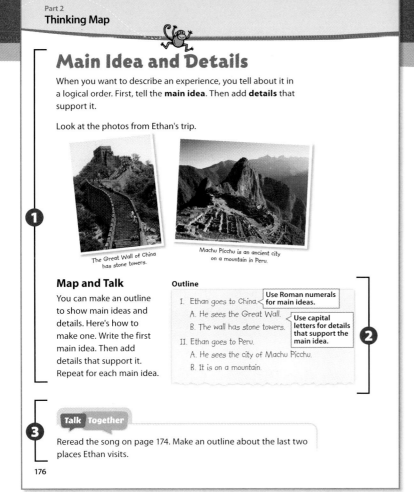

Main Idea and Details

When you want to describe an experience, you tell about it in a logical order. First, tell the **main idea**. Then add **details** that support it.

Look at the photos from Ethan's trip.

The Great Wall of China has stone towers.

Machu Picchu is an ancient city on a mountain in Peru.

❶

Map and Talk

You can make an outline to show main ideas and details. Here's how to make one. Write the first main idea. Then add details that support it. Repeat for each main idea.

Outline

I. Ethan goes to China.　◄ Use Roman numerals for main ideas.

  A. He sees the Great Wall.

  B. The wall has stone towers.

II. Ethan goes to Peru.

  A. He sees the city of Machu Picchu.

  B. It is on a mountain.

Use capital letters for details that support the main idea.

❷

❸

Talk Together

Reread the song on page 174. Make an outline about the last two places Ethan visits.

176

Student Book page 176

Daily Writing

❹ Writing Fluency Use the **Power Writing** routine. (see page PD53). Write the word **plain** and prompt: *What kind of landform is a plain? Think about this word and write about it.*

Power Writing Routine

1. What do you know about the word or picture?

2. Take one minute to write as much as you can, as well as you can.
　B words　　**I** sentences　　**A** **AH** paragraphs

3. Check your spelling and grammar. (Circle) mistakes.

4. Count your words.

NGReach.com eVisual 3.22

❺ Study a Model Research Report Have students review a model of the writing form for their Writing Projects. See pages T206–T207.

CLOSE AND ASSESS

- **Language** *Describe one of the places in Ethan's song.* (Students should use information from the song in their answers.)
- **Reading** *What are two details that tell about the Great Wall of China?*
- **Vocabulary** *Choose one kind of landform and use it to describe a place you know.*

Use **Vocabulary Routine 4** to teach **outline**. (See **Vocabulary Routines, PD40**.

Fold-Up Tab

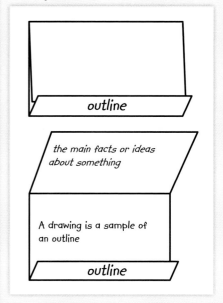

outline

the main facts or ideas about something

A drawing is a sample of an outline

outline

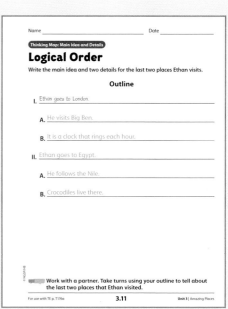

Name _____　　Date _____

Thinking Map: Main Idea and Details

Logical Order

Write the main idea and two details for the last two places Ethan visits.

Outline

I. Ethan goes to London.

  A. He visits Big Ben.

  B. It is a clock that rings each hour.

II. Ethan goes to Egypt.

  A. He follows the Nile.

  B. Crocodiles live there.

Work with a partner. Take turns using your outline to tell about the last two places that Ethan visited.

For use with TE p. T176a　　**3.11**　　Unit 3 | Amazing Places

Practice Master 3.11

Day 2

Day at a Glance:
- ▶ **Language:** Irregular Plural Nouns
- ▶ **Vocabulary:** Academic Vocabulary
- ▶ **Reading:** Visualize
- ▶ **Writing:** Prewrite: Research Report

OBJECTIVES

Vocabulary
- Acquire and Use Academic Vocabulary ⊙
- Use Grade-Level Vocabulary

Grammar
- Irregular Plural Nouns ⊙

Learning and Teamwork Strategies
- Make Connections Across Content Areas

Resources

- ⊙ eVisual 3.23
- ⊙ Practice Master 3.12
- ⊙ Key Word Images

⊙ NGReach.com ❯

See **Technology Station** for digital student resources.

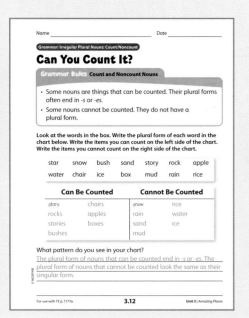

⟲ ⊙ **Practice Master 3.12**

Part 2 Grammar Skills Trace		Page
▶ **Day 2**	**Irregular Plural Nouns: Count/Noncount**	**T177a**
Day 4	Proper Nouns	T196a
Day 7	More Plural Nouns: Irregular	T205a
Day 10	Review Plural Nouns	T206g

T177a Unit 3 | Amazing Places

Language of the Day

Name a place in nature and the things you can see there.

In a _____ you can *see* _____ .

Read the Language of the Day. Model: *In a desert you can see sand and lizards.* Invite students to take turns sharing their own ideas. Note: If students name a **location** that does not fit the language pattern, model the correct usage; for example: *At the* **ocean** *you can see seashells and waves.*

Grammar Irregular Plurals: Count/Noncount B I A AH

① **Teach/Model** Write these sentences and read them aloud.

- *The climbers looked up at the mountains.*
- *Their peaks were covered in snow and ice.*

Have students underline the plural nouns. (climbers, mountains, peaks) Then ask: *Are the nouns* snow *and* ice *plural?* Allow time for partners to discuss answers and offer ideas. Then ask: *Can we count the snow?* (no) Explain: *Some nouns cannot be counted. They have only one form for both "one" and "more than one."* Say: *If I had a strong microscope, I could count snowflakes, but I can't count the snow or ice on the mountains.*

Display the chart. Have volunteers name categories and read the examples.

Nouns That Cannot Be Counted	
Weather Words	snow, ice, thunder, fog
Food	bread, corn, sugar, rice
Ideas and Feelings	fun, health, work, luck
Materials	metal, wood
Activities and Sports	dancing, football, swimming

⊙ NGReach.com ❯ eVisual 3.23

② **Practice/Apply** Have partners begin a t-chart of count and noncount nouns in their journals. Assign **Practice Master 3.12**. Challenge them to add to the chart as they read "Extreme Earth." (Noncount nouns in the article include: sunlight, rain, shade, fur, heat, sand, water, and mist.)

CHECK UNDERSTANDING Write: *Lakes are large bodies of water.* Ask: *Which nouns in the sentence can be counted?* (lakes, bodies) *Which cannot be counted?* (water)

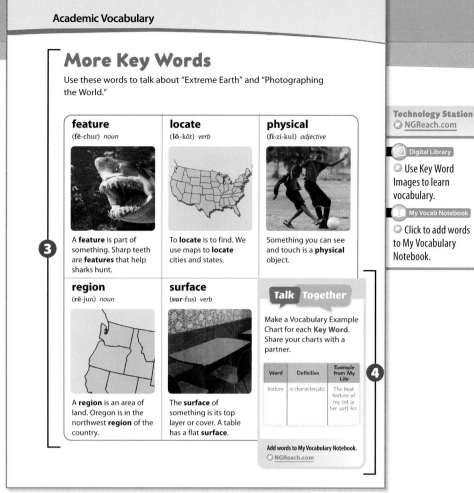

More Key Words

Use these words to talk about "Extreme Earth" and "Photographing the World."

feature
(fē-chur) *noun*

A **feature** is part of something. Sharp teeth are **features** that help sharks hunt.

locate
(lō-kāt) *verb*

To **locate** is to find. We use maps to **locate** cities and states.

physical
(fi-zi-kul) *adjective*

Something you can see and touch is a **physical** object.

region
(rē-jun) *noun*

A **region** is an area of land. Oregon is in the northwest **region** of the country.

surface
(sur-fus) *verb*

The **surface** of something is its top layer or cover. A table has a flat **surface**.

Technology Station
○ NGReach.com

▣ Digital Library
○ Use Key Word Images to learn vocabulary.

■ My Vocab Notebook
○ Click to add words to My Vocabulary Notebook.

Talk Together

Make a Vocabulary Example Chart for each **Key Word**. Share your charts with a partner.

Word	Definition	Example from My Life
feature	a characteristic	The best feature of my cat is her soft fur.

Add words to My Vocabulary Notebook.
○ NGReach.com

Student Book page 177

Academic Vocabulary

3 **Teach/Model** Invite students to discuss each photograph on the page. Read the directions aloud and use **Vocabulary Routine 1** and **Key Word Images** to teach the words.

1. **Pronounce** the word and point to its picture: **feature**.

2. **Rate** the word. Have students hold up their fingers to show how well they know the word. (1 = very well, 2 = a little, 3 = not at all) Ask: *What do you know about this word?*

3. **Define** the word: *A feature is a characteristic of something.*

4. **Elaborate** Relate the word to your experience; for example: *My house has lots of nice features. The windows are the best feature of all. They are big and they let in lots of light.*

4 **Practice/Apply** Use the ratings from step 2 to form pairs. Have partners share their examples with each other.

> **CHECK UNDERSTANDING** Point to the **Key Word Image** of each Key Word and ask students to explain what each word means.

Keys to Efficacy

Connect concepts and Key Words to help activate prior knowledge: *Can you name the features of different* **landforms**?

Differentiate

Spanish Cognates ▶
locate/localizar; physical/físico; region/región; surface/superficie

Part 2 Vocabulary Skills Trace		Page
Day 1	Science Studies Vocabulary	T175
Day 2	**Academic Vocabulary**	**T177**
Day 3	Expand Word Knowledge	T180b
Day 4	Share Word Knowledge	T196b
Day 5	Apply Word Knowledge	T197b
Day 6	Compound Words	T198
Day 7	Compound Words	T205
Days 8–9	Extend Vocabulary	T206e–f
Day 10	Vocabulary Review	T206g–h

Day 2
continued

OBJECTIVES
Vocabulary
• Use Academic Vocabulary ❶
• Use Grade-Level Vocabulary ❶
• Acquire and Use Classroom Vocabulary
Learning to Read
• Words with Long *a, i, e, o, u* in *VCe* Form
• Words with Long and Short Vowel Sounds
Reading Strategy
• Learn to Visualize ❶
Learning and Teamwork Strategies
• Use Personal Experience
• Use Visuals
Writing
• Research report
Social Studies
• Explore Landforms
• Investigate Geography

Resources
   ◎ *eVisual 3.24*
   ✎◎ *Reach Into Phonics TE pages T68,*
       T70, T72

Visualize

❶ Teach Read aloud the introduction. Ask students to picture themselves in Ethan's place. Discuss how they can make a mental picture of this. Make the connection: *When you form a picture in your mind of something, you visualize. You can use these mental pictures to understand what something is like or how someone feels.* Then teach the Classroom Vocabulary word *describe*.

❷ Model Read the chart aloud. To model visualizing details, say:

• *I see how big the Grand Canyon is.*
• *I picture myself sitting in Ethan's place and looking at the* **canyon** .
• *I draw a deep canyon with tall sides.*
• *Now, I understand how small Ethan must feel next to this huge canyon.*

❸ Practice/Apply Read the directions aloud. Point out the **Language Frames.** Read aloud Ethan's story and the sample visualization.

Direct attention to the fourth paragraph and use **Academic Language Frames** to help students at each proficiency level. Ask: *What do you picture?* (dirt trail, clouds of dust, no shade) *What would you draw?* Encourage them to identify words that help them to visualize. *What do you understand about the trail?* (It's hot and dusty climbing down this trail.)

> **CHECK UNDERSTANDING** Reread the fifth paragraph. Ask: *What details help you visualize the place?*

Differentiate

Academic Language Frames

Visualize

■ I read _____.
   I picture _____.
   I draw _____.
   Now I understand _____.
   _____
■ I read _____.
   In my mind, I picture _____.
   I draw a picture of _____.
   Now I understand _____.
   ■ The text says _____.
■ In my mind, I visualize _____.
   Now I understand _____.

◎ NGReach.com ▶ **eVisual 3.24**

Phonics and Fluency

Long *a, i, o, u* in *VCe* form;
Words with Long and Short Vowel Sounds

Display the words: *shade, hike, woke, mule.* Note the *VCe* spelling pattern. Explain: *When a word has the vowel-consonant-e pattern, the vowel has a long sound and the e is silent.* Have students read these word pairs and listen for the vowel sounds. Ask them to identify the long vowel spellings: *rip-ripe, tap-tape, cut-cute, hop-hope.* Display **Transparency 38** from **Reach Into Phonics** and work through the lesson.
Practice Display the sentences:
• Ana made a *kite* from a *kit*.
• We *plan* to take a *plane* on our trip.
• I did *not* write the *note*.
Have partners read the sentences chorally several times to develop fluency.

Learn to Visualize

1

Look at the picture. **Visualize** yourself in Ethan's place. What would it be like?

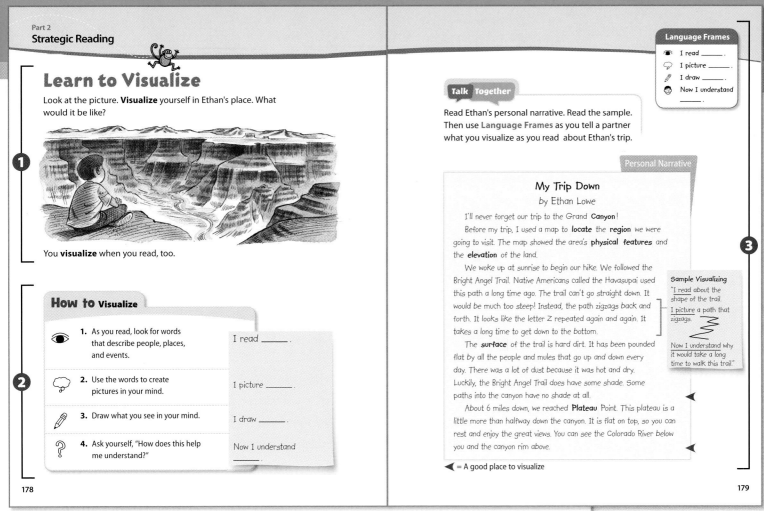

You **visualize** when you read, too.

2

How to Visualize

1. As you read, look for words that describe people, places, and events.

2. Use the words to create pictures in your mind.

3. Draw what you see in your mind.

4. Ask yourself, "How does this help me understand?"

> I read _____ .
>
> I picture _____ .
>
> I draw _____ .
>
> Now I understand _____ .

178

Language Frames

- 👁 I read _____ .
- 💭 I picture _____ .
- ✏ I draw _____ .
- 😊 Now I understand _____ .

Talk Together

Read Ethan's personal narrative. Read the sample. Then use **Language Frames** as you tell a partner what you visualize as you read about Ethan's trip.

3

Personal Narrative

My Trip Down
by Ethan Lowe

I'll never forget our trip to the Grand **Canyon**!

Before my trip, I used a map to **locate** the **region** we were going to visit. The map showed the area's **physical features** and the **elevation** of the land.

We woke up at sunrise to begin our hike. We followed the Bright Angel Trail. Native Americans called the Havasupai used this path a long time ago. The trail can't go straight down. It would be much too steep! Instead, the path zigzags back and forth. It looks like the letter Z repeated again and again. It takes a long time to get down to the bottom.

The **surface** of the trail is hard dirt. It has been pounded flat by all the people and mules that go up and down every day. There was a lot of dust because it was hot and dry. Luckily, the Bright Angel Trail does have some shade. Some paths into the canyon have no shade at all.

About 6 miles down, we reached **Plateau** Point. This plateau is a little more than halfway down the canyon. It is flat on top, so you can rest and enjoy the great views. You can see the Colorado River below you and the canyon rim above.

◄ = A good place to visualize

Sample Visualizing

"I read about the shape of the trail.

I picture a path that zigzags.

Now I understand why it would take a long time to walk this trail."

179

Student Book pages 178–179

Daily Writing

4 **Prewrite: Research Report** Have students plan their Writing Projects. See pages T208a–T210a.

Classroom Vocabulary

Use **Vocabulary Routine 4** to teach the word **describe**.

Wordbench

> describe
> di-<ˈ>skrib
> description
> Meaning: to say what something or someone is like
> Example: Can you describe what the man was wearing?

CLOSE AND ASSESS

- **Language** *Listen to the sentence:* The boys shoveled snow for hours after the storm. *What are the plural nouns in the sentence?* (boys, snow, hours) *Which plural noun cannot be counted?* (snow)

- **Reading** *In his personal narrative, Ethan describes a trail in the Grand Canyon. What details help you visualize the trail?* (zigzags, hard dirt, dusty, no shade)

- **Vocabulary** *What Key Words did you use in your answers?* (Students should use the word *surface* in describing the trail. They may also use the words *canyon, elevation, feature, plateau,* and *physical.*)

Day 3

Day at a Glance:
▶ **Language:** Make and Respond to Requests
▶ **Vocabulary:** Expand Word Knowledge

▶ **Reading:** Read the Selection
▶ **Writing:** Draft a Research Report

OBJECTIVES

Vocabulary
- Use Academic Vocabulary **T**
- Use Grade-Level Vocabulary **T**

Language
- Language Function: Make and Respond to Requests **T**
- Listen to and Imitate Fluent Models
- Use a Variety of Language Structures

Learning and Teamwork Strategies
- Use Media to Build Language
- Use Graphic Organizer: Make a Dictionary Entry Poster

Resources

⊙ ◯ *Sing With Me Language Song CD 2 Tr 7, 8*

◖ ◯ *Sing With Me Language Song Book 15*

⊙ ◯ *eVisual 3.25*

◯ *eVisual 3.26*

• *Chart or poster paper*

◯ NGReach.com ⟩

See **Technology Station** for digital student resources.

Differentiate

Academic Language Frames

Make and Respond to Requests
- ■ Please give me _____.
  Would you help me _____?
  May I see _____?
  _____
- ■ Please tell me _____.
  Would you show me _____?
  May I see _____?
  _____
- ■ Please tell me about _____.
- ■ Would you show me how to _____?
  May I see _____?

◯ NGReach.com ⟩ eVisual 3.26

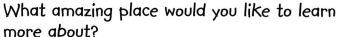

Language of the Day

What amazing place would you like to learn more about?
I would like to learn more about ____.

Read the Language of the Day. Model: *I would like to learn more about the Great Wall of China.* Tell students they will learn how to ask people to tell about places they have visited.

Make and Respond to Requests

1 **Teach** Remind students that they learned how to describe places from "My Travels." Display "My Travels." Then sing the song and invite students to sing along. Introduce: *If you wanted to learn more about Ethan's trip, you could make a request, or ask Ethan to do something.*

Remind students that when they tell someone to do something, they give a command. When they make a request, they politely ask somebody to do something. Activate prior knowledge: *What words might you use to make a request, or ask someone to do something?* Confirm: *The words* May I, Would you, *and* Please *often begin a request.*

Making a Request		
Would you...	**May I...**	**Please...**
Would you show me the pictures from your trip?	May I see the pictures from your trip?	Please show me the pictures from your trip.

◯ NGReach.com ⟩ eVisual 3.25

2 **Model** Making a request: *Would you help me put away these books?* Invite students to make a request using the words *Would you.*

3 **Practice/Apply** Have partners work together to make and respond to requests in the classroom. Use **Academic Language Frames** to encourage students to use language naturally.

> **CHECK UNDERSTANDING** Point to a book on a table and tell one student to request that another student give it to him or her. Allow time for the second student to respond to the request.

Please Tell Me

You traveled to China and saw the Great Wall.
Please show me your photos. I'll look at them all.

You saw Machu Picchu while touring Peru.
Please tell me some stories. Be sure they are true.

When you were in London you went to Big Ben.
Please sing me the song that those bells ring again.

You traveled to Egypt and followed the Nile.
Please answer my question: Do crocodiles smile?

I'll show you my photos and then you can guess.
Do crocodiles smile? My answer is Yes!

Technology Station
⊘ NGReach.com

▸ (MP3) Sing with Me
⊘ Play and sing along.

Tune: "On Top of Old Smokey" | MP3 or Song CD 2 Tracks 7–8 | *Song* | 15

Sing With Me Language Songbook page 15

Expand Word Knowledge

❹ Teach/Model Explain that each student pair will become Key Word experts. They will study one Key Word and create a Make a 4-Corner poster about that word. Use **Vocabulary Routine 2** and model making a dictionary entry about the word *landform*. (See **Vocabulary Routines**, page PD38.)

- Write the word.
- Add the part of speech.
- Add a definition.
- Add a context sentence.

landform	noun
a natural feature of the Earth's surface	You can see the landform as you drive over the hill.

Make a 4-Corner Poster

❺ Practice/Apply Assign a Key Word to each pair of students. Have each pair create a poster for their assigned Key Words. Display the posters on the class word wall.

> **CHECK UNDERSTANDING** Say a Key Word and have the partner experts read the word and definition and sentence from their 4-Corner posters.

Key Words

canyon	physical
elevation	plain
feature	plateau
landform	region
locate	surface
ocean	valley

Differentiate

Newcomer Support
Newcomers can make dictionary entries using words from **Newcomer** picture cards 263–270.

winter   fall   rake leaves

Part 2 Vocabulary Skills Trace		Page
Day 1	Social Studies Vocabulary	T175
Day 2	Academic Vocabulary	T177
Day 3	**Expand Word Knowledge**	**T180b**
Day 4	Share Word Knowledge	T196b
Day 5	Apply Word Knowledge	T197b
Day 6	Compound Words	T198
Day 7	More Compound Words	T205
Days 8–9	Extend Vocabulary	T206e–f
Day 10	Vocabulary Review	T206g–h

Day 3
continued

Day at a Glance:
▶ **Language:** Make and Respond to Requests
▶ **Vocabulary:** Expand Word Knowledge
▶ **Reading:** Read the Selection
▶ **Writing:** Draft a Research Report

OBJECTIVES

Vocabulary
• Use Academic Vocabulary 🅣
• Use Grade-Level Vocabulary 🅣

Reading Strategy
• Plan: Preview

Comprehension and Literary Analysis
• Use Text Features: Graphs and Diagrams
• Analyze Genre: Social Studies Article

Learning and Teamwork Strategies
• Use Prereading Supports
• Build Background Knowledge

Resources

🔘 *Comprehension Coach*

Keys to Efficacy

When students need to be more specific or concentrate on less material, narrow the focus to only one aspect of a topic or one idea.

Preview the Story

1 **Introduce** Tell students to look at the photo on page 181 as you read aloud the title. Have students predict: *What do you think this selection will be about?* Encourage them to think about key words they have already learned as they look at the picture and respond to the question: *What kind of* **landform** *is shown in the picture? What* **features** *does this mountain have?*

2 **Genre and Text Feature** Read aloud the description of a social studies article on page 180. Elaborate: *Social Studies articles tell about real places, people, and events. In this article, we will learn about real places.*

Discuss the text features: graphs and diagrams. Explain: *Graphs and diagrams give information in a visual way.* Ask students to tell how the graph and diagram are alike and different (the diagram is a drawing with labels; the graph includes numbers). Connect to the genre: *As you read, look for graphs and diagrams that provide visual information.*

3 **Preview and Build Background** Use sheltering strategies as you conduct a picture walk.

Pages	Say (and Do)
182–184	*Mount Everest is a mountain in Asia. What can you tell about this* landform *from the pictures? What information does the graph tell you about Mount Everest?*
185–187	*The Sahara is the world's largest desert. What words describe it?* (hot, dry) *Look at the map. Where is the Sahara* **located** *? What do the two graphs show you?* (temperature and rainfall) *The photos on page 186 show some of the animals that live there. Do you know any of these animals? Why do you think the people here live in tents?*
188–189	*A reef is an underwater landform. The reef is built by the tiny animals shown in the photo. What other kinds of marine, or* **ocean***, life do you think live in a coral reef?*
190–191	*The largest river on earth is the Amazon River. How is this river like rivers you have seen? How is it different?*
192–193	*Angel Falls is the tallest waterfall on Earth. It is so tall that most of the water turns to mist before it reaches the ground. Now that's amazing!*
194–195	*Point to the pictures of the* **canyon***. How does a canyon compare to a cave? What do you think is happening in the picture on page 195?*

CHECK UNDERSTANDING Ask: *What kinds of landforms do you learn about in this article?* (a mountain, a desert, a river, a waterfall, a canyon, a cave)

Read a Social Studies Article

Genre
A **social studies article** is nonfiction. It gives facts. Some social studies articles give information about different locations around the world.

Text Features
Look for **graphs** and **diagrams**. They can help you understand the text better.

diagram ▶

Coral Polyp

tentacles (arms)

mouth

outer skeleton

▼ graph

Mountains of the World

Meters above sea level (m)
— 9,000
— 8,000
— 7,000
— 6,000
— 5,000
— 4,000
— 3,000
— 2,000
— 1,000
— 0 (sea level)

Mount Everest 8,850m

Denali 6,194m

Asia

Kilimanjaro 5,895m

Matterhorn 4,478m

North America

Africa

Mount Fuji 3,776m

Europe

Asia

180

Extreme **EARTH**

NATIONAL GEOGRAPHIC

by Beth Geiger

Comprehension Coach

Student Book pages 180–181

Comprehension Coach

Build Reading Power
Assign students to use the software, based on their instructional needs.

Read Silently
- Comprehension questions with immediate feedback
- Vocabulary support

Read Silently

Listen
- Process model of fluent reading
- Text highlighting to facilitate tracking
- Vocabulary support

Listen

Record
- Oral reading fluency practice
- Speech recognition for oral fluency assessment with immediate feedback

Record

Cultural Perpectives: Landforms

Explain that landforms can affect the culture of the people who live on and around them. People who live on mountains have a different kind of life from people who live in deserts. Encourage students to share experiences they have had living in or visiting different places. Ask them to tell how the culture was different from their lives in the United States. Invite students to speculate on how the landforms and features of the place affect the culture of the people who live there.

OBJECTIVES

Vocabulary
- Use Academic Vocabulary ⓣ
- Use Grade-Level Vocabulary ⓣ

Learning to Read
- Phonics: Words with Plurals Formed by Adding -s, or -es
- Concepts of Print: Capitalization

Reading Strategies
- Plan: Set a Purpose, Predict, Confirm Predictions
- Visualize ⓣ

Fluency
- Phrasing ⓣ

Comprehension and Literary Analysis
- Identify Main Idea and Details
- Use Text Features: Graphs and Diagrams
- Analyze Genre: Social Studies Article

Learning and Teamwork Strategies
- Use Reading Supports

Writing
- Connect Reading and Writing
- Draft a Research Report
- Develop Writer's Craft

Resources

◎ ◉ *Read with Me Selection CD*

◐ ◉ *Practice Master 3.13*

◉ *Reach Into Phonics TE page T73*

• Chart or poster paper

ⓃNGReach.com ›

See **Technology Station** for digital student resources.

Key Points Reading

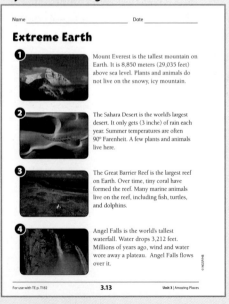

Name _____ Date _____

Extreme Earth

❶ Mount Everest is the tallest mountain on Earth. It is 8,850 meters (29,035 feet) above sea level. Plants and animals do not live on the snowy, icy mountain.

❷ The Sahara Desert is the world's largest desert. It only gets (3 inch) of rain each year. Summer temperatures are often 90° Farenheit. A few plants and animals live here.

❸ The Great Barrier Reef is the largest reef on Earth. Over time, tiny coral have formed the reef. Many marine animals live on the reef, including fish, turtles, and dolphins.

❹ Angel Falls is the world's tallest waterfall. Water drops 3,212 feet. Millions of years ago, wind and water wore away a plateau. Angel Falls flows over it.

For use with TE p. T182   **3.13**   Unit 3 | Amazing Places

◐ ◉ **Practice Master 3.13**

Read the Selection

Suggested Pacing

- Day 3: Read Section 1, pages 182–187
- Day 4: Read Sections 2–3, pages 188–195

Reading Options Scaffold the support for various reading levels.

BELOW LEVEL	ON LEVEL	ABOVE LEVEL
Listen and Read Along	**Read Together**	**Read Independently**
• Have students track the print on the **Key Points Reading** while you read the text aloud. • Use the visuals to support English vocabulary. Say, for example, *Show me where the waterfall turns to mist.* • Check understanding with selected Build Comprehension questions.	• Use section heads to gain an overview of content. • Use Build Comprehension questions to check understanding. • At the end of each section, have students summarize what they learned. • Have students chorally read aloud passages from the selection.	• Have students read each section silently and then discuss the main idea and details with a partner. • Students can discuss the main idea and details as you ask the Build Comprehension questions.

Phonics and Fluency

Words with Plurals Formed by Adding -s or -es

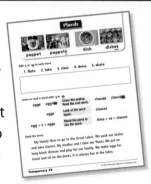

Teach/Model Explain that when students want to talk about more than one thing, they add an -s or an -es to the end of the word. Display the words *sand* and *beach*. Then write the plural of each word: *sands* and *beaches*. Point out that some words only need an -s at the end of the word to make them plural. Other words need an -es to make them plural. Display **Transparency 39** from **Reach Into Phonics** and work through the lesson.

Practice/Apply Display these sentences from "Extreme Earth":

- The hikers can spend weeks trying to reach the top.
- Just eight centimeters (three inches) of rain falls in the Sahara each year…
- Storms here stir up waves as high as a house.

Have partners identify plural nouns in each sentence. Ask them to underline the letters at the end of the word that make the noun plural.

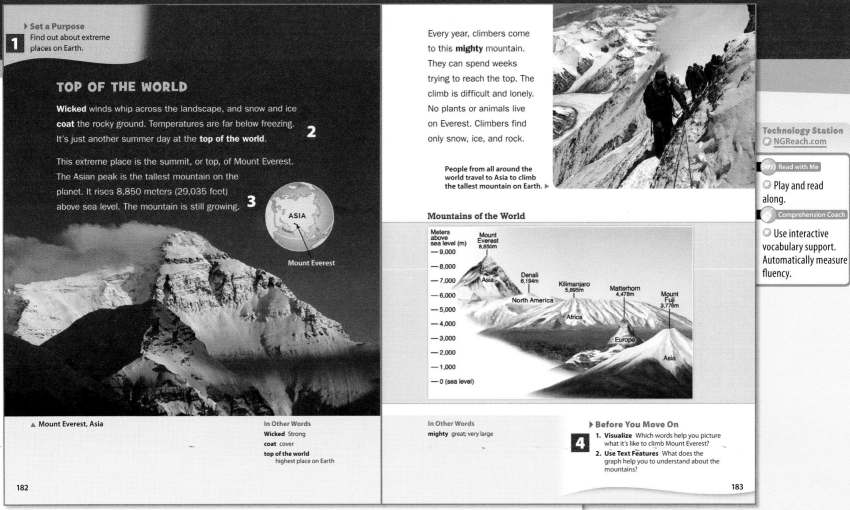

TOP OF THE WORLD

Wicked winds whip across the landscape, and snow and ice **coat** the rocky ground. Temperatures are far below freezing. It's just another summer day at the **top of the world**. **2**

This extreme place is the summit, or top, of Mount Everest. The Asian peak is the tallest mountain on the planet. It rises 8,850 meters (29,035 feet) above sea level. The mountain is still growing. **3**

ASIA

Mount Everest

▲ Mount Everest, Asia

In Other Words
Wicked Strong
coat cover
top of the world highest place on Earth

Every year, climbers come to this **mighty** mountain. They can spend weeks trying to reach the top. The climb is difficult and lonely. No plants or animals live on Everest. Climbers find only snow, ice, and rock.

People from all around the world travel to Asia to climb the tallest mountain on Earth. ▶

Mountains of the World

Meters above sea level (m)
— 9,000
— 8,000
— 7,000
— 6,000
— 5,000
— 4,000
— 3,000
— 2,000
— 1,000
— 0 (sea level)

Mount Everest 8,850m
Asia
Denali 6,194m
North America
Kilimanjaro 5,895m
Africa
Matterhorn 4,478m
Europe
Mount Fuji 3,776m
Asia

In Other Words
mighty great; very large

▶ **Before You Move On**
4
1. **Visualize** Which words help you picture what it's like to climb Mount Everest?
2. **Use Text Features** What does the graph help you to understand about the mountains?

Student Book pages 182–183

Build Comprehension, pages 182–183

1 **Set a Purpose** Read aloud the Set a Purpose at the top of page 182.

2 **Main Idea** MODEL | GUIDE | APPLY What is the main idea for this section? Say: *I read the heading and see a photo of Mount Everest. I read that Mount Everest is the tallest mountain on the planet. I read details that support this idea; Mount Everest is 8,850 meters above sea level. The main idea is that Mount Everest is the highest place in the world.*

3 **Key Words** What is the **elevation** of Mount Everest? (It rises 8,850 meters, or 29,035 feet, above sea level.)

4 **Answers to Before You Move On**

1. Visualize MODEL | GUIDE | APPLY Point out the descriptive words in the first paragraph on page 182. Then use the Language Frames from page 178 to model how to form mental images with these words:

- *I read that the winds are wicked, and snow and ice cover the mountain.*
- *I picture myself hiking in strong, freezing winds and deep snow that make it hard to move. There are no plants or animals, just snow and rock.*
- *I draw a windy snow-covered mountain.*
- *Now I understand why Mount Everest is so difficult to climb.*

2. Use Text Features The graph shows how tall different mountains are and how they compare in height to other mountains.

N B

Concepts of Print: Capitalization

Teach/Model Direct attention to the first sentence on page 182. Point out the capital *W* in *Wicked*. Say: *The first word in a sentence always begins with a capital letter.* Then point to the lowercase *w* in *winds*. Say: *This is lowercase w.* Ask students to tell how the two forms are different. Explain that proper nouns and adjectives also begin with capital letters. Have students find *Mount Everest* and *Asian*.

Practice/Apply As students read, have them think about the use of capital letters in the selection. Ask students to distinguish words that are capitalized because they are proper nouns or adjectives and words that are capitalized because they begin a sentence.

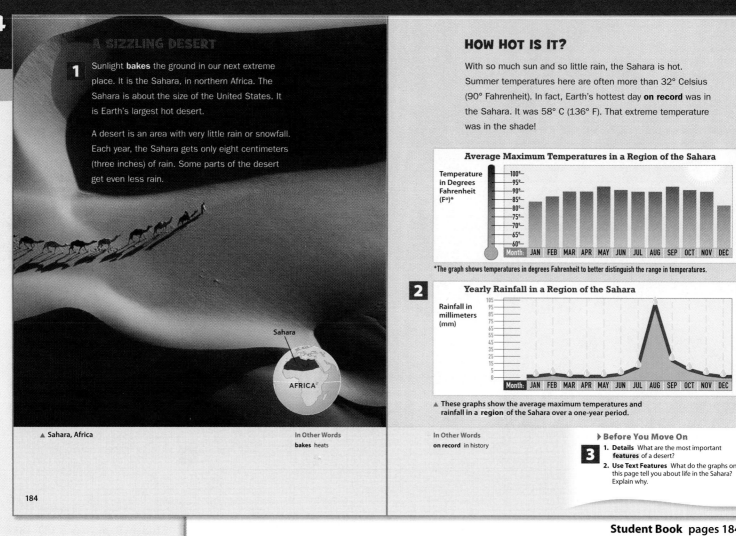

A SIZZLING DESERT

1 Sunlight **bakes** the ground in our next extreme place. It is the Sahara, in northern Africa. The Sahara is about the size of the United States. It is Earth's largest hot desert.

A desert is an area with very little rain or snowfall. Each year, the Sahara gets only eight centimeters (three inches) of rain. Some parts of the desert get even less rain.

▲ Sahara, Africa

In Other Words
bakes heats

HOW HOT IS IT?

With so much sun and so little rain, the Sahara is hot. Summer temperatures here are often more than 32° Celsius (90° Fahrenheit). In fact, Earth's hottest day **on record** was in the Sahara. It was 58° C (136° F). That extreme temperature was in the shade!

Average Maximum Temperatures in a Region of the Sahara

Temperature in Degrees Fahrenheit (F°)*

Month: JAN FEB MAR APR MAY JUN JUL AUG SEP OCT NOV DEC

*The graph shows temperatures in degrees Fahrenheit to better distinguish the range in temperatures.

2 **Yearly Rainfall in a Region of the Sahara**

Rainfall in millimeters (mm)

Month: JAN FEB MAR APR MAY JUN JUL AUG SEP OCT NOV DEC

▲ These graphs show the average maximum temperatures and rainfall in a **region** of the Sahara over a one-year period.

In Other Words
on record in history

▶ **Before You Move On**

3 1. **Details** What are the most important **features** of a desert?
2. **Use Text Features** What do the graphs on this page tell you about life in the Sahara? Explain why.

184

185

Student Book pages 184–185

Home Connection: Family Trips

Explain that many people enjoy going on trips to amazing places.

Have students share something about a trip they have taken. After sharing their findings, help students use push pins to mark the **locations** on a United States or world map.

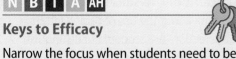

Keys to Efficacy

Narrow the focus when students need to be more specific or focus on less material. *Tell me more about how people might adjust to this environment.*

Build Comprehension, pages 184–185

1 **Figurative Language** Why do you think the author uses the word *bakes*? How does it help you visualize the desert? (It reminds you of an oven.)

2 **Use Text Features** Based on the graph, when is the rainy season in the Sahara? (July, August, September)

3 **Answers to Before You Move On**

1. **Details** MODEL GUIDE APPLY Guide students to identify the **features** of a desert. Ask: *What do the headings and photo tell you about a desert?* (A desert is hot and dry.) Ask: *What details support this idea?* Encourage students to use both graphics and text. (*Temperatures can reach above 90 degrees; it gets very little rain; it is covered with sand; very little grows there.*)

2. **Use Text Features** In reading the graphs, you can see that life in the Sahara would be hard. It is hot all year in the Sahara. It gets little rainfall all year, so there is not much water available, and few plants.

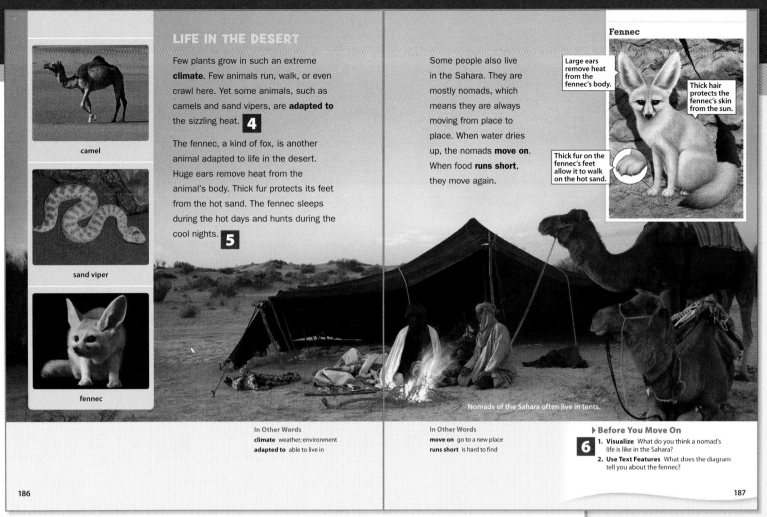

LIFE IN THE DESERT

Few plants grow in such an extreme **climate**. Few animals run, walk, or even crawl here. Yet some animals, such as camels and sand vipers, are **adapted to** the sizzling heat. **4**

The fennec, a kind of fox, is another animal adapted to life in the desert. Huge ears remove heat from the animal's body. Thick fur protects its feet from the hot sand. The fennec sleeps during the hot days and hunts during the cool nights. **5**

Some people also live in the Sahara. They are mostly nomads, which means they are always moving from place to place. When water dries up, the nomads **move on**. When food **runs short**, they move again.

camel

sand viper

fennec

Fennec

Large ears remove heat from the fennec's body.

Thick hair protects the fennec's skin from the sun.

Thick fur on the fennec's feet allow it to walk on the hot sand.

Nomads of the Sahara often live in tents.

In Other Words
climate weather; environment
adapted to able to live in

In Other Words
move on go to a new place
runs short is hard to find

▶ **Before You Move On**
6 1. **Visualize** What do you think a nomad's life is like in the Sahara?
2. **Use Text Features** What does the diagram tell you about the fennec?

186

187

Build Comprehension, pages 186–187

4 **Draw Conclusions** Why is the Sahara an example of an *extreme* climate? (The temperatures are the hottest in the world. Few animals and plants can live here.)

5 **Summarize** What helps a fennec survive in a desert environment? (Its huge ears release heat from its body. Thick fur protects its feet from the hot sand. It sleeps during the day and hunts at night when it is cool.)

6 **Answers to Before You Move On**

1. **Visualize** MODEL GUIDE APPLY Guide students in using the Language Frames from page 178 to form mental images as they read:

   • *What do you read about nomads?* I read that nomads move to a new place when water or food runs out.
   • *What do you picture the nomads doing?* I picture them living in tents; I see them looking for food and water in the hot desert.
   • *What could you draw about their life?* I draw a picture of people living in tents.
   • *What do you understand about their life?* Now I understand that life for nomads in the Sahara is difficult.

2. **Use Text Features** Have students point out callouts that identify adaptations of the fennec. Ask students what feature the diagram mentions that the text does not. (how thick hair protects the fennec's skin from the sun)

I A AH

Social Studies: Geography

Introduce the concept of extreme places around the world: *Extreme places are the biggest, wettest, highest, or driest places on Earth.* Have students go online to find out more about extreme places. Have them research another place that can be called extreme and find out what makes it unique.

UNDERWATER KINGDOM

Our next extreme place is under water. It is the Great Barrier Reef, off the coast of Australia. It is the largest **reef** on Earth. It is bigger than New Mexico. In fact, the Great Barrier Reef is the largest thing ever built by living creatures.

The builders are tiny animals called coral polyps. Each polyp takes **chemicals** from the sea. It uses the chemicals to make a hard **outer skeleton** shaped like a cup. This cup protects the polyp's soft body. **1**

Great Barrier Reef

AUSTRALIA

Coral Polyp
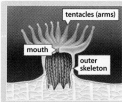
tentacles (arms)
mouth
outer skeleton

polyp

▲ Each of these tiny polyps will help to form the reef.

In Other Words
reef underwater structure
chemicals matter; things
outer skeleton skeleton on the outside of its body

188

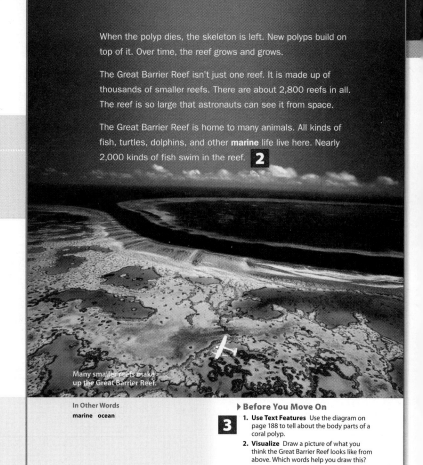

When the polyp dies, the skeleton is left. New polyps build on top of it. Over time, the reef grows and grows.

The Great Barrier Reef isn't just one reef. It is made up of thousands of smaller reefs. There are about 2,800 reefs in all. The reef is so large that astronauts can see it from space.

The Great Barrier Reef is home to many animals. All kinds of fish, turtles, dolphins, and other **marine** life live here. Nearly 2,000 kinds of fish swim in the reef. **2**

Many smaller reefs make up the Great Barrier Reef.

In Other Words
marine ocean

▶ **Before You Move On**
3
1. **Use Text Features** Use the diagram on page 188 to tell about the body parts of a coral polyp.
2. **Visualize** Draw a picture of what you think the Great Barrier Reef looks like from above. Which words help you draw this?

189

Student Book pages 188–189

Literary Analysis: Social Studies Article

Remind students that a social studies article tells about real people, places, and events. Have students look at pages 188 and 189. Point out text **features** that help readers better understand what they read. Have students identify the following features: heading, captions, globe inset, and diagram.

Ask students to look at each feature. Say: *The heading tells you what you will read about next. How does the globe help?* (It shows where the Great Barrier Reef is located.) *What does the diagram show?* (the parts of a coral polyp) *What information do the captions give?* As students continue to read, pause frequently to have volunteers point to or explain various text features.

Build Comprehension, pages 188–189

1 **Ask Questions** What question can you ask about a coral polyp? (Possible answer: How long does it take a coral polyp to grow?)

2 **Author's Purpose** Why do you think the author included the Great Barrier Reef as an extreme place? (It is extreme because it is so large, is built by small animals, and is not a habitat for people.)

3 **Answers to Before You Move On**
1. **Use Text Features** Guide students to use the diagram labels to explain the polyp's body parts. (Possible answer: It has arms that surround its mouth. It has a mouth in the center of the body. It has a skeleton on the outside of the body.)

2. **Visualize** MODEL | GUIDE | APPLY Guide students to use the photo and the text to help them draw. In the text, it tells you that the reef "is made up of thousands of smaller reefs."

Amazon River

SOUTH AMERICA

BIG RIVER

Picture all the **fresh water** that flows into oceans around the world. One in five drops comes from a single river. It is the Amazon River in South America.

The Amazon begins in the mountains of Peru. It stretches across the South American continent. The river ends at the Atlantic Ocean on the coast of Brazil.

Where does all the Amazon's water come from? Much of it comes from rain. More than 1,000 centimeters (400 inches) of rain falls into the river each year. **4**

▲ Amazon River, South America

In Other Words
fresh water water that isn't salty

Some rivers are **pretty calm**, but not the Amazon. Storms here sometimes **stir up** waves as high as a house.

5 As it flows across South America, the Amazon River **winds** through the world's largest rain forest. It is twice the size of all other rain forests combined. More kinds of plants and animals live here than anywhere else on Earth.

Some of the Amazon's animals are pretty extreme. You can find flesh-eating fish and huge snakes. You can also find gentle sloths, monkeys, and even pink dolphins.

sloth

squirrel monkey

pink dolphin

In Other Words
pretty calm slow and quiet
stir up make
winds runs

▶ **Before You Move On**

6
1. **Visualize** If you were in the boat in the photo, tell how would you feel compared to everything around you.
2. **Details** What **features** make the Amazon and its rainforest "extreme"?

190

191

Student Book pages 190–191

Build Comprehension, pages 190–191

4 **Cause and Effect** The area around the Amazon River gets a lot of rain. What effect do you think this has on the river? (The rain makes the river deeper and rougher in stormy weather.)

5 **Homographs** Point to the word *winds* (wīnds) on page 191. Have students compare its spelling and pronunciation to the word *winds* (wĭnds) on page 182. (same spelling; different pronunciation) Discuss the meaning of each word.

6 **Answers to Before You Move On**

1. **Visualize** MODEL | GUIDE | APPLY (Possible response: I read that the Amazon River stretches across the continent. The river is very wide and the trees are huge compared to my boat. I feel very small compared to everything around me.)

2. **Details** MODEL | GUIDE | APPLY Ask: *What are some unusual details about the river and the rain forest?* (One in five drops of **ocean** water comes from the Amazon. The **region** gets more that 1,000 centimeters of rain a year and is home to the world's largest rain forest. More plants and animals live here than anywhere else on Earth. It has extreme animals, such as flesh-eating fish and pink dolphins.)

I A AH

Math: Make a Graph

Have students make a graph that compares the range of temperatures given for different locations in the article. Encourage students to research the temperatures of places mentioned in the article for which an average temperature was not given and add these temperatures to the graph.

WONDERFUL WATERFALL

Water **races** to the edge of a mountain and dives over it. The water drops 979 meters (3,212 feet). During the long fall, it turns into mist. **Barely a drop makes it to** the ground.

To see this, visit Angel Falls, the world's tallest waterfall. It is 17 times taller than Niagara Falls in the United States. Angel Falls is in Venezuela, a country in South America. **1**

Angel Falls

SOUTH AMERICA

◀ Angel Falls, South America

In Other Words
races flows quickly
Barely a drop makes it to Almost no water reaches

192

The falls formed in a special place. Millions of years ago, the land was a large **plateau**. A plateau is an area of flat land that is higher than the land around it. **2**

Over many years, strong wind and water wore away the plateau. They **sliced** the plateau into tall, flat mountains. People call these table mountains because of their flat tops. Angel Falls **plunges** over one of these table mountains.

On average, a plateau that is 1,000 meters (3,280 feet) high would take approximately one to five million years to become a table mountain.

In Other Words
sliced cut
plunges flows

How a Table Mountain Forms

1. A rushing river cuts into the rock at the top of a plateau.

2. Over millions of years, water and wind wear away more and more rock.

3. Eventually, a plateau becomes a table mountain when the rock around it is gone.

▶ **Before You Move On**

3
1. **Make Inferences** At Angel Falls, why do you think barely a drop makes it to the ground?
2. **Summarize** How is a table mountain formed?

193

Student Book pages 192–193

Fluency: Phrasing

Teach/Model Explain the concept: *Fluent readers read with appropriate phrasing. They group and read words that go together. They use punctuation marks such as periods and commas as clues to phrasing. They pause at commas and take a breath at periods.* Direct students' attention to page 188. Say: *Think about how you would say these words if you were speaking them. Which words would you group together when you talk? Where would you pause or take a breath?* Play the selection recording or read aloud the first paragraph of page 188, emphasizing the correct phrasing as you read.

Practice Have partners read the page aloud together several times, mimicking the phrasing you modeled.

Build Comprehension, pages 192–193

1 **Make Comparisons** Compare Angel Falls to the Amazon River. How are the bodies of water different? (Angel Falls is a very high waterfall, and the Amazon is a river that flows across the land.)

2 **Key Words** In what way is a **plateau** similar to a mountain? (Both are areas higher than the ground around them.)

3 **Answers to Before You Move On**

1. **Make Inferences** A drop of water turns to mist as it falls from the top of Angel Falls. Because the water turns to mist, most of it evaporates into the air.

2. **Summarize** Guide students to use the captions to help form their answer: A fast-flowing river cuts into the rock at the top of a plateau. Water and wind wear away rock until it is gone.

EXTREME EXPLORING

Earth has many more extremes, of course. Two of them are in the southwest region of the United States. The Grand Canyon is one of the world's largest **canyons**. It is **located** in Arizona.

In nearby New Mexico, you can find one of the world's longest and deepest caves. It is called Lechuguilla (le-chŭ-gē-u) Cave. Explorers from around the world come to see the unusual rock shapes inside the cave.

The inside of Lechuguilla Cave in New Mexico

Grand Canyon — NORTH AMERICA — Lechuguilla Cave

Grand Canyon

▲ Grand Canyon, Arizona

If you're looking for extreme cold, Antarctica is the place for you. This icy continent is the coldest place on Earth. The lowest temperature ever recorded there was -89° C (-129° F)! Then there's the wettest **spot** in the world: Mawsynram, in India. The town gets 1,187 centimeters (467 inches) of rain a year. By any measure—wettest or driest, hottest or coldest—our Earth is extreme. ❖ **4**

▼ A community in India during the rainy season.

In Other Words
spot place

▶ **Before You Move On**

5
1. **Make Comparisons** How are the Grand Canyon and Lechuguilla Cave alike?
2. **Visualize** What clothes would you wear to visit Antarctica? Why?

194

195

Student Book pages 194–195

Build Comprehension, pages 194–195

4 **Main Idea** MODEL | GUIDE | APPLY What do you think is the main idea of this section? (There are many different extreme places in the world.)

5 **Answers to Before You Move On**

1. **Make Comparisons** Ask students to think and reread before responding. (Both are in the southwest United States, and both are deep.)

2. **Visualize** MODEL | GUIDE | APPLY I picture how cold it is there. I would wear the warmest and heaviest clothes I have.

Daily Writing   A AH

1 **Draft a Research Report** Have students draft their Writing Projects. See pages T210b–T210.

CLOSE AND ASSESS

- **Visualize** *What do you picture it would be like to travel on the Amazon River?* (Students can use the Language Frames on page 178.)

- **Use Text Features** *Look at the diagram on page 187. Why is there a photo of a fennec's foot inside a circle?* (It is to point out a detail of the fennec's foot.)

- **Details** *What details help to describe a* **canyon**? (A canyon is a very large, rocky structure cut out by water. It has very few trees or plant life.)

Keys to Efficacy

Clarify when the student's response is unclear or if you feel a need to change the language of the question to make it more accessible. Say, for example: *Let me say the question another way, how is a plateau like a mountain?*

I A AH

Geography: Research

Extreme places are the biggest, wettest, coldest, hottest, highest, or deepest places on Earth. Have students pick another place that could be called extreme. Ask them to explain why they think this place could be called extreme. Then have students research some facts about the place they chose.

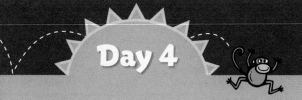

Day at a Glance:
▶ **Language:** Proper Nouns
▶ **Vocabulary:** Expand Word Knowledge
▶ **Reading:** Think and Respond
▶ **Writing:** Write About It; Revise

OBJECTIVES

Vocabulary
- Use Grade-Level Vocabulary ❶
- Use Academic Vocabulary ❶

Grammar
- Proper Nouns ❶

Learning and Teamwork Strategies
- Review
- Collaborate with Peers

Resources

📀 💿 *Practice Master 3.14*

Differentiate

Language Transfer

Challenge In Spanish, the given names of rivers, lakes, mountains, and other geographic features are capitalized, although the initial letter of the place identifier is written in lower case. As an example, the Spanish name for *Mount Everest* is written *monte Everest*. Spanish speakers may tend to transfer this spelling rule when writing place names in English.

Strategy Write these sentences on the board and have students correct the errors in capitalization:

The Amazon river is the largest river in the world.

Niagara falls is a waterfall in New York.

The Grand **canyon** is an amazing place.

Part 2 Grammar Skills Trace		Page
Day 2	Irregular Plural Nouns: Count/Noncount	T177a
▶ Day 4	Proper Nouns	T196a
Day 7	More Plural Nouns: Irregular	T205a
Day 10	Review Plural Nouns	T206g

Language of the Day

What places did you learn about in "Extreme Earth?"
I read about ____.

Read the Language of the Day. Model: *I read about extreme places around the world*. Have each student repeat your sentence and add a particular place from the passage to create a cumulative sentence. Then explain that today students will talk and write about the selection.

Grammar Capitalization of Proper Nouns B I A AH

1 **Teach/Model** Write these sentences and read them aloud.

1. <u>Mount Everest</u> is the tallest <u>mountain</u> on <u>Earth</u>.

2. <u>Mrs. Smith</u> is our <u>teacher</u>.

Ask: *What do we call the underlined words?* (nouns) *Why do some begin with capital letters?* Allow time for students to suggest answers. Then say: *When a noun begins with a capital letter, it names a particular person, place, or thing. We call these nouns "proper nouns." The other nouns are common nouns. They name any person, place, or thing.*

Write these sentences: *3. I will visit a desert. 4. I will visit the Sahara Desert.* Ask: *Which sentence names a particular desert?* (sentence 4) Say: *Yes,* Sahara Desert *is a proper noun.* Ask: *Which sentence names any desert?* (sentence 3) *Yes,* desert *is a common noun.* Display the Noun Chart and call on different students to read each line.

Noun Chart	
Common Nouns	**Proper Nouns**
mountain	Mount Everest
desert	Sahara
teacher	Mrs. Smith

2 **Practice/Apply** Add these common nouns to the chart: *street, city, state, country*. Have a volunteer name a local street. Add it to the chart as a proper noun. Have students suggest proper nouns to complete the chart. Then assign **Practice Master 3.14** for more practice.

CHECK UNDERSTANDING Write: *lake, amazon river, gary soto, writer.* Have students identify and capitalize the proper nouns.

Share Word Knowledge

3 **Teach/Model** To connect concepts, say: *Yesterday you became Key Word experts. Today you will share what you know about your Key Words.* Pair each student with a partner who wrote a poster for a different word. Have partners follow the steps of **Vocabulary Routine 3** to share their word knowledge. (See **Vocabulary Routines,** page PD39.)

- Take turns reading Dictionary Entry posters.
- Talk about how the content sentences help show the meanings of the Key Words.
- Create new sentences for the Key Words and write them in your journals.
- Draw a line under each Key Word.

4 **Practice/Apply** Have each set of partners self-identify as Partner A and Partner 1. Group lettered partners together; group numbered partners together. Form an **Inside-Outside Circle** with numbered partners on the outside (see **Cooperative Learning Routines,** pages PD58–PD59).

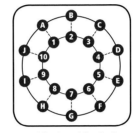

Inside-Outside Circle

Students share the two words they studied and copy the information they learn into their vocabulary journals. Rotate and repeat until each student has a journal entry for each Key Word. Have students take turns reading their dictionary entries again. All students should echo the pronunciation. Correct any mispronunciations.

> **CHECK UNDERSTANDING** Have students write a new sample sentence for their poster with a blank in the place of the Key Word. Have partners trade papers and fill in the blank with the correct Key Word.

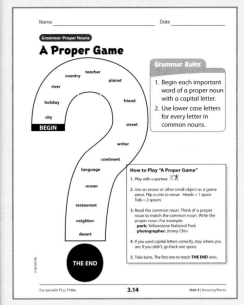

Practice Master 3.14

Part 2 Vocabulary Skills Trace		Page
Day 1	Social Studies Vocabulary	T175
Day 2	Academic Vocabulary	T177
Day 3	Expand Word Knowledge	T180b
Day 4	**Share Word Knowledge**	**T196b**
Day 5	Apply Word Knowledge	T197b
Day 6	Compound Words	T198
Day 7	Compound Words	T205
Days 8–9	Extend Vocabulary	T206e–f
Day 10	Vocabulary Review	T206g–h

Day 4
continued

Day at a Glance:
- ▶ **Language:** Proper Nouns
- ▶ **Vocabulary:** Share Word Knowledge
- ▶ **Reading:** Think and Respond
- ▶ **Writing:** Write About It; Revise

OBJECTIVES

Vocabulary
- Use Grade-Level Vocabulary ⊕
- Use Academic Vocabulary ⊕

Language
- Use Language Function: Describe Places

Reading Fluency
- Phrasing ⊕

Literary Analysis
- Analyze Genre: Social Studies Article

Test-Taking Strategies
- Look for Important Words

Writing
- Write Responses to Social Studies Article
- Revise Research Report

Resources

⊘ eVisual 3.27

⊘NGReach.com ❯

See **Technology Station** for digital student resources.

Fluency: Phrasing

Teach/Model Review phrasing (page T188). Display this reminder: *Look for clues about when to pause as you read.* Remind students that reading with appropriate phrasing helps their reading sound like natural speech.

Practice Have students work with partners to practice reading page T190 with appropriate phrasing. Then have them take turns reading aloud to one another. Encourage partners to offer feedback about their reading.

Think and Respond

1 **Talk About It** Prompt students to cite evidence from the text. Remind students to use Key Words in their answers. If students have difficulty, help them use the sentence starters to form their answers.

1. **Social Studies Article** The author included headings and pictures to help readers locate information. She also included text features such as graphs and diagrams to help give information in a visual way.

2. **Describe Places** Encourage students to review the photos and section heads before they decide on a place to visit. Ask students to visualize the place before giving their descriptions.

3. **Make Comparisons** Use the frame to help you contrast two extreme places. Example: A desert is hot but Mount Everest is cold.

2 **Test-Taking Strategies: Look for Important Words** Explain: *Test questions have important words that tell you what to look for to answer a question.* Read the sample question and point out the important words *Which place* and *hottest.* Explain: *These words tell me that I need to figure out which of the places listed has the hottest temperature.*

> **Which place has the hottest temperature on Earth?**
> A. The Great Barrier Reef
> B. The Amazon
> C. The Sahara *
> D. Antarctica

⊘NGReach.com ❯ eVisual 3.27

Have partners read the answer choices and decide together on the best answer. Tell students that they can go through the choices first and eliminate those that they know aren't correct.

Display the remaining test items and have students look for important words in each question.

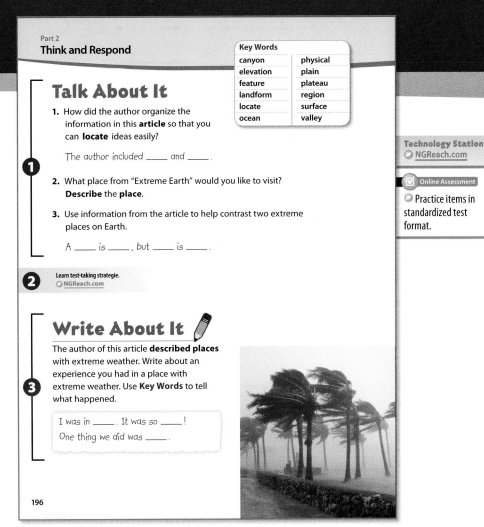

Student Book page 196

Keys to Efficacy

Remind students to use complete sentences when giving answers: *Instead of saying* Mount Everest, *say* The highest mountain on Earth is Mount Everest.

Daily Writing A AH

3 **Write About It** Read the directions aloud. Point out the sentence frames. Use the **Independent Writing Routine** to help students put their thoughts in writing. (See **Writing Routines,** page PD56).

Say 💬	Write ✏️
I was near the ocean during a hurricane. There was a lot of rain and strong wind. The ocean waves washed away the beach.	I was in Florida. There was a hurricane. It was so windy and rainy. Huge *ocean* waves washed away the beach. It was so scary!

Point out the Key Word that you used; **ocean**. Have students use these ideas or their own to write sentences in their journals.

4 **Revise a Research Report** Have students revise their Writing Project compositions. (See pages T211a–T211b).

CLOSE AND ASSESS

- **Language** Name a common noun and challenge students to name a related proper noun. For example: *dog, Lassie; country, Spain; language, French.*
- **Reading** *What is the most interesting extreme location you learned about? Tell why.* (Answers will vary)
- **Vocabulary** *Which Key Words did you use in your answers?* (Answers will vary.)

Day at a Glance:
▶ **Language:** Adjust Speech for Purpose ▶ **Reading:** Reread and Summarize
▶ **Vocabulary:** Apply Word Knowledge ▶ **Writing:** Edit and Proofread a Research Report

OBJECTIVES

Vocabulary
• Use Grade-Level Vocabulary ❶
• Use Academic Vocabulary ❶

Listening and Speaking
• Language Function: Adjust Speech for Purpose

Learning and Teamwork Strategies
• Analyze Expressions
• Follow Instructions
• Review

Social Studies
• Investigate Geography

Resources
• *Markers*
🔘 *eVisual 3.28*
🔘 *Practice Master 3.15*

Differentiate

How to Learn Language

Analyze Expressions Help students develop techniques to analyze expressions. Explain: *Sometimes we do not fully understand something we hear. You might not fully understand a group of words or an expression.* Help students create a strategy for figuring out unknown expressions.

To figure out what "a neat book" means:

• Define "neat" and use the context of the sentence.

• Form a mental picture in your mind.

> If something is neat, it is good or great.

• Make a guess.

Have students suggest other phrases and discuss how they might form mental pictures to figure out and remember their meaning.

Language of the Day

How do you travel to the places you want to go? Sometimes, I _____ to the places I want to go.

Read the Language of the Day. Model: *Sometimes, I follow directions to the places I want to go.* Have students take turns completing the sentence frame, trying not to repeat a previous suggestion. Then explain that today they will learn how to adjust their speech for the purpose, play a word game, retell the story, and write about it.

Adjust Speech for Purpose

❶ Teach/Model Introduce the concept: *Have you ever given a book report? Did you speak differently than if you were talking about the book with a friend?* Explain: *When you speak, you often adjust your speech for your purpose and your audience. You use friendly or informal language with a friend. You use more formal language when speaking to a group or to an adult.*

How to Adjust Speech for Purpose

1. Use words that match the audience and the occasion. • Use formal language and polite words for adults and for presentations. • Use informal language with friends.	**Informal:** Hey, Greta! **Formal:** Good morning, everyone. **Informal:** I read a neat book that you'd like. It's "Extreme Earth." **Formal:** The book I read is called "Extreme Earth."
2. Use facial expressions, body language, tone, and volume to match your audience.	**Informal:** Be relaxed. Speak in a friendly tone. Use informal words. **Formal:** Be serious. Stand straight. Make eye contact. Speak loudly and clearly so the audience can hear you.

NGReach.com ▶ eVisual 3.28

❷ Practice/Apply Have students work with partners to practice giving a formal book report and an informal summary of the selection. Teach the **How to Learn Language** strategy to help students as they listen to their presentations. Have partners offer suggestions and feedback to make more them formal or informal.

> **CHECK UNDERSTANDING** Have partners take turns giving formal and informal presentations about a favorite place they have visited.

Apply Word Knowledge

3 **Teach/Model** Tell students that when people travel to another country, they need a passport. Display **Practice Master 3.15** and explain how to play Around the World.

- *First, write each Key Word on your passport.*

- *I will choose one student to be the traveler. The traveler moves from his or her seat and stands by a student in the next seat. This student is the challenger.*

- *I will read a definition to the traveler and the challenger.*

- *Whoever names the word first, the traveler or the challenger, moves and stands by the student in the next seat. He or she also checks off that word on his or her passport. If neither the traveler nor the challenger can name the word, the next student gets a chance to name it.*

- *The first student to check off all the words on his or her passport, or to travel back to his or her seat, has gone Around the World and wins the game.*

4 **Practice/Apply** Write the Key Words on the board. Distribute **Practice Master 3.15** and have students write each Key Word on their passports. Then play the game with students, verifying as needed that students follow the agreed upon rules.

Monitor students as they follow your instructions. Restate instructions as required.

For vocabulary games, go to NGReach.com.

> **CHECK UNDERSTANDING** Repeat a definition and have students explain how they used their knowledge of the Key Words to name the word.

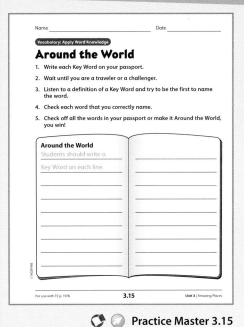

Practice Master 3.15

Part 2 Vocabulary Skills Trace		Page
Day 1	Social Studies Vocabulary	T175
Day 2	Academic Vocabulary	T177
Day 3	Expand Word Knowledge	T180b
Day 4	Share Word Knowledge	T196b
Day 5	**Apply Word Knowledge**	**T197b**
Day 6	Compound Words	T198
Day 7	Compound Words	T205
Days 8–9	Extend Vocabulary	T206e–f
Day 10	Vocabulary Review	T206g–h

Day 5
continued

Day at a Glance:
▶ **Language:** Adjust Speech for Purpose
▶ **Vocabulary:** Apply Word Knowledge
▶ **Reading:** Reread and Retell
▶ **Writing:** Edit and Proofread a Research Report

OBJECTIVES

Vocabulary
• Use Grade-Level Vocabulary ⊖
• Use Academic Vocabulary ⊖

Language
• Summarize the Selection

Learning and Teamwork Strategies
• Use Graphic Organizers: Outline
• Reason Deductively

Reading Fluency
• Read with Accuracy and Rate ⊖
• Read with Appropriate Phrasing ⊖

Literary Analysis
• Identify Main Idea and Details
• Genre: Social Studies Article

Writing
• Edit and Proofread

Social Studies
• Investigate Geography

Resources

◐ ◉ *Practice Master 3.16*

◐ ◉ *Practice Master 3.17*

◉ *Comprehension Coach*

Name _____ Date _____

Reread and Summarize: Outline

Outline the main ideas and details in "Extreme Earth."

Outline

I. Mount Everest is the tallest mountain on the planet.
   A. It is 8,850 meters above sea level.
   B. No plants or animals live there.

II. The Sahara is the largest hot desert on Earth.
   A. Only 8 centimeters of rain fall each year.
   B. Few plants and animals live there.

III. The Great Barrier Reef is the largest reef on Earth.
   A. The reef is built by tiny animals called coral polyps.
   B. The reef is made up of thousands of smaller reefs.

IV. The Amazon River flows through the world's largest rain forest.
   A. One of every five drops of fresh water come from the Amazon.
   B. More than 400 inches of rain fall into the river each year.

V. Angel Falls is the world's tallest waterfall.
   A. The water drops 979 meters.
   B. Angel Falls plunges over a table mountain.

VI. There are many more extreme places in the world.
   A. Lechuguilla Cave is one of the world's deepest caves.
   B. Antarctica is the coldest place on Earth.

Use your outline to summarize "Extreme Earth" with a partner. Include Key Words in your main ideas and details.

For use with TE p. T197c   **3.16**   Unit 3 | Amazing Places

 Practice Master 3.16

Reread and Summarize

1 Main Idea and Details You can use an outline to organize the main idea and details in an article. A social studies article tells about real places and events. Read through the example outline and callouts. Explain: *An outline can help you to summarize information. The detail 8,850 meters supports the idea that Mount Everest is the tallest mountain.*

Have students complete **Practice Master 3.16**.

2 Summarize Read aloud the directions and language frames. Have students summarize the article to their partners. Remind them to include the main idea and important details about each place. Partners reverse roles and repeat. Provide the Key Points Reading (**Practice Master 3.13**) for students who need additional support.

To evaluate students' proficiency levels, use the Summarize rubric.

Summarizing a Selection Rubric		
Scale	**Content**	**Presentation**
B	☐ Misses many important details. ☐ Is unable to identify section main ideas.	☐ Is often hard to hear and understand. ☐ Is uncomfortable summarizing the selection.
I	☐ Includes some details. ☐ Identifies some section main ideas.	☐ Is understood most of the time. ☐ Seems somewhat comfortable with the summarizing task.
A	☐ Cites many of the selection details. ☐ Identifies many section main ideas.	☐ Is clearly and easily understood. ☐ Is comfortable summarizing the selection.
AH	☐ Relates all important details of the selection. ☐ Identifies the main idea of each section.	☐ Speaks clearly and expressively. ☐ Employs eye contact and appropriate gestures while summarizing.

Fluency Accuracy, Rate, and Phrasing ▮I▮ ▮A▮ ▮AH▮

3 Fluency Have students record their reading on the **Comprehension Coach** to assess each student's progress for rate and accuracy. Have students use the passage on **Practice Master 3.17** to record their reading for phrasing. Listen to each recording and assess students' ability to read with appropriate phrasing.

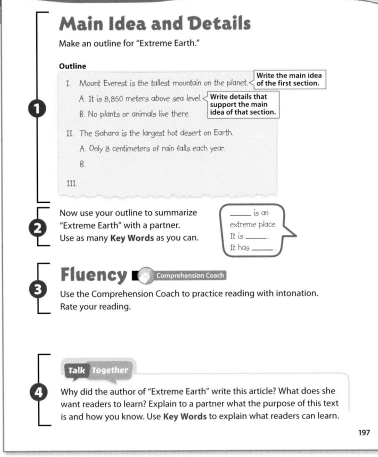

Main Idea and Details

Make an outline for "Extreme Earth."

Outline

I. Mount Everest is the tallest mountain on the planet. ◄ *Write the main idea of the first section.*

   A. It is 8,850 meters above sea level. ◄ *Write details that support the main idea of that section.*

   B. No plants or animals live there.

II. The Sahara is the largest hot desert on Earth.

   A. Only 8 centimeters of rain falls each year.

   B.

III.

2 Now use your outline to summarize "Extreme Earth" with a partner. Use as many **Key Words** as you can.

_____ is an extreme place. It is _____. It has _____.

Fluency ▮ Comprehension Coach

3 Use the Comprehension Coach to practice reading with intonation. Rate your reading.

Talk Together

4 Why did the author of "Extreme Earth" write this article? What does she want readers to learn? Explain to a partner what the purpose of this text is and how you know. Use **Key Words** to explain what readers can learn.

197

Student Book page 197

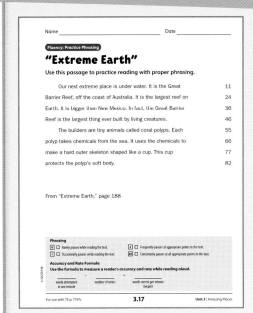

Name _____ Date _____

Fluency: Practice Phrasing

"Extreme Earth"

Use this passage to practice reading with proper phrasing.

Our next extreme place is under water. It is the Great	11
Barrier Reef, off the coast of Australia. It is the largest reef on	24
Earth. It is bigger than New Mexico. In fact, the Great Barrier	36
Reef is the largest thing ever built by living creatures.	46
The builders are tiny animals called coral polyps. Each	55
polyp takes chemicals from the sea. It uses the chemicals to	66
make a hard outer skeleton shaped like a cup. This cup	77
protects the polyp's soft body.	82

From "Extreme Earth," page 188

Phrasing
☐ Rarely pauses while reading the text. ☐ Frequently pauses at appropriate points in the text.
☐ Occasionally pauses while reading the text. ☐ Consistently pauses at all appropriate points in the text.

Accuracy and Rate Formula
Use the formula to measure a reader's accuracy and rate while reading aloud.

_____   _____   _____
words attempted   number of errors   words correct per minute
in one minute   (wcpm)

For use with TE p. T197c   **3.17**   Unit 3 | Amazing Places

 **Practice Master 3.17**

---

4 **Talk Together** Ask students why they think the author wrote this article. What do they think they have learned about extreme places from reading this article? Read aloud the directions and have students jot down notes for their responses. Then have students share their ideas with the class. Students should add their ideas to their Unit concept maps.

Daily Writing

5 **Edit and Proofread a Research Report** Have students edit and proofread their Writing Project compositions. (See pages T211c–T211.)

Keys to Efficacy

Remind students to use content, academic, and/or classroom vocabulary: *How can you use a Key Word to explain your idea?*

CLOSE AND ASSESS

- **Language** *Complete this sentence: When I give a presentation, I should _____.* (decide whether I will use formal or informal language, adjust my speech for my purpose and audiences)

- **Reading** *How can an outline help you?* (Possible answer: It can help you remember details and features about the places in the text.)

- **Vocabulary** *What Key Words did you use to talk about the places you read about?* (Answers will vary.)

Day 6

Day at a Glance:
Language: Describe Places
Vocabulary: Compound Words
Reading: Read the Selection
Writing: Writing Fluency; Publish and Share

OBJECTIVES

Vocabulary
• Use Grade-Level Vocabulary ✪
• Use Academic Vocabulary ✪
• Strategy: Use Structural Analysis (Compound Words) ✪

Language
• Language Function: Describe Places ✪

Learning and Teamwork Strategies
• Relate to Personal Experience
• Adjust Interaction for the Classroom

Resources

📖 🔊 *Language Builder Picture Cards E27–E39*

🔊 *eVisual 3.29*

🔊 *eVisual 3.30*

Language of the Day

Which of Earth's features would you photograph? Why?
I would photograph _____ to show people _____.

Read the Language of the Day. Model how to complete the sentence with a feature you have seen. Ask students to suggest other features they might photograph. Then explain that today students will talk, read, and write about many of Earth's features.

Describe Places

1 Teach/Model Review how to describe places (page T174). Connect concepts: You can respond to a request to describe a place by giving more details about it.

Request Information	Describe a Place
Will you describe Mount Everest?	Yes, I will tell you that Mount Everest is the highest mountain in the world.
Please tell me more about it.	It is cold and windy.

🌐 NGReach.com > eVisual 3.29

Have students take turns asking about a place and responding with a description of it. Encourage students to use common and proper nouns.

2 Practice/Apply Have groups of three form a **Roundtable**. One student asks about a **landform** or feature, for example, *Will you describe a* **canyon**? The next student tells a detail about a canyon. The third student responds with more details. Continue in a similar manner. Use **Academic Language Frames** to provide ideas to support every language level.

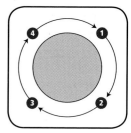

Roundtable

CHECK UNDERSTANDING Have each pair of students select a **Language Builder Picture Card** and make and respond to requests to describe it.

Differentiate

Academic Language Frames

Describe Places
■ The name of this place is _____.
 It is _____. It has _____.

_____

■ One interesting place is _____.
 It is _____ and _____.
 It has _____ and _____.

■ An interesting place is _____.
■ It is in the country of _____.
 It is _____ and _____.
 It has _____ and _____.

🌐 NGReach.com > eVisual 3.30

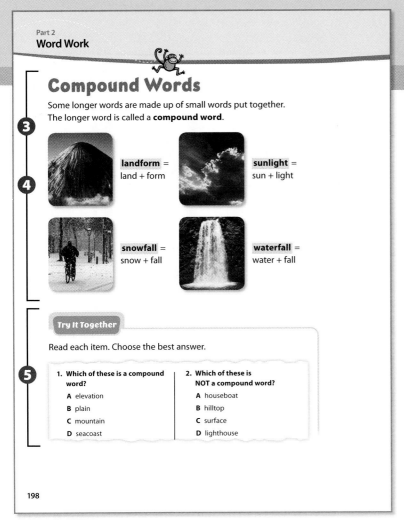

Compound Words

Some longer words are made up of small words put together. The longer word is called a **compound word**.

3
4

landform = land + form

sunlight = sun + light

snowfall = snow + fall

waterfall = water + fall

Try It Together

Read each item. Choose the best answer.

5

1. Which of these is a compound word?
   A elevation
   B plain
   C mountain
   D seacoast

2. Which of these is NOT a compound word?
   A houseboat
   B hilltop
   C surface
   D lighthouse

198

Student Book page 198

Differentiate

Multi-Level Practice Sets

N *bookstore* (a store for books) *backpack* (a pack that is carried on one's back)

B *teamwork* (a group; effort; a group making an effort together), *wildlife* (not a pet; living things; living things that are not pets)

I *earthquake* (surface of the planet, ground; shaking; a shaking of the ground); *wetland* (watery; surface of the Earth; watery place on Earth)

A *foothill* (the bottom; rounded land smaller than a mountain; a hill at the bottom or foot of mountains), *waterway* (a path of water on which a boat travels)

Compound Words

3 Teach Read the introduction aloud and review the two words that make up landform. Explain to students that they can use the meaning of each smaller word to figure out the meaning of the compound word. Activate prior knowledge by having students brainstorm words they know that are made up of two smaller words (Examples include: *toolbox, basketball, raincoat,* and *textbook.*)

4 Model Model how to define *landform* by explaining the meaning of each smaller word and then putting the two meanings together. Point to the first picture and ask: *What does* land *mean?* (Land *is the surface of Earth.) What does* form *mean?* (Form *is shape.) The compound word* landform *means the shape that land can take.* Invite volunteers to repeat the process with *sunlight, snowfall,* and *waterfall.*

5 Practice/Apply Read the directions aloud. Remind students that a compound word combines two whole words to make a new word. Then have partners work together to answer the questions. Use the **Multi-Level Practice Sets** to address varying levels of vocabulary knowledge.

> **CHECK UNDERSTANDING** Say: *Tell me what* mountaintop *means.*
> If students have difficulty, provide a model: *A mountain is a very large hill. The* top *is the highest part. A* mountaintop *is the highest part of a mountain.*

Day 6
continued

Day at a Glance:
Language: Describe Places   **Reading:** Read the Selection
Vocabulary: Compound Words   **Writing:** Writing Fluency; Publish and Share

OBJECTIVES

Vocabulary
• Use Grade-Level Vocabulary
• Use Academic Vocabulary ⊕

Language
• Listen to a Preview

Reading Strategies
• Plan: Preview ⊕
• Make Connections Across Texts
• Visualize

Literary Analysis
• Recognize Genre: Profile
• Interpret Visuals

Learning and Teamwork Strategies
• Use Prereading Supports
• Build Background Knowledge
• Use Reading Supports

Resources

🎧 💿 *Practice Master 3.18*

Reflection Journal

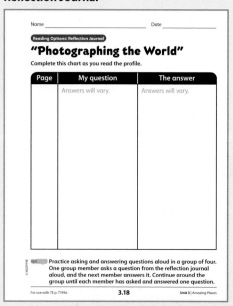

🎧 💿 **Practice Master 3.18**

Read the Profile

1 Connect Across Texts Read aloud the introduction and explain: *As you read the profile, think about the Big Question. Why do people learn about other places?*

2 Genre Read aloud the definition. Say: *Think about the title of the selection and the introduction. What do you think Jimmy Chin does or cares about?*

3 Preview and Build Background Use sheltering strategies as you conduct a picture walk.

Pages	Preview Script
199	*Jimmy learned that he loved the outdoors when he visited a glacier as a child. What do you think a glacier is like? (Pretend to shiver.) Brrr. For one thing, it's cold and icy.*
200–201	*Jimmy is a photographer and a great athlete. He takes pictures in places that would scare many people. Do you think many people have taken photographs like these?*
202–203	*Jimmy takes photographs to help other people learn about places they may never go. He tells stories using pictures instead of words. (Point to the dry mountains, the ice, and the climber at the top of the ice.) What can you learn from this picture? (Point to the zebra.) What about this one?*

4 Read "Photographing the World" Scaffold the support for various reading levels.

BELOW LEVEL	ON LEVEL / ABOVE LEVEL
Listen and Read Along	**Read Silently**
• Have students track the print while you read the text aloud. Pause for students to reflect on the text and photos. • Check understanding with selected Build Comprehension and Before You Move On questions.	• Have students use the **Reflection Journal** as they read silently. Students should write the page number in column 1, a question they have in column 2, and the answer they figure out in column 3. • Meet with students to review their journals and discuss the Before You Move On questions.

CHECK UNDERSTANDING Ask: *Which of Earth's* **physical features** *are you most interested in learning more about? Why?*

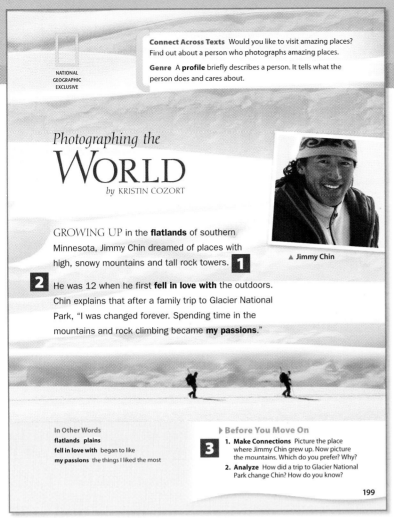

Connect Across Texts Would you like to visit amazing places? Find out about a person who photographs amazing places.

Genre A **profile** briefly describes a person. It tells what the person does and cares about.

Photographing the
WORLD
by KRISTIN COZORT

GROWING UP in the **flatlands** of southern Minnesota, Jimmy Chin dreamed of places with high, snowy mountains and tall rock towers. **1**

▲ Jimmy Chin

2 He was 12 when he first **fell in love with** the outdoors. Chin explains that after a family trip to Glacier National Park, "I was changed forever. Spending time in the mountains and rock climbing became **my passions**."

In Other Words
flatlands plains
fell in love with began to like
my passions the things I liked the most

▶ **Before You Move On**
3 1. **Make Connections** Picture the place where Jimmy Chin grew up. Now picture the mountains. Which do you prefer? Why?
2. **Analyze** How did a trip to Glacier National Park change Chin? How do you know?

199

Student Book page 199

Build Comprehension, page 199

1 **Make Inferences** Why do you think Chin dreamed of mountains? (Possible answer: He lived where it was flat. He had never been to the mountains.)

2 **Clarify Language** What does it mean when the author says Jimmy "fell in love with the outdoors"? (It means he began to really like the outdoors.) Ask students where on the page they could find the meaning for this phrase. (In Other Words feature)

3 **Answers to Before You Move On**
1. **Make Connections** Answers will vary. Students should explain their opinions.
2. **Analyze** Possible response: (Spending time in Glacier National Park made Chin fall in love with the outdoors. I know because he says so.)

Cultural Perpectives

Invite students to tell about trips they have taken and places they have visited. Ask if students took photographs of their trips. Remind students that they are going to read about a photographer who travels around the world and takes pictures. Encourage each student to name a place they would like to visit and photograph.

Getting the Shot

Chin is one of the best extreme photographers in the world. He is also a **world-class** athlete. Chin is an expert skier and climber. His athletic skills help him take photos where few people **dare** to go. "I love to bring back photographs that nobody else could have," he says.

▲ An extreme shot

Chin photographs the **far corners** of the world. He has survived an avalanche and extreme temperatures. He often puts himself in danger to **get the perfect shot**. **1**

Taking risks is part of an extreme photographer's job. ▶

▲ Chin's skill as a climber helps him get amazing shots.

In Other Words
world-class very good
dare are brave enough

In Other Words
far corners faraway places
get the perfect shot take the best photograph

▶ **Before You Move On**
3
1. **Cause/Effect** How do Chin's skills as an athlete help him in his job?
2. **Visualize** Draw a diagram of the top photo showing the positions of the photographer and the climber.

200

201

Student Book **pages 200–201**

Text Features: Captions

Teach/Model Explain that captions describe a visual element of a story or article. They sometimes explain how the image relates to the text or give more detailed information to support the text. Point to the photograph on page 200. Say: *The caption tells me that this photograph shows how Chin uses his skill as an athlete to get photos.*

Practice/Apply Have students explain to a partner what a different caption on page 201 tells them about the photograph and how it supports the text.

Build Comprehension, pages 200–201

1 **Cite Evidence** What evidence can you cite to support that Chin's job is dangerous? (He has been in an avalanche. He has survived extreme temperatures. He climbs steep cliffs to take a photo.)

2 **Make Connections** How does the information shown in the photographs connect to the information given in the text? (The photographs show some of the places described in the text and how Chin has to use his athletic skills to get these photographs.)

3 **Answers to Before You Move On**
1. **Cause/Effect** Possible response: Chin's athletic skills help him get to places that other photographers might not dare go to.
2. **Visualize** Reteach I read the caption. I look at the photo and imagine myself as the climber. Then I make a picture in my mind of where I would be in order to take this photo. I draw a diagram of the two people. This helps me understand how difficult and dangerous Chin's job is.

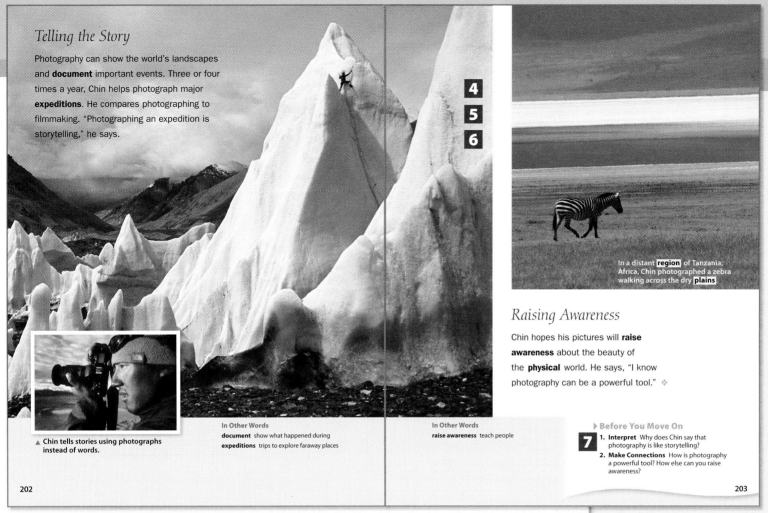

Telling the Story

Photography can show the world's landscapes and **document** important events. Three or four times a year, Chin helps photograph major **expeditions**. He compares photographing to filmmaking. "Photographing an expedition is storytelling," he says.

4
5
6

▲ Chin tells stories using photographs instead of words.

In Other Words
document show what happened during
expeditions trips to explore faraway places

In a distant **region** of Tanzania, Africa, Chin photographed a zebra walking across the dry **plains**.

Raising Awareness

Chin hopes his pictures will **raise awareness** about the beauty of the **physical** world. He says, "I know photography can be a powerful tool." ❖

In Other Words
raise awareness teach people

▶ **Before You Move On**

7 1. **Interpret** Why does Chin say that photography is like storytelling?
2. **Make Connections** How is photography a powerful tool? How else can you raise awareness?

202

203

Build Comprehension, pages 202–203

4 **Ask Questions** What questions could you ask Chin about the photos on these pages? (Sample response: What kinds of expeditions do you go on?)

5 **Key Words** What **features** of the **physical** world do the photographs show? Point to each feature as you identify it. (snow, ice, rocks, mountains, water, grasslands, clouds, sky)

6 **Visualize** [APPLY] How does visualizing yourself in the photos help you understand how Jimmy Chin feels about photographing extreme places? (When I picture myself in these places, I feel a little scared, but excited too. Jimmy might feel that way, too.)

7 **Answers to Before You Move On**

1. **Interpret** Possible response: Chin thinks photographing is like storytelling because he can describe places and events in detail.

2. **Make Connections** Answers will vary. Students should explain that photographs help readers to visualize by showing the actual places and events as they happen. They make the readers feel that they are there. The Internet is another way to help raise awareness. It can show people something as it happens.

Student Book pages 202–203

I **A** **AH**

Science: Glaciers

Introduce the concept: *Glaciers are large bodies of ice that move very slowly across the land. They flow just like rivers do. Glaciers also shrink and grow. When Earth is in a hot phase, glaciers melt and thus shrink. When Earth is in a cold phase, glaciers grow. Because of this behavior, scientists study glaciers to learn about climate change.* Have students go online to learn more about how glaciers behave and why. Encourage them to share and compare their research.

Day 6
continued

Day at a Glance:
▸ **Language:** Describe Places   ▸ **Reading:** Read the Selection
▸ **Vocabulary:** Compound Words   ▸ **Writing:** Writing Fluency; Publish and Share

OBJECTIVES

Vocabulary
• Use Grade-Level Vocabulary ❶
• Use Academic Vocabulary ❶

Language
• Participate in Discussion

Fluency
• Read with Accuracy and Rate ❶

Literary Analysis
• Compare Genres

Learning and Teamwork Strategies
• Use Graphic Organizer: Comparison Chart

Writing
• Develop Writing Fluency
• Monitor and Self-Correct Writing
• Publish and Share

Resources

📄 eVisuals 3.31

📄 eVisual 3.32

✏️📄 Practice Master 3.19

📄 Comprehension Coach

Differentiate

Academic Language Frames

Make Comparisons
■ I see _____ in _____.
  I do not see _____ in _____.

_____

■ I see _____ in _____.
  An example is _____.
  I don't see _____ in _____.

_____

■ Both _____ and _____ have _____, but only
■ _____ has _____.

title	headings	photographs	globes
words	captions	author's purpose	facts
inform	entertain	paragraphs	maps

🌐 NGReach.com ▸ eVisual 3.31

Respond and Extend

❶ Reread As students reread "Photographing the World" on their own, have them think about how the social studies article and the profile go together.

❷ Compare Text Features Read aloud the instructions. Explain: *A comparison chart shows how two or more ideas are alike and how they are different.* Use the instructions to explain how to complete the chart.

Create groups and use the **Numbered Heads**. Focus student thinking: *A genre has certain* **features** *. Sometimes different genres share the same features. Let's compare four features of these selections. What other features can you list?* Ask questions to help guide discussion. Provide **Academic Language Frames** to support students at different language levels.

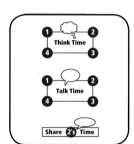

Numbered Heads

Focus	Questions
1. Title	Does each selection have a title? What does the title tell you about the topic of each selection?
2. Section headings	Do the selections have section headings? Where are some examples in the text?
3. Photographs	Do the selections have photographs? How would you compare the photos in Extreme Earth to those in the Chin piece?
4. Captions	Do the photos have captions? What are some examples?

Have partners record their ideas on **Practice Master 3.19**.

❸ Talk Together About the Big Question
Read aloud the question and the directions. Remind students that each selection described some extreme places. Ask follow-up questions to prompt students as they use newly acquired vocabulary and to focus discussion.

• *What makes a place amazing?*
• *What kind of place would you like to learn more about? Why?*

> **CHECK UNDERSTANDING** Have students identify examples of different text features in the selections (heading, caption, graph, etc.)

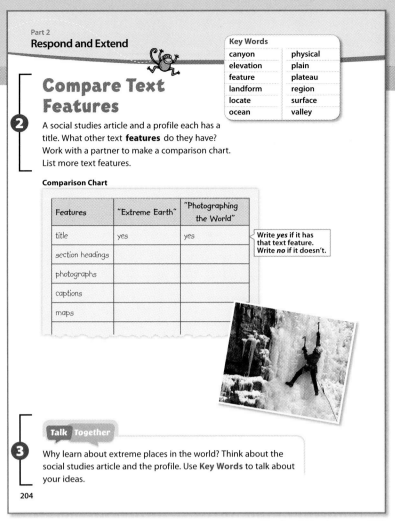

Part 2
Respond and Extend

Key Words

canyon	physical
elevation	plain
feature	plateau
landform	region
locate	surface
ocean	valley

Compare Text Features

2 A social studies article and a profile each has a title. What other text **features** do they have? Work with a partner to make a comparison chart. List more text features.

Comparison Chart

Features	"Extreme Earth"	"Photographing the World"
title	yes	yes
section headings		
photographs		
captions		
maps		

Write *yes* if it has that text feature. Write *no* if it doesn't.

Talk Together

3 Why learn about extreme places in the world? Think about the social studies article and the profile. Use **Key Words** to talk about your ideas.

204

Student Book page 204

Daily Writing

4 **Writing Fluency** Use the **Power Writing Routine** (see page PD53). Write the word **ocean** and prompt: *What do you like about the ocean? Think about this word and write about it.*

Power Writing Routine

 1. What do you know about the word or picture?

 2. Take one minute to write as much as you can, as well as you can.

   B words   **I** sentences   **A** **AH** paragraphs

 3. Check your spelling and grammar. Circle mistakes.

 4. Count your words.

 NGReach.com > eVisual 3.32

5 **Publish and Share a Research Project** Have students publish and share their Writing Project compositions. See page T211.

CLOSE AND ASSESS

- **Language** *What are the* **physical** *features of a place that you learned about?*
- **Vocabulary** *What names of* **landforms** *are compound words?* (Answers will vary but could include mountaintop, seashore, and wetland.)
- **Reading** *Use Key Words to describe the pictures in the selection.*

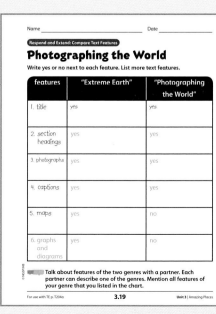

Name _____ Date _____

Respond and Extend: Compare Text Features

Photographing the World

Write yes or no next to each feature. List more text features.

features	"Extreme Earth"	"Photographing the World"
1. title	yes	yes
2. section headings	yes	yes
3. photographs	yes	yes
4. captions	yes	yes
5. maps	yes	no
6. graphs and diagrams	yes	no

Talk about features of the two genres with a partner. Each partner can describe one of the genres. Mention all features of your genre that you listed in the chart.

For use with TE p. T204a   **3.19**   Unit 3 | Amazing Places

 Practice Master 3.19

Day 7

Day at a Glance:
▶ **Language:** More Plural Nouns ▶ **Reading:** Reread the Selection
▶ **Vocabulary:** Compound Words ▶ **Writing:** Writing on Demand: Description

OBJECTIVES

Vocabulary
• Use Grade-Level Vocabulary
• Use Academic Vocabulary
• Strategy: Use Structural Analysis (Compound Words)

Language
• Irregular Plurals

Resources

✎ ⊙ *Practice Master 3.20*

Differentiate

Language Transfer

Challenge Many languages do not make the same distinction that English makes between count and noncount nouns. Students who speak these languages may try to add *-s* or *-es* to noncount nouns to make them plural.

Strategy Provide additional practice sets.

English Words		
Singular	**Plural**	**Sentence with plural**
sheep	sheep	I fed 2 sheep.
not
I fed 2 sheeps.
fish	fish	I fed 20 fish.
not
I fed 20 fishes.

As you write each plural form, point out that it is identical to the singular form. Have students practice with additional nouns, writing singular and plural forms (*money, jewelry, snow*).

Part 2 Grammar Skills Trace		Page
Day 2	Plural Nouns: Count/Noncount	T177a
Day 4	Proper Nouns	T196a
▶ Day 7	**More Plural Nouns: Irregular**	**T205a**
Day 10	Review Plural Nouns	T206g

Language of the Day

Imagine you are flying high in the sky. What landforms do you see?
I see _____.

Read the Language of the Day. Model: *I see waterfalls.* Invite students to add to your example, creating a cumulative sentence. As an added challenge, encourage students to include as many compound words as they can; for example: *I see waterfalls, seashores, mountaintops,* and so on.

Grammar More Plural Nouns ⊞ Ⓐ

1 Teach/Model Remind students that we form the plural of most nouns by adding *-s* or *-es*. Say: *Sometimes we make a spelling change before adding -s or -es.* Have students write the plurals of *peak, fox,* and *body.*

> (1 peak → 2 peaks   1 fox → 2 foxes   1 body → 2 bodies)

Then, read the introduction and first two rules aloud. Have students read the examples, adding numbers: one man, two men; one woman, two women, and so on. Have students identify spelling changes for each word.

Read the rule in the second part of the chart. Explain that some nouns use the same form when they become plural. Ask volunteers to read each example. (one moose, two moose; one sheep, two sheep)

Have students begin a Plural Nouns Chart in their journals. Tell them to include singular and plural forms of any nouns that they find difficult. Model:

Plural Nouns Chart	
country	countries
ox	oxen
deer	deer

2 Practice Read aloud the directions and excerpt from "Extreme Earth." Ask: What is the plural of *foot*?

3 Apply in Writing Read aloud the directions and have partners work together. After they read their sentences, assign **Practice Master 3.20**.

> **CHECK UNDERSTANDING** Ask: *How do you form the plural of* rice? (rice) *How do you form the plural of* sheep? (sheep) *How do you form the plural of* grandchild? (grandchildren)

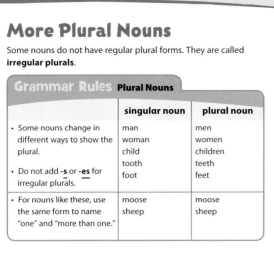

More Plural Nouns

Some nouns do not have regular plural forms. They are called **irregular plurals**.

Grammar Rules Plural Nouns

①

	singular noun	plural noun
• Some nouns change in different ways to show the plural. • Do not add **-s** or **-es** for irregular plurals.	man woman child tooth foot	men women children teeth feet
• For nouns like these, use the same form to name "one" and "more than one."	moose sheep	moose sheep

② **Read Plural Nouns**

Read these sentences from "Extreme Earth." Find the plural nouns. Which one does not follow regular plural rules?

> Huge ears release heat from the animal's body. Thick fur protects its feet from the hot sand. The fennec sleeps during the hot days and hunts during the cool nights.

③ **Write Plural Nouns** 🖉

Look at the pictures on pages 194–195. Write a sentence to tell about one of them. Use as many plural nouns as you can. Show your sentence to a partner.

205

Student Book page 205

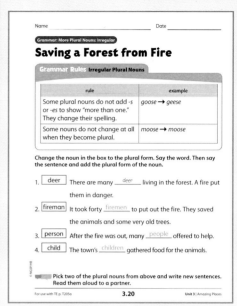

Practice Master 3.20

More Compound Words

④ **Review/Model** Review the Day 6 lesson (page T198). Write the sentences. Model using the definitions of the two smaller words to figure out the meaning of *jellyfish*. Have pairs do a **Three-Step Interview** to determine meanings of the other compound words.

- Some jellyfish shine in the dark. (soft-bodied sea creatures)
- The Great Barrier Reef is an underwater kingdom. (under the water)
- Chin compares photographing to filmmaking. (making a film)
- "Photography is a kind of storytelling." (telling a story)

⑤ **Practice/Apply** Read each sentence. Partners determine the meaning of each underlined word and write a definition.

1. Most fish cannot swim upstream. (against the flow of the stream)
2. Let's jump across the stones in the fishpond. (a pond full of fish)
3. You can write what we see in your notebook. (a book for taking notes)
4. I feel a few raindrops on my head. (drops of water from rain)

> **CHECK UNDERSTANDING** Say: *Give me an example of a compound word. Explain the meaning of each smaller word*. If students have difficulty, have them look back at the definitions they wrote in the practice section.

Part 2 Vocabulary Skills Trace		Page
Day 1	Social Studies Vocabulary	T175
Day 2	Academic Vocabulary	T177
Day 3	Expand Word Knowledge	T180b
Day 4	Share Word Knowledge	T196b
Day 5	Apply Word Knowledge	T197b
Day 6	Compound Words	T198
Day 7	**Compound Words**	**T205**
Days 8–9	Extend Vocabulary	T206e–f
Day 10	Vocabulary Review	T206g–f

Day 7
continued

Day at a Glance:
▶ **Grammar:** Irregular Plurals
▶ **Vocabulary:** Compound Words
▶ **Reading:** Reread the Selection
▶ **Writing:** Writing on Demand: Description

OBJECTIVES

Vocabulary
• Use Grade-Level Vocabulary
• Use Academic Vocabulary

Literary Analysis
• Analyze Genre: Profile ❶
• Analyze Photographs ❶
• Understand a Genre ❶

Learning and Teamwork Strategies
• Make Appropriate Contributions
• Connect Ideas

Writing
• Reproduce Modeled Writing
• Write a Description

Reread: Focus on Genre: Profile

❶ Teach Remind students that they have learned that a profile briefly tells about one person and focuses on one important thing about that person. Ask students to recall what they learned about Jimmy Chin from the profile. (He is a photographer; he loves the outdoors; he uses his athletic skills to take photographs that no one else has taken.) *Today, you will read "Photographing the World" again. This time, think about how the article focuses on Chin as a photographer.*

❷ Model Read the first page of "Photographing the World" aloud and say: *As I read the words, I stop to look at each photograph.* Ask: *What does the photograph of Chin tell you?* (Chin is grown up. He is dressed in clothes for the outdoors.) *The photograph of the two hikers tells me that Chin photographs distant places that few people visit.*

❸ Practice/Apply in Reading Have students read the section of "Photographing the World" titled "Getting the Shot." After reading, have groups use **Roundtable.** Ask the members of each group to discuss what each photograph shows. Ask: *Why does the photograph belong here? What does it tell you about Jimmy Chin?* Allow a representative of each group to answer before you move to the next photograph. Display frames to support students.

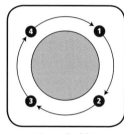

Roundtable

> The photograph shows _____.
> It tells me that Jimmy Chin _____.

> **CHECK UNDERSTANDING** Revisit the photograph of Jimmy Chin on the first page of the selection. Ask: *What can you tell about Jimmy Chin from his facial expression?*

Daily Writing

Writing on Demand: Description Display the writing prompt and have a volunteer read it aloud.

> Write a description of your favorite place and tell why you like it.

Unpack the Prompt Ask: *What is the purpose for writing?* Underline *describe your favorite place).* Then ask: *What form does the writing need to be?* Circle *description* in the prompt.

Explain: A good test-taking strategy is to write your topic sentence based on the prompt. Then add details to support it.

Use the **Modeled Writing Routine** to illustrate how to write a description. (See Writing Routines on page PD54).

Think Aloud	Write
1. Plan	
I will make a web to organize my ideas. I will put my topic in the center of the web.	the old oak tree in my grandfather's backyard
What details can I give to describe the features of my tree? How can I let readers know how special it is?	wide, low branches and thick trunk cool, shady
2. Write	
I will start my paragraph with the main idea.	My favorite place is under the shade of an oak tree in my grandfather's backyard.
Next I will give details about the topic. I will include words that help my reader picture the tree.	The oak tree is the largest tree in the whole yard. One of its features is its thick trunk. Four of us, holding hands, can barely wrap our arms around it.
Model additional details to finish the description. Wrap it up with a concluding sentence.	
3. Read and Reflect	
Model how to proofread the description. Have students identify any plural nouns and see if they have used the right form and spelled them correctly.	

Display the finished description to serve as a model. Use **Multi-Level Strategies** to support students at all proficiency levels in writing the description. After students finish, have them read their descriptions to partners.

CLOSE AND ASSESS
- **Language:** *What regular and irregular plurals did you use in your writing? Did you use any noncount nouns?*
- **Vocabulary:** *How did knowing the Key Words help you in your writing?*
- **Reading:** *How would you compare your description to the selections in "Amazing Places"?*

Differentiate

Multi-Level Strategies

BEGINNING

Use this frame and allow beginners to draw and write familiar words to complete the description.

- My favorite place is ___.
- It is ___
- It has ___

INTERMEDIATE

Have students work in small groups to create a web for a favorite place. Encourage students to work together to list features of the place they want to describe.

ADVANCED

Have students write independently. Then ask them to read aloud their descriptions to partners for feedback. Ask partners to suggest where more details are needed.

ADVANCED HIGH

Encourage students to incorporate proper nouns in their descriptions to tell more about where the place is located.

Days 8–9

Day at a Glance:
▶ **Language:** Oral Language Project: Oral Report
▶ **Vocabulary:** Extend Vocabulary
▶ **Reading:** Read Leveled Books
▶ **Writing:** Paraphrase

OBJECTIVES

Vocabulary
• Use Grade-Level Vocabulary ❶

Language
• Language Function: Describe Places ❶

Listening and Speaking
• Listen and Ask Questions
• Connect to Prior Experience
• Use Visual Aids
• Use Gestures and Expressions

Learning and Teamwork Strategies
• Respond to Questions

Resources

• materials for props such as:
  - construction paper
  - magazines with photographs of extreme places
  - crayons or markers

⟳ ◷ Assessment Handbook page 118

Language of the Day

What did you learn that changed your mind about **landforms**?
I thought ____.
Now I know ____.

Read the Language of the Day. Model: *I thought some landforms were in places no one could get to. Now I know that there are people who go where others would not dare to!* Have students answer the question and encourage them to share their ideas.

Oral Language Project Oral Report

1 **Introduce the Activity** Explain that groups will be giving oral reports on extreme places. Prompt brainstorming: *Imagine you are an explorer who has just returned from an expedition to an extreme place, such as a live volcano. A group of young explorers wants to hear what your trip was like.*

Ask students to think about what happened during their imaginary trip. Encourage them to be creative. Collect responses.

2 **Plan** Form casts of five students each. Have students review "Extreme Earth" and either pick an extreme place from the selection or come up with one on their own. Help students pick roles based on their proficiency levels. Example roles include lead explorer, exploration team, and photographer.

Have casts work together to plan the oral report. Students should write a few sentences describing where they went and what the place is like. They can use the language frames on page 174 to help describe the place. Encourage students to create photographs from their trip with magazine cuttings or original drawings.

3 **Practice** Have students with speaking parts rehearse their lines. Other students can point to photographs or use pantomime to show the extreme weather (wiping weat from their brow) and physical features (trudging uphill). Encourage group members to respond to one another's suggestions so everyone is involved in planning the oral report. Use **Multi-Level Strategies** to help students at each proficiency level.

4 **Explore the World!** Display the photographs and have groups take turns reporting about their extreme place. One group in the audience can act as the young explorers and ask questions to clarify information. Invite family members or another class to enjoy the oral reports. Evaluate the reports using the rubric. For each report, assess the young explorer group's listening skills.

5 **Debrief and Compare** Ask each group to comment on how the imaginary trips remind them of real experiences they have had. Have them add any ideas they learned about why we learn about other places to their unit concept map.

Differentiate

Multi-Level Strategies

BEGINNING

Coach students on how to pantomime actions and use visual aids to communicate ideas.

INTERMEDIATE

Tell students to begin by practicing their parts individually, focusing on using correct sentences. Next, have them rehearse questions and answers with at least one member of their group.

ADVANCED **ADVANCED HIGH**

Encourage students to answer questions that the young explorers ask during the report.

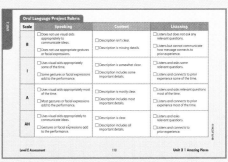

 Assessment Handbook page 118

Days 8-9
continued

Day at a Glance:
▶ **Language:** Oral Language Project: Oral Report
▶ **Vocabulary:** Extend Vocabulary
▶ **Reading:** Read Leveled Books
▶ **Writing:** Paraphrase

OBJECTIVES

Vocabulary
- Extend Vocabulary through Wide Reading

Language
- Participate in Discussion

Reading
- Read Independently
- Summarize Reading
- Make Connections: Text to Text
- Apply Reading Strategies Varied Texts

Writing
- Paraphrase in Logical Order

Social Studies
- Explore the World's Regions

Resources

 Leveled Books:
- *In the Dark Cave*
- *My Little Island*
- *Antarctic Adventure*
- *Places to Visit*
- *Antarctica: Ice-Covered Continent*
- *Matthew Henson*

   Reach Leveled Library Lesson Plans

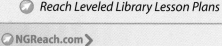
Find more leveled readers about this topic.

Differentiate Read Leveled Books

Group students based on their reading abilities and interests. Use the **Guided Reading** routine (See page PD47) for books at students' instructional level. Use the **Independent Reading Support** (see page PD50) for books at students' independent reading level.

After reading, organize the students into heterogeneous groups to discuss what they read and to use the new information to answer the Big Question. Use these prompts to guide your discussion:

- What new information did you learn about what makes a place amazing?

- What surprised you?

- How did new information change your answer?

Fiction

BEGINNING LEVEL

In the Dark Cave
by Richard Watson

- **Genre:** Animal Fantasy

Some animals are perfectly adapted to living in darkness. Alexander encounters some of these during a visit to the unexplored depths of a cave.

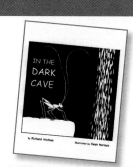

Key Words

creatures

cricket

darkness

depths

shaft

INTERMEDIATE LEVEL

My Little Island
by Frané Lessac

- **Genre:** Realistic Fiction

Two boys visit the Caribbean island where one of them was born. Students learn about the island's culture along with them.

Key Words

dozens

folktales

gobble

square

volcano

ADVANCED   ADVANCED HIGH LEVELS

Antarctic Adventure
by Rebecca L. Johnson

- **Genre:** Realistic Fiction

In this chapter book, four interns travel to icy Antarctica to study Adelie penguins. While they're there, they learn all about the world's coldest continent.

Key Words

icebergs

penguin

predators

scientists

survival

Nonfiction

BEGINNING LEVEL

Places to Visit
by Nick Bruce

- **Genre:** Expository Nonfiction

Learn more about some of America's beautiful natural landmarks, including the Grand Canyon and Yellowstone Park. Maps aid and help to geographically orient students.

Key Words

areas

canyon

marsh

national

volcano

INTERMEDIATE LEVEL

Antarctica: Ice-Covered Continent
by Sherilin Chanek

- **Genre:** Expository Nonfiction

Learn more about the coldest continent on Earth—Antarctica, a land of ice and wind.

Key Words

coldest

continent

explored

icebergs

penguin

ADVANCED   ADVANCED HIGH LEVELS

Matthew Henson
by Maryann N. Weidt

- **Genre:** Biography

In this chapter book, students read about Matthew Henson, an African-American explorer and one of the first people to reach the North Pole.

Key Words

adventure

expedition

friendships

journey

servant

Daily Writing   A AH

Journal Entry Have students write a journal entry in their reading journals. Use "Extreme Earth" to model how to paraphrase in logical order. Provide an example that does not maintain order by skipping the beginning. Have students share their journal entries with others, recommending books they enjoyed.

Same Book / Different Levels

B I A AH

Climbing to Success
by Jacqueline St. Jacques

Explore the dangerous world of the mountain climbers, as they scale the world's tallest mountain, Mount Everest.

Pioneer Edition
Fountas and Pinnell: P-R

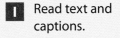

B Conduct a Picture Walk.

I Read text and captions.

Key Words

avalanche	dangerous
guide	Sherpa
skills	summit

Pathfinder Edition
Fountas and Pinnell: Q-S

A Read text and captions.

AH Read and write responses to questions.

Key Words

avalanche	dangerous
expeditions	migrated
scale	summit

Part 2 Vocabulary Skills Trace		Page
Day 1	Social Studies Vocabulary	T175
Day 2	Academic Vocabulary	T177
Day 3	Expand Word Knowledge	T180b
Day 4	Share Word Knowledge	T196b
Day 5	Apply Word Knowledge	T197b
Day 6	Compound Words	T198
Day 7	Compound Words	T205
Days 8–9	Extend Vocabulary	T206e–f
Day 10	Vocabulary Review	T206g–h

OBJECTIVES

Vocabulary
- Review and Use Grade-Level Key Vocabulary **T**
- Review Compound Words

Language
- Review Language Function: Describe Places **T**

Language
- Review Irregular Plurals

Reading Strategy
- Review Visualize

Comprehension and Literary Analysis
- Review Genre: Social Studies Article
- Review Main Idea and Details

Fluency
- Phrasing

Social Studies
- Investigate Geography

Resources

- *Assessment Handbook*
- *Key Word Images*
- *eVisuals 3.33*
- *Comprehension Coach*

Part 2 Grammar Skills Trace		Page
Day 2	Irregular Plural Nouns: Count/Noncount	T177a
Day 4	Proper Nouns	T196a
Day 7	More Plural Nouns: Irregular	T205a
▶ Day 10	**Review Plural Nouns**	**T206g**

Language of the Day

What did you learn? How does it help you in school?
I learned how to ____. ____ means to ____. For example, ____.

Read the Language of the Day. Model: *I learned how to visualize. It means to form pictures in your mind while you read. For example, when I read a description of a beach, I picture how the beach looks, feels, and sounds.* Review the list of skills students learned in Part 2. Prompt students to talk about a skill they have learned.

Review and Assess

Use these interactive review activities to reinforce concepts covered in Part 2. Then use the assessment tools to evaluate students' progress. For more details about assessment, see page T213a.

Language Function

Describe Places

Use a **Fishbowl** to have students take turns describing a place. Display **Key Word Image**. Students on the inside describe the place while students on the outside listen. Display a new image, and have students switch roles.

- **Assessment:** Use the Language Function Rubric on page 110 of the Assessment Handbook.

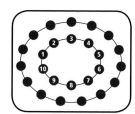

Fishbowl

Grammar

Plural Nouns

Display these words: **ocean**, *explore, beach, city, heavy,* **valley** *, tooth, tiny, sheep.* Have partners determine which words are nouns and then write the plural form of each noun. Challenge partners to create sentences that use two of the plural nouns and read them aloud to the class.

- **Assessment:** Use the Grammar and Spelling Unit Tests on pages 151–157 on of the Assessment Handbook.

Vocabulary

Social Studies and Academic Vocabulary

Form two teams. Show **Key Word Images**. Give clues about the Key Word represented by one of the images. Have teams identify the Key Word and the matching image. When each word has been identified, have the teams use the word in a sentence.

- **Assessment:** Use the Key Words Part 2 Tests on pages 115–117 of the Assessment Handbook.

Key Words	
canyon	physical
elevation	plain
feature	plateau
landform	region
locate	surface
ocean	valley

Vocabulary Strategy

Word Work: Compound Words

Write words on index cards. Include several compound words. Have a player from each team draw a word card and tell whether or not the word is a compound word. Challenge teams to name the two small words in each compound word. The team that gives the most correct answers wins.

> Classroom is a compound word.

> The two small words in *classroom* are *class* and *room*.

- **Assessment:** Use the Reading Unit Tests pages 122–125 of the Assessment Handbook.

Reading Strategy

 Read Aloud

Visualize

Read the first paragraph in "Denali National Park." Have students visualize something described in the text using the **Academic Language Frames:** *I read _____. I picture _____.*

- **Assessment:** Use the Reading Strategy Test page 119 of the Assessment Handbook.

Comprehension

Read Aloud

Literary Analysis

Read the rest of "Denali National Park." Have students identify a main idea from the text and at least two details about it.

Text Structure

Have students identify specific words that describe Denali National Park, using these frames: *I see _____. I hear _____. I feel _____. I smell _____. I taste _____.*

- **Assessment:** Use the Reading Unit Tests on pages 126–150 of the Assessment Handbook.

Fluency

Phrasing

Have students review their own recordings of "Extreme Earth" in the Comprehension Coach. Then have students practice reading **Leveled Library Books** that are appropriate for their reading levels, focusing on accuracy and phrasing.

Read Aloud

Denali National Park

Denali National Park is in Alaska. Mt. McKinley, the tallest peak in North America, towers over the park. Heavy summer rains bring a burst of color. The alpine tundra region looks like a giant green blanket dotted with white, pink, and yellow flowers.

There are no roads or buildings in most of the park. Dall sheep run along the steep cliffs and rocky ledges. The sheep's white coat and curled horns stand out against the gray rock. Grizzly bears search for roots, grasses, and sweet berries. In winter, they escape the extreme cold by sleeping inside warm dens dug into hillsides.

Denali has many glaciers. A glacier is an enormous mass of snow and ice. The ice is smooth, hard, and slippery. The glaciers glisten in the bright sun. Suddenly, a loud *crack* booms through the park as a large chunk of ice breaks off and crashes to the ground.

NGReach.com > eVisual 3.33

Part 2 Vocabulary Skills Trace		Page
Day 1	Social Studies Vocabulary	T175
Day 2	Academic Vocabulary	T177
Day 3	Expand Word Knowledge	T180b
Day 4	Share Word Knowledge	T196b
Day 5	Apply Word Knowledge	T197b
Day 6	Compound Words	T198
Day 7	Compound Words	T205
Days 8–9	Extend Vocabulary	T206e–f
Day 10	**Vocabulary Review**	**T206g–h**

Mode and Form

A research report includes information from a variety of sources that is organized in a new and interesting way. For this project, each student will write about one of the most extreme places in the United States.

Writing Checklist

A good research report

✔ starts with a paragraph that tells what the report is about

✔ has a topic sentence for each paragraph

✔ supports main ideas with facts and details

✔ includes a list of sources.

NGReach.com ▸ **eVisual 3.34**

Connect Reading to Writing Use "Extreme Earth" as a reference for qualities of a research report. Reread the text and point out features of the form.

Writing Trait: Organization

Students will learn how good writers organize and create a research report in which:

• the writing has a clear structure that is appropriate for a research report

• there is a main idea for each paragraph

• ideas flow smoothly from each sentence to the next within a paragraph, and ideas flow smoothly from each paragraph to the next.

Lesson Overview and Pacing

Each lesson in the Writing Project provides detailed instruction. Teach the Writing Project during Part 2 of the unit with this suggested daily sequence and pacing plan, or adjust as your schedule and student needs require.

• Day 1: Introducing the Writing Prompt, Study a Model

• Day 2: Prewrite

• Day 3: Draft

• Day 4: Revise

• Day 5: Edit and Proofread

• Day 6: Publish

Classroom Vocabulary

Use **Vocabulary Routine 4** to teach **organization**. (See **Vocabulary Routines**, page PD40.)

Three-Fold Tab

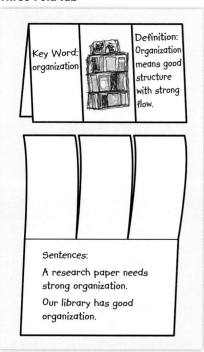

Key Word: organization

Definition: Organization means good structure with strong flow.

Sentences:
A research paper needs strong organization.

Our library has good organization.

Rubric: Research Report

Students use **Practice Master 3.21** to score their own writing on the trait of organization. You can then use the *Reach* Writing Rubric to score each student's project on all traits.

Writing Rubric

Score Point	Focus and Coherence	Organization	Development of Ideas	Voice and Style	Written Conventions
4	**Focus** Paragraphs and the writing as a whole are focused. Ideas are related. Details are relevant. **Completeness** The writing feels complete. The introduction and conclusion are meaningful.	**Structure** The organizing strategy is well-suited to the writer's purpose. **Progression of Ideas** Ideas flow logically and smoothly, with meaningful transitions.	**Content Quality** The writer takes a risk and treats the topic in an interesting way, with insight and thoughtfulness. **Elaboration** Ideas are developed in depth.	**Individuality** The writing sounds genuine and unique. **Word Choice** Words and phrases are interesting and appropriate to the writer's purpose and audience.	**Grammar, Usage, Mechanics, and Spelling** There are only a few errors. **Sentence Fluency** Sentences are varied and effective.
3	**Focus** Paragraphs and the writing as a whole are mostly focused, but there are a few sudden shifts between ideas. Most details are relevant. **Completeness** The writing feels mostly complete. The introduction and conclusion add some meaning.	**Structure** The organizing strategy is generally suited to the writer's purpose. **Progression of Ideas** Most ideas flow logically and smoothly, but there are a few gaps.	**Content Quality** The writer does not take much of a risk, but does treat the topic in a thoughtful way. **Elaboration** Some ideas are more developed than others.	**Individuality** For the most part, the writing sounds genuine and unique. **Word Choice** Words and phrases are mostly interesting and appropriate to the writer's purpose and audience.	**Grammar, Usage, Mechanics, and Spelling** Errors are minor and/or infrequent. **Sentence Fluency** There is some sentence variety. Sentences are generally effective.
2	**Focus** Paragraphs and the writing as a whole are somewhat focused, but there are a number of sudden shifts between ideas. Some details are relevant. **Completeness** The writing feels somewhat complete. The introduction and conclusion may be superficial.	**Structure** The organizing strategy is not clear or does not suit the writer's purpose. **Progression of Ideas** There are breaks in logic and very few transitions.	**Content Quality** The topic is covered, but in an uninteresting way. **Elaboration** Ideas are listed or mentioned superficially.	**Individuality** A few passages sound genuine and unique. **Word Choice** Words and phrases are somewhat interesting and appropriate to the writer's purpose and audience.	**Grammar, Usage, Mechanics, and Spelling** Errors are frequent, but the meaning is clear. **Sentence Fluency** Sentences are somewhat awkward and have simple or inaccurate words.
1	**Focus** The writing is not focused. Ideas are unrelated. Many details are irrelevant. **Completeness** The writing feels incomplete. If there is an introduction and conclusion, they may be perfunctory.	**Structure** No organizing strategy is evident. **Progression of Ideas** Writing is illogical, wordy, and/or repetitious.	**Content Quality** The topic is not really covered. **Elaboration** There is little or no development of ideas.	**Individuality** There is little or no sense of the writer. **Word Choice** Words and phrases are not appropriate to the writer's purpose and audience.	**Grammar, Usage, Mechanics, and Spelling** Errors are severe and/or frequent and are a barrier to understanding. **Sentence Fluency** Sentences are awkward and have missing or misused words.

OBJECTIVES
Writing
- Analyze a Student Model: Research Report
- Trait: Evaluate for Organization ❶
- Use a Rubric to Analyze Writing

Resources

 eVisual 3.34

 Practice Master 3.21

eVisual 3.35

Introduce the Writing Project

❶ Analyze the Prompt Ask a volunteer to read aloud the title of the project and the prompt. As the student reads, have the rest of the class begin to fill out the first three sections of a RAFT:

Role: researcher
Audience: the school community
Form: research report
Topic: _____

Remind students that although they haven't decided on a specific topic for the research report, the prompt gives them a broad subject to begin thinking about. Ask them what that subject is. (one of the most extreme places in the United States) Explain that students will be choosing a topic for the research report when they do the Prewrite step.

Focus on language: *Who is the audience?* (students, teachers, and others in the school building) Guide students in recognizing that formal language is used for a research report.

Study a Model

❷ Focus on Features Read aloud the directions and then have students read the model silently. Remind students to look for a title and introductory paragraph, topic sentences, and main ideas supported by facts and details.

Chorally reread the model, stopping to discuss each callout. Display the **Writing Checklist** and have students find examples of each feature in the model.

> **Writing Checklist**
>
> **A good research report**
>
> ✔ starts with a paragraph that tells what the report is about
>
> ✔ has a topic sentence for each paragraph
>
> ✔ supports main ideas with facts and details
>
> ✔ includes a list of sources.
>
> 🌐 NGReach.com ▶ eVisual 3.34

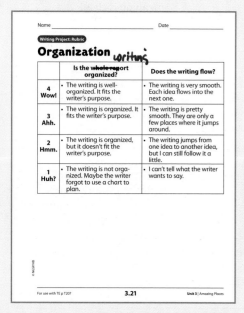

🌐 Practice Master 3.21

Write Like a Researcher

❶ Write a Research Report ✎

Write a report about one of the most extreme places in the United States. You and your classmates will use what you learn to create a display for others to enjoy.

Encourage students to begin thinking of other ways to publish their reports

Study a Model

When you write a research report, you include information from different sources. You organize the facts you find and present them in a new and interesting way.

Read Cheryl's report about Death Valley.

---

❷

Life in Death Valley

Cheryl Lin

It's hard to imagine a place that's more extreme than Death Valley, in California and Nevada. Death Valley is the hottest and the driest place in North America. It also has the lowest spot in the Western Hemisphere! Yet **Death Valley is full of life**.

Death Valley isn't an easy place to live. It gets less than two inches of rain a year, so there isn't much water. It's hot, too. In July, temperatures often climb to over 115 degrees

The title and introduction tell **what the report is about**. *The introduction also gets the reader's attention.*

Each paragraph has a **topic sentence** *that tells the main idea.*

Fahrenheit. The ground is mostly sand and rocks. There is even a dried-up lake that has turned into salt crystals.

None of this stops plants and animals from making Death Valley their home. People have found more than 1,000 types of plants there. It also has 51 types of mammals, 36 kinds of reptiles, 6 types of fish, and more than 300 kinds of birds. The animals aren't all small, either. There are big ones like bighorn sheep, mountain lions, and mule deer.

Water is the biggest challenge for anything that lives in Death Valley. Some plants have roots that go fifty feet beneath the surface to find water. Kangaroo rats get the water they need from the seeds of desert sunflowers. Tiny pupfish can live in water that is 90 degrees Fahrenheit and five times as salty as the ocean!

Every topic sentence is developed with facts and details.

The report is focused. Every paragraph helps to develop the topic.

Sources

"Death Valley." World Book Encyclopedia. 2009. Print.

Death Valley. National Park Service, 11 Jun. 2010. Web. 12 Feb. 2011. <http://www.nps.gov/deva/index.htm>

Hamilton, John. Death Valley National Park. Edina, Minnesota: Abdo Publishing Company, 2009.

A final page lists the sources that Cheryl used for the report.

206 | 207

Student Book pages 206–207

---

❸ Teach the Trait

Ask: *If your closet is organized, how does it look?* (Things are put away neatly, in certain places.) *Writing should be organized, too. In organized writing, all the sentences and paragraphs flow together well.* Find examples of organization in the model:

- *How does the first paragraph set up the organization?* (It clearly tells what the research paper is about. It sets up the flow for the report.)
- *How does the second paragraph show strong organization?* (It begins with a topic sentence and then supports the topic sentence with related details.)
- *How does the entire report show strong organization?* (Each paragraph flows smoothly to the next. All paragraphs tell something about the topic.)

❹ Present the Rubric

Distribute **Practice Master 3.21**. Read aloud the questions and features of each score point. Assign partners the task of telling you the difference between a paper with a score of 2 and 4. Allow time for the partners to review the rubric and then report out. (Students' responses should indicate that a 4-point paper has stronger organization.) Use the **Academic Language Frames** to support students of all proficiency levels.

> **CHECK PROGRESS** Ask students to give one example of how a feature of a research report show strong organization.

Differentiate

Academic Language Frames

Discuss the Rubric
TRAIT: ORGANIZATION

■ 1. It	has / does not have	strong organization.
2. It	does / does not	have a topic sentence for each paragraph.
3. The sentences	do / do not	flow well.

- ■ 1. A four-point research report has _____.
- 2. Each paragraph has a _____ with _____.
- 3. The sentences and paragraphs _____ smoothly.

- ■ A 4-point research report has strong _____, but the
- ■ _____ of a 2-point paper is not as strong.

NGReach.com ▸ eVisual 3.35

OBJECTIVES

Learning and Teamwork Strategies
- Generate Ideas through Brainstorming
- Use Graphic Organizers: Chart

Writing
- Writing Process (Prewrite): Select a Topic, Organize Ideas
- Conduct Research: Locate Information in Texts, Identify Facts and Details

Resources

- *Reference materials such as nonfiction books, magazines, newspapers, encyclopedias, atlases, almanacs, and appropriate online sites*

 eVisual 3.36

Practice Master 3.22

Prewrite

1 Choose a Topic Assemble print materials students can use for their initial planning, such as almanacs, atlases, encyclopedias, geography books, and travel brochures. If possible, arrange for students to have access to the Internet as well. Then review: *What is your research report about?* (one of the most extreme places in the United States)

Display eVisual 3.36. Say: *A chart like this can help you as you choose your extreme place. The extreme place you choose might be very hot or very cold. It might have unusual geographic features, such as high mountains or dense forests.*

Name of Place	State Where It Is Located	Why It Is Extreme

NGReach.com > eVisual 3.36

Display the materials: *Skim the materials for ideas and use your chart to make quick notes about each place that interests you. Skimming means that you quickly look through the materials for information and ideas. You will write the name of the place in the first column. In the second column, you will write the name of the state where the place is located. And in the last column, you will jot quick notes to tell what is extreme about the place.*

Distribute **Practice Master 3.22**. After students have completed their charts, have them select the place that is most interesting to them for their topic.

2 List Your Research Questions Tell students to consider what they already know about the selected topic, as well as what they want to find out. Direct their attention to the questions on page 208. Have a student read the questions aloud.

Have students think of other possible research questions, such as:

- *What is the highest temperature?*
- *What is the lowest temperature?*
- *How much rainfall is there each year?*

Suggest students consider these kinds of ideas as they write their own questions. Allow time for them to create a list of at least four questions.

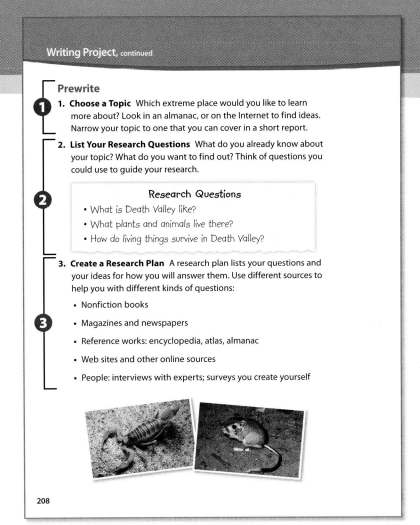

Prewrite

1. Choose a Topic Which extreme place would you like to learn more about? Look in an almanac, or on the Internet to find ideas. Narrow your topic to one that you can cover in a short report.

2. List Your Research Questions What do you already know about your topic? What do you want to find out? Think of questions you could use to guide your research.

Research Questions

- What is Death Valley like?
- What plants and animals live there?
- How do living things survive in Death Valley?

3. Create a Research Plan A research plan lists your questions and your ideas for how you will answer them. Use different sources to help you with different kinds of questions:

- Nonfiction books
- Magazines and newspapers
- Reference works: encyclopedia, atlas, almanac
- Web sites and other online sources
- People: interviews with experts; surveys you create yourself

208

Student Book page 208

Handwritten note: #3 of TE blue heads are dif. from SE - but titles are same

Brainstorm

Use this chart to brainstorm possible topics for your research report. After you complete it, circle the topic that is most interesting to you.

Name of Place	State Where It Is Located	Why It Is Extreme

For use with TE p T208   3.22   Unit 3 | Amazing Places

Practice Master 3.22

3 Create a Research Plan Chorally read the directions. Give examples of each resource so students understand what they are. Ask: *How do you know which references will be useful to answer each type of question?* (You can use what you know about the resource. For example a magazine, newspaper, or Web site has the most current information. An encyclopedia includes historical information.)

Have students write the most helpful resource next to each of their research questions. Use **Multi-Level Strategies** to support students at each proficiency level.

CHECK PROGRESS Have students explain why each research question will be helpful in writing the research report.

Differentiate

Multi-Level Strategies

BEGINNING

Guide students to the most helpful resources for their questions. Check that the resource is appropriate for their proficiency level.

ADVANCED   INTERMEDIATE

To guide students in identifying reference types that have been useful in the past, provide this sentence frame:

The _____ helped me answer the question about _____ because _____.

ADVANCED HIGH

Have partners discuss types of references that have helped them with specific kinds of research in the past.

OBJECTIVES
Learning Strategies
• Locate Information
• Use Graphic Organizers:
  Note Cards
Writing
• Writing Process (Prewrite): Conduct
  Research: Locate Information in Texts,
  Organize Ideas

Resources

• *Index cards for notes*

Gather Information

❶ Identify Sources Explain: *You have worked to think about kinds of resources that will help you answer your research questions. Now, you will find the exact resources to use. How can you quickly check to see if there might be helpful information in them?* (by skimming the table of contents, headings, index, and text features)

Why is it important that every source is up-to-date? (because old information might no longer be correct)

Ask: *Why is important to look for information from experts and others who truly know about the information?* (You want to be sure the information is correct.) *Why is it especially important to be careful on the Web?* (It is easy for people to post information on the Web, and the information might not be true.) Explain that sites run by the government, colleges or universities, and professional organizations usually contain reliable information.

❷ Create Source Cards Go through the features of the source card. Explain that a source card for a Web site would list:

• the title of the article
• the name of the author or organization
• the date the information was retrieved from the Web
• the exact Web address.

Make certain students understand that they will create one of these cards for each source.

❸ Make Note Cards Have students examine the note card on page 209 as they respond to the following questions. *Why do you need to include the title, author, and page number of the source?* (so I can go back to check later and so that others can check the source) *Why do you write facts and details in your own words?* (When I put information in my own words, I understand it better. I should not write the author's words in my report. The words should be my own.)

Encourage students to write one fact per card so that they can more easily organize their ideas later.

Gather Information

1. Identify Sources Choose your sources carefully. Be sure every source is up to date. Also make sure the information is written by an expert in the area.

2. Create Source Cards Keep track of your sources. Use index cards to record important information. Give each card a number.

Source Card for a Book

Death Valley National Park	Card number
John Hamilton	Title of book
Abdo Publishing Company, Edina, Minnesota	Author
2009	Publication information
J917.948	Library call number

3. Make Note Cards As you research, record important words, phrases, and ideas onto note cards. Be sure to put all of the information in your own words.

Note Card

What plants and animals live in Death Valley? — Research question

Death Valley National Park, by John Hamilton, pages 16-17 — Include the title, author, and page number of the source.

--small mammals include kangaroo rats, ground squirrels, and bats

--larger animals include bighorn sheep, mountain lions, and mule deer — Write facts and details in your own words.

Get Organized

1. Sort Your Cards Begin by grouping your cards according to the research questions. Put the cards in an order that makes sense.

2. Organize Information Use an outline or other graphic organizer to help you organize the details. Each group, or category, from your cards can become a main idea. Put the details from those cards under the main idea.

Outline

I. What Death Valley is like
  A. Little water
  B. High temperatures
  C. Rough land
    1. Desert and sand
    2. Rocks

II. Plants and animals — Use Roman numerals for main ideas.
  A. 1,000 types of plants
  B. Small and large mammals
  C. Other animals — Use capital letters for supporting points.

Draft

Use your outline to guide you as you write.

- Begin with an introduction that tells what the report is about.
- Turn each group of ideas from your outline into a paragraph.
- Include maps, photos, or charts to help explain your ideas.
- Put all the information in your own words. Never use words directly from the source. To use someone else's words is to plagiarize (**plā**-ju-riz), which is a type of stealing.

209 210

Student Book page 209–210

Get Organized

4 Sort Your Cards Once students have grouped their cards by research question, discuss possible organization. Suggest that they put all similar facts and examples together. For example, if they talk about the plant and animal life in a place, they should group all the plant life information rather than mixing it up with the facts about the animals.

5 Organize Information Chorally read through the directions. Have a volunteer read the callouts. Then explain that the Roman numerals in the outline will become the topic sentences for each paragraph in the report. Tell students the capital letters in the outline will be the supporting details in the report.

Have students use their sorted cards to create their outlines. Use **Multi-Level Strategies** to support students at each proficiency level.

CHECK PROGRESS Have students explain how each phrase in their outlines supports the main idea that comes before it.

Differentiate

Multi-Level Strategies

BEGINNING

Have students organize their note cards and then write Roman numerals and captial letters next to the facts on the cards to organize their ideas. Encourage them to write short main ideas and then copy their cards for the supporting points.

INTERMEDIATE

Remind students to use their cards and put their details in a logical order. As they create their outlines, they might choose to adjust the order in which they sorted their cards.

ADVANCED ADVANCED HIGH

Before pairs create their outlines, have each partner discuss the way the other partner has organized note cards. Tell students to make suggestions about organization that could help before starting with the outline.

OBJECTIVES

Writing

• Use the Writing Process (Drafting): Write a Research Report

• Use Writing Strategies: Organize Ideas

• Develop Writer's Craft: Support Ideas

Draft

❶ Introduce Drafting Use the **Modeled Writing Routine** (See **Writing Routines**, page PD54.) to show how to turn the outline into a draft. Students will focus on:

• **Writer's Craft: Support Ideas** Remind students: *When you write a research report, it is important to each support topic sentence with details.* Ask: *Why is the support important?* (It makes the writing clearer and more interesting.) *What are some kinds of support you can include in a research report?* (written details, maps, photos, and charts) Have students point out the topic sentence and supporting details in each paragraph in the model on pages 206–207.

• **Writing Strategy: Organize Ideas** Review: *When you write a research report, you should organize ideas by beginning with an introduction that tells what the report is about and then including topic sentences with supporting details in an order that makes sense.* Ask: *What tool do you have to help organize your ideas?* (the outline they created)

Say	Write
My first paragraph should identify the topic and grab the reader's attention.	Death Valley is the hottest and the driest place in North America. Yet Death alley is full of life.
In the next paragraph, I need to begin with a topic sentence to tell the main idea of the paragraph. And it's important for me to support the main idea with details. I will find this information under Roman numeral I in my outline.	Death Valley isn't an easy place to live. It gets less than two inches of rain a year, so there isn't much water.
I've been organizing well. I'll continue by adding more paragraphs. Each paragraph will begin with a topic sentence that comes from a Roman numeral in my outline.	None of this stops plants and animals from making Death Valley their home. People have found more than 1,000 types of native plants.
Pause to review organization. Ask: *Does the research report show strong organization so far?* (yes) *Do the sentences flow smoothly?* (yes)	
Once I have written all my paragraphs, I need a page to show my sources. I will use my Source Cards to do that.	**Sources** "Death Valley." World Book Encyclopedia. 2009. Print.

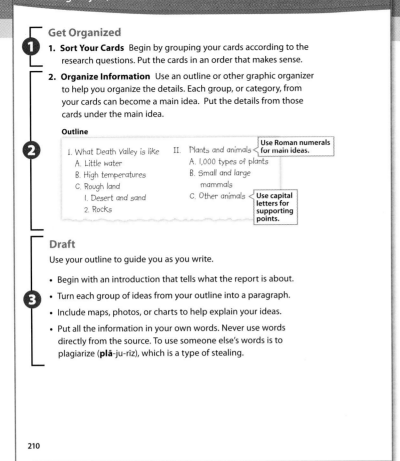

Get Organized

1 1. **Sort Your Cards** Begin by grouping your cards according to the research questions. Put the cards in an order that makes sense.

2. **Organize Information** Use an outline or other graphic organizer to help you organize the details. Each group, or category, from your cards can become a main idea. Put the details from those cards under the main idea.

Outline

2

I. What Death Valley is like
   A. Little water
   B. High temperatures
   C. Rough land
      1. Desert and sand
      2. Rocks

II. Plants and animals
   A. 1,000 types of plants
   B. Small and large mammals
   C. Other animals

> Use Roman numerals for main ideas.

> Use capital letters for supporting points.

Draft

Use your outline to guide you as you write.

3
- Begin with an introduction that tells what the report is about.
- Turn each group of ideas from your outline into a paragraph.
- Include maps, photos, or charts to help explain your ideas.
- Put all the information in your own words. Never use words directly from the source. To use someone else's words is to plagiarize (**plă**-ju-riz), which is a type of stealing.

210

Student Book page 210

2 ## Write the Draft Have students begin their own drafts. Use **Multi-Level Strategies** to support writers at all levels of language proficiency.

Explain: *Before you begin writing, be sure to gather all the things you need: paper, pencil RAFT chart, research questions, note cards, and outline.*

Remind students: *Your chart and notes may contain fragments or incomplete ideas. Check that every sentence in your draft is a complete sentence.*

CHECK PROGRESS Have students point out the information in the outline that will begin the report. Then ask them to point to each paragraph's topic sentence and then to the supporting details.

Differentiate

Multi-Level Strategies

BEGINNING

Provide sentence frames to support students in turning their outlines into sentences:

- _____ is _____ .
- It has _____ .
- There are _____ .

INTERMEDIATE

As students turn their outlines into sentences, remind them to start a new paragraph with each Roman numeral and to include all the details next to each capital letter.

ADVANCED **ADVANCED HIGH**

Encourage students to write an engaging introduction with a variety of sentence types.

OBJECTIVES

Listening, Speaking, and Teamwork Strategies

- Conduct a Peer Conference
- Build on Ideas

Writing

- Writing Process (Revise):
- Revise Drafts for Organization
- Revise Drafts for Facts and Details and Own Words
- Use Revising Marks

Resources

 eVisual 3.37

 Practice Master 3.23

eVisual 3.38

Differentiate

Multi-Level Strategies

BEGINNING

Hold individual conferences with students. Check to be sure all students have written in their own words and have refrained from including unrelated details.

INTERMEDIATE

Tell partners to ask and answer:

- *Have I written the report in my own words?*
- *Have I taken out any unrelated details?*

ADVANCED   ADVANCED HIGH

Have students hold complete peer conferences. Direct them to point out strengths, as well as problems. Also, tell them to provide suggestions for improvement.

Revise

1 Read, Retell, and Respond Review the trait on **Practice Master 3.21**. Then use **eVisual 3.37** to model how to conduct a peer conference. Have students read the paragraphs aloud.

> Some places are really hot
> Death Valley isn't an easy place to live. It gets less than two inches of rainfall a year. My friend likes to read about the desert. The ground is mostly sand and rocks.
>
> The desert environment exhibits characteristics that are not conducive to easy survival. A brutal desert Sun beats down upon all the surroundings.

NGReach.com > eVisual 3.37

Summarize the report and make suggestions:

- *I liked the way you mentioned things being really hot. That can be interesting, but could you clearly identify the topic of the report in the first sentence?*
- *In the second paragraph, you did a good job of stating the paragraph's main idea. But I noticed you wrote about a friend who likes to read about the desert. This sentence is not related to the topic sentence. I think it should come out.*
- *The last paragraph sounds like information from one of your resources. Try rewriting this information in your own words.*

Have pairs discuss their drafts. Use **Multi-Level Strategies** to support students at all proficiency levels.

2 Make Changes Read through the samples. Then use **eVisual 3.37** to model how to revise a draft. Display and use the Revising Marks as you work through the example.

Explain: *During the peer conference, my reader gave me a lot of suggestions. I've also looked at the rubric again to see what a Score 4 should contain.*

Model the first change: *I need to delete details that don't support the topic. So I will delete this sentence:* My friend likes to read about the desert.

Call on students to suggest additional changes that would turn the model into a 4. Have students use **Practice Master 3.23** for additional practice.

Revising Marks	
∧	Add
⌐	Take out
◯⌐	Move to here.

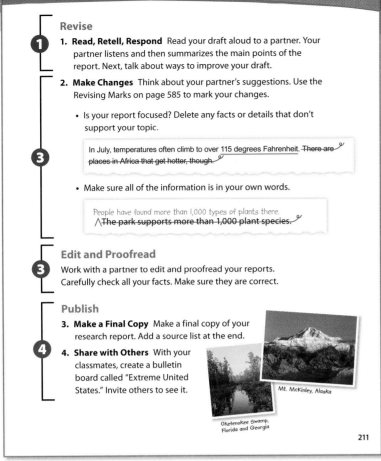

Revise

1. Read, Retell, Respond Read your draft aloud to a partner. Your partner listens and then summarizes the main points of the report. Next, talk about ways to improve your draft.

2. Make Changes Think about your partner's suggestions. Use the Revising Marks on page 585 to mark your changes.

- Is your report focused? Delete any facts or details that don't support your topic.

> In July, temperatures often climb to over 115 degrees Fahrenheit. ~~There are places in Africa that get hotter, though.~~

- Make sure all of the information is in your own words.

> People have found more than 1,000 types of plants there.
> ∧~~The park supports more than 1,000 plant species.~~

Edit and Proofread

Work with a partner to edit and proofread your reports. Carefully check all your facts. Make sure they are correct.

Publish

3. Make a Final Copy Make a final copy of your research report. Add a source list at the end.

4. Share with Others With your classmates, create a bulletin board called "Extreme United States." Invite others to see it.

Mt. McKinley, Alaska

Okefenokee Swamp, Florida and Georgia

211

Student Book page 211

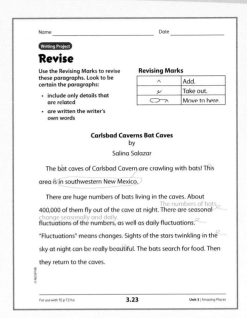

Practice Master 3.23

---

3 Revise the Draft Tell students to use the Revising Marks and begin revising their own drafts. Remind them to review the rubric and notes from their peer conference.

Post examples as a reminder for writers to write in their own words:

Not in the Writer's Own Words	In the Writer's Own Words
The knowledge gained by researchers in regard to the animal life is astounding. Most animals are capable of refraining from water consumption for several days.	Scientists have learned so much about the animals. Most animals can go several days without drinking water.

NGReach.com eVisual 3.38

CHECK PROGRESS As students revise, check to make sure each report is in the student's own words and does not include unrelated details.

OBJECTIVES

Listening and Speaking
- Listen for Main Idea
- Listen and Ask Questions
- Speak at the Correct Pace
- Focus on Pronunciation

Writing
- Writing Process (Edit and Proofread): Edit for Spelling, Grammar, and Mechanics
- Writing Process (Publish and Share): Create a Final Copy; Read Aloud

Grammar, Spelling, and Mechanics
- Plural Nouns With and Without Spelling Changes
- Check Spelling (Irregular Plurals)
- Capitalize and Punctuate Source Materials

Resources

  Practice Master 3.24

eVisual 3.39

Review Grammar: Plural Nouns

Review: *To form the plural of many nouns, add -s to the singular form.* Write *rock.* Below *rock,* write *rocks.* Then have a volunteer write the plural of *flower.* (flowers) Continue by reviewing the rules below.

- To form the plural of nouns that end with: *s, ch, sh, z,* or *x,* add *-es: fox/foxes.*

- a consonant plus *y,* change the *y* to *i,* and add *-es: city/cities.*

- *o,* add *-s* or *-es: zoo/zoos; potato/potatoes.*

- with *f* or *fe,* you might add *s: belief/beliefs.* or you might change the *f* to *v* and add *-s* or *-es: life/lives.*

- Some nouns are the same in the singular and plural forms: *sheep/sheep.*

Have partners write the plural of each of these nouns: *penny* (pennies), *teacher* (teachers), *piano* (pianos), *dish* (dishes), *moose* (moose), *half* (halves).

Assign **Practice Master 3.24** for practice.

Edit and Proofread

❶ Focus on Spelling: Irregular Plurals Remind students: *The plural of all nouns is not formed by adding s or -es. Some nouns have irregular plural forms. You must remember the correct spelling. You can use a dictionary to check the correct spelling of these plural nouns.* On the board, write *child.* Below *child,* write *children.* Point out that the plural form, *children,* is irregular. Then have students provide the plural for each of the following: *woman* (women) and *foot* (feet).

Display the following words. Have partners write the plural for each.

mouse (mice)	man (men)	person (people)
tooth (teeth)	goose (geese)	ox (oxen)

Assign **Practice Master 3.24** for additional practice.

❷ Focus on Mechanics: Punctuation and Capitalization in a Source List Tell students that there is a correct way to punctuate research sources. Direct students' attention to the sources document on page 207. Ask: *What kind of resource is the first item listed?* (encyclopedia) Point out the quotation marks, periods, and underlining. Explain that "Death Valley" is the name of the entry in the encyclopedia. Remind students that all important words in a title should be capitalized. Make certain students understand that 2009 is the copyright date of the encyclopedia. Display a classroom encyclopedia to show students where they can find this date on the copyright page. Explain that "Print" means the information was located in a book, not online.

Repeat the process for the Web entry and the book entry, pointing out the punctuation and capitalization for each.

Assign **Practice Master 3.24** for additional practice.

❸ Edit and Proofread Display the Editing Marks as partners work together to edit and proofread their research reports. Remind students to check their facts against their note cards, too.

Provide and model the editing tip: *Use a sheet of paper to cover the text as you read. Move the paper to uncover one line of text at a time. This will help you pay close attention to each line of text. Stop to correct each error you find.*

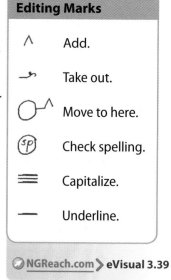

Editing Marks

∧	Add.
⤴	Take out.
◯⌐∧	Move to here.
ⓢⓟ	Check spelling.
≡	Capitalize.
—	Underline.

NGReach.com > eVisual 3.39

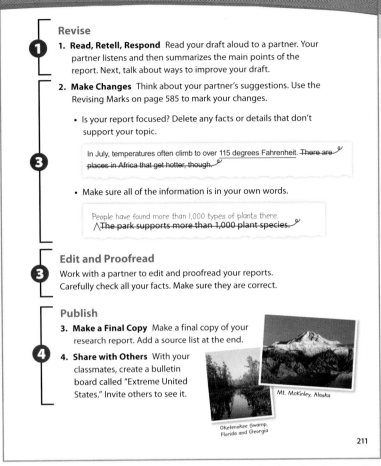

Revise

1. Read, Retell, Respond Read your draft aloud to a partner. Your partner listens and then summarizes the main points of the report. Next, talk about ways to improve your draft.

2. Make Changes Think about your partner's suggestions. Use the Revising Marks on page 585 to mark your changes.

- Is your report focused? Delete any facts or details that don't support your topic.

> In July, temperatures often climb to over 115 degrees Fahrenheit. ~~There are places in Africa that get hotter, though.~~

- Make sure all of the information is in your own words.

> People have found more than 1,000 types of plants there.
> ∧ ~~The park supports more than 1,000 plant species.~~

Edit and Proofread

Work with a partner to edit and proofread your reports. Carefully check all your facts. Make sure they are correct.

Publish

3. Make a Final Copy Make a final copy of your research report. Add a source list at the end.

4. Share with Others With your classmates, create a bulletin board called "Extreme United States." Invite others to see it.

Mt. McKinley, Alaska

Okefenokee Swamp, Florida and Georgia

211

Student Book page 211

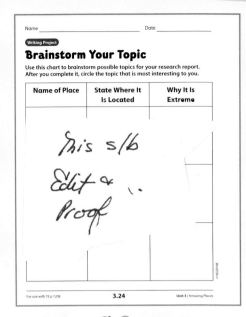

Publish

4 Share Your Research Report Encourage students to make a neat final copy of the research report. Then they may read it aloud or illustrate it and give it to another student to read.

- **Speak at the Correct Pace:** Remind students that research reports often contain new information and terms that listeners do not know well. Demonstrate reading slowly and clearly to help the listener understand new information.

- **Focus on Pronunciation:** Tell students to be certain to correctly pronounce all the place names and other important terms in their papers. Suggest they talk to you about pronunciation of terms if they are unsure.

- **Listen and Ask Questions:** Ask students to listen closely to reports and then ask questions about any details they do not understand.

- **Listen for Main Ideas:** Explain that listening for main ideas will help students better understand and appreciate the information in the report.

Have students create a bulletin board display titled "Extreme United States." Encourage them to create a banner with the title, as well as illustrations for the bulletin board. Tell them to post their reports across the bulletin board.

Add a copy of each research report in the appropriate student's Writing Portfolio.

Unit 3 Wrap-Up

OBJECTIVES

Concepts and Vocabulary
- Use Grade-Level Vocabulary ⓣ
- Use Academic Vocabulary ⓣ
- Use Learning Strategies: Graphic Organizers

Language
- Language Function: Give and Follow Directions; Describe Places
- Discuss Ideas

Social Studies
- Investigate Geography and Landforms
- Explore Well-Known Landforms

Resources

- pens or pencils
- colored markers or colored pencils
- lined and unlined paper
- art materials for constructing a model
- examples of postcards
- unlined index cards

Community Connection

Suggest that tourists, or visitors, might consider some of the places in your community to be amazing. Ask students to list amazing places in their own community. Tell them to circle any they have not visited and discuss with their family whether they might explore one or more of those places.

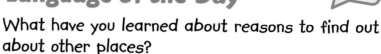

Language of the Day

What have you learned about reasons to find out about other places?

I have learned ____ .

Read the Language of the Day. Model: *I have learned that when we learn about different places, we can find out about the different ways people live.* Have students share other answers to the question.

Talk Together

1 **Complete the Unit Concept Map** Read aloud the introduction. Encourage students to skim the selections in the unit, review the **Leveled Library** books they read, and think about class discussions.

Use these possible answers to the unit concept map to guide the discussion.

Concept Map

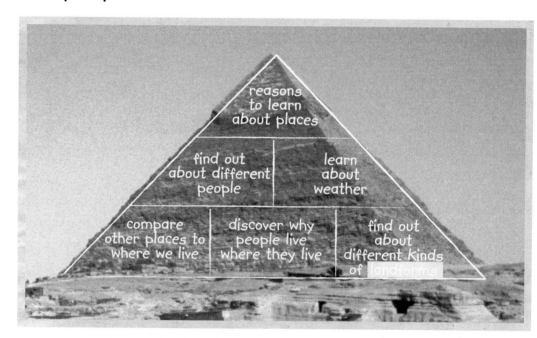

reasons to learn about places

find out about different people

learn about weather

compare other places to where we live

discover why people live where they live

find out about different kinds of landforms

2 **Write a Poem** Read aloud the directions. Have students look back at "A Map to My Home" (page 146). Encourage students to brainstorm some rhyming words and figurative language before they begin to write their poems.

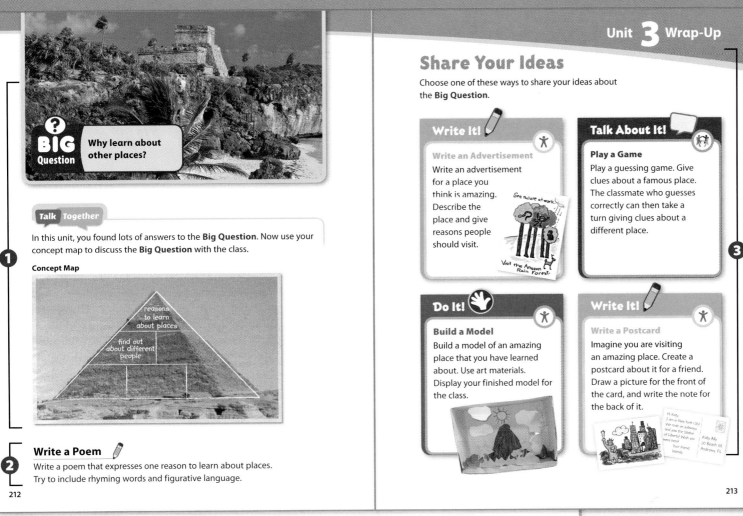

Share Your Ideas

Choose one of these ways to share your ideas about the **Big Question**.

Write It!

Write an Advertisement

Write an advertisement for a place you think is amazing. Describe the place and give reasons people should visit.

Talk About It!

Play a Game

Play a guessing game. Give clues about a famous place. The classmate who guesses correctly can then take a turn giving clues about a different place.

Do It!

Build a Model

Build a model of an amazing place that you have learned about. Use art materials. Display your finished model for the class.

Write It!

Write a Postcard

Imagine you are visiting an amazing place. Create a postcard about it for a friend. Draw a picture for the front of the card, and write the note for the back of it.

212

213

Student Book pages 212–213

Share Your Ideas

 Select and Present Read aloud the presentation options. Explain that some options can be completed alone, but that the others involve working in groups. You may choose to assign students to specific activities or allow them to self-select.

Writing Activity: Write an Advertisement I A AH
Engage students in brainstorming describing words that they might use in an ad to encourage people to visit a place. Give examples to start: *exciting, beautiful, colorful.*

Oral Activity: Play a Game A AH Have students create a chart that gives clues about a place. Ask partners to take turns in giving clues from different columns until their partner guesses the correct place.

 Kinesthetic Activity: Build a Model B I A AH Have students plan their model by telling a partner what they plan to show and how. Encourage partners to discuss specific suggestions about how to make the model using available materials.

Writing Activity: Write a Postcard A AH Show students examples of postcards. Discuss the small amount of space and read examples of messages that use vivid, precise describing words.

Respond and Close Have students share a reason for learning about other places.

Keys to Efficacy

Use think alouds before each activity to give students a model of how to preplan for successful completion of the task. Example: *I will make a model of a volcano. First, I will start a list of the materials I need. I can make a cone from cardboard. I can use cotton for smoke.*

▸ eAssessment
▸ Online Forms
▸ Reteaching Resources

NGReach.com

Administer the assessments below to monitor progress and identify which students will benefit from review, reteaching, or additional practice.

Tested Skills	Assessment Tools	Review and Reteaching
Oral Language		
❶ Give and Follow Directions ❶ Describe Places	• Part 1, Day 10 TE page T174g; ◔ ◔ page 110 • Part 2, Day 10 TE page T206g; ◔ ◔ page 110	◔ Reteaching and Review Activities
❶ Summarize a Story ❶ Summarize a Selection	• Part 1, Day 5 TE page T167c; ◔ ◔ page 114 • Part 2, Day 5 TE page T197c; ◔ ◔ page 118	Preview and model how to complete the graphic organizers. Provide additional books for practice and re-testing. • Leveled Library • Explorer Book Collection ◔ Leveled Book Finder
Vocabulary		
❶ Content Vocabulary ❶ Academic Vocabulary ❶ Word Origins ❶ Compound Words	◔ ◔ ☑ ◉ Part 1 Key Words Test, page 111 ◔ ◔ ☑ ◉ Part 2 Key Words Test, page 115 ◔ ◔ ☑ ◉ Reading Unit Test, page 122 **B I A AH**	Use the Vocabulary Reteaching Routine (PD43). ◔ Vocabulary Games ◔ Reteaching and Review Activities ◔ My Vocabulary Notebook
Reading		
Reading Comprehension ❶ Strategy: Visualize ❶ Literary Analysis: Theme ❶ Text Structure: Main Idea and Details **Reading Fluency** ❶ Intonation ❶ Phrasing ❶ Accuracy and Rate	◔ ◔ Reading Strategy Test, page 119 ◔ ◔ ☑ ◉ Reading Unit Test, page 122 **B I A AH** ■ Comprehension Coach ■ ◔ ◔ Fluency Practice Masters, pages 3.7 and 3.17 ◔ ◔ ☑ Fluency Benchmark Assessment, page 441	**Review Comprehension** Review the test items. Point out the correct response for each item and discuss why it is correct. ◔ Leveled Library lesson plans **Review Fluency** Use Fluency Routines (PD52) and Fluency Passages from Unit 2. Have students listen to the fluency model as they follow along in the text.
Grammar and Writing		
Grammar ❶ Plural Nouns with -s and -es ❶ Nouns and Articles a, an, the ❶ Irregular Plurals: Count/Noncount ❶ Capitalization of Proper Nouns ❶ More Plural Nouns **Writing** ❶ Writing Trait: Focus and Coherence	◔ ◔ ☑ ◉ Grammar Unit Test, page 151 **B I A AH** ◔ ◔ ☑ ◉ Writing Unit Test, page 158 **I A AH** ◔ ◔ Writing Rubrics, Forms, and Checklists, page 469 ◔ ◔ Writing Self-Assessment and Peer Assessments, page 482	**Grammar** Review Grammar Rules boxes and eVisuals from this unit. Use Handbook pages to reteach with additional examples. ◔ Reteaching and Review Activities **Writing** To reteach the writing process or writing traits, use Handbook pages. ◔ Reteaching and Review Activities
Other Measures		
◔ ◔ Unit Self-Assessment, page 121	◔ ◔ Affective Measures, pages 462–465	◔ ◔ Metacognitive Measures, pages 466–468

Key: ❶ Tested Skill ◔ Assessment Handbooks ◔ NGReach.com ☑ eAssessment ◉ ExamView

Power of Nature

? **BIG Question**

How do we relate to nature?

Part 1 **How powerful are wind and water?**

Part 2 **How is nature part of us?**

Curriculum Connections

Content Connection
- Natural Resources
- Wind, Water, Earth, and Air

Unit 4

Theme Connection
- Nature's Power

Reading

Student Anthology
Pages 214–281

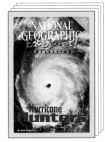

Explorer Books Collection
Hurricane Hunters
Watching Chimps

Non-Fiction Library

Fiction Library

Sing with Me Language Songs
Pages 16–21

Assessment

Assessment Handbook
Pages 167–221

Practice Masters and Manipulatives

Language and Literacy Teamwork Activities
Pages 23–28
Cross-Curricular Teamwork Activities
Pages 23–28

Practice Masters
Pages 4.1–4.27

Language Builder Picture Cards
Pages E40–E52

Newcomer

In The U.S.A.
Resources for Newcomers

Phonics

Reach into Phonics
See Teacher's Edition
Pages T78–T107

NGReach.com

Reach into Teaching

- Online Lesson Planner
- Teaching Resources
- Presentation Tool
- eEdition NG Digital Library
- eAssessment: Online Tests Scan and Score Reports

Reach into Learning

- My Vocabulary Notebook
- Vocabulary Games
- Personalized Dictionaries
- NG Digital Library
- Comprehension Coach

Recordings

- Songs and Chants CD
- Selection Recordings CD
- Fluency Models CD

Unit 4 Planner

Power of Nature

Student Book

UNIT LAUNCH

- Build Background Video
- Introduce the

	LANGUAGE	**VOCABULARY**	**READING**

PART 1

Weeks 1 and 2
Focus: How We Use Natural Resources

LANGUAGE

Language Function
- ❶ Make Comparisons
- Express Certainty, Probability, Possibility

Grammar
- ❶ Present-Tense Action Verbs
- ❶ Present Progressive Tense

Listening & Speaking
- Listen and Learn from Others

How to Learn Language
- Ask for Clarification

Oral Language Project
- Instructions

VOCABULARY

Key Words
❶ Science Vocabulary

convert   generate   renewable
electricity   power   scarce

❶ Academic Vocabulary

available   current   resource
conservation   flow

❶ Basic Vocabulary: Weather

Today is cloudy.
Today is foggy.
Today is rainy.
Today is snowy.
Today is sunny.
Today is windy.

❶ Context Clues

READING

Reading Strategy
❶ Learn to Ask Questions

Genre
- Science Article

Text Structure
❶ Cause and Effect

Text Feature
- Section Headings

Genre
- Persuasive Essay

Literary Analysis
- Persuasive Text

Leveled Library

Reading Fluency
❶ Intonation
❶ Accuracy and Rate

PART 2

Weeks 3 and 4
Focus: Peoples' Connection to the Natural World

LANGUAGE

Language Function
- ❶ Express Needs and Wants
- Ask for and Give Advice

Grammar
- ❶ Forms of *be*
- ❶ Forms of *have* and Modals
- ❶ Forms of *be* and *have*

Listening & Speaking
- Adjust Your Speech for Your Audience

How to Learn Language
- Relate to Personal Experience

Theme Theater
- Story Extension

VOCABULARY

Key Words
❶ Science Vocabulary

atmosphere   landscape   natural
element   material

❶ Academic Vocabulary

benefit   interact   relate
force   modify

❶ Basic Vocabulary: Parts of the Body

arm, elbow	foot, toe, ankle	shoulder
back	hand, finger, thumb, wrist	stomach
body	hip	
chest	leg, knee	

❶ Multiple-Meaning Words

READING

Reading Strategy
❶ Ask Questions

Genre
- Tall Tale

Text Structure
❶ Problem and Solution

Literary Analysis
- Main Character

Genre
- Lyrical Poetry

Literary Analysis
- Sensory Language

Leveled Library

Reading Fluency
❶ Expression
❶ Accuracy and Rate

WRITING	LEARNING STATIONS	REVIEW, ASSESS, RETEACH

Daily Writing
- Writing Fluency
- Instructions
- Support Ideas
- Descriptive Paragraph
- Summary
- Persuasive News Article
- Journal Entry

 Tornado in a Bottle

 Hurricane Winds

 Bodies of Water

 Dust in the Wind

 Compare Resources

 E-mail About Blue Legacy

Oral Language Rubrics
- Make Comparisons
- Retell a Selection
- Oral Language Project: Listening, Speaking, Content

Vocabulary Test
- Key Words: Content Vocabulary
- Key Words: Academic Vocabulary

Daily Writing
- Writing Fluency
- Writer's Craft: Descriptive Sentences
- Paragraph
- Poem
- Journal Entry
- Writing Project: Tall Tale

 Make a Sound Bigger

 Tall Tale Estimates

 My Favorite State Park

 Know Your Nouns

 Talk About Nature

A Poem That's Naturally You

Oral Language Rubrics
- Express Needs and Wants
- Retell a Story
- Theme Theater: Listening, Speaking, Content

Vocabulary Test
- Key Words: Content Vocabulary
- Key Words: Academic Vocabulary

Reading Test
- Reading Strategy: Ask Questions

UNIT WRAP-UP

Answer the
 BIG Question

Unit 4 Assessment
- Self-Assessment
- Reading B I A AH
- Grammar B I A AH
- Writing I A AH

Power of Nature

OBJECTIVES

Listening, Speaking, and Viewing
- Respond to a Video
- Participate in a Discussion

Learning and Teamwork Strategies
- Preview and Predict
- Relate to Personal Experience
- Use Graphic Organizers
- Use Media to Build Concepts

Media
- View and Discuss a Video
- Analyze Media

Resources

- Unit 4 Build Background Video
- Family Newsletter 4
- eVisual 4.1
- Practice Master 4.1

NGReach.com

See **Technology Station** for digital student resources.

Home Connection

Send home **Family Newsletter 4**.
Students look out a window at home and take notes and draw a picture of the "signs of nature" that they see. Students label their drawings. Students' drawings are assembled into a class book.

1 Preview and Predict Read the unit title aloud and encourage students to flip through the unit. Ask: *What do you think you will learn? What makes you think that?*

2 Introduce the Big Question Ask: *What do you think the word* relate *means?* (connect with, get along with, feel friendly toward) *Give an example of how people can relate to each other.* (Sample answer: They can work together on a team project.)

Read aloud the Big Question. Have students share possible answers. Encourage them to provide details. List the answers.

3 Build Background Preview the video: *Now we will play a video that tells us about how we relate to nature. We'll learn why nature is important to us and how we can protect the things in nature.*

Discuss the video:

- *What are some things nature provides that we need to live?*

- *What is an example of something in nature that we could use up so there would be no more? How would this affect us?*

- *What is one way we can protect nature's resources?*

- *Videos are one form of media. What is another form someone could use to convince people about the importance of natural resources? Do you think that would work better than using a video? Why or why not?*

Play the video.

NGReach.com > **Build Background Video**

4 Share What You Know Review the three steps of the directions. Explain: *To complete the activity, you will need to think about:*

- *things in nature*
- *which things in nature are strong and mighty*

If students need help determining which things in nature are strong and mighty, first discuss meanings for the words. Then ask guiding questions, such as: *Which is mighty—a stream or an ocean wave? Which is strong—a tiger or a baby bird?*

Post the class drawings and encourage students to add more drawings throughout the unit.

Power of Nature

1

2

Unit at a Glance
▶ **Language:** Make Comparisons, Express Needs and Wants, Science Words
▶ **Literacy:** Ask Questions
▶ **Content:** Natural Resources

Unit 4

Technology Station
○ NGReach.com

Digital Library
○ Watch the video.

?
BIG Question
How do we relate to nature?

4

Share What You Know ✋
Do It!
❶ **Make** a list of things in nature that are strong and mighty.
❷ **Sort** your ideas into a class list.
❸ **Draw** a picture of something from the list. Show its strength.

Strong Things in Nature
storms
a tiger
the sun
waves

Build Background: Watch a video about natural resources.
○ NGReach.com

3

214

Student Book pages 214–215

❺ Begin the Unit Concept Map Introduce the concept map: *As you go through this unit, it will be helpful to organize your thinking in a concept map.*

Display the unit concept map for the Big Question. Explain: *The Big Question is restated on the river. We'll add our answers to the branches or tributaries.*

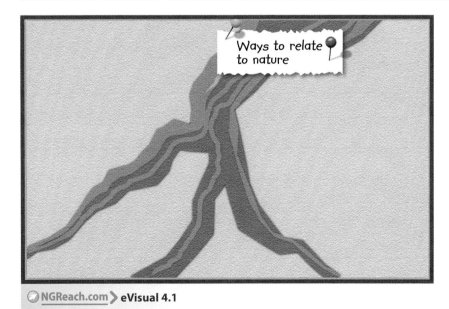

Ways to relate to nature

○ NGReach.com ▶ eVisual 4.1

Have students add the ideas they already listed, and any other ideas they may have, to **Practice Master 4.1**. Explain that they will add more to the concept maps as they read through the unit and learn more about how people relate to nature.

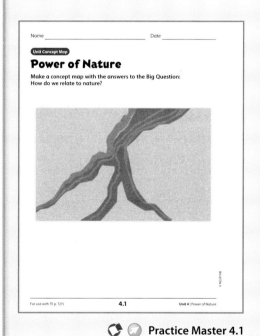

Name _____ Date _____

Unit Concept Map
Power of Nature
Make a concept map with the answers to the Big Question: How do we relate to nature?

For use with TE p. T215   4.1   Unit 4 | Power of Nature

♻ ○ **Practice Master 4.1**

BIG Question How do we relate to nature?

PART 1

Days 1–5

▶ **Main Selection**
Wind at Work, by Beth Geiger

▶ **Genre**
Science Article

▶ **Selection Summary**
This article explains how wind is formed, how wind helps people, and how it causes destruction. Wind can erode mountains, generate electricity, move sailboats, and can also cause tornados and hurricanes. Wind affects many aspects of people's lives.

Wind at Work by Beth Geiger

NATIONAL GEOGRAPHIC

Comprehension Coach

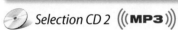
Selection CD 2 (((MP3)))

Skills at a Glance	
Language	Make Comparisons; Express Certainty, Probability, Possibility; Oral Language Project
Grammar	Present-Tense Action Verbs; Present Progressive
Vocabulary	Science Vocabulary: *convert, electricity, generate, power, renewable, scarce* Academic Vocabulary: *available, conservation, current, flow, resource* Context Clues
Reading Strategy	Ask Questions
Text Structure	Cause and Effect
Writing	Writing Fluency; Instructions; Support Ideas; Descriptive Paragraph; Summary; Persuasive News Article; Journal Entry
Newcomer Support	Use *In the USA:* weather words

Days 6–10

► **Companion Selection**
Water: The Blue Gold, by Alexandra Cousteau, with Carol Verbeeck

► **Genre**
Persuasive Essay

► **Selection Summary**
Alexandra Cousteau, the granddaughter of Jacques-Yves Cousteau, explains how people, plants, and animals all depend on water. However, with pollution and the overuse of water, scientists predict that water scarcity will become a major problem in the future. Cousteau wants to preserve and protect our water resources.

Connect Across Texts Read a persuasive essay about another valuable natural **resource**, water.

Genre A **persuasive essay** gives an opinion and tries to get readers to agree with it. The author uses facts to support his or her opinion along with persuasive words like *must* and *should*.

Water
The Blue Gold

by Alexandra Cousteau, with Carol Verbeeck

▲ Alexandra Cousteau

Imagine that you go to brush your teeth one night. You turn on the faucet, but nothing comes out. Then you try to take a shower. There's no water there, either.

We use water for so many things. It's hard to imagine life without it. However, some scientists believe that **in this century**, clean water may become as highly valued as gold.

In Other Words
in this century during the next 100 years

▶ **Before You Move On**
1. **Ask Questions** What is a question you have about the author's opinion of water?
2. **Fact/Opinion** Identify an opinion in the second paragraph and explain how you know it is an opinion.

239

Leveled Library Books

Differentiated Instruction

B | BEGINNING

The Wind Blew
by Pat Hutchins
One day the wind blows away many things. Soon everyone is chasing the wind, as the blows everything out toward the sea.

Wind
by Helen Frost
Simple text and ample visual support show wind, how it's formed, and its effect on Earth and people.

I | INTERMEDIATE

The Wind Eagle
retold by Joyce McGreevy
Gluscabi can't go fishing because the Wind Eagle pushes him back to shore. Gluscabi must find a way to stop the Wind Eagle.

Wind Power
by Pat Malone
Students read about the power of wind, how wind shapes trees, scatters seeds, and shapes sand dunes.

A | ADVANCED   AH | ADVANCED HIGH

The Missing Lighthouse
by Glen Phelan
In this chapter book, a lighthouse disappears. The Sleuths are on the case to track it down.

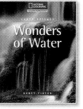

Wonders of Water
by Nancy Finton
In this chapter book, learn about the wonders of water. Water is everywhere and constantly moving through the water cycle.

Unit 4 Daily Planner

BIG Question How do we relate to nature?

PART 1

Core Lessons

	Day 1 Introduce Academic Language	**Day 2** Introduce More Academic Language
Language ⏰ 5–10 minutes	**Language of the Day** T216 ❶ **Language Function: Make Comparisons** T216 🔊 ((MP3)) **Oral Language** • Talk About Energy Resources T217 • Talk Together About the Big Question T217	**Language of the Day** T219a ❶ **Grammar/Spelling: Present-Tense Action Verbs** T219a **Oral Language** • Talk Together About Asking Questions T220
Vocabulary ⏰ 10–15 minutes	❶ **Science Vocabulary** • Introduce Words T217 convert generate renewable electricity power scarce **Classroom Vocabulary** • Introduce Words T218 cause effect	❶ **Academic Vocabulary** • Introduce Words T219 available flow conservation resource current
Reading ⏰ 15–20 minutes	❶ **Text Structure: Cause and Effect** • Introduce Cause and Effect T218a • Use Graphic Organizers: Cause-and-Effect Chart T218 **Read Aloud: "Chloe's Garden"** T218a	❶ **Strategy: Ask Questions** • Introduce and Practice the Strategy T220 **Read "How to Make a Compost Bin"** T221 **Phonics and Fluency** • Long /ā/ai, ay T220
Writing ⏰ 15 minutes	**Daily Writing** • Writing Fluency T218	**Daily Writing** • Friendly Letter T221
Content: Integrated Throughout Each Day	**Science** • Explore Earth's Resources	**Science** • Explore Earth's Resources

Ready-to-Go Plans
▶ Time (20, 30, 40, 60, 90 minutes per day)
▶ Model (Content Focus, Literacy Focus, Dual Language)

Online Lesson Planner
◯ NGReach.com

Day 3

Build Academic Language

Language of the Day *T222a*
⊙ Language Function: Express Certainty, Probability, Possibility *T222a* 🔊 ((MP3))
Listening and Speaking
• Listen to and Sing a Song *T222a*

⊙ Academic and Science Vocabulary
• Expand Word Knowledge *T222b*

Support Newcomers
• Build Basic Vocabulary: Weather Words *T222b*

Read the Selection
⊙ Strategy: Ask Questions *T222–T235*
• Reading Options *T224*
Concepts of Print
• Identify a Sentence *T225*
Text Feature
• Heads *T228–229*
⊙ Fluency: Intonation *T234*

Daily Writing
• Modeled Writing: Support Ideas *T235*

Home Connection
• Class Book *T226–227*
Social Studies
• Renewable Resources *T230–231*
Science
• Tornadoes *T232–233*

Day 4

Build Academic Language

Language of the Day *T236a*
⊙ Grammar: Present Progressive Tense *T236a*
Oral Language
• Talk About the Selection *T236c*

⊙ Academic and Science Vocabulary
• Share Word Knowledge *T236b*

Think and Respond
• Talk About the Selection *T236c*
• Test-Taking Strategy *T236c*
⊙ Fluency: Intonation *T236c*

Daily Writing
• Independent Writing: Write About It *T236*

Science
• Explore Earth's Resources

Day 5

Build Academic Language

Language of the Day *T237a*
Listening and Speaking
• Listen and Learn from Others *T237a*
How to Learn Language
• Ask for Clarification *T237a*
Oral Language
• Talk Together About the Big Question *T237*

⊙ Academic and Science Vocabulary
• Apply Word Knowledge *T237b*

Reread and Explain
⊙ Text Structure: Cause and Effect
• Make a Cause and Effect Chart *T237c*
Retell a Selection *T237c*
⊙ Fluency: Accuracy, Rate, and Intonation *T237c*

Daily Writing
• Interactive Writing: Summary *T237*

Science
• Explore Earth's Resources

| available | convert | electricity | generate | renewable | scarce |
| conservation | current | flow | power | resource | |

PART 1

Core Lessons	Day 6 Expand Academic Language	Day 7 Expand Academic Language
Language 🕐 5–10 minutes	**Language of the Day** *T238a* ❶ **Language Function: Make Comparisons** *T238a* **Oral Language** • Talk Together About the Big Question *T244a*	**Language of the Day** *T245a* ❶ **Grammar/Spelling: Present-Tense Action Verbs** *T245a*
Vocabulary 🕐 10–15 minutes	❶ **Context Clues** *T238* **Support Newcomers:** • Additional Context Clues *T238*	❶ **More Context Clues** *T245* • Context Clues *T245*
Reading 🕐 15–20 minutes	**Read the Persuasive Essay** *T239a* • Reading Options *T239a* ❶ **Strategy: Ask Questions** *T239a—T244* **Concepts of Print** • Identify a Paragraph *T239* **Text Features** • Section Headings *T240–T241* ❶ **Fluency: Accuracy and Rate** *T244* **Respond and Extend** • Compare Genres *T244a*	**Reread the Selection: Focus on Persuasive Text** *T246a*
Writing 🕐 15 minutes	**Daily Writing** • Writing Fluency *T244*	**Daily Writing** • Modeled Writing: Persuasive News Article *T246b*
Content: Integrated Throughout Each Day	**Science** • Explore Earth's Resources	**Science** • Explore Earth's Resources

❶ = Tested Skill

Days 8–9

Apply Academic Language

Oral Language Project
- Introduce the Activity *T246c*
- Plan *T246c*
- Practice *T246d*
- Shoot the Breeze! *T246d*
- Debrief and Compare *T246d*

Read Leveled Books

Fiction *T246e*

 **B**

 **I**

 **A** **AH**

Key Words

newspapers	umbrella
postman	wig
stole	

Key Words

angry	rage
eagle	silence
mighty	

Key Words

erosion	magazine
investigate	platform
lighthouse	

Nonfiction *T246f*

 **B**

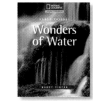 **I**

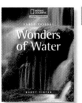 **A** **AH**

Key Words

electricity	pollen
hurricane	tornado
movements	

Key Words

dunes	shore
moving	windmill
scatters	

Key Words

conserve	irrigation
dinosaurs	wetlands
glaciers	

Daily Writing
- Journal Entry *T246f*

Day 10

Review and Assess

Interactive Review *T246g–T246h*
- ❶ Language Function: Give and Follow Directions
- ❶ Grammar: Nouns and Articles *a, an, the*
- ❶ Vocabulary: Social Studies and Academic Vocabulary
- ❶ Vocabulary Strategy: Word Origins
- ❶ Reading Strategy: Visualize
- ❶ Literary Analysis: Setting
- ❶ Text Structure: Theme
- ❶ Fluency: Accuracy and Intonation

Assessment *T246g–T246h*

Same Book, Different Levels

 I **A** **AH**

Key Words

category	data	scientist
damage	eye	thunderstorm
dangerous	hurricane	warning

Reading Station

EXPLORER! COLLECTION
Ladder Text:
- Pioneer edition for below level readers
- Pathfinder edition for on and above level readers

DECODABLE TEXTS

TRADE BOOK COLLECTION
Use the **Leveled Book Finder** at
NGReach.com

Content Stations

Download complete lesson plans **NGReach.com >**

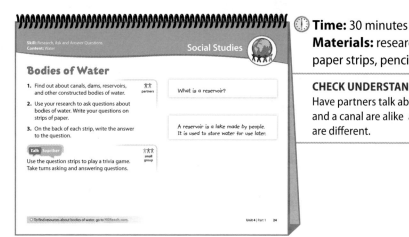

Skill: Make a Model
Content: Tornadoes

Science

Tornado in a Bottle
1. Look at the **Language Builder Picture Card** of a tornado. ★★ partners
2. Fill one 2-liter soda bottle ¾ full of water. Leave the other bottle empty. Screw on the caps with small holes.
3. Line up the holes in the caps. Tape the bottles together. Make sure it's tight.
4. Flip the bottles up. Grip the bottles where they join. Swirl the bottles. Observe.
5. Repeat, using caps with bigger holes.

Talk Together ★★★ small group
Share your observations. How did the size of the hole affect the tornado?

Unit 4 | Part 1   23

🕐 **Time:** 30 minutes
Materials: Language Builder Picture Card E47, 2-liter soda bottles, bottle caps with two sizes of holes, water, duct tape

CHECK UNDERSTANDING
Ask: *What does a tornado look like?*

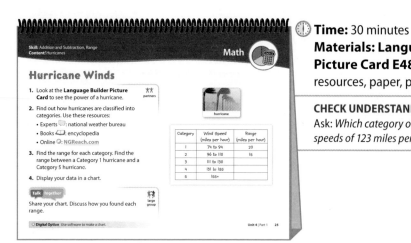

Skill: Research, Ask and Answer Questions
Content: Water

Social Studies

Bodies of Water
1. Find out about canals, dams, reservoirs, and other constructed bodies of water. ★★ partners
2. Use your research to ask questions about bodies of water. Write your questions on strips of paper.
3. On the back of each strip, write the answer to the question.

What is a reservoir?

A reservoir is a lake made by people. It is used to store water for use later.

Talk Together ★★★ small group
Use the question strips to play a trivia game. Take turns asking and answering questions.

To find resources about bodies of water, go to NGReach.com.

Unit 4 | Part 1   24

🕐 **Time:** 30 minutes
Materials: research resources, paper strips, pencils

CHECK UNDERSTANDING
Have partners talk about how a dam and a canal are alike and how they are different.

Skill: Addition and Subtraction, Range
Content: Hurricanes

Math

Hurricane Winds
1. Look at the **Language Builder Picture Card** to see the power of a hurricane. ★★ partners
2. Find out how hurricanes are classified into categories. Use these resources:
   - Experts 💬: national weather bureau
   - Books 📖: encyclopedia
   - Online 💻: NGReach.com
3. Find the range for each category. Find the range between a Category 1 hurricane and a Category 5 hurricane.
4. Display your data in a chart.

Category	Wind Speed (miles per hour)	Range (miles per hour)
1	74 to 94	20
2	96 to 110	15
3	111 to 130	
4	131 to 155	
5	156+	

Talk Together 🧍 large group
Share your chart. Discuss how you found each range.

Digital Option Use software to make a chart.

Unit 4 | Part 1   25

🕐 **Time:** 30 minutes
Materials: Language Builder Picture Card E48, research resources, paper, pencils

CHECK UNDERSTANDING
Ask: *Which category of hurricane has wind speeds of 123 miles per hour?*

Use these resources to provide daily opportunities for students to work individually or in groups at learning stations around the classroom.

Language Stations

Download complete lesson plans  NGReach.com ›

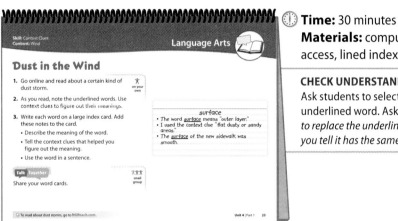

Time: 30 minutes
Materials: computers with Internet access, lined index cards, pencils

CHECK UNDERSTANDING
Ask students to select a sentence with an underlined word. Ask: *Can you find a word to replace the underlined word? How can you tell it has the same meaning?*

Time: 30 minutes
Materials: Language Builder Picture Cards E40–E46, paper, pencils

CHECK UNDERSTANDING
Ask students to name one renewable and one nonrenewable resource.

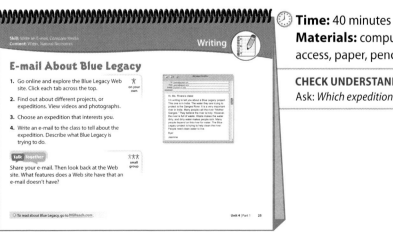

Time: 40 minutes
Materials: computers with Internet access, paper, pencils

CHECK UNDERSTANDING
Ask: *Which expedition did you choose? Why?*

Technology Station

Access resources  NGReach.com ›

((MP3)) Recordings

- A Good Place for a Garden
- Maybe Carrots, Maybe Not
- Wind at Work

Digital Library

Learn vocabulary and practice language

- Key Word Images
- Language Builder Picture Cards

My Vocab Notebook

- Add Words

Comprehension Coach

- Use interactive library support. Automatically measure fluency.

Online Assessment

- Practice items in standardized test format.

Day 1

Day at a Glance:
▶ **Language:** Make Comparisons   ▶ **Reading:** Cause and Effect
▶ **Vocabulary:** Science Vocabulary   ▶ **Writing:** Writing Fluency

OBJECTIVES

Vocabulary
• Acquire and Use Grade-Level Vocabulary ⊤

Language
• Language Function: Make Comparisons ⊤
• Listen to and Imitate Fluent Models
• Use a Variety of Language Structures
• Participate in Discussion

Learning and Teamwork Strategies
• Activate Prior Knowledge
• Use Media to Build Language
• Use Context to Build Concepts and Language

Science
• Explore Earth's resources

Resources

🔄 ⊘ *Sing With Me Language Song Book,* page 16

⊘ *Sing With Me Language Song CD 2 Tr 9,10*

⊘ *eVisual 4.2*

• *eVisual 4.3*

⊘ *Key Word Images*

Language Builder Picture Cards E40, E41

⊘ **NGReach.com** ▶

See **Technology Station** for digital student resources.

Differentiate

Academic Language Frames

Make Comparisons
■ _____ is _____.
  But _____ is _____.
  _____ need _____.
  _____ need _____, too.
  And so do _____.

■ _____ is _____.
  But _____ is / is not _____.
  _____ need _____.
  _____ need _____, and so do _____.

■ _____ is _____.
■ But _____ is / is not _____.
  _____ are _____.
  _____ need _____.
  _____ need _____, too.
  _____ need _____, and so do _____.

⊘ **NGReach.com** ▶ eVisual 4.3

Language of the Day

Name some things from nature.
_____ is a part of nature.

Read the Language of the Day and invite students to take turns naming things from nature. Have students build a cumulative sentence: *The wind is a part of nature. The wind and a rock are parts of nature. The wind, a rock, and a garden are all parts of nature.* Record students' ideas in a semantic web to use when building the cumulative sentence.

Make Comparisons

❶ Teach/Model Display "A Good Place for a Garden." Read aloud the introduction and play the song. Invite students to sing along as you play the song again. Model how to echo and chime in as the audio prompts.

Point out the **Language Frames** and model using these structures to compare different aspects of nature.

How to Make Comparisons	
1. Make a contrast with the word *but*.	The wind is a force of nature. But the wind is not a living thing. Plants and animals are living things.
2. Show similarities with the word *too*. You can also use the phrases *so do* and *so does*.	Plants need water. Animals need water, too. Plants need sunshine, and so do animals.

⊘ **NGReach.com** ▶ eVisual 4.2

Invite a few volunteers to compare different places for planting a garden, such as a sandbox and a hilly plot. Point to each step on the how to card as the students make comparisons. Guide them with questions such as *What is the soil in each place like?*

❷ Practice/Apply Have partners compare two of the items they listed for the class list in Share What You Know. Use **Academic Language Frames** to encourage students to use language naturally to make comparisons with different kinds of sentences.

CHECK UNDERSTANDING Display and have students compare **Language Builder Cards E40 and E41.**

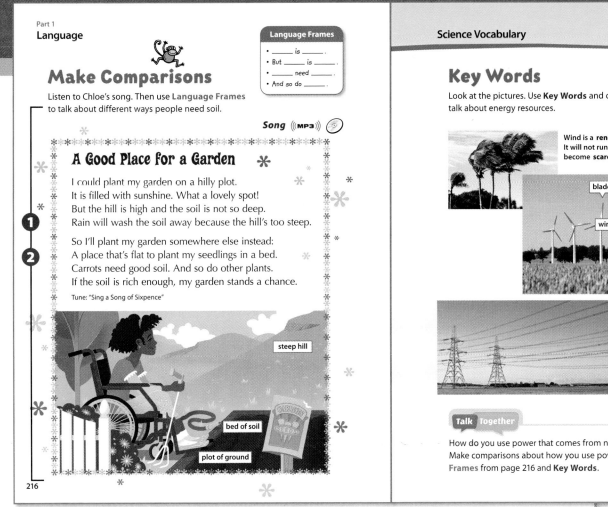

Make Comparisons

Listen to Chloe's song. Then use **Language Frames** to talk about different ways people need soil.

Language Frames
- _____ is _____.
- But _____ is _____.
- _____ need _____.
- And so do _____.

Song ((MP3))

A Good Place for a Garden

I could plant my garden on a hilly plot.
It is filled with sunshine. What a lovely spot!
But the hill is high and the soil is not so deep.
Rain will wash the soil away because the hill's too steep.

So I'll plant my garden somewhere else instead:
A place that's flat to plant my seedlings in a bed.
Carrots need good soil. And so do other plants.
If the soil is rich enough, my garden stands a chance.

Tune: "Sing a Song of Sixpence"

steep hill

bed of soil

plot of ground

216

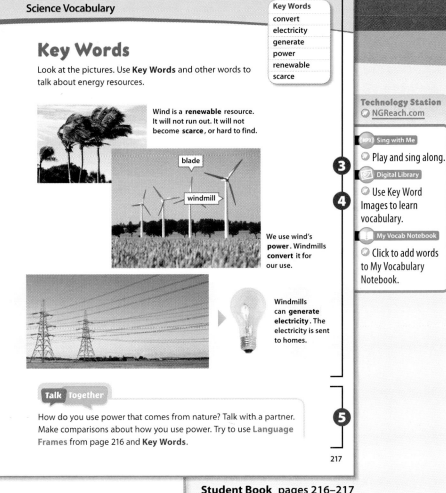

Science Vocabulary

Key Words

Look at the pictures. Use **Key Words** and other words to talk about energy resources.

Key Words
convert
electricity
generate
power
renewable
scarce

Wind is a **renewable** resource. It will not run out. It will not become **scarce**, or hard to find.

blade

windmill

We use wind's **power**. Windmills **convert** it for our use.

Windmills can **generate electricity**. The electricity is sent to homes.

Talk Together

How do you use power that comes from nature? Talk with a partner. Make comparisons about how you use power. Try to use **Language Frames** from page 216 and **Key Words**.

217

Technology Station
○ NGReach.com

(MP3) Sing with Me
○ Play and sing along.

Digital Library
○ Use Key Word Images to learn vocabulary.

My Vocab Notebook
○ Click to add words to My Vocabulary Notebook.

3
4
5

Student Book pages 216–217

Science Vocabulary

3 **Teach/Model** Read the introduction and the captions for each photo. Use **Vocabulary Routine 1** (See page PD37.) and **Key Word Images** to teach the words. Access definitions on pages 616–639.

1. **Pronounce** the word and point to its picture: **electricity**.

2. **Rate** the word. Have students hold up their fingers to show how well they know the word. (1 = very well, 2 = a little, 3 = not at all) Ask: *What do you know about this word?*

3. **Define** the word: *Electricity is a form of energy. We **generate** electricity to provide power to our homes.*

4. **Elaborate** Relate the word to your experience: *I use electricity when I turn on the lights or watch TV.*

4 **Practice/Apply** Have partners take turns repeating the routine for each word, using complete sentences for steps 2, 3, and 4.

5 **Talk Together About the Big Question**
Check Understanding and Connect Concepts Review the **Language Frames** on page 216 and provide an example:

> *Soil is good for flowers. But soil is good for vegetables, too. Flowers need soil. And so do vegetables.*

Have students add ideas to the unit concept map.

Differentiate

Spanish Cognates ▶
convert/convertir;
electricity/electricidad;
generate/generar; power/poder
renewable/renovable; scarce/escaso(a)

Part 1 Vocabulary Skills Trace		Page
Day 1	**Science Vocabulary**	**T217**
Day 2	Academic Vocabulary	T219
Day 3	Expand Word Knowledge	T222b
Day 4	Share Word Knowledge	T236b
Day 5	Apply Word Knowledge	T237b
Day 6	Context Clues	T238
Day 7	Context Clues	T245
Days 8–9	Extend Vocabulary	T246e–f
Day 10	Vocabulary Review	T246g–h

Day 1
continued

Day at a Glance:
► **Language:** Make Comparisons   ▶ **Reading:** Cause and Effect
► **Vocabulary:** Science Vocabulary   ▶ **Writing:** Writing Fluency

OBJECTIVES

Vocabulary
- Acquire and Use Classroom Vocabulary ❶
- Use Grade-Level Vocabulary ❶

Comprehension and Literary Analysis
- Demonstrate Listening Comprehension
- Recognize Cause-and-Effect Relationships ❶

Listening and Speaking
- Listen for Important Details

Learning and Teamwork Strategies
- Use Graphic Organizers: Cause-and-Effect Chart
- Reason Deductively

Writing
- Develop Writing Fluency
- Monitor and Self-Correct Writing

Science
- Explore Earth's Resources

Resources

 eVisual 4.4

·   eVisual 4.5

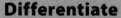 Practice Master 4.2

Differentiate

Multi-Level Strategies

BEGINNING

Have students find illustrations of a cause and effect. Encourage students to say one or two words about each cause and effect.

INTERMEDIATE

Have students state complete cause-and-effect relationships: *Chloe pulled all the weeds so the hill was bare.*

ADVANCED

Encourage students to elaborate on cause and effects. Example: *The weeds no longer hold the soil in place, so the soil is loose. The rain washes the loose soil away.*

ADVANCED HIGH

Have students identify multiple effects for each cause.

Cause and Effect

1 Teach Connect concepts: You learned that wind can cause windmills to turn, which **generates electricity**. Now you will learn how to make a cause-and-effect chart to better understand cause-and-effect relationships.

Read the first paragraph and teach the Classroom Vocabulary words *cause* and *effect*. Point to the illustrations on page 218 as you teach the words that signal a cause-and-effect relationship. *Because Chloe pulled the weeds, _____.* Ask volunteers to use the illustration to respond with an effect.

Read aloud the explanation. Clarify the purpose: *A cause-and-effect chart can show how one event can lead to another.* Remind students to listen for signal words as you read "Chloe's Garden" aloud.

> **Read Aloud**
>
> ### Chloe's Garden
>
> Chloe pulled all the weeds on the slope. As a result, the slope is bare. The weeds no longer hold the soil in place. So when it rains, the rain washes the soil away. Since plants need soil, maybe it wasn't a good idea to pull all of the weeds.

🌐 **NGReach.com** ➤ eVisual 4.4

2 Model Review the first two sentences of "Chloe's Garden." Have volunteers read the first set of boxes in the cause-and-effect chart. Model the process: *I made a box for the cause* Chloe pulls all the weeds. *The next sentence starts with the phrase,* as a result, *so I know that this sentence is the effect. I will add an effect box to my chart. I will draw an arrow from the cause to the effect.* Ask volunteers to repeat for the last two boxes.

3 Practice/Apply Read aloud the instructions. Distribute **Practice Master 4.2** for students to use as they complete their charts. Use **Multi-Level Strategies** to help students at all proficiency levels talk about things that happen to soil. Monitor students' developing proficiency. (See page R2 for **Proficiency Level Descriptions**.)

> **CHECK UNDERSTANDING** *What is the cause of the rain washing the soil away?* (The weeds no longer held the soil in place.)

Cause and Effect

When something happens, you often look for the reason, or cause. What happens is the effect. When you talk about **cause and effect**:

- tell how the events relate
- use words such as *because, since, so,* and *as a result* to connect the cause and the effect.

1 Look at the pictures of Chloe's hill. Read the captions.

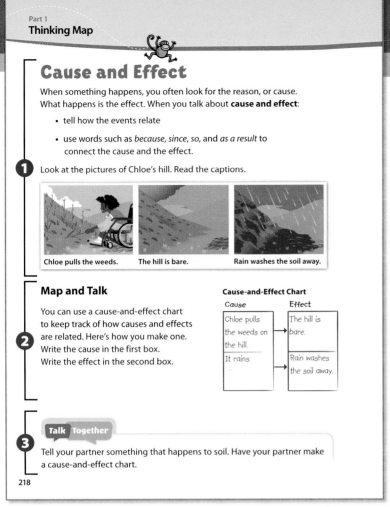

Chloe pulls the weeds.　　The hill is bare.　　Rain washes the soil away.

Map and Talk

2 You can use a cause-and-effect chart to keep track of how causes and effects are related. Here's how you make one. Write the cause in the first box. Write the effect in the second box.

Cause-and-Effect Chart

Cause	Effect
Chloe pulls the weeds on the hill.	The hill is bare.
It rains.	Rain washes the soil away.

Talk Together

3 Tell your partner something that happens to soil. Have your partner make a cause-and-effect chart.

218

Student Book page 218

Daily Writing

4 **Writing Fluency** Use the **Power Writing Routine**. (See page 53.)
Write the word *power* and prompt: *What kind of* power *does water have?*
Think about this word and write about it.

Power Writing Routine

 1. What do you know about the word or picture?

 2. Take one minute to write as much as you can, as well as you can.
B words　　**I** sentences　　**A** **AH** paragraphs

 3. Check your spelling and grammar. (Circle) mistakes.

 4. Count your words.

**NGReach.com** > eVisual 4.5

CLOSE AND ASSESS

- **Language** *Compare the hilly spot and flat area that Chloe thinks about for growing her garden.* (Students should use information from the song in their answers.)

- **Reading** *If soil is not deep enough or rich enough, what will be the effect on the plants?* (They will not grow.)

- **Vocabulary** *Describe a cause-and-effect relationship about wind using the Key Words* generate *and* electricity.

Classroom Vocabulary

Use **Vocabulary Routine 4** to teach **cause** and **effect.** You can add (more sentences inside. (See **Vocabulary Routines**, page PD40.)

Window Graphic

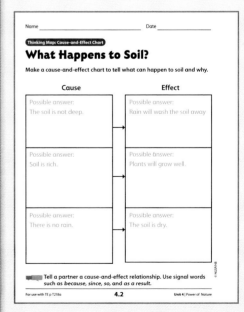

Thinking Map: Cause-and-Effect Chart

What Happens to Soil?

Make a cause-and-effect chart to tell what can happen to soil and why.

Cause	Effect
Possible answer: The soil is not deep.	Possible answer: Rain will wash the soil away
Possible answer: Soil is rich.	Possible answer: Plants will grow well.
Possible answer: There is no rain.	Possible answer: The soil is dry.

Tell a partner a cause-and-effect relationship. Use signal words such as *because, since, so,* and *as a result.*

For use with TE p T218a　　　**4.2**　　　Unit 4 | Power of Nature

 **Practice Master 4.2**

Day 2

Day at a Glance:
▶ **Language:** Present-Tense Action Verbs ▶ **Reading:** Learn to Ask Questions
▶ **Vocabulary:** Academic Vocabulary ▶ **Writing:** Instructions

OBJECTIVES

Vocabulary
• Acquire and Use Academic Vocabulary
• Use Grade-Level Vocabulary

Language
• Recognize Present-Tense Verbs

Learning and Teamwork Strategies
• Make Connections Across Content Areas

Resources

 Practice Master 4.3

NGReach.com

See **Technology Station** for digital student resources.

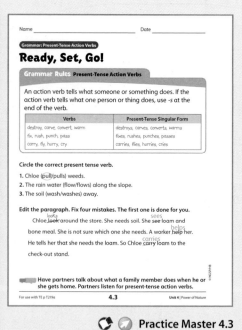

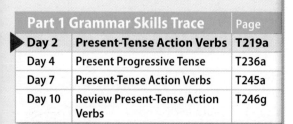

⊙ ⊙ **Practice Master 4.3**

Language of the Day

Pretend you are a natural **resource**.
Say your name. Tell what you do.
I am _____. I _____.

Read the Language of the Day. Model: *I am the rain. I bring water to gardens and fields.* As you "introduce" yourself, make a trickling gesture with your hand. Invite students to take turns pantomiming different natural resources in a similar way.

Grammar/Spelling

Present-Tense Action Verbs B I A AH

1 **Teach/Model** Write the sentences and have volunteers read them aloud.

> 1. *A man plants a garden on a hillside.*
> 2. *The rain washes the garden away.*
> 3. *Chloe studies the power of nature.*

Have students underline the verbs. Say: *These verbs tell what people or things do. They are action verbs, and they tell about an action that is happening now.* Point out the spelling changes (wash/washes, study/studies). Create a chart of singular subjects and verbs.

Singular Subject	Singular Verb
The sun	rushes down the hillside.
The windmill	flows through the streets.
A river	shines on my garden.
The wind	knocks out a power plant.
Rain	makes everything warm.
Electricity	supplies power to our homes.

Call on one student to begin a sentence with a subject from the chart, and another to finish it: *The sun makes everything warm.* Provide opportunities for all students to take part in beginning or ending a sentence. Then say: *When the subject is one person or thing, add -s or -es to the verb to tell what is happening now. We call these verbs "present-tense verbs."*

2 **Practice/Apply** Have partners turn and talk about other things forces of nature can do. Then assign **Practice Master 4.3**.

> **CHECK UNDERSTANDING** Display the words. Have students tell which words are action verbs and have them pantomime each one.
>
> run
> leaf
> hop
> is

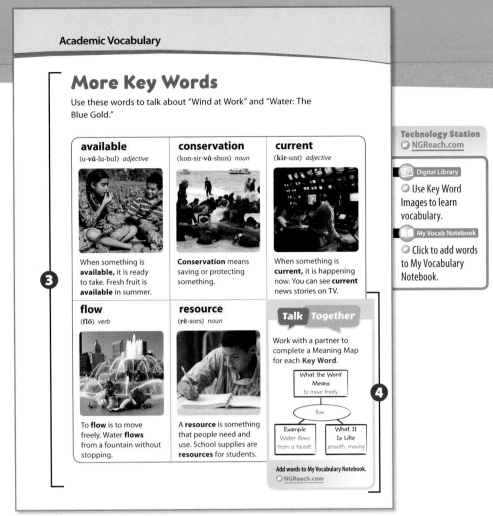

More Key Words

Use these words to talk about "Wind at Work" and "Water: The Blue Gold."

available
(u-vā-lu-bul) *adjective*

When something is **available,** it is ready to take. Fresh fruit is **available** in summer.

conservation
(kon-sir-vā-shun) *noun*

Conservation means saving or protecting something.

current
(**kir**-unt) *adjective*

When something is **current,** it is happening now. You can see **current** news stories on TV.

flow
(flō) *verb*

To **flow** is to move freely. Water **flows** from a fountain without stopping.

resource
(rē-sors) *noun*

A **resource** is something that people need and use. School supplies are **resources** for students.

Talk Together

Work with a partner to complete a Meaning Map for each **Key Word.**

What the Word Means
to move freely

flow

Example
Water flows from a faucet.

What It Is Like
smooth, moving

Add words to My Vocabulary Notebook.
NGReach.com

Technology Station
NGReach.com

Digital Library
Use Key Word Images to learn vocabulary.

My Vocab Notebook
Click to add words to My Vocabulary Notebook.

Student Book page 219

Academic Vocabulary

③ Teach/Model Read the introduction and look at each photograph on the page. Use **Vocabulary Routine 1** and **Key Word Images** to teach the words. Access definitions on pages 616–639.

1. **Pronounce** the word and point to its picture: **available**.

2. **Rate** the word. Have students hold up their fingers to show how well they know the word. (1 = very well, 2 = a little, 3 = not at all) Ask: *What do you know about this word?*

3. **Define** the word: *When something is available, it is ready to take.*

4. **Elaborate** Relate the word to your experience: *Tickets to the new show will be available on Friday.*

④ Practice/Apply Use the ratings from step 2 to form pairs. Have partners complete a Meaning Map for each Key Word. Have volunteers share a Meaning Map with the class.

> **CHECK UNDERSTANDING** Point to the **Key Word Image** of each Key Word and ask students to explain what each word means.

Keys to Efficacy

Model vocabulary acquisition as a lifelong process: *Whenever I see a word I don't know, I look it up in the dictionary.*

Differentiate

Spanish Cognates ▶
conservation/conservacón;
current/corriente; flow/fluir;
resource/recurso

Part 1 Vocabulary Skills Trace		Page
Day 1	Science Vocabulary	T217
Day 2	**Academic Vocabulary**	**T219**
Day 3	Expand Word Knowledge	T222b
Day 4	Share Word Knowledge	T236b
Day 5	Apply Word Knowledge	T237b
Day 6	Context Clues	T238
Day 7	Context Clues	T245
Days 8–9	Extend Vocabulary	T246e–f
Day 10	Vocabulary Review	T246g–h

Day 2
continued

Day at a Glance:
▶ **Language:** Present-Tense Action Verbs
▶ **Vocabulary:** Academic Vocabulary
▶ **Reading:** Learn to Ask Questions
▶ **Writing:** Instructions

OBJECTIVES

Vocabulary
• Acquire and Use Academic Vocabulary
• Use Grade-Level Vocabulary

Learning to Read
• Long *a, ai, ay*

Reading Strategy
• Learn to Ask Questions ⊕

Learning and Teamwork Strategies
• Use Personal Experience
• Use Visuals

Writing
• Write instructions

Resources

🌐 eVisual 4.6

💿 *Reach Into Phonics TE page T80*

Differentiate

Academic Language Frames

Ask Questions

■ I don't understand _____.
   I ask myself _____.
   I read and find _____.

_____

■ I need to understand _____.
   I ask myself _____ and _____.
   I read and find _____.

_____

■ I need to understand _____ and _____.
■ I ask myself _____ and _____.
   I read and find _____ and _____.

🌐 NGReach.com ▶ eVisual 4.6

Learn to Ask Questions

1 Teach Read aloud the introduction. Ask students how they think Chloe feels. Discuss that Chloe looks confused. Make the connection: *When you are confused about something, you can ask questions.* Point out that students ask questions every day in various situations.

2 Model Read aloud the How to chart. Model asking questions about the cartoon:

• *I need to understand <u>why Chloe is confused by what she sees.</u>*

• *I ask myself <u>what is bat guano?</u>*

• *I read and find <u>that Chloe can ask questions at a store to find out.</u>*

3 Practice/Apply Read the directions aloud. Point out the **Language Frames**. Chorally read aloud "How to Make a Compost Bin" and the sample student questions. Listen and note mispronunciations.

Direct students' attention to step 2 in the directions. Use **Academic Language Frames** to help students at each proficiency level ask questions. Students should ask questions about steps 2 and 3. (What does the brown layer add? Why do you need water?) Encourage them to explain why they asked those questions.

> **CHECK UNDERSTANDING** Ask: *What questions do you have about making a compost bin? What answers do you find when you reread?*

Phonics and Fluency

Long *ā, ai, ay*
Display these words: *train* and *day.* Point out the long *ā* sound and explain: *The letters* ai *and* ay *make the long* a *sound.* Write the words *pain* and *pay* on the board. Have students circle the letters that make the long *ā* sound. Display **Transparency 41** from **Reach Into Phonics** and work through the lesson.

Practice Display these sentences from "How to Make a Compost Bin."

• You need a plastic container.
• Start with a layer of brown stuff.
• Then wait as your current garbage is transformed!

Have partners read the sentences chorally several times to develop fluency.

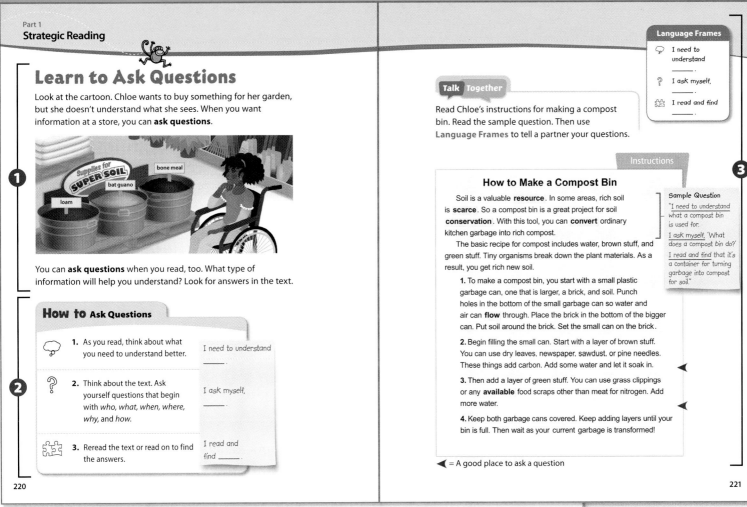

Learn to Ask Questions

Look at the cartoon. Chloe wants to buy something for her garden, but she doesn't understand what she sees. When you want information at a store, you can **ask questions**.

You can **ask questions** when you read, too. What type of information will help you understand? Look for answers in the text.

How to Ask Questions

☁	**1.** As you read, think about what you need to understand better.
❓	**2.** Think about the text. Ask yourself questions that begin with *who, what, when, where, why,* and *how*.
🧩	**3.** Reread the text or read on to find the answers.

I need to understand
————— .

I ask myself,
————— .

I read and find ————— .

Talk Together

Read Chloe's instructions for making a compost bin. Read the sample question. Then use **Language Frames** to tell a partner your questions.

Language Frames

💭 I need to understand
————— .

❓ I ask myself,
————— .

🧩 I read and find
————— .

Instructions

How to Make a Compost Bin

Soil is a valuable **resource**. In some areas, rich soil is **scarce**. So a compost bin is a great project for soil **conservation**. With this tool, you can **convert** ordinary kitchen garbage into rich compost.

The basic recipe for compost includes water, brown stuff, and green stuff. Tiny organisms break down the plant materials. As a result, you get rich new soil.

1. To make a compost bin, you start with a small plastic garbage can, one that is larger, a brick, and soil. Punch holes in the bottom of the small garbage can so water and air can **flow** through. Place the brick in the bottom of the bigger can. Put soil around the brick. Set the small can on the brick.

2. Begin filling the small can. Start with a layer of brown stuff. You can use dry leaves, newspaper, sawdust, or pine needles. These things add carbon. Add some water and let it soak in. ◀

3. Then add a layer of green stuff. You can use grass clippings or any **available** food scraps other than meat for nitrogen. Add more water. ◀

4. Keep both garbage cans covered. Keep adding layers until your bin is full. Then wait as your current garbage is transformed!

◀ = A good place to ask a question

Sample Question
"I need to understand what a compost bin is used for.
I ask myself, 'What does a compost bin do?'
I read and find that it's a container for turning garbage into compost for soil."

220   221

Student Book pages 220–221

Daily Writing 📝

4 **Instructions** Point out the features of the instructions in "How to Make a Compost Bin": an introduction paragraph, steps to follow, and simple sentences. Then write a RAFT for students to follow:

- Role: yourself
- Audience: a friend
- Form: instructions
- Topic: what to do with the compost

Adjust the prompt to include students at all proficiency levels.

B Have students draw simple instructions.

I Have students write sentences.

A Have students write paragraphs

AH Have students create multiple entries.

Invite students to share their instructions with the class.

CLOSE AND ASSESS

- **Language** *Provide singular nouns and have students orally complete sentences with action verbs.* (Examples: *Rain falls. The river rushes. My friend studies.*)

- **Reading** *Reread Step 3 of "How to Make a Compost Bin." What questions can you ask here?* (Possible answers: *How much water do you add? How long do you let it soak?*)

- **Vocabulary** *Why is a compost bin a good project for* **conservation***?* (Possible answer: It **converts** waste into the **resource** soil.)

Day 3

Day at a Glance:
- ▶ **Language:** Express Certainty, Probability, Possibility
- ▶ **Vocabulary:** Expand Word Knowledge
- ▶ **Reading:** Read the Selection
- ▶ **Writing:** Writer's Craft

OBJECTIVES

Vocabulary
- Use Academic Vocabulary ⊕
- Use Grade-Level Vocabulary ⊕
- Acquire and Use Basic Vocabulary

Language
- Language Function: Express Certainty, Probability, Possibility ⊕
- Listen to and Imitate Fluent Models
- Use a Variety of Strategic Learning Techniques

Learning and Teamwork Strategies
- Use Media to Build Language
- Gather Information
- Use Graphic Organizer: 4-Corner Poster

Resources

- ◎ ◯ *Sing With Me Language Song CD 2* Tr 11,12
- ◷ ◯ *Sing With Me Language Song Book,* page 17

  In the U.S.A. Picture Cards 227–232

- • *Chart or poster paper*

◯ NGReach.com ›

See **Technology Station** for digital student resources.

Differentiate

Multi-Level Strategies

BEGINNING

Have students repeat after you as you say sentences such as *I'm sure we are going to read tomorrow; I think we are going to read about the wind; Maybe we will read about hurricanes and tornadoes.*

INTERMEDIATE

Ask students either/or questions such as: *Do you think it's going to be hot or cold tomorrow?* If the student has difficulty, echo his or her response, revising as necessary. For example, if the student says *It can rain tomorrow,* say *Yes, I think it's going to rain, too.*

ADVANCED **ADVANCED HIGH**

Ask students open-ended questions, such as: *What do you think we will do in class tomorrow?* Prompt students to express their degree of certainty by following up with a question such as: *Are you certain about that?*

Language of the Day

What can the wind the do?

The wind can _____.

Read the Language of the Day. Model: *The wind can blow clouds across the sky.* Invite students to share what they know about the wind. If students tend to focus on the wind's destructive aspects *(The wind can blow down houses),* remind them that the wind can carry a seed to an island in the middle of the ocean, or make an airplane go even faster.

Express Certainty, Probability, Possibility

❶ Teach Introduce the language function: *Today you will learn how to express certainty, probability, and possibility.* Play the song "Maybe Carrots, Maybe Not" and invite students to sing along.

Connect: *You can use the words* sure, certain, think, probably, maybe, *and* might *to express certainty, probability, and possibility.* Review the chart:

Express certainty	Express probability	Express possibility
sure, certain	think, probably	maybe, might

❷ Model Put three cups on your desk with an eraser in one of them. Look the other way and "blindly" choose one of the empty cups. Say: *Maybe the eraser is in this cup.* Turn the cup upside down to show that it's empty. Repeat with the other empty cup, saying: *It might be in this cup.* Finally, hold up the last cup and, as you turn it over, say: *I'm sure the eraser is in this cup.*

❸ Practice/Apply Have students work together to look for sentences that express certainty, probability, and possibility in the song "Maybe Carrots, Maybe Not." Then have students make sentences of their own showing certainty, probability, and possibility. Use the **Multi-Level Strategies** to support students at all levels of proficiency.

> **CHECK UNDERSTANDING** Ask students: *What's an expression you can use to show certainty?* (I'm sure, I'm certain) *What words and phrases show probability?* (I think, probably) *What words show possibility?* (maybe, might)

Maybe Carrots, Maybe Not

I will plant some carrots in a
garden row.
If the soil is rich, then maybe
they will grow.
With some sun and water,
probably they'll sprout.
If they grow, I'm pretty sure the
rabbits will find out.

One thing is for certain,
rabbits like a treat.
If they find my carrots,
they are sure to eat.
Maybe planting something
else will ease my doubts.
I bet that even rabbits will not
bother Brussels sprouts!

Tune: "Sing a Song of Sixpence"   MP3 or Song CD 2 Tracks 11–12   **Song** 17

Sing With Me Language Song Book page 17

Technology Station
○ NGReach.com

(MP3) Sing with Me
○ Play and sing along.

Expand Word Knowledge

4 **Teach/Model** Explain that each student
pair will become Key Word experts. They will
study one Key Word and create a Key Word
poster about that word. Use **Vocabulary
Routine 2** and model making a 4-Corner
Poster about the word **resource**. (See
Vocabulary Routines, page PD38.)

- Write the word.
- Add a picture.
- Add a definition.
- Add a context sentence.

5 **Practice/Apply** Assign a Key Word to
each pair of students. Have each pair create a poster for their assigned
Key Word. Display the posters on the class word wall.

CHECK UNDERSTANDING Have the partner experts read their definition
and sentence from their poster. Ask the class to identify the Key Word.

Resource

Sentence:
Books are a
resource for
students at
school.

Definition:
A resource is
something that
people need and
use.

4-Corner Poster

Key Words	
available	generate
conservation	power
convert	renewable
current	resource
electricity	scarce
flow	

Differentiate

Newcomer Support

Newcomers can make 4-Corner Posters
using words from In the **U.S.A. Picture
Cards 227–232**.

Day 3
continued

Day at a Glance:
▶ **Language:** Express Certainty, Probability, Possibility
▶ **Vocabulary:** Expand Word Knowledge
⏵ **Reading:** Read the Selection
⏵ **Writing:** Writer's Craft

OBJECTIVES

Vocabulary
- Use Grade-Level Vocabulary **ⓣ**
- Use Academic Vocabulary **ⓣ**
- Use Classroom Vocabulary **ⓣ**

Reading Strategy
- Plan: Preview

Comprehension and Literary Analysis
- Analyze Text Features: Heads
- Analyze Genre: Science Article
- Analyze Text Structure: Relate Cause and Effect

Learning and Teamwork Strategies
- Use Prereading Supports
- Build Background Knowledge

Resources

 Comprehension Coach

Keys to Efficacy

Encourage elaboration: *Tell me more about the time you saw the wind blow.*

Preview the Science Article

① **Introduce** Have students look at the photograph on page 223 and read the title of the selection: *Wind at Work.* Ask students what they know about the wind, and what they would like to find out about it. Write their questions, and tell students to look for answers as they read the selection.

② **Genre and Text Feature** Read aloud the definition of a science article. Elaborate: *This selection gives facts about the wind. Facts are true statements; they give information, not opinions.* Read the explanation of the section heading. Explain: *A heading tells the main idea of each section. As you read this selection, make a guess about the content of each section, based on the heading.*

③ **Preview and Build Background** Use sheltering strategies as you conduct a picture walk.

Pages	Say (and Do)
224–225	*The diagram on page 224 shows what causes wind. What happens when the sun warms the air? Yes, the air rises.* (Gesture to show air rising.) *Where does cool air go when the warm air rises? Yes, it rushes under the rising air. The diagram on page 225 shows how the sun heats the earth in different places. Point to the picture of the forest. Tell me the names of the other two places.* (desert and prairie)
226–227	*Look at the photos on these two pages. Describe what you see. How are these places different? How are they similar?* (The photo on page 226 shows a big city. The other photo shows a desert. They both show how the wind can affect people and the land.)
228–229	*What do you see on page 228?* (three sailboats) *Why are these pictures in a book about the wind?* (Because the wind makes sailboats move across the water.) *The diagram on page 229 shows wind patterns in different parts of the world.*
230–231	*The photo on page 230 shows a wind farm. The towers are called wind turbines. They have blades that spin very fast in the wind* (make a spinning motion). *Now look at the diagram. What can you tell from looking at it?* (Somehow **electricity** goes from the wind farm to the city.) *We'll find out exactly how a wind farm makes electricity when we read the selection.*
232–233	*Have you ever seen a tornado? What does it look like? How would a tornado sound? The diagram shows what happens during a tornado.*
234–235	*What's this? A hurricane. Hurricanes are even more **powerful** than tornadoes. What do you know about hurricanes? I know that they can cause a lot of damage. They are so strong they can destroy trees and houses. The wind is a powerful force of nature, isn't it? Let's go back to the beginning and learn all about the wind.*

CHECK UNDERSTANDING Ask: *What is the genre of this selection?* (science article). *How do you know?* (It gives facts, not opinions.) *What will this section be about?* (How wind provides power.)

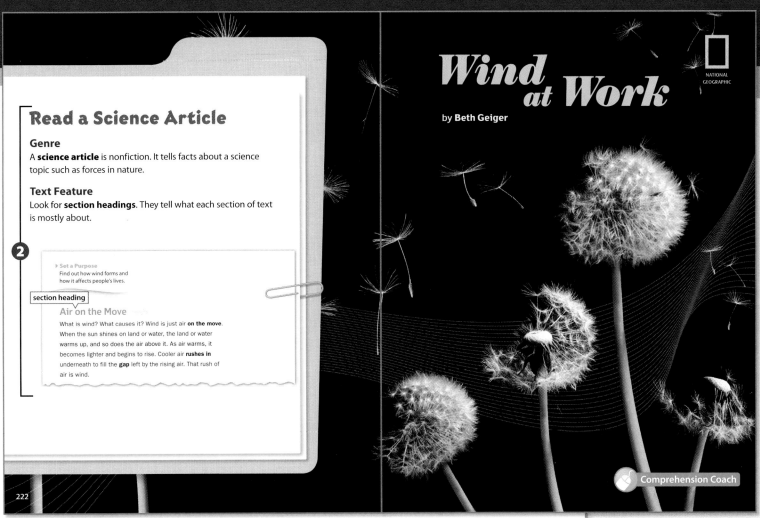

Wind at Work

by Beth Geiger

NATIONAL GEOGRAPHIC

Comprehension Coach

Read a Science Article

Genre
A **science article** is nonfiction. It tells facts about a science topic such as forces in nature.

Text Feature
Look for **section headings**. They tell what each section of text is mostly about.

> **Set a Purpose**
> Find out how wind forms and how it affects people's lives.

section heading

Air on the Move
What is wind? What causes it? Wind is just air **on the move**. When the sun shines on land or water, the land or water warms up, and so does the air above it. As air warms, it becomes lighter and begins to rise. Cooler air **rushes in** underneath to fill the **gap** left by the rising air. That rush of air is wind.

222

Student Book pages 222–223

Comprehension Coach

Build Reading Power
Assign students to use the software, based on their instructional needs.

Read Silently	**Listen**	**Record**
• Comprehension questions with immediate feedback • Vocabulary support	• Process model of fluent reading • Text highlighting to facilitate tracking • Vocabulary support	• Oral reading fluency practice • Speech recognition for oral fluency assessment with immediate feedback

Cultural Perpectives

Explain to students that proverbs are very old sayings that people use to make predictions and give warnings. In English there are numerous proverbs about the weather, such as *A wind from the south has rain in its mouth*. Ask students to "interpret" the proverb. Then, invite them to share other weather-related proverbs that they know. If they share proverbs from other cultures or languages, they will have to interpret them for the class and explain their meaning.

OBJECTIVES

Vocabulary
- Use Grade-Level Vocabulary ⊙
- Use Academic Vocabulary
- Use Classroom Vocabulary

Learning to Read
- Concepts of Print: Identify a Sentence
- Phonics: Words with Long *e: ee, ea* and Long *o: oa, ow*

Reading Strategies
- Plan: Set a Purpose, Predict, Confirm Predictions
- Ask Questions ⊙

Fluency
- Intonation ⊙

Comprehension and Literary Analysis
- Identify Cause and Effect ⊙
- Use Text Structure: Heads

Learning and Teamwork Strategies
- Use Reading Supports

Writing
- Connect Reading and Writing
- Analyze a Professional Model: Article
- Develop Writer's Craft: Support Ideas

Science
- Explore renewable resources

Resources

⊙ *Read with Me Selection CD*

⊙ *Practice Master 4.4*

⊙ *Reach Into Phonics TE page T82*

⊙ NGReach.com ›

See **Technology Station** for digital student resources.

Key Points Reading

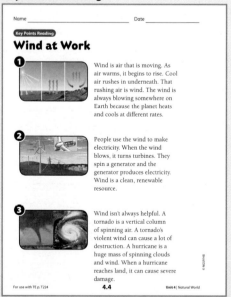

Practice Master 4.4

Read the Science Article

Suggested Pacing

- Day 3: Read Section 1, pages 224–225
- Day 4: Read Sections 2 and 3, pages 226–235

Reading Options Scaffold the support for varied reading levels.

BELOW LEVEL	ON LEVEL	ABOVE LEVEL
Listen and Read Along	**Read Together**	**Read Independently**
• Read the text aloud, while students track the print on the **Key Points Reading** Master. • Use the visuals to support English vocabulary. • Check understanding with selected Build Comprehension questions.	• Have students set a purpose for reading. Have them use the section head to predict what the section is about then read silently and then aloud. • At the end of each section, have students summarize the information in the section. • After reading, have students listen to the Selection Tape/CD and practice reading fluently to a partner.	• Have students set a purpose for reading. Have them choose an appropriate reading rate for the purpose as they read silently. • Ask the Comprehension questions to check understanding. Also have students discuss the effectiveness of the reading rate they chose.

Phonics and Fluency

Words with Long /ē/:. ee, ea and Long /ō/: oa, ow

Teach/Model Explain that the letters *ee* and *ea* make the long /ē/ sound and that the letters *oa* and *ow* make the long /ō/ sound. Write the words *sea, creek, coat,* and *show* on the board and ask students to read them aloud with you. Ask: *Which letters make the long /ē/ sound?* (ee, ea) *the long /ō/ sound?* (oa, ow) Display **Transparency 42** from **Reach into Phonics** and work through the lesson.

Practice/Apply Display these sentences from "Wind at Work."

- The planet's surface heats unevenly.
- Winds blow west near the equator.
- People still sail boats today.

Underline the words *heats, blow* and *boats*. Have students write the words and circle the letters that make the long /ē/ or /ō/ sound. Have partners read the words chorally several times to develop fluency in reading words with long vowels.

► Set a Purpose

1 Find out how wind forms and how it affects people's lives.

Air on the Move

What is wind? What causes it? Wind is just air **on the move**. **2** When the sun shines on land or water, the land or water warms up, and so does the air above it. As air warms, it becomes lighter and begins to rise. Cooler air **rushes in** underneath to fill the **gap** left by the rising air. That rush of air is wind.

What Causes Wind?

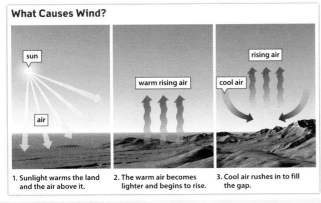

1. Sunlight warms the land and the air above it.
2. The warm air becomes lighter and begins to rise.
3. Cool air rushes in to fill the gap.

In Other Words
on the move that is moving
rushes in moves quickly
gap space

224

3 Wind is always **swirling** around Earth because the planet's surface heats unevenly. For example, water takes longer to heat and cool than land. So air is always rushing between water and land. That's why beaches are often **breezy**!

Different types of places, such as forests, deserts, and prairies, also soak up the sun's heat differently. They cool down at different **rates**, too. Don't forget about the cold places at Earth's North and South Poles and the warm area around the equator, the imaginary line around the planet's middle. Air moves constantly between all these hot and cold spots.

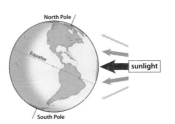

▲ Sunlight usually hits most directly the area near the equator, heating it more than other regions.

In Other Words
swirling moving
breezy windy
rates speeds

forest

desert

prairie

Forests, deserts, prairies, and other types of places soak up heat differently.

► Before You Move On

4
1. **Use Text Features** How does the section heading help you understand the text?
2. **Ask Questions** Choose a photo or diagram on page 224 or 225. What else would you like to know about it?

225

Build Comprehension, pages 224–225

1 **Set a Purpose** Read the introduction at the top of page 224 to help students set a purpose for reading.

2 **Details** What is wind? (Wind is air on the move.) How can you say this a different way? (Possible answer: Wind is moving air.)

3 **Confirm Word Meaning** Wind is always swirling around Earth. What does *swirling* mean? (moving)

4 **Answers to Before You Move On**

1. **Use Text Features** Possible answer: The heading tells what that section will be about. This helps me know that I will learn about how air moves.

2. **Ask Questions** MODEL | GUIDE | APPLY Use the **Language Frames** on page 220 to model how to ask questions about the diagram on page 224.

   - I need to understand why the air is rising in the middle picture.
   - I ask myself, Why is the air rising?
   - I read the caption and find out that warm air becomes light and that is why it rises.

Student Book pages 224–225

N B

Concepts of Print: Identify a Sentence

Teach/Model Turn to page 224. Read the sentence labeled 1 in the diagram. Point to the capital letter at the beginning of the sentence. Say: *A sentence always begins with a capital letter.* Then point to the period at the end of the sentence. Say: *This is a period. It comes at the end of a sentence that tells something.* Read the sentence again with correct intonation and invite students to chime in.

Repeat the process with the question in the first sentence on page 224 and the exclamation in the last sentence in the first paragraph on page 225. Explain: *A question mark comes at the end of a sentence that asks a question. An exclamation point comes at the end of a sentence that shows strong feeling or surprise.*

Practice/Apply Have partners find other examples of sentences that end with a period, a question mark, and an exclamation point.

Different Kinds of Winds

Some winds blow in regular patterns across thousands of miles. Other winds, such as gusts in a thunderstorm, are sudden and **local**. Mountains, islands, and even tall buildings affect how wind moves. **No wonder** wind comes in so many varieties. Gales, gusts, breezes, and puffs are just a few kinds of wind.

1

A Force You Can't See

You can't see wind, but you can see its **handiwork**. Have you seen a tree branch swaying? That's wind. Have you ever watched an umbrella blow inside out? That's wind again.

2

▲ Tall buildings can change the direction of wind.

In Other Words
local stay in one area
No wonder It's not surprising that
handiwork effect

226

Wind does more than just **play with** umbrellas. It **sculpts** rocks and landscapes by tearing away tiny pieces off rocks. Piece by tiny piece, wind can erase a whole mountain. This process of wearing away is called erosion.

Bit by bit, over millions of years, wind carves rock into cool new shapes. What happens to all those loose pieces? Wind piles them into graceful sand **dunes**. That's a lot of **power** for something you can't see.

Wind has helped to slowly wear away rocks and cliffs in Monument Valley, Arizona.

3

In Other Words
play with make trouble for
sculpts shapes; carves
dunes hills ▶

▶ **Before You Move On**

4
1. **Cause/Effect** How does the photo on this page show the wind's effect?
2. **Ask Questions** What is one thing you learned about erosion? What do you still want to know?

227

Student Book pages 226–227

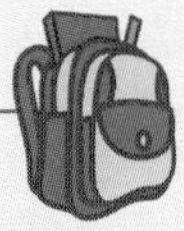

Home Connection: Class Book

Have students share the pictures they drew for the Home Connections activity. Discuss what kinds of things each student saw and why they chose to draw about it. Assemble the pages showing "Signs of Nature" from your neighborhood to make a class book.

Keys to Efficacy

Have students cite evidence from the text to support understanding: *Point to the visual that shows that* or *Read me the sentence that helped you answer that question.*

Build Comprehension, pages 226–227

1 **Make Inferences** How do mountains, islands, and tall buildings affect the way the wind moves? (Possible answer: They block the wind. The wind has to move around them.)

2 **Details** If you can't see wind, how do you know it's there? (Possible answer: You can see branches moving because of the wind.)

3 **Use Text Features** Look at the photo on page 227. Where is this photo taken? How do you know? (Monument Valley, Arizona. I know because I read the caption on the photo.)

4 **Answers to Before You Move On**

1. **Cause/Effect** MODEL | GUIDE | APPLY Model how to identify the effect of the wind. The picture shows the unusual shapes of the rocks in Monument Valley. The wind has slowly worn away the sides of these mountains. Now, what is left is these tall rock towers.

2. **Ask Questions** MODEL | GUIDE | APPLY Discuss an answer to the first part. (I learned that erosion is the process of wearing away.) Guide students to ask questions. Ask: *What else do you need to understand about erosion?* (Possible answers: How long does it take to erase a whole mountain? How big are the pieces of rock that the wind carves away?)

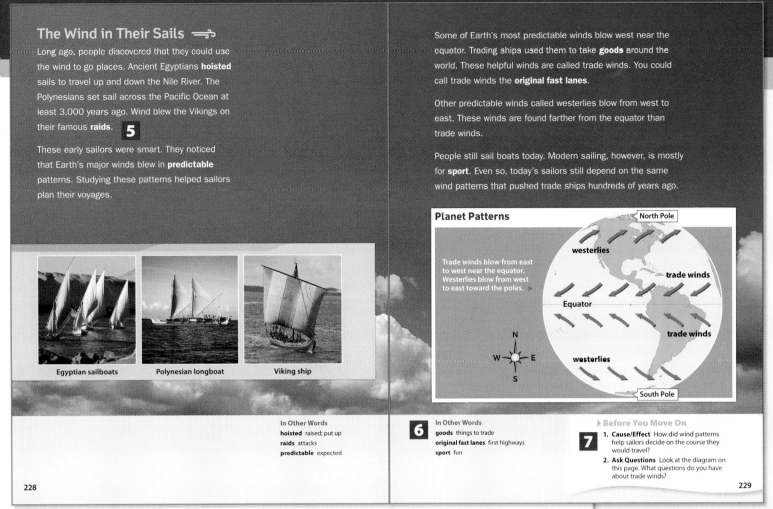

The Wind in Their Sails

Long ago, people discovered that they could use the wind to go places. Ancient Egyptians **hoisted** sails to travel up and down the Nile River. The Polynesians set sail across the Pacific Ocean at least 3,000 years ago. Wind blew the Vikings on their famous **raids**. **5**

These early sailors were smart. They noticed that Earth's major winds blew in **predictable** patterns. Studying these patterns helped sailors plan their voyages.

Some of Earth's most predictable winds blow west near the equator. Trading ships used them to take **goods** around the world. These helpful winds are called trade winds. You could call trade winds the **original fast lanes**.

Other predictable winds called westerlies blow from west to east. These winds are found farther from the equator than trade winds.

People still sail boats today. Modern sailing, however, is mostly for **sport**. Even so, today's sailors still depend on the same wind patterns that pushed trade ships hundreds of years ago.

Egyptian sailboats   Polynesian longboat   Viking ship

Planet Patterns

North Pole
westerlies
trade winds
Equator
trade winds
westerlies
South Pole

Trade winds blow from east to west near the equator. Westerlies blow from west to east toward the poles.

N W E S

In Other Words
hoisted raised; put up
raids attacks
predictable expected

6 **In Other Words**
goods things to trade
original fast lanes first highways
sport fun

▶ **Before You Move On**

7 1. **Cause/Effect** How did wind patterns help sailors decide on the course they would travel?

2. **Ask Questions** Look at the diagram on this page. What questions do you have about trade winds?

228   229

Build Comprehension, pages 228–229

5 **Details** What did the ancient Egyptians, the Polynesians, and the Vikings have in common? (They all used wind to **power** their boats and go places.)

6 **Clarify Language** Look at "In Other Words" to find out what **original fast lanes** means. What does "You could call trade winds the original fast lanes" mean? (The trade winds could be called highways. When people drive on highways they move faster than on streets. This means people sailing with the trade winds move faster than those sailing on other parts of the ocean.)

7 **Answers to Before You Move On**

1. **Cause/Effect** MODEL | GUIDE | APPLY Guide students to use the diagram to help explain the cause-effect relationship. Ask: *If a sailor wanted to travel from east to west, what would he do?* (Look at the wind patterns on the map.) Ask: *Where would he sail to get the best winds?* (near the Equator)

2. **Ask Questions** MODEL | GUIDE | APPLY Student questions will vary. Examples: Do the winds change directions suddenly or gradually? Are the wind directions always the same? Would sailors want to sail near the Poles?

Student Book pages 228–229

B **I** **A** **AH**

Text Feature: Heads

Teach/Model Direct students' attention to the heading on page 228. Tell students that a head signals the start of a new section of text. It tells what the next section will be about.

Ask: What do you think this section will be about? (wind and sailing) What other clues help you? (photos)

Wind farms use the wind's power to make **electricity**.

blade

turbine

tower

Wind Power

People no longer need wind to cross the ocean. They have airplanes for that. Still, wind helps people in other ways. One way is by making electricity.

The Horse Hollow wind farm in Texas doesn't grow wheat or corn. Instead, it has hundreds of steel wind turbines. Each tower is taller than a twenty-story building. If you stood near the towers, you would hear a weird **hum**. That's the sound of the blades spinning in the steady wind. **1**

Wind, after all, is energy. It's clean and **renewable** energy, too. Wind makes the turbines spin. The spinning motion turns a **generator**. Then the generator makes electricity.

In Other Words
hum noise
generator machine

230

Wind farms work best in open places where nothing gets in the wind's way. So far, wind farms in the United States capture enough wind to power about 4.5 million homes. That's only about one percent of the electricity we need. Slowly, though, the role of wind power is growing. More wind farms seem to **crop up** every year. **3** **4**

How a Wind Turbine Works

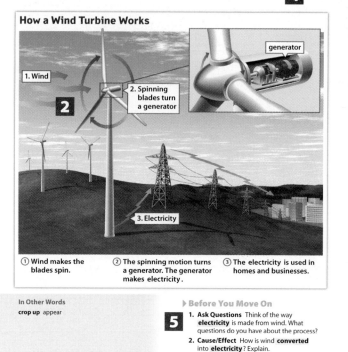

generator

1. Wind

2. Spinning blades turn a generator

2

3. Electricity

① Wind makes the blades spin.

② The spinning motion turns a generator. The generator makes electricity.

③ The electricity is used in homes and businesses.

In Other Words
crop up appear

▶ **Before You Move On**

5
1. **Ask Questions** Think of the way **electricity** is made from wind. What questions do you have about the process?

2. **Cause/Effect** How is wind **converted** into **electricity**? Explain.

231

Student Book pages 230–231

Build Comprehension, pages 230–231

1 **Make Inferences** Why do you think wind turbine towers are so tall? (Possible answer: to make it easier to catch the wind.)

2 **Use Visuals** What part of the turbine spins? (the blades)

3 **Details** Where do wind farms work best? (in open places where nothing gets in the wind's way)

4 **Draw Conclusions** Why do you think the number of wind farms is growing? (Possible answer: Wind is clean and renewable. It's a good way to get energy.)

5 **Answers to Before You Move On**

1. **Ask Questions** MODEL | GUIDE | APPLY Prompt students by saying: *After I read the text and look at the diagrams, I still have questions about wind power. How fast do the blades have to spin to make electricity?* Have students share the questions they have.

2. **Cause/Effect** MODEL | GUIDE | APPLY Have students use the diagram to explain the process step by step and identify the cause-and-effect relationships. For example, in 1, the wind causes the blades to spin.

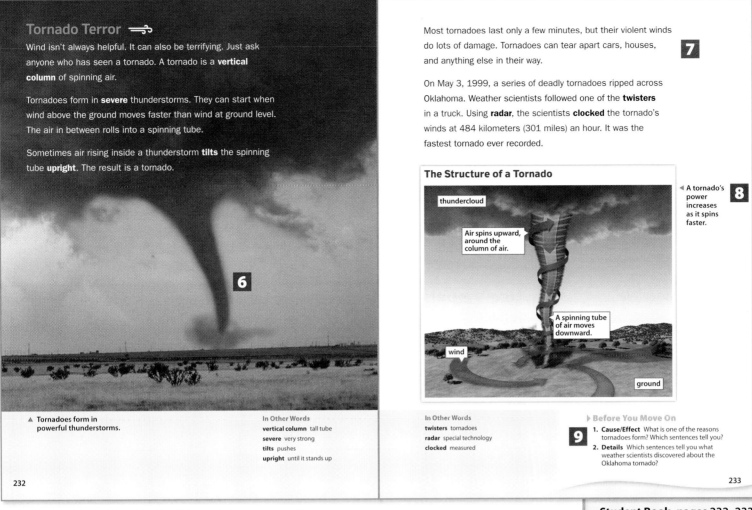

Tornado Terror

Wind isn't always helpful. It can also be terrifying. Just ask anyone who has seen a tornado. A tornado is a **vertical column** of spinning air.

Tornadoes form in **severe** thunderstorms. They can start when wind above the ground moves faster than wind at ground level. The air in between rolls into a spinning tube.

Sometimes air rising inside a thunderstorm **tilts** the spinning tube **upright**. The result is a tornado.

▲ Tornadoes form in powerful thunderstorms.

In Other Words
vertical column tall tube
severe very strong
tilts pushes
upright until it stands up

232

Most tornadoes last only a few minutes, but their violent winds do lots of damage. Tornadoes can tear apart cars, houses, and anything else in their way. **7**

On May 3, 1999, a series of deadly tornadoes ripped across Oklahoma. Weather scientists followed one of the **twisters** in a truck. Using **radar**, the scientists **clocked** the tornado's winds at 484 kilometers (301 miles) an hour. It was the fastest tornado ever recorded.

The Structure of a Tornado

thundercloud

Air spins upward, around the column of air.

A spinning tube of air moves downward.

wind

ground

◀ A tornado's power increases as it spins faster. **8**

In Other Words
twisters tornadoes
radar special technology
clocked measured

▶ **Before You Move On**

9
1. **Cause/Effect** What is one of the reasons tornadoes form? Which sentences tell you?
2. **Details** Which sentences tell you what weather scientists discovered about the Oklahoma tornado?

233

Build Comprehension, pages 232–233

6 **Use Visuals** What does a tornado look like? (Possible answers: It looks like a large, black twirling cloud. It looks like a funnel or cone.)

7 **Details** What part of a tornado causes damage? (The part that touches the ground causes damage.) How long do tornados usually last? (only a few minutes)

8 **Use Key Words** When does a tornado's **power** increase? (A tornado gains power as it spins faster.)

9 **Answers to Before You Move On**

1. **Cause/Effect** `MODEL | GUIDE | APPLY` Any of the following three sentences is acceptable. Tornadoes start when the wind above ground moves faster than the wind below. The air in between rolls into a spinning tube. Sometimes the air rising inside a thunderstorm tilts the spinning tube upright.

2. **Details** The last two sentences on page 233. Scientists clocked the tornado's winds at 484 kilometers (301 miles) an hour. It was the fastest tornado ever recorded.

Student Book pages 232–233

I **A** **AH**

Science: Tornadoes

Tell students that every state is at some risk for a tornado, but states that are in Tornado Alley are at the highest risk. Have students research which states are in Tornado Alley. If possible, mark them on a United States map. Ask: *Is our state in Tornado Alley?*

I A AH

Fluency: Intonation

Teach/Model Explain the concept: *Fluent readers read with intonation. They change the rise and fall in the pitch or tone of their voice.* Direct students' attention to page 234. Say: *If we do not change the pitch or tone of our voice as we read, the reading will be monotone and not very interesting to listen to.* Play the selection recording or read aloud page 234 with intonation.

Practice Have partners read the page aloud together several times, mimicking the intonation you modeled.

Keys to Efficacy

Ask processing questions if a student's answer is incomplete: *Say more about a hurricane's waves. Why might waves flood a coast?*

Build Comprehension, pages 234-235

1 **Clarify Language** What does "pack a major punch" mean? What do these words make you think of? (a physical punch or to hit something or someone) Pack a major punch means "are very strong."

2 **Cause and Effect** MODEL | GUIDE | APPLY What might happen if a hurricane hits land? (The winds can destroy trees and buildings. Huge waves flood coasts.)

3 **Use Visuals** Point out that the photograph on page 234 shows a hurricane from above Earth. Ask: *How does the picture help you understand what a hurricane looks like?* (It shows the swirling clouds and winds.) Identify the Florida peninsula. *How does the photograph help you understand how large a hurricane can be?* (It shows that a hurricane can be almost as big as a state.)

4 **Answers to Before You Move On**

1. Cause/Effect MODEL | GUIDE | APPLY When clouds come together over the ocean, Earth's rotation can cause the mass of clouds to spin. If the winds reach 119 kilometers an hour, the storm becomes a hurricane.

2. Use Text Features The section heading "A World of Wind" tells me that there is wind everywhere in the world. That means that wind probably affects the whole world.

Hurricane Force

Tornadoes may be terrifying, but hurricanes are huge and terrifying. A hurricane can easily stretch across three states with winds that **pack a major punch**. **1**

Hurricanes form over tropical oceans. Warm, **moist** air rises. More air moves in underneath and then rises. Big, wet clouds start to gather.

Over a few days, Earth's **rotation** causes the growing **mass** of clouds to spin. When winds reach 119 kilometers (74 miles) an hour, the storm becomes a hurricane.

Once hurricanes hit land, they can do extreme damage. The winds can destroy trees and buildings, and huge waves flood coasts. **2**

▲ As the earth rotates, clouds that gather over the ocean may start to spin, too. Sometimes the spinning clouds become a hurricane. **3**

In Other Words
pack a major punch are very strong
moist wet
rotation motion
mass group

234

A World of Wind

From gentle breezes to strong gusts, wind is everywhere. It can **sculpt** mountains and tear apart houses. Long ago, wind carried explorers to new places. Now it **helps light** cities.

The next time you are just **shooting the breeze**, think about the many ways that wind changes our world. ❖

In the strongest hurricanes, winds can race at more than 249 kilometers (155 miles) an hour.

In Other Words
sculpt shape
helps light provides **electricity** for
shooting the breeze relaxing and having fun

▶ **Before You Move On**
4
1. **Cause/Effect** How does Earth's motion cause hurricanes?
2. **Use Text Features** What does the section heading tell you about the text on this page?

235

Student Book pages 234–235

Daily Writing A AH

1 **Support Ideas** Explain: *Like Beth Geiger, you can use diagrams, photographs, captions, and facts to support the ideas you present in your selection. Start by thinking about what visuals would help the reader better understand the information you give.* Use the **Modeled Writing Routine** to write sentences that tell which support items help the reader to better understand your writing. (See **Writing Routines,** page PD54).

Think Aloud	Write
Erosion is the process of wearing away.	A photo of a mountain that has eroded is a helpful visual for the reader to understand what erosion is.
Trade winds blow east to west and westerlies blow west to east.	A diagram makes it easier to see where the trade winds occur and how they blow.
Tornado Terror is a good name for this section.	A section heading helps the reader to know what they will be reading about in that section.

Have students write their sentences in their journals.

CLOSE AND ASSESS
- **Language** *How would you compare a tornado and a hurricane?* (Answers will vary.)
- **Vocabulary** *Which Key Words did you use as you read the selection? Give an example.*
- **Reading** *What is a question you can ask yourself about wind? Where will you find the answer?*

Meet the Author

Encourage students to read more books written by Beth Geiger.

-*Strong to the Hoop*
-*Top of the Order*
-*Vroomaloom Zoom*

Day 4

Day at a Glance:
▶ **Language:** Present Progressive
▶ **Vocabulary:** Share Word Knowledge
▶ **Reading:** Think and Respond
▶ **Writing:** Write About It

OBJECTIVES

Vocabulary
• Use Grade-Level Vocabulary ⊕
• Use Academic Vocabulary ⊕

Language
• Use the Present Progressive ⊕

Learning and Teamwork Strategies
• Review
• Collaborate with Peers

Resources

⊙ *eVisual 4.7*

↻ ⊙ *Practice Master 4.5*

Differentiate

Language Transfer

Challenge African-American vernacular English uses the same form of the helping verb *be* in all cases of the present progressive tense.

Strategy Have students take turns performing an action such as running in place. Say: *He/She is running.* Have students repeat after you. Repeat this several times with different students and actions.

Part 1 Grammar Skills Trace		Page
Day 2	Present-Tense Action Verbs	T219a
▶ Day 4	**Present Progressive**	**T236a**
Day 7	Present-Tense Action Verbs	T245a
Day 10	Review Present-Tense Action Verbs	T246g

> # Language of the Day
> What did you learn from "Wind at Work"?
> I learned about _____. I learned that _____.

Read the Language of the Day. Model: *I learned about erosion. I learned that the wind can erase a whole mountain.* Invite students to share what they learned as well. Proficient students can tell what they learned and elaborate using both frames. Beginning students may feel more comfortable using just the first frame. Then explain that today students will talk and write about the selection.

Grammar Present Progressive B I A AH

① **Teach/Model** Write and read aloud these sentences: *Wind is swirling around Earth. I am feeling the wind.* Explain: *When a verb tells about an action as it is happening, the main verb ends in* -ing. Display and read the Grammar Rules.

> ### Grammar Rules Present Progressive
>
> 1. Some verbs show action.
> 2. Present progressive verbs tell about an action as it is happening.
> 3. Present progressive verbs uses *am, is,* or *are* and a main verb that ends in *-ing.*
>
> ⊙ NGReach.com ⟩ eVisual 4.7

Have students identify the helping verbs in the sentences (is, am). Make this chart and say: *The helping verb always agrees with the subject.* Point out the spelling changes (clap/clapping, bake/baking)

Subject	Helping Verb	-ing Verb
I	am	listening
he, she, it	is	clapping
we, you they	are	baking

② **Practice/Apply** Have pairs use present progressive verbs to talk about what is happening on pages 223, 226, and 235. Assign **Practice Master 4.5.**

> **CHECK UNDERSTANDING** Display this sentence: *Dad is running in the cold breeze.*
> Ask: *Which word is the helping verb and which is the main verb?* (helping = *is*, main = *run*)

Share Word Knowledge

3 **Teach/Model** To connect concepts, say: *Yesterday you became Key Word experts. Today you will share what you know about your Key Words.* Group each student with a partner who studied a different word. Have partners follow the steps of **Vocabulary Routine 3** to share their word knowledge. (See **Vocabulary Routines**, page PD39)

- Take turns reading Key Word posters.
- Talk about how the pictures on the posters show the meanings of the Key Words.
- Create sentences using both Key Words and write them in your journals.
- Draw a line under each Key Word.

4 **Practice/Apply** Have each set of partners self-identify as Partner A and Partner B. Have students conduct a **Three-Step Interview** to share their word expertise. First, student A interviews student B about his or her word. Then have partners reverse roles. Student A shares with the class the information from student B. Then student B shares the information from student A. (See **Cooperative Learning Routines**, pages PD58–PD59.)

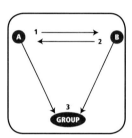

Three-Step Interview

Students share the two words they studied and copy the information they learn into their vocabulary journals. Rotate and repeat until each student has a journal entry for each Key Word. Have students take turns reading the Key Word posters again. All students should echo the pronunciation. Correct any mispronunciations.

CHECK UNDERSTANDING Have students take turns providing a definition of a Key Word. Have the partner name the Key Word being defined.

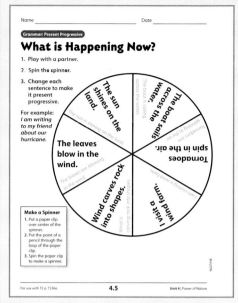

Practice Master 4.5

Part 1 Vocabulary Skills Trace		Page
Day 1	Science Vocabulary	T217
Day 2	Academic Vocabulary	T219
Day 3	Expand Word Knowledge	T222b
▶ Day 4	**Share Word Knowledge**	**T236b**
Day 5	Apply Word Knowledge	T237b
Day 6	Context Clues	T238
Day 7	Context Clues	T245
Days 8–9	Extend Vocabulary	T246e–f
Day 10	Vocabulary Review	T246g–h

Day 4
continued

Day at a Glance:
▶ **Grammar:** Present Progressive
▶ **Vocabulary:** Share Word Knowledge
▶ **Reading:** Think and Respond
▶ **Writing:** Write About It

OBJECTIVES

Vocabulary
• Use Grade-Level Vocabulary ❶
• Use Academic Vocabulary ❶

Language
• Make Comparisons ❶

Fluency
• Intonation ❶

Literary Analysis
• Analyze Genre: Science Article
• Use Text Structure: Headings

Test-Taking Strategies
• Understand the Question
• Practice and Apply Strategies

Writing
• Write Responses to a Science Article

Resources

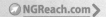 eVisual 4.8

 NGReach.com ❯

See **Technology Station** for digital student resources.

I **A** **AH**

Fluency: Intonation

Review Review intonation (page T234). Display this reminder: *Intonation is the rise and fall in the pitch or tone of your voice as you read aloud.*

Apply Challenge pairs to an intonation reading face-off. Have partners practice reading page 234. Then organize teams of four and have pairs give each other feedback on their reading.

Think and Respond

❶ Talk About It Prompt students to cite evidence from the text. Remind students to use Key Words in their answers. If students have difficulty, help them use the sentence frames to form their answers.

1. **Science Article** Possible answer: I can tell this is a science article because it gives facts about the wind, which is part of the natural world. It includes diagrams and captions.

2. **Make a Comparison** Possible answer: A tornado is started by wind over land. But a hurricane is started by wind over the ocean.

3. **Headings** Possible answers: Air on the move—How does air move? Tornado Terror—Why is a tornado so terrifying? Hurricane Force—How much force does a hurricane have? Asking questions helps me focus on the text and look for answers.

❷ Test-Taking Strategies: Understand the Question

Explain: *When taking a test, it is important to understand the question. Read the question carefully then rephrase the question and put it into your own words. You might even want to say the questions silently to yourself.*

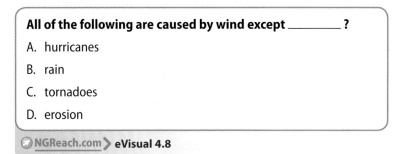

All of the following are caused by wind except _____ ?
A. hurricanes
B. rain
C. tornadoes
D. erosion

NGReach.com ❯ **eVisual 4.8**

Say: *The question is saying that all of the answer choices are caused by wind except for one of them.* Ask: *What is an important word in this question?* (Guide students to the word *except*.) *I can rephrase the question to say, Which of the following is* not *caused by wind. So I have to decide which answer choice is not caused by wind.* (rain)

Display the remaining practice items. Have partners rephrase the questions and then answer the items.

Key Words

available	generate
conservation	power
convert	renewable
current	resource
electricity	scarce
flow	

Talk About It

1. How can you tell that this is a **science article**? Name two features.

   I can tell this is a science article because _____ .

   It includes _____ and _____ .

2. **Make a comparison** between a tornado and a hurricane.

   A tornado is _____ . But a hurricane is _____ .

3. Choose three section headings from "Wind at Work." Change each heading into a question that the section answers. Look for the answers. How does this help you understand the text better?

2 Learn test-taking strategies.
○ NGReach.com

Technology Station
○ NGReach.com

☑ Online Assessment
○ Practice items in standardized test format.

Write About It

Write a paragraph to describe a very windy day. Use **Key Words** and describing words to tell what it is like. Then revise your draft to include describing words that are even more exact.

The day was _____ . The wind _____ .
It was _____ and _____ .

236

Student Book page 236

Daily Writing   A AH

3 Write About It Read aloud the directions. Point out the sentence frames: *You can use the sentence frames and the photograph for ideas.* Use the **Independent Writing Routine** to help students put their thoughts in writing, using the Key Words and the sentence frame. (See **Writing Routines,** page PD56.)

Say	Write
The wind is blowing and snow is everywhere. You can hardly see. People look cold.	The day was cold, and windy. The wind's **power** made it hard to move.
The wind is blowing so hard that it looks like it is pushing people.	It was pushing people and blowing snow everywhere.

Point out the Key Words that you used to complete the sentence frame: *power.* Have students use these ideas or their own to write sentences in their journals.

CLOSE AND ASSESS

- **Language** *Say the present progressive form of each subject and verb: I run, He swims, They eat.* (I am running, He is swimming, They are eating.)
- **Reading** *What is one fact that you learned about wind?* (Answers will vary.)
- **Vocabulary** *What Key Words did you use in your sentences?* (Answers will vary.)

Keys to Efficacy

Remind students to use content, academic, and/or classroom vocabulary. *How can you use a Key Word to explain your idea?*

Day 5

Day at a Glance:
- ▶ **Language:** Listen and Learn from Others
- ▶ **Vocabulary:** Apply Word Knowledge
- ▶ **Reading:** Reread and Explain
- ▶ **Writing:** Write a Summary

OBJECTIVES

Vocabulary
- Use Grade-Level Vocabulary ❶
- Use Academic Vocabulary ❶

Listening and Speaking
- Listen and Learn from Others

Learning and Teamwork Strategy
- Ask for Clarification
- Restate Instructions
- Collaborate with Peers
- Review

Media and Technology
- Build Concepts from Media

Resources

- *Markers for Bingo Game*
- 🔵 *eVisual 4.9*
- ✄🔵 *Practice Master 4.6*
- 🔵 *Unit 4 Build Background Video*

Language of the Day

What are some examples of the power of nature?
_____ is an example of nature's power.

Read the Language of the Day. Have students recall what they learned about nature in the Unit 4 Build Background Video and complete the sentence frame. Add their ideas to the unit concept map. Then explain that today they will learn how to listen and learn from others and play a word game. Then they will write about causes and effects in the selection.

Listen and Learn from Others

❶ Teach/Model Introduce the concept: *When you know how to listen to others, you can learn a lot from them.* Display the how to card and go through the tips and examples with the class.

How to Listen and Learn from Others		
☁	1. Listen carefully. Make a picture in your mind of what you hear.	A hurricane hit the coast last night.
👂	2. Listen for important details.	Heavy rains came down during the hurricane. Some houses were flooded.
❓	3. Ask questions.	What happened to the people whose homes were flooded?
👂	4. Listen for answers to your questions.	Some people had to stay at a nearby school.

🔵 NGReach.com 〉 eVisual 4.9

❷ Practice/Apply Ask students to think of something they know about wind or weather. To prompt them, suggest that they think about weather-related facts and/or news. Form pairs of students and have them take turns listening to and learning from each other.

> **CHECK UNDERSTANDING** Have students switch partners. One partner listens actively while the other relates new information learned from the presentations.

Differentiate

N B I

How to Learn Language

Ask for Clarification Say: *Sometimes you may not understand what another person is saying. When that happens, you can ask for clarification—that is, you can ask them to explain what they mean.*

Brainstorm a list of ways to ask for clarification. Possibilities include:

> Can you repeat that?
> What do you mean by that?
> Can you explain it a different way?

Apply Word Knowledge

3 **Teach/Model** Ask students who have played Bingo to describe the game. Then display **Practice Master 4.6** and explain how to play Vocabulary Bingo:

- *I write the Key Words in any order on the card. I use every Key Word at least once.*

- *I listen to clues or questions about the Key Words. For example: Wind is a natural ___ .*

- *The answer is* **resource**. *I find the word* resource *on my card and place a marker on it.*

- *When I have a row of markers on my card, I call out "Bingo."*

4 **Practice/Apply** Distribute the markers and cards. Students write the Key Words on their cards. Explain that partners will work together to write a clue for each Key Word. Provide an example: *What word means saving or protecting something?* (conservation). Combine all the clues to play the game with the class.

Monitor students as they follow your instructions. Have volunteers restate instructions. Monitor and clarify instructions as necessary; for example: *Make sure you write every Key Word on your card. If you have an extra space, you can use a word again.*

For vocabulary games, go to NGReach.com.

> **CHECK UNDERSTANDING** Call out several clues and have students explain how the clues helped them identify Key Words on their Bingo Cards.

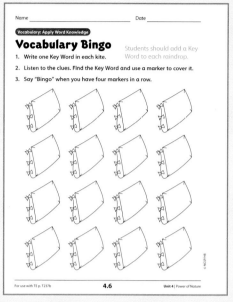

Practice Master 4.6

Part 1 Vocabulary Skills Trace		Page
Day 1	Science Vocabulary	T217
Day 2	Academic Vocabulary	T219
Day 3	Expand Word Knowledge	T222b
Day 4	Share Word Knowledge	T236b
▶ Day 5	**Apply Word Knowledge**	**T237b**
Day 6	Context Clues	T238
Day 7	Context Clues	T245
Days 8–9	Extend Vocabulary	T246e–f
Day 10	Vocabulary Review	T246g–h

Day 5

continued

Day at a Glance:
▶ **Language:** Listen and Learn from Others
▶ **Vocabulary:** Apply Word Knowledge
▶ **Reading:** Reread and Explain
▶ **Writing:** Write a Summary

OBJECTIVES

Vocabulary
• Use Grade-Level Vocabulary ❶
• Use Academic Vocabulary ❶

Language
• Explain
• Participate in Discussion

Learning and Teamwork Strategies
• Use Graphic Organizers: Cause and Effect Chart
• Reason deductively

Fluency
• Read with Accuracy and Rate ❶
• Read with Intonation ❶

Writing
• Write a Summary

Science
• Identify Earth's resources

Resources

🔇 ⊘ *Practice Master 4.7*

🔇 ⊘ *Practice Master 4.8*

⊘ ⊘ *Comprehension Coach*

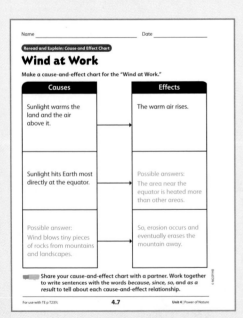

🔇 ⊘ **Practice Master 4.7**

Reread and Explain

❶ Teach Read each question aloud and reinforce that a cause is the reason something happens and an effect is what happens. Read through the example cause-and-effect chart and callouts. Then explain: *The effect* The warm air rises *happens because* Sunlight warms the land and air above it.

Have students complete **Practice Master 4.7**.

❷ Explain Read aloud the directions and language frames. Have students retell the selection to their partners. Remind them to explain how one event affects another. Partners reverse roles and repeat.

To evaluate students' proficiency levels, use the Retelling a Selection Rubric.

Retelling a Selection		
Scale	**Content**	**Language**
B	☐ Omits many important parts. ☐ Includes few cause-and-effect relationships.	☐ Frequently hard to hear or understand ☐ Often seems uncomfortable with the task
I	☐ Covers some important parts. ☐ Includes some cause-and-effect relationships.	☐ Can be understood most of the time. ☐ Seems somewhat comfortable with the task
A	☐ Covers most important parts. ☐ Includes several cause-and-effect relationships.	☐ Is almost always understood ☐ Seems comfortable with the task
AH	☐ Covers all the important parts. ☐ Includes many cause-and-effect relationships.	☐ Is easily understood ☐ Is very comfortable with the task

Fluency Accuracy, Rate, and Intonation I A AH

❸ Fluency Have students record their reading on the **Comprehension Coach** to assess each student's progress for rate and accuracy.

Have students use the passage on **Practice Master 4.8.** to record their reading for intonation. Listen to each recording and assess students' ability to read with intonation.

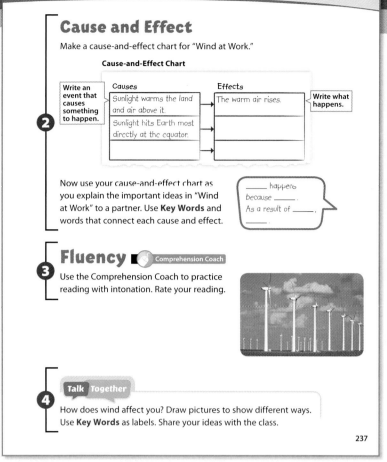

Cause and Effect

Make a cause-and-effect chart for "Wind at Work."

Cause-and-Effect Chart

Write an event that causes something to happen.

Causes	Effects
Sunlight warms the land and air above it.	The warm air rises.
Sunlight hits Earth most directly at the equator.	

2

Write what happens.

Now use your cause-and-effect chart as you explain the important ideas in "Wind at Work" to a partner. Use **Key Words** and words that connect each cause and effect.

_____ happens because _____.
As a result of _____, _____.

Fluency ▮● Comprehension Coach

3 Use the Comprehension Coach to practice reading with intonation. Rate your reading.

Talk Together

4 How does wind affect you? Draw pictures to show different ways. Use **Key Words** as labels. Share your ideas with the class.

237

Student Book page 237

Practice Master 4.8

---

4 **Talk Together** Discuss how wind affects us. Read aloud the directions. Have students draw and label pictures with the Key Words. Then have students share their pictures and explain their labels to the class. Students should add their ideas to their unit concept map.

Daily Writing

5 **Write a Summary** Use the **Interactive Writing Routine** to write a summary about the most interesting idea the students learned about wind. (See **Writing Routines** page PD55.

- As a class, discuss what students learned from the selection.
- Have students take turns building the summary, one word at a time.
- Offer corrective feedback.

Have students copy the summary into their journals.

Keys to Efficacy

Provide prompts students can use to help one another: *You might want to add _____ . You could write _____ .*

CLOSE AND ASSESS

- **Language** *When I listen to others I learn _____ .* (Answers will vary.)
- **Reading** *What does a cause-and-effect chart show?* (It shows what happens and why it happens.)
- **Vocabulary** *How is wind converted into electricity?* (Wind **power** is captured by wind turbines. Generators **convert** the wind to **electricity**.)

Day 6

Day at a Glance:
▶ **Language:** Make Comparisons   ▶ **Reading:** Read the Persuasive Essay
▶ **Vocabulary:** Context Clues   ▶ **Writing:** Writing Fluency

OBJECTIVES

Vocabulary
- Use Academic Vocabulary ⊕
- Use Grade-Level Vocabulary ⊕
- Strategy: Use Context Clues for Unfamiliar Words ⊕

Language
- Language Function: Make Comparisons ⊕
- Use a Variety of Language Structures ⊕

Learning and Teamwork Strategies
- Make Appropriate Contributions
- Build on Ideas

Resources

  Language Builder Picture Card E.46

   eVisual 4.10

Language of the Day

What are different forms of water?
_____ is a form of water.

Read the Language of the Day. Model: *Snow is a form of water.* Record student responses in the form of a web (possible responses include *rain, clouds, ice, dewdrops, fog, mist,* and *steam*). Tell students they are going to compare these forms of water.

Make Comparisons

1 **Teach/Model** Tell students: *When you make a comparison, you tell how things are alike and how they are different.* Model the language function. Follow these steps:

1. Decide what you will compare. Say: *I will compare snow and rain.*

2. Draw a Venn diagram and label it as shown.

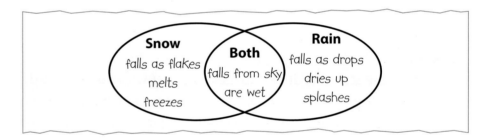

Snow
falls as flakes
melts
freezes

Both
falls from sky
are wet

Rain
falls as drops
dries up
splashes

3. Use the diagram to tell how the two things are alike. Say: *Both snow and rain fall from the sky. Both are wet.* Continue modeling, sharing how the items are different. Elicit suggestions from students.

2 **Practice/Apply** Have groups of four participate in **Team Word Webbing**. Groups can use a Venn diagram to compare two forms of water. (Alternatively, they could compare two different bodies of water, such as an ocean and a lake.) Use **Academic Language Frames** to provide ideas to support every language level.

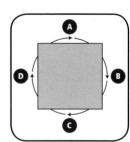

Team Word Webbing

Differentiate

Academic Language Frames

Make Comparisons
- _____ is _____. But _____ is _____.
- _____ is _____. And so is _____.

- Both _____ and _____ are _____.
- _____ are _____, but _____ are _____.

- _____ and _____ are both alike because _____.
- _____ and _____ are different because _____.

NGReach.com ▶ **eVisual 4.10**

CHECK UNDERSTANDING Display **Language Builder Card E46** and have students make comparisons about it.

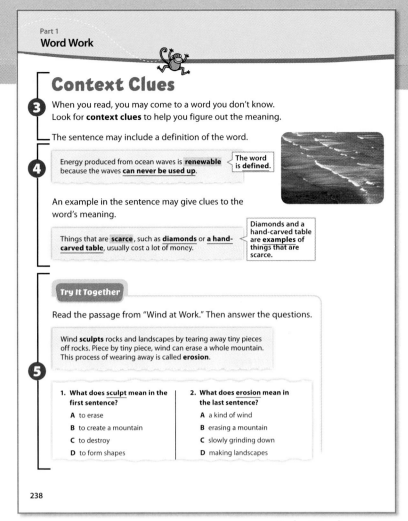

Context Clues

3 When you read, you may come to a word you don't know. Look for **context clues** to help you figure out the meaning.

The sentence may include a definition of the word.

4 Energy produced from ocean waves is **renewable** because the waves **can never be used up**. — The word is defined.

An example in the sentence may give clues to the word's meaning.

Things that are **scarce**, such as **diamonds** or **a hand-carved table**, usually cost a lot of money. — Diamonds and a hand-carved table are **examples** of things that are scarce.

Try It Together

5 Read the passage from "Wind at Work." Then answer the questions.

Wind **sculpts** rocks and landscapes by tearing away tiny pieces off rocks. Piece by tiny piece, wind can erase a whole mountain. This process of wearing away is called **erosion**.

1. What does **sculpt** mean in the first sentence?
   A to erase
   B to create a mountain
   C to destroy
   D to form shapes

2. What does **erosion** mean in the last sentence?
   A a kind of wind
   B erasing a mountain
   C slowly grinding down
   D making landscapes

238

Student Book page 238

Context Clues

3 Teach Read the first two sentences and write this sentence: *Tim **generates** a list of topics and then picks one to write about.* Say: *We can use context clues to figure out the meaning of generates. I know that many people make lists. I think that Tim makes a list of topics first. Then he picks one topic. I think* generates *means "makes."*

4 Model Read the explanation about sentences containing definitions. Have students point to the underlined definition of **renewable**. Then ask: *What word comes right after renewable?* (because) Say: *The word* because *signals that something will be explained. Sometimes a definition of the new word is right there in the sentence.* Renewable *means that something can never be used up.* Repeat for the explanation of context examples and the word **scarce** pointing out the phrase "such as."

5 Practice/Apply Read the directions aloud. Have students look for words that give clues to the words' meanings. (by, is called). Then have partners answer the questions. Use the **Multi-level Practice Sets** to address varying levels of vocabulary knowledge.

> **CHECK UNDERSTANDING** Say: *Tell me what* **flow** *means in this sentence: When water flows, it moves in a constant stream.* (Flow *means to move in a constant stream.*)

Part 1 Vocabulary Skills Trace		Page
Day 1	Science Vocabulary	T217
Day 2	Academic Vocabulary	T219
Day 3	Expand Word Knowledge	T222b
Day 4	Share Word Knowledge	T236b
Day 5	Apply Word Knowledge	T237b
Day 6	**Context Clues**	**T238**
Day 7	Context Clues	T245
Days 8–9	Extend Vocabulary	T246e–f
Day 10	Vocabulary Review	T246g–h

Day 6
continued

Day at a Glance:
Language: Make Comparisons   **Reading:** Read the Persuasive Essay
Vocabulary: Context Clues   **Writing:** Writing Fluency

OBJECTIVES

Vocabulary
• Use Academic Vocabulary
• Use Grade-Level Vocabulary ❶

Language
• Listen to a Preview

Reading Strategies
• Plan: Preview Purpose
• Ask Yourself Questions ❶

Literary Analysis
• Recognize Genre: Persuasive Essay
• Analyze Author's Purpose: Persuade
• Recognize Persuasive Language
• Distinguish Fact and Opinion

Learning and Teamwork Strategies
• Use Prereading Supports
• Build Background Knowledge
• Use Reading Supports

Resources

☝️ 🌐 *Practice Master 4.9*

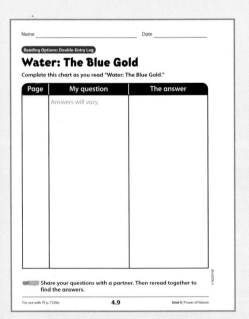

Read the Persuasive Essay

❶ Connect Across Texts   Read aloud the connect feature. Explain: *As you read about water, think about how the* **resources** *, wind and water, are alike.*

❷ Genre   Read aloud the explanation. Explain: *A persuasive essay tries to persuade, or convince, readers to act a certain way. It uses facts and opinions to get readers to agree with the author.* Clarify: *An opinion tells what someone thinks, feels, or believes. Facts are statements that can be proved.* Elaborate: *You can prove facts by reading, observing, or asking an expert.*

❸ Preview and Build Background   Use sheltering strategies as you conduct a picture walk.

Pages	Say (and Do)
239	*Wow! This is a big wave!* (Point to the wave. Gesture with your hands to show "big.") *The ocean has a lot of water. Who has seen the ocean? Tell us what it is like.*
240–241	(Point to the woman.) *This woman loves the water. She thinks water is important. She wants us to think water is important too.* (Read the section heading on p. 241.) *Chemicals and pollution are flowing out of the pipes and into the water. Is this bad for the plants and animals that live in the water? Why?*
242–243	*There is not much clean, fresh water in the world.* (Point to the map.) *This map shows where water is* **scarce***. The author wants us to save water.* (Use a real faucet or act out turning off a faucet.) *Show or tell how you can save water.*

❹ Read "Water: The Blue Gold"   Scaffold the support for varied reading levels.

BELOW LEVEL	ON LEVEL	ABOVE LEVEL
Listen and Read Along	**Read Aloud and Interact with Text**	**Read Silently and Interact with Text**
• Have students track the print while you read the text aloud. • Check understanding with selected Build Comprehension and Before You Move On questions.	• Have partners complete a **Reflection Journal** as they take turns reading the text aloud. • After reading, have partners discuss their questions. Invite them to research unanswered questions.	• Have students ask and list questions in a **Reflection Journal** as they read silently. • After reading, have partners share questions and read aloud to find answers to their questions.

CHECK UNDERSTANDING   Ask: *Why might you write a persuasive essay? What do you want to persuade others to do?* (Responses will vary.)

Student Book page 239

Build Comprehension, page 239

1 **Cause and Effect** What could happen if there is no water? Provide a language frame: *Because there is no water, _____.* (Because there is no water, you can't brush your teeth. Because there is no water, you can't take a shower.)

2 **Recognize Facts** You read that we use water for many things. How do you know that this is a fact? (I know this is a fact because I use water for many things, and I see other people using water for many things too.)

3 **Answers to Before You Move On**

1. **Ask Questions** RETEACH Review with students how to ask questions (page T220). Possible answers: I wonder how the author feels about water? Does the author agree with scientists?

2. **Fact/Opinion** Some scientists believe that in this century, clean water may become as highly valued as gold. I know this is an opinion because the word, *believe,* tells me that this is just an idea or feeling. It's an opinion because it can't be proved or checked.

Cultural Perspectives: Use of Water

Tell students that the ways people use water in their daily lives differ from culture to culture. Have students discuss uses related to needs (such as for drinking and watering gardens), wants (swimming, washing cars), and customs (religious ceremonies, community celebrations).

My Story

Water has always been an important part of my life. When I was seven years old, my grandfather taught me **to scuba dive**. His name was Jacques-Yves Cousteau. He explored the world's oceans. He made films and wrote books to share his explorations with the world.

My grandfather taught me that all living things, inside and outside the oceans, are connected by water. The future of our planet depends on our water **resources**. We must care for Earth's water by protecting and preserving it. Everything we do makes a difference. **1**

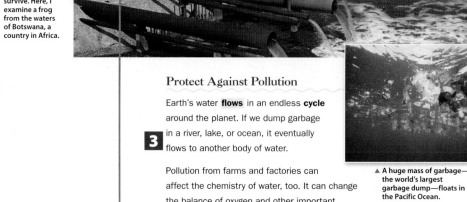

Some factories dump chemicals into water systems.

▲ Water helps all living things survive. Here, I examine a frog from the waters of Botswana, a country in Africa.

▲ I often travel around the world and record water issues through film and photographs.

Protect Against Pollution

Earth's water **flows** in an endless **cycle** around the planet. If we dump garbage in a river, lake, or ocean, it eventually **3** flows to another body of water.

Pollution from farms and factories can affect the chemistry of water, too. It can change the balance of oxygen and other important elements in water. These changes affect plants and animals that live there. To help protect Earth's water, we must stop polluting our water systems. **2**

▲ A huge mass of garbage— the world's largest garbage dump—floats in the Pacific Ocean.

In Other Words
◄ **to scuba dive** how to dive deep in the ocean

In Other Words
cycle pattern; circle

▶ **Before You Move On**
1. **Ask Questions** Look at the photos on this page. What is one question you have about water pollution?
2. **Cause/Effect** Describe some effects of dumping garbage into rivers and lakes. **4**

240

241

Student Book pages 240–241

I **A** **AH**

Analyze Text Features: Section Headings

Teach/Model Review that section headings tell what each section of the text is mostly about. Point to a section heading and read it aloud: *My Story. This section heading tells me that this part of the essay tells about the author's life.* Elaborate: *Remember you can read section headings before you read. The headings will help you predict what you will read about.*

Practice/Apply Have students read the section headings in the rest of the essay and predict what they will read about.

Keys to Efficacy

Guide students to cite evidence from the text: *Read me the sentence that helped you answer that question.*

Build Comprehension, pages 240–241

1 **Details** Why has water always been an important part of the author's life? (Answers will vary: Her grandfather, an expert on oceans, taught her how water connects all living things. He taught her that we must protect and preserve water.)

2 **Recognize Persuasive Language** "We must care for Earth's water by protecting and preserving it." is a persuasive statement on page 240. It is one person's opinion. Find another persuasive statement on page 241. ("To help protect Off a question you have about a photo in the text. For example: *When I look at the photo of garbage in the ocean,* Earth's water, we must stop polluting our water systems.")

3 **Use Key Words** What are some of our planet's water **resources**? (rivers, lakes, the ocean)

4 **Answers to Before You Move On**
1. **Ask Questions** **APPLY** Sample response: When I look at the photo of garbage in the ocean.
2. **Cause/Effect** Possible answers: Garbage or other materials can affect the chemistry of water. It can **flow** to other bodies of water. It can harm plants and animals.

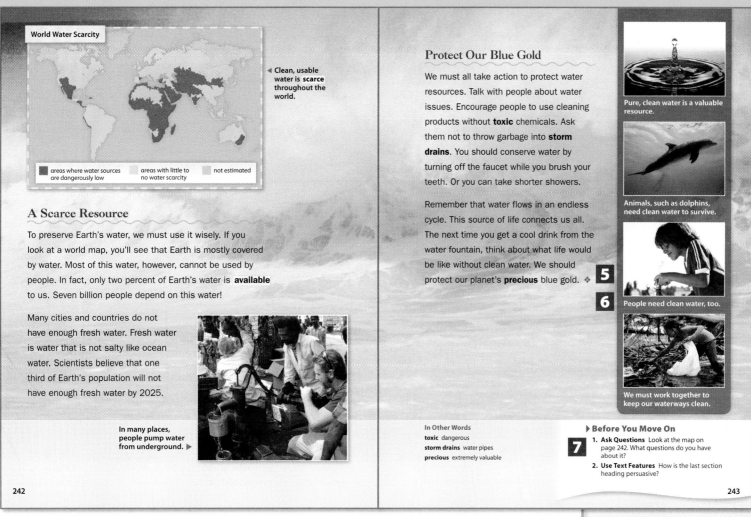

World Water Scarcity

◄ Clean, usable water is **scarce** throughout the world.

areas where water sources are dangerously low

areas with little to no water scarcity

not estimated

A Scarce Resource

To preserve Earth's water, we must use it wisely. If you look at a world map, you'll see that Earth is mostly covered by water. Most of this water, however, cannot be used by people. In fact, only two percent of Earth's water is **available** to us. Seven billion people depend on this water!

Many cities and countries do not have enough fresh water. Fresh water is water that is not salty like ocean water. Scientists believe that one third of Earth's population will not have enough fresh water by 2025.

In many places, people pump water from underground. ▶

Protect Our Blue Gold

We must all take action to protect water resources. Talk with people about water issues. Encourage people to use cleaning products without **toxic** chemicals. Ask them not to throw garbage into **storm drains**. You should conserve water by turning off the faucet while you brush your teeth. Or you can take shorter showers.

Remember that water flows in an endless cycle. This source of life connects us all. The next time you get a cool drink from the water fountain, think about what life would be like without clean water. We should protect our planet's **precious** blue gold. ❖ **5**

6

Pure, clean water is a valuable resource.

Animals, such as dolphins, need clean water to survive.

People need clean water, too.

We must work together to keep our waterways clean.

In Other Words
toxic dangerous
storm drains water pipes
precious extremely valuable

▶ **Before You Move On**

7 1. **Ask Questions** Look at the map on page 242. What questions do you have about it?

2. **Use Text Features** How is the last section heading persuasive?

242

243

Student Book pages 242–243

Build Comprehension, pages 242–243

5 **Analyze Author's Purpose** What is the author trying to persuade readers to do? (Take action to protect water resources.)

6 **Evaluate Author's Purpose** Did the author persuade you to act? Explain. Possible answer: Yes, I will try to save water because everyone on earth uses it for lots of things.

7 **Answers to Before You Move On**

1. **Ask Questions** APPLY Possible questions: Where is water **scarce**? Why is water scarce in these areas? Where is water **available**?

   Focus on metacognition: How did asking yourself questions about the map help you understand what the map shows?

2. **Use Text Features** The heading is a command, telling readers to protect our blue gold. The section heading also suggests that our water is as valuable as gold.

Keys to Efficacy

Encourage students to think about their learning processes: *How did you figure that out? What questions did you ask yourself?*

Day 6
continued

Day at a Glance:
Language: Make Comparisons
Vocabulary: Context Clues
Reading: Respond and Extend
Writing: Writing Fluency

OBJECTIVES

Vocabulary
- Use Grade-Level Content Vocabulary ⊕
- Use Academic Vocabulary ⊕

Language
- Make Comparisons
- Participate in Discussion

Reading Fluency
- Read with Accuracy and Rate ⊕

Literary Analysis
- Compare Genres
- Author's Purpose

Learning and Teamwork Strategies
- Use Graphic Organizer: Comparison Chart

Writing
- Writing Fluency

Resources

- eVisuals 4.11
- eVisuals 4.12
- Practice Master 4.8
- Practice Master 4.10

Differentiate

Academic Language Frames

Make Comparisons

- _____ has/have _____.
  So does/do _____.
  _____ is/are _____.
  But _____ is/are _____.

- _____ and _____ are alike because both _____.
  _____ is different from _____ because _____.

- The selections are different because one is/has _____ and the other is/has _____.

NGReach.com eVisual 4.11

Respond and Extend

① **Reread** As students reread "Water: The Blue Gold" on their own, have them think about how it is the same and different from "Wind at Work."

② **Compare Genres** Tell students that they can use a comparison chart to compare different genres, or forms of writing: *A comparison chart can help you organize how the genres are alike and different.* Read aloud the instructions.

Have groups use the **Numbered Heads** cooperative learning strategy. Help focus students' thinking: *You can ask questions to find out how the genres are alike and different.* Provide **Academic Language Frames** to support students at different levels.

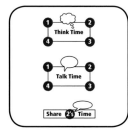

Numbered Heads

Focus	Questions
1. Topic	What is the text mostly about?
2. Point of View	Does the author use first-person words such as *I, my,* or *me?* Does the author write as a third person outside the text?
3. Author's Purpose	Why did the author write this—to inform, to entertain, or to persuade? Does the author have more than one purpose?
4. Statements that Support the Author's Purpose	What facts does the author include? Does the author use opinions to try to persuade you?

As students report their group's ideas, students should record them on **Practice Master 4.10**.

③ **Talk Together About the Big Question**

Read aloud the question and directions. Remind students to use their personal experiences as well as facts from the articles in their responses. Guide students to discuss how the **resources** affect their lives.

Have students add ideas to the unit concept map.

> **CHECK UNDERSTANDING** Make a *Compare* card and a *Contrast* card. Have students name a way the selections are alike or different as you hold up a card.

compare

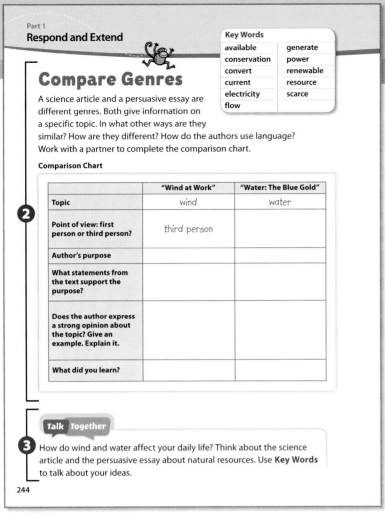

Compare Genres

A science article and a persuasive essay are different genres. Both give information on a specific topic. In what other ways are they similar? How are they different? How do the authors use language? Work with a partner to complete the comparison chart.

Key Words

available	generate
conservation	power
convert	renewable
current	resource
electricity	scarce
flow	

Comparison Chart

	"Wind at Work"	"Water: The Blue Gold"
Topic	wind	water
Point of view: first person or third person?	third person	
Author's purpose		
What statements from the text support the purpose?		
Does the author express a strong opinion about the topic? Give an example. Explain it.		
What did you learn?		

Talk Together

3 How do wind and water affect your daily life? Think about the science article and the persuasive essay about natural resources. Use **Key Words** to talk about your ideas.

244

Student Book page 244

Daily Writing

4 **Writing Fluency** Use the **Power Writing Routine** (see page PD53). Write the word **conservation** and prompt: *What resources do you help conserve when you recycle?*

Power Writing Routine

 1. What do you know about the word or picture?

 2. Take one minute to write as much as you can, as well as you can.
  B words   **I** sentences   **A** **AH** paragraphs

 3. Check your spelling and grammar. (Circle) mistakes.

 4. Count your words.

 NGReach.com > eVisual 4.12

CLOSE AND ASSESS

- **Language** *What action verbs did you use in your speaking and writing?*
- **Reading** *How does* Water: The Blue Gold *connect to a story or article you have already read?*
- **Vocabulary** *Use context clues to tell what* **reduce** *means in this sentence:* You can reduce the amount of water you use by taking shorter showers. (to make less, to conserve)

B **I** **A** **AH**

Fluency: Accuracy and Rate

To activate prior knowledge and practice fluency, conduct timed readings of "Wind at Work." Select an option for recording

- Use the automatic speech recognition on the **Comprehension Coach** to track word count per minute for the entire passage.
- Use **Practice Master 4.8.**

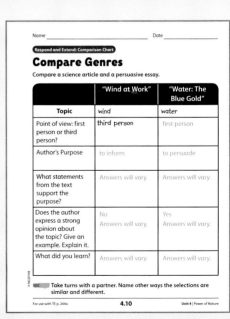

Name _____ Date _____

Respond and Extend: Comparison Chart

Compare Genres

Compare a science article and a persuasive essay.

	"Wind at Work"	"Water: The Blue Gold"
Topic	wind	water
Point of view: first person or third person?	third person	first person
Author's Purpose	to inform	to persuade
What statements from the text support the purpose?	Answers will vary.	Answers will vary.
Does the author express a strong opinion about the topic? Give an example. Explain it.	No Answers will vary.	Yes Answers will vary.
What did you learn?	Answers will vary.	Answers will vary.

Take turns with a partner. Name other ways the selections are similar and different.

For use with TE p. 244o   **4.10**   Unit 4 | Power of Nature

 **Practice Master 4.10**

Day 7

Day at a Glance:
- ▶ **Language:** Present-Tense Action Verbs
- ▶ **Vocabulary:** Context Clues
- ▶ **Reading:** Reread the Selection
- ▶ **Writing:** Writing on Demand: Persuasive News Article

OBJECTIVES

Vocabulary
- Use Grade-Level Vocabulary 🅣
- Use Academic Vocabulary 🅣
- Strategy: Use Context Clues for Unfamiliar Words 🅣

Language
- Present-Tense Action Verbs

Learning and Teamwork Strategies
- Relate to Prior Knowledge
- Make Contributions

Resources

  Practice Master 4.11

🔘 *eVisual 4.13*

Differentiate

Language Transfer

Challenge In Chinese languages, Haitian Creole, Hmong, Korean, and Vietnamese, the verb is not inflected for person and number. Students may say, for example, *The wind blow hard* instead of *The wind blows hard*.

Strategy Write sentence pairs such as these on sentence strips for students to cut apart and reassemble:

> The sun shines in the sky.
> The stars shine in the sky.

> Animals need water to live.
> You need water to live.

Part 1 Grammar Skills Trace

		Page
Day 2	Present-Tense Action Verbs	T219a
Day 4	Present Progressive Tense	T236a
▶ Day 7	Present–Tense Action Verbs	**T245a**
Day 10	Review Present-Tense Action Verbs	T246g

Language of the Day

How does water move? What changes does it go through?

Water ____. It ____, and it ____, too.

Tell students that today they will be learning more about action words like *flow* and how to use them correctly in sentences.

Grammar/Spelling — Present-Tense Action Verbs 🄸 🄰 🄰🄷

1 Teach/Model Read the introduction. Have volunteers read the first rule and examples aloud. Then write these sentences.

> *The river flow**s** through the valley.*

> *It hurrie**s** to the sea.*

Ask: *Does the subject name one person, place, or thing? (one river).* Say: *Yes, the subject is singular, so we add an -s to the verb.*

Ask volunteers to read the second rule and examples aloud. Say: *If the subject names more than one person, place, or thing, we say that the subject is "plural."* Write these sentence frames on the board and call on volunteers to suggest an action word to complete each sentence.

> *The ocean waves _____ onto the beach.* (Possible answers: *crash, roll*)

> *They _____ away the sand.* (Possible answers: *wash, wear*)

2 Practice Ask a student to read aloud the directions and sentence. Have volunteers take turns identifying and spelling the action verb and its subject. Have partners talk about why three verbs have an -s at the end and one verb does not. (*Clouds* is a plural noun, so it takes a plural verb: *threaten.*) Invite pairs to share their answers.

3 Apply in Writing Read aloud the directions and have students work independently. Provide support as necessary. Assign **Practice Master 4.11.**

> **CHECK UNDERSTANDING** List subjects and predicates in a two-column chart: *The wind, People, Dark clouds, Raindrops; hold umbrellas, fill the sky, begin to fall, blows.* Students combine a subject and a predicate to make a sentence.

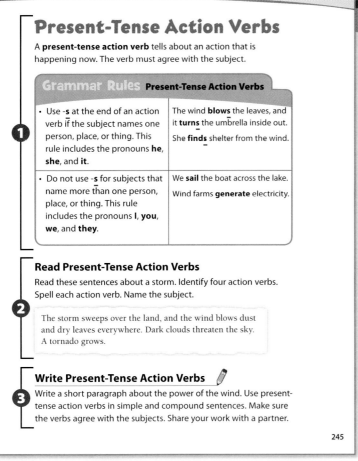

Present-Tense Action Verbs

A **present-tense action verb** tells about an action that is happening now. The verb must agree with the subject.

Grammar Rules Present-Tense Action Verbs

• Use **-s** at the end of an action verb if the subject names one person, place, or thing. This rule includes the pronouns **he**, **she**, and **it**.	The wind **blows** the leaves, and it **turns** the umbrella inside out. She **finds** shelter from the wind.
• Do not use **-s** for subjects that name more than one person, place, or thing. This rule includes the pronouns **I**, **you**, **we**, and **they**.	We **sail** the boat across the lake. Wind farms **generate** electricity.

2 **Read Present-Tense Action Verbs**

Read these sentences about a storm. Identify four action verbs. Spell each action verb. Name the subject.

> The storm sweeps over the land, and the wind blows dust and dry leaves everywhere. Dark clouds threaten the sky. A tornado grows.

3 **Write Present-Tense Action Verbs** ✏️

Write a short paragraph about the power of the wind. Use present-tense action verbs in simple and compound sentences. Make sure the verbs agree with the subjects. Share your work with a partner.

245

Student Book page 245

More Context Clues

4 **Review/Model** Review the Day 6 Lesson Plan (page T238). Write the following sentence and read it aloud.

- *Trash, chemicals, and other kinds of <u>pollutants</u> can harm rivers and lakes.*

Ask: *What clues help you figure out the meaning of the word pollutants?* (Trash, chemicals and other kinds of, can harm) *What do you think the word means?* (things that harm lakes and rivers or the environment)

Display the **Context Clues** sentences and read them aloud. Have students do a **Think, Pair, Share** to determine the meaning of the word *protect* in the first sentence. (to protect is to keep from harm)

5 **Practice/Apply** Have partners use context clues to figure out the meaning of the underlined words in the remaining sentences. Have them work in pairs and then compare answers with another partnership.

1. protect (provide what is needed, keep safe)
2. planets (a large sphere circling a sun)
3. fortune (good luck)
4. trade (to change or exchange)
5. risk (something that puts you in danger of getting hurt)

> **CHECK UNDERSTANDING** Say: *Tell me what* **available** *means in this sentence: If the doctor is available, she will be able to see you.* (*Available means able to be seen.*)

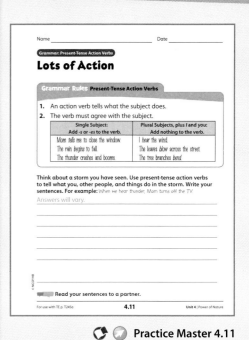

🔄 🕐 **Practice Master 4.11**

Context Clues

1. Birds <u>protect</u> their babies by building nests for them to live in and getting food.

2. I like learning about all the <u>planets</u>, but my favorites are Earth and Mars.

3. I had the good <u>fortune</u> of meeting many nice people on my trip.

4. Ana and Oscar <u>traded</u> seats so Oscar could be closer to the board.

5. If you take a <u>risk</u>, you will be in danger of getting hurt.

🌐 NGReach.com ▶ **eVisual 4.13**

Day 7
continued

Day at a Glance:
► **Language:** Present-Tense Action Verbs
► **Vocabulary:** Context Clues

⊙ **Reading:** Reread the Selection
⊙ **Writing:** Persuasive News Article

OBJECTIVES

Vocabulary
• Use Grade-Level Vocabulary ⊕
• Use Academic Vocabulary ⊕

Literary Analysis
• Analyze Purpose: Persuade
• Identify Author's Position: Identify Arguments
• Genre: Recognize Persuasive Text
• Distinguish between Fact and Opinion

Learning and Teamwork Strategies
• Participate in Discussion

Writing
• Reproduce Modeled Writing
• Write a Persuasive News Article

Practice Master 4.12

Reread Focus on Persuasive Text

① **Teach** Explain to students that persuasive texts give an opinion and try to get readers to agree with it. Authors use facts to support their opinions, along with persuasive words like *must* and *should*. Say: *The author of "Water: The Blue Gold" wants to persuade readers that water is a valuable* **resource** *that we must protect.* Point out some examples from the text:

• page 239: It's hard to imagine life without it (water). Clean water may become as highly valuable as gold.

• page 240: We must care for Earth's water by protecting and preserving it. Everything we do makes a difference.

② **Model** Model how to evaluate how well the author supports her views. Say: *I want to see if the author includes facts to support her opinion that we need clean water.* Point to page 241. Ask: *Can you find facts to support the author's opinion?* (Students should identify how pollution changes water, and affects plants and animals.) *These facts support her statement that we must stop polluting our water.*

Create a persuasive argument chart. Show how you can write a persuasive opinion in the first box and then fill in the supporting fact boxes with examples from the text that support the statement. Explain that if an author hasn't made a strong case for that statement, the supporting fact boxes will remain empty. If there are several supporting facts, the author has made a strong point.

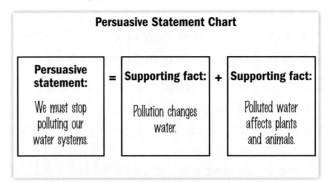

③ **Practice/Apply in Reading** Have students reread "Water: The Blue Gold." Then have them use Think, Pair, Share to complete **Practice Master 4.12.** and find more examples of persuasive statements in the text. After they discuss with a partner and finalize their charts, have students share examples from their discussion.

Daily Writing

Modeled Writing: Persuasive News Article Explain to students that a persuasive news article reports on a current event or issue using someone's opinion or beliefs.

Think Aloud	Write
1. Plan	
I will make a RAFT to plan my writing. I will take on the role of organizer of a campus conservation event, such as a rally about saving local wildlife or protecting local resources.	Role: organizer of a campus conservation event
Who is my audience? I want other students to join the event. My audience will be students.	Audience: students
Repeat the think aloud for form (persuasive news article) and topic (getting other students to join my conservation cause).	
2. Write	
I know I need to make a persuasive point. What is the main point that I want the article to support?	We must stop cutting down trees because it is bad for animals that live in the forest.
I know that to make a persuasive argument, I must support my main point with facts.	Fact: Many trees have been cut down in recent years. Fact: When too many trees get cut down, forest animals have to find new places to live and new sources of food.
I need to include details in the article about the event.	The event: a rally. The purpose: to get more students to support the cause of helping forest animals. The time: the first Saturday of the month
Repeat the think aloud for additional persuasive points to make in the article.	
3. Read and Reflect	
I will read aloud my final news article and check it one more time. *Have I met the plan I made during my RAFT? Yes! Do I want to make more changes? No.* *Now I can share it with my neighbor.*	Read the article, checking for key points addressed during the modeling.

Use **Multi-Level Strategies** to support students at all proficiency levels in writing persuasive news articles.

CLOSE AND ASSESS

- **Language** *Which verb should have an -s at the end? Generators convert wind into power. Wind turn the blades of the turbines.* (turns)
- **Vocabulary** *How can you figure out the meaning of a word you don't know?* (Use clues in the sentence.)
- **Reading** *How do you recognize persuasive writing?* (The selection uses opinion and persuasive words such as *must* and *should* to make a persuasive point. The author provides facts to support his persuasive point.)

Differentiate

Multi-Level Strategies

BEGINNING

Provide a sentence frame for students to express a persuasive point for their article:

- We must stop _____ because it is bad for _____.

Then have students draw pictures and add captions to use as details in their articles.

INTERMEDIATE

Have students work in pairs to plan their persuasive news articles using a persuasive points graphic organizer. Have them include in the organizer as many details as they can.

ADVANCED

Have students plan their persuasive news article using a persuasive points graphic organizer. Have them share their organizer with a partner and then add new details generated by the discussion, using photographs, pictures, words, and phrases.

ADVANCED HIGH

Have students begin their writing by creating a cause-and-effect graphic organizer that explains possible ramifications of not agreeing with their persuasive news article. Then challenge them to write an article that makes the cause-and-effect relationships clear.

Days 8–9

Day at a Glance:
▶ **Language:** Oral Language Project : Instructions
▶ **Vocabulary:** Extend Vocabulary
▶ **Reading:** Read Leveled Books
▶ **Writing:** Paraphrase

OBJECTIVES

Vocabulary
• Use Academic and Grade-Level Vocabulary ⊤

Language
• Language Function: Make Comparisons ⊤

Listening and Speaking
• Listen and Take/Make Notes
• Listen to and Learn from Others
• Present in Sequence
• Give Instructions

Learning and Teamwork Strategies
• Build on Ideas

Resources

• *materials for props, such as:*
  - *metal hangers*
  - *yarn or string*
  - *old silverware, sea shells, old CDs, or other small items*
  - *tape*

⬡ ⬤ *Assessment Handbook page 172*

Language of the Day

Why are wind and water valuable resources ?
Wind and water are valuable resources
because ____ .

Read the Language of the Day. Model: *Wind and water are valuable resources because they* **generate electricity** . Invite students to use the frame in sharing their own ideas with the class.

Oral Language Project Instructions

① **Introduce the Activity** Tap prior knowledge: *What is wind?* Remind students that wind is just moving air. Then ask: *How can you see wind at work?* Collect responses.

Explain that groups of students will create wind chimes that show the power of wind. Display available materials, including coat hangers, yarn, and small items to hang on the wind chimes, such as old silverware, sea shells, and old CDs. Help students create instructions for how to make wind chimes.

② **Plan** Divide the class into small groups. Students should copy the instructions and then take turns reading them out loud. Have each group follow the steps and create a wind chime, using the materials given. As students decide on which items to use, encourage them to make suggestions and build on one another's ideas.

3 **Practice** Have students practice explaining how they created their wind chimes. Ask students to include details about why they chose specific materials and their placement.

Remind students to listen to and learn from others. Model and review:

- As you listen, take notes on important details.
- When you hear something you don't understand, ask questions.

Use **Multi-Level Strategies** to involve students at all proficiency levels.

4 **Shoot the Breeze!** Have groups take turns presenting. Students can blow on the wind chimes to simulate wind. For each presentation, assess one group's listening skills. Invite family members or another class to enjoy the presentations.

5 **Debrief and Compare** Ask students to compare the wind chimes from each presentation. Students should comment on how the wind chimes are alike and how they are different. Then encourage them to add ideas to their unit concept maps, as appropriate.

Differentiate

Multi-Level Strategies

BEGINNING

Have students attach the pieces to the wind chimes and point to each piece during the presentation.

INTERMEDIATE

Ask students to write the instructions in their own words. Provide sentence frames:

- First, _____.
- Then, _____.
- Next, _____.
- Finally, _____.

ADVANCED **ADVANCED HIGH**

Challenge students to explain how the wind chime works. Make sure they include details about how different types of weather would affect the wind chimes.

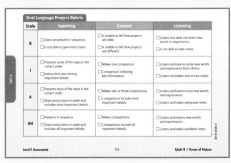

 Assessment Handbook page 172

Days 8–9
continued

Day at a Glance:
▶ **Language:** Oral Language Project: Oral Report
▶ **Vocabulary:** Extend Vocabulary
▶ **Reading:** Read Leveled Books
▶ **Writing:** Paraphrase

OBJECTIVES

Vocabulary
• Extend Vocabulary through Wide Reading

Language
• Participate in Discussion

Reading
• Read Independently
• Summarize Reading
• Make Connections: Text to Text
• Apply Reading Strategies Varied Texts

Writing
• Paraphrase Maintaining Meaning

Science
• Explore Earth's Resources
• Investigate Erosion

Resources

 Leveled Books:
  - *The Wind Blew*
  - *The Wind Eagle*
  - *The Missing Lighthouse*
  - *Wind*
  - *Wind Power*
  - *Wonders of Water*

 Reach Leveled Library Lesson Plans

 NGReach.com ›

Find more leveled readers about this topic.

Differentiate Read Leveled Books

Group students based on their reading abilities and interests. Use the **Guided Reading** routine (See page PD47) for books at students' instructional level. Use the **Independent Reading Support** (see page PD50) for books at students' independent reading level.

After reading, organize the students into heterogeneous groups to discuss what they read and to use the new information to answer the Big Question. Use these prompts to guide your discussion:

• What new information did you learn about the power of wind and water?

• What surprised you?

• How did new information change your answer?

Fiction

BEGINNING LEVEL

The Wind Blew
by Pat Hutchins

• **Genre:** Poetry

One day, the wind blows away many things. Soon everyone is chasing the wind, as it blows everyone's possessions out to sea.

Key Words

newspapers

postman

stole

umbrella

wig

INTERMEDIATE LEVEL

The Wind Eagle
retold by Joyce McGreevy

• **Genre:** Folktale

Gluscabi cannot go fishing because the Wind Eagle pushes him back to shore. Gluscabi must find a way to stop the Wind Eagle.

Key Words

angry

eagle

mighty

rage

silence

ADVANCED   ADVANCED HIGH LEVELS

The Missing Lighthouse
by Glen Phelan

• **Genre:** Realistic Fiction

In this chapter book, the Gulf Point lighthouse has been moved due to beach erosion. The Sleuths are on the case to find out what happened. They simulate the process of erosion to learn more about this phenomenon.

Key Words

erosion

investigate

lighthouse

magazine

platform

Nonfiction

BEGINNING LEVEL

Wind
by Helen Frost

- **Genre:** Expository Nonfiction

Simple text and ample visual support show wind, how it's formed, and its effect on Earth and people.

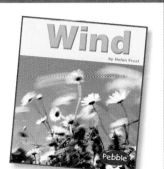

Key Words

electricity

hurricane

movements

pollen

tornado

INTERMEDIATE LEVEL

Wind Power
by Pat Malone

- **Genre:** Expository Nonfiction

Students read about the power of wind, how wind shapes trees, scatters seeds, and shapes sand dunes. Also available in Spanish.

Key Words

dunes

moving

scatters

shore

windmill

ADVANCED   ADVANCED HIGH LEVELS

Wonders of Water
by Nancy Finton

- **Genre:** Expository Nonfiction

Water is everywhere and constantly moving through the water cycle. In this chapter book, learn about the wonders of water and how we harness this powerful natural resource.

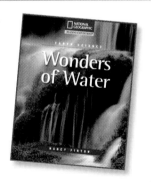

Key Words

conserve

dinosaurs

glaciers

irrigation

wetlands

Daily Writing A AH

Journal Entry Have students write a journal entry in their reading journals. Use "Wind at Work" to model how to write a journal entry. Focus on how to paraphrase maintaining meaning. Say: *Wind happens when hot air sinks under cold air.* Is that right? (no). Then work with students to restate: *Wind happens when hot air rises and cold air rushes down to replace it.* Have students share their journal entries with others, recommending books they enjoyed.

Same Book / Different Levels

B I A AH

Hurricane Hunters
by Beth Geiger

Fly into the heart of a hurricane with fearless scientists who track these powerful storms to keep others safe.

Pioneer Edition
Fountas and Pinnell: P–R

B Conduct a Picture Walk.

I Read text and captions.

Key Words

damage	dangerous
data	eye
hurricane	scientist

Pathfinder Edition
Fountas and Pinnell: Q–S

A Read text and captions.

AH Read and write responses to questions.

Key Words

category	data
hurricane	scientist
thunderstorm	warning

Part 1 Vocabulary Skills Trace		Page
Day 1	Science Vocabulary	T217
Day 2	Academic Vocabulary	T219
Day 3	Expand Word Knowledge	T222b
Day 4	Share Word Knowledge	T236b
Day 5	Apply Word Knowledge	T237b
Day 6	Context Clues	T238
Day 7	Context Clues	T235
▶ Days 8–9	Extend Vocabulary	T246e–f
Day 10	Vocabulary Review	T246g–h

OBJECTIVES

Language
- Review Language Function: Make Comparisons ⊕

Grammar
- Review Present-Tense Action Verbs

Vocabulary
- Review and Use Grade-Level Key Vocabulary ⊕
- Review Context Clues

Reading Strategy
- Review Ask Questions ⊕

Comprehension and Literary Analysis
- Review Text Features: Heads
- Review Cause and Effect

Fluency
- Intonation

Content Area
- Explore Earth's Resources

Resources

- Assessment Handbook
- Key Word Images
- eVisual 4.14
- Comprehension Coach

Part 1 Grammar Skills Trace		Page
Day 2	Present-Tense Action Verbs	219a
Day 4	Present Progressive Tense	236a
Day 7	Present-Tense Action Verbs	245a
Day 10	Review Action Verbs; Present Progressive	246g

Language of the Day

What did you learn? How does it help you in school? I learned how to ____. ____ means to ____. For example, ____.

Model: *I learned how to ask questions as I read. Asking questions as I read it means to stop and ask questions while reading about things I may not understand. For example, I can ask what information I need, and read or reread to find the answer.* Prompt students to talk about a skill they learned.

Review and Assess

Use these interactive review activities to reinforce concepts covered in Part 1. Then use the assessment tools to evaluate students' progress. For more details about assessment, see page T281a.

Language Function

Make Comparisons

Initiate **Numbered Heads** to have students make comparisons. Assign each group two objects to compare. Students create comparison charts before reconvening with the group. Have students use language frames to share their comparisons.

- **Assessment:** Language Function Rubric on page 168 of the Assessment Handbook.

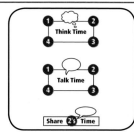

Numbered Heads

Grammar

Present-Tense Action Verbs

Pairs pantomime actions for other pairs. The viewing team uses present-tense action verbs to describe what they see. Performers listen for correct subject-verb agreement. Pairs switch roles. Then have pairs repeat the activity using the present progressive form of action verbs.

Vocabulary

Science and Academic Vocabulary

Show **Key Word Images**. Have partners create sentences that contain as many vocabulary words as they can in one sentence. Invite partners to share their sentences to see which pair was able to correctly include the most vocabulary words in one sentence.

- **Assessment:** Key Word Tests on pages 169–171 of the Assessment Handbook.

Key Words	
convert	available
electricity	conservation
generate	current
power	flow
renewable	resource
scarce	

Vocabulary Strategy

Word Work

Have individuals look for unfamiliar words in a dictionary and challenge them to create context sentences that use the words. Have them share their sentences with partners for the partner to determine the meaning.

> Animals can have spots, stripes, or other markings...

> I think markings are natural patterns on animals.

Reading Strategy

Read Aloud

Ask Questions

Read aloud the title, the first heading, and the first paragraph. Pause for pairs to ask questions. Encourage the use of **Academic Language Frames:** *I need to understand . . . ; I ask myself . . . ; I read and find . . . .* Continue reading, pausing after each paragraph for students to ask questions.

Comprehension

Read Aloud

Literary Analysis

Read "Tornado Safety." Have the student identify a cause-and-effect relationship in the text.

Text Structure

Have the student tell how the headings help organize the text.

Fluency

Intonation

Have students review their own recordings of "Wind At Work" in the Comprehension Coach. Then have students practice reading **Leveled Library Books** that are appropriate for their reading levels, focusing on accuracy, rate, and intonation.

Read Aloud

Tornado Safety

BEFORE A TORNADO

If a tornado is in your area, radio and television stations issue a warning. Do you know what to do if there is a tornado warning for your area? Make a plan with your family. Talk about where you will go and what you will do. Make a tornado kit for your home. Include a first aid kit, some canned food and a can opener, bottled water, and a flashlight. You will need these supplies if the power goes out.

DURING A TORNADO

Go to a basement. If you do not have a basement, go to a room without windows on the lowest floor of the house. This may be a bathroom or a closet. If you can, get under a sturdy piece of furniture, like a table.

If you are in a car, get out. A tornado can move faster than a car. Lie down flat in a ditch or another low area by the side of the road until the tornado passes.

NGReach.com > eVisual 4.14

Part 1 Vocabulary Skills Trace		Page
Day 1	Science Vocabulary	T217
Day 2	Academic Vocabulary	T219
Day 3	Expand Word Knowledge	T222b
Day 4	Share Word Knowledge	T236b
Day 5	Apply Word Knowledge	T237b
Day 6	Context Clues	T238
Day 7	More Context Clues	T245
Days 8–9	Extend Vocabulary	T246e–f
▶ Day 10	Vocabulary Review	T246g–h

PART 2

Days 1–5

▶ Main Selection
Doña Flor, by Pat Mora, illustrated by Raúl Colón

▶ Genre
Tall Tale

▶ Selection Summary
Doña Flor is a giant who lives in a house as big as a mountain. She is friendly with all the villagers and uses her size to help them out with various tasks. She quiets the wind and saves the villagers from the "mountain lion."

 SELECTION AWARDS

- **American Library Association**: Pura Belpré Award Honor Book for both Author and Illustrator, 2006
- **Society of Children's Book Writers and Illustrators:** Golden Kite Award Winner, Picture Book Text, 2005
- **American Library Association:** Notable Children's Books, 2006
- **Bank Street College of Education:** Best Children's Books of the Year, 2005

by **Pat Mora** ♦ illustrated by **Raúl Colón**

Comprehension Coach

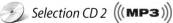 Selection CD 2 (((**MP3**)))

Skills at a Glance	
Language	Express Needs and Wants; Ask for and Give Advice; Theme Theater
Grammar	Forms of *be* and *have;* Modals
Vocabulary	Science Vocabulary: *atmosphere, element, landscape, material, natural*
	Academic Vocabulary: *benefit, force, interact, modify, relate*
	Multiple-Meaning Words
Reading Strategy	Ask Questions
Text Structure	Problem and Solution
Writing	Writing Fluency; Prewrite; Writer's Craft: Human Characteristics; Paragraph; Edit and Proofread; Poem; Journal Entry
Newcomer Support	Use *In the USA:* parts of the body words

Days 6–10

▶ ## Companion Selection
Nature Inside Us, "Comida," by Victor M. Valle and
"The Sun In Me," by Moira Andrew

▶ ## Genre
Lyrical Poetry

▶ ## Selection Summary
Two descriptive poems evoke the feeling that
nature is within the individual. In "Comida," the
author likens some types of food we eat to various
parts of nature. In "The Sun in Me," the author
describes how certain parts of nature are a part of
the narrator. The narrator is affected and enlivened
by nature's presence within.

SELECTION AWARDS

"The Sun in Me"
- *Center for Literacy in Children's Education:*
  CLPE Poetry Award shortlist, 2004
- *H.W. Wilson:* Children's Catalog,
  19th Edition, 2006

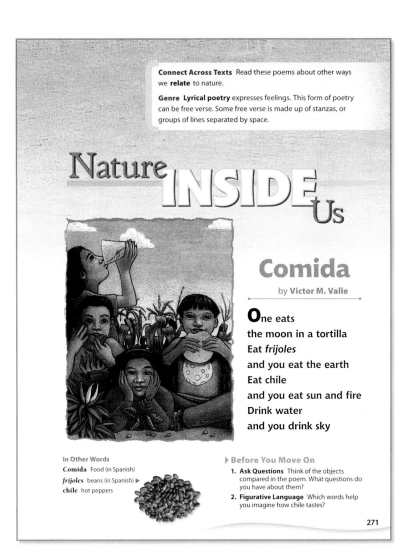

Connect Across Texts Read these poems about other ways we **relate** to nature.

Genre Lyrical poetry expresses feelings. This form of poetry can be free verse. Some free verse is made up of stanzas, or groups of lines separated by space.

Nature INSIDE Us

Comida
by Victor M. Valle

One eats
the moon in a tortilla
Eat *frijoles*
and you eat the earth
Eat chile
and you eat sun and fire
Drink water
and you drink sky

In Other Words
Comida Food (in Spanish)
frijoles beans (in Spanish) ▶
chile hot peppers

▶ **Before You Move On**
1. **Ask Questions** Think of the objects compared in the poem. What questions do you have about them?
2. **Figurative Language** Which words help you imagine how chile tastes?

271

Leveled Library Books

Differentiated Instruction

B | BEGINNING

Dream Weaver
by Jonathan London
A young boy finds a yellow
spider and peers into its
fascinating little world.

I Love Our Earth
*by Bill Martin, Jr. and
Michael Sampson*
Explore the many things to love
about our Earth. From mountains
to sunsets, there is something for
everyone to enjoy.

I | INTERMEDIATE

Prince William
by Gloria Rand
A tanker crashes in Prince
William Sound, spilling oil
everywhere. Denny finds a
baby seal covered in oil and
sets out to save it.

Oil Spill!
by Melvin Berger
Learn about what happened
when the *Exxon Valdez* oil
tanker spilled tons of oil
in Alaska in 1989 and how
people cleaned it up.

A | ADVANCED   AH | ADVANCED HIGH

A River Ran Wild
by Lynn Cherry
Students read about the
environmental history of the
Nashua River, home to native
people and settlers. When the river
becomes polluted, it affects all
those who depend on it.

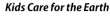

Kids Care for the Earth
by Gare Thompson
In this chapter book, kids take
action to conserve our natural
resources and reduce pollution
and waste.

Unit **4** Daily Planner

PART 2

Core Lessons	**Day 1** Introduce Academic Language	**Day 2** Introduce More Academic Language
Language 🕐 5–10 minutes	**Language of the Day** *T246* ❶ **Language Function: Express Needs and Wants** *T246* 💿 ((MP3)) **Oral Language** • Talk About the Natural World *T247* • Talk Together About the Big Question *T247*	**Language of the Day** *T249a* ❶ **Grammar: Forms of *be*** *T249a* **Oral Language** • Talk Together About Asking Questions *T250*

Vocabulary
🕐 10–15 minutes
	❶ **Science Vocabulary**
	• Introduce Words *T247*
	  atmosphere landscape natural
	  element material
	Classroom Vocabulary
	• Introduce Words *T248*
	  problem solution
		❶ **Academic Vocabulary**
		• Introduce Words *T249*
		  benefit modify
		  force relate
		  interact

Reading 🕐 15–20 minutes	❶ **Text Structure: Problem and Solution** • Introduce Problem and Solution *T248a* • Use Graphic Organizers: Problem-and-Solution Chart *T248* **Read Aloud: "Ethan's Story"** *T248a*	❶ **Strategy: Ask Questions** • Introduce and Practice the Strategy *T250* **Read "Lights Out"** *T251* **Phonics and Fluency** • Verbs Ending in *-ed* *T250*
Writing 🕐 15 minutes	**Daily Writing** • Writing Fluency *T248*	
Content: Integrated Throughout Each Day	**Science** • Explore Elements of Nature	**Science** • Explore Elements of Nature

Day 3

Build Academic Language

Language of the Day *T252a*
Language Function: Ask for and Give Advice *T252a* 🔊 ((MP3))
Listening and Speaking
• Listen to and Sing a Song *T252a*

❶ Academic and Science Vocabulary
• Expand Word Knowledge *T252b*

| atmosphere | element |
| benefit | force |

Support Newcomers
• Build Basic Vocabulary: Parts of the Body Words *T252b*

Read the Selection
❶ Strategy: Ask Questions *T252—T266–267*
• Reading Options T254
Concepts of Print
• Identify Title, Beginning and End, Use Page Numbers *T255*
Literary Analysis
• Genre *T260–261*
❶ Fluency: Expression *T264–265*

Daily Writing
• Modeled Writing: Writer's Craft *T266–267*

Social Studies
• Wild Animals *T258–259*

Day 4

Build Academic Language

Language of the Day *T268a*
❶ Grammar: Forms of *have* and Modals *T268a*
Oral Language
• Talk About the Selection *T268c*

❶ Academic and Science Vocabulary
• Share Word Knowledge *T268b*

| interact | material | natural |
| landscape | modify | relate |

Think and Respond
• Talk About the Selection *T268c*
• Test-Taking Strategy *T268c*
❶ Fluency: Expression *T268c*

Daily Writing
• Independent Writing: Write About It *T268*

Science
• Explore Elements of Nature

Day 5

Build Academic Language

Language of the Day *T269a*
Listening and Speaking *T269a*
• Adjust Your Speech for Your Audience
How to Learn Language
• Relate to Personal Experience *T269a*
Oral Language
• Talk Together About the Big Question *T269*

❶ Academic and Science Vocabulary
• Apply Word Knowledge *T269b*

Reread and Retell
❶ Text Structure: Problem and Solution
• Make a Problem-and-Solution Chart *T269c*
Retell a Story *T269c*
❶ Fluency: Accuracy, Rate, and Expression *T269c*

Science
• Explore Elements of Nature

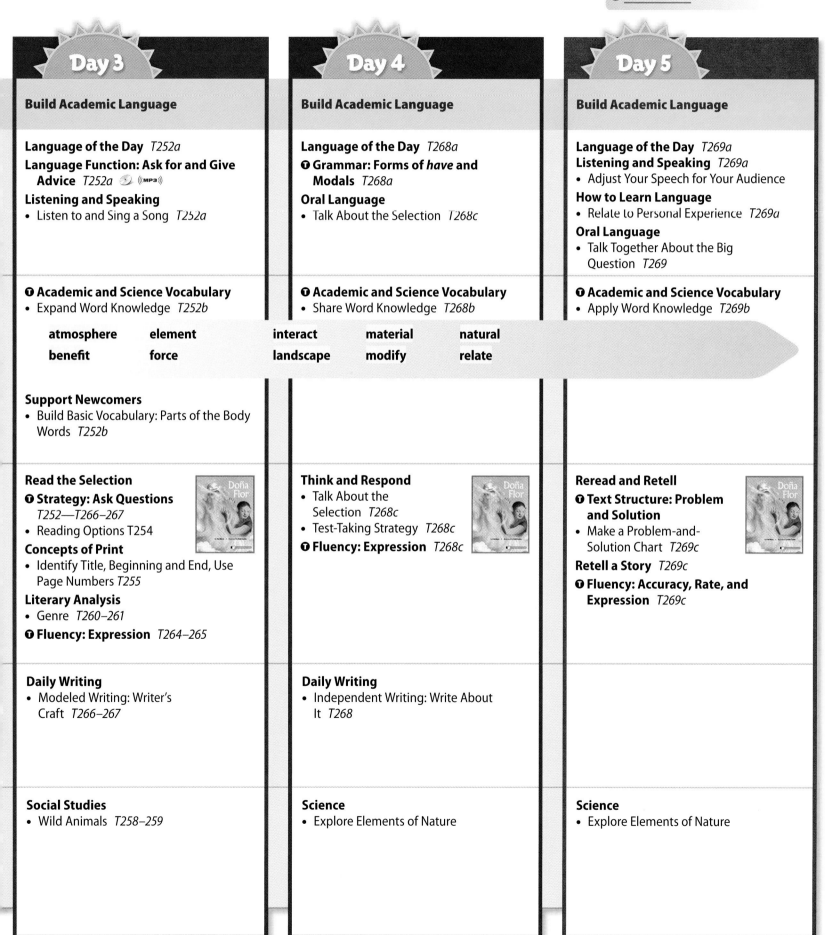

PART 2

Core Lessons	**Day 6**	**Day 7**
	Expand Academic Language	Expand Academic Language
Language 🕐 5–10 minutes	**Language of the Day** T270a ❶ **Language Function: Express Needs and Wants** T270a **Oral Language** • Talk Together About the Big Question T274a	**Language of the Day** T275a ❶ **Grammar: Forms of** *be* **and** *have* T275a
Vocabulary 🕐 10–15 minutes	❶ **Multiple-Meaning Words** T270 **Support Newcomers:** • Additional Multiple-Meaning Words T270	❶ **More Multiple-Meaning Words** T275 • Dictionary Entries T275
Reading 🕐 15–20 minutes	**Read Lyrical Poetry** T271a • Reading Options T271a ❶ **Strategy: Ask Questions** T271a–T272 **Literary Analysis** • Structure and Form T272 ❶ **Fluency: Accuracy and Rate** T274 **Respond and Extend** • Compare Figurative Language T274a	**Reread the Selection: Focus on Sensory Language** T276a
Writing 🕐 15 minutes	**Daily Writing** • Writing Fluency 272	**Daily Writing** • Modeled Writing: Poem T276b
Content: Integrated Throughout Each Day	**Science** • Explore Elements of Nature	**Science** • Explore Elements of Nature

Days 8-9

Apply Academic Language

Theme Theater
- Introduce the Activity *T276c*
- Plan *T276c*
- Plan and Rehearse *T276d*
- Let the Drama Begin! *T276d*
- Debrief and Compare *T276d*

Read Leveled Books

Fiction *T276e*

 **B**

Key Words

creak	weave
pause	web
spider	

 **I**

Key Words

death	volunteers
rescue	wilderness
seal	

A **AH**

Key Words

lumber	rhythm
migration	riverbanks
pollution	

Nonfiction *T276f*

 **B**

Key Words

blossoms	mosses
flicker	sunsets
glow	

 **I**

Key Words

accidents	gallons
chemicals	vacuum
damaged	

 **A** **AH**

Key Words

conserve	pesticide
landfill	resources
natural	

Daily Writing
- Journal Entry *T276f*

Day 10

Review and Assess

Interactive Review *T276g–T276h*
- ❶ Language Function: Express Wants and Needs
- ❶ Grammar: Forms of be and have
- ❶ Vocabulary: Science and Academic Vocabulary
- ❶ Vocabulary Strategy: Multiple-Meaning Words
- ❶ Reading Strategy: Ask Questions
- ❶ Literary Analysis: Tall Tale
- ❶ Text Structure: Problem and Solution
- ❶ Fluency: Expression

Assessment *T276g–T276h*

Same Book, Different Levels

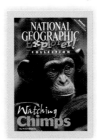 **I** **A** **AH**

Key Words

ape	discovery	social
chimp	grooming	species
chimpanzee	reserve	wildlife

Reading Station

EXPLORER! COLLECTION
Ladder Text:
- Pioneer edition for below level readers
- Pathfinder edition for on and above level readers

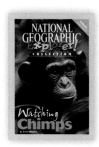

DECODABLE TEXTS

TRADE BOOK COLLECTION
Use the **Leveled Book Finder** at
NGReach.com

Content Stations

Download complete lesson plans NGReach.com

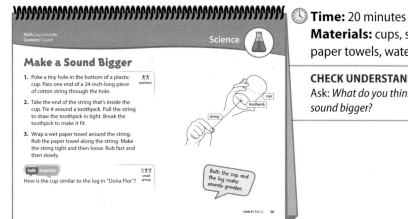

Science

Make a Sound Bigger

1. Poke a tiny hole in the bottom of a plastic cup. Pass one end of a 24-inch-long piece of cotton string through the hole.

2. Take the end of the string that's inside the cup. Tie it around a toothpick. Pull the string to draw the toothpick in tight. Break the toothpick to make it fit.

3. Wrap a wet paper towel around the string. Rub the paper towel along the string. Make the string tight and then loose. Rub fast and then slowly.

Talk Together
How is the cup similar to the log in "Doña Flor"?

Time: 20 minutes
Materials: cups, string, toothpicks, paper towels, water

CHECK UNDERSTANDING
Ask: *What do you think makes the sound bigger?*

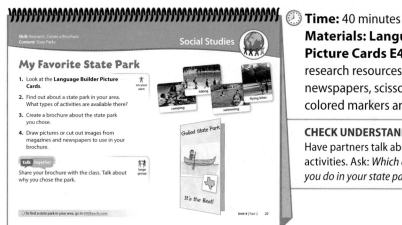

Social Studies

My Favorite State Park

1. Look at the **Language Builder Picture Cards.**

2. Find out about a state park in your area. What types of activities are available there?

3. Create a brochure about the state park you chose.

4. Draw pictures or cut out images from magazines and newspapers to use in your brochure.

Talk Together
Share your brochure with the class. Talk about why you chose the park.

Time: 40 minutes
Materials: Language Builder Picture Cards E49–E52, research resources, magazines and newspapers, scissors, glue, paper, colored markers and crayons

CHECK UNDERSTANDING
Have partners talk about their favorite activities. Ask: *Which of these activities can you do in your state park?*

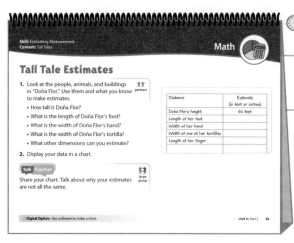

Math

Tall Tale Estimates

1. Look at the people, animals, and buildings in "Doña Flor." Use them and what you know to make estimates.
   - How tall is Doña Flor?
   - What is the length of Doña Flor's foot?
   - What is the width of Doña Flor's hand?
   - What is the width of Doña Flor's tortilla?
   - What other dimensions can you estimate?

2. Display your data in a chart.

Talk Together
Share your chart. Talk about why your estimates are not all the same.

Distance	Estimate (in feet or inches)
Doña Flor's height	60 feet
Length of her foot	
Width of her hand	
Width of one of her tortillas	
Length of her finger	

Time: 20 minutes
Materials: paper, pencils

CHECK UNDERSTANDING
Ask: *How did you estimate the length of Doña Flor's foot?*

Use these resources to provide daily opportunities for students to work individually or in groups at learning stations around the classroom.

Language Stations

Download complete lesson plans  NGReach.com >

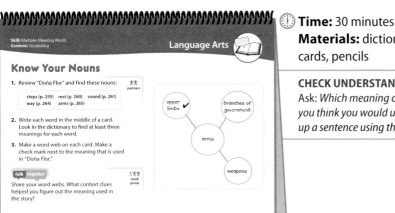

Time: 30 minutes

Materials: dictionary, lined index cards, pencils

CHECK UNDERSTANDING
Ask: *Which meaning of the word* steps *do you think you would use most often? Make up a sentence using that meaning.*

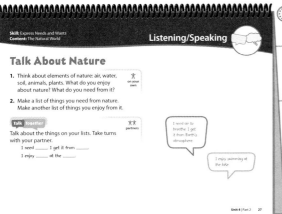

Time: 20 minutes

Materials: paper, pencils

CHECK UNDERSTANDING
Ask students to name three elements of nature.

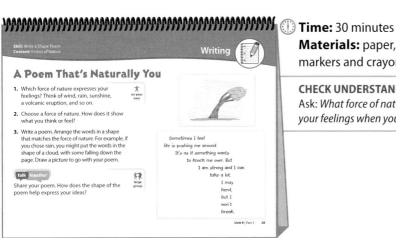

Time: 30 minutes

Materials: paper, pencils, colored markers and crayons

CHECK UNDERSTANDING
Ask: *What force of nature might express your feelings when you are angry? Why?*

Technology Station

Access resources  NGReach.com >

 **Recordings**

- To the Woods
- Where Can I Go?
- Doña Flor

Digital Library

Learn vocabulary and practice language

- Key Word Images
- Language Builder Picture Cards

 **My Vocab Notebook**

- Add Words

 **Comprehension Coach**

- Use interactive library support. Automatically measure fluency.

Online Assessment

- Practice items in standardized test format.

Day 1

Day at a Glance:
- ▶ **Language:** Express Needs and Wants
- ▶ **Vocabulary:** Science Vocabulary
- ▶ **Reading:** Problem and Solution
- ▶ **Writing:** Writing Fluency; Study a Model

OBJECTIVES

Vocabulary
- Acquire and Use Grade-Level Key Vocabulary ❶

Language
- Language Function: Express Needs and Wants ❶
- Listen to and Imitate Fluent Models
- Participate in Discussion

Learning and Teamwork Strategies
- Activate Prior Knowledge
- Use Media to Build Language
- Use Context to Build Concepts and Language

Science
- Explore Elements of Nature

Resources

- 🔖 🅰 *Sing With Me Language Song Book*, page 18
- 💿 🅰 *Sing With Me Language Song CD 2* Tracks 13, 14
- 🅐 eVisual 4.15
- • eVisual 4.16
- 🅐 Key Word Images

🌐 NGReach.com ⟩

See **Technology Station** for digital student resources.

Differentiate

Academic Language Frames

Express Needs and Wants

- ■ I want _____.
  I need _____.

- ■ I want _____ to _____.
  I need _____ to _____.
  _____

- ■ I want _____.
- ■ I would like to have this because _____.
  I need _____.
  I must have this because _____.

🌐 NGReach.com ⟩ eVisual 4.16

Display the Language of the Day. Say: *Wind can blow trees. Water can help trees grow.* Start two webs, one for wind and one for water. Have each student share his or her ideas. Then explain that students will be listening, speaking, and writing more about nature today.

Express Needs and Wants

❶ Teach/Model Display "To the Woods." Read aloud the introduction and play the chant. Invite students to read aloud chorally as you play the chant a second time. Model how to echo and chime in as the audio prompts.

Point out the **Language Frames** and model using these structures to talk about things you need or want. Clarify: Need *means "must have."* Want *means "would like to have."*

How to Express Needs and Wants	
1. Use the word *want* to tell about things you would like to have.	I want to swim in the lake. I want a cookie to eat.
2. Use the word *need* to tell about things you must have.	I need water to drink. I need to rest.

🌐 NGReach.com ⟩ eVisual 4.15

Prompt students to tell about things they need or want. Point to each step on the how to card as students talk. Provide examples as needed. To prompt more participation say: *Tell me why you want that.*

❷ Practice/Apply Have students name a favorite place and tell about things they need and want in this place. Use **Academic Language Frames** to encourage students to use language naturally in expressing their needs and wants.

> **CHECK UNDERSTANDING** Ask students questions such as: *Are food and water needs or wants? Tell me one thing that you need to live. Tell me one thing that you want.*

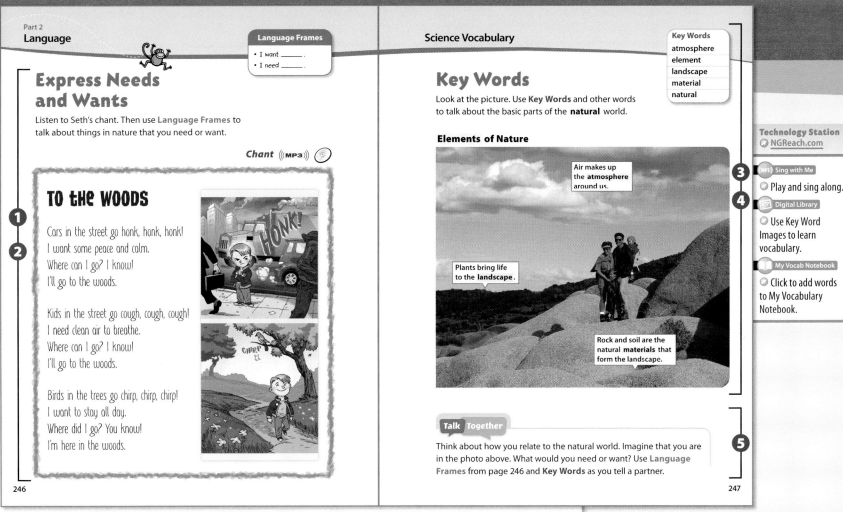

Science Vocabulary

③ Teach/Model Read the introduction and look at the photo with students. Use **Vocabulary Routine 1** and **Key Word Images** to teach the words. Access definitions on pages 616–639.

1. **Pronounce** the word and point to its picture: **landscape**.

2. **Rate** the word. Have students hold up their fingers to show how well they know the word. (1 = very well, 2 = a little, 3 = not at all) Ask: *What do you know about this word?*

3. **Define** the word: *A landscape is a view of an area of land.*

4. **Elaborate** Relate the word to your experience: *The landscape around my home includes a lawn, flowers, and an oak tree.*

④ Practice/Apply Have partners take turns repeating the routine for each word, using complete sentences for steps 2, 3, and 4.

⑤ Talk Together About the Big Question
Check Understanding and Connect Concepts Review the **Language Frames** on page 246. Use these frames with the Key Words. Provide an example:

> The **atmosphere** in the city is smoggy. I need clean air to breathe. I want to go somewhere that's calm and peaceful. Let's go to the flower garden.

Add the ideas to your unit concept map.

Differentiate

Spanish Cognates ▸
atmosphere/atmósfera;
element/elemento;
material/material;
natural/natural

Part 2 Vocabulary Skills Trace	Page
Day 1	**Science Vocabulary**	**T247**
Day 2	Academic Vocabulary	T249
Day 3	Expand Word Knowledge	T252b
Day 4	Share Word Knowledge	T268b
Day 5	Apply Word Knowledge	T269b
Day 6	Multiple-Meaning Words	T270
Day 7	Multiple-Meaning Words	T275
Days 8–9	Extend Vocabulary	T276e–f
Day 10	Vocabulary Review	T276g–h

Day 1 continued

Day at a Glance:
▶ **Language:** Express Needs and Wants
▶ **Vocabulary:** Science Vocabulary
▶ **Reading:** Problem and Solution
▶ **Writing:** Writing Fluency; Writing Project: Study a Model

OBJECTIVES

Vocabulary
- Acquire and Use Classroom Vocabulary
- Use Grade-Level Key Vocabulary ⊕

Comprehension and Literary Analysis
- Demonstrate Listening Comprehension
- Problem and Solution ⊕

Listening and Speaking
- Clarify and support ideas

Learning Strategies and Teamwork
- Use Graphic Organizers: Problem-and-Solution Chart
- Reason Deductively

Writing
- Develop Writing Fluency
- Monitor and Self-Correct Writing
- Writing Project: Study a Model

Science
- Explore Elements of Nature

Resources

- ⊘ eVisual 4.17
- · eVisual 4.18
- ⊙⊘ Practice Master 4.13

Differentiate

Multi-Level Strategies

BEGINNING

Allow students to draw pictures to represent their problem and how they solved it. Provide sentence starters for captions:
- My problem is _____.
- My solution is _____.

INTERMEDIATE

Ask them to make an event box for each action they took and to use complete sentences.

ADVANCED

Encourage students to explain why they took each action and how it helped them solve the problem.

ADVANCED HIGH

Have students discuss alternative solutions they could have used.

Problem and Solution

① **Teach** Connect concepts: *What Key Words have you learned to help you talk about nature? You saw those words used to describe a rocky* **landscape** *where the family hiked. Now you will learn how to make a graphic organizer to identify a problem in the* **natural** *world and how to solve it.*

Read the first paragraph and teach the Classroom Vocabulary words *problem* and *solution*. Use the illustrations to help students identify a *problem* and *solution*. Ask: *What is Seth's problem?* (there's trash in the park) *What does he do?* (First he picks up the trash then he puts up a sign.) Seth's solution is to put a sign for others.

Read aloud the explanation about making a problem-and-solution chart. Clarify the purpose: *I can make a problem-and-solution chart to help me show how to solve a problem. I list the problem first, then the actions taken to solve the problem and finally identify the solution.* Remind students to listen for the problem and solution as you read aloud "Problem at the Park."

> **Read Aloud**
>
> ### Problem at the Park
>
> Seth loves to relax at the park. But today he finds a mess! The landscape is covered with trash. Seth says, "I will clean up the park." He picks up the trash and puts it in a bag. Seth thinks, What else can I do? He hangs up a sign over the trash can that says, "Put Trash Here." Now Seth can enjoy the park. Everyone is helping to keep the park clean.

⊘ NGReach.com ▶ eVisual 4.17

② **Model** Review the first two sentences of "Problem at the Park." Have volunteers read the first two boxes in the problem-and-solution chart and model the process: *I make a box for the problem. I make another box below it to show what Seth does first to solve the problem. I add a box for each new event.* The last box shows the solution to the problem.

③ **Practice/Apply** Read aloud the instructions. Distribute **Practice Master 4.12** for students to use as they complete their charts. Use **Multi-Level Strategies** to help students at all proficiency levels talk about problems and solutions. Monitor students' developing proficiency. (See page R2 for **Proficiency Level Descriptions**.)

> **CHECK UNDERSTANDING** *What is Seth's problem?* (The park is covered with trash.) *What does Seth do to solve the problem?* (He picks up the trash and puts up a sign.)

Problem and Solution.

When you tell a story, you may start with a **problem** and then tell what you did to try to solve it. Finally, you may tell about the **solution**.

Look at the pictures of Seth at the park.

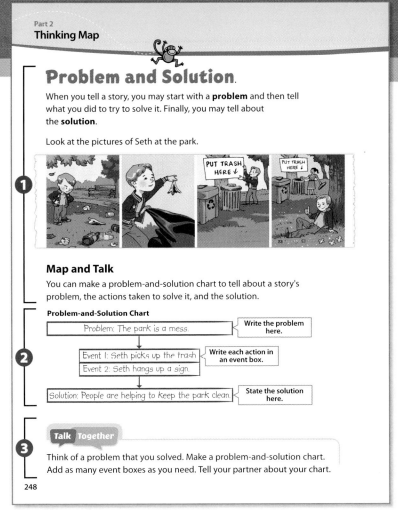

Map and Talk

You can make a problem-and-solution chart to tell about a story's problem, the actions taken to solve it, and the solution.

Problem-and-Solution Chart

Problem: The park is a mess.	Write the problem here.

Event 1: Seth picks up the trash	Write each action in an event box.
Event 2: Seth hangs up a sign.	

Solution: People are helping to keep the park clean.	State the solution here.

Talk Together

Think of a problem that you solved. Make a problem-and-solution chart. Add as many event boxes as you need. Tell your partner about your chart.

248

Student Book page 248

Daily Writing

4 Writing Fluency Use the **Power Writing Routine**. (See page PD53.) Write the word *landscape* and prompt: *What **elements** make up a landscape?* Think about this word and write about it.

Power Writing Routine

 1. What do you know about the word or picture?

 2. Take one minute to write as much as you can, as well as you can.
B words   **I** sentences   **A** **AH** paragraphs

 3. Check your spelling and grammar. (Circle) mistakes.

 4. Count your words.

NGReach.com eVisual 4.18

5 Writing Project: Study a Model Tall Tale Have students review a model of the writing form for their Writing Projects. (See page T276.)

CLOSE AND ASSESS

- **Language** *Tell me about things Seth needs and wants when he is in the woods.* (Students should use information from the chant in their answers.)

- **Reading** *Trash can be a problem for the environment. What are some other things people can do to solve this problem?*

- **Vocabulary** *What are some elements of nature mentioned in Seth's chant?* (woods, air, birds, trees)

Classroom Vocabulary

Use **Vocabulary Routine 4** to teach **problem**. (See **Vocabulary Routines**, page PD40.) Repeat with **solution**.

Fold-Up Tab

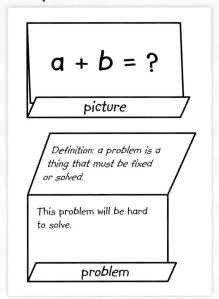

Practice Master 4.13

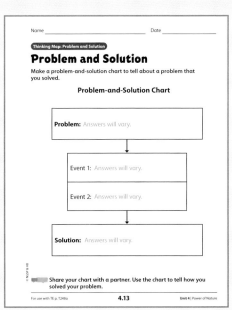

Day 2

Day at a Glance:
▶ **Language:** Forms of *be*   ▶ **Reading:** Learn to Ask Questions
▶ **Vocabulary:** Academic Vocabulary   ▶ **Writing:** Prewrite: Tall Tale

OBJECTIVES

Vocabulary
• Acquire and Use Academic Vocabulary ❶
• Use Grade-Level Vocabulary

Language
• Identify and Use Forms of be ❶

Learning and Teamwork Strategies
• Make Connections Across Content Areas

Resources

📋📀 *Practice Master 4.14*

📋📀 *Practice Master 4.15*

📀 *Key Word Images*

⏺ **NGReach.com** ❯

See **Technology Station** for digital student resources.

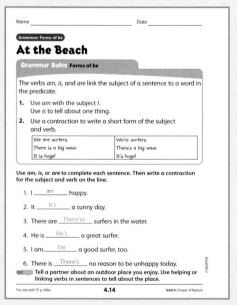

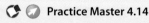

📋📀 **Practice Master 4.14**

Part 2 Grammar Skills Trace		Page
▶ **Day 2**	Forms of *be*	T249a
Day 4	Forms of *have* and Modals	T268a
Day 7	Forms of *be* and *have*	T275a
Day 10	Review Forms of *be* and *have*	T276g

Language of the Day

Think of a **landscape**. Describe the **atmosphere**.
I am thinking of a place with _____ .
It is _____ .
There is/There are _____ .

Read the Language of the Day. Model: *I am thinking of a place with lots of water. It is hot. There is lots of sand, too.* Invite students to guess the place you are describing, and confirm that you are describing a beach. Students can then take turns describing and guessing other locations.

Grammar Forms of *be* 🅱 🅸 🅰 🅰🅷

1 **Teach/Model** Write the sentences and read them aloud.

1. *I am excited.*
2. *We are new hikers.*
3. *There is a park ranger with us, and there are trail markers.*
4. *We are carrying water.*
5. *I'm hiking to the top of the mountain!*

Underline the verbs. Ask: *Do these verbs show action?* (no) *What do they do?* Provide time for suggestions. Then say: *They link the subject with a word in the predicate. The word in the predicate can describe the subject or name it in another way.* Circle *excited* and *hikers*. Have students identify which word describes the subject and which renames it. Say: *The verbs am, is, and are must agree with their subjects.* Draw a chart.

Use for I:	am
Use for one person or thing:	is
Use for more than one person or thing:	are

Say: *These same forms are used in the present progressive. They are helping verbs. They help to tell about an action as it is happening.* Point out *am* in sentence 4 and the contraction of subject-verb in sentence 5. Point to sentence 3: There is/There are *is always followed by a noun.*

2 **Practice/Apply** Have partners pretend they are walking in nature. Have them use forms of the verb *to be* to talk about what they experience. Assign **Practice Master 4.13** for practice with linking and helping verbs.

CHECK UNDERSTANDING *Have students complete the sentence frames:* _____ *is a bird. It* _____ *chirping. I* _____ *happy, too!* (There, is, am)

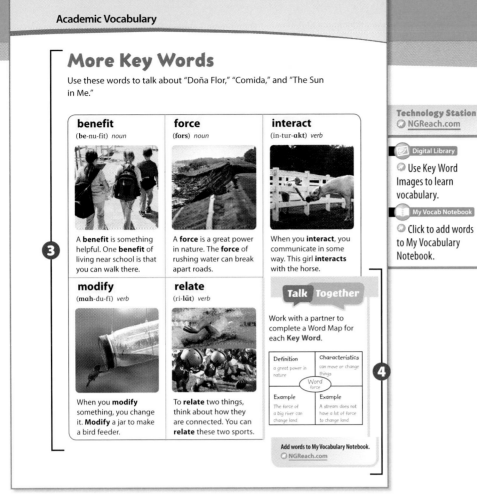

More Key Words

Use these words to talk about "Doña Flor," "Comida," and "The Sun in Me."

benefit
(be-nu-fit) *noun*

A **benefit** is something helpful. One **benefit** of living near school is that you can walk there.

force
(fors) *noun*

A **force** is a great power in nature. The **force** of rushing water can break apart roads.

interact
(in-tur-**akt**) *verb*

When you **interact**, you communicate in some way. This girl **interacts** with the horse.

modify
(**mah**-du-fī) *verb*

When you **modify** something, you change it. **Modify** a jar to make a bird feeder.

relate
(ri-**lāt**) *verb*

To **relate** two things, think about how they are connected. You can **relate** these two sports.

Talk Together

Work with a partner to complete a Word Map for each **Key Word**.

Definition	Characteristics
a great power in nature	can move or change things

Word: force

Example	Example
The force of a big river can change land.	A stream does not have a lot of force to change land.

Add words to My Vocabulary Notebook.
○ NGReach.com

Student Book page 249

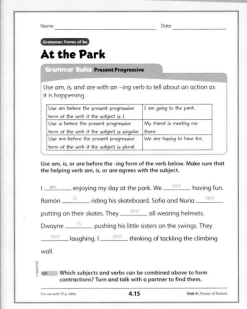

Technology Station
○ NGReach.com

Digital Library
○ Use Key Word Images to learn vocabulary.

My Vocab Notebook
○ Click to add words to My Vocabulary Notebook.

Name _____ Date _____

Grammar: Forms of be

At the Park

Grammar Rules Present Progressive

Use *am, is,* and *are* with an *–ing* verb to tell about an action as it is happening.

Use *am* before the present progressive form of the verb if the subject is *I*.	I am going to the park.
Use *is* before the present progressive form of the verb if the subject is singular.	My friend is meeting me there.
Use *are* before the present progressive form of the verb if the subject is plural.	We are hoping to have fun.

Use *am, is,* or *are* before the *-ing* form of the verb below. Make sure that the helping verb *am, is,* or *are* agrees with the subject.

I ___am___ enjoying my day at the park. We ___are___ having fun. Ramón ___is___ riding his skateboard. Sofia and Nuria ___are___ putting on their skates. They ___are___ all wearing helmets. Dwayne ___is___ pushing his little sisters on the swings. They ___are___ laughing. I ___am___ thinking of tackling the climbing wall.

Which subjects and verbs can be combined above to form contractions? Turn and talk with a partner to find them.

For use with TE p. 249a   **4.15**   Unit 4 | Power of Nature

○ ○ **Practice Master 4.15**

Academic Vocabulary

③ Teach/Model Invite students to discuss each photograph on the page. Read the directions aloud and use **Vocabulary Routine 1** and **Key Word Images** to teach the words.

1. **Pronounce** the word and point to its picture: **benefit**.

2. **Rate** the word. Have students hold up their fingers to show how well they know the word. (1 = very well, 2 = a little, 3 = not at all) Ask: *What do you know about this word?*

3. **Define** the word: *A benefit is something that helps you. Living near your school is a benefit because you can walk to school instead of taking the bus.*

4. **Elaborate** Relate the word to your experience: *I love working with children. One benefit of being a teacher is that I get to work with children every day.*

④ Practice/Apply Use the ratings from step 2 to form pairs. Have partners work together in making word maps for each of the Key Words. Invite partners to share one of their word maps with the class.

CHECK UNDERSTANDING Point to the **Key Word Image** of each Key Word and ask students to use the word in a new sentence.

Keys to Efficacy

Making personal connections can help activate prior knowledge. Ask: *What are ways people **modify** the landscape around their homes?*

Differentiate

Spanish Cognates ▸
benefit/beneficio;
force/fuerza;
interact/interactuar;
modify/modificar;
relate/relacionar

Part 2 Vocabulary Skills Trace		Page
Day 1	Science Vocabulary	T247
Day 2	**Academic Vocabulary**	**T249**
Day 3	Expand Word Knowledge	T252b
Day 4	Share Word Knowledge	T268b
Day 5	Apply Word Knowledge	T269b
Day 6	Multiple-Meaning Words	T270
Day 7	Multiple-Meaning Words	T275
Days 8–9	Extend Vocabulary	T276e–f
Day 10	Vocabulary Review	T276g–h

Day 2
continued

Day at a Glance:
▶ **Language:** Forms of *be*   ▶ **Reading:** Learn to Ask Questions
▶ **Vocabulary:** Academic Vocabulary   ▶ **Writing:** Prewrite

OBJECTIVES

Vocabulary
• Acquire and Use Academic Vocabulary ❶
• Acquire and Use Grade-Level Vocabulary ❶

Learning to Read
• Read Words Ending in *-ed*

Reading Strategy
• Learn to Ask Questions ❶

Learning and Teamwork Strategies
• Use Personal Experience
• Use Visuals

Writing
• Writing Project: Plan a Tall Tale

Resources

⊘ *eVisual 4.19*

⟳ *Reach Into Phonics TE pages T56, T57*

Learn to Ask Questions

❶ Teach Read the introduction aloud. Ask students what questions they have about the picture. Make the connection: *When you do not understand something, ask questions about it. Then find the answers to your questions.* Point out that students ask questions every day in various situations.

❷ Model Read the chart chorally with students. To model asking questions about the picture, say:

• *I do not understand what the boy is watching on TV.* (Shrug your shoulders and look confused.)

• I ask myself, *What kind of TV show has a map and weather symbols?*

• *I think about the images on the TV to help me understand the boy is watching a weather report.*

❸ Practice/Apply Read the directions aloud. Point out the **Language Frames**. Chorally read Seth's story and the sample student question.

Direct students to ask their own questions about the story. Display the **Academic Language Frames** to help students at each proficiency level. Have volunteers ask questions at the end of paragraphs 6 and 7. For example, students can ask how rain could cause a blackout. Encourage them to identify information in the text that helps them answer their questions.

> **CHECK UNDERSTANDING** Ask: *How did asking questions help you better understand the story? What is one question you asked?*

Differentiate

Academic Language Frames

Ask Questions

■ I read _____.
   I do not understand _____.
   I ask myself _____.
   I think about _____ to understand _____.

■ I do not understand _____.
   One question I have is _____.
   I think about _____.
   This helps me understand _____.

▬ I do not understand _____.
■ One question I have is _____.
   I think about _____ and _____.
   Now I understand _____.

⊘ NGReach.com > eVisual 4.19

Phonics and Fluency

Verbs Ending in *-ed*
Display these words: *pick, hop,* and *rake.* Explain as you model each verb: *To make the past tense of most verbs, add* -ed. *If a verb ends with one vowel and a consonant, double the final consonant and add* -ed. *If a verb ends with an* e, *drop the* e *and add* -ed. Read aloud each pair of verbs and have students repeat. Display **Transparency 46** from **Reach Into Phonics** and work through the lesson.

Practice Display these sentences:
• I climb the mountain.
• I stop for a rest.
• I hike up the trail.
Have partners tell how they would change each verb to make it past tense.

Learn to Ask Questions

1

Look at the picture. Sometimes, when you listen to information, you might not understand what you hear. **Ask** yourself **questions**. They might lead you to think about what you already know or feel about the subject.

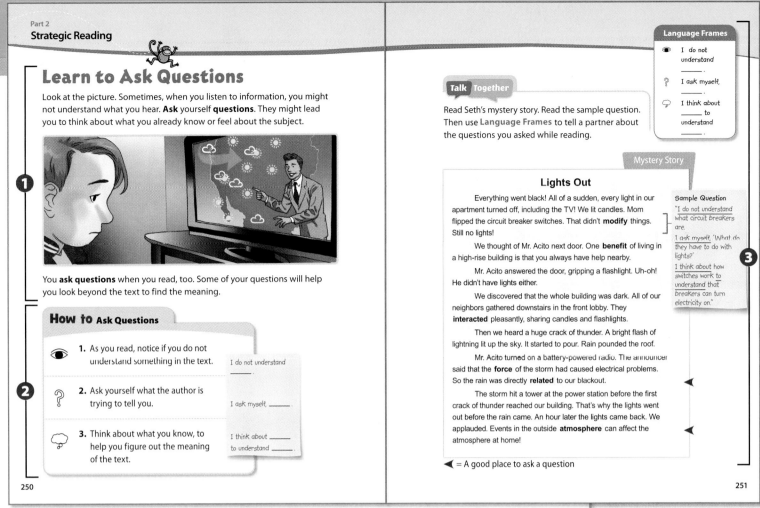

You **ask questions** when you read, too. Some of your questions will help you look beyond the text to find the meaning.

2

How to Ask Questions

1. As you read, notice if you do not understand something in the text.

I do not understand _____ .

2. Ask yourself what the author is trying to tell you.

I ask myself, _____

3. Think about what you know, to help you figure out the meaning of the text.

I think about _____ to understand _____

250

Language Frames

👁 I do not understand _____ .

❓ I ask myself, _____ .

💭 I think about _____ to understand _____ .

Talk Together

Read Seth's mystery story. Read the sample question. Then use **Language Frames** to tell a partner about the questions you asked while reading.

Mystery Story

Lights Out

Everything went black! All of a sudden, every light in our apartment turned off, including the TV! We lit candles. Mom flipped the circuit breaker switches. That didn't **modify** things. Still no lights!

We thought of Mr. Acito next door. One **benefit** of living in a high-rise building is that you always have help nearby.

Mr. Acito answered the door, gripping a flashlight. Uh-oh! He didn't have lights either.

We discovered that the whole building was dark. All of our neighbors gathered downstairs in the front lobby. They **interacted** pleasantly, sharing candles and flashlights.

Then we heard a huge crack of thunder. A bright flash of lightning lit up the sky. It started to pour. Rain pounded the roof.

Mr. Acito turned on a battery-powered radio. The announcer said that the **force** of the storm had caused electrical problems. So the rain was directly **related** to our blackout. ◀

The storm hit a tower at the power station before the first crack of thunder reached our building. That's why the lights went out before the rain came. An hour later the lights came back. We applauded. Events in the outside **atmosphere** can affect the atmosphere at home! ◀

◀ = A good place to ask a question

Sample Question

"I do not understand what circuit breakers are.

I ask myself, 'What do they have to do with lights?'

I think about how switches work to understand that breakers can turn electricity on."

3

251

Student Book pages 250–251

Daily Writing

4 **Writing Project: Prewrite: Tall Tale** Have students plan their Writing Projects. See page T277.

CLOSE AND ASSESS

- **Language** *Use a helping or a linking verb to tell about Seth's story. Provide* sentence frames: *Seth _____ . The people in Seth's building _____ . There _____ .*

- **Reading** *What questions did you have about the story? How did you answer your questions?*

- **Vocabulary** *Explain the meaning of* **interacted** *in this sentence from Seth's story:* They interacted pleasantly, sharing candles and flashlights.

Day at a Glance:
- ▶ **Language:** Ask for and Give Advice
- ▶ **Vocabulary:** Expand Word Knowledge
- ▶ **Reading:** Read the Selection
- ▶ **Writing:** Writer's Craft; Draft

Day 3

OBJECTIVES

Vocabulary
- Use Academic Vocabulary ⊕
- Use Grade-Level Vocabulary ⊕
- Use Classroom Vocabulary

Language
- Language Function: Ask for and Give Advice
- Listen to and Imitate Fluent Models
- Use a Variety of Strategic Learning Techniques

Learning Strategies and Teamwork
- Use Media to Build Language
- Collaborate with Peers
- Gather Information
- Use Graphic Organizers: Three-Quarter Book

Resources

📀 🌐 *Sing With Me Language Song CD 2, Tracks 15, 16*

♻ 🌐 *Sing With Me Language Song Book, page 19*

🌐 *eVisual 4.20*

🌐 *eVisual 4.21*

In the U.S.A. Picture Cards 187–196

- *Chart or poster paper*

🌐 **NGReach.com** ▶

See **Technology Station** for digital student resources.

Differentiate

Academic Language Frames

> **Ask for and Give Advice**
> ■ What should I do?
>   I think you should _____.
> _____
> ■ Do you have any suggestions?
>   I think you should _____.
> _____
> ■ What do you think about _____?
> ■ What advice do you have about _____?
>   I think you should _____ because _____.

🌐 **NGReach.com** ▶ **eVisual 4.21**

> ## Language of the Day
> What do you Know about forces in nature?
> I Know that ____. It can ____.

Read the Language of the Day. Model: *I know that wind is a powerful force in nature. It can lift houses and trees.* Have students share their own ideas. Then explain that students will be listening, speaking, and writing more about nature today.

Ask for and Give Advice

1 Teach Display "Where Can I Go?" Play the song. Invite students to sing along as you play the song a second time. Introduce: *In this song, Seth is asking for and giving advice. If you need advice or help, you can ask someone. When you give advice, you suggest what the person should do.*

Activate prior knowledge: *How do you ask for advice or help? What words do you use?* Connect: *The words* What should I *and* How do I *often begin a request for advice.* Then display the chart:

Asking for Advice	
What should I . . .	**How do I . . .**
The CD will not play. What should I do?	The sound is too low. How do I make it louder?
Giving Advice	
I think you should . . .	I would . . .

🌐 **NGReach.com** ▶ **eVisual 4.20**

2 Model Ask a volunteer to help you do a role-play. Tell the volunteer to think of a problem and use one of the language frames to ask for your advice. Offer some simple advice, using patterns from the chart.

3 Practice/Apply Review the song lyrics. Ask students to offer advice to Seth. *Where should he go to find a peaceful place? What should he do?* Then have partners take turns asking for and giving advice to common problems, such as forgetting your homework, not understanding a word, not knowing how to find something, and so on. Use **Academic Language Frames** to encourage students to use language naturally.

> **CHECK UNDERSTANDING** Ask students to explain the difference between asking for and giving advice.

Technology Station
○ NGReach.com

MP3 Sing with Me
○ Play and sing along.

Birds in the trees go
    chirp, chirp, chirp!
I want to stay all day.
Where did I go? You know!
I'm here in the woods.

CHIRP

MP3 or Song CD 2 Tracks 13–14 **Chant** 19

Sing with Me Language Song Book page 19

Expand Word Knowledge

4 **Teach/Model** Explain that each student pair will become Key Word experts. They will study one Key Word and create an Inside Flap Graphic about that word. Use **Vocabulary Routine 2** and model making a Inside Flap Graphic about the word **benefit**. (See **Vocabulary Routines,** page PD38.

- Write the word.
- Add a definition.
- Write a sentence using the word.

5 **Practice/Apply** Assign a Key Word to each pair of students. Have each pair create a Three-Quarter Book for their assigned Key Word. Display the visuals in the class.

Key word:
benefit

Sentence:
Good health is a
benefit of exercise.

Definition: Sentence:
something   Good health is a
that is   benefit of exercise.
helpful

Inside Flap Graphic

CHECK UNDERSTANDING Say a Key Word and have the partner experts for the word read the definition and examples from their Three-Quarter Book.

Key Words	
atmosphere	landscape
benefit	material
element	modify
force	natural
interact	relate

Differentiate

Newcomer Support

Newcomers can make Inside Flap Graphic Books using words from **In the U.S.A. Picture Cards 187–196**.

Day 3
continued

Day at a Glance:
▶ **Language:** Ask for and Give Advice   ⊙ **Reading:** Read the Selection
▶ **Vocabulary:** Expand Word Knowledge   ⊙ **Writing:** Writer's Craft; Draft

OBJECTIVES

Vocabulary
- Use Academic Vocabulary
- Use Grade-Level Vocabulary

Reading Strategy
- Plan: Preview

Comprehension and Literary Analysis
- Analyze Character
- Analyze Genre: Tall Tale

Learning and Teamwork Strategies
- Use Prereading Supports
- Build Background Knowledge

Resources

   Comprehension Coach

Keys to Efficacy

Encourage students to think collaboratively and build on one another's ideas.

Preview the Story

❶ Introduce Ask students to look at the picture of the woman on page 253. Ask them what they think the woman is doing. Say: *Do you think this could happen in real life? What kind of story do you think this is?* Have a volunteer read aloud the title and ask students to predict what they think the selection will be about, based on the title and picture.

❷ Genre and Main Character Read aloud the definition of a tall tale. Elaborate: *When you exaggerate, you make someone or something seem bigger than real life.*

Read aloud the definition of main character and point to the picture. Explain: *The main character looks much bigger than people in real life do.* Connect to the genre: *Her size is exaggerated because she is a character from a tall tale.*

❸ Preview and Build Background Use sheltering strategies as you conduct a picture walk.

Pages	Say (and Do)
254–255	*This is Flor. She is the hero of the story. How can you tell Flor is "larger than life?"* Point to clues in the picture.
256–257	*Where are the birds in the first picture? Flor is so tall the birds build nests in her hair! Look at the children in the next picture. What are they doing?* (They are floating on one of Flor's tortillas)
258–259	*I see Flor looking in the door of a family's house. They look worried. What do you think they are worried about? In the other picture, Flor is carrying some animals. Do you think she likes animals?*
260–261	Point to the picture of the book on the page. *Why do you think the book is so tiny? Look. Flor tries to cheer up her friends by making them a river with her thumb.*
262–263	*What is Flor looking at? It's called a puma, and it's very dangerous. Do you think Flor is afraid of the puma? Why or why not?*
264–265	*Look at the pictures on this page. How do you think the story ends?*

CHECK UNDERSTANDING Have students look again at the illustration on page 253. Ask: *Is this story going to be about real characters and events? How can you tell?* (No, it's not going to be about real characters and events. Flor is a giant and she does impossible things. That shows it's a made-up story.)

Read a Story

Genre
A **tall tale** is a funny story. Characters and events are exaggerated. The hero may be based on a real person or may be fictional.

Main Character
Often the main character in a tall tale solves problems in an unusual or exaggerated way.

Doña Flor ▶

Doña Flor

by **Pat Mora** ♦ illustrated by **Raúl Colón**

Comprehension Coach

252

Student Book pages 252–253

Comprehension Coach

Build Reading Power
Assign students to use the software, based on their instructional needs.

Read Silently

- Comprehension questions with immediate feedback
- Vocabulary support

Listen
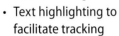
- Process model of fluent reading
- Text highlighting to facilitate tracking
- Vocabulary support

Record

- Oral reading fluency practice
- Speech recognition for oral fluency assessment with immediate feedback

---

Cultural Perspectives
A tall tale is a story about people who are larger than life, sometimes literally. These characters may be make-believe or based on real-life people. They have all kinds of adventures in the stories. People in all cultures have tall tales. Ask students if they can share tall tales that they know from other cultures. Paul Bunyan is one example from American culture.

OBJECTIVES

Vocabulary
- Use Academic Vocabulary ⊕
- Use Grade-Level Vocabulary ⊕

Learning to Read
- Concepts of Print: Identify Title, Beginning and End, Use Page Numbers
- Phonics: Verbs ending in *-ing*

Reading Strategies
- Plan: Set a Purpose, Predict, Confirm Predictions
- Ask Questions ⊕
- Use Text Structure: Problem and Solution ⊕

Fluency
- Expression ⊕

Comprehension and Literary Analysis
- Genre: Tall Tale

Learning and Teamwork Strategies
- Use Reading Supports

Writing
- Develop Writer's Craft
- Connect Reading and Writing
- Writing Project: Draft

Resources

⊘ 🖵 *Read with Me Selection CD*

✎ 🖵 *Practice Master 4.16*

✎ 🖵 *Reach Into Phonics TE T102*

🖵 **NGReach.com**

See **Technology Station** for digital student resources.

Key Points Reading

🖵 **Practice Master 4.16**

Read the Story

Suggested Pacing

- Day 3: Read Section 1, pages 254–257
- Day 4: Read Sections 2 and 3, pages 258–265

Reading Options Scaffold the support for varied reading levels.

BELOW LEVEL	ON LEVEL	ABOVE LEVEL
Listen and Read Along	**Read Aloud**	**Read Independently**
• Read aloud the Key Points Reading while students track the print. • Check understanding with selected Build Comprehension questions. Then include students in Talk About It (page 268).	• Have groups set a purpose for reading—to get information or enjoy a story—and read aloud. • Use Build Comprehension questions to check understanding. • Pause to have students compare Flor and her actions to those of other people.	• Have students set a purpose for reading. Have them read silently and study the illustrations to clarify the text. • Have students read the selection aloud and discuss the Build Comprehension questions. Have students share illustration details that help them understand the text.

Phonics and Fluency

Verbs ending in *-ing*

Teach/Model Explain that verbs that show an action is taking place end in *-ing*, as in *lifting*. Tell students that sometimes the spelling changes when *-ing* is added to a verb. Say: *If a verb ends with a vowel and a consonant, double the final consonant and add -ing, as in skipping. If a verb ends with a silent e, drop the e before adding -ing, as in skating.* Display **Transparencies 51 and 52** from **Reach into Phonics** and work through the lesson.

Practice/Apply Display these sentences from "Doña Flor" and have students identify the verbs ending in *-ing*.

- She started knocking on the doors and calling her neighbors.
- The children have heard a huge mountain lion circling the village.

Then have students preview the story for more examples of *-ing* endings.

▶ Set a Purpose

1 Doña Flor is an unusual person.
Find out about her.

Every winter
morning when
the sun opened
one eye, Doña
Flor grabbed a
handful of snow from the
top of a nearby mountain. "Brrrrrrrr," she said,
rubbing the snow on her face to wake up.

Long, long ago, when Flor was a baby, her mother
sang to her in a voice sweet as river music. When Flor's
mother sang to her corn plants, they grew tall as trees.
When she sang to her baby, her sweet flower, Flor grew
and grew, too.

Some children laughed at her because she was
different. "¡Mira! Look! Big Foot!" they called when she
walked by.

"Flor talks funny," they whispered, because Flor
spoke to butterflies and grasshoppers. She spoke every **2**
language, even **rattler**.

In Other Words
◀ **rattler** rattlesnake

254

But soon Flor's friends and neighbors asked her for
help. Children late for school asked, "***Por favor***, Flor, could
you give us a ride?" She took just one of her giant steps
and was at the school door. **3** **4**

In Other Words
Por favor Please (in Spanish)

255

Technology Station
◉ NGReach.com

(MP3) Read with Me
◉ Play and read
along.

Comprehension Coach

◉ Use interactive
vocabulary support.
Automatically measure
fluency.

Build Comprehension, pages 254–255

1 **Set a Purpose** Read the introduction at the top of page 254 to help
students set the purpose.

2 **Problem and Solution** [MODEL] [GUIDE] [APPLY] What problem
does Flor have when she is young? Model identifying the problem for
students. Create a problem-solution chart to record the problem: The
children laugh at Flor because she is different. Ask students to help you
identify examples of why the children laugh at Flor. Record them in the
chart as examples. (She is very large. They call her big foot. She talks
funny and speaks to the animals.) Together, decide how Flor solves the
problem. (Flor is so helpful that people soon appreciate her size.)

3 **Author's Purpose** Why do you think the author is writing about
Flor? (to entertain or tell an amusing story)

4 **Genre: Tall Tale** What have you read so far that tells you this is a tall
tale? (Possible answers: The author exaggerates Flor's size and actions.
Flor is very, very big and can talk to the animals. She can carry all the
children and take them to school with one of her giant steps.) What other
stories do you know like this? Answers will vary.

Student Book pages 254–255

N **B**

**Concepts of Print:
Identify Title, Beginning
and End, Use Page Numbers**

Teach/Model Tell students to look at
page 253 "Doña Flor." Say "This is the title.
The words of the story are called the text.
That starts on page 254." Turn the page and
point to the page number. Say: "This is page
254." Continue to point to and name the page
numbers until you reach the end of the story.
Say: "This is page 265 where the story ends."

Practice/Apply Ask students to open the
story up to any page and give the book to a
partner. Have the partner use page numbers
and other text clues to identify where they are
in the story.

When Flor finally stopped growing, she built her own house, *una casa* big as a mountain and open as a canyon. She scooped a handful of dirt and made herself a valley for mixing clay, straw, and water. She added some *estrellas*. **1** The stars made the adobe shine. When she worked, Flor sang. Birds came and built nests in her hair. Flor wanted everyone to feel at home in her house. "**Mi casa es su casa**," she said to people, animals, and plants, so they **2** knew they were always welcome. Everyone called her **Doña** Flor because they respected her.

No one needed an alarm clock in Doña Flor's *pueblo*. When her hands, wide as plates, started pat-pat-patting tortillas, everyone in the village woke up. So her neighbors would have plenty to eat, she stacked her tortillas on the huge rock table in front of her house.

Flor's tortillas were the biggest, best tortillas in the whole wide world. People used the extra ones as roofs. *Mmmm*, the houses smelled corn-good when the sun was hot. In the summer, the children floated around the pond on tortilla rafts. **3**

In Other Words
Mi casa es su casa My house is your house (in Spanish)
Doña Lady; Mrs. (a show of respect in Spanish)
pueblo village (in Spanish)

▶ **Before You Move On**
4
1. **Character** What are three things Doña Flor can do that other people can't?
2. **Ask Questions** Look at the pictures on pages 256 and 257. What questions do you have about the story?

256 257

Student Book pages 256–257

B I A AH

Figurative Language: Simile

Teach/Model Remind students that a simile compares two things using the words *like* or *as*. Write common similes on the board, such as *brave as a lion, sick as a dog,* and *eats like a bird*. Explain that this type of language may help an author to exaggerate. Have students look on page 257 to find a simile that describes Flor's hands. Ask them to point to the sentence once they have found it and tell what it means (her hands were big).

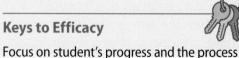

Keys to Efficacy

Focus on student's progress and the process they go through to answer a question—even if the answer to the question is incorrect.

Build Comprehension, pages 256–257

1 **Details** What does Flor add to her adobe mixture to make it shine? (*estrellas,* or stars)

2 **Character's Feelings** What does the phrase, *Mi casa es su casa* say about Flor's feelings toward the people and animals around her? (She was friendly and her home was open to everyone.)

3 **Clarify Language** What do you think the sentence "The houses smelled corn-good when the sun was hot" means? Remind students that some roofs were tortillas. Possible answer: When the sun shone on the roof, it smelled like a corn tortilla baking.

4 **Answers to Before You Move On**

1. **Character** Possible answer: Flor can build a house as big as a mountain. She took stars from the sky to decorate it. She can make giant tortillas the size of a roof.

2. **Ask Questions** MODEL | GUIDE | APPLY Use the Language Frames from page 250 to model how to ask questions about one of the pictures:

   • *I do not understand how someone could make such a big tortilla.*

   • *I ask myself how big Flor's hands are to make a tortilla this size?*

   • *I think about the size of the people to understand how big Flor must be.*

One warm spring day, while a family of lizards swept her house, Doña Flor brought out her stacks of fresh tortillas. Nobody came. *Hmmmmmmm,* thought Flor. She started knocking on doors and calling to her neighbors.

"*¿Qué pasa?* What's the matter?" she asked, bending down to **peer** into their small doors to see where they were hiding.

"*¡El puma!*" they whispered. "The children have heard a huge mountain lion circling the village. Listen!"

In Other Words
peer look
◀ *¡El puma!* The mountain lion! (in Spanish)

258

Doña Flor and her animal friends went out looking for the huge *gato*, but they couldn't find it. That night, she carried her tired friends, the coyotes and rabbits, back home. But just as she started to **tuck them in** and read them a good-night story, they all heard, "*Rrrr-oarrr!*" **6**

"Where *is* that darn cat?" asked Flor, but the scared animals were shaking and shivering under their sheets. **7**

That night, the wind got so angry that he blew the trees and houses first to the left and then to the right. Together, the wind and the giant cat roared all night, and nobody got much sleep.

In Other Words
gato cat (in Spanish)
tuck them in put them in their beds

▶ **Before You Move On**
8 1. **Problem/Solution** What is the problem, and how does Doña Flor try to solve it?
2. **Make Inferences** Why do you think the author describes the wind as if it were a person?

259

Build Comprehension, pages 258–259

5 **Predict** Read aloud the introduction at the top of page 258. Ask students to share their predictions.

6 **Character's Traits** How does Flor **interact** with animals? (She is friends with the animals; she takes care of them and protects them.)

7 **Draw Conclusions** Why do you think the other animals are afraid of the puma? (They may be afraid of being eaten.)

8 **Answers to Before You Move On**

1. **Problem/Solution** MODEL | GUIDE | APPLY Guide students in identifying the story problem. Ask: *Why don't the people want to come out of their homes?* They are afraid of the mountain lion. *What does Flor do about this?* She goes looking for the big cat.

2. **Make Inferences** Possible answer: The author describes the wind as if it were a person to help readers understand how fierce it is. The comparison is also a good exaggeration for a tall tale.

I **A** **AH**

Social Studies: Wild Animals

Introduce the concept: *More and more communities have the problem of wild animals wandering into cities and towns. Why do you think this is?* Many times people have built on the animal's homes and they have no place else to go. Discuss with students what city officials and animal control experts might be able to do to control the problem.

▶ Predict
1 How will Doña Flor find the giant cat?

As the sun rose, Flor's neighbors peered out their windows. Tired-looking Flor was giving that wind a big hug to quiet him down. Then she started her morning **chores**.

Doña Flor had work to do. But first she looked around the village. Where were her neighbors? Then she heard, "*Rrrr-oarrr! Rrrr-oarrr!*"

Flor **stomped off** to find the puma that was bothering her **amigos**. **Exhausted by afternoon**, Doña Flor still hadn't found that cat, so she sat outside the library for a rest.

In Other Words
chores activities
stomped off walked away angrily
amigos friends (in Spanish)
Exhausted by afternoon Tired from the morning activities

260

What can I do to cheer up my friends? wondered Flor. Now, Flor knew that her village needed *un río*, a river, so to make her neighbors happy, Doña Flor scratched **2 3** a new riverbed with her thumb. When the water **trickled** down the stones for the first time, Flor called out, "Just listen to that! Isn't that the prettiest sound you've ever heard?" She smiled, but today her neighbors could barely smile back. They were too worried about the mountain lion. Suddenly there was a terrible "*Rrrr-oarrr! Rrrr-oarrr!*" **4**

In Other Words
trickled flowed gently

261

Student Book pages 260–261

B I A AH

Literary Analysis: Genre

Teach/Model Remind students that tall tales use exaggeration in the story. Ask students how they can tell something is an exaggeration. Point to different illustrations and discuss what is exaggerated in that picture.

Practice/Apply Have student pairs work together to choose an exaggeration from one of the pictures in the story. Ask them to tell what the exaggeration might tell the reader about the character's size, ability, or role in the story.

Build Comprehension, pages 260–261

1 **Predict** Read aloud the question at the top of page 260 to help students make predictions.

2 **Relate to Personal Experience** Flor tries to cheer up her friends by making them a river. What kinds of things do you do to try to cheer up your friends?

3 **Use Key Words** How might a river **benefit** the people of the village? (Possible answers: A river would benefit the villagers because they wouldn't have to go far for water or for fish. They would be able to water their crops.)

4 **Ask Questions** MODEL | GUIDE | APPLY Guide students to ask questions about how the people responded to the river that Doña Flor made. Encourage them to use the language frames. Ask: *What don't you understand about the people's reaction? What could you ask yourself?* (Why didn't the people seem happy? What else were they thinking about?) Ask: *Where could you find the answers to your questions?* (in the text)

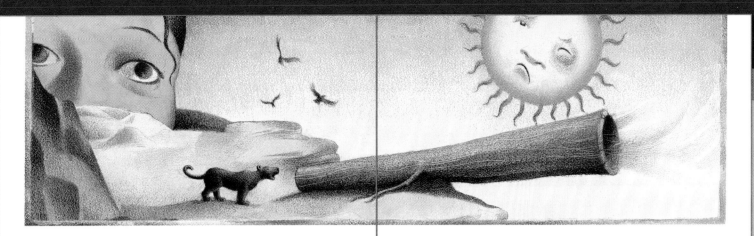

Where is that big monster gato? Doña Flor wondered. *I know,* thought Flor, *I'll go to my animal friends for help.*

"Go quietly to the tallest **mesa**," said the deer. **5**

Doña Flor walked very, very softly up to the tallest mesa. She looked around carefully for the giant cat. Then right near her she heard, "*Rrrr-oarrr! Rrrr-oarrr!*" Flor jumped so high, she bumped into the sun and gave him a black eye. **6**

Flor looked around. All she saw was the back of a cute little puma.

Doña Flor began to **tiptoe** toward the puma when all of a sudden he roared into a long, hollow log. The sound became a huge "*Rrrr-oarrr!*" that echoed down into the valley.

Now, the little puma thought the loud noise was so funny that he rolled on his back and started laughing and laughing—until he saw big Doña Flor.

Aha! thought Flor. "Are you the **chico** who's causing all the trouble?" she asked. The little puma tried to look very fierce. "*Rrrr-oarrr!*" he growled, but without the log, the growl wasn't really very fierce. **7**

In Other Words
mesa plateau

In Other Words
tiptoe walk quietly
chico little one (in Spanish)

▶ **Before You Move On**
8
1. **Problem/Solution** How does Doña Flor find the puma?
2. **Ask Questions** What questions do you have about her behavior towards the puma?

262

263

Build Comprehension, pages 262–263

5 **Use Key Words** Where in the **landscape** was the puma hiding? (The puma was hiding on the tallest mesa.)

6 **Summarize** How did the sun get a black eye in the story? (Flor jumped so high that she bumped into the sun and gave him a black eye.)

7 **Cultural Connections** Why does Flor call the puma *chico*? (Flor is so large that the puma is a "little one to her.")

8 **Answers to Before You Move On**

1. **Problem/Solution** MODEL | GUIDE | APPLY Flor asks her animal friends for help in finding the giant cat. They tell her to go quietly to the highest mesa to find it. Ask a volunteer to read aloud the sentences that show this.

2. **Ask Questions** MODEL | GUIDE | APPLY Possible answers: Why isn't Flor afraid of the puma? What will Flor do with the puma?

▸ **Predict**

1 What will happen to the puma?

Doña Flor just smiled at that brave cat and said, "Why, you're just a kitten to me, **Pumito**." She bent down and scratched that puma behind the ears, and she whispered to him in cat talk until that cat began to purr. **2**

Suddenly Flor heard a new noise. "Doña Flor, *¿dónde estás?* Where are you?" called her worried neighbors. Even though they were frightened, they had all come, holding hands, looking for her.

"Meet my new *amigo*," said Doña Flor.

That evening, Flor **plucked** a star and **plunked** it on the tallest tree so her friends in the *pueblo* could find their way home.

Flor reached up and filled her arms with clouds smelling of flowery breezes. She shaped the clouds into a soft, deep bed and into hills of puffy pillows. "*Mmmm*," said Flor as she snuggled in the clouds.

"Tonight, I'm very tired after my adventure with the giant cat, right, Pumito?" **chuckled** Doña Flor. All the animals **snuggled** down with her, and Pumito stretched out over her big toes. ❖

In Other Words
Pumito Little Puma (in Spanish)
plucked picked
plunked put

In Other Words
chuckled laughed
snuggled lay

▸ **Before You Move On**
3 1. **Confirm Prediction** What happens to the puma after Flor discovers his secret?
2. **Ask Questions** Look at the pictures on this page. What questions do you have about the ending of the story?

264

265

Student Book pages 264–265

I A AH

Fluency: Expression

Teach/Model Explain the concept: *Fluent readers read with expression. They change their voices to show feelings they get from the text.* Direct students' attention to pages 264–265. Say: *How does Flor feel? It must be a relief that the animal did not turn out to be a danger to her friends.* Play the selection recording or read aloud page 264, emphasizing the rhythm and rhyme and the relief of finding that the animal is harmless.

Practice Have partners read the page aloud together several times, mimicking the expression you modeled.

Keys to Efficacy

If students seem overwhelmed, don't overdo it. Too many questions can lead to a loss of comprehension. Focus on the main points that students should know.

Build Comprehension, pages 264–265

1 **Predict** Read the introduction and have students make predictions.

2 **Use Key Words** How does Flor **interact** with the puma? (She treats it like a little kitten. She calls it *chico* and *Pumito*.

3 **Answers to Before You Move On**
1. **Confirm Prediction** The puma becomes friends with Flor. Ask students how the ending compares to their predictions.
2. **Ask Questions** MODEL | GUIDE | APPLY Possible answer: How will the puma get along with the other animals?

Meet the Author/Illustrator, pages 266–267

Have students chorally read the Meet the Author and Illustrator copy.

1 **Writer's Craft** Ask: *What examples can you find where Pat Mora gave nonhuman things human qualities?* Possible answers: *lizards swept Flor's house* (page 258), *the wind got angry* (page 259) *the little puma rolled on his back and started laughing* (page 263).

Pat Mora

"I love landscapes," says Pat Mora. Desert landscapes are a huge theme in her work. That's not surprising. She grew up in El Paso, Texas, a city in the middle of a desert.

El Paso is also near the border between the United States and Mexico. "In my house, we spoke both Spanish and English," she says. Today, her books are published in both languages.

Ms. Mora grew up with tall tales about Paul Bunyan and Babe the Blue Ox. She decided to write this tall tale about a woman named Doña Flor. "The amazing thing about her, was, that she is so connected to the land, and that her heart is so generous," she says.

◄ Pat Mora, like her character Doña Flor, loves to read.

Writer's Craft

On page 262, Pat Mora writes: "Doña Flor jumped so high she gave the sun a black eye." Find other parts of the story where the author gives human qualities to non-human things. Now write your own sentence that gives human qualities to an object or animal.

1

2

Raúl Colón

Meet the Illustrator

What does the wind look like? If you are an illustrator, you ask yourself questions like that. Then you start sketching. Raúl Colón thought a lot about the wind before he began drawing. He says, "I came up with a big open-mouth face, breathing the wind in and breathing the wind out."

Mr. Colón started drawing when he was young. "I learned how to draw the human body using comic books," he says. As a boy, he spent hours copying pictures of superheroes in action.

Today, Raúl Colón makes illustrations with watercolors and colored pencils. He had a lot of fun creating the pictures for *Doña Flor.* "I was fascinated to be able to draw this giant walking around the landscape," he says.

3

As a young boy, Raúl Colón lived in Puerto Rico. Today he lives in New York City. ▶

266   267

Student Book pages 266–267

Daily Writing A AH

2 **Writer's Craft** Explain: *Like Pat Mora, and Raúl Colón, you can give human qualities to nonhuman things. Start by thinking about how your characters will act and speak…* Use the **Modeled Writing Routine** to write sentences that describe these animals or objects in human terms. (See **Writing Routines,** page PD54.)

Think Aloud	Write
I'll write about a tree using its branches as arms. I can draw the tree with arms, too.	The tree creaked when it saw the little bird tumble from the nest. Quickly, it reached out an arm and caught the little bird.

Have students write and illustrate their sentences in their journals.

3 **Writing Project: Draft a Tall Tale** Have students draft their Writing Projects. (See page T277.)

Meet the Author

Encourage students to read more books written by Pat Mora.

-*Tomas and the Library Lady*
-*Birthday Basket for Tia*
-*The Night the Moon Fell*
-*The Rainbow Tulip*

CLOSE AND ASSESS

• **Ask Questions** *What questions did you ask while reading the story?*

• **Vocabulary** *How would you use the Key Word* **benefit** *to talk about Flor's relationship with the people?*

• **Problem/Solution** *What was the main problem in the story? What was the solution?*

Day 4

Day at a Glance:
- ▶ **Language:** Forms of *have* and Modals
- ▶ **Vocabulary:** Share Word Knowledge
- ▶ **Reading:** Think and Respond
- ▶ **Writing:** Write About It; Revise

OBJECTIVES

Vocabulary
- Use Academic Vocabulary ❶
- Use Grade-Level Vocabulary ❶

Grammar
- Identify and Use Forms of *have* and Modals ❶
- Collaborate with Peers

Resources

- ⊘ *eVisual 4.22*
- ↻ ⊘ *Practice Master 4.17*
- 📷 ⊘ *Language Builder Picture Card E51*

Differentiate

Language Transfer

Issue The verb *have* can cause difficulty for English language learners:

- In Chinese languages, Haitian Creole, Hmong, Korean, and Vietnamese, a verb is not inflected for person and number. Students may say *The hat have stripes* instead of *The hat has stripes*.

- In addition, in Korean, the verb *be* is used in place of *have*. Students may say, *I am hat* instead of *I have a hat*.

- In Spanish, the verb *have* is used to express states of being, such as age or hunger. Students may say, *She has ten years* instead of *She is ten years old*.

Strategy Provide practice, having students repeat sentences as you describe the class. *Felix has a red shirt, All the boys have sneakers, Two girls have short hair.*

Language of the Day

What are some **elements** of a tall tale?
A tall tale may have _____ .

Read the Language of the Day. Model: *I tall tale may have unusual characters.* Have each student repeat your sentence and add something they learned about tall tales.

Grammar Forms of *have* and Modals ⬛B ⬛I ⬜A ⬛AH

❶ **Teach/Model** Focus attention: *Like am, is and are, the verbs has and have are not action verbs. Write and read aloud these sentences: Doña Flor has many friends. They have a problem with a puma.* Circle *has* and *have*; then display the chart.

Grammar Rules

1. Use *has* or *have* to tell what belongs to someone or something.	The birds *have* a nest in Flor's hair. The puma *has* a mighty roar.
2. Use *can* plus a main verb to tell what something is able to do.	Flor *can speak* the language of animals.
3. Use *could, may,* and *might* plus a main verb to tell what is possible.	The puma *might harm* the people.
4. Use *should* plus a main verb to tell what is the right thing to do.	Flor *should help* her friends. They *shouldn't* worry.

Ⓝ **NGReach.com** ▶ *eVisual 4.22*

Read aloud rule 1 and have volunteers read the sample sentences. Ask students to provide their own examples. Then call on volunteers to read the other rules and sentences. Point out that these sentences use helping verbs. Help students distinguish between the ability to do something and the possibility of a thing happening. Have students give examples of what they can do and what they could or might do. Discuss also the contraction *shouldn't*. Model how to form negative contractions and how to use them.

❷ **Practice/Apply** Have partners refer to the chart and talk about the characters in "Doña Flor." During their discussion, each pair writes down one sentence that uses *has, have,* or a modal and shares it with the class. Have students play the game on **Practice Master 4.15**.

CHECK UNDERSTANDING Have students respond to these questions: *What can you do? What could you do if you practice more? What should you do?* Have them identify the main verb and the helping verb in each response.

Share Word Knowledge

3 **Teach/Model** To connect concepts, say: *Yesterday you became Key Word experts. Today you will share what you know about your Key Words.* Pair each student with a partner who studied a different word. Have partners follow the steps of **Vocabulary Routine 3** to share their word knowledge. (See **Vocabulary Routine 3**, page PD39.)

- Take turns reading Key Word visuals.
- Talk about how the pictures on the visuals show the meanings of the Key Words.
- Create sentences using Key Words and write them in your journals.
- Draw a line under each Key Word.

4 **Practice/Apply** Regroup students so that each Key Word is represented by a student expert. Have students share what they know about their Key Words and then work with the group to use all the words in different word sorts. Students might, for example, group words by part of speech, number of syllables, or by concept. Then have groups share their word sorts with the class. (see **Cooperative Learning Routines,** pages PD58–PD59.) Repeat until all the words are discussed.

Jigsaw

> **CHECK UNDERSTANDING** Display the **Language Builder Picture Card E51** and ask students to use Key Words to tell about it.

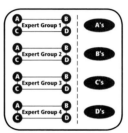

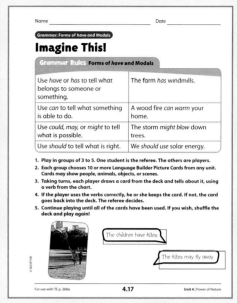

Name _____ Date _____

Grammar: Forms of *have* and Modals

Imagine This!

Grammar Rules Forms of *have* and Modals

Use *have* or *has* to tell what belongs to someone or something.	The farm *has* windmills.
Use *can* to tell what something is able to do.	A wood fire *can* warm your home.
Use *could, may,* or *might* to tell what is possible.	The storm *might* blow down trees.
Use *should* to tell what is right.	We *should* use solar energy.

1. Play in groups of 3 to 5. One student is the referee. The others are players.
2. Each group chooses 10 or more Language Builder Picture Cards from any unit. Cards may show people, animals, objects, or scenes.
3. Taking turns, each player draws a card from the deck and tells about it, using a verb from the chart.
4. If the player uses the verbs correctly, he or she keeps the card. If not, the card goes back into the deck. The referee decides.
5. Continue playing until all of the cards have been used. If you wish, shuffle the deck and play again!

For use with TE p. 268a **4.17** Unit 4 | Power of Nature

Practice Master 4.17

Day 4

continued

Day at a Glance:
▶ **Grammar:** Forms of *have*
▶ **Vocabulary:** Share Word Knowledge
▶ **Reading:** Sequence
▶ **Writing:** Write About It; Revise

OBJECTIVES

Vocabulary
• Use Grade-Level Vocabulary ⊕
• Use Academic Vocabulary ⊕

Language
• Language Function: Express Needs and Wants ⊕

Fluency
• Expression

Literary Analysis
• Analyze Genre: Tall Tale
• Analyze Character

Test-Taking Strategies
• Understand the Question
• Practice and Apply Strategies

Writing
• Write a Response to a Tall Tale
• Writing Project: Revise a Tall Tale

Resources

 eVisual 4.23

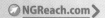 NGReach.com

See **Technology Station** for digital student resources.

 I · A · AH

Fluency: Expression

Teach/Model Review expression (pages T264–265). Display this reminder: *Change your voice to match what you are reading. Think about how the characters might say the words.*

Practice Have partners work together to practice reading pages 264–265. Encourage them to decide how to read Doña Flor's words and the words of her neighbors. After partners have practiced reading the pages, have them take turns reading aloud to other partnerships for feedback.

Think and Respond

① Talk About It Prompt students to cite evidence from the text. Remind students to use Key Words in their answers. If students have difficulty, help them use the sentence frames to form their answers.

1. **Genre** Discuss how a tall tale differs from other fiction stories. Possible answers: This story is a tall tale because Flor is an exaggerated character. Another example is that Flor can **interact** with and **modify** nature in ways that others cannot.

2. **Express Needs and Wants** Prompt students by asking: *What did the children want when they were late for school? What did they need Flor to do for them?*

3. **Ask Questions** Student responses should reflect the idea that, to a normal person, the puma would pose a threat. It is a wild cat, a predator, and could have attacked the children.

② Test-Taking Strategies: Understand the Question Explain: *When taking a test, read each question carefully.* Discuss how to understand the question. Remind students that when they put the question in their own words, it should still ask the same thing.

Understand the Question
1. Read the question carefully.
2. Rephrase the question. Put the question in your own words.
3. Read the question again. Say it silently to yourself.

Read the sample question. Ask: *What is another way to ask this question?* (What did the people do with the extra tortillas?)

How did the people in the village use the extra tortillas that Doña Flor made?
A. They ate the tortillas for breakfast.
B. They used the tortillas as roofs and rafts.
C. They used the tortillas as an alarm clock.
D. They were the best tortillas in the world.

NGReach.com ▶ eVisual 4.23

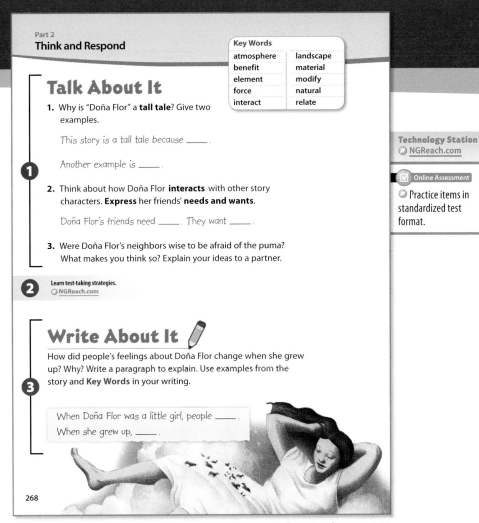

Part 2
Think and Respond

Key Words

atmosphere	landscape
benefit	material
element	modify
force	natural
interact	relate

Talk About It

1. Why is "Doña Flor" a **tall tale**? Give two examples.

This story is a tall tale because _____ .

Another example is _____ .

2. Think about how Doña Flor **interacts** with other story characters. **Express** her friends' **needs and wants**.

Doña Flor's friends need _____ . They want _____ .

3. Were Doña Flor's neighbors wise to be afraid of the puma? What makes you think so? Explain your ideas to a partner.

2 Learn test-taking strategies.
 NGReach.com

Write About It

How did people's feelings about Doña Flor change when she grew up? Why? Write a paragraph to explain. Use examples from the story and **Key Words** in your writing.

> When Doña Flor was a little girl, people _____ .
> When she grew up, _____ .

Technology Station
 NGReach.com

☑ Online Assessment
 Practice items in standardized test format.

268

Student Book page 268

Daily Writing A AH

3 **Write About It** Read aloud the directions. Point out the sentence frames: *You can use these sentence frames to begin your paragraph.* Use the **Independent Writing Routine** to help students put their thoughts in writing, using the Key Words and the sentence frames. (See **Writing Routines**, page PD56.)

Say	Write
I know that some children laughed at Flor because she was different.	When Doña Flor was a little girl, people laughed at her because she was large.

Have students use these ideas or their own to write a paragraph in their journal.

4 **Writing Project: Revise** Have students revise their Writing Project compositions. (See pages PD56.)

Remind students that sometimes they must rephrase their spoken sentences when they write them so they sound better. They should also make sure they use correct grammar when writing their sentences.

CLOSE AND ASSESS

- **Language** *Give me a sentence using* can *and a sentence using* could. *How are they different?*

- **Reading** *What are some questions you can ask about how Doña Flor interacts with the other characters in the story?*

- **Vocabulary** *What are some of the* **elements** *of nature mentioned in the story?*

Day 5

Day at a Glance:
▶ **Language:** Adjust Your Speech for Audience   ▶ **Reading:** Reread and Retell
▶ **Vocabulary:** Apply Word Knowledge   ▶ **Writing:** Edit and Proofread

Objectives

Vocabulary
• Use Academic Vocabulary ❶
• Use Grade-Level Vocabulary ❶

Listening and Speaking
• Adjust Your Speech for Your Audience ❶

Learning and Teamwork Strategies
• Relate to Personal Experience Review

Media and Technology
• Build Concepts from Media

Resources

⊘ *eVisual 4.24*

✎⊘ *Practice Master 4.18*

• *coin and markers for Vocabulary Game*

Differentiate

How to Learn Language

Relate to Personal Experience
Explain: *Your personal experience can help you understand the difference between unfamiliar words, such as* formal *and* informal. *Think about how you talk to your friends. Your language is informal. Think about how you talk to an adult or someone you do not know well, such as a storeowner. Your language is more formal.*

Have students share words and phrases they use with friends and with people they do not know well. Record their responses in a chart and model using the examples of formal and informal language.

Language of the Day

What natural elements do people need and use?
People need and use _____ .

Read the Language of the Day. Model: *People need and use trees for wood.* Have all students complete the sentence frame, trying not to repeat a previous suggestion. Explain that today students will learn how to adjust their speech, play a word game, retell the story, and write about it.

Adjust Your Speech for Your Audience

❶ **Teach/Model** Introduce: *Think about the way you talk with your friends. Do you speak to a friend differently than you speak to an adult?* Explain: *We use informal or friendly language with people we know well. We use formal or polite language with adults and people we do not know well.*

Display the how to card. Show how the speaker would probably talk to a friend's mother, then model the language for a more informal phone call between two friends.

How to Adjust Your Speech for Your Audience

1. Use formal or polite language to speak with adults or people you do not know well.	Hi, Mrs. Reyes. This is Tanya Adams. May I speak with Tina?
2. Use informal or friendly language to speak with friends and people you know well.	Hey, Tina. It's me, Tanya.

⊘ NGReach.com ▶ eVisual 4.24

❷ **Practice/Apply** Have students work with partners to practice adjusting their speech for different audiences. Suggest topics they might discuss and possible audiences. Teach the **How to Learn Language** strategy to help students as they speak.

> **CHECK UNDERSTANDING** Talk to a volunteer about a familiar topic. Ask students if you are talking to a friend or someone you do not know well. Ask them how they could tell if you were using formal or informal language.

Apply Word Knowledge

③ Teach/Model Display **Practice Master 4.16** and explain how to play "Word Race":

- *Write the Key Words in any order on the Practice Master. Use every Key Word at least once.*

- *Flip a coin to see how many spaces to move your marker. Move 1 space for Heads and 2 spaces for Tails.*

- *Read the word on the space. Tell what the word means and use it in a sentence. For example: The word is* **atmosphere***. Atmosphere is the air around Earth. Clouds form in the atmosphere.*

- *Take turns with your partner. The first one to reach the Finish, wins.*

④ Practice/Apply Distribute markers and Practice Masters. Have students write the Key Words on their Practice Masters. Clarify: *Make sure you write every Key Word once. If you have an extra space, you can use a word again.*

Explain that as partners play the game, they should verify their partner's definitions and sentences. Encourage them to offer help or advice in reading, defining, or using Key Words correctly.

Monitor students as they follow your instructions. Restate the instructions as required.

For vocabulary games, go to NGReach.com.

> **CHECK UNDERSTANDING** Call on students, giving each a different Key Word to define and use in an oral sentence.

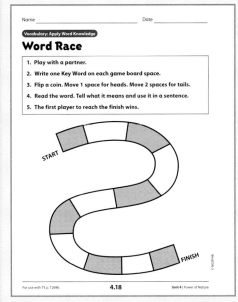

Practice Master 4.18

Part 2 Vocabulary Skills Trace		Page
Day 1	Science Vocabulary	T247
Day 2	Academic Vocabulary	T249
Day 3	Expand Word Knowledge	T252b
Day 4	Share Word Knowledge	T268b
Day 5	**Apply Word Knowledge**	**T269b**
Day 6	Multiple-Meaning Words	T270
Day 7	Multiple-Meaning Words	T275
Days 8–9	Extend Vocabulary	T276e–f
Day 10	Vocabulary Review	T276g–h

OBJECTIVES

Vocabulary
• Use Academic Vocabulary **T**
• Use Grade-Level Vocabulary **T**

Language
• Compare Genres
• Participate in Discussion
• Retell the Story

Learning and Teamwork Strategies
• Use Graphic Organizers: Problem and Solution Chart
• Reason Deductively

Fluency
• Read with Accuracy and Rate **T**
• Read with Expression **T**

Writing
• Writing Project: Edit and Proofread

Social Studies
• Explore Elements of Nature

Resources

📀 🌐 *Practice Master 4.19*

📀 *Practice Master 4.20*

🌐 *Comprehension Coach*

🌐 **NGReach.com** ▶

See **Technology Station** for digital student resources.

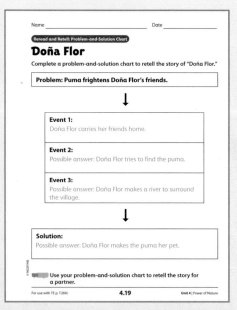

🌐 🌐 **Practice Master 4.19**

Reread and Retell

① **Problem and Solution** Read the introduction and reinforce: *The problem is something a character must solve. The solution tells how the character solves the problem.* Read through the example problem-and-solution chart and callouts. Explain: *When the puma frightens Doña Flor's friends, one action she takes is to carry them home.*

Have students complete **Practice Master 4.19**.

② **Retell** Read aloud the directions and language frame. Display the **Retelling a Story Rubric**. Have partners take turns retelling the story to a friend or an adult. Remind them to include the problem, what Doña Flor did to solve it, and the solution. Provide the Key Points Reading (**Practice Master 4.16**) for students who need additional support.

Retelling a Story Rubric		
Scale	**Content**	**Language**
B	☐ Problem, solution, and events are missing or misstated.	☐ Frequently hard to hear or understand. ☐ Is unable to adjust language for the intended audience.
I	☐ Identifies the problem and some events that lead to the solution.	☐ Is often hard to hear or understand. ☐ Attempts to adjust language for the intended audience.
A	☐ Identifies the problem and most events that lead to the solution.	☐ Can be understood most of the time. ☐ Use some language aimed at the intended audience.
AH	☐ Identifies the problem and all events that lead to the solution.	☐ Speaks clearly and is easily understood ☐ Adjusts language for the intended audience.

Fluency Accuracy, Rate, and Expression I A AH

③ **Fluency** Have students record their reading on the **Comprehension Coach** to assess each student's progress for rate and accuracy. Have students use the passage on **Practice Master 4.20** to record their reading for expression. Listen to each recording and assess students' ability to read with expression.

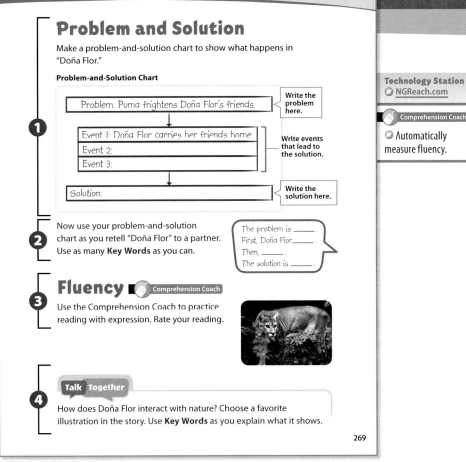

Problem and Solution

Make a problem-and-solution chart to show what happens in "Doña Flor."

Problem-and-Solution Chart

1

| Problem: Puma frightens Doña Flor's friends. | → Write the problem here. |

Event 1: Doña Flor carries her friends home
Event 2:
Event 3:
→ Write events that lead to the solution.

Solution: → Write the solution here.

2 Now use your problem-and-solution chart as you retell "Doña Flor" to a partner. Use as many **Key Words** as you can.

The problem is _____.
First, Doña Flor_____.
Then, _____.
The solution is _____.

Fluency Comprehension Coach

3 Use the Comprehension Coach to practice reading with expression. Rate your reading.

Talk Together

4 How does Doña Flor interact with nature? Choose a favorite illustration in the story. Use **Key Words** as you explain what it shows.

269

Student Book page 269

Technology Station
NGReach.com

Comprehension Coach

Automatically measure fluency.

Practice Master 4.20

4 **Talk Together** Ask students how the main character **interacts** with nature in "Doña Flor." Read aloud the directions and have students jot down notes for their responses. Then have students share their ideas. Students should add their ideas to their unit concept maps.

Daily Writing

5 **Writing Project: Edit and Proofread a Tall Tale**
Have students edit and proofread their Writing Project compositions. (See page T279.)

Keys to Efficacy
Provide prompts students can use to help one another: *You might want to add _____. You could write _____.*

CLOSE AND ASSESS
- **Language** *What did you like about "Doña Flor"? Use appropriate language as you talk.*
- **Reading** *What problem did Doña Flor try to solve?* (People in her village were afraid of a puma.) *How did she solve the problem?* (She made the puma a pet.)
- **Vocabulary** *How do you interact with nature?* (Answers will vary.)

Day 6

Day at a Glance:
- **Language:** Express Needs and Wants
- **Vocabulary:** Multiple-Meaning Words
- **Reading:** Read the Selection
- **Writing:** Writing Fluency; Publish and Share

OBJECTIVES

Vocabulary
- Use Academic Vocabulary ⊕
- Use Grade-Level Vocabulary ⊕
- Strategy: Determine Meaning of Multiple-Meaning Words ⊕

Language
- Language Function: Express Needs and Wants ⊕
- Use a Variety of Language Structures ⊕

Learning and Teamwork Strategies
- Make Appropriate Contributions
- Build on Ideas

Resources

- eVisual 4.25
- eVisual 4.26

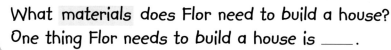

Language of the Day

What **materials** does Flor need to build a house?
One thing Flor needs to build a house is _____.

Read the Language of the Day. Model: *One thing Flor needs to build a house is clay.* Call on volunteers to complete the language frame. Refer students to the selection as needed. Then explain that today students will learn more about expressing needs and wants.

Express Needs and Wants

❶ Teach/Model Review how to express needs and wants. Connect concepts: *Doña Flor needed certain things to build her house. You need tools to build a house. You may want other things, also, like friends to help you build.*

Display the chart and read it aloud.

Tell What You Are Doing	Tell About Your Needs and Wants
I am painting my room.	I need a paintbrush. I would like some help.
We are going to play baseball.	We need a bat. We want a good pitcher.
My sister is playing the drums.	I need earplugs. I want some peace and quiet.

NGReach.com > eVisual 4.25

Brainstorm with students a list of activities or things they might do. Point to an item on the list, for example, *planning a skit.* Say: *We are planning a skit. What do we need?* Call on students to express a need that fits the topic.

❷ Practice/Apply Have groups of four express wants and needs in a **Roundtable**. Ask one student to choose a topic from the list and begin with an opening statement, such as: *The school is having a fair.* Have other students respond with things that are needed for that activity. Continue until each student has a chance to present an opening statement. Use **Academic Language Frames** to provide ideas to support every language level.

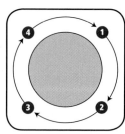

Roundtable

> **CHECK UNDERSTANDING** Call on students to share their weekend plans and tell what they need for that activity.

Differentiate

Academic Language Frames

Express Needs and Wants
- ■ I am _____.
  I need _____.
  I want _____.
- ■ I am going to _____.
  I need _____ to _____.
  I would like _____.
- ▪ I am going to _____.
- ■ I must have _____ because _____.
  We want to _____.
  We need _____.

NGReach.com > eVisual 4.26

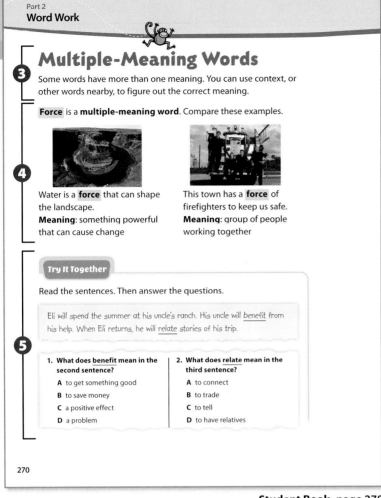

Multiple-Meaning Words

3 Some words have more than one meaning. You can use context, or other words nearby, to figure out the correct meaning.

Force is a **multiple-meaning word**. Compare these examples.

4

Water is a **force** that can shape the landscape.
Meaning: something powerful that can cause change

This town has a **force** of firefighters to keep us safe.
Meaning: group of people working together

Try It Together

Read the sentences. Then answer the questions.

Eli will spend the summer at his uncle's ranch. His uncle will _benefit_ from his help. When Eli returns, he will _relate_ stories of his trip.

5

1. What does **benefit** mean in the second sentence?
   A to get something good
   B to save money
   C a positive effect
   D a problem

2. What does **relate** mean in the third sentence?
   A to connect
   B to trade
   C to tell
   D to have relatives

270

Student Book page 270

Multiple-Meaning Words

3 **Teach** Read the introduction and write these sentences:

The balloon floated over the tree and up into the **atmosphere***.*

The balloons and decorations give the room a happy atmosphere.

Say: *I can use context to figure out the meanings of* atmosphere*. The words* "floated over the tree" *help me decide that* atmosphere *means "the air around Earth." The words* balloons *and* decorations *make me think of a party; they make the room seem happy.* Ask: *What might* atmosphere *mean here?* (the mood or feeling)

4 **Model** Have volunteers read the explanation and first sentence for **force**. Model using context clues to determine meaning. Compare your meaning to the one in the text. Repeat for second meaning of *force*.

5 **Practice/Apply** Read aloud the directions. Have students look for context clues to determine the meaning of the highlighted words. Then have partners work together to answer the questions. Use the **Multi-Level Practice Sets** to help students at varying levels identify multiple-meaning words.

> **CHECK UNDERSTANDING** Ask: *What might the word* current *mean in this sentence: When you flip the light switch,* current *flows through the wires.* (movement of electricity)

Differentiate

Multi-Level Practice Sets

N My new coat is *orange* and black. (color) I picked an *orange* from a fruit tree. (a fruit)

B The frog sat on the *bank* of the river. (edge) I put my money in the *bank*. (a place to keep money)

I Do you have *change* for the snack machine? (coins) I will *change* the light bulb in the lamp. (replace)

A I made a list of the story's *key* events. (main) You need a *key* to open that door. (tool for locking and unlocking)

AH The music teacher will *supply* us with instruments. (provide) The school nurse keeps a *supply* of bandages. (amount)

Use previous Key Words also.

> *express*
> *range*
> *plain*
> *surface*
> *border*

My new coat is *plain* black. (with no pattern or decoration) Large herds of bison covered the *plain*. (large, flat area of land)

Part 2 Vocabulary Skills Trace		Page
Day 1	Science Vocabulary	T247
Day 2	Academic Vocabulary	T249
Day 3	Expand Word Knowledge	T252b
Day 4	Share Word Knowledge	T268b
Day 5	Apply Word Knowledge	T269b
Day 6	**Multiple-Meaning Words**	**T270**
Day 7	Multiple-Meaning Words	T275
Days 8–9	Extend Vocabulary	T276e–f
Day 10	Vocabulary Review	T276g–h

Day 6
continued

Day at a Glance:
▸ **Language:** Express Needs and Wants
▸ **Vocabulary:** Multiple-Meaning Words
⊙ **Reading:** Read the Selection
⊙ **Writing:** Writing Fluency; Publish and Share

OBJECTIVES

Vocabulary
- Use Academic Vocabulary ⊕
- Use Grade-Level Content Vocabulary ⊕
- Use Context Clues for Unfamiliar Words

Language
- Listen to a Preview
- Concepts of Print: Identify a Paragraph

Reading Strategies
- Plan: Preview Purpose
- Make Connections: Text to Self ⊕

Literary Analysis
- Relate Poetic Structure and Form
- Recognize Genre: Lyrical Poetry

Learning and Teamwork Strategies
- Use Prereading Supports
- Build Background Knowledge
- Use Reading Supports

Resources

 Practice Master 4.21

Read Lyrical Poetry

❶ Connect Across Texts Read aloud the introduction. Say: *You read how Doña Flor relates to nature. Now you will read how these poets view the* natural *world.*

❷ Genre Read aloud the explanation. Point to the first stanza of "The Sun in Me." Clarify: *In many poems, lines are grouped into stanzas, just like sentences are grouped into paragraphs.* Use your first finger and thumb to mark the first stanza. Have students follow along, marking off each stanza and counting the stanzas aloud.

❸ Preview and Build Background Use sheltering strategies as you conduct a picture walk.

Pages	Say (and Do)
271	*This poem's title is "Comida." Who can tell me what* comida *means in Spanish? Yes, it means food. The poet compares foods to elements of nature. Look carefully at the picture. What is round like a tortilla?* (the moon) *What is hot like chile peppers?* (fire) *What is brown like frijoles, or beans?* (the earth, soil)
272–273	*The poem "The Sun in Me" is about parts of nature that the poet feels connected to—sun, wind, sea, river, and moon. Where do you see each of these in the artwork?* (Point to the sun, the wind lines near the birds, the waves, and the water.) *What other parts of nature do you see?* (Point to the animals, stars, and ice.) *Are there parts of nature that you feel connected to?*

❹ Read "Comida" and "The Sun in Me" Scaffold the support for varied reading levels.

BELOW LEVEL	ON/ABOVE LEVEL
Listen and Read Aloud	**Read and Grow Vocabulary**
• Ask students to set a purpose for listening. Have them track the print as you read aloud. Then have them read chorally. • Check understanding with selected Build Comprehension questions.	• After you read each poem, have students write one unfamiliar word, what they think it means, and clues to its meaning. See **Practice Master 4.21**. • Use the Build Comprehension questions during the reading. After reading, have students look up their words, write the dictionary definitions, and compare them to their meanings derived from context.

CHECK UNDERSTANDING *What is special about poetry?* (It is grouped into stanzas. The poet uses words to create feelings and images in your mind.)

Name _____ Date _____

Reading Options: Word Detective

"Comida"

Write down a word you don't know from each poem. Write what you think it means and your clues. Then look up the word in the dictionary.

📖 **Word Detective** 📖

New Word: _____
What I think it means: _____
🔍 Clues: _____
📖 Definition: _____

"The Sun in Me"

📖 **Word Detective** 📖

New Word: _____
What I think it means: _____
🔍 Clues: _____
📖 Definition: _____

Work with a partner to learn new words. Take turns reading aloud your words, the clues you used to understand them, and the dictionary definition. Challenge each other to use the new words in sentences.

For use with TE page 271a   **4.21**   Unit 4 | Power of Nature

 Practice Master 4.21

Connect Across Texts Read these poems about other ways we **relate** to nature.

Genre **Lyrical poetry** expresses feelings. This form of poetry can be free verse. Some free verse is made up of stanzas, or groups of lines separated by space.

Nature INSIDE Us

2 Comida
by **Victor M. Valle**

One eats
the moon in a tortilla
Eat *frijoles*
and you eat the earth
Eat chile
and you eat sun and fire
Drink water
and you drink sky **1**

In Other Words
Comida Food (in Spanish)
frijoles beans (in Spanish) ▶
chile hot peppers

▶ **Before You Move On**
3
1. **Ask Questions** Think of the objects compared in the poem. What questions do you have about them?
2. **Figurative Language** Which words help you imagine how chile tastes?

271

Student Book page 271

Build Comprehension, page 271

1 **Poetry** Lyrical poetry expresses feelings. What feelings do you think the poet has about food and nature? (Possible responses: He seems to appreciate food that comes from nature. He feels that food helps him **relate** to nature.

2 **Use Visuals** How does the artwork help you better understand the words in the poem? (It suggests relationships the poet sees between foods and parts of nature. For example, a tortilla and the moon are both round in shape. Beans grow in the earth and are brown like the soil.)

3 **Answers to Before You Move On**
1. **Ask Questions** **RETEACH** Review how to ask questions of the author (page T250). Then guide students in answering the question. I ask myself, How are the sky and water related? I think that some water (rain) comes from the sky.

2. **Figurative Language** sun and fire

Cultural Perspectives: Food
Explain that the poem "Comida" talks about foods that were first eaten in Mexico, Central America, and South America. People from these places brought the foods with them to the United States, where many people now eat them. There are many other foods commonly eaten in the United States that come from a particular culture. Ask students to make a class list of foods and the cultures they come from. Challenge them to include at least one food from each continent.

The Sun in Me
by **Moira Andrew**

The sun is in me,
pale morning flames
setting my still-sleeping
heart alight.

The wind is in me,
clear blue breath
leading my bare feet
into a new day. **1**

The sea is in me,
deep green waves
whispering wild music
in my ears.

The river is in me,
dark brown waters
swirling its questions **2**
around my head.

The moon is in me,
sad silver beams
painting my dreams
with shadows.

In Other Words
setting my still-sleeping heart alight
waking me up from a deep sleep
silver beams moonlight

▶ **Before You Move On**
3
1. **Elements of Poetry** How do the stanzas
help the poet express her feelings about
nature?
2. **Figurative Language** What does the
author mean by "The sun is in me"?

273

Student Book pages 272–273

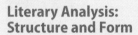

**Literary Analysis:
Structure and Form**

Teach/Model Explain: *The poet uses stanzas
to structure the poem. Each stanza has content
and images that are different from the other
stanzas.* Point to the first stanza and say: *This
stanza tells how the poet feels about the sun.
The imagery is of the sun's flames lighting up
the poet's heart.* Point to the second stanza
and say: *This stanza is also about an element
of nature. But now it talks about the wind. The
imagery is of the wind gently blowing the poet's
feet forward.*

Practice/Apply Have students identify the
content and imagery of the last three stanzas
of the poem. Encourage students to discuss
their ideas with a partner and then write
them down.

Build Comprehension, pages 272–273

1 **Relate to Personal Experience** Ask students to think about
what they have learned about the wind. How might the wind lead you
through your day? (Possible answer: Sometimes, when the wind is strong,
it hurries me along.)

2 **Make Comparisons** How do the sea and the river affect the poet
differently? Prompt students by asking:

- *What does the sea in her do?* (whisper wild music)
- *What does the river in her do?* (swirl questions in her head)
- *How is this different?*

3 **Answers to Before You Move On**

1. **Elements of Poetry** Answers will vary. Each stanza describes a
different **element** and the feelings it gives the poet.

2. **Figurative Language:** Sample response: The poet means she feels
the sun's warmth inside her. It wakes up her heart and feelings.

Plan a Landform Model

Materials: *paper, pencil, calculator*

Science

① Teach Explain: *Landforms are features such as mountains, valleys, and plains that make up earth's surface. Scientists often make small models of landforms.* Activate prior knowledge: *Raise your hand if you have seen a scale model.* Connect concepts: *A scale model is a representation of something. It is like the original thing, except it's smaller.*

Hold up a book. *Let's say I'm making a scale model of this book. My model will be half as long as this book. It will also be half as wide and half as thick. When you make a scale model, all the sizes change by the same amount. If my model is one-tenth as long as the book, how wide will the model be?* Choral response: One-tenth as wide. *How thick will it be?* Choral response: One-tenth as thick.

② Model/Practice Display **eVisual 4.27**, Explain: *I want to make a scale model of Mount Fuji. My model will be one-thousandth the size of the real mountain. I will divide all distances by one thousand. Who can tell me how to find the height?* (Divide 3776 by one thousand).

Using a calculator, show students that 3776 ÷ 1,000 = 3.776 meters. Then explain that 3.776 meters is equal to about 4 yards or a little less than 12.5 feet. Explain: *The width around the base of Mount Fuji is about 40.1 kilometers, or 40,100 meters.* Write "40,100 meters" on the board. Then have students calculate the model's width: 40,100 m ÷ 1,000 = 40.1 meters, which is a bit less than 44 yards or about 131.5 feet.

③ Apply Point out to students that a scale model of Mount Fuji at one-thousandth scale is still very large. Ask: *Who can suggest the scale for a smaller model?* (possible response: one-ten thousandth). Have students use a calculator to determine the size of a model at one-ten thousandth scale. (Height: 3776m ÷ 10,000 = 0.3776, 0.3776m or about 15 inches; Width: 40,100 m ÷ 10,000 = 4.01 meters, or just over 13 feet)

NGReach.com **eVisual 4.27**

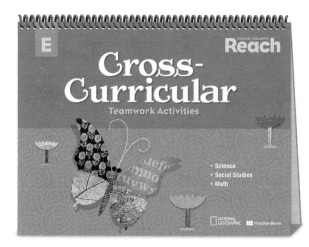

Make more content connections with Cross-Curricular Teamwork Activities (Pages T216g and T246o)

Day 6
continued

Day at a Glance:
Language: Express Needs and Wants
Vocabulary: Multiple-Meaning Words
Reading: Read the Selection
Writing: Writing Fluency; Publish and Share

OBJECTIVES

Vocabulary
• Use Academic Vocabulary 🅣
• Use Grade-Level Content Vocabulary 🅣

Language
• Make Comparisons
• Participate in Discussion

Reading Fluency
• Read with Accuracy and Rate 🅣

Literary Analysis
• Compare Figurative Language

Learning and Teamwork Strategies
• Use Graphic Organizer: Comparison Chart

Writing
• Develop Writing Fluency
• Monitor and self-correct writing

Resources

⊙ eVisuals 4.28

⊙ eVisuals 4.29

✂⊙ Practice Master 4.22

Differentiate

Academic Language Frames

Make Comparisons

■ _____ has/have _____ .
So does/do _____ .
_____ is/are _____ .
But _____ is/are _____ .

■ _____ and _____ are alike because both _____ .
_____ is different from _____ because _____ .

■ The selections are similar because both have
_____ and _____ .
■ The selections are different because one is/has
_____ and the other is/has _____ .

⊙NGReach.com ▶ eVisual 4.28

T274a   **Unit 4** | Power of Nature

Respond and Extend

❶ Reread As students reread "Comida" and "The Sun in Me" on their own, have them think about how the poems are the same and different from "Doña Flor."

❷ Compare Figurative Language Tell students that one way in which the selections are alike is that they all use figurative language to help readers visualize. Read aloud the instructions.

Create groups and have students use **Jigsaw.** Help focus students' thinking: *Figurative language includes metaphors and similes that compare things. Figurative language also includes personification, giving human traits to nonhuman things.* Ask questions to help guide discussion. Provide **Academic Language Frames** to support students at different levels.

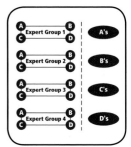

Jigsaw

Focus	Questions
1. Metaphors	What two things are compared? Is the comparison made without using the words *like* or *as*?
2. Similes	What two things are compared? Does the comparison use the words *like* or *is*?
3. Personification	Does an animal or thing have a human trait? What does the animal or thing do?

As students report their group's ideas, students should record them on **Practice Master 4.22**.

❸ Talk Together About the Big Question
Read aloud the question and directions. Encourage students to think how they **interact** with nature. What **materials** do they use? How do they **modify** nature to get the things they need or want?

Have students add ideas to the unit concept map.

> **CHECK UNDERSTANDING** Ask students to share a favorite figurative phrase from one of the selections. *What two things are compared? Why do you particularly like this image?*

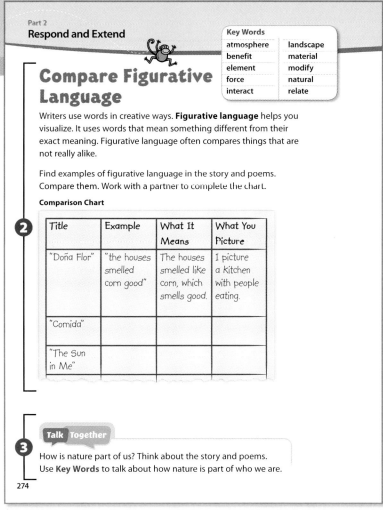

Compare Figurative Language

Key Words	
atmosphere	landscape
benefit	material
element	modify
force	natural
interact	relate

Writers use words in creative ways. **Figurative language** helps you visualize. It uses words that mean something different from their exact meaning. Figurative language often compares things that are not really alike.

Find examples of figurative language in the story and poems. Compare them. Work with a partner to complete the chart.

Comparison Chart

2

Title	Example	What It Means	What You Picture
"Doña Flor"	"the houses smelled corn good"	The houses smelled like corn, which smells good.	I picture a kitchen with people eating.
"Comida"			
"The Sun in Me"			

Talk Together

3

How is nature part of us? Think about the story and poems. Use **Key Words** to talk about how nature is part of who we are.

274

Student Book page 274

Daily Writing

4 **Writing Fluency** Use the **Power Writing Routine**. (See page PD53.) Write the word **benefit** and prompt: *Choose a* **natural** *resource. Tell how you benefit from it.*

Power Writing Routine

 1. What do you know about the word or picture?

 2. Take one minute to write as much as you can, as well as you can.
B words   **I** sentences   **A** **AH** paragraphs

3. Check your spelling and grammar. (Circle) mistakes.

123 **4.** Count your words.

NGReach.com eVisual 4.29

5 **Writing Project: Publish and Share** Have students publish and share their Writing Project compositions. (See page T279.)

CLOSE AND ASSESS
- **Language** *What linking and helping verbs did you use in your writing?*
- **Reading** *Which poem did you* **relate** *to best? Explain your thinking.*
- **Vocabulary** *Choose a Key Word that has a multiple meaning. Use the word in a sentence that shows another meaning for the word.*

Fluency: Accuracy and Rate

To activate prior knowledge and practice fluency, conduct timed readings of "Doña Flor." Select an option for recording

- Use the automatic speech recognition on the **Comprehension Coach** to track word count per minute for the entire passage.

- Use **Practice Master 4.18**.

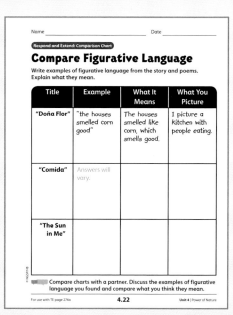

Name _____ Date _____

Respond and Extend: Comparison Chart

Compare Figurative Language

Write examples of figurative language from the story and poems. Explain what they mean.

Title	Example	What It Means	What You Picture
"Doña Flor"	"the houses smelled corn good"	The houses smelled like corn, which smells good.	I picture a kitchen with people eating.
"Comida"	Answers will vary.		
"The Sun in Me"			

Compare charts with a partner. Discuss the examples of figurative language you found and compare what you think they mean.

For use with TE page 274a   **4.22**   Unit 4 | Power of Nature

Practice Master 4.22

Part 2 | Day 6 T274

Day at a Glance:
▶ **Language:** Forms of *be* and *have*   ▶ **Reading:** Reread the Selection
▶ **Vocabulary:** Multiple-Meaning Words   ▶ **Writing:** Poem

OBJECTIVES

Vocabulary
• Use Academic Vocabulary ❶
• Use Grade-Level Vocabulary ❶
• Strategy: Determine Meaning of Multiple-Meaning Words ❶

Grammar
• Forms of *be* and *have*

Learning and Teamwork Strategies
• Relate to Prior Knowledge
• Make Contributions

Resources

 *Practice Master 4.23*

eVisual 4.30

Differentiate

Language Transfer

Issue In Chinese languages, Haitian Creole, Hmong, Korean, and Vietnamese, the verb *be* isn't necessarily used in sentences with adjectives and prepositional phrases. Speakers of these languages may say *Snow on the ground* instead of *Snow is on the ground* and *I cold* instead of *of I am cold.*

Strategy Write the following sentence frames for students to copy and complete:

I _____ in school.
The clown _____ funny.

The clouds _____ are in the sky.

Part 2 Grammar Skills Trace		Page
Day 2	Forms of *be*	T249a
Day 4	Forms of *have* and Modals	T268a
▶ Day 7	Forms of *be* and *have*	T275a
Day 10	Review Forms of *be* and *have*	T276g

Language of the Day

What have you learned about the elements and forces of nature?
I have learned that _____ .

Read the Language of the Day. Model: *I have learned that wind is an element of nature. The force of wind can shape the land.* Make a list of other elements in nature. Ask students to describe the force of each element.

Grammar Forms of *be* and *have* ⒤ Ⓐ ⒜⒣

❶ **Teach/Model** Read the introduction and the first rule aloud. Write these sentence frames. Ask students to use a form of *be* or *have* to complete the sentences.

    I _____ excited. (am)   *I _____ a new friend.* (have)

Have a volunteer read the second rule aloud. Ask: *What other subjects use these same forms of* be *and* have? (we, they) Write these sentence frames and have volunteers use the words to complete the sentences.

    We _____ many friends at school. (have)

    They _____ kind and helpful. (are)

    You _____ a good friend. (are)

Point to the third rule and read it aloud. Call on volunteers to use *is* and *has* with the subjects *he, she,* and *it*. Write their sentences on the board.

❷ **Practice** Read aloud the directions and the excerpt from "Doña Flor." If necessary, help students identify the forms of *be* and *have* (has, are, is) and the contractions (They're, She's).

❸ **Apply in Writing** Read aloud the directions and have partners work together. Provide support as necessary. Assign **Practice Book page 4.23**.

> **CHECK UNDERSTANDING** Write these sentences. Have students supply the correct form of *be*: *I _____ happy. The storm _____ over. The rain clouds _____ gone.*

Grammar and Spelling

Skills Trace: Forms of *be*
Forms of *have*
▶ Forms of *be and have*

Forms of *be* and *have*

The verbs *be* and *have* have irregular forms in the present tense. The subject and verb must agree.

Grammar Rules Present-Tense Action Verbs

❶

	be	have
• Use for **I**:	*am*	*have*
• Use for **you**:	*are*	*have*
• Use for **he**, **she**, or **it**:	*is*	*has*
• Use for **we**:	*are*	*have*
• Use for **they**:	*are*	*have*

Sometimes you can form a contraction with the subject and the verb. For example, you can change *I am* to *I'm* and *you are* to *you're*. An apostrophe shows where one or more letters are left out.

Read Forms of *be* and *have*

❷

Read these sentences about "Doña Flor." Find present-tense forms of *be* and *have*. Identify the subjects. Find two contractions.

> Flor has many friends. Plants, animals, and even the wind are her friends. They're always welcome at her house. Flor is helpful. She's generous, too.

Write Forms of *be* and *have*

❸

Choose an illustration in the story. Write a short paragraph about it. Include present-tense forms of *be* and *have*.

275

Student Book page 275

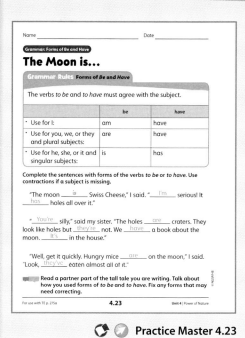

Practice Master 4.23

Dictionary Entries

country *noun* **1** A part of the world with its own borders and government
2 Undeveloped land away from towns or cities

jam *noun* **1** A sweet, thick food made from boiled fruit and sugar
verb **2** To bruise or crush by squeezing
3 To push suddenly or hard

ground *noun* **1** The solid part of Earth's surface
2 Land used for a certain activity
adjective **3** Crushed into small pieces or powder

star *noun* **1** A heavenly body that shines
2 A design or object that has 5 or 6 points
3 An astounding performer, as in sports

pitcher *noun* **1** In baseball, a person who throws the ball
2 A container with a handle and spout for holding and pouring liquids.

NGReach.com eVisual 4.30

More Multiple-Meaning Words

❹ **Review/Model** Review the Day 6 Lesson Plan (page T270). Read this sentence and use the **Dictionary Entries** to model using context to identify which meaning is correct. (2)

- I hurt my finger when I *jammed* it in the front door as the door closed.

❺ **Practice/Apply** Have students do a **Numbered Heads** to find the meaning of the underlined multiple meanings words. (See **Cooperative Learning Routines**, pages PD58–PD59.)

1. We use ground corn to make tortillas. **(3)**

2. The United States flag has stars and stripes. **(2)**

3. Cordell hopes to be a pitcher when she grows up. **(1)**

4. We made jam from our peaches. **(1)**

5. My grandparents have a farm in the country. **(2)**

> **CHECK UNDERSTANDING** Say: *Tell me what* jam *means in this sentence: A deer ran across the road, causing Dad to jam on the brakes.*

Day 7
continued

Day at a Glance:
▶ **Grammar:** Forms of *be* and *have*   ▶ **Reading:** Reread the Selection
▶ **Vocabulary:** Multiple-Meaning Words   ▶ **Writing:** Poem

OBJECTIVES

Vocabulary
• Use Academic Vocabulary ❶
• Use Grade-Level Vocabulary ❶

Literary Analysis
• Identify Sensory Language
• Genre: Identify Elements of Poetry

Learning and Teamwork Strategies
• Relate to personal experience
• Use context

Writing
• Reproduce Modeled Writing
• Write a Poem with Sensory Language

Reread Focus on Sensory Language

❶ Teach Tell students that good writers carefully choose words that will give the reader the ideas or feelings the author wants to share. Write *sensory language* and explain: *Sensory language helps show how things smell, taste, feel, sound, and look.* Introduce the concept: *Today you will read the poems "Comida" and "The Sun in Me" again. This time think about how the poets use sensory language to show the ideas they wanted to share.*

❷ Model Read "Comida" aloud and say: *When I read "eat chile and you eat sun and fire," I imagine the sun and how it warms my whole body. I imagine fire and how it is red and hot. I think of a chile and how it tastes spicy and hot. I think the poet wants me to know that chile is hot like fire and warms him from his head to his toes like the sun.*

Create a web diagram. Show how to organize each image by the senses it refers to. Tell students that not all images relate to all the senses. Similarly, some senses may have more than one image.

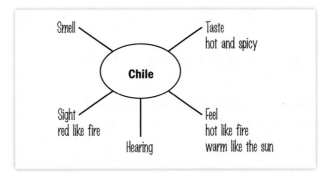

❸ Practice/Apply in Reading Have students chorally reread "The Sun in Me." Then have groups of five use **Team Word Webbing** to list sensory images for the verses of the poem. Each student should add to the part of the web nearest to him or her. Then on cue, students rotate the web and each student adds to the nearest part again. (See **Cooperative Learning Strategies,** pages PD58–PD59.) Last, they individually share points from their discussion with the class.

Daily Writing

Writing on Demand: Poem Display the writing prompt and have a volunteer read it aloud.

> Write a poem describing something in nature. It may be a setting, a **landscape**, an animal, or a **natural** event.

Unpack the Prompt Ask: *What is the purpose for writing?* (to write a poem to describe something in nature) *What does the form of writing need to be?* Circle *poem* in the prompt. Have volunteers underline the Key Words. (landscape, natural)

Initiate brainstorming: Explain that a good test-taking strategy is to think about the subject of a prompt and ask: *What will I write about? What settings do I know? What animals interest me? What natural events can I name?* Then ask: *What kind of poem can I write best?*

Use the **Modeled Writing** routine to illustrate how to write a poem. (See **Writing Routines**, page PD54.)

Think Aloud	Write
1. Plan	
First I want to plan my writing. I will make a web. I will put the topic of my poem in the center circle.	a beautiful sunset
What sensory details could I include? I will add them in circles that surround the topic.	orange and red fiery flames painted clouds
2. Write	
I will start my poem with the main idea.	The sunset is a blazing fire.
Next I will write details about the topic. I will include words that help my reader picture what it was like.	Flames of red and orange spread across the sky.
Go through the remaining details to finish the poem. Then end it with a concluding sentence.	
3. Read and Reflect	
Model how to proofread the poem. Have students point out where you can add sensory images. Have students confirm that you have used correct subject-verb agreement.	

Display the finished poem to serve as a model. Use **Multi-Level Strategies** to support students at all proficiency levels in writing a poem. After students complete their writing, have them read their poem aloud to a partner.

> **CLOSE AND ASSESS**
> - **Language:** *What forms of* be *or* have *did you use in your poem?*
> - **Vocabulary:** *Which Key Words did you use in your writing?*
> - **Reading:** *How would you compare your poem to "Comida" or the "Sun in Me"?*

Differentiate

Multi-Level Strategies

BEGINNING

Provide a sentence frame for students to begin their poem:

- A (The) _____ is a _____ .

Then have students draw pictures to help them compare their topic to another item.

INTERMEDIATE

Have students work in pairs to plan their poems using a web that addresses the senses. Have them include as many details as they can in the organizer.

ADVANCED

Ask students to work individually to plan their poems using a web that addresses the senses. Have them include as many details as they can, pointing out that they don't have to use them all. Have them share their organizer with a partner and then add new details generated by the discussion.

ADVANCED HIGH

Have students begin their writing by creating a comparison chart that explains the relationship between the object in nature and other objects to which it might be compared. Then challenge them to write a poem that uses sensory images to make the comparison clear.

Days 8-9

Day at a Glance:
▶ **Language:** Theme Theater: Story Extension
▶ **Vocabulary:** Extend Vocabulary
▶ **Reading:** Read Leveled Books
▶ **Writing:** Paraphrase

OBJECTIVES

Vocabulary
• Use Academic Vocabulary ❶

Language
• Language Function: Express Needs and Wants ❶

Listening and Speaking
• Watch Actions and Expressions
• Listen Actively
• Speak Clearly
• Adjust Your Speech for Your Audience

Learning and Teamwork Strategies
• Build on Ideas

Resources

•   *materials for props, such as:*
•   *paper and paints*
•   *scissors and glue*
•   *construction paper*
•   *crayons and markers*

⊘   *Assessment Handbook page 176*

Language of the Day

Why do you think people tell stories about the **forces** of nature?

People tell stories about nature because _____ .

Read the Language of the Day. Model: *People tell stories about nature because it helps them to explain how nature works.* Tell students that during the next two days, they will create and act out their own version of "Doña Flor".

Theme Theater Story Extension

❶ Introduce the Activity Ask students to briefly summarize the events in "Doña Flor." Help them focus on key elements of the story: *Who are the important characters? What problem do they have? How does Doña Flor help her neighbors solve that problem?*

Make the connection: *Suppose you want to tell a new Doña Flor tall tale. What problem might the villagers face this time?* Have students brainstorm a list of natural elements or events that might befall the villagers. Add to the list a few ideas of your own: a tornado is heading to the village, the river is rising and may flood, a blizzard has buried the village, and so on. Post sentence frames to help students extend the story:

The villagers need _____ .

The villagers want _____ .

❷ Plan Form casts of five to six students each. Have each cast choose a story extension. Guide students at different proficiency levels to select appropriate roles. For example, more proficient students might take on the role of Doña Flor or the narrator, while less proficient students might take on the role of the natural element, such as a tornado, an advancing river, or an animal.

③ Plan and Rehearse Have casts work together to create a simple story map that outlines the problem the villagers face and what Doña Flor does to help. Encourage students to refer to the story map as they develop their dialogue. As students plan and rehearse, encourage them to build on one another's ideas. Use **Multi-Level Strategies** to help students at each proficiency level.

Have students create or bring props from home. They can make one-dimensional, cardboard representations of props such as trees or mountains.

④ Let the Drama Begin! Clear space and let the dramatizations begin. Invite family members or another class to enjoy the performances. For each performance, assess one group's listening skills.

⑤ Debrief and Compare Ask each group to share what they enjoyed in the performances. Discuss the problems Doña Flor solved in the stories, and invite students to compare and contrast these with the problem in "Doña Flor." Have them add any ideas they learned about the power of nature to their unit concept map.

Differentiate

Multi-Level Strategies

BEGINNING

Coach students in using actions, pantomime, and sound to communicate their roles.

INTERMEDIATE

Suggest that students highlight their parts to make it easier to practice and locate lines. Suggest that they practice their lines slowly, concentrating on speaking clearly and correctly.

ADVANCED   ADVANCED HIGH

Challenge students to think of the problem the villagers will face and how Doña Flor will solve it. Encourage them to provide as much detail as possible.

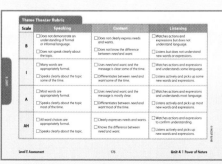

 Assessment Handbook page 176

Days 8-9
continued

Day at a Glance:
▶ **Language:** Theme Theater: Extend the Story　　▶ **Reading:** Read Leveled Books
▶ **Vocabulary:** Extend Vocabulary　　▶ **Writing:** Paraphrase

OBJECTIVES

Vocabulary
• Extend Vocabulary through Wide Reading

Language
• Participate in Discussion

Reading
• Read Independently
• Summarize Reading
• Make Connections: Text to Text
• Apply Reading Strategies Varied Texts

Writing
• Paraphrase in Logical Order

Science
• Explore Our Connection to Nature

Resources

 Leveled Books:
  - *Dream Weaver*
  - *Prince William*
  - *A River Ran Wild*
  - *I Love Our Earth*
  - *Oil Spill*
  - *Kids Care for the Earth*

 *Reach Leveled Library Lesson Plans*

ⓝ NGReach.com ▶

Find more leveled readers about this topic.

Differentiate　Read Leveled Books

Group students based on their reading abilities and interests. Use the **Guided Reading** routine (See page PD47) for books at students' instructional level. Use the **Independent Reading Support** (see page PD50) for books at students' independent reading level.

After reading, organize the students into heterogeneous groups to discuss what they read and to use the new information to answer the Big Question. Use these prompts to guide your discussion:

• What new information did you learn about our connection to nature?

• What surprised you?

• How did new information change your answer?

Fiction

BEGINNING LEVEL

Dream Weaver
by Jonathan London
• **Genre:** Animal Fantasy
A young boy finds a yellow spider and peers into its fascinating little world.

Key Words

creak

pause

spider

weave

web

INTERMEDIATE LEVEL

Prince William
by Gloria Rand
• **Genre:** Realistic Fiction
A tanker crashes in Prince William Sound, spilling oil everywhere. Denny finds a baby seal covered in oil and sets out to save it.

Key Words

death

rescue

seal

volunteers

wilderness

ADVANCED　**ADVANCED HIGH LEVELS**

A River Ran Wild
by Lynne Cherry
• **Genre:** Historical Fiction
Students read about the environmental history of the Nashua River, home to native people and settlers. When the river becomes polluted, it affects all those who depend on it.

Key Words

lumber

migration

pollution

rhythm

riverbanks

Nonfiction

I Love Our Earth
by Bill Martin, Jr. and Michael Sampson

- **Genre:** Poetry

Explore the many things to love about our Earth. From mountains to sunsets, there is something for everyone to enjoy.

Key Words

blossoms

flicker

glow

mosses

sunsets

Oil Spill!
by Melvin Berger

- **Genre:** Expository Nonfiction

Learn about what happened when the *Exxon Valdez* oil tanker spilled tons of oil in Alaska in 1989 and how people cleaned it up.

Key Words

accidents

chemicals

damaged

gallons

vacuum

Kids Care for the Earth
by Gare Thompson

- **Genre:** Expository Nonfiction

In this chapter book, kids take action to conserve our natural resources and reduce pollution and waste.

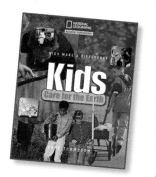

Key Words

conserve

landfill

natural

pesticide

resources

Daily Writing A AH

Journal Entry Have students write a journal entry in their reading journals. Use "Doña Flor" to model how to paraphrase in logical order. Provide an example that does not maintain order by leaving the end out. Have students share their journal entries with others, recommending books they enjoyed.

Same Book / Different Levels

B I A AH

Watching Chimps
by Peter Winkler

Meet world famous scientist Jane Goodall and learn about her work with chimpanzees in the wild.

Pioneer Edition
Fountas and Pinnell: P-R

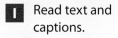

- **B** Conduct a Picture Walk.
- **I** Read text and captions.

Key Words

ape	chimp
discovery	grooming
reserve	wildlife

Pathfinder Edition
Fountas and Pinnell: Q-S

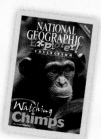

- **A** Read text and captions.
- **AH** Read and write responses to questions.

Key Words

ape	chimpanzee
discovery	reserve
social	species

Part 2 Vocabulary Skills Trace		Page
Day 1	Science Vocabulary	T247
Day 2	Academic Vocabulary	T249
Day 3	Expand Word Knowledge	T252b
Day 4	Share Word Knowledge	T268b
Day 5	Apply Word Knowledge	T269b
Day 6	Multiple-Meaning Words	T270
Day 7	Multiple-Meaning Words	T275
Days 8–9	Extend Vocabulary	T276e–f
Day 10	Vocabulary Review	T276g–h

OBJECTIVES

Language
- Review Language Function: Express Needs and Wants ⊕

Grammar
- Review Present-Tense Action Verbs; Forms of Be/Have; Contractions

Vocabulary
- Review and Use Grade-Level Key Vocabulary ⊕
- Review Multiple Meaning Words

Reading Strategy
- Review Ask Questions ⊕

Comprehension and Literary Analysis
- Review Problem and Solution ⊕
- Review Genre: Tall Tale

Fluency
- Expression

Content Area
- Explore Elements of Nature

Resources

- Key Word Images
- Assessment Handbook
- eVisual 4.31
- Comprehension Coach

Part 2 Grammar Skills Trace		Page
Day 2	Forms of be	T249a
Day 4	Forms of have and Modals	T268a
Day 7	Forms of be and have	T275a
▶ Day 10	Review Forms of be and have	T276g

Language of the Day

What did you learn? How does it help you in school?
I learned how to _____. _____ means to _____.
For example, _____.

Model: *I learned how to express needs and wants. To express needs and wants means to tell what you want or must have. For example, I can ask for things I need in the classroom.* Prompt students to talk about a skill they learned.

Review and Assess

Use these interactive review activities to reinforce concepts covered in Part 2. Then use the assessment tools to evaluate students' progress. For more details about assessment, see page T281a.

Language Function

Express Wants and Needs

Use an **Inside-Outside Circle** to have students express wants and needs. Students outside the circle state something they want to do. Students inside the circle state a thing that the student needs to do the activity. Have students rotate through the circle and then trade inside and outside roles.

- **Assessment:** Language Function Rubric on page 168 of the Assessment Handbook

Grammar

Forms of *be* and *have*

Form small groups. Distribute word cards for *am, is, are, have,* and *has.* Ask each student to choose a card, use the verb in a sentence, and use it again as a contraction in a sentence. Have the rest of the group raise their hands if the verb agrees with its subject. Correct errors as needed. Repeat using the present progressive.

- **Assessment:** Grammar and Spelling Unit Test on pages 207–213 of the Assessment Handbook

Vocabulary

Science and Academic Vocabulary

Show **Key Word Images.** Have pairs prepare clues to the meaning of each word. Then ask pairs to present their clues one at a time, verbally or through pantomime, to another pair. After each clue, have listeners try to guess the word. Once they guess correctly, they must use the word in a sentence. See which pair guesses the word with the fewest clues.

- **Assessment:** Key Word tests on pages 173–175 of the Assessment Handbook.

Key Words	
atmosphere	benefit
element	force
landscape	interact
material	modify
natural	relate

Vocabulary Strategy

Word Work

Have groups use a dictionary to learn the multiple meanings of Key Words. Challenge them to use the words in sentences that reveal another meaning for each word. Students then present their sentences to another group for those students to figure out the meanings.

> We can landscape the bare yard by planting flowers...

> Does landscape mean to make a place look nice?

- **Assessment:** Reading Unit Test on pages 180–181 of the Assessment Handbook.

Reading Strategy

Read Aloud

Ask Questions

Read aloud the first paragraph of "Pecos Bill Rides a Tornado." Pause for students to ask questions. Encourage the use of **Academic Language Frames:** *I do not understand . . . ; I ask myself . . . . I think about _____ to understand . . . .* Continue reading, pausing after each paragraph for students to ask questions.

- **Assessment:** Reading Strategy Test on page 177 of the Assessment Handbook.

Comprehension

Read Aloud

Literary Analysis

Read aloud "Pecos Bill Rides a Tornado." Have the students identify exaggerated elements and events that make this story a tall tale.

Text Structure

Have students identify the problem in the story and its solution.

- **Assessment:** Reading Unit Test on pages 182–206 of the Assessment Handbook.

Fluency

Expression

Have students review their own recordings of "Doña Flor" in the Comprehension Coach. Then have students practice reading **Leveled Library Books** that are appropriate for their reading levels, focusing on accuracy, rate, and expression.

- **Assessment:** Reading Fluency Benchmark Assessment on pages 448–453 of the Assessment Handbook.

Read Aloud

Pecos Bill Rides a Tornado

Long ago, when the West was still wild, there lived a cowboy named Pecos Bill. Now, Bill wasn't just any cowboy. There wasn't a horse in the land that he couldn't ride. He could tame the wildest of the wild from bronco to mountain lion!

One day Bill was out roping cattle when a tornado popped up over the landscape. The other cowboys and the farmers ran for cover like mice running from a cat. The tornado roared and ranted. It twisted and bucked like a wild bronco, tossing trees, barns, and cattle like they were toys. It was causing so much damage that Bill decided right then that he had to tame it.

Bill grabbed a big rattlesnake for a rope and lassoed the tornado's tail. Then he wrestled that tornado to the ground and leapt onto its back. The tornado was fighting mad. It twisted and bucked but it couldn't throw Bill. Bill hung on while that tornado roared through Kansas. He dug in his spurs while the tornado roared through Texas. Still Bill held on, all the way to California before that tornado finally tuckered out.

NGReach.com > eVisual 4.31

Part 2 Vocabulary Skills Trace		Page
Day 1	Science Vocabulary	T247
Day 2	Academic Vocabulary	T249
Day 3	Expand Word Knowledge	T252b
Day 4	Share Word Knowledge	T268b
Day 5	Apply Word Knowledge	T269b
Day 6	Multiple-Meaning Words	T270
Day 7	Multiple-Meaning Words	T275
Days 8–9	Extend Vocabulary	T276e–f
▶ Day 10	Vocabulary Review	T276g–h

Mode and Form

A tall tale is a funny story filled with exaggerated details that could not happen in real life. For this project, students will write a tall tale about someone who battles a force of nature.

> ### Writing Checklist
>
> **A good tall tale**
>
> ✔ opens with a problem and then shows how the character tries to solve the problem
>
> ✔ includes funny, exaggerated details that are unbelievable and could not happen in real life
>
> ✔ ends with the solution to the problem.
>
> ⊘ NGReach.com › eVisual 4.32

Connect Reading to Writing Use "Doña Flor" as a professional model of a tall tale. Reread the text and point out features of the form.

Writing Trait: Voice and Style

Students will learn how good writers use unique voice and style to create writing in which:

- the writing sounds genuine

- words and sentences are interesting and appropriate for the audience

- the dialogue, narration, and characters are appropriate for a tall tale.

Lesson Overview and Pacing

Each lesson in the Writing Project provides detailed instruction. Teach the Writing Project during Part 2 of the unit with this suggested daily sequence and pacing plan, or adjust as your schedule and student needs require.

- Day 1: Introducing the Writing Prompt, Study a Model

- Day 2: Prewrite

- Day 3: Draft

- Day 4: Revise

- Day 5: Edit and Proofread

- Day 6: Publish

Classroom Vocabulary

Use **Vocabulary Routine 4** to teach **voice** and **style**. (See **Vocabulary Routines**, page PD40).

Three-Fold Tab

Rubric: Tall Tale

Students use **Practice Master 4.24** to score their own writing on the trait of voice and style. You can then use the *Reach* Writing Rubric to score each student's project on all traits.

Writing Rubric

Score Point	Focus and Coherence	Organization	Development of Ideas	Voice and Style	Written Conventions
4	**Focus** Paragraphs and the writing as a whole are focused. Ideas are related. Details are relevant. **Completeness** The writing feels complete. The introduction and conclusion are meaningful.	**Structure** The organizing strategy is well-suited to the writer's purpose. **Progression of Ideas** Ideas flow logically and smoothly, with meaningful transitions.	**Content Quality** The writer takes a risk and treats the topic in an interesting way, with insight and thoughtfulness. **Elaboration** Ideas are developed in depth.	**Individuality** The writing sounds genuine and unique. **Word Choice** Words and phrases are interesting and appropriate to the writer's purpose and audience.	**Grammar, Usage, Mechanics, and Spelling** There are only a few errors. **Sentence Fluency** Sentences are varied and effective.
3	**Focus** Paragraphs and the writing as a whole are mostly focused, but there are a few sudden shifts between ideas. Most details are relevant. **Completeness** The writing feels mostly complete. The introduction and conclusion add some meaning.	**Structure** The organizing strategy is generally suited to the writer's purpose. **Progression of Ideas** Most ideas flow logically and smoothly, but there are a few gaps.	**Content Quality** The writer does not take much of a risk, but does treat the topic in a thoughtful way. **Elaboration** Some ideas are more developed than others.	**Individuality** For the most part, the writing sounds genuine and unique. **Word Choice** Words and phrases are mostly interesting and appropriate to the writer's purpose and audience.	**Grammar, Usage, Mechanics, and Spelling** Errors are minor and/or infrequent. **Sentence Fluency** There is some sentence variety. Sentences are generally effective.
2	**Focus** Paragraphs and the writing as a whole are somewhat focused, but there are a number of sudden shifts between ideas. Some details are relevant. **Completeness** The writing feels somewhat complete. The introduction and conclusion may be superficial.	**Structure** The organizing strategy is not clear or does not suit the writer's purpose. **Progression of Ideas** There are breaks in logic and very few transitions.	**Content Quality** The topic is covered, but in an uninteresting way. **Elaboration** Ideas are listed or mentioned superficially.	**Individuality** A few passages sound genuine and unique. **Word Choice** Words and phrases are somewhat interesting and appropriate to the writer's purpose and audience.	**Grammar, Usage, Mechanics, and Spelling** Errors are frequent, but the meaning is clear. **Sentence Fluency** Sentences are somewhat awkward and have simple or inaccurate words.
1	**Focus** The writing is not focused. Ideas are unrelated. Many details are irrelevant. **Completeness** The writing feels incomplete. If there is an introduction and conclusion, they may be perfunctory.	**Structure** No organizing strategy is evident. **Progression of Ideas** Writing is illogical, wordy, and/or repetitious.	**Content Quality** The topic is not really covered. **Elaboration** There is little or no development of ideas.	**Individuality** There is little or no sense of the writer. **Word Choice** Words and phrases are not appropriate to the writer's purpose and audience.	**Grammar, Usage, Mechanics, and Spelling** Errors are severe and/or frequent and are a barrier to understanding. **Sentence Fluency** Sentences are awkward and have missing or misused words.

OBJECTIVES

Writing
- Analyze a Student Model: Tale Tall
- Trait: Evaluate for Voice and Style **T**
- Use a Rubric to Analyze Writing

Resources

 eVisual 4.32

 Practice Master 4.24

eVisual 4.33

Introduce the Writing Project

1 **Analyze the Prompt** Ask a volunteer to read aloud the title of the project and the prompt. As the student reads, have the rest of the class begin to fill out the first three sections of a RAFT:

Role: entertainer
Audience: students at a storytelling festival
Form: tall tale
Topic: _____

Remind students that although they haven't decided on a specific topic, the prompt gives them a broad subject to begin thinking about. Ask them what that subject is. (a tall tale about someone who battles a force of nature) Explain that they will be choosing a topic for their writing when they do the Prewrite step.

Focus on language: *Who is the audience?* (other students) Ask students how knowing their audience will affect the language they use. (It will be more informal, with words that are familiar to kids their age.)

Study a Model

2 **Focus on Features** Read aloud the directions and then have the students read the model silently. Remind students to look for exaggerated details that make the story funny.

Chorally reread the model, stopping to discuss each callout. Display the **Writing Checklist** and have students find examples of each feature in the model.

Writing Checklist

A good tall tale

✔ opens with a problem and then shows how the character tries to solve the problem

✔ includes funny, exaggerated details that are unbelievable and could not happen in real life

✔ ends with the solution to the problem.

NGReach.com > eVisual 4.32

Write Like an Entertainer

1 **Write a Tall Tale** ✏

Write a story about someone who battles a force of nature. Share your tall tale during a storytelling festival.

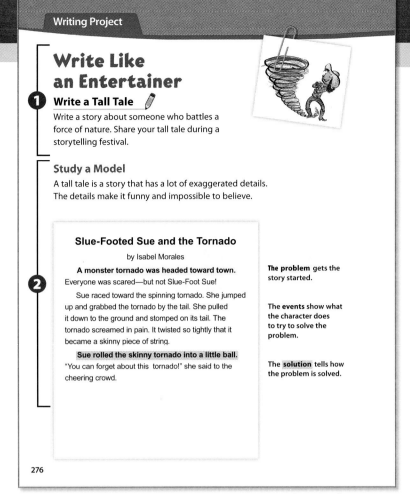

Study a Model

A tall tale is a story that has a lot of exaggerated details. The details make it funny and impossible to believe.

2

Slue-Footed Sue and the Tornado

by Isabel Morales

A monster tornado was headed toward town. Everyone was scared—but not Slue-Foot Sue!

Sue raced toward the spinning tornado. She jumped up and grabbed the tornado by the tail. She pulled it down to the ground and stomped on its tail. The tornado screamed in pain. It twisted so tightly that it became a skinny piece of string.

Sue rolled the skinny tornado into a little ball. "You can forget about this tornado!" she said to the cheering crowd.

The problem gets the story started.

The events show what the character does to try to solve the problem.

The solution tells how the problem is solved.

276

Student Book page 276

Name _____ **Date** _____

Writing Project: Rubric

Voice and Style

	Does the writing sound real and unique?	Is the writing interesting and appropriate?
4 Wow!	• The writing shows who the writer is. • The writer seems to be talking right to me.	• All the words fit the purpose and audience. • The words create clear images.
3 Ahh.	• The writing mostly shows who the writer is. • The writer seems to care about the ideas in the writing.	• Most of the words fit the purpose and audience. • The words create some clear images.
2 Hmm.	• It's hard to tell who the writer is. • The writer doesn't seem to be talking to me.	• Some of the words fit the purpose and audience. • The words do not create clear images.
1 Huh?	• I can't tell who the writer is. • The writer doesn't seem to care.	• The words do not fit the purpose and audience. • It is hard to picture what the writer is describing.

For use with TE p. T276   **4.24**   Unit 4 | Power of Nature

Practice Master 4.24

---

3 **Teach the Trait** Ask: *What does it mean to say your writing has a unique voice and style?* (I have a way of writing that only I can do) Have students explain how they have shown their unique style in a piece they have written. Define: *Writing that engages the reader sounds real and expresses the writer's individual voice and style. The words are powerful and appropriate. The sentences are varied and flow together well.* Find examples in the model:

- *How does the writer capture the reader's interest right away?* (The writer uses powerful, engaging words, such as *monster tornado,* to open the story.)

- *How can you tell that the sentences are varied?* (Some are short, and some are long.)

4 **Present the Rubric** Distribute **Practice Master 4.24**. Read aloud the questions and features of each score point. Assign partners the task of telling you the difference between a paper with a score of 1 and one with a score of 4. Allow time for the partners to review the rubric and then report out. (Students' responses should indicate that a 4-point paper engages the reader, sounds real and unique, and uses powerful, varied, and appropriate words that fit the writer's purpose and audience.) Use the **Academic Language Frames** to support students of all proficiency levels.

Differentiate

Academic Language Frames

Discuss the Rubric

■ 1. It   does / does not   engage the reader.

   2. The words   are / are not   powerful/appropriate.

   3. The writer's voice and style   are / are not   real/unique.

■ 1. A 4-point tall tale _____.

   2. The writer's voice and style _____.

   3. The words are _____ and _____.

■ In a 4-point paper, the writing _____, but in a 1-point paper the writing _____.

■ The words in a 4-point paper are _____, but in a 1-point paper they are _____.

NGReach.com ❯ **eVisual 4.33**

CHECK PROGRESS Ask students to orally provide engaging, powerful words and phrases they would use to describe a rainstorm.

OBJECTIVES

Learning and Teamwork Strategies
- Generate Ideas by Asking Questions
- Use Graphic Organizers: Problem-and-Solution Chart

Writing
- Writing Process (Prewrite): Select a Topic, Organize Ideas
- Conduct Research: Identify a Character, Identify Problem and Solution

Resources

 eVisual 4.34

Practice Master 4.25

Prewrite

1 Choose a Topic Review: *What is the subject of our tall tale?* (a character who battles a force of nature) What *is the force of nature in the tall tale about Slue-Footed Sue?* (tornado) *What are some other forces of nature?* (flood, hurricane, hail, sleet, snow, drought, blizzard, dust storm) *Now, we will brainstorm ideas to select a topic. When you brainstorm, you'll list* What *and* How *questions about forces of nature, for example: What if you could catch a tornado? How could you stop a flood?* Display and discuss the guidelines:

> · Think about events in nature you have seen, heard about, or studied.
> · Write questions about these events.
> · Begin each question with *What* or *How*.

NGReach.com ❯ eVisual 4.34

With a volunteer, model using the **Language Frames** to think of events in nature and list questions. Tell students that their questions can help them think of a character, a problem, and a solution for their tall tale. Then have partners list questions and select a topic.

2 Create Story Elements Tell students to use personal voice and style to describe the story's main character. Remind them to show readers how the main character solves the story problem.

> My main character is a really big man. I will use powerful and engaging words to describe him. *Too-Tall Tommy towers over our city's skyscrapers. He has to duck his head when planes fly near him.*
>
> Something in nature I know about is a flood. The problem could be a flood. What happens in a flood? There is too much water. How can I turn a flood into a tall tale? What will Tommy do to solve the problem? He will solve it by stopping the flood water. *Too-Tall Tommy will gulp the flood water.*

Encourage students to think about what makes the main character special. Then have them review their questions and think about how their character could solve the problem.

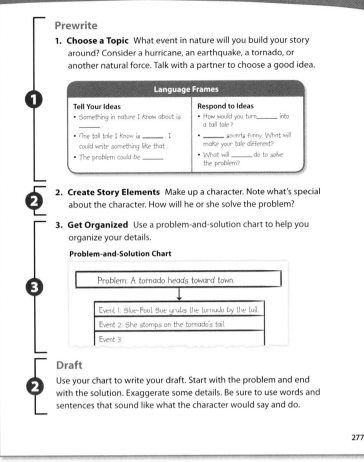

Prewrite

1. **Choose a Topic** What event in nature will you build your story around? Consider a hurricane, an earthquake, a tornado, or another natural force. Talk with a partner to choose a good idea.

Language Frames	
Tell Your Ideas	**Respond to Ideas**
• Something in nature I know about is _____.	• How would you turn_____ into a tall tale?
• One tall tale I know is _____. I could write something like that.	• _____ sounds funny. What will make your tale different?
• The problem could be _____.	• What will _____ do to solve the problem?

2. **Create Story Elements** Make up a character. Note what's special about the character. How will he or she solve the problem?

3. **Get Organized** Use a problem-and-solution chart to help you organize your details.

Problem-and-Solution Chart

> Problem: A tornado heads toward town.
>
> Event 1: Slue-Foot Sue grabs the tornado by the tail.
> Event 2: She stomps on the tornado's tail.
> Event 3:

Draft

Use your chart to write your draft. Start with the problem and end with the solution. Exaggerate some details. Be sure to use words and sentences that sound like what the character would say and do.

277

Student Book page 277

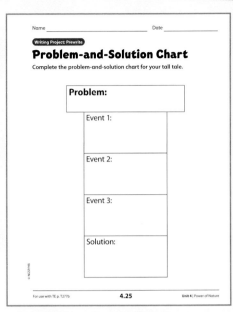

Practice Master 4.25

---

3 **Get Organized** Remind students that tall tales are funny because the characters have unbelievable abilities and do things that could never happen in real life. Review the problem-and-solution chart they created for "Doña Flor" (see page 269c).

Work through the chart on page 277. Reinforce the trait of voice and style by reminding students that they should use powerful words that express their own unique voice and engage their readers.

Distribute **Practice Master 4.25.** Ask: *What do you write in the top box?* (the story problem) *What do you write in the Event 1 box?* (how the character first tries to solve the problem) *What do you write in the Event 2 box?* (the next thing the character does to try to solve the problem) *What do you write in the Event 3 box?* (the next thing the main character does to try to solve the problem) *What do you write in the box at the bottom?* (how the main character finally solves the problem) Have students complete their own charts, using the lists and notes they made earlier. Use **Multi-Level Strategies** to support students at each proficiency level.

CHECK PROGRESS Check problem-and-solution charts. Then ask pairs to trade papers. Have partners check for: a problem in the first box, events in the next three boxes, and a solution in the final box.

Differentiate

Multi-Level Strategies

BEGINNING

Students can write simple words in each event box. They may wish to add pictures to support their ideas.

INTERMEDIATE

Encourage students to write complete sentences in the event boxes.

ADVANCED **ADVANCED HIGH**

Challenge students to include words for each of the five senses in their charts.

OBJECTIVES

Writing

- Writing Process (Drafting): Write a Tall Tale
- Use Writing Strategies: Use Vivid Words
- Develop Writer's Craft: Show Rather Than Tell

Draft

1 Introduce Drafting Use the **Modeled Writing Routine** (See **Writing Routines**, page PD54) to show how to turn the problem-and-solution chart into a draft. Students will focus on:

- **Writer's Craft: Show, Don't Tell** Introduce: _It is much more interesting to show the reader what characters are doing and feeling—instead of just telling the reader._ Direct students' attention to the model on page 276. Ask: _How does the writer show what happens between Sue and the tornado?_ (The writer uses action verbs, such as _raced_ and _screamed_, and vivid phrases, such as _the spinning tornado_ and _in pain_ to show what Sue does to stop the tornado.)

- **Writing Strategy: Use Vivid Words** Explain: _Good writers use vivid words to engage the reader. Vivid words give the reader a clear picture of what you are describing._ Have students identify vivid words in the model on page 276 and tell how these words make the story more engaging.

Say 💬	Write ✏️
I need to begin my tall tale by introducing the character and telling the problem.	A monster tornado was headed toward town. Everyone was scared—but not Slue-Foot Sue!
Then, I'll tell how the main character first tried to stop the tornado.	Sue raced toward the spinning tornado. She jumped up and grabbed the tornado by the tail.
Sue hasn't solved the problem yet, so I need to describe what else she tried. I'll use vivid words to show and not tell, and I'll explain what happened in my own unique way.	She pulled it down to the ground and stomped on is tail. The tornado screamed in pain. It twisted so tightly that it became a skinny piece of string.
Pause to review voice and style. Ask: _Does the writing express a unique voice and style?_ (yes) _Do the words and sentences sound like what the character would?_ (yes) _Are the words vivid and engaging?_ (yes) _Are the sentences varied?_ (yes) _What is the story missing?_ (an ending that tells the solution)	
I'll end my tall tale by telling how Sue solved the problem.	Sue rolled the skinny tornado into a little ball. "You can forget about this tornado!" she said to the cheering crowd.

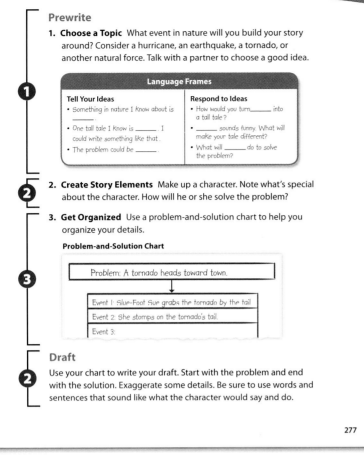

Prewrite

1. **Choose a Topic** What event in nature will you build your story around? Consider a hurricane, an earthquake, a tornado, or another natural force. Talk with a partner to choose a good idea.

Language Frames	
Tell Your Ideas	**Respond to Ideas**
• Something in nature I know about is _____	• How would you turn _____ into a tall tale?
• One tall tale I know is _____. I could write something like that.	• _____ sounds funny. What will make your tale different?
• The problem could be _____.	• What will _____ do to solve the problem?

2. **Create Story Elements** Make up a character. Note what's special about the character. How will he or she solve the problem?

3. **Get Organized** Use a problem-and-solution chart to help you organize your details.

Problem-and-Solution Chart

Problem: A tornado heads toward town.

Event 1: Slue-Foot Sue grabs the tornado by the tail.
Event 2: She stomps on the tornado's tail.
Event 3:

Draft

Use your chart to write your draft. Start with the problem and end with the solution. Exaggerate some details. Be sure to use words and sentences that sound like what the character would say and do.

277

Student Book page 277

---

② **Write the Draft** Have students begin their own drafts. Use **Multi-Level Strategies** to support writers at all levels of language proficiency.

Drafting Tip: It is important to know when your tall tale is done. Your tall tale is done when the answer is *yes* to these questions: *Does my story begin by introducing the main character and the problem and then show how that main character tries to solves the problem? Do I use vivid language and varied sentences to show the reader what happens? Do I present the details with my own unique voice and style? Does the end show how the main character solves the problem?*

Remind students: *Your chart and notes may contain fragments or incomplete ideas. Check that every sentence in your draft is a complete sentence.*

CHECK PROGRESS Have partners read their drafts to one another and then discuss whether the writing is powerful and engaging.

Differentiate

Multi-Level Strategies

BEGINNING

Ask students to draw a picture to illustrate the problem, the events, and the solution. Then have them dictate a sentence that tells about each picture.

INTERMEDIATE

Tell these students to focus on using vivid verbs that describe the character's actions in the draft.

ADVANCED

Ask these students to focus on varying their sentences and showing, rather than telling.

ADVANCED HIGH

Challenge these students to include dialogue at least twice in their stories.

OBJECTIVES

Listening, Speaking, and Teamwork Strategies
- Conduct a Peer conference
- Prompt and Provide Suggestions

Writing
- Writing Process (Revise): ❶ Revise Drafts for Voice and Style; Revise Drafts for Details and Natural Language; Use Revising Marks

Resources

⏺ eVisual 4.35

↻ ⏺ Practice Master 4.26

⏺ eVisual 4.36

Differentiate

Multi-Level Strategies

BEGINNING

Hold individual conferences with students. Check to be sure each student has opened with a problem and closed with a solution.

INTERMEDIATE

Tell partners to ask and answer:
- *Have I added details to help the reader understand the tale?*
- *Have I used natural language and written with my personal voice?*

ADVANCED **ADVANCED HIGH**

Have students hold complete peer conferences. Direct them to point out strong parts as well as problems. Ask them to provide suggestions for improvement.

Revise

❶ **Read, Retell, and Respond** Review the trait on **Practice Master 4.24**. Then use **eVisual 4.35** to model how to conduct a peer conference. Have students read the paragraph aloud.

Slue-Footed Sue and the Tornado

A tornado was coming to town. Everyone was scared. Slue-Footed Sue was not scared. Sue raced toward the tornado. She jumped up and grabbed its tail. She stepped on it. The tornado screamed in pain. It twisted into a piece of string. Sue rolled the skinny tornado into a little ball. "This tornado will not be a problem any more!" she said. The crowd cheered.

🌐 **NGReach.com** ⟩ **eVisual 4.35**

Point to the **Language Frames** as you retell the story and make suggestions:

- *The story takes place in a town.*

- *The main character's problem is a tornado is coming to town. Sue runs toward the tornado. Then she jumps and grabs its tail. Finally, she stomps on it.*

- *The funniest part is when the tornado screams in pain and twists into a piece of string.*

- *It was hard to picture the tornado and what Sue did to it. You could add more details to describe the tornado and use more vivid verbs.*

- *Your story is strong in some parts. Sue's dialogue is one place where you can add different words to sound like she would. That would make it stronger.*

Have pairs discuss their drafts. Use **Multi-Level Strategies** to support students at all proficiency levels.

❷ **Make Changes** Read through the samples. Then use **eVisual 4.35** to model how to revise a draft. Display and use the Revising Marks as you work through the example.

Explain: *During the peer conference, my reader gave me a lot of suggestions. I've also looked at the rubric again to see what a Score 4 should contain.*

Model the first change: *I can revise the beginning of my tale to give details about the problem. Then I can add details to show how Sue tried to solve the problem.*

Call on students to suggest additional changes that would turn the model into a 4. Have students use **Practice Master 4.26** for additional practice.

Revising Marks	
∧	Add.
⌐	Take out.
⟍∧	Move to here.
ⓈⓅ	Check spelling.

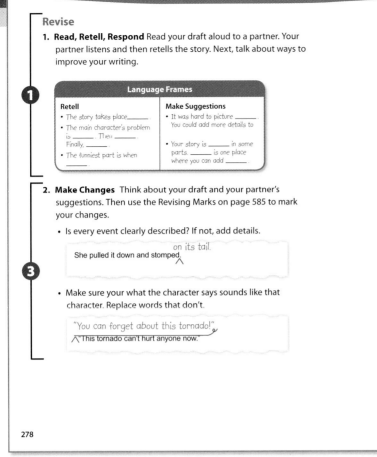

Revise

1. **Read, Retell, Respond** Read your draft aloud to a partner. Your partner listens and then retells the story. Next, talk about ways to improve your writing.

Language Frames	
Retell	**Make Suggestions**
• The story takes place_____.	• It was hard to picture _____. You could add more details to _____.
• The main character's problem is _____. Then _____. Finally, _____.	
	• Your story is _____ in some parts. _____ is one place where you can add _____.
• The funniest part is when _____.	

2. **Make Changes** Think about your draft and your partner's suggestions. Then use the Revising Marks on page 585 to mark your changes.

• Is every event clearly described? If not, add details.

> on its tail.
> She pulled it down and stomped.⌃

• Make sure your what the character says sounds like that character. Replace words that don't.

> "You can forget about this tornado!"
> ⌃"This tornado can't hurt anyone now."

278

Student Book page 278

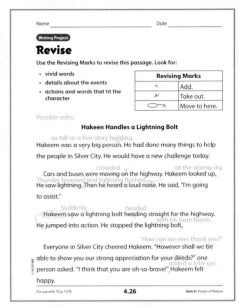

Name _____ Date _____

Writing Project
Revise
Use the Revising Marks to revise this passage. Look for:
• vivid words
• details about the events
• actions and words that fit the character

	Revising Marks
∧	Add.
℘	Take out.
⌒	Move to here.

Possible edits:

Hakeem Handles a Lightning Bolt
as tall as a five-story building.
Hakeem was a very big person. He had done many things to help the people in Silver City. He would have a new challenge today.
crowded   at the stormy sky.
Cars and buses were moving on the highway. Hakeem looked up.
Thunder boomed and lightning flashed.
He saw lightning. Then he heard a loud noise. He said, "I'm going to assist."
Suddenly,   headed
Hakeem saw a lightning bolt heading straight for the highway.
with his bare hands.
He jumped into action. He stopped the lightning bolt.
"How can we ever thank you?"
Everyone in Silver City cheered Hakeem. "However shall we be
able to show you our strong appreciation for your deeds?" one
added a little girl.
person asked. "I think that you are oh-so-brave!" Hakeem felt happy.

For use with TE p. T278   **4.26**   Unit 4 | Power of Nature

 Practice Master 4.26

3 **Revise the Draft** Tell students to use the Revising Marks and begin revising their own drafts. Remind them to review the rubric and notes from their peer conferences.

Post examples as a reminder to use vivid words, such as sensory details, and to show, not tell, what happens.

Telling	**Showing**
There was lightning. She took it out of the sky.	Crackle! She grabbed the jagged bolt of lightning as it blazed through the pitch-black sky.

NGReach.com ▸ eVisual 4.36

> **CHECK PROGRESS** As students revise, check to make sure each tale includes vivid words that engage the reader. Also, check to be certain all tales include exaggerated details, a problem, and a solution.

Writing Project continued

OBJECTIVES

Listening and Speaking
- Read with Expression
- Visualize
- Listen Actively
- Use Gestures and Expressions

Writing
- Writing Process (Edit and Proofread): Edit for Spelling, Grammar, and Mechanics
- Writing Process (Publish and Share): Create a Final Copy; Read Writing Aloud

Grammar, Spelling, and Mechanics
- Use Forms of *be* and *have* Correctly
- Use Subject-Verb Agreement
- Check Spelling (Contractions)
- Capitalize Proper Nouns

Resources

🔹 *Practice Master 4.27*

🔹 *eVisual 4.37*

Review Grammar: Subject-Verb Agreement

Review: *The verbs* be *and* have *tell what a noun is like or what a noun has. They are also helping verbs. Some verbs are action verbs. They tell what a subject does.* Write: *Mia writes a story. Mia and Oscar write together.* Underline the verbs, reminding students that verbs must agree with the subject of the sentence.

Have partners choose the verb that completes each sentence:

Mia and Oscar (is/are) partners.

Mia (has/have) an idea for a story.

Oscar (like/likes) the story idea.

They (work/works) on the story.

They (is/are) excited to share it.

Assign **Practice Master 4.26** for additional practice.

T279a Unit 4 | Power of Nature

Edit and Proofread

1 Focus on Spelling: Contractions Remind students that a contraction is formed by combining two words. Guide them in recalling that letters are left out when the two words are combined, and the letters are replaced by an apostrophe. Suggest students check a dictionary if they are unsure of the spelling of a contraction.

Write: *is not* and *isn't*. Ask: *Which word is a contraction?* (isn't) *What are the two words that have been combined to form* isn't? (is, not) *What was left out when the words were combined?* (the letter *o*) Repeat with *could have/could've*. (contraction: could've/the letters *ha*)

Display the words below. Have students work in pairs. Explain that one student should read the words in the first column aloud, and the other should write the contraction formed by the two words and then read the contraction aloud. Have students switch roles and repeat the process for words in the second column.

I am (I'm)	can not (can't)
here is (here's)	let us (let's)
she would (she'd)	should not (shouldn't)
might have (might've)	who would (who'd)

Assign **Practice Master 4.27** for additional practice.

2 Focus on Mechanics: Capitalization of Proper Nouns

Explain: *A common noun names any person, place, or thing. A proper noun names a specific person, place, or thing. It begins with a capital letter.* Write: *city.* Ask: *Is* city *a common noun or a proper noun?* (common noun) *How can you tell?* (It names any city.) Next, write: *Chicago.* Ask: *Is this a common noun or a proper noun?* (proper noun) *How can you tell?* (It names a specific city. It begins with a capital letter.)

Direct students' attention to "Slue-Footed Sue and the Tornado" on page 276. Have students identify the proper noun and common nouns. Remind students to capitalize proper nouns in their tall tales.

Assign **Practice Master 4.27** for additional practice.

3 Edit and Proofread Display the editing marks as partners work together to edit and proofread their articles.

Provide and model the editing tip: *Use a highlighter or pen to mark things you are not sure about as you edit. Then check a dictionary to determine which of the items you marked might need correction.*

Editing Marks

∧	Add.
‿	Take out.
(sp)	Check spelling.
≡	Capitalize.

NGReach.com ❯ eVisual 4.37

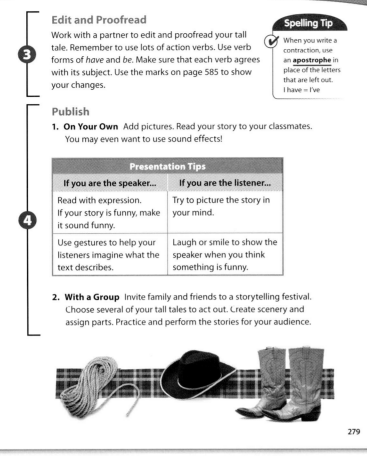

Student Book page 279

Content of Student Book page 279:

Edit and Proofread

3 Work with a partner to edit and proofread your tall tale. Remember to use lots of action verbs. Use verb forms of *have* and *be*. Make sure that each verb agrees with its subject. Use the marks on page 585 to show your changes.

Spelling Tip

When you write a contraction, use an **apostrophe** in place of the letters that are left out.
I have = I've

Publish

1. On Your Own Add pictures. Read your story to your classmates. You may even want to use sound effects!

Presentation Tips	
If you are the speaker...	**If you are the listener...**
Read with expression. If your story is funny, make it sound funny.	Try to picture the story in your mind.
Use gestures to help your listeners imagine what the text describes.	Laugh or smile to show the speaker when you think something is funny.

2. With a Group Invite family and friends to a storytelling festival. Choose several of your tall tales to act out. Create scenery and assign parts. Practice and perform the stories for your audience.

279

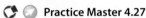

Practice Master 4.27

4 Publish Share Your Tall Tale Encourage students to make a neat copy of the tall tale. They may choose to type it with a word processing program and use clip art to add pictures. Go through the **Presentation Tips** and model the skills for the class:

- **Read with Expression:** Demonstrate the difference between reading funny content with and without expression. Explain that reading with expression engages the audience.

- **Use Gestures:** Reread the student model on page 276, and model using gestures as you read the second paragraph of the story.

- **Visualize:** Remind students to listen for details that help them picture the main character and story action. Explain that picturing these things in their minds will help them better enjoy the story.

- **Listen Actively:** Explain that listeners can show they are enjoying a story by reacting to it. Laughing and smiling are two things listeners can do to show the writer they are enjoying the tall tale.

Have students work in small groups to dramatize one of the tall tales. Encourage them to create scenery, costumes, and props for the tale. Invite students to act out their tall tales for family and friends during a storytelling festival.

Add a copy of each story in the appropriate student's Writing Portfolio.

OBJECTIVES

Concepts and Vocabulary
- Use Grade-Level Vocabulary ⊕
- Use Academic Vocabulary ⊕
- Use Learning Strategies: Graphic Organizers

Language
- Language Function: Make Comparisons; Express Certainty, Probability, Possibility; Express Needs and Wants
- Discuss Ideas

Science
- Identify and Explore Earth's Resources
- Explore Renewable Resources
- Understand Conservation of Natural Resources
- Explore Elements of Nature

Resources

- *pens or pencils*
- *colored markers or colored pencils*
- *lined paper, unlined paper, and poster paper*
- *prerecorded TV weather report or Internet weather site*

Community Connection

Suggest that students take a family member on a tour of their neighborhood and point out elements of nature that they rely on for food, clothing, energy, and other needs.

Language of the Day

What have you learned about how we relate to nature?

I have learned _____.

Read the Language of the Day. Model: *I have learned that one way to* **relate** *to nature is to use* **natural resources** *carefully so they don't become* **scarce**. Have students share other answers to the question.

Talk Together

1 **Complete the Unit Concept Map** Read aloud the introduction. Encourage students to skim the selections in the unit, review the **Leveled Library** books they read, and think about class discussions.

Use these possible answers to the unit concept map to guide the discussion.

2 **Write a Description** Read aloud the directions. If students have trouble getting started, have them look back at the descriptive paragraph they wrote about a very windy day (page 236).

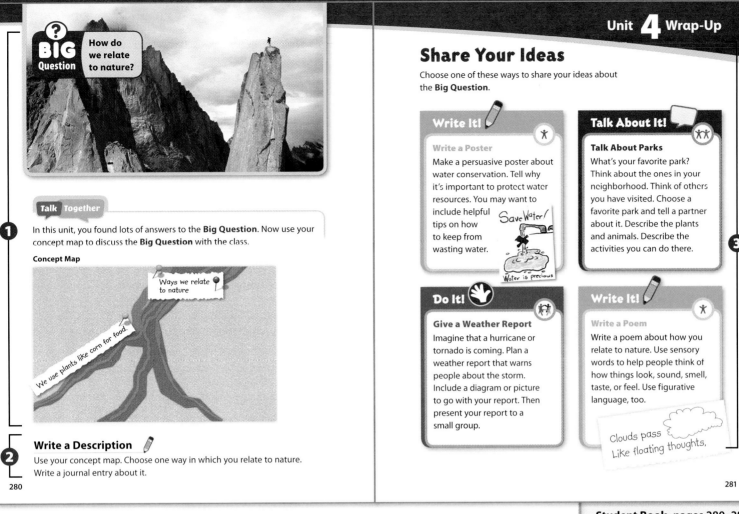

Share Your Ideas

Share Your Ideas

3 **Select and Present** Read aloud the presentation options. Explain that some options can be completed alone, but that the others involve working in groups. You may choose to assign students to specific activities or allow them to self-select.

Writing Activity: Write a Poster A AH Encourage students to create a list of needs and wants that relate to water conservation. Tell them to use a few ideas from their chart on their poster.

Oral Activity: Talk About Parks B I Students may feel more confident speaking about a park if they first draw a picture of the location. Tell them to include details they will discuss with their partner. They can point out the details on the picture as they talk.

Kinesthetic Activity: Give a Weather Report I A AH Have students look at a prerecorded television weather report or an Internet weather site to get ideas for diagrams to make.

Writing Activity: Write a Poem A AH Have students choose an object or place in nature they relate to. Encourage them to use Language Frames to make comparisons using the object or place they have chosen to generate ideas, such as:

- _____ is _____ but _____ is _____ .
- _____ is _____ but _____ is not _____ .

4 **Respond and Close** Have students share a way we relate to nature.

Student Book pages 280–281

Keys to Efficacy

Demonstrate self-questioning to show students how they can prepare for each activity. *What is the task? What materials will I need? What is the first step? What will I do next? What is the last thing I need to do? How will I know if I've done a good job?*

▸ eAssessment
▸ Online Forms
▸ Reteaching Resources

NGReach.com

Administer the assessments below to monitor progress and identify which students will benefit from review, reteaching, or additional practice.

Tested Skills	Assessment Tools	Review and Reteaching
Oral Language		
❶ Make Comparisons ❶ Express Needs and Wants	• Part 1, Day 10 TE page T246g; 🗘 💿 page 168 • Part 2, Day 10 TE page T276g; 🗘 💿 page 168	💿 Reteaching and Review Activities
❶ Retell a Selection	• Part 1, Day 5 TE page T237c; 🗘 💿 page 172 • Part 2, Day 5 TE page T269c; 🗘 💿 page 176	Preview and model how to complete the graphic organizers. Provide additional books for practice and re-testing. • Leveled Library • Explorer Book Collection 💿 Leveled Book Finder
Vocabulary		
❶ Content Vocabulary ❶ Academic Vocabulary ❶ Context Clues ❶ Multiple-Meaning Words	🗘 💿 ☑ 💽 Part 1 Key Words Test, page 169 🗘 💿 ☑ 💽 Part 2 Key Words Test, page 173 🗘 💿 ☑ 💽 Reading Unit Test, page 180 **B** **I** **A** **AH**	Use the Vocabulary Reteaching Routine (PD43). 💿 Vocabulary Games 💿 Reteaching and Review Activities 💿 My Vocabulary Notebook
Reading		
Reading Comprehension ❶ Strategy: Ask Questions ❶ Text Structure: Cause and Effect ❶ Text Structure: Problem and Solution **Reading Fluency** ❶ Intonation ❶ Expression ❶ Accuracy and Rate	🗘 💿 Reading Strategy Test, page 177 🗘 💿 ☑ 💽 Reading Unit Test, page 180 **B** **I** **A** **AH** ■ Comprehension Coach 🗘 💿 Fluency Practice Masters, pages 4.8 and 4.20 🗘 💿 ☑ Fluency Benchmark Assessment, page 441	**Review Comprehension** Review the test items. Point out the correct response for each item and discuss why it is correct. 💿 Leveled Library lesson plans **Review Fluency** Use Fluency Routines (PD52) and Fluency Passages from Unit 3. Have students listen to the fluency model as they follow along in the text.
Grammar and Writing		
Grammar ❶ Present-Tense Action Verbs ❶ Present Progressive ❶ Forms of *be* ❶ Forms of *have* and Modals **Writing** ❶ Writing Trait: Voice and Style	🗘 💿 ☑ 💽 Grammar Unit Test, page 207 **B** **I** **A** **AH** 🗘 💿 ☑ 💽 Writing Unit Test, page 214 **I** **A** **AH** 🗘 💿 Writing Rubrics, Forms, and Checklists, page 469 🗘 💿 Writing Self-Assessment and Peer Assessments, page 482	**Grammar** Review Grammar Rules boxes and eVisuals from this unit. Use Handbook pages to reteach with additional examples. 💿 Reteaching and Review Activities **Writing** To reteach the writing process or writing traits, use Handbook pages. 💿 Reteaching and Review Activities
Other Measures		
🗘 💿 Unit Self-Assessment, page 179	🗘 💿 Affective Measures, pages 462–465	🗘 💿 Metacognitive Measures, pages 466–468

Key: ❶ Tested Skill   🗘 Assessment Handbooks   💿 NGReach.com   ☑ eAssessment   💽 ExamView

Student Book

Picture Dictionary

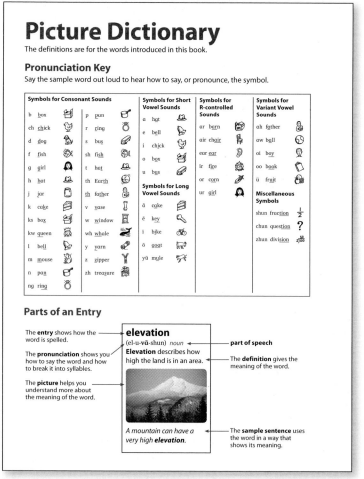

Picture Dictionary
The definitions are for the words introduced in this book.

Pronunciation Key
Say the sample word out loud to hear how to say, or pronounce, the symbol.

Symbols for Consonant Sounds		Symbols for Short Vowel Sounds	Symbols for R-controlled Sounds	Symbols for Variant Vowel Sounds
b box	p pan	a hat	ar born	ah father
ch chick	r ring	e bell	air chair	aw ball
d dog	s bus	i chick	ear ear	oi boy
f fish	sh fish	o box	ir fire	oo book
g girl	t hat	u bus	or corn	ü fruit
h hat	th Earth	**Symbols for Long Vowel Sounds**	ur girl	**Miscellaneous Symbols**
j jar	th father	ā cake		shun fraction ½
k cake	v vase	ē key		chun question ?
ks box	w window	ī bike		zhun division
kw queen	wh whale	ō goat		
l bell	y yarn	yū mule		
m mouse	z zipper			
n pan	zh treasure			
ng ring				

Parts of an Entry

The **entry** shows how the word is spelled.

The **pronunciation** shows you how to say the word and how to break it into syllables.

The **picture** helps you understand more about the meaning of the word.

elevation
(el-u-vā-shun) *noun*
Elevation describes how high the land is in an area.

A mountain can have a very high elevation.

part of speech
The **definition** gives the meaning of the word.

The **sample sentence** uses the word in a way that shows its meaning.

Page 616

A

ability
(u-**bi**-lu-tē) *noun*
An **ability** is a skill.

This girl has the ability to play the flute.

accelerate
(ik-**se**-lu-rāt) *verb*
When someone **accelerates** they move faster.

A racecar accelerates to the finish line.

adaptation
(a-dap-**tā**-shun) *noun*
An **adaptation** is a change that a species develops to live in an environment.

A giraffe's long neck and legs are adaptations so it can eat from tall trees.

adventure
(ud-**ven**-chur) *noun*
An **adventure** is an exciting experience.

Early explorers had many adventures.

ancestor
(an-**ses**-tur) *noun*
An **ancestor** is a family member who lived a long time ago.

The boy is learning about his ancestors.

ancient
(**ānt**-shunt) *adjective*
When something is **ancient** it is very old or it happened in the past.

There are ancient buildings all around the world.

617

Page 617

archaeologist
(ar-kē-**ah**-lu-jist) *noun*
An **archaeologist** is someone who studies old buildings and civilizations.

Archaeologists discover new information about ancient cultures.

artifact
(ar-ti-**fakt**) *noun*
An **artifact** is something that a human made long ago, such as a tool or a weapon.

Artifacts such as these arrowheads were used for hunting.

astronaut
(**as**-tru-nawt) *noun*
An **astronaut** is someone who travels in space.

Astronauts wear special equipment so they can breathe in space.

atmosphere
(**at**-mu-sfear) *noun*
The **atmosphere** is the mixture of gases that are all around a planet.

Clouds form in the atmosphere.

available
(u-**vā**-lu-bul) *adjective*
When something is **available**, it is ready to take.

Fresh fruit is available in summer.

average
(**a**-vu-rij) *noun*
An **average** is an amount that is usual for a group.

Bears have an average of two cubs.

B

balance
(**ba**-luns) *noun*
When something is in **balance**, it is steady.

If she keeps her balance, she will not fall.

behavior
(bi-**hā**-vyur) *noun*
Behavior is how a living thing acts.

You can train an animal to learn a new behavior.

618

Page 618

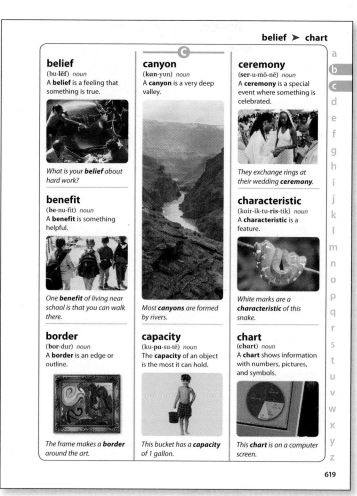

belief
(bu-**lēf**) *noun*
A **belief** is a feeling that something is true.

What is your belief about hard work?

benefit
(**be**-nu-fit) *noun*
A **benefit** is something helpful.

One benefit of living near school is that you can walk there.

border
(**bor**-dur) *noun*
A **border** is an edge or outline.

The frame makes a border around the art.

canyon
(**kan**-yun) *noun*
A **canyon** is a very deep valley.

Most canyons are formed by rivers.

capacity
(ku-**pa**-su-tē) *noun*
The **capacity** of an object is the most it can hold.

This bucket has a capacity of 1 gallon.

C

ceremony
(**ser**-u-mō-nē) *noun*
A **ceremony** is a special event where something is celebrated.

They exchange rings at their wedding ceremony.

characteristic
(kair-ik-tu-**ris**-tik) *noun*
A **characteristic** is a feature.

White marks are a characteristic of this snake.

chart
(chart) *noun*
A **chart** shows information with numbers, pictures, and symbols.

This chart is on a computer screen.

619

Page 619

conservation
(kon-sir-**vā**-shun) *noun*
Conservation means saving or protecting something.

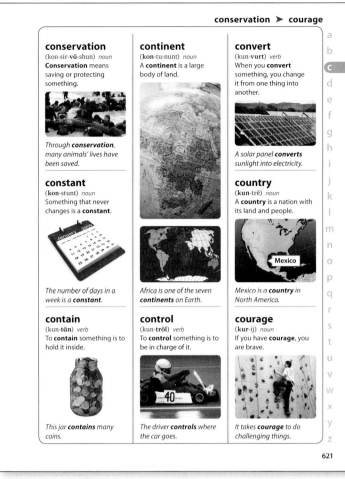

*Through **conservation**, many animals' lives have been saved.*

constant
(**kon**-stunt) *noun*
Something that never changes is a **constant**.

*The number of days in a week is a **constant**.*

contain
(kun-**tān**) *verb*
To **contain** something is to hold it inside.

*This jar **contains** many coins.*

continent
(**kon**-tu-nunt) *noun*
A **continent** is a large body of land.

*Africa is one of the seven **continents** on Earth.*

control
(kun-**trōl**) *verb*
To **control** something is to be in charge of it.

*The driver **controls** where the car goes.*

convert
(kun-**vurt**) *verb*
When you **convert** something, you change it from one thing into another.

*A solar panel **converts** sunlight into electricity.*

country
(**kun**-trē) *noun*
A **country** is a nation with its land and people.

Mexico

*Mexico is a **country** in North America.*

courage
(**kur**-ij) *noun*
If you have **courage**, you are brave.

*It takes **courage** to do challenging things.*

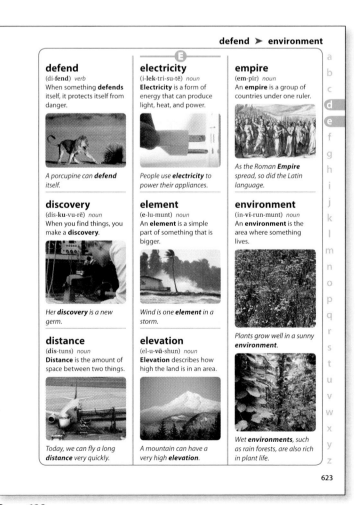

Picture Dictionary, continued

Page 624

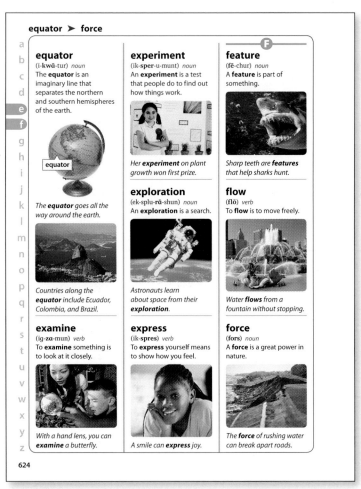

equator
(i-kwā-tur) noun
The **equator** is an imaginary line that separates the northern and southern hemispheres of the earth.

*The **equator** goes all the way around the earth.*

*Countries along the **equator** include Ecuador, Colombia, and Brazil.*

examine
(ig-za-mun) verb
To **examine** something is to look at it closely.

*With a hand lens, you can **examine** a butterfly.*

experiment
(ik-sper-u-munt) noun
An **experiment** is a test that people do to find out how things work.

*Her **experiment** on plant growth won first prize.*

exploration
(ek-splu-rā-shun) noun
An **exploration** is a search.

*Astronauts learn about space from their **exploration**.*

express
(ik-spres) verb
To **express** yourself means to show how you feel.

*A smile can **express** joy.*

feature
(fē-chur) noun
A **feature** is part of something.

*Sharp teeth are **features** that help sharks hunt.*

flow
(flō) verb
To **flow** is to move freely.

*Water **flows** from a fountain without stopping.*

force
(fors) noun
A **force** is a great power in nature.

*The **force** of rushing water can break apart roads.*

624

Page 625

galleon
(ga-lē-un) noun
A **galleon** is a large sailing ship that was used hundreds of years ago.

*In the 17th century, people would sail **galleons** all around the world.*

generate
(je-nu-rāt) verb
To **generate** something, is to make it from other materials.

*Windmills are used to **generate** electricity.*

globe
(glōb) noun
A **globe** is a ball with the map of the earth on it.

*The students studied the **globe** in their social studies class.*

habitat
(ha-bu-tat) noun
A **habitat** is a place where an organism can live and flourish.

*Some snakes live in a hot, desert **habitat**.*

height
(hit) noun
Height is the measurement of how tall someone or something is.

*These boys are different **heights**.*

hemisphere
(he-mu-sfear) noun
A **hemisphere** is one half of the earth.

*The equator separates the two **hemispheres**.*

heritage
(hair-u-tij) noun
Your **heritage** is the traditions, ideas, and language that come from your ancestors.

*Playing a traditional instrument is part of his Indonesian **heritage**.*

625

Page 626

hero
(hear-ō) noun
A **hero** is a person admired by others for being brave.

*When the firefighter rescued the child, everyone said he was a **hero**.*

humid
(hyū-mud) adjective
It is **humid** when there is a lot of moisture in the air.

*A hot and **humid** greenhouse is good for plants.*

imagine
(i-ma-jun) verb
To **imagine** something is to picture it in your mind.

*Your art shows others what you **imagine**.*

imitate
(i-mu-tāt) verb
When you **imitate** something, you try to copy it.

*Babies will try to **imitate** their mothers' smiles.*

influence
(in-flū-unts) verb
To **influence** someone is to affect that person.

*Family members can **influence** your interests.*

inhabitant
(in-ha-bu-tunt) noun
An **inhabitant** is a person who lives somewhere.

*These people are **inhabitants** of Japan.*

inherit
(in-hair-ut) verb
To **inherit** means to get things, usually from parents.

*Skunks **inherit** their stripes.*

interact
(in-tur-akt) verb
When you **interact**, you communicate in some way.

*This girl **interacts** with the horse.*

626

Page 627

interpret
(in-tur-prut) verb
To **interpret** something is to tell what you think it means.

*Can you **interpret** these signs?*

introduce
(in-tru-düs) verb
When people **introduce** themselves, they meet for the first time.

*A handshake is a friendly way to **introduce** yourself.*

invade
(in-vād) verb
To **invade** something is to take it over without permission.

*Sometimes people **invade** natural habitats.*

investigate
(in-ves-tu-gāt) verb
When you **investigate** something, you find out about it.

*The boy **investigates** the cave.*

landform
(land-form) noun
A **landform** is the natural shape of a section of land.

*A mountain is a large **landform**.*

landscape
(land-skāp) noun
A **landscape** is a large area of land.

*These hills are part of this pretty green **landscape**.*

language
(lang-gwij) noun
Language is a way of sharing ideas.

*Writing is a form of **language**.*

627

launch
(**lawnch**) *verb*
When you **launch** something, you send it up into the air.

*This rocket was **launched** into space.*

learn
(**lurn**) *verb*
To **learn** is to gain new skills and information.

*This calf must **learn** to walk.*

legend
(**le**-jund) *noun*
A **legend** explains symbols on a map.

LEGEND
Highway
Road
River
Trees
Swamp

*This **legend** shows blue lines as rivers.*

limit
(**li**-mut) *verb*
To **limit** something is to stop it after a set time or amount.

*Many parents **limit** TV viewing.*

locate
(**lō**-kāt) *verb*
To **locate** is to find.

*We use maps to **locate** cities and states.*

map
(**map**) *noun*
A **map** is a drawing of Earth's surface, or a part of it.

*The class looks at the world **map**.*

marriage
(**mair**-ij) *noun*
A **marriage** is a wedding ceremony that unites a husband and wife.

*They had a lovely **marriage** ceremony.*

Page 628

---

material
(mu-**tear**-ē-ul) *noun*
Materials are the small parts that make up something bigger.

*Sand is a **material** used in cement.*

measure
(**me**-zhur) *verb*
When you **measure** something you find out its size, weight or amount of it.

*The girl is using a ruler to **measure** her cat.*

*The scale **measures** the weight of the orange.*

medium
(**mē**-dē-um) *noun*
A **medium** is a form of communication.

*Radio is one **medium** for news.*

memory
(**mem**-rē) *noun*
Memory is the power to recall or remember events.

*Memory** is stored in the brain.*

merchant
(**mur**-chunt) *noun*
A **merchant** is someone who buys or sells items.

*People buy fish from this **merchant**.*

migration
(mi-**grā**-shun) *noun*
During a **migration**, people or animals move from one place to another.

*These birds fly south in their yearly **migration**.*

mission
(**mi**-shun) *noun*
A **mission** is a job with a goal.

*Their **mission** is to rescue people after an earthquake.*

modify
(**mah**-du-fī) *verb*
When you **modify** something, you change it.

*Modify** a jar to make a bird feeder.*

Page 629

---

mold
(**mōld**) *noun*
Mold is a fungus that grows on old food.

*This bread has a lot of **mold** on it.*

motion
(**mō**-shun) *noun*
Motion is movement.

*A racecar's **motion** is very fast!*

motive
(**mō**-tiv) *noun*
A **motive** is a reason for doing something.

*One **motive** for studying is to get good grades.*

musical
(**myü**-zi-kul) *adjective*
When someone plays an instrument or sings well, they are **musical**.

*It was a very **musical** performance.*

native
(**nā**-tiv) *adjective*
When living things are **native** to an area, they live and grow there naturally.

*In many desert regions, the cactus is a **native** plant.*

natural
(**na**-chu-rul) *adjective*
Something is **natural** if it wasn't made by humans.

*This is a **natural** rock formation.*

navigation
(na-vu-**gā**-shun) *noun*
Navigation is the process of figuring out how to get somewhere.

*With careful **navigation** the boat can pass through the icebergs safely.*

object
(**ob**-jekt) *noun*
An **object** is something that isn't alive that you can touch and see.

clock

remote control

ball glove

*These are all **objects**.*

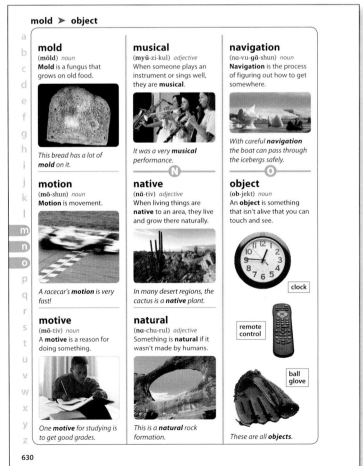

Page 630

---

occasion
(u-**kā**-zhun) *noun*
An **occasion** is a special event.

*The birthday party was a fun **occasion**.*

ocean
(**ō**-shun) *noun*
The **ocean** is the salt water that covers almost three-fourths of Earth.

*Oceans** are very large bodies of water.*

official
(u-**fi**-shul) *adjective*
When something is **official**, it's approved.

*This **official** seal is from the president's office.*

orbit
(**or**-but) *verb*
In space, something **orbits** when it moves around a sun, a moon, or a planet in a predictable path.

*The planets **orbit** around the sun.*

pattern
(**pa**-turn) *noun*
A **pattern** is a design that repeats more than once.

*This floor has an interesting **pattern**.*

perform
(pur-**form**) *verb*
You **perform** when you put on a show for other people.

*These students **perform** for the school.*

physical
(**fi**-zi-kul) *adjective*
Something you can see and touch is **physical**.

*Soccer is a very **physical** sport.*

plain
(**plān**) *noun*
A **plain** is a large area of flat, nearly treeless land.

*Bison live on America's Great **Plains**.*

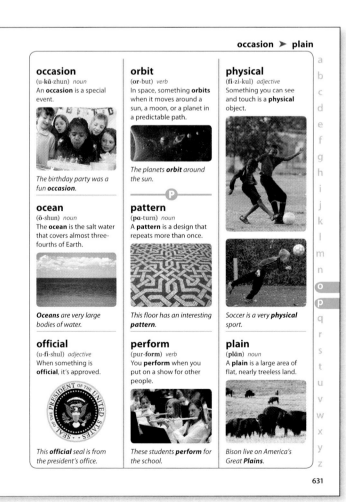

Page 631

Picture Dictionary, continued

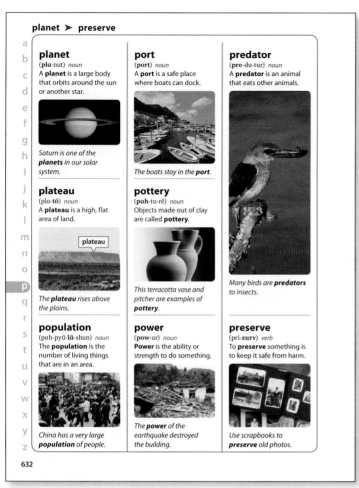

planet
(**pla**-nut) *noun*
A **planet** is a large body that orbits around the sun or another star.

Saturn is one of the planets in our solar system.

plateau
(pla-**tō**) *noun*
A **plateau** is a high, flat area of land.

plateau

The plateau rises above the plains.

population
(pah-pyū-**lā**-shun) *noun*
The **population** is the number of living things that are in an area.

China has a very large population of people.

port
(port) *noun*
A **port** is a safe place where boats can dock.

The boats stay in the port.

pottery
(**pah**-tu-rē) *noun*
Objects made out of clay are called **pottery**.

This terracotta vase and pitcher are examples of pottery.

power
(**pow**-ur) *noun*
Power is the ability or strength to do something.

The power of the earthquake destroyed the building.

predator
(**pre**-du-tur) *noun*
A **predator** is an animal that eats other animals.

Many birds are predators to insects.

preserve
(pri-**zurv**) *verb*
To **preserve** something is to keep it safe from harm.

Use scrapbooks to preserve old photos.

632

Page 632

president
(**pre**-zu-dunt) *noun*
A **president** is an elected leader of a country.

George Washington was the first president of the United States.

prey
(**prā**) *noun*
Prey is an animal that is hunted for food.

The rabbit is prey for the bobcat.

principle
(**prin**-su-pul) *noun*
A **principle** is a rule or law.

Some U.S. laws are based on the principles of freedom.

project
(**prah**-jekt) *noun*
A **project** is a job or activity.

Building a skyscraper is a huge project.

protect
(pru-**tekt**) *verb*
You **protect** something when you guard it against harm.

Seat belts help to protect people in cars.

range
(**rānj**) *noun*
A **range** is a group of things in a certain order.

The Rocky Mountains are a mountain range.

rate
(**rāt**) *noun*
Rate is the speed at which something is happening.

Turtles move at a slow rate.

record
(re-**kurd**) *noun*
A **record** of something is the facts about what happened.

clay tablet

Because many ancient people wrote down information, we have a record of their lives.

633

Page 633

region
(**rē**-jun) *noun*
A **region** is an area of land.

Oregon

Oregon is in the northwest region of the country.

relate
(ri-**lāt**) *verb*
To **relate** two things, think about how they are connected.

You can relate these two sports.

relationship
(ri-**lā**-shun-ship) *noun*
A **relationship** is the way people or things are connected.

Friends have a good relationship.

renewable
(ri-**nyū**-u-bul) *adjective*
Something is **renewable** when you can't use all of it.

Wind is a renewable resource.

resistance
(ri-**zis**-tunts) *noun*
Resistance is a slowing force.

Deep snow creates resistance when you walk in it.

responsible
(ri-**spon**-su-bul) *adjective*
A person who is **responsible** is in charge.

This dad is responsible for his son.

resource
(**rē**-sors) *noun*
A **resource** is something that people need and use.

School supplies are resources for students.

response
(ri-**spons**) *noun*
A **response** is an answer.

These students want to give a response to a question.

634

Page 634

risk
(risk) *noun*
Risk is the possibility of harm.

Wearing a helmet lowers your risk when you ride a bike.

ritual
(**ri**-chu-wul) *noun*
A **ritual** is a special series of events, often done as a ceremony.

Many people have rituals that use water.

role
(**rōl**) *noun*
A **role** is a part or a purpose.

Each actor plays an important role in the school play.

The dog's role is to lead the blind man safely.

rotation
(rō-**tā**-shun) *noun*
The **rotation** of something is how it turns around its axis.

A globe shows the rotation of Earth.

route
(**rūt**) *noun*
A **route** is a path to go someplace.

Do you take the shortest route to school?

scale
(**skāl**) *noun*
A **scale** gives size comparisons.

The scale of this map shows that 1 inch is equal to 1 mile.

635

Page 635

Page 636

a b c d e f g h i j k l m n o p q r **s** t u v w x y z

scarce
(**skairs**) *adjective*
Something is **scarce** if there is not a lot of it.

*Water can be very **scarce** in the desert.*

service
(**sur**-vus) *noun*
When something is of **service**, it is useful.

*A cart is of **service** when you move heavy boxes.*

site
(**sit**) *noun*
A **site** is a special place where something happened.

*People study archeological **sites** to learn about ancient cultures.*

skill
(**skil**) *noun*
A **skill** is the ability that someone has to do something.

*It takes a lot of **skill** to play soccer well.*

solve
(**solv**) *verb*
To **solve** a problem means to figure it out.

*When you **solve** a puzzle, it's done.*

species
(**spē**-shēz) *noun*
A **species** is a group of living things that are very similar and can have offspring.

*Cats and dogs are different **species**.*

speed
(**spēd**) *noun*
Speed is how fast something is going.

*A racecar travels at a very high **speed**.*

636

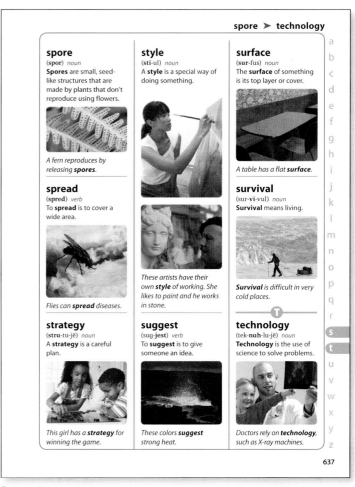

Page 637

a b c d e f g h i j k l m n o p q r **s** **t** u v w x y z

spore
(**spor**) *noun*
Spores are small, seed-like structures that are made by plants that don't reproduce using flowers.

*A fern reproduces by releasing **spores**.*

spread
(**sprēd**) *verb*
To **spread** is to cover a wide area.

*Flies can **spread** diseases.*

strategy
(**stra**-tu-jē) *noun*
A **strategy** is a careful plan.

*This girl has a **strategy** for winning the game.*

style
(**stī**-ul) *noun*
A **style** is a special way of doing something.

*These artists have their own **style** of working. She likes to paint and he works in stone.*

suggest
(sug-**jest**) *verb*
To **suggest** is to give someone an idea.

*These colors **suggest** strong heat.*

surface
(**sur**-fus) *noun*
The **surface** of something is its top layer or cover.

*A table has a flat **surface**.*

survival
(sur-**vī**-vul) *noun*
Survival means living.

Survival is difficult in very cold places.

technology
(tek-**nah**-lu-jē) *noun*
Technology is the use of science to solve problems.

*Doctors rely on **technology**, such as X-ray machines.*

637

Page 638

a b c d e f g h i j k l m n o p q r s **t** **u** **v** w x y z

threatened
(**thre**-tund) *verb*
Something is **threatened** when it is in danger.

*Because of habitat destruction, many rainforest animals are **threatened**.*

tool
(**tül**) *noun*
A **tool** is something that helps you do a task.

*A hammer is a **tool** that helps you pound nails into wood.*

trade
(**trād**) *verb*
To **trade** is to exchange one thing for another.

*The friends **trade** toys.*

tradition
(tru-**di**-shun) *noun*
A **tradition** is a custom or belief shared by a group of people.

*It's a **tradition** to dress up to celebrate the Chinese New Year.*

trait
(**trāt**) *noun*
A **trait** is a characteristic that distinguishes one thing from something else.

*One **trait** of a gazelle is that it can run quickly.*

transport
(trants-**port**) *verb*
To **transport** something is to carry it.

*Large ships **transport** goods across the ocean.*

treasure
(**tre**-zhur) *noun*
A **treasure** is a collection of jewels, money, or other valuable items.

*Gold coins are the **treasure** in this chest.*

valley
(**va**-lē) *noun*
A **valley** is a low area of land between two higher areas.

*This **valley** has a river running through it.*

638

Page 639

a b c d e f g h i j k l m n o p q r s t u **v** **w** x y z

value
(**val**-yü) *verb*
To **value** something is to care about it.

*Many people **value** saving money.*

volunteer
(vah-lun-**tear**) *noun*
A **volunteer** is someone who helps out with a task without being paid.

*This **volunteer** is giving food to people who need it.*

weave
(**wēv**) *verb*
When you **weave**, you lace threads, grass, or other materials together in a pattern.

*She **weaves** thread into beautiful cloth.*

*A tapestry is something people can **weave**. This one was made in Africa.*

639

Contents

Language Development

Language Transfer Supports

Audio Resources

Additional Resources

Stages of Language Acquisition

National Geographic Reach incorporates Academic Language Frames, Multi-Level Strategies, Multi-Level Practice Sets, and more supports to help English language learners move through the stages of language acquisition. As you select strategies and monitor behaviors and progress, keep in mind that stages vary. For example, some students may be beginning speakers and advanced writers while others may be advanced speakers and beginning writers. Use the assessment instruments to measure and monitor language acquisition and adjust scaffolds, grouping, and challenges to support each student. For more information on scaffolding language development, see **Best Practices** (page PD1).

STAGES AND BEHAVIORS	TEACHING STRATEGIES
BEGINNING	
Newcomers & Beginners: • have little or no survival vocabulary or language structures • need to gain familiarity with the sounds, rhythm, and patterns of English • respond non-verbally by pointing, gesturing, nodding, or drawing • have little or no ability to understand spoken English used in academic and social settings • have little or no ability to speak English in academic and social settings • have little or no ability to use English to build foundational reading skills • lack the English vocabulary and English language structures necessary to address grade-appropriate writing tasks • understand new concepts best when previewed in their home language • begin to respond with yes/no or one- or two-word responses • read simple language that has already been experienced orally • write labels, patterned sentences, one- or two-word responses • repeat and recite memorable language; use routine expressions independently • respond with phrases, fragments, and simple subject/verb-based structures • read familiar, patterned text; read language experience texts • begin to apply reading strategies to aid comprehension of text • write patterned text, short captions; complete simple cloze sentences	**Newcomers & Beginners benefit when teachers:** • implement an intensive, individualized or small-group emergent literacy program, starting with the English alphabet • use gestures and other visuals to clarify concepts • provide ample age-appropriate oral-to-print and emergent literacy experiences • use visuals to teach key vocabulary necessary for academic discussion • use simple sentence structures and language patterns during instruction • provide abundant opportunities for active listening, utilizing props, visuals, and real objects • provide opportunities to read literature in short "chunks" • support reading with direct phonics instruction • avoid forcing students to speak before they are ready • model memorable language with songs and chants • pair or group students with more proficient learners • activate prior knowledge, build background, and use visuals before reading activities • ask yes/no, either/or, and Who? What? Where? questions • have students label/manipulate pictures and real objects • provide short frames for students to complete with one- or two-word responses or word banks
INTERMEDIATE	
Intermediate students: • understand simple, high-frequency spoken English used in routine academic and social settings • have the ability to speak in a simple manner, using English commonly heard in routine academic and social settings • have a limited ability to use the English language to build foundational reading skills • have English vocabulary and grasp of English language structures adequate to address grade-appropriate writing tasks in a limited way • understand simple messages with contextual support (gestures etc.) • understand "chunks" or gist of language, and the gist of group reading by relying on picture clues, titles, and summaries • respond to literature with structured support • respond using newly-acquired receptive vocabulary for messages in English • understand more details in spoken English • read resources independently following oral previews or experiences with print • apply reading strategies regularly to aid comprehension of text • write from models for a variety of purposes • respond with connected discourse, using more extensive vocabulary	**Intermediate students benefit when teachers:** • provide direct instruction in key vocabulary necessary for academic discussion • expose students to a variety of understandable texts • have students describe personal experiences, objects, etc. • use graphic organizers or storyboards for retelling or role-plays • structure group discussion to support application of language patterns • structure research projects and guide use of reference resources • ask open-ended questions; model, expand, restate, and enrich student language • provide frames for students to complete with short phrases • provide content-area texts, trade books, newspapers, magazines, etc., to promote conceptual development • respond genuinely to student writing and hold conferences that highlight student strengths and progress • provide frames that support and extend language patterns and structures

STAGES AND BEHAVIORS	TEACHING STRATEGIES

ADVANCED

Advanced students:

- understand, with second language acquisition support, grade-appropriate spoken English used in academic and social settings
- have the ability to speak, with second language acquisition support, using grade-appropriate English in academic and social settings
- have the ability to use English, with second language acquisition support, to build foundational reading skills
- have English vocabulary and grasp of English language structures adequate to address grade-appropriate writing tasks with second language acquisition support
- respond with longer phrases/sentences and increasing grammatical accuracy
- respond to literature by explaining, describing, comparing, and retelling
- participate more fully in discussions, including those with academic content
- understand and respond with increasing levels of accuracy and correctness
- respond with connected discourse, extensive vocabulary, and decreasing grammatical errors
- read and comprehend a wider range of narrative genre and content texts
- apply reading strategies consistently and skillfully
- read, write, and discuss content-area concepts in greater depth
- write connected narrative and expository texts

Advanced students benefit when teachers:

- provide opportunities to create oral and written narratives
- focus on communication in meaningful contexts where students express themselves in speech and print for a wide range of purposes and audiences
- structure group discussion
- guide use of reference resources for research
- facilitate more advanced literature studies

ADVANCED HIGH

Advanced High students:

- understand, with minimal second language acquisition support, grade-appropriate spoken English used in academic and social settings
- have the ability to speak, with minimal second language acquisition support, using grade-appropriate English in academic and social settings
- have the ability to use English, with minimal second language acquisition support, to build foundational reading skills
- have English vocabulary and command of English language structures necessary to address grade-appropriate writing tasks with minimal second language acquisition support
- respond with more complex language structures and patterns
- understand non-literal, idiomatic, everyday, and academic language
- read a wide range of grade-level narrative and expository texts in a variety of subjects, including self-selected resources
- apply reading strategies with automaticity
- write using standard forms with increased depth and breadth of topics and purposes and more creative and analytical writing
- respond using varied grammatical structures and vocabulary
- use a repertoire of language-learning strategies to self-monitor, correct, and further develop English language skills

Advanced High students benefit when teachers:

- facilitate advanced literature studies
- provide opportunities for more sophisticated writing
- continue on-going language development through integrated language arts and content-area activities
- provide opportunities for application of more complex language structures and patterns

Sentence Stems and Activities

Introduction by John Seidlitz

High quality instruction of English language learners (ELLs) involves being intentional about academic language development not only within ESL and language arts courses, but also in content area classes. Educators of ELLs often search for specific ways to have students practice listening, speaking, reading, and writing in math, science, and social studies so they will develop a deeper understanding of language. The following language objectives, frames, and activities are designed to help ELLs develop academic language within content area classes.

How to use the language objectives, frames, and activities:

Teachers can use the academic language objectives, activities, and frames to carefully prepare for and perform instruction for ELLs. Consider the following guidelines when planning and delivering lessons.

Planning

1. Identify a language objective that aligns with lesson goals
2. Identify and adapt specific language frames that correspond with the lesson goals, grade level, and the proficiency levels of your students
3. Choose a teaching strategy or technique that supports your language and content goals for the lesson

Delivering

1. **Introduce:** Provide a clear explanation of the activity. Follow these steps:
   - Display and explain language and content objectives
   - Clearly explain and display instructions
   - Model the activity using materials students will use during the activity
   - Check for understanding and look for opportunities to clarify or correct
2. **Model:** Provide opportunities for students to practice the language they will use during the activity. Use these strategies to scaffold students:
   - Display written examples of language frames
   - Read frames aloud to students and then have them repeat the frame
   - Model the use of the frames prior to the activity
   - Refer to posted word walls and word lists
3. **Support:** Monitor students during the activity and support the use of the scaffolds described above.
4. **Reflect:** After the activity, review content and language goals with questions such as
   - What were our objectives?
   - Did we meet our objectives?
   - What did you learn about ____?

How do they help?

	Help teachers …	Help ELLs …
Language Objectives	Target specific academic language skills	Know their specific language goals for a lesson
Academic Language Frames	Align language practice opportunities to students language proficiency levels	Participate fully in academic discourse
Teaching Strategies and Techniques	Integrate activities that use the language frames	Engage in lessons with a variety of academic language practice opportunities

What are some examples?

Content Area	Language Objective	Academic Language Frames	Activity
Math	L(I) Demonstrate understanding of directions, questions, and conversations by responding orally and taking notes	This problem is about … First… Then… Finally… I would explain how to solve this problem to a friend by …	Keep, Delete, Substitute, Select *Use the Keep, Delete, Substitute, Select, strategy to summarize the main ideas of a word problem and eliminate unnecessary information. Use the frames to summarize their thoughts.*
Science	S(C) Speak using specific words and phrases for emphasis, qualification, and transition	At first…, but now…. Previously… however later….	Experiment/Lab *Have students form a hypothesis before conducting an experiment. After conducting the experiment, have the students compare their hypothesis before the experiment with their conclusion after the experiment.*
Social Studies	W(D) Use appropriate grammar and conventions in writing	The present tense is appropriate because … The past tense is appropriate because …	Contextualized Grammar Instruction *Have students read a social studies text. Identify usage of present and past tenses. Use the stems to justify their answers.*

LANGUAGE OBJECTIVES	LANGUAGE FRAMES	TEACHING STRATEGIES AND TECHNIQUES
Access prior knowledge to learn new language in English.	**Prior Knowledge** **B** 1. I know ____. 2. I want to know ____. **I** 1. This | word / phrase | might mean ____. 2. This | word / phrase | Is like ____. 3. This | word / phrase | reminds me of ____. **A** **AH** 1. This | word / phrase | probably means ____. because ____.	• Anticipation Chat • Anticipation Guides • Free Write • Insert Method • KWL • List/Group/Label • Pretest with a Partner
Use multiple self-corrective methods to monitor English language development.	**Self Corrective Techniques** **B** 1. I mean ____. **I** 1. Let me say that again ____. **A** **AH** 1. I meant to say/write ____. 2. Let me rephrase that ____. 3. How would I be able to check ____?	• Accountable Conversation Questions • Oral Scaffolding • Think Alouds • Total Response Signals
Acquire new grade-level vocabulary through strategic learning strategies such as comparing and contrasting or creating concept maps.	**Memorizing/Reviewing** **B** 1. ____ means ____. **I** 1. I | know / don't know | the words ____. 2. I'm | familiar / not familiar | with ____. **A** **AH** 1. I will need to review ____. **Concept Mapping/Drawing** **B** 1. This shows ____. **I** 1. The | main idea / key term | of my | concept map / drawing | is ____. 2. Some | examples / important details | are ____. **A** **AH** 1. I decided to represent ____ this way because ____. **Comparing/Contrasting** **B** **I** 1. ____ is the same as ____ because they are both ____. 2. ____ is different from ____ because ____. 3. ____ is similar to ____ because ____. **A** **AH** 1. One significant similarity is ____ because ____. 2. One significant difference is ____ because ____.	• Concept Mapping • Creating Analogies • Flash Card Review • Four Corners Vocabulary • Personal Dictionary • Scanning • Total Response Signals • Total Physical Response (TPR) • Vocabulary Games and Drama • Word Map • Word Play

Sentence Stems and Activities, continued

LANGUAGE OBJECTIVES	LANGUAGE FRAMES	TEACHING STRATEGIES AND TECHNIQUES
Demonstrate language learning strategies when speaking, such as non-verbal cues, requesting assistance and employing circumlocution and synonyms.	**Requesting Assistance** **B** 1. Can you help me ____? 2. I don't understand ____. **I A AH** 1. It's similar to ____. 2. It's similar to ____. 3. Let me rephrase that ____. **Synonyms/Circumlocution** **B** 1. It's the same as ____. 2. It has ____. **I A AH** 1. It's similar to ____. 2. It's similar to ____. 3. Let me rephrase that ____.	• Accountable Conversation Questions • Expert/Novice • Instructional Scaffolding • Total Physical Response (TPR) • Think, Pair, Share
Attain and reinforce new language and concepts through meaningful speaking and writing activities.	**Concept Attainment with New Words** **B** 1. I think | is / is not | a ____. 2. All ____ | are / have / are not / do not have / is not | ____. **I** 1. ____ | is / is not | an example of ____ because ____. **A** 1. Another example might be ____ because ____. **AH** 1. One | characteristic / attribute | of ____ is ____. **Language Attainment with New Words** **B** 1. ____ means ____. 2. ____ does not mean ____. **I** 1. I | can / would not | use the word ____ when ____. **A AH** 1. I | might be able to / probably would not | use the word ____ when ____ because ____.	• Concept Attainment • Creating Analogies • Group Response with a White Board • Instructional Conversation • Question, Signal, Stem, Share, Assess • Think, Pair, Share • Whip Around • Word Map
Build on accessible language to acquire new language.	**Using Accessible Language** **B** 1. If I want ____ I need to say ____. **I** 1. To find out how to say ____ I can look at ____. 2. Will you please explain what ____ means? **A AH** 1. I can use resources such as ____ to remember how to say ____.	• Accountable Conversation Questions • CALLA Approach • Expert/Novice • Instructional Scaffolding • Think Alouds

LANGUAGE OBJECTIVES	LANGUAGE FRAMES	TEACHING STRATEGIES AND TECHNIQUES
Distinguish between formal and informal English and determine which to use in the appropriate grade-level settings.	**Formal and Informal English** **B** 1. At school we say _____. **I** 1. When we talk to the whole class we should _____. 2. When we talk with our friends we can _____. 3. Scientists / Historians / Mathematicians / Writers | use the | word _____ / phrase _____ | to say _____. **A** **AH** 1. I would describe that using | scientific / social studies / mathematical / literary | language by saying _____.	• Brick and Mortar Cards • Discussion Starter Cards • Formal/Informal Pairs • Radio Talk Show • Same Scene Twice • Sentence Sort
Employ deductive and inductive reasoning to look for patterns in grade-level language and analyze sayings and expressions.	**Deductive Reasoning** **B** **I** 1. All _____ are _____. **A** **AH** 1. _____ is _____ so it must be an example of _____. **Inductive Reasoning** **B** **I** 1. All the _____ we say | were / had | _____. 2. So all _____ probably | are / have | _____. **A** **AH** 1. Every example we observed | was / had | _____. 2. So we can infer that all _____ | are / have | _____. **Patterns in Language** **Analyzing Sayings/Expressions** **B** 1. I think the | word / expression | means _____. **I** 1. One | word / expression | that was used a lot was _____. 2. The writer chose this | word / expression | because _____. **A** **AH** 1. Another expression the writer could have chosen might be _____ because _____. 2. I noticed the writer tended to use (tense, mood, structure, etc.) _____. 3. One pattern I noticed was _____.	• Guided Reading Routine • Instructional Conversation • Perspective-Based Writing • Question, Signal, Stem, Share, Assess • Structured Conversation (Academic Language Frames)

Sentence Stems and Activities, continued

Language Proficiency Level Key
B Beginner   A Advanced
I Intermediate   AH Advanced High

LANGUAGE OBJECTIVES	LANGUAGE FRAMES	TEACHING STRATEGIES AND TECHNIQUES
Differentiate sounds and intonations of English words, such as tone, pitch, volume, speed and stress patterns.	**Sounds and Intonation Patterns** **B** 1. Point to it. 2. Show it. 3. Write It. *a* **I** 1. You said the word _____. It starts with _____. **A AH** 1. I think that word _____ | starts with the letter _____ | is spelled _____ | because _____. 2. You | stressed | did not stress | the word _____ because _____. 3. To change the meaning of this sentence I could stress _____. 4. To change the tone of this sentence, I could change the | pitch | volume | speed	• CCAP • Segmental Practice • Sound Scripting • Suprasegmental Practice
Identify consonant and vowel sounds, silent letters, and consonant clusters in English words.	**Sound System** **B I** 1. The word _____ has the long/short vowel _____. 2. The word _____ has a silent _____. 3. The word _____ has the consonant blend _____. **A AH** 1. The letter _____ in the word _____ is long because _____. 2. The _____ is silent in the word _____ because _____. 3. The word _____ is pronounced _____ because _____.	• Segmental Practice • Songs/Poems/Rhymes • Systematic Phonics Instruction • Word Sorts • Word Walls
Acquire new language structures, expressions and vocabulary through classroom interactions.	**Language Structures/Expressions during Interactions** **B I** **A AH** 1. I heard the new word/phrase _____. 2. One new phrase I used was _____. 3. I heard _____ use the word/phrase _____. 4. A new word/phrase I heard was _____. 5. I can use that word/phrase when _____. 6. I used the word/phrase _____ when I spoke with _____. 7. I used the word/phrase _____ to express the idea that _____.	• Oral Scaffolding • Personal Dictionary • Scanning • Self Assessment of Levels of Word Knowledge • Think, Pair, Share • Vocabulary Self Collection • Word Sorts
Check understanding of spoken language and seek clarification during instruction and classroom interaction when needed.	**Clarification during Instruction and Interaction** **B** 1. Use gestures I don't understand. I understand. **I A AH** 1. Can you help me to _____? 2. I don't understand what/how _____. 3. Would you please repeat that? 4. So you're saying _____. 5. May I please have some more information? 6. May I have some time to think?	• Inside/Outside Circle • Instructional Conversation • Instructional Scaffolding • Structured Conversation (Academic Language Frames) • Think Alouds • Think, Pair, Share • Total Physical Response (TPR)

LANGUAGE OBJECTIVES	LANGUAGE FRAMES	TEACHING STRATEGIES AND TECHNIQUES
Build understanding of increasingly complex spoken English through linguistic, visual and textual support.	**Linguistic, Visual, Textual Support** **B I** **A AH** 1. If want to find out ____ I can ____. 2. I can use ____ to check if I ____. 3. When I hear ____ it tells me ____. 4. If I don't understand ____ I can say things like ____. 5. Will you please explain what ____ means? 6. Let me see if I understand. You said ____. 7. Would you please show me on the | diagram / picture / organizer / notes | ?	• Graphic Organizers • Inside/Outside Circle • Instructional Conversation • Instructional Scaffolding • Nonlinguistic Representations • Posted Phrases and Stems • Structured Conversation (Academic Language Frames) • Think, Pair, Share

Listen to and understand a variety of multi-media presentations to foster concept and language attainment.	**Concept Attainment from a Variety of Media**
	
	B 1. I notice ____.
	
	I 1. I | heard / saw | a ____.
	
	A 1. I | heard / observed | which makes me think ____.
	     2. I think ____ is an example of ____ because ____.
	
	AH 1. One characteristic of ____ that I heard/observed is ____.
	
	Language Attainment from a Variety of Media
	
	B I 1. I | heard / saw | the | word ____. / phrase ____.
	     2. I think the | word / phrase | | means / does not mean | ____.
	
	A 1. I | heard / saw | the | word ____. / phrase ____. | I can use it when ____.
	
	AH 1. I | can | the | word ____. / phrase ____.
	     2. I | might be able to / probably would not | | use it when ____ / because ____.
		• Chunking Input
		• Concept Attainment
		• Concept Mapping
		• Learning Logs and Journals
		• Pairs View
		• Visual Literacy Frames
		
		Access these media resources
		  NGReach.com
		  InsideNG.com
		
		(((MP3))) Language Songs
		
		(((MP3))) Selection Recordings
		
		(((MP3))) Fluency Models
		
		Build Background Videos
		
		National Geographic Digital Library

Sentence Stems and Activities, continued

Language Proficiency Level Key
B Beginner   **A** Advanced
I Intermediate   **AH** Advanced High

LANGUAGE OBJECTIVES	LANGUAGE FRAMES	TEACHING STRATEGIES AND TECHNIQUES

Construct meaning and identify main points and details in spoken language on familiar and unfamiliar topics.	**Meaning in Spoken Language**
	
	B 1. I think ____ means ____.
	     2. You said ____. I think it means ____.
	
	I 1. I think ____ means ____ because ____.
	
	A AH 1. I heard you say ____. Another way to say that might be ____.
	
	Main Point in Spoken Language
	
	B 1. It's about ____.
	
	I 1. I think the main idea I heard was ____.
	
	A AH 1. Based on the information I heard in ____. I can conclude that the main points were ____.
	     2. (The speaker) said ____. Which supports my view that the main idea is ____.
	
	Details in Spoken Language
	
	B I 1. One thing I heard was ____.
	     2. I heard (the speaker) say ____.
	     3. One thing (the speaker) said was ____.
	     4. One important thing I heard (the speaker) say was ____.
	
	A AH 1. (The speaker) said ____. Which is important because ____.
	     2. I heard (the speaker) say ____. Which supports the idea that ____.
		• IEPT (Inter-Ethnolinguistic Peer Tutoring)
		• Instructional Conversation
		• Literature Circles
		• Question, Signal, Stem, Share, Assess
		• Reciprocal Teaching
		• Story Telling
		• Structured Conversation (Academic Language Frames)
		• Summarization Frames

Make inferences and draw conclusions based on implicit ideas presented in complex spoken language in correspondence with grade-level expectations.	**Implicit Ideas**
	
	B 1. I think ____ probably ____.
	
	I 1. I can infer ____ probably ____.
	     2. I can assume ____ because ____.
	
	A 1. Even though it doesn't say ____ I think ____.
	     2. Based on ____ I can infer that ____.
	
	AH 1. From the information found in ____ I can infer that ____ because ____.
		• Instructional Conversation
		• Literature Circles
		• Question, Signal, Stem, Share, Assess
		• Reciprocal Teaching
		• Story Telling
		• Structured Conversation (Academic Language Frames)
		• Summarization Frames
		• Whip Around

LANGUAGE OBJECTIVES	LANGUAGE FRAMES	TEACHING STRATEGIES AND TECHNIQUES
Demonstrate understanding of directions, questions, and conversations by responding orally and taking notes.	**Following Spoken Directions** **B I** 1. The first step is ____. 2. The next steps are ____. 3. I know when I'm finished when ____. **A AH** 1. The initial step is ____. 2. The next step(s) in the process is/are ____. 3. I know I've completed the task successfully when ____. **Retelling/Summarizing Spoken English** **B I** 1. It is/ It's about ____. 2. The main idea is ____. 3. First ____. Then ____. Finally ____. 4. The general idea is ____. 5. ____ support(s) the main idea. **A AH** 1. I would explain the story/concept to a friend by ____. 2. Some ideas I heard that support the main idea include ____. **Responding to Questions/Requests** **B** 1. You ask ____. I think ____. **I A** 1. You asked ____. I think ____. 2. I heard you say ____, so I need to ____. 3. I think you're asking ____. **AH** 1. One answer to your question might be ____. **Collaborating with Peers** **B I A AH** 1. Can you help me understand ____? 2. Would you please repeat that? 3. Who's responsible for ____? 4. Who should ____? 5. My job/part/role is to ____. 6. So I should ____. 7. I'm responsible for ____. **Taking Notes** **B** 1. I write ____. **I A** 1. I noted ____. 2. The main ideas I wrote down were ____. 3. Some details I wrote down were ____. **AH** 1. I can organize the ideas I wrote by (making an outline, concept map, Venn diagram, chart, etc…)	• Framed Oral Recap • Keep, Delete, Substitute, Select • IEPT (Inter-Ethnolinguistic Peer Tutoring) • Instructional Conversation • Literature Circles • Note Taking Strategies • Outlines • Question Answer Relationship (QAR) • Question, Signal, Stem, Share, Assess • Reader/Writer/Speaker Response Triads • Reciprocal Teaching • ReQuest • Story Telling • Structured Conversation (Academic Language Frames) • Summarization Frames • Tiered Questions • Tiered Response Stems • W.I.T. Questioning • Word MES Questioning

Sentence Stems and Activities, continued

Language Proficiency Level Key
B Beginner   **A** Advanced
I Intermediate   **AH** Advanced High

LANGUAGE OBJECTIVES	LANGUAGE FRAMES	TEACHING STRATEGIES AND TECHNIQUES
Practice articulating consonant and vowel sounds in English with increasingly accurate sound production.	**Producing Sounds** **B** 1. The letter(s) ____ make(s) the ____ sound. 2. The word ____ begins with the letter ____. 3. The word ____ has the long/short vowel ____. 4. The word ____ has a silent ____. 5. The word ____ has the consonant blend ____. **I A AH** 1. The letter ____ in the word ____ is long because ____. 2. The ____ is silent in the word ____ because ____. 3. The word ____ is pronounced ____ because ____.	• Fluency Workshop • List Stressed Words • Recasting • Segmental Practice • Suprasegmental Practice
Employ routine classroom language and simple, high-frequency vocabulary for describing, retelling simple stories and basic information that is depicted visually.	**Description and Simple Story Telling with High Frequency Words and Visuals** **B I** 1. I see ____. 2. I hear ____. 3. I observe ____. **I** 1. ____ | heard / saw | a ____. 2. The picture(s) show(s) ____. 3. The first thing that happened was ____. Then ____. Finally ____. **A** 1. ____ | probably also | has / is | ____. **AH** 1. ____ could be described as ____ because ____. **Routine Language for Classroom Communication** **B I A AH** 1. Where | is / are | ____. 2. Where do I ____? 3. How do I ____? 4. Can you help me ____? 5. May I please have some more information? 6. May I ask someone for help? 7. May I go to ____? 8. May I sharpen my pencil? 9. When is it time to ____?	• Accountable Conversation Questions • Conga Line • Expert/Novice • Inside/Outside Circle • Instructional Conversation • Literature Circles • Numbered Heads Together • Partner Reading • Question, Signal, Stem, Share Assess • Retelling • Summarization Frames • Think, Pair, Share

LANGUAGE OBJECTIVES	LANGUAGE FRAMES	TEACHING STRATEGIES AND TECHNIQUES

As more English is acquired, practice using a variety of grammatical structures when speaking, including; description, sequence, cause and effect, comparison, qualification, emphasis and conclusion with increasing accuracy.

Speak using a variety of Structures

Description

B

1. ____ | is / has / looks like | ____.

I

1. ____ | tends to be / seems / becomes / is able to / appears to be | ____.

2. ____ is an example of ____ because ____.

A **AH**

1. ____ | shows / is / has | which means ____

2. ____ | for example / for instance / such as | ____.

Sequence

B

1. ____ | while / before / after | ____.

I

1. First ____, second ____, finally ____.
2. At first ____ but ____

1. Now / Later | ____.

A **AH**

1. Previously / Initially / Earlier | ____ however | now / later

Cause and Effect

B

1. ____ causes ____.
2. When ____then ____.

I **A** **AH**

1. Not only ____ but also ____.
2. ____ was one of the causes of ____however ____.
3. ____ contributed to ____due to ____.

Comparison

B

1. ____ | while / before / after | ____.

2. ____ is the same as/is different from ____.
3. ____ differs from/is similar to ____ in that ____.
4. Although ____ still/yet ____.
5. ____ however/whereas/nevertheless ____.
6. ____ on the other hand/on the contrary

Teaching Strategies and Techniques:

- Canned Questions
- Discovery Learning
- Experiments/Labs
- IEPT (Inter-Ethnolinguistic Peer Tutoring)
- Instructional Conversation
- Literature Circles
- Numbered Heads Together
- Question, Signal, Stem, Share, Assess
- R.A.F.T.
- Reader/Writer/Speaker Response Triad
- Signal Words
- Story Telling
- Structured Conversation (Academic Language Frames)
- Summarization Frames

LANGUAGE OBJECTIVES	LANGUAGE FRAMES	TEACHING STRATEGIES AND TECHNIQUES
As more English is acquired, practice using a variety of grammatical structures when speaking, including; description, sequence, cause and effect, comparison, qualification, emphasis and conclusion with increasing accuracy. (continued)	**Speak using a variety of Structures (continued)** *Qualification* **B** 1. Sometimes/few/many _____. 2. Occasionally/often/seldom/rarely _____. **I A AH** 1. Sometimes/often _____ because _____. 2. Many/few _____ however/due to _____. 3. Rarely/seldom _____ yet _____. *Emphasis* **B** 1. _____ is important. **I** 1. _____ is significant due to _____. 2. _____ is especially relevant due to _____. **A AH** 1. Above all/of course/remember _____ because _____. *Conclusion* **B** 1. Finally/therefore _____. **I A AH** 1. As a result _____ should/it is necessary to _____. 2. _____ proves _____ because _____.	See page R13
Speak using specific words and phrases for emphasis, qualification, and transition	**B** 1. This word/phrase means _____. 2. This word/phrase is like _____. **I** 1. This word/phrase reminds me of _____. **A AH** 1. I think this word probably means _____ because _____.	• Content-Specific Stems • Creating Analogies • Instructional Conversation • Literature Circles • Question, Signal, Stem, Share, Assess • Reciprocal Teaching • Self Assessment of Levels of Word Knowledge • Structured Conversation (Academic Language Frames)
Give input and express ideas in cooperative learning activities.	**Share in Cooperative Interactions** **B** 1. _____ feel / think / believe _____. **I** 1. In my opinion _____. 2. I wonder _____. 3. I like the idea that _____. 4. The way I would _____. **A AH** 1. My suggestion would be _____ because _____. 2. I agree / disagree that _____ because _____. 3. After considering _____ I think _____.	• Instructional Conversation • Interview Grids • Literature Circles • Pairs View • Partner Reading • Peer Editing • Question, Signal, Stem, Share, Assess • Structured Conversation (Academic Language Frames) See **Teaching Strategies and Routines** for more information on cooperative learning.

LANGUAGE OBJECTIVES	LANGUAGE FRAMES	TEACHING STRATEGIES AND TECHNIQUES
Ask questions and share information using methods ranging from using a high frequency, concrete vocabulary bank to applying abstract vocabulary in extended conversations when participating in classroom discussions.	**Ask and Give Information** **B** 1. What is _____? 2. _____ is _____. 3. How do you _____? 4. First you _____ then _____. **I** 1. What did you notice about/in _____? 2. I noticed _____. 3. Why do you think _____ is important? 4. _____ is important because _____. 5. What are the characteristics of _____? 6. One of the characteristics of _____ is _____. **A** **AH** 1. What do you think caused _____? 2. I think _____ caused _____ because _____. 3. In my opinion _____ happened due to _____.	• Instructional Conversation • Interview Grids • Literature Circles • Question, Signal, Stem, Share, Assess • Structured Conversation (Academic Language Frames) • Think, Pair, Share

Express ideas, feelings and opinions using methods ranging from single word responses, short phrases and sentence stems to extended conversation when participating in grade-appropriate classroom discussions.	**Express Opinions, Ideas, and Feelings**
	
	B **I**
	1. How do you feel when/about _____?
	   I feel _____.
	2. What do you think about _____?
	   I think _____.
	3. What is your opinion about _____?
	   In my opinion _____.
	4. My view on the matter is _____.
	   I agree / disagree that _____ because _____.
	5. Why do you think _____?
	   I think _____ because _____.
	
	A **AH**
	1. Is there another _____.
	   Another _____ might be _____ since _____.
	2. What else can you tell me about _____?
	   Another _____.
		• Anticipation Chat
		• Instructional Conversation
		• Literature Circles
		• Question, Signal, Stem, Share, Assess
		• Reciprocal Teaching
		• Structured Conversation (Academic Language Frames)
		• Think, Pair, Share
		• W.I.T. Questioning

In discussions, use increasingly specific language when narrating, describing or explaining.	**B** **I** 1. This is a _____. 2. _____ is about _____. 3. The main idea is _____. 4. It's important to remember _____. 5. First _____, then _____, finally _____. 6. Initially _____ then _____ ultimately _____. **A** **AH** 1. It's significant that _____ because _____. 2. Some of the supporting ideas are _____. 3. Some of the important details include _____.	• Instructional Conversation • Literature Circles • Numbered Heads Together • Question, Signal, Stem, Share, Assess • Story Telling • Structured Conversation (Academic Language Frames) • Summarization Frames

LANGUAGE OBJECTIVES	LANGUAGE FRAMES	TEACHING STRATEGIES AND TECHNIQUES
Select formal or informal language as it corresponds to appropriate settings.	**B** 1. At school we say _____. **I** 1. When we talk to the whole class we should _____. 2. When we talk with our friends we can _____. **A** 1. I would explain this | story / concept | to a friend by _____. 2. Scientists / Historians / Mathematicians / Writers | use the | word _____ / phrase _____ | to _____. 3. I would describe _____ to someone outside of school by _____. 4. I would describe _____ using | scientific / social studies / mathematical / literary | language by _____.	• Expert/Novice • Oral Scaffolding • Radio Talk Show • Sentence Sort • Word Sorts
Discuss information presented in a variety of formats, including print, visual, audio and electronic to emphasize content and language attainment to improve conversational skills.	**Concept Attainment from a Variety of Media** **B** 1. I notice _____. **I** 1. I | heard / saw | a _____. **A** 1. I | heard / observed | which makes me think _____. 2. I think _____ is an example of _____ because _____. **AH** 1. One characteristic of _____ that I heard/observed is _____. **Language Attainment from a Variety of Media** **B** 1. I | hear / see | a _____. **I** 1. I | heard / saw | the | word _____. / phrase _____. 2. I think the | word / phrase | means / does not mean | _____. **A** 1. I | heard / saw | the | word _____. / phrase _____. | I can use it when _____. **AH** 1. I | can | the | word _____. / phrase _____. 2. I | might be able to / probably would not | use it when _____ because _____.	• Chunking Input • Concept Attainment • Learning Logs and Journals • Pairs View • Visual Literacy Frames • Word Map Access these media resources NGReach.com InsideNG.com Language Songs Selection Recordings Fluency Models Build Background Videos National Geographic Digital Library

LANGUAGE OBJECTIVES	LANGUAGE FRAMES	TEACHING STRATEGIES AND TECHNIQUES
Apply letter-sound correspondence and word analysis skills to affixes, roots, and cognates in decoding and sounding out words.	**Decoding** **B I** 1. The letter(s) _____ make(s) the _____ sound _____. 2. The word _____ has the long/short vowel _____. 3. The word _____ has a silent _____. 4. The word _____ has the consonant blend _____. **A AH** 1. The letter _____ in the word _____ is long because _____. 2. The _____ is silent in the word _____ because _____. 3. The word _____ is pronounced _____ because _____. **Cognates and False Cognates** **B** 1. A cognate is _____. **I** 1. The word _____ sounds like _____ in my language and means _____. 2. The word _____ sounds like _____ in my language, but does NOT mean _____. **Affixes, Roots, and Base words** **B** 1. A ⎧prefix / suffix / root⎫ is _____. 2. A base word is _____. **I** 1. The word _____ has the ⎧prefix / suffix / root⎫ which means _____. 2. Some other words with this ⎧prefix / suffix / root⎫ are _____. **A AH** 1. The word _____ is common in ⎧history / geography / science / math / language arts⎫ because _____. 2. This word probably means _____ because _____.	• Direct Teaching of Affixes • Direct Teaching of Cognates • Direct Teaching of Roots • Self Assessment of Levels of Word Knowledge • Word Generation • Word Sorts • Word Study Books • Word Walls
Understand concepts of print, including directionality and spacing of English text.	**Directionality of English Text** **B** 1. In English, words go _____ (students can use gestures to indicate directionality) **I A AH** 1. In _____ (Chinese/Arabic/Hebrew etc.) words to _____, but in English words go _____. 2. In _____ (Spanish/French/Russian etc.) words go _____ and in English words also go _____.	• Directionality Sort • Total Physical Response (TPR)

LANGUAGE OBJECTIVES	LANGUAGE FRAMES	TEACHING STRATEGIES AND TECHNIQUES
Incorporate English vocabulary and language structures commonly used; such as sight words, high frequency words and environmental print.	**Sight Vocabulary/Environmental Print** **B** **1.** When I see the word/phrase ____ it means ____ (*students demonstrate actions with gesture* or use simple phrases to explain classroom vocabulary) **2.** This sign says ____ it tells me ____. (students demonstrate actions with gesture or use simple phrases to explain classroom vocabulary) **3.** My friend's name is ____. **4.** Our logo/mascot/team is ____.	• Expert/Novice • Oral Scaffolding • Total Physical Response (TPR)
Increase comprehension of written text through before reading strategies such as graphic organizers, picture walks and frontloading vocabulary.	**Pre Reading Supports** **B** **1.** This story/article is about ____. **I** **1.** This wordlist tells me this story is about ____. **2.** The illustrations tell me this story is about ____. **3.** The diagram tells me the story is about ____. **4.** The organizer tells me that I should pay attention to ____. **5.** The organizer shows me that ____ is significant because ____. **A AH** **1.** The strategy that will help me to understand this text the best is probably ____. (note taking, scanning, surveying key test features such as bold words illustrations and headings, using *the wordlist, etc.*)	• Advance Organizers • Anticipation Guides • Backwards Book Walk • Comprehension Strategies • DRTA • Scanning • SQP2RS • Visuals • Word Walls
Extend independent reading and gradually release dependence on linguistic accommodations as more English is acquired.	**Use of Linguistically Accommodated Material** **B I** **1.** The (native language summary, native language wordlist, picture dictionary, outline, simplified English text, sentence starters, etc.) helped me to understand/write/say ____. **A AH** **1.** I should use ____ when ____. **2.** I don't need to use ____ when ____.	• Adapted Text • Comprehension Strategies • Graphic Organizers • Insert Method • Margin Notes • Native Language Texts • Outlines • Related Literature • SQP2RS

LANGUAGE OBJECTIVES	LANGUAGE FRAMES	TEACHING STRATEGIES AND TECHNIQUES
Construct meaning, develop vocabulary and background knowledge, learn and grasp language structures through visual and contextual support, peer support and teacher support to confirm understanding.	(see below)	(see below)

LANGUAGE FRAMES

Using Visual/Contextual Support to Understand Text

Reading

B **I**
1. The illustrations tell me this text is about ____.
2. The diagram tells me the text is about ____.
3. The organizer tells me that I should pay attention to ____.

A **AH**
1. The organizer shows me that ____ is significant because ____.

Confirming Understanding

B
1. I raise my hand when ____.
2. I don't understand ____.

I **A**
1. I can check if I understand what I'm reading by ____.

AH
2. The strategy that will help me to understand this text the best is probably____ (note taking, scanning, surveying key text features such as bold words illustrations and headings, using the wordlist, etc.) because ____.

Developing Vocabulary and Background Knowledge

B **I**
1. I use the word wall/word list while I read to ____.

A **AH**
1. When I come across an unfamiliar word or phrase, I can ____.

Grasp of Language Structures

B **I**
1. When I see ____ in a text, it tells me ____.

A **AH**
1. I noticed a lot of ____ in the text. It probably means ____.
2. I also noticed ____ in the text. I was wondering ____ because ____.
3. I noticed the writer tended to use (tense, mood, structure, etc.) ____.

Using Teacher/Peer Support to Understand Text

Reading

B **I** **A** **AH**
1. What is the main idea of ____?
2. What should I write down about ____?
3. What should I pay attention to in ____?
4. Would you please show me on the (diagram/picture/organizer/notes/ etc.) ____?

Confirming Understanding

B **I** **A** **AH**
1. It seems like ____. Is that right?
2. Can you help me understand ____?
3. Can I please have some more information about ____?
4. Where can I find out how to ____?
5. Can I ask someone for help with ____?

Developing Vocabulary and Background

B **I** **A** **AH**
1. Will you please explain what ____ means?
2. Does ____ also mean ____?
3. Why does the text have ____?

Grasp of Language Structures

B **I** **A** **AH**
1. One word/expression that I saw was ____.
2. What does the word/expression ____ mean?
3. Why is there a lot of ____ in the text?

TEACHING STRATEGIES AND TECHNIQUES

- Anticipation Chat
- Comprehension Strategies
- DRTA
- Graphic Organizers
- Improv Read Aloud
- Insert Method
- Nonlinguistic Representations
- QtA
- Question, Signal, Stem, Share, Assess
- Scanning
- SQP2RS

Sentence Stems and Activities, continued

Language Proficiency Level Key
B Beginner   A Advanced
I Intermediate   AH Advanced High

LANGUAGE OBJECTIVES	LANGUAGE FRAMES	TEACHING STRATEGIES AND TECHNIQUES
Use shared reading, retelling, summarizing, responding to questions and taking notes to demonstrate comprehension of grade-level text.	**Shared Reading** **B I / A AH** 1. Can you help me understand _____? 2. Would you please repeat that? 3. Who should read _____? 4. I will read _____. 5. My job/part/role is to _____. 6. So I should _____. 7. I'm responsible for _____. **Retelling, Summarizing** **B I / A AH** 1. It's about _____. 2. The main idea is _____. 3. First _____ Then _____ Finally _____. 4. I would explain _____ to a friend by _____. 5. The story is about _____. 6. What happened was _____. 7. The general idea is _____. Some ideas I heard that support the main idea include _____. **Responding to Questions/Requests** **B I** 1. I heard you say _____, so I need to _____. 2. You asked _____. I think _____. 3. I think you're asking _____. **A AH** 1. One answer to your question might be _____. **Taking Notes** **B I / A AH** 1. I noted _____. 2. The main ideas I wrote down were _____. 3. Some details I wrote down were _____. 4. I can organize the ideas I wrote by _____ (making an outline, concept map, Venn diagram, chart, etc.)	• Cornell Notes • Guided Notes • Instructional Conversation • Keep, Delete, Substitute, Select • Literature Circles • Numbered Heads Together • Question, Signal, Stem, Share, Assess • Reciprocal Teaching • Story Telling • Structured Conversation (Academic Language Frames) • Summarization Frames
Increase the rate, duration, and ease of comprehension when reading silently.	**Responding to Questions/Requests** **B I** 1. I read about _____. 2. I { liked / didn't like } _____. 3. The text I read today described _____. **A AH** 1. I would describe what I read today as _____ because _____.	• Book Reviews • Dialog Journal • Double Entry Journals • Idea Bookmarks • Interactive Reading Logs • SSR Program • Structured Conversation (Academic Language Frames)

LANGUAGE OBJECTIVES	LANGUAGE FRAMES	TEACHING STRATEGIES AND TECHNIQUES

LANGUAGE OBJECTIVES

Demonstrate understanding of main ideas, details in text and graphic sources, and summarize to increase reading comprehension in correspondence with grade-level expectations.

LANGUAGE FRAMES

Supporting Ideas

B **I**
A **AH**

1. The text talked about things like _____.
2. The text discussed different topics, for example _____.
3. _____ supports the idea that _____.
4. _____ resulted in _____.
5. I | caused / led to | _____.

Details

B

1. This talks about | things / people / events | like _____.

I

1. _____ could be described as _____.
2. I would describe _____ as _____ because _____.

A **AH**

1. Some significant features/facts about _____ include _____.

Graphic Sources

B

1. The illustrations tell me this text is about _____.
2. This | illustration / chart / diagram | shows _____.

I

1. The illustrator showed _____ by _____.

A **AH**

1. The author(s) included a(n) | diagram / graph / chart | showing _____ because _____.
2. The | illustration / diagram / graph / chart | is significant _____ because _____.

Summarizing

B

1. This is about _____.
2. The main | characters / ideas | are _____.

I **A**

1. The main | actions / arguments / problems | discussed in the text are _____.

AH

1. In my opinion, the most significant | idea / conflict | In this text is _____ because _____.

Distinguishing Main Ideas and Details

B **I**

1. This text is about _____.
2. The main idea of this text is _____.
3. One detail that supports the main idea is _____.

A **AH**

1. _____ supports the idea that _____.
2. _____ is an example of a detail because _____.
3. _____ is an example of a main idea because _____.

TEACHING STRATEGIES AND TECHNIQUES

- Comprehension Strategies
- DRTA
- Graphic Organizers
- Learning Logs and Journals
- Nonlinguistic Representation
- Numbered Heads Together
- QtA
- Question, Signal, Stem, Share, Assess
- Scanning
- SQP2RS
- Structured Conversation (Academic Language Frames)
- Summarization Frames

Sentence Stems and Activities, continued

LANGUAGE OBJECTIVES	LANGUAGE FRAMES	TEACHING STRATEGIES AND TECHNIQUES
Make predictions, connections, and inferences from text, pictures, graphs, tables and charts to increase comprehension in correspondence with grade-level expectations.	**Predicting** **B I** 1. I think _____ will _____. **A AH** 1. I predict _____ will happen next because _____. 2. Based on the information in the passage, it seems that _____ will probably _____. 3. _____ supports the idea that _____ might _____. **Making Connections Between Ideas** **B** 1. _____ reminds me of _____. 2. _____ is similar to _____. 3. _____ is different from _____. **I A AH** 1. _____ relates to what happened when _____ because _____. 2. _____ is the result of _____ because _____. **Drawing Inferences and Conclusions** **B I** 1. I think _____ probably _____. 2. I can infer _____ probably _____. 3. I can assume _____ because _____. **A AH** 1. Even though it doesn't say _____ I think _____. 2. Based on _____ I can conclude that _____. 3. From the information found in _____ I can infer that _____ because _____. **Finding Supporting Text Evidence** **B I** 1. I think _____ because _____. 2. _____ supports the idea that _____. 3. I think _____ is evidence that _____. **A AH** 1. Based on the information found in _____ I can conclude that _____ because _____.	• Comprehension Strategies • DRTA • Graphic Organizers • Learning Logs and Journals • Nonlinguistic Representations • Prediction Café • QtA • Question, Signal, Stem, Share, Assess • Scanning • SQP2RS • Structured Academic Controversy • Structured Conversation (Academic Language Frames) • Summarization Frames

LANGUAGE OBJECTIVES	LANGUAGE FRAMES	TEACHING STRATEGIES AND TECHNIQUES
Analyze literary elements such as characters, setting, plot, theme and author's point of view to increase reading comprehension in content areas and grade-level expectations.	**Evaluating Written Information** **B** 1. The theme of this text is ____. 2. The ⎰ setting / plot / conflict / genre ⎱ of this text is ____. **I** 1. Some ⎰ Characters / ideas / symbols / metaphors / similes ⎱ found in this text include ____. **A AH** 1. I would describe ____ as ____ because ____. 2. The author used ____ in order to ____. 3. The author could have used ____ in order to ____. **Performing Critical Analysis** **B I** 1. The author wrote this to ____. 2. The author used the ⎰ word / phrase ⎱ to ____. **A AH** 1. The intended audience of this text is ____. 2. The writer's motive for ____ was probably ____. 3. The writer tried to prove ____ by ____. 4. ____ is an example of ⎰ bias / propaganda ⎱ because ____. 5. The author was ⎰ successful / unsuccessful ⎱ because ____. 6. I would ⎰ agree / disagree ⎱ with the author that ____ because ____.	• Book Reviews • Comprehension Strategies • Dialog Journal • Double Entry Journals • DRTA • Graphic Organizers • Instructional Conversation • Learning Logs and Journals • Nonlinguistic Representations • QtA • Question, Signal, Stem, Share, Assess • Scanning • SQP2RS • Structured Academic Controversy • Structured Conversation (Academic Language Frames) • Summarization Frames
Apply letter-sound relationships to compose written English.	**Letter/Sound Relationships in Writing** **B** 1. The letter(s) ____ make(s) the ____ sound. 2. The word ____ has the long/short vowel ____. 3. The word ____ has a silent ____. 4. The word ____ has the consonant blend ____. **I A** 1. The letter ____ in the word ____ is long because ____. 2. The ____ is silent in the word ____ because ____. 3. The word ____ is pronounced ____ because ____.	• Use Reach Into Phonics • Word Sorts • Word Study Books • Word Walls
Employ newly learned basic and academic vocabulary in writing.	**Write Using New Vocabulary** **B I** 1. I learned the word ____. 2. ____ means ____. 3. I can use the word ____ to ____. **A AH** 1. I can use the phrase ____ in order to show ____. 2. The phrase ____ can be used to help the reader ____. 3. The ⎰ word / phrase ⎱ ⎰ would / would not ⎱ be appropriate for ____. 4. I can ____ using the ⎰ word / phrase ⎱ ____.	• Choose the Words • Cloze Sentences • Dialog Journal • Double Entry Journals • Field Notes • Letters/Editorials • Learning Logs and Journals • Read, Write, Pair, Share • Self Assessment of Levels of Word Knowledge • Think, Pair, Share • Ticket Out • Word Sort • Word Wall

Sentence Stems and Activities, continued

Language Proficiency Level Key
B Beginner   **A** Advanced
I Intermediate   **AH** Advanced High

LANGUAGE OBJECTIVES	LANGUAGE FRAMES	TEACHING STRATEGIES AND TECHNIQUES
Apply correct English spellings patterns and rules when writing in English	**English Spelling Patterns and Rules** **B** 1. ____ is spelled ____. 2. ____ begins with the letter ____. **I** **A** **AH** 1. In this set of words I notice ____. 2. These words are all similar because ____. 3. The spelling rule that applies to this word is ____ because 4. The spelling rule that applies to this word is ____ because ____. 5. This word is spelled correctly/incorrectly because ____. 6. I can check my spelling by ____.	• Peer Editing • Personal Spelling Guide • Word Analysis • Word Sorts • Word Walls
Use appropriate grammar and conventions in writing in correspondence with grade-level expectations	**Grammar and Usage** **B** **I** **A** **AH** 1 Pronouns agree when ____. 2. The subject | agrees/disagrees | with the verb ____ because ____. 3. The pronoun | agrees/disagrees | with ____ because ____. 4. The (present/past/future/conditional) tense is appropriate/inappropriate in this sentence because ____.	• Contextualized Grammar Instruction • Daily Oral Language • Oral Scaffolding • Peer Editing • Reciprocal Teaching • Sentence Mark Up • Sentence Sort
Apply developmentally appropriate grammatical structures, including subject-verb agreement, correct usage of possessives, contractions, apostrophes and negatives in written works in correspondence with grade-level expectations.	**Using Correct Verb Tenses** **B** **I** **A** **AH** 1. A subject of a sentence is ____. 2. A verb is ____. 3. A subject and a verb agree when ____. 4. A verb tense is ____. 5. A tense is appropriate when ____. **Using Possessive Case/Contractions Correctly** **B** **I** **A** **AH** 1. An apostrophe is ____. 2. Apostrophes are used to show ____. 3. A contraction is ____. 4. The apostrophe in this contraction is correct/incorrect because ____. 5. The apostrophe correctly/incorrectly shows a contraction because ____. **Using Negatives** **B** **I** **A** **AH** 1. The word (no/not/none) is used when ____. 2. An example of a sentence with (no/note/none is ____. 3. Neither is used when ____. 4. An example of a sentence with neither is ____. 5. Hardly, scarcely, and barely are used to show ____. 6. Nothing/nowhere and nobody are used to show ____.	• Contextualized Grammar Instruction • Daily Oral Language • Peer Editing • Reciprocal Teaching • Sentence Mark Up • Sentence Sort

LANGUAGE OBJECTIVES	LANGUAGE FRAMES	TEACHING STRATEGIES AND TECHNIQUES
Compose grade-appropriate sentences of varied types and lengths, including compound and complex sentences; such as cause and effect, comparison, qualification, emphasis and conclusion in correspondence with grade-level expectations.	**Sentence Writing Using a Variety of Structures** *Cause and Effect* **B I** 1. ____ caused/led to ____. 2. When ____ then ____. **A AH** 1. ____ was brought about by ____. 2. ____ was one of the causes of ____ however ____. 3. ____ contributed to ____ due to ____.. *Comparison* **B** 1. ____ is the same as / different from ____. **I A** 1. ____ differs from / is similar to In that ____. 2. Although ____ still/yet ____. 3. ____ however / whereas / nevertheless ____. **AH** 1. ____ on the other hand / on the contrary ____. *Qualification* **B** 1. Sometimes / Few / Many ____. **I** 1. Sometimes / Often ____ because ____. 2. Many / Few ____ however / due to ____. **A AH** 1. Occasionally / Often / Seldom / Rarely ____. 2. Rarely / Seldom ____ yet ____. *Emphasis* **B** 1. ____ is important. **I** 1. ____ is significant due to ____. 2. It's important to note ____ since ____. **A AH** 1. ____ is especially relevant due to ____. 2. Above all/of course/remember ____ because ____. *Conclusion* **B** 1. Finally/therefore... **I A** 1. As a result ____ /it is necessary to ____. **AH** 2. ____ proves ____ because ____	• Dialog Journal • Double Entry Journals • Draw & Write • Field Notes • Free Write • Genre Analysis/Imitation • Hand Motions for Connecting Words • Letters/Editorials • Learning Logs and Journals • Perspective-Based Writing • R.A.F.T. • Read, Write, Pair, Share • Summarization Frames

Sentence Stems and Activities, continued

Language Proficiency Level Key
B Beginner   A Advanced
I Intermediate   AH Advanced High

LANGUAGE OBJECTIVES	LANGUAGE FRAMES	TEACHING STRATEGIES AND TECHNIQUES

Write in various formats, using narrative, descriptive and explanatory to fulfill specific content areas needs.	**Narration**
	
	 B 1. First, ____ second ____ finally ____.
	
	 I 1. ____ | while / before / after | ____.
	
	    2. At first ____ | but now / later | ____.
	
	 A **AH** 1. Previously / Initially / Earlier | ____ | however | now / later | ____.
	
	 Description & Explanation
	
	 B 1. ____ | is / has | ____.
	
	 I 1. ____ | tends to be / seems / becomes / is able to / appears to be | ____.
	
	    2. ____ is an example of ____ because ____.
	
	    3. ____ | shows / is / has | which means ____
	
	    4. ____ | for example / for instance / such as | ____.
	
	 A **AH** 1. ____ is a characteristic or attribute of ____.
		• Book Reviews
		 • Dialog Journal
		 • Double Entry Journals
		 • Draw & Write
		 • Field Notes
		 • Free Write
		 • Genre Analysis/Imitation
		 • Learning Logs and Journals
		 • Letters/Editorials
		 • Perspective-Based Writing

Guide to Terms, Teaching Strategies, and Activities

Accountable Conversation Questions: Place the following poster in your room:

> ### What to say instead of "I Don't Know"
> - May I please have some more information?
> - May I have some time to think?
> - Would you please repeat the question?
> - Where could I find information about that?
>
> **Please speak in
> complete sentences.**

Model for the students how to use the questions when they are unsure what to say when called on by a teacher (Seidlitz & Perryman 2008). Explain that when they are called on for a response, they can respond, or ask for help and then respond. Newcomer English learners should not be pressured to speak in front of the class if they have not yet begun to show early production levels of speech proficiency. Students should be encouraged, but not forced to speak when in the silent period of language development (Krashen 1982).

Adapted Text: Techniques for making the content presented in texts available to students who are not able to fully comprehend the level of academic language including: graphic organizers, outlines, highlighted text, audio recordings of texts, margin notes, native language texts, native language glossaries, chunked text with frequent opportunities to check comprehension, and word lists (Echevarria et al. 2008).

Advance Organizers: Information given to students prior to reading or instruction that helps them organize the information they will encounter during instruction (Mayer 2003). Advance organizers should involve both activating prior knowledge and organizing new information. Examples include: graphic organizers, anticipation guides, KWL, guided notes, etc.

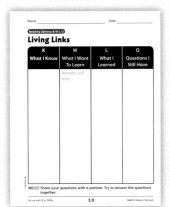

Anticipation Chat: Prior to instruction, a teacher facilitates a conversation between students about the content to be learned. The teacher opens the discussion by having the students make inferences about what they are going to learn based on their prior knowledge and experiences and limited information about the new concepts (Zwiers 2008).

Anticipation Guides: A structured series of statements given to students before instruction. Students choose to agree or disagree with the statements either individually or in groups. After instruction, students revisit the statements and discuss whether they agree or disagree with them again after having learned about the topic (Head & Readence 1986).

Backwards Book Walk: Students scan a non-fiction text briefly looking at headings, illustrations, captions, key words, and other text features. After the scan, students discuss what they believe they will learn from the text (Echevarria & Vogt 2008).

Book Reviews: After being immersed in the book review genre, English learners write short reviews which can then be published so that others can have access to them (Samway 2006).

Brick and Mortar Cards: Students are given five "brick" cards with academic vocabulary (content area terms) and are instructed to organize them however they think makes sense. Afterward, they have to link the cards together using language. They write the language they are using on "mortar" cards that they then use to tie the concepts together. Students may need lists of sentence terms and connecting words to facilitate the process (Dutro & Moran 2003; Zwiers 2008).

CALLA Approach: An approach to teaching English learners which involves the explicit teaching of language learning strategies and academic content and language skills through scaffolding and active engaged learning and language use (Chamot & O'Malley 1994).

CCAP (Communicative Cognitive Approach to Pronunciation): A five step process for assisting English learners in improving pronunciation (Celce-Murcia et al. 1996 as cited in Flores 1998):

- Description and analysis of the pronunciation feature
- Listening/Discrimination activities (see segmental/supra segmental practice below)
- Controlled practice and feedback
- Guided practice and feedback
- Communicative practice

Canned Questions: Students are given a series of question stems ranging from the lowest to the highest level of Blooms taxonomy so that they can participate in discussions about a topic (Echevarria et al. 2008). For example:

- "What is …?"
- "How do…?"
- "What would be a better approach to…?"
- "How do you know that…?"

Choose the Words: Students select words from a word wall or word list to use in a conversation or in writing.

Chunking Input: Breaking up material into smaller units for easier comprehension. Text, visual and auditory information can be chunked so that students have time to discuss new information, pay attention to details, and create schema for organizing new information.

Cloze Sentences: Fill in the blank sentences used to help students process academic text (Taylor 1953; Gibbons 2002).

Guide to Terms, Teaching Strategies, and Activities (continued)

Compare, Contrast, Analogy & Metaphor Frames: Sentence frames used to help students organize schema for new words (Marzano 2001; Hill & Flynn 2006). For example:

- Compare: _____ is similar to _____ in that both…
- Contrast: _____ is different from _____ in that …
- Analogy: _____ is to _____ as _____ is to _____
- Metaphor: I think _____ is like/is…
- because…

Comprehension Strategies: Strategies used by proficient readers to understand what they read. These strategies are used in different kinds of text, can be taught, and when they are taught, students are likely to use them. Strategies include: plan and monitor, ask questions, make inferences, synthesize, visualize, make connections, and determine importance (Echevarria et al. 2008; Dole et al. 1991; Baker 2004). See the **Best Practices** section of this Teacher's Edition for more information on Comprehension Strategies.

Concept Attainment: A strategy based on the theories of Jerome Bruner in which the teacher gives students examples and non examples of a concept and has students categorize them. Over time students develop conceptual categories at increasing levels of depth and understanding (Boulware & Crow 2008; Bruner 1967).

Concept Mapping: A technique for making a visual diagram of the relationship between concepts. Concept maps begin with a single concept which is written in a square or circle. New concepts are listed and connected with lines and shapes creating a web showing the relationship between the ideas (Novak 1995). See the **Teaching Routines and Strategies** section of this Teacher's Edition for more information about Concept Mapping

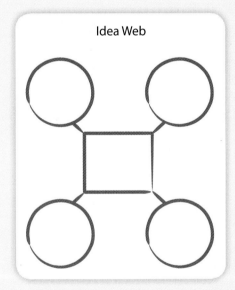

Idea Web

Conga Line: Students form two lines facing one another. Students in each row share ideas, review concepts, or ask one another questions. After the first discussion, one row moves and the other remains stationary so that each student now has a new partner (Echevarria et al. 2008).

Content-Specific Stems: Sentence stems using content specific vocabulary. For example, instead of a general stem such as _In my opinion…_ a content specific stem would be _In my opinion the Declaration of Independence is significant because…_

Contextualized Grammar Instruction: Teaching grammar in mini-lessons that apply to specific, meaningful tasks students will perform. The purpose of the grammar instruction is to enable students to communicate verbally or in writing more effectively (Weaver 1996).

Cornell Notes: A method of note taking in which a paper is divided into two columns. In one large column students take traditional notes in modified outline form. In the other column, students write key vocabulary terms and questions (Paulk 2000).

Creating Analogies: Generating comparisons using the frame: _____ is to _____ as _____ is to _____ (Marzano et al. 2001).

Daily Oral Language: A strategy for teaching English usage which involves five minute mini lessons where students view a list of sentences that have incorrect English usage. Students learn correct usage by correcting the mistakes in the sentences (Vail & Papenfuss 1993).

Dialog Journal: A journal that is exchanged between the student and teacher or between two or more students. The journal focuses on academic topics and the language used by the teacher and student should be content focused and academic (Samway 2006).

Direct Teaching of Affixes: Lessons on prefixes and suffixes to build knowledge of English word structure (White, Sowell, & Yanagihara 1989).

Direct Teaching on Cognates: Lessons on words that sound the same in the primary language and the target language. For a list of Spanish and English cognates see: page T000. Go to www.NGReach.com or www.InsideNG.com for translations of program key words in eight different languages.

Direct Teaching of Roots: Teaching students Greek and Latin roots that form the base of many words in English.

Directionality Sort: Students are given copies of texts in various languages in groups. Each group must sort the tests based on perceived directionality. Is the text written from top to bottom then left to right? Is the text right to left, then top to bottom? For newspapers showing letters and characters used in a variety of languages see: www.newoxxo.com.

Discussion Starter Cards: Small cards containing sentence starters for students to use when beginning an academic conversation, or seeking ways to extend a conversation. For example: _In my opinion…, I think…, another possibility is…,_ etc. (Thornburry 2005). Sentences starters appear in the Student Editions to support expression.

Double Entry Journals: A two column journal used for reflective writing about texts. In one column students write words, phrases, or ideas that they found interesting or significant. In the other column, students write the reasons they found them significant or ways they could use them in their own writing (Samway 2006).

Draw & Write: Allowing English learners to express their knowledge of academic content using both drawing and writing. Students may use their native language to express ideas but are encouraged to express new concepts using English (Adapted from: Samway 2006).

DRTA: Directed Reading-Thinking Activity. This activity involves the teacher stopping regularly before and during reading to have the students make predictions and justify their predictions. Questions might be: *What do you think is going to happen? Why do you think that will happen next? Is there another possibility? What made you think that?* (Echevarria et al. 2008).

Experiments/Labs: A form of hands-on learning in science where students directly encounter the scientific process: Making an observation, forming a hypothesis, testing the hypothesis, and coming to a conclusion. Teachers of ELLs need to make sure to preteach necessary content and functional vocabulary to enable full participation of English learners.

Expert/Novice: A simulation involving two students. One student takes on the role of an expert and the other a novice in a particular situation. The expert responds to questions asked by the novice. The procedure can be used for lower level cognitive activities such as having students introduce one another to classroom procedures, and higher level activities such as explaining content area concepts at greater degrees of depth. The procedure can also be used to model the difference between formal and informal English, with the expert speaking formally and the novice informally (Seidlitz & Perryman 2008).

Field Notes: Students take notes and write in a journal and write reflections about what they are learning and experiencing. Field journals should be content focused yet can contain both social and academic language as well as drawing (Samway 2006).

Flash Card Review: Students make flash cards, preferably including images with explanations of the meanings of words. Students study, play games, and sort the flash cards in various ways.

Fluency Workshop: Students have three opportunities to talk and listen to another student talk about the same topic. They alternate roles back and forth from listening to speaking. When listening, they may ask questions, but cannot contribute an opinion on what the speaker has said. After the activity students reflect on their level of fluency in the first discussion and the third discussion (Maurice 1983).

Formal/Informal Pairs: The teacher provides strips of paper with pairs of statements written in formal English and in informal English. The papers are distributed to the students and students have to find the student who has their match. Students can also be given sets of all the pairs in small groups and sort them into two stacks.

Four Corners Vocabulary: A way of processing vocabulary with a paper or note card divided into four sections: The term, a definition, a sentence, and an illustration (Developed by D. Short, Center for Applied Linguistics. Described in Echevarria et al. 2008). See the **Teaching Routines and Strategies** section of this Teacher's Edition for more information about Four Corners Vocabulary.

Framed Oral Recap: An oral review involving two students using sentence starters. Students are given stems such as: *Today I realized…, Now I know…,* and *The most significant thing I learned was…* They pair up with a partner to discuss what they have learned in a lesson or unit (Adapted from: Zwiers 2008).

Free Write: Students write nonstop about a topic for five to ten minutes. The goal is to keep writing, even if they can't think of ideas. They may write *I don't know what to write* if they are unable to think of new ideas during the process. English learners can use sketching and write in the native language during the process although they can be encouraged to write in English (Elbow 1998).

Genre Analysis/Imitation: Students read high quality selections from a genre of literature. They note particular words, phrases and ideas they found interesting or effective and record those in a journal. Students then use their notes and observations as a resource when writing in that genre (Adapted from Samway 2006).

Graphic Organizers: A way of developing a learner's schema by organizing information visually. Examples include the T-Chart, Venn diagram, Concept Map, Concept Web, Timeline, etc. Graphic organizers are a form of nonlinguistic representation that can help students process and retain new information (Marzano et al. 2001).

Group Response with a White Board: Students write responses to questions on white boards using dry erase markers. These can be made from card stock slipped into report covers, or with shower board cut into squares able to fit on student's desks. White boards are a form of active response signal that research has shown to be highly effective in improving achievement for struggling learners.

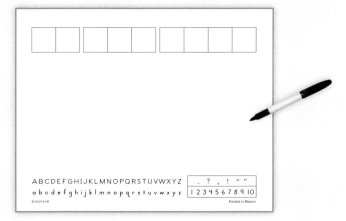

Guided Notes: Teacher prepared notes used as a scaffold to help students take notes during a lecture and learn note taking skills. For examples of guided note formats see: www.NGReach.com or www.InsideNG.com.

Hand Motions for Connecting Words: Gestures representing transition/signal words that students use to visually model the function of connecting words in a sentence. For example students might bring their hands together for terms like: also, including, as well as, etc. For terms such *as excluding, neither, without, no longer,* etc., students could bring their hands together. Students can come up with their own signals for various categories including: comparing, contrasting, cause and effect, sequence, description, and emphasis (Adapted from: Zwiers 2008).

Guide to Terms, Teaching Strategies, and Activities (continued)

Hi-Lo Readers: Readers published on a variety of reading levels while having the same content focus and objectives. For example National Geographic Explorer Collection Books found at www.NGSP.com.

Homophone/Homograph Sort: Teacher prepares cards with words that sound or are written the same but are spelled differently such as *know* and *no* or *rose* (a flower) and *rose* (past tense of rise). The teacher asks the students to group the words that sound the same together and then explain the meanings of each.

IEPT: Inter-Ethnolingusitic Peer Tutoring: A research based method for increasing fluency in English learners by pairing them up with fluent English speakers. Tasks are highly structured and fluent English speakers are trained to promote more extensive interaction with English learners (Johnson 1995).

Idea Bookmarks: Students take reflective notes on bookmark size pieces of paper. The bookmarks include quotes, observations, and words that strike the reader as interesting or effective. The bookmarks can be divided into boxes as quotes are added with page numbers written in each box (Samway 2006).

Improv Read Aloud: Students act out a story silently while the teacher or another student reads aloud. Each student has a role and has to discover how to act out the story while it is being read. Afterward, students discuss how each student represented their part during the improv (Zwiers 2008).

Insert Method: Students read text with a partner and mark the texts with the following coding system: a check to show a concept or fact already known, a question mark to show a concept that is confusing, an exclamation mark to show something new or surprising, or a plus to show an idea or concept that is new (Echevarria et al. 2008).

Inside/Outside Circle: A way of facilitating student conversations. Students form two concentric circles facing one another, an inside circle and an outside circle. Students can then participate in short, guided discussion or review with their partner. After the discussion, the outside circle rotates one person to the right while the inside circle remains still. All students now have a new partner to speak with (Kagan 1990). See the **Teaching Routines and Strategies** section of this Teacher's Edition for more information about Inside/Outside Circles.

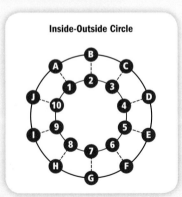

Inside-Outside Circle

Instructional Conversation: A way of engaging students in conversation about literature through open ended dialog between the teacher and students in small groups. Instructional conversations are open ended, have few "known answer" questions, and promote complex language and expression (Goldenberg 1992).

Instructional Scaffolding: A model of teaching where students achieve increasing levels of independence following the pattern: teach, model, practice, and apply (Echevarria et al. 2008).

Interactive Reading Logs: Reading journals where students write reflections to texts read silently. These logs can be exchanged with other students or with the teacher who can write questions or responses to what students have written. These logs are ideal components of an SSR program.

Interview Grids: A grid used to get students to record other students' responses to various questions. Students wander around the room and search for their partners who will respond to their questions (Zwiers 2008).

Keep, Delete, Substitute, Select: A strategy for summarizing developed by Brown, Campoine, and Day (1981) discussed in *Classroom Instruction That Works* (Marzano et al. 2001). Students keep important information, delete unnecessary and redundant material, substitute general terms for specific terms (e.g. birds for robins, crows, etc.) and select or invent a topic sentence. For ELLs, Hill and Flynn (2006) recommend using gestures to represent each phase of the process and clearly explain the difference with high frequency and low frequency terms.

KWL: A pre-reading strategy used to access prior knowledge and set up new learning experiences (Ogle 1986). The teacher creates a chart where students respond to three questions. The first two are discussed prior to reading or the learning experience, and the third is discussed afterward.

Learning Logs and Journals: Students record observations and questions about what they are learning in a particular content area. The teacher can provide general or specific sentence starters to help students begin their reflections (Samway 2006).

Letters/Editorials: Students write letters and editorials from their own point of view or from the point of view of a character in a novel, person from history, or a physical object (sun, atom, frog, etc.). Teachers of ELLs should remember to scaffold the writing process by providing sentence frames, graphic organizers, wordlists, and other supports. Newcomers may use the Draw/Write method discussed above.

List Stressed Words: Students take a written paragraph and highlight words that would be stressed, focusing on stressing content English words such as nouns, verbs, adverbs over process words such as articles, prepositions, linking-verbs/modals and auxiliaries.

List/Group/Label: Students are given a list of words or students brainstorm a list of words. They then sort the words into similar piles and then create labels for each pile. This can be done by topic (planets, stars, scientific laws etc.) or by word type (those beginning with a particular letter, those with a particular suffix, and those in a particular tense) (Taba 1967).

Literature Circles: Activity through which students form small groups similar to "book clubs" to discuss literature. Roles include: discussion facilitators, passage pickers, illustrators, connectors, summarizers, vocabulary enrichers, travel tracers, investigators, and figurative language finders. ELLs will need to be supported with sentence starters, wordlists, and adapted text as necessary depending on language level (Schlick & Johnson 1999). For support in starting literature circles see: www.litcircles.org.

Margin Notes: A way of adapting text. Teachers, students, or volunteers write key terms, translations of key terms or short native language summaries, text clarifications, or hints for understanding in the margins of a textbook (Echevarria et al. 2008).

Native Language Texts: Native language translations, chapter summaries, word lists, glossaries, or related literature that can be used to understand texts used in content area classes. Summaries of selections in this program in 8 languages can be found online. Go to www.InsideNG.com or www.NGReach.com.

Nonlinguistic Representations: Nonverbal means of representing knowledge including illustrations, graphic organizers, physical models, and kinesthetic activities (Marzano et al. 2001). Hill and Flynn (2006) advocate integrating Total Physical Response (Asher 1967) as a means of integrating nonlinguistic representations because of its unique way of engaging learners, especially those in the early stages of language development.

Note Taking Strategies: Strategies for organizing information presented in lectures and in texts. English learners at the early stages of language development benefit from guided notes (see above), native language word lists, summaries, and opportunities to clarify concepts with peers. Strategies include informal outlines, concept webbing, Cornell Note taking, and combination notes. Research seems to indicate that students should write more rather than less when taking notes (Marzano et al. 2001). ELLs in pre-production phases can respond to teacher notes through gesture. Those in early production and speech emergent phases can communicate about information in teacher prepared notes using teacher provided sentence frames (Hill & Flynn 2006).

Numbered Heads Together: A strategy for having all students in a group share with the whole class over time. Each student in a group is assigned a number (1, 2, 3 and 4). When asking a question the teacher will ask all the ones to speak first, and then open up the discussion to the rest of the class. For the next question the teacher will ask the twos to speak, then the threes, and finally the fours. The teacher can also randomize which number will speak in which order. When doing numbered heads together with English learners, teachers should provide sentence starters for the students (Kagan 1992). See the Teaching Routines and Strategies section of this Teacher's Edition for more information about Numbered Heads Together.

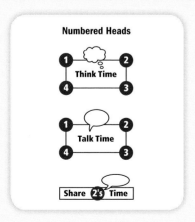

Numbered Heads

Think Time

Talk Time

Share Time

Oral Scaffolding: The process of:
- Explicitly teaching academic language
- Modeling academic language
- Providing opportunities in structured ways for students to use language orally
- Write using the language they have ready seen modeled and have used (Adapted from: Gibbons 2002)

Outlines: Traditional note taking method involving roman numerals, Arabic numerals, upper and lowercase letters.

Pairs View: A strategy for keeping students engaged and focused while they process viewed material at a deeper level. When watching a video clip or movie, each pair is assigned a role. For example, one partner might be responsible for identifying key dates while another is listing important people and their actions (Kagan 1992).

Partner Reading: A strategy for processing text where two students read a text. Each can alternate a paragraph while the other summarizes or one can read and the other student summarize and ask questions (Johnson 1995).

Peer Editing: Students review one another's work using a rubric. Research shows that English learners benefit from peer editing when trained on specific strategies for participating in peer response to writing (Berg 1999).

Language Frames	
Retell	**Make suggestions**
• The topic is _____ . • Most of the facts and details tell about _____ .	• I like the examples you used to tell about _____ . • The detail about _____ does not tell about _____ . Can you take out that detail?

Personal Dictionary: Students choose words from the word wall, other wordlists, and words encountered in texts to record on note cards or in a note book which become a personal dictionary. Students are encouraged to use drawing, reflection, and their native language when explaining the meaning of terms (Adapted from: Echevarria et al. 2008). Students can use **My Vocabulary Notebook** at www.NGReach.com to create an electronic Personal Dictionary.

Personal Spelling Guide: Students record correct spellings of misspelled words on note cards. As the number of cards grows, students sort the words based on characteristics of the words. Students should generate the categories for example, students may develop lists like: contractions, big words, words with "ie" or "ei", words that are hard to say, words I will never use. Encourage students to look for patterns in the spellings of the words. Students can select a number of words to review and have a partner quiz them orally over their self-selected words.

Guide to Terms, Teaching Strategies, and Activities (continued)

Perspective-Based Writing: Writing from an assigned point of view using specific academic language. For example, students in a social studies class could write from the perspective of Martin Luther King, Jr. writing a letter explaining his participation in the Montgomery bus boycott to a fellow pastor. Students should be given specific words and phrases to integrate into the writing assignment. Students can also write from the point of view of inanimate objects such as rocks, water, molecules, etc. and describe the processes from an imaginative perspective as if they were that object. In addition, students can take on the role of an expert within a field: math, science, social studies, literature and use the language of the discipline to write about a particular topic. Genre studies can be particularly helpful as a way of preparing students for perspective-based writing activities (Seidlitz & Perryman 2008).

Posted Phrases and Stems: Sentence frames posted in clearly visible locations in the classroom to enable students to have easy access to functional language during a task. For example, during a lab the teacher might post the stems: *How do I record…, Can you help me (gather, mix, measure, identify, list)…, Can you explain what you mean by…?* Frames should be posted in English but can be written in the native language as well. **Academic Language Frames** are available to put this strategy into practice.

Academic Language Frames

Make Inferences

■ I read _____.
  I know _____.
  And so _____.

_____

■ I read _____.
  Because I know _____, I can infer _____.

_____

■ The text says _____.
■ That relates to what I know about _____.
  I can infer _____ because _____.

Prediction Café: A way of having students participate in mini discussions about what will happen or what students will learn about in a text. Pick out important headings, quotes, or captions from a text (about eight quotes for a class of 24). They may only speak with one student at a time. Some students may have the same card. Either way, they will discuss with that student what they think the text is about or what they think will happen in the text. Students should be given frames to facilitate the development of academic language during the activity such as: _____ *makes me think that…, I believe _____ because…,* etc.) (Zwiers 2008).

Pretest with a Partner: Students are given a pretest in pairs. Students take turns reading the questions. After each question they try to come to consensus before recording an answer (Echevarria et al. 2008).

QtA (Question the Author): A strategy for deepening the level of thinking about literature (Beck et al. 1997). Instead of staying within the world of the text, the teacher prompts the students to question the author. For example:

- *What do you think the author is trying to say?*
- *Why do you think the author chose that word or phrase?*
- *Would you have chosen a different word or phrase?*

Question Answer Relationship (QAR): A way of teaching students to analyze the nature of questions they are asked about a text. Questions are divided into four categories (Echevarria et al. 2008):

- Right There (found in the text)
- Think and Search (require thinking about relationships between ideas in the text)
- Author and Me (require me to form an inference about the text)
- On My Own (requires me to reflect on my own experience and knowledge)

Question, Signal, Stem, Share, Assess: A strategy to get students to use new academic language during student-student interactions. The teacher asks a question and then asks students to show a signal when they are ready to respond to the question with a particular sentence stem provided by the teacher. When all students are ready to share, they share their answers. Students are then assessed either through random calling on individual students after the conversation or through writing assignments that follow the conversation (Seidlitz & Perryman 2008).

Radio Talk Show: Students create a radio talk show about a particular topic. This can be a good opportunity for students to practice using academic language as they take on the role of an expert. It can also provide an opportunity for students to identify the distinctions between formal and informal use of English as they take on different roles (Wilhelm 2002).

R.A.F.T.: A social studies writing strategy that enables students to write from various points of view (Fisher & Frey 2007). The letters stand for **R**ole (the perspective the students take), **A**udience (the individuals the author is addressing), **F**ormat (type of writing that will take place), **T**opic (the subject).

Read, Write, Pair, Share: A strategy for getting students to share their writing and ideas during interactions. Students read a text, write their thoughts on it using a sentence starter, pair up with another student and share their writing. Students can also be given suggestions on how to comment on one another's writing (Fisher & Frey 2007).

Reader/Writer/Speaker Response Triad: A way of processing text in cooperative groups. Students form groups of three. One student will read the text aloud; one will write the group's reactions or responses to questions about the text, a third will report the answers to the group. After reporting to the group, the students switch roles (Echevarria et al. 2008).

Recasting: Repeating an English learner's incorrect statement or question correctly without changing the meaning in a low risk environment where the learner feels comfortable during the interaction. Recasts have been shown to have a positive impact on second language acquisition (Leeman 2003).

Reciprocal Teaching: A student-student interaction involving collaboration in creating meaning from texts (Palinscar & Brown 1985). Hill and Flynn (2006) suggest adapting reciprocal teaching for use among English learners by providing vocabulary, modeling language use, and using pictorial representation during the discussion. Reciprocal teaching involves a student leader that guides the class through stages: Summarizing, Question Generating, Clarifying and Predicting.

Recorded Text: Recordings of text used as a way of adapting text for English Learners (Echevarria et al. 2008).

Related Literature: Connecting and supporting texts used in content areas. These texts can be fiction or nonfiction, in the native language or the target language (Echevarria et al. 2008). Use the **Leveled Library** books available and the Leveled Book finder online to locate appropriate texts.

ReQuest: A variation of reciprocal teaching (see above). The teacher asks questions using particular stems following a period of silent reading. After another period of silent reading, the teacher provides the stems for the students and has them ask the questions over the text (Manzo 1969; as cited in: Fisher & Frey 2007).

Retelling: Students retell a narrative text in their own words or summarize an expository text in their own words.

Same Scene Twice: Students perform a skit involving individuals discussing a topic. The first time through, the individuals are novices who use informal language to discuss the topic. The second time through they are experts who discuss the topic using correct academic terminology and academic English (adapted from: Wilhelm 2002).

Scanning: Students scan through a text backwards looking for unfamiliar terms. The teacher then provides quick brief definitions for the terms giving the students only the meaning of the word as it appears in context. Marzano, Pickering and Pollock (2001) state that "even superficial instruction on words greatly enhances the probability that student will learn the words from context when they encounter them in their reading" and that, "the effects of vocabulary instruction are even more powerful when the words selected are those that students most likely will encounter when they learn new content."

Segmental Practice: Listening/Discrimination activities that help learners listen for and practice pronouncing individual combinations of syllables. There are several ways to engage in segmental practice. Tongue twisters and comparisons with native language pronunciations can help English learners practice English pronunciation. The activity "syllable, storm, say" involves students brainstorming syllables that begin with a particular sound for example: *pat pen pal pas pon pem*, etc. Long and short vowel sounds can be used as well as diphthongs. Students then practice in partners pronouncing the terms (Celce-Murcia et al. 1996).

Self Assessment of Levels of Word Knowledge: Students rank their knowledge of new words from the word wall and other word lists using total response signals (see below) or sentence starters. Responses range from no familiarity with the word to understanding a word well and being able to explain it to others (Diamond & Gutlohn 2006; as cited in: Echevarria et al. 2008). See the **Teaching Routines and Strategies** section of this Teacher's Edition for more information about rating word knowledge.

 I have never seen or heard this word before

 I have seen the word before but I can't use it in a sentence

 I can use it in a sentence or give a definition

Sentence Mark Up: Method of using colored pencils to mark texts to indicate cause and effect, opposing thoughts, connecting words, and other features of a sentence to understand the relationship between clauses (Zwiers 2008)

Sentence Sort: Sorting various sentences based on characteristics. The teacher provides the sentences and students sort them. This can be done with an open sort where students create the categories or a closed sort where the teacher creates the categories. It can also be done by taking a paragraph from a textbook or a piece of literature the students are going to read and using sentences from the text. Possible categories include:

- Description sentences
- Complex sentences
- Simple sentences
- Sentences connecting ideas
- Sentences comparing ideas
- Sentences opposing ideas
- Sentences with correct usage
- Sentences with incorrect usage
- Sentences in formal English
- Sentences in informal English

Sentence Stems: Incomplete sentences provided for students to help scaffold the development of specific language structures and to facilitate entry into conversation and writing. For example *In my opinion…* and *One characteristic of annelids is …*

Signal Words: Words that determine a text pattern such as generalization, cause and effect, process, sequence, etc. A sample of signal words can be found at: www.nifl.gov/readingprofiles/Signal Words.pdf.

Six Step Vocabulary Process: Research based process developed by Marzano (2004) that teachers can use to develop academic vocabulary. The steps are:

- Teacher provides a description
- Students restate the explanation in their own words
- Students create a nonlinguistic representation of the term
- Students periodically do activities that help them add to their knowledge of vocabulary terms

Periodically students are asked to discuss the terms with each other. Periodically, students are involved in games that allow them to play with the terms.

Sound Scripting: A way for students to mark text showing pauses and stress. Students use a writing program to write a paragraph and then enter a paragraph break to show pauses and capital and bold letters to show word stress (Powell 1996).

Guide to Terms, Teaching Strategies, and Activities (continued)

SQP2RS (Squeepers): A classroom reading strategy that trains students to use cognitive metacognitive strategies to process nonfiction text. The following steps are involved (Echevarria et al. 2008):

- **S**urvey: students scan the visuals, headings, and other text features
- **Q**uestion: students write what questions they might find answers to
- **P**redict: student write predictions about what they will learn
- **R**ead: students read the text
- **R**espond: revisit your questions and think through how you respond to how you read
- **S**ummarize: Students restate key concepts either individually or on groups

SSR Program (Sustained, Silent Reading): A program used by schools to encourage students to read silently to develop literacy where students read whatever they wish for fifteen to twenty minutes during a school day. Pilgreen (2000) discusses eight features of high quality SSR programs: Access to books, book appeal, conducive environment, encouragement to read, non-accountability, distributed reading time, staff training, and follow up activities (Pilgreen 2000).

Story Telling: Students retell narratives in their own language.

Structured Academic Controversy: A way of structuring classroom discussion to promote deep thinking and the taking of multiple perspectives. Johnson & Johnson (1995) outline five steps.

- Organizing information And Deriving Conclusions
- Presenting And Advocating Positions
- Uncertainty Created By Being Challenged By Opposing Views
- Epistemic Curiosity And Perspective Taking
- Reconceptualizing, Synthesizing, and Integrating

Structured conversation: Student-student interaction where the language and content are planned. Students are given sentence frames to begin the conversation and specific questions and sentence starters to extend the conversation.

Summarization Frames: A way of structuring summaries of content area text. The frames involve specific questions that help students summarize different kinds of texts. Marzano (2001 p. 27-42) and Hill & Flynn (2006) discuss seven frames:

- narrative frame
- topic restriction frame
- illustration frame
- definition frame
- argumentation frame
- problem solution frame
- conversation frame

Suprasegmental Practice: Pronunciation practice involving groups of syllables. Some techniques include: sound scripting (see above), recasting (see above, a pronunciation portfolio, and content/function word comparisons (Wennerstrom 1993).

Systematic Phonics Instruction: teaching sound-spelling relationships and how to use those relationships to read. The national literacy panel (Francis et al. 2006) reported that instruction in phonemic awareness, phonics, and fluency had "clear benefits for language minority students."

Think Alouds: A way for teachers to scaffold cognitive and metacognitive thinking by saying aloud the thinking involved in solving problems and making decisions (Bauman et al. 1992).

Think, Pair, Share: A method of student-student interaction. The teacher asks a question and then provides wait time. The students then find a partner and share their answers. Afterward, selected students share their thoughts with the whole class (Lyman 1981). See the **Teaching Routines and Strategies** section for more information about Think, Pair, Share.

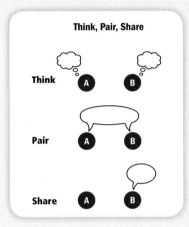

Ticket Out: A short reflection written at the end of a lesson. Teachers can use tickets out as an opportunity for students to reflect on what they have learned and use new vocabulary by specifying specific words and phrases for students to use.

Tiered Questions: Asking varying the type of questions students are asked based on their level of language development (Hill & Flynn 2006).

Tiered Response Stems: Asking a single question but allowing students to choose from a variety of stems to construct responses. Students choose a stem based on their level of language knowledge and proficiency (Seidlitz & Perryman 2008). ***National Geographic Reach*** and ***Inside*** provide **Academic Language Frames** to support this strategy.

Total Physical Response (TPR): A way of teaching using gesture and movement so that content is comprehensible to ESL newcomers (Asher 1967).

Total Response Signals (Also called active response signals): Active responses by students such as thumbs up/down, white boards, and response cards. Response signals enable teachers to instantly check for understanding and allow students to self assess current levels of understanding.

Unit Study for ELLs: A modified approach to writers workshop advocated by Samway (2006). The steps involve:

- Gathering high quality samples of the genre
- Immersion in the books
- Sifting between books that students can model and those that they can't
- Students immerse themselves a second time in the books
- Students try out using the "writing moves" they find the accomplished writers using
  - Writing and publishing
  - Reflecting and assessing

Visual Literacy Frames: A framework for improving visual literacy focusing on affective, compositional, and critical dimensions of processing visual information (Callow 2008).

Visuals: Illustrations, photographs, graphic organizers, manipulatives, models, and real world objects used to make content comprehensible for English learners.

Vocabulary Games: Use games to have students practice academic vocabulary. Specific game ideas are provided in the **Teaching Routines and Strategies** section.

Vocabulary Self Collection: A research based method of vocabulary instruction involving student collection of words for the class to study. Students share where the word was found, the definition and why the class should study that particular word (Ruddell & Shearer 2002).

W.I.T. Questioning: A questioning strategy involving training the students to use three stems to promote elaboration in discussion (Seidlitz & Perryman 2008):

- **W**hy do you think…?
- **I**s there another…?
- **T**ell me more about…

Whip Around: A way of getting input from all students during a class discussion. The teacher asks students to write a bulleted list in response to an open ended question. Students write their responses to the question and then stand up. The teacher then calls on students one at a time to respond to the question. If students have the same answer they mark it off on their papers. The teacher continues to call on students and students continue to mark through their answers. When all their answers have been marked through the students sit down. The activity continues until all students are seated (Fisher & Frey 2007).

Word Analysis: Studying the parts, origins, and structures of words to improve spelling (Harrington 1996).

Word Generation: Students brainstorm words having particular roots. Teachers then have students predict the meaning of the word based on the roots (Echevarria et al. 2008).

Word Map: A visual organizer that enables students to process a term (Echevarria et al. 2008).

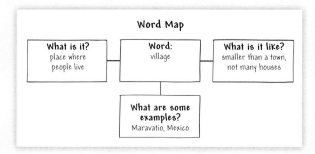

Word MES Questioning: A method of differentiating instruction for ELLs developed by Hill & Flynn (2006). The mnemonic device stands for "Word, Model, Expand, and Sound." Teachers work on word selection with pre-production students. "*Model* for early production. *Expand* what speech emergence students have said or written and help intermediate and advanced fluency students *sound* like a book" by working on fluency.

Word Play: Manipulating words through various word games to increase understandings. Johnson, von Hoff Johnson, & Shlicting (2004) divide word games into eight categories; onomastics (name games), expressions, figures of speech, word associations, word formations, word manipulations, word games, and ambiguities.

Word Sorts: Sorting words based on structure and spelling to improve orthography (Bear & Invernizzi 2004). See the **Teaching Routines and Strategies** section of this Teacher's Edition for more information on Word Sorts.

Word Study Books: A way of organizing words into a notebook based on spelling and structures such as affixes and roots (Bear & Invernizzi 2004).

Word Walls: A collection of words posted in a classroom organized by topic, sound, or spelling to improve literacy (Eyraud et al. 2000). See the **Teaching Routines and Strategies** section of this Teacher's Edition for more information about Word Walls.

Introduction to Language Transfer Issues

English learners arrive at the doors of our schools from many different countries and every walk of life. With them, they bring a wealth of linguistic and cultural diversity that transforms the simplest classroom into a unique cultural experience.

Regardless of previous educational experiences, second-language learners have a developed sense of how language operates. Through home-language experiences, they understand how sounds combine to form words and how words combine to convey meaning, sense, and ideas. Students' understanding of their first language serves sometimes to accelerate and other times to detour their acquisition of similar skills in English.

When you learn to identify and capitalize on students' existing language skills, you use positive transfer to accelerate progress. For example, you can use explicit instruction to develop pronunciation skills by explaining how sounds are the same or approximate. Once you know which grammatical structures transfer negatively to academic English conventions, you can adjust instruction to provide maximum reinforcement for skills lessons on these structures.

The charts on the following pages address language transfer issues between English and six of the most common languages spoken by English learners in U.S. schools.

- The **Language Structure Transfer Chart** explains grammar differences between English and six other languages to identify points of negative transfer. Compare students' errors to the transfer errors on the chart. This will help you understand why the error is occurring so that you can design appropriate instruction. You may also wish to encourage students to identify and share ways in which English parallels or differs from their own home languages.

- The **Phonics Transfer Chart** compares the sounds of English to those of the same six languages. As you work with students to teach phonics or develop pronunciation skills, use the chart to identify which sounds students may already know and which are new. In your instruction, devote particular practice to sounds that do not exist, or exist with different symbols, in students' primary languages.

We recognize that more than 150 languages are spoken by English learners in our schools. We hope this section, though it addresses just six languages, is a good start on the transfer issues involved in the education of our English learners. For languages other than those shown in the charts, make use of the resources in your district (including community volunteers, district language translators, and in-class primary language support) to identify the points of positive and negative transfer for your students.

Transfer Charts

The following charts are designed to help teachers locate potential transfer issues in a simple, practical way. We recognize that language structures and pronunciation can vary based upon multiple factors, including region, dialect, and even sociological issues. For this reason, we have enlisted the aid of the following language consultants, educators, linguists, and phonologists to compile and review information about each of the six target languages. We gratefully acknowledge their assistance and appreciate the contributions they made to the compilation of the Transfer Charts. We especially acknowledge the assistance of OMA Graphics, Inc., in Fremont, California, in locating language consultants throughout the United States.

In a few cases, the language consultants were unable to reach a consensus on specific items. The resulting charts show our best attempt to reconcile the information in a clear and consistent fashion. We welcome additional input and suggestions that will assist us in updating this information and in adding information for other languages in future publications.

Cantonese Language Consultants

Dr. John Whelpton
English Instructor
Baptist Lui Ming Choi Secondary School
Shatin, Hong Kong, PRC

Jihua Zhou
Cantonese Professor
Defense Language Institute
Monterey, California

Haitian-Creole Language Consultant

Dr. Jean-Robert Cadely
Associate Professor
Florida International University
Miami, Florida

Hmong Language Consultants

Max Leyang
ELL Community Specialist
St. Paul Public School District
St. Paul, Minnesota

Brian McKibben
Author, English-White Hmong Dictionary, 1992
Bridgeport, West Virginia

Korean Language Consultants

Koong-Ja Lauridsen
Assistant Principal and Education Technology Consultant
Alexandria Avenue Elementary School
Los Angeles, California

Jewel H. Lee
Assistant Professor
Defense Language Institute
Monterey, California

Saekyun Harry Lee
Assistant Professor
Defense Language Institute
Monterey, California

Spanish Language Consultants

Lada Kratky
Author
Carmel, California

Guadalupe López
Senior Editor
Carmel, California

Dr. Josefina Tinajero
Associate Dean, Professor of Education
University of Texas at El Paso
El Paso, Texas

Vietnamese Language Consultants

La Ba Nhon
Associate Professor
Defense Language Institute Foreign Language Center
Monterey, California

Mai Tran
Translator for Asian Pacific and Other Languages Offices
Los Angeles Unified School District
Los Angeles, California

Language Structure Transfer Chart

ENGLISH STRUCTURE	LANGUAGE TRANSFER ISSUE	LANGUAGES	SAMPLE TRANSFER ERRORS IN ENGLISH
Articles	There are no indefinite articles.	**Chinese** **Hmong** **Korean** **Vietnamese**	He goes to one class on Wednesdays. = He goes to a class on Wednesdays. I bought one cake from bakery. = I bought a cake from a bakery.
	The definite article can be omitted.	**Hmong**	Do you have book? = Do you have the book? Do you have a book?
	The indefinite article is not used before a profession.	**Chinese** **Haitian Creole** (article is optional if the predicate contains the verb *be*) **Korean** **Spanish** **Vietnamese**	He is teacher. = He is a teacher. My sister is famous doctor. = My sister is a famous doctor.
	The definite article is used before a title.	**Spanish**	The Professor Ruiz is helpful. = Professor Ruiz is helpful.
	Singular and plural definite articles follow the noun.	**Haitian Creole** **Examples:** zanmi an = friend (the) zanmi yo = friends (the)	***Note:*** *Students may place definite articles incorrectly.*
Nouns	There is no plural form for nouns (plurals can be expressed through an adjective quantifier).	**Chinese** **Hmong** **Korean** (plurals are usually used for "people" nouns, such as *my friends*, and other nouns) **Vietnamese**	I have many good idea. = I have many good ideas. The paper has several problem. = The paper has several problems.
	There is no plural form after a number.	**Chinese** **Haitian Creole** (plural form is often omitted) **Hmong** **Korean** **Vietnamese**	There are three new student. = There are three new students. Vacation is four week. = Vacation is four weeks.

ENGLISH STRUCTURE	LANGUAGE TRANSFER ISSUE	LANGUAGES	SAMPLE TRANSFER ERRORS IN ENGLISH
Nouns, *continued*	A plural is formed by placing a plural marker after the noun.	**Haitian Creole** (indefinite plurals are unmarked) **Korean**	*Note: Students may add an additional word rather than adding -s to the noun.*
	In English, *-es* is added only after the consonants *s, x, ch, sh,* and *z.* Also, *y* is changed to *i* before adding *-es.* In other languages, *-es* is added to nouns that end in *y* or any consonant to form the plural.	**Spanish**	*walles* = walls *rayes* = rays
	English contains noncount nouns that do not have a plural form (for example: *fishing, money, bread, honesty, water, snow*).	**Chinese** **Haitian Creole** **Hmong** **Korean** **Vietnamese**	I like dancings. = I like dancing. She wears jewelrys. = She wears jewelry.
	Proper names can be listed last-name first. *Chinese example:* Chan Fu Kwan is written last-name first without a comma. *Vietnamese example:* Tran My Bao is written last, middle, first.	**Chinese** (always last name first) **Hmong** (in Asia) **Korean** **Vietnamese**	*Note: Teachers and students may confuse first and last names.*
	A first name is preferred when repeating a person's name.	**Hmong** **Vietnamese**	Mr. Kou Xiong is a teacher. Mr. Kou (first name) speaks many languages.
	Possessive nouns are formed with an *of* phrase.	**Haitian Creole** (Southern Haiti only) **Spanish** **Vietnamese**	This is the chair of Jamie. = This is Jamie's chair.
Pronouns	There is no distinction between subject and object pronouns.	**Chinese** **Haitian Creole** **Hmong** **Vietnamese**	I gave the forms to she. = I gave the forms to her. Him helped I. = He helped me.

Language Structure Transfer Chart, continued

ENGLISH STRUCTURE	LANGUAGE TRANSFER ISSUE	LANGUAGES	SAMPLE TRANSFER ERRORS IN ENGLISH
Pronouns, *continued*	There is no gender difference for third person singular pronouns.	**Chinese** (spoken language only) **Haitian Creole** **Hmong** (uses the pronoun *it*) **Vietnamese** (uses familiar form of third person singular)	Talk to the girl and give it advice. = Talk to the girl and give her advice.
	There is no distinction between simple, compound, subject, object, and reflexive pronouns.	**Hmong**	The book is I. = The book is mine. She is I sister. = She is my sister. I go I. = I go by myself.
	There are no relative pronouns.	**Korean** (modifying clause can function as a relative clause) **Vietnamese**	Look at the backpack is on the floor. = Look at the backpack that is on the floor.
	It is possible to omit the pronoun *it* as a subject.	**Chinese** **Hmong** **Korean** **Vietnamese**	What time? = What time is it? Three o'clock already. = It is three o'clock already.
	A possessive pronoun is formed by placing a separate word or character before the pronoun.	**Vietnamese**	This car is (of) him. = This car is his.
	A possessive pronoun is placed after the noun.	**Haitian Creole**	That book is (for) me. = That is my book.
Verbs	The verb *be* can be omitted with adjectives and prepositional phrases.	**Chinese** **Haitian Creole** **Hmong** **Korean** **Vietnamese**	We always cheerful. = We are always cheerful. I hungry. = I am hungry. You at home. = You are at home.
	The verb *be* is not used for adjectives or places.	**Hmong** **Vietnamese**	She beautiful. = She is beautiful. The book on the table. = The book is on the table.

ENGLISH STRUCTURE	LANGUAGE TRANSFER ISSUE	LANGUAGES	SAMPLE TRANSFER ERRORS IN ENGLISH
Verbs, *continued*	A verb is not inflected for person and number.	**Chinese** **Haitian Creole** **Hmong** **Korean** (verbs are inflected to reflect age or status) **Vietnamese**	That house have a big door. = That house has a big door. Everyone like you. = Everyone likes you.
	Several verbs can be used together with no words or punctuation to separate them.	**Hmong** **Vietnamese**	I cook eat at home. = I cook and eat at home.
	There is no gerund form (-*ing*) and/or no distinction between gerunds and infinitives.	**Chinese** (no form to show that an action is ongoing) **Haitian Creole** **Hmong** **Korean** **Spanish** **Vietnamese**	She hates to read. = She hates reading.
	The verb *be* can be used in place of *have*.	**Korean**	I am car. = I have one car.
	Infinitives are not used to indicate purpose.	**Haitian Creole**	I want learn English. = I want to learn English. I go to the library for study. = I go to the library to study.
	A *that* clause is used rather than an infinitive.	**Hmong** **Spanish**	I want that they try harder. = I want them to try harder.
	Have is used in place of *there is, there are,* or *there was, there were.*	**Hmong** **Vietnamese**	In the library have many books. = In the library, there are many books.
	The verb *have* is used to express states of being (such as age or hunger). Have *(tener)* is followed by a noun.	**Spanish**	She has ten years. = She is ten years old. I have hunger. = I am hungry. I have heat. = I am hot.

Language Structure Transfer Chart, continued

ENGLISH STRUCTURE	LANGUAGE TRANSFER ISSUE	LANGUAGES	SAMPLE TRANSFER ERRORS IN ENGLISH
Verbs, *continued*	Two-word verbs, or phrasal verbs, exist in very few languages. (In addition to English, they are found in a few other languages, such as Dutch, German, and Scandinavian languages.)		***Note:*** *Most ESL students find two-word verbs difficult, but it is necessary to learn them in order to understand informal, conversational English.*
Verb Tense	There are no tense inflections. Tense is usually indicated through context or by adding an expression of time.	**Chinese** **Hmong** (infinitive form of the verb is used with an expression of time) **Vietnamese**	When I am small, I ask many questions. = When I was small, I asked many questions. She teach math next semester. = She will teach math next semester.
	Verb tense does not change within the same sentence.	**Haitian Creole** **Hmong**	When we finish, we leave. = When we finish, we will leave.
	Present perfect tense can be used in place of past tense.	**Haitian Creole**	I have seen Lucas yesterday. = I saw Lucas yesterday.
	Present tense can be used in place of future tense. The present tense is used in place of the present perfect.	**Haitian Creole** **Hmong** **Spanish**	I finish it tomorrow. = I will finish it tomorrow. I live here a long time. = I have lived here a long time.
Adverbs	Adverbs are not used. Two adjectives or two verbs can be used to describe an adjective or verb.	**Hmong**	I run fast fast. = I run really fast. I run run to school. = I run quickly to school.
Adjectives	Adjectives follow the nouns they modify.	**Hmong** **Spanish** (The position of the adjective can also indicate meaning. In Spanish, limiting adjectives go before the noun, descriptive adjectives go after the noun) **Vietnamese**	They have a house big. = They have a big house. We live in a village Laotian. = We live in a Laotian village.
	Adjectives can reflect number and gender.	**Spanish**	I have kinds parents. = I have kind parents.

ENGLISH STRUCTURE	LANGUAGE TRANSFER ISSUE	LANGUAGES	SAMPLE TRANSFER ERRORS IN ENGLISH
Adjectives, *continued*	Some nouns and adjectives share the same form.	**Chinese**	***Note:*** *Students may have difficulty choosing between noun and adjective forms.* She wants to be independence. = She wants to be independent.
	Comparative adjectives do not change form. They are expressed with the equivalent of *more* and *most*.	**Hmong** (add adverbs after the adjective) **Korean**	She is fast more. = She is faster. She is more old than you. = She is older than you.
	A definite article is used in place of a possessive adjective.	**Spanish** (definite article used for parts of the body and articles of clothing)	Ana broke the leg. = Ana broke her leg.
	A possessive adjective is formed by placing a separate word, character, or article between the pronoun and the noun.	**Chinese** (suffix may be omitted in some cases) **Hmong**	he (possessive character) book = his book
	Possessive adjectives are omitted when the association is clear.	**Korean** **Vietnamese**	He raised hand. = He raised his hand.
	There is no distinction between personal pronouns and possessive adjectives.	**Vietnamese**	It is book I. = It is my book.
Prepositions	Meanings of prepositions do not always correspond to those in English.	**Spanish**	I like the songs in the CD. = I like the songs on the CD.
Word Order (Statements)	The verb may precede the subject.	**Spanish**	Arrived the teacher late. = The teacher arrived late.
	Verbs are placed last in a sentence. The usual word order is subject-object-verb.	**Korean**	The teacher the assignment gave. = The teacher gave the assignment.
	Subject and verb order is rarely changed.	**Chinese** **Haitian Creole** **Korean**	She is content and so I am. = She is content and so am I.

Language Structure Transfer Chart, continued

ENGLISH STRUCTURE	LANGUAGE TRANSFER ISSUE	LANGUAGES	SAMPLE TRANSFER ERRORS IN ENGLISH
Word Order (Statements), *continued*	A subject pronoun can be omitted when the subject is understood.	**Chinese** **Korean** (can omit the subject pronoun *you*) **Spanish**	Is crowded. = It is crowded. Am hungry. = I am hungry.
	A direct object precedes an indirect object when the indirect object is a pronoun.	**Chinese** (Cantonese only)	I gave an apple him. = I gave him an apple.
	Adverbs and adverbial phrases can precede verbs.	**Chinese** **Korean**	I hard study. = I study hard. He by train goes to school. = He goes to school by train.
Questions	*Yes/No* questions can be formed by adding an element to the end of a declarative statement.	**Chinese** **Hmong** **Korean** **Vietnamese** (statement followed by phrase *"or not"*)	The book is interesting, yes? = Is the book interesting? You like that color, no? = Do you like that color?
	Yes/No questions can be formed by adding a verb followed by its negative within a statement.	**Chinese** **Vietnamese**	You want not want watch movie? = Do you want to watch a movie or not?
	Yes/No questions can be formed by adding the question word between the pronoun and the verb.	**Hmong**	You (question word) like the school? = Do you like the school?
	Question words are placed according to the position of the answer. For example, if the answer functions as an object, the question words are placed in the regular object position.	**Chinese** **Korean**	He told you what? = What did he tell you? Tell me he is where? = Tell me where he is.

ENGLISH STRUCTURE	LANGUAGE TRANSFER ISSUE	LANGUAGES	SAMPLE TRANSFER ERRORS IN ENGLISH
Questions, *continued*	The answers *yes* and *no* vary depending upon the verb used in the question.	**Hmong**	***Note:*** *Students may substitute a verb for a yes-or-no answer.* Do you speak English? Speak. = Do you speak English? Yes. Do you speak English? No speak. = Do you speak English? No.
Commands	Commands can be formed by adding an adverb after the verbs to be emphasized.	**Hmong** (add the adverb *now*) **Vietnamese** (add the adverb *right now*)	Do now. = Do it!
	Commands can be formed by adding a time indicator after the verbs to be emphasized.	**Hmong**	Fix the car at 3:00. = Fix the car.
	Commands can be formed by adding the verb *go* for emphasis at the end of the sentence.	**Vietnamese**	Buy my groceries, go! = Buy my groceries.
	Commands can be formed by changing the verb ending.	**Korean**	Bring(ing) it over here. = Bring it over here.
Negatives and Negative Sentences	Double negatives are routinely used.	**Haitian Creole** **Spanish**	They don't like nothing. = They don't like anything.
	The negative marker goes before the verb phrase.	**Korean** (especially in informal situations) **Spanish** (when using perfect tense)	Joey not has finished the homework. = Joey has not finished the homework.
Subjects and Predicates	Sentences do not always include a subject.	**Spanish**	Is fun cook? = Is it fun to cook? Is raining. = It is raining. Is your mother? Yes is. = Is she your mother. Yes, she is.

Phonics Transfer Chart

	ENGLISH		SPANISH		CANTONESE		VIETNAMESE	
Phoneme	Grapheme	Key Word	Sound Transfer?	Sound-Symbol Match?	Sound Transfer?	Sound-Symbol Match?	Sound Transfer?	Sound-Symbol Match?
/b/	b	book	yes	yes	approx.	no	approx.	yes
/k/	c	carrot	yes	yes	yes	no	yes	yes
	k	key	yes	yes	yes	no	yes	yes
	ck	check	yes	no	yes	no	yes	no
/d/	d	desk	approx.	yes	approx.	no	approx.	yes
/f/	f	fish	yes	yes	yes	no	yes	no
/g/	g	girl	yes	yes	approx.	no	yes	yes
/h/	h	hand	yes	no	yes	no	yes	yes
/j/	j	jacket	no	no	approx.	no	approx.	no
	g	cage	no	no	approx.	no	approx.	no
	dge	badge	no	no	approx.	no	approx.	no
/l/	l	lamp	yes	yes	yes	no	yes	yes
/m/	m	map	yes	yes	yes	no	yes	yes
/n/	n	newspaper	yes	yes	yes	no	yes	yes
/p/	p	pizza	yes	yes	yes	no	yes	yes
/kw/	qu	quarter	yes	no	approx.	no	yes	yes
/r/	r	red	approx.	approx.	no	no	no	yes
/s/	s	seed	yes	yes	yes	no	yes	yes
	c	city	yes	yes	yes	no	yes	yes
/t/	t	ten	yes	yes	yes	no	approx.	yes
/v/	v	van	yes	yes	no	no	yes	yes
/w/	w	window	yes	yes	yes	no	no	no
/ks/	x	six	yes	yes	no	no	no	yes
/y/	y	yellow	yes	yes	yes	no	no	yes
/z/	z	zero	no	no	no	no	yes	no
/ch/	ch	chin	yes	yes	approx.	no	no	yes
	tch	match	yes	no	approx.	no	no	no
/sh/	sh	shell	no	no	no	no	yes	no
/hw/	wh	whisk	no	no	no	no	no	no
/th/	th	bath	approx.	no	no	no	approx.	yes
/th/	th	this	approx.	no	no	no	no	yes
/ng/	ng	ring	yes	yes	yes	no	yes	yes
/a/	a	map	approx.	no	no	no	approx.	yes
/e/	e	ten	yes	yes	approx.	no	approx.	yes
/i/	i	lid	approx.	no	approx.	no	no	yes
/o/	o	dot	approx.	no	approx.	no	approx.	yes
/u/	u	cup	approx.	no	approx.	no	yes	no

ENGLISH			HMONG		KOREAN		HAITIAN CREOLE	
Phoneme	Grapheme	Key Word	Sound Transfer?	Sound-Symbol Match?	Sound Transfer?	Sound-Symbol Match?	Sound Transfer?	Sound-Symbol Match?
Consonants								
/b/	b	book	approx.	no	approx.	no	yes	yes
/k/	c	carrot	yes	no	yes	no	yes	yes
	k	key	yes	yes	yes	no	yes	yes
	ck	check	yes	no	yes	no	yes	yes
/d/	d	desk	yes	yes	approx.	no	yes	yes
/f/	f	fish	yes	yes	no	no	yes	yes
/g/	g	girl	approx.	no	approx.	no	yes	yes
/h/	h	hand	yes	yes	yes	no	approx.	yes
/j/	j	jacket	no	no	approx.	no	yes	yes
	g	cage	no	no	approx.	no	yes	yes
	dge	badge	no	no	approx.	no	yes	yes
/l/	l	lamp	yes	yes	yes	no	yes	yes
/m/	m	map	yes	yes	yes	no	yes	yes
/n/	n	newspaper	yes	yes	yes	no	yes	yes
/p/	p	pizza	approx.	yes	yes	no	yes	yes
/kw/	qu	quarter	no	no	yes	no	yes	yes
/r/	r	red	no	no	no	no	yes	yes
/s/	s	seed	yes	no	yes	no	approx.	approx.
	c	city	yes	no	yes	no	approx.	approx.
/t/	t	ten	approx.	yes	yes	no	yes	yes
/v/	v	van	yes	yes	no	no	yes	yes
/w/	w	window	no	no	yes	no	yes	yes
/ks/	x	six	no	no	yes	no	yes	yes
/y/	y	yellow	yes	yes	yes	no	yes	yes
/z/	z	zero	yes	no	no	no	yes	yes
Digraphs								
/ch/	ch	chin	yes	no	yes	no	yes	yes
	tch	match	yes	no	yes	no	yes	yes
/sh/	sh	shell	yes	no	yes	no	yes	yes
/hw/	wh	whisk	no	no	yes	no	yes	yes
/th/	th	bath	no	no	no	no	yes	yes
/th/	th	this	no	no	yes	no	yes	yes
/ng/	ng	ring	yes	no	no	no	approx.	approx.
Short Vowels								
/a/	a	map	yes	yes	yes	no	yes	yes
/e/	e	ten	no	no	yes	no	no	no
/i/	i	lid	no	no	yes	no	yes	yes
/o/	o	dot	approx.	yes	approx.	no	yes	yes
/u/	u	cup	no	no	no	no	no	no

Phonics Transfer Chart, continued

ENGLISH			SPANISH		CANTONESE		VIETNAMESE	
Phoneme	Grapheme	Key Word	Sound Transfer?	Sound-Symbol Match?	Sound Transfer?	Sound-Symbol Match?	Sound Transfer?	Sound-Symbol Match?
Long Vowels								
/ā/	a_e	cake	yes	no	approx.	no	approx.	no
	ai	sail	yes	no	approx.	no	approx.	no
	ay	tray	yes	no	approx.	no	approx.	no
/ē/	ee	feet	yes	no	approx.	no	yes	no
	ea	sea	yes	no	approx.	no	yes	no
	y	happy	yes	no	approx.	no	yes	no
/ī/	i_e	bike	yes	no	approx.	no	yes	no
	ie	tie	yes	no	approx.	no	yes	no
	igh	night	yes	no	approx.	no	yes	no
	y	sky	yes	no	approx.	no	yes	no
/ō/	o_e	globe	yes	no	approx.	no	approx.	no
	oa	boat	yes	no	approx.	no	approx.	no
	ow	rowboat	yes	no	approx.	no	approx.	no
/ū/	u_e	flutes	yes	no	approx.	no	yes	yes
	ui	suit	yes	no	approx.	no	yes	no
	ue	blue	yes	no	approx.	no	yes	no
/yo͞o/	u_e	mule	yes	no	approx.	no	no	no
	ue	rescue	yes	no	approx.	no	no	no
R-Controlled Vowels								
/är/	ar	star	approx.	yes	approx.	no	no	no
/ôr/	or	horn	approx.	yes	approx.	no	no	no
/ûr/	er	fern	approx.	yes	approx.	no	no	no
	ir	bird	approx.	no	approx.	no	no	no
	ur	curb	approx.	no	approx.	no	no	no
/âr/	air	chair	no	no	no	no	no	no
	ear	bear	no	no	no	no	no	no
/îr/	eer	deer	no	no	no	no	no	no
	ear	tear	no	no	no	no	no	no
Variant Vowels								
/oi/	oi	coin	yes	yes	approx.	no	approx.	yes
	oy	boy	yes	yes	approx.	no	approx.	no
/ou/	ou	cloud	yes	no	approx.	no	yes	no
	ow	crown	yes	no	approx.	no	yes	no
/ô/	aw	saw	approx.	no	yes	no	yes	no
	au	laundry	approx.	no	approx.	no	yes	no
/ôl/	al	salt	approx.	no	approx.	no	no	no
	all	ball	approx.	no	approx.	no	no	no
/o͞o/	oo	moon	yes	no	approx.	no	approx.	no
	ew	screw	yes	no	approx.	no	approx.	no
/o͝o/	oo	book	no	no	approx.	no	approx.	no
/ə/	a (initial syllable)	asleep	no	no	no	no	approx.	no

ENGLISH			HMONG		KOREAN		HAITIAN CREOLE	
Phoneme	Grapheme	Key Word	Sound Transfer?	Sound-Symbol Match?	Sound Transfer?	Sound-Symbol Match?	Sound Transfer?	Sound-Symbol Match?
Long Vowels								
/ā/	a_e	cake	approx.	no	yes	no	yes	yes
	ai	sail	approx.	no	yes	no	yes	no
	ay	tray	approx.	no	yes	no	yes	no
/ē/	ee	feet	yes	no	yes	no	yes	yes
	ea	sea	yes	no	yes	no	yes	no
	y	happy	yes	no	yes	no	yes	no
/ī/	i_e	bike	yes	no	yes	no	yes	yes
	ie	tie	yes	no	yes	no	yes	yes
	igh	night	yes	no	yes	no	yes	yes
	y	sky	yes	no	yes	no	yes	yes
/ō/	o_e	globe	no	no	yes	no	yes	yes
	oa	boat	no	no	yes	no	yes	yes
	ow	rowboat	no	no	yes	no	yes	yes
/ū/	u_e	flutes	yes	yes	yes	no	yes	yes
	ui	suit	yes	no	yes	no	yes	yes
	ue	blue	yes	no	yes	no	yes	no
/yōō/	u_e	mule	no	no	yes	no	no	no
	ue	rescue	no	no	yes	no	no	no
R-Controlled Vowels								
/är/	ar	star	no	no	no	no	no	no
/ôr/	or	horn	no	no	no	no	no	no
/ûr/	er	fern	no	no	no	no	no	no
	ir	bird	no	no	no	no	no	no
	ur	curb	no	no	no	no	no	no
/âr/	air	chair	no	no	no	no	no	no
	ear	bear	no	no	no	no	no	no
/îr/	eer	deer	no	no	no	no	no	no
	ear	tear	no	no	no	no	no	no
Variant Vowels								
/oi/	oi	coin	no	no	yes	no	yes	yes
	oy	boy	no	no	yes	no	yes	yes
/ou/	ou	cloud	approx.	no	yes	no	yes	yes
	ow	crown	approx.	no	yes	no	yes	no
/ô/	aw	saw	approx.	no	approx.	no	yes	no
	au	laundry	approx.	no	approx	no	yes	yes
/ôl/	al	salt	no	no	approx.	no	yes	yes
	all	ball	no	no	approx.	no	yes	yes
/ōō/	oo	moon	yes	no	yes	no	yes	yes
	ew	screw	yes	no	yes	no	yes	yes
/ŏŏ/	oo	book	no	no	approx.	no	no	no
/ə/	a (initial syllable)	asleep	no	no	yes	no	yes	yes

Articulation of English Consonant and Vowel Sounds

How Are Consonant Phonemes Classified?

Consonant phonemes are generally classified according to manner of articulation (type of consonant sound), place of articulation (position in the mouth), and whether they are voiced or voiceless. Consonant sounds are also classified as either a continuous sound or a complete stop. When a consonant phoneme is produced, the air flow is cut off either partially or completely.

CONSONANT PHONEME CLASSIFICATIONS

Manner of Articulation
How is the sound produced?
- **Plosives:** formed by closing or blocking off the air flow and then exploding a puff of air; for example, /b/ as in *box*.
- **Nasals:** formed when the mouth is closed, forcing air through the nose; for example, /m/ as in *man*.
- **Fricatives:** formed by narrowing the air channel and then forcing air through it, creating friction in the mouth; for example, /v/ as in *voice*.
- **Affricatives:** formed by a stop followed by a fricative; for example, /ch/ as in *chip*.
- **Glides:** formed in similar ways as vowels; for example, /y/ as in *yes*.
- **Lateral:** formed by interrupting the air flow slightly, but no friction results; for example, /l/ as in *line*.

Place of Articulation
Where in the mouth is the sound produced?
- Lips (bilabial)   • Roof of mouth (palatal)
- Lips and teeth (labiodental)   • Back of mouth (velar)
- Tongue between teeth (dental)   • Throat (glottal)
- Tongue behind teeth (alveolar)

Voiced or Voiceless
- **Voiced:** the vocal cords vibrate; for example, /z/ as in *zoo*.
- Voiceless: the vocal cords do not vibrate; for example, /s/ as in *sit*.

Continuous or Stop
- **Continuous:** a sound that can be produced for several seconds without distortion; for example, /s/ as in *sun*.
- **Stop:** a sound that can be produced for only an instant; for example, /p/ as in *pop*.

CONSONANT PHONEME ARTICULATION

Place ▶ / ▼ Manner	Lips	Lips and Teeth	Tongue Between Teeth	Tongue Behind Teeth	Roof of Mouth	Back of Mouth	Throat
Plosives	/p/ /b/*			/t/ /d/		/k/ /g/	
Fricatives		/f/ /v/	/th/ /th/	/s/ /z/	/sh/ /zh/		/h/
Affricatives					/ch/ /j/		
Nasals	/m/			/n/		/ng/	
Lateral				/l/			
Glides	/hw/ /w/			/r/	/y/		

* Boldface indicates a voiced phoneme. Note the voiceless-voiced consonant pairs.

CONSONANT PHONEMES

Continuous Sounds
/f/, /h/, /l/, /m/, /n/, /r/, /s/, /v/, /w/, /y/, /z/

Stop Sounds
/b/, /d/, /g/, /j/, /p/, /t/, /k/, /ch/

Some students may need extra practice in producing consonant sounds that do not transfer from their native languages. Use the scripts and information below to model and discuss the English consonant sounds.

/m/

Place of Articulation: Lips

Manner of Articulation: Nasal

Voiced

Say the sound /m/. Pay attention to your mouth. What part of your mouth moves? (*lips*) How do they move? (*They are pressed tightly together.*) Does any air come out? (*yes*) Now hold your nose. Can you still say /m/? (*no*) That's because air comes out through your nose.

/p/

Place of Articulation: Lips

Manner of Articulation: Stop

Voiceless

Now say /p/. What part of your mouth moves? (*lips*) The lips help make /p/ also. Close your lips and then open them quickly. Does any air come out? (*yes, a lot*) When you say a /p/, you stop the air for a moment, and then you let the air rush out. Put your hand in front of your mouth and feel the air when you say /p/.

/t/

Place of Articulation: Tongue Behind Teeth

Manner of Articulation: Stop

Voiceless

Try making the sound /t/. Put your hand in front of your mouth. Do you feel a lot of air coming out? (*yes*) Now try to close your lips and say /t/. Does it work? (*no*) Another part of your mouth makes /t/. Can you feel what part? (*the tongue*) Where does it stop the air? (*on the hard ridge behind your top teeth*)

/b/

Place of Articulation: Lips

Manner of Articulation: Stop

Voiced

Do you remember saying the /p/ sound? Say /p/. What makes the air stop? (*lips*) Do you feel a lot of air come out? (*yes*) Now use your mouth in the same way, but use your voice also. This sound is /b/. Do you think you really use your voice? Cover your ears and say /p/ and /b/. Which one sounds louder? (*/b/*) That is because you are using your voice. Say *pit, bit*. Notice that when you change only one sound, you can get a different word.

/k/

Place of Articulation: Back of Mouth

Manner of Articulation: Stop

Voiceless

Now try saying /k/. Put your hand in front of your mouth. Do you feel a lot of air come out? (*yes*) What stops the air? Do your lips move? (*no*) Do you put your tongue up behind your top teeth? (*no*) Where is your tongue? (*The front is low because the back of the tongue stops the air.*) Where? (*in the back of the mouth*) The /k/ is pronounced in the back of the mouth.

/n/

Place of Articulation: Tongue Behind Teeth

Manner of Articulation: Nasal

Voiced

Let's say the sound /n/. Keep on saying /n/, and put your hand in front of your mouth. Does any air come out? (*no*) Now hold your nose. Can you say an /n/ now? (*no*) What other sound did we practice where air came through the nose? (*/m/*) Say an /m/ now. What part of your mouth did you use? (*lips*) We don't use our lips for the /n/ sound. Say /m/ and /n/. Where does your tongue move to? Say *meat, neat*. The tongue is behind the teeth for *neat*, and air still comes out the nose.

/d/

Place of Articulation: Tongue Behind Teeth

Manner of Articulation: Stop

Voiced

Now let's say /d/. Does a lot of air come out? (*yes*) How do you know that? (*I put my hand in front of my mouth.*) Cover your ears when you make /d/. Do you use your voice in making this sound? (*yes*) Say /t/, /d/, /t/, /d/. How are these sounds different? (*We use our voice for /d/ but not for /t/. That is the only difference.*)

/g/

Place of Articulation: Back of Mouth

Manner of Articulation: Stop

Voiced

Watch my face as I say a /g/ sound (as in *get*). Does any part of my face move? (*no*) (If someone does notice your throat, you should recognize the good observation and come back to it later.) Now let's make the sound and see if a lot of air comes out. (*yes*) You should have put your hand up to be sure. Do you use your voice? How do you know? (*cover your ears*) Notice where your tongue stops the air when you start to make the sound. Is it in the front of your mouth or the back? (*in the back*) Now say /k/, /g/, /k/, /g/. These sounds are pronounced in the same place, but we use our voice for one. Which one? (*/g/*)

/l/

Place of Articulation: Tongue Behind Teeth

Manner of Articulation: Lateral

Voiced

Say an /l/. Does a lot of air come out? (*no*) The air is not stopped for /l/, so you don't feel a puff of air when you make this sound. Keep saying /l/. Can you say /t/ and hold it? (*no*) The air stops on /t/ and then rushes out. For /l/, the air flows out at both sides of the tongue. Can you tell me where the tip of the tongue is for /l/? (*on the upper ridge behind the front teeth*)

Consonant Sounds, continued

/f/

Place of Articulation: Lips and Teeth **Manner of Articulation: Fricative** **Voiceless**	Try saying an /f/ sound. Can you keep saying this sound? (*yes*) Watch my face as I say the sound /f/. What part of my mouth moved? (*Students may say lips.*) Watch again closely. Do both lips move? (*no, just one*) Which? (*the lower lip*) Say the sound /f/ yourself. The lower lip comes up close to your upper teeth and makes the air sound noisy. Keep saying the /f/ and listen to the noise of the air.

/h/

Place of Articulation: Throat **Manner of Articulation: Fricative** **Voiceless**	Now say /h/, /h/, /h/ and hold your hand in front of your mouth. Do you feel a puff of air? (*yes*) Now say *eee*. Then say *he, he, he*. Did you feel a difference from when you said *eee*? (*yes*) Now say *ooo, ho, ho, ho*. When we put a small puff of air before another sound, it is the /h/ sound. Say *I, hi,* or *it, hit*. Does the /h/ sound make a difference in the meaning? (*yes*)

/r/

Place of Articulation: Tongue Behind Teeth **Manner of Articulation: Glide** **Voiced**	Try saying the sound /r/. Can you keep saying this sound for a long time? (*yes*) /r/ does not stop the air. Now stop making /r/, but keep your tongue ready to say the sound. Take a deep breath. The part of your tongue that feels cool is the part that helps to make this sound. It is under part of the tip of your tongue. This part comes close to a part of your mouth. What part of your mouth does the tongue come close to? (*the roof of the mouth*) Say *at*. Now put the /r/ first and say *rat*. Do *at* and *rat* mean different things? (*Yes, the /r/ makes a difference in meaning.*)

/w/

Place of Articulation: Lips **Manner of Articulation: Glide** **Voiced**	For the next sound, I am going to get ready to say it, but I won't say it. Can you guess what sound it is? (Round your lips to pronounce /w/, but do not say it.) Can you tell me what sound I was going to make? (*/w/*) Now let's all make the /w/ sound. Which part of your mouth moves? (*lips*) What do they do? (*get round and tight*) Do you use your voice to say the /w/ sound? (*yes*) Say *itch*, then *witch*. Does the /w/ sound make a difference in meaning? (*yes*)

/sh/

Place of Articulation: Roof of Mouth **Manner of Articulation: Fricative** **Voiceless**	Next, we are going to make another sound where the lips are round but not as tight. Try /sh/. Can you keep saying this sound? (*yes*) (Have a student stand in the corner of the room and make the /sh/.) Could everyone hear (student's name) make the /sh/? (*yes*) The air is very noisy. Remember, the air gets noisy when it rushes past a close or narrow place. The lips help make this narrow place, and so does the top of the front part of the tongue. The tip of the tongue comes close to the roof of your mouth.

/s/

Place of Articulation: Tongue Behind Teeth **Manner of Articulation: Fricative** **Voiceless**	Watch my lips as I change from making /sh/ to /s/. How do my lips change? (*They are no longer rounded.*) Does the air make a lot of noise in /s/? (*yes*) Are your teeth close together or far apart? (*close together*) The top of your tongue makes this sound also, but it has moved from the ridge to come close to another part of your mouth. Can you tell where? (*It comes close behind your teeth.*) Say *she, see,* or *ship, sip*. Does /s/ make a difference in meaning? (*yes*)

Source

This material was adapted from *Phonological Awareness Training for Reading* (pp. 7, 32, 33–34) by Joseph K. Torgesen and Bryan R. Bryant, 1994, Austin, TX: PRO-ED. Copyright © 1994 by PRO-ED, Inc. Adapted with permission.

How Are Vowel Phonemes Classified?

When a consonant phoneme is produced, the air flow is cut off either partially or completely. When a vowel phoneme is produced, however, the air flow is unobstructed, or continuous. Vowel phonemes are all continuous sounds. They are classified according to tongue position and mouth position. All vowel sounds are voiced.

VOWEL PHONEME CLASSIFICATIONS

Tongue Position
1. Is the tongue high, in neutral position, or low in the mouth?
2. Is the tongue near the front, center, or back of the mouth?

Mouth Position
1. How rounded are the lips?
2. How tense are the mouth and jaw muscles?

In the chart below, the most common English spellings are listed under each vowel sound. Notice that to produce the /ē/ sound in the word *tree*, the mouth position is wide and smiling; the jaw muscles are tense. To pronounce the /o/ sound in the word *lot*, the mouth position is round and wide open; the jaw muscles are relaxed. To pronounce the /oo/ sound in the word *boot*, the mouth position is round and partially open; the jaw muscles are tense.

VOWEL PHONEMES BY MOUTH POSITION

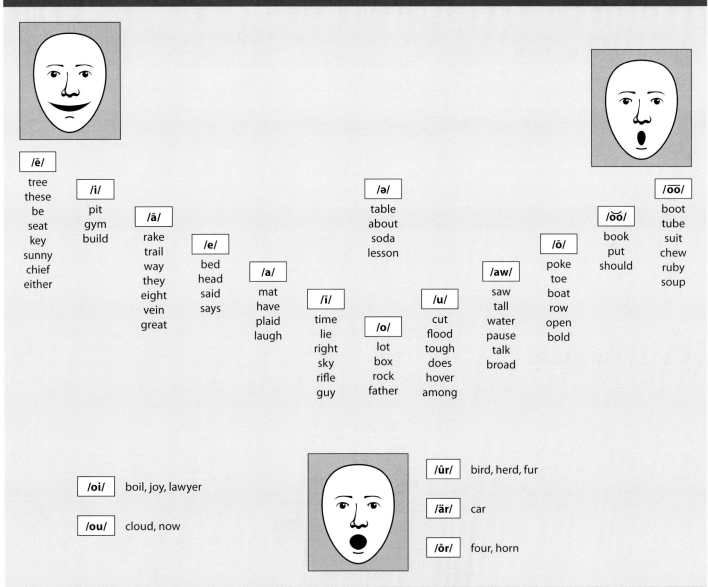

/ē/
tree
these
be
seat
key
sunny
chief
either

/i/
pit
gym
build

/ā/
rake
trail
way
they
eight
vein
great

/e/
bed
head
said
says

/a/
mat
have
plaid
laugh

/ī/
time
lie
right
sky
rifle
guy

/ə/
table
about
soda
lesson

/o/
lot
box
rock
father

/u/
cut
flood
tough
does
hover
among

/aw/
saw
tall
water
pause
talk
broad

/ō/
poke
toe
boat
row
open
bold

/o͝o/
book
put
should

/o͞o/
boot
tube
suit
chew
ruby
soup

/oi/ boil, joy, lawyer

/ou/ cloud, now

/ûr/ bird, herd, fur

/är/ car

/ôr/ four, horn

Using the Language Songs

Introduction

The goal of the audio program is to help English language learners (ELLs) develop their listening and speaking skills and improve their English proficiency. Students are encouraged to be active participants in improving their listening and speaking skills.

Sing with Me Language Songs audio includes a rich variety of opportunities for students to listen to language models and interact with various genres ranging from songs, and chants to telephone conversations, discussions, interviews, explanations, stories, speeches, and presentations. These lessons provide a starting point for modeling language and having students practice the language functions and patterns.

Teaching with the Language CD Lessons

The **Language Function** lessons are introduced in the **Student Book** and the **Sing with Me Language Songs Big Book**. Engaging visuals support the content and language of the song. Follow the teaching instructions on the accompanying Teacher's Edition page to support student learning.

The audio models the language sample that appears on the page. For most songs, chants, and dialogs, the narrator will follow a consistent instructional path:

1. Prompt students to listen
2. Invite students to listen and echo (repeat) the song or chant or to listen and sing along or chime in (say at the same time)
3. To support independence, the students are then asked to sing the song or say the chant on their own with the music or beat

As you use the Language audio, you will discover new ways to enhance the lessons for your students, depending on their level of language proficiency. These include:

- provide more repetitions of the audio track, as the needs of your students dictate
- have students write down words or phrases for the language function or use the Language Frames to create alternative verses
- play the audio again with an additional purpose for listening
- read from the student book page for further practice in speaking
- set up listening stations or provide access to recordings for independent work
- encourage families to log into NGReach.com to connect in-school and out-of-school literacy experiences

Audio Formats

The audio is provided in several formats. These various formats enable students to access the activities at listening centers or share the songs at home, extending language practice opportunities to families.

Interactive eEditions

 **Audio CD**

MP3 Downloads

 Go to NGReach.com for more information about how to access online audio resources.

Audio Tracks for **Sing with Me Language Songs**
Level E

CD	Unit	Track #	Title	Language Function	Listening Genres
1	1	1–2	Fresh Hot Corn Tamales	Express Feelings	Song
		3–4	Too Many Tamales!	Agree and Disagree	Song
		5–6	A Tooth Tradition	Ask for and Give Information	Song
		7–8	What Happened to Your Tooth?	Ask for and Give Information	Dialogue
	2	9–10	Raccoon Talk	Express Ideas	Dialogue
		11–12	A Discussion	Engage in Discussion	Chant and Discussion
		13–14	Let's Talk About Pets	Engage in Conversation	Dialogue
		15–16	The Smartest Dog	Tell an Original Story	Song
2	3	1–2	A Map to My Home	Give and Follow Directions	Chant
		3–4	One Way to Make a Map	Give, Restate, and Follow Instructions	Chant and Restatement
		5–6	My Travels	Describe Places	Song
		7–8	Please Tell Me	Make and Respond to Requests	Song
	4	9–10	A Good Place for a Garden	Make Comparisons	Song
		11–12	Maybe Carrots, Maybe Not	Express Certainty, Possibility, and Probability	Song
		13–14	To the Woods	Express Needs and Wants	Chant
		15–16	Where Can I Go?	Ask for and Give Advice	Song
3	5	1–2	Flowers or Weeds?	Retell a Story	Song
		3–4	Try a Summary	Summarize	Chant and Summary
		5–6	Nowhere to Hide	Define and Explain	Poem
		7–8	If We Want to Survive	Elaborate	Song
	6	9–10	My Treasure Hunt	Express Intentions	Chant
		11–12	Treasure Hunting Tips	Make and Accept Suggestions	Song and Response
		13–14	Bongo's Treasure Hunt	Restate an Idea	Song, Summary, and Restatement
		15–16	What a Dog!	Verify or Confirm Information	Song
4	7	1–2	Star Search	Ask and Answer Questions	Dialogue
		3–4	Three Stars	Evaluate	Chant
		5–6	Let's Go to the Moon	Clarify	Song
		7–8	Captain's Orders	Give and Carry Out Commands	Dialogue
	8	9–10	One Kid Can	Express Opinions	Song
		11–12	Here's My Opinion	Express Opinions	Song and Opinion
		13–14	Who Gets the Prize?	Justify	Dialogue
		15–16	Prize Persuasion	Persuade	Dialogue

Scope and Sequence

Language Development and Communication

	Grade						In the U.S.A.
	K	1	2	3	4	5	2–5
ACADEMIC AND SOCIAL LANGUAGE FUNCTIONS							
Listen actively	●	●	●	●	●	●	●
Repeat spoken language	●	●	●	●	●	●	●
Give personal information	●	●					●
Make introductions	●	●					●
Express social courtesies	●	●	●	●	●	●	●
Ask and answer questions	●	●	●	●	●	●	●
Talk about school-related activities	●	●	●	●	●	●	●
Use a telephone							●
Conduct a transaction							●
Agree and disagree	●	●	●	●	●	●	●
Ask for and give advice		●	●	●	●		
Make and accept suggestions	●	●	●	●	●	●	●
Make and respond to a request (including ask for help)	●	●	●	●	●	●	●
Demonstrate nonverbal communication			●	●	●	●	●
Interpret nonverbal communication	●	●	●	●	●	●	●
Express likes and dislikes	●	●	●	●	●	●	●
Express feelings, needs, opinions, intentions, ideas, or wants	●	●	●	●	●	●	●
Express certainty, probability, or possibility					●	●	
Give and carry out commands	●	●	●	●	●	●	●
Describe people, places, things, events, ideas, feelings, experiences	●	●	●	●	●	●	●
Listen to and derive meaning from a preview	●	●	●	●	●	●	●
Listen to and derive meaning from a song, chant, poem, selection	●	●	●	●	●	●	●
Recite using clear diction, tempo, volume, and phrasing	●	●	●	●	●	●	●
Read a text	●	●	●	●	●	●	●
Read online content		●	●	●	●	●	●
Retell a story	●	●	●	●	●	●	●
Tell an original story	●	●	●	●	●	●	●
Restate an idea (paraphrase)	●	●	●	●	●	●	●
Give and follow directions	●	●	●	●	●	●	●
Give and follow instructions	●	●	●	●	●	●	●
Role-play	●	●	●	●	●	●	●
Dramatize	●	●	●	●	●	●	●
Ask for and give information	●	●	●	●	●	●	●
Make comparisons	●	●	●	●	●	●	●
Summarize		●	●	●	●	●	●
Engage in conversation	●	●	●	●	●	●	●
Engage in discussion (academic)		●	●	●	●	●	
Level	A	B	C	D	E	F	Newcomer Level

Language Development and Communication, continued

ACADEMIC AND SOCIAL LANGUAGE FUNCTIONS, continued

	K	1	2	3	4	5	In the U.S.A. 2–5
Seek clarification		•	•	•	•	•	•
Define and explain		•	•	•	•	•	
Elaborate				•	•	•	
Persuade				•	•	•	
Justify or negotiate				•	•	•	
Verify or confirm information					•	•	
Evaluate			•	•	•	•	
Write		•	•	•	•	•	•
Adjust communication to the audience, purpose, and occasion	•	•	•	•	•	•	•

LANGUAGE PATTERNS AND STRUCTURES

	K	1	2	3	4	5	In the U.S.A. 2–5
Basic Sentence Patterns (I like _____; This is _____; etc.)	•	•	•	•	•	•	•
Language structures 　See Grammar and Sentence Structure (page S&S 19)	•	•	•	•	•	•	•

Concepts and Vocabulary

VOCABULARY

	K	1	2	3	4	5	In the U.S.A. 2–5
Greetings and other social courtesies	•	•					•
Personal information (name, address, etc.)	•	•					•
Categories: clothing, food, school, etc.	•	•	•	•	•	•	•
Academic vocabulary in Language Arts and Literature	•	•	•	•	•	•	•
Academic vocabulary in Science, Social Studies, Mathematics	•	•	•	•	•	•	•

VOCABULARY STRATEGIES

	K	1	2	3	4	5	In the U.S.A. 2–5
Relate Words	•	•	•	•	•	•	•
Word categories		•	•	•	•	•	•
Synonyms and antonyms		•	•	•	•	•	•
Analogies					•	•	
Distinguish shades of meaning					•	•	
Cognates	•	•	•	•	•	•	•
Use Structural Clues		•	•	•	•	•	
Compound words		•	•	•	•	•	
Prefixes and suffixes		•	•	•	•	•	
Latin, Greek, and other roots					•	•	
Determine the Meaning of Figurative Language					•	•	
Idioms, sayings, adages, or expressions					•	•	
Similes and metaphors					•	•	
Level	A	B	C	D	E	F	Newcomer Level

Scope and Sequence, continued

Concepts and Vocabulary, continued

	Grade						In the U.S.A. 2–5
	K	**1**	**2**	**3**	**4**	**5**	
VOCABULARY STRATEGIES, continued							
Use Context Clues		•	•	•	•	•	
Unfamiliar words		•	•	•	•	•	
Multiple-meaning words			•	•	•	•	
Homophones and homographs					•	•	
Idioms, sayings, adages, or expressions			•	•	•	•	
Figurative language			•	•	•	•	
Use Tools and References		•	•	•			•
Locate words using alphabetical order		•	•	•	•	•	•
Dictionary and glossary		•	•	•	•	•	
Thesaurus					•	•	
Technology and online tools	•	•	•	•	•	•	•
Apply Learning Strategies	•	•	•	•	•	•	•
Pronounce words correctly	•	•	•	•		•	•
Associate words and images (create images, find images)	•	•	•	•	•	•	•
Use graphic organizers to learn and relate words	•	•	•	•	•	•	•
Use peers, adults, and the teacher to establish, clarify, or extend understanding	•	•	•	•	•	•	•
Maintain vocabulary notebooks, journals, word cards, and word maps	•	•	•	•	•	•	•
Compare and contrast words	•	•	•	•	•	•	•
Use language patterns	•	•	•	•	•	•	•
Use nonverbal cues	•	•	•	•	•	•	•
Use prior knowledge and experience	•	•	•	•	•	•	•
Engage in wide reading to grow vocabulary			•	•	•	•	

Learning Strategies

STRATEGIES FOR LEARNING LANGUAGE							
Listen to and imitate others	•	•	•	•	•	•	•
Recite songs, chants, dialogs and poems	•	•	•	•	•	•	•
Practice new language (repeating, reciting, etc.)	•	•	•	•	•	•	•
Rehearse, review, and memorize	•	•	•	•	•	•	•
Use learning tools and resources	•	•	•	•	•	•	•
Take notes		•	•	•	•	•	•
Gather information		•	•	•	•	•	
Outline					•	•	
Use graphic organizers	•		•		•	•	•
Interact with peers	•	•	•	•	•	•	•
Level	**A**	**B**	**C**	**D**	**E**	**F**	**Newcomer Level**

Learning Strategies, continued

	K	1	2	3	4	5	In the U.S.A. 2–5
STRATEGIES FOR LEARNING LANGUAGE, continued							
Self-Monitor and Self-Assess	●	●	●	●	●	●	●
Plan	●	●	●	●	●	●	●
Set goals and monitor progress		●	●	●	●	●	●
Ask questions	●	●	●	●	●	●	●
Visualize	●	●	●	●	●	●	●
Paraphrase or restate			●	●	●	●	
Summarize		●	●	●	●	●	●
Connect new information to known information	●	●	●	●	●	●	●
Self-Correct	●	●	●	●	●	●	●
Verify language usage or spellings through dictionaries, etc.		●	●	●	●	●	
Determine appropriate language use (formal/informal)	●	●	●	●	●	●	●
Use visuals and media to construct or clarify meaning	●	●	●	●	●	●	●
Use Multiple Strategies	●	●	●	●	●	●	●
Use nonverbal cues to get across an idea	●	●	●	●	●	●	●
Respond to nonverbal cues	●	●	●	●	●	●	●
Ask for help, feedback, and clarification	●	●	●	●	●	●	●
Say things another way (circumlocution)		●	●	●	●	●	●
Test hypotheses about language (take risks)			●	●	●	●	
Incorporate language "chunks"		●	●	●	●	●	●
Reflect on learning and strategies		●	●	●	●	●	●
Analyze and Connect Ideas	●	●	●	●	●	●	●
Generate and organize ideas	●	●	●	●	●	●	●
Make predictions	●	●	●	●	●	●	●
Use prior knowledge and experience	●	●	●	●	●	●	●
Reason inductively and deductively		●	●	●	●	●	●
Compare and contrast language and identify patterns in language	●	●	●	●	●	●	●
Make connections across content areas	●	●	●	●	●	●	●
Collaborate with peers	●	●	●	●	●	●	●
Use graphic organizers	●	●	●	●	●	●	●
Reproduce teacher-modeled writing	●	●	●	●	●	●	●
STRATEGIES FOR TAKING TESTS							
Read directions carefully			●	●	●	●	
Know the test format			●	●	●	●	
Plan time for each item/selection			●	●	●	●	
Clarify vocabulary in passages/questions			●	●	●	●	
Look for important words			●	●	●	●	
Rephrase the question			●	●	●	●	
Level	A	B	C	D	E	F	Newcomer Level

Learning Strategies, continued

	Grade						In the U.S.A. 2–5
	K	1	2	3	4	5	
STRATEGIES FOR TAKING TESTS, continued							
Predict the answer			●	●	●	●	
Read all choices			●	●	●	●	
Skip and return to questions			●	●	●	●	
Strategies for Writing Tests			●	●	●	●	
Unpack a writing prompt			●	●	●	●	
Brainstorm topics			●	●	●	●	
Make a plan for writing			●	●	●	●	
Choose the type of language to use			●	●	●	●	
Write with focus and coherence			●	●	●	●	
Write fluent sentences			●	●	●	●	
Use correct grammar, mechanics, usage, and spelling			●	●	●	●	
Revise and edit your work			●	●	●	●	
RESEARCH SKILLS							
Organize prior knowledge	●	●	●	●	●	●	●
Formulate and revise research questions		●	●	●	●	●	
Plan research methods				●	●	●	
Use the research process				●	●	●	
Gather Information		●	●	●	●	●	
Use alphabetical order		●	●	●	●	●	
Look up key words		●	●	●	●	●	
Use parts of a book	●	●	●	●	●	●	
Use print resources: books, maps, dictionary, etc.	●	●	●	●	●	●	
Use electronic resources	●	●	●	●	●	●	
Conduct observations, experiments, and interviews	●	●	●	●	●	●	
Take and compile notes		●	●	●	●	●	
Organize information	●	●	●	●	●	●	
Analyze and evaluate notes			●	●	●	●	
Draw conclusions			●	●	●	●	
Present research findings	●	●	●	●	●	●	
Prepare a research report					●	●	
Level	A	B	C	D	E	F	Newcomer Level

Listening, Speaking, Viewing and Representing

	Grade						In the U.S.A. 2–5
	K	1	2	3	4	5	
LISTENING AND SPEAKING							
Determine the purpose for listening	●	●	●	●	●	●	●
Listen actively	●	●	●	●	●	●	●
Associate speech with actions, expressions, context, and visuals	●	●	●	●	●	●	●
Listen for the main idea and important details	●	●	●	●	●	●	●
Listen for implicit ideas			●	●	●	●	
Listen to take notes				●	●	●	
Listen to follow instructions or directions	●	●	●	●	●	●	●
Listen critically to determine author's purpose, interpret a message			●	●	●	●	
Listen and respond to a poem, song, selection	●	●	●	●	●	●	
Listen and speak effectively in a discussion or peer conference		●	●	●	●	●	
Listen and ask questions	●	●	●	●	●	●	●
Listen and speak effectively to work with a partner or on a team	●	●	●	●	●	●	●
Listen and connect ideas to prior experiences or knowledge	●	●	●	●	●	●	●
Listen and summarize or paraphrase		●	●	●	●	●	
Monitor understanding of spoken messages	●	●	●	●	●	●	●
Ask for clarification	●	●	●	●	●	●	●
Evaluate or appreciate spoken messages	●	●	●	●	●	●	
Speak at an appropriate rate and volume	●	●	●	●	●	●	
Speak clearly	●	●	●	●	●	●	
Demonstrate and respond to nonverbal communication	●	●	●	●	●	●	●
Organize Ideas Effectively	●	●	●	●	●	●	
with a clear beginning, middle, and end	●	●	●	●	●	●	
in chronological order	●	●	●	●	●	●	
around a main idea		●	●	●	●	●	
with a clear focus		●	●	●	●	●	
Deliver Ideas Effectively	●	●	●	●	●	●	
Stay on topic	●	●	●	●	●	●	
Include relevant details or examples		●	●	●	●	●	
Use visuals, gestures, and expression to clarify or enhance ideas	●	●	●	●	●	●	
Make eye contact	●	●	●	●	●	●	●
Use language appropriate to the audience, purpose, and occasion		●	●	●	●	●	
Use correct speech and pronunciation	●	●	●	●	●	●	●
Vary words and sentences		●	●	●	●	●	
Self-monitor and self-assess oral communication		●	●	●	●	●	●
Level	A	B	C	D	E	F	Newcomer Level

Scope and Sequence, continued

Listening, Speaking, Viewing and Representing, continued

	K	1	2	3	4	5	In the U.S.A. 2–5
Grade							
REPRESENTING IDEAS AND INFORMATION							
Create graphic organizers	●	●	●	●	●	●	●
Create visuals and graphic displays	●	●	●	●	●	●	●
Create multimedia presentations			●	●	●	●	
Represent ideas with movement and gestures	●	●	●	●	●	●	●
SPEAKING APPLICATIONS							
Read aloud	●	●	●	●	●	●	●
Role-play or dramatize	●	●	●	●	●	●	●
Retell a story or spoken message	●	●	●	●	●	●	●
Tell a story	●	●	●	●	●	●	●
Give an explanation			●	●	●	●	
Give an oral report		●	●	●	●	●	
Participate in and initiate a conversation or discussion	●	●	●	●	●	●	●
Participate in choral reading	●	●	●	●	●	●	●
Participate in Reader's Theater	●	●	●	●	●	●	
Give and restate instructions and directions		●	●	●	●	●	●
Relate events or experiences in sequence	●	●	●	●	●	●	●
Deliver an oral summary or oral response		●	●	●	●	●	
Conduct an interview			●	●	●	●	
Participate in a panel or conference			●	●	●	●	
COLLABORATION (TEAMWORK)							
Adjust interaction for the context (classroom, social)	●	●	●	●	●	●	●
Agree on discussion rules	●	●	●	●	●	●	●
Speak when recognized	●	●	●	●	●	●	●
Interrupt politely	●	●	●	●	●	●	●
Listen to others	●	●	●	●	●	●	●
Make appropriate contributions	●	●	●	●	●	●	●
Respond to questions	●	●	●	●	●	●	●
Prompt and provide suggestions		●	●	●	●	●	●
Consider and respond to suggestions		●	●	●	●	●	●
Connect and build on one another's ideas			●	●	●	●	
Support and defend ideas			●	●	●	●	
VIEWING TEXT AND MEDIA							
Respond to visual images and multimedia content	●	●	●	●	●	●	●
Comprehend and interpret visual images and multimedia content	●	●	●	●	●	●	●
Compare information across media	●	●	●	●	●	●	
Use media to confirm and enhance understanding		●	●	●	●	●	●
Level	A	B	C	D	E	F	Newcomer Level

Reading

	Grade						In the U.S.A. 2–5
	K	1	2	3	4	5	
READING STRATEGIES							
Plan Your Reading	●	●	●	●	●	●	
Build background knowledge	●	●	●	●	●	●	●
Activate and share prior knowledge and experience	●	●	●	●	●	●	●
Preview to anticipate content, purpose, and organization	●	●	●	●	●	●	
Make and confirm predictions	●	●	●	●	●	●	
Set a purpose for reading	●	●	●	●	●	●	
Monitor Your Reading	●	●	●	●	●	●	
Clarify ideas and vocabulary	●	●	●	●	●	●	
Adjust reading rate	●	●	●	●	●	●	
Ask Questions	●	●	●	●	●	●	
Visualize	●	●	●	●	●	●	
Determine Importance	●	●	●	●	●	●	
Identify the main idea and details	●	●	●	●	●	●	
Summarize	●	●	●	●	●	●	
Make Connections	●	●	●	●	●	●	
Connect text to world	●	●	●	●	●	●	
Connect text to self	●	●	●	●	●	●	
Connect text-to-text	●	●	●	●	●	●	
Make Inferences	●	●	●	●	●	●	
Synthesize			●	●	●	●	
Draw conclusions			●	●	●	●	
Make generalizations			●	●	●	●	
Relate and Compare Texts	●	●	●	●	●	●	
Apply Strategies	●	●	●	●	●	●	
Use strategies before, during, and after reading	●	●	●	●	●	●	
Use strategies flexibly and self-monitor use of strategies	●	●	●	●	●	●	
READING FLUENCY							
Read with appropriate accuracy and rate		●	●	●	●	●	
Read with correct phrasing		●	●	●	●	●	
Read with expression		●	●	●	●	●	
Read with correct intonation		●	●	●	●	●	
Reread and rehearse to build oral and silent reading fluency		●	●	●	●	●	
READING BEHAVIORS							
Engage in varied reading experiences	●	●	●	●	●	●	●
Listen to text readings or recordings and follow along	●	●	●	●	●	●	●
Participate in shared reading	●	●	●	●	●	●	●
Read independently for sustained periods			●	●	●	●	
Level	A	B	C	D	E	F	Newcomer Level

Scope and Sequence, continued

Reading, continued

	K	1	2	3	4	5	In the U.S.A. 2–5
READING BEHAVIORS, continued							
Read a variety of texts for a variety of purposes			●	●	●	●	
Read texts from diverse cultures and authors		●	●	●	●	●	●
Respond to Reading	●	●	●	●	●	●	●
Respond through talk, movement, music, art, drama, writing	●	●	●	●	●	●	●
Respond in ways that reflect understanding and interpretation		●	●	●	●	●	●
Offer observations, make connections, react, speculate, interpret, and raise questions		●	●	●	●	●	
Connect and compare ideas, themes, and issues across texts		●	●	●	●	●	
Apply Reading to Personal and Academic Life		●	●	●	●	●	●
Identify personal interests and related literature		●	●	●	●	●	●
Develop personal preferences in reading		●	●	●	●	●	●
Recognize how literature expands viewpoints, experiences		●	●	●	●	●	●
Recognize that literature may elicit a variety of valid responses	●	●	●	●	●	●	●
Recognize how informational text expands knowledge, viewpoints				●	●	●	●
Relate own experiences to authors and illustrators	●	●	●	●	●	●	●
COMPREHENSION AND CRITICAL THINKING							
Follow directions	●	●	●	●	●	●	●
Classify	●	●	●	●	●	●	●
Categorize	●	●	●	●	●	●	●
Relate Ideas		●	●	●	●	●	●
Sequence of events or ideas	●	●	●	●	●	●	●
Steps in a process	●	●	●	●	●	●	
Cause and effect	●	●	●	●	●	●	
Problem and solution		●	●	●	●	●	
Goal and outcome				●	●	●	
Main idea and details	●	●	●	●	●	●	
Compare and contrast	●	●	●	●	●	●	
Analyze Information	●	●	●	●	●	●	●
Interpret visuals	●	●	●			●	●
Distinguish fact from opinion			●	●	●		
Identify the topic	●	●	●	●		●	●
Identify facts and information		●	●	●	●	●	●
Analyze story elements (character, setting, plot)	●	●	●	●	●	●	●
Paraphrase			●	●	●	●	
Interpret figurative language			●			●	
Identify sensory details	●	●	●	●	●	●	
Form opinions			●	●	●	●	
Level	A	B	C	D	E	F	Newcomer Level

	Grade						In the U.S.A. 2–5
	K	**1**	**2**	**3**	**4**	**5**	

COMPREHENSION AND CRITICAL THINKING, continued

	K	1	2	3	4	5	In the U.S.A. 2–5
Support inference, conclusion, judgment, generalizations, connections with text evidence, examples, experience			●	●	●	●	
Identify text evidence, examples, and experiences to support visualizations, connections, and monitoring strategies		●	●	●	●	●	●
Analyze Facts		●	●	●	●	●	
Determine author's purpose and perspective		●	●	●	●	●	
Determine author's point of view				●	●	●	
Distinguish fact from opinion				●	●	●	
Evaluate relevance						●	

ANALYZE STORY ELEMENTS

	K	1	2	3	4	5	In the U.S.A. 2–5
Characterization	●	●	●	●	●	●	●
Describe characters	●	●	●	●	●	●	●
Character's traits and feelings		●	●	●	●	●	
Character's roles, motives, changes, and relationships			●	●	●	●	
Character's conflicts and points of view					●	●	
Character's actions		●	●	●	●	●	●
Setting	●	●	●	●	●	●	
Plot	●	●	●	●	●	●	
Sequence of events	●	●	●	●	●	●	
Relationship of events				●	●	●	
Goal and outcome					●	●	
Problem and solution		●	●	●	●	●	
Conflict and resolution					●	●	
Theme, lesson, or moral	●	●	●	●	●	●	

RECOGNIZE LITERARY DEVICES

	K	1	2	3	4	5	In the U.S.A. 2–5
Description		●	●	●	●	●	
Sensory details and sensory language		●	●	●	●	●	
Dialogue			●	●	●	●	
Literary language			●	●	●	●	
Figurative language				●	●	●	
Imagery				●	●	●	
Narrator's point of view (first-person, third-person)				●	●	●	
Repetition, rhyme, and rhythm	●	●	●	●	●	●	

Level	**A**	**B**	**C**	**D**	**E**	**F**	**Newcomer Level**

Reading, continued

	Grade						In the U.S.A. 2–5
	K	1	2	3	4	5	
RECOGNIZE GENRES							
Recognize Kinds of Fiction	•	•	•	•	•	•	•
Drama			•	•	•	•	
Fiction (story) or fantasy	•	•	•	•	•	•	
Folk tales, fairy tales, fables, tall tales, myths, and legends	•	•	•	•	•	•	
Realistic fiction	•	•	•	•	•	•	
Recognize Kinds of Nonfiction	•	•	•	•	•	•	•
Article			•	•	•	•	
Biography, autobiography, or profile		•	•	•	•	•	
Description				•	•	•	
Diary, journal, notebook, or blog	•	•	•	•	•	•	
Essay				•	•	•	
How-to article or experiment		•	•	•	•	•	
Instructions or directions		•	•	•	•	•	
Interview or online bulletin board				•	•		
Fact sheet or fact book	•	•			•	•	
Letter, postcard, or e-mail	•	•	•	•	•	•	
Literary nonfiction		•	•	•	•	•	
Magazine, newspaper, or online article		•	•	•	•	•	
Memoir/personal narrative	•				•	•	
Photo essay or book	•	•	•	•	•	•	
Web site		•	•	•	•	•	
Recognize poems, proverbs, riddles, and songs	•	•	•	•	•	•	
Distinguish Between Forms and Genres		•	•	•	•	•	•
Fiction and nonfiction		•	•	•	•	•	•
Fantasy and reality/fact		•	•	•	•	•	
Literary forms, genres			•	•	•	•	
Connect knowledge of different genres to writing activities		•	•	•	•	•	
EVALUATE TEXTS							
Identify examples of author's/illustrator's craft		•	•	•	•	•	
Connect the author's time, culture, and experiences to writing				•	•	•	
Evaluate impact of illustrations on text		•	•	•	•	•	
Evaluate impact of literary devices/medium on text					•	•	
Evaluate impact of author's perspective/point of view on text					•	•	
Level	A	B	C	D	E	F	Newcomer Level

Reading, continued

	K	1	2	3	4	5	In the U.S.A. 2–5
COMPARE TEXTS							
Compare fiction and nonfiction	●	●	●	●	●	●	
Compare forms of fiction		●	●	●	●	●	
Compare forms of nonfiction		●	●	●	●	●	
Compare texts from different cultures			●	●	●	●	
Compare writing on the same topic	●	●	●	●	●	●	
Compare ideas in different texts	●	●	●	●	●	●	
Compare literary elements (character, setting, plot, theme)		●	●	●	●	●	
Compare author's purposes			●	●	●	●	
Compare genres		●	●	●	●	●	
Compare texts and dramatic interpretations		●	●	●	●	●	
ANALYZE TEXT STRUCTURES							
Identify structural patterns used by writers to organize ideas		●	●	●	●	●	
Cause and effect		●	●	●	●	●	
Chronological or sequential order		●	●	●	●	●	
Comparison and contrast		●	●	●	●	●	
Logical order or main idea and details		●	●	●	●	●	
Problem and solution					●	●	
Steps in a process or procedure		●	●	●	●	●	
USE TEXT FEATURES							
Locate text features, identify their functions, and use the feature to build understanding		●	●	●	●	●	●
Bold, print, italics, and key words		●	●	●	●	●	
Captions, labels, and callouts	●	●	●	●	●	●	
Charts and tables					●	●	
Diagrams and timelines		●			●	●	
Headings, subheadings, and titles	●	●	●	●	●	●	●
Illustrations	●	●	●	●	●	●	●
Maps	●	●	●	●	●	●	
Sidebars					●	●	
Table of contents		●	●	●	●	●	●
Index					●	●	●
Stage directions					●	●	
Level	A	B	C	D	E	F	Newcomer Level

Multicultural Awareness and Appreciation

	K	1	2	3	4	5	In the U.S.A. 2–5
Connect personal experiences, information, ideas, and insights with those of others		•	•	•	•	•	•
Compare oral traditions, language, and sayings across regions and cultures		•	•	•	•	•	•
Read to Compare		•	•	•	•	•	•
Personal experiences, language, customs, or culture		•	•	•	•	•	•
Characters across cultures				•	•		
Characteristics of cultures			•		•	•	
Cross-cultural themes and/or connections			•		•	•	
Identify language related to regions, cultures, or customs			•	•	•	•	•
Appreciate the diversity of cultures and/or generations	•	•	•	•	•	•	•
Appreciate and Share Aspects of Home, U.S., and World Culture	•	•	•	•	•	•	•
History					•	•	
Language	•	•	•	•	•	•	•
Folklore and literature		•	•	•	•	•	•
Symbols		•	•	•	•	•	•
Holidays, customs, and traditions, music, and dance	•	•	•	•	•	•	•
Determine common and distinctive characteristics of cultures				•	•	•	•

Reach into Phonics

Beginning Reading Use these resources for comprehensive instruction in beginning reading

CONCEPTS OF PRINT	K Alphachants	1 Reach into Phonics	2 Reach into Phonics	3–5 Reach into Phonics
Know the order of the alphabet	•	•		
Identify letters	•	•	•	•
Match capital and lowercase letters	•	•	•	•
Identify a word	•	•	•	•
Recognize sentence punctuation	•	•	•	•
Identify title	•	•	•	•
Hold a book/turn pages	•	•	•	•
Directionality	•	•	•	•
Identify a sentence	•	•	•	•
Use parts of a book	•	•	•	
Identify author		•	•	
Use page numbers		•	•	•
Identify dialogue			•	•
Identify indentation of paragraphs				•
Use captions and labels	•			•
Use print from the environment				•

Level	A	B	C	D	E	F

Beginning Reading, continued

	Grade			
	K Alphachants	**1** Reach into Phonics	**2** Reach into Phonics	**3–5** Reach into Phonics

PHONOLOGICAL AWARENESS

Skill	A	B	C	D	E	F
Isolate words in a sentence	○	●	●		●	
Identify syllables	○	●	●		●	
Blend syllables to form a word	○	●	●		●	
Segment a word into syllables	○	●	●		●	
Identify rhyming words	○	●	●		●	
Generate rhyming words	○	●	●		●	
Match initial, medial, and final sounds	○	●	●		●	
Identify and isolate initial, medial, and final sounds	○	●	●		●	
Blend onset and rime	○	●	●		●	
Blend sounds to form a word	○	●	●		●	
Segment a word into sounds	○	●	●		●	
Manipulate sounds in words (add, delete, substitute)	○	●	●		●	

ASSOCIATE SOUNDS AND SYMBOLS

Skill	A	B	C	D	E	F
Consonants	○	●	●		●	
Short vowels	○	●	●		●	
Consonant blends and digraphs		●	●		●	
Word Patterns						
CVCe word patterns with *a, i, o, u, e*		●	●		●	
CV word patterns with *o, e*		●	●		●	
Short and long vowels in CVC and CVCe word patterns		●	●		●	
CVVC word patterns		●	●		●	
Vowel digraphs: *ai, ay, ee, ea, ie, igh, oa, ow, oo, ou, ui,*		●	●		●	
r-Controlled vowels: *ar, or, -ore, er, ir, ur, air, -are, eer, ear*		●	●		●	
Sounds for *-y*: /ē/, /ī/		●	●		●	
Diphthongs: *oi, oy, ou, ow*		●	●		●	
Variant vowels: *aw, au, al, all, oo, ew, ea,*		●	●		●	
Vowel patterns: *-igh, -old, -alk*		●				
Vowel patterns: *o, i, -ight*			●			
Schwa			●		●	
Soft c		●	●		●	
Soft g		●	●		●	
Silent consonants *kn, wr, gn, mb*		●	●		●	
Plurals *-s, -es, -ies*		●	●		●	
Inflected forms		●	●		●	

Level	A	B	C	D	E	F

Scope and Sequence, continued

Beginning Reading, continued

	K Alphachants	Grade 1 Reach into Phonics	Grade 2 Reach into Phonics	3–5 Reach into Phonics
ASSOCIATE SOUNDS AND SYMBOLS, continued				
Multisyllabic Words				●
Compound words		●	●	●
VCCV syllable division (bas/ket, kit/ten)		●	●	●
VCCCV syllable division (hun/dred)		●	●	●
VCV syllable division (mu/sic, cab/in)		●	●	●
Words with consonant + *le*		●	●	●
Schwa *a* in the first syllable			●	●
Schwa + *r, n,* or *l*			●	
Suffixes *-ful, -less, -er, -ly*		●	●	
Suffixes *-y, -er, -or, -ness*			●	
Suffixes *-ful, -less, -ly, -y*				●
Prefixes *un-, re-*		●	●	●
Prefixes *mis-, dis-, pre-, in-, im-*			●	
Syllable Types: *r*-controlled, consonant + *le*, vowel team, vowel + silent *e*		●	●	●
Final syllables with *-tion, -ture, -ent, -ant*			●	
IDENTIFY WORD PARTS				
Inflectional endings (*-s, -ed, -ing*)		●	●	●
Suffixes		●	●	●
Prefixes		●	●	●
IDENTIFY AND READ SPECIAL FORMS				
Contractions		●	●	
Abbreviations			●	
DECODING STRATEGIES				
Blend sounds to decode words	○	●	●	●
Use context to support decoding	○	●	●	●
Recognize word families	○	●	●	●
Use structural clues		●	●	●
Identify syllable types		●	●	●
READING FLUENCY				
Recognize high frequency words	○	●	●	●
Read with accuracy		●	●	●
Use phrasing		●	●	●
Read with expression		●	●	●
Read with correct intonation		●	●	●
Read regularly in instructional level materials	○	●	●	●
Level	A	B	C	D E F

Beginning Reading, continued

	K Alphachants	1 Reach into Phonics	2 Reach into Phonics	3–5 Reach into Phonics
SPELLING				
Spell CVC and CVCe words with consonants and consonant blends		•	•	•
Spell words with complex consonants, r-controlled vowels, long vowels, vowel digraphs, and vowel diphthongs		•	•	•
Spell high frequency words	•	•	•	•
Spell base words with inflectional endings		•	•	•
Spell simple contractions		•	•	
HANDWRITING				
Directionality	•	•	•	•
Form capital and lower-case letters correctly	•	•	•	•
Form letters correctly	•	•	•	•
Use beginning strokes	•	•	•	•
Use consistent letter and word spacing	•	•	•	
Write legibly	•	•	•	•

Writing

	K	1	2	3	4	5	In the U.S.A. 2–5
WRITING TRAITS							
Focus and coherence	•	•	•	•	•	•	
Organization	•	•	•	•	•	•	
Development of ideas	•	•	•	•	•	•	
Voice and style	•	•	•	•	•	•	
Written conventions	•	•	•	•	•	•	
WRITER'S CRAFT							
Write strong beginnings and endings		•	•	•	•	•	
Word choice		•	•	•	•	•	
Use literary devices (dialogue, figurative language, etc.)				•	•	•	
Write Effective Sentences		•	•	•	•	•	•
Complete sentences		•	•	•	•	•	•
Combine sentences				•	•	•	
Break up run-on sentences						•	
Use sentence variety		•	•	•	•	•	
Write Effective Paragraphs		•	•	•	•	•	
Topic sentence and supporting details		•	•	•	•	•	
Transition words		•	•	•	•	•	
Progression of ideas				•	•	•	
Relevant details				•	•	•	
Level	A	B	C	D	E	F	Newcomer Level

Scope and Sequence, continued

Writing, continued	Grade						In the U.S.A. 2–5
	K	1	2	3	4	5	
WRITER'S CRAFT, continued							
Show, don't tell		●	●	●	●	●	
Tell what's helpful, important, or interesting	●	●	●	●	●	●	
Exclude unnecessary details			●	●	●	●	
Elaborate		●	●	●	●	●	
Use visual and organizational aids			●	●	●	●	
Develop a personal voice or style		●	●	●	●	●	
Develop characters		●	●	●	●	●	
Appeal to logic or emotions				●	●	●	
Support ideas		●	●	●	●	●	
WRITING PURPOSES, MODES, AND FORMS							
Write for a variety of purposes	●	●	●	●	●	●	●
Write for a variety of audiences	●	●	●	●	●	●	●
Choose the mode and form of writing that works best for the topic, audience and purpose					●	●	
Write in a Variety of Modes		●	●	●	●	●	
Descriptive		●	●	●	●	●	
Narrative		●	●	●	●	●	
Expository		●	●	●	●	●	
Persuasive			●		●	●	
Expressive			●		●	●	
Write in a Variety of Forms	●	●	●	●	●	●	
Captions, labels	●	●	●	●	●	●	●
Description			●	●	●	●	●
Diary/journal entry		●	●	●	●	●	●
Instructions/directions		●	●		●	●	●
Innovation on a story or poem		●	●	●	●	●	
Letter invitation or e-mail	●	●	●	●	●	●	
List	●	●	●	●	●	●	●
Literary response			●	●	●	●	
News article, newscast, newspaper, or newsletter		●	●	●	●	●	
Paragraph			●	●	●	●	
Personal narrative			●	●	●	●	
Poem/rhyme/song	●	●	●	●	●	●	
Report			●			●	
Sentences	●	●	●	●	●	●	●
Story			●		●	●	
Summary			●	●	●	●	
Words/word list	●	●	●	●	●	●	●
Level	A	B	C	D	E	F	Newcomer Level

Writing, continued

WRITING PROCESS				Grade				In the U.S.A. 2–5
		K	1	2	3	4	5	
Prewriting		●	●	●	●	●	●	●
Analyze professional models and student models		●	●	●	●	●	●	●
Determine the purpose, form, audience		●	●	●	●	●	●	●
Generate ideas		●	●	●	●	●	●	●
Choose a topic		●	●	●	●	●	●	●
Gather information		●	●	●	●	●	●	●
Organize ideas		●	●	●	●	●	●	●
Drafting		●	●	●	●	●	●	●
Develop drafts			●	●	●	●	●	●
Categorize ideas			●	●	●	●	●	
Organize ideas into sentences or paragraphs		●	●	●	●	●	●	●
Blend paragraphs into larger units of text					●	●	●	
Evaluate the draft for completeness and effectiveness				●	●	●	●	
Use resources for writing drafts (dictionary, thesaurus, writing handbook)				●	●	●	●	
Revising			●	●	●	●	●	
Evaluate the draft			●	●	●	●	●	
Participate in peer-conferencing			●	●	●	●	●	
Identify revision needs			●	●	●	●	●	
Add, delete, combine, and/or rearrange text			●	●	●	●	●	
Use revising marks			●	●	●	●	●	
Editing and Proofreading			●	●	●	●	●	●
Check and correct writing for correct conventions of written English		●	●	●	●	●	●	●
Select and use reference materials (dictionary, etc.)					●	●	●	
Publishing		●	●	●	●	●	●	●
Create the final version of the work and prepare it for publication		●	●	●	●	●	●	●
Use visuals or multimedia to complement or extend meaning		●	●	●	●	●	●	●
Read writing aloud		●	●	●	●	●	●	●
Conduct presentations			●	●	●	●	●	●
Enhance work with graphics or media			●	●	●	●	●	●
Reflect and Evaluate			●	●	●	●	●	●
Use rubrics to evaluate the writing			●	●	●	●	●	
Monitor growth as a writer			●	●	●	●	●	
Self-assess			●	●	●	●	●	
Use evaluations to set goals as a writer			●	●	●	●	●	
Keep a writing portfolio			●	●	●	●	●	●
Level		A	B	C	D	E	F	Newcomer Level

Scope and Sequence, continued

Grammar, Usage, Mechanics, and Spelling

	K	1	2	3	4	5	In the U.S.A. 2–5
SENTENCES							
Sentence Types	•	•	•	•	•	•	•
Statements, questions, exclamations, and commands	•	•	•	•	•	•	•
Negative sentences			•	•	•	•	•
Sentence structures	•	•	•	•	•	•	•
Simple sentences	•	•	•	•	•	•	•
Compound sentences with coordinating conjunctions				•	•	•	
Complex sentences					•	•	
Subjects and Predicates		•	•	•	•	•	•
Complete subject		•	•	•	•	•	•
Simple subject		•	•	•	•	•	
Compound subject					•	•	
Complete predicate		•	•	•	•	•	•
Simple predicate (verb)		•	•	•	•	•	
Compound predicate					•	•	
Complete sentences		•	•	•	•	•	•
Subject-verb agreement	•	•	•	•	•	•	
PARTS OF SPEECH							
Nouns	•	•	•	•	•	•	•
Common and proper		•	•	•	•	•	
Count and noncount		•	•	•	•	•	
Plurals	•	•	•	•	•	•	•
Possessive			•	•	•	•	
Articles		•	•	•	•	•	•
Pronouns		•	•	•	•	•	•
Subject		•	•	•	•	•	•
Object		•	•	•	•	•	•
Possessive		•	•	•	•	•	
Demonstrative					•	•	
Pronoun agreement		•	•	•	•	•	•
Adjectives	•	•	•	•	•	•	•
Adjectives that compare					•	•	
Verbs	•	•	•	•	•	•	•
Action		•	•	•	•	•	•
Linking			•	•	•	•	
Modals (can, could, would, might, must, etc.)			•	•	•	•	•
Helping			•	•	•	•	
Level	A	B	C	D	E	F	Newcomer Level

Grammar, Usage, Mechanics, and Spelling, continued

	Grade						In the U.S.A. 2–5
	K	1	2	3	4	5	
PARTS OF SPEECH, continued							
Verb tenses	●	●	●	●	●	●	●
Present tense	●	●	●	●	●	●	●
Past tense (regular and irregular)	●	●	●	●	●	●	
Future tense	●	●	●	●	●	●	
Present-perfect tense					●	●	
Past-perfect tense					●	●	
Progressive forms of verbs					●	●	
Contractions			●	●	●	●	●
Adverbs		●	●	●	●	●	
Adverbs that compare					●	●	
Prepositions	●	●	●	●	●	●	●
Prepositional phrases		●	●	●	●	●	
Conjunctions					●	●	
CAPITALIZATION							
First word of a sentence	●	●	●	●	●	●	●
Pronoun I	●	●	●	●	●	●	●
Proper nouns		●	●	●	●	●	●
Abbreviations of proper nouns			●	●	●	●	
Salutation and closing of letters	●				●	●	
Important words in titles					●	●	
PUNCTUATION							
Sentence punctuation (comma, period, exclamation point)	●	●	●	●	●	●	●
Period in abbreviations			●	●	●	●	
Comma					●	●	
Apostrophe			●	●	●	●	
Quotation marks					●	●	
SPELLING *See Beginning Reading (page S&S 16)*							
Level	A	B	C	D	E	F	Newcomer Level

Language Builder Picture Card Index

Level E Index
Unit Order

UNIT	CARD	LABEL
Unit 1: Living Traditions	E1	Pueblo pottery
	E2	Hopi baskets
	E3	Navajo blankets
	E4	ancient cliff homes
	E5	pueblo
	E6	hogan
	E7	Loy Krathong Festival
	E8	Thanksgiving
	E9	Children's Day
	E10	Noche de Rabanos (Night of the Radishes)
	E11	Earth Day
	E12	Teuila Festival
	E13	Carnival
Unit 2: Animal Intelligence	E14	A fox steals an egg.
	E15	A bear looks for food.
	E16	Bees work together.
	E17	A squirrel buries food.
	E18	A beaver builds a dam.
	E19	A cat drinks from a sink.
	E20	A dog brings a newspaper.
	E21	Ants find food.
	E22	A dog herds sheep.
	E23	guide horse
	E24	police dog
	E25	search-and-rescue dog
	E26	helping-hand monkey
Unit 3: Amazing Places	E27	Rapa Nui National Park
	E28	Nile River
	E29	Dead Sea
	E30	Royal Gorge
	E31	Mammoth Cave
	E32	North Pole
	E33	Antelope Canyon
	E34	Yellowstone National Park
	E35	Mount Fuji
	E36	stone towers in Madagascar
	E37	Bear Glacier
	E38	cone houses in Goreme Valley
	E39	floating market in Bangkok

UNIT	CARD	LABEL
Unit 4: Power of Nature	E40	Wind is an energy resource.
	E41	Water is an energy resource.
	E42	Oil is an energy resource.
	E43	Coal is an energy resource.
	E44	Wood is an energy resource.
	E45	solar power panels
	E46	power plant
	E47	tornado
	E48	hurricane
	E49	camping
	E50	hiking
	E51	swimming
	E52	flying kites
Unit 5: Invaders!	E53	penicillin mold
	E54	blue cheese mold
	E55	yeast cells
	E56	penicillin shot
	E57	blue cheese
	E58	fungi
	E59	Stir yeast in water.
	E60	Make the dough.
	E61	Let the dough rise.
	E62	Bake the bread.
	E63	locusts
	E64	termites
	E65	mice
Unit 6: Treasure Hunters	E66	gold
	E67	silver
	E68	silver mine
	E69	The Endeavor
	E70	The Half Moon
	E71	cannons
	E72	shipwreck
	E73	sea chest
	E74	ship's logbook
	E75	pewter mugs
	E76	pocket sundials
	E77	coins and leather pouch
	E78	ivory carving

UNIT	CARD	LABEL
Unit 7: Moving Through Space	E79	100-meter race
	E80	high jump
	E81	long jump
	E82	hurdles
	E83	shot-put
	E84	egg race
	E85	sack race
	E86	zero-gravity training
	E87	spacewalk
	E88	moon walk
	E89	space camp
	E90	lunar rover
	E91	view from space
Unit 8: Saving a Piece of the World	E92	protecting dunes
	E93	climate researchers
	E94	Mary Ann Goodnight
	E95	Palenque
	E96	terra-cotta soldiers
	E97	Iron Age village
	E98	ancient ruins in Mali
	E99	citizen scientists
	E100	wildlife conservationist
	E101	park ranger
	E102	firefighter
	E103	rescuer workers
	E104	teacher

Note: Page numbers in boldface type indicate main discussion.

Skills Index, continued

independent PD62, T26, T58, T129, T196, T212, T213, T268, T302c, T336c, T378, T423, T444, T514, T548, T564, T565
interactive PD61, T27, T303, T379, T445, T515
journal T97, T423
letter T565
modeled PD60, T24–T25, T36b, T38, T56–T57, T66b, T66k, T67c, T95, T106b, T138b, T138k, T165, T166c, T176, T206b, T206, T235, T246b, T266–T267, T276b, T276k, T277c, T300–T301, T314b, T316, T346b, T377, T386b, T388, T408, T418b, T419c, T442–T443, T454a, T484j, T485c, T512–T513, T526b, T560a, T561c
note T488
packing list T489
paragraphs T57, T138b, T165, T167, T236, T245, T268, T275, T301, T313, T350, T378, T453, T476, T483, T525, T548, T559
persuasive essay T564
play T351
poetry T174b, T212, T281
postcard T213
poster T281
power writing T6, T34, T38, T64, T76, T104, T108, T148, T172, T176, T204, T218, T244, T248, T274, T286, T312, T316, T344, T356, T384, T388, T416, T428, T452a, T494, T524, T528a
publish and share **T279**
RAFT T9, T66k, T151, T179, T206b, T206, T221, T276k, T289, T346k, T359, T418k, T431, T484j, T497, T560k
science experiment T351
sentence frames T128, T166, T268
sentences T35, T65, T77, T95, T96, T105, T148, T165, T173, T196, T205, T236, T345, T429, T548
  complete T35
  compound T65, T137
  questions T336
  simple T148, T173, T205
  topic T548
  variety T105, T245
sentence stems R4–R26
shared T565
short story T106b
song T422
story T489
structured responses PD63
tall tale T269
  see also Writing forms

Writing checklist T66i, T66k, T138i, T138k, T206i, T206, T276i, T276k, T346i, T346k, T418i, T418k, T484i, T484j, T560i, T560k

Writing fluency *see Writing: power writing*

Writing forms
advertisement **T26**, T213, T565
advice column T71
biographic article T36b
book report T431
business letter **T138**
comic book T423
comic strip T143
conversation T385
description T70, T95, T165, T196, T280, T377, T476, T513
e-mail T96, T142
essay T408
figurative language T512–T513
friendly letter T58, T166, T565
historical fiction **T418i–T421**, T418
instructions T221, T444, T497
interview **T66i–T69**, **T66**
interview questions T27
journal T9, T36f, T66f, T106f, T138f, T174f, T206f, T246f, T276f, T280, T314f, T346f, T417, T423, T454f, T484f, T560f
letter T126–T127, T128, T129, T136, T151, T565
letter of inquiry **T138i–T141b**
list T128, T215, T489
literary response **T560i–T563a**, **T560**
message with directions T386b
news report T303
note T488
packing list T489
paragraph response T515
paragraphs T66b, T379, T560a
personal narrative **T484i–T487**, **T484**
persuasive essay **T346i–T349**, **T346**, T564
persuasive news article T246b

persuasive poster T281
play T351
poem T174b, T212, T276b, T281, T514
postcard T213
poster T281
research report **T206**
review T445
science experiment T351
song T422
story **T489**, T489
summary T237, T346f, T359, T418f, T526f
tall tale T251, T269, **T276i–T279**, T276
  see also Research

Writing models
biography T391
book report T431
business letter **T138**
e-mail T96
essay T359
fairy tale T289
friendly letter T151, T166
historical fiction **T418**
instructions T221
interview T41, **T66**
journal T9
literary response **T560**
mystery story T251
news story T319
personal narrative T179, **T484**
persuasive essay **T346**
poem **T497**
report T111, **T206–T207**
speech T531
story T79, T459
tall tale **T276**
web site T141

Writing process T278a, T319
draft T56–T57, T67c–T67, **T67**, T126–T127, **T139c–T139**, **T139**, T194–T195, **T210b–T210**, **T210**, T266–T267, **T277c–T277**, **T277**, T334–T335, **T347c–T347**, **T347**, T406–T407, **T419c–T419**, **T419**, **T485c–T485**, **T485**, T546–T547, **T561c–T561**, **T561**, T584
edit and proofread T59, **T69a**, **T69**, T128, T129, **T141a**, **T141**, T197, **T211c**, **T211**, T269, **T279a**, **T279**, T337, **T349a**, **T349**, T409, **T421a**, **T421**, **T487a**, **T487**, **T563a**, **T563**, T586
organizing **T67**, **T139**, **T210**, T277, **T347**, **T419**, **T485**, **T561**, **T578**, T583
prewrite T41, **T67a–T67b**, **T67**, **T139a–T139b**, **T139**, **T208a–T210a**, **T208**, **T277a–T277b**, **T277**, **T347a–T347b**, **T347**, **T419a–T419b**, **T419**, **T485a–T485b**, **T485**, **T531a–T531b**, **T531**, **T561a–T561b**, **T561**, T578
plan **T67**, **T139**, T179, **T208**, **T277**, **T347**, T391, **T419**, **T485**, **T561**, T578
proofread T129, T197, T269
publish and share T64, **T69**, T69, T136, T141b, **T141**, T204, **T211**, T211, T274, **T279**, T344, **T349**, T349, T416, **T421**, T421, **T487**, T487, **T563**, T563, T587
revise T58, **T68a–T68**, **T68**, T128, **T140a–T140b**, **T140**, T196, **T211a–T211b**, **T211**, T268, **T278a–T278**, T336c, **T348a–T348**, T408, **T420a–T420**, **T486a–T486**, T548, **T562a–T562**, T585

Writing projects T108, T111, T487
advertisement T213
comic book T423
debate T565
historical fiction **T418i–T420**
instructions T221
interview T66i–T69
letter of inquiry **T138i–T141b**
literary response **T560i–T563**
modeled T176, T248, T528a
packing list T489
paragraph T167
personal narrative **T484i–T487**
persuasive essay **T346i–T349**, T564
poem T174b, T212, T276b, T281
postcard T213
poster T281
research report **T206i–T211**
song T422
summary T237

tall tale T251, T266–T267, T269, **T276i–T279**
  see also Writing Process
Writing prompts T66b, T66k, T138b, T138k, T206, T276b, T276k, T346b, T346k, T418b, T418k, T484j, T560a, T560k
Writing routines PD54–PD56, PD59–PD63, T24–T25, T26, T27, T36b, T58, T67c, T95, T97, T139c, T165, T167, T174b, T196, T206b, T235, T236, T237, T266–T267, T268, T277c, T336c, T347c, T377, T378, T379, T386b, T408, T409, T419c, T442–T443, T454a, T512–T513, T514, T515, T526b, T548, T561c
  see also Modeled writing routine; Power Writing Routine
Writing strategies
develop characters **T419c**
develop personal voice **T485c**
organize ideas **T210b**
organize information **T139c**
support ideas with relevant details **T561c**
support opinions **T347c**
use vivid words **T277c**
write a strong beginning **T67c**
Writing traits
conventions *see Conventions, in writing*
development of ideas T138i, T138, **T346i**, **T346**, T589
focus and coherence T66i, **T66**, **T418i**, **T418k**, T588
organization **T206i**, T207, **T210b**, **T277b**, **T419a**, **T485b**, **T560i**, **T560**, T590
voice and style T139c, **T276i**, **T276**, **T484i**, T484, T591

Z

Index of Authors
Agra Deedy, Carmen T43, **T56–T57**
Andrew, Moira T272
Batten, Mary T321
Cousteau, Alexandra T239
Cozort, Kristen T199
Dorros, Arthur T291, T300–T301
Falstein, Mark T361
Fern, Tracey E. T499, **T513**
Finlayson, Christy T339
Geiger, Beth T181, T223, T235
Hall, Leslie T113
Hiebert, Fredrik T533
Hutts Aston, Dianna T461
Jafar, Ramona T11
Knutson, Barbara T81, **T94**, **T95**
Millman, Patricia T29
Mora, Pat T253, T266–T267
New England Pirate Museum Web Site T381
Science Explorer, The T305
Scro, Ronald T533
Sengel, Elizabeth T131
Shepard, Aaron T99
Shulevitz, Uri T153, **T164**, T165
Soto, Gary T169
Stevenson, Robert Louis T361, **T376**, T377
Valle, Victor M. T271
Verbeeck, Carol T239
Wells, Robert T433
Winter, Jeanette T551

Index of Illustrators
Brady, Shannon T61
Burr, Dan T321
Catrow, David T291
Colon, Raul T253, **T267**
Foley, Tim T361
Knutson, Barbara T81, **T95**
Nakamura, Joel T169
Pinkney, Jerry T461, **T475**
Shed, Greg T499
Shulevitz, Uri T153, **T164**, T165
So, Meilo T99
Winter, Jeanette T551

see Reach Into Phonics for early reading skills and strategies

Acknowledgments

Acknowledgments, continued

Text Credits

Unit One

Peachtree Publishers: *Martina the Beautiful Cockroach* by Carmen Agra Deedy. Text copyright © 2007 by Carmen Agra Deedy. Reprinted by permission of Peachtree Publishers.

Highlights for Children: "Shaped by Tradition," from *A Touch of Genius* by Patricia Millman, November 2000, Volume 55, Number 11, Issue No. 589. Copyright © 2000 by Highlights for Children, Inc., Columbus, Ohio. Reprinted by permission.

Skipping Stones: Adaptation of "Coming of Age" by Jyotsna Grandhi, from *Skipping Stones*, January/February 2009. Copyright © 2009 by Skipping Stones. Reprinted by permission of Skipping Stones, www.skippingstones.org.

Unit Two

Lerner Publishing Group, Inc.: *Love and Roast Chicken* by Barbara Knutson. Copyright © 2004 by Barbara Knutson. Reprinted with the permission of Carolrhoda Books, a division of Lerner Publishing Group, Inc. All rights reserved. No part of this excerpt may be used or reproduced in any manner whatsoever without the prior written permission of Lerner Publishing Group, Inc.

Shepard Publications: Excerpt adapted from *The Adventures of Mouse Deer: Tales of Indonesia and Malaysia* told by Aaron Shepard from www.aaronshep.com/stories/RO1.html, April 9, 2009. Copyright © 1995 by Shepard Publications. Reprinted by permission.

Unit Three

Farrar Straus & Giroux, LLC: *How I Learned Geography* by Uri Shulevitz. Copyright © 2008 by Uri Shulevitz. Reprinted by permission of Farrar, Straus and Giroux, LLC.

Houghton Mifflin Harcourt: "Tortillas like Africa" from *Canto Familiar* by Gary Soto. Copyright © 1995 by Gary Soto. Reprinted by permission of Houghton Mifflin Harcourt Publishing Company. All rights reserved.

Unit Four

Random House, Inc.: *Doña Flor* by Pat Mora, illustrated by Raúl Colón. Text copyright © 2005 by Pat Mora. Illustrations © 2005 by Raúl Colón. Reprinted by permission of Random House, Inc.

Victor M. Valle: "Comida," by Victor M. Valle from *Fiesta in Aztlan: Anthology of Chicano Poetry*. Text copyright © 1981 by Victor M. Valle. Reprinted by permission of the author. All rights reserved.

Moira Andrew: "The Sun in Me," by Moira Andrew. First published by Barefoot Books. Copyright © 2003 by Moira Andrew. Reprinted by permission of the author. All rights reserved.

Unit Five

Scholastic, Inc.: Adapted from *The Fungus that Ate My School* by Arthur Dorros, illustrated by David Catrow. Text copyright © 2000 by Arthur Dorros. Illustrations © 2000 by David Catrow. Reprinted by permission of Scholastic Inc., Scholastic Press.

Exploratorium: Excerpt from "Mold Terrarium" from www.exploratorium.edu, September 9, 2009. Copyright © 1998 by Exploratorium. Reprinted by permission.

Peachtree Publishers: Excerpt from *Aliens from Earth: When Animals and Plants Invade Other Ecosystems* by Mary Batten. Text © 2003 by Mary Batten. Illustrations © 2003 by Beverly J. Doyle. Permission to reprint granted by Peachtree Publishers.

Unit Six

New England Pirate Museum: Excerpt from "Make a Treasure Map" by the New England Pirate Museum from www.piratemuseum.com, March 5, 2009. Copyright © 2009 by New England Pirate Museum. Reprinted by permission.

National Geographic Books: Adaptation from *Real Pirates: The Untold Story of the Whydah from Slave Ship to Pirate Ship* by Barry Clifford, illustrated by Gregory Manchess. Text copyright © 2008 by Barry Clifford. Illustrations © 2008 by Gregory Manchess. Reprinted with permission.

Texas Archeological Research Laboratory: "La Belle Shipwreck" by the Texas Historical Commission. Copyright © Texas Archeological Research Laboratory, University of Texas, Austin. Original article from the Texas Beyond History website www.texasbeyondhistory.net, March 2009. Reprinted with permission of the Texas Archeological Research Laboratory.

Unit Seven

Albert Whitman & Company: *What's Faster than a Speeding Cheetah?* by Robert E. Wells. Copyright © 1997 by Robert E. Wells. Used by permission of Albert Whitman & Company.

Penguin Group (USA) Inc: Excerpt from *The Moon Over Star* by Diana Hutts Aston, illustrated by Jerry Pinkney. Text copyright © 2008 by Diana Hutts Aston. Illustrations © 2008 by Jerry Pinkney. Used by permission of Dial Books for Young Readers, a division of Penguin Young Readers Group, a member of Penguin Group (USA) Inc., 345 Hudson Street, New York, NY 10014. All rights reserved.

Unit Eight

Houghton Mifflin Harcourt: Abridged from *Buffalo Music* by Tracey E. Fern. Copyright © 2008 by Tracey E. Fern. Used by permission of Clarion Books, an imprint of Houghton Mifflin Harcourt Publishing Company. All rights reserved.

Houghton Mifflin Harcourt Company: Excerpt from *The Librarian of Basra: A True Story from Iraq* by Jeanette Winter. Copyright © 2005 by Jeanette Winter. Reprinted by permission of Houghton Mifflin Harcourt Publishing Company. All rights reserved.

NATIONAL GEOGRAPHIC SCHOOL PUBLISHING

National Geographic School Publishing gratefully acknowledges the contributions of the following National Geographic Explorers to our program and to our planet:

Joshua Ponte, 2007 National Geographic Emerging Explorer
Jill Pruetz, 2008 National Geographic Emerging Explorer
Jimmy Chin, 2004 National Geographic Emerging Explorer
Alexandra Cousteau, 2008 National Geographic Emerging Explorer
Christy Finlayson, National Geographic grantee
Constance Adams, 2005 National Geographic Emerging Explorer
Fredrik Hiebert, National Geographic Fellow

Photographic Credits

iv (tl) Jacqui Hurst/Corbis. v (tl) Mattias Klum/National Geographic Image Collection. vi (tc) Jimmy Chin/National Geographic Image Collection. vii (tl) DigitalStock/Corbis. viii (tl) Christy Finlayson, Ph.D.. ix (tc) Bill Curtsinger/National Geographic Image Collection. x (tc) Andy Rouse/Getty Images. xi (tc) Larry Gerbrandt/Getty Images. 2-3 Purestock/Alamy Images. 3 Sankar

Page 656

Page 657

Page 658

Page 659

Acknowledgments, continued

Text Credits

Highlights for Children: "Shaped by Tradition," from *A Touch of Genius* by Patricia Millman, November 2000, Volume 55, Number 11, Issue No. 589. Copyright © 2000 by Highlights for Children, Inc., Columbus, Ohio. Reprinted by permission.
Skipping Stones: Adaptation of "Coming of Age" by Jyotsna Grandhi, from *Skipping Stones*, January/February 2009. Copyright © 2009 by Skipping Stones. Reprinted by permission of Skipping Stones, www.skippingstones.org.

Unit Two

Lerner Publishing Group, Inc.: *Love and Roast Chicken* by Barbara Knutson. Copyright © 2004 by Barbara Knutson. Reprinted with the permission of Carolrhoda Books, a division of Lerner Publishing Group, Inc. All rights reserved. No part of this excerpt may be used or reproduced in any manner whatsoever without the prior written permission of Lerner Publishing Group, Inc.
Shepard Publications: Excerpt adapted from *The Adventures of Mouse Deer: Tales of Indonesia and Malaysia* told by Aaron Shepard from www.aaronshep.com/stories/RO1.html, April 9, 2009. Copyright © 1995 by Shepard Publications. Reprinted by permission.

Unit Three

Farrar Straus & Giroux, LLC: *How I Learned Geography* by Uri Shulevitz. Copyright © 2008 by Uri Shulevitz. Reprinted by permission of Farrar, Straus and Giroux, LLC.
Houghton Mifflin Harcourt: "Tortillas like Africa" from *Canto Familiar* by Gary Soto. Copyright © 1995 by Gary Soto. Reprinted by permission of Houghton Mifflin Harcourt Publishing Company. All rights reserved.

Unit Four

Random House, Inc.: *Doña Flor* by Pat Mora, illustrated by Raúl Colón. Text copyright © 2005 by Pat Mora. Illustrations © 2005 by Raúl Colón. Reprinted by permission of Random House, Inc.
Victor M. Valle: "Comida," by Victor M. Valle from *Fiesta in Aztlan: Anthology of Chicano Poetry*. Text copyright © 1981 by Victor M. Valle. Reprinted by permission of the author. All rights reserved.
Moira Andrew: "The Sun in Me," by Moira Andrew. First published by Barefoot Books. Copyright © 2003 by Moira Andrew. Reprinted by permission of the author. All rights reserved.
Pages R4 – R35 of this resource are adapted from pages 41-59 and pages 79-89 of *Navigating the ELPS: Using the New Standards to Improve Instruction for English Learners, 2nd Ed.*, by John Seidlitz, © Canter Press, 2008. This content is the sole property of Seidlitz Education, Inc. and is licensed for use specifically within the confines of the agreement in place between NGSP and Seidlitz Education, Inc. These pages cannot be reproduced, adapted, redistributed, or republished without the express written permission of Seidlitz Education, Inc. For additional information regarding Seidlitz Education and its suite of products designed for "Giving Kids the Gift of Academic Language," please visit Seidlitz Education on the Web at www.seidlitzeducation.com.

☐ NATIONAL GEOGRAPHIC SCHOOL PUBLISHING

National Geographic School Publishing gratefully acknowledges the contributions of the following National Geographic Explorers to our program and to our planet:
Joshua Ponte, 2007 National Geographic
   Emerging Explorer
Jill Pruetz, 2008 National Geographic
   Emerging Explorer
Jimmy Chin, 2004 National Geographic
   Emerging Explorer
Alexandra Cousteau, 2008 National Geographic
   Emerging Explorer
Christy Finlayson, National Geographic grantee
Constance Adams, 2005 National Geographic
   Emerging Explorer
Fredrik Hiebert, National Geographic Fellow

Photographic Credits

Cross Curricular Teamwork

5 Artville. 11 Alan D. Carey/PhotoDisc/Getty Images. 31 Stephen Aaron Rees/Shutterstock. 33 lemonlight features/Alamy. 38 (tc) Linda & Colin McKie/iStockphoto, (tr) C Squared Studios/PhotoDisc/Getty Images, (mc, mr) PhotoDisc/Getty Images. 48 Werner Pfunder/Photolibrary.

Language Builder Picture Cards

E1-E2 Marilyn Angel Wynn/Nativestock Pictures. E3 Hemis.fr/SuperStock/SuperStock. E4 Robin Nelson/PhotoEdit. E5 Rolf Richardson/Alamy Images. E6 Nancy Carter/North Wind Picture Archives. E7 Andrew Woodley/Alamy Images. E8 Radius Images/Alamy Images. E9 Gary Conner/PhotoEdit. E10 Olga Rosario Avendano/epa/Corbis. E11 Todd Gipstein/Corbis. E12 Bob Krist/Corbis. E13 V1/Alamy Images. E14 Marsha Goldenberg/Shutterstock. E15 Mihai Dancaescu/Shutterstock. E16 Radius Images/Alamy Images. E17 Cindy Haggerty/Shutterstock. E18 Corel. E19 David G. Miller/Getty Images. E20 Masterfile. E21 Susan E. Degginger/Alamy Images. E22 Nick Koudis/Digital Vision/Getty Images. E23 Steven Senne/AP Images. E24 moodboard/Alamy Images. E25 Jim Parkin/iStockphoto. E26 David H. Wells/Corbis. E27 Alexander Chaikin/Shutterstock. E28 Richard T. Nowitz/Corbis. E29 Arthur Tilley/Jupiterimages. E30 Cindy Miller Hopkins/Danita Delimont/Alamy Images. E31 David S. Boyer and Arlan R. Wiker/National Geographic Image Collection. E32 Sue Flood/Getty Images. E33 Jason Gilmore/National Geographic Image Collection. E34 Richard Coomber/Taxi/Getty Images. E35 Kiyomasa Miyashita/Yamanashi Fujicolor/Dex Image/Getty Images. E36 Stephen Alvarez/National Geographic Image Collection. E37 Bill Brooks/Alamy Images. E38 Frank and Helen Schreider/National Geographic Image Collection. E39 W. Robert Moore/National Geographic Image Collection. E40 Glen Allison/Photodisc/Getty Images. E41 Belinda Pretorius/Shutterstock. E42 Luc Novovitch/Alamy Images. E43 James P. Blair/National Geographic Image Collection. E44 Norbert Michalke/imagebroker/Alamy Images. E45 Nobor/Shutterstock. E46 Brittany Courville/Shutterstock. E47 Corbis Premium RF/Alamy Images. E48 Mike Theiss/National Geographic Image Collection. E49 Masterfile. E50 Karl Weatherly/Getty Images. E51 Matt Carr/Getty Images. E52 Jim Cummins/Taxi/Getty Images. E53-E54 Dennis Kunkel Microscopy, Inc./Phototake/Alamy Images. E55 Steve Gschmeissner/Science Photo Library/Alamy Images. E56 Louise Gubb/Corbis Saba/Corbis. E57 Igor Dutina/Shutterstock. E58 Bettmann/Corbis. E59 Daniel Dillon/Alamy Images. E60 Schieren - StockFood Munich/StockFood America. E61 Foodcollection/Alamy Images. E62 Tim Pannell/Corbis Premium RF/Alamy Images. E63 Gianni Tortoli/National Geographic Image Collection. E64 Dr. Morley Read/Shutterstock. E65 blickwinkel/Alamy Images. E66 George F. Mobley/National Geographic Image Collection. E67 Charles E. Rotkin/Corbis. E68 Paul Springett 08/Alamy Images. E69 BMCL/Shutterstock. E70 The Granger Collection, New York. E71 Artefficient/Shutterstock. E72 IIC/Axiom/Getty Images. E73 Bill Curtsinger/National Geographic Image Collection. E74 DK Limited/Corbis. E75-E78 Victor R. Boswell, Jr./National Geographic Image Collection. E79 Michael Newman/PhotoEdit. E80 Jose Carillo/PhotoEdit. E81 max blain/Shutterstock. E82 Louis Fox/Getty Images. E83 Gordon Scammell/Alamy Images. E84 Dave Nagel/Getty Images. E85 Bob Daemmrich/PhotoEdit. E86 James A. Sugar/National Geographic Image Collection. E87 Stockbyte/Getty Images. E88 NASA - Image of the Day Gallery. E89 Richard T. Nowitz/Corbis. E90 Stockbyte/Getty Images. E91 NASA Image Exchange. E92 C. C. Lockwood 2004. E93 Maria Stenzel/National Geographic Image Collection. E94 The Granger Collection, New York. E95 Kenneth Garrett/National Geographic Image Collection. E96 O. Louis Mazzatenta/National Geographic Image Collection. E97 Cindy Miller Hopkins/Danita Delimont/Alamy Images. E98 Sarah Leen/National Geographic Image Collection. E99 Bob Daemmrich/PhotoEdit. E100 Natalie Fobes/Corbis. E101 Patrick Ward/Corbis. E102 PhotoDisc/Getty Images. E103 Jocelyn Augustino/FEMA. E104 Stretch Photography/Blend Images/Corbis.

Language and Literacy Teamwork

30 Accent/Shutterstock.

Marketing FM

vii Design Pics/Jupiterimages. viii Andy Dean/iStockphoto. xi Thomas Perkins/iStockphoto. xiii Catherine Yeulet/iStockphoto. xv (l) Yevgen Timashov/Shutterstock, (r) Obvious/Shutterstock.

Tab Photo Credits

Unit 1 Purestock/Alamy. Unit 2 Reuters/Corbis. Unit 3 VisionsofAmerica/Joe Shom/Getty Images. Unit 4 Jimmy Chin/Focus Productins Inc. Unit 5 Johnny Haglund/Lonely Planet Images/Getty Images. Unit 6 Borut Furlan/WaterFrame-Underwater Images/Photolibrary. Unit 7 NASA Marshall Space Flight Center (NSAS-MSFC)/NASA Image Exchange. Unit 8 O. Louis Mazzatenta/National Geographic Image Collection.